Volume 84

Woodworker Annual

12 monthly copies January 1980-December 1980

 Model & Allied Publications, Argus Books Ltd.

The Woodworker 1980　　　Index

References prefixed by January, April, July or October indicate the article was published in the Woodworker Record.

ADVERTISERS INDEX

Published by
Model & Allied Publications
Argus Books Ltd.,
14 St. James Road, Watford, Herts.

Model & Allied Publications Ltd.
First Published 1980

Printed in Great Britain

Distributed solely by Argus Books Ltd., Watford, Herts.

ISBN 0 85242 738 7

THE MAGAZINE FOR THE CRAFTSMAN IN WOOD

JANUARY 1980   VOL. 84   NO. 1034

Woodworker Record: 8-page supplement includes: Equipment you can make, Violin woods, Looking at wood, Teaching them to be self-starters, Jobs to spare, Music and models, Work from schools.

FRONT COVER: 'Jack' Goodchild, famous Windsor chairmaker of High Wycombe, Bucks (see article on page 18). *(Photo: David Askham)*

Editor	Geoffrey Pratt
Production Editor	Polly Curds
Group Advertisement Manager	Michael Merrifield
Managing Director	Gospatric Home
Editorial Director	Ron Moulton

SUBSCRIPTION DEPARTMENT: Remittances to MODEL AND ALLIED PUBLICATIONS, P.O. Box 35, Hemel Hempstead, Herts HP1 1EE. Price per copy 50p plus postage 21p. Subscription queries: Tel: Hemel Hempstead 51740. Subscription rate £8.40 per annum; overseas sterling £8.40; $19.00 U.S. for overseas dollar subscribers. Second class postage paid at New York, NY North American enquiries regarding news stand sales should be sent to: Eastern News Distribution, 111 Eighth Avenue, New York, NY 1011, USA. Telephone (212) 255-5620 and craft and hobby sales to Bill Dean Books Ltd., 166-41 Powells Cove Boulevard, Whitestone, New York 11357, USA. Telephone (212) 767-6632.

Model & Allied Publications Ltd

P.O. Box 35, Bridge Street, Hemel Hempstead, Herts HP1 1EE. Telephone: Hemel Hempstead (0442) 41221.

The music goes round . . .

Is there something in the air? Is it the time of the year? Or the TV 'interregnum'? Whatever the cause there is a remarkable upsurge in the interest in making musical instruments of all kinds. For several months past this office has been hard put to meet the requests from readers for backnumbers of WOODWORKER carrying articles on making string and wind instruments.

That most useful piece of office equipment — the photocopier — has enabled us to meet these requests at a modest cost to readers and we are pleased to continue this service as an interim measure.

For those who may wish to have more than the printed word to aid them in making musical instruments, West Dean College, West Dean, Chichester PO18 0QZ, is arranging another of its courses. This will be from 3 — 12 April next year under the direction of Robert Kerr, who is also one of the tutors along with Gordon Jones, John Watkins and Simon Skinner.

The course is primarily for teachers in primary, middle and upper schools and covers a range of instruments, especially those that could be made and used in schools. Applications will also be accepted from those interested in making instruments for themselves.

The instruments that can be made are in the following categories: proficient craftsmen — lute; guitar; Celtic harp; tenor viola de gamba; treble viola da gamba; spinet (4½ octaves table model). Moderate ability — trapezoidal violin/viola; trapezoidal ½-size cello; mandolin; Celtic harp; tenor viola da gamba; treble viola da gamba. Beginners — Appalachian dulcimer; mandolin; Roberts instruments such as tubular bells, alto glockenspiel, chordal dulcimer, Nordic lyre, bowed psaltery.

West Dean College points out that tools and equipment are provided in the workshop but those wishing to bring their own may do so. It may be possible to include some basic tuition on the instrument being made and there will be opportunities for music-making but, of course, the main aim of the course is the making of the instruments.

It is understood that teachers applying for the course should be able to claim financial help from their LEAs and certificates of attendance can be supplied by West Dean at the end of the course. The charge for full board and tuition will be £120.

West Dean courses are always popular so early application (with a £10 deposit) is advised to Miss Sue Overman at West Dean College.

Topical notes

First, WOODWORKER wishes readers a Happy Christmas and a good New Year. Our hope is that 1980 will be a successful 12 months for all craftsmen and craftswomen who work with wood. We thank readers for their interest and support and look forward to developing in the 1980 issues a still wider range of topics associated with timber usage.

Second, the Woodworker Show, which closed as this page goes to press, was a success due to the support of visitors, competitors, judges, exhibitors, stewards and those who worked behind the scenes. WOODWORKER thanks them all. It was also a great pleasure to meet and talk with so many of the visitors. There will be an illustrated report of the Show in the February issue.

Who's seasoning his own timber then?

Actually they both are, but the chap on the right has discovered how simple an Ebac Mini Timber seasoner is. It should be, it was designed for him. In fact the Ebac Mini is the only timber seasoner specially designed for the needs of the smaller woodworking business the sort of business which sells its reputation with its woodwork and doesn't like the idea of both cracking up in somebody's living room.

The Mini is a refrigeration dehumidifier which fits into a drying cabinet of whatever size is needed, where it will season all varieties of wood - even from green - with a minimum of degrade. There's no noise, no fuss and not much heat.

Furthermore, the system's inexpensive to buy, install and run, saving money on ready - seasoned timber and ensuring better quality.

If you're interested in an alternaive to cracked woodwork, contact Dept. TSS, Ebac Ltd., Greenfields Industrial Estate, Bishop Auckland, Co. Durham.
Tel: (0388) 5061

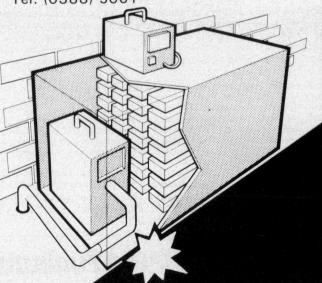

Ebac Limited

Our Agents cover all of England, Scotland, Wales, Southern & Northern Ireland.

our locking system may not look much

but it certainly makes life a lot simpler.

With any combination woodworking machine, one has to consider the possible disadvantages of changing from one operation to another against individual machines. In an age where time means money one cannot be satisfied with outdated methods of unbolting this or that when setting up for a particular operation.

That is why, over a decade ago, Joseph Scheppach designed and patented his "Universal Adaptor 4-Point Locking System" on his Combined Planing and Thicknessing Machine. Since then some 10,000 users every year discover that with the Scheppach System one does not have to sacrifice the advantages gained by low initial outlay with hours of frustration afterwards when it comes to setting up.

With the Model PRIMA HM1 the customer has the distinct advantage of adjusting his inital purchase to suit his budget or work requirement, and then add to at a later date as required.

New from Scheppach

The Universal woodworking machine with separate drives.

This is where the Scheppach Universal Adaptors really begin to make life a lot simpler. When it comes to fitting the **Sawbench, Spindle Moulder, Mortiser, Sander, Lathe or Grinder Attachments** they are all designed to simply locate on four fixing points and then lock with the twin Universal Adaptor Locking Discs. Nothing could be simpler!

And that isn't all. By combining the Locking System to the thicknessing table all attachments have automatic rise and fall facilities with handwheel adjustment.

This year Scheppach have come up with another "first". On the new Model PRIMA HM2 only the required tooling operates when the machine is running. When using the planer, the fitted attachment is idle. When using an attachment the planer is idle — thus offering complete ate safety. In addition, the automatic feed of the thicknesser is controlled separately by lever adjustment.

Do not let the fact that the machine is not of cast construction mislead you. The Scheppach machine will perform accurately, all day long if needs be, on long lengths, both soft and hard timbers. When it comes to a modular system there is nothing to touch Scheppach for large working capacity at such low price!

FREE GIFT with every FULL RANGE CATALOGUE

PRIMA HM2 Illustrated

4

Prices quoted are those prevailing at press date and are subject to alteration due to economic conditions.

Woodworker, January 1980

Prices quoted are those prevailing at press date and are subject to alteration due to economic conditions.

CORONET

complete Home Workshop
— comprising:-

1 ELF WOODTURNING LATHE
4 speeds
12" between centres
14" Bowl Turning (as illustrated)

 IMP BANDSAW
3 speeds
12" throat
5" (approx.) Depth of cut
Table tilts to 45°

 SOVEREIGN 4½" PLANER
½" rebate
Fence tilts 45°

 CONSORT SAW/SPINDLE MOULDER
4 speeds
2¼" depth of cut
Table tilts to 45°
Spindle Moulding (See separate leaflet)

Each unit comes complete with its own motor, press button starter and cabinet stand.

Each unit can be purchased separately — if required for bench mounting (without cabinets)

Illustration shows:-
1. 14" plaque being turned
2. Preparing disc for turning
3. 4½" surface planing
4. Spindle moulding shelf mould

MAJOR CMB 500

MAJOR CMB 600

MINOR MB 6

7" PLANER CAP 300

PRACTICAL COURSES
in WOODMACHINING AND WOODTURNING
for owners or intending purchasers of

Universal WOODWORKING MACHINES & LATHES

GAIN PRACTICAL EXPERIENCE UNDER EXPERT GUIDANCE

The Courses, in our modern, fully equipped Training School offer tuition in the use of Woodworking machines — for owners, stockists, instructors and trainee tradesmen. Regular (½/1/1½ and 2 day) courses cover a wide range of woodworking operations, with individual tuition in woodmachining & woodturning on universal & independent machines. Courses are for day visitors or residential.

Send coupon or phone for details
LEARN-A-CRAFT LTD.
Monk St., Derby. Tel. 0332-364384

LEARN A CRAFT

NAME _____
ADDRESS _____
_____
_____ L.C./W.1.80

BEDSIDE CABINET

A. Yarwood describes how he made a pair of cabinets for the bedroom. One cabinet has a door opening to the left, the other has its door opening to the right. The cabinets are in sapele with doors and drawer fronts veneered in zebrano. The different colours of the streaky zebrano veneers provide an interesting contrast to the sapele of the carcases.

This bedside table is one of a pair which I made to stand beside twin beds in our main bedroom. Each cabinet comprises a carcase mounted on a stool. Each carcase contains a drawer and a cupboard. The only difference between the two cabinets is that one has a door opening to the left, the other has a door opening to the right. Each carcase contains a drawer and a cupboard. The cabinets are made from sapele with doors and drawer fronts veneered in zebrano. Sapele is one of the African 'mahoganies'. The trees from which this wood is produced grow in the belt of tropical rain forests which stretch across central Africa. The boles of the trees produce some huge, clean logs of up to 30m in length and up to 1m in diameter. As a result, very wide boards of sapele can be obtained.

Apart from its rich 'mahogany' colour, a feature of sapele is the interlocking grain. When the boards are cut on the quarter the interlocking grain produces a striking, regular pattern of streaks of alternating light and dark grain, which change in colour as the wood is viewed from different directions.

Fully polished with a french polish finish, sapele is a truly beautiful material. The different colours of the streaky zebrano veneers on drawer and door fronts provide an interesting contrast to the sapele of the carcases.

As is my usual practice when working in solid wood, all the pieces for the carcases, stools and drawers were planed to their finished sizes before any constructional work commenced. All sizes can be obtained from the cutting list. As I had purchased some boards of sapele which were very wide, there was no need for edge jointing to obtain the 305mm (12in.) pieces for the boxes of the carcases.

Planing quarter-sawn sapele demands a sharp blade and constant maintenance of that sharpness if tearing of the interlocking grain is to be avoided. With the heavy task of planing out of the way, the construction of the carcase boxes could commence.

As can be seen in Fig. 2, the carcases are made with secret lap dovetails at their top corners and lap dovetails at their bottoms. A drawer rail is mortised and tenoned into each carcase and drawer runners are tongued into grooves at the rear of the rails. The runners are also fitted into grooves cut across the insides of the carcase ends. Plywood backs are glued and screwed into rebates in the carcase ends and tops and screwed flush against the rear of the carcase bottoms. Note that the front edges of the carcase members are chamfered at 45°, this angle being repeated on the fronts of the stool legs.

The four pieces for each carcase box were planed to their exact finished lengths, taking great care to ensure that the ends were precisely square in both directions. After gauging the appropriate shoulder lines for all the dovetail joints, the rebates at the ends of the carcase tops (which form part of the secret laps) were planed out with the aid of a sharp shoulder plane.

Next stage was to mark and cut the pins for the secret laps on the upper end of the carcase ends. This is the usual practice when marking any form of secret dovetail. It is an easy matter to mark from the pins to find the tails' shape, whereas with other forms of dovetail it is easier to mark the pins from the tails.

After marking and cutting the secret lap tails on the undersides of the tops, the joints were tested for fit. The pleasure obtained from finding that the results of your labours result in a well-fitted joint, is well worth the effort of making this quite difficult jointing construction.

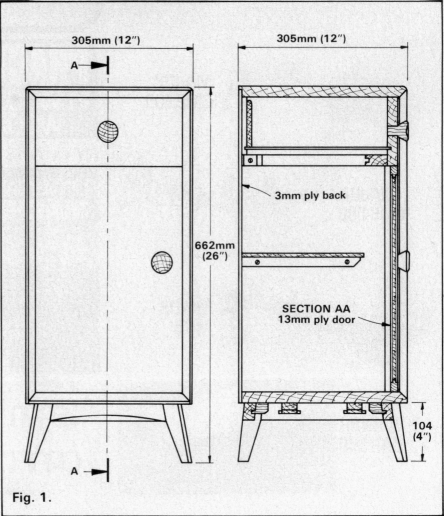

Fig. 1. Front and sectional end views.

Fig. 1.

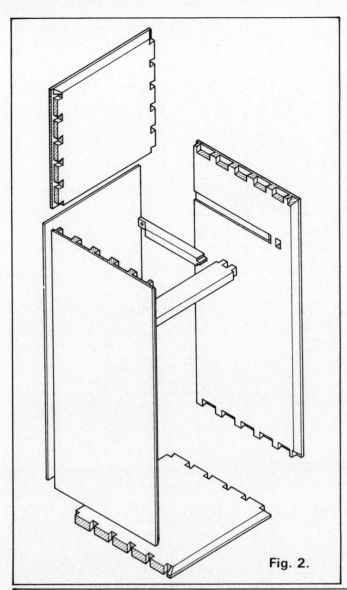

Fig. 2. Left: Exploded drawing showing carcase construction

Fig. 3. Below: Exploded drawing showing rails to front leg construction in stools.

Fig. 2.

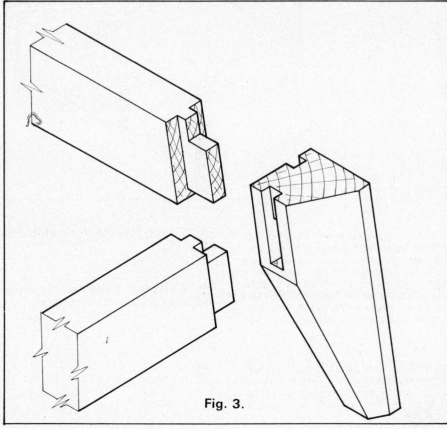

Fig. 3.

Next, the standard lap dovetails joining the carcase ends to the bottoms were made. In both upper and lower sets of dovetail joints, allowances for the chamfers along the fronts of the carcase edges had to be made. These chamfers form mitres at the fronts of the dovetails. Each of these mitres needs careful chiselling to ensure an exact fit at the fronts of each corner.

With the carcase box corner jointing completed, the drawer rail mortise and tenons could be cut and fitted. Grooves were ploughed along the back edges of these rails — 6mm cutters, 6mm deep (¼ x ¼ in.). Grooves across the insides of the carcase ends to receive drawer runners could then be cut and the runner tongues sawn to fit into the grooves in the rails. Grooves could also have been cut in the edges of the runners and dustboards fitted, if thought necessary.

I did not fit dustboards. These seem to me to be necessary only where fairly large chests of drawers are being made. In such large drawers dust filters downwards as drawers are slid in and out and such dust can indeed be a nuisance. With the small drawers of these cabinets the extra refinement of dustboards seemed unnecessary.

Note that when gluing-up the tongues of the runners are glued into the drawer rail grooves. The runners must not be glued into the grooves cut across the carcase ends, but only screwed at the rear. If the runners are glued into these grooves there is a risk of the carcase end splitting lengthwise. This comes about because the ends will shrink and expand slightly across their grain in response to fluctuations in atmospheric humidity. If held rigid with the runners glued into their grooves, this movement will be restricted and splitting of the ends could well occur in time. Before gluing-up, shelf supports were glued to the inner face of the carcase ends.

To complete the carcases, rebates were planed in the back edges of the ends and tops to receive the ply backs. All interior surfaces of the carcases could now be sanded smooth and the boxes glued-up. I always firmly cramp secret dovetails when gluing-up making sure of clean joint lines along the laps. When the glue had set quite firmly, ply backs were sawn and planed to fit into their rebates and over the back of the rear edge of the carcase bottoms. These backs were then glued and screwed in place.

Now the stools could be made. The two front stool legs of each cabinet contain chamfers to match the carcase front edge chamfers. This means that these legs are pentagonal (five-sided) in section — see Fig. 5. Because of this the front rails are set flush with the rear of the front legs as shown in the exploded drawing Fig. 3.

On the other hand, there is no need for the rear legs to be formed to this pentagonal shape, so the jointing of the rear legs is slightly different (see Fig. 4). All stool legs slope outwards in both directions. This slope is 19mm in the 104mm of the leg height (¾in. in 4in.). Note that the cutting list shows a finished leg length of 110mm (4¼in.). This allows for the tops and bottoms of the legs to be cut at an angle to ensure they are flush with the top edges of the stool rails and flat with the floor.

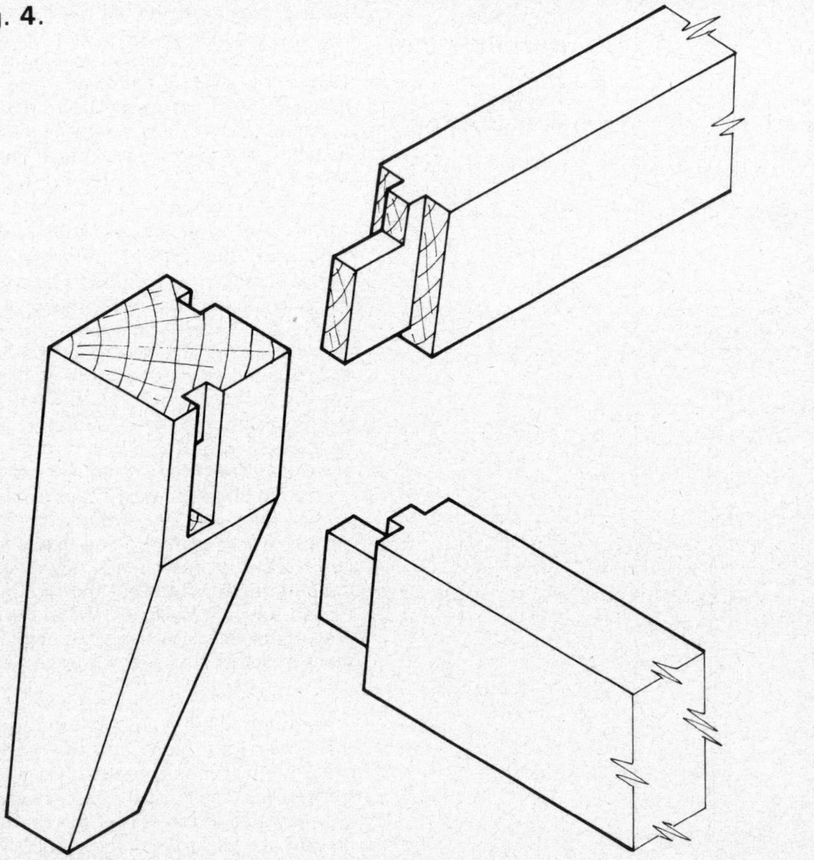

Fig. 4.

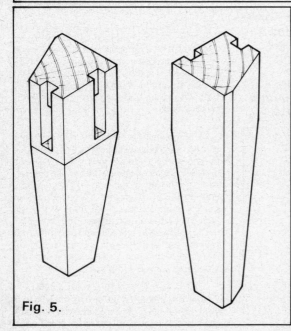

Fig. 4. Exploded drawing showing rails to back legs construction in stools.

When all the dovetailing of the drawer boxes had been completed their inner surfaces were sanded smooth, a groove ploughed in the back of the front for the drawer bottom and the boxes glued-up. Drawer slips were made and fitted and a drawer bottom from 3mm ply also fitted to the slips and into the groove earlier cut in the front.

When the glue had set hard the drawers were planed to an easy sliding fit in their carcases. The drawer sides were liberally coated with candle wax to ensure smooth sliding for a long time to come.

The doors consist of pieces of 12mm thick plywood lipped on all four edges (see Fig. 7). The plywood was first planed to size with edges quite square. Grooves were then planed in all four edges of each door. The lippings were made and their tongues cut.

Fig. 5.

Fig. 6.

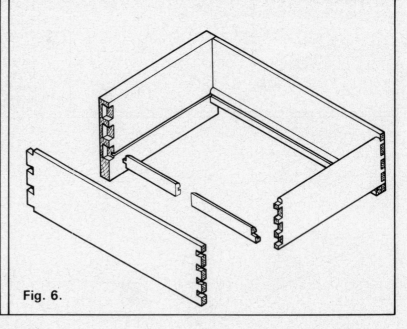

After making allowances for all these design features, the mortise and tenons of the stool could be marked and cut and the frame joined together dry to check the fit of the joints. When satisfied, the legs were shaped and the mortises, to receive buttons for holding the stool to the carcase, were cut on the insides of the four rails. The stool parts could then be cleaned-up and the stool glued and cramped. When the glue had set hard the top edges of the rails were planed level and the tops of the legs squared-off. Buttons for fixing the stool to the underside of the carcase were made and the stool screwed to the carcase using 40mm gauge 8 (1¼in. x 8) brass countersunk screws.

Making the drawers was the next task. Drawer fronts were planed to fit into their respective openings in the carcases. Drawer backs were planed to the same length as the fronts but minus about 0.5mm (approx ¹⁄₆₄in.) This slightly shorter length of the back allows for easier sliding when the drawer has been made and fitted to its compartment.

Drawer sides were planed to a tight sliding fit in their respective places. Then the drawer boxes could be jointed using standard traditional dovetailing methods as shown in Fig. 6.

Fig. 5. Left: Two views of left front stool leg.

Fig. 6. Above: Exploded drawing showing drawer construction.

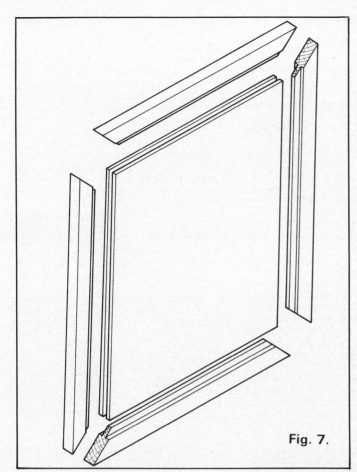

Fig. 7. Exploded drawing showing door construction.

Fig. 7.

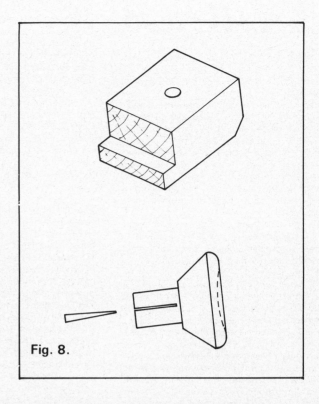

Fig. 8.

Fig. 8. Above: Button end view of a handle.

The corner mitres for the lippings were cut with the aid of a mitre box and the doors were glued-up. When this glue had set the doors were planed to fit in their compartments and hung with 40mm solid drawn brass butts. A door stop made from a strip of sapele 10 x 6mm (³⁄₈ x ¼ in.) was glued and pinned to the inside of the carcase end in its correct place to stop the door. A nylon door catch was also fitted to hold the door in its closed position.

Now the door could be removed and its front and the drawer front veneered with zebrano veneer. As can be seen in the photograph the grain of the veneer continues from the drawer to the door. Care in cutting and laying the veneers was essential to achieve this. Veneering was carried out in the traditional manner of hot scotch glue and a veneering hammer.

As a precaution against possible warping or twisting the rear surfaces of the doors were also veneered, using a cheaper mahogany veneer. When the glue was quite dry and hard the surfaces were scraped and sanded to smooth finish.

Door and drawer handles were turned from short lengths of 38mm square (1½in.) sapele and fitted into holes bored in doors and drawer fronts. These handles were glued into the holes and also held with wedges let into saw kerfs cut into the dowels of the handles.

The carcases were thoroughly cleaned-up by scraping and sanding. The two cabinets were finished with Furniglas polyurethane french polish. First the grain was filled-in with Furniglas filler. This was followed by two brush coats of clear polyurethane varnish, thinned to about half its normal consistency. Then three full bodyings of french polish were applied. A final glossing coat, followed by dulling with pumice powder, completed the finish.

CUTTING LIST

Dimensions in mm and in.
Note: Allowances have been made as follows: length: an extra 13mm (½in.); width: an extra 6mm (¼in.); thickness: an extra 3mm (⅛in.). Plywood is shown as finished manufactured thickness.

CARCASE

2 ends	568 × 310 × 22	(22³⁄₈ × 12¼ × ⅞)
1 top	316 × 310 × 22	(12½ × 12¼ × ⅞)
1 bottom	310 × 310 × 22	(12¼ × 12¼ × ⅞)
1 drawer rail	305 × 58 × 22	(12 × 2¼ × ⅞)
2 runners	240 × 38 × 22	(9½ × 1½ × ⅞)
1 back	568 × 305 × 3	(22³⁄₈ × 12 × 3mm ply)

STOOL

4 legs	120 × 38 square	(4¾ × 1½ square)
4 rails	260 × 38 × 22	(10¼ × 1½ × ⅞)
8 buttons	52 × 38 × 22	(2 × 1½ × ⅞)

DRAWER

1 front	280 × 126 × 22	(11 × 5 × ⅞)
2 sides	280 × 108 × 13	(11 × 4¼ × ½)
1 back	280 × 89 × 13	(11 × 3½ × ½)
2 slips	273 × 32 × 13	(10¾ × 1¼ × ½)
1 bottom	273 × 254 × 3	(10¾ × 9¾ × 3mm ply)

DOOR

1 panel	388 × 248 × 12	(15¼ × 9¾ × 12mm ply)
2 lippings	412 × 26 × 16	(16¼ × 1 × ⅝)
2 lippings	280 × 26 × 16	(11 × 1 × ⅝)

SHELF

1 shelf	280 × 210 × 13	(11 × 8¼ × ½)
2 supports	197 × 27 × 13	(7¾ × 1 × ½)

ALSO REQUIRED

Veneer for door and drawer front
2 handles
1 pr 40 (1½) solid drawn brass butts

Letters

From: Bruce Boulter, London SE9 4RP
Dear Sir,
With reference to the article The World's Timber Trees (Indian rosewood: 6) in the October issue, I would take issue with the author's penultimate paragraph. I am a worker of *Dalbergia* in various forms and also sell these timbers. I have a number of very satisfied customers from age 14 to over 70 all of whom work these woods (and buy more) without becoming faint from the scent given off.

I appreciate the author indicates that there are many species but I think the paragraph in question is misleading to those aspiring to work in exotics who could be 'put off' by what he says there.

I have taken a sample of 10 of my customers and all agree with my comments and I feel you do readers a disservice by not amplifying the author's remarks on scent etc.
Yours faithfully, **Bruce Boulter**

Mr Boulter has declared his interest and we would point out that there are restrictions on space. Indeed, the author of The World's Timber Trees series (C.W. Bond) comments: 'A volume could be written on the subject.' He goes on to say: 'I am delighted and encouraged to hear of so many of Mr Boulter's satisfied customers of all ages. Long may they prosper in the working of these beautiful woods. I do not for one moment think that these artists are likely to be "put off" by my descriptions. The true craftsmen, surely, will bear with any adversity for the sake of the pleasure of future fulfilment.

'Everything is comparative, and I still think that the various species of *Dalbergia* are not by any means the pleasantest of woods to work with. Opinions differ. Personally I do not like the smell of any of them; and as for the dust . . . ! Perhaps my membranes are hypersensitive.

'May I, in conclusion, urge readers to explore the wonderful harvest of the world's forests by whatever means they can find. Mr Boulter can be sure that he is doing a great service by supplying these exotic woods.'

Referring to Mr Bond's remarks on dust, we point out that prolonged inhalation or contact with any dusts, including wood dusts, is undesirable for health reasons and should be avoided. For more information on dust hazards see the article on page 579 of the October issue.

From: J. Lane, Welford, Northants
Dear Sir,
In the article 'Carver chair in iroko' by A. Yarwood (WOODWORKER for November 1979, page 620), I was surprised to see disc sanding being carried out on the assembled piece. I have always understood this operation to be used on less refined pieces than the one shown and would have thought that orbital sanding prior to hand-finishing is to be preferred.

In his article 'Setting up a workshop' (page 678) in the same issue, Gordon Stokes refers to disc sanders as 'useful for rough trimming though of little value for finishing sanding.'

I have found that machined orbital finish before assembly results in the final handwork kept to a minimum.
Yours faithfully, **J. Lane**

The author comments: 'Mr Lane raises some points of considerable interest. To cover his 'surprise to see disc sanding being carried out on an assembled article': the reason for using this tool was to finish off and shape the rounded and curved parts of the framework, particularly at those points where bridle joints broke through. I find a disc sander with fine grade aluminium oxide sandpaper, say, grade 200, to be a valuable shaping tool, which produces a reasonably smooth sanded finish if handled with care and dexterity, when finishing such work as the fairly complex frame of this carver chair with its variety of curves. Mr Lane will have noted that the disc sanding was followed by "a final careful sanding with fine sandpaper worked by hand along the grain of each part" (text of article).

'I would thoroughly agree with the statement that orbital sanding is to be preferred to disc sanding, particularly when finishing flat surfaces. However, using an orbital sander on the frame of this carver chair would be rather impractical, even before assembly, due to the narrow and sometimes complex shapes of its parts. I don't think one should rule out any tool, hand or powered. They all have their uses under some conditions and varying circumstances.'

WOODWORKER INDEX
We have had numerous enquiries from readers of WOODWORKER on the subject of an index for each year. Those readers who have a subscription with us will know that an annual index is published and that it is sent to them with one of their copies early in the following year. Those who buy the Woodworker Annual rather than monthly copies will know that a index is incorporated. Other readers may like to know that the index can be obtained each year from our sales department.
As soon as the 1979 index is available we will put the details of price and the address to contact in the WOODWORKER.
Some indexes for previous years may still be available.

From: Capt W. J. Wooldridge REME RNZEME (retd), London
Dear Sir,
The letter from Hugh Blogg in the August issue describing his method of storing tools by hanging from hooks, is most interesting. I feel however that the method I adopted many years ago in army workshops and elsewhere, is a superior one.

The disadvantages in hook-hung tools (I had tried them) is in: (a) engaging and disengaging the hook; (b) the tendency for the tool to swing in any direction when touched, unless hung close to the wall and, of course, the unsatisfactory feature of hooks screwed into end grain.

My method is this: The heads of sufficient 1 — 1½in. nails are snipped off and the stumps nicely rounded. These pins are driven into prepared holes set at 45° to the vertical surface intended for stowing the tools, leaving approximately ½in. of pin protruding.

Thereafter the wooden tool handles have ³/₁₆-¼in. diameter holes drilled at an upwards angle of 45° to a depth of ⅝ - ¾in. from a

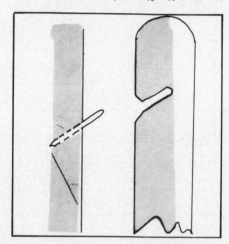

centre 1 - 1½in. down from the top end of the handle. The holes are then given a generous counter sink and the job is finished.

The prime advantages of this system are the ease with which the countersunk hole is located on the pin; the straight-off withdrawal action; and the way the tool snugs-up to the backboard without further movement.
Yours faithfully, **W.J. Wooldridge**

From: R.D. Henderson, Marlow, Bucks
Dear Sir,
I was interested in the paragraph on early ratchet screwdrivers which was part of the article on woodscrews in the September issue (page 500).

I have in my possession one of these early screwdrivers but the patent date is 1890 and not 1897. The tool was brought from America by William Small of Brechin (my wife's grandfather) who emigrated at the beginning of the century but returned after a few years.

The screwdriver is still in working condition but is somewhat worn having been used regularly for many years. I enclose a sketch — the detail may be of some interest.
Yours faithfully, **R.D. Henderson**

Thanks to Mr Henderson for his letter and sketch which will also be of interest to Stanley Tools Ltd which issued the leaflet quoted in the article in the September issue giving the patent date of 1897.

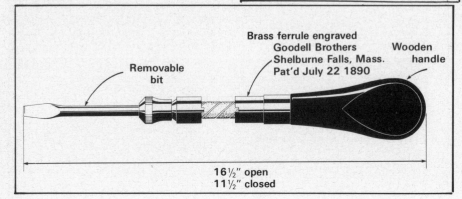

Removable bit

Brass ferrule engraved
Goodell Brothers
Shelburne Falls, Mass.
Pat'd July 22 1890

Wooden handle

16½" open
11½" closed

Take the 'Aggro' out of changing blades.

Use the Elu One-Handed Planer and dispense with Sharpening and Setting ✳

- **Side Fence**
- **Bevel Fence**
- **Tungsten Carbide Blades**
- **Dust Bag**
- **Steel Case**

Completes the Kit

ONLY

£89.00 +
£13.35 VAT

✳ Since the MFF 80 uses throw—away TC Blades.

Powerful planing

This powerful Elu planer MFF 80, really moves material, a real »goer« but so simple to use. It rebates to 22 mm depth and takes 2.5 mm off in one go! Its child's play to set up and use, but designed for the builder and home craftsman alike. This is a must for all those who need to plane, rebate or clean up edges fast. This 650 watt planer is fitted out with an adjustable side fence, spare set of blades, and a handy carrying case too! It's a planer to see. Try it for yourself. Contact your local dealer now.

50 Years Elu

Elu – have been your partner for 50 years now. Tradesmen, Hobbyists, as well as the woodworking and metal working industry are guided by the motto: "Quality with guaranteed service".

Coupon

Please send more information on Elu Portable Electric Tools

Name _____

Company _____

Street _____

Place _____

Phone _____   80 10

Elu Machinery Limited, Stirling Way, Stirling Corner, Borehamwood, Herts, WD6 2AG. Tel.: 01-953 0711

workpieces

Replacing the elm

According to an article in the *Financial Times* of 4 October, Pitney Bowes, the mailing and paper-handling group, is to plant six disease-resistant elms around its headquarters at Harlow, Essex. This is the first step in an experiment which the company hopes will help restore the elm to the British countryside and eventually blossom into an international Elms across Europe campaign.

Mitsui, the Japanese corporation, is running a similar scheme to bring several thousand elm saplings of different strains from Japan and North America and distribute them among local authorities.

Pitney Bowes' plan is based on a strain believed by the Forestry Commission to have the best chance of survival here. The strain is reported to be Sapporo autumn gold, developed in Wisconsin from the seed of a Siberian elm growing in the garden of a Japanese university. Sapporo is not quite the same as the trees which have dominated the British skyline in the past; it is not as big.

There is the risk that a single species might in the future fall prey, as the traditional elm has done, to some as yet unknown blight. If Sapporo proves a success it would take half a century to replace the 15m elms which have died in the past 10 years of the so-called Dutch elm disease.

Peculiar attitude

Commenting on the above, W.H. Brown FIWSc points out that Britain has adopted a peculiar attitude to the elm tree for many years. Its timber was thought suitable for coffins and fence posts but no one thought seriously of using it for high-class furniture until a few years ago. On the one hand, elm trees are unpopular for a number of reasons, — mainly because they are shallow-rooted and easily blown down, and liable to shed their limbs during gales. On the other hand, because they appear everywhere as hedgerow trees and have a beautiful form when mature, no painter or photographer of note would envisage a pastoral scene without one or more elms being in evidence.

Over the last 100 years or more, there has never been any official attempt at perpetuating elms of any species in Britain in the sense of afforestation. Even now, 10 years after the last epidemic of Dutch elm

disease, it is a private company taking the initiative of experimental planting of possible disease-resistant species, with the blessing of the Ministry of Agriculture and Forestry Commission.

Whether of indigenous or introduced species, elm trees have been in Britain since the Roman occupation and, until the present time, elm timber has been one of the least costly hardwoods with a multitude of uses — from water conduit pipes laid down by the Romans to beautiful furniture. Is it not strange that a wood capable of being buried in the soil for centuries as a water pipe and finally dug up sound (as was the case in London's Euston Road and Tottenham Court Road) a few years ago; and encouraging a move to solid wood suites instead of veneered chipboard (as was the case once it was appreciated that by proper handling and design elm made fine furniture), that no special attempt has been made to ensure elm trees, and their timber, for the future?

It is true that due to the Dutch elm disease, there is available in Britain many thousands of cum of good elm timber and, despite the wide range of potential use, insufficient demand to utilise the wood quickly. But this is a problem of today and not of the future. We use elm for dock and harbour work; sea defences; boat building; vehicle bottoms; flooring; furniture; turnery; woodware; fencing and constructional purposes. It does not mean these uses cannot be fulfilled by alternative timber species — they can, but generally by imported hardwoods. It seems to be a straight choice between spending more money in the future to import more costly hardwoods, or spending a little extra money now to help support our own economy by calling for experimental work to be carried out, possibly by one of the universities on hybrid forms of elms or suitable alternative species, in order to help future generations.

For hundreds of years (and despite epidemics) we have fared very well from a tree which has appeared, almost like a weed, in our hedgerows; and where the most ambitious planting has been on large estates where avenues of elms have been grown.

Footnote: There is a further problem which the authorities seem loath to tackle. With all the elm timber lying around they are doing nothing about the young, but dead, elms left standing. These will progressively become host to all sorts of beetle pests, including *Lyctus* and *Anobium* (furniture beetle).

Kity distributors

More distributors have been appointed by Kity (UK) (WEF Woodworking Machinery Ltd), Sizer's Court, Henshaw Lane, Yeadon, Leeds LS19 7DP. The firms are: George Gardiner, Ballymoney Street, Ballymena, Co Antrim; Steenwise Ltd, James Street, Harrogate; Cecil W. Tyzack Ltd, Kingsland Road, London E2; Kenterprise Ltd, Camden Road, Tunbridge Wells; and Trend Machinery & Cutting Tools Ltd, Penfold Works, Imperial Way, Watford.

For its northern area Kity has appointed Wayne Given as salesman-demonstrator.

DRAT THAT DOOR!

G. R. Melton pays a snap visit to the merchant

I arrived home to find the door had been delivered while I'd been away on-site. But unfortunately it was not of the type I'd ordered. So here we were, faced with a bank-holiday weekend, no deliveries for nearly a week, pressing jobs waiting. I decided to nip in and change it on the Friday afternoon.

The day was sultry and oppressive. Black clouds loomed up but the journey was uneventful. I marched into the merchant's office and was confronted by staff scurrying back and forth. The 'looming-up of the holiday weekend' was much in evidence.

I explained to the nearest assistant my mission: I merely wished to exchange the door. How innocent I must have been.

'Where is your green slip,' he asked? To which I replied that I had had no time to change and had come in dressed for work as usual. The assistant remained completely unmoved by such frivolity but condescended to look it up later.

He despatched me to the door department. Here I was confronted by banks of doors, masses and masses, seried ranks of them. 'I want a solid door, no openings for glass,' I explained. 'Yes,' said the storekeeper, 'hardboard flush?' 'No,' I replied, 'I need an exterior door.' 'Oh yes, pattern 50.' This turned out to be a Georgian 15-light door — worse and worse. 'But we don't get asked for solid doors now,' he said.

Anyway I prowled around and found a heap of what they laughingly call 'framed, ledged and braced.' These have to be seen to be believed. No wonder Britain is on the long downhill run. 'Why don't we get them from Japan,' I asked? This time I extracted a loud guffaw from the storekeeper, evidently made of sterner stuff than his office colleague.

I resigned myself to accepting the only apparent solution to the problem and returned to the office. I explained to the sober-faced assistant what I had done. 'We shall have to adjust it on our invoice so I must check the details and price.' Whereupon he reached for an imposing catalogue. Minutes ticked by, pages flicked back and forth. Eventually he looked up bewildered. 'I can't find it,' he confessed.

The clock was ticking on. 'Let me have a look,' I said. He pushed it across to me with that 'I suppose there is nothing to lose' look on his face. The others were clearing desks and counters. A man rattled a bunch of keys impatiently.

Eventually I found the door in question, only to discover that it was not on the price list at all.

I'd spent nearly a whole hour on the premises changing one door. I departed bewildered — and clutching several different coloured forms!

workpieces

Adhesives directory

In pocket-size the *Adhesive Directory 1979-80* contains 206 pages and an adhesives selection chart. More than 50 different adhesives classified by basic types are listed, together with nearly 200 end uses and over 1,000 different trade names. Other sections deal with plant and equipment and raw materials.

Published by A.S. O'Connor & Co Ltd, 26 Sheen Park, Richmond TW9 1UW, the directory costs £4.25 inclusive of postage.

Hardware fittings

General hardware fittings are listed in a booklet issued by B. Lilly & Sons Ltd, Baltimore Road, Birmingham B42 1DJ. Details are given of bolts, hooks, hinges, window stays and handles, letter plates, finger plates, numerals, door handles, escutcheons, card frames and cupboard latches and fittings. Lilly supplies to builders merchants and hardware wholesalers.

Wrap up well—and not for winter only!

Those who read the following remarks may at first be inclined to recall the old saying about bolting the stable door . . . But to parry that we are, in a way, taking time by the forelock. What we want to do is to mention the packaging of entries received for the 1979 Ashley Iles — Woodworker carving competition.

It is unfortunate that several entries were received in damaged condition and therefore we remind future entrants that the Post Office has issued a leaflet *Wrap up well* which gives useful hints on packing for inland post. Copies are available from head postmasters.

For such items as carvings the box or container should be large enough to allow you to pack plenty of cushioning material round the carving on all sides. Crushed newspaper, corrugated cardboard, sawdust, wood wool, foamed plastics such as polystyrene are all good for this. Sponge rubber or plastics foam of the type used in upholstery are good too. Make a layer about 2in. thick between the carving and the sides of the box.

Fasten the package with adhesive tape and then with string. Make sure that it is clearly and accurately addressed and if you use a tie-on label use a stick-on label as well. Write your own name and address on the package (at right angles to the destination address). The cover of the package should be clearly marked FRAGILE HANDLE WITH CARE (you can get labels from your post office).

It is advisable to pay a compensation fee at the time of posting and obtain the appropriate document from the counter clerk. A compensation fee is not in itself a safeguard against damage in course of transmission. 'Compensation fee' parcels are carried in mail bags like other postal packages and therefore must be packed carefully.

If you are in any doubt about packing do have a word with your post office first.

We hope these remarks will help to avoid disappointment in any future competitions which involve the sending of readers' work through the post.

Musical guild

With an address at Chester Walk, Cheltenham, Glos, the Guild of Luthiers & Pipemakers has been formed on a commercial basis. Retail and exhibition facilities are being established together with a register of members and a slide register of members' work. The guild embraces all musical instruments and seeks to promote the use of contemporary quality instruments. It is also stated to be 'an information-sharing system.'

Disabled professionals

Disabled people are reliable, loyal, conscientious and productive workers. This is one of the general conclusions in a review of research into the performance of disabled people. It has been carried out by Dr Melvyn Kettle of the University of Aston in Birmingham for the Association of Disabled Professionals. Copies of the review can be had from the association's general secretary at The Stables, 73 Pound Road, Banstead, SM7 2HU, at £2.50 including postage.

Fairs this year

Woodworking machinery fairs loom large in 1980. The 4th International Woodworking Industries Exhibition (IWIE) takes place between 25 and 29 November in hall 1 of the National Exhibition Centre, Birmingham. In adjacent halls 6 and 6A the specialist ASFI show will be held. This will feature materials, accessories, components and services to the furniture, upholstery and bedding industry.

At the same time the BFMA furniture show will be held at the National Exhibition Centre.

European woodworking machinery fairs this year include France (April), Italy (Interbimal) (May), Denmark (September), Switzerland (October), Spain and Austria (November). There are something like 800 firms in Europe making woodworking machinery. In North America there are two shows during 1980 — Atlanta and Louisville — to cater for the large number of manufacturers in that continent. The Japanese also have a machinery show.

Model vehicles

The September-October 1979 issue of the Model Horse-Drawn Vehicles Club *Newsletter* (no. 41) gives useful hints on coopering in connection with making a model water cart. There is also a reference to protection against inhaling wood dust (a subject considered in WOODWORKER for October 1979 on page 579). The *Newsletter* mentions an old rully 'in very good condition and still being used' near Kirkbymoorside which was seen by a member of the club who made a note of the dimensions and constructional details.

Secretary of the MH-DVC is John Pearce, 4 Brentlea Crescent, Higher Heysham LA3 2BY, Lancashire.

Kitchen furniture

Draft code of practice for kitchen furniture has been finalised by the kitchen furniture liaison committee which meets under the auspices of the British Woodworking Federation. General objects of the code, which has been sent to the OFT for approval, are given as: to set out guidelines relating to good trading practices; to enhance product quality and service given to customers; to provide practical guidance in relation to manufacture and trading.

British Woodworking Federation has its office at 82 New Cavendish Street, London W1M 8AD.

Uses for wood byproduct

Mention on page 495 of September 1979 WOODWORKER relating to the number of wood-processing plants using byproducts such as sawdust, chips and offcuts as fuel, has prompted Parkinson Cowan GWB Ltd., PO Box 4, Dudley, West Midlands DY3 2AD, to send details of a system supplied to Worcester Furniture Co to generate 15,000 lb/hr of steam.

The boiler was installed in October 1978 to be fired by byproduct and fuel saving over the winter of 1978-9 is claimed to be in excess of £50,000.

At every point throughout the factory where byproduct is created in the manufacture of lounge furniture, sawdust and sander dust is collected by pneumatic suction and delivered to a 10ton capacity overhead bunker from where it is fed pneumatically to the boiler 200ft away. Offcuts are hogged to small size and fed into the system at the same time as the dust.

Some 30-40ton/wk of byproduct is used and the boiler is provided with alternative oil firing for start-up. Worcester Furniture is considering using steam from the boiler for process work and thus effecting further energy saving by reducing the amount of electricity at present used.

On the same page in September we also referred to sawdust briquettes as a possible addition to the solid fuel source. A machine for making briquettes is produced by the Swiss firm of F. Hausmann AG, Hammerstrasse 46, CH-4005, Basle. In smaller workshops the woodburning stoves (now widely advertised for domestic heating) could have application for disposal of, for example, offcuts. But before making an installation it is well to check with one's insurers, and to have the job done by a reputable heating firm.

1½in. blade chisel

The Marples 1½in. blade Blue Chip chisel is re-introduced to the M444 bevel-edge range. Thus Blue Chip chisels are now available in individual sizes from ⅛in. to 1½in., the most popular sizes being also offered in sets of four or five.

The blades are designed to give clearance for fine cabinet work while being of sufficient strength for general purpose work. Handles are of square section — to prevent rolling off the bench — and contoured for comfort in the hand.

The Marples brand name is in the Record Ridgway Tools Ltd 'family'. Full details from the company at Parkway Works, Sheffield S9 3BL (0742 449066), or stockists.

The company has issued a leaflet featuring selected Record and Marples tools most likely to be appreciated as Christmas gifts.

49th Model Engineer Exhibition, Wembley.

AN IMPORTANT MESSAGE FOR VISITORS.

If you are thinking about buying a machine tool, don't, until you have visited <u>Cowells Machine Shop</u> at Wembley.

You'll find high quality precision-engineered machines and accessories on show.

We will as usual have something new for you to see.

It may well be what you are looking for. Come along and see, you'll be very welcome.

Cowell Engineering Limited

Stand 24

MINIATURE CHAIRS FROM THE CHILTERNS

Stuart King makes for world markets
David Askham has been to find out something of the techniques used by Stuart in 1/12 scale furniture-making

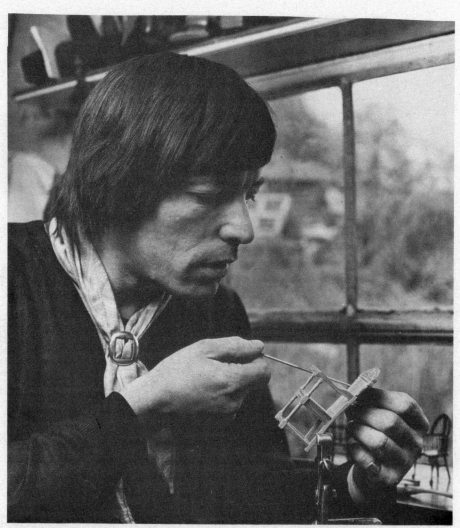

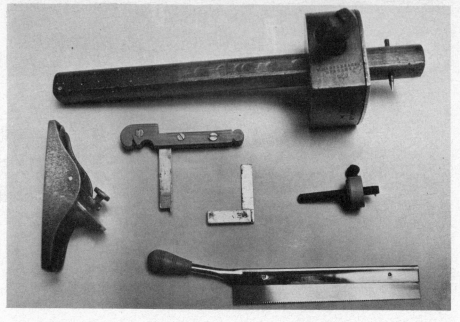

Top right: Stuart King putting the finishing touches to a chair in Japanese oak; a copy of a late Elizabethan/early Jacobean design. Above: A thimble gives an idea of the size of this classical Windsor chair, circa 1760-1780, made of yew. Right: Selection of Stuart King's tools showing centre left: a miniature scratch stock, centre right: a marking gauge with the full-size version above.

Right: Stuart King turning tiny utensils for a miniature dresser. Below: A dresser made of North American pencil cedar; a copy of a German Pennsylvanian dresser, although it is very similar in style to the Welsh dresser. On the shelves stand miniature yewtree turned objects, bowls, spoons and cups, turned on his lathe.

Above: A miniature chair of modern design — Jubilee chair.

Right: Worktable with hinged top inlaid with various woods; notably a miniature marquetry shell with rosewood cross banding around the edges of the table top. A copy of a Regency table.

Above: Stuart King's hat, worn at shows and exhibitions, typically decorated with some of his miniatures.

Above: A 150-year-old marquetry cutter's donkey in use cutting a back piece for a settee. Top right: Miniature saw cutting a piece of mahogany moulding. Below: Stuart King operating the 150-year-old marquetry cutter's donkey.

Most woodworkers are inspired to their craft by the need for functional furniture or a special design unobtainable from commercial sources. Rising costs are also a factor but, primarily there is the joy of fashioning an article whether it is for utility or pleasure, with their own hands from wood. Chairmaking appeals to many people but the replication of antique furniture calls for rather more than novice skills if the end results are to bear comparison with the renowned originals. But what about miniature versions; are they easier? I recently went to find out from Stuart King of Holmer Green near High Wycombe in Buckinghamshire. He is one of the experts in this country whose products are sought by discerning buyers at home and abroad.

Born in the Chilterns he became interested in local history at an early age. He was fascinated by the famous Windsor chairs for which the High Wycombe manufacturers

had earned an enviable name for quality. Stuart traced the origins of the craft from the chair bodgers who operated as two or three-man concerns with their woodland workshops and foot-driven pole lathes. While the beechwoods remain, the chair bodgers have been overtaken by modern methods of furniture making.

As a result of his interest and research, Stuart developed an expertise which led to a demand for his services as a lecturer to local colleges, schools and business groups. At the same time he engaged in restoring antique furniture as a pastime, and thus his first-hand knowledge grew. He illustrated his lectures not only with photographs but with full-size specimens of furniture so as to bring the subject 'alive'.

Then it occurred to him that the transport of his specimens could be eased if he could obtain scale models. These were not readily available at a price he could afford so he resolved to make some for himself. Hence his first ¼-scale model of a comb-back Windsor chair. Further models followed and, somewhat to his surprise, audiences became very interested in them and a demand steadily grew for copies. So, from that unpredictable beginning 15 years ago, his miniature furniture making activities expanded until in 1973 he left his employment as a marquetry veneer matcher and set up a one-man enterprise near Holmer Green, in the Chiltern woodlands.

Stuart is proud that he is self-taught in his craft. But do not underestimate the long hours of study and hard work that go into perfecting his miniatures. Good design is the essential starting point and this calls for a thorough understanding of the design, materials and constructional techniques of the originals. As most of his work is based on precise scaling-down of antique furniture, he has pored over old books, especially those written at the beginning of this century, and visited museums to examine rare specimens.

Originally he built to ¼-size scale but since 1977 he has concentrated on the scale of $1/12$ which is popular in this country and the US. Queen Anne, Chippendale, Hepplewhite, Sheraton and Robert Mainwaring are the principal designs he builds. Modern furniture does not feature in his range. Indeed nothing later than the Regency period is built. His models are mainly English, a few Welsh and some American designs for trans-Atlantic customers.

Traditional furniture-making wood is used: oak, walnut, mahogany, boxwood, ebony, rosewood, cherry and elm. About half his wood Stuart obtains from old furniture which has the matured colour that comes, convincingly, with age. Some of the oak comes from old beams. But it is not always possible to scale-down the grain size of English oak, so where this feature is important he uses Japanese oak which looks more authentic.

Finish of the furniture is important. Not only must the pieces look attractive, they must be pleasant to touch and feel. An authentic and distinctive finish marks out the superlative from the commonplace; highly varnished miniatures lack the patina of quality antiques. (He has developed a formula for finishing but, since his livelihood depends upon holding his place in a discerning market, he is understandably reluctant to reveal one of this trade secrets.) The workshop contains the basic woodwoorking tools and a collection of antique tools which, he claims, provide the authentic touch of nostaligia to inspire him in his work. But neither modern nor antique tools are sufficient in themselves. The cutting and shaping of tiny pieces of wood calls for tiny tools which are not stocked by dealers. Some modelling tools like the X-Acto range he has adapted to suit his purpose better, but a number of tools he has designed for his special needs, such as a miniature scratch stock, marking gauge, spokeshave and saw. The marking gauge is 5cm long.

In the scaling down of traditional joints Stuart says that economics have a big influence on whether the more complicated joints are replicated in scale, exactly like the originals. All visible joints are always accurately scaled, but the cost of doing so for hidden joints can seldom be justified. If customers wish to pay the extra cost he can use scale joints throughout. His Windsor chairs all have authentic joints but since load-bearing is not a consideration with miniature furniture adapted joints cause no impairment to the final product.

How long does it take to make a miniature chair or table? There is no simple answer to this question because designs vary so much; chairs can take anything from one to 14 days depending upon the degree of complexity.

Who buys miniature furniture? 'No one type of person', says Stuart King. 'A football team bought some to present to their continental opponents; specimens have been commissioned to give to royalty and other famous people and many become personal souvenirs'. Waiting time is about three months at present but some pieces are held in stock by The Singing Tree in London's New Kings Road, by an antique shop in Los Angeles and a boutique in Pasadena, US. Prices range from £7.50 to £50 and nearly half his production goes overseas.

His personal collection includes many for exhibition purposes, such as a set-piece illustrating one of his ¼-scale Windsor chairs purporting to be the handiwork of a figurine representing 'Jack' Goodchild, acknowledged as one of the most outstanding Windsor chair-makers in the Chilterns. He lived at Naphill near High Wycombe and died in 1950 at the age of 65. Stuart commissioned this figure from Bedford craftsman Dennis Fairweather. There is also a set-piece model drawing room, mid-18th century, commissioned by the Central Office of Information for use overseas.

Stuart King's love of wood and fine craftsmanship is evident in the way he has tastefully integrated some old timbers into his living room. His skill and example has not gone unnoticed by his two young sons who, having acquired their own tools have already started to make small items for themselves.

TIMBER TOPICS 6

W.H. Brown FIWSc continues his series on the conditioning of timber. In part 5 (October 1979 issue) he explained the reasons why wood tends to distort and split during drying and below he enlarges on this aspect insofar as it applies to round sections sawn from the ends of logs, or tree discs. The next Topic will give details of the drying method based on research carried out in the US and said to produce excellent results.

In preceding Topics we have referred to the development of stresses in wood both as the result of growth and of removal of moisture and have said that unbalanced stresses are responsible for distortion and splitting in wood as it dries. It is now pertinent to the general discussion to enlarge a little on this aspect insofar as it applies to round sections sawn from the ends of logs, or tree discs.

Tree discs are much sought after and are used for steak plates; salad and fruit bowls; flower pots; ash trays; and other novelty items — and when large enough for table tops. The biggest problem in trying to dry these sections is their distinct liability to spilt. Since the problem is universal, experiments have been carried out at the University of Wisconsin in the US to try to find a method of drying these sections without the use of a drying kiln in such a way as to prevent degrade occurring.

The research was carried out under the direction of associate Professor Hans Kubler and was based on the thesis that when a tree stem is crosscut, this relieves longitudinal growth stresses and converts them into tangential tension forces near the ends of logs: consequently, discs cut from the ends of logs usually develop V-shaped splits (Fig. 1a).

In theory, drying tree discs without defects should be easy as moisture can diffuse evenly in the fibre direction to the cut faces; but in practice, the wood around the pith of the tree does not shrink by the same percentage tangentially and radially (Fig. 2); and significant circumferential or tangential tension occurs which can trigger-off the forming of V-shaped cracks.

During the growth of a tree complicated stresses build up, and what are called primary tangential growth stresses in the direction of the growth rings, create compression near the bark. This causes tension in the core (Fig. 3). The tension stress in the inner third of the stem increases toward the pith and becomes greater as the tree grows in diameter until the material fails (Fig. 1b), usually when the diameter reaches about 2ft (60cm) in dense wood species and 3 or 4ft (91 or 121cm) in low density species.

It is essential at this point to understand that primary tangential growth stresses contribute to the formation of heart checks (Fig. 1b). These run from the pith outwards toward the bark, as opposed to the V-shaped cracks which start from the bark and extend inwards (Fig. 1a) and which are produced, or are initiated, by secondary longitudinal growth stresses.

It should be noted that failure of the wood due to tension stress in the centre portion of the stem begins the formation of a heart check when the stem is about 2ft (60cm) in diameter in dense wood species. This would be rather small for, say, a table top, but it is probably larger than the average size generally used by the comparative amateur. One must not be misled into thinking that tree discs of smaller diameter will not develop heart checks, because the stress is still present.

Hearts checks may be present in the growing tree and be visible on the end of a felled log, or they may occur when the tree is felled and hits the ground. On the other hand there may be no visible sign of heart checking; but this natural tendency for tangential growth stresses to develop in a tree must be taken into account and the potential breaking force countered by appropriate measures designed to prevent splitting, when considering suitable methods of drying.

We have mentioned that the difference between tangential and radial shrinkage in the centre portion of the core of the wood plays a large part in starting off V-shaped cracks. Beech and elm are awkward timbers in that sense, beech shrinking by 9.5% tangentially and 4.5% radially, and elm 6.5% and 4.5% respectively, by comparison with teak whose shrinkage values are 2.5% and 1.5% respectively.

In the context of sawn wood, ie in board form, if its wide surface is truly tangential (with the growth rings roughly parallel with the surface), then its shrinkage potential from the green, wet state to a dry one is greater than if that same wood was cut to give a surface with a true radial plane, ie with the growth rings roughly vertical to the wide

surfaces, approximately to the values given above.

In the sense of sawn boards, however, although beech would be said to have large movement and teak small movement, this can quite easily be taken into account and allowed for in use, because all the major growth stresses have been broken down or relieved by sawing the boards from the log; and any splitting or cracking of the wood during conversion would have been rejected by cutting out or by grading.

With round discs sawn from the end of logs it is a different matter: the greatest force exerted by differences in tangential and radial growth is potentially much higher in the smaller area of the inner portion of the tree stem, roughly one-third of the stem area. Accordingly, either the stem develops a heart check while growing or it does not. In this much depends upon the tree species and the diameter of the tree, but even with a seemingly sound disc free from visible checks, the growth stresses are still present particularly the primary tangential stress. It is this that has especially to be subdued in drying in order to prevent heart checks to occur and so weaken the wood and open up the way for V-shaped cracks to start.

In Kubler's experiments, studies were first made of the method of cutting discs from a log in order to ascertain whether or not this had much effect on relieving stress. It was found that sawing the logs into short sections relieved some of the growth stresses, so that when these were now cut into discs alternately from either end there was less tendency for heart checks to occur. This was only a partial help. It was also found that ellipse-shaped sections cut obliquely to the stem axis checked and cracked less than circular discs, as checking increases with the angle between the plane of the cut and the stem axis (Fig. 4).

Thickness, too, was found to be important; discs dry with least defects if they are small in diameter and thin although there is a limit. Very thin discs will warp even under the most equable drying conditions, while in thick discs the slow drying of the deeper wood layers restrains surface shrinkage and causes surface stresses. The minimum thickness recommended is approximately ½in. (12.5mm) for discs 1ft (30cm) in diameter; 1in. (25mm) for 2ft (60cm) discs; and 1½in. (38mm) for 4ft (120cm) discs.

In the next Topic we will give details of the drying method which was said to produce excellent results.

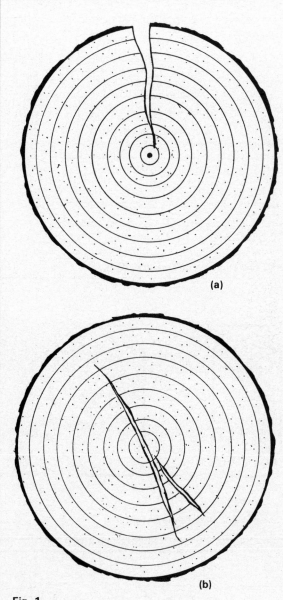

Fig. 1.

(a) V-shaped drying crack; (b) heart check. Heart checks are initiated in the tree in the inner part of the stem: if the stresses that cause them are not subdued during drying, they encourage the development of V-cracks.

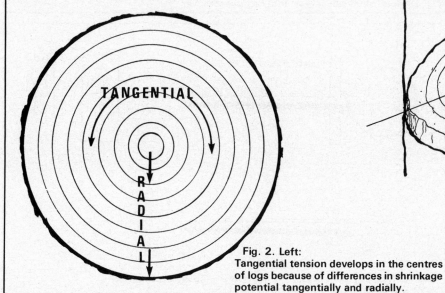

Fig. 2. Left:
Tangential tension develops in the centres of logs because of differences in shrinkage potential tangentially and radially.

BARK

TENSION

COMPRESSION

PITH

Fig. 3.
Trees develop primary tangential growth stresses, ie in the direction of the growth rings; compression is created near the bark thus causing tension in the core.

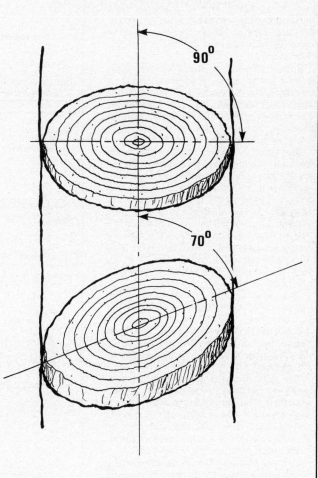

Fig. 4. Above:
By reducing the angle between the plane of the cut and the axis of the tree, splitting and cracking of discs is reduced during drying.

The Yorkshire Light

The Yorkshire light is not a variation of the *aurora borealis,* nor is it a local delicacy! It is a window often used in the bedrooms of that county's dale cottages. Charles Cliffe describes here how to make this window which, he says, is perfectly weather-tight and when secured by a thumbscrew cannot be forced as easily as a vertically sliding sash.

The Yorkshire light is a straightforward window to make and is thoroughly satisfactory in use. It comprises an outer frame set in the brick or stonework in the usual way. One half of the frame is glazed while the other half is a sliding sash running on a metal bar let into the sill. It is perfectly weathertight and when secured by a thumbscrew cannot be forced as easily as a vertically-sliding sash. As the window is much wider than it is high the sash could not operate vertically and is made to slide horizontally. Such windows are often used in the bedrooms of dales cottages, the more usual vertical sash being fitted to ground-floor rooms.

Both the head and the sill of the main frame run through and the stiles are tenoned into them. The sill should be of hardwood but the other components are usually of softwood. A rebate is worked in the head and stiles for the sash to slide in and the sill is ploughed to take the metal runner.

The sash is made from 2 × 2in. sash material. The stiles run through and the top and bottom rails are tenoned into them and scribed to fit the mouldings. A putty groove is usually worked in the left-hand stile of the sash instead of a rebate; this simplifies glazing. If the upright bar in the centre of the frame and the left-hand stile of the sash are constructed as in Fig. 2 (a) or splayed as in (b) they will need to be planed from 2 × 2½ in. stuff. If using 2 × 2in. it will be necessary to nail beads as in (c).

To enable the sash to slide easily in the frame, metal shoes (Fig. 3) are let into the bottom rail which is ploughed to accommodate the metal runner. The shoes ride on this runner and save wear and tear of the sill and the sash. The runner also acts as a water bar.

The main frame is made from 5 × 2in. material mortised, tenoned and scribed shoulders. The upright bar is stub-tenoned and scribed. It was usual to paint the joints and wedges with red lead just prior to assembly but as red lead is now rarely seen a good waterproof glue should be used.

The sash is retained by beads, mitred at the corners, being nailed to the inner faces of the main frame.

When closed the sash is securely fastened by a thumbscrew and front plate (Fig. 4) which passes through the centre of the left-hand stile of the sash and screws into a plate and nut let into the fixed upright bar.

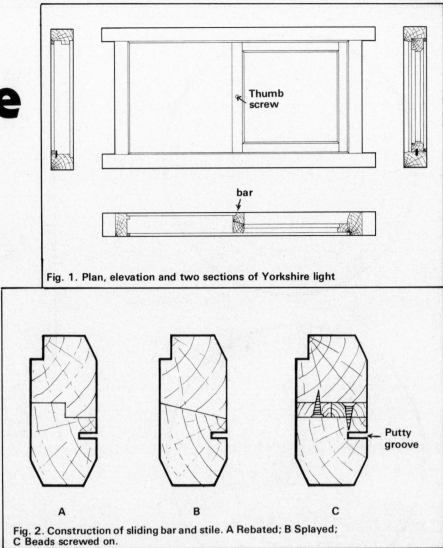

Fig. 1. Plan, elevation and two sections of Yorkshire light

Fig. 2. Construction of sliding bar and stile. A Rebated; B Splayed; C Beads screwed on.

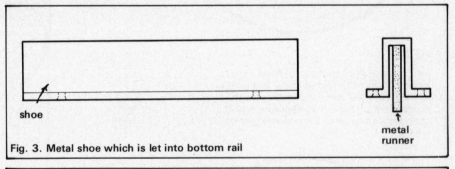

Fig. 3. Metal shoe which is let into bottom rail

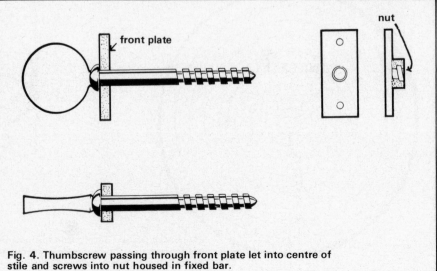

Fig. 4. Thumbscrew passing through front plate let into centre of stile and screws into nut housed in fixed bar.

Steenwise Ltd.

TOOLS FOR CRAFTSMEN

Steenwise policy is to supply high quality machines, produced in UK and Europe, by well known manufacturers at the best possible price.

We normally deliver within seven days from receiving your order. Payment can be cash with order, cash on delivery, or any of the well known credit cards and we also operate a confidential hire purchase scheme with attractive rate of interest.

We will be pleased to quote for any machine or accessory, and we are sure you will be surprised at the prices we can offer. Trade enquiries will be most welcome.

Below are some examples from our current price list. For further information send the coupon or 'phone us direct on Harrogate (0423) 61403.

Planer Thicknesser
10'' × 6'' Scheppach HM1 2 H.P. Motor, Floor Standing – £399.00.
10'' × 6'' Kity 7136 1½ H.P. Motor, Floor Standing – £564.00.
6'' × 4'' Kity 7139 1½ H.P. Motor, Floor Standing – £339.00.

Band Saws
Kity 7212 – £299.00.

Circular Saws
Kity 5017 2¼'' depth of cut ¾ H.P. – £169.00.
Maffell Site Saw 3½'' depth of cut 2.3 H.P. (Galvonised) – £159.00.

Special Offer
● Kity 5020 Combination – consisting of a planer thickness or spindle moulder and slot mortiser. Recommended man. price £662.40, Steenwise price £500 including free double ended 5'' bench grinder.

● Kity Lathe 6636 3 speed, floor standing model. Recommended man. price £358.80, Steenwise price £312.00 including six free Sorby wood turning tools.

● Kity 6646 variable speed, floor standing, recommended man. price £481.85, Steenwise price £449.00 including a free 5'' double ended bench grinder and six Sorby wood turning tools.

● Kity 10 × 6 planer thicknesser 7136 and dust extractor 695, recommended man. price £940 .81, Steenwise price £647.50 including hose and attachments. All prices include VAT at 15%.

- -

Please send me more information about Steenwise stocks and prices.

Name ....

Address ....

....

36b James Street, Harrogate HG1 1RF Telephone (0423) 61403
Showroom & warehouse
Limefield Mills, Wood Street, Crossflats, Bingley, West Yorks.

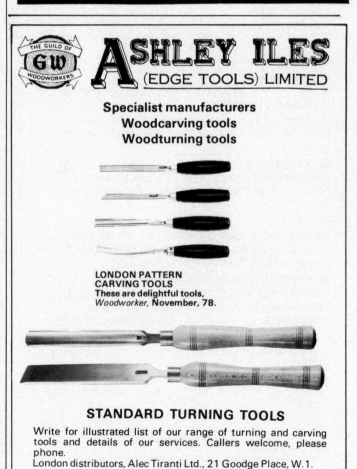
Prices quoted are those prevailing at press date and are subject to alteration due to economic conditions.

A -- Z OF HAND TOOLS

In the December issue John Sainsbury dealt with the various types of cramps. In this part of the series he explains the different kinds of cutting gauge. The next part will consider dowel bits.

Wherever possible in the series references have been made in general terms as regards manufacturers' products. Readers wishing to add to the information published are invited to write to the editor.

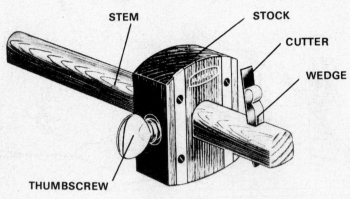

STEM   STOCK

CUTTER

WEDGE

THUMBSCREW

CUTTING GAUGE

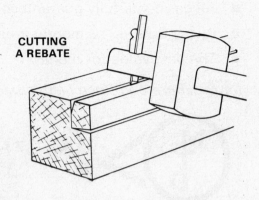

CUTTING A REBATE

The cutting gauge is a little used, but extremely useful tool, not only for marking-out but for a number of other applications. It consists of a stem near one end of which is fitted a tiny cutter held in place by a brass wedge. A stock slides along the stem and can be fixed in any position relative to the cutter by means of a small plastics thumbscrew. The timber used is beech and the face of the stock is protected against wear with two brass strips.

Unlike the spur of the marking gauge, the cutter of the cutting gauge is designed to sever the fibres across the grain. It is therefore ideal for marking lines which have to be cut with the saw or chisel as in dovetailing. It is also an excellent tool for marking lines across end grain.

Position of the cutter depends on the job, but flat edge should be vertical in the stem.

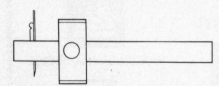

When veneering, inlaying or banding, by reversing the cutter for the second cut, the gauge cuts perfect limit lines and the waste between is removed with a small chisel or scratch stock, to receive the inlay, banding or stringing.

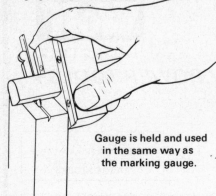

Gauge is held and used in the same way as the marking gauge.

Cutting gauge used for cutting and gauging across the grain of timber, eg depth of dovetails in a half lap dovetail joint, trimming veneer, small rebates, cutting strings, or for cutting difficult grain before rebating.

When marking out a groove the cutter is reversed.

Small rebates can also be cut to receive decorative edging strips.

As with all other cutting tools, the cutter must be perfectly sharpened. Many users re-shape the cutter. The essential feature is that it should cut with a slicing action.

GRINDING OF CUTTER BLADE

The blade can be ground with a curve as A and B to give a diamond point C as needed.

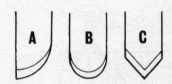

A   B   C

HISTORICAL

Cutting gauges a 100 years ago were made in beech and rosewood. The Marples M2096 was hooped at the working end in brass to reduce wear. The cutter was firmly held by a screw inserted at the end of the stem. The oval stock was faced completely in brass; ebony was used throughout.

2096 — Ebony improved cutting gauge.

2110 — Beech combined pencil-marking and cutting gauge.

An interesting gauge having the cutter held with a wedge permitted the holding of a pencil, using the end screw similar to the 2096.

WORK WITH
ELEKTRA

Bench Grinders with Drill

Bench Saws

Nail Guns

Lathes

RECOMMENDED RETAIL PRICE
ONLY £515.00 + V.A.T.

Planer - thicknessing machine HC 260

■ Die cast aluminium body throughout.
Webbed surfacing table for strength (10″ x 6″).

■ Twin knife cutter block.

■ Easy conversion from surfacing to thicknessing.
No tools required.

■ Easy adjustment of thicknessing bed by handwheel via 4 spindles.

■ Anti-kick back fitted for safety.

■ Powerful single-phase 2½ H.P. integral induction motor.
Interchangeable with other ELEKTRA woodworking machines.

■ Bench or stand mounted for site working.

This planer-thicknesser is just one of a range of fine quality, competitively priced, ELEKTRA woodworking machines that offer the craftsman greater scope in project design and construction.

The TOOLMARK for quality

ELEKTRA BECKUM

For further information and the name of your nearest stockist please write to the address below.

ELEKTRA BECKUM U.K.

(A division of the J.O.C. Group of Companies)
184/185 Headquarters Road, West Wilts Trading Estate, Westbury, Wiltshire.
Telephone: (0373) 865017   Telex 995701.

SHAVINGS FROM A VILLAGE WHEELWRIGHT'S SHOP

Traditional milking stools, left and right, the centre one is suitable for milking a goat.

The old-time craftsman who could undertake all sorts of jobs around the village and neighbourhood is still very much with us. Here Mrs Jocelyn Bailey tells of some jobs which her husband has done in his wheelwright and carpenter's shop in an east Kent village.

In my husband's family wheelwright and carpenter's shop a great variety of jobs is undertaken. Recent ones have included traditional-style milking stools for a collector of bygones; a Wendy house for a customer's grandchildren; entrance gates and fencing for a riding school.

However, it is stories of long-past domestic and agricultural needs which hold even more appeal today. For example, the simple wooden copper-lids once needed in every country home. Not so simple, though, to make. Wooden pegs had to be used in constructing them, as screws would stain the clothes being washed in the copper. The specialist carpenter would like to taper and dovetail the crossboards and handle. The lid would be made up in a rough square or oblong to start with, and then the whole assembly cut to a round with a pad or bandsaw at final stage. The diameter had to be accurate so that the lid would just fit over the rim of the copper but not on to the brick surround. Apprentices were often set to making copper-lids because they could learn a number of woodworking skills without too much outlay of expensive wood, deal being suitable for copper lids.

On the agricultural side, making the early horse-drawn seed-drills was just one part of the wheelwright's contribution to farming history. Jethro Tull's 18th century idea of a machine to bury the seed in rows was to eventually become acceptable in farming circles so displacing the somewhat wasteful broadcast method of sowing.

Old-time copper-lid seen recently at a farmhouse.

Suffolk drill in action. *By courtesy of The University of Reading, Museum of English Rural Life.*

COPPER LIDS AND SEED DRILLS

Individually-designed versions of the seed-drill were made by village wheelwrights and blacksmiths. Even when patented drills were made by factory methods they would subsequently need attention at the wheelwright's shop or the forge. The Suffolk drill, for example, was a large, heavy machine, and the big wooden wheels would be sent to the local shop for repairs.

Some early drills had large square brushes in the seed box to control the flow of seed being picked up by little brass cups set in a wooden roller; often the brushes needed renewing and the carpenter did this by wiring-in hog bristle imported from Russia. This bristle later became unobtainable and ordinary paint-brush bristle had to be used instead, but this was never so hardwearing. The basic ideas built into the old seed-drills can often be clearly traced in today's all-metal, all-purpose drills.

Agricultural history is now explained so delightfully at farm museums and farm parks dotted about the country. One useful guide is *Farm Museums and Farm Parks* by Shirley Toulson, published by Shire Publications Princess Risborough, Bucks, at 60p. The visitor who inspects the wheelwrighting or blacksmithing exhibits at some of these museums will reflect on the many different things the village craftsmen had to make or repair for customers in addition to the more obvious jobs of making and maintaining horse-drawn vehicles or shoeing horses. The old domestic scenes, too, are often set up in folk museums, and reflect the myriad of utilitarian objects made by carpenter and smith.

Broken wheel from an old Suffolk drill awaiting restoration.

Looking into the detachable seed-box of a very old Kent pattern seed-drill. Brass cups set in the wooden pick-up roller can just be seen; they collect seed and drop it down the spouts leading to the shares which cut rows through the soil. (Bottom left).

Close-up view of two of the brushes on the same Kent drill. (Bottom right).

Hugh Blogg explains how he OVERCOMES A TURNING PROBLEM

JURY-RIG

There are times when jobs are too long for your lathe. If you do not have access to another with a longer bed then the thing to do is to jury-rig a substitute tailstock.

This I have done on more than one occasion. I have fixed a chock, carrying a live or dead centre, to an adjacent wall. The only means of tightening the job between centres has been to tap the feet of the lathe towards the wall.

When I have needed to bore a 5ft hole through the length of a job I have fitted a hollow centre (a short length of threaded steel or brass tubing suffices, fashioned as in Fig. 1) into a stout board mounted in the bench vice. The lathe is slewed round on the floor to line-up with the hollow centre, the work set-up between centres and the boring done with the auger over the top of the bench as in Fig. 2.

The lathe and bench were necessarily heavy in this case. If turning had to be done, then an extended T-rest had to be made from a stiff batten fixed at the tail end to the board carrying the hollow centre.

Photographs show how a job, just an inch or so too long for the lathe was tackled. The job was the *lignum vitae* staff (placed against a grid of ½in. squares). The handle is separate from the shaft which was made on the bench using only a trying plane and a smoother; it was not turned in the lathe as many would think to be the obvious thing to do. (I once had a would-be student join my class solely to turn a fishing rod. He left when I advised against. He thought I was a 'nut'. I wish now I'd let him try!)

The only turning done on the shaft of the staff was for the pin which fitted into the turned handle; and at the bottom for the fitting of a ferrule 2½in. long in steel. The set-up for this is shown in the photograph, along with the extemporary tail centre.

The tail stock was removed and a chock of pine substituted. It carries a morse taper dead centre fitting tightly into a hole at centre height. The chock is 2 x 5 x 8in. with a 1½in. hole bored to take the head of a G-clamp which passed down between the ways and screws up against a pad of wood bridging the underside of the ways. Adjustment for tightening the work is achieved by judicious taps with the hammer at the foot of the chock.

Left: Lignum vitae staff. Right: showing temporary tailstock.

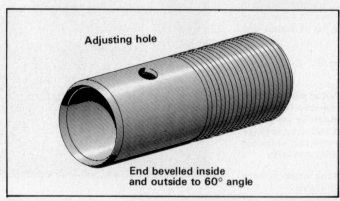

Adjusting hole

End bevelled inside and outside to 60° angle

Fig. 1. Threaded tube hollow centre.

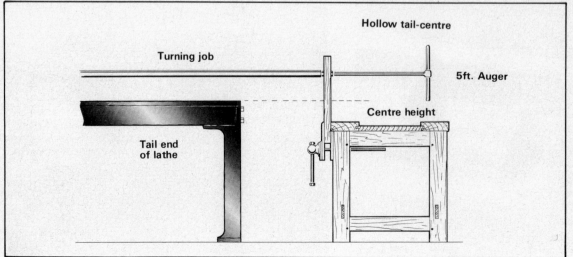

Turning job

Hollow tail-centre

5ft. Auger

Centre height

Tail end of lathe

Fig. 2. Showing jury-rigged extension tail-centre.

Woodworker

Record

Co-Editors: John Sainsbury
Geoffrey Pratt

No. 10 JANUARY 1980

A quarterly supplement for all in craft education

This supplement is issued free with WOODWORKER, the leading magazine for all concerned with traditional crafts in woodwork. Published monthly, annual subscription £8.40 ($19); Subs Dept, PO Box 35, Hemel Hempstead, Herts, HP1 1EE.

CORRESPONDENCE FOR THE ATTENTION OF JOHN SAINSBURY to: Record Ridgeway Education Dept, Parkway, Sheffield, Yorks, or for GEOFFREY PRATT to: Woodworker, PO Box 35 Bridge Street, Hemel Hempstead, Herts. All schools' Question Box correspondence should be sent direct to Mr. Sainsbury.

EQUIPMENT YOU CAN MAKE

by H. W. Gates

A setting-out pencil gauge is useful for making parallel lines of some length or lines greater than the range of a T-square. Another use is in marking the width of panels on plywood.

The gauge is made from two pieces of mahogany glued or screwed together. With plywood for the lath this can be varied in length to suit a larger dimension. Constructing the guide from two pieces enables the slot to be cut very neatly. The alternative method is using one piece and mortising.

Another item is the large square. For this sound, straight-grained hardwood such as mahogany is often used. The joint usually employed is a glued wedged mortise and tenon. The blade projects above the stock for marking-out purposes and so that the square can be re-trued if this becomes necessary.

A nib is shown at the lower end of the stock; this rests on the material to keep the square level.

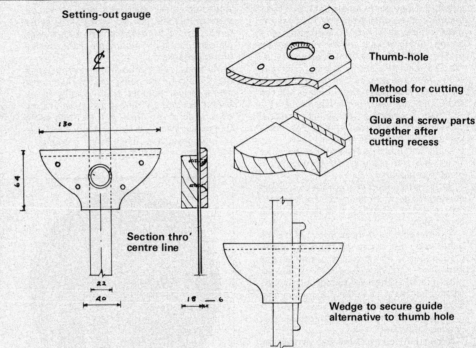

Setting-out gauge

Thumb-hole

Method for cutting mortise

Glue and screw parts together after cutting recess

Section thro' centre line

Wedge to secure guide alternative to thumb hole

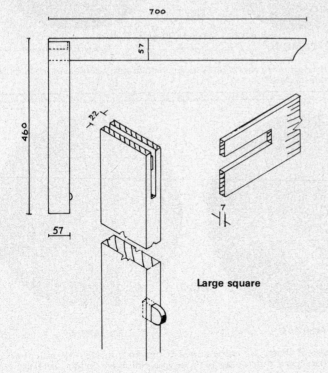

Large square

Above: The setting out gauge.
Left: The large square which can be made in mahogany.

VIOLIN WOODS

One afternoon 50-odd years ago, I was looking through a microscope at a section of wood I had laboriously cut and stained. I was startled by the voice of one of my superiors asking: 'How are these sections coming?' My answer was: 'Well, sir, this one is not perfect.' I remember his comment: 'Nothing is perfect, Bond.'

Many years later I made two ranks of organ pipes and, being fond of music, thought I had realised the ultimate in my woodworking ambitions. The pipes ranged from about 1in. to 8ft in speaking length and I thought they looked and sounded fine. But my sense of perfection was short-lived. The more I listened the more they seemed to vary among themselves in tonal quality and I was forced to the conclusion that it is easy to make a pipe, be it a flute, a diapason or a 'string'; but to make C and then C♯ in perfect tonal accord with each other is an art beyond me. However this, surely, is what craftwork is all about: and if we cannot reach the end of the rainbow of perfection I believe we can sometimes approach pretty close to it.

I had a passing sense of personal achievement in completing the pipes. Some years later, after making a third violin, I had to admit that much as I loved the 'organ', the violin and the making thereof gave even greater personal joy.

So I can heartily recommend violin making. To get a chunk of wood and carve it into a violin scroll is a most satisfying experience.

Another popular stringed instrument is the guitar and presumably the same, or similar, graduations in tonal quality are detectable here also. The plucked string, of course, gives a more evanescent sound; but a highly-trained ear must be equally discriminating, be the instrument played with a bow or a plectrum. My lack of familiarity forbids more positive comment.

Motivation comes to the fore in planning the making of any musical instrument. My interest was sparked off by work with different woods and I found myself asking the question: 'Now that we have the whole world's supply of many hundreds of woods to choose from, is there any guarantee that the old masters Stradivarius, Amati and the rest, really used the best toned wood for their violins?' Presumably they made those fine instruments out of what grew locally: maple, sycamore and the so-called Swiss pine, in reality a spruce.

Much has been written on the 'secret' of the ever-famous 'Strad' violins. Is it the wood, the varnish, the measurements, the climate, Antonio's skill or the happy convergence of them all? Perhaps both sentiment and cold cash come into it, too, not to mention personal idiosyncrasies; for what may be a source of profound inspiration to one listener may be commonplace to his neighbour.

Even so the wonderful variations to be seen in the anatomical structure of wood must surely have a bearing on the tone of a masterpiece which is (or should be?) every craftsman's dream.

I obtained a book as long ago as 1947 but soon found, indeed it was repeatedly stressed by the author, that only practical experience can make a violin; and no amount of detached reading can make up for 'having a go.'

Referring to wood structure and its relation to music, readers may care to have my view for what it is worth. I cannot help but think that the ray structure in wood has a bearing on vibration and tonal properties. Everyone knows that the large rays of oak form the 'figure' for which oak is so famous. Beech also has a finer, more subdued figure on radial or quarter-sawn surfaces and the same feature is quite readily seen, though even more subdued, in sycamore.

Now the rays of the rosewoods, African blackwood, the padauks and others of the Leguminosae, all noted for their tonal properties, are extremely small and regularly disposed. This led to the making of two violins the back plate and sides of which were of merbau, another wood of the same family, and a third instrument with a back plate of m'ninga or muninga a sister species of the padauks.

Muninga is very difficult to obtain but it has the distinction of being the world's most stable wood, another point, surely, in its favour for violins. (There is a story behind my own piece of muninga. A friend had some things sent to him from Africa and the packing-case was made from muninga! I soon made an offer for it.)

Since this violin's completion — it took me two years, I have sought to have it fairly assessed by competent judges. Perhaps they are too polite to be candid, after all, my name is not Antonio.

For an amateur, violin making is a very time-consuming hobby but for anyone in whom the urge is strong enough, research on the question of alternative species of wood might possibly be rewarding. It is of interest to note that one wood which was singled out as promising by me here in England had been likewise noted by a professional guitar maker who lives and works in the sunshine of the Mediterranean. Unfortunately, of all the irritating woods to work with this is one of the worst. Anyone who has used an abrasive paper on mansonia will know only too well what I mean. Even so mansonia has been noted for its resonance by the two of us working independently of each other, and if the rays of mansonia and the traditional sycamore are compared (Fig. 1), there is seen to be quite a difference. These photographs are from tangential sections ×60.

A few other woods come to my mind as possibilities worthy of trial. The two photographs (Fig. 2) are of merbau and

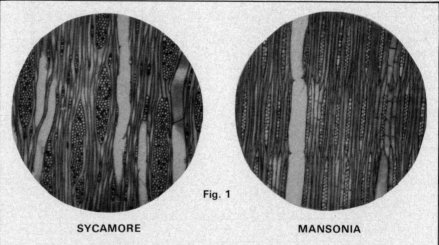

Fig. 1

SYCAMORE **MANSONIA**

The vessels of mansonia are very slightly larger in diameter, but the two would both be classed as fine-textured.

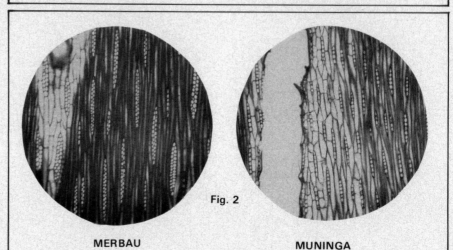

Fig. 2

MERBAU **MUNINGA**

The open texture of these two woods does not make for ease of working! What bearing the conspicuous thin-walled parenchyma cells have on tone, who knows?

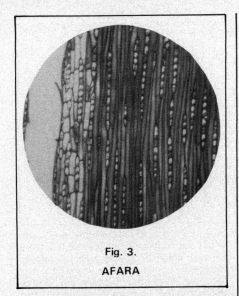

Fig. 3.

AFARA

LOOKING AT WOOD

W. H. Brown FIWSc discusses gymnosperms versus angiosperms

muninga, both of which illustrate the small rays characteristic of many woods of the Leguminosae. In the latter they are very small indeed and, like those of mansonia, arranged in storeys.

Another wood which on test suggested a high degree of resonance was afara, and it is worth noting that the rays of afara are also very fine and, like those of muninga, would be described as 'uniseriate', that is only one cell wide. (Fig. 3).

So much for four woods which may (or may not) show promise as alternatives for violin making. Merbau is from Sabah and elsewhere in the far east; mansonia and afara are west African, all three being available; but muninga, which occurs rather sparsely over equatorial Africa, may prove somewhat elusive.

The first violin, made as a trial instrument, was of merbau throughout except that the traditional Swiss 'pine' was used for corner blocks and for the soundboard or front plate or belly as it is variously called.

I understand that a hard back plate must be balanced against a softer front plate to give good tone, and wonder how this long-standing practice came about. Perhaps Jubal (*Genesis* chap. 4 verse 21) as 'the father of all such as handle the harp and organ' had something to do with it. Or it might have been before his time.

The extra weight of merbua (some 40% heavier than sycamore) proved eventually to be something of a problem, and this must be borne in mind; but any resourceful maker will have the wherewithal to minimise this drawback.

I decline to include in this article any practical suggestions on violin making for three reasons. Firstly, there are books available for those wishing to 'have a go'; secondly, every craftsmen has his own way of mastering the details of methods and tool operations; and thirdly, there are no doubt many readers of WOODWORKER who know more about this fascinating craft than I do.

One more point: old wood is generally considered to be preferable to new: and I have heard it said that mellowed wood is at its best for violins when it is 100 to 150 years old. At this rate should we find a better wood; our great-great-grandsons might well have their own secret!

However I personally consider the world-wide choice of woods now available, coming as it has long after the old masters' time, to be worthy of systematic experiment.

by C. W. BOND FIWSc

If we want to view wood with an intelligent eye, then we have to learn to relate common-place terms to meaningful understanding of scientific expression. Softwoods and hardwoods, for example, are meaningless terms since a hardwood may be softer than a softwood and a softwood may be harder than a hardwood.

Balsa *(Ochroma pyramidale)* is a hardwood by classification but is actually very soft and light in weight, while yew *(Taxus baccata)* although classified a softwood is harder than some hardwoods. There are very sound scientific reasons for these timbers being drawn from different types of trees but to understand this we must start at the beginning.

The dominant plants today are the seed plants or Spermatophytes. They represent the highest form of plant specialisation, bearing true roots, stems and leaves, and producing seeds which are dormant structures representing a pause in the development of the new infant plant, designed by nature to insure perpetuation of the species in question.

The Spermatophytes are divided into two classes, the gymnosperms and the angiosperms, each distinguished by the manner in which the seeds are borne. The word gymnosperm is derived from the Greek gymnos, or uncovered, and sperma, seed; seeds not enclosed in a true ovary, ie the seeds are borne naked, subtended by scales as in the pines *(Pinus)* or in fleshy structures as in the podocarps *(Podocarpus)*. Angiosperm is derived from the Greek anggeion, vessel, and sperma, seed; having seeds in a closed case, the ovary.

Gymnosperms form a relatively small part of the seed plant vegetation but they are generally regarded as the surviving remnant of a vast group which originated in the Carboniferous period and flourished particularly in the Triassic period.

Angiosperms evolved much later and are represented today by some 125,000 species. They have been able to attain and hold the ascendency over other groups because of their ability to adapt to ever-changing environmental conditions.

The Gymnospermae comprise trees commonly known as conifers, although the typical woody cone is not found in yew *(Taxus)*, nor in juniper and pencil 'cedar' *(Juniperus)*; in these the seed is contained in a fleshy berry. The group is represented by 40 genera and approximately 350 species, mainly found growing in temperate, alpine or sub-boreal regions.

Coniferous tree species produce the so-called softwoods and include the true pines *(Pinus)*; Parana 'pine' *(Araucaria)*; spruces *(Picea)*; true cedars *(Cedrus)*; western red 'cedar' *(Thuja)*; true fir *(Abies)*; Douglas 'fir' *(Pseudotsuga menziesii)*; hemlock *(Tsuga)*; larch *(Larix)*; and others.

In contrast to gymnosperms, the angiosperms are more of a heterogeneous group containing a vast assemblage of plants, lianas, shrubs and trees, intermixed in bewildering confusion and widespread throughout the world. As a group, however, the Angiospermae is divided into two sub-classes; the monocotyledons and the dicotyledons, characterised by differences in growth form leading to two very different groups of trees. The basic differences are indicated by the classification thus: a cotyledon is a seed leaf, while the Greek móno or monos, means alone (one); di (two) means that when the seed germinates two leaves push up to the light as opposed to the single leaf that first appears in a monocotyledonous plant. There are other morphological differences, but let it suffice to say that the monocotyledons produce bamboos and palms and in the sense in which we interpret the meaning of timber, their trunks cannot be utilised for this purpose.

Dicotyledonous timber, or hardwood as it is known, is the product of trees which exhibit great diversity of form and habitat. They attain their best development in terms of species in tropical regions, but many are found in temperate and sub-arctic zones. There is less tendency for hardwood trees to develop pure stands than with the conifers.

Reverting now to economic differences, coniferous trees have what are called excurrent stems. This word deriving from the Latin ex (out) and currere (to run) meaning the stem runs on undivided, as opposed to hardwood trees whose stems are said to be deliquescent, a word derived from the Latin deliquescere, meaning to become fluid. This refers to the habit of hardwood tree stems to divide into a number of irregular branches.

Throughout the world today, much criticism is levelled at governments whose tree-planting programmes involve mainly coniferous trees. In general, there is wisdom in this except, of course, where hardwood planting for posterity is completely ignored. However, when the different growth habits of softwoods and hardwoods are taken into account with other factors, the economics of modern forestry methods become a little clearer.

Conifers grown under ideal conditions

attain very large sizes, eg Douglas fir and western hemlock, so with their straight stems very little is wasted during conversion into timber; they can be grown in pure stands, they mature quickly, thinnings and small diameter stock have immediate uses, particularly for paper pulp and chipboard; and largely due to their preponderance in temperate zones, they grow where there is the greatest impetus on industrial activity.

In contrast although many hardwood species are gregarious, with few exceptions they do not tend to form pure stands and in some cases a particular species may dominate growth in a particular area but with very few of saw-log size at any given time. In many cases they occur in remote areas and have to be hauled and shipped great distances thus increasing their cost. As we have already mentioned, the angiosperms have held their ascendency over the gymnosperme because of an ability to adapt to changing environments and, accordingly, where hardwood trees occur in relative isolation they tend to develop more branches and distorted forms, often reducing the potential timber yield and its quality.

Although we have two clearly defined botanical classes of timber tree, all the wood substance produced is basically cellular and relatively porous and is the same for softwoods and hardwoods. Trees are woody plants, that is to say they possess vascular tissue (specialised water-conducting tissue) which becomes 'lignified' or woody as it matures. This process of lignification is brought about by certain chemical and physical processes which take place in the woody part of the vascular tissue whereby its cell walls are rendered harder, stronger and more durable than before.

The woody tissues become lignified soon after attaining ultimate growth, ie in the first year of growth of the tree, the process continuing each year. This aspect should not be confused with changes which occur in the wood tissues when they pass from sapwood to heartwood. Thickening of the wood cell walls due to lignification in effect means that besides conducting watery sap, the cells can now cope much better with the job of supporting the weight of the crown of the tree, and can exert a greater resistance to bending forces when the tree is exposed to storms and gales.

The features which characterise sapwood and heartwood are those of colour, weight and durability; heartwood is generally darker, heavier and more durable than sapwood. But the colour character must be used with reservation since in some trees there is no clearly defined heartwood; for example in spruce, silver fir and obeche. As the term implies, sapwood is concerned with the movement of sap (dilute aqueous solutions of mineral and organic food) up the stem; heartwood performs purely a mechanical function in the core of the stem. Sapwood possesses living cells which make up much of its bulk. In heartwood the cells are dead to all intents and purposes, and play no part in sap conduction.

Caricature drawings of end grain:
(a) Oak x10 showing typical pore arrangement;
(b) *Drimys winteri* x10 showing absence of hardwood pores, but with prominent tracheids;
(c) Typical softwood x100, no pores but prominent tracheids.

Monkey puzzle

Although wood substance is basically the same for both softwoods and hardwoods, the shape, size, distortion and amount of characters or components vary in terms of proportional representation, not only by genera and species but from tree to tree. The basic cells are variable in their shape in the hardwoods but are commonly referred to as pores or vessels; whereas in the softwoods the structure is less complex and composed of almost square-shaped cells know as tracheids.

While there are many differences in the appearance of coniferous and broad-leaved hardwood trees, it is on the structural features alone that a piece of wood can be examined. The first action a wood anatomist takes when presented with a small piece of unknown wood and a request for identification, is to ascertain whether the wood is a softwood or hardwood. In preliminary investigation the end grain is examined through a hand lens with ×8 or ×10 magnification. While some specimens can be classified immediately others, particularly small thin pieces coated with paint or coloured with stain need closer scrutiny. Having decided on its origin, normal procedures can then be followed either with the continued use of the hand lens or with the aid of a microscope, essential for most softwood identification.

Seen through a hand lens the end grain of hardwood exhibits various patterns of different size pores, quite different from the difficult to see, regular rows of tiny tracheids making up the end grain of softwoods. The timber technology student should be aware of the test sample sometimes put up for identification of a S American hardwood known as canelo: this is the product of the winter's bark tree *(Drimys winteri)*. The wood has no pores as in hardwoods generally, but a vertical arrangement of tracheids as in softwoods. The rays, however, are

quite prominent, much more so than in softwoods and sufficiently noticeable to enable a proper distinction to be made. A further species of *Drimys* grows in Australia.

In tree form, the conifers are readily distinguishable from the dicotyledons. The leaves are linear or needle-like and most conifers are evergreen; larch is an exception being deciduous. While many conifers look alike closer observation will reveal many distinctive features. The true pines have linear leaves, like blades of grass, while Parana 'pine', closely related to the monkey puzzle tree, has awl-shaped leaves. The leaves in the true pines are carried in bundles of two to five; Scots, maritime and contorta pine have two needles; radiata and ponderosa pines have leaves in threes, Quebec yellow pine and sugar pine are examples of 5-needle pines.

The spruces may have flattened 2-edged leaves as in sitka spruce, or quadrangular in section as in Norway spruce. The juvenile leaves in cypress are awl-shaped but when adult become scale-like and press closely to the stem.

Dicotyledonous trees have many leaf forms but all are broad by comparison with conifers. Most hardwood trees are deciduous, a few evergreen.

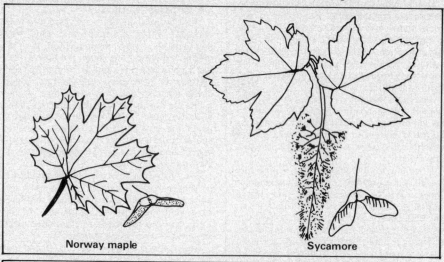

Norway maple   Sycamore

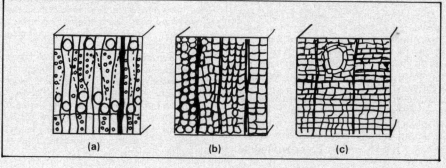

(a)   (b)   (c)

TEACHING THEM TO BE SELF-STARTERS

S. Heighington of the Industrial Arts Department at Cosburn Avenue Junior High School,
Toronto, gives a light-hearted report of his summer enrichment course. 'Not the ideal
programme,' he says, 'but it provided an insight into the ability and independence of our
so-called unemployable students.' He will be pleased to exchange a detailed description
of his programme for whatever teachers care to offer in the way of project plans, model
construction materials, curriculum guides and suchlike.

In the summer of 1979 I took no courses. I taught what was to have been an enrichment or fun course in industrial arts with the primary object of making the school a more useful and visible place to the community. An enrichment course suggested it would be for the better students, but this was not so as the school office gave hints of 'let them do their own thing . . . make it fun.'

I do not see industrial arts as being an enrichment course nor just a 'fun' programme. Industrial arts is an integral part of today's technological society.

I looked at the time allotment: the course would encompass four weeks or 19 days or 57 hours. What could be accomplished in that time? The age group was limited to students between 12 and 15. The experience or aptitude for technology was non-existent. I was to have any child opting for the programme. And if I wanted to run the programme 18 students was the minimum enrolment.

I read. I looked. I searched. I talked. I schemed. Eventually the thing evolved as 'an industrial experience for students unable to obtain summer employment because of age'. The objects were to teach them about the world of work; and to make money. What could be more straightforward? But what could be produced that would involve a large number of students with a wide range of abilities, bearing in mind that the school had a composite workshop with limited space? I finally hit on the idea of wooden toys which involved numbers of parts and numbers of repetitive operations as well as child appeal — and if all else failed the students could give the toys away!

Student numbers were obtained through a public relations campaign; notices were put in local libraries and student summer employment offices and the local newspapers willingly provided space. Students were also 'enticed' — I described how dull the mornings of July would be if they stayed home and, of course, how empty their pockets would be.

Before the numbers were assembled I had to know what materials would be necessary. I gambled on the amount of wood to be used and ordered it through the regular budget. The whole thing was designed to cost nothing but obviously a grubstake was necessary, and since I was teaching in my regular school it was possible to borrow materials for later replacement.

What toys were to be made? Teaching a quasi-design programme I am aware of the time required for sketches, prototypes, models, decisions, patterns and so forth. Fortunately, over the year I had a number of toys designed and built of which I selected the best. During the month of June templates were made by the students in readiness for the start.

We were all set to go. Materials had been pre-ordered, designs drawn; and all I needed was the appropriate number of students. There are always those who want to be different of course: two students wanted to mass-produce lamps, so as well as a toyworks I had a lampworks! Day 1 came (and went) and with it safety first: spectacles, dust masks, ear protection, safety seminar — and a box of bandages. Then within the span of four days, 20 cranes were completed, pieces of a large traction engine were being assembled, wheels by the 100 were cut with a holesaw. It was machine-intensive with the first two-and-a-half weeks spent in cutting, turning, drilling, sanding, and gluing. There was a job for everyone and little time in which to wander. Things went well and the quality, quantity and variety of toys increased. As the preconceived toys ran the gamut students' designs were encouraged. This brought a renewed spirit and July began to look like Christmas.

Marketing. Yes, but where, when, how much? In prearranged meetings students took samples to various toy shops where the comments ranged from: 'Oh you have the

Mercedes Benz of toys,' to a negative from the lady who owned her own factory in Vermont and mistook beech for cedar. As the four weeks drew to a close the students wanted a share of the dividends. (By the way, the two lampworkers were still turning out lamps and had by this time obtained Ontario Hydro approval of their electrical works.)

Our instant cash was obtained through an in-school sale and a full Sunday sale at the harbour front market. (I might add that the lampworkers sold most of their lamps.) But there was still a lot of toys left so we took them to the Guild Craft shop in a wealthy district — and watched the prices triple. We were also fortunate that the Ontario Science Centre was featuring a special wood show. At the present time the remainder of the toys are being distributed through the science city shops within the centre.

The toymakers made money. The initial dividend paid 20 cents an hour and it is anticipated that the second dividend will be 30 cents an hour. Incidentally, the lampworkers' gross revenue and shared profit leave serious doubts in my mind as to the personal monetary value of teaching a summer programme!

It all made for an eventful and interesting summer. With the knowledge and experience gained these students will enter the world of work as beneficial employees or, better still, they'll apply for government grants and become selfstarting and self-employed entrepreneurs.

I would not say that this is the ideal programme but it provided an insight into the ability and independence of our so-called unemployable students. They can do it. Just give them the opportunity.

'JOBS TO SPARE'

Craft, design and technology —
the image and the reality

Two main themes came out of International Craft, Design & Technology Education exhibition; every lecturer, student and teacher had the same story: 'There are plenty of jobs to spare'; and 'We are not dummies.'

The picture is perfectly clear that the newly-qualified teacher can take his pick of half-a-dozen jobs and it was emphasised over and over again that the old way of teaching craft subjects is moving away from 'Here is a drawing, make it' to 'Here is a problem, solve it.'

Together with these facts came the figures that showed there are plenty of vacancies in colleges for young and old people — men or women — who like the look of the new approach.

I looked at this exhibition as a sympathetic and reasonably well-informed outsider for I trained as a handicraft teacher before moving into journalism and, without wishing to sound too pompous about it, I think it reflects the changing attitudes in society towards authority. It is part of the swing away from a blind acceptance of habits to an individual summing-up of situations and problems and taking the responsibility for acting on them.

So, who said what?

Bob Millard, head of creative design at Loughborough University department of creative design, said that the number of entrants had been declining for 15 years. This year he has 15 to 18 places vacant for people wishing to become teachers although the quality is still high.

He blamed the comprehensives for their emphasis on the traditional academic subjects to the detriment of CDT. Another factor which he mentioned was the wider choice of job opportunities for pupils.

Principal lecturer in craft and design studies at the City of Liverpool College of Higher Education, R. J. Hunt, also put the blame for the decline in numbers of students wishing to become CDT teachers on to the headmasters of comprehensives. He said that since re-organisation, the more able students had been streamed away from craft studies because the heads wanted to have good examination results in the academic fields of study. He said that he needed more candidates and that the decline had been going on for 10 to 15 years. Some practising teachers were being lost to administration, lecturing and pastoral work in schools and some, because of increased money, to industry.

The second International Craft, Design & Technology Education exhibition was held at the National Agricultural Centre at Stoneleigh at the end of October.

There was much to learn about tools, timbers and techniques but the most exciting — and disturbing — message came from the colleges directly concerned with training teachers of craft, design and technology: CDT as it is now being known.

Former WOODWORKER editor Peter Scaife went to the exhibition to see how the image — and the reality — is changing.

His report must be of interest to teachers, whether just beginning their careers or near retirement. It is of interest to anyone thinking of changing his career in mid-stream.

If you are interested in training — or re-training — as a teacher, get the booklet entitled *Teaching Craft, Design and Technology*. It is available free from room 2/11, Elizabeth House, Department of Education & Science, York Road, London SE1 7PH. It gives most of what you will need to know at first about courses ranging from one to four years, grants, qualifications and college addresses.

If in Scotland write to the Scottish Education Department, New St Andrews House, St James Centre, Edinburgh. If in Northern Ireland write to the Department of Education, Rathgael House, Balloo Road, Bangor, Co Down.

He stressed that promotion chances were good and said that there was hope in the spread — and acceptance — of A level design courses and exams.

I spoke to Gordon McGowan, from Hatfield, on the stand of Middlesex Polytechnic, of which the old Trent Park College is now part. He is in his fourth year there hoping to get an honours classification in his Bachelor of Education degree course in CDT.

He said, 'I took three A levels — sociology, English literature and design technology — and it was the last of these which was the most intellectually demanding.

His fourth year at Middlesex is being spent in design education which, he said, was very theoretical but very valuable for it crossed boundaries and applied a variety of disciplines.

'I don't like and don't want the image of dummies,' he said. 'With an honours degree, you can hold your own in any staff room.' He feared the possibility of a vicious circle developing: fewer pupils, fewer classes, fewer teachers, and so on.

Malcolm Johnston, industrial designer and part-time lecturer, was on the stand of Goldsmiths' College of the University of London.

He thought government spending cuts had given some people the wrong idea about the situation but felt that it was picking up. He

Rt hon Baroness Young, Minister of State at the Department of Education and Science, watches the school demonstration woodworking class at the International Craft, Design and Technology Education exhibition at the National Agricultural Centre, Stoneleigh, Coventry.

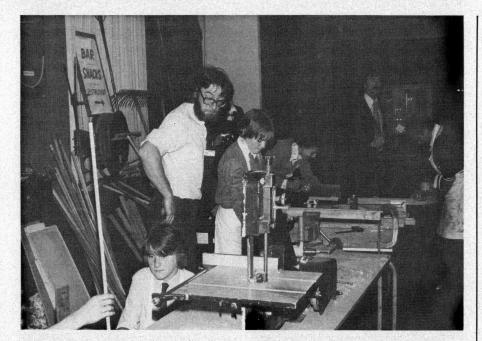

School exhibition of woodworking.

MUSIC AND . . .

H. C. King reports

West Dean College was founded to foster crafts of all kinds and offers weekend, five day, nine and 10 day courses in a wide range of arts and crafts.

From 3-12 April 1980 there will be one of particular interest to teachers of crafts and music and others on the making of musical instruments. Many schools have had to abandon instrumental work owing to the prohibitive costs of instruments, making this course an answer to the problem. Meagre skills with tools need not be deterent as the projects are so cleverly designed and graded that many of them can be made in a school workshop. They range from simple percussion items to trapezoidal violins and violas with celtic harps, table spinets and lutes for the more skilled craftsmen. I have seen and heard the work produced at three previous courses and can vouch for the craftsmanship and musical tone.

Tuition is by Robert Kerr, the course director, and his three assistants, and all four are experts in this field of work and have been involved in all the courses since 1973. Stocks of materials will be available for sale to students for use in the fully equipped workshop complex.

The College is part of the Edward James Foundation and is housed in a beautiful mansion set in extensive gardens and grounds off the A286, about six miles north of Chichester. Accommodation and catering are of a high standard as are the other facilities. The latter include the oak room with bar, the library and the music room. West Dean is approved by the Dept of Education & Science and students should be able to claim financial help from their local authorities.

Further details are available from Peter Sarginson, Principal, West Dean College, West Dean, Chichester, West Sussex, PO18 0QZ.

Keyboard instruments

For those who would like to make their own early keyboard instrument in the company of like minded people, or who want to increase their knowledge of instrument making, John Storrs, Hunston, Chichester, Sussex PO 20 6NR (phone 0243 789605) runs residential courses several times a year in Chichester. The courses he hopes to run in 1980 are Friday 11 to Monday 21 April for spinet and clavichord making and from Friday 4 to Monday 21 of July for harpsichord making.

Each course is limited to 10 participants who stay at Chichester Theological College a few minutes walk from the cathedral and town centre. The course also includes a visit to one or more of the following — the Festival Theatre, the Open Air museum at West Dean and Fishbourne Roman palace. The evenings give opportunities for informal music making and discussion.

. . . MODELS

Model Engineer Exhibition

The 1980 Model Engineer Exhibition will take place at Wembley Conference Centre from January 2 — January 12 (closed Sunday 6 Jan). There will be regular daily displays and demonstrations and many clubs and societies will also be represented.

---

praised the quality of his fellow-lecturers there and said that students leaving Goldsmiths' could take the cream of the jobs. Usually, the students were recommended to apply for jobs where the teaching would be mainly at a first- or second-year level. 'We and Loughborough are still the big two,' said Ms Val Powley, lecturer in educational psychology at Shoreditch College, Egham, Surrey. 'There are dozens of jobs waiting for our students and they can have virtually anything they like. The prospect is quite rosy but we must go out and sell our wares.' Now that rumours of the closure of Shoreditch were finally quashed it was 'full steam ahead.'

Although students were not able to bargain over the money paid in individual jobs, they were able to take those where the promotion prospects were best and quickly move into head of department jobs.

'But there are still blackspots,' said Ms Powley, citing one comprehensive with an academic bias away from CDT and with workshop classes of 28.

Two newly-qualified teachers from Shoreditch, one working in London and the other in Warwickshire, confirmed Ms Powley's comments on attitudes and promotion. Alan Dickson, in Brent, said he was now getting more money to spend on running photographic and jewellery studies; Andy Williams had had the offer of five different jobs in Birmingham.

Keith Renton is administration officer for CDT with the associated examining board for the GCE. He said: 'The AEB has been giving a lead in the movement since the mid-50s by introducing a design element. With problem-solving exam questions, we have had 3,600 different answers to the same stimulus. But there is some lack of security, particularly among older teachers, and they need some support.'

He also pointed out the change in emphasis from a single-material course, ie wood or metal work, to multi-material where the choice is much freer.

Alan Brown, tutor in charge of CDT at Leeds Polytechnic, felt that the parents of pre-third year pupils were the ones who most needed their prejudices changing. Heads, he felt, were being convinced, but he confirmed the hundreds of vacancies now available. He was optimistic that the university recognition of the A level

examinations for entry requirements would help.

Director of studies in the department of design at Bristol Polytechnic is Geoff Hawes. 'We are haunted by the ghosts of Plato and Aristotle,' he said. 'Visual education is just as important — it is essential — and we must break down the prejudices of parents and head teachers. The old image was poor; too many teachers were dull with no inspiration.'

He, too, was hopeful of the university acceptance of design and technology A levels, but blamed heads for not getting enough recruits.

'We are moving out of woodwork and metalwork and into design education with a sequence of design projects while retaining the quality of making. More can be done in the primary schools; more can be done in the comprehensives to encourage the more able pupils. Positive encouragement is needed because the situation is getting worse numerically.

'There are not enough recruits and we are welcoming women and mature students onto the courses.'

He quoted approvingly Prof Denis Lawton, deputy director of London University Institute of Education, who in a recent speech said that it was essential for CDT to be included in the core curriculum.

One college where the number of entrants is against the general trend is de la Salle, at Hopwood Hall, affiliated to the University of Manchester.

'We are full and turning away students,' said Michael John, head of the department of design and technology. 'With university college status, we are moving into the status of being one of the top colleges and students here work alongside those who will be employed full-time in design or industrial jobs.' He said the staff were highly qualified with, say, a master's degree in engineering or a PhD in metallurgy.

A couple of lecturers said to me that I could get an overall picture of the scene from the stand run by the Department of Education and Science. So to get the last round-up, I went to speak to one of Her Majesty's Inspectors.

And he said: 'An HMI does not make statements to the press on behalf of the DES!'

Work by the schools

Left: Electric guitar: african walnut body, african sapele neck and african mansonia finger board with inlay inserts. Metal folding guitar stand *(David Greasley)*.
Right: Record display cabinet for music centre in african mahogany *(Duncan Burton)*.

Examples of work done in the technical studies department of George Spencer Comprehensive School, Stapleford, Nottingham, are illustrated on this page.

R.N. Williamson who is head of technical studies and assisted by a staff of three, says the school became comprehensive in September 1978 and for 18 years prior to this was a secondary modern (mixed) school of approximately 450 pupils. 'Over that time it has I believe built up a reputation for the variety and excellence of its craft work,' says Mr Williamson.

About five years ago the technical studies department was responsible for building a new technical drawing room and boys from the 4th and 5th years were involved in every stage of construction. In 1973 the school was chosen by the LEA to display its craft work, and to represent the work done in county schools, at the Nottingham County Show.

'Today, in new buildings, the craft areas in the lower school give younger pupils the opportunity to work on simple projects in a range of materials,' says Mr Williamson. 'In the upper school the crafts are separated in preparation for examinations. Besides normal school work, the staff in the department run extra-tuition groups and school clubs. All these are well attended,' adds Mr Williamson, 'and reflect the enthusiasm of both staff and pupils for the subjects involved.'

Above: Coffee table in brazilian freijo with ceramic tiled top *(Stephen Poyser)*.

Below left: Selection of turned work by 4th and 5th year students.
Below right: Cabinet in african sapele *(Gordon Tomlinson)*.

THE WORLD'S TIMBER TREES

C. W. Bond continues his series with a study of paduak. Last month he discussed African blackwood: 7 and in the October issue Indian rosewood: 6 The next tree to be considered will be Berlinia: 9.

PADAUK: 8

Pterocarpus spp. *Pterocarpus* — having a winged seed.

Leguminosae (Papilionaceae) Among the 24 species of *Pterocarpus* there are five which supply the woodworking world with some of the most impressive of woods. Andaman padauk (*P. dalbergioides*) (resembling *Dalbergia*) from the Andaman islands is perhaps the most striking. This is a large tree giving large sizes of extremely handsome deeply red-coloured, hard, heavy, stable, lustrous timber of great value in the highest class of decorative fittings. It is also available in veneer form.

Pterocarpus indicus (from India) is a smaller tree which supplies, in burr form, the veneer known as amboyna.

Pterocarpus macrocarpus (large seeded) is a tall tree from Burma, which also supplies a handsome wood, not quite so deeply coloured and a little less imposing in appearance. It is a hard, heavy and strong timber used for construction and decorative work. Padauk is a Burmese word.

African padauk or camwood (*P. soyauxii*) is similar to the Andaman species, bright, hard, heavy and deeply coloured. It is in demand for parquet flooring, various fancy articles carved and turned, and decorative work generally.

Under this heading mention must be made of the world's most stable wood, m'ninga or muninga (*P. angolense*) (from Angola). It is a wood less hard than the above species and with much more agreeable working qualities. These trees occur over something like 1,000,000 sq. ml of equatorial Africa, but only at the rate of about one tree sq. ml. This species is the world's 'Number 1'!

The photomicrographs show vessels large but rather sparsely distributed, rays numerous and extremely small — not discernible with a lens — and parenchyma cells are conspicuous in wavy tangential bands.

5 cm

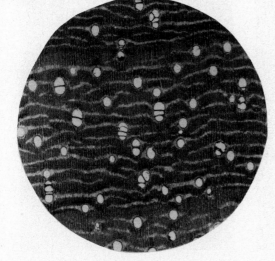

Pterocarpus macrocarpus. **Drawn from material in the Forest Herbarium, University of Oxford, with acknoweldgments to the curator.**

Left: Cross section x 10 lineal.
Above: Cross section x 3.3.

VISITORS WELCOME

H. C. King has been to see a business which puts emphasis on quality and workmanship — and not just on the ring of the till

Alan Holtham is a modest young man who enjoys his work throughly. That satisfies him and he does not seek fame. But he won the first prize for woodturning at the Woodworker Show in 1976, thus making a name for himself. Since then he has set up in business.

His knowledge and love of wood stems from his mother's family who have been in the timber trade for many years. A BSc degree in forestry plus practical information gathered over the years helps him in choosing his timber and getting the best out of it.

A search for suitable premises for his business led him to a Co-op store which had been empty for some time. With the help of his father he set about turning it into a very different place. Now he has a spacious, well-lit workshop, showroom for turnery and a sales display room for machinery, tools and equipment. A further room is used for final drying-off of blocks and blanks for bowls and dishes. In the yard timber is stored under cover. One valuable stack of mahogany had been rescued just before it was to be sawn up for firewood. The premises are known as the Old Stores Turnery, Wistaston Road, Willaston, Nantwich, Cheshire.

Pride of place in the workshop is the lathe Alan won as his prize in 1976. 'The best lathe I have ever used', is his comment. A smaller lathe is part of a universal woodworking machine, and for bowl turning he has a

Above: Timber stored under cover.
Below left: The room used for the final drying-off of blocks and blanks for bowls and dishes.
Below right: Consignment of trophy truncheons for the local police sports day.
Bottom right: Demonstrating a combination machine to a prospective customer.

Below: Sycamore planks.
Centre: A corner of the machinery and equipment showroom.

home-made power driven head which is very efficient. A bandsaw and saw bench are used for converting big stuff, and a pillar drill completes his workshop machinery. A sturdy bench occupies the length of one wall. Alan is interested in the history of wood turning and when he can find the time, he intends to make a chair bodger's pole lathe 'just for fun'.

The display in the turnery showroom is an indication of Alan's skill, artistic flair and the high standard he sets himself. Of the wide variety of products on show at the time of my visit, the most outstanding items were his prizewinning wassail bowl in laburnum and a lovely English walnut spinning wheel. The finish as well as the turning and woodwork were superb. Shelves were lined with table lamps, bowls, boxes and dozens of examples of his work. A graceful standard lamp was also on show. A consignment of truncheons had just been finished for the local police. No, they were not regulation size but 6 in. long. Each was mounted on a stand as a trophy for the sports day.

Next was the machinery, tool and equipment showroom. Firms whose products he handles include Elu, Coronet, Arundel, Startrite, Ajax, Trend and Sorby. Alan does

not sell any machine or tool with which he is not happy to work. An extensive range of fittings such as clock and barometer movements, condiment liners, lampholders and switches is also stocked. A turner's smock designed by Alan finds a ready sale.

Visitors are always warmly welcomed, whether they come to buy, to ask advice (which is readily given) or just for a chat. During the short time I was there, several people came in to admire and to buy. Many an amateur turner has cause to thank Alan for his help, advice, and encouragement.

Choosing the timber and its preparation for use are very important at the Old Stores where the stock includes sycamore, elm, oak, mahogany, walnut, ash, damson and several exotics. To augment his natural seasoning facilities, Alan recently installed an Ebac dehumidifier and made the necessary cabinet. From the first full load of partially-dried timber, 8½pt of water was extracted. He intends to review the Ebac in a future issue of WOODWORKER. I found the visit interesting and enjoyable. It is also pleasant to find a young man so dedicated to his work, and a business which puts emphasis on quality and workmanship and not just on the ring of the till.

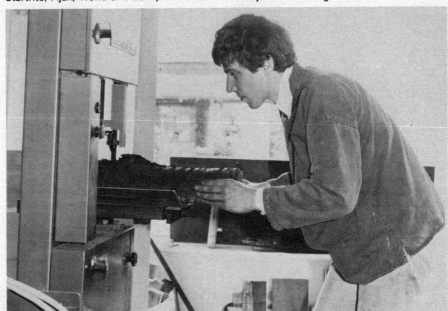

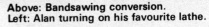

Above: Bandsawing conversion.
Left: Alan turning on his favourite lathe.

Below: Happy customers.

KITY SERVICE

A new concept in after sales back-up

Like other manufacturers, Kity guarantee their machines, provide spares and a maintenance service, but Kity plan sheets go one step further, they help you exploit the full potential of your machines.

Kity plan sheets give detailed specification about materials, design, cutting and machining for all kinds of woodworking projects. Fill in the coupon and we will send you a free 44 page book all about this invaluable and unique Kity service.

BOOK REVIEW
RESTORING DECORATION

Revised edition in paperback form of *Early American Decorating Techniques* by Mariette P. Slayton, offers a teach-yourself guide to the art of restoring and reproducing stenciled and painted decoration on antique furniture, tinware and glass with a glance at the treatment of walls and floors. The tradition of producing gaily painted trays, boxes and other household articles flourished more vigorously in America than England and this branch of popular folk art still enjoys greater appeal in the States than Britain. Nevertheless a comprehensive practical treatise on this decorative idiom is a welcome addition to the literature of fringe furniture crafts.

The book opens with sensible hints on types of brushes, how to choose, clean and store them, advice on where and what to buy in the way of paints and the best kind of varnish. Old hands, we are told, always breathe into the storage bottles before replacing the cap — carbon dioxide apparently retards the formation of a skin on the varnish. Basic information is also provided on such mundane subjects as paint rags, palettes and worktables.

A description of the seven basic brush strokes and how to combine them to create ornamental patterns, prefaces an advanced technical discussion which may bewilder the amateur enthusiast. However, the more primitive designs display an effective simplicity of character often more congenial than elaborate compositions (here quaintly called 'Chippendale') akin to the ostentatious decoration of Victorian papier-mâché work.

The accurate reproduction of original painted surfaces by tracing and colour matching; how to execute stems; veins squiggles or curleycues; accomplish transparent overstrokes; achieve floating colours; blend hues and apply bronze powders is all explained in telling detail. Peasant art is, as one always suspected, hard to copy well.

There is also an interesting section on stencils as opposed to free-hand painting — a technique which, if used with skill and flair, can be visually exciting. The celebrated Hitchcock family of American chairs relies for its glamour on an imaginative union of stenciled and free-hand painting. Approved methods of preparing grounds, cutting stencils, bronzing, gilding, applying pearl-shell and related processes are included in the course of study. One cannot help feeling that it would be more fun to practice this art in a class rather than learn it from a book.

The third part illustrates an anthology of 27 full-size patterns copied from original American decoration on chairs, trays, tin trunks, canisters, bellows, looking-glasses, etc.

For a furniture historian the book is shallow on the historical side; it is a product of the middle class cult of antiques/craft revival and the author performs competently.

Publisher is Collier Macmillan Ltd, Stockley Close, Stockley Road, West Drayton UB7 9BE. The book is priced at £5.25. **C.G.G.**

Woodcarving course

A woodcarving course is being arranged by Guild of Woodworkers from 23-25 May 1980, at West Dean College, Chichester. This is the first weekend event organised by the guild and numbers are restricted to 25 to ensure adequate instruction and participation.

The cost will be approximately £48 for each member attending and this charge includes accommodation and meals at the College and use of the facilities.

Members wishing to attend are advised to make early reservation with the administrator of the guild. The address is Guild of Woodworkers, PO Box 35 Bridge Street, Hemel Hempstead HP1 1EE. When writing please give membership number. Further details will be available later.

Interbimall '80

The International Biennial Exhibition of Woodworking Machinery and Tools — will take place at the Milan Fair, from the 15-21 May 1980.

Model Engineer Exhibition

The 1980 Model Engineer Exhibition will take place at Wembley Conference Centre from January 2-January 12 (closed Sunday 6 Jan). There will be regular daily displays and demonstrations and many clubs and societies will also be represented.

Japan style

An exhibition presented by the Victoria and Albert museum and the Japan Foundation to show objects never before seen outside Japan. Areas of interest will include craft masterpieces in lacquer, bamboo, ceramics, wood and textiles, designer crafts, International fashions, graphics, industrial design, paper kites, and traditional Japanese tea houses and temple arches. Admission will be £1.25 at the Victoria and Albert museum from 12 March to 22 June, 1980.

WHAT'S ON IN WOODWORKING

Below: A stringing operation at West Dean musical instrument making course.

Guild of Woodworkers

Catalogue

Members may like to know that the current catalogue issued by Craft Supplies, The Mill, Millers Dale, Buxton SK17 8SN, lists a new copying attachment designed to facilitate production of a complicated turned shape 'quickly and accurately and where uniformity of design is important. For example, turning matched articles and repairing turned furniture.'

The catalogue also illustrates the sizing tool for reproducing a diameter without the need of callipers. It is said to fit most parting tools but is recommended for use with Sorby ⅜in. beading and parting tool.

Craft Supplies runs a mail order business but the shop is open at Millers Dale from Monday to Saturday, 9.00am to 5.00pm (other times by appointment).

Beware of thieves

One member unfortunate enough to have his workshop broken into and some £500-worth of tools stolen, asks us to remind others who have their workshop situated some distance from the house, that a very loud bell or alarm is a worthwhile investment.

'In my case,' says the member, 'it's rather like locking the stable door after the horse has bolted, but the alarm I have now put in makes a very loud noise indeed. The first time I opened the door (forgetting that I had not switched it off) I frightened myself stiff. I reckon the noise would put any thief off.'

Guild of Woodworkers is hoping to arrange a special insurance so that members can cover loss etc of tools and equipment from workshops. But prevention is better than cure and an alarm could prevent theft of treasured items that no amount of money can replace.

Insurance

For small businessmen in particular, the cost of getting legal advice and the cost of taking disputes to court often means that suitable redress is not obtained for wrongs that have been suffered. The legal aid scheme is being affected by inflation which means that fewer people can claim the help of public money to pursue lawsuits.

However there is such a thing as legal expenses insurance and one company — DAS Legal Expenses Insurance Co Ltd of Bristol — offers several policies covering disputes in personal, motoring, employment and property matters. Policies can also be tailor-made to meet the specific needs of individuals or firms.

While on the subject of insurance, it is appropriate to mention pensions for the self-employed whether running their own businesses or as a partner in a firm. In this context self-employed means those employees in the state pensions scheme only.

There are a number of such schemes available and one that has been recommended to the writer as being best suited to his requirements is that of the Equitable Life Assurance Society which has its registered office at 4 Coleman Street, London EC2R 5AP. The important things to remember in all these schemes are the benefits at retirement, the tax advantages; and of course choosing a scheme to suit one's particular needs.

Why a router?

Use of a router is now open to the more ambitious craftsman, according to a 12-page booklet called *Routing Techniques* which is available at 50p from Elu Machinery Ltd, Stirling Way, Stirling Corner, Borehamwood WD6 2AG. The applications recommended in the booklet are for the Elu MOF96 model, though the techniques used can be applied to the other models in the company's range of plunging routers.

The hints given on page 12 are useful. For example: *Do* maintain the cutting edges of your cutter in good condition. Working with a dull cutter overloads the motor as well as the operator. *Do* feed the hand router in the opposite direction to that in which the router bit is rotating. *Do* stand the router, when you are not using it, high up on a shelf to avoid dust from the workbench falling on to the top of the air intake mesh of the machine.

Do not rout to a greater depth than twice the diameter of the cutter; make several routing passes. *Do not* overload the motor. Listen to the tone of the motor. This indicates if there is an unusual drop in rpm.

On re-sharpening the booklet says that a fine honing tool can be used to maintain cutters in sharp condition. This must be done regularly and with care to see that the same angle is maintained on the cutting edges as when purchased. It is normally recommended to send these to a reputable cutter-grinder who has sharpening facilities with the right equipment to ensure the cutters are ground in an efficient manner.

GUILD OF WOODWORKERS
APPLICATION FORM

Cut out and send this coupon to: The Guild of Woodworkers, PO Box 35, Hemel Hempstead, HP1 1EE, England.

Name ....

Name of business (if applicable) ....

Address ....

....

Annual subscription enclosed (cross out which does not apply).
(a) I enclose £2: individual craftsman.
(b) I enclose £5: trading craftsman.
(Equivalent currency please for subscribers outside UK).

For new subscribers to Guild of Woodworkers:
I enclose £1 registration fee (equivalent currency for subscriptions outside UK).

I specialise in (eg cabinetmaking, woodturning, etc) ....

Signature .... Date ....

PLEASE USE BLOCK CAPITALS

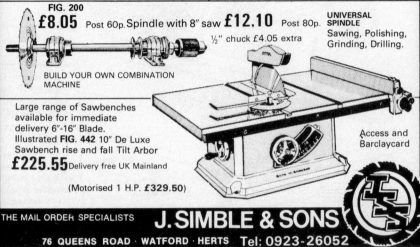

48

Prices quoted are those prevailing at press date and are subject to alteration due to economic conditions.

Woodworker, January 1980

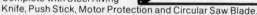

SETTING UP A WORKSHOP

CIRCULAR SAWBENCH

Gordon Stokes continues his series by advising on the selection of a circular sawbench. No recommendation is made as to specific makes or models. The object is to discuss outstanding features and attempt to guide intending purchasers so that they may know what to look for.

The range of machinery available to the craftsman or small commercial workshop, is quite vast. Some confusion is inevitable when beginning to equip the workshop with circular saw, planer, spindle moulder, bandsaw, abrasive machinery, and so on. It is not the function of this series to recommend specific makes. Rather it is to point out outstanding features and attempt to guide intending purchasers so that they may know what to look for. By helping them to decide which machines will best suit their purpose, it is hoped that costly mistakes in the choice of machinery can be avoided.

I have some sympathy with those who scorn machinery and consider the only real woodwork to be that done with hand tools; but only insofar as I agree that there is nothing quite like the feel of a sharp hand tool in operation. Against this, we must accept that power woodwork is extremely interesting, and that the built-in accuracy and speed of good machinery cannot be ignored. Whatever may be the reasons which prompt the change to power, however, care should be taken in selecting the machines, and, initially, some thought given to the order of priority.

Without doubt the majority of woodworkers will put a circular saw at the top of the list, followed by a planer or a planer/thicknesser. The decision to purchase a sawbench rather than a radial-arm saw, or *vice versa*, must be made by the individual in the light of his specific requirements. Both types will be considered in this series so that the merits and demerits of each will be apparent.

For the moment we can look at the sawbench as such, and its important features. Later we will return to the many operations of which it is capable, and the jigs and fixtures which can be made in the workshop to extend its capabilities, or set it up for repetition work.

There are various types of sawbench, having slightly different facilities; but the heart is the spindle and bearings which carry the blade. If these are of a cheap nature the machine is likely to be inaccurate and will certainly give trouble. The bearings on modern benches are packed with grease and sealed for life, so no maintenance is called for. The table itself is frequently a source of argument and there are those who prefer to have a castiron table, rather than a diecast alloy or pressed steel version.

Dramatic improvements have been made in the newer types of table, while in some cases today the castings from which the iron tables are made are not given sufficient time to weather in the open air prior to being machined. Unless sufficient weathering has taken place such tables can warp and become inaccurate. Good quality, heavy pressed steel tables are quite satisfactory, but light ones should be avoided except for rough sawing. Some of the diecast tables now manufactured are first-class.

Tables on circular saws are normally equipped with slots which run parallel to the blade. Ideally there should be one to right and one to left of the saw slot. This facilitates use of the mitre guide which slides in the slots and enables more accurate home-made jigs to be employed.

The rip fence should be examined carefully, particularly if the bench is to handle fairly heavy timber. Some rip fences are very light. Although they work well enough with light workpieces they tend to move when heavier timbers are passed along them. A rip fence should be drilled to accept screws so that a wooden sub-fence can be fitted by the purchaser if necessary. The problem with light rip fences can be overcome by fitting a sub-fence which has a small block of wood at its far end, and extends right across the table. It can be clamped at the far end by means of a G-clamp and so provide adequate support. Some sawbenches are made with rip fences which are clamped at front and back of the table, but these fall into the expensive bracket.

Standards laid down for guarding woodworking machinery have been tightened considerably in recent years, but accidents are to be avoided, so it is vital to check with suppliers that all machinery complies with current requirements as to safety. (See note on safeguarding machinery.) On some saws the guard is carried on the riving knife, which is the curved piece of metal fitted in line with the blade and immediately behind it, designed to prevent wood from closing up onto the back of the blade when being ripped. This is not a good system, since much of the work done on circular saws calls for the removal of the riving knife — and with it the guard. A riving knife, by its very nature, cannot be left in position unless the blade is to pass right through the wood. In the cutting of joints, grooves, housings and the like, this does not happen, so an unguarded blade must be used. Therefore, the guard should be mounted on an overhead arm.

It is important to bear in mind that the riving knife fitted to a sawbench when purchased will work satisfactorily with the blade provided. However, other blades are likely to be used as time goes on and, if they are thicker than the original, a new and thicker riving knife will be needed.

Depth of cut on circular saws is varied either by altering the height of the table in relation to the saw, or by moving the saw relative to the table. The latter method is preferable since it leaves the table at a constant height — which is a big point when home-made panel supports or take-off rollers are used.

The cutting of angles other than 90° can be arranged by having a table which will tilt to 45°, or by mounting the saw on a spindle which can be tilted. The best benches have 'rise and fall tilt arbor' facilities, the table always remaining at the same height and in the horizontal plane. The mechanism provided for tilting table or blade, and for altering depth of cut, should be checked for smoothness of operation. Benches on which the blade cannot be taken fully below the table surface should be avoided.

Power is important with circular saws. Even when freshly sharpened the saw draws a great deal of power from the motor in a deep cut on hardwood. At a pinch 1 hp will do for a 10 in. diameter blade, but 1½ hp is more satisfactory. If much cutting of man-made boards is envisaged, a blade with tungsten carbide tipped (TCT) teeth should be purchased. Materials such as chipboard will blunt a steel blade in very short time. It may be possible to deal with the sharpening of circular saw blades later in this series, but readers with no knowledge of the process should send their blades to a saw doctor.

Safeguarding machinery

On safeguarding machinery, a report by HM factory inspectorate (*Furniture & Woodworking: health and safety 1977*), points out that the basic machines, particularly the circular saw, the vertical spindle moulding machine, the overhand planer and the bandsaw continue to account for most of the accidents in the woodworking industries.

Regulation 5 of the WWM regulations requires that the cutters of a woodworking machine be enclosed by a guard or guards to the greatest extent that is practicable. A simple example of this is that a large part of the blade of a circular saw could be enclosed when being used on repetitive production on a crosscutting operation, where only a small part of the front edge of the saw had to be exposed.

It should be noted that an accident involving a circular saw without a top guard or riving knife resulted in the operative losing two fingers. The operative had been given no training on woodworking machines and was, in fact, a self-employed person. Nevertheless, the factory occupier was prosecuted under section 4 of the HSW Act. He pleaded guilty.

Inspections made during the year covered by the report suggest that designers, manufacturers and users of machinery are failing to meet the more onerous requirements placed on them by the recent significant changes in the law.

The report stresses that if certain measures which reduce severe risks to safety and health are well-known and are practicable in factories, then such measures are reasonably practicable to adopt on machines in premises not subject to the Woodworking Machines Regulations 1974, unless there are special reasons indicating otherwise. These regulations are mainly aimed at serious risks and can be regarded as a reasonably practicable minimum standard in other places.

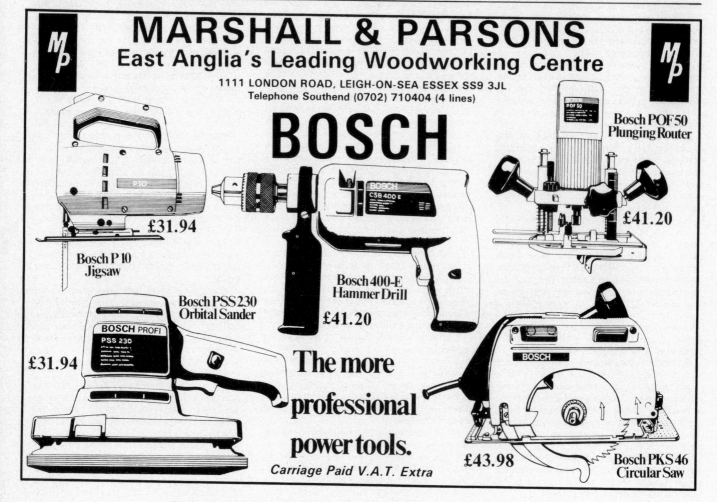

Room divider

From: Bernard Tate, Wistaston, Cheshire

Can you please give me assistance over a room divider based on spindle woodturning. The divider would be between two rooms having a 7 × 7ft opening which at present has a metal french-type window ensemble. I want to remove this and substitute an all-wood structure with fixed ends and a free central opening of about 3ft.

It would appear that the french window is in an external wall with an extension added to form the other room. It is difficult to advise without a detailed drawing of the existing work. However, the following notes and accompanying sketches may be helpful:

If there is an existing timber frame and this is to be removed, first ascertain that a lintel is supporting the wall above the opening; this applies to internal and external walls. If you are not sure the local planning officer's department will be able to advise.

The sketches show two methods of finishing the soffit and the jambs of the opening with: (a) a lining projecting beyond the wall face and; (b) a lining set inside the wall face.

The frame of the room divider should have mortised and tenoned joints, a raised and fielded panel is shown at the bottom part of the room divider. This can be omitted and the turnings continued down to the bottom rail. If the section of the intermediate rails as shown is used, drill the holes before working the bevels.

It is better to leave sufficient clearance on the height and width of the frame so that it is easily placed into position, particularly if dowels are used to fix the bottom rail as shown. Distance pieces or packings are required at the fixing points of the frame. The space is covered by using a scotia or quadrant moulding.

Finish for a boat

From: John Catmull, New South Wales, Australia

I have a sailing boat and after five years of sanding and varnishing the exterior woodwork twice yearly, I have just reached the stage where I can make it last 12 months! The timber is oak. Is there something I can use, perhaps ordinary linseed oil, that will preserve the wood in a fairly hostile environment of sun and salt a little longer than 12 months?

I actually enjoy applying the varnish but do object to the job of sanding and scraping. And at the present rate there soon will be no timber left!

There are three aspects concerned with the maintenance of your boat finish: preserving the wood; its appearance; but most of all the time-consuming task of

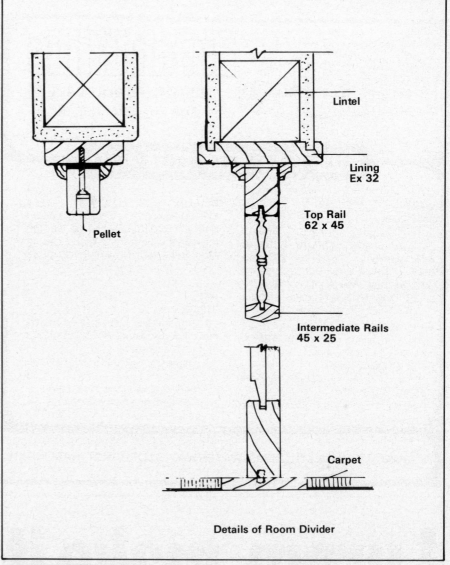

Details of Room Divider

(labels: Pellet, Lintel, Lining Ex 32, Top Rail 62 × 45, Intermediate Rails 45 × 25, Carpet)

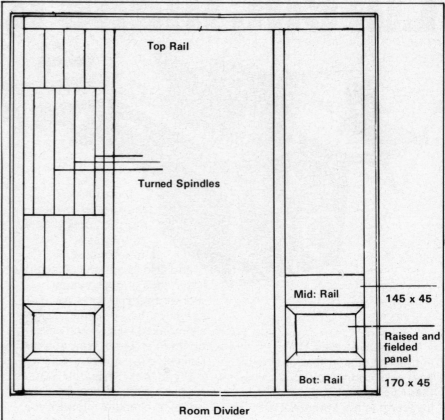

Room Divider

(labels: Top Rail, Turned Spindles, Mid: Rail, 145 × 45, Raised and fielded panel, Bot: Rail, 170 × 45)

cleaning-off the old flaking varnish and making good. Since you refer to the possibility of using linseed oil as a complete answer to the problem, it suggests you are not too fussy about the lack of a final gloss finish.

If this is the case, and since linseed oil would contribute nothing to preservation but would only tend to collect dirt, we would suggest a simple alternative: Obtain what is known as a water-repellent preservative stain pigmented in a suitable shade and, after stripping the wood bare, apply three coats of the fluid. Ultimate maintenance would be to wash-down the wood and apply one or two additional coats.

You will see that labour is reduced to a minimum and several things are achieved: the material does not flake or craze; it imparts a preservative to the wood; it adds colour and adds water-repellency to the surface; and these factors are progressively increased year after year.

Various brands are on the market made by people like Solignum and Cuprinol. If this type of finish appeals to you, before buying anything we further suggest you have a word with your CSIRO Division of Building Research at PO Box 56, Highett, 3190 Victoria, and find out whether its new water-repellent finish is available. We have had advice on this but are not sure if it is ready for the market. If you wish to telephone CSIRO on (03)95 0333 please speak to Mrs E. Bolza.

If you insist upon varnishing, then a phenolic-based type would last a little longer than an alkyd one; polyurethane, while initially giving a marvellous finish, would be the hardest to remove once it failed. Oak, and we assume you refer to true oak (Quercus spp.), is not a good wood for varnishing for external exposure; the wood tends to surface check very easily soon fracturing the varnish film and allowing moisture to penetrate.

There is also the probability of moisture vapour or air bubbles becoming trapped in the large pores of the wood when the varnish is applied. These make for tiny pinhead blisters in the varnish which are easily penetrated through movement of the wood or from abrasion. We think a water-repellent finish would suit you best.

Making a ship's wheel

From: J. Fleck, Godalming, Surrey
I would like to turn a ship's wheel about 12 — 14in. in diameter in hardwood and would be glad to have advice on appropriate construction and turning methods to be used for this.

In the days of sail the rim would no doubt have been shaped with an adze in the same way wheelwrights chopped the felloes of wagon wheels. However, turning on the faceplate should be easier and will result in a round wheel,

In view of the small diameter of the ship's wheel it is suggested that Mr Fleck makes it with four spokes drilled centrally into four felloes. Draw the wheel full size either on paper or scrap ply to ascertain the width of the felloes. Having mitred the ends, dowel them and glue with waterproof glue. Let the glue thoroughly set and then screw the rim to a plywood faceplate at least ½in. thick and a little larger than the diagonals of the square rim. Fig. 1 shows the rim screwed through the wastewood to the ply

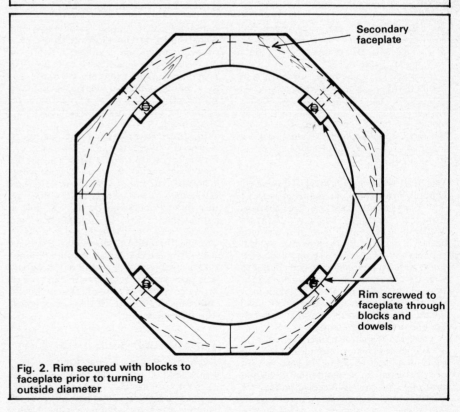

Fig. 1. Rim mounted centrally on ply faceplate

Fig. 2. Rim secured with blocks to faceplate prior to turning outside diameter

which is mounted centrally on the rear turning attachment. The inside diameter is first turned to the correct size, then the face is trued up and the rim edges shaped as required.

Unscrew the rim and saw off the four corners close to the finished size. Reduce the faceplate diameter to slightly less than that of the finished rim. Fit four dowels into blocks of wood the same thickness as the finished rim and insert the dowels into the holes bored through the felloes as in Fig. 2. Accurately centre the rim on the faceplate to which it is secured by screwing through the blocks. Run the lathe fairly slowly and turn the outside diameter. True-up the second face with the lathe running at normal speed.

The boss of the wheel is turned to the required size and shape and the spoke holes drilled. Turn four spokes long enough to fit well into the boss and to enter the rim to about a third of its width. The outer ends of the spokes are turned to fit the holes in the rim and are made parallel so that they can be inserted into the rim about ¾in. deeper than their ultimate position.

Work plenty of waterproof glue into the spoke holes of both rim and boss and insert the spokes into the rim as deep as they can go. Position the boss in the centre of the wheel and draw in the spokes until they 'bottom' in the boss. Check the wheel for true running and adjust it by tapping the rim before the glue sets.

The ends of the spokes which are held in the hand are turned to a comfortable shape with the inner ends reduced to fit the holes in the rim into which they enter for about two-thirds of the rim's width.

Ship's wheels are usually made from teak and finished with yacht varnish. Occasionally they are made from Australian black bean. The wheel is mounted so that one spoke is upright when steering dead ahead and on this spoke is worked a Turk's head knot.

Finishing veneer

From: H. R. Leach, North Nibley, Glos

I am restoring a 24ft circus living wagon and re-panelled the bedroom in veneers of English elm, the main living room in walnut and the ceiling throughout in sycamore. So far all the veneers are untreated; they are mounted on 6mm ply, except the sycamore which is on 4mm ply. I wish to finish the veneers to give as antique a look as possible and would prefer not to stain them as I think this would spoil the excellent grain effect they already have.

I would like all three veneers, and particularly the sycamore and the walnut, to have a 'yellow' effect. Could you please advise on the best way of polishing these woods. Would wax polishing be best? Could the veneers be treated with Cuprinol before the finishing is started, or might this affect the final result?

The question of final finishing of the veneer is not difficult since you could use wax as you suggest, or one of the Sterling Roncraft products such as Ronseal Mattcoat. The appearance you want to obtain is another matter however. All the veneers will, of course, take on a yellowish tint with time. It would have been better to have used weathered sycamore veneer for the ceiling: this is more buff in colour than the normal whitish sycamore and its use would have reduced the contrast between the elm and walnut veneer.

Reverting to your last query, Cuprinol in a clear or transparent grade and indeed, most if not all of these organic solvent preservatives can be painted or varnished over once the solvent has evaporated. We mention this now for several reasons: if you think it necessary to preserve the veneered panels, then the Cuprinol would be ideal but, although practically colourless in the can, the pentachloro-phenol content does tend to darken the wood, and it is possible that such initial treatment of the veneer would give the antique appearance you want. We can only suggest you try it out on an odd piece of similar material.

We must warn that all these wood preservatives are highly inflammable,

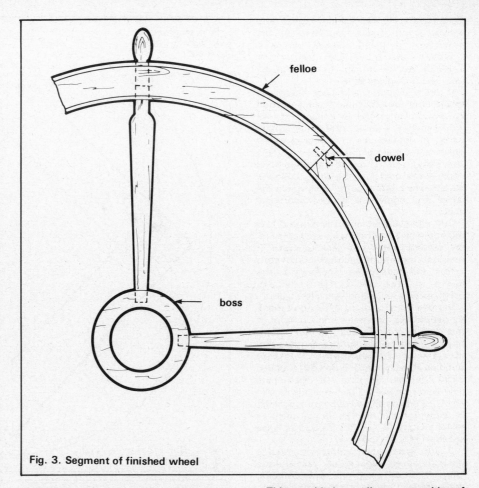

Fig. 3. Segment of finished wheel

particularly their fumes, so smoking and naked lights in the close confines of a caravan must be avoided. There is absolutely no problem after the spirit has evaporated and the fumes vented off, say, in 48hr. Should you decide to use the preservative, then no top finish must be applied before the spirit (solvent base) has evaporated.

Ignoring the aspect of using a preservative, we feel that the use of a Colron wood dye (and a light oak one all over might give the effect you want) followed by three coats of Ronseal Satincoat or Ronseal Mattcoat, allowing a day interval between coats will give a satisfactory finish by appearance and resistance to wear. If you care to write to Sterling Roncraft, Chapeltown, Sheffield S30 4YP, and ask for the colour brochure on Ronseal, wood dyes and woodshades, you can obtain a good idea of the type of appearance likely by use of these products. Alternatively, you could use a wax polish over a dyed veneer.

Treatment for pine

From: A.T. Wilkins, Hythe, Kent

I have been asked to make up new bits for old stripped pine furniture — legs, knobs, drawer fronts and suchlike. What sort of treatment can I give to the new pine to make it blend with the old?

When old pine furniture is stripped down the rather dull, aged appearance is as much due to the stripping process as to age. In other words the wood is more bleached than stripped. Usually, too, there is a faint residue of stain, not entirely removed by stripping. We suggest you experiment with some odd pieces of pine using a bleaching agent first of all.

This could be ordinary peroxide of hydrogen or oxalic acid crystals mixed in the proportion of 1oz of crystals dissolved in ½pt of hot water. Apply to the wood with a rag, using as many applications as necessary. Wipe over with vinegar and finally with clean water, and dry.

You might find that a light oak stain applied to the wood and then bleached-out might give a good result but this only makes more work, and we think that simple bleaching would be best. The avoidance of sharp arrises on replacement wood parts likewise encourages an aged appearance, but doubtless you know this.

Do not neglect to use rubber gloves when using strong chemicals like bleach. Strong soda solution could be used as an alternative to bleach.

What timber?

From: C.P. Burges, Exeter, Devon

I wonder if you would be so good as to identify the enclosed sample of wood? It has been used extensively in railway wagon-building, both for framing and lining purposes.

We have examined the wood sample and would say it appears typical of the various species of *Dipterocarpus* which occur throughout SE Asia. The different countries of growth do not differentiate between these species but sell their timber collectively under the commercial names of keruing and gurjun.

It is, therefore, impracticable to attempt a specific identification and we accordingly advise that the sample is keruing/gurjun *(Dipterocarpus* spp.). The wood has excellent strength properties and is used for constructional purposes, decking, flooring, sills and, of course, for vehicle bodies, wagon sides and floors etc.

WHAT'S NEW IN EQUIPMENT

The value for money deluxe twin-vice workbench, launched by Rawdon of Yeadon, West Yorkshire, has a large tool cupboard and a bank of five drawers.

Workbenches

Kiln-dried and selected African hardwood is used in the Rawdon workbenches introduced by Rawdon Machine Sales Ltd (WEF Woodworking Machinery Ltd), Sizers Court, Henshaw Lane, Yeadon, Leeds LS19 7DP (0532 504456). There are two models (both supplied in KD flat-pack form for self-assembly): the deluxe twin-vice, and standard twin-vice. The metal screw tail and front vices can be extended by bench dogs fitting in square mortise holes to the full length and width of the benches.

The deluxe incorporates tool cupboard with pegboard tool hanging on the inside of the door; alongside is a bank of five drawers one of which has a tray with compartments for smaller tools.

The standard bench is intended for the workshop having tool storage, so the cupboard and drawers are omitted. Price of the deluxe is given as £125 and the standard £85 (both prices exclusive of VAT).

Rawdon states that its benches are of attractive appearance and have a high level of dimensional stability.

Chainsaw from Sweden

Described as a lightweight chainsaw the Partner Mini from Sweden is introduced to the UK market by C. D. Monninger Ltd, Overbury Road, London NI5 6RJ (01-800 5435). Weighing 7.9lb and powered by an air-cooled 34cc two-stroke it is designed for two-handed operation but can be worked with one hand.

The saw is said to incorporate an inertia-type automatic chain braking system to reduce the dangers arising from kick-back. Pullcord start, electronic ignition and sealing against moisture and dirt are claimed to ensure easy starting in all weather conditions. Price is given as approximately £117 plus VAT. Illustrated booklet is available and Monninger states that it is seeking distributors.

Above: the Partner mini chainsaw and below the Lurem ME40 panelsaw.

Panelsaw with 10ft carriage

The Lurem ME40 panelsaw has a 10ft (3200mm) carriage and mirco-setting fence for accuracy. The scoring unit eliminates spelching to give a professional finish to veneered and plastics-coated panels. Other features include the cam type carriage lock, fence sizing stops and a blade speed chart.

Machinery Plus Ltd, 9 Biggin Hill Road, Evington, Leicester LE5 6HQ (0533 735554), which is Lurem agent in UK, says the saw has a wide variety of uses in furniture making and joinery shops or diy stores.

Glue pot and glue

The old-fashioned glue pot necessary when using Scotch glue is available from R. Oldfield, 143 Cotefield Drive, Leighton Buzzard LU7 8DN (052-537 3976). The 1pt capacity cast aluminium inner pot is fitted with brush support and wiper bar while the outer pot is also of cast aluminium for use on electric or gas ring heating source. Handles of inner and outer pots have heat-resistant sheathing. Price inclusive of post and packing is £13 and this covers a pack of best Scotch glue and glue brush. Mr Oldfield also supplies Scotch glue separately (best golden grain animal glue) at £1.60 a lb inclusive of post and packing.

Cast aluminium glue pot of 1pt capacity.

More shade

From Sterling Roncraft Ltd, Chapeltown, Sheffield S30 4YP (074-15 3171), comes information of a new shade in the Hi-Build Woodshades range of polyurethane varnish. This is chestnut and described by the company as midway between the existing dark oak and antique oak finishes. It is available in 250 and 500ml containers.

No rusting

Stainless steel hinges with single and double spring action are offered ex-stock by Charles P. Moody, Broadford Mills, Shalford, Guildford, Surrey (0483 77161). Sizes are 3 to 8in. and the finish is either bright or satin. The springs are described as being 'totally rust-free' and specially suitable for marine application.

Eclipse Little Beaver saw and storage tray.

Multi-purpose small saw

Described as a multi-purpose small saw which will deal with most materials likely to be encountered in modelmaking, the Eclipse Little Beaver is from Neill Tools Ltd, Napier Street, Sheffield S11 8HB (0742 71281). It comes with three interchangeable blades of 150mm length having respectively 32 teeth per in. (tpi) for cutting soft metal, plastics, etc; 14 tpi for hardwood and softwood; and 7tpi for rough wood cutting.

The saw is said to be perfectly balanced, with pistol-grip handle and screw and knurled nut assembly for speedy blade change and accurate tensioning.

Included in the package is a three-section storage tray for nuts and bolts, washers, screws and such like. Recommended retail price from stockists is £3.98 inclusive of VAT.

Noise reduction by B & D

The industrial division of Black & Decker Ltd, has been renamed the professional division and continues to handle the tradesman and industrial ranges of power tools and accessories. Marketing and technical departments are at Bath Road, Harmondsworth, Middlesex and distribution and customer service at Cannon Lane, Maidenhead, Berks.

The division has recently issued a four-page leaflet illustrating and describing products in the tradesman and industrial ranges. New point-of-sale stands in large and small versions are available to stockists for showing the various products.

New items introduced include the BG10/M and BG10 10in. bench grinder, the latter being the three-phase model. A 1½hp motor is fitted and fine or medium grinding wheels are available, also wire wheel brushes. A new accessory is the bi-metal holesaw with HSS teeth and diameters of 20, 25, 32, 38 and 51mm all fitted with the extra length pilot drill.

The company has paid particular attention to reducing the noise level of its new power tools. This is in line with current thinking by the health and safety agencies in this country.

It is expected that the company will announce during 1980 the introduction of further power tools specifically for woodworking processes.

250mm bench grinder for Black & Decker's industrial range. 1½hp machine available in single or three-phase.

Packaging changes

Following the take-over of Furniglas Ltd by Evode Ltd, Common Road, Stafford (0785 57755), the former's wood finishing products have been given new packaging designs. The Furniglas fadeless wood dyes are now known as Long-life wood colours. These are water-based and can be diluted or intermixed to provide the desired shade. The Furniglas PU-15 polyurethane varnishes include exterior and interior gloss formulations, satin and matt clear finishes and transparent coloured varnishes in light, brown and dark oak, teak, red cedar and mahogany shades.

New livery for Furniglas.

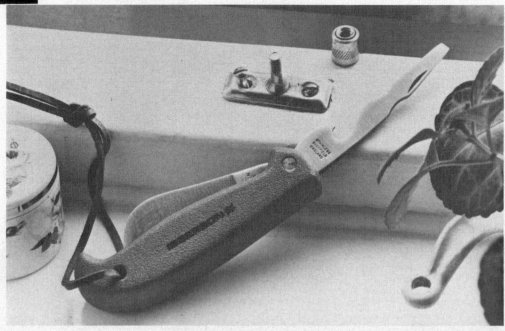

George Ibberson & Co Ltd Handyman's knife showing screwdriver blade. The cutting blade is of stainless steel.

Handyman's knife

With a curved stainless steel blade and also a blade having tapered blunt end for use as a screwdriver and curved indentations for wire-stripping, the Handyman's knife from George Ibberson & Co Ltd, Violin Works, Scotland Street, Sheffield S3 7DE (0742 731621), is available from ironmongers and hardware stores at £4.64 plus VAT. The handle is of plastics material fitted with leather thong. The company manufactures a variety of 'pocket' knives, details of which are given on the Handyman's knife packaging.

Finger-jointing

Marketed in conjunction with C. D. Monninger Ltd, Overbury Road, London N15 6RJ (01-800 5435), is a 10mm finger-jointing machine made by Ladbourne Engineering of Ware. It is said that the machine can joint timber even down to 150mm long such as, for example, offcuts. Monninger is also introducing more tooling from Leitz of West Germany. Included is a solid multi-profile cutter with HSS-tipped teeth for producing mouldings; quick-change adaptor for dowel boring and hinge boring bits; and a range of knives for most of the well-known names of portable electric planers.

Door openings

All the components for constructing internal door openings come in two shrink-wrapped packs branded Dorkit. There is a choice of five doors in three different sizes and four different frame depths. One pack contains the door frame (factory-jointed and machined) with the keep plate and hinges fixed in place. The other pack contains the door fitted with mortise latch and recessed for hinges, with the architraves mitred and pre-assembled into 'goal posts'. Architraves and frame are primed ready for painting.

Dorkit is a product of John Carr Joinery Sales Ltd, Watch House Lane, Doncaster DN5 9LR (0302 21333), which has issued a leaflet giving specification, sizes and finishes. Copies of the leaflet can be had from the company's stockists.

John Carr has introduced the Carr-Regency six-panel moulded door in a range of sizes for internal use. The door is of one-piece construction which is claimed to prevent joint separation and grain rise common in traditionally constructed panel doors.

Spraying equipment

Three compressor-type sprayers in the Sprayit range distributed by Burgess Power Tools Ltd, Sapcote LE9 6JW (045-527 2292), are the WOB.L 708, 808 and 1008, all for 220/240V supply and rated respectively 325W, 1.57A; 400W, 2.1A; and 525W, 3.2A; Free air delivery is given as 3.7, 4 and 4.4cfm.

The company states that each sprayer is supplied with gun, hose, internal and external mix nozzles and instructions; the compressor can also be used as an air source. RRP are respectively £138.60; £150; and £176.50 plus VAT in each case.

One of the compressor-type spraying units now available from Burgess Power Tools Ltd.

Plate jointing

For joining timber together in the construction of sheds, fences, gates, framework and suchlike, the OBO timber connector is offered in two sizes: one for 2 and 2½in., the other for 3in. connections. Douglas Kane Ltd, Carlyon Road, Atherstone CV9 1LQ (08277 4511), states that the OBO connector is made of treated mild steel with teeth and the plate is driven in across the two timbers being joined by means of a hammer and a block of wood.

Plated joints are used extensively in roof-truss manufacture though in such instances the plates are driven in by power. To ensure a tight connection in roof-trusses the members are clamped together while the plate is being driven in.

OBO timber connectors join wood quickly, simply and strongly, no nailing, gluing, screwing or dowelling required. Available in two sizes for 2"/2½" joints and 3" joints.

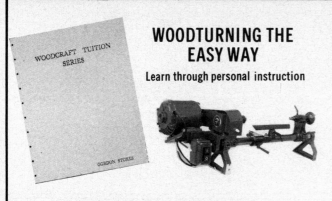

Universal woodworking machine

Zinken Compact 21 (ZC-21) universal woodworking machine with 'monobloc' construction is said to offer six individual machines in one unit. Changing of belts is no longer necessary. Indeed, 'the operative simply turns the ignition key, alters a gear selection lever to the required operation, engages the motor and all the power is directed to the single operation pre-selected.' This information is supplied by Sumaco Machinery & Tools Division of Susemihl (UK) Ltd, Newcombe Street Works, Elland HX5 0EG (0422 75491).

Above: Zinken compact 21 universal woodworker imported by Sumaco Machinery & Tools.

Wadkin bandsaws

At Loftus, Co Cleveland, Wadkin Bursgreen division of Wadkin Ltd, Green Lane Works, Leicester LE5 4PF (0533 769111), has set up a new factory to manufacture bandsaws. Virtually the whole of this 12,500sq ft factory is engaged in producing bandsaws so as to achieve economies of scale. First machines to come from Loftus are the series C. These are said to have larger worktables than usual with

tilting facility from 0-35°, V-belt drive; heavy main frames; top slide adjustment of 100mm thus allowing 200mm blade variance; sealed-for-life bearings on top and bottom wheels; Carter guides with replaceable shoes; comprehensive guarding; starters with 'no-volt' protection; and a wide range of optional extras.

Series C comprises five models: C9, C8, C7, C6 and C5 with wheel diameters of 900, 800, 700, 600 and 500mm respectively and maximum cutting widths of 880, 780, 680, 580 and 480mm.

Portable tools from Wadkin

With its reputation established on high-production machines for wood processing, Wadkin Ltd of Leicester, has made what deputy chairman Michael Goddard describes as a 'logical diversification and one complimentary to our existing business' by introducing a range of industrial portable power tools. This will be handled by the newly formed portable power tool division at Trent Lane, Castle Donington, Derby DE7 2PU (0332 812267), under the general managership of J. W. Nutt.

Initially 14 tools are being offered with those for woodworking predominating. All are made by the Japanese Ryobi concern to meet Wadkin requirements and those of BSI. Several of the tools carry the Kite-mark.

The range comprises: belt sander B-7200A (4in.) and B-7075 (3in.) with dust bag and abrasive belt as standard accessories and a bench stand as an extra (this is for sanding short pieces); both models have belt speed of 350m/min. There are also orbital sanders LS-35 medium duty and SU-6200 wide pad size both operating at 10,000 orbits/min with a $^5/_{64}$ in. diameter of orbit.

Hand planer L-1512 has cutter blade $3^5/_8$ in. wide, $^3/_{64}$ in. planing depth and quick blade replace-

ment facility; sharpening attachment is a standard accessory. Machined groove on front and rear shoes acts as a guide when chamfering and edge planing. The heavy-duty router R-500 has a 2hp motor and plunge capacity of 0-2⅜in. No-load speed is 22,000rpm and collet capacity ½in. Standard accessories include guide holder, straight guide, roller attachment, template guide, bit adaptors, spanners and straight bit.

Impact drill PD-1920 has two speeds for both rotary and percussion drilling and is provided with depth adjustment stop bar. Chuck capacity is ½in. and weight 4.6lb. There are two models of circular saw — W-6502 and W-8502 having blades of 7⅛in. and 9¼in. diameter respectively. Maximum cutting capacity at 90° is given as $2^{31}/_{64}$ and $3^{11}/_{32}$ in. respectively. Both models are fitted with anti-kickback riving knife and powerful motor. There is also a chainsaw (model CS-360) and this is

said to be the lightest in its class. The 240V version has chain speed of 530m/min. Maximum cut-off length is 14in.

Included in the range are models G-1000 and G-1150 grinder and G-1800 and G-2300 angle grinder, the latter machines having a 1,700W motor.

Illustrated leaflets can be had on application to Wadkin portable power tools division at the address given above. A number of distributors have been appointed and service and spares facilities arranged. At Castle Donington there is a permanent showroom, spares depot and service centre.

Mr Nutt describes the new machines as essentially operators' tools — easy to set, well balanced and extra powerful which have already been extensively 'user tested' by firms in the Leicester area. It is understood that other models will be brought on to the market during the next 12 months.

Above: Wadkin hand planer, model L-1512.
Left: Wadkin plunge router, model R-500.

WOODTURNING LATHE BY LUREM

NEW MODEL!

SPECIAL PRICE £275 + VAT

HEIGHT ABOVE BED : 120mm (4½")
MAXIUM TURNING ø : 240mm (9")
DISTANCE BETWEEN CENTRES : 800mm (31")
3 SPEEDS : 1200/1500/2700r.p.m.

Standard Accessories:
Rotating centre, 4-spike centre, Screw centre
& Cone punch

Optional Attachments:
Faceplate ø 200mm, 3-jaw chuck ø 100mm, 13mm chuck for
drilling extra long tool rest (500mm), Faceplate turning
attachment (ø 400mm), Table for lathe and motor, Motor O,
75HP — single or 3-phase Woodturning tools Clamps for adapting
lathe to JUNIOR machine table.

**WOKINGHAM TOOL CO. LTD.,
99 Wokingham Road, Reading, Berks.
Tel. Reading 661511**

A Meddings Jig Sawing machine cuts costs and corners

*MK. IV MODEL
(with 25" throat)*

Meddings Scroll
and Jigsawing
Machines not only
provide the accuracy
required by professional
sign manufacturers, stand-fitters and carpenters employing high-cost modern materials but the robustness, reliability and reasonable pricing essential for widespread
use in schools and training colleges. Floor or bench
models available.
Other Meddings products include Drilling Machines,
pneumatic Sanding Drums & Wet Sandstone grinders.

MEDDINGS

BUY BRITISH BUY MEDDINGS

W. J. Meddings (Sales) Ltd., Lee Mill Industrial Estate,
Ivybridge, Devon. Tel: Ivybridge (075 54) 3277.

A NEW DIMENSION IN ROUTING!

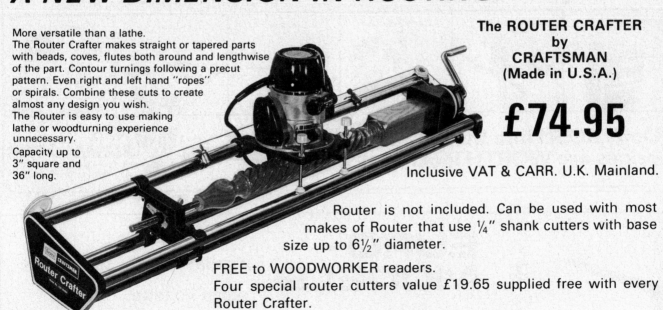

More versatile than a lathe.
The Router Crafter makes straight or tapered parts
with beads, coves, flutes both around and lengthwise
of the part. Contour turnings following a precut
pattern. Even right and left hand "ropes"
or spirals. Combine these cuts to create
almost any design you wish.
The Router is easy to use making
lathe or woodturning experience
unnecessary.
Capacity up to
3" square and
36" long.

**The ROUTER CRAFTER
by
CRAFTSMAN
(Made in U.S.A.)**

£74.95

Inclusive VAT & CARR. U.K. Mainland.

Router is not included. Can be used with most
makes of Router that use ¼" shank cutters with base
size up to 6½" diameter.

FREE to WOODWORKER readers.
Four special router cutters value £19.65 supplied free with every
Router Crafter.

We can also supply CRAFTSMAN Routers — All ¼" shank and 240 volt.
½ H.P. Router : ⅞ H.P. Home Craftsman Router
1 H.P. Heavy Duty Router (Illustrated).
SEND NOW for details and current prices of the range of CRAFTSMAN Tools

AVON TOOL CENTRE 6a HAYMARKET WALK, BRISTOL BS1 3LN
Telephone: (0272) 298947

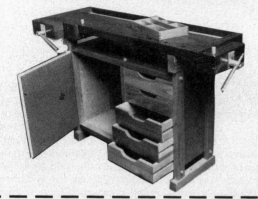

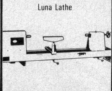

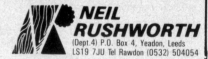

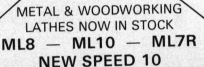

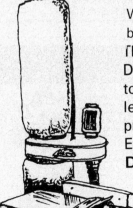

Prices quoted are those prevailing at press date and are subject to alteration due to economic conditions.

Classified Advertisements

FOR SALE

Snooker & Pool
Build your own table plans. Chipboard, Slate. (Send £1.50). Cloth, Rubber Balls, Materials etc. Snooker, Pool Coin-op. tables Bought/Sold. New/Reconditioned.
"HIGH POINT" Garstang Road East, Singleton, Blackpool, Lancs. FY6 7SX. Tel: 0253-883426
Advice Centre

EMCOSTAR — Ideal for model maker or handyman. Combination circular and bandsaw. Attachments include fret and jigsaws, grinding wheel, circular saw sharpener, spare blades all saws. Worth over £500 new. Will sell £350 or sensible offer. Edward-Collins, Bodmin 850502. L

FOR SALE

Coronet Major as new, many accessories. Cabinet mounted, value £1,000 — Accept £750.
Tel: 021-784-0826 or call:
88 Stechford Road, Hodge Hill, Birmingham.

BRASS OR ALUMINIUM plates for your project. Letters block or script, example 3" x 1" brass plate with 20 block letters £1.10p plus post, plus VAT. Also engraved badges, name plates, numbers, labels etc. in coloured plastic. Trade enquiries welcome. Brian J. Bowman Trophies Limited, "Anela", Lower North Street, Cheddar, Somerset. Tel: Cheddar 742774. LMN

FOR SALE: ML8 wood turning lathe rear turning attachment face plates sanding table, ½ h.p. motor. Offers over £150. 8 Vine Farm Close, Kirk Hallam, Ilkeston, Derbyshire. L

CORONET minor planer attachment, little used £60. Variety old woodworking tools. Power drill rebating attachment. Offers? Maidenhead 39498. L

'NORRIS' shoulder plane 1¼" rosewood and dovetailed steel. Offers? Ashton, 15 Victoria Street, Barnsley, S. Yorkshire. L

FOR SALE Stanley 45 multiplane with cutters £35. Tel: Norwich 413011. L

YOUR advertisements are seen every month FOR A MONTH. Why not ring GILL for details on: 0442-41221 Ext. 241.

HOBBYIST has surplus mouldings and timber for sale. P. H. Manning, 387 Liverpool Road, Southport, Merseyside. L

MYFORD 4½" PLANER — complete — thicknesser — stand — ½ h.p. motor. Excellent condition — buyer collects. £65.00. Mason, 11 Woodlands Road, Lepton, Huddersfield. L

UNUSED mortice attachment and bits for coronet minor lathe £40. Tel: Storrington 3120, Sussex. L

CARNAUBA WAX, green baize, S.A.E. for List, Blands, Oldbury-on-Severn, Glos. T/C

MATERIALS

FIRST QUALITY 8 day weight driven grandfather clock movements, break arch dials, battery grandfather clock movements 24" and 28" pendulum, battery clock movements from £3.70. All clock accessories. SAE please: Timecraft, 164 Park Road, Formby, Liverpool. T/C

VENEERS, all types, S.A.E. List — S. Gould (Veneers) 342, Uxbridge Road, W.12. Tel: 01-743.2561. T/C

G. K. HADFIELD

Immediate despatch from stock, of materials for clock restoration. Finials, hands, keys, pendulums, suspensions, weights, pulleys and hundreds of other items.

Write, phone or call. Peaceful parking!

Send large SAE 16p for free lists of materials and new/old horological books.

Blackbrook Hill House, Tickow Lane, SHEPSHED, Loughborough LE12 9EY. Phone: Shepshed (05095) 3014.

VENEERS

SHORT AND FULL LEAVES
In all popular timbers. Send S.A.E. for FREE price list or 45p for samples of 12 pieces 4" × 3" to:
ELLIOTT BROS.
Four Winds, Moorwoods Lane, Dore
All letters to PO Box No. 6, Glossop, Derby. Reg. No. 2064782

WOODTURNERS' SUPPLIES

Ceramic tiles, Table-lighter inserts, Egg timers, Hour glasses, Barometers, Nut Bowl Hardware, Rubber Stoppers, Peppermills, Cheese Knives, Polishes and waxes, etc. Catalogue S.A.E.

COUNTRY CRAFT STUDIO
Lawshall, Bury St. Edmunds, Suffolk.

TROLL

For
STEEL WOOL
TROLLULL (U.K.) LTD
16 Richfield Avenue, READING, Berks. RG1 8HH Tel: Reading (0734) 596464

HARDWOOD OFFCUTS in seasoned English Oak, Iroko, Mahogany etc. Trial pack for £9.50 including mainland carriage and V.A.T. Traditional Doors, Biddenden, Ashford, Kent. LNPRTVX

MANCHESTER 061-236 2477

FRED ALDOUS LTD
37 LEVER STREET

Supply materials for Basketry, Stool Seating, Lampshade making, Marquetry, Modelling, Pewter, Copper, Enamelling, Leather Work.

SEASONED RUSSIAN PINE 17 x 7cm (7" x 3"), 15', 11' 6", and 8' lengths. Only 5000ft available, ideal for sauna cabins, pine furniture etc. From £1.30 per foot. Tel: Wix (Essex) 616. KLM

Rustic woodslices for house signs, wall plaques etc.
Seasoned hardwoods with bark on, sawn obliquely up to 30" long. £1.75 each or 3 for £4.25. Post paid. Special price for quantities.

A. CRACKNELL
Bromeswell
Woodbridge,
Suffolk.
Tel: Eyke 574.

MUSICAL INSTRUMENT MAKERS

Send for *Free Catalogue* of imported tonewood for Lute, Guitar, Violin and Keyboard.

A. HIGHFIELD & COMPANY
Rosewood House, Bridge Road, Downham Market, Norfolk, PE38 0AE

SEASONED English Hardwoods. Air and kiln dried timbers for the discerning craftsman. P. Smith, Furniture Makers, Chapel Workshops, Kirkburn, Driffield, E. Yorkshire. Tel. Driffield 89301. T/C

HEGNER UNIVERSAL SAWS

The world's first universal precision saw cuts 50mm wood, 10mm steel, plastics, rubber etc. Very safe in use. Not to be compared with a fretsaw. 8p stamp, for Brochures.

36 Great Eastern Road, Hockley, Essex. Tel: Hockley 5669

See these machines in action at the Model Engineer exhibition. Wembley Conference centre. Stand A11 Avon Suite. 2nd to 12th January, 1980, excluding Sundays.

WANTED: Boxwood (or similar) stringing, quantity of reproduction brass gallery, large sheet old mahogany for table leaf. Coventry, 8 New Acres, Newburgh, Parbold, Lancs. WN8 7TU. L

Materials for the
Amateur and Professional
VIOLIN & GUITAR MAKER

Send S.A.E. 11p
plus 50p for either cat.
50p deductable
from purchase £5.00 or over

SYDNEY EVANS LTD.
45 Regent Place,
Birmingham, B1 3BN
Tel: (021) 233-1741

Suppliers of all types of woodworking equipment.
Stockists of Elu and Bosch tools and complete range of fixings.
Opening hours:
Mon-Fri 8.00-6.00 Sat 9.00-12.00
Send today for our free catalogue
**The R.M. Tool and Fixing Co. Ltd.,
17 Hollybush Lane, Penn,
Wolverhampton.
Tel. 37015**

MAKE HANDSOME CLOCKS
for Pleasure or Profit . . . with
. . . our superb electronic and quartz battery movements from the world famous KIENZLE Works. With every one we include a traditional style dial beautifully screened on metallic gold card. The quality of our movements can be judged by the repeat orders we enjoy. SAE details now: SMS/Kingswoode (W1), 24 Holwood Road, Bromley, Kent. BR1 3EB.

SCALE MODEL AXLES FOR WAGON MAKERS

A large range of purpose-made cart half-arms, collinge and other special axles for popular models available by mail order together with coach bolts and square nuts, model makers' materials and wood. Send 3 first class stamps for coloured brochure illustrating horses and full price lists:
**Lenham Pottery (WW)
215 Wroxham Road,
Norwich, NR7 8AQ**

MINIATURE 1" to 1' scale Chippendale drawer pulls, Butts, and H. Hinges all in Brass. Send £1.50 for samples. Bailey, 131 Centre Drive, Newmarket, CB8 8AP, Suffolk. J-L

HARDWOODS: Rosewood, Imbuya, Folh-Ade-Bolo, Yew, Teak, Walnut. Other species. Rio Rosewood veneer £1.00 per sq. ft. Tel: Reading 695336 (evenings/Saturdays). L

Cabinet Makers, Woodcarvers, Woodturners, Luthiers, etc.
PERSONAL TUITION WITH A DIFFERENCE
We specialise in supply of small quantities
EXOTIC WOODS
and no order is too small!
Send s.a.e. for our descriptive list of: Indian Rosewood, Laurel, Indian Ebony, Macassar Ebony, Satin-wood, Tulipwood, Grande Pallisander, Cocobolo, Lauro Preto, Teak, Andaman Padauk, etc. . .

bruce boulter
12 Colview Court,
Mottingham Lane,
London SE9 4RP
Tel: 01-851-0590

COURSES

BE YOUR OWN CRAFTSMAN
with a little help from us . . .

HARPSICHORDS SPINETS AND CLAVICHORDS FOR SELF ASSEMBLY

residential instrument making courses in Chichester

**JOHN STORRS
HUNSTON,
CHICHESTER, SUSSEX**

WOODTURNING: Personal 2-day courses by a professional woodturner, in fully equipped workshop within a 13th century priory, set in the heart of Newcastle. Accommodation provided. SAE for details to: Peter Dickinson, Blackfriars, Stowell Street, Newcastle-upon-Tyne. K-Q

WOODCARVING — a course in carving with expert tuition. For overseas clients, a four course by post £20. F. W. Miles, 23 Rands Estate, Preston, Hull, N. Humberside. Tel: Hull 896441. LM

WOODTURNING: come to historic Ironbridge — birthplace of British industry. Professional craftsman John Murtha offers expert tuition. Please telephone Telford 883364 for details. L

Prices quoted are those prevailing at press date and are subject to alteration due to economic conditions.

There is a national shortage of teachers of
Design, Craft and Technology

At **Crewe + Alsager College of Higher Education** you can study courses in Design, Technology and the Crafts of working wood, metal, plastics and other 2 and 3 dimensional materials which will qualify you to teach Design, Craft and Technology in secondary schools.

These courses are available in the following qualifications:

(a) 3yr and 4yr Dip. H. E./B.Ed. and B.Ed. Honours degrees for students with two 'A' levels or equivalent experience

(b) One-year Special Course in Design, Craft and Technology for students with H.N.C. or City & Guilds full technological certificate or equivalent

(c) One-year retraining course for qualified teachers of other subjects.

We have a modern outlook, a modern campus, first class study and recreational facilities, easy access by road and rail, plenty of attractive accommodation and a developed social environment.

For further details contact the Academic Office (Admissions), Crewe + Alsager College of Higher Education, Crewe. CWI 1DU.

Crewe+Alsager College
of Higher Education

Bind it

It's so easy and tidy with the Easibind binder to file your copies away. Each binder is designed to hold approximately 12 issues and is attractively bound and blocked with the WOODWORKER logo.

Price UK £3.20 including postage, packing and VAT, overseas orders add 40p. Why not place your order now and send the completed coupon below with remittance to:

it's easy with EASIBIND

Easibind Ltd., 4 Uxbridge St., London, W8 7SZ.

Order Form Woodworker

I enclose PO/cheque value .... for

.... binders.

Years required ....
(BLOCK LETTERS PLEASE)

Name ....

Address ....

....

....

Date ....

Registration No. 307469

WOODMEN

WEEKLY DELIVERIES TO ALL PARTS OF THE U.K. BY OUR OWN TRANSPORT

WADKIN QUALITY WITHIN YOUR REACH! A new range of top quality, superb value power tools from the country's best known and most reputable manufacturers of industrial woodworking machines. EXAMPLES: Wadkin 2 h.p. plunging router £128; Wadkin 3⅝" hand planer £73; Wadkin orbital sanders £39 or £86; Wadkin 4" belt sander £135. (Ask for full details of the range or send your order for immediate dispatch).

IS £365 TOO MUCH TO PAY FOR THE STARTRITE INCA 3-SPEED BANDSAW? Yes or no, you'll be delighted to learn we are offering a new single speed version of this proven machine for just £199.90 (+ £9 delivery). Fitted with heavy-duty TONVR push button starter and 3/4 h.p. motor, the INCA offers a working capacity that simply cannot be equalled for this price.

ELEKTRA HC260 FULLY CAST SURFACE PLANER & 10"×6" CAPACITY AUTO-FEED THICKNESSER, INCREDIBLE VALUE AT £379 + £9 delivery. (M.R.P. £598) The tables and bed are ground to an exceptionally fine and accurate finish. The integral motor generates an output of nearly 2½ H.P. making it the most powerful unit fitted to a machine of this size and type. FREE COLOUR CATALOGUE of this and other planers on request.

CORONET MAJOR CMB500 UNIVERSAL WITH SAW-TABLE, REBATING SURFACE PLANER, A SET OF 6 ASHLEY ILES PROFESSIONAL TURNING TOOLS AND A HEAVY DUTY T.C.T. SAWBLADE UNBEATABLE AT £616 + £9 delivery. (M.R.P. £738). The MAJOR is the *only* universal that successfully combines turning with the other principal wood-machining operations. The unique swivelling headstock enables "feed" and takeoff areas to be re-located in a few seconds, invaluable wherever workshop space is restricted. FREE CATALOGUE on request covering the complete CORONET range.

DeWALT'S NEW RADIAL ARM SAW, THE DW125, HIGH PRECISION, MULTIPURPOSE, VIRTUALLY A COMPLETE WORKSHOP IN ONE QUALITY MACHINE. OUR PRICE: £329 + £9 delivery. DELIVERED THIS MONTH WITH A FREE FLOORSTAND. (Total M.R.P. £467). Safely cross-cuts the heaviest timber sections at an infinite variety of angles. Tenons, rebates, grooves, bevels, etc. etc. with equal facility. Converts timber and sheet materials into the exact sizes required. The DW125 also offers a comprehensive range of attachments for moulding, routing, drilling, sanding and jig-sawing. ALSO IN STOCK, THE NEW 12" RADIAL ARM SAW FROM DeWALT: £419 + £9 delivery. (M.R.P. £517).

THE LATEST 3 H.P. FLOORSTANDING SAWBENCH WITH WHEEL OPERATED RISE & FALL, TILTING ARBOR, FENCES & T.O.N.V.R. PUSH BUTTON STARTER FOR ONLY £169 + delivery. (M.R.P. £221). Exceptionally high power output enables you to use the full 3¾" depth of cut without overloading. The basic saw is complete with wired switch and motor, all above and below table guards, blade, etc. (Also in stock for this model are: a FULL SIZE PANEL EXTENSION for handling 8' + 4' sheets £25.38 and a 6 BEARING SLIDING DIMENSION TABLE at £64.87)

WOODTURNING IS A PRACTICAL PROPOSITION FOR EVERYONE WITH THE NEW "ELF" LATHE FROM CORONET. COMPLETE, COMPACT AND INVITINGLY PRICED AT £159 + £9 delivery. Substantially built from cast iron and offering a full range of chucks and fittings at very reasonable cost, the ELF will enable you to tackle full scale turning projects for the minimum possible outlay. (Ask for details of all our heavy duty lathes, including machines from MYFORD, ARUNDEL, KITY AND HARRISON.)

ELU 600 WATT PLUNGING ROUTER COMPLETE WITH FENCES, CUTTERS ETC., STILL ONLY £75 + £3 delivery. (M.R.P. £99.50). Supplied with an illustrated manual to lead you through the potentially limitless workshop and site applications for this uniquely versatile tool. (ELU saws, sanders, grinders, timbers, trimmers and production routers always available for immediate dispatch.)

A BANDSAW TO DEEP CUT MORE THAN 6" OF HARDWOOD WITH POWER TO SPARE! NOW, only £229 + £9 delivery. (M.R.P. £298). DeWALT'S FAMOUS BS1310IS NOW FITTED WITH A SILENT RUNNING BUT POWERFUL INDUCTION MOTOR TO COPE WITH THE TOUGHEST CUTTING PROBLEMS. Rigid frame, above and below table guides and thrust rollers, efficient lateral blade support and sensitive tracking control combine to ensure accuracy when shaping delicate contours or cutting large tenons etc. (Bandsaws up to 24" throat capacity can be seen at our showrooms at any time.)

HEAVY WORKSHOP MACHINERY, MORTISERS, TENONERS, PANEL SAWS, MOULDERS, EXTRACTORS, GUILLOTINES ETC. ALL IN STOCK FOR IMMEDIATE DELIVERY. RING FOR FULL DETAILS OF ANY MACHINE YOU REQUIRE.

To take advantage of any offer, simply post or telephone your order direct to us today.

You can pay by cheque (payable to WOODMEN), by BARCLAYCARD or ACCESS, or we will collect C.O.D. Alternatively, we can arrange credit at a very attractive annual interest charge of just 12%.

Our vehicles now operate a weekly delivery service to every part of the U.K. mainland. Frustrating delays and any danger of damage in transit are therefore avoided.

FULL CASH REFUND GUARANTEE ON ANY MACHINE SUPPLIED BY US IF YOU ARE NOT COMPLETELY SATISFIED

---

43 CRWYS ROAD, CARDIFF CF2 4ND
TEL: (0222) 36519/373793/35221

Woodworker

THE MAGAZINE FOR THE CRAFTSMAN IN WOOD

FEBRUARY 1980   VOL. 84   NO. 1035

FRONT COVER: Hal Brooks in his clown costume (photo: *Sylvia Hayes*) pictured with the first and second prize winning clowns from the 1979 Ashley Iles/Woodworker carving competition (photo: *Brenda Norrish*).

Editor	Geoffrey Pratt
Production Editor	Polly Curds
Group Advertisement Manager	Michael Merrifield
Managing Director	Gospatric Home
Editorial Director	Ron Moulton

MEMBER OF THE AUDIT
BUREAU OF CIRCULATIONS

SUBSCRIPTION DEPARTMENT: Remittances to MODEL AND ALLIED PUBLICATIONS, P.O. Box 35, Hemel Hempstead, Herts HP1 1EE. Price per copy 50p plus postage 21p. Subscription queries: Tel: Hemel Hempstead 51740. Subscription rate £8.40 per annum; overseas sterling £8.40; $19.00 U.S. for overseas dollar subscribers. Second class postage paid at New York, NY North American enquiries regarding news stand sales should be sent to: Eastern News Distribution, 111 Eighth Avenue, New York, NY 1011, USA. Telephone (212) 255-5620 and craft and hobby sales to Bill Dean Books Ltd., 166-41 Powells Cove Boulevard, Whitestone, New York 11357, USA. Telephone (212) 767-6632.

Model & Allied Publications Ltd

P.O. Box 35, Bridge Street, Hemel Hempstead, Herts HP1 1EE. Telephone: Hemel Hempstead (0442) 41221.

AN APPROACH TO QUALITY

A visitor's remark at the Woodworker Show last November sums up a paradoxical situation. He said: 'It amazes me what a high standard of skill is shown by people who do woodwork purely as a hobby ...' The craftsmanship displayed in the competitive classes was certainly high and proves that skills today are no less than in former times, as is sometimes averred.

Yet despite the skills that exist (and woodworking is by no means the sole activity displaying skills), Britain's products do not rate so highly in the quality stakes. Indeed, it has been found necessary to issue BS5750 *Quality systems* which, if applied could help provide this country with a new reputation for quality in industry.

British Standards Institution emphasises that BS5750 makes no reference to any specific product or industry. The aim is to present practical requirements of quality assurance that are fundamental. The standard may be used as the yardstick against which a firm's capability of undertaking a contract is assessed. 'Quality for an organisation working to the standard will not mean just the assiduous correction of defects and failures but a practical discipline which integrates objectives throughout the industrial process from design to marketing and servicing.'

BSI has been tackling quality systems for some time by formalising terminology and recommending systematic procedures wherever possible. BS5750 specifies requirements for three levels of system for the assurance of quality of products or services, or both. It can be used in a number of ways: it may form the basis for evaluating a supplier's quality management system or be invoked in a contract to specify appropriate quality assurance requirements. It may be used in other documents such as product standards, where reference to a quality management system is appropriate.

Disciplined and properly integrated requirements can help to bring under control the high variability in quality which is now so common, states BSI. Indeed, it has been suggested that quality and reliability are critical factors absent from most costing and economic evaluation systems and that this is due, no doubt, to the fact that they demand technical rather than financial competence.

BS5750 is obtainable from BSI sales department, 101 Pentonville Road, London N1 9ND, at £2.60 for each of the three parts comprising the standard.

After the Show

'One of the finest things that has begun to happen is that craftsmen inclined to self-discovery are beginning to get together. They tend to bump into one another, quite casually, almost by accident. A few people meet, and suddenly one person is saying to another: "Hey, you live only 20 miles down the road from me. I didn't know you existed. I thought I was alone in these parts." Next thing you know these two people are talking, exchanging ideas, taking up practical problems: where to get wood, tools, machines, and so on. An exchange begins; it's like rings on water ... I see this as one of the most positive forces at work.' James Krenov in his new book *The Impractical Cabinetmaker* (Van Nostrand Reinhold Co Ltd, Wokingham), £8.50.

Lurem, make it so easy

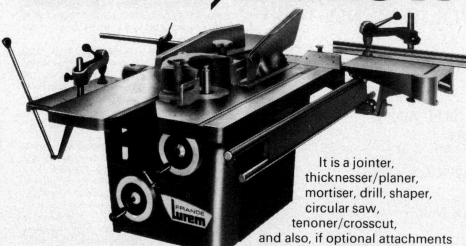

Whether you are a DIY enthusiast or a professional with your own commercial business, there are ten good reasons for investing in the Lurem C210B.

It is a jointer, thicknesser/planer, mortiser, drill, shaper, circular saw, tenoner/crosscut, and also, if optional attachments are used, a grinder, sander, woodturner and bandsaw. You can have this combined facility or a simplified version with less operations. Either way, you get real value for money.

If you look closer, the features are even more impressive. Solidly built for reliability intended for hard and continuous work with minimum maintenance. Rugged castings are extensively used yet it is highly manoeuvreable. Individual components are easily accessible. Adjustments are positive and effective. In fact, the C210B is both functional and practical. And safe.

Fortunately, it is inexpensive too. So for your home workshop, professional business or for schools and technical training, it is a sound and safe investment with twelve months guarantee.

lurem For Reliability and Service

For full details write to:
Lurem Machines
9 Biggin Hill Road, Evington,
Leicester, LE5 6HQ.
Telephone: (0533) 735554.

74

Prices quoted are those prevailing at press date and
are subject to alteration due to economic conditions.

Woodworker February 1980

Alan Holtham

Woodturner
Woodturner Supplier
Light Woodworking Machinery Specialist

THIS MONTH SPECIAL OFFER!

THE NEW MkII Bench and Pedestal Drilling Machines with 7 ★ Features . . .

£220 Delivered

★ Crank handle operated rack and pinion rise and fall table

★ ''Dial in'' Depth stop

★ No volt release overload protection, P6 starter

★ Simple lever belt release for speed change. 5 speeds

New Mk.II AJBD16 ⁵⁄₈"
bench drilling machine
with star features

★ Swivelling and tilting table

★ Externally fan-cooled motor

★ ⁵⁄₈" capacity chuck, standard

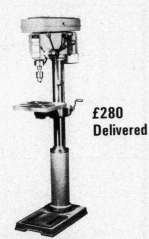

£280 Delivered

The New Mk.II AJPD.16 ⁵⁄₈" Pedestal Drilling Machine

We are also Main Stockists for: CORONET, ARUNDEL, ELU, DEWALT, SCHEPPACH, SUSEMIHL, ZINKEN, BOSCH, TREND router cutters and CUT sawblades. Please write or call for details of any machines of interest.

THE OLD STORES TURNERY
WISTASTON ROAD
WILLASTON
NANTWICH
CHESHIRE   Tel: CREWE 67010

MULTI-TOOLS
OF HARROGATE

SPECIALISTS IN SUPPLY AND DISTRIBUTION OF ALL TYPES OF WOODWORKING AND ENGINEERING HAND AND MACHINE TOOLS STOCKISTS OF DUST EXTRACTORS FOR LIGHT INDUSTRIAL USE. *NOW IN STOCK:* 'ELU & CRAFTSMAN' PORTABLE POWER TOOLS

SERVICE AND TECHNICAL BACK-UP WITH ALL SALES.

Permanent Demonstration Machines on Display.

JUST QUOTE YOUR ACCESS AND BARCLAYCARD NOS.

 KITY WOODWORKING MACHINES

 **Black & Decker**

INDUSTRIAL
LIGHT MACHINE TOOLS AND
WOODWORKING MACHINE
SPECIALISTS

158 KINGS ROAD, HARROGATE, N. YORKS. HG1 5JQ
TELEPHONE: HARROGATE (0423) 55328 66245

emcostar

The Emco Star is matched in its superb looks only by its versatility, ease of operation and ease of maintenance. The standard machine performs many different Sawing and Sanding operations all to the same high standards. Additional operations include moulding, planing, thicknessing, working with flexible shaft and many others. The machine has a powerful 2-speed motor and is fitted with safety clutches. And the complete miracle fits into mere 40" x 28" of space.

OUR PRICE **£469** inc. VAT carriage £3 List Price £514 inc. VAT.

emco BS2 Bandsaw

Unique in its price class, the BS2 has three speeds and is suitable for wood, metal and plastic. Large size upper and lower bandsaw guide, tilting table and torsion resistant band-saw frame ensure clean, accurate cuts, even on large workpieces. The BS2 is easy and safe to operate and has extra large bearings for long life.

OUR PRICE **£235** inc. VAT. Carriage £3.00 List Price £270 inc. VAT.

Write or Telephone NOW for details:
A. MILLS (ACTON LTD.)
32-36 Churchfield Road, Acton, London W3
Telephone: 01 992 4835 Telex: 24224-305
Easy access M1/M3/M4 Motorways
Opening hours: .... *ACCESS AND*
Monday-Friday 9 a.m.-5 p.m. .... *BARCLAY CARDS*

PLUNGING ROUTERS

FROM V.H.

& Co. Ltd.

190 West Street,
Bedminster, Bristol.
Tel. Bristol (0272) 667013

✳ **Send for cutter chart** ✳

PLUNGING ROUTERS IN STOCK:

NEW! BOSCH POF50 320 WATT
Plunging router, including many standard accessories **£55.00** incl. VAT/carr.

ELU-MOF96 600 WATT
Plunging router, our most popular router, very versatile, **£92.88** incl. VAT/carr. Write for details of our special offer.

MOF96 ACCESSORY KIT
Comprehensive kit to convert a portable machine to a stationary machine plus many other features. **£53.46** incl. VAT/carr.

ELU MOF31 1200 WATT
Plunging router, combines power with light weight, a rare combination **£130.00** incl. VAT/carr.

WRITE NOW FOR OUR SPECIAL OFFERS ON ROUTERS!

ROUTER CUTTERS

Prices include post, packing & VAT	All ¼" shank — send for leaflet with ¼", ⅜" & ½" shanks			
Description	Dia.	Ref.	HSS	TCT
Straight cutters all with plunge bottom cut	3/16"	TR4.8	1.50	8.69
	¼"	6.3	3.25	7.00
	5/16"	T8.0	3.60	7.45
	⅜"	T9.5	3.85	9.50
	½"	T12.7	4.50	8.40
	⅝"	T16.0	50.0	9.20
	¾"	T19.0	7.00	13.47
A range of cheaper TCT cutters available.				
'V' groove	—	TRV	4.75	8.64
Radius (U)	3/16"	RU	3.80	—
Radius (U)	5/16" rad	TU	6.80	15.00
Laminate bearing trim	18mm	T2	—	11.00
Ogee + pin	13mm depth	T/E1	11.50	—
Ogee + pin	20mm depth	T/E2	14.85	—
Ovolo	5mm rad	TO2	6.80	—
Ovolo	8mm rad	TO4	8.40	—

Over 150 different cutters in stock

Prices quoted are those prevailing at press date and are subject to alteration due to economic conditions.

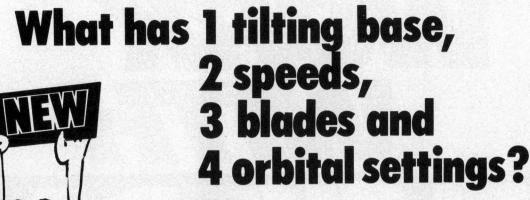

What has 1 tilting base, 2 speeds, 3 blades and 4 orbital settings?

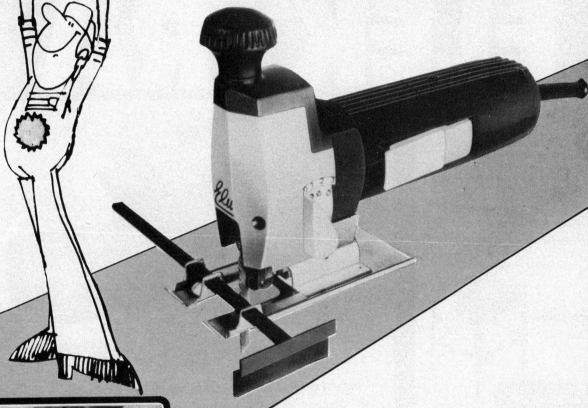

The New Elu ST142/11 Jigsaw has it all. Furthermore there are 7 additional Jigsaw blade types to choose from. This will enable you to cut efficiently all types of materials to give a finish you desire, for example, at the higher speed with the orbit position set at number three using the wood-cutting blade, this will give you a fast rough cut on timber. Set the speed to the higher speed, select the O position of orbital action, and using a narrow wood-cutting blade, this will enable you to cut intricate shapes in timber giving an excellent finish.

The base plate can be adjusted to cut angles up to 45°, and the universal blade holder enables the fitting of different makes of jigsaw blades, so as not to restrict you in times of emergency.

This machine is being introduced at a special price of £94.00 plus £14.10 VAT and will be supplied in a steel carrying case, for a limited period only.

142/11

50 Years Elu

Elu – have been your partner for 50 years now. Tradesmen, Hobbyists, as well as the woodworking and metal working industry are guided by the motto: "Quality with guaranteed service".

Coupon

Please send more information on Elu Portable Electric Tools

Name _____
Company _____
Street _____
Place _____
Phone _____

Elu Machinery Limited, Stirling Way, Stirling Corner, Borehamwood, Herts, WD6 2AG. Tel.: 01-953 0711

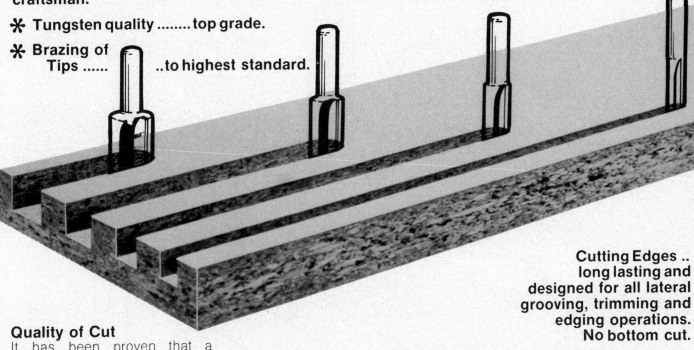

WOODWORK BENCH

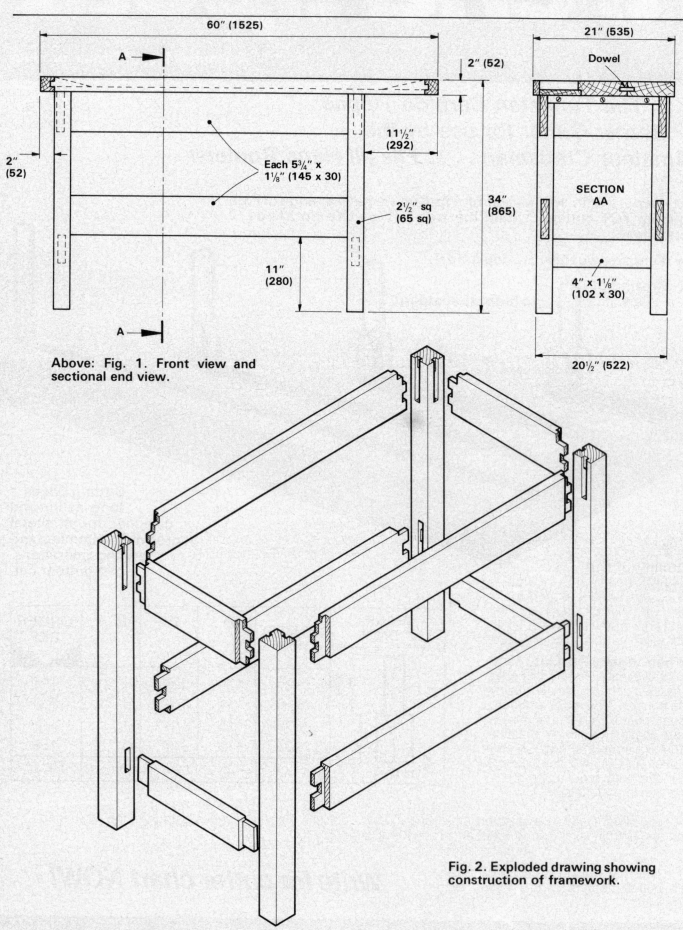

60" (1525)

A

2" (52)

11½" (292)

Each 5¾" x 1⅛" (145 x 30)

2" (52)

2½" sq (65 sq)

34" (865)

11" (280)

A

21" (535)

Dowel

SECTION AA

4" x 1⅛" (102 x 30)

20½" (522)

Above: Fig. 1. Front view and sectional end view.

Fig. 2. Exploded drawing showing construction of framework.

'The height of the bench top is critical for comfort when working.' A. Yarwood tells how he made a bench in European beech:

It seemed about time I made a new bench. My old one has been in almost daily use for the 35 years since it was made. While in the process of designing a new bench I came across an advertisement for the Record 42D vice and thought this would make an admirable end vice. The Record 42D would also give me a second vice which could provide a range of functions, quite apart from its value as an end vice.

European beech is the obvious choice for a woodworker's bench. It is a tough and hard wood which can be obtained in the thick planks of good straight grained material necessary for the making of a bench. The wood will finish to a smooth, clean surface which will resist considerable wear, shock and abrasion. European beech is common in southern England. It also grows in great quantities over most of the continent, except in northern Scandinavia. Considerable stands of beech grow in Austria, France, Germany, Czechoslovakia, Denmark, Poland and Yugoslavia.

The tree grows to quite large sizes, heights up to 150ft and boles up to 4ft in diameter being quite common. The wood produced from these trees is a tough, strong hardwood with an even, fine texture. Its colour varies from almost white to a pale brown darkening with age to a pale reddish brown.

In parts of the continent it is common practice to steam beech during the conversion from tree to plank. Steamed beech is always a light red-brown colour. Beech tends to split and warp during seasoning and even when seasoned, has a tendency to shrink if placed in dry conditions. This means that constructions made from solid beech must be designed to allow for shrinkage. The beech from which my bench was made came from a variety of sources. I was able to obtain steamed beech in boards of 2in. thickness and in 2½in. squares. The 1¼in. boards for the rails and the 1in. boards for other parts were made from unsteamed English beech. Personally I don't think the steaming makes much difference. Steamed beech is usually easier to work than white beech, but this is more likely to be due to the fact that English beech tends to be harder than continental beech anyway.

All the wood purchased for the bench had been machine-planed. Despite this and because it was essential for the framework of the bench to be square, legs and rails were hand-planed straight and square before commencing the cutting of the mortises and tenons joining rails to legs. The construction of this framework is quite straightforward and is shown in the drawings.

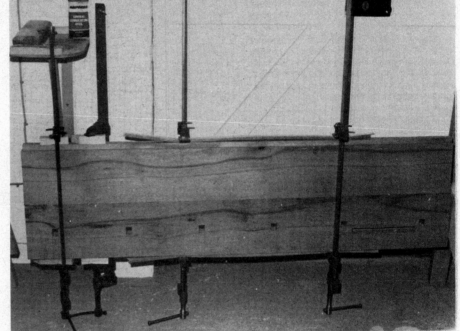

Top: Sawing tops of legs level with rails.

Centre: Top glued and cramped.

Below: Sawing top tongues with aid of power saw.

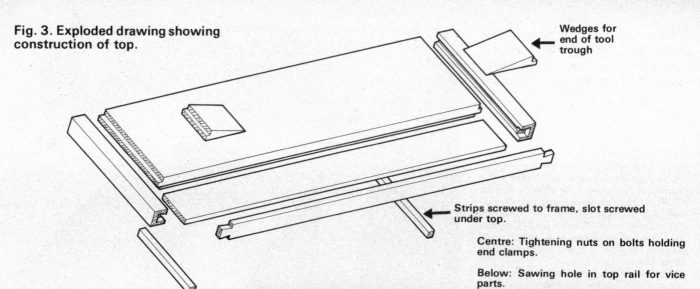

Fig. 3. Exploded drawing showing construction of top.

Wedges for end of tool trough

Strips screwed to frame, slot screwed under top.

Centre: Tightening nuts on bolts holding end clamps.

Below: Sawing hole in top rail for vice parts.

The front and back rails are very wide with the tenons of the top rails interlocking within their mortises (see Figs. 4 and 5). This construction was designed to give maximum strength to the frame to allow it to withstand the considerable forces exerted when working at a woodwork bench. All the tenons are 'barefaced' on the insides of the rails to allow the mortises to be placed as near the centres of the legs as possible, yet retaining a goodly length of tenon. The mortises were cut with the aid of a ¾in. (19mm) Slickbit in a hand power drill, finishing removal of the waste with a heavy-duty chisel. The tenons were cut on a circular saw to avoid the extremely hard work of sawing them by hand. When the mortises and tenons had been cut, the frame was assembled dry to test whether the joints fitted. The frame could then be glued up. The two end frames were glued and cramped together and then these were glued and cramped to the front and back rails.

To add to the strength of the frame, each tenon was double-pinned with two ½in. (13mm) dowels glued into holes bored through legs and tenons after the frame had been glued. When all the glue had set quite firmly the frame was cleaned-up by planing and sanding.

At this stage it is advisable to determine the height required for the bench. I stand 6ft 1½in. in my socks, so the height of my bench is 34in. This height is possibly about the maximum for a woodwork bench. A more usual height would be 30in. — for the average 5ft 9in. person. It should be remembered, however, that the height of the bench top is critical for comfort when working. Having decided on the bench height, the tops of the legs were sawn and planed flush with the tops of the rails and the floor ends of the legs sawn square.

Now work on the top could be started. This was made from two lengths of board each measuring 57½in. (1460mm) × 8in. (204mm) × 2in. (51mm), edge joined with ½in. (13mm) dowels set at intervals of 4in. (102mm) along the length of the join. Before gluing the two boards together, a slot for the front vice and holes for bench stops were cut in the front board. The bench stop holes were spaced at intervals equal to the maximum opening of the Record 42D vice. A rebate to receive the bottom of the tool trough was also cut in the rear board before gluing the two parts of the top together. This construction can be seen in the exploded drawing of the top. Fig. 3.

our locking system may not look much

but it certainly makes life a lot simpler.

With any combination woodworking machine, one has to consider the possible disadvantages of changing from one operation to another against individual machines. In an age where time means money one cannot be satisfied with outdated methods of unbolting this or that when setting up for a particular operation.

That is why, over a decade ago, Joseph Scheppach designed and patented his "Universal Adaptor 4-Point Locking System" on his Combined Planing and Thicknessing Machine. Since then some 10,000 users every year discover that with the Scheppach System one does not have to sacrifice the advantages gained by low initial outlay with hours of frustration afterwards when it comes to setting up.

With the Model PRIMA HM1 the customer has the distinct advantage of adjusting his inital purchase to suit his budget or work requirement, and then add to at a later date as required.

New from Scheppach

The Universal woodworking machine with separate drives.

This is where the Scheppach Universal Adaptors really begin to make life a lot simpler. When it comes to fitting the **Sawbench, Spindle Moulder, Mortiser, Sander, Lathe or Grinder Attachments** they are all designed to simply locate on four fixing points and then lock with the twin Universal Adaptor Locking Discs. Nothing could be simpler!

And that isn't all. By combining the Locking System to the thicknessing table all attachments have automatic rise and fall facilities with handwheel adjustment.

This year Scheppach have come up with another "first". On the new Model PRIMA HM2 only the required tooling operates when the machine is running. When using the planer, the fitted attachment is idle. When using an attachment the planer is idle — thus offering complete ate safety. In addition, the automatic feed of the thicknesser is controlled separately by lever adjustment.

Do not let the fact that the machine is not of cast construction mislead you. The Scheppach machine will perform accurately, all day long if needs be, on long lengths, both soft and hard timbers. When it comes to a modular system there is nothing to touch Scheppach for large working capacity at such low price!

PRIMA HM2 Illustrated

Prices quoted are those prevailing at press date and are subject to alteration due to economic conditions.

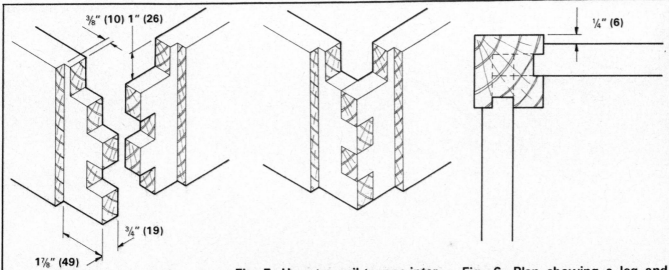

Fig. 4. Details of top rail tenons.

Fig. 5. How top rail tenons interlock within legs.

Fig. 6. Plan showing a leg and position of rails.

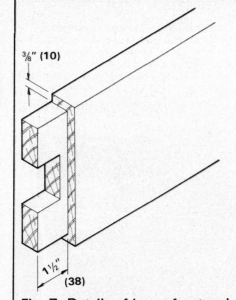

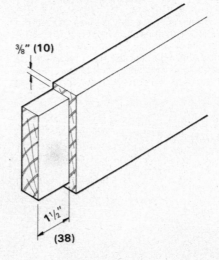

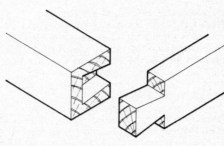

Fig. 7. Details of lower front and back rail tenons.

Fig. 8. Details of lower end rail tenons.

Fig. 9. Details of lap dovetail of back top rail.

After sawing and planing the jointed boards to their correct length (57in.), tongues were cut on the ends to receive the top end clamps. Groves ⅝in. (16mm) wide × ½in. (13mm) deep were cut in the 2in. square (51mm) clamps to fit over the tongues. The clamps were fixed to the top with the aid of coach bolts and nuts as shown in Fig. 10.

Before finally fixing the clamps to the top, the back rail of the top was fitted with single lap dovetails to the rear ends of the clamps. The top could then he assembled, the back rail glued and screwed in place and the tool trough bottom glued and screwed into its rebate under the back edge of the top. Screws along the back rail into the rear edge of the tool trough base hold the tool trough firmly in place. Finally, to facilitate easy sweeping out of waste from the tool trough, two wedges were shaped and glued into its ends. It should be noted that these wedges have tongues which fit into the grooves cut in the clamps.

Before the top can be fixed to its framework, a wooden block to receive the front vice (a Record 9in.) should be screwed in position under the top. This block holds the vice in its correct position in relation to the bench top. The method adopted was to fit

Screwing front vice wooden jaw to bench.

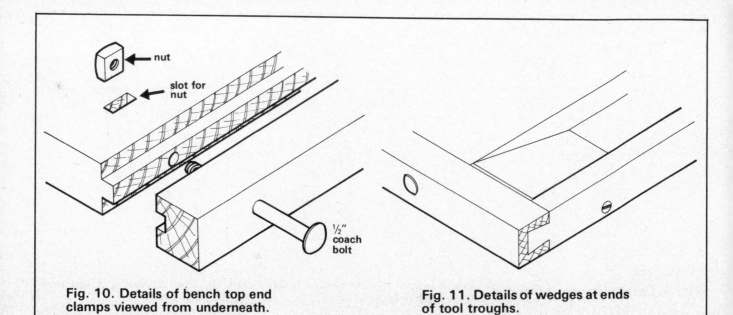

Fig. 10. Details of bench top end clamps viewed from underneath.

Fig. 11. Details of wedges at ends of tool troughs.

four 3in. coach bolts into a 2in. (51mm) thick block and screw this block to the underside of the top, just behind the recess already cut to receive the vice casting.

This method leaves the screw threads of the coach bolts standing proud. The vice casting is then bolted on these screws. A shaped hole must be cut in the front rail through which the screw slides and quick-release rod of the vice can be passed. Two pieces of wood are needed to provide a vice jaw on the front of the bench and a second vice jaw bolted to the rear of the vice jaw metal casting. The details of this method of fitting the vice are shown in a series of drawings (Figs. 12 to 15).

The bench top could now be fixed on its frame. Two strips of beech each 1½in. square (38mm) were glued and screwed in between the legs of the end frame and slot screwed to receive screws up into the bottom of the top. This holds the top in place and allows for shrinkage that might occur across the bench top. The front vice fitting could now be completed and the bench top hand-planed quite flat.

Right: Planing bench top flat.

Below: Completed bench ready for end vice.

Bottom right: Cutting recess in vice jaw for end vice.

Fitting of the end vice was carried out using the method shown in Figs. 16 and 17. A piece of wood to position the vice casting was screwed under the top. A wooden vice jaw behind which the vice casting was fitted is screwed to the end clamp. The vice was then bolted in place using coach screws.

Finally the top was sanded smooth and the bench given two brush coats of clear polyurethane varnish. When this was quite hard the top was again sanded with fine paper.

WOOD WORK BENCH

The completed bench

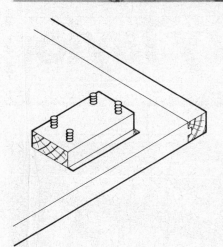

Fig. 12. Stage 1 of fitting front vice.

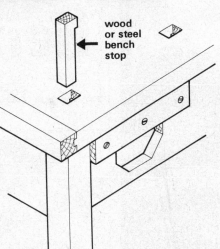

wood or steel bench stop

Fig. 13. Stage 2 of fitting front vice.

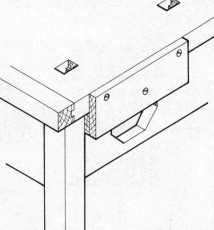

Fig. 14. Stage 3 of fitting front vice.

Cutting List		
(Dimensions in in. and mm). Finished sizes not including waste.		
4 legs	32 × 2½ × 2½	840 × 65 × 65
2 top rails	45¼ × 5¾ × 1⅛	1150 × 145 × 30
2 top rails	19¼ × 5¾ × 1⅛	490 × 145 × 30
2 bottom rails	18½ × 4 × 1⅛	470 × 102 × 30
2 bottom rails	44½ × 5¾ × 1⅛	1130 × 145 × 30
16 dowels	2 × ½ diameter	51 × 13 diameter
1 top	57 × 16 × 2	1448 × 407 × 51
2 top clamps	21 × 2 × 2	533 × 51 × 51
1 back rail	59 × 2 × ⅞	1500 × 51 × 22
1 tool trough	56 × 5½ × ⅝	1423 × 140 × 16
2 wedges	8 × 5 × 1⅜	204 × 127 × 40
2 top strips	17¾ × 1½ × 1½	450 × 38 × 38

Also required: Pieces of wood for vice fitting, bolts and screws for vice fitting.

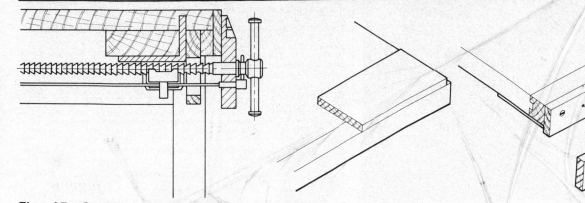

Fig. 15. Section through fitted front vice.

Fig. 16. Stage 1 of fitting end vice.

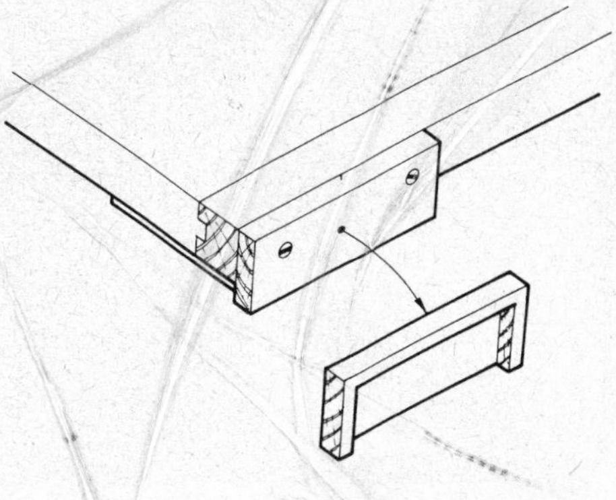

Fig. 17. Stage 2 of fitting end vice.

Cowells Jigsaw
Rugged, trouble-free design

Widely accepted by educational
authorities for use in schools,
this jigsaw is indispensable for
the modelmaker and handyman
who are looking for a no-nonsense,
hard working machine.

- One piece body casting
- Balanced crankshaft to minimise
  vibration
- Built-in safety features
- Large diameter spindles and bearings for
  long, continuous trouble-free work
- A price anyone can afford
- Cuts wood, plastics, metal, slate, bone etc.
- Continuously rated motor

Write to us **now** for details, and address
of your nearest stockist

Cowell Engineering Limited

Oak Street Norwich NR3 3BP England
Telephone (0603) 614521 Telex 975205

Don't settle for less.

Great British Engineering from the COWELLS Collection

Prices quoted are those prevailing at press date and
are subject to alteration due to economic conditions.

workpieces

Hints and tips

Tricks of the Trade is the title of a pocketbook issued by Cintride Ltd, Ashford Road Works, Bakewell DE4 1GL. Copies are obtainable from the company (send your address and a 10p stamp). Although of more value to beginners the pocketbook contains plenty of tips that will be useful to experienced craftsmen and in the working with wood section there are sound remarks on safety with power tools as well as hints on sawing and sanding. Drilling techniques (and drills) are also covered.

With each pocketbook there is a pocket calculator to provide the user with a means of checking screw lengths, drill diameters and wall plug gauges.

Woodcraft advice

Catalogue from Allan McNair Woodcraft, 28 Paignton Avenue, Whitley Bay, Co Tyne & Wear, lists machine tools and hand tools primarily intended for woodcarvers and woodturners. Turning and other accessories as well as abrasives, finishes and waxes are included.

The catalogue points out that the object is to provide the professional and amateur craftsman with the best of tools, materials and information. Over the past two years Allan McNair has been buying quality home-grown hardwood in the butt. This timber, of various species, is still drying-out but 'as soon as we can provide continuity, we will offer it for sale.'

The catalogue states: 'We offer a free advisory service and will be pleased to help you with any problems, be it in timber, turning or techniques.' There is no charge for the catalogue which runs to nine pages plus order form.

Tools and books

From Roger's, 47 Walsworth Road, Hitchin SG4 9SU, comes *Tool & Book Catalogue No. 2* which runs to 120 pages of descriptions, pictures and diagrams.

The sections cover: turning and accessories; gluepots and woodscrew sets; planes (metal and wood); speciality planes and drawknives; spokeshaves; scrapers and scraper burnishers; veneering tools; screwdrivers; hammers etc; vices; cramps; books; handsaws; portable circular saws and bandsaws; jigsaws; circular saw blades and jigsaw blades; mitring equipment; bench accessories; chisels and gouges; carving tools; sculptors' tools; rasps and files; routers and attachments etc; Dremel tools; measuring and marking tools; braces, drills and awls; machine, drill and brace bits; dowelling equipment; mortise and drill stands and electric drills; whetstones; grinders; and sharpening equipment.

There is also an index. Cost of the catalogue (95p incl. p&p) is refunded on purchases over £30.

Timber preservation

Data sheets on bulk water-borne and organic solvent wood preservatives for use in commercial timber preservation, and details of treatment plants are available from Rentokil Wood Preserving Division, Felcourt, East Grinstead, Sussex.

British craftsmen show in Paris

Display of the work of 15 craftsmen took place during November at the Galerie J. Kraus in rue Faubourg St Honoré, Paris. Arranged by Charles de Temple of London the exhibition included woodturning and carving by David Hensel, Cecil Jordan, Ray Key, David Pye and Howard Raybould. Pieces ranged from jewellery in wood to turned boxes, bowls and dishes, carvings, mirror frames and games boards. The emphasis was on exotic and rare woods though, for example, Howard Raybould uses fruit wood where weight, strength or working qualities require it.

Cecil Jordan frequently uses burrs and all his pieces have beeswax finish or blend of natural waxes. Ray Key turns his boxes from a single block so that the grain flows throughout and the lid is an integral part of the piece as a whole. David Pye makes fluted bowls and dishes as well as turned boxes, while David Hensel carves much of his jewellery in European box, African blackwood and ebony.

Back row left: platter of oak burr by Cecil Jordan.
Front row left: handturned bowl and boxes in yew by Ray Key; wooden bracelet inlaid with silver and awabi shell by David Hensel.

Heat from wood

References to energy in WOODWORKER for September 1979 considered the uses of wood byproduct for heating and process steam generation. The catalogue issued by the Danish firm Passat which produces solid fuel burners suggests that the 'cheapest, most practical way to reduce heating costs is by using solid fuel.'

The catalogue describes how wood can be used in the Passat system and quotes Danish experience in which a six-room house needs about 6-8 cords of wood (one cord equal to a pile 4 x 4 x 8ft, roughly equivalent to 83cu ft of solid wood) during the six months' cold season. Passat burners also take straw, peat, paper and wood byproduct such as chips and shavings.

Fuel must be dry to assist efficient combustion. At 200°C, for example, tars and gases will be generated and evaporated from the fuel, whereas at about 450°C, these will burn productively, adding to the heat. Equally important, there will be a cleaner discharge with less risk of building-up tar and pyroligneous acids in the chimney.

In this country Passat is represented by Lodebrook Ltd, Watergate Lane, Bulford, Salisbury SP4 9DY.

Interested in doll's houses?

We have just received the first issue of a new newsletter/journal for those interested in doll's houses and their furniture and fittings. *Home Miniaturist* published and edited by Mary Churchill will be published quarterly (Nov, Feb, May and Aug) priced at 75p per issue. It is available from specialist doll's house shops and craft shops or by post at £1.00 from Holly House, Hasle Drive, Hedgehog Lane, Haslemere, Surrey GU27 2PL. Each issue claims to contain instructions, plans and helpful hints plus kits, historical details, stockists and book reviews. It aims to combine the diy aspect of creating a doll's house with the collecting of miniatures made by professionals. Issue number 2 will include furnishing a bedroom, peg dolls, diy ideas and constructing a doll's house.

Days of yore for modellers

Models makers and horse-drawn vehicle enthusiasts will find much to interest them in *The Model Wheelwright Yearbook 1980*. This is produced by John Thompson, I Fieldway, Fleet, Hants, and costs 30p. Contents include advice to the model maker; details of more than 50 plans; guide to suppliers of parts and materials; books; and lists of museums, clubs and postcards.

The *Yearbook* indicates that John Thompson's new book on carriages is due for publication at an early date. I hope it will inspire more modelling of these beautiful vehicles. I am grateful that my years and upbringing in a fairly remote part of the country provide memories of a landau or two, and a victoria with coachman and footmen in livery, when the grand jury assembled on commission day at the county assises. I felt let down by our local magnate when she (yes it was the *lady* of the manor) invested in a motor car, though she retained the liveries. But flat caps were poor substitues for toppers and cockades!

In the miscellany of plans on page 26 of the *Yearbook* there is an illustration of a Shand Mason steamer. These splendid appliances gradually faded-out from 1920 though we kept our Shand Mason until the early 30s. Of course by that time it was horse-drawn on ceremonial occasions only. 'On the run' we were towed by a motor tender carrying crew, ladders and small gear.

Most of our 'shouts' were farm fires usually requiring long hoselines from the nearest pond or brook. The engineer screwed down the safety valve and we never failed to give the men on the branches the water they needed. Our more up-to-date neighbouring brigades who prided themselves on their motor appliances often had trouble when 'water on' was the command. I've seen faces red as Braidwood bodywork.

Those were the days — but oh! the brass to be cleaned. I know now why our captain (we did not have chief fire officers in those days) persuaded the joint fire committee to introduce a scheme for cadets. But we were not allowed to wear the helmets we'd cleaned. 'London round caps for you lads,' was our reward!

G.P.

Cosmetic wooden box, duck feeding ducklings with a fish. (About 6in. long) © British Museum.

MORE BEAUTY ON THE NILE

P. R. Rostron discusses the wooden boxes used by ancient Egyptians to hold their cosmetics and unguents.

In ancient Egypt people used lots of cosmetics and ungents which they kept in wooden boxes often shaped as fruit, fish, birds or animals. Animals were popular; one cosmetics box was carved in the shape of two kneeling antelopes; the lid of another box had a formal design based on two calves playfully butting each other — this box measured about 9 × 3in. wide.

A cucumber-shaped box to hold rouge for the cheeks dates from around 1250BC. The cucumber measured some 6-7in. long and the curves contained a green pigment. Another container was in the form of the squat little god Bes (guardian of perfumes and cosmetics). This container was to hold ointments and the god had a mirror in its head.

Men and women of ancient Egypt spent hours at their dressing tables, which usually displayed kohl pots made of acacia and were about 4-5in. high. Some popular shapes were a goat, pomegrante and a Nubian slave carrying a pot on her back. All these containers displayed considerable artistry and ingenuity in manufacture. Around the period 1200BC the variety of designs reached new levels.

The cult of personal adornment probably had something to do with the hot climate of the Nile delta and valley and oils and unguents were used instead of soap. An intment such as qemi softened the skin. Scent bottles held perfumes such as kyphi and sesame which were very expensive.

Egyptian pharmacists were skilled in mixing powders and ointments. Their green and black eye powders were believed to possess magical properties but they also protected the eyes from the sun's rays. The ingredients were malachite and galena. Egyptian beauties liked their eyes to resemble pearls hidden in shells. Queen Cleopatra painted her eyebrows and lashes black, the top lids dark blue and the lower lids dark green. This colour scheme evidently appealed to such notables as Julius Caesar and Mark Anthony!

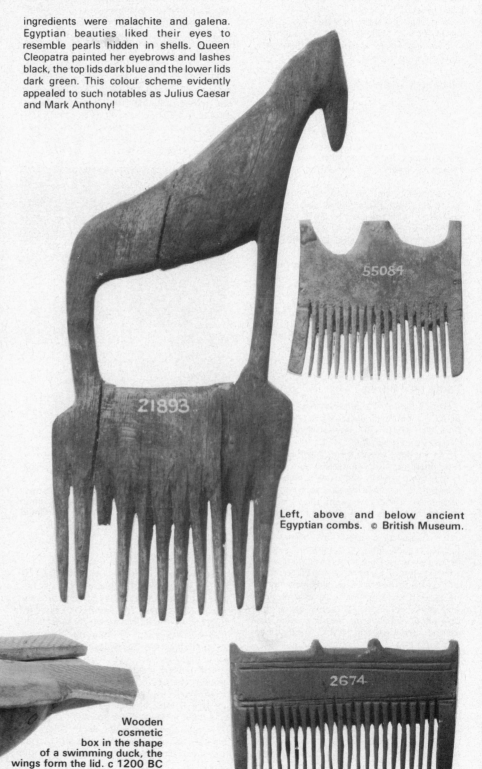

Left, above and below ancient Egyptian combs. © British Museum.

Wooden cosmetic box in the shape of a swimming duck, the wings form the lid. c 1200 BC (5-6in. long) © British Museum.

Wooden spoon in the form of a dog seizing a fish by the tail. The fish forms the bowl of the spoon, c 1300 BC © British Museum.

Ethiopean princess accompanied by slaves or porters carrying cosmetics. (Thebes fresco from the 18th dynasty).

To mix the powders and other ingredients every dressing table had a variety of wooden spoons. These were in various shapes, such as a girl swimming and pushing an ointment box in the form of a duck; or a dog seizing a fish by the tail, the fish forming the bowl. Spoons in the form of the lotus flower were also popular.

Pharoah used cosmetics and unguents daily and the director of the royal hairdressers department was a most important official. Baldness was to be avoided at all costs and eminent physicians were called in to prescribe. One remedy known as 'Pharoah's hair restorer' was sold in wooden boxes. The ingredients were a mixture of animal fats. For white hair the blood of a black bull boiled in oil was a prescription!

During the long periods at their dressing tables the ancient Egyptians probably played various kinds of board games and in many households there would be a wooden box to hold the game pieces. The top of one such box was divided into squares by thin pieces of ivory for games such as Senet and Tjau, known also as 30 squares and 20 squares. Moves were decided by the throw of a dice or knuckle bones. The pieces were often in the shape of reels or similar to modern halma men.

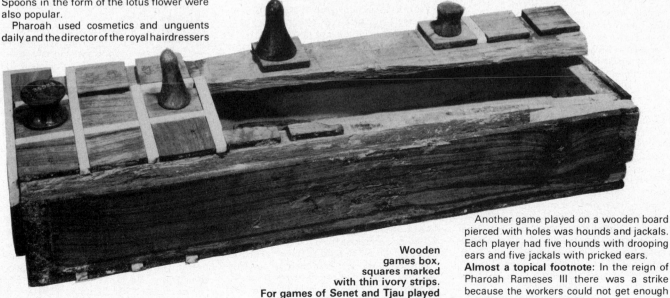

Wooden games box, squares marked with thin ivory strips. For games of Senet and Tjau played on the board, box about 1 m long.

Another game played on a wooden board pierced with holes was hounds and jackals. Each player had five hounds with drooping ears and five jackals with pricked ears.

Almost a topical footnote: In the reign of Pharoah Rameses III there was a strike because the workers could not get enough cosmetics and unguents!

Letters

From: L. R. Noblett, Cardiff, S. Wales
Dear Sir,

With reference to the query by R. T. Cox of Caterham (block for a kitchen, page 686 of the November 1979 issue), if the block that he has acquired has been used for hand 'clicking' (cutting), it will most likely have been treated with an oil. This would usually be a mixture of linseed and driers to keep the surface soft and close-up the grain after use.

This could account for the sweet smell that Mr Cox mentions and this in my opinion would make it unsuitable for his intended purpose, since in course of time the oil would have penetrated deeply into the wood. However, linseed has such a characteristic smell that it would be readily recognisable by anyone familiar with that oil, although if it had not been used for a long time the smell would be much less pronounced.

If the block has been used for machine clicking it would not have received this treatment. The surface would be relatively rough and hard from the multitude of criss-crossing impressions left by the cutters in which would be embedded fibres from whatever materials had been cut on it. Provided that the marred surface is planed-off this would be suitable for his purpose.

Regarding his query as to the type of wood used for these blocks, I can add little to your consultant's remarks except to say that I doubt very much that it would be cedar. More likely it would be one of the softer, close-grained 'hardwoods', possibly lime or poplar. Neither of these has a strong or very characteristic odour.

Yours faithfully, **L. R. Noblett**

From: D. Tasker, Farnham, Surrey
Dear Sir,

Having read 'Have you stepped away?' in the December 1979 issue I feel I must write what I really feel. I am sure there are many like me who have the urge to do something, but for various reasons have never been able to do that 'something.'

I left school in 1955 knowing what I wanted to do and that was cabinet making. The youth employment officer said at the time that it was a dying trade and what I could do in wood I could do in metal. My father tried to find me a job with a high-class carpenter and joiner, but to no avail.

So I started work as an engineering craft apprentice and have tried ever since to work my way up the ladder in a job which I regard as being second best. I am continually frustrated, without really a sense of job satisfaction. This is because I would rather do a creative job.

After all these years I would like to make a break and do what I originally wanted; but there is the risk of giving up a secure job when I have a wife, two children — and a mortgage.

I would like to know how other people have managed to take the plunge and how they have fared. I might add that I have been trained in industrial management. I believe that many small business fail because they lack management know-how.

Yours faithfully, **D. Tasker**

From: D.S. Cotter, Welling, Kent
Dear Sir,

I read with interest your comment and the article by W.F. Nesbit in WOODWORKER for December 1979 and I wholeheartedly agree.

However, the largest single obstacle facing the would-be craftsmen in setting up his business has not been mentioned. Readers contemplating such a course of action should be warned that finding a suitable workshop property will be by far their biggest headache. No doubt the problem varies across the country but not everyone wants, or is able, to move to Wales, Norfolk or areas where the problem is apparently far less.

I have been trying to find a property in the home counties for longer than I care to recall and my efforts have included approaches to the following: Department of Industry; Department of the Environment; Small Firm's Bureau; London Enterprise Agency; Crafts Advisory Council; CoSIRA; county and district councils — including surveyor's and planning departments; and various estate agents.

If there is any avenue I have not yet explored I should very much like to know as so far all my enquiries have been to no avail. Most of the organisations mentioned either do not deal with questions of property or, in the case of local authorities, the attitude is one of disinterest and even discouragement. To its credit, only CoSIRA totally appreciated my problem, but holds out little hope.

The basic problem is that the individual craftsman is included in the broad category of light industry and it is high time pressure was brought to bear on the government to have a separate class formulated. Until then (and coupled with some degree of relaxation in the rules pertaining to planning consent which, in my experience, are rigidly enforced by the authorities), there is little chance of new firms being established in the home counties except parts of central London (often inconvenient and always expensive) or on a vast industrial estate (almost certain sudden death).

We are simply not wanted. I only hope that the declared attitude towards private enterprise by the present government will have an effect. But I suspect it will be a long, long wait.

Yours faithfully, **D.S. Cotter**

Can you help him?

A reader who lives in Scotland is extremely interested in learning the craft of woodturning. However, he is having difficulty in finding a teacher and would be grateful for any 'leads.' His name is John Ferguson and he is 22. He writes: 'I have tried to find a 10-day course on woodturning locally but as yet to no avail. Somewhere reasonably near to St Andrews would be convenient and if any reader can help I would be pleased to have details of costs and of accommodation in the vicinity.' Mr Ferguson's address is: 2 Stonywynd Cottages, Boarhills, by St Andrews, Fife.

From: T.S.A. Seager, West Chadsmoor, Staffs
Dear Sir,

In reply to your note on page 638 of the November 1979 issue about the reader who is seeking a source of supply for straight shafts for making shepherd's crooks, he does not say if his market is for the decorative or the functional article. Ramin would be suitable (and obtainable) for the former but not ideal for the latter.

If ramin is used I suggest that with the crook at the top the grain should run down to the butt. Holes, if any, to locate the crook should be drilled and not nailed through; ramin does splinter easily and is prone to splitting when nailed. Beech would be better and is also obtainable as dowelling.

As an ex-forester and timber-feller I recall that rakes were always made from young rowan/mountain ash plants. A seven-year plant was suitable for the shaft and the rake. I think that growing from seed would give a suitable shaft in four year's time. The pruned shoots would also give a good appearance for whatever purpose the crook was intended. It is also fair to say that a functional crook would require a taper to the top so as to give a better 'grip', especially on cold, wet days.

Most manufacturers who use timber have offcuts and byproduct and would possibly be able to supply these quite cheaply for purchasers themselves to saw to size required.

Yours faithfully, **T.S.A. Seager**

The subject of shepherd's crooks has been taken a step further with publication of the article on page 727 of the December 1979 issue about Harry Binns. He uses hazel and blackthorn which he selects and cuts in the woods near his home. The sticks are bundled and stored in the workshop for at least two years, but often much longer.

From: Dr J. M. Macpherson, 19 The Struet, Brecon, Powys LD3 7LS
Dear Sir,

I'm another of the legion turning from other occupations to woodworking — a PhD geologist setting up a small workshop in mid-Wales, aiming to specialise in small, quality cabinet work. Within months this will be my sole source of income.

I am keen to contact other professional or part-time woodworkers in mid-Wales, with the intention of developing some sort of co-operative system for buying, storing and seasoning wood; for swopping advice and ideas; and perhaps for utilising expensive but underused machines. For example, there is a great potential in this part of the country for the co-operative use of a chainsaw mill for *in situ* conversion of logs to planks; and the accumulation of a stock of cheap, good-quality otherwise unobtainable timber.

Would anyone interested please get in touch with me at the above address.

Yours faithfully, **J.M. Macpherson**

We wish Dr Macpherson well in his enterprise. No doubt he will have seen the reference to the facilities offered by the Development Board for Rural Wales published on page 748 of last December's issue. The same issue also gave details of a 'co-operative' established at Royston, Herts, by David Gratch, to condition timber (page 739). Of course, Royston is a long haul from Brecon.

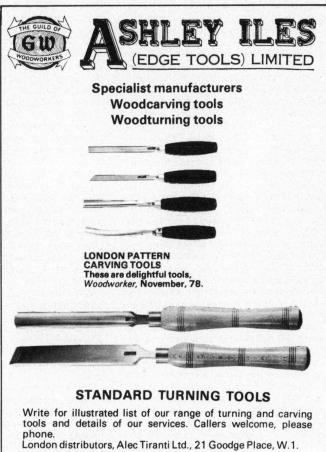

WOODTURNING
for PLEASURE or PROFIT

In my previous article on woodturning (page 724 of the December 1979 issue), I recommend a set of nine tools for beginners. Later in this series I hope to discuss in detail the uses of each of these. Meanwhile it may help if I deal with some examples of the ancillary equipment offered for lathe work.

Measuring devices are important, more so to beginners than to experienced turners who do a great deal of work by eye. Calipers are used widely in turning. For our purposes they fall into three categories; outside caliper; inside caliper; and Columbus vernier caliper.

Outside calipers as used in spindle and chuck work for checking diameters at specific points, are of two versions. The cheaper has two curved legs held together by a friction nut and washer. The stiffness of the opening and closing movement can be regulated by tightening or loosening the nut. I find this type useful for measurements which are taken with the workpiece stationary, but not too reliable when used for measurements on rotating work. This kind of measurement is common in furniture work, where calipers are used for sizing purposes, riding on the wood as its diameter is decreased by a parting tool. This type of caliper can open slightly during the cut, so giving rise to inaccuracies; whereas the more expensive version has its legs joined at the top by a strong spring, the opening and closing action being controlled by a knurled knob on a threaded bar which runs across the tool.

The purpose of inside calipers is obvious, but it is worth noting that such calipers should *never* be used to check rotating workpieces, except by experienced turners. Inside calipers are available in the two versions described above, and the same remarks apply. The legs of inside calipers are straight, with the ends turned outwards. They have a wide variety of applications where uniformity is required, as in sets of egg cups, goblets, wine glasses and such like.

The Columbus pattern vernier caliper is a cheap but effective version of the engineer's vernier — which can cost up to £100. As the jaws are opened by means of the knurled wheel the gap between the forward jaws will always equal the distance between the rearward facing points. This means that the diameter of the spindle can be compared accurately with the diameter of a recess. This is extremely useful when joining spindles by means of round tenons, as in the making of standard lamp stems.

Another use is the fitting of the pin on the end of a table lamp to the hole which is bored in the base. Here the pin is first turned to a suitable diameter — without measuring — then the jaws are closed over the pin. The setting which this produces on the points which face rearwards can now be used to mark the disc which is to form the base. This marking is done as the disc rotates and I will describe this procedure in detail in the appropriate section. I, personally, would not like to be without this type of caliper.

A good pair of dividers is essential in the turner's shop. Two are better; one small pair for fine work, one robust and fairly large pair for marking-out larger discs. Dividers are the same in principle as those used in geometry, but for turning they need to be more rugged. A common use is in the marking-out of discs prior to bandsawing, and here the leg, about which the scriber pivots, will leave the centre of the disc clearly marked, thus facilitating centring on the lathe.

Dividers are used extensively in furniture work and in the copying of spindles generally, measurements being taken from drawing or pattern and transferred to the rotating blank in the lathe by means of the divider points. The process is simple, but can be dangerous if not fully understood. The main factor is that *both* points of the dividers must be firmly on the tool rest before they touch the wood, and the legs should point slightly downwards — never up. A sharp pencil with a fairly hard lead is useful though most turners carry out line marking with the point of a skew chisel, pencils being easily mislaid in a workshop full of shavings.

Numerous other items used in woodturning shops may seem rather insignificant, but each is part of the whole, and every item makes life a little easier.

A small bradawl with a sharp point is handy for marking centres of spindles when mounting them in the lathe. The normal pattern will do though I prefer what used to be known as the birdcage maker's awl. This has a tapered square shank and was once used for making small holes in thin wood near the edge, as in fitting bent bamboo strands. The awl was rotated as it was pushed in, so making a hole without splitting the wood. The pattern is now sometimes referred to as an auger awl and is handy when mounting small blanks on woodscrew chucks.

I frequently receive queries about copying devices. In my view their value in woodturning is minimal, since although they will reveal an error in turning they do little to help in getting the shape right. These devices consist of a central 'sandwich' of rubber between metal with a large number of thin metal rods pushed through crosswise. The metal rods can slide in the central bar. Thus when pressed against a shape, some rods move more than others and produce the outline of the turning. At the same time the reverse of this shape appears at the other side of the tool.

I find these devices useful for fitting tiles or floor covering round doorposts, but am not greatly impressed by their value in turning. But there are two devices which will help very much indeed in copy turning, and I hope to describe these in a later article. Both can be made in the workshop from odds and ends.

There are a number of jigs for various purposes which turners can construct. The true origins of most of these jigs are lost in history, but they are still being 'invented' and hailed as new. As the saying goes — there is nothing new under the sun!

A drill of some kind is worth keeping handy for the various lathemounting operations which employ screws. Holes should be pre-drilled, or driving screws will be hard work in many of the harder timbers. In bowl turning care should be taken over the depth to which faceplate screws are pre-drilled. If the drilling is too deep, holes may be uncovered at the bottom of the bowl as it is hollowed out. I like the type of drill which is operated by a handwheel on the side. If a broken drill bit of suitable length is used, drilling can continue until the chuck touches the surface of the blank, thus ensuring uniformity of depth and preventing over-penetration.

Another item which I always keep close to the lathe is a small hacksaw or, at least, a hacksaw blade. This is for final separation of a turning from its waste section or sections. In many cases if separation is completed with a parting tool there is some tearing at the centre, tufts of fibres being ripped out leaving small holes in the wood. This can be avoided by parting down to about ¼in. diameter and completing the operation with the hacksaw.

Some turners may want to construct special racks for tools. These are useful, but the bottom of the racks must be left open to permit egress of shavings; and tool racks should never be located at the rear of the lathe. The risk of clothing being caught up by machine or work as the turner leans over is obvious. The location of the on-off switch is equally important. It should be reached without having to lean over the machine. And even more important, the switch must be instantly accessible. In more than 30 years of woodturning I have had no occasion to use the switch but I like to know that I can stop the lathe with my knee or hip if necessary.

Now that the equipment and impedimenta of the woodturner have been discussed in broad terms, the time has come to consider turning itself. For the present I will do this in general terms. If readers have specific problems and would like any advice I will be pleased to assist. But please do enclose a stamped envelope; my post bag is weighty!

Just what is woodturning? Somewhat to my surprise the *Concise Oxford Dictionary* appears not to have heard of it. Perhaps this is as well and for the purpose of this series it may be better if I provide my own definition, which is the concept of woodturning upon which I base all my tuition and instructional writing. I define woodturning as 'the cutting to shape of wood which is rotating under power'.

In this series I am not attempting to deal with ornamental turning, the principles of which are entirely different and much more closely allied to those of the metal turner. It is sometimes confused with laminated, post-blocked or built-up work. These are subjects very much within our province, but ornamental turning is totally unrelated.

I have never been happy about the arbitrary subdivisions of woodturning into (a) spindle turning; and (b) faceplate work. These can cause confusion since spindle turning is taken to refer to work supported by both headstock and tailstock, while faceplate turning refers to work supported by only the

(continued on p.96)

The DeWalt 1370 Radial Arm Saw is quite simply the best on the market. It gives you high-speed cutting, up to 50 planks a minute.

It gives you hairline accuracy, and you can cut at any angle, either lengthways or crossways.

You can bevel and mitre.

And, by adding the attachments, you can whistle through the boring, routing, housing, sanding, jointing, moulding, grooving and rebating.

For the large-volume user, the new DeWalt 1370 (single phase) gives greater capacity.

And we're launching it with the special offer of a DW30 Dust Extractor at the package price of £656. A saving of £64.00.

So you cut the costs while you cut out the dust.

For the low-volume user, the famous DeWalt 125 is still the best on the market and we're currently offering it with a free leg-stand worth £37.00.

So whether your living depends on your saw or just your new fitted kitchen, find out more about DeWalt.

You'll cut out the time-wasting if you cut out the coupon now.

Subject to availability.

If your saw can't cut 50 planks a minute, use a pair of scissors.

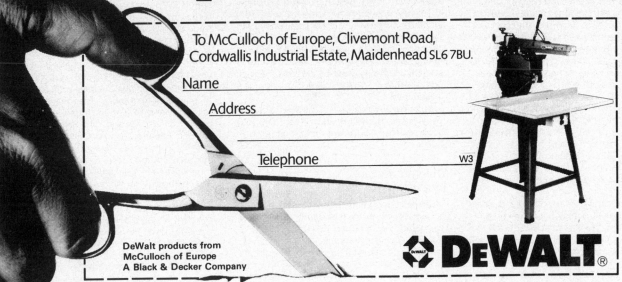

To McCulloch of Europe, Clivemont Road, Cordwallis Industrial Estate, Maidenhead SL6 7BU.

Name

Address

Telephone   W3

DeWalt products from
McCulloch of Europe
A Black & Decker Company

◆ **DeWALT** ®

(Continued from page 94)

headstock, so embracing work supported on a faceplate or any form of chuck. It may be simpler for beginners to use a rather different subdivision, considering their blanks as either discs or sticks. A disc, cut from a plank, will have the grain running across it, and when mounted in the lathe the grain will be rotating in a plane at 90° to the bed of the lathe. A stick may be taken to be a workpiece in which the grain runs lengthwise and for successful turning different techniques must be used.

Beginners in woodturning normally feel some apprehension when first using the lathe, particularly if they are not accustomed to machinery. Those who feel no such apprehension are either qualified woodturners of considerable experience, or fools. Some apprehension is normal and natural, since the instinct of self-preservation is high in all living things. It should, however, be stressed that the woodturning lathe is probably the safest of all woodworking machines, and those who have acquired a fundamental knowledge of the principles are unlikely to be involved in accidents.

I will deal first with the turning of sticks — or spindle turning — leaving chuck work and the turning of discs until later. Note that chuck work falls between the two, since the material will sometimes be mounted with its grain running across, as in a disc, while for other purposes the grain direction will be as in a stick.

Spindle turning is where the beginner should begin because the diameters of workpieces can be kept between reasonable limits; the work is securely held by headstock and tailstock; and the dreaded 'dig-in' is less spectacular — and much less nerve-shattering than with a large disc.

Spindle and chuck work is more demanding of the turner's skill than the turning of discs, at least in my opinion. There are those who hold that the man who can produce a first-class large bowl has achieved the ultimate.

A little consideration will show this to be nonsense, however. The turning of bowls calls for mastery of one gouge — and the use of a scraper. The skill, if such it can be called, needed to use a scraper is on a par with that required to open a can of beans, and 10-15 minutes' instruction should be adequate.

If the correct technique has been learned of using gouges between centres, there will be a few problems in using one on a bowl, since the techniques are identical. In bowl turning the blank usually has considerable mass and weight and vibration problems are more obvious. I have always felt that beginners need courage rather than skill.

In chuck work and in spindle turning most of the tools in the kit of nine tools discussed in my December 1979 article will be used, some of them performing several different cuts; and the difference between a good operator and a bad one will soon be apparent. After all, a bowl is only a block of wood with a curve on both inside and outside, but a good deal of skill is needed to produce four nicely-turned legs for a piece of furniture.

In this series the emphasis is on cutting with sharp and correctly presented tools wherever possible, leaving the use of scrapers for situations where there is no hope of cutting. To me a scraper is not a woodturning tool. It is a substitute for one and to be used only where it is difficult or dangerous to cut.

It is important for beginners to understand the procedures for mounting woodturning blanks in the lathe — a blank is a rough piece of timber from which some item is to be produced. Wood which has been properly mounted will not fly from the lathe, though this can easily happen when the mounting is incorrect. There is considerable danger; therefore it is vital that there be adequate penetration of both drive and tailstock centres into the wood and that all clamps on the machine be tightened securely. Sufficient drive centre penetration can be achieved by pushing the wood on by means of the tailstock. However, this is not good practice since it can impose great strain on the bearings. A two-pronged drive centre should be used for all but very thin workpieces, since the desired depth of penetration is easier to achieve than with the four-pronged variety.

An old chisel or, better still, an old chisel of similar size to the drive centre, should be driven into the end of the blank to a depth of about ½in., and removed. The wood can then be pushed onto the drive centre of the lathe by means of the tailstock without undue strain. The drive centre itself should not be hammered into the wood, as the metal is soft and hammering will distort it quite easily.

The centre of the workpiece can be found by drawing in the diagonals, but its location can normally be estimated by eye for practice blanks. When the material has been pushed onto the drive centre by means of the tailstock, the latter can be backed-off by about a quarter of a turn of the handwheel to ease the strain. Immediately prior to starting the lathe all clamps must be checked for security, and the workpiece rotated by hand to ensure that it does not foul the tool rest. Speed is not critical but it is best for beginners to keep below about 1500rpm.

Many suggest that the corners of square blanks should be removed by means of a planer or circular saw before mounting in the lathe. Such advice comes usually from those with little experience. The roughing gouge is the safest and most efficient tool for the removal of the corners, if the operator knows how to use it. Having given personal tuition to hundreds of beginners, I state categorically that all have taken to the tool at once, experiencing few difficulties. This is a basic technique which I hope to cover in detail later.

Emphasis on projects

Large and lavish is *The Book of Furniture Making;* almost I feel to the extent of being intended for the 'coffee table' range of publications carelessly, but thoughtfully, scattered along with a galaxy of glossy magazines on homemaking themes.

A little less extravagance in the production would surely have lowered the cost and brought it within the range of those of us who have to budget to buy not only books on our chosen craft but tools, timber and all the other numerous items connected therewith.

Nevertheless, Alf Martensson has done a good job in showing how to make a comprehensive range of woodwork items for the home covering a spectrum that spans chopping boards to bunk beds. Each piece is thoroughly dealt with and includes cutting lists, descriptions of making and assembling; and all accompanied with a profusion of photographs (colour and monochrome) and drawings.

At their best, Mr Martensson's projects reflect the eminent design sensitivity of his native Sweden (he was raised in the US and now lives in London), but other pieces fall short of the mark. Items employing solid timber and man-made materials are shown and the various chapters deal with a room at a time.

BOOK REVIEWS

The latter part is almost a complete monograph on tools, materials, construction and finishes. It could hold its own with many another textbook on the same subjects. Yet I wonder, with my earlier reservations about the price, whether it would not have been better to divide the whole into two leaving the customer to decide whether he wants to buy a book of designs or a working manual, and still have enough money for glue and glasspaper!

Published by Wm Collins Sons & Co Ltd, 14 St James's Place, London SW1A 1PS, the book costs £7.95. It runs to 252 pages with index. **R.W.G.**

Designs for bygone furniture

Latest in a long line of authoritative books on woodworking by that distinguished and respected writer Charles H. Hayward, is *Antique Furniture Designs.* As a craftsman, author and illustrator he has remained the doyen of his craft over a considerable period of time and he was for many years the editor of WOODWORKER.

As might be expected, therefore, the book displays throughout a depth of accuracy and information on bygone furniture, accompanied not only with photographs but by measured line drawings as well. Supplementary drawings show, where necessary, specific points of construction and technique; and many are the tricks of the trade thereby revealed!

Thus, the book has a dual appeal: To the craftsman who wants to make reproduction furniture, a varied and sensible selection of some 24 items spanning the ages are dealt with, all of which would have a practical use in a household of today. To those who are in the business of antique dealing, whether buying or selling and who seek to gain a greater knowledge and understanding of how these pieces were constructed, there is set out in straightforward and clear language the intricacies of each design. More difficult and technical terms are explained in an illustrated glossary at the back of the book.

The pages of this excellent publication contain a distillation of cabinet making practice and tradition and it will prove delightful reading to all who have a sympathy and interest in antique furniture.

Publisher is Evans Brothers Ltd, Montague House, Russell Square, London WC1B 5BX. The price is £6.95. **R.W.G.**

NOW..... you can make your circular saw do the work of an expensive radial arm or table saw

RIP CUTS! CROSS CUTS! STRAIGHT CUTS! ANGLE CUTS!

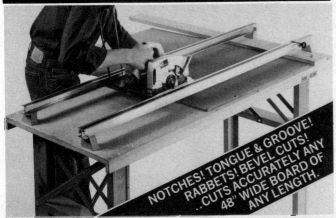

NOTCHES! TONGUE & GROOVE! RABBETS! BEVEL CUTS! ...CUTS ACCURATELY ANY 48" WIDE BOARD OF ANY LENGTH.

CROSS CUTS 4'x 8' CHIPBOARD AND PLYWOOD WITH EASE.

RIP CUTS PANELLING AND WOOD/ PLASTICS ETC. TO ANY LENGTH.

MAKES ANGLE CUTS (MITRE, BEVEL ETC) WITH EASE.

SAW GUIDE CAN ALSO BE USED WITH YOUR ROUTER.

Heavy steel saw plate — accommodates circular saws from 4½" to 8¼" blade size. Can also be used with your router (extra plates available if you wish to permanently mount your router). Six nylon bearings assure easy movement. ¾" thick chipboard top with 22¼" x 60" work surface supports almost any material... i.e. 4' x 8' chipboard for accurate cutting. 60" structural aluminium I-beam shaped rails give support in every direction. Angle degree indicator shows position for angle cuts. Saw guide fence is 48" long — assuring accurate cuts in both large and small projects. Anti-kick spring and cord-holder for safety. Folding legs and floor protectors. Overall size: 60" wide 34" high 24" deep. Weight 70 lbs. Saw not included unless ordered. Easily assembled — instructions included.

SPECIAL INTRODUCTORY PRICE
£135.00 Inc. VAT (Plus £6.00 P & P) R.R.P. £178.00
or together with Shopmate 7¼" 1.6 HP Heavy Duty Circular Saw
£176.00 Inc. VAT (Plus £7.40 P & P) SAW R.R.P. £56.00
JEMCO TOOLS 32 Baker Street, Weybridge, Surrey. Tel: Weybridge 54896-7

ORDER TODAY
JEMCO TOOLS
32 Baker Street, Weybridge, Surrey. Tel: Weybridge 54896-7

☐ Send......Portable saw guides at £135.00 each plus £6.00 p & p

☐ Send......Portable saw guides plus a Shopmate 7¼" heavy duty saw at £176.00 each plus £7.40 p & p

☐ Please send me literature on the portable saw guides and your range of discount power tools.

Credit Card Holder can order by phone at any time:
Access ☐   Barclaycard ☐

No ☐☐☐☐☐☐☐☐☐☐☐☐☐☐☐☐

Name _____

Address _____
_____

My satisfaction guaranteed or I may return in 15 days for refund.

SHOW REPORT
'Craftsmanship is alive and well'

Left: The winners (l to r) Nicholas Bott, Ralph G. Fellows, A. J. Lown, J. G. Brundrit, E. Ives, J. Oxlade, E. Paris, J. S. Ambrose, and H. W. Heasman. Centre left: Musical instrument class judges (l to r) C. W. Bond, I. Owen, and R. Rose. Below: Cabinet making class judge John Price and two of the clocks. Bottom: Two of the judges in the model horse-drawn vehicle class, David Wray (left) and John Thompson.

The importance of small businesses to the woodworking sector was stressed by managing director Gospatric Home of Model and Allied Publications Ltd when he presented trophies to winners of the competitive classes at the Woodworker Show in November. 'It is evident from the high standard of entries, numbering more than 160 examples of fine woodwork that craftsmanship is indeed alive and well,' declared Mr Home. The enquiries received by the Council for Small Industries in Rural Areas (CoSIRA) at its exhibition stand and the interest shown by so many of the 10,200 visitors in the demonstrations arranged by Rycotewood College and in the exhibits of Bucks College of Higher Education and Shrewsbury Technical College, gave some indication of the potential which exists for linking craftsmanship with business.

Mr Home who was accompanied on the platform by the Swedish Trade Commissioner (Johan Dahl), Ashley Iles, Derek Simble, Harold Derbyshire, David Rodgers and David Whitehouse (MAP marketing manager), presented trophies to: Ralph G. Fellows for his carved oak chest (cabinet making class WA) (Robbins rose bowl and Trend Machinery cutting tools); H.W. Heasman who submitted a coat of arms of the London borough of Hillingdon (woodcarving class WB) (Henry Taylor award and cheque); J.S. Ambrose for a laminated bowl with lid (woodturning class WC) (Henry Taylor award and cheque); R.G. Hargrave who entered a violin (musical instruments class WD) (WOODWORKER challenge cup); E. Ives for his picture 'The Craftsmen' in marquetry (marquetry inlay class WD) (World of Wood cup); E. Paris for a half-size spinning wheel (miscellaneous class WF) (Brian Bowman trophy); A.J. Lown who submitted a Glamorgan farm waggon model (horse-drawn vehicle models class WG) (John Thompson trophy); J. Oxlade who submitted a glass-topped coffee table (junior section class WH) (WOODWORKER special prize).

Junior Woodworker of the Year challenge shield (donated by J. Simble & Sons) was presented by Derek Simble to Paul Underwood who entered a laminated long bow. He also received a case of Stanley woodworking tools from the company's technical lecturer Harold Derbyshire.

The Swedish trade commissioner handed token awards to Nicholas Bott winner of the Sjöberg family crafts competition organised by WOODWORKER in conjunction with Olro Group Scotland (Wood Products Division) which handles sales of Sjöberg woodworking benches in UK). Mr Bott's prize is a holiday for two in Sweden.

Top right: Woodcarving class judges (l to r) John Sainsbury, T.A. Woolhouse and Ashley Iles. Centre left: N. Martyr and John Gould judging the miscellaneous class. Centre right: I. Owen marking the winning violin. Below left: Two of the junior class judges, left K. Riseborough and right S. Cliffe Ashworth.

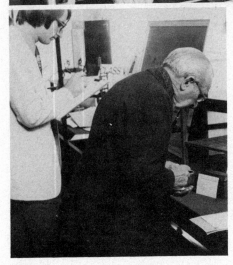

Right: Cabinet making class judges John Price (left) H. C. Triggs (centre) and S. Mackilligin.

Prizes donated by Ashley Iles (Edge Tools) Ltd for the Ashley Iles/WOODWORKER 1979 international woodcarving competition (43 entries) were presented by Ashley Iles to: (1) J.G. Brundrit (Coventry), (2) E. Green (St Helier) and (3) A. Flanaghan (Leicester) winners in the figure carving section. They received respectively 30 carving tools, 12 tools and six tools all in presentation cases. Winners of the relief carving section were (1) C.T. Roe (Chichester), (2) J. Murphy (Dun Laoghaire, Co Dublin) and (3) J. Reside (Newtownards, Co Down) who received 12 carving tools in presentation cases, six tools in a box and a lignum vitae mallet and set of three slipstones respectively.

This year's Woodworker Show was the first to be held as a separate event. More than 160 entries were received and standards of craftsmanship were generally high. The classes were: WA1 — cabinet making, WA2 clocks; WB1 — carving (architectural), WB2 — figure carving, WB3 — relief carving; WC1 — woodturning (spindle), WC2 — faceplate, WC3 — segmental; WD1 — musical instruments (wind), WD2 — musical instruments (string); WE1 — marquetry and inlay (picture), WE2 — Marquetry and inlay (inlay); WF1 — fretwork, pyrography, toys, miscellaneous; WG1 — horse-drawn vehicle models (agricultural), WG2 — passenger, WG3 — model vehicles made from a kit; WH — junior section.

Judging of the exhibits was performed by H.G. Triggs, J. Price, S. Mackilligin (class WA); Ashley Iles, T.A. Woolhouse, J. Sainsbury (class WB); P. Child, E. Doulton, G. Stokes, A. Holtham (class WC); Ieuan Owen, R. Rose, C.W. Bond (Class WD); C. Simpson, J. Bowles, C.H. Good (class WE); J. Thompson, D.C. Wray, B. Voisey (class WG); J. Gould, N. Martyr (class WF); S. Cliffe Ashworth, K. Riseborough, M.P. Bulger (class WH).

In addition to trophy and prize winners named previously, certificates of merit were recommended by the judges for the following: Class WA1 — 2 P. St Pier (yew low table); 3 B. Bostock (writing/work table). class WA2 — 1 R. Palmer (bracket clock); 2 G.R. Bailey (longcase clock); 3 W. Cox (longcase clock). Class WB1 — 2 M. Lund

B. Voisey, one of the judges in the model horsedrawn vehicles class.

(carved wall clock); 3 Edina McGuire (St Francis of Assisi). Class WB2 — 1 R. Moll (nude female with robe); 2 Miss I. Neel (two shoals of fish forming a spherical shape); 3 Dr M.A. Bacon (Henry VIII); highly commended P.G. Garbett (lady's fashion sandal). Class WB3 — 1 Edina McGuire (the Skater); 2 G.F. Castle (Christmas bouquet); 3 R.G. Fellows (three-legged stool). Class WC3 — 1 J.S. Ambrose (wine ladle). Class WD1 — 1 H.G. McCarthy (Irish bagpipes). Class WD2 — 2 Maggie Ridout (classical guitar). Class WE1 — 2 E. Ives (the Alchemist); 3 R.J.H. Miller (borough of Southwark armorial bearings). Class WF1 — 2 R.F. Street (classic design rolling pin); 3 D.J. Moody (pyrographic engraving). Class WG1 2 P. Cooper (Oxfordshire wagon); 3 E.H. Horne (Lincolnshire hermaphrodite); very highly commended P. Pratley (Buckinghamshire wagon). Class WH — 2 M. Wale (jewellery box); 3 B. James (large technical drawing board).

The exhibition section of the Show proved to be extremely popular and the 75 stands attracted a great deal of attention. Standholders reported a high level of enquiries and good business for all types of machinery and hand tools. One hand tool manufacturer had to arrange daily deliveries from his works to the stand in order to maintain stocks. Another manufacturer was pleasantly surprised by the demand for relatively large machines and anticipated being able to secure a large contract from overseas as a result of enquiries.

Above: Two shoals of fish by Iris N. Neel, Maidstone. Bottom left: Timer glass by G. Wrench, Thetford. Bottom centre: Walnut bracket clock by W.E. Landon, Bozeat. Bottom right: Forklift truck by T. Wood, Ilkley.

Books and plans sold well and additional supplies had to be rushed through. Guild of Woodworkers administrator David Whitehouse and his colleagues had the pleasure of meeting a large number of members and processing applications from visitors wishing to join the guild.

Upstairs in the lecture theatre the Woodworker-Record 'answer station' and lectures on wood carving and wood turning had capacity audiences. In fact, John Sainsbury who organised this feature in conjunction with his colleagues from Record Ridgway Tools Ltd, had to hang up 'house full' notices on several occasions.

Though the bulk of visitors were from the British Isles, continental countries were represented along with Africa and India. A party of 24 Americans took the opportunity of Russ Zimmerman's organisation to make the Woodworker Show the centrepiece of their week's tour of UK.

Summing up the 1979 event, Model and Allied Publications managing director Gospatric Home, said: 'We have had tremendous support from distributors. In the future we hope that this support will be complemented by manufacturers. We know the Woodworker Show was weak in some areas so our aim for the future is "attraction in depth". We want the Show to be a meeting place for manufacturers, distributors and end users.'

Plans for the 1980 Woodworker Show are already being discussed. Provisional arrangements are for a five-day event in the first week of November.

Top: Chest by Ralph G. Fellows, Dudley, best in class cabinet making. Right: Ships wheel by C. Deeley, Rugeley. Left: Old woodsman in lime by R.D. Scott, Peacehaven. Left bottom: Borough of Hillingdon coat of arms by M.W. Heasman. Below: Chalice by G. Wrench, Thetford.

Judges' reports

Cabinet making — class WA: We were pleasantly surprised by the magnificent response in WA1 and WA2 and the high standard of work entered. Our main problem was to equate the diverse nature of the work: reproduction, contemporary, amateur and professional.

Some entries were impressive at first sight but did not stand up to close inspection. Veneers were often badly layed although the folding-top Georgian table was excellent. Most pieces were well-finished to a high standard but some ignored the finish of backs and bottoms; others had polyurethane spread like marmalade.

It would be unfair to make comment on the design. Design is, after all, personal and often controversial; and we were assessing a wide range. But we were unanimous in selecting the three winners in WA1 and WA2. The outright winner displayed such a wide range of ability in cabinet making and woodcarving that his oak chest could not be faulted.

Far left: Chair in teak by R.A. Fuller, Goring-on-Sea. Left: The laminated bowl and lid in teak and sycamore which won woodturning best in class for J.S. Ambrose, Ely. Below: Glamorganshire farm waggon (first prize) by A. J. Lown of Croydon.

Judges' reports

Model horse-drawn vehicles — class WG: An impressive display of farm waggons provided an interesting contrast between the various regional types. As well as winning the John Thompson trophy for the best model in the class, W.G. Lown had three other farm waggons on display. It would be hard to fault the impeccable craftsmanship in these models, built in the original wheelwright's timbers of oak, ash and elm, although it might be considered that a less conspicuous grain is more appropriate in a model.

Eric Horne had shown a lot of imagination in displaying his Lincolnshire hermaphrodite in a wheelwright's shop setting, jacked-up and with a broken axle. A couple of out-of-scale features relegated this to third place behind the mahogany Oxfordshire waggon made by Peter Cooper.

It was difficult to decide on the models to be highly commended as there was defects in workmanship and, in particular, in finish. The fact that no painted model was among the prizewinners does not mean that a natural wood finish is necessarily expected in competitions. But if the model is to be painted the painting must be done to a high standard.

It was encouraging to see a model from a female modelmaker. Although it had technical faults the brewer's dray by Carole A. Feasey was neatly made and finished. Incidentally, all the award-winning models were built to a scale of 1½in. to 1ft.

Entries in the subclasses for carriages and caravans and for models made from kits were disappointing; no awards were given.

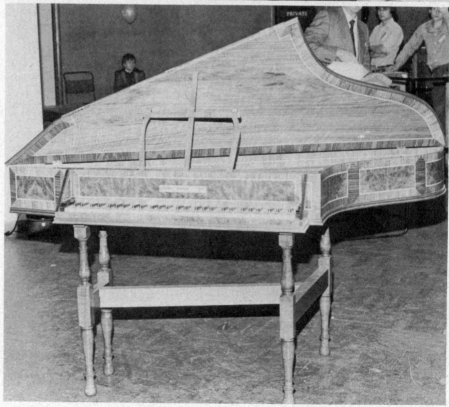

Centre: Oxfordshire waggon which won second prize for P. Cooper in the model horse-drawn vehicles class. Brewers dray by Carole A. Feasey in the background. Right: Spinet by A.J. Dunhill of Barking.

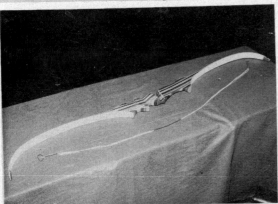

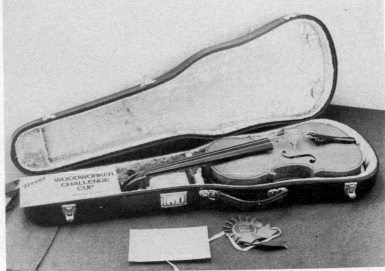

Top left: Regency style sofa table by J.R. Bowser, Luton. Top right: The Craftsmen by E. Ives, Ipswich, best in class marquetry section. Above left: Laminated long bow by Paul Underwood, London W, junior woodworker of the year, Centre right: Violin by R.G. Hargrave, Aylesbury, best of class musical instruments. Below right: Lincolnshire hermaphrodite by E.H. Horne, Essex.

Judges' reports

Junior section — class WH: We were disappointed by the small entry but unanimous in our selection. The glass-topped coffee table had good jointing of the bottom rails and in particular the mitre/mortise joints on the glass surround were well executed. The redeeming feature of the jewellery box was the ebony/sycamore inlay on the top, though the dovetails were not a neat design and the hinges were poorly executed. The support frame of the large technical drawing board was weak in construction design and the Perspex moveable draughting cross-member was not stable. More care could have been given to the finish, including the metal fittings.

CORONET WOODWORKING MACHINES

Universal & Independent models for Woodworking & Woodturning

Judges' reports

Musical instruments — class WD: It was not difficult to choose the winners, the standard of craftsmanship of the violin and Irish bagpipes being especially high. The violin was given the overall prize for the class.

An instrument is sometimes a piece of furniture as well as a musical instrument; it must be aesthetically attractive as well as being playable. We judged the instruments not only for workmanship but for their musical function.

We hope that this class becomes more popular at future Woodworker Shows; musical instruments are so fascinating that we are sure more people would enjoy making them.

Top: David Rodgers (Henry Taylor Tools) with left M.W. Heasman and right J.S. Ambrose with their awards. Centre left: R.G. Fellows receiving the Robbins rose bowl from G.D.L.R. Home, managing director MAP. Centre right: J.G. Brundrit, Coventry, winner of the figure carving section in the 'Clowns' competition receiving his award from Ashley Iles. Left: Nicholas Bott who won the Sjöberg trip to Sweden prize, pictured with the Swedish trade commissioner Johan Dahl and Mr and Mrs Bott.

Below: The winning entry in the figure carving section of the Ashley Iles/Woodworker competition 'Clowns' carved by J.G. Brundrit of Coventry.

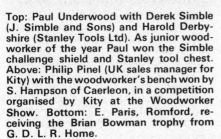

Top: Paul Underwood with Derek Simble (J. Simble and Sons) and Harold Derbyshire (Stanley Tools Ltd). As junior woodworker of the year Paul won the Simble challenge shield and Stanley tool chest. Above: Philip Pinel (UK sales manager for Kity) with the woodworker's bench won by S. Hampson of Caerleon, in a competition organised by Kity at the Woodworker Show. Bottom: E. Paris, Romford, receiving the Brian Bowman trophy from G. D. L. R. Home.

Judges' reports

Pyrography, toys, miscellaneous — class WF: We found the class somewhat difficult to judge because of its miscellaneous nature. It would be exciting one day to see a toymaking section with the criterion of 'tools for play' which is what most toys really should be. In the pre-school period of child development the use of wood as a material for toys, its 'feel' and robustness and the necessary simplification of shapes and forms that it dictates, is seen by many to be of inestimable value. Such a section would seem to provide a number of useful points on which meaningful judgement could be made.

CLOWNS

The Ashley Iles/Woodworker wood-carving competition was again divided into two sections: one for relief carving and one for figure carving. The subject chosen was 'Clowns' — circus clowns or any clown or clowning activity which, it was hoped, would allow for a great deal of artistic and original experiment, as well as wide interpretation.

Choosing a subject for this competition is not easy ... it is difficult to cater for all abilities and styles of carving: an expert animal carver may have no hope of a prize if the subject specifies the human form. Again an expert figure carver may fall down if faces are important. Often the expression on the face of the carving is very important. The response seems to have justified the choice of clowns. There were 43 entries (35 in the figure section eight in the relief).

As in previous years the competition attracted entries from overseas. Our furthest travelling clown came from Gooseberry Hill, Australia; several entries crossed the Irish Sea; and two came over from Jersey.

We were pleased to have two entries from schoolboys: 14-year-old Martin Czerniuk and Alan Necchi. Alan entered the competition for the third time and seems to improve with every competition. His clown was precariously balanced on a bucket. Both boys showed a fine sense of humour in their carvings. The baggy trousers and outsize bowtie on Martin's entry was a classical study.

Several of the entries followed the 'bucket of water' theme so beloved of the circus clown, including those of Ron Morgans and L.K. Nixon. The balancing theme was also popular: P.J. Watson's clown was balancing upside-down on a ball; Brian Ackrill's clown was on a drum; and A. Collis had his clown teetering on a wall. Among other humorous touches were shaving with a meat cleaver, playing violins with saws, dogs being enticed through hoops and doing what comes naturally.

Mr Petrie was highly commended for his imaginative use of a yew root in the production of 'Yewi '79'. Actual people also became the subject of carvings; Charlie Chaplin and the American clown Lou Jacobs among them.

There was little hesitation in choosing the winner of the figure section. J.G. Brundrit produced the most elegant violin-playing clown with his coat tails swirling around him. His left foot was almost visibly tapping to the music and the pied piper quality of this piece gave a feel of lightness and movement. The long fingers so daintily holding the bow and neck of the violin looked sensitive. Indeed, the piece was much commented and remarked upon.

Prize winners were (figure carving): 1 J.G. Brundrit, Coventry; 2 E. Green, St Helier, Jersey; 3 A. Flanaghan, Leicester; highly commended H. Petrie, Manchester; (relief carving) 1 C.T. Roe, Chichester; 2 J. Murphy, Dun Laoghaire; Co Dublin; 3 J. Reside, Newtownards, Co Down.

CLOWN MEETS CLOWNS

When we chose 'Clowns' as the subject for the Ashley Iles/Woodworker 1979 international carving competition we did not expect an association with a real life clown. Then Sylvia Hayes sent in a story and pictures about Kerby Drill the road safety clown who appears on the front cover of this issue with two of the prize winning carved clowns displayed at the Woodworker Show last November.

Out of the ring or off TV, Kerby Drill is Hal Brooks who, with his wife Deena, has a shop in Bognor Regis, Sussex, trading under the name of Home & Garden Centre. Here he also sells the name sculptures and other items such as candelabras and wooden ornaments which he makes in his workshop. He has always been interested in woodwork and after war service started up in business as a carpenter, builder and decorator. It was during this time that Mrs Brooks, who comes from a theatrical family, persuaded her husband to make props and costumes for local pantomines.

From this it was but a short step to entertaining and he says: 'More and more I felt I would like to become a clown because above all I enjoyed making people laugh.' Subsequently he devised Kerby Drill the road safety clown and presented his own show all over England and Wales. During 16 years in show business he also made many TV appearances.

Two years ago Mr Brooks decided to give up full-time 'clowning' and concentrate on his name sculptures and other woodworking activities and on painting in oils — not surprisingly his most popular subject is clowns.

The name sculptures, hand worked in laminated pine and clear finished, use a person's name, sometimes in humour and other times linked to work or hobby, and are completely individual and original.

With his retail shop and workshop Mr Brooks is a busy man though he still finds time for occasional 'clowning' when asked to appear for a local event as Kerby Drill.

Above and left: Hal Brooks (Kerby Drill) with some of his name sculptures.

The clown that won first prize in the relief section for C.T. Roe of Chichester

Pepi who won second prize in the figure carving section for Eric Green of St Helier

Below: Pagliacci by C.J. Fisher of Abergavenny

Third prize in the figure section by A. Flanaghan of Leicester

Above: Second prize in the relief section carved by John Murphy

Yewi '79 by H. Petrie was highly commended by the judges.

Left: Alan Necchi's balancing clown.

Left: R. Riddell's 'close shave.'

Above: Charlie Chaplin by John Murphy. Below: Ron Morgans' water throwing clown.

Below right: 14 year old Martin Czerniuk's amusing entry.

CLOWNS

Below: Father and son by John Reside, which won 3rd prize in the relief carving section.

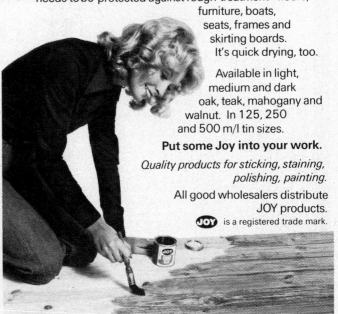
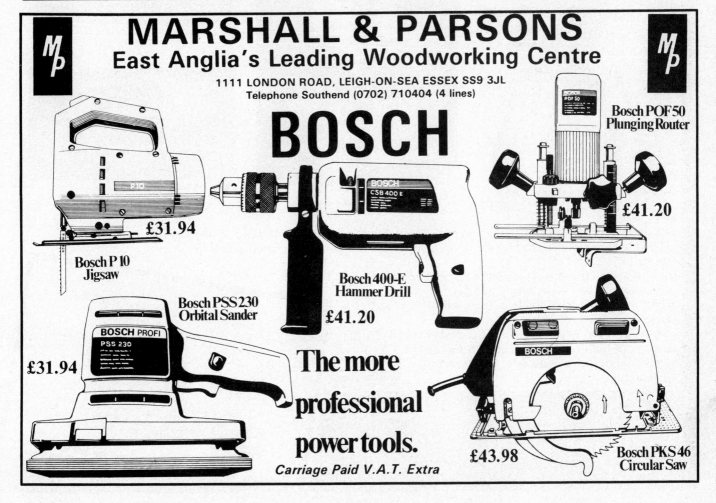

W.H. BROWN FIWSc

discusses

BRAZILIAN HARDWOODS AND STRESS-GRADING

One of the many problems of forestry in tropical areas of the world is how to conserve the preferred tree species and at the same time encourage greater utilisation of less preferred or secondary species. When surveys of these forests are made, generally on a 10 acre assessment, enumeration of trees from 1ft to 10ft in girth will usually disclose 1,000 or more trees of different species with only a small proportion of preferred species, often with no more than two or three of these ready for felling at any given time. Thus in many tropical countries the major priority is trying to create world-wide markets for the disposal of hundreds of different species of hardwoods lesser known to consumers.

In the main the markets sought for these woods are those concerned with appearance. That is to say uses where appearance is the attraction, eg veneers, furniture and cabinet making; high-class joinery; shop and bank fitting; turnery etc, because other outlets, principally of a structural nature, are often closed due to what might be termed spheres of interest. For example, western Europe including UK, draws its structural softwoods from Scandinavia, Russia and Canada, and turns to west Africa firstly for structural hardwoods, and secondly to SE Asia and tropical America. Oceania relies more upon Australia, New Zealand and Papua-New Guinea.

Tropical America and the Caribbean islands look more to North America for additional outlets for their woods, but US and Canada are self-supporting in structural softwoods. Very few hardwoods for building and engineering are brought in from else-where. Thus the surplus woods of the tropical rain forests are difficult to dispose of economically.

In what used to be called the emerging nations the need for urban expansion is still great, particularly in Brazil, where on the one hand agriculture is demanding expansion into forest clearings, where roads bisect forest areas; and on the other hand, where the need to extract more timber is aided by increasingly better communications and greater timber exports are essential to help balance trade figures, the very timber being extracted has no ready market.

To offset this, Brazil has been turning its attention to the greater utilisation of its secondary hardwoods for building and civil engineering projects. The first step was for the Federal University of Vicosa in Brazil to liaise with Purdue University in Lafayette, Indiana, US, in the development of machine stress-grading methods for some of its more predominant hardwoods.*

When a timber species is tested for strength, this is done by using small clear specimens of wood, ie without knots and other strength limiting features. The results of these tests, expressed in appropriate values, become the basic stresses of that particular wood. Strange as it might seem, very few timbers have unknown strength properties because every new wood discovered is subjected to much research.

Basic strength properties are indeed basic, ie for practical purposes it would be entirely uneconomic to try to use timber without a blemish as is the case in determining the basic stresses, so working stresses are needed. Put another way, if a given size of clear, knot-free timber used as a beam was known to be capable of supporting a given load, if only half this load was to be applied then either the beam need be half the size, or it could be the same size but of poorer quality.

For a good number of years now, many countries have stress-graded their structural softwoods by visual means, and UK has been a leader in the field. By admission of certain strength limiting features, grades of timber have been established which give only a percentage of the basic stresses. For example, if the wood only has a few defects it could be deemed to have, say, 75% of the basic stresses and would be referred to as 75 stress-grade. For most of our roof timbers in domestic housing we use a 50 stress-grade.

Subsequently, machines have been developed where a whole plank of wood is passed through and the stresses measured automatically, generally by deflection (ie bending). This has been particularly relevant to the stress-grading of hardwoods. It is by this method the present work on some of the secondary woods of Brazil is taking place. Actually the idea is to establish the proportion of different stress-grades obtainable from a given parcel of timber and relate this to the basic stresses. There is invariably a degree of opposition to the use of structural hardwoods in building, general on the basis of unwanted weight, but while in the main most hardwoods are heavier than softwoods, they are also generally much stronger. Therefore smaller sizes of hardwoods can be used to provide suitable strength.

It is to be hoped that Brazil will eventually find an outlet for many of her secondary hardwoods in domestic housing, and in civil and naval engineering projects.

*'Increased utilisation of tropical hardwoods through species-independent structural grading.' By John F. Senft and Ricardo M. Della Lucia. Copyright Forest Products Research Society 1979 (US).

114

Prices quoted are those prevailing at press date and are subject to alteration due to economic conditions.

THE WORLD'S TIMBER TREES

C.W. Bond FIWSc continues his series with a description of berlinia, a timber strong enough for structural work. It is very decorative for interior fittings on an imposing scale. Veneer may be known by the name of rose zebrano. Last month the author described padauk and in December 1979 African blackwood: 7.

BERLINIA: 9

Berlinia spp. *Berlinia* — probably in honour of Anders Henricsson Berlin (pupil of Linnaeus) 1746 — 1773. Leguminosae (Caesalpiniaceae).

Right: *Berlinia grandiflora* cross section × 3.3.
Below right: Cross section ×10 lineal.

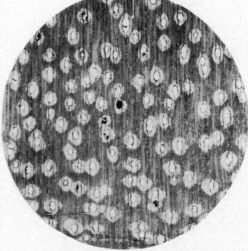

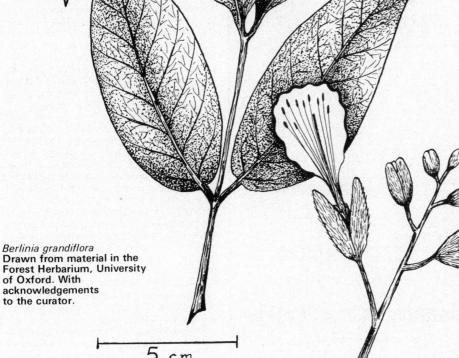

Berlinia grandiflora
Drawn from material in the Forest Herbarium, University of Oxford. With acknowledgements to the curator.

5 cm

This is another instance of the botanical name of the tree being adopted as the commercial name of the timber. Two allied genera, *Isoberlinia* and *Tetraberlinia,* may appear from time to time. There are 18 species of berlinia and the wood comes from either *B. confusa* or *B. grandiflora* (large-flowered) illustrated here.

The wood is highly attractive with its pale brown background handsomely marked with wavy red-brown or purplish streaks. The general appearance is somewhat variable. In hardness and weight it compares with oak but may be somewhat harder. In hand-working it is fairly resistant but presents no special difficulty. The vessels are large, giving a rather coarse texture; they are comparatively numerous, solitary and show a tendency to occur in oblique lines. Seasonal growth is faintly marked.

The photomicrographs show all this with unusual clarity, the parenchyma cells surrounding the vessels in almost perfect circles. This is a classic example of 'vasicentric parenchyma'. On the other hand the rays are so fine as to be almost invisible with a × 10 hand lens.

The timber is strong enough for structural work and is very decorative for interior fittings on an imposing scale. Veneer may be known by the name of rose zebrano.

A--Z OF HAND TOOLS

Oak was used for this table by D. R. Sage, but any home-grown timber is suitable.

The previous article (in the January issue) discussed the cutting gauge which author John Sainsbury described as 'little used but extremely handy not only for marking-out but for a number of other applications.' This month he deals with dowel bits.

Readers are invited to add to the information already published. Wherever possible in the series references have been made in general terms as regards manufacturers' products.

Cutting dowel holes in solid timber is best carried out using the Jenning's pattern dowel bit in a hand brace. This bit is precision ground to exact size at its boring diameter and is about 5in. in length. Its form is exactly similar to the normal Jenning's bit, having a fine screw nose, two spurs and cutters and a finely-finished twist through which the chips are passed.

R241 dowel bit
(Far right)

The dowel bit is also available with a machine shank and a choice of brad point or screw nose. The brad point should also be selected for fast machine work.

R302 Jenning's pattern machine dowel bit. (Right)

This bit is best not used in particleboard (chipboard). The craftsman should use a wood drill and be prepared to sharpen it frequently, since the abrasive character of particleboard tends to quickly blunt cutting edges. The wood drill is ground accurately to size, has adequate chip clearance and a pointed nose to give perfectly accurate location. The engineer's drill should *not* be used since it has none of these essential features, although its edge may well stand up to the task.

Historical

Early dowel bits were spoon type with round noses, shell form and with both flat and square tang-

(Top and centre right)

Those of twisted form were of Gedge's pattern, permitting the cutting of angled dowel holes.

(Bottom right)

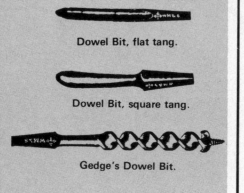

Dowel Bit, flat tang.

Dowel Bit, square tang.

Gedge's Dowel Bit.

The requirement was to produce a cottage-style occasional table of traditional design. Oak has been used but any home-grown timber such as elm, ash or chestnut is suitable and in keeping. The table is well within the scope of the non-power tool craftsman.

Timber for the top was chosen for the best figure and made up from two pieces 8 × 7/8 × 30in. long. After shooting the butting edges true and square they were dowel jointed, glued with Cascamite and cramped together until the adhesive had set. Both ends were squared-up and the chamfers marked out. Using a finely set jack plane both ends were chamfered first so that any splitting-out would be removed when chamfering the sides. The long chamfers were planed with care so that they matched the end chamfers. Both sides of the top were then cleaned-up with a scraper.

The stretcher was made from a piece 4 × 2 × 26in. long, the tenons marked out on both ends and the waste cut with a tenon saw. The tenons were cleaned-up and the shoulders pared square and true with a bevel-edge chisel, and the ends of the tenons rounded. A template was made from cardboard for the shape, positioned on the stretcher and drawn round. After cutting off the waste at the ends of the outer curve planing to shape was done with a smoothing plane. The waste was cut out from the inner curve with a coping saw and finished with a spokeshave, care being taken not to pick-up the grain at the bottom of the curve.

The legs were made from two pieces 8 × 7/8 × 14½in. Tenons were marked out on both pieces and, using a temporary fence clamped along the shoulder line, worked with a rebate plane. When all four tenons were true and square the waste was cut out at each end and the shoulders pared square with a bevel-edge chisel. A centre line was drawn along the length of each piece and the positions of the mortises marked in relation to the bottom tenon shoulders. The waste was drilled out and the mortises cut to fit the stretcher tenons. A template of cardboard was made for the shape, positioned on the legs and drawn around. The curves were cut with a coping saw and finished with a spokeshave, again taking care not to pick-up the grain at the bottom of the curves.

Two leg wedges were marked-out, cut and planed to size. The position of the tapered wedge hole in the stretcher was determined by fitting the stretcher to the leg and placing the wedge in mid-position against the leg

Cottage-style occasional table

and stretcher tenon and marking on both sides of the tenon the degree of taper. The stretcher was removed from the leg and a line marked ¾in. from the shoulder of the tenon. The width of the wedge hole was then marked and the hole cut out. After re-assembly and trying the wedge for fit, the wedge was trimmed to length as necessary and the operation repeated for the other end.

Feet and top supports are almost identical and made from four pieces 2 × 1⅛ × 10in. long. The mortises were marked, waste drilled out to depth and the supports cut to fit the leg tenons. The chamfers were then marked out on the bottom feet and worked with a small block plane. The ⅝in. radii was marked out on the top supports for working either with a block plane or a spokeshave.

The screw fixing holes were drilled for No. 8 brass woodscrews and counterbored for ⅜in. diameter dowel plugs.

All parts were cleaned-up with a scraper and fine glasspaper and all edges slightly rounded to remove sharpness. Top supports and the feet were glued with Cascamite, fitted on to the legs, then cramped, checked for squareness and set aside for the adhesive to dry.

The stretcher was fitted into both legs and held in position with the wedges. The top was upturned, the leg/stretcher assembly placed on in its correct position and the fixing holes spotted through. The top was drilled to take the No. 8 brass woodscrews taking care not to break through to the surface.

Before final assembly all parts were fumed with 8/80 ammonia in a large sealed polythene bag for 24hr. After fuming the legs and stretcher were assembled and retained with the wedges, and the assembly glued with Cascamite and screwed to the top. Dowel plugs were cut from ⅜in. diameter dowel rod and glued in position to cover the screw heads.

The table was given two coats of linseed oil which turned it a golden-brown colour. Each coat was well rubbed in and allowed to dry after which the table was polished with home-made beeswax-based polish and burnished up to a shine. An alternative, and more durable finish, would be polyurethane varnish rubbed down with wirewool and then wax polished. But, of course, the final finish is a matter of personal preference.

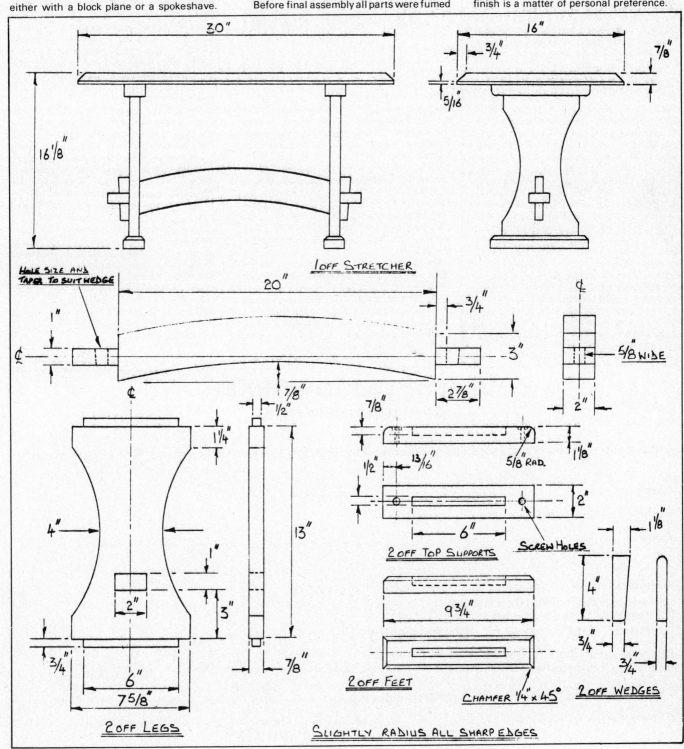

1 OFF STRETCHER

HOLE SIZE AND TAPER TO SUIT WEDGE

2 OFF TOP SUPPORTS

2 OFF FEET

2 OFF LEGS

2 OFF WEDGES

CHAMFER ¼" × 45°

SLIGHTLY RADIUS ALL SHARP EDGES

Business expands

Eric Swain who operates Periwinkle Press at Doddington in Kent is one of the guild's trading craftsmen. He specialises in picture frame making and also restores old prints. He has a gallery and bookshop dealing in antiquarian, historical and general titles as well as leather bindings.

Mr Swain's workshop is on the site of Doddington windmill which was built in 1816 and demolished some 40 years ago. Much of his picture framing is to special order and he carries a stock of more than 80 different mouldings. He is now expanding activities to include the manufacture of individual display cases and cabinets.

In addition to prints (about which he has issued an interesting leaflet) and books Mr Swain caters for postcard collectors. He has thousands of indexed cards on all subjects from c1900 onwards.

Uncertain prospects

A state of trade enquiry carried out by the British Woodworking Federation, 82 New Cavendish Street, London W1M 8AD, shows that the industry is becoming increasingly concerned about the prospects for 1980. In the individual joinery manufacturing sections, standard joinery output for private housing held up well in the first nine months of 1979, together with the manufacture of kitchand and bedroom fitments. This was offset by cut-backs in the public housing sector. Timber-frame housing is steadily assuming a higher percentage of the housing market.

Firms throughout the country, except in the Liverpool area, report severe shortages of skilled labour, particularly joiners and wood machinists. Nevertheless the BWF considers that the majoring of woodworking firms will achieve a higher workload this year than in 1979.

Carving a favourite eagle

A Woodcarver's Primer written by John Upton, an American woodcarver of many years' standing, should prove helpful to the beginner. It is profusely illustrated with clear, close-up photographs showing the progress through various woodcarving projects.

The author describes and illustrates a selection of woodcarving tools and bench tools suitable for the aspiring carver. Methods for sharpening chisels and gouges are shown in detail — from the use of the sharpening stone, slips and hone, to the final leather strop to put a really fine edge on the tool.

A sea scallop is the first project, which illustrates step-by-step the procedure to adopt for carving a simple relief design. This popular woodcarving motif is a good example for the novice as it embodies many of the fundamental techniques used by the woodcarver. The author then goes on to a larger more involved carving of an eagle, again carved in relief.

The simple shape of a leaping dolphin is used as an example of in-the-round carving. This appears to be the only three-dimensional carving described in the book. It would have been helpful to follow this with a further, more ambitious, sculpture. Instead the author demonstrates how to carve another eagle very similar to the one already mentioned.

In succeeding passages the carving of decorative mouldings is explained; laurel leaf and rope designs are applied as decoration for mirror frames, and relief and intaglio designs are used as decoration on a yacht's transom and trailboards. The author's favourite eagle crops up yet again in the design.

The final chapters deal with the various ways in which woodcarvings can be finished. There are instructions on how to mix your own stains and apply them, the use of colour on carvings and the preparation of the wood, and types of paint for indoor and outdoor use. Finally the author gives a short description on the use of gold leaf for gilding.

Except in certain instances, such as coats of arms, or outdoor signs which will be subjected to weathering, the use of paint will not recommend itself to the budding sculptor. Those who sculpt in wood usually regard the intrinsic beauty of their material — its colour and figure — as an integral part of the finished piece. Apart from mahogany and pine the woods recommended by the author are difficult to obtain in Britain, and there are a great many other woods eminently suitable for carving which have not been mentioned. Some advice on seasoning green timber and on the characterisitics of various woods, ie colour, density and workability, would have been helpful.

Throughout the book the use of power tools is included, namely the bandsaw, rotary saw and pillar drill. The amateur might find this somewhat daunting for power tools are certainly not an essential part of the woodcarver's tool kit; all the pieces in the book could be made entirely with the use of hand tools. Also, some of the uses of the rotary saw described do not adhere to the British standards of safety, and are not to be recommended.

Some of the designs could, perhaps, have been more graceful and the finish on some of the carvings could have been better. It might have been helpful to include photographs of other craftsmen's work to show the different styles of woodcarving, and to provide a source of inspiration. And being an American publication some of the terminology may be unfamiliar to the English reader.

Although the book is somewhat limited, in that the carving is mainly of a decorative nature rather than sculptural, it explains the fundamental techniques of woodcarving and should be of help to the beginner. It is distributed in Britain by Oak Tree Press, Ward Lock Ltd, 116 Baker Street, London W1M 2BB, at £4.50 hardback and £2.50 softback. The US publisher is Sterling Publishing Co Inc, New York.　　　　　　　　**K.S.**

GUILD OF WOODWORKERS
APPLICATION FORM

Cut out and send this coupon to: Guild of Woodworkers, PO Box 35, Hemel Hempstead, HP1 1EE, England.

Name ....

Name of business (if applicable) ....

Address ....

....

Annual subscription enclosed (cross out which does not apply).
(a) I enclose £2: individual craftsman.
(b) I enclose £5: trading craftsman.
(Equivalent currency please for subscribers outside UK).

For new subscribers to Guild of Woodworkers:
I enclose £1 registration fee (equivalent currency for subscriptions outside UK).

I specialise in (eg cabinetmaking, woodturning, etc) ....

Signature .... Date ....
PLEASE USE BLOCK CAPITALS

Fine woodworking demands a fine bench

A) Lervad bench No. 610CU with two integral vices, double row bench dog system and built-in cupboard. **B)** Carving between single row bench dog system on Lervad bench No. 600. **C)** Commodious shoulder vice, one of the three ways of work holding on models 610 and 611. **D)** Exclusive Lervad pattern tail vice which also operates with bench dog clamping system running full length of top (Models 610 & 611)

- Danish made woodwork benches of superb quality, chosen by craftsmen woodworkers and craft teachers the world over.
- Made from solid kiln dried Danish beech. Precision machined and sanded tops are oiled and sealed against warping etc.
- Unique multiple vice holds for secure, comfortable and accurate working at all angles. On principal models this includes exclusive Lervad double row bench dog clamping system running full length of bench top.
- Varied choice of models to suit every woodworkers need. Built in cupboards or moveable cupboards and tool racks available.

Lervad are also leading school workshop suppliers of both wood and metalwork benches and storage units.
If you are involved in teaching please ask for School Workshop catalogue.

Made by craftsmen for craftsmen

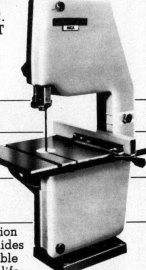

Danish oil

From: W.A. Kinsman, Oulton, Staffs

Frequently I see references in woodturning books to Danish oil. Could you kindly tell me what this is exactly, how it is used and how it can be made up, and from which suppliers it can be purchased?

It seems that many years ago teak oil was imported from Denmark and came to be known as Danish oil. It is a thin oleo resinous varnish applied with a cloth or piece of flannel and is readily available in tins of various size from paint shops and builders merchants. It is beyond the scope of the home craftsman to make up such oils.

Raw linseed oil applied with a cloth and vigorously rubbed in with a clean duster will give a similar finish although the build-up of polish may be a little slower.

Afrormosia dining table

From: A.M. Bone, Epsom, Surrey

I bought an afrormosia dining table some 17 years ago and it has been treated periodically with refined linseed oil. The surface has darkened unevenly and when water has been spilled some of the surface comes away leaving a light-coloured mark.

I wonder if you could recommend a method of cleaning the whole surface to give as far as possible the original light colour of the wood.

In addition a surface crack of about 1ft in length has appeared in the table running with the grain of the wood. Can this be filled with a wood filler?

There are several aspects of your problem we are unsure about. Firstly, whether the table was bought 'in the white', ie unpolished, hence the use of linseed oil. Secondly, whether the top is solid afrormosia or veneered chipboard or block-board. Thirdly, why the top has now split 17 years after purchase.

We would recommend the following: clean-off the surface with white spirit and the use of a nylon washing-up pad; do not use wire wool and do not use a metal scraper since afrormosia is liable to develop black ink stains if iron and water are in contact with the wood; even perspiration from the hands can cause this to happen.

Clean-off, wiping the surface with clean rag after each scrubbing action in the direction of the grain. Treatment after this would depend on what is underneath the oily build up. If veneer, it is probable this was bonded with a poor adhesive, say urea

formaldehyde extended with starch, because you mention if water is spilled on the top 'some of the surface comes away'. This would suggest water is locally breaking down the glue line and a piece of veneer is peeling off disclosing the substrate underneath.

If the top is solid wood then we can only conclude that it was originally polished or varnished, that spilled water has locally penetrated the surface film and laid there for a time before eventually forcing off a flake of the finish, the light-coloured mark being due to water staining of the wood.

However, by use of the white spirit and by sanding, the top could be prepared for refinishing. The crack could be filled with a matching filler such as Brummer, and a suitable finish finally applied to the wood. What finish you decide upon would be a matter for individual taste: it could be wax (probably the best for your particular case), an oil finish or one of the synthetic finishes like Ronseal.

We would comment that linseed oil tends to quite rapidly collect dust particles from the air; the more oil used the worse the appearance of treated wood becomes. On the other hand, linseed oil used simply as an aid to burnishing the surface of wood is an ideal wood-finishing medium. The important aspect of this is energetic rubbing of the wood over many months, using only a tiny amount of oil each time.

It would appear to suggest that your wood split badly due to environmental changes. This would be likely where central heating was suddenly installed or where the table was moved to warmer premises. We regret we have had to conjecture somewhat on the circumstances governing your problem.

Polishing yew

From: J.B.A. Davies, Redruth, Cornwall

It would be appreciated if you could give details of the best way of polishing yew.

Common yew (Taxus baccata), although inclined to be oily can nevertheless take a high polish. Basically we would suggest you use one of the Sterling Roncraft products readily obtainable from retail stockists, eg Ronseal Mattcoat, Ronseal Hardglaze or Ronseal Satincoat. Here are three types of final finish, easily applied and capable of standing up to hard wear and resistance to water and heat.

However you give no details of the item you wish to polish and we are wondering whether you are experiencing difficulty in getting a good surface on the wood: if this is the case and the item has relatively wide surfaces with perhaps some slightly torn grain then the polyurethane-type finishes might not be the best to use. An alternative would be wax polish which would give a fairly dull finish. Finishes such as Ronseal form a surface film on the wood whereas wax penetrates the wood slightly but fills the pores, building up to a coated finish.

Yew is sometimes an awkward wood to plane and even when a recommended cutting angle of 15° is used the grain will tend to tear. You will appreciate that unless the wood surface is reasonably smooth, finishes that need not only to adhere to the surface but depend upon polymerisation to form a film cannot be expected to give their best performance. Wax then becomes a better alternative.

You can make up a wax polish by shredding a cake of beeswax very finely and letting it dissolve slowly in pure turpentine, stirring with a stick until the polish takes on the consistency of soft butter. The polish is best applied to the wood with a rag rubbing well into the grain. A second rag is used vigorously to build up a shine and a third is used for polishing.

A lot of friction is needed in wax polishing and it is obviously time-consuming, but if your wood does not respond to good preparation of its surface it would be better than Ronseal which, however, would be our first choice.

QUESTION BOX

Carvings

From: T.R. Beveridge, Lartington, Co Durham

I recently found some carvings in the loft of my home. They were covered in dust and dirt and had evidently been there for some considerable time and were badly broken. I hoped to be able to reassemble them but many of the smaller pieces are missing. I am particularly impressed by the fact that each piece is carved from one block of timber and yet in places there are three overlapping layers of leaves.

Although I have never done any woodcarving the standard of workmanship appears to me to be very high. I would appreciate any information as to the possible time period of the pieces and what they would originally have been. The carvings are about 1ft 10in. high and 2ft 2in. wide. The wood is not very heavy. Perhaps from the small sample I am sending you could identify the species.

I might add that the loft of my home was used many years ago as an estate workshop, with living accommodation underneath.

The wood used for the carvings is lime *(Tilia* spp.), a traditional wood for this work: it has good strength properties but is soft and light in weight and easy to work. Sharp, thin-edged tools are needed to obtain a smooth finish.

Grinling Gibbons (1648 — 1720) was probably the earliest exponent of the use of lime for fine carvings, principally based on foliage, fruit, birds and game and examples of his work can be seen in many Wren churches and stately homes, including Windsor castle, Blenheim palace, Chatsworth, Petworth, and St Paul's cathedral.

From what you say of the probable history of your home, It seems feasible that the carvings you have found were produced a long time ago for the anticipated embellishment of some local building. Planted-on carvings have been used for centuries for panelling in large houses in dining and ante-rooms, and in churches on choir stalls and screens.

It is possible they were surplus to requirements or, more likely, they were accidentally damaged and therefore became moribund. It is not possible to give an indication of age; lime trees in this country, if allowed to reach maturity have a maximum diameter of about 36in. and since this dimension would only cover the centre portion including the pith, it follows that a large tree of this size would be needed to provide suitable wood to finish 2ft 2in. wide, free of centre, the width you say of some of the carvings.

Lime trees began to get scarce round about the 1920s and have become scarcer still since then. During the last 50 or 60 years to produce large sized, one-piece carvings from lime would have been difficult, unless you were an estate owner with your own specially available trees. It seems highly probable that the wood was obtained this way and could, therefore, have been used for the work at any time prior to your occupation of the house. You might be able to obtain more information from your local parish records or country record office.

Matching a finish

From: E. Holt, Dalserf, Lanarkshire, Scotland

I am building a grandmother clock in oak and would like the finish to match our recently purchased dining room suite. The maker thereof has kindly provided a sample piece of the timber showing the finish and I send this sample to you. Can you please help by giving ideas on stains, suppliers and polishing.

It was helpful to receive the wood sample from the furniture maker, though presumably he is not disposed to divulge recipes for a Jacobean finish. However, I think the following suggestions will enable a good match to be made.

The sample piece has a Jacobean finish which can be obtained in several ways. Whatever the stain it is advisable to test for colour on waste wood from the job in hand. This will help to avoid mistakes which cannot easily be rectified. Here are some suggestions:
(1) Mix 2oz Vandyke brown in 1pt of ammonia and add 1oz bichromate of potash.
(2) Spirit stains are made by dissolving 1oz of spirit-soluble powder in 1pt of methylated spirit. When the powder has dissolved and the mixture has settled pour off the clear stain into a clean bottle. For a Jacobean finish spirit black

and spirit red are needed; a mixture of roughly 2/3rd black and 1/3rd red should be satisfactory.
(3) Oak crystals soluble in water are obtainable and the stronger the solution the darker the stain.

Identifying which polish has been used on a piece of furniture is not too difficult but requires a little experimenting on an unseen part. If french polish is suspected moisten a small area with methylated spirit and if the finish softens it is french polish. Meths will not affect cellulose or varnish. With a chisel held nearly upright scrape the polished surface and if a yellow shaving curls up varnish has been used. If a white dust comes off the surface has been cellulosed. Yellow shavings indicated that the sample has been varnished.

A recommended finish would be to brush on two coats of transparent white polish with a bear hair mop. When hard, ease down with fine glasspaper and then wax polish.

Transparent varnish would also give a pleasing effect. Use either a new brush or one that is perfectly clean; work in a warm well-lit room and keep the atmosphere dust free.

All the above stains and finishes can be obtained from James Jackson (London) Ltd, Major Works, 76-89 Alscot Road, London SE1

Timber identification

From: A.F. Wareham, North End, Portsmouth

Could you please give me information about the sample of timber enclosed with my letter. You can bend it without heating. I would also be glad to know of a source of supply.

The wood is beech *(Fagus sylvatica)* and appears to be of the continental steamed variety. Beech, which is a whitish-brown colour when freshly cut, will retain much of its colour when dried slowly in the open air followed by kiln-drying. This type is referred to as white, or unsteamed beech. Even white beech will however darken perceptibly after exposure.

On the continent, particularly in Yugoslavia, to save air-drying space beech is more often converted from the log to meet shipping orders and is then kiln-dried green. Temperature and high humidity react with the colouring pigments in the wood and by hydrolysis, (which means decomposition of a chemical compound by addition of water), the wood turns a reddish-brown colour, and is now referred to as steamed.

Some people prefer to use steamed beech contending it to be of milder texture, although there is no real evidence to support this. All beech lends itself to steam bending, often to quite sharp radii. Cold bending is often satisfactory for less acute bends and by the use of thinner stock. Beech, square edged or waney edged, steamed or unsteamed, is readily available from hardwood merchants everywhere.

Noise reduction

From: David Brown, Pontefract, Yorks

My problem is noise. Use of machinery in the home workshop means that the noise produced reaches a level where complaints from neighbours are justified. Knowing that the noise I make can disturb my neighbours, severely detracts from the pleasure of working with wood. To reduce this nuisance as much as possible I intend to build an 8 x 6ft timber shed. I intend to double-glaze the window and would appreciate your advice on insulating the walls, floor and roof to contain the noise generated by my band-saw, drills and router.

Sound insulation in buildings falls into two categories: (a) minimising unwanted sound through partitions and floors; and (b) isolation of machinery vibration and noises. Your problem is associated directly with (a). The sensation of sound is due to stimulation of the auditory nerves of the ear by sound waves. Hence to introduce suitable sound insulation it is essential to interpose discontinuities in the paths of the disturbances in order to reduce the range of sounds to a comfortable level on the opposite side of the walls and floors, ie considered as partitions.

To appreciate what represents a loudness level, the threshold of audibility is considered as O decibels (dB(A)) while the rustle of leaves is 10. The approximate threshold of hearing, a most unpleasant stage, is 120. Thinking in terms of a domestic nature a loud radio equals about 80, a pneumatic drill 90 and a loud car horn 100.

Trying to relate your machinery noises to this it is probable that your panels, ie walls, roof and floor must attempt to reduce the sound value from, say, 80 to something like 30 or 40dB(A) (the former equals to a library reading room the latter to ordinary conversation in the home). In other words you need a reduction by insulation of about 40/50dB(A). Taking your floor first of all, 3×2in (75×50mm) joists set at 18in. (450mm) centres and covered on one side with $\frac{7}{8}$in. (22mm) t&g boarding cramped tight, is deemed to give an approximate sound reduction of 21dB(A), but this value is assumed for a partition.

Contact with the ground would produce a dampening effect and might raise the 21 a little but, if necessary, a mineral fibre blanket draped loosely over the joists would increase sound insulation to perhaps 38 or thereabouts. The walls and roof should be lined on the inside with sheets of insulating fibreboard or low-density chipboard either of wood or flax; $\frac{1}{2}$in. (12.5mm) thick fibre insulation board will give an approximate sound reduction of about 21dB(A) when nailed to a wood frame.

You must remember that sound reduction is governed by the weakest link in the construction. If a wall is insulated to give, say, a reduction of 40 but the door is only rated at 20 the overall sound reduction is reduced to something like 29 dB(A). Obviously, an acceptable amount of sound outside the building would depend upon the ambient noise level, eg passing traffic. But our recommendations would be that a fibre insulation board lining gives a reasonable reduction of sound acceptable outside the workshop, if you consider your machining activities to create no more noise than, say, in a noisy office with talking, telephoning, typing etc going on: (70dB(A). If you are doubtful about the efficiency of this insulation, then you would need to fix a mineral fibre blanket (such as used for loft insulation) between the studs before fixing the insulation board inner cladding.

Exterior finish

November Question Box p. 687. We are grateful to Mr Allday for taking the time to see us at the recent Woodworker Show to point out that in the answer we should have specified Ronseal *outdoor* finish as this product is not widely stocked and an indoor quality finish would not obviously be suitable.

Qualities that matter

Printed in the Netherlands for Mitchell Beazley Ltd, Artists House, 14-15 Manette Street, London W1V 5LB, *The Finishing Touch* at £13.95, is about one's personal imprint on our homes.

The author, Robin Guild, acquired his taste for 'things' early in his mother's antique shop. By the late '60s Robin had built up a reputation as a decorator who put the client's taste first; a respector of people and their possessions.

This book encourages you to take a fresh look at the contents of your home to decide whether you are doing them justice. Your home can become an original showcase that reflects your personality and taste.

Recognising this, the book asks questions but does not give answers and dictate rules. You establish your own environment once your mind is questioning along the right lines.

Chapters include living with things; show-off; hang-it; on the shelf; out of sight and (most importantly to my mind) back-up; a glossary; and index.

The author says 'this isn't a book for copycats'. It is basically a book of ideas, a large number of photographs mostly in colour with comments and questions: 'Do you like this arrangement?' 'How would you alter it?' 'React to the pictures'.

Shelves are for storage and display — although traditionally the storage function is the dominant one in most homes. This section discusses the shelving in association with the architectural features of the room under such headings as made-to-measure, shelf-adjusting, furniture shelves, walls of shelves and fit that space.

'Back-up' is an essential information source, design says the author being a marriage of taste and technique. It is a wealth of practical reminders and tricks of the trade. There are notes on furniture surfaces; recognising finishes; stains and blemishes; woodworm; chipped or bubbled veneer; stripping wood; bleaching; staining; varnishing; beeswaxing; and french polishing.

Under miscellaneous are included ivory; leather; cane and wicker; musical instruments; clocks and guns. Picture care; restoration; handling and hanging; framing; mouldings; cutting mitres; and alternative framing are discussed. Hanging methods also includes positioning on the wall and display in groups or singly to give maximum impact.

The qualities that matter are taste, colours, conviction, patience, perfection, proportion, texture, style . . . read the book, look at the many pictures and develop your own personal 'finishing touch'. **C.R.C.**

Armchair journey into the past

The author of *The Complete Practical Book of Country Crafts* (published by David & Charles, Brunel House, Newton Abbot, Devon (1979) at £7.50), Jack Hill, though raised in industrial Lancashire has always loved the countryside and open spaces. This love comes through in his book on country crafts which is not just a nostalgic appraisal of dying and forgotten skills but a personal experience and sympathetic appreciation by one craftsman of many another's work.

Over 50 photographs illustrate the text and are an historical record in their own right. But what makes this book such a delight are the author's own line drawings which profusly illustrate and complement the text.

Jack Hill teaches rural studies and crafts to children and adults, as well as exhibiting and selling his own traditional hand-made furniture. He is also a contributor to WOODWORKER. This personal involvement is obvious in the book; here is a practical man talking and writing of the things he has experienced and grown to love.

There are full details of how to obtain and prepare materials, including 'harvest-it-yourself' of which tools are still available; which you can make yourself and which are the modern equivalents of others.

Comprehensive step-by-step line drawings illustrate the individual processes and selected work projects.

The crafts dealt with are too numerous to list but besides the more usually met ones of wheelwrighting, basket-making, pottery, spinning and weaving a host of others are covered; like rake and besom making, clog making, sticks and crooks, rushwork, hornwork, hedging and walling, wood carving and turning plus many more.

Additional information is listed at the end of the book on displays, courses, suppliers, demonstrations, museums and further reading so that the many people who now want to practise self-expression in the old crafts can use this book as a stimulus and as a source of sound practical guidance.

Each chapter of the book deals with a particular craft and of course each chapter could be twice or three times as long. It is only possible in an encyclopedia of crafts to touch on some processes; Jack Hill has managed, however, with an economy of words to say enough to stimulate, not too much to bore the expert, and sufficient to produce thought and further research if the reader becomes interested.

The book's main purpose is to contribute to the craft revival by giving a better understanding of the work and way of life of our country forebears. It succeeds. It is a real armchair treasury for the winter evenings ahead, even if one's own 'craft revival' gets no further than a passive armchair variety, or a purely amateur beginner's approach. **P.C.**

TS-5 circular saw

With maximum cutting depth of up to 55mm and 500×400mm wide table at height of 230mm, the EMCO TS-5 table saw is powered by a 1.2hp motor coupled to a sawblade of 203mm maximum diameter. Cutting speed is given as 24m/sec. Maximum cutting width with rip fence and extension tables (optional extra) is 420mm.

Made in Austria by Maier & Co the machine is imported by EME Ltd, BEC House, Victoria Road, London NW10 6NY (01-961 0120), and was mentioned briefly on page 650 of the November 1979 issue.

Other features are welded construction and large base area with provision for fixing to workbench, table tilting to 45°, mitre gauge with graduated scale (accessory) and simple changing of sawblade.

The blade is said to have maximum over-run time of 10 sec and the operating switch is provided with low-volt release to prevent unintentional restarting after power failure. Guarding is arranged so that the saw teeth are covered in every cutting depth.

Basic machine includes housing, saw table, rip fence with gib, guarding, motor, switch, 203mm diameter universaw saw blade, service tools, instruction manual and parts list. A leaflet is available on application to EME Ltd at the address above or stockists.

Protective coating

Protective coating which is said to double as a primer is introduced by Yewpalm Technical Developments Ltd, Penfold Industrial Estate, Imperial Way, Watford WD2 4JD (Watford 35511). Known as OKO it is available in 4.5 litre tins at £22 rrp exclusive of VAT. The coating is a polymer resin for application to most materials and common surfaces.

Surface treatment

An American-made high-gloss polymer coating known as EnviroTex is available through House of Broomfield, Fan Court, Longcross, Chertsey KT16 ODJ (Ottershaw 3811). A booklet describing and illustrating applications of the product states that it can be poured on to the surface and then spread before leaving to cure. EnviroTex is said to give protection against alcohol, heated containers and the effects of spillage of food and beverages.

Emco TS-5 table saw. The 500 x 400mm table can be extended.

Saw kit

A 10in. diameter circular saw in kit form is available from Sarjents Tools 62-4 Fleet Street, Swindon, Wilts (0793 31361), and the firm's branches at Reading and Oxford. Specification is given as follows: table size 29 × 19in. (larger if required); table height 12½in.; saw diameter 10in.; drive-single A-section V-belt; rise and fall maximum depth of cut 3¹⁄₁₆in.; maximum table tilt 45°; shaft ½in. diameter mounted on ball bearings with ½in. capacity chuck and clamping flanges at free end; saw speed with 2,800rpm motor 8,377ft/min. A 550w 220/240v single-phase motor is recommended. Price without motor is £41.40 including VAT.

More from B&D

There are several items added to the product range of Black & Decker Ltd, Cannon Lane, Maidenhead SC6 3PD (Littlewick Green 2130). For example, the Jobber which is described as a portable worktop, vice and tool caddy, weighing 11lb and consisting of a 16in. vice mounted over a base incorporating a 12 × 13in. tool tray. The price is given as £19 with VAT. Another item is the D600 Majorvac suction cleaner mounted on a three-wheeled trolley and said to be suitable for collection of wood shavings.

Among new saws are the DN56, DN57 and DN59 with 5, 6 and 7¼in. blades and cutting capacities respectively of 1⅜in., 1¹⁵⁄₁₆in. and 2⁷⁄₁₆in. Blowers are provided to keep the cutting line clear. There is also the DN39 pendulum-action jigsaw which B&D states has improved cutting speed. Four settings of the pendulum-action are provided through the medium of a control switch. Cutting depth is 2½in. in wood and angle cutting up to 45° on either side is afforded by an adjustable saw shoe. Speed of cut is variable between 500 and 3,000 strokes/min according to changes in the workload. Price is £80 including VAT.

In drills there are the H40 and H40S, claimed to be more compact that previous rotary-hammer drills, but with chuck capacity of ⅜in. The former is a single-speed model, the latter a two-speed. For larger capacity chucks (½in.) B&D offers the D222, D223 and D226 Mastercraft versions, all two-speed with rotary-hammer action.

The D226 has a device which the maker calls 'electronic feedback' whereby the motor provides a constant speed when drilling. Price of this drill is £65.50 with VAT.

Canoes

The Kayel Tripper 16 and 18 are canoes of the Canadian type available from Granta Boats Ltd, Ramsey, Huntingdon (0487 813777). The former is 15ft 7in. long and has a carrying capacity of up to three adults and associated equipment. It weighs 35lb. The latter is 17ft 7in. and weighs 40lb. Both canoes have a 3ft beam and each is packed in an 8ft × 17 × 4in. carton containing all the materials needed to build and varnish the craft.

Pulleys

Aluminium V-pulleys and timing pulleys from Aluminium Pulleys Ltd, Albion Street, Chipping Norton OX7 5BJ (0608 3311), are described and illustrated in an interesting catalogue which also gives specifications and information relating to service factors, belt selection, power ratings for various types of belts, pulley dimensions, belt section and pitch lengths etc.

Mini orbital sander

Developed in collaboration with the 3M Co specifically for use with Stikfit self-adhesive coated abrasives, the Super Stork LE7 is described as a mini orbital sander having pad size 80 × 130mm, overall height 136mm and weight of 1.2kg. Orbital action is 2mm diameter at 11,000 orbits/min. A toggle switch positioned on the top of the machine provides finger-tip control and the rubber soleplate is a self-adhesive fit for ease of replacement.

Stikfit abrasive is available in a variety of grit sizes, in packs or sheets or in a perforated roll. Sheet size is 81 × 153mm. When change of sheet is necessary, the old abrasive is peeled off and replacement fitted using the built-in lugs on the LE7 as a guide to accurate positioning. Once fitted the abrasive sheet remains perfectly flat and ensures an even sanding pressure, states Super Stork (Industrial Power Tools) Ltd, Queensbury Station Parade, Edgware HA8 5NN (01-952 5642).

WHAT'S NEW

Halve-joint cutter

Type KSF machine by Stegherr has been developed to produce closed halve-joints on Georgian-type doors and windows. The mitred edges are cut simultaneously with an upper and lower cutting unit and at the same time a third unit finishes the flat portion in between.

The machine table is moved hydro-pneumatically and feed and return speeds can be regulated. The cutting units are in two parts and are adjustable in width; they also have vertical and depth setting. Type KSF is introduced to the UK market by Interwood Ltd, Stafford Avenue, Hornchurch RM11 2ER (Hornchurch 52591).

Electric chainsaw

Supplied with 10in. bar and chain and weighing 6lb, the A100 chainsaw is powered by a 1100W motor for 220/240V supply. Chain speeds up to 28.5ft/sec give efficient cutting with bevel drive gear to the bar allowing the motor to be mounted longitudinally in line with the chain. The tool is double insulated and fitted with guarded front and rear handles, chain catcher and double-action on/off control.

It is available initially from the distributors of products handled by C.D. Monninger Ltd, Overbury Road, London N15 6RJ (01-800 5435), but eventually it will be sold through other retail outlets. The price is given as £51.75 inclusive of VAT.

The A100 electric chain saw from C. D. Monninger Ltd.

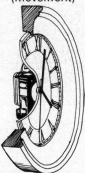

Prices quoted are those prevailing at press date and are subject to alteration due to economic conditions.

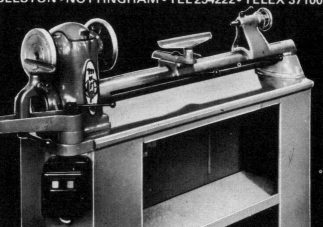

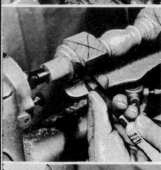

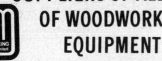

Classified Advertisements

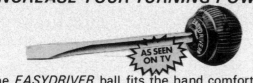

Classified Advertisements

FOR SALE

LEATHER APRONS
For the Craftsman & Handyman

Strong, hard-wearing aprons with leather thong fastenings. Choice of two side pockets or one in centre.
Size 25" x 32". £9.30 including P&P. Larger sizes or special requirements to order at extra cost.

Moor Cote Workshops, Ellingstring, Ripon, North Yorkshire.
Tel: Bedale (0677) 60282

BRANDING IRONS

Made from solid steel with 15" handle, to last a lifetime. Now you can permanently identify your tools and production pieces. We can quote for special styles for a professional look. Price guide — 3 x 3/8" characters **£6.95p.**

SAE details – WHS, 38 Summercourt Way, Brixham. TQ5 0DY.

HARPSICHORDS, spinets and clavichords: World-famous kits. Competitive prices. Hardware and strings for small harps. Alan & Helen Edgar, 49 Tranby Avenue, Hessle, East Yorkshire. Tel: 0482-640330. MN

MYFORD ML8A with saw table sanding table mortising attachment, tenoning attachment, chucks, plus many smaller parts. One owner. Little used £650. Current price £1,100. Tel: 061-432-1740. MN

RAPIER radial arm saw tipped blade hardly used nearest £160. Buyer collects. Smith, 2 Hurst Beaminster. Tel: Beaminster 862-042. M

ROY STARTIN LTD.

134 Wood Street, Earl Shilton, Leicester
Tel: 0455 43254

Electra HC260 10" x 6" Planer & Thicknesser **£379.00.** Stand £25.00 extra.

Electra 12" Combi-Saw Bench, rise and fall, tilt blade **£152.00.**

Kity 612 Bandsaw on Stand with 1.5 H.P. motor **£270.00.**

Kity 636 Planer complete with Kity Dust Extractor and fittings **£648.00.**

Kity 627 Spindle Moulder on Stand with 1.5 H.P. motor complete with *FREE* Cutters RRP £113.85. Our price complete **£380.00.**

Electra Dust Extractor complete with hose and fittings **£195.00**

All prices include VAT at 15%

TOOLS TO TREASURE
First quality cabinetmaker's HIDE GLUE fine ground for easy mixing. **£2.48** per kilo.
BRIDLED GLUE BRUSHES pure grey bristle set in rubber. British made. 1/2" **£1.83** 1" **£2.84** 11/2" **£5.07**
All prices include postage in U.K.

Adzes, Drawknives, Inshaves and other tools for the craftsman Woodworker send foolscap S.A.E. for details.

CORBETT TOOLS

Dept. WW/1, 224 Puxton Drive, Kidderminster, Worcester.

THREE NORRIS PLANES panel 131/2" smoother and shoulder offers over £300 for the lot. Stanley mitre box with Disston saw £75. Wooden plough plane 7 irons £25. Many more old tools for sale. Tel: 01-570-5909. M

Fine Period Furniture
for you to make by hand at home
Large selection of 17th C copies in solid oak or elm for simple home assembly without special tools.

- All materials supplied
- All parts cut, planed and jointed
- Simple instructions
- Save up to 60% on retail prices

Send large SAE for brochure and price list

JACOBUS WORKSHOP
South Road, KIRKBY STEPHEN, Cumbria

Equipping a workshop?
Call and see demonstrated or write for details (25p stamps) of quality machines of the popular Kity range or by Startrite, Sedgwick, De Walt, Lurem and most others: Elu Routers and Power Tools; Arundel, Myford, Kity Woodturning Lathes, accessories etc.
Trymwood Services, 2A Downs Park East (near the Downs), Bristol. 629092 2-6pm, Mondays to Fridays.

WOODTURNERS' DREAM! Genuine South American mahogany, 4" depth, lengths and widths various at reasonable prices. Trymwood Services, 2A Downs Park East, Bristol, BS6 7QD. Tel: 629092. M

CORONET CMB 517 planer with thicknesser fits maroon or blue Major lathe £130. Tel: Nottingham 786417 evenings. M

OFFERS: Norris A3 adjustable plane 9" x 2⅝" in mahogany brass and steel. Tel: 0283-46970 Ferryden, 2 Waverley Lane, Burton, Staffordshire. M

DEWALT 110 radial arm saw plus extras, chuck sander drills, seven years old, but only used twice. £200 ONO. Tel: Watford 24889. M

WALL CLOCKS
an exciting new look!
colourful decorative ceramic clockfaces, guaranteed quartz battery movements, ensure that the wall clocks you make will be elegant and reliable. Attractive designs and range of styles. Featured by Woodcraft Supply Corp.
SAE details – WHS, 38 Summercourt Way, Brixham. TQ5 0DY.

BRASS OR ALUMINIUM plates for your project. Letters block or script, example 3" x 1" brass plate with 20 block letters £1.10p plus post, plus VAT. Also engraved badges, name plates, numbers, labels etc. in coloured plastic. Trade enquiries welcome. Brian J. Bowman Trophies Limited, "Anela", Lower North Street, Cheddar, Somerset. Tel: Cheddar 742774. LMN

WORKSHOP EQUIPMENT

LEISURECRAFT IN WOOD WITH CORONET
The full range of these universal and independent machines on show.
Demonstrations and lessons.
Full back-up of tools and accessories for Turning, Carving and Marquetry.

**KENTERPRISE LTD.
122 & 124 Camden Road, Tunbridge Wells**
Tel. Tunbridge Wells 23475

WOODCARVING tools

Ashley Iles & Henry Taylor
Arkansas Bench & Slip Stones
Bench Screws, Carvers Vices
Professional Turning Tools
Send 20p in stamps for illustrated catalogue
ALEC TIRANTI LTD
70 High St., Theale, Reading, Berks
21 Goodge Place, London W.1.

TUNGSTEN CARBIDE TIPPED CIRCULAR SAWS
Leading UK suppliers Govt., Industry & DIY. 24 hr despatch most sizes/types. Overseas orders: free air despatch at approx half N. American prices. SAE lists.
**TLC WORLD TRADING LTD.
32/34 Craven Street, London WC2 Tel: 01-930 1942**

A. POLLARD & SON

De-Walt, Shopmate, Kity, Elu, Susemihl
We offer good service, good stocks and low prices
Dust extractors
A. Pollard & Son, 51 Queensway, Bletchley, Milton Keynes.
Tel: 0908-75221

ACCESS — BARCLAYCARD
Business established over 50 years.

WASHITA & ARKANSAS whetstones now readily available from importer. Large selection. S.A.E. for lists. C. Rufino, Manor House, South Clifton, Newark, Notts. T/C

TOOLS OF QUALITY
for Craftsmen and Handymen

We also supply a wide range of British-made screws: steel, brass, plated., Pozi-driv, etc.
Send for our free illustrated lists before you buy. You'll be glad you did!

BENMAIL SUPPLIES
St. Georges, Weston-s-Mare, Avon

HAMPSHIRE WOODWORKING MACHINERY

**HOE FARM HOUSE
HOE ROAD
BISHOPS WALTHAM
SOUTHAMPTON
HAMPSHIRE**

OPEN MON.-SAT.
for
SALES AND DEMONSTRATIONS OF

CORONET

STARTRITE

KITY

Telephone:
B.W. (04893) 2275

SHERWOOD TURNING LATHES

All cast iron constructed. 3¾"CH 24" or 36" B.C. 3 or 4 speed, bowl turning up to 14" dia. ball bearing spindle c/w face plate, centres etc. Prices from **£46.97** inc. VAT.

Send stamp for leaflets and details of above and other machines and motors.

**James Inns (Engs),
Main St., Bulwell, Nottingham.**

Prices quoted are those prevailing at press date and are subject to alteration due to economic conditions.

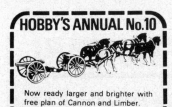

Prices quoted are those prevailing at press date and are subject to alteration due to economic conditions.

Woodworker

THE MAGAZINE FOR THE CRAFTSMAN IN WOOD

MARCH 1980 VOL. 84 NO. 1036

FRONT COVER: The lifting bridge at lock no. 5, Blisworth, Northants Arm, Grand Union Canal *(photo: H. W. Gates).*

Editor	Geoffrey Pratt
Production Editor	Polly Curds
Group Advertisement Manager	Michael Merrifield
Managing Director	Gospatric Home
Editorial Director	Ron Moulton

MEMBER OF THE AUDIT BUREAU OF CIRCULATIONS

SUBSCRIPTION DEPARTMENT: Remittances to MODEL AND ALLIED PUBLICATIONS, P.O. Box 35, Hemel Hempstead, Herts HP1 1EE. Price per copy 50p plus postage 21p. Subscription queries: Tel: Hemel Hempstead 51740. Subscription rate, including index £9.00 per annum; overseas sterling £9.00; $20.00 U.S. for overseas dollar subscribers. Second class postage paid at New York, NY North American enquiries regarding news stand sales should be sent to: Eastern News Distribution, 111 Eighth Avenue, New York, NY 1011, USA. Telephone (212) 255-5620 and craft and hobby sales to Bill Dean Books Ltd., 166-41 Powells Cove Boulevard, Whitestone, New York 11357, USA. Telephone (212) 767-6632.

WOODWORKER is printed by New Avenue Press Ltd, Pasadena Close, Pump Lane, Hayes, Middlesex. (Mono origination by Multiform Photosetting Ltd, Cardiff), for the proprietors and publishers, Model & Allied Publications Ltd (a member of the Argus Press Group). Trade sales by Argus Distribution Ltd, 12-18 Paul Street, London EC2A 4JS. WOODWORKER is published on the 3rd Friday of the month.

Model & Allied Publications Ltd

P.O. Box 35, Bridge Street, Hemel Hempstead, Herts HP1 1EE. Telephone: Hemel Hempstead (0442) 41221.

FURNITURE DESIGN

Our contemporary publication in the United States *Fine Woodworking* has sent us a copy of its *Design Book Two*. This runs to 228 pages of photographs of 'the best work in wood by 1,000 craftsmen' and costs $11.95.

The editor makes some interesting comments in his introduction on the subject of techniques and their effects on design and construction. In an 18th century cabinet shop, as he says, trees were sawn into boards and the boards planed smooth by muscle power. The man-driven lathe was likely to be the only machine tool. The easiest way to make a finished leg for a table or chair was to turn it . . .

Conversely, with a motorised bandsaw and planer, and with modern cramps and glues, it is almost as easy to make a curved leg or stretcher, or a whole curved panel. Our ancestors knew how to make these things but chose not to on account of the back-breaking labour involved.

Similarly, our ancestors festooned their furniture with elegant mouldings and carvings, not only for decorative effect but also to conceal the joints that held it together. Contemporary craftsmen are likely to leave the joinery exposed, and rarely use mouldings. The reason is that when all joints were cut by hand, there was nothing special about them. They were the untidy skeleton, best hidden behind an attractive moulding, so the work would appear perfect. Today machines routinely achieve apparent perfection without the intervention of skill. What machines cannot do is to imitate the minute imperfections that give character to a hand-cut joint. Exposed joinery thus becomes the special mark of the craftsman.

Design Book Two makes the point that it is easy to forget that Chippendale and Sheraton and their contemporary followers were all the modern rage, in their day. They were also as far removed — or as close, depending on how you look at it — from their predecessors as today's artisans are from theirs.

These comments serve as an introduction to the article in this issue on exhibition standards for furniture making. The author — John Price, furniture tutor at Shrewsbury Technical College, and one of the judges at last year's Woodworker Show — discusses some of the faults in entries submitted for the cabinet making classes and explains how to avoid, correct and so improve the general standard of work. As Mr Price says: 'It is one thing to recognise a fault, another to know how to correct it and yet another to understand why the fault has occurred . . . Do not try to improve on Chippendale or Sheraton. Make a true copy. Use modern technology if modern methods will achieve a better result. Do not copy the mistakes of earlier cabinet makers who were spared the trials of central heating.'

While on the subject of the Woodworker Show we acknowledge with thanks the numerous comments that readers have been kind enough to make, favourable and not so favourable. Taking the latter first, the organiser of the Show is conscious of the fact that visitors would have been happier had more machinery manufacturers been present along with suppliers of the raw material. It is hoped that future Shows will be supported by more manufacturers and timber suppliers. Firms may be encouraged by one of the favourable comments made by an exhibitor. This is to the effect that the 1979 Show was the best so far and there is a need for it to expand so as to bring together those who work in wood and also to show the public that there is still an abundance of craftsmen.

 **interbimall '80**

7th INTERNATIONAL BIENNIAL EXHIBITION OF
WOODWORKING MACHINERY AND ACCESSORIES

MILAN
15 - 21 MAY 1980
IN THE MILAN FAIR GROUNDS

635 exhibitors from 21 European and non-European countries in 7 pavilions on a net display area of 45,000 sq.m.

SPECIALISED EXHIBITION
OF MACHINES AND ACCESSORIES
FOR THE WORKING OF WOOD,
FOR FURNITURE, DOOR-AND WINDOW-FITTINGS,
FLOORS, PLYWOODS, WOOD SHAVING PANELS,
PACKAGING, SAWMILLS, ETC.

FOR INFORMATION : INTERBIMALL - 76, VIA VARESINA - I-20156 MILANO (ITALY)
PHONES 3271841 - 2 - 3 - 4
TELEX 331215 ACIMAL I

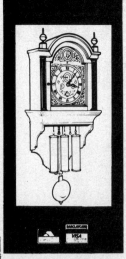

Fine woodworking demands a fine bench

A B C D

A) Lervad bench No. 610CU with two integral vices, double row bench dog system and built-in cupboard. **B)** Carving between single row bench dog system on Lervad bench No. 600. **C)** Commodious shoulder vice, one of the three ways of work holding on models 610 and 611. **D)** Exclusive Lervad pattern tail vice which also operates with bench dog clamping system running full length of top (Models 610 & 611)

- Danish made woodwork benches of superb quality, chosen by craftsmen woodworkers and craft teachers the world over.
- Made from solid kiln dried Danish beech. Precision machined and sanded tops are oiled and sealed against warping etc.
- Unique multiple vice holds for secure, comfortable and accurate working at all angles. On principal models this includes exclusive Lervad double row bench dog clamping system running full length of bench top.
- Varied choice of models to suit every woodworkers need. Built in cupboards or moveable cupboards and tool racks available.

Lervad are also leading school workshop suppliers of both wood and metalwork benches and storage units.
If you are involved in teaching please ask for School Workshop catalogue.

 *Made by craftsmen for craftsmen*

LERVAD (UK) LTD, 18, CRENDON STREET, HIGH WYCOMBE BUCKINGHAMSHIRE HP13 6LS. TEL: (0494) 32561
Please send me full details of Lervad work benches.

Name _____

Address _____

_____ W.3.0

---

140   **Prices quoted are those prevailing at press date and are subject to alteration due to economic conditions.**

Roger's for the next time you need a clean shave and a fine scrape!

GERMAN DRAW-KNIVES

These drawknives of traditional design, are manufactured of high quality steel. The hand forged blades are hollow backed, slightly carved and bevelled on the front edge. The offset of the hardwood handles gives good control whilst keeping the hands clear of the work.

Cat. No.	Size	Price £
103773	200mm	8.40
103774	250mm	8.62
103775	300mm	9.54

INSHAVE

The traditional chairmakers tool for the manufacture of chair seats. They are also useful wherever a concave shape is required. The blade is made from high quality German tool steel and fitted to unfinished hardwood handles to give a firm non-slip grip.

Cat. No.	Price
103776	£9.20

CHAMFER SPOKESHAVE

Chamfers from 0-1½″ wide can be produced with this spokeshave by means of two adjustable fences.
Length 10½″ Blade width 1½″

Cat. No.	Price
103791	£5.52

Spare iron for the above

| 103792 | £1.03 |

COOPERS SPOKESHAVE

This heavy-duty tool was traditionally used in coopering for smoothing the outside of barrel staves after assembly. In the United States it became popular for log house buildings for chamfering the ends of round and square timbers. It has one flat face, overall length
(Continued top of column four)

GERMAN CHIP CARVING KNIVES

Chip carving is an old craft entailing the cutting of geometric patterns into flat surfaces. The blade styles shown below were developed to meet the chip carver's needs, they are equally suitable as Whittling knives and general cabinet makers bench knives, the handle styles are designed to match the blade styles to give the best tool control.

Style	Cat. No.	Price	Style	Cat. No.	Price
A	111020	£1.89	F	111026	£1.89
B	111021	£2.30	G	111026	£1.89
C	111022	£2.76	H	111027	£2.76
D	111023	£2.30	I	111028	£2.76
E	111024	£2.42	J	111029	£1.89

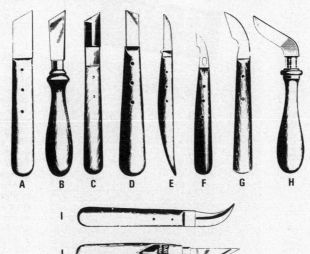

ITALIAN HAND-CUT RIFFLERS

For woodcarvers and sculptors these hand-cut rifflers are invaluable tools, available in eight different shapes as illustrated below. Approximate length 8″ and are double-ended.

Style	Cat. No.	Style	Cat. No.
A	111032	E	111036
B	111033	F	111037
C	111034	G	111038
D	111035	H	111039

Price £3.11 each.

18″ (480mm). Blade width 2⁹⁄₁₆ (65mm). Manufactured in West Germany.

Cat. No.	Price
103787	£5.98

Spare Iron for the above

Cat. No.	Price
103788	£1.10

CABINET SCRAPERS

Roger's shaped cabinet scrapers come in three different styles to accommodate all manner of convex and concave shapes of varying radii and are manufactured of properly tempered high quality steel.

Cat. No.	Square	Price
103768	4″ x 2½″	£0.45p
103769	4½″ x 2½″	£0.45p
103770	5″ x 2½″	£0.49p
103771	6″ x 3″	£0.52p

Cat. No. 103908
Price
£0.75
Convex/Concave
Cat. No. 103907
Price £1.03
Goose Neck

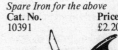

SCRAPING PLANE No. 112

The large plane type sole of this scraper makes it well suited for large areas. The angle of the blade may be set at any angle between 80 degrees and 90 degrees.

Cat. No.	Price
103915	£17.94

Spare Iron for the above

Cat. No.	Price
10391	£2.20

POSTAGE AND PACKING
Goods up to the value of

£2.00 = 20p	£25.00 = £1.05
£2.00 = 20p	£30.00 = £1.35
£5.00 = 30p	£38.00 = £1.75
£9.00 = 40p	£48.00 = £2.00
£12.00 = 55p	£55.00 = £2.30
£12.00 = 55p	£75.00 = £3.00
£16.00 = 75p	£85.00 = £3.20
£20.00 = 90p	£100.00 + £3.40

All orders over £100 free of charge.

Roger's
47 Walsworth Road, Hitchin, Herts. Tel: Hitchin 4177

OVERSEAS CUSTOMERS
Please contact us for quotation on postage and packing.

Send today for your Mail Order Catalogue No. 2 only 75p Plus 20p P&P.
U.K. Residents only.

DISTRIBUTION — WOODWORKING & EQUIPMENT SPECIALISTS

★ SPECIAL INTRODUCTORY OFFER!

HANNING ELECTRICAL EQUIPMENT

£106.50 INC. VAT

£106.50 INC. VAT

£145.00 INC. VAT

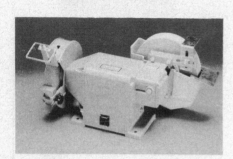

As in earlier days, with the sandstone turning slowly in a water bath, the component is ground without thermal influence (no annealing of the edges).

During the sharpening process, in which the grinding disc turns slowly in a water bath, the cutting edge is additionally consolidated.

The best fine finish is obtained with natural sandstone. To date, there were hardly any tools available for this purpose, that showed the quality and ease of operation that can be expected of todays grinding machines.

Pre-grinding:
rough grinding disc, 175mm ø, 3000 rpm, 36 grit

Fine grinding:
rotating disc in water bath, 200 × 40mm, 120 rpm, 150 grit

Technically refined construction with maintenance-free worm gear.
Multiple applications in industry, handicraft and household.

Joineries, schools, training workshops, agriculture, butcher's shops, restaurants, hotel kitchens, fish processing firms etc.

Technical data
Grinding and sharpening combination

	SSK 18/20	
Voltage:	220V, single-phase 50 cycles	
Capacity:		
input/output	450/300W	
Current input:	2.1 Amp.	
Measurements:		
height, total mm	230	
width, total mm	490	
depth, total mm	250	
weight, kg	16.3	
Grinding wheels	**Grinding stone**	**Sharpening stone**
Speed:	3000 rpm	120 rpm
Circumferential speed	27.5 m/s	1.25 m/s
Disc diameter:	175mm	200mm
Boring	16mm	16mm
Bond:	vitrified	vitrified
Grain:	36	150
Hardness:	medium	medium

Solid construction for workshop, building site, etc.

Sturdy, inclined angle sections with transverse stiffening in the lower third ensure stability. The table is of galvanised steel plate. All other components are primed and durably coated.

The circular saw is equipped with cutting depth regulation, by which the riving knife remains equidistant to the highest point of the saw blade.

Basic equipment includes a parallel stop. An angle stop can be supplied upon request.

The HTK 315 is powered by a sturdy, powerful, directly driven special motor. Motor, switch/plug combination and on/off switch are connected ready for immediate operation.

The motor is supplied with a built-in undervoltage release. The undervoltage release ensures that the saw does not start-up again after a power failure.

Technical data: HTK 315

Table:	770 × 560mm 800mm high
Saw blade ø:	315mm
Cutting depth:	85mm
Speed	3000 rpm

The HTK 315 can be supplied with the following motors:

4,1/3.0 hp 3.0/2.2 kw	220V

The belt grinding facility allows table-top grinding of flat surfaces.
Radii, curvatures or any other shapes can be ground on the rubber-covered drive shaft.
The grinding belt measures 80mm in width and is therefore quite large enough.
An 80 grit grinding belt is supplied as standard equipment. Grinding belts of 120 and 100 are available
The belt grinding facility allows table-top grinding of flat surfaces.
Radii, curvatures or any other shapes can be ground on the rubber-covered drive shaft.
The grinding belt measures 80mm in width and is therefore quite large enough.
An 80 grit grinding belt is supplied as standard equipment. Grinding belts of 120 and 100 grit are available.
The grinding machine is supplied complete with cable and mains connection.

Technical data:	BSK 175/80
Motor:	220V, a/c. 50 cycles power input: 450W power output: 300W speed: 2800 rpm
Grinding disc:	175 ø × 30mm, boring 16mm ø normal corundum, 36 grit
Belt grinding facility:	contact roll 120 ø × 80mm, vulcanized rubber coating grinding belt measurements 822 × 80mm
Belt speed:	18 m/sec.

ALSO FROM STOCK

RECORD	AMER. SAW
PARAMO	ELU
FOOTPRINT	HITACHI
BARRUS	HANNING
VERMONT AMER.	METABO
SANDVIC	PEUGEOT
FOLEY	HENDRICK
LUREM	ELSWORTH
SUMACO	TIVOLI-KAY
STARTRITE	MARPLES
LUNA	DISTON
SCHEPPACH	ZINKEN
MAFELL	HEMPE
DURANTIK	RICO
RIDGWAY	

ACS DISTRIBUTION

PARK FARM INDUSTRIAL EST., STUDLEY RD., REDDITCH, WORCS. Tel: Redditch 27058 27083 26983 21220

Prices quoted are those prevailing at press date and are subject to alteration due to economic conditions.

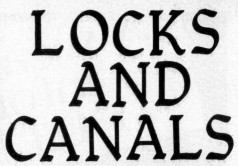

LOCKS AND CANALS

'As one walks along the tow-path of a canal . . . the years roll back and one enters an earlier time. The world of the tow-path is a world that began about 1760 and on the whole ended about 1850. The warehouses may be of old dark brick, designed with an eye which looked to the appearance as well as the use of a practical building . . .'

This quotation from Charles Hadfield's *Introducing Canals* aptly sums up the subject which H. W. Gates portrays in his pictures taken by courtesy, and with the co-operation, of British Waterways. The scenes are of the Grand Union canal formed by the merger in 1929 of the Grand Junction and various other canals. The Grand Junction was authorised in 1793 from Brentford on the Thames to Braunston in Northants where it joined the Oxford canal.

The Grand Union passes through Hemel Hempstead less than a mile from WOODWORKER office and climbs over the Chilterns by locks at Tring. In the neighbourhood are several large reservoirs to maintain the water level. Just beyond Tring is Bulbourne where there is a splendid group of buildings serving as the canal works These buildings were certainly 'designed with an eye which looked to the appearance as well as the use . . .'

The works house some interesting woodworking machines of considerable age and of a size capable of dealing with large timbers such as are used for the construction and repair of lock gates. The planing machine, probably from the early years of last century, was renovated quite recently and seems likely to go on working for a long time to come.

Wherever you go on the canals you see timber being used: lock gates, bridges, especially in the delightful lifting bridges that are characteristic of the Llangollen canal, in warehouse and building construction and, of course, in the narrow boats and cruisers for holidaymakers. Here and there you can still see wharf cranes made of timber.

Many readers of WOODWORKER are, like the editor, canal enthusiasts who enjoy seeing Britain from her 'roads of water', and who have spent happy and industrious hours 'locking' up and down, for example, the Bingley five-rise and Bingley three on the Leeds and Liverpool, or making the vertiginous passage across the Pontcysyllte aqueduct more than 120ft above the river Dee in North Wales. This must surely be the crowning glory of Thomas Telford and justification for his sobriquet of Pontifex Maximus!

This article will, we hope, encourage you to enjoy your waterways and to follow the advice of Eric de Mare: . . .' Build a small boat to adventure on them. Fish in them, or walk beside them along the tow-paths, watching their wild life and contemplating their serenity. As nowhere else in the muddle of the modern world, peace and pleasure, use and beauty, there go hand-in-hand'. *(Your Book of Waterways).*

Top: Old timber crane at Aylesbury basin on the Grand Union canal.

ROADS OF WATER

H. W. Gates pictures the beauty and interest of the canals

Left: Totem pole of red cedar *(Thuja plicata)* which stands in the premises of Alford Ltd, timber merchants on the canal bank at Berkhamsted.

The pole was carved by Henry Hunt, a Kwakuitl Indian carver from Fort Rupert which is on the NE tip of Vancouver Island. Henry Hunt has been carving for over 20 years and the tools that he uses are curved knives, adze, mallet, chisels, axe, hatchet and a crosscut saw.

Figures on the pole are known as crests and a chief can only use the figures he has a right to display. The figures on the top and bottom of this pole are the raven and the sun. The sun is frequently personified and on totem poles it is shown as a human body. The sun on this pole holds a coffer to his chest denoting wealth. Among the Kwakuitl the raven was a culture and stories about it are legion. The raven was one of the first inhabitants of the coast, and it is believed he could assume a human form at will; with this ability he helped to set up the world for man who was to follow.

Above: Lock No. 45 Marsworth. Hydraulic lifting gear is fitted to some of the replacement lock gates to raise and lower the paddles which adjust the water level.
Top right: South Oxford canal bridge 186.
Right: The planing machine which is over 100 years old (thought to be about 130 years old by Bill Mew). The machine is still in the Bulbourne works. It is 20ft long and planed a maximum section of 18 x 18in. It was made by Charles Powis & Co of Millwall Vale Pier, London, a firm no longer in existence.
(WOODWORKER thanks Mr Mew who is in charge at Bulbourne for his help in preparing this article).

Left: Oak inner and outer posts of a lock gate. They are shaped by hand with the aid of portable electric machines. Lifting gear is required to manoeuvre the English oak.
Right: Triple head combination mortise and drilling machine at Bulbourne works.

This portable hand drilling machine is part of British Waterways' maintenance equipment and although still in a workable condition it is not in normal use. A later machine, similar in appearance but with modified gearing that automatically withdraws the auger bit has superseded this model.

It is interesting to note that a hand-operated machine of this type is still the most economical and simplest way of carrying out work on those sections of the canals that are a considerable distance from a road and an electricity supply. The difficulty of transporting generating plant, to say nothing of the cost, would prohibit use of power-operated drilling machines for all minor projects.

The auger bit used in this machine does not have projecting side cutters, this reduces surface damage when drilling straight through from one side; the bit also has a better cutting action in end grain.

Intended for drilling holes in large timbers the machine can be adjusted to drill holes at any required angle to the surface of the work. The base frame and the standards of the drill are made from greenheart which is extremely strong and durable. An ingenious idea is incorporated in the design so the auger can be removed from the drilling. This is accomplished by a sliding cogwheel that is free-running when the tool is in use to cut a hole. To withdraw the bit from the timber the cogwheel is slid along the spindle where it engages with a key and the rack attached to the left-hand standard. Rotation of the drill handles then, in addition to turning the bit, raises it from the timber.

BRITAIN'S LARGEST PERMANENT DISPLAY & DEMONSTRATION CENTRE FOR LIGHT WOODWORKING MACHINERY

OPENING: TUESDAY 4TH MARCH — SATURDAY 8TH MARCH 1980

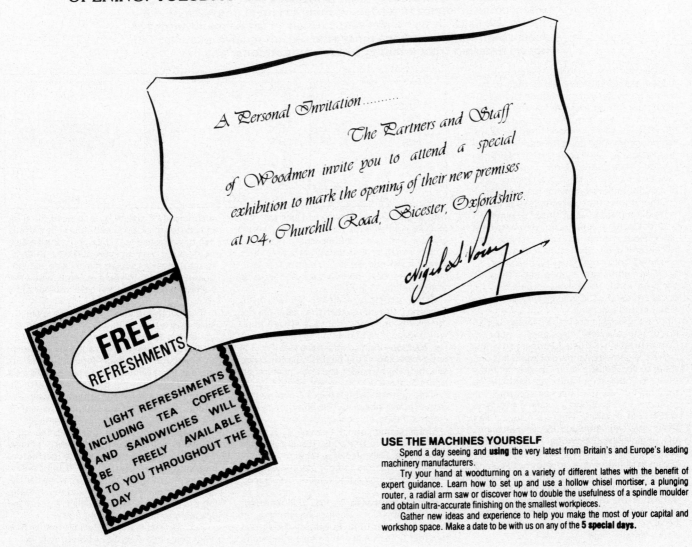

A Personal Invitation..........

The Partners and Staff of Woodmen invite you to attend a special exhibition to mark the opening of their new premises at 104, Churchill Road, Bicester, Oxfordshire.

FREE REFRESHMENTS

LIGHT REFRESHMENTS INCLUDING TEA COFFEE AND SANDWICHES WILL BE FREELY AVAILABLE TO YOU THROUGHOUT THE DAY

USE THE MACHINES YOURSELF

Spend a day seeing and **using** the very latest from Britain's and Europe's leading machinery manufacturers.

Try your hand at woodturning on a variety of different lathes with the benefit of expert guidance. Learn how to set up and use a hollow chisel mortiser, a plunging router, a radial arm saw or discover how to double the usefulness of a spindle moulder and obtain ultra-accurate finishing on the smallest workpieces.

Gather new ideas and experience to help you make the most of your capital and workshop space. Make a date to be with us on any of the **5 special days.**

WITH YOUR PLANS IN MIND

From mini-bandsaws at £49 to giant panel saws with contra-rotating scribing heads at around £2500, you can be confident of finding the exact machine to suit your plans and pocket, be it a lathe, a hand planer or the brand new K5 — a truly amazing cabinet mounted universal at the incredible price of £499!

Senior representatives from every company will be on hand and delighted to discuss, demonstrate, and advise on the full exciting range of their machinery. With your own needs in mind, take advantage of this marvellous opportunity to use and compare a range of purpose-built equipment from the world's best known manufacturers.

Prices will never be lower and we will be happy to arrange credit over any period up to 3 years at an exceptional flat rate interest charge of just 13%. (You can of course pay by cash, cheque or credit card.) And remember that you are totally safeguarded by our **full cash refund guarantee.**

ON HAND FOR EXPERT GUIDANCE

You cannot fail to benefit from the guidance and expertise of no fewer than 28 of the nation's leading authorities on woodworking machinery. They are the top men in their field who have made their companies successful because of concern for and total identification with your needs.

Who could better explain the advantages of the various CORONET systems than Chris Parker, managing director and innovator in this world famous company? Think what you can learn from John Farrar, architect and principal behind the explosive growth of KITY in the U.K. market, or John O'Connor, who with an incredible £1,000,000 worth of ELEKTRA sales to his credit this year, has brought large capacity machinery well within reach of every home woodworker.

In fact, whether you want to solve a production problem, take advantage of temporary price reductions or simply enjoy a rare opportunity to become familiar with the full spectrum of machinery in use today, we know your visit will be enjoyable and well worthwhile.

WOODMEN

All machines are delivered by our own transport to your home or workshop within 7 days.

Contact us today for free colour catalogues and price lists.

43, CRWYS ROAD, CARDIFF, GLAM. (0222) 36519/373793
General Manager, John Fox. Branch Manager, Michael Holiday.

104, CHURCHILL ROAD, BICESTER, OXON. (08692) 3218/9
Branch Manager, Michael Boden.

27, NEWGATE, BARNARD CASTLE, CO. DURHAM. (0833) 38442
Branch Manager, Bob Beveridge.

49, NEATH ROAD, BRITON FERRY, WEST GLAM. (0639) 820803/4
Branch Manager, Jim Blakeney.

Making to Exhibition Standards

John Price, furniture tutor at Shrewsbury Technical College, and one of the cabinet making class judges at last year's Woodworker Show, offers some guidance to readers wishing to enter competitions in the future. He says: 'It was a pleasant surprise to see so many entries of such a high standard. I hope those who did not receive an award will not be deterred from entering future competitions.'

Naturally the personal preferences of judges has some influence on their judgements, particularly in the reproduction v contemporary furniture controversy; in an open competition it is virtually impossible to be impartial. It is recommended that in future, reproduction and contemporary furniture and amateur and professional work be judged separately. Many entries not awarded a prize were of outstanding merit and ought to be given some recognition.

Other entries that were impressive at first sight did not stand up to close inspection — poor dovetailing, veneers uneven, long-case clock hoods wrongly moulded to shape, split panels and so on. Most faults found could be classified under the following headings: (1) joint setting-out, cutting and fitting; (2) bending and veneering problems; (3) peculiarities of solid wood; (4) cleaning-up, staining and polishing.

It is impossible to list all faults, but in discussing the few mentioned I hope to demonstrate how to avoid, correct and so improve the general standard of work. It is one thing to recognise a fault, another to know how to correct it and yet another to understand why the fault has occurred.

Joints Fig. 1 shows a common fault in setting-out dovetails where the layout has been reversed. Although the dovetails lock the proportions are wrong. Instead of end pins, half tails appear and abut end grain. It is common practice never to rely on glue alone for strength where end grain is involved. If the drawer back subsequently cups as in Fig. 3 the glue line will break, whereas if the joint is laid out as in Fig. 2 the joints are secure because side grain abuts side grain, where pins and tails meet.

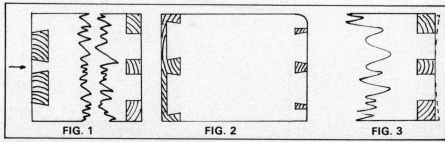

FIG. 1   **FIG. 2**   **FIG. 3**

was angled when sawing. To correct, the mortise is filled with a waste piece of wood glued-in and recut, whereas both sides of the tenon have to be built-up with veneer or thick waste wood and recut. An alternative is to cut off the tenon and insert a false tenon, or use dowelling (Fig. 9).

When panels are being jointed, it is necessary to ensure that the plane shoots the boards uniformly and thus avoid bumps which when glued leave hollows as shown in Fig. 10. Plane both boards in the vice (Fig. 11) and before taking the boards out of the vice see that two complete shavings have rolled from the plane over the length of the boards. A slight gap at both ends (Fig. 12) may pull together when glued, but as they are under stress splitting may occur at a later date.

Start shooting from the centre of the board and work out to the ends, leaving a slight hollow (the thickness of a sheet of WOODWORKER). Use the largest plane available; small planes create undulations over a long board.

Bending and veneering Fig. 13 illustrates a coopered hood for a longcase clock made up of small angular jointed pieces of wood glued together on a mould and shaped afterwards

techniques. If animal glue is used the glue may be too thick, or chilled before the surplus can be squeezed out. Thick contact glue also produces a very uneven surface. (Rubber-based adhesives should not be used on high-quality work for in years to come, when the rubber perishes, the veneers will certainly lift).

If a contact adhesive is to be used be sure it is a thin solution recommended for veneering by the manufacturers. A hot-melt glue is a far better modern adhesive. It is easy to apply, but not easily obtainable, and its storage life is limited. The paper-backed glue film is applied to the ground work with an electric iron and the paper peeled away. The veneer is placed over the film which is reheated and then sticks to the veneer.

When using animal glue get the consistency of the glue right so that it flows evenly off the brush. If the glue gels before the surplus can be hammered out, melt it with a hot iron and, working from the centre, squeeze it out. Avoid using too much water on the veneer as water swells the grain and leaves a shrinkage gap when dry.

Peculiarities of solid wood. No matter how well seasoned a piece of timber may be, or

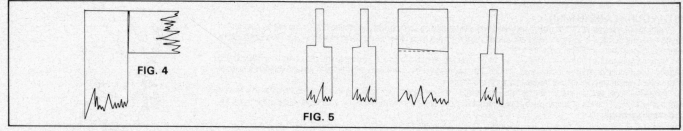

FIG. 4

FIG. 5

Fig. 4 illustrates a badly-fitted mortise and tenon joint filled with veneers, plastics wood or stopping which is invariably the wrong colour. The gap is often caused by poor sawing of the tenon or chiselling of the mortise out of square. Variations are shown in Figs. 5, 7,8. Most of these are shoulder defects that can be corrected by re-squaring a knife around the wood at the lowest point of defect and paring back to the line (Fig. 6), using a square-edged piece of wood cramped-up to the line as a guide. Wide-shouldered tenons can be cut back to the line using a shoulder plane.

Fig. 7 is a section through a mortise joint cut out of square by tilting the chisel. Fig. 8 is a tenon parallel in thickness but angled to the rail. The tenon in Fig. 8 would result if the saw was held at a slight angle or the timber

to the exact curve. These could either be finished as they are or veneered to match the case.

Another method would be to build a mould as for Fig. 13, then glue together two pieces of 1½mm ply cut on the cross and staple them both to the mould to set. When set remove staples and cover with decorative matching veneer or stain. If 1½mm ply is difficult to obtain, 4mm ply cut on the cross will bend reasonably well. Constructional veneers may also be built up in a similar way as in Fig. 15, and pulled over the mould with sheet metal or canvas attached to strips of wood. Either polish the mould or place paper on it to prevent the laminates sticking.

Faults in the laying of veneers (easily seen when light reflects from a polished surface) are probably the result of poor gluing

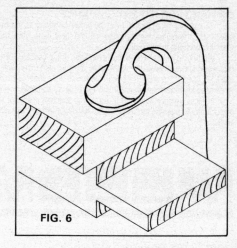

FIG. 6

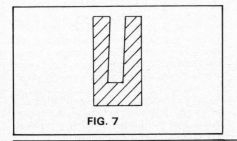

FIG. 7

checking surface before polishing is to hold it so that a light source reflects from the wood. Try passing your fingers over the wood and feel the irregularities either from the plane or scraper. Badly-set planes leave ridges across the grain, whereas a scraper will pull out the softer fibres and leave a rough finish which is emphasised when polish is applied.

When setting a smoothing plane ensure that the blade is sharpened square and

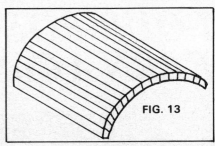

FIG. 13

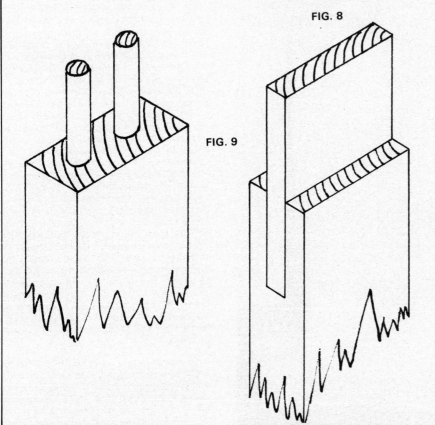

FIG. 8

FIG. 9

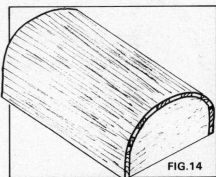

FIG.14

Mould

Base Board

FIG. 15

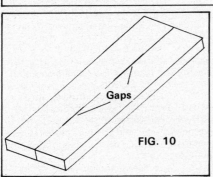

Gaps

FIG. 10

FIG. 11

FIG. 16   FIG. 17

FIG. 12

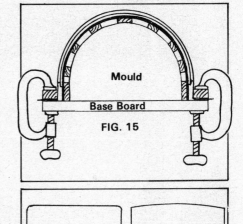

how low its moisture content (m.c.) it will absorb moisture in humid weather and lose it in dry weather. Unless allowance is made for this movement in constructing a piece of furniture the timber will split. Solid panels should be free to move and not be fixed with pins, screws or glue. Solid drawer bottoms need to expand and contract from front to back and should therefore be fixed with slotted screws. Similarly solid table tops must have slotted screw fittings or buttons mortised into the rails.

Cleaning-up, staining and polishing. The same care and attention must be given when finishing as in the construction of furniture. With experience you develop a certain sensitivity to surfaces of wood which involves all the senses. Light will reflect from poorly-planed (and polished) wood and show up all irregularities. A simple way of

straight but rub off the corners to 'fade out' the ridge (Fig. 16). Use the lever to centralise the blade in the plane mouth. A blade sharpened as in Fig. 17 is for roughing only and will produce waves over the surface, these must be cleaned-up with the smoother as described above.

A blunt plane gives a poor surface. It will only cut hardwood when great force is used — and it 'hops' along the wood. Reflect light on the cutting edge and note how it is polished. Listen to the sound it makes — a dull scrape when blunt and a crisp note when sharp. Difficult, cross-grained timber pulls-out or tears when the plane is blunt or incorrectly set. A sharp plane gives a superior finish which requires very little glasspapering. So keep it sharp and save money.

Very coarse-grained hardwood requires some form of filling before staining. Otherwise the open grain will absorb more stain and over-emphasise the grain pattern. However an even colour can be obtained when fuming oak or mahogany with ammonia and no preliminary filling is necessary.

Polish used to finish the piece of furniture may be traditional or modern and the choice is often personal. There is a danger that if the finish is built-up to such an extent as to act as a mirror it reflects the light and masks the natural beauty of the wood. Polyurethane

FOUR-POSTER BEDS EARN A CoSIRA PRIZE

Sympathy for small businesses faced with current high rates of interest was expressed by David Mitchell, minister at the department of industry responsible for small firms, recently. Presenting prizes to the winners and runners-up of the Council for Small Industries in Rural Areas (CoSIRA) national new starters competition, in London on 17 December, Mr Mitchell said it was not an easy time for starting new businesses but high interest rates were inevitable when the government was giving priority to tackling inflation. Once inflation had been conquered the way would be clear for a massive increase in the number of small businesses.

The CoSIRA competition was divided into two categories: A — for businesses committed to starting, but which had not started trading until after 1 April 1979; and B — those which started business within the 12 months preceding 1 April 1979. The winners and runners-up in each category received £2000 and £250 respectively.

Main criteria by which entries were judged were: prospect of viability and permanence; prospect of good profit performance and security of employment; and contribution to the local community.

The competition in 1979 was arranged by CoSIRA in association with *The Guardian* newspaper.

In category B the winner was Manor Lodge Furniture Ltd, Little Downham, Ely, Cambs, established by ex-Royal Air Force pilot John Cross and his wife Julia in January 1978. After a careful appraisal of the furniture market they decided that there was a demand for four-poster beds. Mr Cross then went to the drawing board and prepared five different designs which could be adjusted to suit individual customer requirements. The beds are in solid timber, either oak or mahogany incorporating hand-carved work and complete with hand-sewn drapes and covers to match.

Principal customers are hotels — and now

discerning individuals who are happy to pay for high-quality work and, very often, personalised carving on headboards and top rails, and superb finish. Manor Lodge produces bedroom furniture to complement the four-posters and offers a complete furnishing service for bedrooms including curtains, pelmets as well as wardrobes and dressing tables. It also makes occasional tables and 'monk's seats' in oak and mahogany.

Mr Cross told WOODWORKER that personalisation of each piece, coupled with the highest standards of workmanship and finish and careful selection of materials ensured a steady flow of orders executed from the bench, not from stock. 'We adhere strictly to delivery dates,' said Mr Cross.

By the middle of the year Manor Lodge expects to have moved into larger premises constructed by CoSIRA. With the additional workshop space the company will be able to develop into export markets from which enquiries are already being received.

Runner-up in category A was Creative Wood of Sydling St Nicholas, Dorchester, Dorset. This began trading in May 1979 as a result of the combined skills of Denis Buckland and his wife Valerie and Christopher and Heather Robinson. They decided there was a market for top-quality wooden toys of original design as well as carved and turned items for the home. In the toys range, rocking animals such as a lion, elephant, dog and giraffe have proved popular with several of the top London department stores. The design side of the business is in the hands of Mrs Buckland who is an artist, woodcarver and sculptress with a studio in Dorchester.

Mr Buckland told WOODWORKER that he had established connections with local mills and suppliers of hard and soft woods. Having decided which of the many prototypes offered the best chance of success, he would be investing in more woodworking machinery and larger premises.

In category B the runner-up was Creative Cane, Gimingham, Norfolk, started in October 1978 by Richard Parker, an engineer, and Malcolm Hastings, a carpenter and joiner, to make cane headboards and occasional and bedside tables. Four months later the premises were involved in a fire which destroyed stock, materials and equipment. Undeterred by this setback the partners re-invested previous profits in new materials and equipment and in renting new premises.

Now they are producing eight styles of headboards in 3ft, 4ft 6in. and 5ft sizes as well as tables in four different designs. Some 40% of the cane production is sold through manufacturing agencies with the remainder being taken by department stores and shops specialising in cane work.

Future proposals for Creative Cane include moving to new premises and probably expanding production to other lines of furniture.

Continued from page 149

varnish is criticised because it sometimes appears like marmalade spread on the surface. It should be applied thinly with a rubber, not a brush, and worked well into the grain. When successive layers have filled the grain, cut back with wet and dry paper 400 grit lubricated with water. Thoroughly clean the water and dust particles off the surface before applying the next coat; any dust

trapped in the grain will show up as white flecks.

Polish inaccessible parts of furniture before gluing. Modern glues are difficult to clean-off when set. They also fill the pores of the wood. This is not always visible until after the polish is applied. Then it shows up as a cream or gold patch under the polish.

Finally, a comment on the ethics of making

reproduction furniture. Do not try to improve on Chippendale or Sheraton. Make a true copy. Use modern technology if modern methods will achieve a better result. Do not copy the mistakes of earlier cabinet makers who were spared the trials of central heating. Why reproduce mistakes unless the intention is to deceive people into thinking the piece is an original?

Cowells Jigsaw
Rugged, trouble-free design

Widely accepted by educational
authorities for use in schools,
this jigsaw is indispensable for
the modelmaker and handyman
who are looking for a no-nonsense,
hard working machine.

- One piece body casting
- Balanced crankshaft to minimise vibration
- Built-in safety features
- Large diameter spindles and bearings for long, continuous trouble-free work
- A price anyone can afford
- Cuts wood, plastics, metal, slate, bone etc.
- Continuously rated motor

Write to us **now** for details, and address
of your nearest stockist

Cowell Engineering Limited

Oak Street Norwich NR3 3BP England
Telephone (0603) 614521 Telex 975205

Don't settle for less.

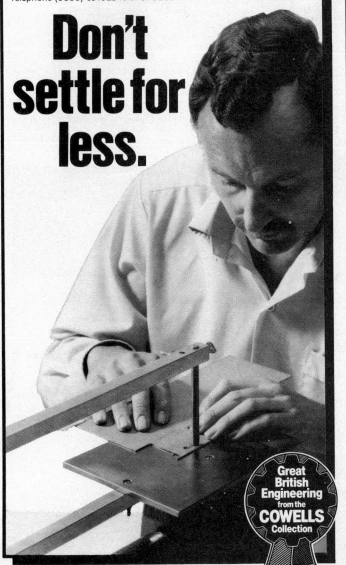

Great British Engineering from the COWELLS Collection

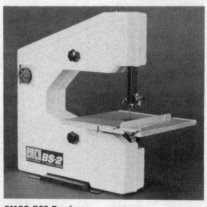

WOODTURNING AIDS NO 5

Alan Holtham has been testing high-speed steel (HSS) turning tools made by Robert Sorby Ltd. He finds that HSS takes a very fine edge from the grindstone; and that edge lasts very much longer since it is much less susceptible to the damaging effects of heat generated when turning.

This month we take a look at some recent additions to the tools produced by Robert Sorby Ltd, 817 Chesterfield Road, Sheffield S80SR, namely a set of four highspeed steel-tipped scrapers, and the highspeed steel fluted parting tool. The tipped scrapers are perhaps the most interesting of the two, and I shall discuss these first.

The standard boxed set consists of four tools which are shaped to give six different cutting applications: right skew, left skew, round nosed and quarter round, the left skew and quarter round being hooked (Fig. 1). The tools are basically long and strong heavy section scrapers, but the difference is that a high-speed steel tip of about 1½ in. has been brazed into the end (Figs. 2 and 3).

This small section of high-speed steel (HSS) is all that is necessary since it is only the top edge of the scraper that is used during a cut. HSS takes a very fine edge from the grindstone; and that edge also lasts very much longer since it is much less susceptible to the damaging effects of heat generated when turning. A solid HSS tool would be prohibitively expensive, besides being unnecessary.

In use, a very light touch on the grindstone is all that is required to bring up a superb burr on the edge of the tool. To make maximum use of this the tools should be used pointing well down. Fig. 4 shows the recess for a small ceramic tile being scraped flat with the skew ended/hooked tool. This to my mind is the most useful of the four shapes. I use it a lot when making the recess for the 6 in 1 chuck.

(Continued on page 154)

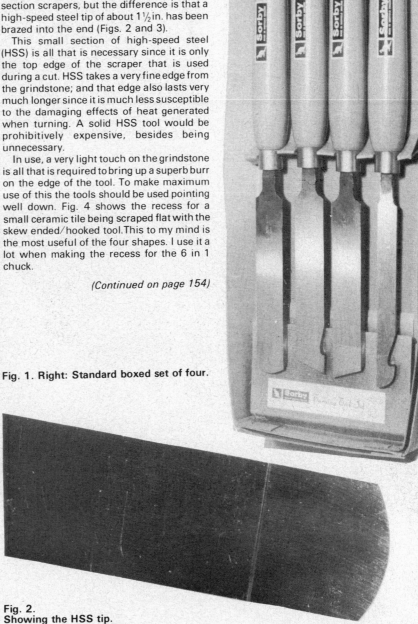

Fig. 1. Right: Standard boxed set of four.

**Fig. 2.
Showing the HSS tip.**

The hooked round shape is ideal for those deep hollowing jobs (Fig. 5). The thick section makes it very safe when there is a lot of overhang on the rest but, on the other hand, heavy tools are rather awkward when working very small diameter recesses. A complementary set of standard strength tools might be a good idea here.

To really put the tools to the test, I next tried the round nosed version in a large bowl turned from a rather spectacular piece of burr elm (Fig. 6). Despite what the books say you should do, I nearly always seem to end up using scrapers in the final stages of bowl work, mainly to remove those persistent ridges left by the gouge. And this piece was no exception, since the very uneven texture of the burr timber had induced considerable vibration to the bowl gouge.

This vibration becomes most noticeable down the sides of very thin walled bowls, and once there it seems to get worse the more you try to remove it. Normally when a scraper is introduced at this stage, some deterioration of the wood surface is inevitable no matter how light the cuts are. You really have to decide whether you are going to try and sand out the gouge marks, or scrape them out and then sand out the end grain roughness caused by the scraper!

Salvation is at hand, though, since the very fine wire edge taken by the HSS tools does seem to minimise tearing of the end grain, and the final result on my piece of burr certainly surprised me. I have always felt that scrapers are an essential finishing tool rather than a shaping tool, and if used accordingly they are quite acceptable, the HSS tools being a distinct improvement on conventional tools.

The other skew ended shape is designed for those with outboard turning facilities, though I must admit that I reprofiled it to be square across, which I find a more versatile shape.

Fig. 3. Showing HSS tip brazed into end of scraper.

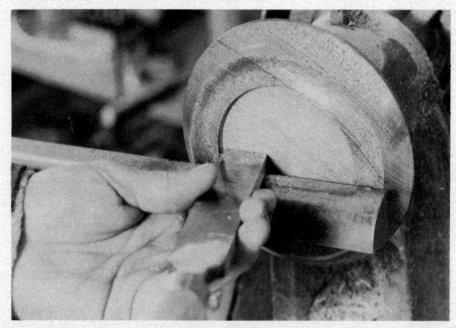

Fig. 4. Above: Shows the recess for a small ceramic tile being scraped flat with the skew ended/hooked tool.

Fig. 5. Below: The hooked round shape is ideal for those deep hollowing jobs.

The tools are available either as a complete boxed set at £30.50 or separately at approximately £7.60 each from your Sorby dealer. The loose tools are also available unhandled, so if you know of a good turner who can make you some handles . . . !

The other new tool is the HSS fluted parting tool (Fig. 7). This is a piece of solid HSS ground to a taper, and with a flute machined along the bottom edge. (Figs. 8 and 9). The end result of all this is to leave a cutting edge with two projecting spurs and a central cutting edge. In use the theory is somewhat similar to an auger bit as used in a carpenter's brace. The outer spurs slice through the wood defining the cut and the central portion then removes the waste. The surface is thus left with a much cleaner finish since it has been cut rather than scraped, as with a conventional parting tool.

This is shown very clearly in Fig. 10 on the end grain of a piece held between centres. The resulting surface resembles that left by the normal cleaning up cut of the skew. This photo confirms that the tool is used fluted side down, something which seems to surprise those seeing it for the first time. The taper ground across the blade ensures that overheating does not occur when making deep partings. The only possible criticism of the tool is that the sharp edges of the flutes sometimes dig into the tool rest, making it difficult to manoeuvre the tool onto the work. This is unavoidable and you have occasionally to dress the top of the rest with a flat file.

Fig. 6. Round nosed version in a large bowl turned from burr elm.

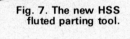

Fig. 7. The new HSS fluted parting tool.

Fig. 8. HSS fluted parting tool, the tool is ground to a taper with a flute machined along the bottom edge.

Fig. 9. Left: Section showing taper ground blade.

Fig. 10. Left: The surface is left with a much cleaner finish since it is cut rather than scraped as is shown on this end grain of a piece held between centres.

This is perhaps one tool that does not require sharpening on the grindstone. Just a few strokes with an oilstone along the diagonal edge are usually sufficient to keep it cutting cleanly unless, of course, you bang the end on the lathe bed when putting the tool down. (How many times have you done that with a freshly sharpened tool?) If damage does occur a little light grinding followed by a rub with a tiny slipstone in the flute will restore respectability. This is a tool that should, therefore, last forever which is just as well since it is priced at £8.35. However, its thin section will save you a little money by reducing the waste when parting-off!

THE WORLD'S TIMBER TREES

Last month C. W. Bond FIWSc discussed berlinia: 9. Next month he will write about agba. Here he describes ayan which is a moderately hard wood and highly attractive with either a matt or full polish. Figured examples are manufactured into veneer which may be met under the French name movingui.

AYAN: 10

Distemonanthus benthamianus. Distemonanthus — having a two-stamen flower; *benthamianus* — after George Bentham, a famous English botanist. Leguminosae (Caesalpiniaceae).

This is a moderately hard wood and its chief characteristic is its pale but bright yellow colour. The texture is medium, the vessels being fairly large but they are rather sparsely distributed and finished surfaces have a glossy and satiny character. The wood, therefore, has been aptly named Nigerian satinwood. But in spite of this and the pronounced yellow colour there is little similarity between it and the famous east Indian satinwood from Sri Lanka which is much harder, somewhat deeper in colour, and which belongs to a different botanical family, the Rutaceae, famous for the citrus fruits.

The rays are small and have little affect on appearance. Seasonal growth is faintly in evidence and the most obvious feature is formed by the broad bands of parenchyma cells which are conspicuous in cross section and have a definite bearing on the character of tangential (flat-sawn) surfaces.

Ayan is highly attractive with either a matt or full polish, and the uniformity of colour permits freedom of outline in the design of small articles. The colour, though modest, might prove to be somewhat monotonous over a large area, but handsome effects could be produced with contrasting woods in a decorative scheme. Figured examples are manufactured into veneer which may be met under the French name movingui.

The photomicrographs show the prominent parenchyma cells but the rays are too small to be clearly seen even with a x10 lens.

Nigerian satinwood (ayan)
Distemonanthus benthamianus
Drawn from material in the Forest Herbarium, University of Oxford, with acknowledgements to the curator.

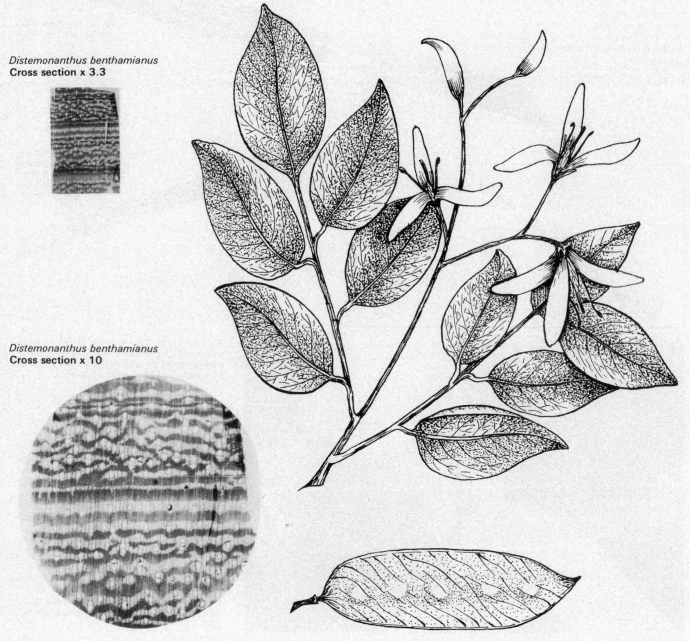

Distemonanthus benthamianus
Cross section x 3.3

Distemonanthus benthamianus
Cross section x 10

What has 1 tilting base, 2 speeds, 3 blades and 4 orbital settings?

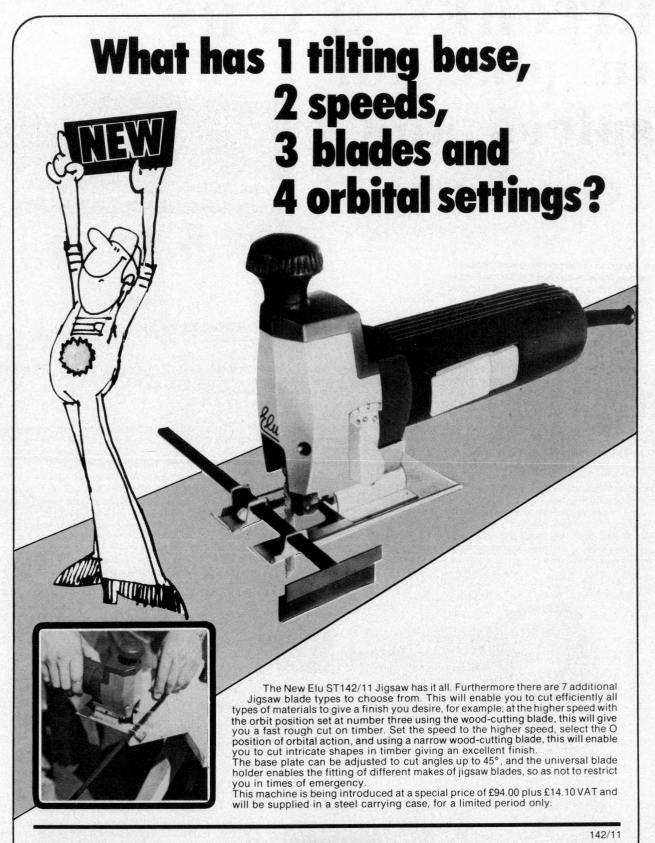

NEW

The New Elu ST142/11 Jigsaw has it all. Furthermore there are 7 additional Jigsaw blade types to choose from. This will enable you to cut efficiently all types of materials to give a finish you desire, for example, at the higher speed with the orbit position set at number three using the wood-cutting blade, this will give you a fast rough cut on timber. Set the speed to the higher speed, select the O position of orbital action, and using a narrow wood-cutting blade, this will enable you to cut intricate shapes in timber giving an excellent finish.

The base plate can be adjusted to cut angles up to 45°, and the universal blade holder enables the fitting of different makes of jigsaw blades, so as not to restrict you in times of emergency.

This machine is being introduced at a special price of £94.00 plus £14.10 VAT and will be supplied in a steel carrying case, for a limited period only.

142/11

50 Years Elu

Elu – have been your partner for 50 years now. Tradesmen, Hobbyists, as well as the woodworking and metal working industry are guided by the motto: "Quality with guaranteed service".

Coupon

Please send more information on Elu Portable Electric Tools

Name _____

Company _____

Street _____

Place _____

Phone _____

Elu Machinery Limited, Stirling Way, Stirling Corner, Borehamwood, Herts, WD6 2AG. Tel.: 01-953 0711

KITCHEN RACKS in pine for spices and crockery

A. Yarwood gives drawings and details for making traditional-style kitchen wall racks in pine *(Pinus sylvestris)*; and a method for boring angled holes.

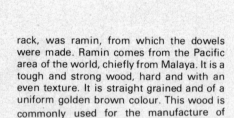

The spice rack

Traditional-style kitchen racks made from pine finished natural colour and grain, make attractive wall features in the modern kitchen. They form pleasing contrasts to the straight lines, square edges and plain colours of so many kitchen fitments. Here are two such racks, one designed to hold spices, the other to contain plates, cups and saucepans.

The term pine is used here to describe the wood from Scots pine *(Pinus sylvestris)*. This common building timber comes under the guise of a variety of names — yellow deal, red deal, Scots pine and redwood — to name a few. British Standard specifications recommend the use of redwood to describe the timber from Scots pine.

Indeed the term redwood or red deal is commonly used in the Scandinavian countries from which this timber is often exported. The term deal refers to the size of the planks into which the logs from the trees are sawn. A deal is usually 9 × 3in. or 11 × 3in. The deals are re-converted by sawing into the market sizes we use in the workshop.

Good quality redwood is a joy to work with. Providing all tools are very sharp it planes sweetly, saws easily and cleanly and chisels quite freely. As you work with this timber, the workshop becomes redolent of the forests from which the wood was obtained. As the tiny resin canals of the wood are cut, so the air becomes scented with the sweet smell of resin. The second wood used, in the wall

rack, was ramin, from which the dowels were made. Ramin comes from the Pacific area of the world, chiefly from Malaya. It is a tough and strong wood, hard and with an even texture. It is straight grained and of a uniform golden brown colour. This wood is commonly used for the manufacture of dowels.

The spice rack was made first. To find suitable dimensions for this rack, all the spices (in their containers) from our kitchen cupboard were placed in lines on the kitchen worktop. This allowed measurement of the lengths which each row would take up in the rack. After measuring this length and the required depths, a drawing of the design for the rack was made. This is given in Fig. 1. Then all parts for the rack were planed to their finished width and thickness and the ends of the side pieces shot to their final length in a shooting board. The construction of this rack can be seen in Fig. 3. After making the dovetails by which the box corners are jointed, its front rails and shelf were jointed to the sides with mortise and tenons and stopped housings respectively. The tenons are only ¼in. (6mm) long and the housing grooves only ⅛in. (3mm) deep.

When satisfied that all the jointing fitted well, the curves on the front edges of the ends were sawn, filed to shape and sanded. Now the various parts of the assembly could be sanded clean and the rack glued together, taking the precaution of ensuring all was square before putting the glued-up work to one side for the glue to set hard. A final planing and sanding of the outer surfaces of the construction completed the work. More about finishing and fitting to the wall later.

Dimensions for the second rack were obtained by measuring such items as plates, saucers, cups and saucepans. When satisfied that suitable sizes had been found a working drawing was made (Fig. 2). Again apart from the dowels which were purchased, all parts for the rack were planed to finished widths and thicknesses before work on the jointing commenced.

The wall rack

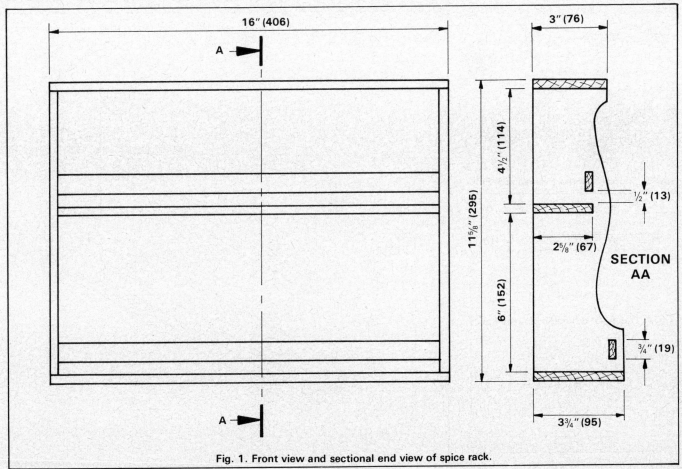

Fig. 1. Front view and sectional end view of spice rack.

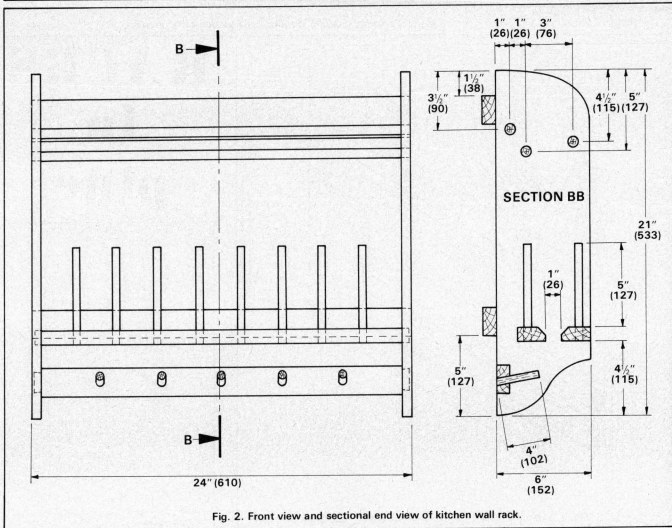

Fig. 2. Front view and sectional end view of kitchen wall rack.

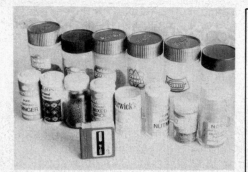

How to find the length of the spice rack.

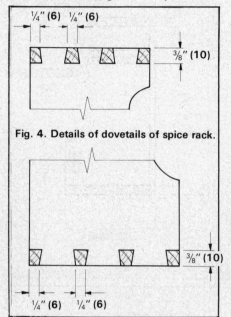

¼" (6) ¼" (6)

⅜" (10)

Fig. 4. Details of dovetails of spice rack.

⅜" (10)

¼" (6) ¼" (6)

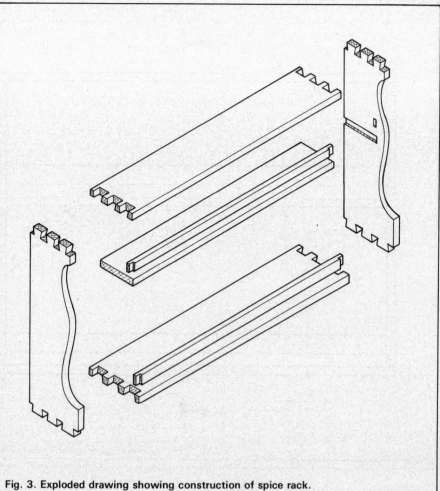

Fig. 3. Exploded drawing showing construction of spice rack.

RACKS
in
pine

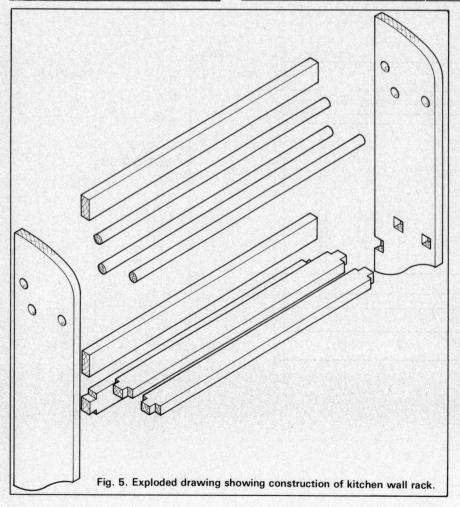

Fig. 5. Exploded drawing showing construction of kitchen wall rack.

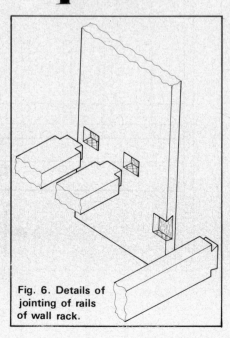

Fig. 6. Details of
jointing of rails
of wall rack.

Fitting one of the corner dovetails of the spice rack

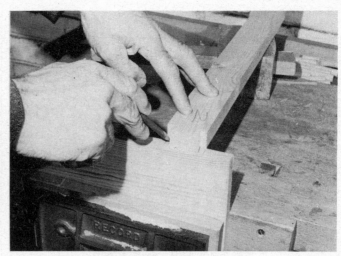
Marking lap dovetail of wall rack plate rail

Sawing the curve on bottom of end of wall rack

Screwing home a wall rail of the wall rack

Then the mortise and tenons of the plate rails were marked and cut, followed by the marking and cutting of the lap dovetails joining the cup rail to the rack sides. Holes of ¾ in. (19mm) diameter could then be bored for the saucepan rack and cup rack and a test made to find whether the assembly fitted together well. After taking this assembly apart holes for the plate and cup dowels were bored in their respective rails. (Note a method of boring the angled holes for the cup dowels shown in Fig. 7).

Bevels had to be planed on the inside of the plate rails and the inner surfaces of the parts of the rack cleaned by sanding before gluing rails and dowels to the two sides. When the glue on this assembly had set, the outer surfaces were planed and sanded. Now the rear wall rails could be glued and screwed in position, using 1¾ in. (45mm) brass CS screws of gauge 8. The dowels for plates and cups were cut to length and glued in their holes to complete the construction of this rack.

To ensure a smooth, easily cleanable, yet tough smooth surface finish both racks were given three brush coats of clear polyurethane varnish. The spice rack was hung on a wall with the aid of two brass wall plates (often also called mirror plates). The wall rack was hung in position on a wall by screwing through the wall rails into wall plugs set in the wall.

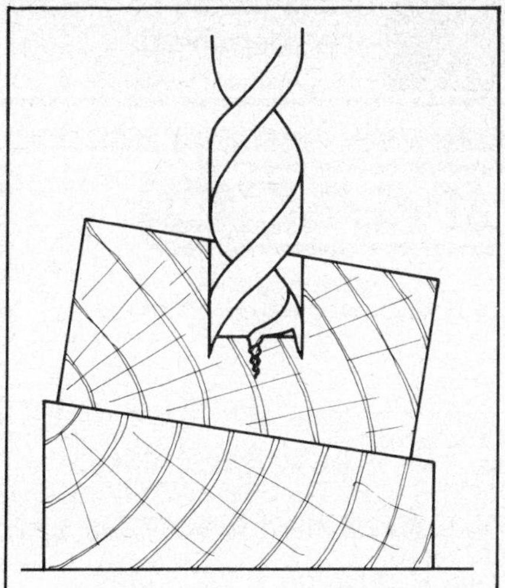

Fig. 7. Boring dowel holes for cup rack.

CUTTING LIST

Dimensions in in. and mm. Allowances to length — ½ in. (13mm); allowances to width — ¼ in. (6mm); allowances to thickness — ⅛ in. (3mm); dowel diameters are as purchased.

Spice rack

2 ends	12⅛ × 4 × ½	308 × 102 × 13
1 bottom	16½ × 4 × ½	420 × 102 × 13
1 top	16½ × 3¼ × ½	420 × 89 × 13
1 shelf	16 × 3⅛ × ½	407 × 83 × 13
2 front rails	16¼ × 1 × ⁷⁄₁₆	413 × 26 × 10

Wall rack

2 ends	21½ × 6¼ × ¾	546 × 158 × 19
2 plate rails	24¼ × 2 × 1	616 × 51 × 26
1 cup rail	24¼ × 2 × 1	616 × 51 × 26
2 wall rails	24½ × 2 × 1	622 × 51 × 26
3 pan rails	24½ × ¾ dia. dowel	622 × 19 dia dowel
16 plate dowels	6⅜ × ½ dia. dowel	162 × 13 dia dowel
6 cup dowels	4½ × ½ dia. dowel	108 × 13 dia dowel

For spice rack — 2 brass wall plates for securing to wall

After 130 years you'd expect us to come up with something different.

We've been selling tools to craftsmen for well on 130 years.

In that time we've grown to know every woodwork and metalwork tool there is.

You'd also expect us to stock the vast bulk of them.

We do, including the more unusual ones like those we've shown here.

Write off and we'll send you our literature, or arrange for you to come for a demonstration.

You'll be shown proudly over our huge range of tools and accessories by one of our Branch Managers who will talk to you like seasoned experts.

And with 130 years experience behind them, would you expect anything less?

Arundel J3 Lathe long series
An economical small lathe, ideal for all turners, especially beginners.
Motor recommended: ⅓ or ½ H.P.
180mm (7″) swing over bed
750mm (30″) between centres
300mm (12″) bowl turning capability supplied with 2 faceplates, centres, tool rest, motor pulley belt, etc. £90.00 inc. VAT

Inca Bandsaw
Two versions of this precision built machine at a very special price: motorized £225.98 inc. VAT or pulley driven (to fit motor) £129.37 inc. VAT

Wood Screw Sets
For smooth accurate threads in all woods. Tap and die box with full instructions. ½″ up to 1½″. From £21.27 inc. VAT

Prices liable to change without notice, but are subject to carriage charges.

Australian agents for Woodscrew Sets and Bandsaw Kits.
Woodwork Tool Supplies, Camberwell 3124, Victoria.

New Zealand Agent for Woodscrew Sets
R. Cameron & Co. Ltd., P.O. Box 30-345, Lower Hutt.

Emir Wooden Planes
Super quality wooden planes with screw adjustable blades and lignum vitae bases. Four models to choose.
600mm Try plane with 60mm cutter £42.85 inc. VAT
225mm Smoothing Plane with 48mm cutter with adjustable throat £42.85 inc. VAT
240mm Jack Plane with 48mm cutter £33.92 inc. VAT
280mm Rabbet Plane with 30mm cutter £36.22 inc. VAT

Terms available. Barclaycard, Access.

South African agent of Bandsaw Kits
K & A Services Ltd., P.O. Box 17148. Congella 4013.

U.S. agent for Woodscrew Sets
Leichtung Inc., 4944 Commerce Parkway, Cleveland, Ohio 44143.

SARJENTS TOOLS

62-64 Fleet Street, Swindon, Wiltshire. Tel: 0793 31361. Telex 449485.
44-52 Oxford Road, Reading, Berkshire. Tel: 0734 586522. Telex: 848695.
150 Cowley Road, Oxford. Tel: 0865 45118.

Luna wood-turning lathes

One small step in outlay one giant leap in production

Whether turning is a hobby or a profession, LUNA of Sweden offer a machine to suit you and your budget.

From the SP600 Bench Model without electrics for the very cost conscious, to the motorised SP800 and SP1000 Models, Luna Lathes are competitively priced without sacrificing the quality associated with Swedish engineering.

NEW

For repetition turning with minimum outlay LUNA now offer the new Automatic Copying Device.

Luna-always one step ahead

◄ Luna Automatic Copying Device

SUMACO

Please send 10p for Luna Lathe Literature ☐
Please send 50p for Full Sumaco Range Catalogue ☐

Name _____
Address _____
Tel _____

Post to Sumaco Ltd Dept (L1)
Newcombe St. Elland W. Yorks. Tel. (0422) 75491/2
FREE GIFT SENT WITH EVERY FULL SUMACO RANGE

Post to Sumaco Ltd Dept ( )
Newcombe St. Elland W. Yorks. Tel. (0422) 75491/2

162

Prices quoted are those prevailing at press date and are subject to alteration due to economic conditions.

Woodworker, March 1980

Alan Holtham

Woodturner

Woodturner Supplier

Light Woodworking Machinery Specialist

THIS MONTH SPECIAL OFFER!

THE NEW MkII
Bench and
Pedestal Drilling

Machines with 7 ★ Features . . .

£220 Delivered

★ Crank handle operated rack and pinion rise and fall table

★ ''Dial in'' Depth stop

★ No volt release overload protection, P6 starter

★ Simple lever belt release for speed change. 5 speeds

**New Mk.II AJBD16 ⁵⁄₈''
bench drilling machine
with star features**

★ Swivelling and tilting table

★ Externally fan-cooled motor

★ ⁵⁄₈'' capacity chuck, standard

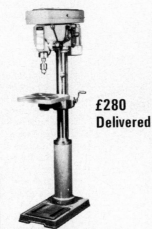

£280 Delivered

The New Mk.II AJPD.16 ⁵⁄₈'' Pedestal Drilling Machine

*We are also Main Stockists for:
CORONET, ARUNDEL, ELU,
DEWALT, SCHEPPACH,
SUSEMIHL, ZINKEN, BOSCH,
TREND router cutters and CUT
sawblades. Please write or call
for details of any machines
of interest.*

**THE OLD STORES TURNERY
WISTASTON ROAD
WILLASTON
NANTWICH
CHESHIRE**

Tel: CREWE 67010

SEND FOR **Cost Cutting** TUNGSTEN CARBIDE TIPPED **RAZEDGE SAWS** *Patented*

- ● 'TC' tipped blades stay sharper longer than steel plate saws.
- ● Razedge 'TC' tipped blades have PTFE anti-friction coating.
- ● More versatile—no need to change blades with materials.

Razedge blades give a fast, super finish cut on all usual materials and last up to 200 times the life of a plate saw. They rip and cross cut soft and hardwoods, chipboard, blockboard, plys. They cut laminated plastics, perspex, cork, asbestos, etc. A regrind service is available.

Money Back Guarantee!

ELLIS SAWS,
CANAL STREET, LONG EATON,
NOTTS. NG10 4GA. Tel: LE 5850

	A2 General Purpose Hand and Bench Machines Wood and Boards		B3 General Purpose Superior Natural Wood Laminate and Ply		C4 Super Cut Hand Tools Laminated Boards, Plastics Ply	
Dia.	Teeth	£ p	Teeth	£ p	Teeth	£ p
5"	12	12.00	20	17.15	30	20.35
6"	14	13.55	24	19.15	36	22.20
7"	14	14.90	28	21.65	42	25.60
8"	16	17.05	32	24.75	48	30.25
9"	18	18.80	36	26.30	54	32.70
10"	20	19.95	40	28.95	60	35.95

Quality Industrial Saws at Discount Price
Prices inclusive of V.A.T. and Packing & Postage

ELLIS SAWS, Canal Street, Long Eaton, Notts. NG10 4GA. Tel: Long Eaton 5850.

Please send ....Saw Blades ....diameter

................teeth. Bore size ....

I enclose cheque/Postal Order for £....

Send SAE for full list of T.C.T. Circular saws and standard bandsaws.
WW

SUPPLIERS OF ALL TYPES OF WOODWORKING EQUIPMENT

Stockists of ELU and Bosch Tools and complete range of fixings

ELU Orbital Sander MVS 93

*MOF 96
The Professional Plunging Router MOF 96 a Router and Moulder complete in two cartons.*

Opening hours:
Mon-Fri: 8.00-6.00
p.m. Sat: 9.00 a.m.-
12.00

ELU Jig saw ST142 with tilting base and orbit action.

ELU Portable Circular Saws MH 155 and MH 182

24 hour service: free delivery to all areas: ample car parking.

THE R.M. TOOL AND FIXING CO. LTD.

17 HOLLYBUSH LANE, PENN, WOLVERHAMPTON.
Telephone: 37015

AN AID TO MAKING THE SECRET MITRE DOVETAIL JOINT

by R. W. Grant DLC FRSA MSIAD

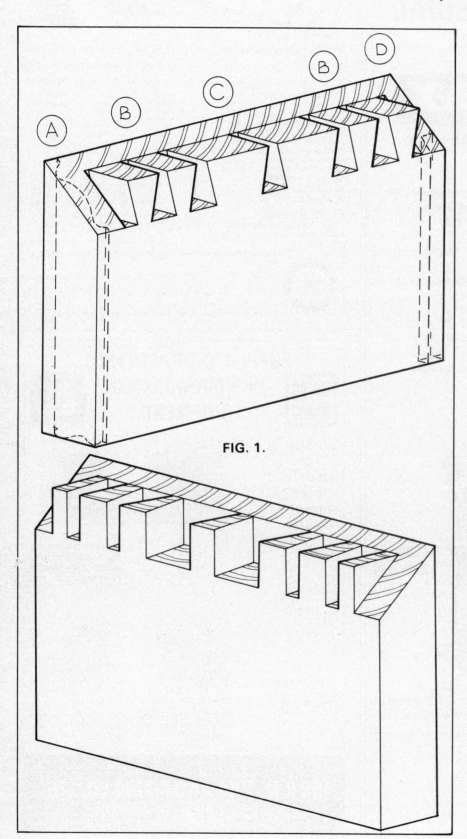

FIG. 1.

The secret mitre dovetail is often held to be the supreme test of cabinet making skill because of the need to cut not only an accurate set of dovetails but to fit a mitre in combination as well.

Recent articles in WOODWORKER have referred to secret mitre dovetails and the object here is to give further information on the practice to be followed on large carcassing jobs. There is also a description of a technique of forming the mitres with the aid of a side rebate plane which instantly removes much of the bogey of making the joint.

When making corner joints in wide boards there is always the tendency of the boards to curl across their width, unless quarter-sawn stock can be obtained. To allow for this possible movement two baby dovetails (Fig. 1(B)), are placed as near the extremities of the board as is possible. This increases the gluing area at these vulnerable points.

The central section (Fig. 1 (C)) may be more widely spaced out. Extra wide mitres may have to be provided (Fig. 1(A) and (D)) to allow for face moulding and grooves and rebates for the fitting of a back. Again, the practice of increasing the gluing area as near as possible to these areas will prevent the face mitres from opening.

Most difficult part of the secret mitre dovetail joint is found in the final fitting of the mitres. Fig. 2 shows a method that the author has found to be totally effective. It should be noted that the assembly has been reversed against the bench and supplementary G-cramps to pinch the pieces together omitted for reasons of clarity. In actual practice it will be found best to work 'overhand' with the mitres sloping away from the body.

A sound piece of stock, larger than the joint, should accurately be shot at 45° along one edge and then cramped to the joint. This ensures that the mitre lines register. Much of the mitred lap can be removed with a chisel and the final trimming can be achieved by the use of a side rebate plane as shown. (Both Record Ridgway and Stanley Tools make such a plane). With the use of this tool, unlike the shoulder plane often employed, no damage will occur to the guide piece, particularly if the non-cutting blade is withdrawn.

While the assembly is still in position the face mitres can be trimmed. At first sight the method indicated would seem literally to be against the grain, but in practice the results obtained are excellent. The knack is to have a wide, razor-sharp chisel approaching the work at a skew angle while exerting heavy pressure with the hand at the point arrowed in Fig. 2, where the back of the chisel is bearing on the guide piece.

Light paring cuts should only be attempted and with the more open-grained woods a scrap piece temporarily jammed in the socket next to the mitre will prevent any breaking-out.

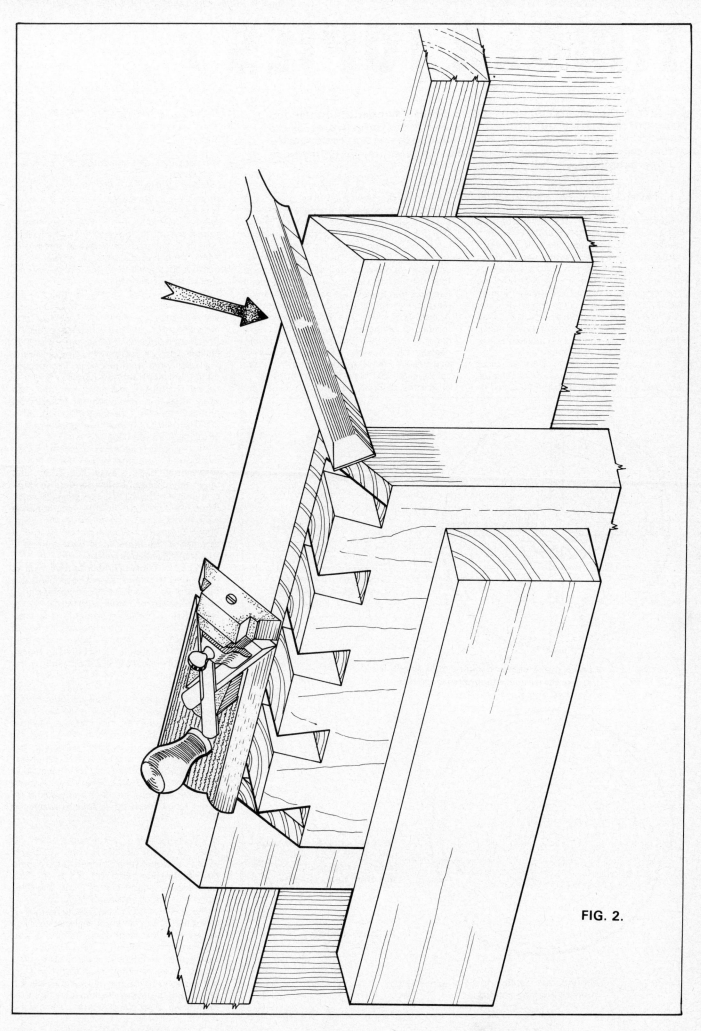

FIG. 2.

TIMBER TOPICS 7

Here W.H. Brown FIWSc gives details of the drying method used in experiments carried out in the US on wood sections (round discs) sawn from logs of Douglas fir. He concludes that it would be worth-while following the lines set out by the experiments since they have proved satisfactory.

In Timber Topics 6 (WOODWORKER for January 1980 pages 22-3), we referred to experimental work on the drying of tree discs, carried out in the US at the University of Wisconsin. The objective was to find a satisfactory way of drying wood discs without use of a kiln, in such a way as to prevent or reduce the tendency for cracking and splitting to occur, a difficult thing to achieve normally. We have already described and explained the technical reasons for this type of material to develop defects and now refer to the actual method of drying used in the experiments.

The wood sections used were round discs sawn from logs of Douglas fir *(Pseudotsuga menziesii)* 1 ft (30cm) in diameter and 1 in. (25mm) thick. The wood was green and therefore very wet. The drying was carried out at room temperature, ie below 100°F (38°C) but with fairly well-controlled relative humidity, in three phases, as follows:

Phase 1 Because green wood cross-sections are under strong tangential tension near the pith due to growth stresses, these had to be minimised. This was done by taping plastics film over the inner one-third of the disc on both sides, in order to prevent the formation of heart checks if this were possible. The outer portion of the disc especially the sapwood, needed to be dried rapidly so the air relative humidity (R.H.) was selected at 65%. The duration of phase 1 was three days at the end of which time the sapwood had dried to 30% moisture content (m.c.).

Phase 2 The plastics film was now removed from the samples and all the wood was exposed to ambient air containing 75% relative humidity (R.H.). These conditions gave moderate drying conditions which were held for a further three days at the end of which time the m.c. of both sapwood and heartwood was down to 25%. No heart checks had developed.

Phase 3 In this final stage differential shrinkage stresses increase substantially, so surface stresses must be kept low and reduced to zero as the wood approaches its final m.c. In phase 3 the discs were placed in plastics bags perforated with tiny openings. The bags were then placed in a room containing only 40% relative humidity.

Under these conditions the moisture evaporated from the wood and provided an atmosphere within the bags of around 80 to 90% R.H., with only small amounts of vapour escaping from the bags.

As drying proceeded less moisture was evaporated from the discs, the humidity within the bags slowly decreased and approached equilibrium with the surrounding air. Drying was complete (8% m.c.) when the moisture in the wood reached equilibrium with the humidity in the room. Phase 3 took four weeks and at the end of this period the dried wood was practically free from objectional defect.

Under laboratory conditions proper control of the air R.H., would present no problem, but for the private person with limited facilities this could prove rather difficult at times. Nevertheless, these experiments could form a sound basis for simple drying: the key to success revolves around a few aspects only.

As we have mentioned in previous Topics, temperature is not as important when drying wood as is air R.H. In phase 1 the R.H. was 65% and with a wide range of room temperatures this equals an equilibrium m.c. for wood of around 12%, ie if the wood was left in that air for long enough. In the experiment, phase 1 took only three days for the green wood, and in particular the sapwood, to dry to 30% m.c. This suggests the temperature was fairly high because at low temperature moisture would be removed more slowly from the wood and would have taken longer than three days to reach the 30% m.c. value.

The same remarks on time apply to phase 2 where 75% R.H. was used and which at normal room temperatures equals an equilibrium m.c. of 15%. In the experiments, at the end of phase 2 all the wood was dry to a value of 25% m.c.

Phase 3 provides a very simple method of controlled drying in the sense that if the air of the room has R.H. of 40% the equilibrium m.c. for wood is roughly 7 to 8%. Therefore, if within the bag there is R.H. of 80 or 90% (which equals an EMC for wood of 16 to 21%) but the holes in the bag allow a slow escape of vapour, then provided the movement of moisture is steady and progressive, and the

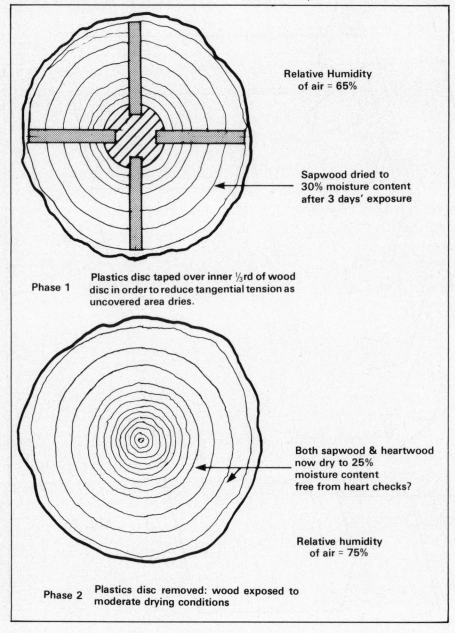

Relative Humidity of air = 65%

Sapwood dried to 30% moisture content after 3 days' exposure

Phase 1 Plastics disc taped over inner ⅓rd of wood disc in order to reduce tangential tension as uncovered area dries.

Both sapwood & heartwood now dry to 25% moisture content free from heart checks?

Relative humidity of air = 75%

Phase 2 Plastics disc removed: wood exposed to moderate drying conditions

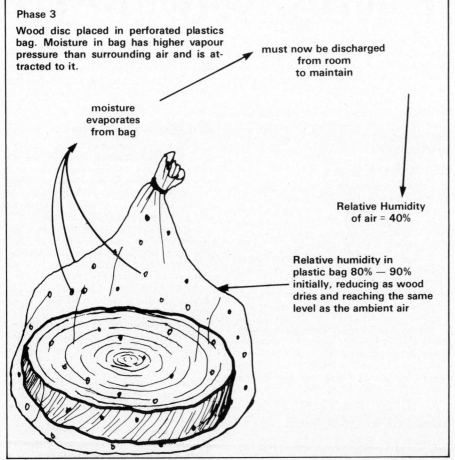

Phase 3

Wood disc placed in perforated plastics bag. Moisture in bag has higher vapour pressure than surrounding air and is attracted to it.

moisture evaporates from bag

must now be discharged from room to maintain

Relative Humidity of air = 40%

Relative humidity in plastic bag 80% — 90% initially, reducing as wood dries and reaching the same level as the ambient air

vapour is discharged from the surrounding air so as to maintain the 40% R.H. all the time, then the wood should dry slowly and carefully.

Time is an essential element. If softwood or low-density hardwood discs are dried too slowly in phases 1 and 2, then blue sapstain could occur. Unless the m.c. level of around 25% is reached uniformly, at the end of phase 2 there is a distinct possibility of surface mould forming on the wood in the high humidity conditions of phase 3, particularly with hardwoods like oak and beech. Although these furry moulds are harmless and can be brushed off the dry wood, they do tend to slow down evaporation by blocking air spaces; and since evaporation in this experiment depended upon perforations in the plastics bag, obviously they must be able to breathe.

Reverting to phase 1, the essential aspect here was to slow down the drying in the centre of each disc while the outer two-thirds dried rapidly. For this the centres were covered with the plastics film. There were alternative ways of regulating the drying: by coating each side of the discs with paraffin wax, using a single coat for the outer third of the diameter, two coats for the next third, and three coats for the centre third, but this created problems of removal later.

We preferred the alternative of liberally brushing the centre portion of the discs with water, particularly for the person wishing to dry a relatively few sections. By wetting each piece in the centre at regular intervals closer examination is possible and any signs of heart checks developing can be spotted and a greater effort made to reduce the tendency. Unless tangential tension near the pith is minimal then defects in the form of splits and cracks can become apparent later on.

As we have said, temperature is not too important but, obviously a high temperature will dry wood more rapidly if the R.H. remains the same. Quite often high temperature used to dry wood increases the R.H. and therefore slows the drying until the excess moisture is vented off. The biggest problem is in trying to control R.H. over several days or weeks. During the period of March to late September in Britain it would be practical to carry out phases 1 and 2 in the open air, provided there was some top cover to give a little shelter from rain, but which could be removed if a shower was likely to prove helpful.

A relative R.H. of 40% is a bit of a tall order in most rooms and is more likely to be around 50%. This would be alright and would permit the wood in the bags to dry down to about 10% m.c. but there would be rather less R.H. created within the bags which might be too drastic.

However, it would be worthwhile following the lines set out by the experiments since they have proved satisfactory.

The appeal of fine furniture

Most people at some time or other, aspire to make something worthwhile from wood. Quite often, and perhaps due to lack of suitable tools, the desire to progress beyond simple forms of carpentry has had to be satisfied by making something from veneered chipboard, already cut to size and lipped on the edges, fixed together by means of patent jointing devices.

There is, of course, nothing wrong with this but as a rule these materials are engineered so as to enable simple units to be erected with a minimum of fuss and bother and little imagination is needed: frequently, enthusiasm for woodworking is confined to getting the job finished over a wet weekend.

Few people, however, can resist the appeal of fine furniture made from exotic wood and in lots of cases where a successful project has been produced from man-made materials, the appetite has been whetted and there is an urge to try one's hand at something ambitious. The problem is that suitable guidance on how to proceed is not readily forthcoming unless it is in the form of a well-illustrated book that can be kept for reference.

Such a book has been published recently, written by an amateur for amateurs, on the subject of furniture making. David Johnston who wrote the book, is an ardent timber man,

combining a professional interest in the proper growth of trees with the spare-time occupation of furniture maker to himself, a pursuit that has been aptly justified when one considers the illustrated examples of his work. There is an example, for instance, of a small occasional table carried out in yew and inlaid with mahogany. It does not require much imagination to visualise the slow, careful, methodical fashioning of the wood and finally the pleasure of regarding the finished article.

In this book, the author has quite adequately covered the various aspects of selecting suitable wood, preparing it for use, choosing the right tools, how to use them and how to sharpen and set them. He has provided chapters on the basic principles of constructing carcases, doors, drawers and plinths and passes on many tips that result from his personal methods and techniques. There is even a chapter on how to correct mistakes which, the author quite rightly contends, frequently arise from the sporadic working time available to the true amateur, and not always because of lack of expertise.

The Craft of Furniture Making (David Johnston), is published by B. T. Batsford Ltd, 4 Fitzhardinge Street, London W1H 0AH, at £5.95 in hardback. It is a book which will offer much encouragement to everyone who likes wood and likes making things from wood.   **W.H.B.**

Sale of tools

At the Grove House hotel in Norwich on 15 April, Tyrone R. Roberts will conduct a sale of more than 650 lots of tools including a collection of British metal planes by Spiers of Ayr, Norris of London and other noted makers such as Kimberley, Slater, Miller, Preston, Mathieson, Holland and Stanley, as well as craftsman-made examples. A Howkins A1 gunmetal patent plough complete with fences, cutters and a dovetailing arrangement is also included.

In the sale will be a varied selection of brass and ebony-type braces, an 18th century bitstock complete with 12 bits and 18th century wooden planes including nine hollows and rounds from the same set by I. Cogdell who started his business in 1750.

Carving and turning tools by Addis, Holtzapffel, Herring Bros, saws by Diston and Atkins as well as quality tools, watchmakers' equipment, engravers' and other craftsman tools are among the lots to be offered.

The illustrated catalogue costs £1.50 (including postage) from Tyrone R. Roberts, La Corbiere, Watton Road, Swaffham, Norfolk. There are special facilities for postal bidders.

Guild of Woodworkers

Residential courses

Micklethwaite is a village on the edge of the Yorkshire dales countryside. It has an early 19th century textile mill which is being restored to provide space for a small group of craftsmen who will combine the making of high-quality craftwork with the teaching of crafts and design to residential groups.

Robert and Jan Ellwood are established in the mill and offer workshop courses in woodturning, carving and furniture making as well as clock making and the construction of portative and positive organs.

Courses during 1980 (the Ellwood's sixth season) cover either a week, weekend or mid-week (Monday to Thursday) and the fees are respectively £82, £40 and £55; an intensive woodturning course of two days is £80 with the number of students on this course limited to three. The other courses are limited to eight to 10 adults so that individual tuition can be given. Fees cover accommodation, meals, tuition and use of workshop facilities.

Accomodation is on two floors in the former mill owner's house which has been modernised; there are single, double and twin-bedded rooms all with h&c. Booklet giving full details is available from Micklethwaite Studio Workshops, Holroyd Mill, Beck Road, Micklethwaite, Bingley, West Yorks.

Using the bank

Trading craftsmen members in particular may be interested in three leaflets issued by Williams & Glyn's Bank Ltd under the general title of *Good business from the bank.*

Leaflet no. 4 is on the subject of equipment leasing (did you know this was practised in the Middle East some 5,000 years ago?); no. 5 deals with loans for small businesses; and no. 6 covers sales finance and factoring.

Copies of the leaflets can be had from Williams & Glyn's branches or from the bank's marketing department at New London Bridge House, 25 London Bridge Street, London SE1 9SX.

Operating lift trucks

Those who operate — or who are responsible for operating — lift trucks (LTs) will find useful information in a booklet titled *Safety in working with lift trucks* issued by the Health & Safety Executive and published by HMSO at £1.

Though dealing mainly with conventional reach and counter-balanced trucks equipped with forks, special LTs such as sideloaders (extensively used in timber handling) and rough-terrain LTs are mentioned in the booklet.

The important thing is that truck operators should be properly trained to meet the particular conditions and nature of the work, and that proper systems of work (eg procedures for training, for traffic and pedestrian movements, for control and maintenance of trucks) should be adopted.

Local help for small firms

Coventry chamber of commerce and the city council are to establish a centre of innovation. It will concentrate on helping one-man and other small businesses either to start or to expand. This initiative is believed to be the first of its kind and has been put on a two-year experimental basis. The chamber of commerce will provide offices and staff and the city council is initially allocating £8,000.

Safety with chainsaws

Those who use chainsaws regularly should remember that if the saws are not fitted with anti-vibration mountings it is important to maintain good blood circulation to the hands. Sufficient clothing to keep the operative warm, and dry gloves designed for use with chainsaws should be worn.

Such precautions are necessary to guard against vibration-induced white finger (vwf), a condition which is less common today than formerly. Indeed, a sample survey by the Forestry Commission of chainsaw users showed a reduction in operatives affected by varying degrees of vwf from 87% in 1970 to 50% in 1976.

The vibrations of a chainsaw are absorbed mainly by the tissue of the hand and wrist, resulting in distortion of the blood supply, leading to loss of sensation in the fingers. The symptoms may be either pins-and-needles or varying degrees of blanching of the fingers, especially in cold conditions. This can extend to total loss of use of the fingers.

This warning is given in *Health & Safety (Agriculture) 1977* published by the Health & Safety Executive, 25 Chapel Street, London NW1 4DT, and available from HM Stationery Office at £1.25 plus postage.

FURNITURE

Buildings and equipment that can be seen today in such places as Old Chatham Shaker museum, New York; Hancock Shaker village, Pittsfield, Mass; and Canterbury Shaker village, New Hampshire, all possess a uniformity in standards of workmanship, utility of design and painstaking perfection for purpose. These ideals of purity and simplicity evolved a distinct style of furniture. Living in communal buildings necessitated furniture for large numbers of people, but the Shakers managed to avoid the stereotyped design and finish that makes the institutional equipment of the machine age so ugly.

The rooms of their buildings were light, airy and functional. There were large built-in cupboards for orderliness, narrow-framed windows for maximum light, uniquely designed woodstoves for maximum efficiency of heat; and everywhere, even in corridors, horizontal peg boards on the walls to hang anything from furniture to clothes to baskets to mirrors.

Corridors and stairways, unlike most contemporary buildings of the era, were wide and well-lit by borrowed natural light. Trestle tables, some as much as 20ft long, were built with a central vertical board of some 9in. in depth for the underframing and just two trestles, one at either end. Thus there was abundant knee room and provision for storage of chairs or benches when not in use. The chairs often had low backs, stick or single slat, so that they, too, could be stored away under the tables, or hung on the pegboards around the walls for cleaning purposes. Size of wood used in the construction of the furniture was scaled down for lightness. Shaker full-sized rocking chairs, for instance, weighed under 10lb. All ornamentation was discarded as superfluous, and the earlier heavy colonial furniture was refined and simplified.

The range of products made in wood by the Shakers was enormous. Besides tables, chairs and cupboards, either built-in or free-standing, they designed or invented all manner of items neccessary for their many activities. Pedestal tables for candle stands, or with a raised lip on the tops, with one scalloped exit in the rim for counting seeds and packing them in their garden seed industry. Sewing tables with a drawer at either end so that two sisters could use one table together for their work. Step-stools for reaching cupboards. Firewood boxes to stand near wood stoves, with small compartments incorporated for kindling wood. Oval-lidded boxes made with thin bands of maple on wooden formers, so that all boxes could be duplicated. Woven wooden splint baskets, again made on formers. Looms and original wool winders for the weaving shops. Benches and lathes for the cabinet shops. Long counters and cupboards for sewing and cutting tables in the sewing shops, and ironing tables for the same.

Heading picture reproduced by permission of The American Museum in Britain, Bath. *(Photo: Derek Balmer).*

If a need arose for a particular design to fulfill a purpose in order to increase or ease production, the Shakers evolved a unique and specialised solution to the problem.

Material used was wood grown within the community. The Shakers were shrewd in their choice of sites, making sure they had abundant timber for their needs, and water power for the machines they invented for the conversion of the timber. They were among the first users of the circular saw in America and devised t&g machinery and planers powered by water turbines. Local timbers in New England were pine, maple, poplar, birch, hickory, ash, cherry and butternut. In the western communities in Ohio and Kentucky walnut was available. Woven seats on chairs were of hickory or ash splint, cane, rush and woven tapes. The latter became distinctive of Shaker chairs.

Visitors and neighbours of the communities naturally sought to purchase items of furniture. Elder Robert Wagan of the New Lebanon (NY) community established a thriving business with the 'outside' world, especially for chairs. At the Philadelphia centennial exhibition of 1876 the Shaker products of R. M. Wagan & Co were honoured with a medal and diploma for their 'strength, sprightliness and modest beauty'.

As the numbers in the communities began to decline items of furniture began to disappear or were sold as they were no longer required. The furniture would probably have vanished into obscurity had it not been for the work of Edward Deming Andrews and his wife, Faith, who in the 1930s, began an exhaustive search into the life and times of the Shakers. The Andrews amassed a vast collection of Shaker furniture and artifacts, thereby saving much of the culture from oblivion.

During the last 20 years there has been a resurgence of demand for original Shaker furniture, to such an extent that earlier this year in America, a chair of scroll-arm, slat-back design dating around 1860 realised a price equivalent to £800. A settee, with tape woven back and seat, one of only four known to be in existence, sold for the equivalent of £3,250.

A number of craftsmen in New England today have made a success of reproducing Shaker furniture: Alejandro de la Cruz, David and Susan Margonelli, Joel Seaman, North Family Joiners, Thomas Moser, to name a few. As befitting the Shaker ideals these craftsmen also go on to create new designs in the Shaker idiom. Which goes to show that even in today's materialistic society, we appreciate the qualities and craftsmanship engendered in the furniture made by this monastic sect over 100 years ago.

In Britain the American Museum at Bath has a beautiful collection of Shaker furniture and artifacts that embody the Shaker philosophy of 'Hands to work and hearts to God'.

Pageant of the Horse

This year's Pageant of the Horse organised by South Yorks CC will be on Sunday, 20 April at Doncaster racecourse. The Model Horse-Drawn Vehicles Club has again been invited to participate in the event. Hon secretary John Pearce reports in the club's *Newsletter no. 42* (Nov-Dec 1979) that the same pattern as in previous years will be followed, ie a large display area with trestle tables for models.

The pageant is a one-day affair usually attracting around 80,000 visitors and the model horse-drawn vehicles display is an exhibition, not a competition, though the SYCC presents each exhibitor with a commemorative plaque. There is no entrance charge and no limit on the number of models each exhibitor can enter.

Club members wishing to take part should get in touch with Mr Pearce at 4 Brentlea Crescent, Higher Heysham LA3 2BT, as soon as possible please.

Forthcoming exhibitions and congresses

America

May 5-9 International Research Group on Wood Preservation. AGM. At North Carolina State University, Raleigh, further details from IRG Secretariat, Drotting Kristinas väg 47C, S-11428, Stockholm.

Australia

April 15-17 FIME 1980. Forest Industries Machinery Exposition. The 1980 FIME will be the largest in-forest demonstration in the world. At Myrtleford, Victoria. Hardwood and softwood harvesting, saw milling, processing and forestry equipment will be displayed and demonstrated.

Italy

May 15-21 INTERBIMAL '80. The biennial international exhibition for woodworking machinery and tools from forest to manufactured product. At Milan Fair Grounds. Further details from Via Varesina 76, Milan 20156, Italy.

South Africa

February 18-23 Italian Machinery Exhibition. The first major exhibition of Italian industrial machinery for woodworking packaging and other industries. At Milner Park Showgrounds, Johannesburg.

College exhibition

Shrewsbury Technical College exhibition of work will be from 14-26 June.

Instrument making course

John Storrs, Hunston, Chichester, Sussex PO20 6NR (phone (0243) 789605) hopes to run two courses in early keyboard instrument making: Friday 11 to Monday 25 April for spinet and clavichord making and Friday 4 to Monday 21 July for harpsichord making.

West Dean music course

An extended nine day course open to all interested in musical instrument technology will be held at West Dean College from 3-12 April. For further details write to Peter Sarginson, West Dean College, West Dean, Chichester, W Sussex PO18 0QZ.

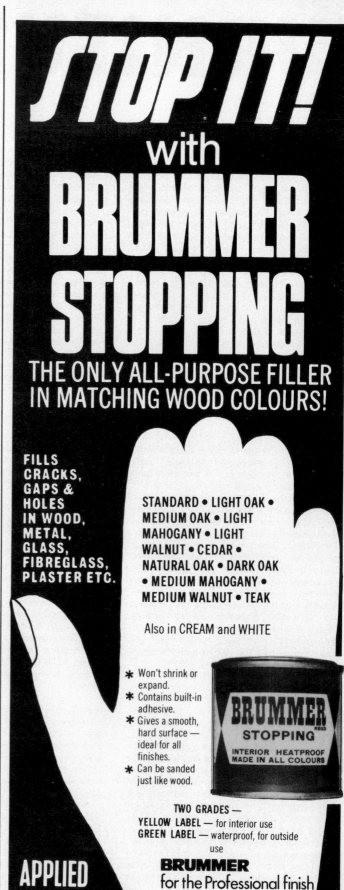
Prices quoted are those prevailing at press date and are subject to alteration due to economic conditions.

PROTECTIVE GARMENTS

A COMPLETE RANGE FOR ALL PRACTICAL PURPOSES

- Direct from manufacturer to Education and Industry
- 7 Day dispatch from receipt of order
- All garments fully guaranteed
- Prices firm for 12 months from January 1st
- The best value for money

for Brochure and Price List contact:

MOORFIELD
of LANCASHIRE

PERSEVERENCE MILL
OLIVE LANE DARWEN
LANCASHIRE BB3 3DS
TEL. 0254 - 74131-2-3

DOWELLING HELPFUL HINTS

Dowelled joints are firm and strong if made correctly. Here Charles D. Cliffe advises on getting good results.

Dowelled joints are made by drilling holes in line at right angles to the faces to be joined and fitting wooden pins into these holes. The resulting joint is firm and strong if made correctly. If the holes are not accurately bored or the dowels are slack the joint will soon fail.

Dowel rods are usually made of beech and are obtainable in various sizes. As a general guide the size of dowel to be used is usually half the thickness of the wood to be joined. Thus if two pieces ¾ in. thick are to be joined use ⅜ in. dowels.

Marking-out for dowelling must be accurate; it may be done in a variety of ways. If the edges of two boards are to be dowelled together it is first necessary to ensure that the two surfaces fit properly. Put the two boards back to back and clamp them together in the vice. Set a marking gauge to half the board's thickness and, working from the two outer face sides, gauge a line down the

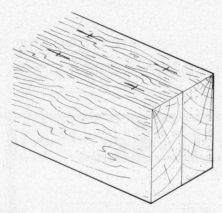

Fig. 1   Marking dowel holes in butt joint.

centre of both boards. Measure off the positions for the dowels at equally spaced intervals and square these marks across both edges. The dowel holes are drilled where the lines cross (Fig. 1).

Sometimes when a job is partly made-up it is not possible to mark the two edges together. In these cases ordinary pins, spaced at the required intervals, are laid along the halfway gauge line as in Fig. 2. The two edges are offered together and when correctly positioned are tapped with a mallet so that the impression of the pinhead is made half in each edge. Boring takes place at these marks.

Fig. 3   Dowel pop and method of use.

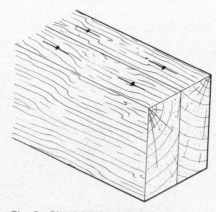

Fig. 2   Pins laid along halfway line.

A third method of marking out can be effected by using dowel pops (Fig. 3). These are made from brass and come in various sizes. Dowel holes are bored where required and the pops inserted in the holes so that their flanges seat on the edge of the work. Correctly position the mating piece of wood and tap the two pieces together so that the points of the pops mark the edge and show where to bore the dowel holes.

If a number of light doors such as for sideboards or cupboards are to be made, the work of marking out can be greatly reduced by means of a template as shown in Fig. 4. The template is made the same width as the rails and small holes are drilled in the template tongue at the precise centre of the dowel holes. Place the template over the end of the rail as in Fig. 5 (a) and with a scriber inserted through the holes in the tongue mark the positions for boring. The template tongue is then placed level with the end mark of the stile as in Fig. 5(b) and the scriber again used to mark for boring.

Before boring the dowel holes see that the bit is sharp. Twist bits are used in preference to centre bits because they drill true holes.

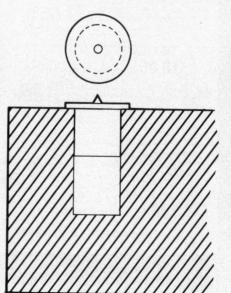

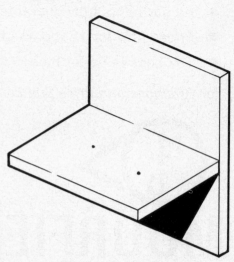

Fig. 4   Template for making dowel holes.

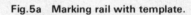

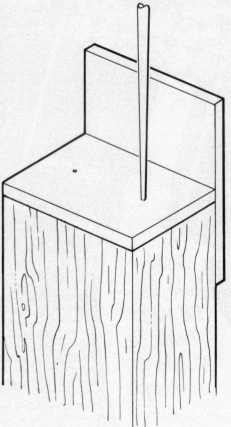

Fig.5a   Marking rail with template.

Centre bits are inclined to wander. It is essential to keep the bit at 90° to the surface otherwise a bad joint will result. Checking the direction of the bit with a trysquare helps in this respect. Fig. 6(a) shows the two holes correctly bored as to direction and depth so that the dowel is at maximum efficiency.

At (b) one hole is slightly out of 90° and the dowel is distorted, thereby weakening the joint. In (c) although the dowel is straight it will have to be bent to persuade it to enter and at (d) the holes are misaligned and will have to be plugged and rebored.

All the dowel holes should be bored to the same depth, namely slightly over half the length of the dowel. For 2in. dowels the holes should be 1⅛in. deep. If the holes are not deep enough the dowel will 'bottom' and keep the joint apart. Boring to the correct depth can be achieved in several ways. Counting the number of turns of the brace gives an approximate depth but sticking a piece of tape the correct distance from the bit's cutters is more reliable. A cylindrical piece of hardwood drilled down the middle and fitted with a grub screw is better as is a wooden depth gauge (Fig. 7).

To assist in assembling the joint the ends of the dowels should be slightly pointed. A special dowel sharpener which fits into a brace can be bought if a large quantity have to be shaped. A saw kerf should be cut the length of the dowel to let surplus glue escape. If this is not done the dowel will act like a piston in a cylinder and may prevent the joint from meeting properly. The tops of the holes should be slightly countersunk as this helps the joint to come together as well as forming a reservoir for surplus glue. Fig. 8 shows a joint ready for assembly.

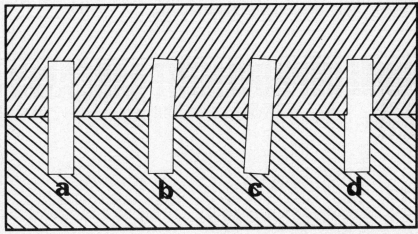

Fig. 5b   Marking stile with template.

Fig. 7   Wooden depth gauges.

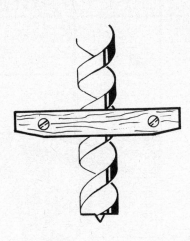

Fig. 6   (a) Correct dowelling; b, c and d are dowelling faults.

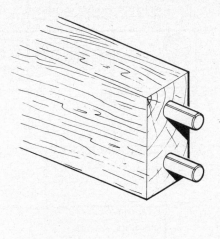

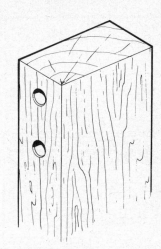

Fig. 8   Joint ready for assembly.

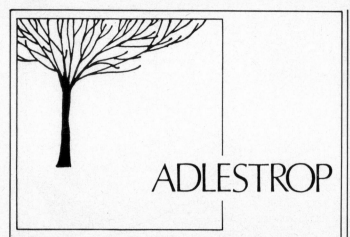

ADLESTROP

NEW FURNITURE WORKSHOP TO HOLD EXHIBITION AT SCOTTISH DESIGN CENTRE

Adlestrop is the name of the workshop. It comprises just four young men who qualified at the John Makepeace School for Craftsmen in Wood, in Dorset, and who now have their workshop at 8 Bernard Terrace, Edinburgh.

The exhibition which runs from 26 February to 15 March, at Scottish Design Centre, 72 St Vincent St, Glasgow (gallery opening times 9.30-5.30 Monday to Friday, 9.00-5.00 Saturdays), features a selection of recent work, and the first designs to be realised by the four as a Scottish workshop. These consist of specially commissioned individual pieces and also examples of contract work designed for specific settings.

Prices quoted are those prevailing at press date and are subject to alteration due to economic conditions.

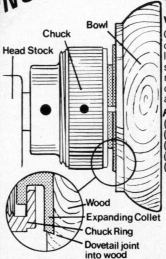

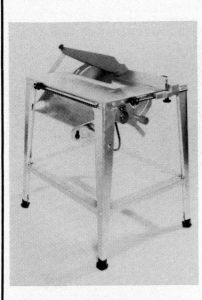

The Child Coil Grip Chuck

A COMBINATION CHUCK FOR HAND WOODTURNERS   (copied but not improved on)   Patented

COIL GRIP ASSEMBLY

This unique chuck is the outcome of many years experience by a professional woodturner and teacher, and the patented coil grip method together with the many extra modes of operation safely and neatly overcome the chucking problems encountered by amateur and professional turners. The coil grip, supplied ONLY WITH THIS CHUCK, together with the large (4½") diameter heavy duty body offers unbeatable strength and rigidity for gripping end grain work of ANY size. It grips by compression on the outside of the work so there is no danger of splitting the wood by excessive outward pressure. It holds staved work safely. An almost limitless variety of home-made wooden adaptors can be made which will grip any shape or size of work, internally, externally, dovetail grip, plain grip, or as required. The coil grip feature makes this chuck by far the most versatile of its kind. Made for most lathes (state model) £30.00 post free.

WOODTURNERS' SPECIALIST SUPPLIER

The most comprehensive range of tools available. The new ROY CHILD parting tool. Chucks, centres, fittings, drills. Flexicramps. Many types and sizes glass inserts, barometers, hygrometers, thermometers, eggtimers, hourglasses, condiment liners, 160 circular tile patterns, lighters, pens, flower vase tubes, peppermills, STAINLESS saltmills, knives, clocks, pencil sharpeners, silver-plate salt and pepper tops. Abrasives, waxes, finishes. Speed-n-Eze, Rustings. WOOD for turning. MYFORD agents. ROY CHILD pyrography machines. Post Office Parcel Contract for most quick and direct delivery service. Send S.A.E. for catalogue, or FREE to overseas enquirers. We EXPORT worldwide.

WOODTURNING AND FINISHING

Two-day intensive course and personal tuition at 17th century Essex-Suffolk farmhouse. Fully equipped workshops. Maximum of two guests for any one course.

PETER CHILD

THE WOODTURNER CRAFTSMAN
The Old Hyde, Little Yeldham, Halstead, Essex. Tel. Gt. Yeldham (0787) 237291

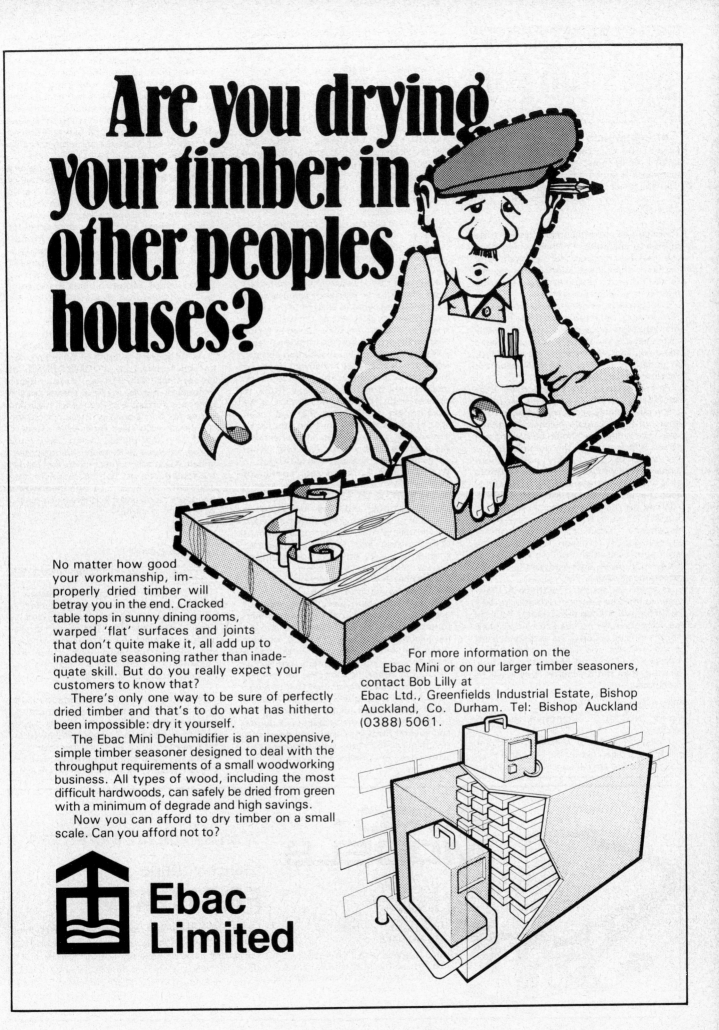

Are you drying your timber in other peoples houses?

No matter how good your workmanship, improperly dried timber will betray you in the end. Cracked table tops in sunny dining rooms, warped 'flat' surfaces and joints that don't quite make it, all add up to inadequate seasoning rather than inadequate skill. But do you really expect your customers to know that?

There's only one way to be sure of perfectly dried timber and that's to do what has hitherto been impossible: dry it yourself.

The Ebac Mini Dehumidifier is an inexpensive, simple timber seasoner designed to deal with the throughput requirements of a small woodworking business. All types of wood, including the most difficult hardwoods, can safely be dried from green with a minimum of degrade and high savings.

Now you can afford to dry timber on a small scale. Can you afford not to?

For more information on the Ebac Mini or on our larger timber seasoners, contact Bob Lilly at Ebac Ltd., Greenfields Industrial Estate, Bishop Auckland, Co. Durham. Tel: Bishop Auckland (0388) 5061.

Ebac Limited

QUESTION BOX

Turning speeds
From: L. Barker, Darlington, Co Durham
What are the most suitable speeds for a woodturning lathe from, say, 1in. up to 18in. diameter? Also should a variation be made for soft or hardwood? Thanking you in anticipation.

There can be no hard and fast speeds to be quoted for diameters in woodturning since the variable factors such as weight of material, thickness, balance and species render the provision of set speeds for given diameters quite impossible.

Charts are from time to time printed for this process, but it must always be borne in mind that figures given are intended purely as guide lines and that the speeds will need to be adjusted according to the workpiece in question. The value of such charts is therefore dubious.

Any workpiece on a woodturning lathe should be run fast enough to provide a clean cut without excess speed which can spoil the cut and create excessive frictional heat. The workpiece should be running at a speed which enables the operator to use his tools to cut cleanly and without unnecessary vibration. It follows therefore that once the operator has appreciated this fact, he will soon get into the habit of running his machine at speeds which suit his style of work. It would be wrong for an experienced turner or instructor to quote specific speeds for given diameters, since although these might well suit Mr Barker they could prove unsatisfactory for a less experienced turner.

It must be assumed with both these queries that the reference is to the cutting of timber rather than the scraping. If this is so, there is really no need to adjust speed for the cutting of softwood as distinct from hardwood or *vice versa*. If however a scraper or some form of scraping method, is used, then slightly higher speeds will be beneficial.

Work bench in iroko
From: Dr C. A. J. Brightman, Hampton Wick
I wish to make a workbench and am proposing to use iroko for the top rather than beech. Is there any reason why I should not use iroko? Do you know where I might obtain plans for making a wooden vice to go at the end of the bench? Since I already have pieces of iroko suitable for the frame of the bench I have considered buying a ready-made top; I should be grateful for your advice on this.

Recent issues of WOODWORKER have mentioned use of neatsfoot oil for use on oilstones. I can only purchase this oil in 1gal containers which will last me for many years. Will the oil keep so long? Should it be diluted with paraffin before use and can it be used on an Arkansas stone?

I have been recommended to use pearl glue rather than synthetic glue for joinery. Is this sound advice and could you tell me briefly how to prepare this (Scotch) glue? I am using an India oilstone for finishing the cutting edge of my tools but would it be worth investing in an Arkansas stone?

Taking your queries as follows: 1 Iroko has been found to be perfectly adequate for bench tops, proving in service to be stable and hardwearing. It has, by the way, found favour in laboratories for worktops in place of the more expensive and traditional teak. 2 We are not aware of any existing plans of wooden vices but they are straightforward in construction and reference could be made to existing examples as fitted to commercial benches. The only part of the construction of the vice that will need special tools will be the cutting of the lead screw and its housing in the outer jaw. Woodscrew sets are available from specialist tools dealers who advertise in WOODWORKER. These sets consist of taps and dies ranging in diameters from $\frac{1}{2}$ up to 2in. These are of a double Whitworth thread pattern and the operation is identical to the cutting of a thread in metal. A little tallow may be used as a lubricant while cutting and thereafter blacklead should be used on the thread during service. Hornbeam is reckoned to be the best timber for the lead screw while the jaws may be made of beech.

In regard to your query 3 we were not previously aware that ready-made bench tops are available but since you already have access to iroko (see 1 above), why not make the whole bench in this timber? 4 Neatsfoot oil is upheld by many traditionalists as the superfine lubricant for honing; but it should be remembered that in times gone by it was probably the only fine oil that craftsmen had access to. Modern thin machine oils are in many respects superior and several firms manufacture honing oils specifically for the woodworker (see references in previous issues of this magazine).

Neatsfoot oil is an organic substance and is much used in the leather-working trades. It should be obtainable from reputable saddlers in small quantities and should not require thinning. It is interesting to note that many modern craftsmen eschew the use of neatsfoot oil for honing, preferring to use water and paraffin when they want the stone to cut 'fast' and hydrocarbon oil when the action at the stone needs to be retarded.

On the subject of pearl glue (your query 5), this is only a specific form of animal or Scotch glue, being made up of small beads or pearls rather than in cake form and this makes the glue easier to prepare. However, modern glues specifically developed for joinery work are generally superior in quality to the old Scotch glue type. These are easier to apply (usually cold), often ready mixed, have a high resistance to mould and fungal attack, are impervious to moisture and have enhanced strength. But they are generally not reversible and hence Scotch glue still finds favour in veneering work where it is sometimes necessary to soften the glue bond with hot water or steam.

As to query 6 relating to oilstones, the natural stones (see WOODWORKER for November 1979) are much more expensive that the artificial stones but the latter are incapable of producing superfine edges to tools because of their comparative large grain size. Those who aspire to producing the highest-quality work must possess good-quality tools and equipment and an Arkansas stone could be included in the toolkit. It must be said, however, that excellent results can be obtained with a fine India stone and a leather strop dressed with crocus powder.

Elm and beetle
From: Dr M. H. K. Haggie, Shuknall, Hereford
I am at present making various pieces of furniture out of elm. Elm is suceptible to attack by furniture beetle and may well be already infected as it has been air-dried. Will it affect the final finish if I treat both exposed and hidden surfaces with colourless Cuprinol or Rentokil before staining and finally oil and wax finishing?

Before you decide the best treatment for your elm it would be appropriate to consider what the potential beetle hazard might be. Elm might be attacked by furniture beetle (*Anobium*) because this is a possibility with a great many hardwoods and softwoods, though elm is by no means

more susceptible. It is, however, susceptible to attack by powder post beetle. *(Lyctus)* which poses a rather different problem.

Lyctus beetle attack is more of a problem of stored timber in the sense that if the wood is kiln-dried prior to sale, the heat and humidity involved in the process tend not only to kill-off any grubs and sterilise any eggs that might be present but, furthermore, tend to deplete the starch content of the wood, this being the beetle's chief nutrient.

Accordingly, any *Lyctus*-susceptible timber seasoned in the open air runs the risk of infection although, of course, this is by no means automatic. Since *Lyctus* beetle attack is confined principally to those areas of wood containing most starch, ie the sapwood, and occasionally round ingrown knots, it is relatively simple to discard sapwood and to cut out knots during conversion into woodwork.

Largely, where *Lyctus* beetle is found in wood it has become infected from a common source such as a timber yard; by comparison furniture beetle more often attacks wood from other infected timber in a building, or from old dead tree stumps outside the home; and in that sense while furniture beetle will attack sapwood, it may not confine its attack to this.

Organic solvent-based unpigmented insecticidal fluids are very efficient in preventing or remedying attack by both *Lyctus* and *Anobium;* and generally they are said to be satisfactory for painting or varnishing over once the solvent base has evaporated, say, after 48hr.

In this type of use if light-coloured paint, for example, is applied too soon, unsightly oxidative stains are liable to occur under the paint; and we are wondering what sort of chemical reaction might occur in your wood when the pigments of your penetrating stain came in contact with the toxic chemicals in the insecticide.

We would suggest that if you prefer to apply the fluid as a safeguard, it would be advisable to take up the question of chemical reaction with the manufacturer. Otherwise cutting off all sapwood will reduce much of the potential liability to beetle attack.

Condensation problems
From: D. R. Chapman, Ashburton, Devon
I have a serious problem of condensation in my garage-workshop built in 1970 and not lined with felt and wiremesh as to the roof which is flat and of asbestos cement sheeting on 4 x 2in. purlins spanning 9ft. I have fixed 3in. thick Poron sheets between

the purlins (brush-treated with Protim) but this has not stopped condensation. Yet in my garden shed of 2 x 1in. studding covered in 6mm external grade marine ply and with roof similar to that of the garage, I do not have the problem. Any advice will be welcome.

Your problem of condensation is concerned initially with particular atmospheric conditions, eg warm, muggy weather following rapidly after a frost can cause the humidity of the air in an unheated garage to contact the cold asbestos roofing which now acts as a condenser, converting the vapour in the air to liquid water (condensate). If this is not vented or evaporated off it will not only stain surrounding materials, but will create conditions suitable for the decay of organic materials such as wood.

Fixing felt and wire mesh beneath the corrugated asbestos would only hide condensation not prevent it, although with a fall to the roof the felt might be expected to collect the condensate and carry it along to the guttering.

There are several aspects concerning condensation which must be understood before any remedial action is taken. When warm air strikes a cold surface condensation is likely to form on that surface, so one way of reducing this would be to increase the temperature of the air adjacent to the cold surface so as to warm this. The trouble with this is that warm air can hold much more moisture vapour than cold air and since night external air temperatures are invariably several degrees colder than the interior of the building, you will see that with a material like relatively thin asbestos, it is almost impossible to keep its surface warm by heating the area below.

To some extent you have aggravated the problem by installing the Poron insulation since this has had the effect of keeping any heat from the garage from warming the asbestos. What is lacking is a suitable vapour barrier and insulation in the right place.

We suggest you remove the Poron and when the asbestos and wood is dry, review the wood joists/purlins in the following light: You say the wood was brush-treated with Protim but it would help to give the members additional treatment as a safeguard. The 2 x 4in. timbers are rather skimpy in relation to the 9ft span and while they are no doubt capable of supporting the asbestos they will not take the additional material we suggest you should use to put the job right.

It is essential to isolate the garage air from the roof and this can be done by

fastening 500 gauge (minimum) polythene over all the roof soffit, ie by stapling to the underside of the joists. When this has been done the whole should be lined with ½in. thick fibre (insulation) building board.

However, since the joists need stiffening we suggest 1 x 7in. boards be nailed to the joists, working from inside the garage, the 3in. extra wood coming below the level of the existing joists. This will do three things: (a) stiffen the joists to enable them to take the weight of the insulation boards (these would be low density, but would still be too heavy for the 2 x 4in.); (b) give 3in. to take your Poron if you want to replace it; and (c) leave adequate space below the corrugated asbestos for ventilation. The 1 x 7in. boarding would also need to be liberally brushed with Protim or similar organic solvent preservative before fixing.

You must now consider the following point: If the joists are set more than at 24in. centres, the insulation boards, say, 8 x 4ft will not match up for nailing. Should this be the case it would be necessary to nail 2 x 1in. nominal battens, at not more than 24in. centres, to the underside of the joists, ie at right angles to their line.

When the roof members are suitably adjusted, the Poron could be replaced, and then the polythene vapour barrier fastened to the underside of the joists or battens. Any joins that have to be made in the polythene should be in the form of folded overlaps and where it meets the walls, again it should be folded and concealed by fixing a quadrant or scotia moulding. The building board should be fixed over the polythene for insulation. When this has been done you will have sealed and insulated the garage from the roof void, and if the Nuralay flashing is altered, perhaps by boring a few holes, through ventilation under the asbestos roofing will eliminate the tendency for condensation to occur.

In passing, should you wish to remove the large-headed nails used to fasten down the corrugated asbestos sheets this can usually be done by judicious use of a Mole grip tightly fastened to the heads, the nails then being 'unwound' without damage to the sheets.

The reason why your garden shed is free from condensation is that wood substance is warmer than bricks and cement, and there is adequate ventilation in your shed. In other words, it is in effect, a large roof void similar to the one in your house which, doubtless, is free from condensation. This is vastly different from the conditions in your garage, with its probable dampness, particularly if you also put your wet car inside and close the door.

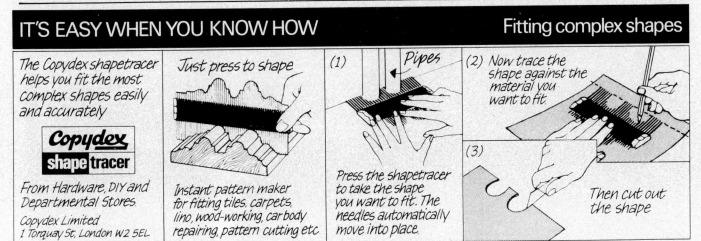

Jack Hill starts an interesting series on

COUNTRY CHAIRS AND CHAIRMAKING STOOLS

1: in the beginning there were

Country chairs, those traditionally hand-made by village craftsmen and intended originally for use by the local community, are basically of two types. First, those made in one of the many Windsor-type variations in which the shaped seat (from a solid piece of wood) has legs and back parts socketed into it; and second, those made frequently with rush or cane seats, in which a pair of legs extend upwards to form either a ladderback or a spindleback. Since the late 19th century many such chairs have been factory-made and used in urban homes. But their design is basically 'country' in origin.

Origin of the name Windsor is uncertain. The popular story of how George III, sheltering from a thunderstorm in a cottage near Windsor sat in such a chair and, liking it, ordered similar ones for Windsor castle, is erroneous; the chairs had the name long before any of the Georges reigned. A possible explanation lies with the fact that such chairs became more widely known when bought by London furniture dealers in the Windsor area during the late 17th century. (See page 212 of WOODWORKER for April 1979). But they were in common use in the villages before this, presumably without having any special name. In addition they were made in various styles throughout rural Britain and not just in the Windsor area.

Ladderbacks take their name from the ladder-like arrangement of shaped, horizontal rails between the two upright back parts. Spindlebacks have vertical rows of short, turned spindles held between pairs of horizontal back bars.

Both types of chair evolved from the simple stools which, together with low benches once formed the principle means of seating.

Chairs did not come into general use in Britain until Elizabethan times. Before this only the most important member of important households owned and used a chair. It is from this that we retain the customary title of chairman for the person who presides at a meeting. Usually this single chair was of a heavy throne-like appearance, of box construction, having been developed from the medieval chest by the simple addition of panelled back and arms.

Elaborate and often quite elegant chairs were known to the ancient Egyptians and to the Romans, too, but like so much else, chairs had to await rediscovery in the period following the so-called Dark Ages in Europe.

The stools and benches in common use were of three kinds. In rural cottages and farms stools were frequently three-legged — angled out or splayed in tripod fashion so as to be more stable on the uneven stone or hard floors of early dwellings. Each leg, round at the top, was socketed directly into a hole through the solid wooden seat which was often circular or semi-circulcular in shape.

Legs were usually of local-grown ash or beech, cut and used in the round or cleft and shaped by hand. This material was obtained from coppicing, a type of woodland husbandry once widely practiced, in which close-grown trees of certain species, cut back almost to ground level when young, produce a number of separate upright stems rather than a single trunk. These straight stems were cropped at intervals of from seven to 20 years to provide poles of various diameters, suitable for a variety of purposes from fencing posts to rake handles, ladder rungs and chair parts.

When used in the round for legs, coppice poles need only to have the bark removed — and even this can be dispensed with. Cleft material from larger diameter butts was split with an axe or with a cleaving tool known as a froe. Cleft pieces, roughly triangular in section, would then be trimmed approximately round with a drawknife the round end joint being left oversize at this stage. All this work is best carried out while the wood is green — that is, unseasoned; left to dry out thoroughly, winter-cut coppice depending on thickness, needs up to a year of seasoning after rough shaping.

Final shaping was with a spokeshave or perhaps a stail or rung engine — hand-operated in spite of its name and used to make rake handles (stails) and ladder rungs. This tool would have made the task easier and the result more accurate. A modern version of this type of tool is available and known as a rotary plane or rounder. (See WOODWORKER for January 1974) and *Woodworker Record* supplement for July 1979, page 389(7).

Seats were most often cut from thick planks of elm or oak which, in those days would have been sawn at the sawpit by a two-man team. Using a 7ft saw one man stood on top of the trunk to be sawn placed over a 6ft deep trench in the ground and guided and lifted the saw while the other, in the trench, pulled the saw downwards on each cutting stroke. This method of converting large timbers continued from

Modern copies of a three-legged stool with wedged joints visible and a woven seat stool made by J. Hill (photo: D. Yaffe and Son).

MAKING STOOLS

Legs made 'in the round' or cleft from coppice ①. Straight grained sawn material can be used ②. Cut roughly hexagonal ③. Shape with drawknife or rotary plane (1³/₈") (35), approx 10" (255) long ④. Joint tenon formed ~ use 1" (25) rotary plane or turn to size ⑤. Bottom end of leg is rounded over; leg may be tapered along its length or left plain ⑥. Alternatively, decorative or plain legs may be lathe turned

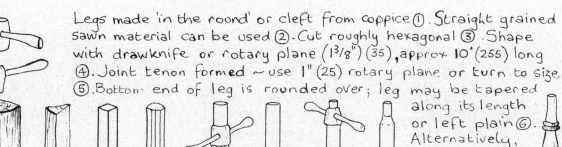

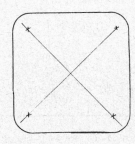

Three legged stools

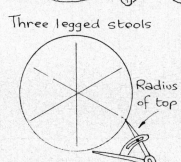

Radius of top

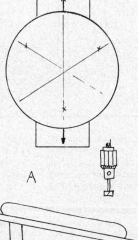

A

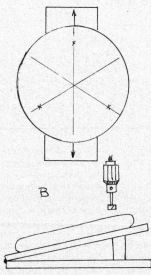

B

Seat cut from 1½" (38) elm, ash or beech, approx diameter 12" (300). Mark out as shown. Drill leg holes 1" (25) diam. using a sloping platform jig to splay legs at about 106°

For wedged joint mark TOP of seat & drill from the TOP, going right through

For 'blind' joint mark & drill UNDERSIDE & drill only part way through

Four legged stools, rectangular or round, are marked out & drilled in same manner. It is important to align guide lines to centre line of jig to ensure correct splay of legs

Details of wedged & 'blind' seat joints

For stool A make a 1" (25) saw cut in leg tenon as shown. Cut three hardwood wedges to fit. Assemble so that wedges are at right angles to grain of seat. Cut stub ends flush & clean-off surface

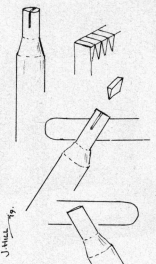

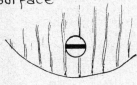

For stool B joint must be a tight push fit. Secure all joints with a suitable adhesive

Woven seat stools. Make in various sizes using ash or beech 'sticks'. All cut 12" (300) long is a suitable size. Four legs, 1³/₈" (35), four top rails, ¾" (19) & four stretchers, ¾" (19), are required. Drill & socket all parts together as shown below

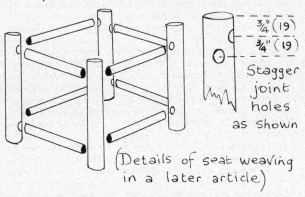

¾" (19)
¾" (19)

Stagger joint holes as shown

(Details of seat weaving in a later article)

All construction methods applicable to chair making described later

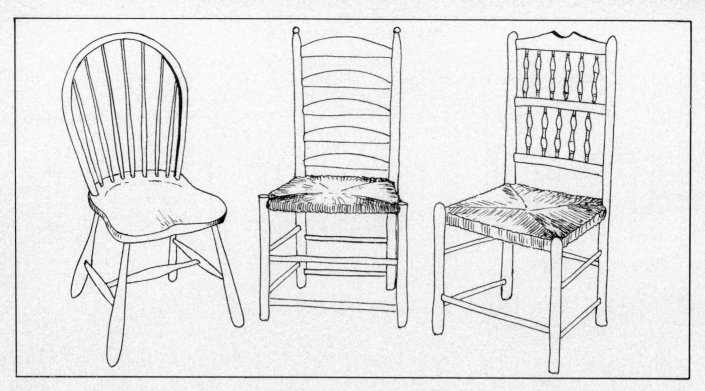

medieval times to well into the present century. Now power-driven saws do the work in a fraction of the time.

A shell or auger bit, turned by hand with the aid of a wooden stock brace, would have been used to bore holes for the legs, each one at the required angle. These were bored right through the seat. The joint was secured by means of a hardwood wedge which when, driven down into a saw cut made in the top of the leg prior to fitting, effectively spread and thus tightened the socketed end. An important precaution with this type of joint is to ensure that the wedge lies at right angles to the grain of the seat (see diagram). A wedge put in along the grain could cause the seat to split.

This simple round wedged joint which requires no complicated marking out or great skill in the manipulation of a chisel, was widely used by those who made these early stools, it being more simple to use wood roughly round than to make it accurately square. Later, when the round joint could be made more precise, it could be used without the wedge and socketed and glued into a blind hole of sufficient depth. Even today the turned parts of chairs are fitted together in these ways.

Four-legged stools and benches were constructed in this same manner, their sturdy legs often being drawknifed to a tapered hexagon section but round at the top to form the joint with the seat.

The second distinctive type of seat in use in country districts was the more lightly made woven-seat stool. This had round or turned parts throughout, each joined to its neighbour by means of the round joint to form a box-like framework. The seat was more often than not woven with rush *(Scirpus lacustris)*, a once prolific aquatic plant in many rivers and along the margins of lakes throughout the country. These were closely woven between and across the top rails of the stool framework to form a comfortable and fairly durable seat. (A later article will describe rush seat weaving in detail).

The third type of seating was known as the joyned stool or bench. These were in widespread use, both in towns and villages

and consisted generally of an oak framework of thick rails and legs. The former were rectangular and heavily carved, the latter elaborately turned but left square where they joined (or 'joyned') the cross rails by means of square, pegged mortise and tenon joints. This heavy underframe, fitted with a seat of thick boards, formed a sturdy though somewhat cumbersome piece of furniture. These stools and benches, together with tables of the same period, had heavy bracing rails or stretchers purposely placed low down so that the sitter might use them to keep his feet clear of the dirty, rush or straw-strewn floor.

Gradually these joyned stools lost some of their earlier heaviness and at some stage — and it is difficult to say when with any degree of certainty — two of the legs were extended upwards to form a backrest. This was usually panelled and frequently elaborately carved as was the fashion at that time. This mode of construction continued to be developed. Ultimately it was to form the basis of much of the stylish furniture made fashionable by numerous big-name furniture designers which graced the dining rooms and drawing rooms of the wealthy.

In more humble circumstances, however, it was the parallel development of the three- and four-legged socketed seat stool and the woven seat stool which was to lead to the true country-style chairs. Like the joyned stools, those with woven seats were at some time provided with backrests by a similar upward extension of two of their legs, the space between being filled with horizontal bars or combinations of bars and spindles.

It was the further development of this style which gave us the ladderback or spindleback styles as we know them today. Solid seat stools had backs added, too, separately socketed into the upper surface of the seat in the same manner as described for legs. This particular back design, which eventually was to lead to the so-called Windsor-style of chairs, consisted at first of a simple arrangement of rods or back sticks surmounted by a single horizontal rail or comb.

Whatever the style or arrangement of these significant changes in design the results were not regarded as chairs to begin

with, being merely considered to be stools fitted with backrests. As such they became known as backstools or occasionally backchairs. This terminology was apparently adopted so that there would be no confusion with the elaborate armchairs of the period. But partly it was to avoid offending the dignity of the owners of chairs of status! Gradually, however, as backstools became more widely used they came to be accepted as true chairs. And while some modern designs appear to owe little to these humble beginnings, the traditional styles of the country chair, as popular today as ever, still retain many of their original features. Further articles will discuss these and describe details of their construction.

Oak 'joyned' stool c1600 (copyright Victoria and Albert Museum).

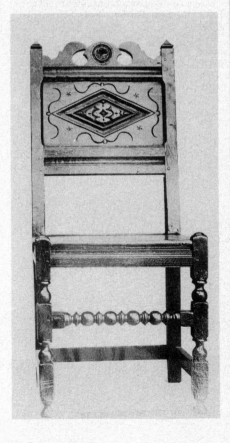

Letters

From: Hugh Blogg, Broadstairs, Kent

Dear Sir,

The reference in Question Box to bobbins for lace making (December 1979 issue p 759) pleased me immensely. Only a few weeks ago I turned 12pr of bobbins out of Cuban mahogany for a friend, promising her more later made from laburnum, boxwood *(Buxus)*, lignum vitae and Mozambique mahogany. Because of their weight she will probably use them without the need for the traditional beaded spangles.

As indicated by WOODWORKER consultant, Cuban mahogany is, without doubt, superior to all others including the so-called 'mahoganies' like khaya. Its specific gravity (SG) is quoted as 0.8 and its comparative workability (CW) as 3.5. This means that it is $3\frac{1}{2}$ times as difficult to work as Weymouth pine *(Pinus strobus)* which is CW1 (or unity). By way of interest and comparison, lignum vitae has CW 5.5 and SG 1.2 indicating, of course, that it promptly sinks in water, as does ebony and many other timbers.

Today I tested my mahogany and was pleased to find it has SG of 0.9. Readers may

be interested to know how this was done: I took an odd piece at random and using a hollowground circular saw blade for a smooth accurate finish, I prepared the specimen piece $1 \times 1 \times 20$cm long. This I weighed using laboratory weights, and found it to be 18gr, thus giving SG 0.9.

Knowing this figure I then squared lines on one face of the specimen at points 17, 18, 19cm from one end. This end was lowered into a glass measuring cylinder about $\frac{2}{3}$ filled with water until the wood floated. The water line came to a point midway between the 17 and 18cm lines, thus showing the SG to be 0.875. The tiny bubbles which adhered to the immersed surface accounted for the disparity in the two SG figures.

I still have three lengths cut from a squared flitch of this Cuban or Spanish mahogany, which I consider to be of San Domingo quality. Black with age and bearing adze marks of the native foresters, they average around $7 \times 11 \times 39$in. and are more than I can manage to lift. Imagine the fun I have converting one of these on my small 1hp sawtable with a depth of cut of only $3\frac{1}{2}$in. But I manage it and being so valuable I cut it as I like it to be cut.

I think this timber I have is about all that remains of what was imported to make propellors for our early aircraft before, and about the time of, World War I, it being the wood *par excellence* for this purpose.

Bobbin maker D.G. Francis would have no need to stain Cuban mahogany; it has the pleasing property of darkening, under the influence of light, to that lovely warm-brown colour that I always associate with fresh,

new conkers — horse chestnuts. It will do this in a month or two, even under white french polish. If Mr Francis is at a standstill I may be able to spare some of this rare wood, since only short sections are needed.

It may be of interest to refer to deeping a flitch of Cuban mahogany. The photograph shows the short flitch deeped, the cut having been completed by hand sawing. The fourfold rule indicates the measurement.

It is strictly forbidden in industry to invert to complete the cut. I follow this ruling in my home workshop and therefore completed the cut by hand sawing. But the whole of the flitch weighed almost 100lb and needed quite a bit of unaided manhandling!

Yours faithfully, **Hugh Blogg**

Mr Blogg kindly sent with his letter what he describes as a 'bit of treen.' This is an egg and eggcup approximately $2\frac{3}{8}$in. high overall and $1\frac{1}{16}$in. in diameter. He points out that the treen demonstrates two of the virtues of Cuban mahogany. First, how the wood has darkened since last Easter when he made it, among several others much smaller. 'Where the light has not contacted the wood it has not darkened. If you wet the wood with your finger you will see that exquisite colour of Chippendale's and Gillow's furniture,' says Mr Blogg. Second, the extreme stability: both egg and cup are still perfectly round.

From: John C. Allison, Bath, Co Avon

Dear Sir,

With reference to the article on sharpening stones (page 725 of the December 1979 issue), I have for some time been using a similar system. I find that a Norton (fine) stone works very well if followed by stropping on a piece of coach hide or any thick leather offcut from the shoemaker's on to which has been smeared a small amount of Solvol Autosol (the car chrome cleaner). The advantage is that this seems very much easier to obtain (and cheaper) than crocus or jewellers rouge.

I think it is important to state that for a perfect edge the back of the chisel or plane iron should have as much attention as the cutting side.

I would also like to thank you for the article on the Bristol firm of Robbins Ltd (pages 722-3 of the same issue). I was introduced to Robbins some years ago, as a young teacher, and have been taking advantage of the firm's vast experience, excellent service and friendly, helpful manner ever since.

Yours faithfully, **John C. Allison**

From: William Sinnott, Coatbridge, Lanarkshire

Dear Sir,

Reader A. C. Weller asks if anyone can identify the Stanley plane he has (page 739, WOODWORKER for December 1979). I have one like it which I bought second-hand when I was an apprentice in the 1930s.

There are a great number of irons for this tool. A set of plough irons from $\frac{1}{8}$in. upwards, bead irons the same, flute irons from $\frac{1}{8}$ to $\frac{3}{4}$in. and a great many moulding irons. They all have a 'holding groove' cut in the back face.

I'm afraid I can't give Mr Weller much help as to the history of this very versatile tool, but if he examines the handle closely he will find that it has 'Miller's patent June 28th 1870' stamped on it. My plane is in original condition but differs from Mr Weller's in one respect: the decorated fence is malleable iron and not brass.

I haven't used this tool in years.

Yours faithfully, **William Sinnott**

Top and above: Typical back chairs of the 17th century (copyright Victoria and Albert Museum).

A SHORTER GUIDE TO
MACHINES AND ACCESSORIES

One of the interesting exhibits at Interbuild (National Exhibition Centre, Birmingham) last December, was the Total Hobby universal which has two tool spindles belt driven from a 0.736kW motor. The spindles act as power take-offs for the various tools which are available. The machine is produced by AMRP Handels AG, Leonhardstrasse 38, Postfach 112, 4003 Basle, Switzerland, and distributed by Carmichael Engineering Ltd, Burkitt Road, Earltrees Industrial Estate South, Corby NN17 2DT.

Another European exhibitor was W. Altendorf, Wettiner Allee 45, PO Box 2009, D-4950 Minden, W Germany, which manufactures sizing circular saws of various dimensions for trimming lengths between 1350 and 5000mm.

Well-known British firms were at Interbuild: Atkin & Sons (Birmingham) Ltd, 110 Bradford Street, Birmingham 12, which trades in most aspects of woodworking machinery and tools and offers service on all types of saws and blades; Autool Grinders, Padiham Road, Sabden, Blackburn BB6 9EW, specialising in grinding machines for edge tools, including a grinder to handle bandsaws up to 45mm wide and a fully automatic TCT circular saw grinder to resharpen both the faces and tops of the tips completely without reset; E. P. Barrus Ltd, Launton Road, Bicester OX6 OUR, showing for the first time the Hitachi U210 universal for which a mortising kit is also available.

For spraying components such as handles for drawers, tools and brushes, Charvo Ltd, Snay Gill, Keighley Road, Skipton BD23 2QR, introduced an automatic spray line which is equally at home with stains, clear lacquers, tinted lacquers or pigment materials.

Supplier of new and reconditioned machinery for woodworking is A. L. Dalton Ltd, Crossgate Drive, Queens Drive Industrial Estate, Nottingham NG2 1LW. Part-exchange facilities is another feature of Dalton's activities; this gives firms the opportunity to trade-in surplus or outdated equipment against either new or rebuilt replacements. Danckaerts Woodworking Machinery Ltd, 2-6 East Road, City Road, London N1 6AG, is an international company established on all five continents. At its London showrooms there are to be seen Danckaerts machines and others from a Danckaerts agency covering the range of woodworking operations.

A spindle moulder type BCB incorporating variable speed drive between 3,000 and 9,000 rpm was shown by Dominion Machinery Co Ltd, Denholmegate Road, Hipperholme, Halifax HX3 8JG, together with the FM four-sided planing and moulding machine and other equipment including the Elliot universal. The associated Dominion Agencies handles numerous machines such as the DeWalt 12 crosscut type 1370; it also supplies works reconditioned machines including the Elliot universals.

Another continental exhibitor was Festo Maschinenfabrik Gottlieb Stoll, Ulmer Strasse 48, 7300 Esslingen, W Germany, with equipment for manufacturing mouldings and also for the line production of louvre doors.

Ott junior press model 90 is open on all four sides for ease of installation.

The Holzma model 26-3/2500 hinge and KD insertion automat which was shown by Jaydee (Machine Sales) Ltd, agents for Holzma in the UK.

edge banding machines and the Lamello system for jointing chipboard); and Jaydee (Machine Sales) Ltd, Copyground Lane, High Wycombe, Bucks, (Holzma, Brandt, Weeke and Grum-Schwensen equipment for specialist applications in wood processing). Another well-known firm is Lohmann & Co Ltd, Lohmann House, Horton Bridge Road, West Drayton UB7 8HS, which showed Griggio dimension saw, combination machine, thicknesser, planer knife grinder, spindle moulder, multi-ripsaw, lathe, and combined planer/thicknesser and planer.

Chain mortise gear is made in this country by MW Equipment Ltd, Progress Works, Shawcross Street, Stockport SK1 3HA, which also supplies the Orteguil twin bladed mitre machines for cutting window beads, picture frames etc. Adler 2000 portable edge planer, Hebor P72 laminate trimmer and Hebor clamping system for cabinet assembly are other products handled by MW Equipment.

Wood preservatives and primers as used in the building and joinery industries are supplied by Macpherson Industrial Finishes Ltd, Kelvin Way, West Bromwich B70 7JZ. A. & K. Marshall, Unit 8, Walkers Road, North Moons Moat Industrial Estate, Redditch, Worcs, showed electrically operated and foot operated mitre cutters as well as sharpening machines and the Arminius T20 profile sander for mouldings. C. D. Monninger Ltd, Overbury Road, London N15 6RJ, showed a new finger-jointing machine using Leitz 10mm mini finger-jointing cutters as well as Leitz TCT circular saws for which low noise figures are quoted, typically 5dB(A) lower than for ordinary blades when cutting compressed laminated wood up to 60mm thick. Monninger also handles Haffner portable electric tools — routers, saws, hand planers and belt and orbital sanders.

A planer rebating to a depth of 22mm (⅞in.) which can be provided with an attachment to enable tenons to be cut efficiently and quickly, as well as an attachment to allow the user to square materials accurately, is produced by Multico Co Ltd, Brighton Road, Salfords, Redhill RH1 5ER; there are 230mm (9in.) and 300mm (12in.) models in the range. Sawbenches, mortisers, single ended tenoner, a range of six bandsaws from 400 mm (16in.)

Below: Now available in the UK from Gerd C. Ney Jun Ltd, of Marlow, Bucks, is Vertongen's automatic belt sanding machine. The firm claims that features like sealed-for-life bearings and self-cleaning guides keep maintenance to a minimum.

Festo produces the FKV finger-jointing line by means of which a greater use of offcuts can be made. Hot-melt guns for applying adhesive to V-groove joints, draw slots, edgings and mouldings for door panels are supplied by GS Airmatics Ltd, 31 Liverpool Road, Kingston upon Thames KT2 7SX; the company additionally handles compressed air tools suitable for the woodworking industries. Noise reduction is an important factor in woodworking operations and Gomex Tools Ltd, Orchard Road, Finedon, Wellingborough, Northants, has introduced a surface planer with spiral cutter head said to offer a reduction in noise level. The Gomex Minibel circular saw offers a noise reduction in sawing machines from as much as 42%. The company supplies a variety of cutting tools.

Supplier of hand tools and machinery is John Hall Tools Ltd, 23 Churchill Way, Cardiff CF1 4UE. Its stand at Interbuild featured the Elektra Beckum range of machines and accessories. John Hall has 12 industrial branches and five retail branches and an export department.

Preservative treatment of timber and surface finishes for exterior and interior application are among the activities of Hickson's Timber Impregnation Co (GB) Ltd, Castleford WF10 2JT. Its Vac-Vac treatment is used by many manufacturers of standard exterior joinery; smaller manufacturers can send pre-cut material to a large number of Vac-Vac service plants.

Among suppliers of industrial woodworking machinery are JKO Cutters Ltd, Hughenden Avenue, High Wycombe HP13 5SQ, (Holz-Her panel saws and

to 900mm (36in.), and dust extraction equipment are among the other products from this company.

The Orma universal comprising surface planer, thicknesser, spindle moulder, circular saw, mortiser, cutter sharpener and tenoner, is among the range of woodworking machines handled by Gerd C. Ney Jun Ltd, 31 Dedmere Court, Marlow SL7 1PL. Newly introduced are the Hafele jig systems for easy and accurate assembly of cabinets and carcasses.

Hydraulic veneering and hot platen presses made in Germany by Paul Ott GmbH, include the Junior 40S school press having platen size 1500 x 850mm and four 60mm diameter hydraulic cylinders providing total pressure of 40ton. This single daylight press is available in bolted construction version for ease of transport and installation. Through its British company (Paul Ott Ltd, 5 The Rickyard, Ashwell, Herts), a variety of veneering presses and edge banding machines is available.

The stand of Record Ridgway Tools Ltd, Parkway Works, Sheffield S9 3BL, exhibited a selection of Record, Gilbow, Marples and Ridgway tools with emphasis on Ridgway woodboring tools for machine use. Sacme Ltd and Benview Ltd, Unit 38, Sittingbourne Industrial Park, Crown Quay Lane, Sittingbourne, Kent, showed byproduct and dust extraction equipment from single-bag units to the Modulare multi-bag range. Another item on the stand was the Sacme combination router/spindle moulder which has a variety of applications.

SCM International SpA of Italy, claims to manufacture 20,000 woodworking machines a year. Its products are handled in Britain by J. J. Smith (Woodworking Machinery) Ltd, Melling, Liverpool L31 1DX.

TCT sawblades to suit all types of machines are made by Scott Saws Ltd, 84 Easton Street, High Wycombe, Bucks, which has produced a leaflet *Choosing the right sawblade* describing the type of saws for particular materials such as softwood, hardwood and exotics. An interesting device, a hot air paint stripper was demonstrated by Sikkens UK Ltd, Didcot Industrial Estate, Station Road, Didcot OX11 7NQ. With air temperature adjustable between 20-600°C the stripper consists of two double-insulated units: the blower which is left lying on the ground and the heater which is directed at the surface to be stripped with one hand, leaving the other hand free to use a scraper. The paint stripper was devised for removing old and hardened layers of paint during renovation of the Noordeinde royal palace in the Netherlands. Sikkens is, of course, well-known for its interior and exterior wood finishes.

Another company from the Netherlands at Interbuild was Verboom BV, PO Box 1, 3927 ZL Renswoude, which manufactures sanding machines of the wide belt type, as well as automatic moulders and tenoning machines for industrial applications.

From Stanley Power Tools, Nelson Way, Cramlington, Northumberland, there is a new router — the 1287 heavy-duty plunge base model powered by a ½hp motor; in addition to the standard equipment there is a 1287K kit of extras. The range of router bits and cutters has been increased by the introduction of a series of production bits having mirror-finish.

The portable power tool division of Wadkin Ltd, Trent Lane, Castle Donington, Derby DE7 2PU, showed the tools described in WOODWORKER for January 1980. Belt and orbital sanders, hand planer, plunge router, chain and circular saws, impact drill and angle grinders are available. 'Demand for the initial range (other tools are to follow this year) has been high,' reports the division's general manager J. W. Nutt. Wegoma UK Ltd, Paynes Lane, Rugby, Warwickshire, supplies radial saws, a thicknesser, universals, tilting arbor and double mitre saws; these and other machines are also on display at the Rugby showroom.

Wide belt sanders are made in this country under licence agreement by Thomas White & Sons Ltd, Laighpark, Paisley PA3 4DA, and the company supplies in addition panel and radial arm saws, thicknessers, knife grinders and lathe with copying attachment in which an existing component or template can be used as the master. Large and small plants for byproduct and dust extraction and installation of trunking systems are among the activities of Wood Waste Control Ltd, Unit 75, Soho Mills, Wooburn Green, High Wycombe HP10 0TF. Also supplied are wood-fired low pressure hot water or steam generators for factory heating or process requirements.

Copy shaping of wooden components in a wide variety of patterns from an enlarged cast iron master is carried out on a machine known as the Challenger type 1:1 which accepts a workpiece up to 42 x 8½ x 8½in., though versions able to handle up to 12ft long workpieces are available. The Challenger is made by Zuckermann KG, 22-4 Anastasius Gruengasse, A-1181, Vienna.

Above: Multico type TM Mk IV single-ended tenoner incorporates a cabinet stand. The machine is provided with standard 1½ in. cutter head.

Two Sheffield firms — Tyzack Sons & Turner Ltd and Record Ridgway Tools Ltd — have signed a sales, marketing and distribution agreement whereby the latter, subject to certain exclusions, will have sole selling rights in England, Scotland and Wales for the hand, tenon, specialist and circular saws made under the Tyzack name.

The agreement became effective from 1 January this year and means that Record Ridgway 'offers the widest range of top-quality woodworking tools available from one manufacturer in UK.' Correspondence to Record Ridgway Tools Ltd, Parkway Eorks, Sheffield S9 3BL (0472 44 9066).

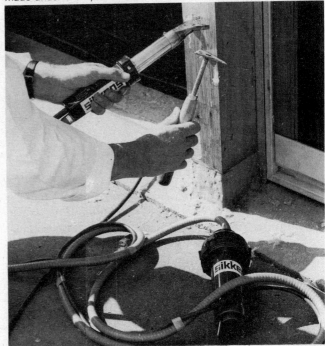

Right: The Sikkens hot air paint stripper.

If the Americans couldn't have made the most versatile woodworking machine in the world they wouldn't have made the SHOPSMITH MARK V

The SHOPSMITH Mk V is the only machine in the world to combine a lathe, sawbench, disc sander, horizontal boring machine and vertical drill press in a single unit taking up no more space than an ordinary bicycle!

More than 350,000 Americans have chosen the 'Smith' as the ultimate solution for their home workshop and currently around 500 customers are choosing the SHOPSMITH **every week!** It is easy to understand why.

No other machine offers all these unique features:

- Five basic machines including vertical drill press.
- Special Add-To Machines include Bandsaw, Planer, Belt Sander and Fret Saw plus accessories enabling a total of 16 different machine operations.
- Automatic speed dial from 700 rpm to 5200 rpm without even turning the machine off. Just dial the correct speed for whatever operation is required.
- With SHOPSMITH'S exclusive Quill Feed Control any required depth of feed is pre-set, locked and absolute accuracy is guaranteed.

Whether you are just starting in woodwork or been at it for years the SHOPSMITH Mk V will give you the home workshop you have always wanted – to build the projects you have always dreamed of.

The Shopsmith makes virtually everything - including sense!

CROSSCUTTING

SANDING

HORIZONTAL BORING

VERTICAL DRILLING

The SHOPSMITH is now available from SUMACO – the UK's leading importer of the world's finest smaller woodworker machines, and their appointed distributors.

Suma House, Huddersfield Road, ELLAND, W. Yorkshire
Tel. (0422) 75491/2

Please send: Further information on the
Shopsmith Mk 5 ☐ (Enclose 10p stamps)
The full Sumaco catalogue ☐ (Enclose 50p stamps)

NAME _____

ADDRESS _____

_____

SS2

Prices quoted are those prevailing at press date and are subject to alteration due to economic conditions.

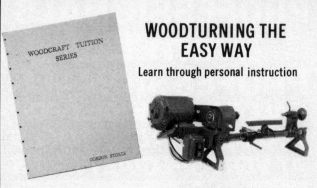
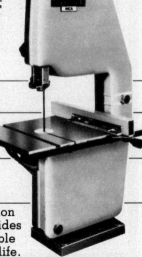

Prices quoted are those prevailing at press date and are subject to alteration due to economic conditions.

TENTBROOK
LIMITED

Offer this new range of 'Wadkin' super quality power tools for home and industry at special introductory prices – **they are the best – we are the cheapest** – compare our prices!

Model	Description	Power input	M.R.P.	Our Price*
B-7075	**BELT SANDER**, 75mm wide, inc. dust bag	850W	£126.50	**£94.30**
B-7200A	**BELT SANDER**, 100mm wide, inc. dust bag	980W	£155.25	**£115.00**
LS-35	**ORBITAL SANDER**, 93mm × 185mm pad	180W	£44.85	**£33.35**
SU-6200	**ORBITAL SANDER**, 112mm × 226mm pad	300W	£98.90	**£73.60**
L-1512	**HAND PLANER**, 92mm wide, inc. blade sharpening jig	550W	£83.95	**£63.25**
R-500	**PLUNGE ROUTER**, 12mm collet chuck	1500W	£147.20	**£109.25**
W-6502	**CIRCULAR SAW**, 180mm blade, 240V only	1400W	£102.35	**£77.05**
W-8502	**CIRCULAR SAW**, 235mm blade	1700W.	£147.20	**£109.25**
CS-360	**CHAIN SAW**, 355mm cut-off length	1250W	£105.80	**£79.35**
PD-1920	**IMPACT DRILL**, 2-speed, 13mm chuck	550W	£98.90	**£73.60**
G-1000	**ANGLE GRINDER**, 100mm wheel, 240V only	480W	£60.95	**£44.85**
G-1150	**ANGLE GRINDER**, 115mm wheel	480W	£67.85	**£50.60**
G-1800	**ANGLE GRINDER**, heavy duty, 180mm wheel	1700W	£113.85	**£85.10**
G-2300	**ANGLE GRINDER**, heavy duty, 230mm wheel	1700W	£120.75	**£89.70**

* Our prices include p/p and VAT. Detailed leaflet on request.

- **Quality built to BSI standards**
- **Double insulated ● Radio suppressed**
- **12 months guarantee**
- **comprehensive after-sales service**

Order with remittance (State voltage 110V/240V)

TENTBROOK LIMITED
14 Church Road, Great Glen, Leicester

Full cash refund if not completely satisfied. Allow 21 days for delivery

---

Illustrated here is the recently introduced type M230 lathe — developed from the highly successful and popular type J4 MkII which continues in production. The M230 incorporates a heavy-duty spindle to metric dimensions, ball-bearing headstock and five-speed drive. The lathe is available as a cabinet stand motorised ready to run unit or for those wishing to utilise their own work bench, the machine and a range of accessories and electrical items can be purchased separately. Obtainable from a limited number of stockists or direct from us.

In addition to the M230, we have other wood-turning lathes in our own range, whilst we also stock Myford ML8 series, various makes of bandsaws, grinders, turning tools, motors, books, etc. For leaflets and current price list, please send 30p in stamps to:

Arundel
WOOD TURNING LATHES AND ACCESSORIES

D. ARUNDEL & COMPANY LIMITED,
Mills Drive Farndon Road
Newark,
Nottinghamshire.
NG24 4SN

Tel. Newark (0636) 702382

FANTASTIC
Spindle Moulder Offer!

When you buy our superb Kity 7227 Spindle Moulder price £432.32* we'll send you, completely free of charge, a Kity 2180 moulding block and a full set of cutters value £113.85*. This offer is available now, for a limited period only at selected Kity distributors. For more information about this offer fill in the coupon and post it to Kity without delay.

*All prices include VAT.

Name ....

Address ....

Please send me Spindle Moulder offer Information.

KITY
UNITED KINGDOM

Sizer's Court, Henshaw Lane, Yeadon, Leeds LS19 7DP.

---

emcostar

The Emco Star is matched in its superb looks only by its versatility, ease of operation and ease of maintenance. The standard machine performs many different Sawing and Sanding operations all to the same high standards. Additional operations include moulding, planing, thicknessing, working with flexible shaft and many others. The machine has a powerful 2-speed motor and is fitted with safety clutches. And the complete miracle fits into mere 40" x 28" of space.

OUR PRICE **£469** inc. VAT carriage £3
List Price £514 inc. VAT.

emco BS2 Bandsaw

Unique in its price class, the BS2 has three speeds and is suitable for wood, metal and plastic.

Large size upper and lower band-saw guide, tilting table and torsion resistant band-saw frame ensure clean, accurate cuts, even on large workpieces. The BS2 is easy and safe to operate and has extra large bearings for long life.

OUR PRICE **£235** inc. VAT. Carriage £3.00
List Price £270 inc. VAT.

Write or Telephone NOW for details:

A. MILLS (ACTON LTD.)

32-36 Churchfield Road, Acton, London W3
Telephone: 01 992 4835 Telex: 24224-305
Easy access M1/M3/M4 Motorways

Opening hours: ....
Monday-Friday 9 a.m.-5 p.m. ....

ACCESS AND
BARCLAY CARDS

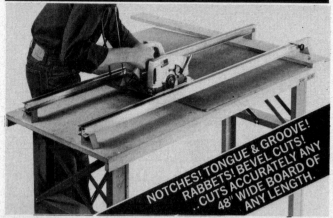

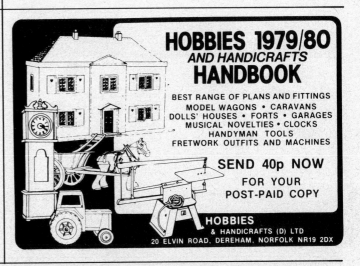
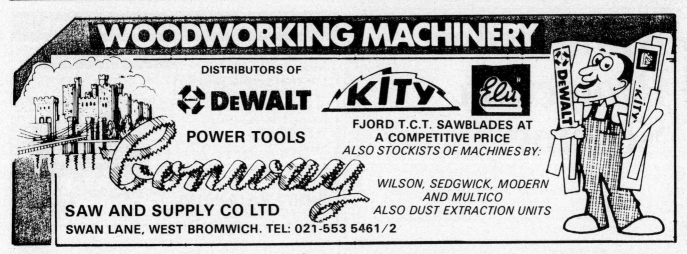

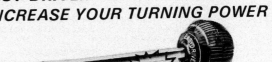

Mail Order Protection Scheme

If you order goods from mail order advertisers in this
magazine and pay by post in advance of delivery, this
publication *(Woodworker)* will consider you for
compensation if the advertiser should become insolvent or
bankrupt, provided

1. You have not received the goods or had your money
   returned; and
2. You write to the publisher of this publication
   (Woodworker) explaining the position not earlier than 28
   days from the day you sent your order and not later than
   2 months from that day.

Please do not wait until the last moment to inform us. When
you write, we will tell you how to make your claim and what
evidence of payment is required.

We guarantee to meet claims from readers made in
accordance with the above procedure as soon as possible
after the advertiser has been declared bankrupt or insolvent
up to a limit of £1350 per annum for any one advertiser so
affected and up to £4050 p.a. in respect of all insolvent
advertisers. Claims may be paid for higher amounts, or
when the above procedure has not been complied with, at
the discretion of this publication *(Woodworker)*; but we do
not guarantee to do so in view of the need to set some limit
to this commitment and to learn quickly of readers'
difficulties.

This guarantee covers only advance payments sent in *direct*
response to an advertisement in this magazine (not, for
example, payments made in response to catalogues, etc.,
received as a result of answering such advertisements).
Personal advertisements are excluded.

Something to sell?
Something to buy?
Try a **WOODWORKER**

Classified Advertisement

Lineage for only **14p** per word min. **£2.40** or
display classified **£3.00** per single column centimetre, min. **£7.50**. Box numbers **£1.00** extra.
Use the coupon on page 204 of this issue or
phone Gill (0442) 41221 extn. 241.

All advertisements are inserted in the first available issue.

200
**Prices quoted are those prevailing at press date and
are subject to alteration due to economic conditions.**
Woodworker, March 1980

Classified Advertisements

FOR SALE

Fine Period Furniture
for you to make by hand at home

Large selection of 17thC copies in solid oak or elm for simple home assembly without special tools.

- All materials supplied
- All parts cut, planed and jointed
- Simple instructions
- Save up to 60% on retail prices

Send large SAE for brochure and price list

JACOBUS WORKSHOP
South Road,
KIRKBY STEPHEN,
Cumbria

WALL CLOCKS
an exciting new look!

colourful decorative ceramic clockfaces, guaranteed quartz battery movements, ensure that the wall clocks you make will be elegant and reliable. Attractive designs and range of styles. Featured by Woodcraft Supply Corp.
SAE details – WHS, 38 Summercourt Way, Brixham. TQ5 0DY.

HARPSICHORDS, spinets and clavichords: World-famous kits. Competitive prices. Hardware and strings for small harps. Alan & Helen Edgar, 49 Tranby Avenue, Hessle, East Yorkshire. Tel: 0482-640330. MN

PLANS FOR ADVANCED MODELLERS. "Roll-top Desk", 1/12th scale, 300 pieces, £1.50 ($4), "Mini Chartwell House" 150 pieces, £1.50 ($4). Other plans with Churchill connections, 50p ($1.50). W.E.H. 1, Hollytree Gardens, Frimley, Surrey. N

TOOLS TO TREASURE
First quality cabinetmaker's HIDE GLUE fine ground for easy mixing. £2.48 per kilo.
BRIDLED GLUE BRUSHES pure grey bristle set in rubber. British made. ½" £1.83; 1" £2.84; 1½" £5.07; *All prices include postage in U.K.* Adzes, Drawknives, Inshave and other tools for the craftsman Woodworker send foolscap S.A.E. for details.
CORBETT TOOLS (Dept. WW/2) 224 Puxton Drive, Kidderminster, Worcs.

BRASS OR ALUMINIUM plates for your project. Letters block or script, example 3" x 1" brass plate with 20 block letters £1.10p plus post, plus VAT. Also engraved badges, name plates, numbers, labels etc. in coloured plastic. Trade enquiries welcome. Brian J. Bowman Trophies Limited, "Anela", Lower North Street, Cheddar, Somerset. Tel: Cheddar 742774. LMN

FARNWORTH 4" bench plane/rebater including motor/stand £70. Tel: 01-361-1685 (London, Southgate). N

MYFORD ML8A with saw table, sanding table, mortising attachment, tenoning attachment, chucks, plus many smaller parts. One owner. Little used £650. Current price £1,100. Tel: 061-432-1740. MN

FOR SALE: 25 Boxwood moulding planes and one Boxwood rebate plane. All in good condition. Any offers: Tel: 01-340-2711 (anytime). N

MAKITA 1085B 6" planer plus stand and spare blades £125. Ring Disley 4014. N

BRANDING IRONS
Made from solid steel with 15" handle, to last a lifetime. Now you can permanently identify your tools and production pieces. We can quote for special styles for a professional look. Price guide — 3 x ⅜" characters £6.95p.
SAE details – WHS, 38 Summercourt Way, Brixham. TQ5 0DY.

FOR SALE
CORONET MAJOR. 48" lathe bed, with 10" saw table, planer, thicknesser, mortiser, grinding set, turning chisels. Mounted on strong purpose-made bench. All as new. Makers list price £975. Accept £750.
Phone New Milton 613637. Denham, 2 Waverley Road, New Milton, Hants.

COLLECTION of cabinetmaker's and designer's tools used over three generations to be sold individually or as lot. L. Keep, 45 Hamilton Road, High Wycombe. Tel: H.W. 30524. N

KITY 535 independent planer/thicknesser, grinding table/honer attachments. Motor 4 months old, can deliver. Offers: Eastergate 2216. N

SUPERB Victorian church pew timber. Mainly pitch pine/Douglas fir. 12" x 1¼" 75p ft, 5" x 1¼" 10p ft, T and G boards 12" x 4" 7p each. Various mouldings and architectural pieces. S. Noble, Tel: 01-460-9073 (evenings). N

Snooker & Pool
"High Point" Garstang Rd. East, Singleton, Blackpool, Lancs. FY6 7SX
Tel: 0253-883426
Table Plans. Chipboard/Slate. State size, send £2 + SAE. Cod service on cloth, balls, rubber, etc. New and reconditioned Snooker and coin-op Pool tables sold/bought.
Advice Centre

WORKSHOP EQUIPMENT

WOODCARVING tools

Ashley Iles & Henry Taylor Arkansas Bench & Slip Stones Bench Screws, Carvers Vices Professional Turning Tools
Send 20p in stamps for illustrated catalogue
ALEC TIRANTI LTD
70 High St., Theale, Reading, Berks
21 Goodge Place, London W.1.

WASHITA & ARKANSAS whetstones now readily available from importer. Large selection. S.A.E. for lists. C. Rufino, Manor House, South Clifton, Newark, Notts. T/C

SHERWOOD TURNING LATHES
All cast iron constructed. 3¾" CH 24" or 36" B.C. 3 or 4 speed, bowl turning up to 14" dia. ball-bearing spindle c/w face plate, centres etc. Priuces from £58.92 inc. VAT.

Send stamp for leaflets and details of above and other low-priced machines and motors.
JAMES INNS (Engs), Main St., Bulwell, Nottingham.

CLASSIFIED
Telephone Gill Dedman (0442) 41221 Ext. 241

Equipping a workshop?
Call and see demonstrated or write for details (25p stamps) of quality machines of the popular Kity range or by Startrite, Sedgwick, De Walt, Lurem and most others: Elu Routers and Power Tools; Arundel, Myford, Kity Woodturning Lathes, accessories etc.
Trymwood Services, 2A Downs Park East (near the Downs), Bristol. 629092 2-6pm, Mondays to Fridays.

A. POLLARD & SON

De-Walt, Shopmate, Kity, Elu, Susemihl
We offer good service, good stocks and low prices
Dust extractors
A. Pollard & Son, 51 Queensway, Bletchley, Milton Keynes.
Tel: 0908-75221

ACCESS — BARCLAYCARD
Business established over 50 years.

BANDSAWS
The BIRCH 16" throat 2-speed BANDSAW, LINISHER and SANDER with fence, all attachments, two blades, two bands, complete, ready to plug in, £146 plus VAT. Send for illustrated details.
HAB Eng., Fardons Ind. Est., Glover Street, Birmingham 9 Tel. 021-772 2699

Sorby WOODTURNING TOOLS
Also peppermills, barometers, thermometers, lighters, hourglasses, eggtimers, sealers and polishes, sawtooth bits, screwboxes and taps, ceramic tiles, spinning wheel plans, P.E.G. Stockists of Kity, Myford and Arundel lathes. S.A.E. for list.
ERIC TOMKINSON 86 Stockport Road, Cheadle, Cheshire SK8 2AJ
Tel: 061-491 1726 & 061-428 3740
Now open every Wednesday, Thursday, Friday and Saturday

ELU 600 WATT PLUNGING ROUTER KIT COMPLETE WITH FENCES, CUTTERS, ETC. PLUS FREE TREND ROUTER. CUTTERS TO THE VALUE OF £5.00 inc. WITH EVERY PURCHASE. £76.00 inc. VAT (P&P, Ins. £2.50).

For further details and other special offers, send 3 x 10p Stamps to: W. THATCHER & SON LTD. Est. 1934, 221A Kilburn High Road, LONDON N.W.6, or Telephone 01-624-5146. Day St. Albans 32350 Evenings.

Callers welcome by appointment please.
ORDERS ALSO TAKEN BY BARCLAYCARD.

HAMPSHIRE WOODWORKING MACHINERY
HOE FARM HOUSE HOE ROAD BISHOPS WALTHAM SOUTHAMPTON HAMPSHIRE

YOUR LOCAL STOCKISTS FOR:

Arundel

CORONET

Elu

KITY

STARTRITE

Tel: B.W. (04893) 2275
Demonstrations: Mon., Wed., Sat.

PETER CRISP OF RUSHDEN THE CARPENTER'S SHOP

Hand Tools by leading makers. Stockists of:
Craftsmen, Coronet, Elu, Kity, Woodworking Machinery. Sorby Turning Chisels Taylor Carving Chisels Gomex T/Carbide Circular Saws

Stock list 25p
Illustrated Catalogue — 75p
(Refundable on first order over £10)

Tel. 093 34 56424-7
High Street, Rushden, Northants.

CIRCULAR and band saw blades for all applications from: A. A. Smith of Lancing Ltd., Churchill Industrial Estate, Lancing, Sussex. Tel: 09063-4474. L-R

TOOLS OF QUALITY
for Craftsmen and Handymen

We also supply a wide range of British-made screws: steel, brass, plated, Pozidriv, etc.
Send for our free illustrated lists before you buy. You'll be glad you did!

BENMAIL SUPPLIES
St. Georges, Weston-s-Mare, Avon

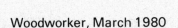

QUESTION BOX COUPON

★

MARCH

THIS COUPON MUST BE CLIPPED AND INCLUDED WITH YOUR QUERY

SEND SAE

FOR OVERSEAS READERS THIS COUPON IS VALID FOR 6 MONTHS

Something to sell?
Something to buy?
Try a **WOODWORKER**
Classified Advertisement
Lineage for only 14p per word min. £2.40 or display classified £3.00 per single column centimetre, min. £7.50. Box numbers £1.00 extra. Use the coupon on page 204 of this issue or phone Gill (0442) 41221 extn. 241.

All advertisements are inserted in the first available issue.

Classified Advertisements

From:

....

....

....

I enclose remittance value........................to cover ....

Insertions under the heading:

WORKSHOP EQUIPMENT	☐	BOOKS, PUBLICATIONS, ETC	☐
COURSES	☐	GENERAL	☐
CRAFT AND ANTIQUE TOOLS	☐	MATERIALS	☐
WANTED	☐	FOR SALE	

To: **WOODWORKER**
CLASSIFIED ADVERTISEMENT DEPT.
P.O. BOX 35, 13 BRIDGE STREET,
HEMEL HEMPSTEAD, HERTS. HP1 1EE

- ★ **Lineage rate 14p a word. Minimum charge £2.40**
- ★ **Semi display single column cm= £3.00 (Minimum £7.50 which is 2.5 cm. Maximum 5 cm)**
- ★ **Box number 50p extra**

Name and address if to appear must be paid for

BLOCK CAPITALS PLEASE

....	....	....	....	....
....	....	....	....	....
....	....	....	....	....
....	....	....	....	....
....	....	....	....	....

Prices quoted are those prevailing at press date and are subject to alteration due to economic conditions.

Woodworker

THE MAGAZINE FOR THE CRAFTSMAN IN WOOD

APRIL 1980   VOL. 84   NO. 1037

FRONT COVER: Violin repair clamp that won a prize in last year's Schools Design Prize competition for David Morton of Colchester. Details of this year's competition see page 228 (photo: courtesy *The Design Council*).

Editor	Geoffrey Pratt
Production Editor	Polly Curds
Advertisement Manager	Terence M. Healy
Group Advertisement Manager	Michael Merrifield
Managing Director	Gospatric Home
Editorial Director	Ron Moulton

MEMBER OF THE AUDIT
BUREAU OF CIRCULATIONS

SUBSCRIPTION DEPARTMENT: Remittances to MODEL AND ALLIED PUBLICATIONS, P.O. Box 35, Hemel Hempstead, Herts HP1 1EE. Price per copy 50p plus postage 21p. Subscription queries: Tel: Hemel Hempstead 51740. Subscription rate, including index £9.00 per annum; overseas sterling £9.00; $20.00 U.S. for overseas dollar subscribers. Second class postage paid at New York, NY North American enquiries regarding news stand sales should be sent to: Eastern News Distribution, 111 Eighth Avenue, New York, NY 1011, USA. Telephone (212) 255-5620 and craft and hobby sales to Bill Dean Books Ltd., 166-41 Powells Cove Boulevard, Whitestone, New York 11357, USA. Telephone (212) 767-6632.

Model & Allied Publications Ltd

P.O. Box 35, Bridge Street, Hemel Hempstead, Herts HP1 1EE. Telephone: Hemel Hempstead (0442) 41221.

TIMBER SUPPLIES

Total amount of softwood available for sale in Britain through the Russian selling organisation will probably be around 1.1m³, a reduction of about 20% on 1979. The first offer for 1980 shipment to our importers is reported to show a rise of around 14% averaged over the five main grades. Increased handling costs through the trade will also have to be taken into account when pricing through to users.

Sweden is another important supplier of softwood to Britain. A recent report by that country's forestry and national industrial boards states that the upsurge in world oil prices has made wood more competitive as a source of fuel and could threaten supplies of round wood. In fact, wood could contribute some 7-8% of Sweden's total energy output by 1990 and help to reduce oil imports by about 4m tonnes a year.

To limit the conflict of interest the two boards recommend that the Swedish government should control the use of wood as a fuel and that forest owners be induced to take more timber from their holdings by improving forestry methods and developing techniques which would make it more profitable for them to harvest more wood.

In previous issues of WOODWORKER over the past year we have drawn attention to the importance of developing Britain's forest resources as well as considering alternative species — and sources — of the raw material. There is plenty of timber in the world and it is a renewable resource but, as a contributor in the August 1979 issue pointed out, some shortages are certain to become acute over the coming 20 years.

Last year we spent more than £2.4bn on imported timber and wood-based products and as George Holmes, the Forestry Commission's director-general told the British Association meeting at Edinburgh, last year, action is required 'right away' if difficulties in wood supply are not to be exacerbated in the next century. He said our forests would double in area to nearly 8m acres over the next 45 years and that we should be able to continue expanding our forests while maintaining agricultural production.

International events have moved swiftly since Mr Holmes made his speech and these, coupled with the long lead times of forestry, make it all the more important for the government to give prompt attention (and active encouragement) to improving and enlarging our own timber resources.

Small firms in Scotland

Through its small business division the Scottish Development Agency offers technical assistance to woodworking firms. The SDA woodworking officer can give advice and instruction over a wide range of subjects. These include: maintenance of machinery; sharpening tools; supply of plant and materials; investigation of faulty operating equipment; workshop layout; safety considerations; jigs and tooling for repetitive work; timber condition; optimum production methods; individual tuition for employees; and product design.

No charges are made for short advisory visits (up to 4hr in a firm's premises) by the woodworking officer, though a small charge is made for longer or multiple visits.

Leaflets giving details of these services as well as publications on assistance for craftworkers; finance; counselling; and technical instruction can be had from the Scottish Development Agency (small business division), 102 Telford Road, Edinburgh.

THE CHEPSTOW 17-37 'GAP BED' LATHE

FROM

V. H.

Willis

& CO. LTD.

190-2 West St., Bedminster,
BRISTOL
Tel. (0272) 667013

YOU CAN EASILY MAKE:

WINE GOBLETS, TABLE LAMPS,
NAPKIN RINGS, PEPPERMILLS, SALT
SHAKERS, EGG CUPS, POTS, TOBACCO JARS,
FRUIT BOWLS, ORNATE TABLE LEGS, ETC., ETC.

CREATE YOUR OWN DESIGNS!

THE BASIC SKILLS OF WOODTURNING ARE EASILY MASTERED TO
OPEN UP A NEW SIDE OF WOODWORKING.

LOOK AT THESE INCLUSIVE FEATURES!

KIT A

BOWL TURNING FACILITIES INCLUDING FACEPLATE TO MAX. DIA. 17"
DRIVING CENTRE AND TAILSTOCK CENTRES GIVING 37" BETWEEN
    CENTRES
WOODSCREW CHUCK 30mm DIA.
WOODSCREW CHUCK 60mm DIA.
SET OF SIX SORBY WOODTURNING CHISELS
SEALED BEARINGS — DOUBLE SHEILDED, DEEP GROOVE WITH NO
    MAINTENANCE
FIVE SPEEDS WITH 'POLY VEE' DRIVE. 530-3325r.p.m.

(LIST PRICE £235.25
£195.00
INCLUDING V.A.T.

KIT B

AS ABOVE, BUT WITH ½ h.p. BROOKES MOTOR, BELT TENSION BRACKET
AND NO VOLT OVERLOAD SWITCH.

(LIST PRICE £308.85
£265.00
INCLUDING V.A.T.

★ FREE CARRIAGE — U.K. MAINLAND ★

HOW TO ORDER:
    SEND CHEQUE OR CREDIT CARD NO.
To: V. H. WILLIS & CO., LTD.
   190-2 West Street, Bedminster, Bristol
   Telephone: 0272-667013
★ *Barclaycard or Access Numbers taken by Phone*

The CHEPSTOW 17-37 we believe to be the best
value for money on the market, it combines performance and specification with low price. The deep
groove thrust bearings are fully enclosed for maintenance-free operation. Bed of Lathe is of two lengths
of 1" solid cold rolled steel, essential other parts cast.

SEE US AT BRISTOL IDEAL HOMES EXHIBITION
APRIL 4-12 INCLUSIVE

Prices quoted are those prevailing at press date and
are subject to alteration due to economic conditions.

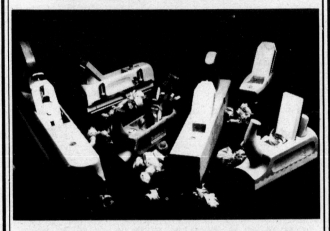

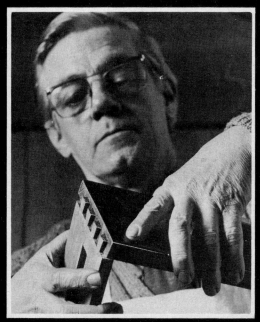

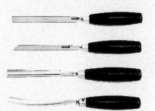

208

Prices quoted are those prevailing at press date and are subject to alteration due to economic conditions.

Woodworker, April 1980

Prices quoted are those prevailing at press date and are subject to alteration due to economic conditions.

GARDEN TABLE AND CHAIR IN AFRORMOSIA

With spring on the way now's the time to make furniture for outside. A. Yarwood designed and made these pieces

This table and chair were designed and made to enable me to make better use of the garden when the weather is good enough to continue in the open air with work usually carried on indoors. The following details of the design of the two pieces should be noted: The table, at 735mm (28⅞in.) is of a normal table height, as is the chair seat at 450mm (17⅞in.) a common dining chair height. Both the table top and the chair seat are slatted to allow rainwater to pass through and so not form as pools on flat surfaces. The chair seat tilts to the back 13mm (½in.) and the chair back also tilts from the seat to allow a comfortable seating position. There are no arms to the chair because it was designed as a working chair.

Frames for table and chair are of simple design relying, in part, on the slats of their tops to form part of the construction. The wood chosen for making the two items was afrormosia. Dimensions for the table and chair can be taken from Figs. 1 and 2 and from the cutting lists.

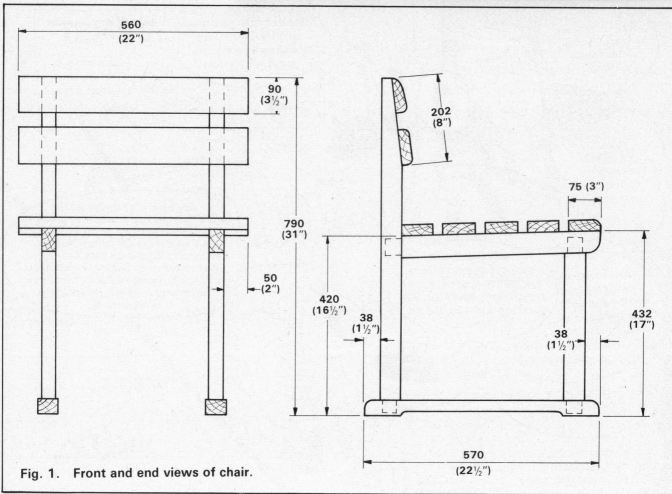

Fig. 1.   Front and end views of chair.

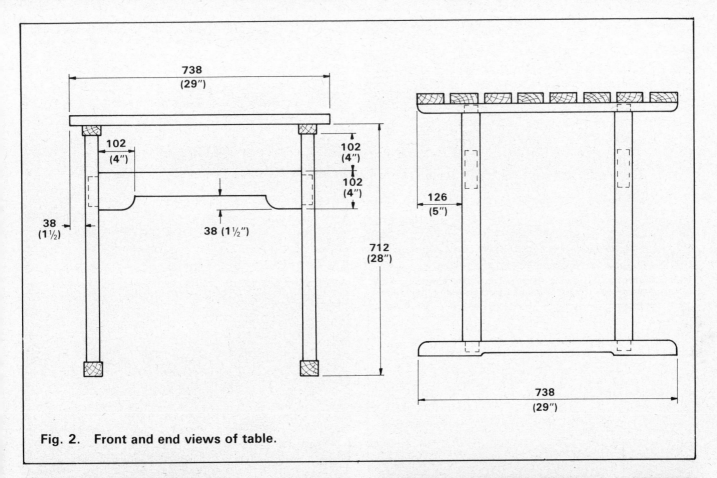

Fig. 2.   Front and end views of table.

738
(29")

102
(4")

102
(4")

102
(4")

38
(1½)

38 (1½")

712
(28")

126
(5")

738
(29")

Afrormosia is an African hardwood. The tree is found growing in the drier parts of the W African forests — Ivory Coast, Ghana, parts of Nigeria and in the central African state (formerly the Congo). The tree grows to large sizes, logs of 5m (15ft) long and 1m (3ft) in diameter being quite common. When freshly sawn the wood is a yellow-brown colour which darkens on exposure to the atmosphere to a deeper brown. The seasoned wood is fairly hard and dense, although it works well with sharp and well-adjusted tools. Surfaces with interlocking grain are common. Grain figure can be very good. The wood is classified as very durable which suggests it will not deteriorate if left out in all weathers. This last characteristic makes afrormosia a very suitable choice for garden furniture. Its cost is about 50% to 60% that of teak.

I bought two sawn boards of afrormosia for this job. One board was 40mm (about 1½in.) thick, the other 25mm (about 1in.) thick.

After marking out the various parts for both table and chair on the two boards the pieces were sawn to size. This was followed by a session of planing during which all pieces were planed to their final widths and thicknesses.

Care was taken throughout the planing to ensure that each piece was straight and square. All pieces were then sawn to their finished lengths. Work on the construction started by marking out and cutting the joints for both the chair side frames and the table side frames. The constructions for these frames can be seen in Figs. 3 and 4. All the joints are mortises and tenons and it should be noted that the tenons marked A on Fig. 3 are 13mm (½in.) thick, while those marked B (Figs. 3 and 4) are 19mm (¾in.) thick. The reason for using two different thicknesses of tenon are clear when you consider that some of the mortises (those marked A) are cut into the 35mm (1⅜in.) edge of the chair rear legs and chair seat rails. All other

mortises are cut into the 51mm (2in.) width of the other frame members.

All tenons were cut with a tenon saw. Waste from the mortise holes was partially removed with the aid of a 13mm (½in.) bit in a power drill before being finished with an appropriate size of mortise chisel. None of the mortises are worked right through, all being stopped.

After checking that all joints fitted well the rear chair legs were sawn and planed to the taper required for the seat back, and the recesses along the bottom of all ground rails were sawn and chiselled out. The four frames could then be glued and cramped together. The chair frames were glued first, using my four sash cramps. When the glue on these two frames had set hard the table

Above: Cramping and gluing frames. Top right: Screwing back slats of chair to legs. Right: Using bandsaw to shape table rails.

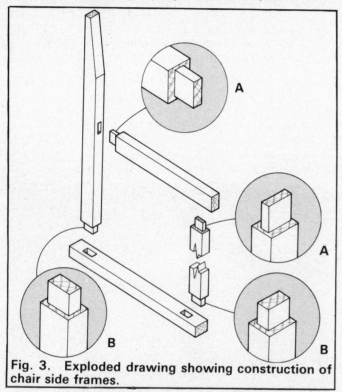

Fig. 3. Exploded drawing showing construction of chair side frames.

Below: Screwing table top slats to framework.

Cutting Lists

Dimensions in mm and in. Some metric dimensions are rounded to the nearest 5 mm. No allowance for any waste. Finished sizes only given.

Chair

2 rear legs	785 × 50 × 35	$30\frac{7}{8} \times 2 \times 1\frac{3}{8}$
2 front legs	425 × 50 × 35	$16\frac{3}{4} \times 2 \times 1\frac{3}{8}$
2 ground rails	570 × 50 × 35	$22\frac{1}{2} \times 2 \times 1\frac{3}{8}$
2 seat rails	520 × 50 × 35	$20\frac{1}{2} \times 2 \times 1\frac{3}{8}$
5 seat slats	560 × 75 × 22	$22 \times 3 \times \frac{7}{8}$
2 back slats	560 × 90 × 22	$22 \times 3\frac{1}{2} \times \frac{7}{8}$
26 screws	50 × gauge 10	2 × gauge 10
2 screws	45 × gauge 10	$1\frac{3}{4}$ × gauge 10

Table

4 legs	705 × 50 × 35	$27\frac{3}{4} \times 2 \times 1\frac{3}{8}$
2 top end rails	738 × 50 × 22	$29 \times 2 \times \frac{7}{8}$
2 ground rails	738 × 50 × 35	$29 \times 2 \times 1\frac{3}{8}$
2 top rails	650 × 100 × 35	$25\frac{1}{2} \times 4 \times 1\frac{3}{8}$
8 top slats	738 × 75 × 22	$29 \times 3 \times \frac{7}{8}$
32 screws	35 × gauge 10	$1\frac{1}{2}$ × gauge 10

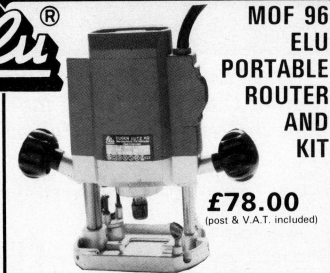

'trend tipcut

The Tungsten Carbide Tipped Router Cutter for use by the Amateur Craftsman .... Fits all Hand Routers!

At last ... with the arrival of Tip-Cut, we have a range of high quality TCT cutters, 'within the pocket' of the amateur craftsman.

✳ Tungsten quality .... top grade.

✳ Brazing of
   Tips ....to highest standard.

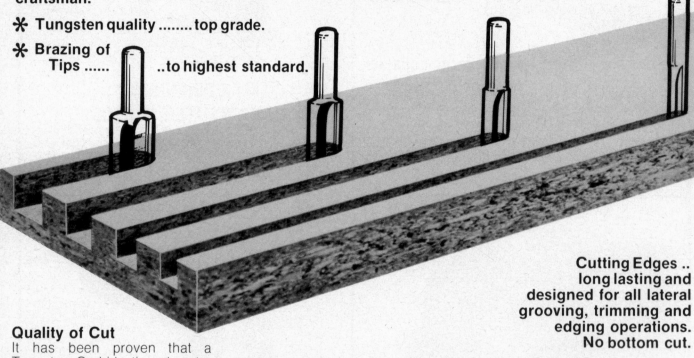

Cutting Edges ..
long lasting and
designed for all lateral
grooving, trimming and
edging operations.
No bottom cut.

Quality of Cut

It has been proven that a Tungsten Carbide tipped router bit will outlast normal HSS cutters many times, when abrasive materials are involved.

When to use Tip-Cut

Abrasive materials which require tungsten tipped tools are mainly: Chipboard, Plywood, Hardboard, Conti-board. Plastic Laminates, and Glass Reinforced Plastics. Routing from the edge of the work, Tip-Cut two flute cutters will efficiently groove and profile the above materials.

SHANK ¼" DIAM.	PRICES 1979	D	C	B	ORDER REF
	£4.95	1/4"	5/8"	1"	T14
	£5.30	3/8"	5/8"	1"	T38
	£5.75	1/2"	5/8"	1"	T12
	£6.35	5/8"	5/8"	1"	T58
	£21.50	Set of Four above			Set TA

A Cutter Wall Chart is available from Trend Cutter stockists, which describes a large range of shaped cutters, both in High Speed Steel and Tungsten Carbide.

If in difficulty, write in or phone for details of cutter dealers who stock Trend Products.

Write for cutter chart NOW!

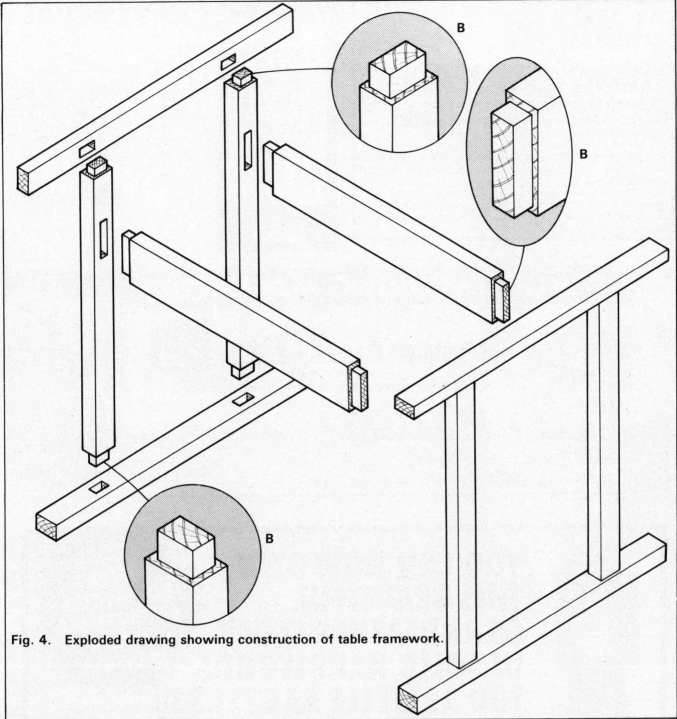

Fig. 4. Exploded drawing showing construction of table framework.

Completed chair.

frames were glued and cramped. Cascamite glue was used because of its water-resistant properties.

As each frame was released from its cramps, the top corners of all ground rails and the lower corners of the chair seat rails were rounded by chiselling and sanding. The outer surfaces of each frame were cleaned-up with a finely set and sharp smoothing plane. All corners of the various parts of the frames were then rounded slightly by sanding.

The five seat rails could now be secured to their end frames with two 50mm (2 in.) gauge 10 brass CS screws at each end. These screws were fitted from underneath the chair seat rails. The back slats of the chair were secured to their tapers of the back legs with either 50mm or 45mm (2 in. or 1¾ in.) gauge 10 brass CS screws — two screws at each end of each slat from the rear of the chair legs. This completed the construction of the chair.

Before fixing the table top slats in place, the two rails joining the two end frames to each other had to be completed. After cutting tenons at the ends of these rails their lower edges were shaped as shown in Fig. 2. After cleaning up both rails they were glued and cramped to the two end frames. Upon releasing the glued-up frames from the cramps the table top slats could be fixed to them. Two 35mm (1½ in.) gauge 10 brass CS screws at each end of each slat, driven in from underneath the top frame rails, secured the slats to the frames. A final sanding of corners, edges and ends completed the table.

No finish was applied to the two pieces. Afrormosia, like teak, weathers to a pleasing golden brown if left out in all weathers. However, you may wish to retain the original brown colouring of the wood. In this case two or three brush coats of a good-quality, clear polyurethane varnish would seem appropriate.

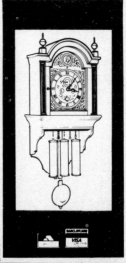
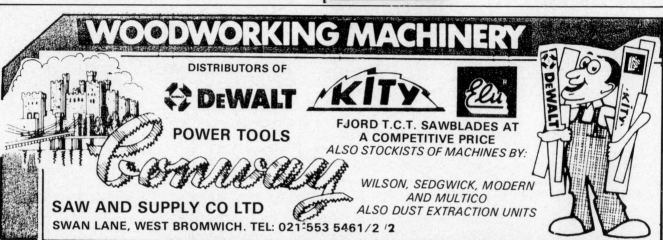

218

Prices quoted are those prevailing at press date and
are subject to alteration due to economic conditions.

Woodworker, April 1980

Guild of Woodworkers

Carving seminar at West Dean

Guild of Woodworkers carving seminar (intermediate level) will be held at West Dean College, West Dean, Chichester, Sussex, from Friday evening 23 May to Sunday evening 25 May inclusive. There has been an enthusiastic response to earlier announcements and it has been decided that as members will wish to have the benefit of individual tuition numbers should be restricted to 24 for this residential seminar. Applications will therefore be considered in order of receipt though a reserve list will be kept. Booking forms can be had from the guild's administrator David Whitehouse at PO Box 35, Bridge Street, Hemel Hempstead HP1 1EE. Early application is advised to avoid disappointment. Lecturers include Phillip Bentham of West Dean College and John Sainsbury, Record-Ridgway education advisor until his retirement at the end of last year.

Provisional programme for the seminar is as follows: Friday 23 May 6.30 pm — members assemble at the College for informal dinner at 7.00pm followed by discussions. Saturday 24 May 9.30am-12.30pm courses and lectures; lunch 1.00pm; 2.30pm-4.30pm courses and lectures; 4.30pm afternoon tea; 7.00pm dinner; 8.00pm special film show at the College. Sunday 24 May 9.30am-12.30pm courses and lectures; lunch 1.00pm; 2.30pm-4.30pm courses and lectures; 4.45pm seminar closes. The provisional programme has been arranged to allow members ample time for informal discussions among themselves and with the lecturers. All courses and lectures will be to groups of 12.

West Dean College has a limited number of sets of carving tools but members may bring their own if they so wish. Materials will be available from the College shop at extra cost, though members may bring their own materials.

Cost of the weekend seminar is £52 (plus VAT) per person. This includes: full board accommodation, membership of the College social club for the weekend; full tuition and use of College workshop facilities; and lecture and course fees.

There is a supplementary charge of £2 (plus VAT) payable by those wishing to have a private bathroom. The accommodation at West Dean comprises single and/or double rooms of which a certain number have bathrooms *en suite*.

Further seminars and courses on carving and other subjects are being planned for various locations throughout the country.

If you intend coming to West Dean in May to enjoy meeting your fellow members, taking part in an interesting seminar and seeing something of the delightful surroundings of the College, write to David Whitehouse for an application form.

Crafts by post

There are three shops where a substantial part of the Dryad range is available: Reeves-Dryad, 178 Kensington High Street, London; Binns, Paragon Square, Hull; and Dryad, Cumberland Street, Leicester. Over the next few years the number of stockists throughout the country will be increased. Meanwhile Dryad has issued its mail order catalogue *Dryad Crafts* running to 96 pages of high-quality printing with the illustrations in colour. (Cost £1.50 redeemable on orders over £10).

Company director M. Waddington writes in his foreword: 'This catalogue is unique in that it is specially designed with both the beginner and expert in mind and contains many of the suggestions that have been put forward to us over the past few months . . . . We have tried to give as accurate a description of the articles as possible so that everyone can be sure they are purchasing exactly what they want.'

Nearly 40 different crafts are covered including woodwork, marquetry and veneers, stool seating and cane work, spinning and weaving, toymaking, gold tooling and leatherwork. There is also a books section with titles on musical instruments, toys and woodworking. Dryad is at PO Box 38, Northgates, Leicester LE1 9BU.

Reduced charges

Members are reminded that a special facility has been arranged with Model and Allied Publications Ltd whereby they can obtain reduced entry charges at the following shows organised by MAP: Clocks for Everyman, Kensington Town Hall, London 3-6 July; Gem Craft Summer Expo, Crown Hotel, Harrogate 23-25 August; Old Motor Festival, Queens Hall, Leeds 12-14 September; Craft in Action, Kensington Town Hall, London 26-28 September; Woodworker Show, RHS New Hall, London 4-9 November; 50th Model Engineer Exhibition, Wembley Conference Centre 1-10 January 1981.

All that is necessary is for members to show their Guild of Woodworkers identity card at the entrance and thus obtain a reduction on the quoted 'gate price' at each of the shows.

Insurance of tools

David Whitehouse has been able to arrange an insurance 'all risks' scheme at advantageous rates. It covers members' woodworking tools and machinery at an average cost of 2½% of total value, though in certain high-risk areas this may be subject to variation.

Underwriters will require an excess of £5-£10 to obviate a large number of small claims, though under the guild's special scheme provision can also be made for the insurance of valuable collections of antique woodworking tools.

Of course the success of the 'all risks' scheme depends on maximum support and Mr Whitehouse looks forward to as many members as possible writing to him for details. His address is: Guild of Woodworkers, PO Box 35, Bridge Street, Hemel Hempstead HP1 1EE.

Membership

There has been a splendid response to the new concept of the guild as announced in the November issue of WOODWORKER last year. Currently membership is more than 900 — and increasing. Obviously, the greater number of woodworkers who enrol the more the guild will be able to achieve for its members.

Addresses please

Guild of Woodworkers administrator David Whitehouse comments that several new subscribers to the guild have either not given their correct addresses or their addresses have been incomplete. Thus their indentures forwarded by post have been returned to the guild office marked 'gone away.' Will new subscribers to the guild who have not yet received their indentures please write to Mr Whitehouse, Guild of Woodworkers, PO Box 35, Bridge Street, Hemel Hempstead HP1 1EE, and give their full postal address.

Subscribers who change address are asked to notify Mr Whitehouse as early as possible so that guild records can be kept up-to-date.

Homeworkers

Proposals for new regulations to replace outdated sections of the Factories Act and other legislation dealing with the registration of homeworkers have been published for consultation. The document *Homeworkers – draft regulations* is available from the Health & Safety Commission, HSE Enquiry Point, Baynards House, 1 Chepstow Place, London W2 4TF, at 50p. Comments should be sent not later than 30 June this year to: J. Renton, HSE Resources & Planning Division, Branch A1, Baynards House, 1 Chepstow Place, London W2 4TF.

The proposals aim to control risk from materials or equipment provided for homeworkers at source. Firms or individuals putting work out to homeworkers would send information to their local factory inspectors twice a year about the nature of the work and the materials or equipment used. A record of the names and addresses of homeworkers would be kept by the firms or individuals concerned.

By definition homeworkers would not include self-employed craftsmen and would cover only those who do not market their own product. Routine inspections of domestic premises would not be made; inspectors would assess potential risks from the returns of the type of work put out and the materials and equipment used. They would take up any question of risk to homeworkers with the supplier of the work.

The consultative document points out that craftsmen are distinct from homeworkers in that they work on their own initiative and are themselves responsible for marketing their product. It follows that they should be primarily responsible for health and safety conditions in the course of their work. Homeworkers, properly speaking, work for the person who puts out the work to them in the sense that they contribute to products which he markets. For this reason those who put out work to homeworkers bear the prime responsibility for ensuring that, so far as is reasonably practicable, no risks to health and safety arise.

'. . . bloom in the spring tra-la . . .'

Spring is here and now is the time for those outside jobs. For example, a garden shed. Here H. W. Gates gives constructional notes for such a building; he has also supplied the drawings.

Whether for storage of tools or use as a workshop the basic construction of the garden shed is similar, with some refinements when required for workshop use.

Figs. 1 and 2 show two types of building: a lean-to and a couple roof having two slopes. Which to choose is influenced by the size required. As the parts are made up in sections and assembled on site these buildings are termed portable, and erection and dismantling is a simple procedure.

Joints used in the construction are usually of the type shown in Fig. 3: slotted mortise and tenon, halved or housed or a combination of these. Assembly of the sections after the joints are prepared is simplified if four stools and some boards are available to bring the work up to a convenient height.

For small sheds 50 x 50mm material is sufficient for the construction, and two purlins will be adequate in each roof slope. There are two methods for marking up the roof sections: (a) the boards are fixed directly to the purlins; and (b) using separate battens to hold the boards together; these battens rest against the purlins when the roof sections are in place, see Figs. 6 and 7.

Door end or side This can be as shown in Fig. 5, with the bottom plate in one piece, or the piece across the opening can be omitted to allow for the movement of a heavy lawn-mower. In the case of a lean-to the door can be placed in the end or highest side. Another consideration if the shed is for workshop use is the size of the doorway; it can be increased in width to accommodate double doors.

Windows As the position of the studs controls the window sizes consideration must be given to this when designing the framework. The size of the window is governed by whether the building is to be used as a workshop or for storage. For both purposes an opening is necessary to provide ventilation.

In Fig. 4. a roof light is incorporated, this being ideal for a workshop or studio and provides the maximum amount of available light. Sawn material is used for the framework but the window linings, stops etc should be prepared timber. The casements are usually top hung and have stays fitted at the bottom. The sills are either bevelled to form the weathering with a stop planted on, or worked from the solid (Fig. 9).

Boarding There are various ways to cover the frames such as t&g matched boards, weather boards, but for a superior finish timber 'siding' is obtainable in several different sections. Suitable timbers are cedar, pine and redwood. Exterior grade plywood can also be used.

Doors These consist of vertical t&g boards with ledgers and braces. A door superior in appearance and with improved security is a framed ledged and braced door. This is the type of door I would personally recommend for a workshop. Boards, ledgers and braces should be carefully selected, the component parts must be flat and true, otherwise the door will be in wind (or twisted). Once this occurs the condition cannot be rectified.

Floors A timber floor provides a better surface to stand on when the building is used as a workshop and assists in the prevention of damp conditions. The floor can be built as a complete unit or in sections. The sides and the ends stand on the floor and their boarding projects to cover the floor.

To provide under-floor ventilation the building should be raised above the slab or paving by standing the floor section on sleepers. All timber in contact with the base and the underside of the floor should have a thorough treatment of wood preservative.

Finishing The other parts of the building can be treated with wood preservative to maintain the natural colour of the timber. Certain types of preservative can also be painted or varnished over after they have dried. This method will protect the timber against attack by insects and rot. (See reference to exterior finish on page 687 of November 1979 issue).

Barge boards improve the appearance and help to keep the weather out. These are fixed to the ends of the boards and to the ends of the purlins, if these are extended. Insulation is improved by lining the inside of the shed with thin t&g boards, hardboard or plywood. (See also reference to noise insulation on page 123 of February 1980 issue, and to heat insulation on page 398 of July 1979 issue). (Fig. 8 refers).

Site preparation – concrete slabs Having selected the site for the shed, there are several basic site works to be carried out:

1 Remove the vegetation and top soil. Any roots in the subsoil should be taken out so that a smooth, firm surface is provided. Tamping will be beneficial.
2 For a large shed to be used as workshop a base of hardcore is necessary if machines are to be installed. The hardcore should be laid to a depth of 125mm, and the concrete should be 75mm to 100mm in thickness.
3 Finished height of the slab should be above the level of the surrounding soil.
4 A vapour barrier to prevent rising moisture from entering the slab can be laid over the hardcore. Polyethylene film, bitumen-coated papers and metal foil are used for this purpose.
5 When a timber floor is to be used, an alternative to the slab is brick walls or piers, supporting plates or sleepers to carry the floor. The soil beneath the building will require treatment to prevent the growth of weeds. 'Blinding' with ashes or gravel or a chemical treatment are all effective measures.

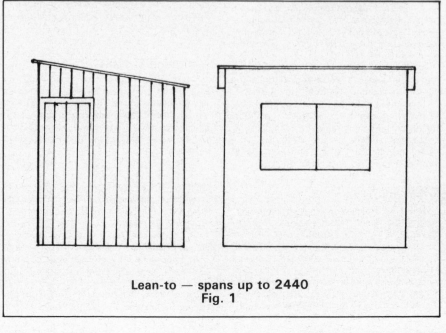

GARDEN SHEDS

Lean-to — spans up to 2440
Fig. 1

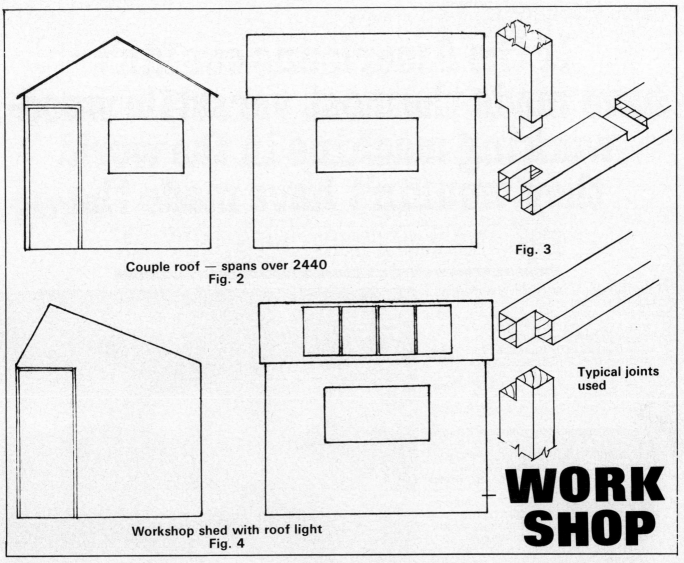

Couple roof — spans over 2440
Fig. 2

Fig. 3

Workshop shed with roof light
Fig. 4

Typical joints
used

WORK SHOP

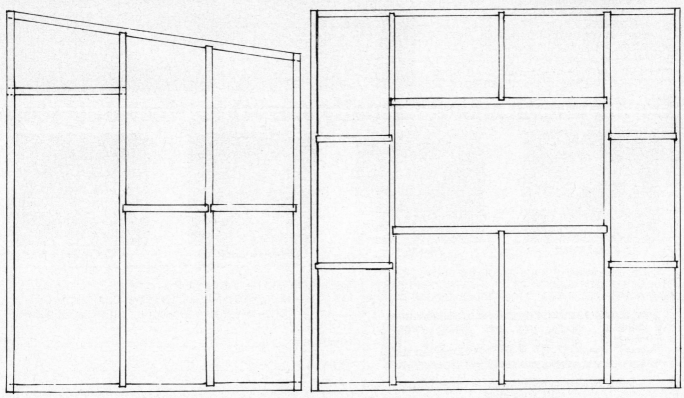

Typical frame construction
Fig. 5

If the Americans couldn't have made the most versatile wood-working machine in the world they wouldn't have made the

SHOPSMITH MARK V

The SHOPSMITH Mk V is the only machine in the world to combine a lathe, sawbench, disc sander, horizontal boring machine and vertical drill press in a single unit taking up no more space than an ordinary bicycle!

More than 350,000 Americans have chosen the 'Smith' as the ultimate solution for their home workshop and currently around 500 customers are choosing the SHOPSMITH **every week!** It is easy to understand why.

No other machine offers all these unique features:

- Five basic machines including vertical drill press.
- Special Add-To Machines include Bandsaw, Planer, Belt Sander and Fret Saw plus accessories enabling a total of 16 different machine operations.
- Automatic speed dial from 700 rpm to 5200 rpm without even turning the machine off. Just dial the correct speed for whatever operation is required.
- With SHOPSMITH'S exclusive Quill Feed Control any required depth of feed is pre-set, locked and absolute accuracy is guaranteed.

Whether you are just starting in woodwork or been at it for years the SHOPSMITH Mk V will give you the home workshop you have always wanted – to build the projects you have always dreamed of.

The Shopsmith makes virtually everything - including sense!

CROSSCUTTING

SANDING

HORIZONTAL BORING

VERTICAL DRILLING

The SHOPSMITH is now available from SUMACO – the UK's leading importer of the world's finest smaller woodworker machines, and their appointed distributors.

Suma House, Huddersfield Road, ELLAND, W.Yorkshire
Tel. (0422) 75491/2

Please send: Further information on the
Shopsmith Mk 5 ☐ (Enclose 10p stamps)
The full Sumaco catalogue ☐ (Enclose 50p stamps)

NAME _____

ADDRESS _____

_____
SS2

Prices quoted are those prevailing at press date and are subject to alteration due to economic conditions.

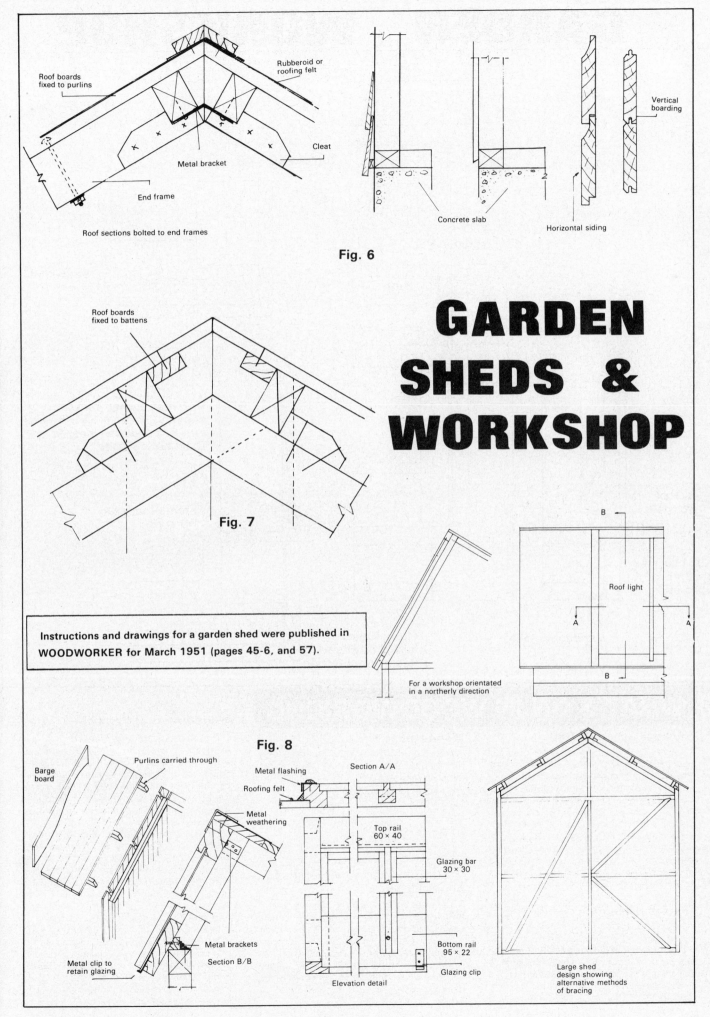

Roof boards fixed to purlins

Rubberoid or roofing felt

Metal bracket

Cleat

End frame

Roof sections bolted to end frames

Fig. 6

Concrete slab

Horizontal siding

Vertical boarding

Roof boards fixed to battens

Fig. 7

GARDEN
SHEDS &
WORKSHOP

Instructions and drawings for a garden shed were published in
WOODWORKER for March 1951 (pages 45-6, and 57).

For a workshop orientated in a northerly direction

B

Roof light

A

A

B

Fig. 8

Barge board

Purlins carried through

Metal flashing

Roofing felt

Section A/A

Metal weathering

Top rail 60 × 40

Glazing bar 30 × 30

Bottom rail 95 × 22

Metal clip to retain glazing

Metal brackets

Section B/B

Glazing clip

Elevation detail

Large shed design showing alternative methods of bracing

GARDEN WORKSHOP

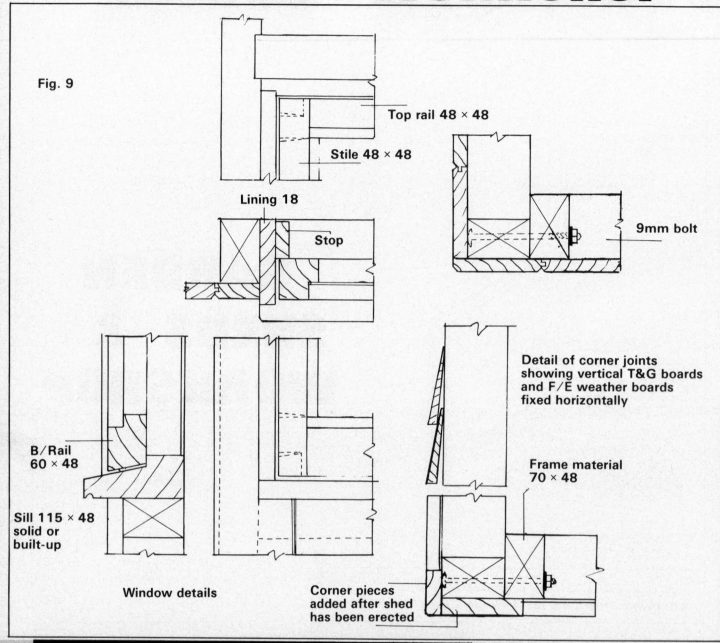

Fig. 9

Top rail 48 × 48

Stile 48 × 48

Lining 18

Stop

9mm bolt

Detail of corner joints
showing vertical T&G boards
and F/E weather boards
fixed horizontally

B/Rail
60 × 48

Frame material
70 × 48

Sill 115 × 48
solid or
built-up

Window details

Corner pieces
added after shed
has been erected

WHAT'S ON IN WOODWORKING

Summer Schools 1980

Interested in a summer school? Send 10p stamp for full details to the Registrar, 35 Park Road, Hemel Hempstead, Herts HP1 1JS if you are interested in courses at West Dean College, Chichester, Sussex from July 28-August 8 (these include: a short course in traditional clockmaking), or at Leeds Polytechnic, Becket Park, Leeds from July 20-August 2 (these include one or two-week courses in cane basketry, rural crafts, wood and allied materials, woodturning and foundation design studies).

Dial an exhibition

If you are looking for something to do in London or want to make sure you do not miss a major exhibition Dial an exhibition will give you plenty of ideas. It is a service provided by the Inter-Museums Public Relations Group in association with the London Tourist Board. The number to dial is 01-730 0977.

Woodworker Show 1980

From November 4-9 inclusive at the Royal Horticultural Society's New Hall, Westminster, London SW1.

Clocks for Everyman

Kensington Town Hall, London 3-6 July.

Craft in Action

Kensington Town Hall, London 26-28 September.

Day lectures at the Victoria and Albert Museum

Tuesdays at 13.15. March 18 in the lecture theatre: The furniture of the '60s (lecturer Leela Meinertas); March 25 in the lecture theatre. Modern architecture — second thoughts? (lecturer Launce Gribbin).

Saturdays at 15.00. March 22 gallery lecture on Seventeenth-century continental cabinets (lecturer Anne Manningham-Buller).

Woodturners at Parnham

An international two day seminar for woodturners will be held at Parnham House, Beaminster, Dorset on 14 and 15 June. Organised by Parnham House and supported by the World Crafts Council, the Crafts Council of Great Britain and the Furniture Industry Training Board, the seminar will be conducted by Stephen Hogbin of Canada, Neville Neal and Richard Raffan of Britain and Bob Stockdale of the US. Other speakers will include Paul Smith, director of the Museum of Contemporary Crafts in New York and the design critic Professor Stephen Bayley. Running concurrently with the seminar will be a series of one-man exhibitions of wood turnery, including a selection from the late Edward Pinto's collection of treen. Those interested in places for the seminar should contact: Brian James, Arts Administrator, Parnham House, Beaminster, Dorset DT8 3NA (phone Beaminster (0308) 862204). Places are strictly limited; early application is urged.

BOOKS, REVIEWS, GUIDES...

Something for everyone

Woodworker Annual Vol. 83 is comprised of the 12 monthly issues of WOODWORKER magazine for 1979, and as such contains more than 700 pages of well-illustrated and informative articles on a wide range of subjects. For example, how to build and erect a timber-framed house porch; how to make a sewing cabinet; start wood sculpture; how to use various tools; and many more.

A good magazine is one which by its editorial content encourages a lively response from its readers and WOODWORKER is a leading one in this respect: articles written by knowledgeable people are frequently commented upon, the supposition, the moot point, the argument and the field of enquiry figuring often in readers' letters and enquiries.

Accordingly, *Woodworker Annual* is a work of reference to a wide range of wood and allied subjects sometimes reflecting more than one point of view, and also providing a convenient basis of study for the newcomer to craft and leisure woodworking.

It is easy to enthuse over the general excellence of this annual but rather more difficult to offer constructive criticism. However, bearing in mind the value of easy reference, some thought could be given to extending the index so as to cover all references under a common heading. For example, under the heading 'finishing' would be page references covering articles devoted to the subject (probably also included under a more obscure title), broken down into sub-headings, say, oil, french, polyurethane, paint, varnish etc and including readers' letters and enquiries where applicable. Stains as a heading would have sub-headings such as: water, water-based, spirit-based, fungal, chemical etc.

Question Box, for examples, has 15 entries in the current index but over 100 different questions and answers. It also seems a pity that the front cover coloured pictures cannot be included in the annual since these are invariably excellent. Since space is at a premium, would it not be possible to exclude the advertisement pages from, say, the first six monthly issues in order to accommodate some changes as suggested for 1980?

Woodworker Annual Vol. 83 is published by Model and Allied Publications Argus Books Ltd, 14 St James Road, Watford, Herts, at £7.95 (UK only). It is a must for the woodworker, be he a professional craftsman or a mere dabbler in wood. **W.H.B.**

Whither woodworking?

For those of us who aspire to things above the ordinary in woodworking James Krenov has written *The Impractical Cabinetmaker*, though you cannot help feeling that a knowledge of his two earlier books on the subject would help to put this one into prospective.

Its enigmatic title is explained in the opening chapters in what is an inspiring essay on the author's philosophy of craftwork. His is a highly individual approach and you can sense through his words the integrity and honesty of the man and at the same time respond to his rare sympathy for wood.

James Krenov is in the top, and international, flight of contemporary designer-craftsmen, yet in his modesty denies that there is such an animal! He quotes instead his own maxim for success: 'Try to live the way you are, be the person in your work that you are in the rest of your life.'

Yet this is no book full of personal theorising; there is much knowledge and know-how contained in its pages. Fine photographs throughout show not only finished pieces but useful techniques of manufacture as well, and these are accompanied in some instances by the author's original design sketches.

The designs themselves owe nothing to the English tradition of cabinet making and by comparison appear bald and approaching the monolithic. Hints of starkness, however, are relieved by some very subtle curving, and careful selection of the wood for each individual piece yields distinctive results. You are taken along the steps by which these pieces were designed then made, providing unique insights into the principles and methods by which this superb artist works.

It is all most enjoyable and instructive reading and provides a significant signpost to those of us who ponder the directions that the craft of hand woodworking might follow. Publisher is Van Nostrand Reinhold Co Ltd, Molly Millars Lane, Wokingham, Berks, and the price is £8.50. **R.W.G.**

Directory of craftsmen

Craftsmen in the building and allied trades as well as other crafts, and artist craftsmen are listed in the *Directory of Members 1979-80* of the Guild of Master Craftsmen which has its administrative office at 10 Dover Street, London W1X 3PH. In the first section names are listed alphabetically by county and alphabetically by name within counties. In the second section they are arranged alphabetically by craft and alphabetically by county within crafts. In the last section the names are arranged alphabetically by county. The directory costs £4.75.

Buyer's guide

The Educational Institute of Design, Craft and Technology *Craft Buyer's Guide 1980* of some 136 pages is published by Kogan Page Ltd, 120 Pentonville Road, London N1 9JN, at £4.95. First part of the book consists of topical articles on the subject of craft education, a useful one being devoted to adhesives for school use. Second part of the book is a directory listing manufacturers, suppliers of tools, machines and materials for some 46 different crafts including carpentry and joinery; woodworking; treen and woodturning; pyrography; leatherwork; rural crafts; and children's crafts.

The Guide also refers to safety training for teachers in school workshops for which subject course elements have been prepared by the Association of Advisers in Design & Technical Studies in consultation with the Health & Safety Executive.

Acknowledgement

WOODWORKER wishes to thank H. G. Harrison for the colour picture of Tea Break sculpted by S. Cliffe Ashworth to be found on page 240 of this issue.

Edward Barnsley

Readers will join WOODWORKER in wishing many happy returns to Edward Barnsley who celebrated his 80th birthday on February 9. Mr. Barnsley, probably the country's most distinguished furniture maker, has had his workshop at Froxfield, Hants, since he took over from Geoffrey Lupton, to whom he was apprenticed, in 1923. It is understood that plans are being made to turn the business into a charitable trust so that the traditions of design and workmanship can be upheld and new master-craftsmen trained. At the present time the staff numbers four, including foreman 'Bert' Upton who has been with Mr. Barnsley since 1924, all but one of whom are of retiring age. Orders are as good as ever but it has been impossible to take on the many would-be apprentices who present themselves at Froxfield.

STANDARDISATION OF SANDING BELTS

The Machine Tool Trades Association (MTTA), 62 Bayswater Road, London W2 3PH, believes that a greater degree of standardisation in abrasive belts for sanding machines would be beneficial to users and manufacturers alike. The considerable variety of non-standard sizes currently in use clearly indicates the international standards now available are either not meeting the needs of users and manufacturers, or are not well known enough, states the association in a recently — published note.

There are in fact two standards published by the International Organisation for Standardisation some years ago: ISO1929 *Abrasive - selection of width/length combinations* which in Germany is adopted as DIN69130: 1976 *Abrasive belts, dimensions;* and in this country as BS5367: 1976 *Dimensions of coated abrasives.* MTTA points out that there may of course be other similar national standards but these are difficult to identify as woodworking standards and are probably more likely to be listed under subject headings such as 'grinding' or 'abrasives.'

A recent survey of the sizes of abrasive belts used in Europe by manufacturers of sanding machines indicates that of 227 different width and length combinations only 21 are in agreement with international standards.

If the international standards were more widely adopted there should be not only a reduction in costs but improved availability and delivery, says MTTA.

Schools Design Prize 1980

The Schools Design Prize is organised by The Design Council and since its inception in 1977 has been sponsored by the General Electric Company Ltd. For the next two years the Prize will be sponsored by Rolls-Royce. This was announced by Keith Grant, director of The Design Council on 24 January. Baroness Young, Minister of State for Education spoke in support of the scheme.

The Schools Design Prize which is now in its fourth year, aims to find Britain's 'designers for tomorrow' the students in schools throughout the UK who have the imagination and ability to identify a problem, design and evaluate a solution and see the project through to a prototype which could be manufactured. Keith Grant stressed what the competition means to school children; it is total design not just an aesthetic or technological achievement.

Design covers the whole spectrum from the art based to the technological. Not all those who enter will find a career in design but everyone, whether man, woman or child, is affected by design; the future of the whole manufacturing industry of this country is based on design, imagination and the creative ability of the people.

The Design Centre stress that more time should be spent in learning how to convey to school children the importance of design. A report is due to be published shortly on 'Progress in Secondary Education' which will highlight this problem.

The Schools Design Prize is a prestigious competition which rewards and recognises excellent design project work. Each year has seen an improvement in both quality and quantity of entries. Beyond the prizes which are awarded to the gifted few who are nationally rewarded, the whole exercise is very valuable and the general spin-off effect into the various fields of design is very important. School children with imaginative ideas for new or improved products which they think would be suitable for manufacture are invited, through their teachers, to enter the scheme. Their design projects may stem from the arts and humanities, or from science and technology; entries from art, craft, design and technology and science departments are welcomed and may come from individuals or from teams of children from single or mixed disciplines. Twelve cash prizes totalling £3,200 are offered to the winners and their schools. Projects undertaken for GCE 'O' and 'A' level exams are eligible for entry. Purely decorative designs, or 2D designs will not be eligible. To encourage more of the younger designers to enter, an extra group for under 14-year-olds has been added to the two original groups for under and over 16-year-olds.

Donald J. Pepper, vice-chairman of Rolls-Royce, speaking of the sponsorship, said that the company saw the competition not as a do-gooding exercise, but as investment in the future of British industry to develop products for world markets. Design takes many forms, the quality of development must take place in schools. Engineering design has been neglected in the past; there are unlimited opportunities for creative designers in industry. Creative talent needs encouraging at an early age. Sponsorship gives

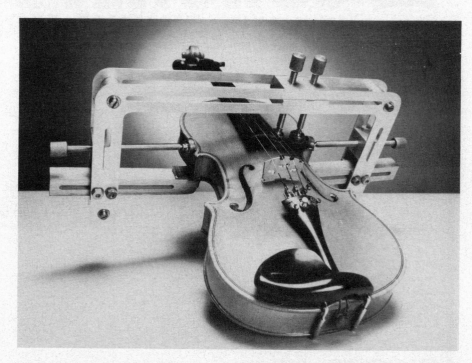

Clamp to aid violin repair designed by David Morton of Philip Morant School, Colchester. ©*Design Centre.*

practical help and cash. He went on to say 'We think it is important that industry should make it known that design is a vital factor for commercial success and will support schemes to encourage young people to take up careers in industrial and engineering design. One of the long-term aims of the Schools Design Prize is to strengthen links between schools and their local industries'.

Rolls-Royce have promised a very close link with the schools that give notice of 'intent to enter': they undertake that a design representative of the company will visit each school.

Baroness Young expressed her support for the scheme and also a desire to see within the framework of the school curriculum participation and interaction between the craft, design and technology and science departments. The economic future of the country depends on this, CDT is not a soft option, it is a key factor in the prosperity of the country. Baroness Young congratulated Rolls-Royce on their initiative in sponsoring the prize and was impressed by the commitment to the scheme that was being offered. Mutual understanding and two-way exchange between schools and industry was important. The Minister offered support and encouragement to The Design Council in its attempts to advance design education in schools. She recognised the shortage of craft teachers and mentioned the retraining schemes open to men and women over 28 years. There should be a clear route in schools to 'A' level for design related studies for the more able pupils.

Last year 79 schools entered the competition, two of them are pictured here. In group 1 (under 16) David Morton of Philip Morant School, Colchester, Essex received

£100 for his violin repair clamp. His project simplified workshop operation for a violin repairer. The clamp can be finely adjusted to fit the curved surfaces so that very fine cracks can be mended. Also in the under-16 age group Michael Gascoyne and Andrew Watts of Wymondham College, Norfolk received £100 for their versatile radio-controlled model aeroplane kit. Various wings, tail planes and nose cones can be fitted onto a basic body to make a glider, bi-plane, basic trainer or aerobatic aircraft.

Further competition details and entry forms should be obtained from The Design Council by 28 March '80. All correspondence should be addressed to Margaret Bradbury, Schools Design Prize, The Design Council, 28 Haymarket, London SW1Y 4SU (01-839 8000).

Michael Gascoyne and Andrew Watts of Wymondham College with their multi-purpose aeroplane. ©*Design Centre.*

BLC WOODTURNING LATHE

I have the enviable job of testing and reviewing new machinery for WOOD-WORKER, but sometimes this causes minor disruption in my workshop. The disruption occurs not because a machine is unsatisfactory, but because it performs far better than expected. Occasionally I am sent a machine that appears to have no serious vices, is easy to use and does a good job. So good in fact and I get so used to it, that when the time comes for it to go back, the loss is all the more keenly felt. Hence the disruption.

This happened recently when I was asked to look at the BLC woodturning lathe manufactured by G. B. Luck Engineering, Fakenham Road, Beetley, Dereham, Norfolk. (This machine was announced in the October 1979 issue of WOODWORKER). Being a woodturner I have quite definite ideas as regards lathe design, and am a bit set in my ways so any 'radical' new models are usually shoved away in a corner of my over-crowded workshop, and left until the editor chases me into some sort of action. (No editorial comments please!) From the literature I had previously received I assumed that this would be the case with this particular model.

But there was a rude awakening when BLC arrived on one of the biggest articulated lorries I have ever seen. Not, I hasten to add, because the machine itself is so big but because the 'artic' was the only vehicle the carrier had available. It took the combined efforts of myself, the lorry driver and several unsuspecting customers to get the lathe off the lorry and onto the pavement, at which point the driver decided enough was enough and disappeared rapidly in a cloud of exhaust fumes, leaving us to manhandle it into the workshop.

As you will have gathered from this preamble, BLC is a lot more substantial than first appears! However, we eventually managed to get it into place, and I was then able to have a better look at the machine as a whole. And there were certainly some rather interesting features to look at (Fig. 1).

My first impression was one of superb quality, the actual paint finish of the machine being of a heavy enamel type which looks very well, but which I later found was rather prone to chipping. The lathe is designed with mounting brackets giving a three-point fixing to eliminate any problem of distortion or twisting brought about by uneven bench tops. This also means the lathe sits very firmly. Like several other features I shall describe in due course this is certainly unconventional but seems to work very well in practice.

The bed is of the twin-bar type which is very rigid and also has the advantage of allowing the shavings to fall clear between the two bars. The BLC standard model gives a distance between centres of 38in, a feature I wish other lathe manufacturers would imitate.

The heavy-duty spindle has a totally enclosed four-speed belt drive, access being via the very snug fitting hinged drive cover (Fig. 2). The belt tension is controlled by the vertical lever fitted to the headstock (Fig. 3). This activates a rod-and-cam system which hinges the motor back and tightens the belt. Such a system allows the lever to be used as a clutch if desired, which cuts out all the stopping and starting necessary with most

Fig. 1. BLC lathe.

Alan Holtham reports on a machine with some rather interesting features. He says it arrived at his workshop on one of the biggest articulated lorries he had ever seen. 'Not, I hasten to add, because the lathe itself is so big but because the "artic" was the only vehicle the carrier had available. It took the combined efforts of myself, the lorry driver and several unsuspecting customers to get the lathe off the lorry and on to the pavement'.

lathes. After only a few hours' use I found myself using this clutch feature more and more.

To change speed though, the lathe must first be stopped and then all you have to do is push the lever back to release the tension, slide the belt across onto the appropriate pulleys and relock the tension with the lever. The knurled knob visible in Fig. 3 in line with the clutch lever allows fine adjustments to be made to the tension obtained in the locked position. I found the smoothest running was obtained with the belt just tight enough to give a positive drive to the work without slip. Generally speaking it should be possible to move the clutch lever to its locked position without undue strain.

Fig. 3 Also shows the integral on-off starter which incorporates both overload and no-volt release protection. A reversing switch is fitted as standard. This is electrically interlocked so that the switch may safely be operated while the machine is in motion; the motor will not reverse until it has been stopped and restarted.

Probably you will have noticed by now the rather funny business at either end of the main spindle where you normally expect to see a screwed spindle nose. On BLC this has been done away with and replaced by a protruding centre boss and drive flange, the latter having two tapped bolt holes. To attach faceplates or chucks to the machine, these are firstly slid over this boss (Fig. 4) and then secured with the two fixing bolts (Fig. 5). This system is possible due to the fact that the machine is fitted with the reversing switch.

On a conventional lathe there is always the danger of faceplates unscrewing themselves when the machine is operated in reverse. The bolt-on system of BLC overcomes this danger. Although appearing rather cumbersome you soon get used to it and, at least, there is no possibility of the faceplate getting stuck! It also has the advantage that faceplates can be fitted on either end of the spindle, ie on both inboard and outboard ends (Fig. 6). The headstock spindle is bored No. 1 Morse taper allowing conventional centres to be used (Fig. 7).

The spindle bearings are angular contact bearings. Oil cups are provided to keep these lubricated, provision having been made to allow excess oil to drain away without contaminating the drive housing and belt.

The tailstock takes some getting used to, appearing at first to be rather light. However, this is all part of the clever design in that the offset barrel without a handwheel allows toolrests to be moved in really close to small diameter work (Fig. 8); it also allows the full length rest to be used irrespective of the length of the work between centres. This is another feature that you only appreciate as you use the machine. The tailstock barrel is similarly bored No. 1 MT and is self-ejecting when the barrel is fully retracted.

Now for another nice touch. How many of us have struggled when trying to completely remove either the tailstock or the toolrest saddle? On BLC removal of these is easily accomplished by slackening the clamp handle sufficiently to allow the clamp bar to

Fig. 2. **Totally enclosed four-speed belt drive.**

Fig. 3. (Left) Belt tension is controlled by the vertical lever fitted to the headstock. Fig. 4. (Above left) and Fig. 5 (Above right) To attach faceplates or chucks these are first slid over the centre boss and then secured with the two fixing bolts.

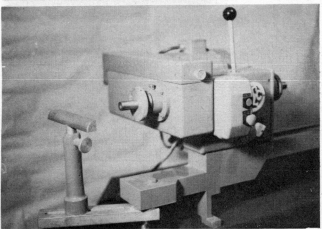

Fig. 6. (Above left) Faceplates can be fitted on either end of the spindle. Fig. 7. (Above right) Headstock spindle bored No. 1 Morse taper. Fig. 8 (Far left) Toolrests can be moved in close to small diameter work. Fig. 9 (Left) Bar and handle can pass through the bed bars. Fig. 10 (Below) The full length toolrest is drilled and tapped at 6in. intervals to take the vertical fixing post.

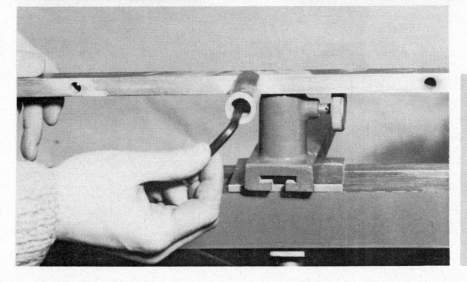

BLC LATHE

SPECIFICATION

Distance between centres .... 38in.
Swing over bed .... (diameter) 9in.
Left-hand swing .... (diameter) 20in.
Single phase motor .... ¾hp
Starter with no-volt and overload safeguard
Four spindle speeds ..... 550, 980, 1660, 2860 rpm
Hand rest lengths ...... Full, 13, 8, 4½in.
Spindle bored both ends No. 1 Morse taper
Tailstock bored .... No. 1 Morse taper
Tailstock travel .... 2in.

BLC LATHE

Fig. 11. (Above) The BLC motor is mounted on rubber bushes. Fig. 12 (Above left) Knurled knob acts as dividing plunger. Fig. 13 (Right) Standard equipment. Fig. 14 (Below) Optional extras.

turn through 90° and then both bar and handle can pass through the bed bars (Fig. 9). There is no need to remove clamp nuts completely. So simple. Yet I have never seen it before.

The full length toolrest is drilled and tapped at 6in. intervals to take the vertical fixing post (Fig. 10). This enables the mounting saddles to be positioned along the bed to best advantage, depending on what you have between centres. These vertical posts of the long rest are also free to revolve to allow the banjos to be moved without having to disturb the setting of the knurled locking nuts. These are the sort of touches you see only on such top-of-the-market machines. While on the subject of the toolrest banjos you may notice that on the BLC they have an inverted T-slot to prevent shavings clogging the slides — which often occurs on saddles with the slot milled right through the top.

The motor is a totally-enclosed ¾hp job giving spindle speeds of 550, 980, 1660 and 2860rpm. BLC is very quiet in operation since every effort has been made to eliminate vibration, the motor itself being mounted on rubber bushes (Fig. 11). Note also in the photo how all the cabling is run into the machine through very neat brass fittings. On the left of the picture you can see clearly the inverted T-slot of the toolrest banjo. One other feature I have used before on a few lathes is a dividing head for marking off divisions round a workpiece. On this model the rim of the largest pulley is drilled with a series of holes round the circumference; and a knurled knob is fitted along the back of the headstock to act as the dividing plunger (Fig. 12).

BLC is well provided for in the way of standard equipment, this being a four-pronged centre, tailstock centre, rear turning assembly, 5in. faceplate, 1½in. screwchuck, 13in. toolrest, 8in. toolrest and a cranked

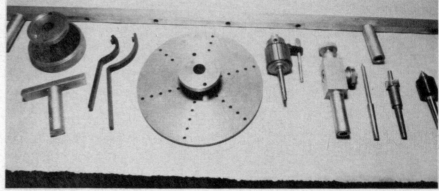

toolrest for bowl turning (Fig. 13). Optional extras are a 10in. faceplate, drill chuck, revolving centre, long hole boring kit, full length toolrest, 4½in. toolrest, 2in. screwchuck and a coil grip chuck (Fig. 14).

I always feel that stability when turning large diameter work is a good indication of the performance of a machine as a whole, so I started by turning some large elm blanks for heavy lampbases from 4x4in. and 5x5in. stock (Fig. 15). In this situation I really appreciated the tripod type fixing of the lathe which, despite its rather top-heavy appearance, does nevertheless provide a very firm support. Conventional turning on the outboard end was easy since the arrangement of the rear turning assembly allows the rest to be kept close to the work at all times (Fig. 16). Notice that all the toolrests are of the much favoured quadrant section type.

Long hole boring is carried out using the normal type of boring jig (Fig. 17), though for most jobs I prefer a hollow tailstock barrel and hollow ring centre. The latter arrangement saves all the fiddling about setting up jigs and centre finders.

BLC really came into its own when I had to turn three batches of staircase spindles, the last being a set of 70 with barley sugar twists. Any long repetition work is much simplified if you can set out the main dimensions on the long rest (Fig. 18) and I found the smoothness and stability of the machine a great asset, since the long, spindly nature of the work always causes vibration and whipping problems. (By the way, more about the barley sugar twists in a later article).

Overall, I found BLC very nice to use. Everything about it seems to have been designed to make the turners' job as problem-free as possible. But it is only fair to say that it is a machine aimed at the top end of the lathe market, and therefore you would expect something pretty outstanding. This one certainly is! Niggles? There are a few. For instance, the toolrest banjos have only one locating hole for the tightening screw; the tailstock winder seems rather light; and the faceplate locking system although a very good idea in principle could possibly be simplified. These are minor points though.

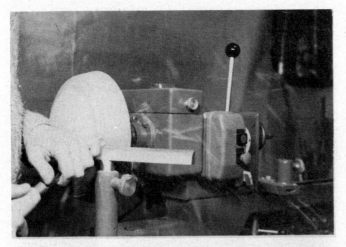

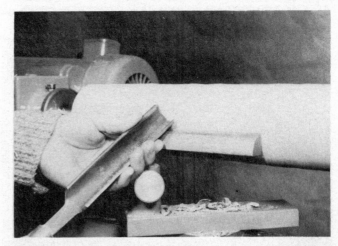

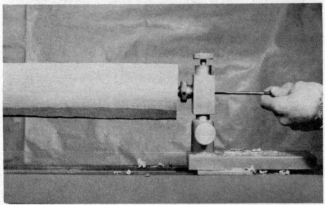

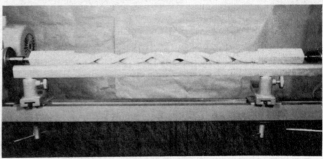

Fig. 15. (Top left) Turning large elm blanks. Fig. 16. (Top right) Conventional turning. Fig. 17 (Left) Long hole boring. Fig. 18 (Above) Barley sugar twists.

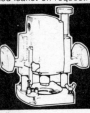

Prices quoted are those prevailing at press date and are subject to alteration due to economic conditions.

MARSHALL & PARSONS
East Anglia's Leading Woodworking Centre

1111 LONDON ROAD, LEIGH-ON-SEA ESSEX SS9 3JL
Telephone Southend (0702) 710404 (4 lines)

We stock an excellent range of Hand Tools, Portable Power Tools and Woodworking Machinery including: Barrus. Black & Decker. Bosch. Burgess. Coronet. Cowell. De-Walt. Elektra. Elu. Kango. Kity. Makita. Meddings. Multico. Myford. R.J.H. . Shopvac. Stanley. Startrite. Sumaco. Wolf.

Elektra 12" Sawbench

85mm depth of cut, 3hp motor
Fully guarded.

£158.70 inc. V.A.T. Carr. £8

Delivery normally within 14 days unless otherwise advised.

The NEW and versatile ELU ST 142/11 Jigsaw is available direct from us at the SPECIAL INTRO-DUCTORY OFFER PRICE £81. inc. VAT (plus £2.50 P&P) supplied in a steel carrying case complete with 3 blades and fitted with a tilting base to cut angles up to 45⁰. The 2 cutting speeds plus the 4 orbit settings make it possible to cut all types of Wood, Metals and Plastics. Only available until 30th April or while stocks last.

Established ELU Dealers for over 20 years

NEW FROM CRAFT SUPPLIES

WOODTURNING COURSES

Our two-day intensive courses in woodturning provide you with expert tuition, good food and comfortable accommodation in the Mill situated in the heart of the beautiful Peak District National Park.

From ONLY £55 inclusive.
Send S.A.E. for full details.

QUARTZ CLOCKS
(movement)

Highest quality W.German movement **£6.00 each** + 90p V.A.T. **£5.00 each** for 10. Selection of metal hands available.

CERAMIC FACES
85p + 13p VAT

CUTLERY BLANKS

Highest quality — Sheffield made stainless steel — 19 patterns available — all illustrated in our catalogue.

WOODTURNING ACCESSORIES

Largest range of woodturning accessories available — and still expanding — Pepper mills from 50p — Time glasses — nearly 200 patterns of circular tiles from 20p and an excellent range of finishing materials including CRAFTLAC and now RUSTIN'S finishes. Stockists of ARUNDEL, CORONET, KITY machines and largest range of SORBY tools available.

Postage paid on orders over £30.
Delivery within 28 days

6-in-1 UNIVERSAL CHUCK

NOW WITH 12 DIFFERENT USES makes it "the best combination chuck that I have ever seen or used in all the twenty-plus years of my woodturning experience" quotes one American owner — one of over 3,000 satisfied users. Send for our 6-in-1 Chuck on 30 days approval. If not entirely satisfied it is the *BEST* Chuck available we will refund your money immediately.

£29.50 + £4.42 VAT

ALSO AVAILABLE:
WOODTURNING MANDRELS FROM £2.75 + 41p VAT
CRAFT COPYING ATTACHMENT **£13.50 + £2.03 VAT**

CRAFT SUPPLIES
Specialists in woodturning tools
THE MILL, MILLER'S DALE, BUXTON
DERBYSHIRE SK17 8SN
TEL. 0298 871636

Send 40p stamps for 24 page fully illustrated catalogue — with voucher for 40p refund on your first order.

---

workpieces

John Sainsbury retires

After 16 years as education adviser to Record Ridgway Tools Ltd, Parkway Works, Sheffield S9 3BL, John Sainsbury retired with effect from 1 January 1980. His successor is his assistant A.G. (Tony) Walker, who is already well-known in the education field.

Mr Sainsbury, although retiring from 'active service' with the company, intends to continue his writing and lecturing activities. He hopes to move to Devonshire and set up his studio for woodturners. He told WOODWORKER recently: 'I would like to say how mindful I am of the kindness and help which has been extended to me. I have many pleasant memories to look back on and I am grateful for the host of friends I have made.'

Before joining C. & J. Hampton, he was a teacher and training college lecturer. He set up the Record Marples Ridgway education service in 1964. This became the Record Ridgway education service upon the merger of C. & J. Hampton and William Ridgway & Son.

Tests for timber

From British Standards Institution comes notice of BS5820 *Methods of test for the determination of certain physical and mechanical properties of timber in structural sizes.* These tests aim at a level of repeatability which is desirable particularly in view of the adoption of limit state design and with the development of visual and machine stress-grading (WOODWORKER for February 1980).

The test procedures apply to rectangular and square sections of solid timber and are presented in three sections: physical properties; grade determining properties and mechanical properties. Copies of BS5820 are obtainable from BSI Sales Department, 101 Pentonville Road, London N1 9ND, at £4.50.

Carving and turning tools

Well-produced catalogues illustrating and describing carving and wood turning tools are issued by Henry Taylor (Tools) Ltd, The Forge, Lowther Road, Sheffield S6 2DR. The former catalogue also lists adzes, tool handles, rifflers, slipstones and canvas tool rolls, as well as woodcarvers's punches, woodcarvers' screw, chip knives and mallets with lignum vitae or beech heads. (It is sometimes advised that lignum vitae mallets be kept in a polythene bag when not in use to avoid splitting).

Taylor has also issued a small 'mailer' leaflet listing all its specialist tools including long thin paring chisels, registered chisels double steel hooped for mortise and general heavy-duty work and cranked neck paring chisels (all with beech handles).

A further publication is the 20-page booklet *How to make a start in woodcarving* which is intended to help in the choice of wood, tools and techniques. The booklet also gives information on the sharpening of chisels and gouges and suggests that household abrasives such as Ajax or Vim are good substitutes for crocus powder as a dressing on leather strops.

Sales manager of Henry Taylor (Tools) Ltd, David W. Rodgers says: 'This literature "package" is available to WOODWORKER readers at a special price of £1 (post free) against the normal price of £1.36.'

Multiple drill system

Selfeedrils, the complete multiple drill system evolved by R. S. Brookman Ltd, Parkside Works, Rothley, Leicester LE7 7NS (0533 302323), can be applied to a wide variety of applications in woodworking. For example, the production of pallet parts, KD chairs, garden seats and toy components. For each of these special arrangements of Selfeedrils were prepared with associated equipment. For the toy components (wooden blocks of a building set requiring holes bored at right angles in the same plane, into cubes and spheres of varying size), a free-standing machine was evolved. This has four Selfeedrils and two spindle units all mounted in a common plane with all the axes pointing to a common centre.

At this centre a workholding device is provided with interchangeable jaws to suit the different shaped components and the walls of the jaws incorporate drill bit guide bushes. A hopper to feed the components was supplied though this is dispensed with when hand-loading applies.

For the garden seats the problem was to drill the two components of the pegged mortise and tenon joint separately but with

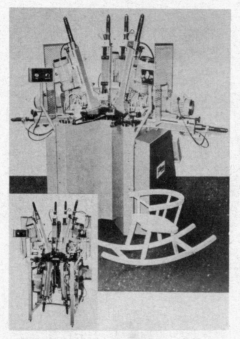

Upper picture shows the machine with covers and guards *in situ*. Inset picture shows the borer with casings removed to show the lower boring heads. In this set-up the eight bores in the seat component (four upper and four under) are drilled at a single operation.

such a degree of accuracy that the peg holes would align precisely and pull the tenons firmly into the mortises when the seats were assembled by customers.

To overcome the problem Brookman used its Preset system involving a series of mounting jig plates, locating spigots and drill bit guides.

Full details of these various applications are given in illustrated leaflets available from the company.

The company has recently supplied a custom-built version of its chair seat borer modified to accommodate components which go together to make a child's rocking chair. The machine employs the Neulectric electric motor drive rather than the pneumatic version of the Selfeedril, and can be set to bore all the components which comprise the rocking chair. It bores eight holes into the seat component (four into each of the upper and under faces). It bores the rockers in pairs, two holes in each. It bores six holes into the arm, four to take the spindles and two horizontally for the safety hand bar.

All the boring heads are set at angles, no one bore is parallel to any of the others. Setting the heads at these angles is made possible by the completely self-contained self-functioning properties of the Selfeedril and by the spigotted nose flange mounting of the Neulectric. The heads can be relocated with repetitive accuracy in a matter of minutes.

Workpiece cramping is automatic. The drilling cycle is initiated by double push buttons and thus complies with current safety requirements.

Exterior finish

With reference to the note on exterior finish given on page 687 of the November 1979 issue, Roger's, 47 Walsworth Road, Hitchin, Herts, advises that one of its customers has been using for many years a mixture of boiled linseed oil and terebine (or terebene) one of the driers used in paint etc. For further details of this substance see pages 104-10 of WOODWORKER for March 1978.

The proportions of boiled linseed oil and terebine are adjusted to suit the particular work being treated and it is understood that the mixture gives protection for a number of years.

Boiled linseed oil and terebine are stocked by Roger's but cannot be supplied other than to customers calling at the Hitchin premises.

Mixing for colour

Flat wood stains under the Joy brandname can be mixed to obtain the particular colour requirements of most wood shades. The nine colours that can be mixed are light, mid, dark, Jacobean and golden oak and walnut, teak, mahogany and ebony. Joy stains can be applied by brush or cloth and are said to be suitable for french polishing or varnishing. They are supplied in 125, 250 and 500ml capacity tins. Manufacturer is Turnbridges Ltd, 72 Longley Road, London SW17 (01-672 6581).

Timber from old churches

Reader S. Noble, 49 The Chase, Bromley, Kent, says he trades in timber from old churches. This is mostly pine and Douglas fir though perhaps once a year or so he may have hardwood such as oak. The timber is generally varnished and comes from fittings such as pews and pulpits. Mr Noble has a stripping tank installed.

Booklet by Barrus

Third edition of the booklet *This is Barrus* has been published by E. P. Barrus Ltd, Launton Road, Bicester OX6 0UR. This deals with the activities of the company in its three main divisions — marine, tools and farm and garden equipment. Hand and power tools, including a range for the woodworking industries, takes in the products of Hitachi and Diston as well as the Barrus own brandname Shapercraft lines together with measuring instruments and auger bits.

NESTING BOX for wild birds

Tom Pettit poses a design problem for 12—13 year-olds.

Two recent publications, one from the Department of Education & Science and one from the Design Council, re-emphasise the importance of teaching design in schools. They suggest that perhaps our future well-being as an industrial nation may depend upon it.

Craft, design and technology is now expected to teach not only basic tool skills, but how materials can be used effectively and aesthetically in solving design problems. This concept is particularly important to those students who wish to become technicians, engineers, craftsmen or designers. All students, however, learn from making the best use of available materials as solutions to problems; in making the piece of work designed further skill in the use of tools is achieved.

The selection of a design problem will involve the teacher in much careful thought. It will have to fit neatly into his scheme of work, so meeting the needs of a particular child or group of children at a specific stage of their craft education. Because problem-solving caters so well for children of varying ability, no matter what their level of attainment might be, this approach to craft education is advantageous. A successful problem will be one for which many alternative satisfactory solutions are possible, each within the particular ability of an individual child.

Each design brief set should in extending the child's previous craft experience have the following objectives:

a Improve the student's design ability requiring greater consideration to be given to the choice of materials and dimensions, including any of a particularly specific nature to ensure efficiency; constructional details including joints and fastenings; the final finish to be given to the work; its cost and the final evaluation of the completed piece — will it perform the function efficiently for which it was designed?

b Teach further craft skills and techniques, ie jointing of materials; use of nails and screws; use of metal and plastics fittings etc.

c Teach further tool skills so improving the child's craft ability.

d Should involve some personal research either by observation of from reference material.

e Should excite and interest. Therefore for any particular age group the problem must be carefully chosen to ensure the necessary enthusiasm.

Such a problem might be stated as follows: You are to design a nesting box for wild birds. The box is for use at your home and you wish to attract birds (other than sparrows and starlings) to use it. Show by means of simple freehand sketches and accompanying notes how you would develop the design for such a box. Alternative methods of jointing and fixing the corners should be shown. Also how the bottom would be fitted, what provision you would have for cleaning, how it would be mounted and how the birds would have access. A particular size of hole will be necessary — how can you find out what this is?

There are other special problems to consider because the box is to be used out of doors. Can you say what these are?

Before the work is commenced you must show on your design sheet all necessary details of construction; a materials list including any nails, screws, glue or other fittings to be used; and what finish you propose to employ.

By discussion between teacher and child, the various combinations of methods of construction should be considered and sketches made of these so that comparisons may be made and decisions taken. Reference material in the form of books, wall charts, photographs and other similar pieces of work should be studied. It is during this stage (as alternatives are being considered) that the teacher will pay particular attention to the known ability of the child. Although the work should extend the child's craft experience, the design should be within his or her ability to complete the work sucessfully. This will inspire confidence, the teacher knowing the child's strengths and possibly avoiding known weaknesses at that stage. There will be a logical sequence by which the design can be approached, which in this case could take the following pattern:

Initially it will be necessary to study box constructions. How will the corners be joined? Will this be by simple butt joints or with lap joints? Might finger or even dovetail joints be used? In any case which way will the grain of the wood run and what kind of wood will be best? Will it be necessary to strengthen the corners by the use of nails, screws or glue? How big should the box be?

Many of these questions can be applied to the fitting and fixing of the bottom, and the lid. How will the lid itself be weatherproofed? Might the lid be arranged to give access to the box which is necessary for cleaning? If so how will it be opened and held firmly closed? How will the bird enter the box? What size of hole is required to encourage particular species and will a perch be provided to assist access? Once the construction is decided upon consideration must be given to how it is to be hung on the chosen wall, tree or post. Will it be screwed

A compact box secured by a batten screwed to a conifer. The bottom is fitted inside the box and is secured with glue and nails. Bitumen felting waterproofs the sloping roof. A block of wood, glued and nailed to the underside of the lid is held by two brass screws, one through each side of the box so holding it firmly in place.

directly to its support; or to a batten which in turn is fixed to the support; or might some form of metal fitting such as a bracket or hooks and eyes be used?

Having completed this basic designing process it is essential that the child realises the importance of choosing the correct finish for the type of timber employed and the situation in which it is being used. Similarly the importance of using non-rusting nails, screws and other metal fittings should be emphasised as the work is intended for out-of-doors.

The child's final satisfaction, however, should not be simply in completing the work. The thrill of fixing; of seeing the first occupants take up residence; in providing a service to nature which will give many years of pleasure to young and old, is ample evaluation of a very valid piece of work.

The extended back of the box provides a means of hanging up. Of much more spacious size it has been painted to preserve the wood, and in this case the top has been hung on a strip of leather which provides an effective weatherproof hinge.

What has 1 tilting base,
2 speeds,
3 blades and
4 orbital settings?

NEW

The New Elu ST142/11 Jigsaw has it all. Furthermore there are 7 additional Jigsaw blade types to choose from. This will enable you to cut efficiently all types of materials to give a finish you desire, for example, at the higher speed with the orbit position set at number three using the wood-cutting blade, this will give you a fast rough cut on timber. Set the speed to the higher speed, select the O position of orbital action, and using a narrow wood-cutting blade, this will enable you to cut intricate shapes in timber giving an excellent finish.

The base plate can be adjusted to cut angles up to 45°, and the universal blade holder enables the fitting of different makes of jigsaw blades, so as not to restrict you in times of emergency.

This machine is being introduced at a special price of £94.00 plus £14.10 VAT and will be supplied in a steel carrying case, for a limited period only.

142/11

50 Years Elu

Elu – have been your partner for 50 years now. Tradesmen, Hobbyists, as well as the woodworking and metal working industry are guided by the motto: "Quality with guaranteed service".

Coupon

Please send more information on Elu Portable Electric Tools

Name _____

Company _____

Street _____

Place _____

Phone _____

Elu Machinery Limited, Stirling Way, Stirling Corner, Borehamwood, Herts, WD6 2AG. Tel.: 01-953 0711

THE PLEASURES OF WOODWORKING

'I enjoy every minute of teaching woodcarving, woodsculpture and general woodwork,' says S. Cliffe Ashworth, who is an energetic 74-year-old now living in the Cheadle (Cheshire) area. He is also in demand as a lecturer, one of his special subjects being sculpture in retirement. His audiences include members of the Rotary and Probus clubs. 'I do this to show my gratitude for the wonderful work these organisations do,' Mr Ashworth told WOODWORKER recently.

His working life started at the age of 14 when he was apprenticed as a patternmaker with a firm at Rochdale, Lancs. Subsequently he became a foreman and it was during this period that he had to undertake a variety of work for textile machinery, gear wheels and general engineering. In 1936 he joined the famous A. V. Roe aircraft firm at Newton Heath where for the seven years prior to his retirement in 1971 he served as technical assistant to the design and research director. 'My time with A. V. Roe covered the war years and there was never any time for hobbies,' says Mr Ashworth.

So when he finished work he took up woodsculpture with enthusiasm — and success. A number of his works have been accepted by the Manchester Academy of Fine Arts exhibitions. One of these was his robin on a post which was a runner-up in the 1976 Ashley Iles/Woodworker woodcarving competition.

Though carving is his love, he also makes furniture. For example, a wardrobe in Austrian oak to a design published in WOODWORKER 50 years ago.

Mr Ashworth, who was one of the judges in the junior section at last year's Woodworker Show, attributes his skills to the valuable instruction he received from the craftsmen with whom he worked. And like so many woodworkers he is always happy to pass on his knowledge. 'I implore young and old, experienced and inexperienced to enjoy the pleasures of woodworking,' he told WOODWORKER.

Left: Tea Break sculpted from a 6in. square old oak gate stump by S. Cliffe Ashworth, stands 11½ in. high.

COUNTRY CHAIRS AND CHAIRMAKING

2: then came

WINDSOR CHAIRS ...

The first Windsor-type chairs as we know them today date back probably to the second half of the 17th century. Early types were almost certainly in use before then, but few examples survived the rough rural use to which they were put and fewer still were cherished as collectors' items later on.

There were — and still are of course — a number of different styles, each one having the solid, wooden seat with all four legs socketed into it which is characteristic of the true Windsor. Although there is some confusion in terminology, each style is distinguished by the design and construction of the back.

One of the earliest known is the comb-back which has two uprights or stiles arising from the seat surmounted by a cresting rail or comb. Within this framework are arranged a number of turned spindles or back sticks; or perhaps a combination of sticks and a carved and pierced central splat or baluster. Where the two stiles angle noticeably outwards with sticks fanned out into a wider comb the chair is appropriately called the fanback. A late 19th century varient of this style, the latheback, has flattened bars instead of turned sticks which are often curved to follow the shape of the sitter's back.

Chairs without arms are known as single or side chairs. When fitted, arms are either separately tenoned into the stiles and supported at the front on short sticks socketed into the seat; or a one-piece horizontal arm bow may be used, supported at the front as before but extending in a continuous curve around the back of the chair. In this case the back sticks may either pass through or be socketed into the bow.

The true bowback Windsor has a hooped or semi-circular bow arising from the seat and this is infilled with sticks or sticks and centre splat. This type of chair can also be made with or without arms; when fitted they are tenoned into the upright portion of the bow as in the comb-back. Alternatively the back bow may be socketed into a horizontal arm bow rather than into the seat; this is known as the double bow armchair — and it can be made only as an armchair. A popular 19th century introduction known as the smokers' bow has a substantial horizontal bow, sometimes shaped and carved but without the bow above it. The American name low-back is a more descriptive name for this particular type of chair.

Few country chairs were ever made complete from start to finish by one craftsman. Most were made piecemeal by a number of different men, the work being normally divided between that done in the woods among the growing trees, usually by one or two men; and that done, perhaps by several, in a workshop.

Comb-back Windsor armchair known as the Goldsmith chair c 1750. *(Copyright Victoria and Albert Museum).*

MAKING WINDSOR CHAIRS

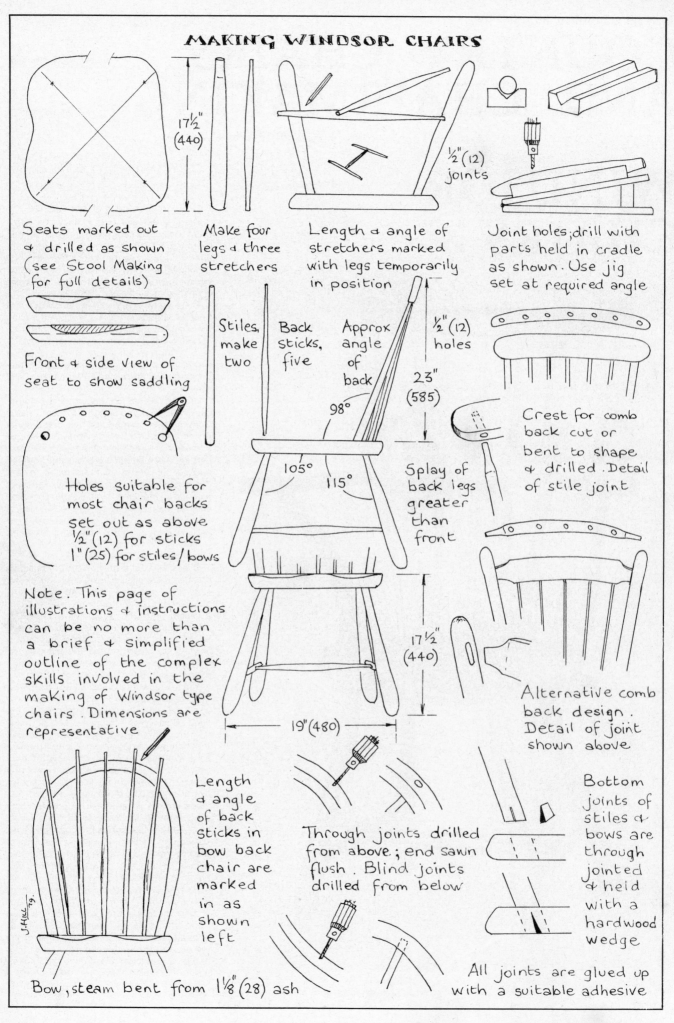

Seats marked out & drilled as shown (see Stool Making for full details)

Front & side view of seat to show saddling

Holes suitable for most chair backs set out as above ½" (12) for sticks 1" (25) for stiles/bows

Note. This page of illustrations & instructions can be no more than a brief & simplified outline of the complex skills involved in the making of Windsor type chairs. Dimensions are representative

Make four legs & three stretchers

17½" (440)

Stiles, make two

Back sticks, five

Approx angle of back

98°

105°   115°

Length & angle of stretchers marked with legs temporarily in position

½" (12) holes

23" (585)

Splay of back legs greater than front

17½" (440)

19" (480)

Joint holes; drill with parts held in cradle as shown. Use jig set at required angle

½" (12) joints

Crest for comb back cut or bent to shape & drilled. Detail of stile joint

Alternative comb back design. Detail of joint shown above

Length & angle of back sticks in bow back chair are marked in as shown left

Through joints drilled from above; end sawn flush. Blind joints drilled from below

Bottom joints of stiles & bows are through jointed & held with a hardwood wedge

Bow, steam bent from 1⅛" (28) ash

All joints are glued up with a suitable adhesive

The first of these, the bodgers as they were called, selected and cut down suitable beech or ash trees which, after being sawn to length, were cleft to make turned parts for all kinds of chairs. Cleaving was done first with a beetle (a heavy mallet) and wedges and then with a side axe or sometimes a froe. Individual clefts were further trimmed into leg pieces or spindle pieces with the axe, then, held in the vice-like grip of a shaving horse, drawknifed almost to their finished size.

Skilful work produced little wastage and left the minimum of wood to be removed at the lathe during the final turning. Indeed, plain legs and stretchers on some early chairs were not turned but merely drawknifed to their 'round' shape. Turning in the early days would be done on the primitive but efficient pole lathe.

All this work was carried out shortly after the tree was felled — wood cleaves more easily while it is still green and the bodgers preferred turning it in this condition also, allowing it to season outside while awaiting transport to a workshop. For the modern craftsman leaving the cleft and roughly trimmed pieces to season before turning is advised as is the use of a powered lathe if one is available. Alternatively the use of the rotary planes referred to in the previous article is recommended.

In the workshop seats were cut to shape from elm planks, this timber being preferred to all others. Its wild grain is best able to withstand without splitting the hollowing-out which it receives and the several holes which are bored into it, plus the stresses to which it is subjected during use. (It is for these same qualities that elm was always used for the nave or hub of the best cart-wheels). The hollowing-out process, which creates the comfortable dished or saddle shape which is an important feature of a good Windsor chair, was done with a long handled, razor-sharp adze.

Working with the seat blank on the floor and held firm with his feet, the bottomer, as

Turning a chair leg on the pole lathe. *(Copyright Museum of English Rural Life).*

he was known, with each calculated cut across the grain, removed waste wood with great skill to make the rough hollow shape. This roughness was later cleaned-off with a series of shaves and scrapers, each not unlike the modern spokeshave in function but with a wooden stock and blade shaped to fit the hollow of the seat.

Machines now do what the adze once did and not nearly so successfully. The modern factory-made chair is never as deeply bottomed as it ought to be. Where an adze (or the expertise to use one) is lacking a large but shallow carver's gouge may be used for

Above left: Cleaving chair legs with axe and beetle. *(Copyright Museum of English Rural Life).*
Above right: Roughing out a chair leg, using a drawknife; piece held in a shaving horse. *(Copyright Museum of English Rural Life).*

roughing-out. With the seat blank clamped firmly to the bench the gouge is struck with a mallet to begin with as in carving a shallow bowl, working outwards from the centre. A modified round bottom spokeshave is used for further contouring and cleaning-up, together with a curved steel scraper.

A benchman made the non-turned parts such as some back stiles, combs and centre splats and he was usually responsible also for shaping back and arm bows. The latter, most often of cleft ash or beech but sometimes of yew or fruit woods, were first cut to size then after boiling, or more likely steaming, to render them pliable, bent round a suitable former clamped to a bending table or bench. When dry after several days these retained their new shape and were ready to be fitted into a chair. (Steam bending methods will be considered in a subsequent article).

All these various parts now came into the skilled hands of the framer. It was he who bored the many holes for jointing and for this he used wooden stock braces fitted with spoon bits. Each hole bored had to be not only in its proper place but at the correct angle to take account of the splay of the legs and the rake of the back etc. To increase pressure without injury when using the brace he wore a breast bib — a recessed wooden block held across the chest by a leather strap into which the head of the brace fitted. When the boring was finished he prepared all the other parts, cutting each to its required length, checking joints for fit and so on and finally cleaning-up their surfaces with scrapers and glasspaper.

It is easier to make holes with a power drill, of course. The old craftsmen accepted this and most went over to drilling machines as they became available. Using simple jigs, the modern pillar or stand drill can be used effectively for drilling accurate holes at any angle without recourse to eye judgement alone — which is what guided the old chairmakers. (See drill system on page 236).

Assembly began with legging-up — fitting the four legs and leg stretchers into the seat. The method used holds good today. Leg tenons go right through the seat, glued and knocked in tight with the framer's hammer or a mallet. The tenons are further secured with hardwood wedges driven into saw cuts made in their ends at right angles to the grain of the seat so as not to cause splitting. The legs — a back and front pair — and a side stretcher are assembled to make two leg units and these are placed temporarily into the seat sockets. This enables the central cross-stretcher to be cut after being checked for length and fit.

After applying glue to all the joints the underframe is reassembled into the seat in the same order as before, the cross-stretcher being sprung into position before the legs are pushed fully home. The leg joints are wedged as described and when the glue is well set stub ends are cleaned-off flush with the seat using first a tenon saw and then a sharp chisel or spokeshave. If the seat is of substantial thickness, at least 1½in. (38mm) at the joint, a stopped or blind tenon may be used.

Stiles for comb-backs and bows for bowbacks should go right through the seat and be wedge-jointed like the legs. Back sticks are then fitted into holes bored in the back edge of the seat and either into the lower edge of a previously drilled comb, or arranged fanwise to lean against a wider fanback comb. In this way their position and drilling angle can be marked-off on the comb and with these holes drilled the back can then be glued-up and assembled.

Back sticks are arranged around the top curve of a bowback in a similar way and for the same purpose as above. In this case normal practice was to bore right through the bow from the top and fit and wedge the back sticks, rather as spokes were jointed into the felloes of a wheel. The visible joint mattered little for many early Windsors were painted and the joints concealed. For a neater appearance with a varnished or waxed finish blind holes may be drilled into the bow from below. Where a centre splat is fitted narrow mortises are cut to accommodate it.

Arm bows are bored and assembled along with back sticks or sticks and splats, their forward facing arm ends being supported on short arm sticks arising from holes in the seat. Where arms are tenoned into the stiles are fitted. Then when in position the arm tenons are inserted and the arms brought down on to the arm sticks.

Finishing consists mainly of thorough scraping and sanding. Many old Windsors were painted and some were stained — often to conceal a variety of different woods used in their construction. The best were polished with beeswax and this method is recommended here; seal the grain with a good sanding sealer and apply the first polish of beeswax and turpentine with fine grade wire wool. Apply subsequent polish with a soft cloth.

It has been correctly said that the Windsor chair is full of hidden skills. It has only been possible to outline some of them here but the main secrets lie in the choice of sound material, in properly aligned parts and especially in tight joints. It is the tension built into the chair during its assembly which gives the Windsor its considerable strength.

Bowback Windsor armchair with wheel splat c 1850. *(Copyright Victoria and Albert Museum).*

The old chairmakers, who a century ago received as little as 12s 6d (65p) for a 'half dozen bundle of single Windsors', made their chairs to last. That so many of them did (and are now being resold by antique dealers at prices beyond the wildest dreams of their makers) is testimony to their sound design and method of construction.

Left: Legging up. Right: Almost completed Windsor bow back. *(Both photos copyright C. F. F. Snow, School House, Old Windsor, Berks).*

The first article in the series (March 1980) explained how chairs evolved from stools and gave instructions for making various kinds of stools. The next article will be about ladderbacks and spindlebacks.

workpieces

Wadkin chairman retires

Chairman of Wadkin Ltd, Leicester, since 1970, William L. Sims OBE has retired and has been appointed hon president of the company. He joined Wadkin in 1927 as an electrical engineer, became a director in 1942 and joint managing director in 1961. He has been a member of many industrial committees and associations and was president of the Machine Tool Trades Association (MTTA) in 1969-71. He is a former president of the European Committee for Woodworking Machinery Manufacturers (Eumabois).

Mr Sims is succeeded as chairman by Michael H. Goddard who has been deputy chairman and joint managing director. D. A. Hancock has been appointed joint managing director in succession to Mr Goddard.

Another Wadkin appointment is that of George A. Steel who has joined the company's portable power tools division based at Trent Lane, Castle Donington, Derbyshire. Mr Steel has had 20 years' experience in power tools and was previously sales director of Gittings Tools Ltd, Leicester.

John Nutt who is general manager of Wadkin agencies division and of the portable power tools division, has been appointed an associate director of the company and will be additionally responsible for the development of certain new product lines. Mr Nutt has been with Wadkin Ltd for 25 years on sales and export marketing and has been general manager of the agencies division since 1977.

Stain finish for windows

Many timber windows are now being finished with decorative exterior wood stains such as coloured water-repellent finishes, preservative stains, pigmented finishes and microporous finishes. The decorative finish is essentially a surface treatment, which contributes little in terms of preservation within the body of the timber but improves the water-repellency of the surface.

Provided these frames are properly designed and the correct specifications are followed; that the necessary care and control is applied to their preparation, storage and fixing; and that glazing is carried out correctly, there should be no serious problems with such installations.

If the necessary care is not maintained excessive movement of timber may occur, causing frame joints to open and the glazing system to break down.

Curable sealant and compound glazing systems will accommodate a greater degree of movement than conventional systems; traditional type linseed oil putties are not recommended.

To assist those involved in both the manufacture, fixing and glazing of stain-finished timber windows the Glass & Glazing Federation has produced a detailed instruction sheet and this is available on request to the federation at 6 Mount Row, London W1.

Halifax heck cart

With *Newsletter no. 43* (January-February), John Pearce. hon secretary of the Model Horse-Drawn Vehicles Club, 4 Brentlea Crescent, Higher Heysham LA3 2BT, has enclosed drawings of a barouchette sent by one of the club's members in the Netherlands. Member Ted Fox reports that his wheelwrighting venture with his blacksmith partner is getting off the ground. They have to repair seven hay waggons, three tip carts, an old bicycle with wooden wheels and an 1880 fire appliance. They have made two 4ft diameter wheels for a period field piece and are now engaged in producing replacements of the hobby horses on a steam-driven roundabout.

The *Newsletter* also gives details of the Halifax heck cart developed to meet the requirements of moving loads in the hilly area of Halifax. One of these carts was in use up to the 1950s. Mr Pearce has details and sketches.

Member Don Wheels has developed a self-contained jig for drilling the holes in wheel hubs. This and other devices will be shown at the Pageant of the Horse MH-DVC exhibition at Doncaster racecourse in April.

HERE COMES THE BRIDE'S COG

From the 'top end' of Britain, Robert Towers who lives at St Ola, Orkney, tells you how he makes a bride's cog. He does not say how you should make the potion that fills this wooden vessel. Indeed, he warns: 'All recipes have one thing in common: they are lethal if you are inclined to over-indulge!'

Here in these northern islands at wedding receptions we have a somewhat strange and ancient custom. It is the use of a wooden drinking vessel know as the bride's cog.

Origin of the cog goes back to our links with Scandinavia. The shape and size of the cog is very similar to that of the Swedish horned kasa, though the kasa is often carved from the solid and some have the handles extended to about 18in. and jointed at the top like a collar.

The cog is built on the lines of a cask and those made today are similar to those of early times with the possible exception of the hoops. These are now made of copper or brass rather than of willow as was used on herring barrels in times past.

Cogs differ from maker to maker. Some have handles on the sides. Others, my own included, have the handles as a continuation of the stave and on the top.

As to the filling of the cog, this is usually done by one of the guests at the wedding, who will assure you that the recipe is the proper one (all recipes for the filling have one thing in common: they are lethal if you are inclined to over-indulge!) The first drink is taken by the bride, then the groom, the bridesmaid, and the best man, then the guests. But always the cog should go round the hall in the direction of the sun.

As to the making, you can have any number of staves you wish provided the number divides by two for the placing of handles. I use 24 as this number can be used for a cog having two or three handles, ie 24 divided by 2 = 12 = 11 staves 1 handle; or 24 divided by 3 = 8 = 7 staves 1 handle.

Timber can be anything the maker wishes, though I prefer to use teak and oak. As well as the wood you will require some 6ft of brass strip and four brass rivets.

Having selected your timber the first thing to do is to plane it to the thickness required (16mm). After this it is ripped to 130 and 38mm for the bottom and the staves respectively. It is then cut to the lengths required for bottom, staves, handle staves and handle sides.

After this the bevelling and tapering is done, both in one go using purpose-built jigs. Bevels are very carefully planed by hand to ensure a perfect fit. Handle sides are glued on and the two pieces used for the bottom are glued as well. When the glue is dry you can 'try' the cog together dry. This is done around a wastepaper bin using two elastic bands.

Next stage is the turning of the handles and here you may use your own ideas as to the shape etc, though I suggest you refrain from anything too elaborate. Then comes the marking-off of the waste from the top inside of the staves. Note that this tapers upwards and inwards on the two staves at the side of each handle. Cut away the waste.

Now cut the groove for the bottom; this groove is some 22mm from the bottom. I use a C.K. cutter in the electric drill in a home-made stand but there are any number of ways you can do this.

Next is to measure for the bottom of the cog and here again 24 staves is a good number as the radius of your circle is approximately 1/6th of its distance in the round. Set your compass to the distance of four of your staves (1/6th of 24) on the groove and this is the radius.

The bottom is cut to its shape on the edge on the spindle moulder on the Emco Star and I cut mine to have a tongue to fit in the groove. After careful dry fitting of the bottom glue the cog together. After gluing, plane and sand the cog to a good finish; or if you have a lathe that is big enough the cog can of course be turned.

For making the brass hoops, position two elastic bands on the cog with their lower edges just where the *bottom edge* of the hoop is to be. Take a measurement, plus 1½in. for overlap for the rivets, and this is the size of the hoops. Always use the same tape to measure both the cog and the brass. In the making of these hoops file the inside edge to stop 'dig-in' when driving them on. Also they are not dished but flat (this is why we measure where the bottom of the hoop will be).

After making the hoops drive them on evenly. When putting on the hoops have the riveted joints at opposite sides but travelling in the same direction. Add a name plate if required. Give the cog five to six coats of matt varnish, sanding down well each time.

Cogs have been made with two bottoms and a marble placed between. I have no doubt this caused the user some concern as he heard the marble rattle while he drank!

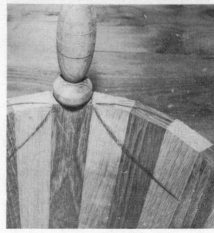

This page, top to bottom: Alternate three handle cog in the rough. Checking diameter of handle. Marking out of handle shape. Marking out of inside for the cutting away of waste.
Facing page, top to bottom: Measuring for size of bottom. Cog glued showing building hoops. Measuring for hoops. Driving on of hoops.

CUTTING LIST

2 of handle staves teak 300 x 38 x 16mm
10 of handle staves teak 175 x 38 x 16mm
12 of handle staves oak 175 x 38 x 16mm
4 of sides for handles teak 125 x 38 x 16mm
2 of bottom oak 130 x 300 x 16mm

Machines that I use in making the cog are a 10in. Shopmate radial arm saw, Emco Star and Rex planer, along with the usual assortment of hand tools.

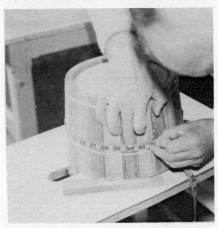

BRIDE'S COG

Letters

From: C. W. Bond, Leamington Spa, Warwickshire
Dear Sir,

I was once instructed to visit a veneer manufacturer in the east end of London to see how a certain wood behaved in veneer-cutting processes. 'See if you can bring a sheet of veneer back with you,' was Major J. R. Cosgrove's final order. I duly arrived in a somewhat unsavoury atmosphere where a sheet was selected and rolled up for me to take back to Trafalgar Square.

I held it at arm's length and placed it under the stair of the bus, sitting just inside from where I could keep an eye on it. I noticed the bus conductor sniffing and with a disgusted look on his face he eventually confronted me with the question: 'What the hell is it?' I pointed to the roll of veneer.

Travelling westwards the passengers increased in number and sophistication; and the conductor and I were highly amused when smart ladies, one after another, turned up their shoes to see what it was they had stepped in!

The wood was kabukalli *(Goupia glabra)* and looking it up in *Timbers of South America* (TRADA) I see it is reported as possessing 'an unpleasant odour.'

I recounted this incident to B. J. Rendle a few years ago after looking at a display panel at Princes Risborough (from the identical sheet). His only comment was: 'It never took on, did it?'

Yours faithfully, **C. W. Bond**

From: H. Reynolds, Cromer, Norfolk
Dear Sir,

In reply to D. Tasker's letter on page 92 of the February 1980 issue, I too was employed in the engineering trade for a number of years without really a sense of job satisfaction. In 1976 I took the plunge and applied for a TOPS course in carpentry and joinery and, after 12 months wait, I was accepted.

The training, although geared to the construction industry, was excellent. I had some previous experience of woodwork — as a hobby — and was able to take full advantage of the course. In the event, on completion of the course I obtained a job as maintenance carpenter at a private school. I plan to work for myself some day but I get a lot more job satisfaction than I ever had before.

So, I would say to Mr Tasker: Take the plunge and do a TOPS course. The training allowance will enable you to keep your family and pay your mortgage for six months. Then you will have no difficulty in finding a job in one of the woodworking industries and in consequence, increasing your job satisfaction. I certainly have.

Yours faithfully, **H. Reynolds**

Manpower Services Commission is sponsoring a 10-week small business course in May. This is under TOPS (the training opportunities scheme). Details from: Manpower Services Commission (training services division), District Office, 93 Southchurch Road, Southend-on-Sea, Essex.

From: P. de Berker, Ilford, Essex
Dear Sir,

I read about David Brown's noise problems (page 123 of the February issue) with considerable sympathy as in the course of my hobby I, too, was driving my neighbour to distraction. At one point I had a lathe, a surface planer and a circular saw in an upstairs back bedroom of a terraced house. Matters were made worse because the floor and the room beneath acted as a soundbox for the noise; and my neighbour's small daughter slept just the other side of the wall.

As a short-term expedient I agreed not to run the machines after the child's bed-time.

In the long run I agreed to build a shed.

When designing my shed I took the advice of two friends, one a structural engineer, the other a specialist in accoustics. The burden of their advice was: First, about half the sound was transmitted by the structure so that by removing the machines from the house I would lose about half the noise. Second, that noise approximately obeys the inverse square law which, in practical terms, means that if Mr Brown doubles the distance between his machines and his neighbours, the noise will fall, not to half but to one quarter; and if the distance is trebled the perceived noise will fall to one-ninth etc. Thus it pays to build the shed as far away from neighbours' houses as possible. (I built mine right at the bottom of the garden). Third, I was advised to build the shed as solidly as possible. I built on a solid base with 9in. building blocks, externally rendered and with a tiled roof. From the noise point of view it works — the only problem I had was that of damp, despite having a proper damp course. I cured this by running an electric oil-filled radiator three hours a night. This is rather expensive of course.

I hope my experience will be of some use to anyone who is thinking of doing the same. But don't forget that most permanent structures need either planning permission or consent under the current regulations.

Yours faithfully, **P. de Berker**

Wymondham market cross modelled in US

In WOODWORKER for December 1979 we published a note from Charles A. Knapp of Akron, Ohio, about the miniature Tudor-style house he had made to the plans given in the December 1978 issue. Mr Knapp now tells us that he has made a model of the market cross at Wymondham, Norfolk, solely from the picture on the cover of last July's issue and description in the October issue, (see below).

Letters

From: Walter E. Mason, Arcadia, California USA
Dear Sir,

I am writing in reply to A. C. Weller's remarks on page 739 of the December 1979 issue. I believe his plane to be a No. 42 Miller's Patent Adjustable Metallic Plow, Filletster, Rabbet & Matching plane. This tool is the same as the No. 41 except that the stock gauge and fence are made of gunmetal, the gunmetal referred to here being a copper alloy akin to bronze.

These planes were offered by Stanley from 1871 until 1895. They are 9⅞in. long and had 10 cutters, eight plow bits (⅛, 3/16, ¼, 5/16, ⅜, 7/16, ½ and ⅝in.), one tonguing cutter and one filletster cutter 1⅝in. The filletster bed piece provided is quickly detached by means of the two screws. Later on a slitting cutter was added to make a total of 11 irons. None of these early planes by Stanley had the model numbers on the tools.

Yours faithfully, **Walter E. Mason**

From: John Ryan, Tullamore, Co Offaly
Dear Sir,

In reply to A. C. Weller's letter in the December 1979 issue, regarding a plane made by the Stanley Rule & Level Co, his plane is known as Miller's Patent Combined Plow, Filletster & Matching plane. It was patented by Charles Miller of Vermont, USA, in 1870. The Stanley company immediately acquired the patent and produced two versions: No. 41 with iron stock and fence; and No. 42 which had a gunmetal stock and fence and was the more expensive version.

Charles Miller afterwards joined the Stanley Rule & Level Co and together with Leonard Bailey introduced further improvements to other planes in the Stanley range. Nos 41 and 42 planes were sold with a tonguing tool ¼in., a filletster cutter and eight plough irons in ⅛, 1/16, ¼, 5/16, ⅜, 7/16, ½ and ⅝in.

On studying the illustration of Mr Weller's plane I would say he is correct in concluding that the set screws of the fence are not original. The original setscrews were flat-topped and knurled, similar to but smaller than the depth control screw on the Stanley 45. Apart from this his plane seems to be fully intact as Nos 41 and 42 were not fitted with any front handle or knob.

Yours faithfully, **John Ryan**

From: R. Candy, Wells, BC, Canada
Dear Sir,

With reference to A. C. Weller's enquiry on page 739 of the December 1979 issue, I believe his plane to be a Miller's Patent Adjustable Metallic Plow, Filletster, Rabbet & Matching plane. This was patented by Charles G. Miller of Brattleborough, Vermont, in 1870 and manufactured by the Stanley Rule & Level Co by 1871.

The plane was accompanied by a ¼in. tonguing tool and eight plow bits plus a bed piece for filletster and rabbet operations. The bed piece fastened to the plane body by means of two screws whose heads passed through slots both front and rear of the plow. The bed then passed through the fence. The copy of an illustration from the Kenneth Roberts publication *Reprint of Stanley Rule & Level Co supplement for 1871* will explain the function of the plane and, I trust, answer Mr Weller's questions.

Yours faithfully, **Ron Candy**

From: E. Hemmingsen, Manlius, NY, USA
Dear Sir,

In response to the enquiry of A. C. Weller on page 739 of the December 1979 issue, it can be said that the plane illustrated is the Stanley no. 42 (Miller's Patent Adjustable Metallic Plow, Filletster, Rabbet & Matching plane), whose stock and sliding fence were of a bronze-like metal known as gunmetal. It came with a detachable steel bed called a filletster bed and with 11 cutters (eight plain bits, one tonguing tool, one filletster cutter and one slitting cutter).

It was manufactured from 1871 to 1892 and was the first of the Stanley combination planes. It is entirely similar to the Stanley no. 41 which, however, is made of iron instead of gunmetal. The two rods and the base of the no. 42 are of iron and steel respectively.

It might be of interest to mention that a Stanley no. 42, complete with filletster bed and all cutters and in excellent condition, sold at auction for $2100 in the summer of 1979. In October last year a catalogue of an antique tool dealer in Vermont offered a Stanley no. 42 (which had the filletster bed but lacked all but one cutter) at $1295.

Yours faithfully, **Erik Hemmingsen**

See also page 187 March 1980 Letters page where the reply by William Sinnott, Lanarkshire, is published.

---

8 MILLER'S PATENT ADJUSTABLE PLOW, ETC.

Miller's Patent Adjustable Metallic Plow, Filletster, Rabbet, and Matching Plane.

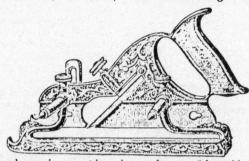

This Tool embraces in a most ingenious and successful combination, the common Carpenter's PLOW, a FILLETSTER, an adjustable RABBET PLANE, and a perfect MATCHING PLANE. The entire assortment can be kept in smaller space, or made more portable, than an ordinary Carpenter's Plow.

Each Tool in this combination is complete in itself, and is capable of more perfect adjustment, for its specific uses, than the most improved form of the same Tool as manufactured separately by any other party.

The above drawing represents the FILLETSTER, which may be readily adjusted to cut any required width, by regulating the horizontal Guage which slides upon the two bars on the front side of the Stock. The depth to be cut can be adjusted by use of the upright Guage, with a Thumb-screw, on the back side of the Stock.

The Bed-piece represented above can be fastened to the Stock instantly, by means of two screws, projecting from the back of the same. The heads of the screws being passed through the front end of the slots, as shown in the cut of the Plow, and then brought back to the rear end of the slots, a single turn will secure the Bed-piece to the Cast Steel Base-piece with perfect firmness; and it can be released at any time with equal facility. The horizontal Gauge may be easily secured at any point upon the bars projecting from the Stock, by its Thumb-screws, and a RABBET PLANE of any desired width, up to 1¼ inches, be obtained.

FIRST ILLUSTRATED January 1871 SUPPLEMENT

PROTECTIVE GARMENTS

A COMPLETE RANGE FOR ALL PRACTICAL PURPOSES

- Direct from manufacturer to Education and Industry
- 7 Day dispatch from receipt of order
- All garments fully guaranteed
- Prices firm for 12 months from January 1st
- The best value for money

for Brochure and Price List contact:

MOORFIELD
of LANCASHIRE

PERSEVERENCE MILL
OLIVE LANE DARWEN
LANCASHIRE BB3 3DS
TEL. 0254 - 74131-2-3

THE WORLD'S TIMBER TREES

Here C. W. Bond FIWSc describes agba which is popular for a wide range of work in the furniture industry. It has excellent working qualities. Last month the author discussed ayan: 10, and in the next issue he will deal with merbau.

AGBA: 11

Gossweilerodendron balsamiferum – named in honour of Johann Gossweiler, a collector in W Africa; *dendron* — tree; *balsamiferum* — bearing balsam. Leguminosae (Caesalpiniaceae).

This wood is too well-known to need description, being deservedly popular for a wide range of work in the furniture industry.

The tree is one of the real jungle giants, 200ft and more in height, with an unbuttressed cylindrical bole. Compared with many leguminous woods agba is considerably lighter in weight (similar to the mahoganies) and has excellent working qualities. If stained to match mahogany the two woods look very similar indeed. There is a marked difference, however, in that agba (as the specific name indicates) is a resinous timber and this is evident in working, but is not sufficiently pronounced to be troublesome.

The writer used agba for many years in school and found it beyond criticism except in the case of a school lectern made in the woodwork room and polished with linseed oil. This method can hardly be recommended as the oil did not result in a pleasant finish; it made the wood a rather unpleasant brown in colour and produced a somewhat artificial look about the surface. A coat of white polish and a wax finish gave a second lectern a much better appearance.

The photomicrographs show the reason for agba's comparatively light weight. The parenchyma cells, although numerous, do not show up so clearly because the surrounding fibres have thinner walls; and the structure is more lace-like compared with the padauks and the rosewoods and many other woods of the Leguminosae. Growth rings are faintly evident and, as with keruing and others of the dipterocarps, some of the large cells are resin canals.

Cross section × 3.3 as seen with a × 10 hand lens.

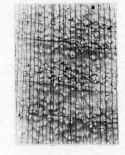

Gossweilerodendron balsamiferum. **Drawn from material in the Forest Herbarium, University of Oxford. With acknowledgements to the curator.**

5 cm

Cross section × 10 lineal.

Steenwise Ltd.
TOOLS FOR CRAFTSMEN

Steenwise policy is to supply high quality machines, produced in UK and Europe, by well known manufacturers at the best possible price.

We normally deliver within seven days from receiving your order. Payment can be cash with order, cash on delivery, or any of the well known credit cards and we also operate a confidential hire purchase scheme with attractive rate of interest.

We will be pleased to quote for any machine or accessory, and we are sure you will be surprised at the prices we can offer. Trade enquiries will be most welcome.

Below are some examples from our current price list. For further information send the coupon or 'phone us direct on Bradford (0274) 560699.

Planer Thicknesser
10'' × 6'' Scheppach HM1 2 H.P. Motor, Floor Standing – £399.00.

10'' × 6'' Kity 7136 1½ H.P. Motor, Floor Standing – £564.00.

6'' × 4'' Kity 7139 1½ H.P. Motor, Floor Standing – £347.00.

Band Saws
Kity 7212 – £299.00.

Circular Saws
Kity 5017 2¼'' depth of cut ¾ H.P. – £169.00.

Elektra Site Saw 3½'' depth of cut 2.3 H.P. (Galvonised) – £159.00.

Special Offer
● Kity 5020 Combination – consisting of a planer thickness or spindle moulder and slot mortiser. Recommended man. price £662.40, Steenwise price £500 including free double ended 5'' bench grinder.

● Kity 6646 variable speed, floor standing, recommended man. price £517.50, Steenwise price £469.00 including a free 5'' double end bench grinder and six Sorby wood turning tools.

● Kity 10 × 6 planer thicknesser 7136 and dust extractor 695, recommended man. price £1,018.57, Steenwise price £647.50 including hose and attachments. All prices include VAT at 15%.

Please send me more information about Steenwise stocks and prices.

Name ....

Address ....

....

Showroom & warehouse
Limefield Mills, Wood Street, Crossflats, Bingley, West Yorks. C

NOW..... you can make your circular saw do the work of an expensive radial arm or table saw
RIP CUTS! CROSS CUTS! STRAIGHT CUTS! ANGLE CUTS!

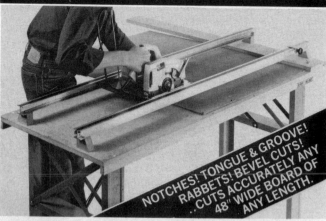

NOTCHES! TONGUE & GROOVE! RABBETS! BEVEL CUTS! ...CUTS ACCURATELY ANY 48" WIDE BOARD OF ANY LENGTH.

 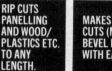

CROSS CUTS 4' x 8' CHIPBOARD AND PLYWOOD WITH EASE.

RIP CUTS PANELLING AND WOOD/ PLASTICS ETC. TO ANY LENGTH.

MAKES ANGLE CUTS (MITRE, BEVEL ETC) WITH EASE.

SAW GUIDE CAN ALSO BE USED WITH YOUR ROUTER.

Heavy steel saw plate — accommodates circular saws from 4½" to 8¼" blade size. Can also be used with your router (extra plates available if you wish to permanently mount your router). Six nylon bearings assure easy movement. ¾" thick chipboard top with 22¼" x 60" work surface supports almost any material ... i.e. 4' x 8' chipboard for accurate cutting. 60" structural aluminium I-beam shaped rails give support in every direction. Angle degree indicator shows position for angle cuts. Saw guide fence is 48" long — assuring accurate cuts in both large and small projects. Anti-kick spring and cord-holder for safety. Folding legs and floor protectors. Overall size: 60" wide 34" high 24" deep. Weight 70 lbs. Saw not included unless ordered. Easily assembled — instructions included.

SPECIAL INTRODUCTORY PRICE
£135.00 Inc. VAT (Plus £6.00 P & P) R.R.P. £178.00
or together with Shopmate 7¼" 1.6 HP Heavy Duty Circular Saw
£176.00 Inc. VAT (Plus £7.40 P & P) SAW R.R.P. £56.00
JEMCO TOOLS 32 Baker Street, Weybridge, Surrey. Tel: Weybridge 54896-7

ORDER TODAY
JEMCO TOOLS
32 Baker Street, Weybridge, Surrey. Tel: Weybridge 54896-7

□ Send......Portable saw guides at £135.00 each plus £6.00 p & p

tick

□ Send......Portable saw guides plus a Shopmate 7¼" heavy duty saw at £176.00 each plus £7.40 p & p

□ Please send me literature on the portable saw guides and your range of discount power tools.

Credit Card Holder can order by phone at any time:
Access □   Barclaycard □

No ☐☐☐☐☐☐☐☐☐☐☐☐☐☐☐☐

Name ....

Address ....

_____

Delivery within 14 days

252

Prices quoted are those prevailing at press date and are subject to alteration due to economic conditions.

Woodworker, April 1980

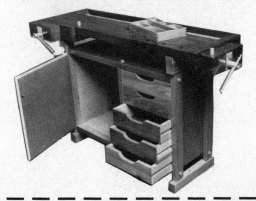

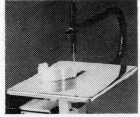

Illustrated here is the recently introduced type M230 lathe — developed from the highly successful and popular type J4 MkII which continues in production. The M230 incorporates a heavy-duty spindle to metric dimensions, ball-bearing headstock and five-speed drive. The lathe is available as a cabinet stand motorised ready to run unit or for those wishing to utilise their own work bench, the machine and a range of accessories and electrical items can be purchased separately. Obtainable from a limited number of stockists or direct from us.

In addition to the M230, we have other wood-turning lathes in our own range, whilst we also stock Myford ML8 series, various makes of bandsaws, grinders, turning tools, motors, books, etc. For leaflets and current price list, please send 30p in stamps to:

Arundel
WOOD TURNING LATHES AND ACCESSORIES

D. ARUNDEL & COMPANY LIMITED,
Mills Drive Farndon Road
Newark,
Nottinghamshire.
NG24 4SN

Tel. Newark (0636) 702382

Sale of Antique Woodworking & Craft Tools
Tyrone R. Roberts

on Tuesday, April 15th at 10.30 a.m., viewing Monday, April 14th
from 12 noon to 9 p.m.
at The Grove House Hotel, Newmarket Road, Norwich, Norfolk

The Sale will comprise of over 650 lots of interest to the collector and craftsman and will include items used by Wheelwrights, Coopers, Cabinet Makers, Shipwrights, Patternmakers, Joiners, Watchmakers, gunsmith and Leatherworking tools.

Illustrated catalogue with estimated prices and facilities for postal bidders, prices by post, U.K. £1.50; Europe £1.75; International £2; U.S.A. $4.50. (U.K. Subscribers please send S.A.E. if "Prices realised" list is required). Overseas subscribers will automatically receive list.

Tyrone R. Roberts, Auctioneers Office, Watton Road,
SWAFFHAM, Norfolk.

Telephone: 21767 STD 0760

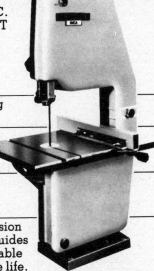

WHAT'S NEW

Grinders from Cowell

Additions to the powered workshop equipment from Cowell Engineering Ltd, 95-101 Oak Street, Norwich NR3 3BP (Norwich 614521), are a wetstone grinder (25-200) and a linisher-grinder (25-300). The former has a 100mm diameter aluminium oxide wheel for rough grinding and a 250mm wet sandstone wheel. The 100mm wheel runs at 2,750 rpm and the 250mm wheel at 60rpm. The single phase motor is for 220V, 50Hz, 170W supply. Weight of the grinder is 15kg complete with tool rest for both wheels.

The linisher-grinder is based on the motor of an 8in. grinder and combines a 6in. grinding wheel and an 800 x 50mm linisher. It accepts standard linisher belts which are available in a range of grades. No. 25-301 is a grinder only fitted with two 6in. diameter wheels.

Cowell has also restyled the motorised version of its model 10-200B lathe.

The company reports that the trade has forward ordered a major portion of the 1980 production.

Router cutters

Tungsten carbide tipped (TCT) router cutters branded Trend/Tipcut are marketed by Trend Machinery & Cutting Tools Ltd, Unit N, Penfold Works, Imperial Way, Watford WD2 4YY (0923 49911). They are said to fit all hand routing machines and to be suitable for routing in abrasive materials such as particleboard. Four standard diameters are offered through Trend cutter stockists — 1/4, 3/8, 1/2 and 5/8in. and all but the largest will perform plunge drilling operations. Prices range from £4.95 (1/4in.) to £21.50 for a set of four (exclusive of VAT).

Stick-on abrasives

Stick-on abrasive papers in 60, 100 and 150 grits with self-adhesive backing are produced by the 3M Co Ltd, PO Box 1, Bracknell RG12 1JU. A peel-off protective backing protects the adhesive which although it holds the paper in place firmly during sanding, nevertheless allows it to be removed when worn out. Papers will be supplied for application to plain-faced 5in. rubber sanding discs made by the company and for a 5¼ x 2¼in. hand sanding block.

The paper which uses aluminium oxide in the two coarser grades and silicon carbide in the finer, is described as 'open-coated' and likely to become clogged less quickly than normal types. It is less likely to tear in use and is damp-proofed.

The rotary disc paper needs no centre fixing and is therefore less likely to mark the workpiece. On orbital sanders the paper can be used providing an initial vinyl pad is fixed using the sander's clips.

Bevel edge chisels

Bevel edge chisels from E. Germany (brandname Smalcalda) are imported by The Goport Co Ltd, York House, Empire Way, Wembley HA9 0QH (01-903 2065). Fitted with a shock washer the handles are of beech protected with a steel impact ferrule. There are 15 sizes from 6mm (1/4in.) to 32mm (1¼in.).

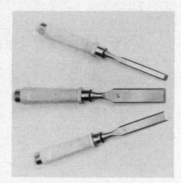

Ratchet screwdriver 3½in. long

A ratchet screwdriver with 5/16in. point on a 1/4in. square shank mounted in a plastics handle and 3½in. long overall, is manufactured by J. Stead & Co Ltd, Greenland Road, Sheffield S9 5BW. The ratchet system utilises roller bearings which are allowed to freewheel or jam between flat surfaces on the blade and the outer casing. This provides drive and freewheel, full lock and unscrew and freewheel positions.

While the blade has the resistance of a screw slot to hold it, the three positions marked forward, neutral and reverse on a rotating sleeve where handle meets shaft, can be selected at a touch of the finger of the hand grasping the handle. The maker claims that greater torque can be applied with this type of screwdriver than any other. Price is given as approximately £2.25.

Grinder and drills

A redesigned angle grinder (GD3116) and three pistol-grip drills (GD3094, 3096 and 3098) are introduced by Black & Decker Professional, Bath Road, Harmondsworth UB7 0BX (01-759 2411). In the drills GD3094 is a 420W tool with 10mm chuck while GD3096 has a 450W motor and 13mm chuck. These two are rotary models and GD3098 (with 450W motor) is a rotary-percussion model. All have two speeds of 1,225 and 2,900rpm (no load) and are listed respectively at £47.50, £53 and £59.50 exclusive of VAT.

Measuring devices

New introductions by Fisco Products Ltd, Brook Road, Rayleigh, Essex, include Trimatic side locking pocket measuring tapes, with ½in. (13mm) wide yellow blade in 2m (6ft), 3m (10ft) and 3.5m (12ft) lengths housed in a chromium-plated case fitted with brake.

Recent additions to the company's range include 6in. (15cm) and 8in. (20cm) plastics stock squares and the multi-purpose 12in. square with angle-finder which can be used as an outside or inside try square, mitre square, level finder, plumb level, 45° level, depth or height gauge, marking gauge, steel rule, scriber and straight edge.

Dust extraction

Equipment to filter dust from smaller machine tools such as grinders, circular saws and linishers, is handled by Environetics Ltd, 505 Daimler House, 33-4 Paradise Circus, Queensway, Birmingham B1 2BJ (021-632 6341). The equipment comprises the Aerodyne mobile Mk II Midget and Mini-dyne models, the former having capacity of 250cfm and the latter 500cfm. Both incorporate manual shaker assembly, quick-release dust tray and are mounted on nylon castors so as to be capable of movement from one machine tool to another.

Prices range from £345 to £380 and a leaflet giving technical details and illustration showing position of fan and motor and filter bags etc is available on application to Environetics at the address given above.

Spiral staircase

Spiral staircase in hardwood and supplied sanded is available in three diameters: 1532mm (5ft 0½in.); 1832mm (6ft 1in.); and 2072mm (6ft 9in.) with standard rise of 200mm (8in.) tread. There is a centre core to permit multi-storey installation with rigidity with or without a handrail. 'This gives the customer flexibility in the balustrading with choice of straight or turned,' states Albion Design (Kaytree Ltd), 12 Flitcroft Street, London WC2H 8DJ (01-836 0151), from which further details are available.

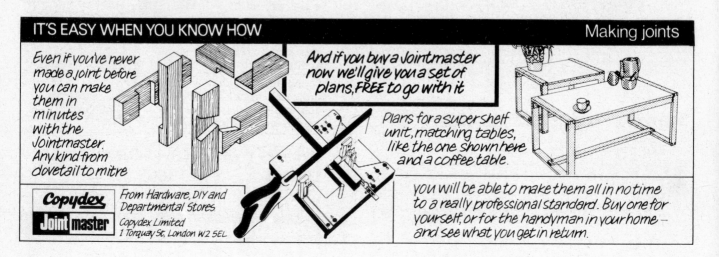

WHAT'S NEW IN EQUIPMENT

Stains and finishes

Butinox preservative timber finish is described as an organic solvent containing safe fungicides for interior or exterior use. Covering capacity is given as approximately 10m²/litre by brush or spray with initial application of two coats and a single coat for maintenance. Enquiries to Butinox Division of Nodest AS, c/o Monzie Joinery Ltd, Crieff, Perthshire, Scotland (0764 2740).

Floor lacquer, paint and wood-preservative coating known as Oxan, together with Demi-Dekk opaque wood stain and Benar hardwood protective coating, are products of Jotungruppen A/S of Norway. The company is represented in Britain by Stanleys (Stratford) Ltd, Warton Road, Stratford, London E15 2JY (01-534 2145). Sadolin (UK) Ltd, Shirehill, Saffron Walden, Essex (0799 23490), is another producer of timber preservatives and sealants. Preservatives are available in clear and colours for interior and exterior application. Water-repellent PX-65 protects against blue stain and mould growth.

Prices down

Average price reductions of 20% are announced by CeKa Works Ltd, Pwllheli, Gwynedd (0758 2254), in respect of its concealed cabinet hinges. For example a bubble-packed pair of standard non-sprung 35mm hinges now retails at £1.05 (plus VAT) a pair. The price reductions also apply to bulk packs of 20, 50 and 100 hinges. Reductions averaging around 10% on ex-VAT prices of several micrometers and Vernier caliper gauges in the CeKa range are also being made.

Finest grade abrasive

From English Abrasives Ltd, PO Box 85, Marsh Lane, London N17 0XA (01-808 4545), there is information about 1000 and 1200 grits in Supraflex waterproof silicon carbide paper. Grades now range from 60 to 1200 grits, the latter being for use on high-quality lacquering in furniture production. This is the finest grade available, allowing hand finishes finer than ever previously obtainable with this type of coated abrasive material, states the company.

Jacobs' open mesh sanding disc.

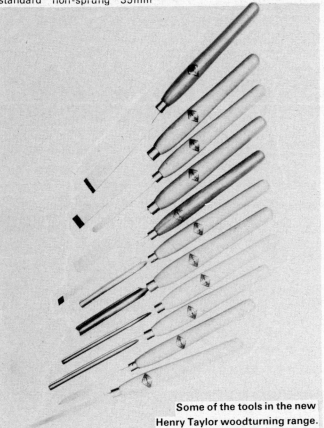

Some of the tools in the new Henry Taylor woodturning range.

Regulator ready to build

Emperor's new regulator clock kit is an authentic reproduction of a popular late 1800s design. It is simple to build. The decorated glass door is pre-assembled, all kit pieces are pre-cut from solid ½in. oak. The kit includes complete instructions, screws, hardware and clock movement. This solid brass movement is completely assembled, it strikes and counts each hour, strikes each half hour and carries a one year warranty. The clock can be purchased completely assembled and finished with the movement installed. For a new furniture kit colour brochure and all details send $1.00 to Emperor Clock Company, Dept FS Fairhope, Alabama 36532, US.

Equipment for the home handyman

An extensive range of quality accessories, to increase the versatility of industrial or home power tools, has been released by Jacobs Manufacturing Co Ltd, Archer Road, Millhouses, Sheffield, South Yorks.

For intricate and detailed work, Jacobs' extensive range of rotary cutters save time when shaping difficult curves and removing burrs to give a truly professional finish. Like all Jacobs' tools they can be used with any make of drill or with Jacobs' own flexible drive shaft. A wide range of shapes, including two countersinks are available, and they are suitable for an extensive variety of materials including formica, wood and soft metals. A range of six miniature cutters is also available for model makers or extra delicate work.

Diamic woodturning

A comprehensive range of woodturning tools has been released with the Diamic label following detailed research by Henry Taylor Tools of Sheffield, into the need for rationalisation of the overwhelming array of shapes and styles stocked by the woodturning industry. There is a basic range of 40 tools now being marketed in traditional sets of 3, 5 and 8. All blades are hand forged at Sheffield using traditional methods and tooling. Henry Taylor have been forging tools in Sheffield since 1834 (with the exception of two short breaks during the two World wars.) Export accounts for 80% of production and the accent is still on producing for the specialist and artistic craftsman. For further information contact Sales Dept. Henry Taylor Tools Ltd, The Forge, Lowther Road, Sheffield, South Yorks.

Emperor's new regulator clock available in kit form or fully assembled.

New and reconditioned machinery

With workshop and machining facilities at Unit 3a Mill Lane Industrial Estate, Glenfield, Leicester, 5 Tudor Square, West Bridgford, Nottingham, and Browns Lane, Stanton-on-the-Wolds, Keyworth, Notts, Poole Wood Equip Ltd and its associated companies has more than 350 new, used and reconditioned woodworking machines in stock. Managing director Ken Poole advises that his companies are also agents for Apollo spray plant, Oppold and Micor tooling etc and dust control systems and equipment.

New from Italy is the Pisani four side planer and the Alpha universal machine, and from Germany the Bolman timber dryer. The company also handles Sumaco, Wadkin Evenwood, Startrite, Multico, DeWalt and other woodworking machines.

Repair service

Retoothing of hand and tenon saws, pitch alterations, resetting and sharpening for small or large quantities are among the services offered by Conway Saw & Supply Co Ltd, Swan Lane, West Bromwich B70 0NU (021-553 5461). The company also services circular and bandsaws and carries out machinery overhauls, repairs and breakdowns. It is stockist of woodworking machinery, circular saws and cutters.

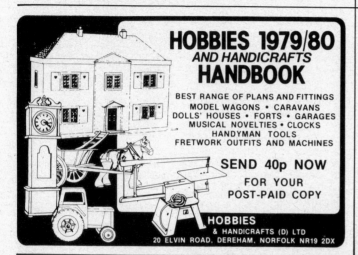

260

Prices quoted are those prevailing at press date and are subject to alteration due to economic conditions.

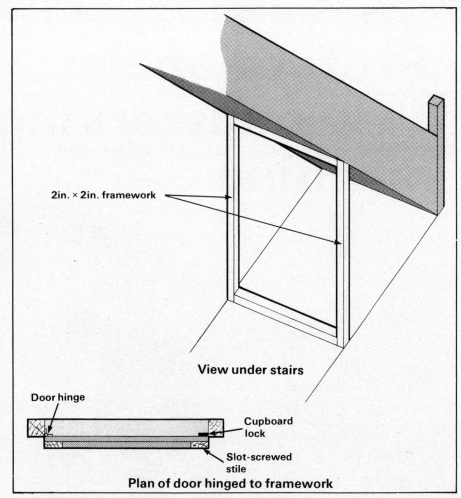

2in. × 2in. framework

View under stairs

Door hinge

Cupboard lock

Slot-screwed stile

Plan of door hinged to framework

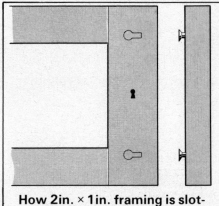

How 2in. × 1in. framing is slot-screwed to conceal keyhole

Understairs cupboard

From: J. C. Delvoir, Welling, Kent
I have the normal cupboard under the stairs and would like to make an inconspicuous small compartment with a hidden lock at the back of the cupboard about 18-24in. from the foot of the stairs. Any advice that you can offer would be most appreciated.

It is assumed that a place is wanted which would be overlooked by intruders rather than a strongbox. This would be akin to the secret compartments found in old desks and bureaux. Their value lay not in their security so much as in the fact that their presence was not immediately apparent.

It is suggested that a 2 x 2in. framework be constructed as shown in the sketches about 2ft 6in. high by 2ft 9in. wide. Plain halving or notched joints can be used. The cupboard door made from stout ply can be hinged on one of the uprights to open outwards and if the hinges are screwed behind

the door as shown their presence will be concealed. A good-quality cupboard lock should be fitted to the right-hand edge of the door and the keyhole cut.

In order not to give the game away, the keyhole must be concealed and it is suggested that a 2 x 1in. framing be glued and nailed to the top, bottom and left-hand faces of the door. The right-hand piece is slot-screwed to the door so that it appears to be firmly fixed and it conceals the keyhole. By sliding it a little way to the left this piece can be lifted away and the door unlocked. The sketches also show the method of slot-screwing.

Brass on walnut doors

From: H. B. Forster, Blackpool, Lancs
I have two doors in walnut which have brass kicking plates and hand protective plates on both sides of the doors. Some time in the past cleaners have polished the various brass decoration with a particular polish and the polish has badly stained the walnut wood on both sides of the doors. Various acids, thinners, solvent, turps, etc have been tried, but nothing seems to clean the surface for a re-french polishing. The old french polish was ruined and has been taken off. Before re-polishing I am anxious to have some advice on how to deal with the stain.
Principal constituents of polish are water, white spirit and polishing chalk, with a small amount of emulsifier to hold the chalk in suspension; there would therefore seem to be no intense form of stain involved. It is most likely that over a long period, water staining of the surface of the wood under the polish has occurred, with some penetration of dirt due to the spirit content. If this theory is correct, it would

explain why the various solvents you have used have had no effect. It would seem that the only effective way of cleaning up the doors is by sanding the wood. This would not be difficult were the doors solid, but if they are veneered, then sanding might not be the answer if the veneer is grimed through. In this case, the alternative would be to try to clean up the dirty patches by rubbing these with a cork dipped in oxalic acid, wiping over with a clean, wet rag. This would of course bleach the treated area which would need eventual staining. Care would be needed to 'kill' the acid with water, otherwise it could affect the final finish. Sanding the wood is really the best answer.

English oak church doors

From: D. P. Craven, Winterbourne, Bristol
Could you please recommend a suitable finish for a pair of solid English oak church doors which I am making. We wish to preserve the beauty of the figured oak while giving a weather-proof finish. We also wish to reduce annual maintenance to a minimum.

The material that meets your requirements is produced by the firm of Sadolins (UK) Ltd, Shire Hill Industrial Estate, Shire Hill, Saffron Walden, Essex, under the trade name Sadolins PX65, and by Sikkens (UK) Ltd, Didcot Industrial Estate, Station Road, Didcot, Oxon OX11 7NG, under the trade name Sikkens Rubbol TXB. We suggest you ask both companies to send you their colour charts because you will need to select the most suitable shade. These formulations (and others like them) consist of a spirit base, toxic agents such as pentachlorophenol for protection against fungi and most beetles (important in new oak if sapwood is present, as a safeguard against *Lyctus* beetle) and containing a small amount of wax and resin for water-repellency. Depending on type, pigments are included, small amounts which do not obscure the grain, large or heavy amounts that do. Application is simplicity itself: an initial three-coat finish will give a good appearance, and successive maintenance by a single coat every so often will increase water-repellency and improve the colour. Colour selection is very important; you might find it expedient to choose a 'natural' oak finish at first, changing over (or recommending to the customer) to a slightly darker version in two or three years' time. It must be remembered that the natural colour of wood is fugitive and, depending on exposure will progressively be lost, the pigments in the applied fluid being the compensating factor. There is no degradation of these finishes by breakdown, and while annual inspection is essential if the doors are to look their best at all times, it is possible simply to wash down the wood, using a detergent at some periods of maintenance. Generally speaking, eighteen months to two years ought to be the maximum period left between maintenance coats.

Lathe attachment

From: G. Roche, Ashbourne, Co Meath
I am having some problems turning small bowls on a lathe attachment powered by a portable drill. I am using a ¾in. round nosed spindle gouge with a steepish bevel, but the results are not good. Should I use a bowl turning gouge? What tool is used in reducing the hexagon shape to circular, ie roughing-down?

The machine you are using is by no means suitable for the turning of bowls; an electric drill is not intended for woodturning purposes, there being both end and side float present in the bearings.

The only tool which can satisfactorily be used in the turning of a bowl of any description is the deep fluted gouge ground with a square end; this is commonly referred to as a bowl gouge. Use of tools of this type calls for a considerable amount of power, more than is required for the turning of a spindle. If work of this nature is carried out on a lathe attachment the life of the drill will be shortened appreciably.

A gouge with a curved end should not be used, a spindle gouge (by definition) being intended for the turning of a spindle. Standard strength bowl gouges are available though not very common, but use of a standard strength gouge will not improve your situation.

Regarding the reduction of hexagonal blank to a circular form, this would be carried out with a ⅜in. deep fluted long and strong gouge but, once again, adequate power and good bearings are essential. The process can be performed by means of a scraper, but the surface of the material is likely to be badly torn. This is undesirable since it calls for extensive repair work at a later stage.

To sum up: while a drill lathe attachment has its merits and, indeed, is quite a good method by which to get started, it does have definite limitations. For anyone wishing to enter into faceplate turning — such as bowls, plaques, picture frames and so forth, a rather better type of machine which is of sturdy construction is strongly recommended.

Staining spruce

From: W. J. Barrow, Otley, West Yorks
I make model scale furniture and am having a lot of trouble with staining the wood to the correct shades of dark Jacobean oak, mahogany and walnut. The wood I use is Solarbo spruce and I find that some stains are not consistent and do not colour different batches of wood the same. Could you give any advice on how to get an even and also consistent colour?

Spruce is a difficult wood insofar as its ability to accept liquids uniformly is concerned: it is classified as resitant in terms of preservative treatment, ie it is difficult to penetrate the wood through side grain, even under vacuum pressure, to more than 3mm to 6mm; obviously, a liquid applied by hand is more likely to soak in fairly well in the areas of thin-walled early-wood tracheids, while tending to sit on the surface so to speak on the more resistant areas of thick-walled late-wood tracheids, the overall effect being eventual non-uniform penetration in each growth ring. Spirit-based stains tend to penetrate a little better than water stains, and it might help to brush the surface of the wood with white spirit prior to applying the stain to try to assist penetration and achieve greater uniformity. Failing this, we would suggest you change over to a more permeable wood. European redwood (Scots pine) is classified as being moderately resistant to the passage of liquid; and alder beech, lime, poplar and sycamore, all hardwoods, are permeable species.

Turning a holly log

From: J. C. Beharrell, Chigwell, Essex
I have been given a holly log about 7in. diameter and 4ft. long. One end is covered with tar and the log has been seasoned in a moderately warm garage for 3½ years. The cross-section appears to be uniform, ie no sap wood. There is a radial crack which is less than half the diameter of the log; the crack appears to finish at about half the length.

What would be the way to have this log cut to make best use of the wood? I'd like to make a bowl, but is end-grain turning satisfactory?

Holly is fairly difficult to dry, especially in the round, due to its tendency to distort and split at the ends. Best results are obtained by converting the log to the smallest sizes permissible and drying them slowly with the wood weighted down.

Although the wood has a fine, even texture its grain is often irregular. This latter aspect contributes to distortion tendencies and to the usual planing and moulding recommendations that the cutting angle be reduced from the more normal 30° to 15 or 20°.

Since your log is already showing a long split, part at least of the log could not in any case be used for whole diameter end-grain turning. The best treatment we would recommend would be to saw the log through the central pith, following the line of the split approximately, so as to provide two 4ft half-rounds. These could then be used for long-grain turning.

Alternatively, you could experiment with the sound end by cutting this clear of the split. Although the log may be relatively dry its moisture content (m.c.) is probably no drier than 16 or 18%, so if you do decide to use the whole diameter try rough turning so as to remove some of the surplus wood, especially from the centre. This will reduce any further tendency to splitting.

For a bowl the m.c. will need reducing to 12% or less; therefore before final turning the wood will need to be kept in a warm room for a couple of weeks or so, ie in the roughed-out state. The wood is hard and compact so end-grain turning could give good results: cutting edges must be kept sharpened and bearing in mind cutting angles for planing, the tool should be offered to the wood as soon as convenient to give more of a scrape than a cut.

Holly is often used as a substitute for boxwood — and for ebony when dyed black. Otherwise it is used for engraving blocks, inlaying and general turnery.

SHOP GUIDE

The quickest and easiest method of reaching all Woodworkers is to advertise in SHOP GUIDE.
Telephone Gill Dedman (0442) 41221 Ex. 241.
Rate: £5.00 per unit. Minimum of 6 months.
★ Mail Order

AVON

BATH   Tel. Bath 22617
GORDON STOKES (office anytime)
WOODCRAFT SUPPLY   ★
110 MOUNT ROAD, WHITEWAY
Open: 9.30 a.m.-5.00 p.m.
Wednesday and Saturdays only

BRISTOL   Tel. (0272) 311510
JOHN HALL TOOLS LIMITED   ★
CLIFFTON DOWN SHOPPING
CENTRE, WHITELADIES ROAD
Open: Monday-Saturday
9.00 a.m.-5.30 p.m.

BRISTOL   Tel. 0272-629092
TRYMWOOD SERVICES   ★
2a DOWNS PARK EAST,
(off North View) WESTBURY PARK
Open: 9.00 a.m.-5.30 p.m.
Monday to Friday

BRISTOL   Tel. 0272-667013
V. H. WILLIS & CO. LTD.   ★
190-192 WEST STREET
BEDMINSTER
Open: 8.30 a.m.-5.00 p.m. Mon-Fri.
Saturday 9.00 a.m.-1.00 p.m.

BERKSHIRE

READING   Tel. (0734) 586522)
SARJENT'S TOOL STORES   ★
LTD.
44-52 OXFORD ROAD
Open: 8.30 a.m.-5.30 p.m.
Monday-Saturday

BUCKINGHAMSHIRE

MILTON KEYNES   Tel:
A. POLLARD & SON   0908-75221
LTD.   ★
51 QUEENSWAY, BLETCHLEY
Open: 8.30 a.m.-5.30 p.m.
Monday-Saturday

CAMBRIDGESHIRE

CAMBRIDGE   Tel: 0223-353091
H.B. WOODWORKING
69 LENSFIELD ROAD
Open: 8.30 a.m.-5.30 p.m.
Monday-Friday
8.30 a.m.-1.00 p.m. Saturday

PETERBOROUGH   Tel:
PETERBOROUGH   0733-62800
TOOL CENTRE
16 WESTGATE
Open: Mon.-Sat. 9.00am-5.30pm
Thursday 9.00 am-1.00 pm

CHESHIRE

CHEADLE   Tel. 061-491-1726
ERIC TOMKINSON   ★
86 STOCKPORT ROAD
Open: 9.00 a.m.-4.00 p.m.
Wednesday-Saturday
Closed all day Monday & Tuesday

STOCKPORT   Tel:
M.W. EQUIPMENT   061-480-8481
LIMITED
SHAWCROSS STREET
Monday-Friday
9.00 a.m.-4.45 p.m.

CLEVELAND

MIDDLESBROUGH   Tel. 0642-
WINTZ   460035/83650
INDUSTRIAL SUPPLIES   ★
2 BESSEMER COURT,
GRANGETOWN
Open: Mon.-Fri. 8.30 a.m.-5.00 p.m.

CORNWALL

HELSTON   Tel.03265-4961
SOUTHWEST POWER TOOLS   ★
MONUMENT ROAD
Open: 8.00 a.m.-5.00 p.m.
Monday-Friday
Saturday 8.00 a.m.-12.30 p.m.

LAUNCESTON   Tel. 0566-3555
SOUTHWEST POWER TOOLS   ★
6 WESTERN ROAD
Open: 8.00 a.m.-5.00 p.m.
Monday-Friday
Saturday 8.00 a.m.-12.30 p.m.

DERBYSHIRE

BUXTON   Tel. 0298-871636
CRAFT SUPPLIES   ★
THE MILL
MILLERSDALE
Open: Monday-Saturday
9.00 a.m.-5.00 p.m.

DEVON

AXMINSTER   Tel. 0297-33656
POWER TOOL CENTRE   ★
STYLES & BROWN
CHARD STREET
Open: 9.00 a.m.-5.30 p.m.
Monday-Saturday

BIDEFORD   Tel. 023-72-3513
NORTH DEVON TOOLS   ★
7-9 MEDDON STREET
Open: Monday-Friday
8.00 a.m.-6.00 p.m.
Saturday 8.30 a.m.-5.00 p.m.

EXETER   Tel. 0392-73936
WRIDES TOOL CENTRE
147 FORE STREET
Open: 9.00 a.m.-5.30 p.m.
Monday-Saturday
Wednesday 9.00 a.m.-1.00 p.m.

CO. DURHAM

DARLINGTON   Tel. 0325-53511
PERCY W. STEPHENSON & SON
171/179 NORTHGATE
Open: 8.30 a.m.-5.30 p.m.
Monday to Saturday

ESSEX

SOUTHEND ON SEA   Tel.
MARSHALL &   0702-710404
PARSONS LIMITED
1111 LONDON RD., LEIGH ON SEA
Open: 8.30 a.m.-5.30 p.m. Mon.-Fri.
Open: 9.00 a.m.-5.00 p.m. Sat.

GLOUCESTERSHIRE

TEWKESBURY   Tel. 0684-
TEWKESBURY SAW CO.   293092
LIMITED   ★
TRADING ESTATE, NEWTOWN
Open: 8.00 a.m.-5.00 p.m.
Monday-Friday

HAMPSHIRE

ALDERSHOT   Tel. 0252-28088
BURCH & HILLS LTD.   ★
BLACKWATER WAY TRADING
ESTATE
Open: 8.30 a.m.-5.30 p.m. Mon.-Fri.
8.30 a.m.-12.00 Saturday

SOUTHAMPTON   Tel.
HAMPSHIRE   0703 77672
WOODWORKING MACHINERY   ★
297 SHIRLEY ROAD, SHIRLEY
Open: Tuesday-Saturday
9.30 a.m.-6.00 p.m.

HERTFORDSHIRE

HITCHIN   Tel. 0462-4177
ROGER'S
47 WALSWORTH ROAD
Open: 9.00 a.m.-6.00 p.m.
Monday-Saturday
Closed all day Wednesday

WATFORD   Tel. (0923) 49911
TREND MACHINERY & CUTTING
TOOLS LTD.
UNIT N, PENFOLD WORKS,
IMPERIAL WAY
Open: 9.00 a.m.-5.00 p.m. Mon.-Fri.

LANCASHIRE

LANCASTER   Tel. 0524-2886
LILE TOOL SHOP
43/45 NORTH ROAD
Open: 9.00 a.m.-5.30 p.m.
Monday-Saturday
Wednesday 9.00 a.m.-12.30 p.m.

MERSEYSIDE

LIVERPOOL   Tel. 051-263-1359
TAYLOR BROS. (LIVERPOOL) LTD.   ★
5/9 PRESCOTT STREET
Open: 8.30 a.m.-5.30 p.m.
Monday-Friday

LEICESTERSHIRE

LEICESTER   Tel. 0455-43254
ROY STARTIN LTD.
134 WOOD STREET   ★
EARL SHILTON
Open: Mon.-Fri. 8.00 a.m.-5.30 p.m.
Saturday 8.00 a.m.-1.30 p.m.

LONDON

      Tel. 01-739-7126
CECIL W. TYZACK   ★
79-81 KINGSLAND ROAD
Open: 8.45 a.m.-5.15 p.m.
Monday-Friday — Closed Saturday

      Tel.
GENERAL   01-254-6052
WOODWORK SUPPLIES
76-80 STOKE NEWINGTON
HIGH STREET, N16
Mon-Sat 9.00-6.00. Thur 9.00-1.00

NORFOLK

NORWICH   Tel. 0603 898695
NORFOLK SAW SERVICES
DOG LANE, HORSFORD
Open: 8.00 a.m.-5.00 p.m.
Monday-Friday
Saturday 8.00 a.m.-12.00 noon

NORTHAMPTONSHIRE

RUSHDEN   Tel. 093-34-56424
PETER CRISP LIMITED   ★
7 HIGH STREET
Open: 8.30 a.m.-5.30 p.m.
Monday-Saturday
Thursday 8.30 a.m.-1.00 p.m.

NOTTINGHAMSHIRE

NOTTINGHAM Tel. 0602-811889
THE WOODCUTTER   ★
5 TUDOR SQUARE,
WEST BRIDGEFORD
Open: Tues.-Sat. 9.00 am-5.30 pm
Fri. 9.00 am-7.30 pm. Closed Mon.

OXFORDSHIRE

OXFORD   Tel. (0865-45118/9)
SARJENT'S TOOL STORES LTD.   ★
150 COWLEY ROAD
Open: 8.30 a.m.-5.30 p.m.
Monday-Saturday

SUFFOLK

BURY ST. EDMUNDS   Tel.
TOOLS & THINGS   0284-62022
21 CHURCHGATE   ★
Open: 9.00 a.m.-5.30 p.m.
Monday-Saturday

SURREY

CROYDON   Tel. 01-688-5513
L.H. TURTLE   ★
6-12 PARK STREET
Open: 8.30 a.m.-5.30 p.m.
Monday-Saturday

GUILDFORD   Tel. 0483-61125
MESSINGERS FOR TOOLS
14-18 CHERTSEY STREET
Open: 8.30 a.m.-5.30 p.m.
Closed all day Monday

EAST SUSSEX

HASTINGS   Tel. 0424-423072
THORCROFT   ★
181/182 QUEENS ROAD
Open: 8.30 a.m.-5.30 p.m.
Monday-Saturday
Closed all day Wednesday

WEST SUSSEX

WORTHING   Tel. 0903-38739
W. HOSKING (TOOLS &   ★
MACHINERY)
96a MONTAGUE STREET
Open: 8.30 a.m.-5.30 p.m. Mon-Sat
Wednesday 8.30 a.m.-1.00 p.m.

WILTSHIRE

SWINDON   Tel. (0793-31361)
SARJENT'S TOOL STORES LTD.   ★
64 FLEET STREET
Open: 8.30 a.m.-5.30 p.m.
Monday-Saturday

NORTH YORKSHIRE

HARROGATE   Tel.
      0423-66245/55328
MULTI-TOOLS   ★
158 KINGS ROAD
Open: 8.30 a.m.-6.00 p.m.
Monday-Saturday

WEST YORKSHIRE

LEEDS   Tel. 0532-79-507
GEORGE SPENCE & SONS LTD.
WELLINGTON ROAD
Open: Monday-Friday
8.30 a.m.-5.30 p.m.
Saturday 9.00 a.m.-5.00 p.m.

CLEVELAND

MIDDLESBOROUGH   Tel.
REM ELECTRIC   0642-248460
POWER TOOLS
89 PARLIMENT ROAD
Open: 8.30 a.m.-5.00 p.m.
Monday-Saturday

Lurem, make it so easy

Whether you are a DIY enthusiast or a professional with your own commercial business, there are ten good reasons for investing in the Lurem C210B.

It is a jointer, thicknesser/planer, mortiser, drill, shaper, circular saw, tenoner/crosscut, and also, if optional attachments are used, a grinder, sander, woodturner and bandsaw. You can have this combined facility or a simplified version with less operations. Either way, you get real value for money.

If you look closer, the features are even more impressive. Solidly built for reliability intended for hard and continuous work with minimum maintenance. Rugged castings are extensively used yet it is highly manoeuvreable. Individual components are easily accessible. Adjustments are positive and effective. In fact, the C210B is both functional and practical. And safe.

Fortunately, it is inexpensive too. So for your home workshop, professional business or for schools and technical training, it is a sound and safe investment with twelve months guarantee.

lurem For Reliability and Service

For full details write to:
Lurem Machines
9 Biggin Hill Road, Evington,
Leicester, LE5 6HQ.
Telephone: (0533) 735554.

266

Prices quoted are those prevailing at press date and are subject to alteration due to economic conditions.

Woodworker, April 1980

A Meddings Jig Sawing machine cuts costs and corners

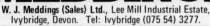

MK. IV MODEL
(with 25" throat)

Meddings Scroll and Jigsawing Machines not only provide the accuracy required by professional sign manufacturers, stand-fitters and carpenters employing high-cost modern materials but the robustness, reliability and reasonable pricing essential for widespread use in schools and training colleges. Floor or bench models available.

Other Meddings products include Drilling Machines, pneumatic Sanding Drums & Wet Sandstone grinders.

MEDDINGS

BUY BRITISH BUY MEDDINGS

W. J. Meddings (Sales) Ltd., Lee Mill Industrial Estate, Ivybridge, Devon. Tel: Ivybridge (075 54) 3277.

𝕎𝕠𝕠𝕕𝕥𝕦𝕣𝕟𝕚𝕟𝕘 Courses

four days with
MIKE LAW
(Thos Harrison & Sons)

Relax into a four-day long woodturning course in the informal atmosphere of our farmhouse home. We offer comfortable accommodation, good food, and professional tuition in the heart of this beautiful countryside.
Please write or telephone for details: Mike Law, The Longhouse, Maxworthy Cross, North Petherwin, Launceston, North Cornwall. Tel: STD (056685) 322.

Mike Law,
The Longhouse,
Maxworthy Cross,
North Petherwin,
Launceston,
North Cornwall

Dear Customer,

The business formerly known as Thos. Harrison & Sons of Bishop's Waltham has become Hampshire Woodworking Machinery, and is now established in larger premises (and more accessible) in Shirley Road, Southampton.

A large range of woodworking machinery, lathes and hand tools are stocked and on display, and if you have any doubts about the particular machine best suited to your needs, Mr. Brian Botto (already known to many of you) who has many years of experience in the use of these machines will be glad to help.

As I shall be in Cornwall by the time you read this, devoting my time to woodturning, I take the opportunity of thanking all past customers for their business, and of assuring you that your future requirements will be well catered for by H.W.M.

Yours sincerely,
Mike Law

$H \underset{M.}{\overset{W}{\sim}}$

HAMPSHIRE WOODWORKING MACHINERY

297 SHIRLEY ROAD, SHIRLEY SOUTHAMPTON
Telephone: Southampton 776222

Note the new address and number

Lathes, Bandsaws, Hand Power Tools, Grinding Wheels, Woodturning Tools and Carving Tools.

♛ **CORONET**

Sorby

Wadkin

Elu ®

KITY

Arundel

Henry Taylor

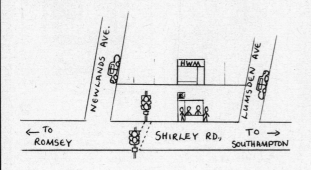

The complete centre for your woodworking needs.
Quality machinery, tools, abrasives and finishes.
OPEN TUESDAY TO SATURDAY — 9.30 a.m. - 6.00 p.m.

STARTRITE

Mail Order - 14 days delivery.

Prices quoted are those prevailing at press date and are subject to alteration due to economic conditions.

Classified Advertisements

Telephone Gill Dedman (0442) 41221 Ex.241

All classified Advertisements must be pre-paid.
Private and trade rate 14p per word (minimum £2.40).
Box Numbers £1.00 extra. Display box rates s.c.c. £3.00 (min. £7.50). All advertisements are inserted in the first available issue.
Box replies to be sent care of Advertisement Department, P.O. Box 35, Bridge Street, Hemel Hempstead, Herts, England HP1 1EE. There are no reimbursements for cancellations.

FOR SALE

Fine Period Furniture
for you to make by hand at home
Large selection of 17thC copies in solid oak or elm for simple home assembly without special tools.

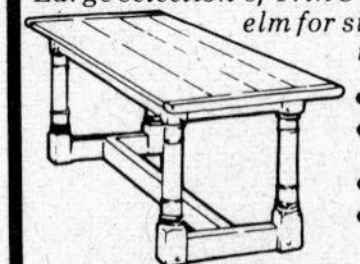

- All materials supplied
- All parts cut, planed and jointed
- Simple instructions
- Save up to 60% on retail prices

Send large SAE for brochure and price list

JACOBUS WORKSHOP
South Road,
KIRKBY STEPHEN,
Cumbria

ULMIA 6ft. German Red Beech woodwork bench. 3" top and underframe, front and end vices, excellent condition, buyer collects. £200 o.n.o. Richards, 'Arosfa', Beacon Road, West End, Southampton. Tel: 24218-2931. O

Brass or aluminium plates for your project. Letters block or script, example 3" x 1" brass plate with 20 block letter £1.10p, plus post, plus VAT. Also engraved badges, name plates, numbers, labels, etc. in coloured plastic. Trade enquiries welcome.

BRIAN J. BOWMAN TROPHIES LTD.
"Anela" Lower North Street, Cheddar, Somerset. Tel. Cheddar 742774

BUSINESS FOR SALE: Manufacturing opportunity leading branded name laminated timber sports equipment. Box No. 464 (Somerset), c/o Woodworker, MAP Limited, 13-35 Bridge Street, Hemel Hempstead, Herts. HP1 1EE. O

FOR SALE: Coronet minor lathe, 36" bed complete with stand, saw table, planer attachment, grindstone and several tools etc. £400 o.n.o. Contact Mr. Ward Louth (0507)-604875. O

EBAC 'MINOR' timber dryer and proportional timber, almost new, £500. Tel: Okehampton 2579. O

TOOLS TO TREASURE
Cabinetmakers' twine — strained Bowsaws with lacquered hardwood frames.
10" **£10.84** 14" **£11.76**
Rosewood handled cabinetmakers' marking knifes £1.20. All prices include P&P in U.K.
Adzes, Drawknives, Inshaves and other tools for the craftsman woodworker, send large S.A.E. for details.

CORBETT TOOLS
(Dept. WW/3),
224 Puxton Drive, Kidderminster, Worcester.

BRASS ELECTRICAL FITTINGS. Switches, Power Points, Dimmers, T.V. and Telephone Outlets, etc. Choice of three different designs on all models. Produced in heavy gauge solid brass. Polished, and treated with transparent lacquer to preserve high finish indefinitely. Also French Gilt, Wrought Iron, and a nine difference decorator colour range. All designed for simple replacement of existing plastic Models. Full compliance with British Safety Standards. Illustrated colour catalogue FREE from the Classic Brass Co., Dept. WE, 429/431 London Road, Westcliff, Essex. Personal Shoppers welcome. OPQ

VIOLIN KIT
Pre-shaped scroll, back and front, all material and accessories.
Detailed instruction manual and drawings £57.00.

C. JOHNSTON,
Violin Maker,
Manor Road, Wrea Green,
Preston. PR4 2PB.
V

WOLF 4" belt sander with dustbag, 9 months old, hardly used £90.00. Tel: Swindon 39332 after 6.00 p.m.

CLEARING antique tools. Marples 'Ultimatum' brace, planes, etc., etc. Tel: 01-876-9654. O

BRANDING IRONS
Made from solid steel with 15" handle, to last a lifetime. Now you can permanently identify your tools and production pieces. We can quote for special styles for a professional look. Price guide — 3 x 3/8" characters **£6.95p.**

SAE details — WHS, 38 Summercourt Way, Brixham. TQ5 0DY.

Snooker & Pool
"High Point" Garstang Rd. East, Singleton, Blackpool, Lancs. FY6 7SX
Tel: 0253-883426
Table Plans. Chipboard/Slate. State size, send £2 + SAE. Cod service on cloth, balls, rubber, etc. New and reconditioned Snooker and coin-op Pool tables sold/bought.
Advice Centre

WELSH SLATE sharpening stones for sale at very competitive prices. Send SAE for details: Inigo Jones and Co. Limited, Groelon, Caernarfon, Gwynedd. Tel: 0286-830242. O-U

GERMAN KARGER c.i. woodturning lathe, complete with face-plates, centres, chuck, motor, grindstone, new parts and 4" planer attachment. All excellent condition. Price £175.00. Tel: 01-876-9654. O

SHOPMATE 10" radial arm saw condition as new, hardly used. First offer £240 secures. Tel: 01-958-5116. O

CARVING/TURNING BLOCKS
Ready to use Iroko, Mahogany, Utile, Sapele and other imported hardwoods for bowls, lamps, etc. 1¼" to 4" thick up to 12" diameter as available. Mixed parcel of 1cft. before cutting into discs. Send SAE for details and prices.
For quantities of more than 5cft. ask for quotation. Enquiries for other sizes and species welcomed.

BERRYCROFT PRODUCTS
P.O. Box 2, Lydney, Glos.

MYFORD ML7 with motor, chuck, changewheels etc. £325. Also manual bar cropper £15. Tel: 01-476-4050 (evenings). O

ROYALE 10" tilt arbour saw table, cast base, 20 x 30 table, micro-fence, 1hp motor, blades, jigs inc. comb jointer £160. Tel: 051-727-5761. O

WALL CLOCKS
an exciting new look!
colourful decorative ceramic clockfaces, guaranteed quartz battery movements, ensure that the wall clocks you make will be elegant and reliable. Attractive designs and range of styles. Featured by Woodcraft Supply Corp.
SAE details — WHS, 38 Summercourt Way, Brixham. TQ5 0DY.

WORKSHOP EQUIPMENT

WOODCARVING tools

Ashley Iles & Henry Taylor
Arkansas Bench and Slip Stones, Bench Screws, Carvers, Vices, Professional Turning Tools.
send 20p in stamps for illustrated catalogue
Alec Tiranti Ltd
70 High St., Theale, Reading, Berks.
21 Goodge Place, London W1

LEISURECRAFT IN WOOD WITH CORONET
The full range of these universal and independent machines on show.
Demonstrations and lessons. Full back-up of tools and accessories for Turning, Carving and Marquetry.

KENTERPRISE LTD.
122 & 124 Camden Road, Tunbridge Wells
Tel. Tunbridge Wells 23475

TOOLS OF QUALITY
for Craftsmen and Handymen
We also supply a wide range of British-made screws: steel, brass, plated, Pozidriv, etc.
Send for our free illustrated lists before you buy. You'll be glad you did!
BENMAIL SUPPLIES
St. Georges, Weston-s-Mare, Avon

BANDSAWS
The BIRCH 2-speed BANDSAW, SANDER and LINISHER 16" throat, 6" depth, tilt. ½ h.p. single phase. Ready to plug in. Stamp illustrated details. Prices.

HAB ENGINEERING (Unit C)
Fardons Ind. Est., 113 Glover Street, Bordesley, Birmingham 9.
Tel: 021 772 2699

TUNGSTEN CARBIDE TIPPED CIRCULAR SAWS
Leading UK suppliers Govt., Industry & DIY. 24 hr despatch most sizes/types. Overseas orders: free air despatch at approx half N. American prices. SAE lists.
TLC WORLD TRADING LTD.
32/34 Craven Street, London WC2 Tel: 01-930 1942

Equipping a workshop?
Call and see demonstrated or write for details (27p stamps) of quality machines of the popular Kity range or by Startrite, Sedgwick, De Walt, Lurem and most others: Elu Routers and Power Tools; Arundel, Myford, Kity Woodturning Lathes, accessories etc.
Trymwood Services, 2A Downs Park East (near the Downs), Bristol. 629092 2-6pm, Mondays to Fridays.

Sorby WOODTURNING TOOLS
Also peppermills, barometers, thermometers, lighters, hourglasses, egg-timers, sealers and polishes, sawtooth bits, screwboxes and taps, ceramic tiles, spinning wheel plans, P.E.G. Stockists of Kity, Myford and Arundel lathes. S.A.E. for list.
ERIC TOMKINSON
86 Stockport Road, Cheadle, Cheshire SK8 2AJ
Tel. 061-491 1726 & 061-428 3740
Now open every Wednesday, Thursday, Friday and Saturday

SHERWOOD TURNING LATHES
All cast iron constructed. 3¾" CH 24" or 36" B.C. 3 or 4 speed, bowl turning up to 14" dia. ball-bearing spindle c/w face plate, centres etc. Prices from **£58.92** inc.VAT.

Send stamp for leaflets and details of above and other low-priced machines and motors.

JAMES INNS (Engs),
Main St., Bulwell, Nottingham.

PETER CRISP OF RUSHDEN THE CARPENTER'S SHOP
Hand Tools by leading makers. Stockists of:
Craftsmen, Coronet, Elu, Kity,
Woodworking Machinery.
Sorby Turning Chisels
Taylor Carving Chisels
Gomex T/Carbide Circular Saws

Stock list 25p
Illustrated Catalogue — 75p
(Refundable on first order over £10)

Tel. 093 34 56424-7
High Street, Rushden, Northants.

Now in CLEVELAND!
WOODWORKING MACHINERY
by Lurem, Emco, Elektra, etc. Arundel woodturning lathes. Wadkin portable power tools. Kef bench grinders.
Abrasive Specialists
Bandsaw and circular sawblades. Also — hand tools, chisels, etc.
Catalogue 25p.

WINTZ INDUSTRIAL SUPPLIES
2 Bessemer Court, Grangetown, Middlesborough
Phone: 0642-460035 Mon.-Fri.

A. POLLARD & SON
De-Walt, Shopmate, Kity, Elu, Susemihl
We offer good service, good stocks and low prices
Dust extractors
A. Pollard & Son,
51 Queensway,
Bletchley, Milton Keynes.
Tel: 0908-75221

ACCESS — BARCLAYCARD

Business established over 50 years.

BLACK & DECKER
7¼" Circular Saw (No. 7308)

Cutting depth up to 2.7/16" (not metal/masonry).
Angle adjustment 0-45° 5300 Rev/Min. 1⅓ h.p.

R.R.P. **£42.50**   **OUR PRICE £32.50**

Prices include V.A.T. Carriage: £1.00. Offer applies U.K. Mainland only. Delivery within 28 days.

JOHN HALL TOOLS
23 CHURCHILL WAY, CARDIFF. Tel. (0222) 373007

270

Prices quoted are those prevailing at press date and are subject to alteration due to economic conditions.

An exciting prospect for the constructive thinker!
Give shape to your ideas in nature's most beautiful and challenging medium with the new K5 Universal Woodworker

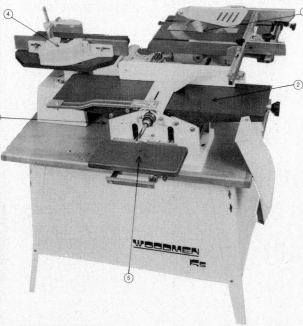

This amazingly versatile companion in your workshop for less than £3.50 per week

DIRECT TO YOUR HOME

Within just a few days the K5 can be working for you. Our vehicles now operate a weekly delivery service to all parts of the U.K. mainland thereby eliminating frustrating delays and any possibility of damage through careless handling.

Simply post or telephone your order today. You can pay by cheque (payable to WOODMEN), by BARCLAYCARD or ACCESS, or we will collect your payment at time of delivery.

HAND BUILT BY ENGINEERS

From thoughtful design and energetic quality control to final assembly and testing by production engineers, your K5 comes with a guarantee of satisfaction.

Sealed, maintenance free bearings on all spindle and shaft assemblies. Heavy cast alloy tables machined to fine limits and electrically processed to provide a hard polished work surface that gives exceptional wear and greatly reduced drag characteristics. Distortion free sealed and coated hardwood mounting base for resilience and strength. Rigid steel floor stand (with integral storage cabinet) to bring every unit to the most convenient working height. Simple and precise quickchange blade and cutter system.

Features that add up to a machine which looks after itself while you discover the immense satisfacton of creating, planning and working with wood.

AUTOMATIC PLANING TO A PRE-SET THICKNESS ON THE K5

SWITCHING ON

Each inviting step into the fascinating world of woodworking at this rewarding level is clearly laid out for you to follow. The illustrated manual supplied explains in simple terms all you need to know.

Clean lined hardwood and pine kitchen furniture, traditional joints for door and window construction, intricate mouldings for clock cases and other reproduction cabinet work — each technique and machining operation is dealt with in easily assimilated stages that will immediately enable you to give shape to your ideas .

FROM ROUGH TO SMOOTH

More than just a versatile machine, the K5 replaces the need for years of practical experience with traditional hand woodworking techniques.

Rough timber is quickly converted into the sizes and lengths you require. Automatic feed through the thicknessing unit ensures that every piece of wood is reduced without effort to a completely uniform section size throughout ts length.

Surfaces are planed satisfyingly true and square revealing the silky texture and unique grain structure of every individual piece. Functional grooves, rebates and chamfers are cut with speed and accuracy where the design calls for them

Ornate or simple mouldings are chosen and machined effortlessly to complement the rich tones of mahogany, draw the eye to the ageless strength of oak or enhance the supple clean lines of ash.

Joints are prepared, end-grain and complex contours sanded, tenons cut and holes bored — all with consistent accuracy and ease. In fact, the K5 will help you to achieve almost anything with wood you have a mind to.

EFFICIENCY GAIN

Sliding and locking at the touch of a lever, the K5's powerful motor provides smooth and positive drive to any machining head in a matter of seconds. Also, because the modular design allows all the units to be permanently mounted, you can enjoy the significant working advantages of fully independent machines at a fraction of their cost.

No time is wasted in moving from sawing to planing or moulding and the tremendous work potential of the K5 quickly becomes apparent. Valuable workshop space is conserved without sacrificing performance or efficiency — you are equipped to tackle the most demanding projects and still achieve the greatest economy in space and cash.

UNIQUE SERVICE COVER

No matter how hard you work the K5, any defect which occurs during the first **2 years** is speedily dealt with under the full parts and labour guarantee — We don't just claim the K5 is top quality, we have the organization and confidence to back it with a truly marvellous insurance that covers you against all service costs (due to manufacturing fault) for a really exceptional period. Even more, our policy ensures that service requirements are always effected within one week.

PERFORMANCE SUMMARY

1 CIRCULAR SAW: adjustable angle (0-45°) and depth of cut (max. 2¼''). Choice of 2 speeds (3750/6200 rpm) giving cleanest possible cut on a wide variety of materials. Eccentric collars for variable width grooving. Rip and protractor fence (180°) with cut length gauge for repetition work.
2 SURFACE PLANER: 27½'' x 8 ' bed to aid true finishing of long edges (max. planing width 6''). Tilting fence for bevel planing and transverse adjustment for utilizing full width of table. Quick-set spring loaded knives and dynamically balanced cutter block giving 11,400 cuts per minute.
3 THICKNESSER: fully automatic thicknessing of timber up to 6'' x 4'' (feed rate 24' per minute). Fitted auto-feed isolator, anti-kick back fingers, calibrated scales, wheel operated thickness adjustment.
4 SPINDLE MOULDER: 1¾'' vertical adjustment by finely geared handwheel and corresponding fence depth adjustment to give infinite range of positive settings for moulding and rebating up to full capacity (max. rebate in single pass — 1'' sq. approx.) 15¾'' x 11'' table swivels to clear surface planer. 6400 r.p.m. shaft speed gives exceptional finish on simple and intricate mouldings.
5 SLOT MORTISER: 4'' rise and fall of table with adjustable depth control. Chuck accepts milling and boring bits up to 12mm dia. Accurate mortising and horizontal boring for dowel jointing etc. Accessories (extra) include disc sander, planer knife grinding jig and tool grinding attachment.

FULL CASH REFUND GUARANTEE ON ANY MACHINE SUPPLIED BY US IF YOU ARE NOT COMPLETELY SATISFIED

WOODMEN

43, CRWYS ROAD, CARDIFF, CF2 4ND
TEL: (0222) 36519/373793/35221
Contact us today for informative lists and full details of all our special offers

HOW LITTLE IT COSTS

WW 01

PAYMENT WITH ORDER OR ON DELIVERY
K5 WOODWORKER WITH ALL STANDARD EQUIPMENT £499.00
DELIVERY BY OUR TRANSPORT £9.00

CREDIT TERMS
DEPOSIT .... £99 (plus std. delivery charge)
+36 MONTHLY PAYMENTS OF .... £15.12 .. (total cost £643.32)
or 24 MONTHLY PAYMENTS OF .... £20.67 .. (total cost £595.08)
or 12 MONTHLY PAYMENTS OF .... £37.34 .. (total cost £547.08)

272

Prices quoted are those prevailing at press date and are subject to alteration due to economic conditions.

Woodworker, April 1980

Woodworker

THE MAGAZINE FOR THE CRAFTSMAN IN WOOD

MAY 1980   VOL. 84   NO. 1038

Front cover: Not a house falling down but Ballingdon Hall in Suffolk being prepared for its move on a 26-wheel 'chassis' to a new site 350 years after it was built. The substantial timber-frame building weighs some 175 tons. See also story on page 282.

Editor	Geoffrey Pratt
Production Editor	Polly Curds
Advertisement Manager	Terence M. Healy
Group Advertisement Manager	Michael Merrifield
Managing Director	Gospatric Home
Editorial Director	Ron Moulton

ABC
MEMBER OF THE AUDIT
BUREAU OF CIRCULATIONS

SUBSCRIPTION DEPARTMENT: Remittances to MODEL AND ALLIED PUBLICATIONS, PO Box 35, Hemel Hempstead, Herts HP1 1EE. Price per copy 75p includes p&p. Subscription queries: Tel: Hemel Hempstead 51740. Subscription rate, including index £9.00 per annum; overseas sterling £9.00; $20.00 U.S. for overseas dollar subscribers. Second class postage paid at New York, NY. North American enquiries regarding news stand sales should be sent to: Eastern News Distribution, 111 Eighth Avenue, New York, NY 1011, USA. Telephone (212) 255-5620 and craft and hobby sales to Bill Dean Books Ltd, 166-41 Powells Cove Boulevard, Whitestone, New York 11357, USA. Telephone (212) 767-6632.

WOODWORKER is printed by New Avenue Press Ltd, Pasadena Close, Pump Lane, Hayes, Middlesex. (Mono origination by Multiform Photosetting Ltd, Cardiff), for the proprietors and publishers, Model & Allied Publications Ltd (a member of the Argus Press Group). Trade sales by Argus Distribution Ltd, 12-18 Paul Street, London EC2A 4JS. WOODWORKER is published on the 3rd Friday of the month.

Model & Allied Publications Ltd

MAP

PO Box 35, Bridge Street, Hemel Hempstead, Herts HP1 1EE. Telephone: Hemel Hempstead (0442) 41221.

WOOD FOR THE TREES

'You can't see the wood for the trees' is an old saw (and readers are quite at liberty to groan over the pun!). But wood for the trees takes on a new meaning in this day and age. We have commented in this column (November last year and April this year) on the importance of expanding the country's forests. That forest planting must be stepped up if a serious and expensive shortfall in timber supplies by the end of this century is to be avoided, is emphasised in a report prepared by the Centre for Agricultural Strategy at Reading university. (*A Forest Strategy for the UK,* price £8.50).

Quick and sustained action to improve forest yields and to plant new areas is called for. The report reminds us that in 1978 we imported no less than 92% of our timber needs at a cost of £2.37bn and 'even if the maximum feasible planting rate was achieved Britain would still be supplying only half its needs by 2030.' By that year timber prices are likely to have risen by at least 30% in real terms.

While the report has been welcomed by timber growers, some environmentalists are not pleased. Apparently they would like control of afforestation to be brought under the normal planning processes rather than left with the Forestry Commission. Environmentalists are entitled to their opinions of course but the FC has had 60 years of experience in improving our woodlands — and helping private owners to do likewise — so it is questionable if changes in planning procedures would result in more trees being planted. And it is the trees that are needed, not bureaucratic growth.

Though economic circumstances have encouraged the planting of large areas of softwood species we would now like to see greater emphasis given to hardwood which would also improve the environment. It is really time for practical measures rather than exhortation. And one very practical measure would be greater financial incentives for all who grow timber, even on a small scale.

However, tree plantings by the Forestry Commission fell below target last year. According to the commission's annual report 11,842 hectare of new plantations were established in 1978-9, 2,552 hectare below the budgeted programme. Main trouble was the inadequate area of land obtained for planting and the commission has revised its future programmes to take account of its falling land reserves. The report says that unless there is a dramatic improvement in the amount of land acquired, planting programmes will decline by about 1,000 hectare a year over the next few years.

We are interested to note that the 3,000 hectare woodlands on the crown estate at Windsor which was planted with Scots and Corsican pine in a ratio of 9 to 1 during 1946-61, is producing from an area of just over 1,000 hectare a steadily increasing quantity of good sawlogs expected to reach a figure about double the present volume of 12,000m³ by the end of the century.

In the meantime WOODWORKER will continue to help readers make best use of their increasingly expensive raw material.

Steenwise Ltd.
TOOLS FOR CRAFTSMEN

GORDON STOKES INVITES YOU TO VISIT HIS NEW STEENWISE WORKSHOP IN BATH

Centrally placed to service Wiltshire, Gloucestershire and South Wales, this new Workshop is equipped with a large range of woodworking machinery, ready for immediate demonstration by specialist craftsmen. Each demonstrator will give you impartial advice on the choice and price of machinery, and help with any technical problems you may have.
The Workshop is open from Tuesday to Saturday – 9.30am to 6.0pm. We are not offering a beautiful showroom, but a real woodworking environment, so come and see for yourself, if the machine of your choice will really do what you want.

Gordon Stokes (Steenwise) Ltd., 110A Mount Road, Whiteway, Bath. Tel: Bath (0225) 22617.

Steenwise policy is to supply machines produced in the U.K. and Europe, by well-known manufacturers, at the best possible prices. Our pricing policy is fair to both customer and manufacturer, we buy at the best possible prices, add a small fixed percentage to cover our costs, we then sell to you at this price, which is often less than the manufacturers recommended price.

We normally despatch direct to your door within seven days from receiving your order. Payment can be made cash with order, cash on delivery or credit card. A confidential hire purchase scheme with attractive rates of interest is also available. Leasing is possible if you are V.A.T. registered. A full cash refund is guaranteed if your goods prove to be defective.

Gordon Stokes says,
"I have always tried to maintain the highest possible standards in this wonderful craft. My training courses offer the woodworker instruction in techniques, intended to develop the individual's ability to the absolute maximum. I decided to become a Steenwise operator because it offers the best of both worlds to my customers – a broad selection of demonstration machinery, some of the finest manufactured in the U.K. and Europe. Together with a mail order system that allows the customer to buy at the best possible price. By selling through Steenwise, I can aid the craftsman in his choice of machinery, knowing that he will have excellent value for money".

We will be pleased to quote for any machine or accessories, and we are sure you will be surprised at the prices we can offer. Trade enquiries will be most welcome. Below are some examples of our current price lists.

Planer Thicknesser
● 10″ × 6″ Scheppach HM1 2 H.P. Motor, Floor Standing – £399.00.
● 10″ × 6″ Kity 7136 1½ H.P. Motor, Floor Standing – £564.00.
● 6″ × 4″ Kity 7139 1½ H.P. Motor, Floor Standing – £347.00.

Band Saws
● Kity 7212 – £299.00.

Circular Saws
● Kity 5017 2¼″ depth of cut ¾ H.P. – £169.00.
● Elektra Site Saw 3½″ depth of cut 2.3 H.P. (Galvanised) – £159.00.

Special Offer
● Kity 5020 Combination – consisting of a planer thickness or spindle moulder and slot mortiser. Recommended man. price £662.40, Steenwise price £500 including free double ended 5″ bench grinder.
● Kity 6646 variable speed lathe, floor standing, recommended man. price £517.50 Steenwise price £469.00 including a free 5″ double end bench grinder and six Sorby wood turning tools.
● Kity 10″ × 6″ planer thicknesser 7136 and dust extractor 695, recommended man. price £1,018.57, Steenwise price £647.50 including hose and attachments.
All prices include VAT at 15%.

For further information about Steenwise stocks and prices, return the coupon to our Head Office in Bingley, West Yorkshire, or telephone us direct on Bradford (0274) 560699 or Bingley (09766) 69136.

Please send me more information about Steenwise stocks and prices

Name . . . .

Address . . . .

. . . .

. . . .

Showroom and warehouse Limefield Mills, Woods Street, Crossflats, Bingley, West Yorkshire.

All orders placed before 7 May '80 with Gordon Stokes (Steenwise) Ltd. above the value of £700 will include a free 7″ double wheeled grind stone, recommended selling price £120.00.

Prices quoted are those prevailing at press date and are subject to alteration due to economic conditions.

When you're woodworking for a living do it with Wadkin.

When an amateur is let down by a power tool, it's a darned nuisance.

But, for the pro, breakdowns can be nothing short of disastrous.

So, of all the features we build into Wadkin power tools, far and away the most important is reliability. It comes as standard. Whether you buy an orbital or belt sander, hand planer, circular saw, plunge router, handy trimmer, drill/screwdriver, or any other tool in the range.

And if the sheer quality, extra power and rugged construction of Wadkin power tools demonstrates our perfect understanding of the professional's needs, so does the way our tools are designed.

Wadkin. The power tools of the trade. At the right price. Buy one from your nearest distributor or direct from us.

Wadkin
PORTABLE POWER TOOL DIVISION
Built to last, made to work.

Trent Lane, Castle Donington, Derby. DE7 2PU.
Tel: Derby (0332) 812267/8 Telex: 37191

MAIN DISTRIBUTORS

Avon
V. H. Willis & Co. Ltd., Bristol
E. Cheshire
H. V. Hird & Son Ltd., Hyde
Cleveland
Wintz Industrial Supplies, Cleveland.
Derbyshire
J. W. Tomlinson & Sons Ltd., Derby
Co. Durham
Woodmen (Barnard Castle) Ltd., Barnard Castle.
Dyfed
Scimitar Engineering Co. Ltd., Swansea.
S. Essex
Cutwell Tools Ltd., Goodmayes.
S. Glamorgan
Woodman Ltd., Cardiff.

W. Glamorgan
Woodmen (Briton Ferry) Ltd., Briton Ferry.
Mid. Hampshire
Hampshire Woodworking Company, Southampton.
Humberside
F. J. Elvin, Hull.
Jersey C.I.
Norman Ltd., St. Helier.
E. Lancashire
J. B. Electrics, Bolton
N. Leicestershire
David Taylor Ltd., Thurmaston, Leicester.
S. Leicestershire
Tentbrook, Great Glen, Leicester.
N. W. London
E. R. Cole, Neasden Lane, London. NW10

Northamptonshire
Electool, Rushden.
Nottinghamshire
A. L. Dalton Ltd., Nottingham.
Oxfordshire
Woodmen (Bicester) Ltd., Bicester.
S. Yorkshire
George Marshall Power Tools Ltd., Sheffield.
W. Yorkshire
Midhage Tools Division of Foundrometers Ltd., Leeds.
Eire
Modern Tool & Equipment Co. Ltd., Dublin.
N. Ireland
Modern Tool & Equipment Co. Ltd., Lisburn.

PRICE LIST

MODEL	DESCRIPTION	INCREASED POWER INPUT	PRICE PLUS VAT
L-1512	Hand Planer, 92mm wide blade	550W	£73.00
R-500	Plunge Router, 60mm capacity	1500W	£128.00
SU-6200	Orbital Sander, 112×226mm pad	300W	£86.00
LS-35	Orbital Sander, 93mm×185mm pad	180W	£39.00
PD-1920	Impact Drill, 13mm chuck	550W	£86.00
B-7075	Belt Sander, 75mm wide belt	850W	£110.00
B-7200A	Belt Sander, 100mm wide belt	980W	£135.00
CS-360	Chain Saw, 355mm cut-off length	1250W	£92.00
W-6502	Circular Saw, 180mm blade	1400W	£89.00
W-8502	Circular Saw, 235mm blade	1700W	£128.00
TR-30	Handy Trimmer, 29000 rev/min	430W	£62.00
D-1015	Drill/Screwdriver, 10mm chuck	380W	£83.00
G-1000	Angle Grinder, 100mm wheel.	480W	£53.00
G-1800	Angle Grinder, heavy duty, 230mm wheel	1700W	£99.00

A new House, A new Factory

£25

per week in Mid Wales

We have "starter factories" available at **Aberystwyth, Cardigan, Lampeter, Dolgellau, Ystradgynlais, Newtown, Welshpool, and Llandrindod Wells.**

Starter factories of 500 and 700 sq ft are ideal for the expanding small company or the new business starting up.

We can offer housing to go with them - the combined rental, factory **and** house, will only be £25 per week!

As well as providing a new factory, the Development Board for Rural Wales can help businesses in other ways:

Business Advisory Service - provides expert advice on all aspects of running a business.

New Enterprise Promotion - is a course run in conjunction with the Manchester Business School to help people put their business ideas into practice.

Send the coupon for further details.

Development Board for Rural Wales

Ladywell House, Newtown, Powys SY16 1JB.
Telephone: 0686 26965

Please send details of your Starter Factories and other Development Board for Rural Wales services for small businesses.

Name _____

Address _____

_____

_____

To Marketing Director, Development Board for Rural Wales, Ladywell House, Newtown, Powys SY16 1JB.

CLOCKS

For Everyman Exhibition

sponsored by CLOCKS magazine An exhibition for clock lovers

"We've been waiting for this for 30 years"

"Nothing like it has ever been staged before"

"What a marvellous show"

Comments from last year's visitors

Well it's coming again – Bigger – Better – Longer

If you – Buy – Make – Restore – Collect – Read about or just like looking at or "Talking" clocks, come along to the comfort of the modern Kensington Town Hall – Enjoy the atmosphere of beautiful clocks.

You can even park your car if you come early!

Access to the hall

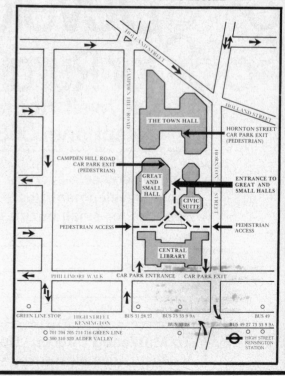

KENSINGTON TOWN HALL,
Hornton St. Kensington, London W8.
Thursday to Sunday 3rd to 6th July 1980. 10 am to 6 pm.
Refreshments are available. Tickets at the door £1.25.

If the Americans couldn't have made the most versatile wood-working machine in the world they wouldn't have made the

SHOPSMITH MARK V

The SHOPSMITH Mk V is the only machine in the world to combine a lathe, sawbench, disc sander, horizontal boring machine and vertical drill press in a single unit taking up no more space than an ordinary bicycle!

More than 350,000 Americans have chosen the 'Smith' as the ultimate solution for their home workshop and currently around 500 customers are choosing the SHOPSMITH **every week!** It is easy to understand why.

No other machine offers all these unique features:

* Five basic machines including vertical drill press.
* Special Add-To Machines include Bandsaw, Planer, Belt Sander and Fret Saw plus accessories enabling a total of 16 different machine operations.
* Automatic speed dial from 700 rpm to 5200 rpm without even turning the machine off. Just dial the correct speed for whatever operation is required.
* With SHOPSMITH'S exclusive Quill Feed Control any required depth of feed is pre-set, locked and absolute accuracy is guaranteed.

Whether you are just starting in woodwork or been at it for years the SHOPSMITH Mk V will give you the home workshop you have always wanted – to build the projects you have always dreamed of.

The Shopsmith makes virtually everything - including sense!

CROSSCUTTING

SANDING

HORIZONTAL BORING

VERTICAL DRILLING

The SHOPSMITH is now available from SUMACO – the UK's leading importer of the world's finest smaller woodworker machines, and their appointed distributors.

SUMACO

Suma House, Huddersfield Road, ELLAND, W. Yorkshire
Tel. (0422) 75491/2

Please send: Further information on the
Shopsmith Mk 5 ☐ (Enclose 10p stamps)
The full Sumaco catalogue ☐ (Enclose 50p stamps)

NAME _____

ADDRESS _____

_____

SS2

Ways with tambours

Here Charles Cliffe explains how to make horizontally sliding tambour doors and the vertically sliding tambour fall as used in roll-top desks.

Fig. 5. Boring cord holes in strip.

Wanted by collector: American roll-top desk!. Advertisements like this appear frequently in my local paper. These fine old pieces of oak furniture must have a greater appeal than the present-day chipboard or steel constructions.

As a matter of fact the description 'American' is incorrect for this type of shutter was used by Sheraton and continental cabinet-makers long before it became popular in the US. Furthermore, 'roll-top' is a misnomer for the correct name is tambour. There are horizontally sliding tambour doors and the vertically sliding tambour fall.

Tambours are sometimes used in radio-gram and television cabinets and I once saw a vertically sliding tambour on a drinks cupboard in a doctor's study. There was a slight fault in its construction and it used to jam open at the shelf where the beer was kept. He refused to allow the trouble to be rectified because when he pushed the tambour further down it revealed bottles of scotch on the lower shelf!

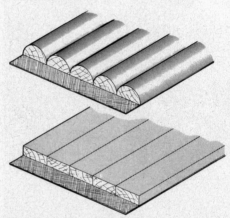

Fig. 1. Simple forms of tambour.

A tambour consists of a series of strips of wood glued to a canvas backing with the ends of the strips sliding in grooves. The groove can follow any reasonable convex curve but cannot become concave because the canvas backing will not allow the strips to hinge in that direction. The simplest form of tambours comprise plain strips or slightly rounded ones (Fig. 1). Such shapes will be adequate when the visible strips run in a flat or slightly curved groove, but if a sharp curve were on view the canvas would be seen as the strips opened up. The appearance would be even worse as time went on and the canvas stretched.

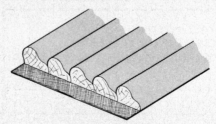

Fig. 2. Modified form of bead.

A modified form of bead is shown in Fig. 2. Here a small projection on one strip fits beneath a hollow worked on the adjoining piece. Consequently, the canvas backing cannot be seen even when the tambour passes round a curve. The most straight-forward method of preparing these moulded strips is to plane up a straight-grained well seasoned board to a thickness slightly more than the width of the finished strips. Then by adjusting the shape of the cutter of a bead plane, work the thicker edge of the strip as in Fig. 3. The front of the strip is shaped with a round plane to which a fence has been

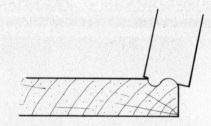

Fig. 3. Moulding thick edge of strip.

screwed. Finally the thin edge is shaped with a small bead plane. Using the quirk of the bead as a guide, saw off the strip and plane up the edge of the board ready to mould the next strip.

To enable the backs of the strips to be planed to precisely the same thickness a cradle is made by ploughing and splaying a board so that the strips can sit in it to the required depth (Fig. 4). The top surface of the cradle acts as a guide for planing the strip to the correct dimensions.

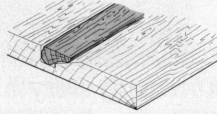

Fig. 4. Strip resting in cradle.

When making a tambour for a large desk it is advisable not to rely solely on the canvas backing to keep the laths together. Either of the two following methods of reinforcement can be used: All the laths can be bored with three or four holes (depending on the length of the laths) and cords passed through. Each of the holes will have to be at the same distance in all the laths and to achieve this we adopt the planing cradle. With a fine bit bore holes correctly spaced and at the same distance from the top. Secure each lath in turn in the cradle by cramping a piece of wood over the top as in Fig. 5 and drill through. The second and simpler method is to obtain three or four strips of steel about ½in. wide and 1/16in. thick. Drill holes the same distance apart as the width of the laths and screw the metal strips to the laths as in Fig. 6.

When gluing the canvas to the back of the laths, care must be taken not to let glue run

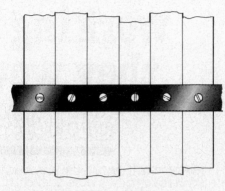

Fig. 6. Steel strip screwed to back of laths.

between the joints of the strips. One way of preventing this is to brush thin glue on one side of a sheet of drawing paper. Allow the glue to dry and cut the paper into ¼in. wide strips. Lay out the tambour on a flat surface and damp the glued side of the paper strips and stick them over all the joints on the back face. Allow two or three hours for the paper to dry. Then glue on the canvas backing, being careful not to disturb the strips.

With a fine-toothed saw, cut the ends of the tambour to size and slide the completed roll into its grooves. Provision has to be made for the roll to be inserted after the carcass of the desk or cabinet has been assembled. This is accomplished by running the grooves out at the back of the cabinet as in Fig. 7. If you

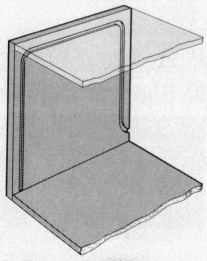

Fig. 7.
Grooves in cabinet
run out at back.

have to repair a desk where the grooves are not run out you will probably find that grooved inner ends were screwed in after the carcass was put together. In this case the ends will have to be unscrewed and the entire fitment removed in one operation.

When designing a tambour some important features should be borne in mind.

First, ensure there is sufficient room for the entire length to fold away when the tambour is opened. Second, the length of the roll (measured across the strips) should be as long as possible in proportion to its width (along the strips). Failure to do this will render the tambour liable to skew sideways in its grooves and jam instead of moving smoothly. Third, keep the width of the individual strips as small as practicable and thereby avoid having to greatly enlarge the width of the grooves at the curves. Fourth, the end strip which has to stand up to a fair amount of pushing and pulling should be made somewhat stouter in section than the

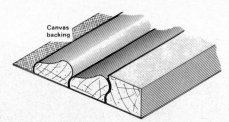

Fig. 9. Shape of tambour strips and end strip.

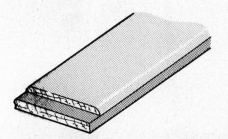

**Fig. 8.
Ends of closing strip reduced to fit groove.**

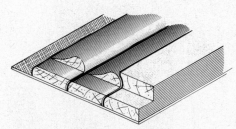

Fig. 10. Ends of strips rebated.

other strips. To enable it to negotiate the curved grooves the ends of this strip are reduced to the same dimensions as the others (Fig. 8).

Polishing of the strips should be carried out before the tambour is assembled and the canvas glued on; otherwise it is almost impossible to achieve a really satisfactory result.

While on this subject it is of interest to mention an enquiry received from a reader who wanted to make vertical tambour doors for an opening about 3ft 6in. wide in a fitment some 24in. deep. On the basis of information supplied, the author suggested that if the strips making up the tambour were, say, 1¼in. wide and about ½in. thick they could be worked to the shape shown in Fig. 9. This contour is recommended because the canvas backing glued to the backs of the strips remains concealed even when the tambour passes round a curve.

The two ends which meet when the doors are closed are wider and thicker to enable them to withstand the strain of being pulled and pushed. The ends of all the strips are rebated (Fig. 10) to the same thickness to allow them to slide in the grooves. The grooves are made slightly wider at the curves to enable the folded tambour to negotiate smoothly.

OLD BARN CONVERTED

At Wilmington near Eastbourne, one of the barns at Priory farm has been bought by a local architect for conversion into a dwelling. The building 85 x 28ft had open storage space, framed and supported by timber posts, for carts and implements while the roof space served as a granery.

The new owner has been anxious to retain, and emphasise, the timber structure, principally of oak members in sound condition. Old oak was used to replace the few timbers which were unsound and the entire roof structure of beams, purlins and crossties has been left exposed. Externally, the supporting posts are also exposed, the framework having been filled in with weatherboard.

All timber, including new softwood joinery and elm doors, has been treated with transparent protective finishes manufactured by Sikkens (UK) Ltd, Station Road Industrial Estate, Didcot OX11 7NQ. The full range of finishes — Rubbol THB, Cetol transparent and Ceta-Bever transparent satin — has been used to suit each particular application.

The finishes provide a microporous coating which keeps out moisture but allows excess water in the timber to pass through as vapour. This eliminates cracking and flaking and ensures an easily maintained and attractive finish. Another barn on the farm, also being converted into a residence, is being similarly treated with Sikkens products.

Priory farmhouse itself has been taken over by the Sussex Archaeological Society as a permanent museum.

Sikkens decorative transparent wood finishes have been used externally and internally on timber at Priory Barn, Polegate, for the conversion to a private dwelling. Top: the barn before conversion and bottom the timber roof structure.

MOVING HOUSE

ALL 175 TONS OF IT

After 350 years Ballingdon Hall in Suffolk was transported intact on a 26-wheel 'chassis' to a new site half a mile away.

Moving house takes on a new dimension when you not only pack up the contents and go but take the complete structure with you. This is more or less what happenened to Ballingdon Hall near Sudbury, Suffolk, when Mr and Mrs John Hodge decided to move their home to a new site.

The house, a substantial timber-frame building about 350 years old, is some 27m long and 6.5m wide and estimated to weigh 175 tons. The new site, half a mile away, was considered by Mr and Mrs Hodge to provide a more suitable setting for their home. Though the planning and other authorities (Ballingdon Hall is a listed building) were not agreeable to the house being dismantled and re-erected on a new site, they agreed to the building's 'bodily' removal. Why not dismantle and re-erect? The reason given was that once the stresses had been removed the timbers had a tendency to revert to their original shape making it impossible to re-create exactly the original house.

For the move it was necessary to build a steel frame made up of Bailey bridge components around the house which was cross-braced internally with steel trusses. At critical positions support shoring was provided. The building was then raised 2.9m above the original foundations by means of hydraulic jacks and purpose-made wheels 1.6m diameter were positioned at the jacking points. The wheels had timber treads on steel frames and were placed in sets of three and four at the corners of the main frame. A total of 26 wheels were used.

The 'chassis' was towed by trackless tractors across the fields and up a 1 in 10 slope to the new site.

It is interesting to recall that timber-framing is so strong, yet flexible that a building — and an old building too — could be moved 'lock, stock and barrel' across fields and up slopes to a fresh site. That the work could be successfully accomplished is a tribute to the craftsmen who erected it three and a half centuries ago.

The photographs were taken by WOOD-WORKER contributor H. W. Gates who also supplied the details of the operation.

Footnote: Some years ago an old half-timbered building in Hereford was moved from one part of a street to another. This operation was also carried out by means of a specially built 'chassis' on which the building had been placed intact. The Hereford move was, however, carried out over level ground and along a surfaced street.

Above: Some of the support and chassis members are shown, these were removed as the foundation was placed in sections. A preservation order applies to this old house.

Below: Three of the wheels used to carry the house to its new home. (Photographs taken by H. W. Gates).

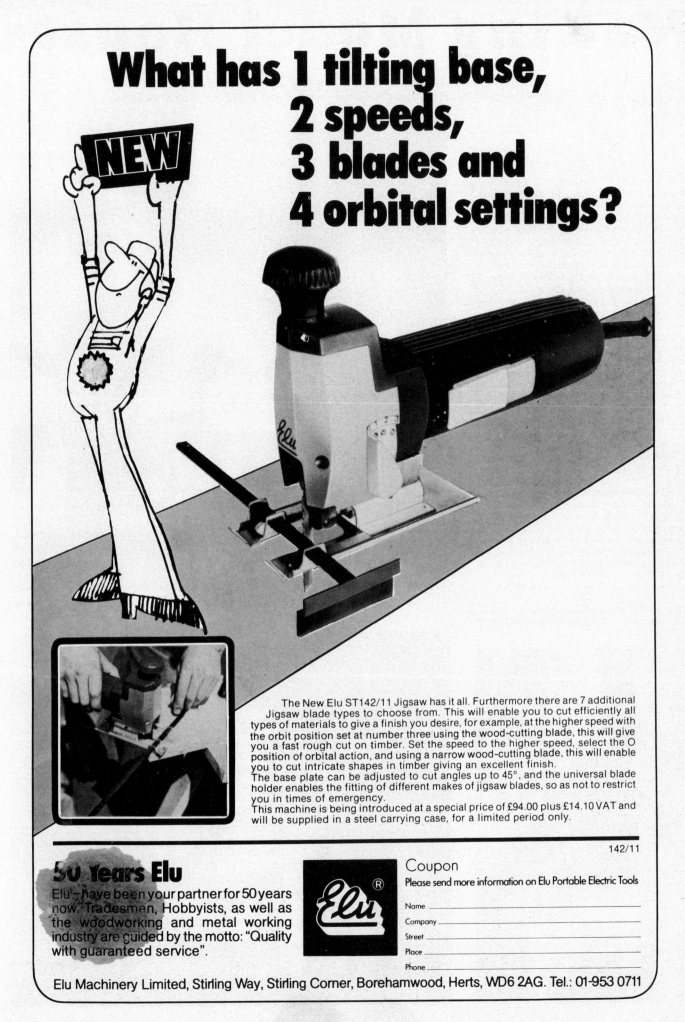

What has 1 tilting base, 2 speeds, 3 blades and 4 orbital settings?

NEW

The New Elu ST142/11 Jigsaw has it all. Furthermore there are 7 additional Jigsaw blade types to choose from. This will enable you to cut efficiently all types of materials to give a finish you desire, for example, at the higher speed with the orbit position set at number three using the wood-cutting blade, this will give you a fast rough cut on timber. Set the speed to the higher speed, select the O position of orbital action, and using a narrow wood-cutting blade, this will enable you to cut intricate shapes in timber giving an excellent finish.

The base plate can be adjusted to cut angles up to 45°, and the universal blade holder enables the fitting of different makes of jigsaw blades, so as not to restrict you in times of emergency.

This machine is being introduced at a special price of £94.00 plus £14.10 VAT and will be supplied in a steel carrying case, for a limited period only.

50 Years Elu

Elu – have been your partner for 50 years now. Tradesmen, Hobbyists, as well as the woodworking and metal working industry are guided by the motto: "Quality with guaranteed service".

142/11

Elu ®

Coupon
Please send more information on Elu Portable Electric Tools

Name _____

Company _____

Street _____

Place _____

Phone _____

Elu Machinery Limited, Stirling Way, Stirling Corner, Borehamwood, Herts, WD6 2AG. Tel.: 01-953 0711

Making Model Houses

You may not be able to build a 'half-timbered' house to live in but you can build one to scale. Here Ian Thwaites gives some hints on model buildings.

Fig. 1 (Above) General view of the prototype shows overall shape, form and character.

Timber-frame buildings of past centuries make interesting subjects for modelling. Before starting on the actual work information has to be gathered: a suitable prototype found; details obtained of how it was constructed; photographs taken; and plans prepared. Information can often be obtained from local sources such as the curator of the building; county record offices; museums; libraries; and books and magazines.

If it is not possible to find plans of the prototype the alternative is to prepare your own and for this you need a set of good photographs in black and white. These you can take yourself (with owners' permission). You will need a general view of the prototype to show the overall shape, form and character (Fig. 1), photographs of interesting features (Fig. 2), and detail photographs (Fig. 3). If the prototype is a distance from your home make your photographic session thorough — you will not want to rush back to check on something you forgot!

The detail photographs (Fig. 3) are taken as square-on as possible to minimise the effects of perspective; no attention is paid to artistic merit. In this case a photograph is required of each flank. Fig. 3 also shows a ranging rod (under the left-hand edge of the jetted storey). The rod is a 6ft. length of 1in. square timber with each ft. painted alternatively black and white. The last ft. is divided into 3in. sections and both ends of the rod are white which makes it easier to see in a photograph.

Fig. 2 (Below) Interesting detail of the prototype such as this jetted storey should be photographed.

The rod is placed against the wall of the building to give a fixed dimension in each photograph which, itself, is not subject to much perspective distortion. By setting a pair of dividers against the rod in the photograph it is possible to measure off the dimensions of the building. For drawing the plan on paper, cardboard or artboard a rule, set-square, dividers, H-grade pencil and rubber are sufficient. The plan gives the detail needed to make the model and it does not have to be a work of art. Fig. 4 shows the principle. Begin by drawing in the outline and add the detail later. It is convenient to lay the whole structure out on one sheet in a straight line — this makes for quicker drawing. Spread all the photographs out before you and gradually build-up the 'picture' of the structure. Drawing your own plan gives you an idea of how the original was made and also an idea of how you are going to make your model.

As to the scale the choice depends on the size of the prototype and the size of your model. I use 4mm to 1ft. It is an easy scale when making a closed model (Fig. 5) but a larger scale is better for an open model (one which is cut-away or has see-through sides showing the interior and construction (Fig. 6). Choose a scale that is easy and convenient; ¾in. to 1ft. is easier than, say, $^{11}/_{16}$in. to 1ft.

Whenever possible draw the plan to full scale size. Calculations have only to be done once and it is easier to lay a length of material on the plan and mark-off direct than to look at the plan and then multiply by two or whatever. There is also less chance of mistakes. I always measure direct from the plan instead of using a rule. When it is not convenient to lay the material on the plan I use dividers and measure-off this way.

Fig. 3 (Left) Detail photograph of prototype. Note the ranging rod (left) which gives a fixed dimension.

Another reason for drawing the plan to full scale size is that if you know what material you are going to use in construction, take a small offcut and draw round it. Suppose a beam is to be fashioned from ¼in. square strip of wood. If you draw round an offcut (and the loss of accuracy will be slight), when the model is being made the strip wood cut to length will form the beam without having to be planed or fashioned to size.

Keep the plan clean and either pinned to the wall of the workshop or on a board. If it is kept on the bench it will get soiled and crumpled. A plan is accurate only when kept flat.

In modelling buildings few special tools are required. I use a modelling knife such as an X-Acto. When joining small-section timbers it is sometimes useful to pin the

joint. To avoid splitting I drill a pilot hole and as many of the drills are less than $^1/_{16}$in. they are easily broken. To avoid this I use a pin vice. For cutting the small timbers I favour either a junior hacksaw or a razor saw. But you can always begin with your normal set of tools and add as necessary.

As regards materials balsa is particularly useful, the standard grade being quite satisfactory. I normally use ⅛in. and $^1/_{16}$in. Beamed timber models can be constructed in hardwood strip obtainable from most diy shops which usually offer different sections of mouldings, rectangular and square sections being most useful. Ordinary wood-working or impact adhesives give the best results.

It is tempting to make your model using the timber of the prototype. But bear in mind that the model is in scale. It is possible to cut small beams from almost any timber but not possible to reduce grain and texture to scale. Thus a large-grain timber such as oak will look unrealistic. A more realistic appearance is obtained by using close-grained hardwood strip. For glazing windows I use clear plastics sheet.

There are basically two types of model buildings that you can make: the closed and the open. The closed model is complete in every detail and looks exactly like the prototype. The open model is cut-away or has see-through sides.

In the closed model it does not really matter what technique you use in making it providing the final result is satisfactory. For a Tudor-style cottage that I made recently I adopted the technique of a ⅛in. thick balsa shell cut to the full height but less in width all the way round by the thickness of the beams. Erected, the shell was smaller than it should be. I then photocopied the plan and cut out each beam and numbered it, these cutouts forming templates which were stuck on to $^1/_{16}$in. balsa sheet. With a craft knife I cut the individual timbers from the balsa sheet. Following the plan I stuck the individual timbers on to the basic shell as a kind of overlay (Fig. 5) and this overlay on the shell resulted in the overall dimensions being the same as on the plan. (continued p.286)

Fig. 5 Detail of a closed-type model of the building shown in Fig. 1.

For infilling I used Polyfilla leaving it slightly below the level of the timbers to represent the shrinkage evident on the prototype. The model was subsequently glazed, an interior light added and also a plywood base. The roof could be either cardboard or balsa, depending on the span, and tiled with strips of 'tiles' cut from graph paper. It is important to paint tiles and any brick-work just the right shade so as to give the 'weathered' appearance of the prototype. But I did not paint the beams black or the infilling white; a better effect was obtained by using grey-brown for the timbers and grey-cream for the infilling.

As explained earlier the open type of model shows not only the exterior shape but the interior and the manner of construction. There is no attempt to include every exterior detail nor to 'weather', though the model is of course to scale and correct in both shape and dimensions. This type of model calls for an understanding of how the prototype was constructed and of the original methods, joints and materials used.

Whatever type of model you decide to make it needs to be well presented. This means not only finishing it to a high standard but setting it off effectively. A base and a case are necessary. A closed type model can be placed on a landscaped base, for example, whereas an open type tends to look better on a plain board, perhaps laminated with a fine layer of cork on a nicely polished base of hardwood. To keep out dust a case can be made of Perspex assembled with appropriate adhesive and of a size to fit over the model and on to the base.

Fig. 6 Open type of model gives detail of the constructional timbers as used in the original building. (The prototype of this model is not that shown in Fig. 1). Note how the model becomes more 'open' towards the centre. Model supplied by West Galer and Partners, architects to Whitehall museum Cheam. Photograph reproduced by permission of the curator.

Work by the Colleges

Last year's furniture course at Shrewsbury Technical College ended with a very encouraging exhibition of work and good examination results. Most of the one-year mature students have now set up in business. We hope that dreams may become reality, that the books balance and customers will be satisfied with a job well done. One student has been invited to undertake restoration work for the National Trust.

The younger students who remained at college to take City & Guilds 555 (furniture and advanced level) have been joined by some mature students who because of their existing qualifications are eligible to take the examination in one year. In addition, 16 students have started their first year of training for City & Guilds 555 (furniture part II).

As a result of Philip Cole's demonstration of the Sperber slabbing mill at the College (WOODWORKER for November 1978), the local authority purchased one for use within Salop. Trees felled by the county council will be offered to the nearest school or college and be converted by the ground maintenance staff. This will save a valuable resource and supplement existing limited timber supplies.

All students have an opportunity of working in the engineering workshops one afternoon a week. This gives them the chance to make special tools necessary for their craftwork, including Norris-type smoothing or jack planes. Some have made patterns for casting the planes, others are prefabricating the planes from channel section.

Oak desk, stool and chair in laminated beech.

Above: Table in oak by Steve Barker.
Below: Desk/table by Nigel Rickets. Top inlayed with laburnum oysters and elm burr.

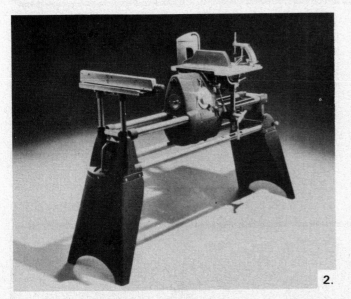

Woodworker PLANS SERVICE
CONSTRUCTION PLANS FOR CRAFTSMEN

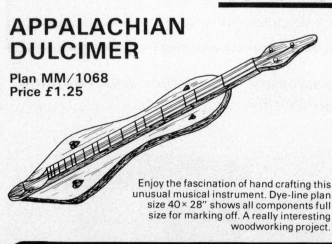

APPALACHIAN DULCIMER

Plan MM/1068
Price £1.25

Enjoy the fascination of hand crafting this unusual musical instrument. Dye-line plan size 40 × 28" shows all components full size for marking off. A really interesting woodworking project.

ZODIAC TABLE MATS
Plan MM/1106 Price 95p

A complete set of full-size patterns showing all the Zodiac signs. Dye-line plan size 33" x 22" provides step-by-step written instructions, with recommendation for veneer combinations for each of the Zodiac patterns. A practical project for those who enjoy the challenge of marquetry.

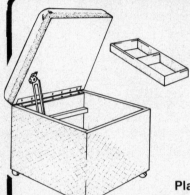

POUFFE

A simple project for less experienced woodworkers looking for a practical project in furniture making. Dye line drawing size 30 × 22" is simple but explicit, showing all parts half size and dimensioned.

Plan MM/1129 Price 95p

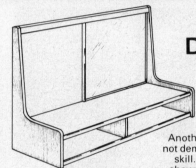

DRESSING TABLE

Another furniture project which does not demand too much in woodworking skill. Dye-line drawing size 26 × 18" shows complete project drawn ¼ full size, with full dimensioned details.

Plan MM/1130 Price 95p

ROCKING ELEPHANT

Plan MM/1122
Price £2.85

A simple project which will repay the effort in the hour of enjoyment it can bring for children — and a refreshing change from the usual rocking horse. Big dye line print size 54 × 38" provides a complete full size pattern for marking out.

Dolls House

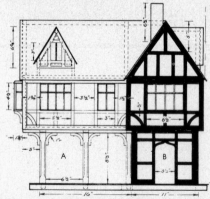

Plan WW/101
Price 55p

An Elizabethan style dolls' house. Built to overall dimensions 31" high × 34" × 27", the model features Elizabethan style half timbered effect and ground floor arcade, 4pp. Instruction leaflet includes full description of all constructional stages and cutting list.

Upright Spinning Wheel

Upright style spinning wheel. A fascinating woodworking project with emphasis on woodturning work.

Plan MM/1109
Price £2.85

Model & Allied Publications Ltd, PO Box 35, Bridge Street, Hemel Hempstead, Herts HP1 1EE. Delivery 21 days.

DANCE

The 1980 competition is figure carving only. This follows the indications of previous years that figure carving is more popular than relief. The organiser has therefore, agreed that this year's competition shall be for one section only, namely figure carving.

Subject is The Dance which will allow entrants the widest choice of design, expression and finish for their work. The subject also allows for a great deal of artistic and original experiment.

Ashley Iles (Edge Tools) Ltd, East Kirkby, Spilsby, Lincs, is co-sponsor of the competition and has generously agreed to award prizes.

The attention of entrants is drawn to the importance of correctly packaging their work, a subject explained in some detail on page 16 of WOODWORKER for January this year. The GPO has issued a leaflet *Wrap up well* (copies can be obtained from head postmasters) which tells how parcels should be packed to minimise damage during transit. Adequate packaging is essential to avoid disappointment.

Closing date is Friday, 24 October 1980. This will enable entries to be sent to WOODWORKER, PO Box 35, Bridge Street, Hemel Hempstead HP1 1EE, in time for judging to take place at the Woodworker Show which is being held at the RHS New Hall, Greycoat Street, Westminster, London SW1, from 4-9 November inclusive.

General conditions of entry

1. Entry is open to professional and amateur craftsmen. There is no entry fee.
2. The decision of the judges shall be final.
3. Entries must be received by Friday 24 October 1980 at the latest.
4. Entries must not be submitted before Monday 22 September 1980.
5. Maximum dimensions of figure carvings: 8 × 4½ × 4½ in.
6. Entrant's full name, address and telephone number must be securely attached to each piece submitted.
7. Each entry must include the appropriate return postage, and packing should be of adequate quality to allow for safe return of the piece.
8. Each entry must be accompanied by a statement of its approximate value. (This is required for insurance purposes.)
9. Each entry will be acknowledged on receipt.
10. *Pieces entered in the Ashley Iles competition are not eligible for entry in the woodcarving classes of the Woodworker Show.*
11. Pieces may be coloured using conventional water or spirit-based woodstains and may be finished using a clear transparent sealer if desired, but no opaque paints or finishes of any description may be applied.
12. Model and Allied Publications Ltd reserves the exclusive rights to describe and photograph any piece entered for this competition and to make use of any such photograph or descriptions in any way the company may think fit.

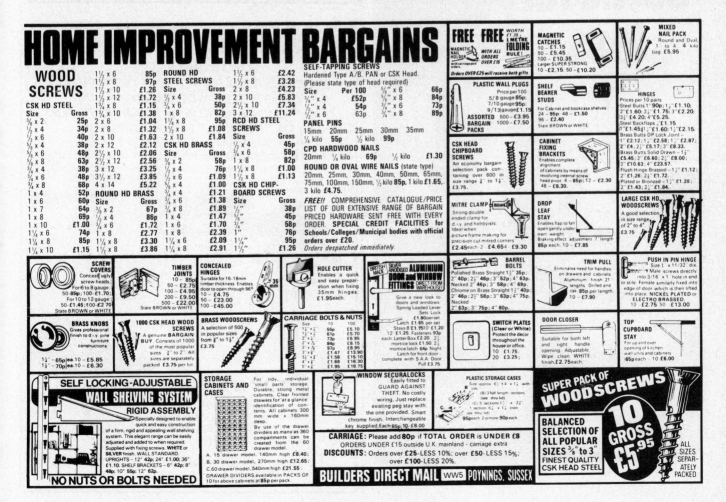

MAKE MINE MUSIC

We greatly admire the energy and the skill of Jessie Heard who lives in Bristol. At the age of 73 Miss Heard, who says she had no tuition of any kind in woodwork but 'I enjoy working with wood', started to make musical instruments. At the editor's invitation Miss Heard sent her story about making a violin, viola, lyre and harp. Here it is. But before reading it note her last paragraph: 'At the harp's completion I decided to study it and used it for my first year's study. Later I acquired a larger harp and continued until the sudden death of my teacher in December 1979.'

♯ ♯ ♯ ♯

There's more to the saying 'ship-shape and Bristol fashion' than you think!

♪ ♪ ♪ ♪ ♪

In the first instance I bought a book *Violin and Cello Making* by Robert Alton. I had but a minimum of tools; no bending rod for rib making, no reamer large or small for peg holes. I purchased a large quantity of sand-paper and three sanders.

I worked out the design on paper in 1in. squares, also the sound holes and made a careful study from an old violin that I had. This applied to the making of the viola. Each instrument gave quite a good tone when completed, which came from tomato boxes from which they were made and not from the usual sycamore.

The lyre was of my own design which again had to be worked out in 1in. squares on a large sheet of strong brown paper and later transferred to white Canadian wood. The lyre has 19 strings of music wire, with a large deep sound box which produces a sound similar to that of a harpsichord. The strings are plucked without the use of a plectrum, and can be played in an upright or flat position. The height of the lyre is 37in. and its width 21in. Each instrument is varnished.

♪♪ ♪♪ ♪♪

There was a certain music store in Bristol which I could not pass without taking note of what lay inside. The window displayed a beautifully illustrated book *Folk Harps* with instructions on how to make them by the author Gildas Jaffrennou.

I purchased the book and decided to make a Minstrel harp of 34 strings. At no time had I received tuition in woodwork but learned by my mistakes. I studied the book well and learned that I must work in mm. This was a problem which had to be overcome somehow. I learned, too, that the requirements for the harp could be obtained from the author, such as bridge pins, brass bridge pins, large and small taper reamers, eyelets, semi-tone systems and 34 strings. The total cost with postage was £32.17.

At this stage I had no intention of studying the harp as I had previously studied the piano, violin and organ. I simply wished to make a harp.

At the local diy store I was able to buy off-cuts of Columbian pine quite cheaply. (The wood stated in the book was beyond my purse). Having no means of transport I was rather limited to the quantity of wood I was able to carry on each journey that I made.

Regarding tools, here again I had only a minimum which were non-electric. I had no vice, no bench; but the strong kitchen table stood in good stead. No nails at all were used in any of the instruments. Evo-stik proved to be sufficient. The harp I was to make had now taken over my life and the household chores and continued to do so for the next 14 months which was the time of its completion.

Every part of the harp had to be designed on paper and later transferred to the wood. At one early stage the harp resembled the structural body of a boat before taking on its own bodily shape. I was now fully and enjoyably launched on a fascinating project. Of course there were days when things went wrong and had to be overcome.

♪ ♪ ♪ ♪ ♪

At the harp's completion I decided to study it and used it for my first year's study. Later I acquired a larger harp and continued until the sudden death of my teacher in December 1979.

Photo by courtesy of Bristol United Press Ltd.

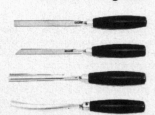
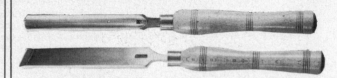

TIMBER FORECAST

Arthur Jones forecasts a bleak outlook for supply of some home-grown hardwood and discusses the new regulations governing the import of red and white oak from America.

Inflation is just as much a part of the timber trade as in other industries. It is not possible to promise the woodworker that this rising price tendency has come to an end, though there are signs that the pace of price increase might be easing.

Confirmation can be found in the official wholesale price index of the prices charged by timber importers. This index is based on the 1975 price being 100. We started 1979 with the index at 157.2 for softwood, 184.6 for hardwood and 157.7 for plywood. We ended the year with the index at 178.5 for softwood, 203.5 for hardwood and 183.1 for plywood.

In all three categories the increase over the last three months of the year was three points, although for the year as a whole softwood rose by 21 points, hardwood by 19 points and plywood by 26 points.

Slowing down of the timber inflation rate maybe, but a halt has certainly not yet been called. Take the new Russian softwood prices for 1980. Most of the increase has actually taken place in the lower grades of fourths and fifths, which can have little interest for the woodworker, but the handyman is a good user of unsorted Kara Sea and Archangel redwood and whitewood.

Unsorted Archangel redwood up to 175mm wide, sold in deals and battens, is now priced at £123/m³ and the whitewood is £103. In the case of redwood this is an increase of £12/m³ on the last Russian offer of 1979 and a rise of £14 for the whitewood.

Put this way it might seem that the Soviet sellers have made a massive price jump, but it must be remembered that they have not sold on the market since the early summer of 1979, whereas all the other main softwood producers — Sweden, Finland and Canada — have been selling steadily all the time and at ever-increasing prices. Finland and Sweden had sold heavily for 1980 before this first Russian offer was made. The Soviet sellers are really doing little more than catch up with their competitors, though they might have given the others a basis for yet another advance in prices (which is the usual trend).

Importers have bought heavily at these higher prices because they knew that a second Russian softwood offer was being made by April for shipments in the last quarter of this year — and that the prices for this wood would be higher again in view of the over-subscription for the first offer.

If there is likely to be some relief for the woodworker it will come in the need for timber merchants to keep up turnover at a time of impending recession and substantial stocks.

They can do this only by cutting prices; and some may be under severe pressure to do this at a time of high interest rates when they have to pay at least 18% on bank loans and inflation is hitting their operating costs. This means there could be some wide variations in prices asked for similar specifications from different wood stockists. The woodworker will find that shopping-around can be profitable at this time.

But this discovery of the occasional bargain offer should not lead to the impression that the market is about to collapse; nothing could be farther from the truth. In the international timber market prices are firm and still moving upwards. There is nothing the British importer can do to alter this pattern. We are no longer the world leaders able to break the market.

Woodworkers will have noted the continued rise in some of their favourite imported hardwood. Teak is now so expensive that even the manufacturers of high-quality furniture seem to be deserting this wood.

One of the favourites in the past few months has been mahogany from Brazil. It is much cheaper than mahogany from W Africa and woodworkers have discovered that it is a good timber which can be readily accepted for many uses. There has been a boom in its sales and this high demand (not merely from Britain) has had the inevitable effect of pushing up prices. The situation is not helped by a new export tax on the timber and a rise in freight costs.

Stocks of most hardwood species favoured by the handyman are reasonable in the country. There have been some good shipments from the Far East in the opening months of this year to replenish stocks. But prices are likely to be up by as much as 10% over the first quarter of this year to cover higher costs involved in getting tropical hardwood to the distribution outlets in sawn timber form.

Some temporary relief in the market might come from the massive over-buying of hardwood logs by Japan, which has effectively removed this major buyer from the world market until they use up their stocks.

Home-grown hardwood has continued to increase in price on the back of the higher cost of imported hardwood, which is understandable. There have been grumbles over quality of some of the native hardwood stocks. This is something which is likely to get worse rather than better, if only because there is so little hardwood planting in Britain (and this has been the case for the past 50 years) that the outlook is bound to be bleak. The oak which we see in the yard today was planted well before and there is little to take its place.

This gives an added interest to the new regulations which came into force in April governing imports of red and white oak from America. The milder American oak was once a favourite with our furniture manufacturers and was imported in large volume. But fashion changed. Now it is becoming more popular again, though the oak wilt scare has handicapped development of the market of late.

The agreed regulations will require that sawn oak imports are certified to be free of bark, and generally it will be sufficient if it is squared edge. If kiln-dried down to no more than 20%m.c. this will also satisfy the regulations. But generally it will be the sawn material that will be available rather than the 20% limit material. A lot of kiln-dried oak is imported from the States, but it is impossible to fill the demand entirely from this material because there is a limit to the kilning capacity.

Woodworker, May 1980

Texprint 80

Britain's textile design trade show is to have a new venue. It will be held at the Royal College of Art, Kensington Gore, SW7 from Wednesday 1 October to Friday 3 October inclusive. Texprint is organised by the Design Council in association with the SIAD. Space is available for 50 top freelance designers and design groups plus 30 of the best graduate designers of 1980 to present designs suitable for furnishings, fashions and flooring.

Crafts Fair

From 17-20 April at the Camden Arts Centre, Arkwright Road, London NW3 6DG.

Exhibitions

Prescote Gallery, Cropredy, Banbury from 6-27 April, an exhibition of wood sculpture and toys by Peter Markey.

Central Library, Lion Yard, Cambridge from 2-10 May, woodturning by Jean Whitaker, furniture by David Whitaker.

Cale Art Gallery, 17 Cale Street, London SW3 from 2-29 April, drawings, painted scarves, ceramics and furniture by Steve Wright.

Horniman Museum, London Road, London SE23 in May, June and July, woodcarving from Macedonia.

Victoria and Albert Museum, London SW7 from March to May, Heal & Sons: work from company archives; 12 March-22 June Japan Style.

Manor House Craft Gallery, Sandhurst from 1-30 April, musical instruments, including work by John Paul, Malcolm Rose and S. C. Grigg.

Courses at West Dean

These are a varied mixture and comprise weekend one and four day courses, five, six and seven day courses plus a 10 day course. Details should be obtained from the college at West Dean, Chichester, West Sussex PO18 0QZ but a brief summary follows to whet the appetite: The 9th to 15th August has been set aside as a family week with a combination of tutors and crafts including clay, sculpture, spinning and weaving, drawing and painting, making simple musical instruments and music making. Experienced workers in wood might be interested in the cottage furniture stage 2 course in June (15-20) which will include drawing, solid geometry, setting out, chair design and anthropometrics, drilling aids, steam bending, design and making of formers.

Much of the time will be spent out of doors on the appreciation of trees course taken by Ivan Hicks in July (4-6). Other courses specialise in mounting and framing pictures, woodcarving, making tools for cottage furniture, caring for antique furniture, cane seating, English furniture, and upholstery at various levels of competence.

THE EMCOSTAR

More Craft . . . Less Space!!

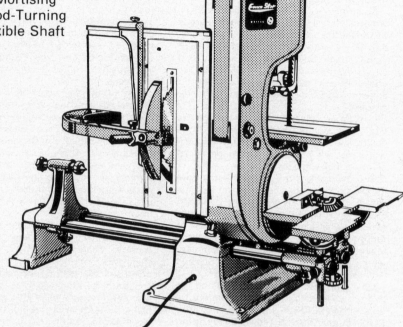
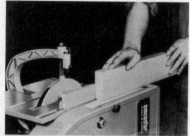

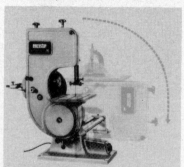
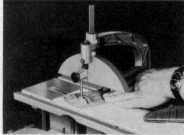

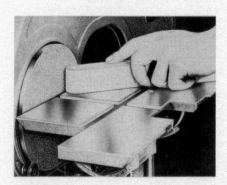

Guild of Woodworkers

Woodworker Show 1980

Elsewhere in this issue we give details of the competitive classes at the Woodworker Show to be held at RHS New Hall, Westminster, London SW1, from 4-9 November inclusive. To meet some of the suggestions made by the judges at last year's Show we have re-arranged several of the classes. The age limit of the junior section is raised to 18 (as on 1 November 1980) and it is hoped that this will encourage greater participation by schools.

Exhibition manager Peter Freebrey will be glad to hear from readers willing to act as stewards at the Show. Please let Mr Freebrey have names and availability (days, times etc) as soon as possible. His address is: PO Box 35 Bridge Street, Hemel Hempstead, Herts.

Apprenticeships

From time to time Guild of Woodworkers is asked for information about training schemes, particularly openings for apprentices, in the wood and wood-based industries. Members able to take apprentices now or in the future, or who could offer other training facilities to school leavers are asked to sent details to guild administrator David Whitehouse at PO Box 35, Bridge Street, Hémel Hempstead HP1 1EE. The aim is to compile a register on a geographical basis. If, however, members prefer their addresses not to be given in the first instance will they please indicate accordingly.

Business move

Member Phillip R. Barnes who is principal of Forest Glade Craftsman Woodturners Ltd, has moved the business to Unit 11, Wimbledon Avenue, London Road Industrial Estate, Brandon IP27 0NZ. He says: 'In this small factory unit of 3,000 sq ft hand-turned craftware is produced for sale on the home market through trade fairs and county shows. A new venture, and one that I believe may be of interest to some readers, is the production in small numbers of turned components for carpenters and joiners. For example, finials and fluted pillars for long-case clocks, table and chair legs, in pine as well as many hardwood species.'

Mr Barnes says that fluting and spiralling is possible on most types of work and he is always happy to give quotations for any turned work. His telephone number is Thetford 811025 and he would be delighted to make contact with other members.

Woodmachining courses

At the beginning of this year member Roy Sutton (0888) from Herne Bay in Kent, started a two-day woodmachine course. He tells us: 'To date I have had a total of eight students and all have been very satisfied with the results. For my part I find the work rewarding and interesting.' Mr Sutton is a joiner and cabinet maker who has spent 40 years in the trade, 25 as a self-employed craftsman. He holds C & G certificates in carpentry and joinery and woodcutting machinists' work.

Mr Sutton's courses, normally on Fridays and Saturdays, have been devised to give beginners the opportunity to study and operate most of the commonly-used machines. They are also flexible enough to enable those with some experience to have special tuition on one or two machines, should they so desire.

Cost per person is £75 which includes all materials as well as lunches and refreshments. At present Mr Sutton is unable to offer accommodation but he will provide a list of hotels and guesthouses in the area. He says: 'We start at 9.00am and I will collect you from your hotel at 8.50am. We take a short mid-morning break for tea or coffee (this time will not be wasted as we shall have plenty to talk about). Lunch is from 1.00 to 2.00pm (if you have any dietary problems, please mention them). We finish around 5.30pm and I take you back to your hotel.'

Members can get in touch with Mr Sutton at 14 St George's Avenue, Herne Bay, Kent (Herne Bay 3297) or in the evening on Whitstable 272136. We are glad to note from the leaflet which he issues about the courses that he places great emphasis on safety and safe working practices.

Back numbers

Following the death of her husband, Mrs F. M. Seward, Glenderry, 20 Tower Street, Alton GU34 1NU, has a number of copies of WOODWORKER from 1952 to 1968 for disposal. Most are complete bound volumes but in those for 1962, 1966 and 1968 some issues are missing.

Carving seminar at West Dean

Guild of Woodworkers carving seminar (intermediate level) will be held at West Dean College, West Dean, Chichester, Sussex, from Friday evening 23 May to Sunday evening 25 May inclusive. As members will wish to have the benefit of individual tuition numbers are restricted to 24 for this residential seminar. Booking forms can be had from the guild's administrator David Whitehouse at PO Box 35, Bridge Street, Hemel Hempstead HP1 1EE. Lecturers include Phillip Bentham of West Dean College and John Sainsbury, Record-Ridgway education adviser until his retirement at the end of last year.

West Dean College has a limited number of sets of carving tools but members may bring their own if they so wish. Materials will be available from the College shop at extra cost, though members may bring their own materials.

Cost of the seminar is £52 (plus VAT) per person. This includes: full board accommodation, membership of the College social club for the weekend; full tuition and use of College workshop facilities; and lecture and course fees.

There is a supplementary charge of £2 (plus VAT) payable by those wishing to have a private bathroom. The accommodation at West Dean comprises single and/or double rooms of which a certain number have bathrooms *en suite*.

SIDEBOARD IN

Malcolm Ward says: 'This is not a project that can be knocked-up in a couple of weekends. The period from conception to completion covered two or three years, largely because of interruptions when the work had to be laid aside for business or personal reasons. But what does it matter how long it takes? Every hour spent on a job like this is rewarding'

Fig. 1 The finished sideboard.

Aim of the design is to produce a strong, sturdy piece of furniture on modern lines and not appearing too heavy. Much use is made of the decorative effect of the chamfer. The drawer fronts are chamfered and set back in a chamfered surround. The cupboard doors are chamfered at the edges, but these are set forward.

As a variation, the outer edges of the door could be left square, and the door set back in a chamfered door opening similar to that surrounding the drawers. The panels on the end finish flush with the frame. The sides of the panels are beaded, not only for decoration, but also to mask the gap that would occur when the inevitable shrinkage takes place. The door panels rely for decorative effect on the selection of quarter-sawn timber showing that figure that can be so rich on English oak. The handles are of Indian rosewood which contrasts with the light oak waxed finish adopted. However, there is scope for personal variation here.

Timber English oak is not easy to come by and is expensive. If you can get it air-dried you are lucky. I had to use kiln-dried timber. Buy enough to allow for having to discard parts because of hidden shakes that appear in working. To save cost some of the pieces that do not show can be made from beech, ash or chestnut. I used beech. However, I have some doubt as to whether this is worth while as you will get pieces of oak with shakes or burrs which are not suitable for show timber, but adequate for hidden members.

For partitions, shelves, drawer bottoms, dust panels, and the back the purist will use thin, solid timber; the more practical person will use plywood; or, as a compromise, oak-faced plywood for the parts that show inside. I thought oak-faced plywood expensive and used birch ply. This I stained in areas that could be seen, as near as possible to the colour of the main timber.

The oak should preferably be stored inside for a few months to ensure that it is thoroughly dry, then cut to size according to the parts list, noting that finished sizes are given. The usual allowance (which I regard as a minimum) is $\frac{1}{8}$in. on thickness, $\frac{1}{4}$in. on width and $\frac{1}{2}$in. on length except on parts like door stiles where 'horns' are to be left until after gluing and an allowance of 1 in. or more should be made. The timber should be carefully selected so as to show good grain and the minimum of burrs on show parts. Cuts more or less radial to the original log will show figure, and other cuts will show grain.

Having cut the timber lay it aside for two or three months, inside, to settle. This is important because it takes a long time to shape all the parts and cut the joints. It is annoying to find when you come to assemble them, that a part which was cut perfectly true is now quite out of shape.

Finish It may seem strange to discuss the finishing process at this stage but as the panels have to be polished before assembling them in their frame it is as well to decide the finish early on. The first decision to be taken is whether to stain and, if so, what colour. I like my oak light, but I did use a light oak stain. This hardly had any darkening effect, but it unified the colour between the various pieces and enhanced the grain. Use a spirit stain, as a water stain raises the grain,

necessitating dampening and papering before staining, and the chamfers look best straight from the tool.

To my mind there is only one finish for oak, and that is wax. It can be applied direct, or the wood can be sealed first. Use two or three applications of white polish applied with a rubber, or two applications of polyurethane diluted 50:50 with white spirit and applied with a cloth. Rub down lightly with fine, worn

Fig. 2 Showing the use made of decorative chamfers.

ENGLISH OAK

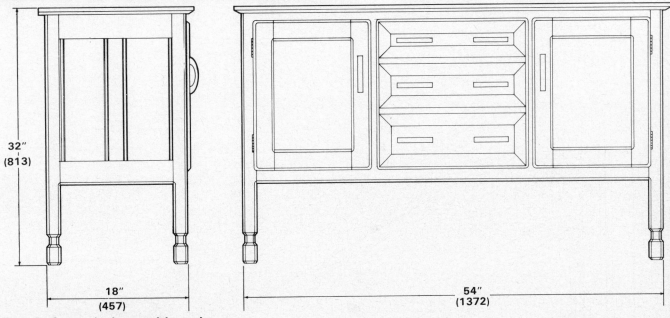

32"
(813)

18"
(457)

54"
(1372)

Fig. 3 General view, with main dimensions.

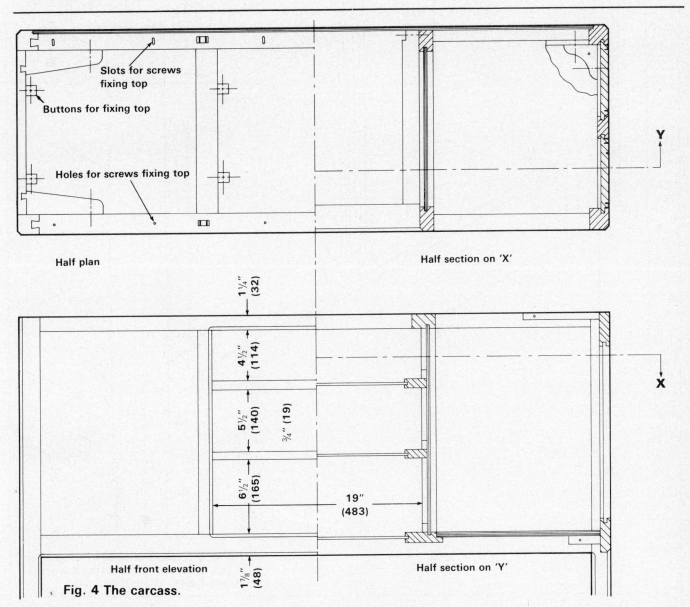

Slots for screws fixing top

Buttons for fixing top

Holes for screws fixing top

Y

Half plan

Half section on 'X'

1¼"
(32)

4½"
(114)

5½"
(140)

¾" (19)

6½"
(165)

19"
(483)

X

Half front elevation

1⅞"
(48)

Half section on 'Y'

Fig. 4 The carcass.

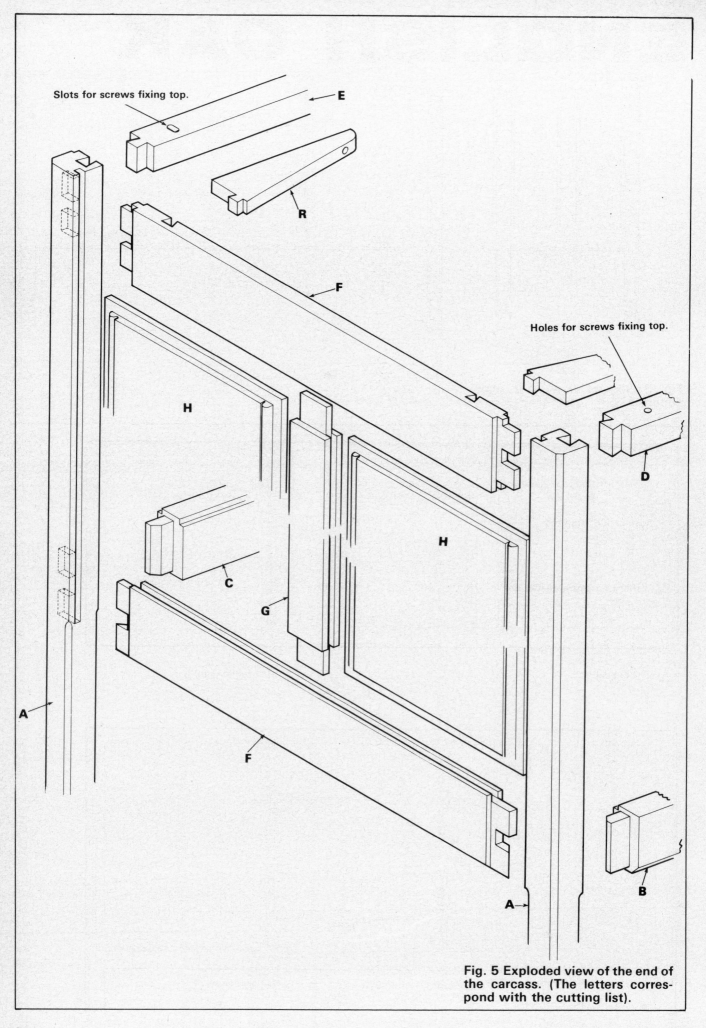

Slots for screws fixing top.

E

R

Holes for screws fixing top.

F

H

D

H

C

G

F

A

B

A

Fig. 5 Exploded view of the end of the carcass. (The letters correspond with the cutting list).

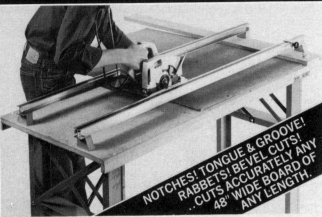

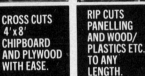

Woodworker, May 1980

Prices quoted are those prevailing at press date and are subject to alteration due to economic conditions.

303

abrasive paper between coats, and go over the final coat with 000 grade steel wool.

The wax may be applied with a shoe brush (kept solely for this purpose) or a cloth. Work the wax in well, remove surplus with a separate cloth, leave for the solvent to evaporate, and polish with a soft cloth. If you have not sealed, this procedure has to be repeated several times.

Try out the finishing process on an offcut. Do not use too small a sample — nothing less than 6in. square — or it is difficult to judge the effect.

Carcass Plane and thickness all parts, taking care that all the face surfaces and edges are true. The general arrangement of the carcass is shown in Fig. 4, and the joints for the ends in Fig. 5. The tenons in the end rails and the muntins, and the grooves for the panels are $\frac{5}{16}$in. (8mm). The grooves in the legs are stopped at the lower mortise.

The procedure for making the panels is: cut the rebates at each side; cut the beads, using a scratch stock (unless you have a beading plane); cramp-up the frame and mark off the length of the panel between rebates carefully, leaving it a little full rather than too short; cut the rebates at the ends using a fillister plane with a spur. Draw the plane back a few times before planing to avoid breaking out at the end of the stroke. It is best to cut the beads rather below the surface of the panel so that, after assembly, the panel can be planed flush with the frame without spoiling the beads.

The panels should be polished on the insides and in the rebates and beads so that if any shrinkage occurs it does not 'show white'. It is convenient to polish the insides of the division panels at the same time. They should be cut slightly over-size as they can be trimmed up without spoiling the polish.

The tenons on the ends of the front and back lower rails are $\frac{1}{2} \times 1\frac{1}{2}$in (12 × 38mm). These tenons and the corresponding ones on the end rails are bevelled to give maximum length without interference. Cut and fit the dovetails on the front and back rails; do not fit the triangular strengthening pieces at this stage.

Mark out and cut the mortises and tenons joining the front and rear centre uprights to the top and bottom rails. Note that the rear uprights are set forward $\frac{5}{16}$in. (8mm) from the back of the back rails to allow for the back. The tenons are $\frac{1}{2} \times 1$in. (12 × 25mm) and are wedged. Assemble the front centre uprights and the front top and bottom rails and mark off the lengths for the drawer rails. Note that the drawer rails are set back $\frac{1}{4}$in. (6mm) so that the front edge is level with the inner edge of the chamfer. The joints are shown in Fig. 7.

Mark off the housings for the drawer rails in the rear centre uprights from the front uprights. Cut the housings; do not cut the notches at the back of the drawer runners until the exact length can be marked off after assembly of the carcass.

Mark out and cut the mortises and tenons for the bottom drawer runners and the top cross rails. These are stub tenons $\frac{5}{16}$in. (8mm) thick by $\frac{1}{4}$in. (6mm) long.

Cut a $\frac{5}{16} \times \frac{3}{8}$in. (8 x 10mm) rebate for the back in the lower back rail, and in the back legs (stopped). Cut a stopped rebate in the front and back lower rails and in the bottom drawer runners to take the bases of the cupboards. Cut a groove in the bottom drawer runners and a groove (stopped at each end), in the front and back lower rails for the lowest dust panel. Groove the intermediate

drawer rails and runners for dust panels. Cut the housings for the buttons which hold the top. Drill holes for the top fixing screws in the front upper rail and slots in the back rail (to allow for shrinkage of the top).

Work the chamfers $\frac{1}{4}$ x $\frac{1}{4}$in. (6 x 6mm). Where the chamfer is stopped it is to show in the finished assembly as a quarter-circle running into the through chamfer in the adjoining member (See Fig. 2). I found it best to stop the chamfer a little short and complete the curve after assembly and cleaning up the face. A $\frac{1}{4}$in. skew carving chisel will do the job.

The feet are a matter of individual preference. They can be carved (as shown) or turned, or the legs can be left plain.

Assembly begins with the end frames. With a finely set smoothing plane clean up all inside surfaces that cannot be run through after assembly. Glue and cramp-up the end frames, testing for squareness and winding before putting on one side for the glue to set.

A word about gluing. With an adhesive such as Cascamite wiping-off surplus adhesive with a damp cloth is not good on oak. Water tends to stain oak and the adhesive fills the grain. This is all right if the surface can be run through afterwards; but if it is on an inside surface it is almost impossible to remove and leaves an ugly mark because of its different acceptance of

stain and polish. I use adhesive sparingly. If a small amount squeezes out at a joint I leave it to harden, then remove it with a sharp chisel. If I have to wipe away adhesive on oak I use a dry cloth.

When the end frames are set, clean up the outside and inside surfaces. The next stage of assembly takes in the lower rails, the bottom drawer runners and the bottom dust panel, so clean up inside surfaces of these. You will need a pair of sash cramps which will span 54in. (1372mm) plus allowances for softwood pads. I bought lengthening bars for my existing cramps. Assemble first the bottom drawer runners in the lower rails, not forgetting to insert the dust panel. Insert the lower rails into the end frames. Insert the dovetails of the top rails into the end frames *dry* so that they act as spacers. Cramp across the lower rails (you will need an assistant with such long cramps), test for squareness and winding, and correct if necessary.

On the next stage of assembly glue the drawer rails into the front centre uprights, then insert the uprights into the lower rail. Do the same with the rear centre uprights and insert the cupboard division panels. Add the front and back upper rails, inserting the cross rails. Cramp across the drawer rails, then across the centre uprights. The dovetail joints only need light cramping; I used rubber luggage straps. Wedge the tenons at the

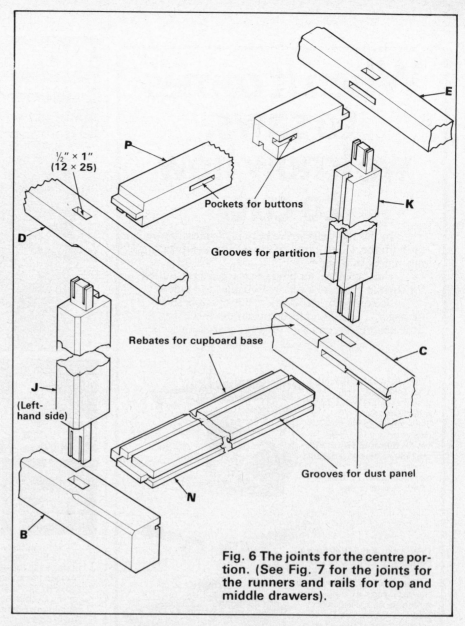

½" × 1" (12 × 25)

Pockets for buttons

Grooves for partition

Rebates for cupboard base

(Left-hand side)

Grooves for dust panel

Fig. 6 The joints for the centre portion. (See Fig. 7 for the joints for the runners and rails for top and middle drawers).

P D E K C J B N

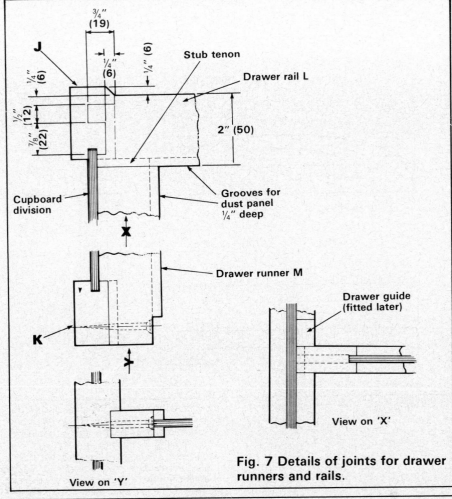

Fig. 7 Details of joints for drawer runners and rails.

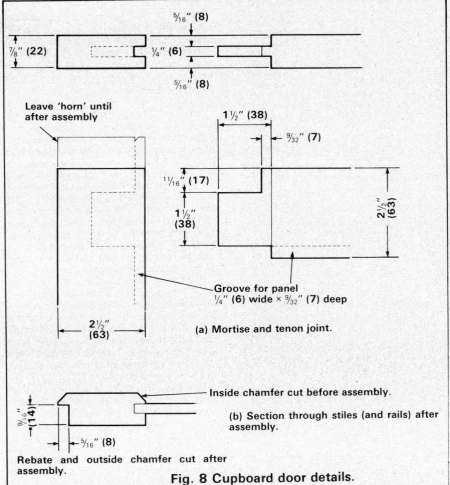

(a) Mortise and tenon joint.

(b) Section through stiles (and rails) after assembly.

Rebate and outside chamfer cut after assembly.

Fig. 8 Cupboard door details.

ends of the uprights, after which the cramps can be removed.

Fit the triangular strengthening pieces at the top corners and the 'knees' at the lower corners. These knees support the cupboard bases and should be fixed with the tops level with the bottom of the rebate.

The top and middle drawer rails can now be fitted. They are notched on both sides at the back; on the outside to fit into the housings on the uprights, and on the insides so that the fixing screws allow the dust panels to be inserted. The stub tenons are glued at the front, the rail inserted and fixed by a screw at the back.

The drawer guides should now be planed up and glued in. Check them carefully, one pair at a time, before gluing in. The best procedure is to cut a strip of wood (about 1/4 in. square) so that it will just go in the drawer opening. Use this as a feeler gauge to check the distance between the guides right to the back. For good drawer action the opening must not be narrower at the back than it is at the front, and may with advantage be, say, 1/32 in. (1mm) wider. Apply a similar test vertically.

Fit the bases of the cupboards, which are fixed by screwing up from underneath. I fitted a shelf in the right-hand cupboard, supported on corner blocks. The front of the shelf should be lipped with oak. There is no shelf in the left-hand cupboard so that it can take bottles.

This completes the carcass, except for cleaning up the front, which can be done just before polishing.

Drawers The drawers are of conventional construction. The oak fronts are 1 1/8 in. (28mm) thick to allow for the chamfers. The sides and backs are of beech, or other suitable hardwood, and finish 3/8 in. (10mm) thick. I do not like the excessively thin pins for the front dovetails which were fashionable at one time; 1/8 in. (3mm) wide at the narrow end with a slope of 1 in 8 seems appropriate. The dovetails should be 5/8 in. long. Cut and fit the dovetails at the front and back and plough the groove in the fronts for the base before working the chamfers on the fronts. These are 1 1/2 x 1/4 in. It is convenient to drill the fixing holes for the handles at this stage. After assembly, fit the drawers carefully.

Cupboard doors The cupboard doors are of framed construction with a flat panel. The joints are shown in Fig. 8. Chamfers are worked both inside and outside the stiles and rails, those inside before assembly and those outside after, together with the rebates.

For the panels, which finish 1/4 in. (6mm) thick, select a handsome piece of figured oak. I cut mine from a single piece 1 in. thick by slicing through the middle. This was done by taking a cut with a circular saw all round to maximum depth (2 1/8 in. in my case), then sawing the rest with a hand rip saw. (A tough assignment but not so tough as it sounds). The idea was to open out the pieces 'book fashion' so as to have matching figure, but of opposite hand, on each side. However, it did not quite work out like that as the cut disclosed a knot running parallel to the surface which was not visible in the original board. This was unsightly and had to placed on the inside and then the outside faces, being displaced nearly 1 in., showed slightly different figuring.

There is a little problem about the hingeing of the doors because of the rebate. Ideally, cranked hinges should be used, I was not able to obtain these so used brass butts as shown in Fig. 9. A triangular packing piece is

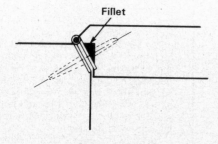

Fig. 9 Hingeing of cupboard doors

Fillet

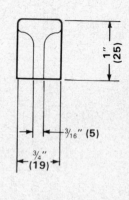

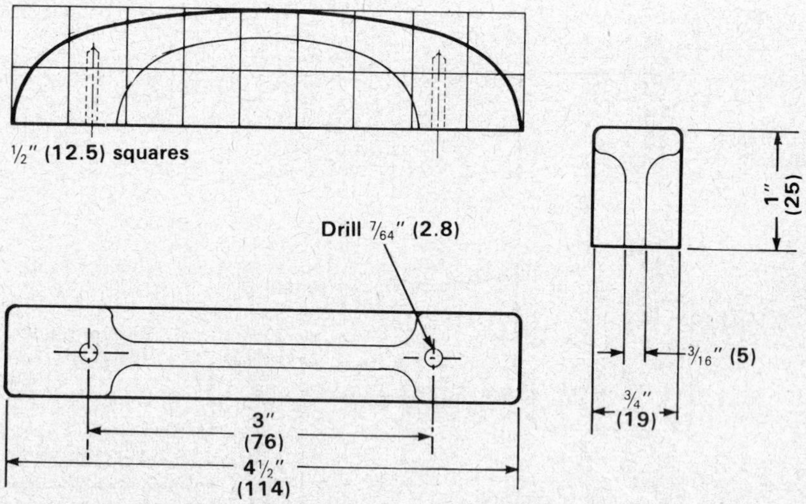

½" (12.5) squares

Drill ⁷⁄₆₄" (2.8)

Fig. 10 Handles

1" (25)

³⁄₁₆" (5)

3" (76)

4½" (114)

¾" (19)

Ref	No. off	Description	Dimensions In.	mm	Material
Carcass					
A	4	Legs	1¾ × 1¾ × 31¼	44 × 44 × 794	Oak
B	1	Front lower rail	1¾ × 1⅞ × 53½	44 × 48 × 1359	Oak
C	1	Back lower rail	1¾ × 1⅞ × 53½	44 × 48 × 1359	Hardwood
D	1	Top front rail	1¼ × 1¾ × 51¾	32 × 44 × 1314	Oak
E	1	Top back rail	1¼ × 1⁷⁄₁₆ × 51¾	32 × 37 × 1314	Hardwood
F	4	End rails	⅞ × 3 × 16¼	22 × 76 × 413	Oak
G	2	Muntins	⅞ × 2 × 17⅛	22 × 51 × 435	Oak
H	4	End panels	⅝ × 7 × 15⅞	16 × 178 × 403	Oak
J	2	Front centre uprights	1¼ × 2 × 21¼	32 × 51 × 540	Oak
K	2	Rear centre uprights	1¼ × 1¾ × 21¼	32 × 44 × 540	Hardwood
L	2	Drawer rails	¾ × 2 × 20½	19 × 51 × 521	Oak
M	4	Drawer runners	¾ × 1¾ × 15¹¹⁄₁₆	19 × 44 × 398	Hardwood
N	2	Bottom drawer runners	⅞ × 3½ × 15½	19 × 89 × 394	Hardwood
P	2	Top cross rails	1¼ × 2 × 15½	32 × 51 × 394	Hardwood
Q	6	Drawer guides	½ × ¾ × 14¼	12 × 19 × 362	Hardwood
R	4	Corner pieces	⅝ × 2 × 7½	16 × 50 × 190	Hardwood
S	4	Knees — four from:	¾ × 2½ × 12	19 × 64 × 305	Hardwood
T	1	Dustboard	15 × 15½	381 × 394	4mm ply
U	2	Dustboard	16 × 15½	424 × 394	4mm ply
V	2	Divisions	14⁷⁄₁₆ × 18½	367 × 470	6mm ply
W	1	Back	20½ × 51¾	52 × 1315	6mm ply
X	2	Cupboard bases	15⁷⁄₈ × 15½	403 × 394	12mm ply
Y	1	Shelf	16 × 15½	406 × 394	12mm ply
Z	1	Top	⅞ × 19⅞ × 56	22 × 505 × 1422	Oak
Drawers					
AA	1	Drawer front	1⅛ × 4½ × 19	28 × 114 × 483	Oak
AB	1	Drawer front	1⅛ × 5½ × 19	28 × 140 × 483	Oak
AC	1	Drawer front	1⅛ × 6½ × 19	28 × 165 × 483	Oak
AD	2	Drawer sides	⅜ × 4½ × 16	10 × 114 × 422	Hardwood
AE	2	Drawer sides	⅜ × 5½ × 16	10 × 140 × 422	Hardwood
AF	2	Drawer sides	⅜ × 6½ × 16	10 × 165 × 422	Hardwood
AG	1	Drawer back	⅜ × 4 × 19	10 × 102 × 483	Hardwood
AH	1	Drawer back	⅜ × 5 × 19	10 × 127 × 483	Hardwood
AJ	1	Drawer back	⅜ × 6 × 19	10 × 152 × 483	Hardwood
AK	6	Drawer slips	⅜ × ¹¹⁄₁₆ × 16½	10 × 21 × 419	Hardwood
AL	3	Drawer base	16¼ × 18	413 × 457	4mm ply
Cupboard doors					
BA	4	Stiles	⅞ × 2½ × 18½	22 × 64 × 470	Oak
BB	4	Rails	⅞ × 2½ × 13	22 × 64 × 330	Oak
BC	2	Panels	¼ × 10½ × 14	6 × 267 × 114	Oak
Handles					
	8	Handles	¾ × 1 × 4½	19 × 25 × 114	Rosewood
Fittings					
	4	Brass butt hinges	2¼ × 1¼		
	2	Brass ball catches			
	16	Plastics screw cups with snap covers			

glued into the rebate at the hinge position to bring the hinge axis to the correct position. This is trimmed to size after gluing so that the hinge comes in the position shown. This allows the door to open through about 150°. It does necessitate a rather deep housing in the door frame. I had misgivings about this method, but it seems to have worked out all right.

Top The top overhangs the carcass by ⅞in. at the back and 1in. at the front and sides. It is made from two boards joined. I planed mine by hand from the sawn timber, but if I had to make another I would enlist the help of someone with a large planer to do the initial planing.

After the boards are planed (check for winding if you hand plane), plane the joint edge using the longest and most accurate plane you can lay your hands on, and test until you have a perfect fit. Then plough a ⅛in (or, say, 4mm) wide groove for a loose tongue. Plywood can be used for the tongue but a crossgrained tongue is better. The latter will have to be made in several short pieces as it is impossible to obtain, or plane, a long length crossgrained. In either case, make the last 2in. or so at each end of oak in lengthwise grain so that it shows end grain at the end, the same as the top.

After the joint is glued, trim the ends and finish off the top with a finely set smoothing plane and a cabinet scraper. Round the front corners and chamfer the underneath at the front and ends so as to show a ⅝in. edge, taking the chamfer back about ¾in. The arris should be rounded. The top is fixed by 1¾in. x no. 10 brass screws and by wooden buttons to allow for any shrinkage.

Handles The handles on the original were carved from Indian rosewood to the shape shown in Fig. 10. They are fixed from the inside with no. 8 zinc-plated steel screws in plastics screw cups with snap covers.

Back The back is of 6mm plywood fixed in the rebate by ⅝in. x no. 4 brass or plated screws. Slide in the dust panels between the drawers before fixing the back.

MAKING MINIATURES

Mastercrafting Miniature Rooms and Furniture (Ann Kimball Pipe) is fascinating — at least that is the word which comes to mind in a preliminary look-through; but as you read on you agree whole-heartedly with the authoress who in her introduction uses the word 'enchanting'.

The book consists of eight sections: 1 Planning; 2 Building a room; 3, 4 and 5 Electrical wiring, tools and supplies; use of electric tools; 6 Making furniture; 7 Cloth, glass and metals; 8 Finishing touches. In the introduction stress is laid on imagination and accuracy: 'Instructions in this book, therefore, are for making miniatures not doll-houses.' It is not difficult to sense this distinction.

Planning. This brief section discusses separate rooms, houses and miniatures as a decoration in their own right. Attention is drawn to the creation of period rooms from early Gothic to contemporary styles, the Georgian and Victorian eras being perhaps the richest. There is useful advice on the importance of detail and especially on scales, 1/12th and 1/16th being the most popular. An illustration clearly shows the difference between 1in. to 1ft. and ¾in. to 1ft. A metric conversion table is included as an appendix.

Building a room. Full and concise instructions are given here for the making of rooms, attention being drawn to the necessity for 'channels' giving glimpses of adjoining rooms and their use in lighting arrangements. This is a very comprehensive chapter and it includes what might be considered the climax of the subject — over 20 coloured illustrations.

These pictures are, indeed, enchanting and in themselves an inspiration to a serious reader of this satisfying hobby. They include a living-room and kitchen in the early 1920s, a Victorian bedroom, a student's room (not too tidy), a formal dining-room, an attic sewing-room, office, playroom, upstairs hall, bathroom and numerous items of furniture from an office desk to a grand piano. The section is well illustrated with numerous photographs and drawings; and clear instructions are given for the making of windows, panelled doors, fire places, wood and tiled floors, wall decorations, skirting, brickwork, staircases and balusters. (The engineer's hammer shown in use on page 38 looks to be over-hefty, but no doubt it is a matter of choice.)

The three following sections also are profusely illustrated. Electric wiring is adequately dealt with and shows that much can be done to enrich a miniature room with imaginative lighting. Useful hints for work with a small jigsaw, miniature circular saw, lathe and drill are dealt with at some length. Carving small shapes with an electric drill must be fascinating provided safety is borne in mind!

Making furniture. Much work is done from 'commercial patterns' which can be 'bought individually or in book form', but the authoress stresses the desirability of making your own. Instructions are given for drawing patterns with graph paper and calculator, selecting suitable wood, sawing furniture parts, sanding and filing, gluing, filling and staining, types of adhesives; and there is a note on wood bending. There are many references to improvising. For instance toy hats to serve as cane seats for chairs.

Cloth, glass and metals. This section and the one on *Finishing touches* are masterpieces in the art of improvisation and serendipity. Curtains from various fabrics, bedspreads from paper towels, patchwork quilts from pieces glued to a background, settees upholstered with embossed paper, glass for curved doors from plastics bottles are just a few examples. This aspect of the craft becomes highly individual.

At the very outset Ann Kimball Pipe states: 'This book has been written for the craftsman who would like to go beyond the building of a simple dollhouse . . .' Such work may not be meet for us all. But how many times has an ageing craftsman been asked to make a 'dollhouse' for a sophisticated grand-daughter? And who would not be pleased to see the young lady's expression of delight? To the average reader of WOODWORKER much of the text of this book would appear elementary in style but making miniatures is a sphere of its own; and if patience and finicality add up to enchantment who can criticise?

Publisher is Van Nostrand Reinhold Co Ltd, Molly Millars Lane, Wokingham, Berks, and the price is £8.95.

C.W.B.

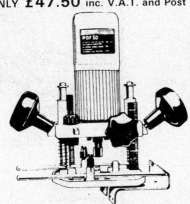

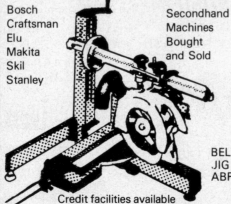
Prices quoted are those prevailing at press date and are subject to alteration due to economic conditions.

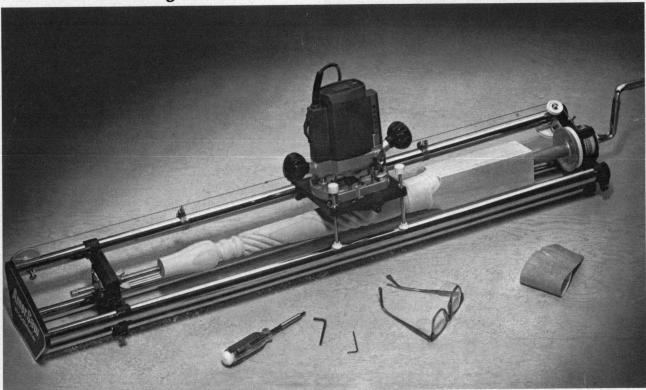

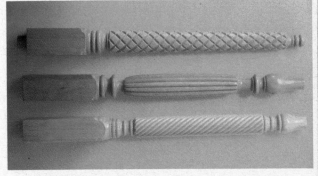

TOOL WORKS
on a GREEN FIELD SITE

When a Sheffield craftsman moved to rural Lincolnshire everybody was pleased. And they're even more pleased now that he has built new works to cope with a bulging order book

High quality hand tools such as the woodcarving and turning chisels made by Ashley Iles (Edge Tools) Ltd are usually associated with Sheffield rather than the rural area of Spilsby, Lincolnshire, where the firm has been located since 1967. But there were solid reasons for the move to a truly 'green field' site and solid reasons for staying there and, indeed, for building a larger factory which is now in full production.

In 1949 Ashley Iles started a one-man workshop in Sheffield where his family had been associated with tools for generations. He was one of the band of master craftsmen known colloquially as 'little mesters' and business prospered. But when the time came for the first of his three sons to join him, Mr Iles realised there was no way to expand in his small workshop so he began to look for suitable premises in the industrial area of Sheffield. But there was no joy.

Then on a visit to his father, who had retired to a Lincolnshire village, he noticed a one-man workshop nearby making wood saws. The occupier told him of the assistance he had received from the local authority and of the absence of opposition by people in the neighbourhood to the setting up of a workshop.

This encouraged Mr Iles to search the area for a suitable site and he found one: 1½ acres with farmhouse and outbuildings suitable for conversion to a forging and grinding shop. The local authority was most helpful so the property was bought and work on foundations for the machinery from the Sheffield shop started. Then the machinery was installed and a start-up made. Unskilled local labour was recruited and trained by Mr Iles to his exacting standards. Business expanded at home and overseas as more and more woodworkers appreciated the quality of tools made in the old way.

Two years ago it was decided to build a larger factory on the site. The grinding

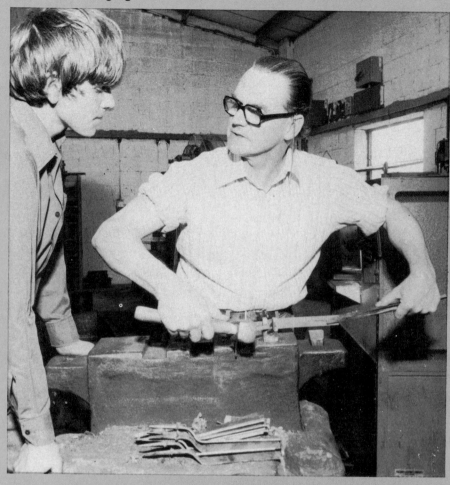

Above: Ashley Iles training an apprentice in the making of cranked neck paring chisels.
Below left: forging carving tools.
Below right: forging turning gouges using spring hammer.

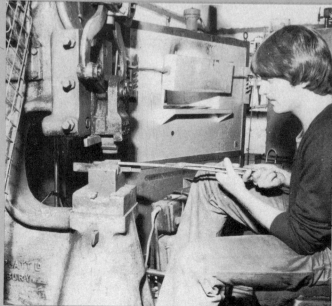

Turners at work in Darlington note their caps . . .

The original photograph from which this illustration was taken shows the turning shop of Wm Brown's sawmills at Darlington, Co Durham. The date? Possibly around 1910-14 to judge by the head-dress of the operatives! The picture is reproduced from a copper halftone as used in the letterpress process of printing formerly employed by WOODWORKER. Some of the detail is inevitably lost as WOODWORKER is now printed by the offset process.

The halftone was kindly loaned by reader D. White of Brompton-on-Swale, North Yorkshire (the old North Riding), who tells us that the firm, established in 1856, was taken over by Magnet Joinery in 1965 (Magnet merged with Southerns Evans in 1975) but Wm Brown's Sawmills Ltd is still trading as a subsidiary of Magnet-Southerns.

Mr White served his time in this turning shop, starting in 1949 under the late Stan Henderson, a well-known Darlington turner. Mr Henderson is believed to be the young boy on the far right of the illustration.

The shop was some 25ft square. Down the front wall was a double wooden bed on which headstocks and tailstocks were fitted to make as many as three lathes, or one lathe taking between centres 18ft. There were another two shorter sets of beds fitted with headstocks and tailstocks, and at the height of the turning as many as seven turners worked in the shop at one time.

Ultimately the shop was pulled down to make way for a liftshaft. This has now been pulled down to make room for storage.

FACE-LIFT FOR MINERVA

York Civic Trust has provided £300 for a bit of cosmetic surgery to one of the city's most famous woodcarvings — Minerva, goddess of wisdom and drama. The old girl is perched on a pile of books above Minster Gates, once the home of the city's booksellers and she has kept her solitary vigil in the face of all kinds of weather for nearly 180 years.

First carved in 1801 by local woodcarver Mr John Wolstenholme, Minerva was beginning to show signs of age on her shapely frame. Mr John Shannon, chairman of York Civic Trust said: 'She is sorely in need of some attention as she was beginning to look a little washed out'. The face-lift will include expert painting to make the carving once again a focal point at one of the busiest tourist spots in the city.

IVAN E. BROADHEAD

✦ CORONET
complete Home Workshop
— comprising:-

 ELF WOODTURNING LATHE
4 speeds
12" between centres
14" Bowl Turning (as illustrated)

 IMP BANDSAW
3 speeds
12" throat
5" (approx.) Depth of cut
Table tilts to 45°

 SOVEREIGN 4½" PLANER
½" rebate
Fence tilts 45°

 CONSORT SAW/SPINDLE MOULDER
4 speeds
2¼" depth of cut
Table tilts to 45°
Spindle Moulding (See separate leaflet)

Each unit comes complete with its own motor, press button starter and cabinet stand.

*Each unit can be purchased separately —
if required for bench mounting
(without cabinets)*

Illustration shows:-
1. 14" plaque being turned
2. Preparing disc for turning
3. 4½" surface planing
4. Spindle moulding shelf mould

MAJOR CMB 500

MAJOR CMB 600

MINOR MB 6

7" PLANER CAP 300

SHAKER

Three years ago Mrs Jane Pullen of Liss in Hampshire, went on a course at West Dean, taken by Fred Lambert on making cottage furniture. She writes: 'Using the round planes that Fred has developed (page 389/7 *Woodworker Record supplement* for July 1979), I learnt how to make stick-back chairs.

'I have been happily producing chairs, stools and tables with these tools ever since. In 1979 I was fortunate enough to be awarded a Winston Churchill travelling fellowship to go to New England and study Shaker and early American colonial furniture. These styles of furniture are applicable to the use of the round planes.

'Having seen the furniture in the flesh, so to speak, I intend to use the Shaker example to enhance my future designs. The other attribute, applicable to today's scarcity of wood, is that the stick construction uses very little wood and also wood that conventional furniture manufacturers discard as poor quality. I can work round shakes and knots.

'So much wood is being cut and burnt when it could be utilised for furniture and allied wooden ware. If only the public could be educated into not cutting tree trunks into nice round chunks, and would leave the trunk in one piece for a woodworker to look at before it is cut into firewood.'

The reference to the Shakers and Shaker furniture in *Woodworker Record supplement* for October 1979 (page 578/8), is taken further by Mrs Pullen. A Shaker quote which embodies their philosophy is 'That which has in itself the highest use possesses the greatest beauty.'

The United Society of Believers in Christ's Second Appearing, or the Shakers as they came to be known due to the fervour of their religious ritual, originated in Manchester. In 1774 Ann Lee and eight followers sailed to the New World hoping to find freedom from persecution of their religious beliefs, as had so many other such sects.

The Shakers were far removed from the society of the time. Marriage, private property, competitive industry were all held in disfavour. To combat the evils of worldliness they separated from the world and set up communities that became totally interdependent and self-sufficient. During the first 20 years in the New World they were involved in establishing their settlements and forming the ideals and laws that made the pattern of their way of life.

They attracted a growing number of converts, largely common people of the countryside of puritan/protestant stock, who brought with them skills and trades they had

learnt. Eventually 19 communities were established and at their peak in the 1850s they had a membership of 6,000 throughout New England, New York and as far west as Pleasantville, Kentucky.

After 1876 the communities went into a gradual decline, due in part to their celibacy and the increased mobility and industrialisation of the time. Today two communities remain, with only nine elderly women. The few survivors at Canterbury, New Hampshire, and Sabbathday Lake, Maine, have voted to discontinue admitting new members. They are custodians of a movement out of America's past.

The furniture industry of the Shakers grew out of the necessity to furnish buildings erected by the growing membership during the first half of the 18th century. The most skilled and idealistic members set the standards that elevated uninspired provincial woodworkers to the position of fine craftsmen, with a guild-like pride in accomplishment.

Within each community they built meeting houses, dwelling houses and workshops all to be equipped with furnishings, tools and artifacts required by large numbers of people living together in a communal society devoid of outside attachments.

machines have now been moved in and new electric furnaces are taking the place of the oil-fired furnaces previously used. In this project Mr Iles was greatly helped by the Council for Small Industries in Rural Areas (CoSIRA). 'A splendid service' is how he describes it.

Ashley Iles (Edge Tools) Ltd employs 16 people including Mr Iles, two of his sons and his daughter-in-law who runs the office. He does all hardening and tempering of the tools — and makes the final inspection. He and his son Anthony also carry out training of employees. 'I give any would-be apprentice a one-day trial and let him loose in the place to try our various jobs,' he says. 'I can soon assess if he has the necessary ability and co-ordination to make a success of it. I recently advertised for two craft apprentices and 40 young men applied. It was tragic having to select two out of such a number knowing full well that there must have been many a potential craftsman among the other 38.'

Though there are no problems in getting labour the move from Sheffield to rural Lincolnshire created one — water. In Lincolnshire it is so hard that it is impossible to suitably harden with it so oil has to be used. 'That, of course, is why Sheffield sprang up by the soft waters of the river Don,' says Mr Iles.

Demand for high-class woodcarving and turning tools continues upwards. Overseas the US, Canada, Australia and New Zealand are important markets with France showing considerable potential. At home trade is good. Indeed, at last year's Woodworker Show in London, Mr Iles had to arrange daily stock deliveries by Securicor from the Lincolnshire works to satisfy sales from his stand.

His interest in hand tools does not finish with making them. He takes a delight in the end results and is a co-sponsor of the annual Ashley Iles/Woodworker international carving competition.

Above: cannelling 2in. skew turning tool. Wheel 42 × 6 running in water.
Below left: general view of wet grinding.
Below right: forging bolster and tang on spring hammer. Note work in electric furnace.

Jack Hill extends his series on

COUNTRY CHAIRS AND CHAIRMAKING

In spite of documentary evidence which illustrates a ladderback-style chair in use as early as 1340 there is little proof that the design survived the Dark Ages. Its development (or redevelopment?) is generally thought to have taken place during the early part of the 17th century, probably in Holland where the style was known as a rushback chair.

Ladderbacks and spindlebacks as we know them today are linear descendants of the 'joyned' back stool or back chair of the early 16th century and the simple rush bottomed stool once popular in country districts. The solid back rests of the former gradually gave way to a back consisting of one or two richly carved horizontal rails, then to combinations of carved rails and turned spindles or half panels and rails.

These chairs remained richly ornamented and heavily built, with solid boarded seats however; the choice of the better-off townsfolk. It seems likely, therefore, that the final transition came with the adaption of the back rest idea to the rush seated stool to produce a more lightly built and less elaborate country chair. In addition, the rush seat could be woven by women and even children thus reducing the cost of making the chair.

Making full use of plain-turned parts and the simple but effective round joint throughout almost its entire construction, the rush seated chair became popular with the country carpenters who, before the advent of specialist chair makers, made chairs along with their other work in wood.

Frames were made from the most suitable local timbers, usually ash or perhaps beech cut annually from nearby coppice or woodland. Parts were always cleft from straight-grained material, thus ensuring the maximum strength in legs and spindles which, in later years, were made smaller and smaller in cross-section, almost to the point of appearing too fragile one might think. Clefts cut roughly to length as required were trimmed almost to their finished size with a drawknife and then turned to shape on a lathe.

After turning, parts would be put aside to season thoroughly, although some makers apparently assembled chairs before this process was entirely complete, the simple joint remaining secure due to even shrinkage which left both parts of the joint oval in section.

The strength of these chairs lies in the material used in the box-frame arrangement of parts. Although design details may vary considerably most are constructed as shown in the accompanying diagrams so that all components contribute something to the total strength and rigidity.

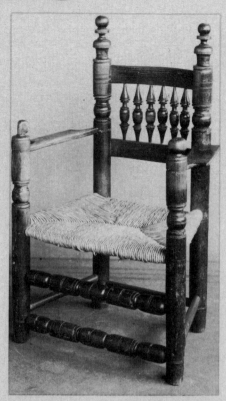

3: on to LADDERBACKS

In particular the importance of sound joints is emphasised. The round or dowel end should be a good push fit into its drilled socket and this in turn must be of adequate depth. The joint is further secured by glue, of course, but adhesives should not be relied upon as gap filling agents. Minimum depth of joint sockets is based on the diameter of the dowel plus at least ⅛in. (3mm).

After preparing the various parts to length and marking in the position of joint sockets these are bored out. In the simplest chairs this is a comparatively simple task as the frame, being square, has all joints at right angles. Some chairs, however, are shaped and have parts of different length and sockets bored at various angles. Some chairs have their two back uprights shaped, leaning slightly backwards towards the top for added comfort and splayed outwards at the bottom for the sake of stability; others have seats wider at the front than at the back.

Above right: early rush bottomed chair with spindle back, probably late 17th or early 18th century.
Left: an old ladder back with rush seat, probably about 1900. Note the bar across the top. Acknowledgements to Shibden Hall, Halifax.

Both these features were, and still are, frequently combined in one chair and call for extra care in measuring and boring. Working by hand and eye alone the old craftsmen accurately made these angled sockets with a wooden stock brace and bit. The work can be simplified, however, by use of a power drill and simple jigs as shown in the sketches. The drilling cradle is basically a wooden V-block and drilling angles are obtained by measuring between the drill and a dowel placed temporarily into the adjacent socket. Note that adjacent holes are staggered to retain the maximum strength of the upright.

The slight curve of the back uprights is formed by steam-heating the parts after turning but before being bored. Some chairs are fitted with arms, or arm rests to be precise, by the simple upward extension of the two front legs to form arm supports. The arms themselves, sawn to shape and trimmed with a spokeshave, are socketed onto these supports and into the back upright or stile.

While most country-made ladderback and spindleback chairs have plain turned parts below the seat, others are found with decorative turning ranging from the very simple to the highly ornate, including some with heavy cabriole legs. Ocasionally such chairs are found with components, in particular the two long back members, part

AND SPINDLEBACKS

LADDERBACKS & SPINDLEBACKS

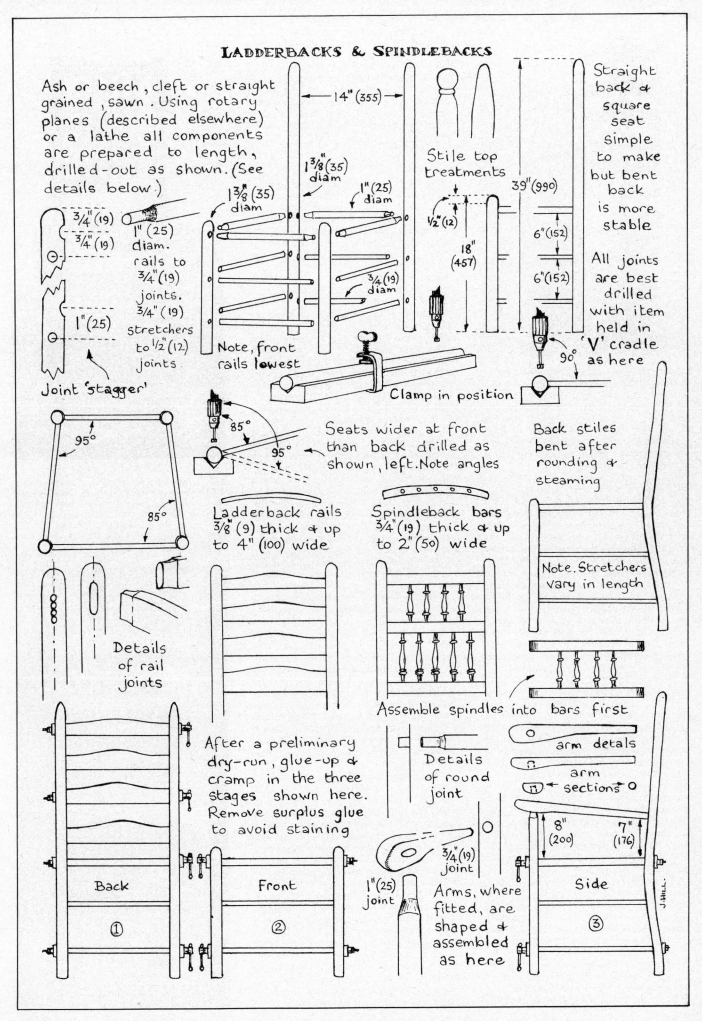

Ash or beech, cleft or straight grained, sawn. Using rotary planes (described elsewhere) or a lathe all components are prepared to length, drilled-out as shown. (See details below.)

3/4" (19)
3/4" (19)
1" (25) diam. rails to 3/4" (19) joints. 3/4" (19) stretchers to 1/2" (12) joints.

1" (25)

Joint 'stagger'

14" (355)

1 3/8" (35) diam

1 3/8" (35) diam

1" (25) diam

3/4" (19) diam

Note, front rails lowest

Stile top treatments

1/2" (12)

18" (457)

39" (990)

Clamp in position

6" (152)

6" (152)

90°

Straight back & square seat simple to make but bent back is more stable

All joints are best drilled with item held in 'V' cradle as here

95°

85°

85°

95°

Seats wider at front than back drilled as shown, left. Note angles

Back stiles bent after rounding & steaming

Details of rail joints

Ladderback rails 3/8" (9) thick & up to 4" (100) wide

Spindleback bars 3/4" (19) thick & up to 2" (50) wide

Note. Stretchers vary in length

Assemble spindles into bars first

After a preliminary dry-run, glue-up & cramp in the three stages shown here. Remove surplus glue to avoid staining

Back ①

Front ②

Details of round joint

3/4" (19) joint

1" (25) joint

Arms, where fitted, are shaped & assembled as here

arm details

arm sections

8" (200)

7" (176)

Side ③

J. HILL.

turned and part rectangular. Differences such as these were no doubt originally of a regional nature. Although certain styles may be attributed to specific areas of the country, and even to specific craftsmen in some cases, with the wide interchange of ideas which came later, it is wise to tread with some caution when designating these various styles and designs.

As is the case with the various Windsor-style chairs it is the construction of the back which is the most distinguishing feature of these chairs. The ladderback, so named from the ladder-like arrangement of horizontal bars or slats between the two back uprights or stiles, may have these bars quite plain or elaborately shaped and, occasionally, pierced also. They can vary in number from three to seven with five generally quite common. Each may be of equal width or varied, usually decreasing in size from top to bottom. Some chairs have distinctive turned decoration on the top ends of their back stiles. Others, in addition to the ladder rails, have an extra bar joining these terminal ends together.

Spindlebacks, which seem to have been most popular in the northern countries of England, consist of combinations of narrow horizontal bars supporting rows of vertical-turned spindles. The horizontal bars may be three or sometimes four in number, the top one often wider and perhaps shaped on its top edge to form a decorative comb. Some designs have their horizontal bars turned to match their vertical back spindles. Every possible number and arrangement of bars and spindles seems to have been used, from two bars and a single row of three or four spindles up to three separate rows totalling some 17 or 18 spindles. Most spindles are turned in the vase and ring or bobbin designs.

Horizontal bars for both types of chair were steam-bent to a slightly curving shape to fit the roundness of the sitter's back. This can be done either before or after cutting to pattern. The extreme ends of these bars were usually trimmed to form a full width tenon, ie without shoulders, although many of the later spindlebacks did have shouldered tenons. Positions for matching mortice slots were marked out on the stiles and, working at the bench, these were cut by drilling a line

of holes inside the pencilled marks and finishing to size with a bevel chisel.

The bar which joined the tops of certain ladderbacks was bored out so that it could be socketed down on to the top of the back stiles. The horizontal bars of spindlebacks were drilled to accommodate their rows of spindles, bars and spindles being assembled together before fitting to the back stiles. All drilling can, of course, be done with a power drill.

With all the preliminary work of turning, shaping etc completed it is advisable to have a dry run. That is, to assemble the chair without glue. to check that everything fits and that the chair 'shapes-up' properly. As already stated joints should be tight but not so tight as to cause splitting. Do not try the joints for fit too often as this may cause them to become too loose.

When all is well, assembly takes place in stages. The correct sequence is of great importance. In the case of ladderbacks all back members, ie two uprights or stiles together with stretchers, rear seat rail and ladder bars are glued and assembled together as one unit and cramped-up. When cramping, ensure that cramps are placed opposite and in line with stretchers and other horizontal cross-members, otherwise breakages will occur. Protect cramping points with softwood blocks.

For spindlebacks spindles are first glued into their respective horizontal rails, then the complete back is assembled and cramped as described. Similarly, front members for both types of chair, ie two front legs, stretchers and front seat rail, are assembled and cramped-up. When the glue is set the cramps are removed and separate back and front units joined together with their side members, ie stretchers and side seat rails, and the whole chair cramped-up again 'fore and aft'. Check that the chair stands square and leave under pressure until the glue is set.

It was usual at this stage to do the rushing of the seat, work more often than not carried out by outworkers (people working part-time in their own homes). Seats were rushed or matted, to use the original name for this work, using the English freshwater rush *Scriptus lacustris,* common throughout the country at one time. A traditional geometric pattern was, and still is, used in most seats of this kind. Before the seat is rushed it is wise to clean-up the chair and apply a sealing coat to the wood leaving the final polishing stages until after completion of the seat. (Rush seating methods will be considered in a subsequent article).

These simple country styles were made, quite literally, by the thousand, Many, later on, were produced by factory methods to satisfy the demands of an ever-increasing population. It was not uncommon for a manufacturer to receive orders for several gross at a time (a gross is 144 for those who have forgotten or never knew) for use in church halls, public meeting places and so on. They were just as popular in the home, and not just in the cottages of country folk. A number of famous-name furniture designers of the mid-18th century borrowed the simple country styles and many an elegant, though somewhat ornate, ladderback with upholstered seat was to be found in the drawing rooms of the wealthy. These same styles figured prominently in the late 19th century design movement started by William Morris and remain popular even today.

Left: ladderback armchair by Gimson about 1880 now in the Victoria and Albert Museum, London. Above: spindleback chair at Shibden Hall, Halifax. Late 19th century? Below: ladderback chair in beech with rush bottom made by the author in 1978.

workpieces

Selling on safety

Some 4,000 sq ft of showroom space in which woodworking machinery and equipment is laid out for demonstration purposes, is a feature of the premises of the ACS Distribution subsidiary of Accurate Cutting Services Ltd at Park Farm Industrial Estate, Studley Road, Redditch, Worcs. Director Charles Thirtle-Watts tells WOODWORKER: 'At the moment our coverage is for people who require equipment up to small workshop size and during this year we will be adding to the range a number of very interesting machines. Our showroom is laid out so that would-be buyers can see items being demonstrated and receive adequate training in the use of any equipment which may be selected.

'We regard this as being a very important factor since most woodworking machines are dangerous, and with the number of accidents in small workshops, it is evident that these accidents occur through lack of knowledge of the equipment. Our demonstrators are employed to instruct in the correct use of the equipment and above all else to make the would-be buyer safety conscious.'

Mr Thirtle-Watts says that during the past year a machine tool rebuilding division has been established within ACS Distribution. This specialises in woodworking machines, tools and equipment. On the service side ACS is manufacturing bandsaw blades and reconditioning circular saw blades as well as re-tipping and re-grinding TC blades. He adds: 'For the larger workshop we handle the whole range of Foley equipment from the US. Apart from the possibilities of servicing cutting tools *in situ*, this range is ideal for anyone to set up a small workshop offering saw re-grinding or tooth re-cutting, re-setting and finishing services.'

ACS Distribution also handles the Woodmaster lathe from the Vermont American Corporation. Eventually the company intends to add to its ranges some of the large machines for industrial outlets.

2nd Stanley lecture

Britain's industrial and economic decline is linked with deficiencies in our educational system though education changes alone will not solve our problems. This was one of the conclusions of the 2nd Stanley lecture (1979) delivered by Professor Denis Lawton BA PhD, last October. The full report of the lecture and discussions thereon is available without charge from the PR department of Stanley Tools Ltd, Woodside, Sheffield S3 9PD.

Points arising from the lecture are also considered in the spring 1980 issue of the *Stanley Link Bulletin in Craft Design & Technology* published from the same address. It stresses that there are many signs of curriculum change and goes on to study the opportunites for action for those who feel strongly about the contribution which craft, design and technology can offer within the curriculum.

Old into new

Plans for making various items of furniture (repro and contemporary) as well as wooden toys and garden sundries are available from Mrs Diana Hamlyn, 57 The Green, Lyneham, SN15 4PH. A list of the plans costs 60p inclusive of postage. Mrs Hamlyn who describes herself as 'an ordinary housewife with some knowledge of the antique trade' supplies with the plans (which are full-size) notes and hints on construction. 'Each plan is really rather like a dressmaking pattern for wood as it is full-sized for each piece required, not only the shaped pieces, so this should present no problem in setting out and cutting,' says Mrs Hamlyn.

She also gives hints on using wood from old furniture but wisely advises: 'Think carefully before breaking up a large old piece of furniture. If you are not sure of its value take advice. It would be heart-breaking to destroy a large piece of valuable furniture to make something less valuable.'

Courses

City and Guilds of London Art School is offering a three year diploma course in stone and wood restoration; a two year certificate course in wood and gesso carving; oil and water gilding and decorative techniques and a two year certificate course in lacquer work, gilding, painting furniture, faux marbre, faux bois, frescoes, etc. SAE to the secretary, 124 Kennington Park Road, London SE11 4DJ (phone 01-735 2306).

Interbimall '80

The International Biennial Exhibition of Woodworking Machinery and Tools will take place at Milan Fair from 15-21 May.

Living Crafts

The sixth in the series of annual 'Living Crafts' exhibitions will take place in the park and grounds of Hatfield House, Herts from 8-11 May, when some 200 specialist and professional craftsmen will be demonstrating about 80 different crafts.

These will include, a Sussex maker of room settings of miniature funiture; a carver in bas-relief on wood panels; a sculptor of life sized birds; a Kent maker of wooden toys for adults and a Hampshire wheelwright who makes farm implements in miniature among many others.

Exhibition hours 11-6 daily, admission, adults £1.50, children 85p.

Collection of eggcups

Wood finishing techniques of Willie Levine is one of the contributions by Cyril Brown to the Society of Ornamental Turners *Bulletin No. 61* (September 1979), recently received from the editor (A. Mayor, Kenilworth, Hayesfield Park, Bath BA2 4QE). The article includes a table showing sanding procedure following turning of huge vases and bowls in circular and oval patterns in choice hardwoods.

Cyril Brown has also contributed a description of his collection of eggcups in different woods and patterns. 'The total has passed 350 .... which includes most of the world's rare, elegant and oldest wood species not likely to be obtained again by one turner', he writes.

Another article is based on correspondence between Mr Levine and the *Bulletin* editor on the problems of larger-scale elliptical turnery.

Mechanical handling

In the past Wadkin Ltd of Leicester has depended on European firms for the mechanical handling and inter-process mechanisation used in conjunction with its woodworking machines. Now Wadkin has linked with Torvale Engineering, Pembridge, Herefordshire, for the supply of handling equipment which ranges from simple powered roller conveyors to sophisticated inter-process lines and computer-controlled bulk handling systems. Torvale also provides standard one-off conveyor equipment or specially designed items for high-production handling.

From 29 April to 5 June Wadkin and Torvale will have an exhibition at the latter company's works showing a one-man sawing and planing line with an output of 50m/min. A Torvale mechanised line will provide destacking and feeding to a Stenner band resaw with sequential control of cut pieces to a fast feed table and a type FBN moulder by Wadkin.

The exhibition is intended to demonstrate the scope for increasing mill efficiency. The line will be operated on Tuesdays, Wednesdays and Thursdays of each week and technicians will be present to advise.

Jointing methods

On the subject of joints (pages 148-9 of WOODWORKER for March 1980), a reader has sent illustrations from the July 1953 issue, Figs. 2 and 11 of which are reproduced here. He says that during his apprenticeship 1926-30 'we jointed thicknesses up to $\frac{5}{8}$ in. × 3ft on the shooting board (Fig. 2) and when jointing table tops up to 4ft × $8\frac{3}{4}$ × $\frac{7}{8}$ in. the joints were made and glued as shown in Fig. 11. No cramps were ever used and two pieces were not planed together as illustrated in Fig. 11 on page 149 of the March issue.'

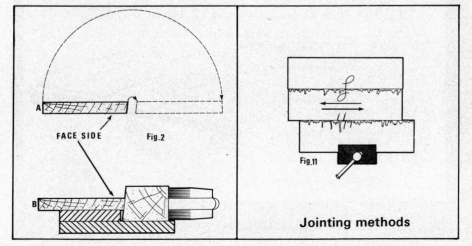

FACE SIDE   Fig.2

Fig.11

Jointing methods

workpieces

Book catalogues

The 1980 catalogue of titles published by Evans Brothers Ltd, Montague House, Russell Square, London WC1B 5BX, lists a number of forthcoming books of interest to all woodworkers, in addition to the well-known series by Charles H. Hayward. Wooden toys and art and craft subjects are also included.

Oak Tree Press Co Ltd, c/o Ward Lock Ltd, 116 Baker Street, London W1M 2BB, has issued its 1980 catalogue of titles several of which are on carving and whittling, wood block cutting and printing, building Shaker furniture and wicker and cane furniture making. There are also craft books and in the pastimes section is a title on furnishing a dolls house.

More magazines

New monthly magazines launched by the publisher of WOODWORKER (Model and Allied Publications Ltd), are *Popular Crafts* and *Model Maker*. Cover price of the former is 60p and the latter 55p. As its title implies *Popular Crafts* covers a great variety of subjects including enamelling, china painting, pottery, jewellery, gems, weaving, soft toy making. *Model Maker* is basically a 'how-to' guide dealing with the widest range of modelling in all materials.

Fireside bellows

We understand that ornamental brass nozzles suitable for fireside bellows (pages 324-5 of WOODWORKER for June 1979) can be supplied by Sweetman & Thompson Ltd, 127 Soho Hill, Handsworth, Birmingham B19 1AT. This firm specialises in the manufacture of brassware and director N. G. Thompson says that the minimum order would be 10 nozzles.

Catalogues

From Rabone Chesterman Ltd, Whitmore Street, Birmingham B18 5BD, is catalogue No. 7 (spring 1980) running to 48 pages of colour illustrations with descriptions of linear measuring and other equipment. There are separate sections devoted to carpenters tools and hand tools; precision tools; spirit levels; and hole saws.

GKN Screws & Fasteners Ltd., PO Box 77, Heath Street, Smethwick B66 2RA, has issued a number of publications relating to its products. One leaflet is *Woodscrews & Allied Products* (A500 revised) and another is *DIY Fasteners Handbook* (A409 revised). The Supadriv woodscrews and Twinfast woodscrews (for particleboard) are the subject of publication A501 revised and A502 revised respectively.

High-performance windows (those which have achieved severe exposure rating in accordance with BS4315) and have weather-stripping as an integral feature, are the subject of a leaflet from Market Harborough Joinery Co Ltd, Riverside, Market Harborough LE16 7PT. The various types and sizes are described and their applications reviewed. The windows are available in either preservative-treated softwood or in hardwood, or a combination of both and are suitable for staining. Softwood windows can also be supplied with one coat of lead-free paint primer.

Sound insulation

What is described as a simple sound insulation rating which architects and designers may specify for the structure of buildings and for building elements, is given in BS5821 *Rating sound insulation in buildings and of building elements*. Copies of the standard can be had from British Standards Institution sales department, 101 Pentonville Road, London N1 9ND at £4.50 (or £2.70 to BSI subscribing members).

BSI states that the new system, which replaces the averaging procedure previously used, will enable building elements such as partitions, doors and floors to be put into rank ordering sequence in accordance with their ability to attenuate sound.

Heat insulation

Several enquiries in Question Box recently have been on the subject of insulating workshops both for heat and sound. Now Celotex Ltd, Warwick House, 27-31 St Mary's Road, London W5, has issued a booklet called *Keep Heat in its Place* for those interested in how to save energy.

Available free of charge from Celotex the booklet advises on the terminology used in calculating thermal conductivity, thermal resistance and thermal transmittance. It explains how suspended ceilings work and gives details concerning the thermal insulation of industrial buildings, the availability of lining insulation and grid systems used to support these linings in over and under purlin situations.

1 2 3 4

complete Home Workshop

CORONET
WOODWORKING MACHINES

Universal & Independent models for Woodworking & Woodturning 👑

SAWING ● BOX COMBING ● WOBBLE SAWING ● SPINDLE MOULDING ● PLANING THICKNESSING ● REBATING ● MORTICING ● SLOTTING & GROOVING ● DISC SANDING BELT SANDING ● GRINDING & POLISHING ● TURNING ● LONG HOLE BORING

Bench mounted & Cabinet models ideal for . . .
PROFESSIONALS AND D-I-Y ENTHUSIASTS

Whatever woodworking operation you need — Coronet have the ideal machine.

Since 1946 Coronet have achieved a world wide reputation as leading designers and manufacturers of Quality woodworking machines with production of castings, machining and assembly being carried out in our modern factory — to achieve essential standards of accuracy.
Today our extensive range includes universal machines with fitments and attachments which can be purchased as and when required. — to suit your particular needs.

Send Now for
BROCHURE
on all models

CORONET
TOOL CO LTD
Alfreton Road
Derby DE2 4AH

WOOD WORKING WOOD TURNING CORONET

see the Coronet Range in action

—at Coronet Works and Learn-a-Craft Training Centre in Derby
—by arrangement
Telephone: 0332-362141

—at Stockists. Coronet Demonstrators visit main Stockists throughout the year.
Send for details.

Please send me brochure, price list & my local stockists address.
I enclose stamps, value 15p for p & p.

NAME _____

ADDRESS _____

_____

_____ C/W 5.80

👑 CORONET
complete Home Workshop
— comprising:-

1 ELF WOODTURNING LATHE
4 speeds
12" between centres
14" Bowl Turning (as illustrated)

2 IMP BANDSAW
3 speeds
12" throat
5" (approx.) Depth of cut
Table tilts to 45°

3 SOVEREIGN 4½" PLANER
½" rebate
Fence tilts 45°

4 CONSORT SAW/SPINDLE MOULDER
4 speeds
2¼" depth of cut
Table tilts to 45°
Spindle Moulding (See separate leaflet)

Each unit comes complete with its own motor, press button starter and cabinet stand.

Each unit can be purchased separately — if required for bench mounting (without cabinets)

Illustration shows:-
1. 14" plaque being turned
2. Preparing disc for turning
3. 4½" surface planing
4. Spindle moulding shelf mould

MAJOR CMB 500

MAJOR CMB 600

MINOR MB 6

7" PLANER CAP 300

Woodworker Show
Royal Horticultural Society's New Hall
4-9 November, 1980

Royal Horticultural Society's New Hall, London SW1 — 4-9 November inclusive (10.00am to 7.00pm each day)

COMPETITION RULES:
All correspondence and entry forms to: P. D. Freebrey, Exhibitions Manager, Model and Allied Publications Ltd, PO Box 35 Bridge Street, Hemel Hempstead HP1 1EE.

GENERAL CONDITIONS OF ENTRY

1. Each entry shall be made separately on the official form and every question must be answered. Be sure to include the estimated value of your model. LAST DAY OF ENTRY WILL BE FRIDAY, 5 SEPTEMBER 1980.
2. All entry forms must be accompanied by a remittance for the appropriate entry fee(s).
3. The competition entry fee will be £1.25 for seniors, 75p for juniors.
4. A junior shall mean a person under 18 years of age on 1 November 1980.
5. No exhibit which has previously won a bronze medal, rosette or higher award at any of the exhibitions promoted by this company shall be accepted for these competitions. The organisers reserve the right to transfer an entry to a more appropriate class.
6. Entries may be submitted by amateur or professional workers.
7. The decision of the judges shall be final.
8. Competitors shall state on the entry form:
   (a) that the exhibit is their own work and property;
   (b) any parts or kits which were purchased or were not the outcome of their own work.
   (c) the origin of the design.
9. Exhibits will be insured for the period during which they will be at the exhibition. Insurance of exhibits in transit to and from the exhibition is the responsibility of the competitor.
10. Model and Allied Publications Ltd reserves the right to refuse any entry or exhibit on arrival at the exhibition and shall not be required to furnish any reason for doing so.
11. Model and Allied Publications Ltd reserves the exclusive rights to describe and photograph any exhibits entered for competition or display and to make use of of any such photograph or descriptions in any way the company may think fit.
12. Competitors will be issued with a free non-transferable competitors pass to the exhibition on presentation of their exhibit to the organisers.

RECEPTION

13. All exhibits must be delivered to Royal Horticultural Society's New Hall, Greycoat Street, Westminster, London SW1 (near Victoria station) on Sunday, 2 November between 10.30am and 4.00pm. Exhibitors must take away all empty cases, packing materials etc.

COLLECTION

14. Exhibits can only be reclaimed on the presentation of a Control Card, and this cannot be done before the end of the exhibition. They may be removed from the New Hall between 7.00pm and 9.00pm on Sunday, 9 November or between 10.00am and 4.00pm on Monday, 10 November. Any remaining uncollected exhibits will be removed to the offices of Model and Allied Publications Ltd and the organisers reserve the right to dispose of any for which collection arrangements have not been made by 30 November 1980.

AWARDS

15. All awards are made entirely at the discretion of the judges who may deem a particular class or section to be not worthy of any particular award.

16. A challenge cup will be awarded for the best entry in each of the following classes:
    - WA — Cabinet making
    - WB — Woodcarving
    - WC — Woodturning
    - WD — Musical instruments
    - WE — Marquetry and inlay
    - WF — Toys
    - WG — Model horse-drawn vehicles
    - WH — Junior (under 18) section
    - WJ — Clocks

17. Awards of 1st, 2nd and 3rd will be made in each section. The awards will take the form of Certificates of Merit.

18. Any additional prizes may be made by personal donation of individuals or companies but are, as such, not part of the official WOODWORKER show award schedule.

COMPETITION CLASSES

CABINET MAKING

WA1 Furniture: Any piece of work of any size and style. Finish to entrants' choice.

These may be individual pieces such as dining or card table, display cabinet, armchair, etc., each of which would represent one entry.

If, however, the exhibit were to be a dining suite, a maximum of three entries may be made: entry would be accepted on the following basis: dining chair — one entry; dining table — one entry; carver chair — one entry.

WOODTURNING

WC1 Any piece of spindle turning, or set of pieces.
WC2 Any example of face plate turning including laminated work.
WC3 Any segmental turned item.

MUSICAL INSTRUMENTS

WD1 Any wind instrument.
WD2 Any string instrument.

MODEL HORSE-DRAWN VEHICLES

WG1 Any farm cart or waggon or agricultural implement, drawn by horses, or horse-drawn vehicles for industrial purposes such as brewers' dray, coal cart, delivery vehicle etc.
WG2 Any caravan, coach, carriage or horse-drawn vehicle used for passenger transport (public and private).
WG3 Any horse-drawn vehicle made up from a kit. Horses that are carved or modelled or made in ceramics may be included with the exhibit but they will be disregarded in judging.

WOODCARVING

Exhibits in this class may be coloured using conventional water- or spirit-based woodstains and may be finished using a clear transparent sealer if desired, but no opaque paints or finishes may be applied.

WB1 Architectural: Any piece of architectural carving such as fireplace surround panel, church carving. A complete fireplace surround (three panels) would represent three entries.
WB2 Figure carving: Any sculpture not more than 24in. high. Abstract forms will not be acceptable neither will, for example, polished branch or driftwood. The forms must be fully representational.
WB3 Relief carving: Any subject, overall size not to exceed 18 × 12in.

MARQUETRY AND INLAY

WE1 Any marquetry picture of any subject.
WE2 Any miniature marquetry picture of any subject, size 3 × 3in.
WE3 Any piece of inlay work such as decorative top to a box or table.

TOYS

WF1 Toys made in solid timber or wood-based sheet material.

JUNIOR SECTION

WH1 Any item of woodwork made by a junior under the age of 18 on 1 November 1980.

CLOCKS

WJ1 Longcase clocks.
WJ2 Bracket clocks.

Royal Horticultural Society's New Hall
4-9 November, 1980

Royal Horticultural Society's New Hall, London SW1 — 4-9 November inclusive (10.00am to 7.00pm each day)

COMPETITION RULES:
All correspondence and entry forms to: P. D. Freebrey, Exhibitions Manager, Model and Allied Publications Ltd, PO Box 35 Bridge Street, Hemel Hempstead HP1 1EE.

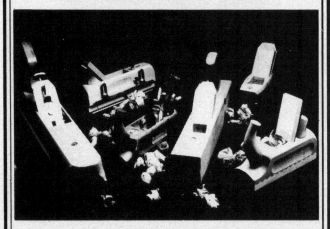

322

Prices quoted are those prevailing at press date and are subject to alteration due to economic conditions.

Woodworker, May 1980

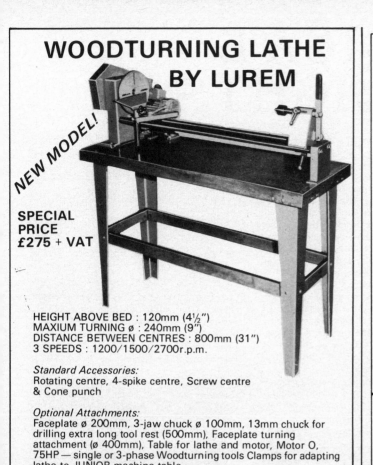

MUSICAL HIGHLIGHTS

A 'Celebration of Skills' was the theme chosen by this year's Ideal Home Exhibition to herald the new decade. Traditional skills and craftsmanship were seen flourishing alongside new technological skills that will change all our lives.

The Skills in Action Pavilion was a major feature designed to show how some traditional skills are surviving in the 80s. Exhibitors included the Embroiderers' Guild, the Royal College of Art silversmithing and jewellery students, the Canterbury Company of Stained Glass Craftsmen, the British Model Soldier Society and students from the London College of Furniture.

These latter were making stringed and woodwind instruments. At the college they learn the skills involved in making instruments as varied as lutes and harpsichords. The LCF, as it is affectionately known, is situated in the unfashionable East End of London. It is not far from old dockland into which once poured precious raw materials which the college craftsmen, like their predecessors in the furniture trade, use in the many sided craft of woodworking.

Putting aside commerce, the East End is probably the craft capital of Europe, if not the world and the LCF has been part of that scene since its establishment during the last century. Even the college's output of qualified students has an effect on the area too. Many have set up their workshops within the vicinity of the LCF and are now running thriving concerns.

The origins of the LCF go back to around 1889 when the college was originally created to provide further education for operatives in the furniture industry. By 1959, the college was rapidly surging ahead, as probably, one of Britain's key educational establishments for musical instrument making. At that time the accent was very

much on violins and general stringed instruments.

The Department of Musical Instrument Technology now deals, as the name implies, with the making of a great variety of instruments of all kinds. The department is concerned with providing education in musical instrument technology by full-time, block release, part-time day and evening courses. The range of studies is broad and covers keyboard, fretted and bowed stringed instruments as well as woodwind and electronic musical instruments. The department has well-equipped workshops for instrument making and electronics laboratories equipped with musical synthesizers and a harmonic analyser as well as a comprehensive range of test gear related to electronic musical instruments and the relevant ancillary equipment.

There are piano tuning cubicles expressly designed for that purpose ensuring adequate facilities for prospective piano tuners. There is also an electronic music studio.

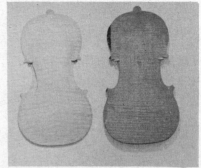

For further details of the college and the various courses offered write to the head of the department: P. L. Shirtcliff CIMIT, London College of Furniture, 41/71 Commercial Road, London E1 1LA (phone 01-247 1953).

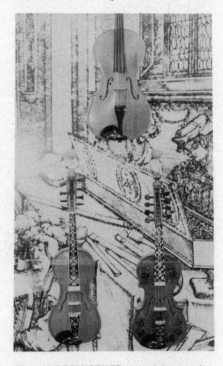

When WOODWORKER visited the stand at the Ideal Home Exhibition, Malcolm Parrish, a 4th year diploma student was busy making a hardanger. Malcolm has already completed the three-year course in violin making at the college and became very interested in the highly decorative hardanger. With a local education authority grant to support him he has spent a month of his diploma year in Norway studying the instrument which he says is usually made in maple and pine with traditional patterns in shell, mother of pearl and occasionally ivory decorating the neck and scroll regions.

Malcolm had two hardangers on display incorporating his own decorative patterns. He hopes to find employment in this country or in Norway making these beautiful instruments when he leaves the college in July.

Malcolm Parrish making a hardanger at the London College of Furniture stand in the Skills in Action Pavilion. Two of Malcolm's finished hardangers can be seen in the picture above.

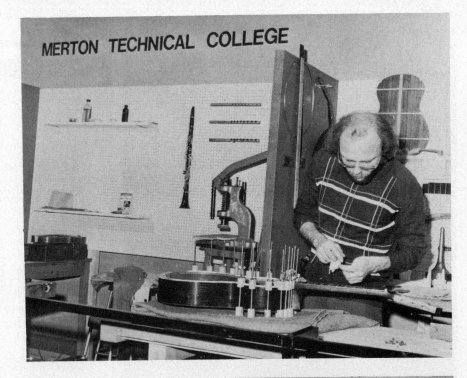

MERTON TECHNICAL COLLEGE

Other instruments on display included a piano and various woodwinds.

Part-time courses in musical instrument technology (woodwind, brass, strings and organ) are being offered from September by Merton Technical College, Merton Park, London Road, Merton, Surrey. Duration is one full day a week per specialism for a minimum of one academic year.

WOODWORKER understands that applicants must be over 18 at the start of the course and ideally will have successfully completed a course leading to a recognised qualification in musical instrument crafts. Those having other craft qualifications or experience and an interest in musical instruments will be required to satisfy the college authorities of well above average craft ability, for example by showing recently personally-

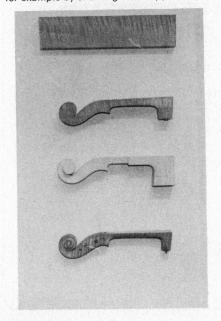

made relevant workpieces. Applicants will be interviewed at the college prior to acceptance and should bring examples of recently completed work.

Students work individually in the musical instrument workshops under the overall supervision of P. Chambers, the lecturer-in-charge. They will be able to call upon the

expertise of specialist instructors as required. The timetable is:

Monday: brass and organ;
Tuesday woodwind, non-fretted strings;
Thursday: woodwind, fretted strings;
Friday: brass, non-fretted strings.

Repair and restoration is covered, with making of fretted and non-fretted strings.

Merton Technical College has been offering courses in musical instrument technology since 1972 and the two-year full-time course leads to the City & Guilds certificate in musical instrument repair. The course is general and as such gives a broad training in the basic repair of most classes of instrument, chiefly woodwind and brass, with both fretted and non-fretted strings. A student

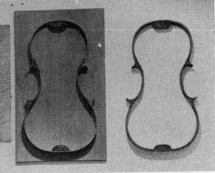

completing the course is expected to reach such a standard that he (or she) could work competently and efficiently in a general musical instrument repair workshop. There is an opportunity to work with pipe organs and certain small keyboard instruments but piano work is not part of this course.

The college was newly built in 1971 and in its open-plan workshops almost all the equipment, tools and materials used for work in this field have been provided. Tuition is in groups of about 10 students; many of the instructors have their own workshops and businesses in the musical instrument repair trade.

Further details of the courses at Merton can be had on application to D. S. Tulloch MSc who is head of the Department of General Education & Science.

In Wales the School of Musical Instrument Making & Repair offers a three-year course in stringed instrument making and repair and a two-year course in piano tuning and repair. The courses emphasise practical work but include theory and various related studies: toolmaking, acoustics, drawing, instrumental tuition, history and business studies. The workshops are well equipped, though students are advised to try and build up their own collection of tools during the courses. Wood and other materials are supplied by the School which is part of the Ystrad Mynach College of Further Education.

Details are available from the principal, School of Musical Instrument Making & Repair, Thomas Street, Abertridwr, Caerphilly, Mid Glamorgan.

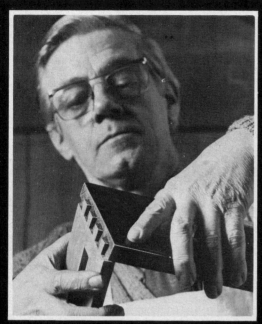

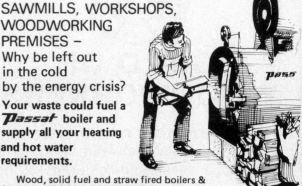
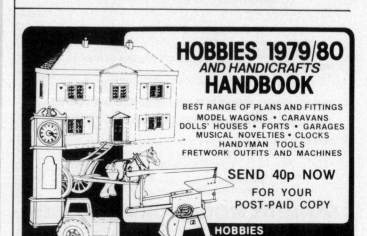
328   Prices quoted are those prevailing at press date and are subject to alteration due to economic conditions.

Woodworker, May 1980

Steam bending

From: D. J. Parsons, Dronfield, Sheffield

I would appreciate some advice on steaming and bending yew. The section I need to bend is approximately 1¼in. sq and 4ft 6in. long. I have a 3in. diameter pipe with one end blanked off and I can get a good boiling action with a wood fire underneath and this lasts about 2hr on a 5ft length. I have tried a piece of dry timber which went rather black on the outside after 2hr though inside colour was satisfactory. However, the piece would not bend to the required shape. Would green timber be more satisfactory? I want to bend the timber for making a Windsor chair back.

The wood of a yew tree *(Taxus baccata.* L.) although botanically a softwood species can, like most of the English hardwoods, be bent to the inverted U-shape required in the bow back of a Windsor chair. Indeed, yew was a wood much favoured by the old chairmakers for this very purpose. Often it seems they used yew in the round, that is straight grown, coppice-like poles having a diameter a little over the required section to which the bent piece would later be trimmed.

Alternatively the yew might be cleft along the grain from straight poles of larger diameter. Mostly the wood was green, ie unseasoned when bent. In this state it would be bent cold or, more successfully, after being subjected to heat treatment by means of boiling or steaming.

Bending yew cut from sawn boards presents a number of problems. Yew is a very slow growing tree and its stems are often deeply fissured. As a consequence knots and other defects such as twisted grain and ingrown bark are often present in sawn boards which make successful bending almost impossible.

All wood for bending must be straight grained and free from even the smallest defects. And, again speaking in general terms, green wood bends well but so does timber air-dried down to a moisture content (m.c.) of about 25%. Kiln-dried stuff is generally too dry for successful bending.

The question of whether to boil or steam wood for bending is one of those problems to which everyone has a different answer and no one answer is really incorrect. The object of both is to *heat* the wood to the boiling point temperature (100°C). Total immersion in water is not necessary and does often lead to staining and discolouration of the wood as you have experienced. I prefer to steam as this presents fewer technical problems in actually applying the required heat to the wood, less discolouration; and the drying-out time of the finished bend is much reduced also.

Therefore, may I suggest that the 3in. pipe would be better employed as a steam tube rather than as a boiler. The wood for bending should be hung inside from a loose-fitting lid through which excess steam can escape.

Using water inside the blanked-off pipe depends upon whether there would be sufficient capacity below the wood for bending to maintain the steaming temperature for up to 1½hr (which is the time required for material of 1¼in. square section). If not the tube could be connected to an external boiler (such as a large kettle) by means of a short length of rubber pipe. Or an open-ended pipe could be fitted over a suitable boiler, the tube with the wood inside thus forming a sort of chimney through which the steam has to pass. It might be found necessary to lag the pipe in order to maintain the required temperature.

Finally, remember it is heat which softens the wood fibres and makes them bendable. Therefore no time should be lost between getting the steamed piece out of the steamer and round the former. If it is allowed to cool too much the bend will almost certainly fail. And failures are not uncommon when bending wood so don't despair if you spoil a few in the process of making your chair!

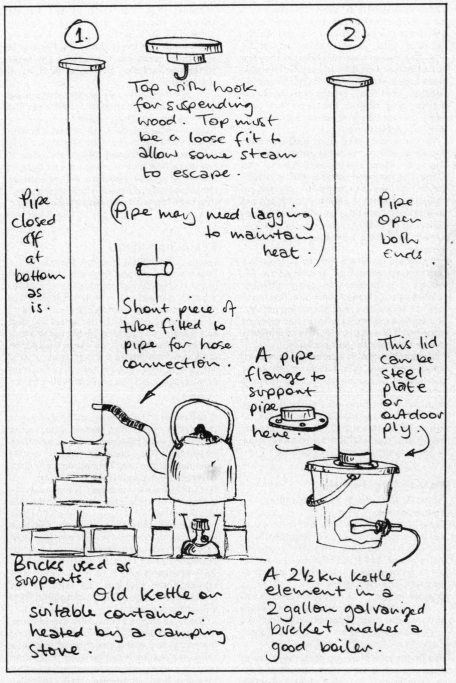

① Pipe closed off at bottom as is.

Top with hook for suspending wood. Top must be a loose fit to allow some steam to escape.

(Pipe may need lagging to maintain heat.)

Short piece of tube fitted to pipe for hose connection.

A pipe flange to support pipe here.

Bricks used as supports.

Old kettle on suitable container heated by a camping stove.

② Pipe open both ends.

This lid can be steel plate or outdoor ply.

A 2½kw kettle element in a 2 gallon galvanized bucket makes a good boiler.

Stained ceiling

From: J. A. Foster, Bellanaleck, Northern Ireland

I stained a t & g ceiling with Sadolins dark oak and applied one coat of matt clear varnish. But the ceiling is much darker than I want and I have tried sanding it. However it is a large ceiling and the sander keeps clogging-up.

Could you please advise if there is an easy method of removing the varnish by either machine or chemical stripper; or if there is a treatment I could apply either to bleach or lighten the colour of the stain; or could I apply a lighter stain to the existing one (after having first removed the varnish)?

Your problem is a difficult one. Short of taking down the ceiling, turning it over and starting again, there is no suitable method of restoring its natural lightness. Formulations such as Sadolins PX65 are produced really for external wood cladding where the exposure might be severe. Accordingly, the pigmented stain is designed not only to penetrate deep into the wood but for the salts to become 'fixed' and to resist all solvents, acids and alkalis.

Oxalic acid, caustic soda or similar bleaches are not recommended as they are not effective against the resins and pigment contained in the formulation and, in addition, they may, unless completely removed, give rise to problems due to a chemical reaction with subsequent stain or lacquer applications.

We have discussed your problem with Sadolins which confirms what we say. The firm's recommendations are that the varnish be removed using Sadolins Hydrosolver, or similar chemical stripper, in conjunction with a Skarsten scraper; and then to try to sand the wood back using an initial cut of a P60 grade abrasive and final cut with a P120 grade abrasive to remove the stain.

We would go along with this except we can foresee difficulties at the joints. Although it is possible to apply different colours over a cleaned-back one, this is not very attractive as a rule, appearing patchy. You could experiment with an odd piece of wood but it seems to us there is no straightforward answer to your problem.

You could possibly overlay the darkened wood with very thin matching placed at right angles or diagonally (if the joists will bear the additional weight without sagging), finishing-off with a clear polyurethane type matt or gloss varnish; or you could do this if you removed the dark ceiling and replaced it after cleaning it up by sanding or reversing the boards.

Making finger-joints

From: Dr Malcolm F. Fuller, Kintore, Aberdeenshire
Could you please advise on methods of making finger-joints to join long lengths of timber? I have seen how neat and strong the result is and had thought of doing it with a jigsaw followed by a router, using a guide or template. Do you think this method is feasible (in $\frac{7}{8}$ in. thick hardwood) and do you know if such templates are available? I seem to have seen them for dovetailing. The long lengths are required for the rails of a boat.

The finger-joint that you describe is one of a number of splicing joints developed for the lengthening of timber stock and in this instance originally applied to veneer splicing.

With the ever-increasing need to economise on solid timber usage commercial finger-jointing machines are now available for the manufacture, for instance, of skirting boards from short ends; and there are many other such non-structural applications. The timbers so joined possess about 75% of the original strength. One such machine is made by Ladbourne Engineering Ltd, Phoenix Works, Star Street, Ware, Herts, and marketed through C. D. Monninger Ltd, Overbury Road, London N15 6RJ. It is also possible to buy solid profiling blocks to fit on a spindle moulder which will produce the same result. These are available in different sizes to accommodate various widths of stock and are supplied by Monninger.

We are not aware of any commercial templates for use with the hand router to make a finger-joint but see no reason why one should not be made up for the purpose mentioned in your enquiry. Hardboard of $\frac{1}{8}$ in. thickness or Tufnol plastics would be suitable, with the ends of the fingers equalling the radius of the router cutter employed. A 1 in 12 gradient would be appropriate for the slope of the fingers. In $\frac{7}{8}$ in. thick hardwood it would be advisable to take several step cuts to avoid burning the cutter.

In commercial machines the stock to be cut is 'packeted' together; in the case of a hand-produced finger-joint it would be best to machine each piece individually. Needless to say the template must be made with extreme accuracy. As you suggest it would be best to remove the waste first on a band or jigsaw, cutting a V-piece out on the waste side of the joint line before accurate profiling with the template and router.

Restoring a floor

From: C. P. Burges, Exeter, Devon
I have softwood board floor in the kitchen of about 100 sq ft which needs to be restored to a clean natural state. It is unfinished at present and is dark and soiled with wear. I could use a drill with flapwheel or disc attachment, an orbital or a barrel sander but wonder whether or not these would be sufficient to penetrate the ingrained surface. Any advice that you can give on restoration or a durable finishing process would be appreciated.

A softwood board floor is ranked as solvent tolerant as opposed to certain other forms which are water tolerant. It is essential to remember this because warm water, especially when used in conjunction with a detergent and vigorous scrubbing, will tend progressively to break down the wood surface. Any initial cleaning must take this into account.

You could lightly mop the wood surface with a damp mop to take off any fine dust or you could use a floor sweeping compound made up from 38 to 45% sawdust, 25% fine sand and 5 to 12% water contained in the sawdust and sand; or you could obtain a proprietary compound from a flooring company.

The next step is to consider the removal of ingrained dirt. This can be done by hand (kneeling) and doing a section of floor at a time, or a machine can be used. But either way, if the dirt is badly ingrained a special cleaning fluid should be used. This also could be obtained from a flooring company, a typical formulation being made up from white spirit, gum spirits of turpentine and oil of mirbane (nitrobenzene).

At this point we must mention cleaning pads; although nylon or steel wool pads can be used, for domestic work small, round, nylon pads are best. These come in a variety of sizes and types: thick, circular pads for commercial polishing machines, and thin and smaller pads for household polishers. The main types are: (a) coarse, used for stripping built-up polish off floors; (b) medium, used for general maintenance work; and (c) fine, used for burnishing.

To clean the ingrained dirt a little cleaning fluid should be placed on the floor (a small section at a time) and with either a coarse or medium nylon pad, by hand or machine, the wood should be worked in the direction of the grain. The dirty cleaning fluid should be wiped off frequently and the process repeated until the floor is satisfactorily clean. Incidentally, a good cleaning fluid will not remove paint from wood skirtings. When this has been done sufficient time must be allowed for the cleaning fluid to evaporate, about 48hr as a rule, and the floor surface should be protected from traffic during this time.

A further sanding with a medium nylon brush on the machine may be necessary, but once the floor is clean and smooth it can be finished. There are various ways of doing this: A wax finish could be applied, a solid paste wax is rubbed into any worn or roughened patches by hand, allowed to dry and then polished by machine with hard brushes only. This process is repeated three or four times with a rub over with 00 sandpaper between coats before more wax is applied all over and polished, again sanding lightly between coats. When the whole area has been gone over a number of times in different directions with the brushes on the polisher (and left overnight for the wax to harden), the medium nylon pads should be fixed to a mechanical polisher and the whole floor polished to and fro a number of times.

This type of finish needs little upkeep. In fact too much wax afterwards will only build up and collect dirt. The axiom to be followed is infrequent wax sparingly applied. The alternative is to apply by hand using a brush, a plastics-type floor seal, eg Ronseal in matt, semi-matt or gloss.

With all synthetic floor seals their success depends upon proper preparation of the floor initially, with subsequent maintenance of the film. You could use the orbital sander but you would probably make a better job by borrowing a floor sander with nylon pads from your local flooring company.

The Charnley forest stone

From: G. A. Taylor, Billingham, Co Cleveland
I was very interested in the article on sharpening stones in the December 1979 issue and wonder if you could describe the appearance of the Charnley forest stone in its undressed and dressed state. Could you also say how this stone is dressed and with what tools?

The stone itself is of rare occurrence, being formed of a type of solidified volcanic ash known as Harnstone. This word is a corruption of Honestone. The Charnley forest varies from a dirty, dark green colour to a rosey hue and is hard and finely textured.

An unflawed lump can best be dressed to the familiar oilstone shape with a masonry saw (such as builders use for cutting bricks etc). A final accurate working surface can then be obtained by rubbing with a coarse then fine carborundum brick using water as a lubricant.

The cutting quality of the stone will only be discovered in use. If, with a light oil, the sharpening seems to be inordinately slow, substitute water as a lubricant, being mindful that Charnley forests although excellent, were notorious for their slow action.

We are indebted to H. P. Powell of the University Museum at Oxford for certain geological information contained in this reply.

A -- Z OF HAND TOOLS

In the February issue John Sainsbury dealt with dowel bits and here he describes the draw knife (sometimes called drawing knife or draw shave) and the hand drill. His next article will be about dowel jigs which are increasingly popular these days.

Wherever possible in this series references have been made in general terms as regards manufacturers' products.

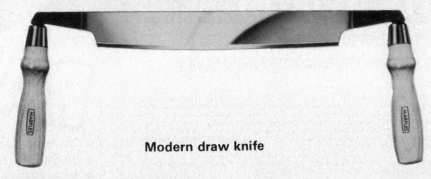

Modern draw knife

Sometimes called drawing knife or draw shave, this tool is in many forms some of which have been in existence for 2000 years. A smaller range is presently seen. The tool consists of a flat blade up to 18in. in length, bevelled on its forward edge with tangs bent at 90° and passed through the handles to be rivetted over a small steel washer.

Draw knives are used with the bevel side up for roughing work, bevel side down for more skilled applications and drawn toward the user. They were varied in shape and size to suit many trades and often used in conjunction with a shaving horse, where the action of sitting served to hold the timber firmly in place.

Draw knives for mastmakers, hoopmakers, coachbuilders, saddle tree makers, shipwrights, coopers and wheelwrights, all carried variations of shape and size. These were added to with American, French and Spanish patterns.

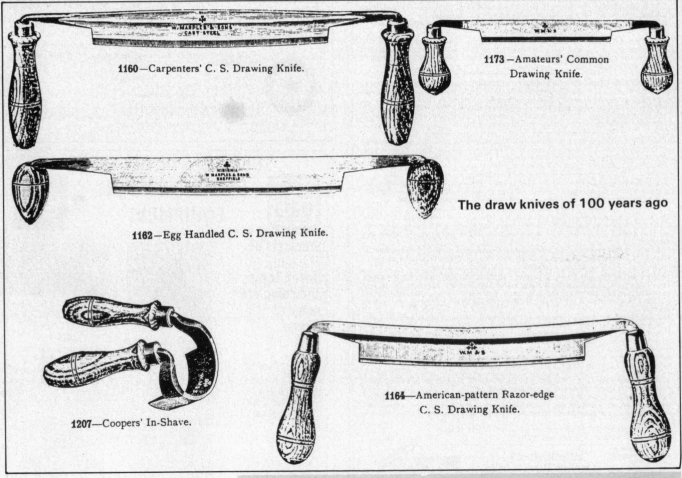

1160—Carpenters' C. S. Drawing Knife.

1173—Amateurs' Common Drawing Knife.

1162—Egg Handled C. S. Drawing Knife.

The draw knives of 100 years ago

1207—Coopers' In-Shave.

1164—American-pattern Razor-edge C. S. Drawing Knife.

Hand Drill

The hand drill is a tool more usually associated with the metalworker, but one often resorted to by the woodworker when the need for small holes arises. These drills usually have a three-jaw self-centring chuck which is actuated by a geared wheel and two pinions. Engineers jobbers drill bits up to $5/16$in. are used. The drill has a side handle; its back handle can usually be unscrewed and repositioned to convert the drill to a pistol grip.

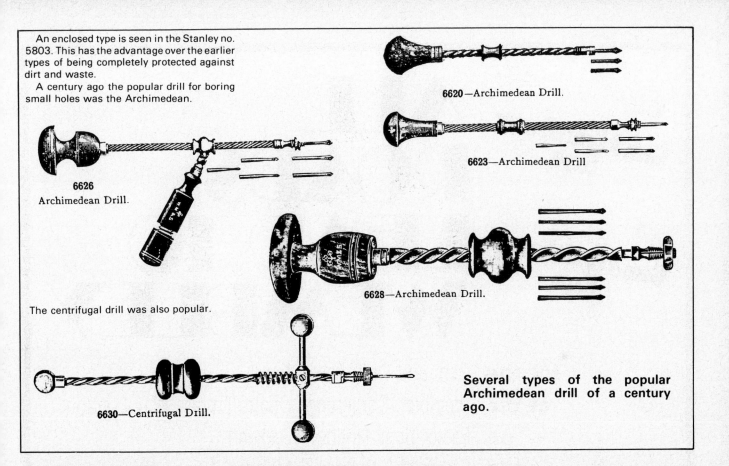

An enclosed type is seen in the Stanley no. 5803. This has the advantage over the earlier types of being completely protected against dirt and waste.

A century ago the popular drill for boring small holes was the Archimedean.

6626
Archimedean Drill.

The centrifugal drill was also popular.

6630—Centrifugal Drill.

6620—Archimedean Drill.

6623—Archimedean Drill

6628—Archimedean Drill.

Several types of the popular Archimedean drill of a century ago.

FROM MILLSTONE GRIT TO CARBORUNDUM

R. W. Grant traces developments in the techniques of putting the edge on cutting tools

Use of grinding as a technique in engineering for shaping metals is now well established but formerly grindstones were solely used for the preparation of edge tools. It is in this role that the woodworker still has an interest in them.

For centuries the Millstone Grit moors of the Pennines have been the site of the quarrying of suitable sandstone to make grinding stones where the occurrence of grains of angular silica within the sandstone make the substance ideal for cutting metal. Throughout this area during the 17th century the manufacture of grindstones and the use of the coarser beds for millstones became a flourishing business. It is recorded that grindstones were one of the principal exports of Tyneside while the area around Sheffield also became famous and took on a national importance; doubtless in more remote areas such as the Forest of Dean and parts of Wales, where suitable stones could be found, local needs were met from these sources.

The honey-coloured stones from Yorkshire were claimed to be the finest obtainable. Those from Derbyshire had the reputation of being somewhat coarser but harder, often having a blue tinge to them and the name Derby Blue may still be remembered by an older generation of woodworkers.

The introduction around 1850 of artificial grindstones using emery and corendum not only spelt the death knell of many of those bleak moorland industrial sites but accelerated the development of all sorts of grinding

machines, culminating with the introduction of an American universal grinder in 1876. In this most of the features of modern grinders were incorporated. The durability and cutting power of manufactured grinding wheels was greatly improved by the innovation in 1891 of A. E. Acheson's carborundum wheel. This name he gave to artificially produced silicon carbide which is formed by the reaction of coke and silica sand at very high temperatures. Thus, grinding by the early 1900s had become an important engineering process.

Nevertheless, not all quarrying was finished off in the Pennines and there is still a demand for the natural stones, the Kirkwood Brown being among the most notable. These grindstones should be treated with care and will produce excellent results on modern tool steels with the stone running in a trough of cooling water and turning at about 95rpm for an 18in. stone. This steady abrasion of the cooled metal will obviate any tendency to 'burn' the most delicate of edge tools.

The stone should never be left standing partly immersed in water as this will inevitably soften the material while, conversely, a stone left standing in the open (like the old-fashioned hand-cranked grindstones often seen outside the country workshops of yesteryear) will become hard and lose its cut. A stone that loses its concentricity or becomes grooved by the grinding of narrow tools and gouges in one spot can easily be trued and resurfaced by holding a coarse grade carborundum rubbing brick against the running stone.

Modern high-speed grinding wheels really have little place in the amateur woodworker's shop; the attractiveness of a quick result seductively easily done on a bench

grinder often in reality means overheating the tool and drawing the fine temper of the cutting edge thereby rendering it useless for further work. Frequent dipping in water is often advised to cool the edge, but just as frequently the overheating occurs the instant before the tool can be plunged into the relieving coolant.

However, there are manufacturers who make excellent grinding machines for the woodworker using both silicon carbide and aluminium oxide wheels. A feature of a number of these machines is that the wheel is mounted horizontally and the grinding is done on the flat of the wheel with the revolutions considerably reduced and a stream of coolant constantly provided. The addition of a holding jig for the tools is another useful item that ensures a correct grinding bevel being maintained. It is also possible to obtain conical grinding 'points' for the grinding of scribing gouges.

There is now a bewildering complexity of artificial grinding materials and wheels (many of which have been developed for specific purposes); a universal coding system for identifying abrasive agent, grit-size, structure and bonding material is in use. There are also important factors to be considered in the mounting, balancing and trueing of high-speed wheels, while safety aspects are covered by the Abrasive Wheels Regulations 1970. Those readers who wish to delve deeper into these aspects of the subject will find comprehensive information in a booklet obtainable from Norton Abrasives Ltd, Welwyn Garden City, Hertfordshire.

WOODWORKER is indebted to H. P. Powell of the University Museum, Oxford, for verifying certain geological information about natural grindstones mentioned in this article.

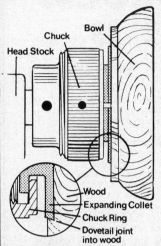

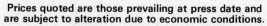

Letters

From: J. E. Durey, Kenterprise Ltd, Tunbridge Wells, Kent
Dear Sir,

I had a number of mahogany button-shaped ornaments about 1⅜ in. × ⅜ in. to turn for an antique dealer. Each required a dowel on the back ⁵⁄₁₆ × ½ in. long for fixing like a drawer knob. My usual way of tackling these had been by turning up a number of blanks in a row, only finishing the dowel part a little oversize and tapered. Then with a piece of wood on the screw chuck drilled to take the peg I could, with care, execute the work, relying on friction.

This time, however, the things kept skidding. (I have had collet chucks on order for a long time as these provide a complete answer to this type of work).

An idea came: Acquire a ½ in. bolt only partially threaded, cut off the head and leave about 1 in. of the unthreaded portion for the chuck to grip. I was fortunate in having a second chuck which I put in the tailstock with a ⁵⁄₁₆ in. HSS twist bit. Then with my Coronet Major on its slowest speed I drilled right through the length of the piece of bolt, a matter of about 2 in. o/a.

Removing the piece of bolt from the chuck I put it upright in the vice and with a hacksaw cut right across the centre down ⅝ in. I quarter-turned it in the vice and again cut down ⅝ in. This divided the threaded part into four equal portions. I then screwed a nut on as far as it would go.

The home-made collet now being ready I put it into the chuck on the headstock. Having pushed the dowel of one of the button-shaped ornaments into the quartered aperture I used a spanner to tighten the nut. This had the effect of clamping the button firmly in place — and there was room to work all around it.

It has been so successful that I intend making smaller ones in the same way. Larger bolts would need to have a shank reduced to fit anything above the chuck capacity.

By the way, drilling right through the bolt allows any work that will not pull out easily after the nut has been moved to be driven through from the rear.

Yours faithfully,   J. E. Durey

From: H. Nicholas, Wymondham, Norfolk
Dear Sir,

Some time ago a friend asked me to repair an ebony hand mirror. I have tried to find out how it was actually constructed but in spite of the fact that it was made in Wymondham many years ago I have been unable to get any information. I thought that if I could find out how the glass is put into the frame in the first place, this would help.

Perhaps readers may be able to give some suggestions.

Yours faithfully, H. Nichols

From: V. J. L. Weeks, Cirencester, Gloucestershire
Dear Sir,

As the only impractical carpenter in my family, I was asked to build a strong toybox for my one-year-old grandson. I agreed. As the measurements were written down for purchasing the timber, I thought that as a toybox is usually empty all day I would include a daytime use for it. A rocking horse seemed to be the best idea.

I designed and built the box in the simplest way I could, ie with 6 and 10mm ply and various hardwood beadings and quarterings that are readily available even in a small country town. The horse's head was cut with a jigsaw from 10mm ply and let into the front sliding part of the lid and strengthened with an extra wood surround at the base. All joints were glued as well as being fastened with brads or screws.

The box was well sanded and two coats of polyurethane varnished brushed on, giving a durable and easily-cleaned surface inside and out. The padding and covering of the horse's head was beautifully done by a member of the crafts section of the local Townswomen's Guild.

It gave me pleasure that the toy was acclaimed both by my grandson and his parents and I thought these details might interest other readers who, like myself, find difficulty in making desks, sofa tables and other pieces with joints needing patience and skill.

Yours faithfully,   V. J. L. Weeks

From: H. H. Bridge, Southport, Merseyside
Dear Sir,

Having read the letters from D. Tasker and D. S. Cotter on page 92 of the February issue I am reminded of the words of a well-known conductor interviewed on radio recently. Having said he would most likely settle finally

in the United States, he was asked why? 'Because its a ''yes'' country,' he replied.

I lived in Canada for a couple of years and remember going on a job-finding course sponsored by the government. It emerged that the best way to find a job was to knock on doors. I guess its the same here and might well work for Mr Cotter in his search for premises.

I suggest that he studies a large-scale OS map beforehand and notes any small buildings behind other premises. If his area is as rich in them as is this part of the world, he could be lucky.

A lot of money has gone to the Arts Council in years past for what I can only describe as 'mucking about'. I only hope that the different attitude and realism of the present administration at Whitehall will result in encouragement for more worthwhile forms of individual and corporate effort. We should be lobbying on behalf of those like Mr Tasker and Mr Cotter, especially in view of the budget.

Might I offer an extra word of encouragement to Mr Tasker: At Samlesbury Hall a few months ago I met a successful violin maker. He was trained as an engineer. In east Lancashire some time later I met a successful furniture maker. Seven years ago he was a mill manager in one of our cotton towns.

Perhaps we can make Britain a 'yes' country and lobby for the money — and move away from the pessimism that so many have felt for so long.

Yours faithfully,   H. H. Bridge

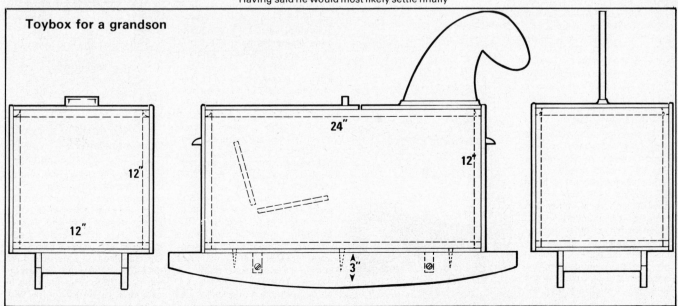

Toybox for a grandson

24"

12"

12"

12"

12"

3"

New 17-37 lathe
from Chepstow
Woodturners Ltd.

Lathe for skilled amateurs

Newly established company Chepstow Woodturners Ltd, 8 Rowan Drive, Chepstow NP6 5RQ (029-12 6641), with John Stamford as managing director, is manufacturing what it describes as a large diameter lathe designed to meet the needs of the skilled amateur turner. Known as the 17-37 it has a turning diameter up to 17in. and a 37in. maximum between centres and can be stand or bench mounted.

It has five-speed operation: 3325, 2300, 1600, 730 and 530rpm and the sealed-for-life deep-groove thrust bearings securely housed in the headstock castings are claimed to give a vibration-free operation. Need for maintenance or adjustment of these bearings is obviated and no damage can be caused to the machine through forgetfulness or continuous high-speed running, states the maker.

Essential parts of the lathe are in cast metal and the bed is of solid 1in. cold-rolled steel bars supported on a 1in. steel hollow section with the gap bed.

Before joining Chepstow Woodturners Mr Stamford was sales manager of Kity (UK); he has had many years' experience in marketing woodworking machinery.

Start button on saw

Model 082-2 is a 7¼in. portable circular saw powered by a 1 2/3hp motor operating at 5200rpm and selling at approximately £56.48 (VAT extra). The blade is fitted with an external clutch and standard equipment includes blade wrench and 3¼in. faced rip fence guide. From Craftsman Tools Division of Hagemeyer (London) Ltd, 25-33 Southwark Street, London SE1 1RQ (01-403 0680), the saw is said to be capable of cutting timber to a depth of 2¼in. at 90° or up to 1¹⁵⁄₁₆in. at 45°.

It is provided with blade and swing guards with a rear position sawdust chute and blower to clear the cutting line. A 'non-accidental' start button is fitted into the left-hand side of the handgrip and is an additional control to the standard on/off trigger switch on other models, states Hagemeyer. Before the motor can be started the start button must be depressed firmly. Otherwise it is impossible to pull the trigger switch into the 'on' position.

Timber seasoning

Suitable for drying approximately 250cu ft of timber, the Minor dehumidifier is the latest production of Ebac Ltd, Greenfields Industrial Estate, Bishop Auckland, Co Durham (0388 5061). It supplements the smaller capacity Mini model and is intended for small businesses. Weighing 70kg the machine is 530 x 1087mm high. It will dry most European hardwoods, states Ebac, and works by removing moisture from the atmosphere. By enclosing the timber in a chamber with the dehumidifier (power consumption 1.5kW), a drying cycle is set up which is natural and controllable. Running costs are said to be low.

Price of the Ebac Minor is given as £626 ex-works. Full details are available on application to the company at the address given above.

The Ebac Minor.

Angle drilling

The Hico precision drill guide that can be used with most domestic power drills is said to give 90° as well as angle drilling, edge drilling, hole saw drilling and drilling round stock. It can be used for smaller routing jobs, shaping and sanding. In conjunction with the guide there is a range of 10 shaper bits which can be used with power drills at speeds under 4,000rpm. Hico is introduced by Filegold Ltd, 243-45 Horn Lane, Acton, London W3 9ED (01-993 4242), which has produced an illustrated leaflet describing and illustrating the uses to which the guide can be put; the leaflet includes a chart of drilling angles from 45 — 80°. Recommended retail selling price £8.99 including VAT.

Filegold has also introduced the Hico power screwdriver attachment with built-in depth adjustment to give a choice of eight different depth settings. It takes screws with shank diameters from 2.9 to 5mm and head diameters up to 9.5mm. It can be used in reverse action and is complete with slot bit and Philips cross-recess bit. The attachment is said to be suitable for use with softwood and plywood without pre-drilling and with hardwood when round-head screws are required. Pre-drillling is required with hardwood when using countersunk screws. RRSP is £12.99 including VAT.

Another item is the Hico drill press stand which can be used in the horizontal position for grinding, polishing and disc sanding. It incorporates a swing-away tilt table, 18in. tubular steel column with throat depth of 4½in. The 6 × 6in. cast aluminium base has holes for bench mounting. 90° and angle drilling is possible, also routing, and the stand accepts most ¼in. (6mm), ⅜in. (10mm) and ½in. (13mm) electric drills. RRSP is £19.99 including VAT.

In addition to the illustrated leaflet Filegold has produced a well-illustrated spiral bound instruction manual for all the items mentioned above.

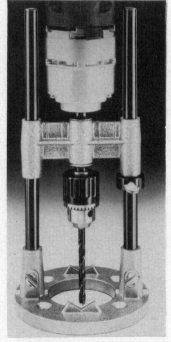

Mini-bandsaw

Powerline Mini-bandsaw said to cut regular or irregular shapes in hardwood, softwood and other materials up to 76.2mm (3in.) in thickness, has been selected by Design Council for the Design Centre in London. It has been designed by Burgess Power Tools Ltd, Sapcote, Leicester LE9 6JW (045-527 2292), and is now in full production. The machine is additional to the Powerline BK1 and BK2 two-speed bandsaws.

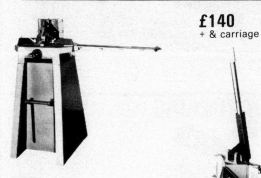
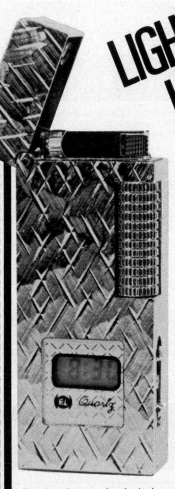

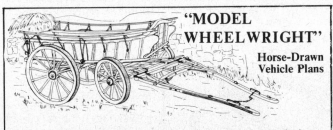

"MODEL WHEELWRIGHT"
Horse-Drawn Vehicle Plans

Would you like to build a model farm waggon, using the same methods as original craftsman? Such a project is much more satisfying than the assembly of plastic parts, and is within the capability of any competent modelmaker. My "Catalogue and Yearbook" gives all the advice needed to start the hobby and I recommend the Monmouthshire waggon (above) as a suitable first project. You can go on to build a collection of the many regional types.

Monmouthshire waggon plan in ⅛ scale, (five sheets), wheel construction chart and catalogue, £2.90 post free. Or send four first class stamps for catalogue only.

John Thompson, (Ref. WW), 1 Fieldway, Fleet, Hants.

DeWalt DW125 (10") Radial Arm Saw

Please write for our latest Price List!!

Please write for free leaflet and price list

Motor	240v
Cross Cut Cap	15"
Depth of Cut	2¾"
Ripping Cap	25"

COLIN M. GRANT LIMITED
33 Balmore Road, Glasgow G22 6RJ Tel: 041-336-8741

TOP QUALITY MODEL WHEELWRIGHT SUPPLIES

Build this splendid Olde English Stage Coach from our highly detailed plan or complete kit. Kit contains selected ply and Jelutong cut to section, plus pre-marked ply panels and templates. Over 80 difficult to make parts precision etched in solid brass, ready shaped axles, nuts, bolts, screws, pins, brass rod, strip, tube, cushion coverings, foam for seat padding, plus plan and instructions.

Stage Coach Plan only £4.33
Complete Kit £34.32
Solid brass fittings available separately £7.20

Our catalogue details complete range of products — over 60 plans of carts, waggons, carriages, plus David Wray's complete range including farm implements and windmill. Several complete kits, wooden wheels and wheel kits, hubs, axles, knave bonds, washers, brass strip, rod, tube, barrels, carriage lamps, harness accessories, horses, books, etc.

Illustrated catalogue: 50p; USA: $2.00 from:
BARRIE VOISEY PLANS (WW), 205 CITY ROAD, FENTON, STOKE ON TRENT, ST4 2SW ENGLAND

GORDON STOKES

★ Two-day intensive woodturning courses in rural workshop, cutting techniques, tool grinding, and points of difficulty for beginners.

★ Comprehensive woodturning courses in book form. Now very popular around the world. Illustrated, and with tutorial facility.

★ Professional woodturning tools, waxes, polishes, abrasives, calipers, dust masks, sealers, etc. Mail order a speciality.

★ *Books by Gordon Stokes:*
  Modern Woodturning, Woodturning for Pleasure, Beginner's Guide to Woodturning, Manual of Woodturning, Beginner's Guide to Power Tools, Toymaking in Wood, etc., etc.

Send 11p large s.a.e. for full details to:

Gordon Stokes, 202 The Hollow, Bath, Avon, or visit our showroom at 110A Mount Road, Whiteway, Bath.
Telephone: Bath 22617

No time like this present!

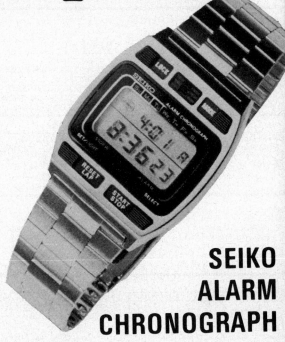

SEIKO ALARM CHRONOGRAPH

For the first time M.A.P. brings its readers a Seiko Alarm Chronograph for under £50. Just check the following super functions for value:

(i) Full time display including seconds
(ii) Calendar indicator showing day of week
(iii) Two part stop watch — function time, hours, minutes and seconds up to 20 hours and minutes, seconds and 1/100 secs. up to 20 mins.
(iv) Audio Alarm Function:
  (a) Can be set to operate any desired hour and minute
  (b) Time signal can be set to ring every hour on the hour

The Seiko Alarm Chronograph features a liquid crystal display. It is water and shock resistant, anti-magnetic and temperature stable through the normal range of 5°C-35°C. Battery life is approximately 2 years.

Price to readers £49.95 incl. V.A.T. P&P.

N.B. (i) Please make cheques, etc., payable to Model & Allied Publication Ltd.
(ii) Allow 21 days for delivery.
(iii) Goods found to be faulty will be replaced immediately.
(iv) Please add 20% to our Special Prices if outside the U.K. Delivery could be up to 8 weeks.

Model & Allied Publications Ltd.,
P.O. Box 35, Bridge St., Hemel Hempstead, Herts. HP1 1EE.

To: **Model & Allied Publications Ltd.**

Dept. EO,
13/35 BRIDGE STREET,
HEMEL HEMPSTEAD, HERTS.

Please supply .... SEIKO ALARM CHRONOGRAPH(S) for which I enclose cheque/postal order value ....
(Please write in BLOCK CAPITALS)

Name ....

Address ....

....

....

Barclaycard ☐ ☐ ☐ ☐ ☐ ☐ ☐ ☐ ☐ ☐ ☐ ☐ ☐ ☐ ☐ ☐

Signature .... WW

SHOP GUIDE

The quickest and easiest method of reaching all Woodworkers is to advertise in SHOP GUIDE.
Telephone Gill Dedman (0442) 41221 Ex. 241.
Rate: £5.00 per unit. Minimum of 6 months.
★ Mail Order

GREATER MANCHESTER

ST. HELENS   Tel. St. Helens
ROBERT KELLY   58672
5 BRIDGE STREET
Open: Mon.-Sat.
9.00-5.30 p.m.

MERSEYSIDE

LIVERPOOL   Tel: 051-709-5341
ROBERT KELLY
28/32 RENSHAW STREET
Open: Mon.-Sat.
9.00 a.m.-5.30 p.m.

AVON

BATH   Tel. Bath 22617
GORDON STOKES (office anytime)
WOODCRAFT SUPPLY   ★
110 MOUNT ROAD, WHITEWAY
Open: 9.30 a.m.-5.00 p.m.
Wednesday and Saturdays only

BRISTOL   Tel. (0272) 311510
JOHN HALL TOOLS LIMITED   ★
CLIFFTON DOWN SHOPPING
CENTRE, WHITELADIES ROAD
Open: Monday-Saturday
9.00 a.m.-5.30 p.m.

BRISTOL   Tel. 0272-629092
TRYMWOOD SERVICES   ★
2a DOWNS PARK EAST,
(off North View) WESTBURY PARK
Open: 9.00 a.m.-5.30 p.m.
Monday to Friday

BRISTOL   Tel. 0272-667013
V. H. WILLIS & CO. LTD.   ★
190-192 WEST STREET
BEDMINSTER
Open: 8.30 a.m.-5.00 p.m. Mon-Fri.
Saturday 9.00 a.m.-1.00 p.m.

BERKSHIRE

READING   Tel. (0734) 586522)
SARJENT'S TOOL STORES   ★
LTD.
44-52 OXFORD ROAD
Open: 8.30 a.m.-5.30 p.m.
Monday-Saturday

BUCKINGHAMSHIRE

MILTON KEYNES   Tel:
A. POLLARD & SON   0908-75221
LTD.   ★
51 QUEENSWAY, BLETCHLEY
Open: 8.30 a.m.-5.30 p.m.
Monday-Saturday

CAMBRIDGESHIRE

CAMBRIDGE Tel: 0223-353091
H.B. WOODWORKING
69 LENSFIELD ROAD
Open: 8.30 a.m.-5.30 p.m.
Monday-Friday
8.30 a.m.-1.00 p.m. Saturday

PETERBOROUGH   Tel:
PETERBOROUGH   0733-62800
TOOL CENTRE
16 WESTGATE
Open: Mon.-Sat. 9.00am-5.30pm
Thursday 9.00 am-1.00 pm

CHESHIRE

CHEADLE   Tel. 061-491-1726
ERIC TOMKINSON   ★
86 STOCKPORT ROAD
Open: 9.00 a.m.-4.00 p.m.
Wednesday-Saturday
Closed all day Monday & Tuesday

CHESTER - Tel: Chester 42082
ROBERT KELLY
19 NEWGATE ROAD
Open: Mon.-Sat.
9.00 a.m.-5.30 p.m.

CHESHIRE

STOCKPORT   Tel.
M.W. EQUIPMENT 061-480-8481
LIMITED
SHAWCROSS STREET
Monday-Friday
9.00 a.m.-4.45 p.m.

CLEVELAND

MIDDLESBOROUGH   Tel.
REM ELECTRIC   0642-248460
POWER TOOLS
89 PARLIMENT ROAD
Open: 8.30 a.m.-5.00 p.m.
Monday-Saturday

MIDDLESBROUGH   Tel. 0642-
WINTZ   460035/83650
INDUSTRIAL SUPPLIES   ★
2 BESSEMER COURT,
GRANGETOWN
Open: Mon.-Fri. 8.30 a.m.-5.00 p.m.

CORNWALL

HELSTON   Tel.03265-4961
SOUTHWEST POWER TOOLS   ★
MONUMENT ROAD
Open: 8.00 a.m.-5.00 p.m.
Monday-Friday
Saturday 8.00 a.m.-12.30 p.m.

LAUNCESTON   Tel. 0566-3555
SOUTHWEST POWER TOOLS   ★
6 WESTERN ROAD
Open: 8.00 a.m.-5.00 p.m.
Monday-Friday
Saturday 8.00 a.m.-12.30 p.m.

DERBYSHIRE

BUXTON   Tel. 0298-871636
CRAFT SUPPLIES   ★
THE MILL
MILLERSDALE
Open: Monday-Saturday
9.00 a.m.-5.00 p.m.

DEVON

AXMINSTER   Tel. 0297-33656
POWER TOOL CENTRE
STYLES & BROWN
CHARD STREET
Open: 9.00 a.m.-5.30 p.m.
Monday-Saturday

BIDEFORD   Tel. 023-72-3513
NORTH DEVON TOOLS   ★
7-9 MEDDON STREET
Open: Monday-Friday
8.00 a.m.-6.00 p.m.
Saturday 8.30 a.m.-5.00 p.m.

EXETER   Tel. 0392-73936
WRIDES TOOL CENTRE
147 FORE STREET
Open: 9.00 a.m.-5.30 p.m.
Monday-Saturday
Wednesday 9.00 a.m.-1.00 p.m.

CO. DURHAM

DARLINGTON   Tel. 0325-53511
PERCY W. STEPHENSON & SON
171/179 NORTHGATE
Open: 8.30 a.m.-5.30 p.m.
Monday to Saturday

ESSEX

SOUTHEND ON SEA   Tel.
MARSHALL &   0702-710404
PARSONS LIMITED   ★
1111 LONDON RD., LEIGH ON SEA
Open: 8.30 a.m.-5.30 p.m. Mon.-Fri.
Open: 9.00 a.m.-5.00 p.m. Sat.

WESTCLIFFE-ON-SEA   Tel:
CLASSIC   0702-354055
BRASS COMPANY
429/431 LONDON ROAD
Open: 9.00 a.m.-5.30 p.m.
Mon.-Sat.

GLOUCESTERSHIRE

TEWKESBURY   Tel. 0684-
TEWKESBURY SAW CO.   293092
LIMITED
TRADING ESTATE, NEWTOWN
Open: 8.00 a.m.-5.00 p.m.
Monday-Friday

HAMPSHIRE

ALDERSHOT   Tel. 0252-28088
BURCH & HILLS LTD.   ★
BLACKWATER WAY TRADING
ESTATE
Open: 8.30 a.m.-5.30 p.m. Mon.-Fri.
8.30 a.m.-12.00 Saturday

SOUTHAMPTON   Tel.
HAMPSHIRE   0703 776222
WOODWORKING MACHINERY   ★
297 SHIRLEY ROAD, SHIRLEY
Open: Tuesday-Saturday
9.30 a.m.-6.00 p.m.

HERTFORDSHIRE

HITCHIN   Tel. 0462-4177
ROGER'S
47 WALSWORTH ROAD
Open: 9.00 a.m.-6.00 p.m.
Monday-Saturday
Closed all day Wednesday

WATFORD   Tel. 0923-26052
J. SIMBLE & SONS LTD   ★
76 QUEENS ROAD
Open: 8.30 a.m.-5.30 p.m.
Mon.-Sat. Closed Wednesday

WATFORD   Tel. (0923) 49911
TREND MACHINERY & CUTTING
TOOLS LTD.
UNIT N, PENFOLD WORKS,
IMPERIAL WAY
Open: 9.00 a.m.-5.00 p.m. Mon.-Fri.

LANCASHIRE

LANCASTER   Tel. 0524-2886
LILE TOOL SHOP
43/45 NORTH ROAD
Open: 9.00 a.m.-5.30 p.m.
Monday-Saturday
Wednesday 9.00 a.m.-12.30 p.m.

GREATER MANCHESTER

MANCHESTER   Tel.
ROBERT KELLY   061-832-9920
UNIT 143, UPPER MALL
ARNDALE CENTRE
Open: Mon.-Sat.
9.00 a.m.-5.00 p.m.

LIVERPOOL

LIVERPOOL Tel. 051-263-1359
TAYLOR BROS. (LIVERPOOL) LTD.
5/9 PRESCOTT STREET
Open: 8.30 a.m.-5.30 p.m.
Monday-Friday

LEICESTERSHIRE

LEICESTER   Tel. 0455-43254
ROY STARTIN LTD.
134 WOOD STREET   ★
EARL SHILTON
Open: Mon.-Fri. 8.00 a.m.-5.30p.m.
Saturday 8.00 a.m.-1.30 p.m.

LONDON

Tel. 01-624-5146
W. THATCHER & SONS LTD.   ★
221A KILBURN HIGH ROAD NW6
(1st floor above travel agency)
Open Monday-Saturday 9.00-5.30
Closed Wednesday

Tel. 01-739-7126
CECIL W. TYZACK   ★
79-81 KINGSLAND ROAD
SHOREDITCH E2
Open: 8.45 a.m.-5.15 p.m.
Monday-Friday — Closed Saturday

Tel.
GENERAL   01-254-6052
WOODWORK SUPPLIES   ★
76-80 STOKE NEWINGTON
HIGH STREET, N16
Mon-Sat 9.00-6.00. Thur 9.00-1.00

NORFOLK

NORWICH   Tel. 0603 898695
NORFOLK SAW SERVICES
DOG LANE, HORSFORD
Open: 8.00 a.m.-5.00 p.m.
Monday-Friday
Saturday 8.00 a.m.-12.00 p.m.

NORTHAMPTONSHIRE

RUSHDEN   Tel. 093-34-56424
PETER CRISP LIMITED
7 HIGH STREET
Open: 8.30 a.m.-5.30 p.m.
Monday-Saturday
Thursday 8.30 a.m.-1.00 p.m.

NOTTINGHAMSHIRE

NOTTINGHAM Tel. 0602-811889
THE WOODCUTTER   ★
5 TUDOR SQUARE,
WEST BRIDGEFORD
Open: Tues.-Sat. 9.00 am-5.30 pm
Fri. 9.00 am-7.30 pm. Closed Mon.

OXFORDSHIRE

OXFORD   Tel. (0865-45118/9)
SARJENT'S TOOL STORES LTD. ★
150 COWLEY ROAD
Open: 8.30 a.m.-5.30 p.m.
Monday-Saturday

STAFFORDSHIRE

TAMWORTH   Tel. 0827-56188
MATTHEWS BROTHERS. LTD
KETTLEBROOK ROAD
Open: Mon.-Sat.
8.30 a.m.-6.00 p.m.
Demonstrations Sunday mornings

WOODWORKER SHOW

Royal Horticultural Society's New Hall, Greycoat Street, Westminster, London SW1

The year's show will be held from 4-9 November inclusive and entries for the competition classes must be made on the official form not later than 5 September, 1980. Forms are obtainable from Peter Freebrey, Exhibition Manager, Model and Allied Publications Ltd, PO Box 35, Bridge Street, Hemel Hempstead HP1 1EE.

There are nine classes: WA — Cabinet making; WB — Woodcarving; WC — Woodturning; WD — Musical instruments; WE — Marquetry and inlay; WF — Toys; WG — Model horse-drawn vehicles; WH — Junior (under 18) section; WJ — Clocks.

Full details of the classes, awards, conditions of entry, reception and collection of exhibits are given elsewhere in this issue.

Entries in the Woodworker/Ashley Iles international carving competition will be judged at the Woodworker Show. Conditions of entry and other information relating to this competition appear on page 289.

Prices quoted are those prevailing at press date and are subject to alteration due to economic conditions.

Classified Advertisements

Telephone Gill Dedman (0442) 41221 Ex.241

All classified Advertisements must be pre-paid.
Private and trade rate 14p per word (minimum £2.40). Box Numbers £1.00 extra. Display box rates s.c.c. £3.00 (min. £7.50). All advertisements are inserted in the first available issue.
Box replies to be sent care of Advertisement Department, P.O. Box 35, Bridge Street, Hemel Hempstead, Herts, England HP1 1EE. There are no reimbursements for cancellations.

FOR SALE

Brass or aluminium plates for your project. Letters block or script, example 3″ x 1″ brass plate with 20 block letter £1.10p, plus post, plus VAT. Also engraved badges, name plates, numbers, labels, etc. in coloured plastic. Trade enquiries welcome.

BRIAN J. BOWMAN TROPHIES LTD. "Anela" Lower North Street, Cheddar, Somerset. Tel. Cheddar 742774

BRASS ELECTRICAL FITTINGS. Switches, Power Points, Dimmers, T.V. and Telephone Outlets, etc. Choice of three different designs on all models. Produced in heavy gauge solid brass. Polished, and treated with transparent lacquer to preserve high finish indefinitely. Also French Gilt, Wrought Iron, and a nine difference decorator colour range. All designed for simple replacement of existing plastic models. Full compliance with British Safety Standards. Illustrated colour catalogue FREE from the Classic Brass Co., Dept. WE, 429/431 London Road, Westcliff, Essex. Personal Shoppers welcome. OPQ

MEDDINGS wet sandstone grinding machine. Very little used, £150.00. Tel: 0702-547029 (Southend). Mornings and evenings. P

BRANDING IRONS

Made from solid steel with 15″ handle, to last a lifetime. Now you can permanently identify your tools and production pieces. We can quote for special styles for a professional look. Price guide — 3 x 3/8″ characters **£6.95p.**

SAE details - **Woodcraft Supply (U.K.) Ltd., 38 Summercourt Way, Brixham, TQ5 0DY**

COLLECTION of WOODWORKERS, October 1947 to December 1962 inclusive. Offers wanted. Tel: 051-424-7513. P

NORRIS adjustable 14″ panel plane (£125) adjustable smoother. Smoother no handle type, Spiers panel plane and smoother. Brass — ebony — bullnose etc, etc. Mike Wills 021-421-2529. P

Snooker & Pool

"High Point" Garstang Rd. East, Singleton, Blackpool, Lancs. FY6 7SX
Tel: 0253-883426

Table Plans. Chipboard/Slate. State size, send £2 + SAE. Cod service on cloth, balls, rubber, etc. New and reconditioned Snooker and coin-op Pool tables sold/bought.

Advice Centre

WOODTURNER'S DREAM! Genuine South American mahogany, 4″ depth, lengths and widths various at reasonable prices. Trymwood Services, 2A Downs Park East, Bristol, BS6 7QD. Tel: 629092. P

PLANS for advanced wood modellers. 1/12th scale 19th Century roll-top desk, £1.50. Miniature 'Chartwell House' £1.50. Other plans for 1/12th scale 'Churchill' furniture 50p each. From: W.E.H.3, 1 Hollytree Gardens, Frimley, Surrey. P

FOR SALE: complete woodturner's workshop Myford ML8A bench, 3/4hp motor, mortising, tenoning attachment, cross slide both with tools. Grinder, chucks, face plates, accessories, woodturning tools. Willow 6″ bench sander 1hp motor, lamp drilling machine £900.00 o.n.o. Tel: Mickleton 418 (Glos.). P

Fine Period Furniture

for you to make by hand at home

Large selection of 17thC copies in solid oak or elm for simple home assembly without special tools.

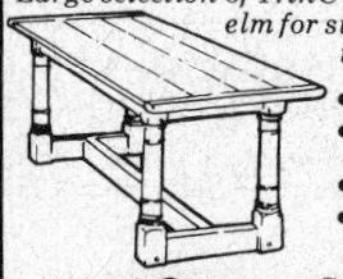

- **All materials supplied**
- **All parts cut, planed and jointed**
- **Simple instructions**
- **Save up to 60% on retail prices**

Send large SAE for brochure and price list

JACOBUS WORKSHOP

JACOBUS WORKSHOP DEPT. W1, South Road, *KIRKBY STEPHEN, Cumbria*

WALL CLOCKS

Quartz battery movements	**£5.95**
Pendulum movements	**£5.75**
Clock hands — Black **55p**; Brass **75p** pair	
Colourful ceramic clockfaces	**£1.25**
Assorted plastic clockfaces	**55p**

Prices including post. Full guarantee.

SAE - **WOODCRAFT SUPPLY (U.K.) LTD. 38 Summercourt Way, Brixham TQ5 0DY**

MINIATURE carving tools for the finest detail in sets or singles. Designed and made by woodcarvers (work and tools exhibited WOODWORKER, November 1978). Also retempering, sharpening service. J. Mitchell, 65 Parkhurst Road, Norris Green, Liverpool L11 1DZ. PQR

ROUTERS

If you are thinking of buying a Router, we offer Bosch/Elu range at unbelievable prices.
If you already own a Router Send for our Free Cutter Wall Chart.

**BARRIE IRONS MACHINERY
106A Aldenham Road,
Bushey, Herts.
Tel. Watford (0923) 30422**

OFFERS? Norris 2 1/8″ smoothing plane. 2 1/4″ beech badger. Record 020 compass plane. All in good condition. Tel. Cleethorpes (0472) 67444. P

EXCITING IDEAS IN FURNITURE-MAKING FOR NEWLYWEDS, D.I.Y. AND UNSKILLED

ALL you need are a few SIMPLE tools to make your own REPRODUCTION, MODERN AND GARDEN FURNITURE etc., from our EASY TO COPY PLANS and SIMPLE CLEARLY MARKED assembly instructions. EACH PLAN is FULL-SIZED. Just trace the plan on wood etc., similar to a dressmaking pattern. SO SIMPLE over 60 plans to choose from. FREE plumbing hints leaflet with each catalogue. Many satisfied customers who re-order once they try the plans. Send 60 p&p inc. TODAY for catalogue to Hamlyn Dept. D.W. 57 Lyneham, Wilts, SN15 4PH.

Chair illus. made in less than a day from plan No. 35 price only £1.99.

SET of 14 patternmakers cranked paring gouges with Boxwood handles 1/8″-1 1/4″ Marples/Sorby £80. Tel: Witney 4170. P

WELSH SLATE sharpening stones for sale at very competitive prices. Send SAE for details: Inigo Jones and Co. Limited, Groelon, Caernarfon, Gwynedd. Tel: 0286-830242. O-U

MYFORD 5″ planing machine on stand with 1/2hp single phase motor and thicknesser attachment £200 o.v.n.o. Tel: 0604-858470. P

BD DN 75 power plane little used. £35. Rockwell 1/2″ variable speed and reversing drill as new £20. Tel: 021-743-9890 (evenings). P

CORONET CMB 518 combination table and GPB 728 thicknesser for sale. Both unused new price £65.00 accept £45.00. Hindmarch, Thack Dene, Thacka Lane, Penrith, Cumbria. P

CORONET major lathe with 10″ saw table, planer, thicknesser, morticer and turning chisles. All as new. Offers? Tel: 0734-733352 (nr. Wokingham). P

WORKSHOP EQUIPMENT

SHERWOOD TURNING LATHES

All cast iron constructed. 3 3/4″ CH 24″ or 36″ B.C. 3 or 4 speed, bowl turning up to 14″ dia. ball-bearing spindle c/w face plate, centres etc. Prices from **£58.92** inc.VAT.

Send stamp for leaflets and details of above and other low-priced machines and motors.

JAMES INNS (Engs), Main St., Bulwell, Nottingham.

LEISURECRAFT IN WOOD WITH CORONET

The full range of these universal and independent machines on show.
Demonstrations and lessons.
Full back-up of tools and accessories for Turning, Carving and Marquetry.

**KENTERPRISE LTD.
122 & 124 Camden Road,
Tunbridge Wells**
Tel. Tunbridge Wells 23475

CIRCULAR and band saw blades for all applications from: A. A. Smith of Lancing Ltd, Churchill Industrial Estate, Lancing, Sussex. Tel. 09063-4474. L-R

Equipping a workshop?
Call and see demonstrated or write for details (27p stamps) of quality machines of the popular Kity range or by Startrite, Sedgwick, De Walt, Lurem and most others: Elu Routers and Power Tools; Arundel, Myford, Kity Woodturning Lathes, accessories etc.
Trymwood Services, 2A Downs Park East (near the Downs), Bristol. 629092 2-6pm, Mondays to Fridays.

HAMPSHIRE WOODWORKING MACHINERY

HWM

297 SHIRLEY ROAD, SHIRLEY, SOUTHAMPTON
Telephone: 0703-776222

Open: Tuesday - Saturday
9.30 a.m. - 6.00 p.m.

Stockists for:
Wadkin, Elu, Startrite, Coronet, Kity, Arundel, Henry Taylor & Sorby.

Everything for the carpenter, joiner, turner and carver.

Ask for price list for tools, polishers, finishers, books, etc. *(S.A.E. Please).*

Demonstrations, personal service, mail order (14 days delivery).
Access, Barclaycard and Mercantile Credit.
Answering service day and night.

WASHITA & ARKANSAS whetstones now readily available from importer. Large selection. S.A.E. for lists. C. Rufino, Manor House, South Clifton, Newark, Notts. T/C

BELT SANDERS

Craftsman 3 ins. 1.hp. One year guarantee. Great value at **£65.00** incl. VAT.

**CRAFTOOLS
100A Alexandra Road, Newport, Gwent.**
Tel: (0633) 842996

A. POLLARD & SON

De-Walt, Shopmate, Kity, Elu, Susemihl
We offer good service, good stocks and low prices
Dust extractors
A. Pollard & Son, 51 Queensway, Bletchley, Milton Keynes. Tel: 0908-75221

ACCESS — BARCLAYCARD

Business established over 50 years.

Classified Advertisements

348

Prices quoted are those prevailing at press date and are subject to alteration due to economic conditions.

Woodworker, May 1980

Woodworker
THE MAGAZINE FOR THE CRAFTSMAN IN WOOD

JUNE 1980   VOL. 84   NO. 1039

Front cover: Geraldine Gilbert is 18 and the only girl apprentice gunsmith registered with the Gun Trade Association. She works at the Penthalon sports shop in Great Harwood, Blackburn, Lancs. See also story page 356. *(Photo: W. Wilkinson).*

Editor	Geoffrey Pratt
Production Editor	Polly Curds
Advertisement Manager	Terence M. Healy
Group Advertisement Manager	Michael Merrifield
Managing Director	Gospatric Home
Editorial Director	Ron Moulton

ABC
MEMBER OF THE AUDIT
BUREAU OF CIRCULATIONS

SUBSCRIPTION DEPARTMENT: Remittances to MODEL AND ALLIED PUBLICATIONS, PO Box 35, Hemel Hempstead, Herts HP1 1EE. Price per copy 75p includes p&p. Subscription queries: Tel: Hemel Hempstead 51740. Subscription rate, including index £9.00 per annum; overseas sterling £9.00; $20.00 U.S. for overseas dollar subscribers. Second class postage paid at New York, NY. North American enquiries regarding news stand sales should be sent to: Eastern News Distribution, 111 Eighth Avenue, New York, NY 1011, USA. Telephone (212) 255-5620 and craft and hobby sales to Bill Dean Books Ltd, 166-41 Powells Cove Boulevard, Whitestone, New York 11357, USA. Telephone (212) 767-6632.

MAP

Model & Allied Publications Ltd
PO Box 35, Bridge Street, Hemel Hempstead, Herts HP1 1EE. Telephone: Hemel Hempstead (0442) 41221.

'Small is preferable . . .'

This is the current political philosophy, according to one of the commentators in the *Financial Times* on budget day + 1 (which should there be any doubt was Thursday 27 March). It seems to be generally agreed that the chancellor of the exchequer produced the most useful package of measures aimed at boosting industrial enterprise in general — and encouraging small businessmen in particular — since the current political interest in small firms started nearly three years ago.

For example, changes in capital taxation and the increase in the capital transfer tax threshold; measures aimed at easing the tax or administrative burdens of small businesses; provisions for unincorporated small businesses, plus proposed concessions for the cost of raising business loan finance, and relief for pre-trading expenses. VAT administration is also being eased.

Linked with these measures are two property innovations. First, a small workshop scheme is being introduced. For a period of three years capital expenditure on the construction of industrial buildings providing working space of less than 2,500sq ft will qualify for a 100% allowance, instead of the usual arrangements of an initial allowance of 50% followed by annual writing down allowances of 4%. Second, the provision of £5m for the construction of 1,000 nursery units in assisted areas in co-operation with the private sector.

The chancellor put forward proposals for setting up about six zones — each averaging 500 acres — in areas of 'urban dereliction' and designated as zones for an initial period of 10 years, subject to renewal. Businesses established in the zones will be exempt from development land tax and general rates; they will benefit from 100% capital allowances on industrial and commercial property; simplified planning procedures; exemption from training board levies; abolition of industrial development certificates; and reduction to a 'bare minimum' of government requests for statistical information.

Budget proposals in relation to personal taxation and other charges are controversial, of course, but for the self-employed (and those not in company pensions schemes) there is a useful uplift. As from 1980-1 the contributions limit goes from 15 to 17½% of net relevant earnings and the overriding ceiling of £3,000 on premium contributions is abolished.

Rural industries

Head office and training centre for the Council for Small Industries in Rural Areas (CoSIRA) was officially opened in March. Now the separate centres from London, Wimbledon and Salisbury have come together at Salisbury with workshops, engineering machine shop, display workshop, photographic studio, two lecture rooms equipped with projection facilities and office accommodation for staff and field services.

Eventually there will be 160 staff about half being specialist advisers in technical matters and business management. However this figure represents less than half the total as the remainder are operating throughout England's rural areas.

Registered office of CoSIRA is Queen's House, Fish Row, Salibury SP1 1EX (0722 24411).

An Invitation...

to visit the opening of our new showroom during the six days 2nd – 7th June

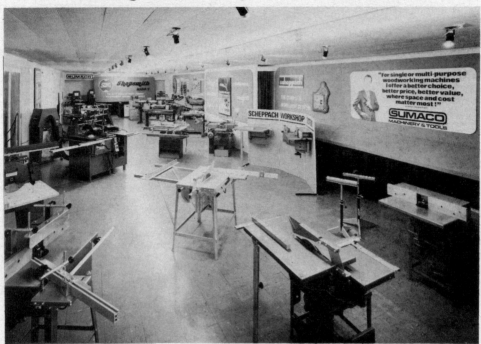

Sumaco invite both trade and woodworking enthusiasts to call at their new extensive showroom of SUMACO products. On display and available for demonstration will be:

Scheppach Workshop system & individual machines

Mafell Tilting Arbor Sawbench & Power Tools

Eumenia Universal Radial Saw

Luna Woodturning lathes & Universal Woodworker

Zinken Universal Woodworker "Compact 21"

Alfa Radial Arm & Mitre Saws

Shopsmith The World's Most Versatile Home Workshop System

Weber Consult Accessories TCT Tooling & Sawblades

Sumaco Library Woodworking Publications and Project Plans

This is one event you cannot afford to miss. Any time between 9 am and 9 pm, 2nd – 7th June at
Suma House, Huddersfield Road. Elland, W. Yorkshire HX5 9AA Tel. (0422) 75491/2

1¼ miles from junction 24 M62

SUMACO
MACHINERY & TOOLS

50 GAMMA 7 ROUTERS TO BE GIVEN AWAY

Details on request.

Name _____

Address _____

Post to SUMACO Suma House, Huddersfield Road. Elland, W. Yorkshire

Prices quoted are those prevailing at press date and are subject to alteration due to economic conditions.

KITY SERVICE

A new concept in after sales back-up

Like other manufacturers, Kity guarantee their machines, provide spares and a maintenance service, but Kity plan sheets go one step further, they help you exploit the full potential of your machines.

Kity plan sheets give detailed specification about materials, design, cutting and machining for all kinds of woodworking projects. Fill in the coupon and we will send you a free 44 page book all about this invaluable and unique Kity service.

KITY UNITED KINGDOM

Kity U.K., Sizers Court, Henshaw Lane, Yeadon, Leeds LS19 7DP. West Yorkshire.

MARSHALL & PARSONS
East Anglia's Leading Woodworking Centre

1111 LONDON ROAD, LEIGH-ON-SEA ESSEX SS9 3JL
Telephone Southend (0702) 710404 (4 lines)

We stock an excellent range of Hand Tools, Portable Power Tools and Woodworking Machinery including: Barrus. Black & Decker. Bosch. Burgess. Coronet. Cowell. De-Walt. Elektra. Elu. Kango. Kity. Makita. Meddings. Multico. Myford. R.J.H.. Shopvac. Stanley. Startrite. Sumaco. Wolf.

£158.70
inc. V.A.T.
Plus Carr. £8

Elektra 12″ Sawbench

85mm depth of cut, 3hp motor
Fully guarded.
Strong galvanised steel construction.
Hand wheel rise and fall for accurate
height adjustment 0-85mm.

Special Offer Limited Period
- REDUCED PRICE
- STEEL CARRYING CASE

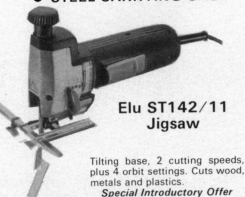

Elu ST142/11 Jigsaw

Tilting base, 2 cutting speeds,
plus 4 orbit settings. Cuts wood,
metals and plastics.
Special Introductory Offer

Price **£83.00** inc. V.A.T.
and Post

Elu MOF 96 Plunging Router

650 watt Motor, 24,000 r.p.m. No load
speed. Maximum depth of plunge 2″-50mm
Collet size ¼″.
This power tool is a breakthrough for the
ambitious craftsman and is very versatile.

Only **£78.00** including V.A.T.
and Postage

NEW FROM CRAFT SUPPLIES

WOODTURNING COURSES

Our two-day intensive courses in woodturning provide you with expert tuition, good food and comfortable accommodation in the Mill situated in the heart of the beautiful Peak District National Park.

From ONLY £55 inclusive.
Send S.A.E. for full details.

QUARTZ CLOCKS
(movement)

Highest
quality
W.German
movement
£6.00 each
+ 90p V.A.T.
£5.00 each
for 10.
Selection of
metal hands
available.

CERAMIC FACES
85p + 13p VAT

CUTLERY BLANKS

Highest quality — Sheffield
made stainless steel — 19 patterns available — all illustrated
in our catalogue.

WOODTURNING ACCESSORIES

Largest range of woodturning
accessories available — and
still expanding — Pepper mills
from 50p — Time glasses —
nearly 200 patterns of circular
tiles from 20p and an excellent
range of finishing materials including CRAFTLAC and now
RUSTIN'S finishes. Stockists
of ARUNDEL, CORONET, KITY
machines and largest range of
SORBY tools available.

Postage paid on orders over
£30.

Delivery 10 to 14 days

6-in-1 UNIVERSAL CHUCK

NOW WITH 12 DIFFERENT USES
makes it "the best combination
chuck that I have ever seen or
used in all the twenty-plus years
of my woodturning experience"
quotes one American owner —
one of over 3,000 satisfied users.
Send for our 6-in-1 Chuck on 30
days approval. If not entirely
satisfied it is the *BEST* Chuck
available we will refund your
money immediately.

£29.50 + £4.42 VAT

ALSO AVAILABLE:
WOODTURNING MANDRELS
FROM £2.75 + 41p VAT
CRAFT COPYING ATTACHMENT
£13.50 + £2.03 VAT

CRAFT SUPPLIES
Specialists in woodturning tools
THE MILL, MILLER'S DALE, BUXTON
DERBYSHIRE SK17 8SN
TEL. 0298 871636

Send 40p
stamps for 24
page fully
illustrated
catalogue —
with voucher for
40p refund on
your first order.

352
Prices quoted are those prevailing at press date and
are subject to alteration due to economic conditions.
Woodworker, June 1980

MOF 96 SPECIAL OFFER

THE HOME CRAFTSMAN TOOL OF THE 80's

MOF 96 Router with standard accessories as below also

INCLUDING SIX ROUTER CUTTERS

★Cast side fence
★Template guide
★Instruction booklet
★Spanners, rods etc.

Only £86.00
★Free carriage★

Also £5.00 voucher for next Elu purchase.
(Accessory kit now only £43.00 with voucher, £48.00 without)

Routers cutters can be expensive so Willis have put together an attractive offer including six router cutters to give you tremendous versatility with your router for only **£86.00**. The cutters are high speed steel, suitable for hard and soft natural timber.

CHEPSTOW WOODTURNING LATHE LOOK AT THESE INCLUSIVE FEATURES

1. Faceplate and large diameter turning to 17" dia.
2. Long 37" between centres.
3. Five speeds 530-3325 rpm.
4. Sealed bearings.
5. ½hp Brookes motor and switch.
6. Tilting motor platform.

ONLY
£269.00
INCLUDING VAT
CARRIAGE £8.00 (UK)

YOUR IMAGINATION IS YOUR ONLY LIMIT WITH A WOODTURNING LATHE FROM

FREE SET OF SIX TURNING TOOLS

OFFER ENDS JUNE 28

Turning between centres.

Bowl turning.

The Chepstow 17-37 we believe to be the best value for money on the market. This up to the minute design combines performance and specification with low price. The deep groove thrust bearings are fully enclosed for maintenance free operation.

SEND YOUR ORDER TO:

V. H. WILLIS & Co. Ltd.,
190-2 WEST STREET,
BEDMINSTER, BRISTOL.

Tel. (0272) 667013

Make cheque payable to: V. H. Willis & Co. Ltd. or phone through Barclaycard/Access number for immediate despatch. Full money back refund if not satisfied within 14 days of receipt of goods.

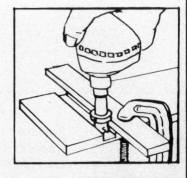

Fine woodworking demands a fine bench

A) Lervad bench No. 610CU with two integral vices, double row bench dog system and built-in cupboard. **B)** Carving between single row bench dog system on Lervad bench No. 600. **C)** Commodious shoulder vice, one of the three ways of work holding on models 610 and 611. **D)** Exclusive Lervad pattern tail vice which also operates with bench dog clamping system running full length of top (Models 610 & 611)

- Danish made woodwork benches of superb quality, chosen by craftsmen woodworkers and craft teachers the world over.
- Made from solid kiln dried Danish beech. Precision machined and sanded tops are oiled and sealed against warping etc.
- Unique multiple vice holds for secure, comfortable and accurate working at all angles. On principal models this includes exclusive Lervad double row bench dog clamping system running full length of bench top.
- Varied choice of models to suit every woodworkers need. Built in cupboards or moveable cupboards and tool racks available.

Lervad are also leading school workshop suppliers of both wood and metalwork benches and storage units.
If you are involved in teaching please ask for School Workshop catalogue.

LERVAD *Made by craftsmen for craftsmen*

WOODTURNING LATHE BY LUREM

NEW MODEL!

SPECIAL PRICE £275 + VAT

HEIGHT ABOVE BED : 120mm (4½")
MAXIUM TURNING ø : 240mm (9")
DISTANCE BETWEEN CENTRES : 800mm (31")
3 SPEEDS : 1200/1500/2700r.p.m.

Standard Accessories:
Rotating centre, 4-spike centre, Screw centre & Cone punch

Optional Attachments:
Faceplate ø 200mm, 3-jaw chuck ø 100mm, 13mm chuck for drilling extra long tool rest (500mm), Faceplate turning attachment (ø 400mm), Table for lathe and motor, Motor O, 75HP — single or 3-phase Woodturning tools Clamps for adapting lathe to JUNIOR machine table.

**WOKINGHAM TOOL CO. LTD.,
99 Wokingham Road, Reading, Berks.
Tel. Reading 661511**

JOY teak oil
protects for a finer finish

For an oiled finish to all hard woods. You can apply it with a cloth or a brush, it'll penetrate deep into the grain to give waterproof dirt-shrugging siliconized protection — and yet it allows wood to breathe. In tins from 125 m/l upwards.

For staining new wood use Joy Wood Dye or Joy Stained Glaze.

Put some Joy into your work

quality products for Sticking Staining Polishing Painting

You will find Joy products at all good stores, ironmongers, paint and D.I.Y. shops.

JOY is a registered trade mark

GERALDINE MAKE YOUR GUN

While it is by no means uncommon for women to take up shooting, as distant from gun-toting, it is unusual to find a woman who actually makes guns. However the duchy and county palatine of Lancaster can always produce surprises and at Great Harwood near Blackburn 18-year-old Geraldine Gilbert is the only girl apprentice gunsmith registered with the Gun Trade Association. She works with Leslie Meggison at the Pentathlon sports shop in Great Harwood, which makes complete guns. These are hand-built to the specific requirements of shooting men throughout the north of England.

At the present time Geraldine is concentrating on producing the stock fashioned from a solid block of Kashmir walnut *(Juglans regia* Linn.) The stock is first marked out then cut to take the action and finally shaped. This work can take three days.

According to *Timbers of the World* (A.L. Howard) 1934, although walnut requires some time to season, and shrinks considerably during the process, yet when subsequently exposed to drying or moistening influences it stands excellently, and it is exceedingly difficult, if not impossible, to find another wood possessing this attribute to the same degree. For this reason it is the best-known wood for gun and rifle stocks. After the stock has been cut out and shaped, the wood retains its form and shape exactly, so that the barrel and locks will drop into their position and rest, without bending the locks or throwing the barrel out of the straight. No variation in climate affects this wood; it is also of appropriate weight which gives proper balance to the firearm; is readily cut to shape; and gives a good surface for polishing.

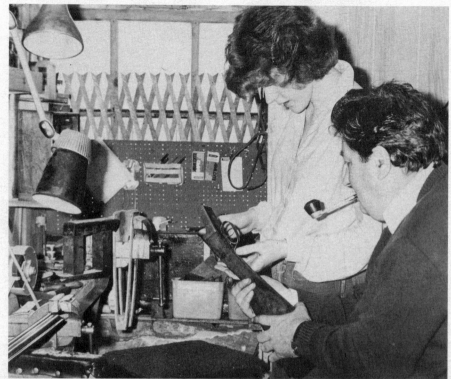

On the opposite page W. H. Brown FIWSc describes experiments carried out in the US to try and stabilise gunstocks made from black walnut *(Juglans nigra)* by using polyethylene glycol (PEG).

TIMBER TOPICS 8

Here W. H. Brown FIWSc considers polyethylene glycol (PEG) which was described in WOODWORKER last November as a treatment for unseasoned wood so as to reduce shrinking and swelling tendencies. He describes experiments carried out in the US to try to stabilise gunstocks made from black walnut *(Juglans nigra)* by using PEG and in his next Topic will discuss how PEG works with other species.

In November 1979 WOODWORKER carried an excellent article by Brian Howarth entitled *Improving the Dimensional stability of Wood.* This described the possibilities of using PEG (polyethylene glycol) for the purpose of treating unseasoned wood so as to reduce shrinking and swelling tendencies. Since in the last two Timber Topics we have been dealing with the awkward problem of attempting the drying of tree discs, and have referred to some American experiments in this direction, it is important that the possible use of PEG for this purpose ought not to be ignored if, indeed, it could be used successfully.

It is intended therefore to expound a little further on the basis of cause and effect in the use of PEG in order to give the widest possible coverage to its possibilities.

Use of PEG for stabilising wood is not new; the first serious experiments were carried out by Dr A. J. Stamm in 1934 while on the staff of the Forest Products Research Laboratory at Madison, US, and subsequently at North Carolina State College where he concentrated solely on pioneering the further use of the chemical. Probably the earliest account published by Stamm on his work was in 1959: *Effect of Polyethylene Glycol on the Dimensional Stability of Wood* (Forest Products Journal; 9 (10) 375).

This coincided with his first major assignment, ie to try to stabilise gunstocks made from black walnut *(Juglans nigra).* It will be appreciated that any movement of a gunstock will throw the barrel out of alignment; and since competition rifle shooting is a major occupation in America (quite apart from hunting activities), the amount of wood used for rifles is very high.

In the first phase of the experiments, two walnut logs were freshly sawn into 63mm (2½ in.) thick planks and these were bandsawn into 28 standard gunstock blanks. These were then divided into two groups: 14 blanks were sealed in polythene bags to prevent moisture loss, and were stored in a conditioning room maintained at a constant 4°C (35°F) with 82% RH. The remaining blanks were soaked for 39 days in a vat containing a 30% (by weight) aqueous solution of polyethylene glycol-1000 maintained at room temperature of about 24°C (73°F). While these were being treated, eight pieces were taken from the polythene bags and sent to a gunstock manufacturer, where they were machined for a Springfield action.

Machining to shape was carried out to within 3mm (⅛ in.) of the desired final dimensions. They were then soaked in a similar 30% solution of PEG for 24 days. These precarved stocks were much smaller in diameter than the blanks; and the machining out for the action, barrel groove and magazine block allowed much more diffusion of the chemical to take place in a shorter soaking time than would be required for solid blanks.

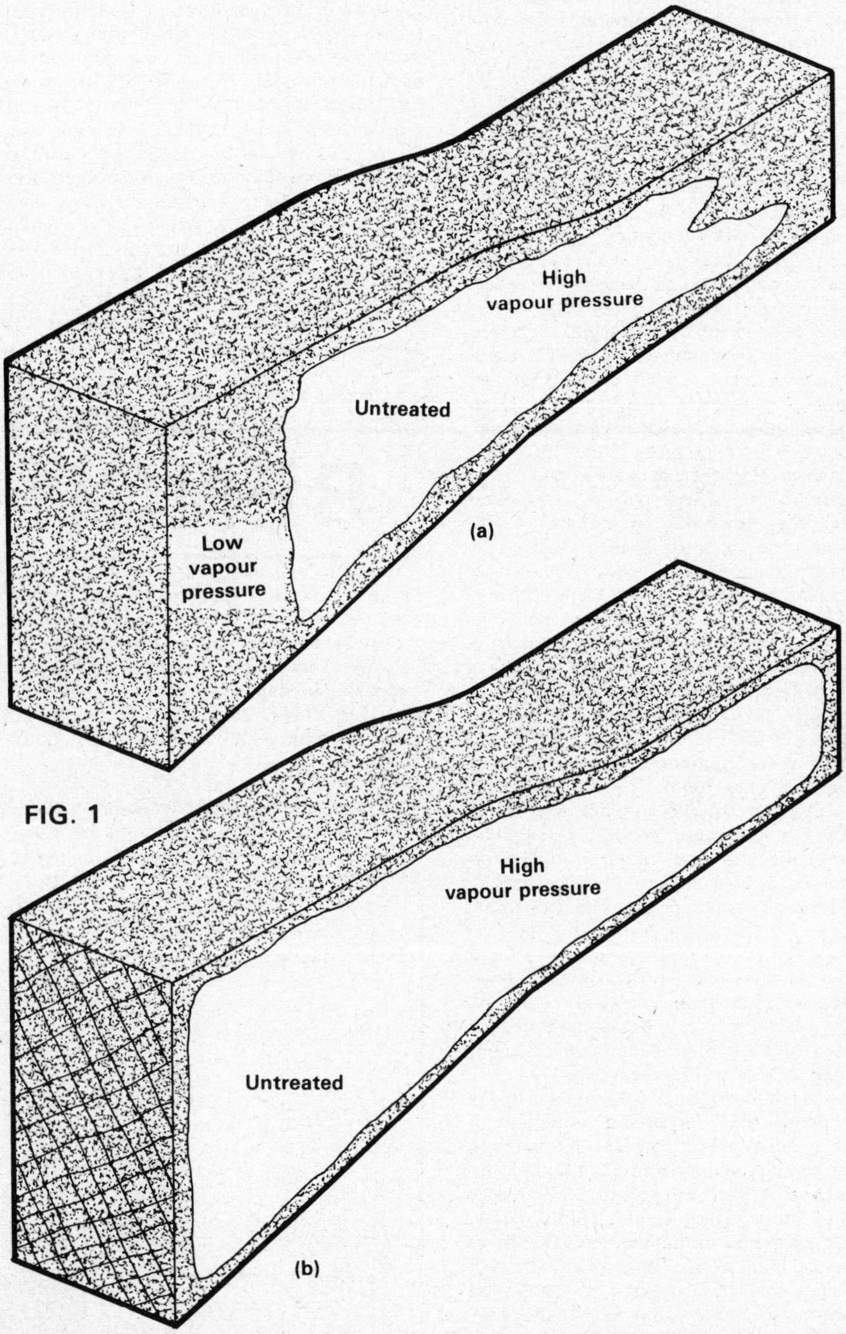

FIG. 1

At the end of the soaking period the chemically treated blanks and precarved stocks, together with the untreated blanks from the polythene bags, were accurately measured with a micrometer at several marked spots, and the green dimensions recorded. The entire quantity was then divided into two equal groups and placed to dry in two separate drying kilns. One kiln was operated on a normal drying schedule for black walnut, and took 57 days to reduce the m.c.

In (a) there has been a greater diffusion of PEG through end grain. The treated wood has a lower vapour pressure than the untreated core, thus when subjected to drastic drying conditions, severe stress is created between the two zones. In (b), by coating the ends with a moisture-resistant seal diffusion of PEG is more uniform through side grain, vapour pressure is more regular and drying stresses are reduced.

Swelling in untreated walnut blanks was 2.6% at (a), 3.6% at (b) and 3.6% at (c). In PEG-treated blanks swelling was reduced to 1.2%, 2.2% and 1% respectively.

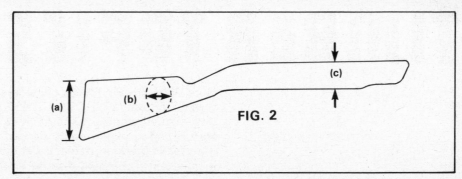

FIG. 2

from the green state to an average m.c. of 6% including five days at the end of the drying run for equalising and conditioning, ie to level out the extremes of m.c. between the pieces and to eliminate or relieve stress.

The other kiln was operated on a schedule much more drastic in its drying effect than would normally be recommended for commercial drying of walnut. This time the m.c. of the wood was reduced to 6% in 44 days, ie 13 days less than would be required in a normal kilning run. At the end of both drying runs, the whole quantity was re-measured at the same points as before.

A number of significant features now became apparent: all the treated precarved stocks were in perfect condition after kilning by both drying schedules; even the drastic treatment had failed to degrade the wood. There were no surface splits or checks nor internal honeycomb checks. It was therefore obvious that by suitable use of PEG black walnut was enabled to dry easily. This was encouraging because all the true walnuts produce timber that needs to be dried slowly, particularly in thick sizes, since the wood tends to develop internal checks if the drying is forced.

Before commenting on stability of the treated wood, we must refer to another significant feature. Of the original 28 blanks, six were kept in the polythene bags until the final kiln drying when three were placed in each kiln run. All these untreated blanks had their ends coated with a mixture of coal tar pitch and asphalt before kilning. The pieces that were subjected to the drastic drying, despite the end coating were, in fact, badly surface and end checked and had internal honeycomb checking.

Subsequent studies proved that thick walnut blanks treated with PEG can also be dried by the drastic schedule, but unlike the precarved smaller blanks, it is necessary to apply an end coating prior to chemical treatment.

The point of coating the ends of the wood with a moisture-retardent seal is to prevent a severe stress developing between the ends of the pieces, which could become heavily treated, and the interior fibres which might contain little or no chemical (Fig. 1).

In this pilot field test of 20 years ago it was established that the drying properties of black walnut for a single specific purpose were definitely improved by treating the wood with polyethylene glycol-1000. It was now essential to discover what effect, if any, was contributed to dimensional stability of the wood in question. The only way to check on this was by exposure to controlled atmosphere. First of all, the PEG-treated precarved stocks, together with an equal number of untreated stocks, machined to shape and recessed to take the fittings and manufactured from kiln-dried walnut blanks, were placed in a conditioning room maintained at a constant 27°C (80°F) and 30% RH. This equalled an equilibrium moisture content (EMC) for the wood of 6%. They were weighed weekly until they showed no significant change in weight, indicating they had attained equilibrium with the air conditions.

They were then carefully measured with a micrometer at several points. All were then transferred to another conditioning room, this time maintained at the same temperature as before but with 90%RH, or an EMC for the wood of 20.5%. In five weeks the pieces had picked up sufficient water vapour to come to equilibrium conditions with the air, so any swelling of the wood due to the change in atmosphere should now have occurred. Accordingly the pieces were again measured and the dimensions recorded. The results (taken at the same points, ie butt from heel to toe; butt thickness midway between heel and toe; and across forearm (Fig. 2)) were as follows:

PEG-treated 1.2% 2.2% 1.0% respectively
Untreated 2.6% 3.6% 3.6% respectively

When the pieces were returned to the low humidity room they lost the picked-up moisture and returned to their original dimensions.

It was obvious that polyethylene glycol-1000 could under certain circumstances, reduce movement in black walnut by around one-half of its normal movement potential, not eliminate it entirely. But what of other timber species and how does PEG work? We will continue the discussion in the next Timber Topic.

VARIABLE BENCH HEIGHTS

Readers will recall the problem John Parkinson of Northern Ireland has always experienced with benches in as much as they never seem to be the right height for the boy. We have had a number of helpful suggestions sent to us by readers of WOODWORKER, one of which comes from Keith Newbury of Morphettville, South Australia.

He prepares two pieces of timber 3 × 3in. of length equal to the width of his benches. These he hinges to the bottom of the legs at each end. To raise the height the bench is lifted, one end at a time, and the 3 × 3in. moved under the legs. The addition of a small cupboard bolt could serve to lock the 3 × 3in. in place. Sizes could be varied to suit the height of the worker.

Keith writes in his penultimate paragraph of his love of woodturning and his use of Tasmania timbers like blackwood, Huon pine, celery-top pine, King William's pine and sassafras. We have asked him for some notes. Are there other readers with information about lesser-known timbers?

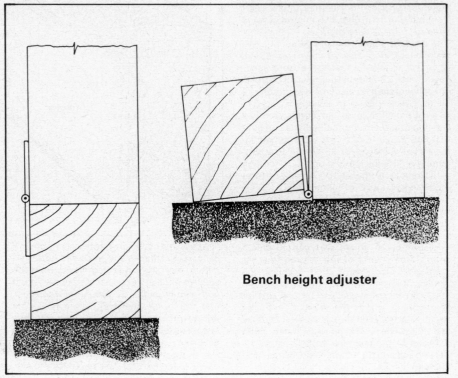

Bench height adjuster

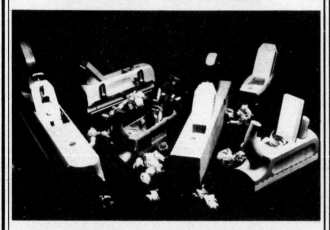

STORING YOUR BANDSAW BLADES

To facilitate the storage of bandsaw blades such as are used in home workshops, R. W. Grant describes and illustrates a method that makes use of the flexible nature of the blades, accompanied by a little manual dexterity. The author advises that industrial-type gloves should be worn to prevent scratches or, even worse, gashes on your hands.

Stage 1 With the hands held roughly opposite one another, grasp the blade with the left hand as you would to hold a car steering wheel and the right hand gripping downwards. It makes little difference if the teeth of the blade are pointing upwards or downwards.

Stage 2 Twist the wrists, with the left hand coming upwards towards the body and the right hand passing down and away from its starting position.

Stage 3 Continue the twisting action with the left hand passing across the front of the body and the right hand continuing down and under the left hand.

Stage 4 The coils will gather together with the completion of stage 3 and the palms of the hands are opened with the thumbs clearing the closing coils.

Although for convenience sake the operation has been described in four stages in actual fact the whole is carried out as one smooth movement.

Uncoiling Hold the coils in both hands and open them slightly to find the 'loose' loop. Take hold of this loop and release the other hand. The band will then spring open ready for fitting on to the machine. Always hold the blade to be coiled or uncoiled well away from the body.

Dealing with longer blades Longer blades that cannot easily be handled in the manner shown can, nevertheless, be dealt with by holding the band in the right hand and trapping the bottom of the loop on the floor with the right foot. With the palm of the right hand facing outwards grip the band and twist the hand in an anti-clockwise direction spiralling downwards at the same time. This action causes the band to form a coil as before. But remember to keep the blade anchored with your shoe during the operation.

If you happen to have a well-blunted bandsaw blade it is a good idea to use this for practise purposes before trying with a sharp blade.

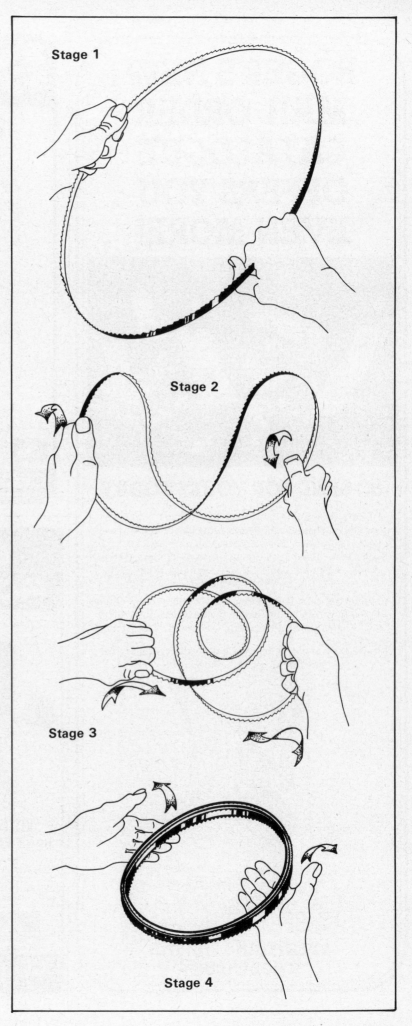

Stage 1

Stage 2

Stage 3

Stage 4

STARTRITE INCA

LEFT: Model AF 186S Motorised 230-250V with push button starter. A quality bench model bandsaw giving a high standard of finish. 320 mm square table will tilt through 45°. With rip fence depth stop and slotted for a mitre gauge. Complete with blade tension indicator upper blade guides and guard. Easily adjustable guides ensure max. blade life.

RIGHT: Floor model AF 190 M combined 10¼'' planer and 6¼'' thicknesser. Two rates of power feed 11 and 16 ft.-min. Surface tables are 31½'' long. Front table adjustable by handwheel against scale for cuts up to 1/8' deep. Fabricated steel stand houses a 1¼ hp motor protected by a thermal overload no volt release starter. Models available to suit single or three phase electrics.

STARTRITE
MACHINE TOOL CO LTD

PARRY & SON (Tools) LTD

LONDON
325/329 OLD ST.
LONDON
TEL 01-739 9422-3-4

KENT
Branch at 186/188 MAIN RD. BIGGIN HILL
WESTERHAM, KENT TN16 38B
TEL: Biggin Hill 73777 & 73800

GEO. SPENCE & SONS LTD. LEEDS

Plunging Router MOF 96

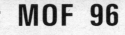

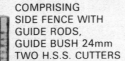

COMPRISING
SIDE FENCE WITH
GUIDE RODS,
GUIDE BUSH 24mm
TWO H.S.S. CUTTERS

PLUS
A £5 + VAT
VOUCHER WHICH
CAN BE USED
AGAINST ANY
OTHER ELU
MACHINE

OUR PRICE
£66.00
INC. V.A.T.
+ £3 CARRIAGE

Shopsmith

MARK 5

KITY
STOCKIST

STANLEY
ROUTER CENTRE

105 WELLINGTON ROAD
LEEDS LS12 YORKS. Tel: 790507

SUPPLIERS OF ALL TYPES OF WOODWORKING EQUIPMENT

Stockists of
ELU and
Bosch Tools
and complete
range of
fixings

ELU Orbital Sander
MVS 93

MOF 96
The Professional Plunging Router MOF 96 a Router and Moulder complete in two cartons.

Opening hours:
Mon-Fri: 8.00-6.00
p.m. Sat: 9.00 a.m.-12.00

24 hour service: free delivery to all areas: ample car parking.

ELU Jig saw ST142
with tilting base and
orbit action.

ELU Portable Circular
Saws MH155 and
MH182

THE R.M. TOOL AND FIXING CO. LTD.
17 HOLLYBUSH LANE, PENN, WOLVERHAMPTON.
Telephone: 37015

Woodworker, June 1980   KINDLY MENTION 'WOODWORKER' WHEN REPLYING TO ADVERTISEMENTS   361

CORONET WOODWORKING MACHINES

Universal & Independent models for Woodworking & Woodturning ♔

SAWING ● BOX COMBING ● WOBBLE SAWING ● SPINDLE MOULDING ● PLANING THICKNESSING ● REBATING ● MORTICING ● SLOTTING & GROOVING ● DISC SANDING BELT SANDING ● GRINDING & POLISHING ● TURNING ● LONG HOLE BORING

Bench mounted & Cabinet models ideal for . . . PROFESSIONALS AND D-I-Y ENTHUSIASTS

Whatever woodworking operation you need — Coronet have the ideal machine.

Since 1946 Coronet have achieved a world wide reputation as leading designers and manufacturers of Quality woodworking machines with production of castings, machining and assembly being carried out in our modern factory — to achieve essential standards of accuracy.
Today our extensive range includes universal machines with fitments and attachments which can be purchased as and when required. — to suit your particular needs.

Send Now for BROCHURE
on all models

CORONET
TOOL CO LTD
Alfreton Road
Derby DE2 4AH

see the Coronet Range in action

—at Coronet Works and Learn-a-Craft Training Centre in Derby
—by arrangement
Telephone: 0332-362141

—at Stockists. Coronet Demonstrators visit main Stockists throughout the year.
Send for details.

Prices quoted are those prevailing at press date and are subject to alteration due to economic conditions.

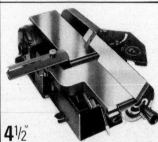

IDEAL FURNITURE

It is recorded that Stephen de Parnham had a house 'in the valley of pear trees' during the reign of Richard the Lionheart (1189-1199).

Parnham has many gardens both formal, kitchen and coppice woodland. The historic house is a fitting base for John Makepeace and the eight cabinet-makers and apprentices who use fine woods and traditional methods to bring alive unique designs that are very much part of the 20th century. Eighteen students at a time can follow an intensive two-year course to learn the skills of cabinet-making, turnery, marquetry, inlaying and gilding, carving, lacquering and polishing.

Parnham House featured at this year's Ideal Home Exhibition in London (at the invitation of the organisers) on a massive stand that conveyed the atmosphere of Parnham — tall 'yew' hedges, stripes of mown grass and a blue 'sky' surrounding displays of recent work. The 10 students who started their two-year course last September were showing some of their early products including a range of bathroom accessories and a series of cabinets with pivoted drawers. Some of last July's graduates also had work on display and there, too, were examples of a new collection known as Parnham Editions.

Each piece is individually signed by the craftsman who made it and will normally be in cherrywood, oak or muninga according to individual taste and preference. Some of the pieces on show were a circular drop-leaf dining table, a dining chair and a folding chair with a coach-hide seat and back. Smaller pieces are made in a variety of timbers, sycamore, ash, elm, satinwood and rosewood in particular.

(See also Focus on Design, WOODWORKER September 1979, pp 505-6).

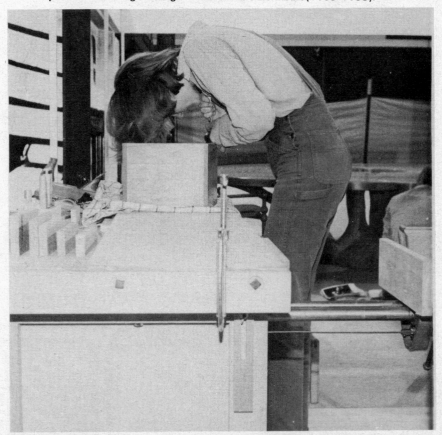

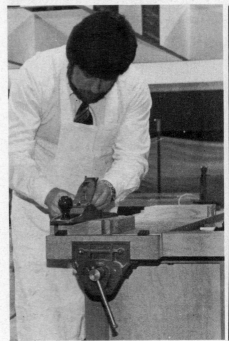

Above and below left: two students 'working' on the Parnham House stand at the Ideal Home exhibition. Below right: Some of the range of Parnham Editions *(acknowledgements John Makepeace);* chairs and stool in solid timber and coach-hide, circular dropleaf dining table in oak with satin finish, seats six people.

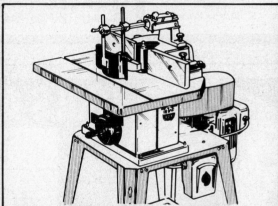

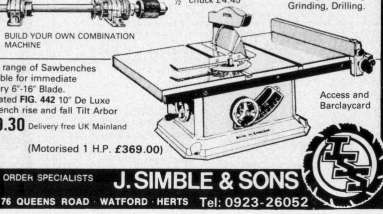

BOOK REVIEWS

Colonial comes home

Most pieces of colonial furniture will not be out of place in British homes where the 'country' style is favoured. The straight, clean lines of trestle tables, ladderback chairs, beds, benches, chests, cabinets and smaller items such as stands and mirrors in the colonial idiom have contributed to its growing popularity in American homes of today and it may well be that we shall see a return journey for colonial furniture to Britain.

Early American craftsmen, many of whom had learned their skills here, were inspired by early Jacobean and Cromwellian furniture. They did not, however, duplicate these heavy and ornate styles but using them as a basis developed designs of a simpler and more practical kind.

Franklin H. Gottshall, a craftsman and teacher of carpentry for 40 years in America and author of several books on furniture making, has written *How to make Colonial Furniture*. He gives details, cutting lists and measured drawings for no less than 44 pieces including chairs; dressing tables; mirrors and benches; chests; beds; desks; sideboards; settles; dressers; gun cabinets; candlestands; tables; floor lamps.

He favours the American timbers — pine, poplar, cedar and walnut — used by the colonial craftsmen and their jointing methods. He recommends the finishes that enhance the natural beauty of the grain. 'In view of my dedication in creating only furniture that in construction, style and materials is faithful to the originals built by our colonial forebears', writes the author in his preface, 'it will not surprise the reader to learn that I do not believe in mutilating new pieces of furniture to simulate antiques. This, I think, is a misguided practice; if comfort or improvement in design resulted, it might be justifiable but this is seldom the case. Therefore, I would advise using the greatest discretion concerning the "antiquing" or "distressing" of new furniture'. Wise words indeed.

The book is a handsome production running to more than 180 pages in hardcovers. It is profusely illustrated with excellent black and white photographic reproductions and measured drawings. Some of these may be a little difficult to follow on account of the detail but obviously the publisher has had to take account of the limitations imposed by the size of the pages — 12 × 8¾ in. Nevertheless, to put such a book on the market at £5.75 is a most creditable achievement by Macmillan Publishing Co Inc in New York and Collier Macmillan Ltd (Stockley Close, Stockley Road, West Drayton UB7 9BE) in Britain.

Many of the pieces illustrated were made by students of the Berry College near Rome in Georgia and the Boyertown area schools, Pennsylvania, where the author taught industrial arts. Three pieces in walnut were built by Robert T. Hogg who has a workshop near Oxford, Pennsylvania.

With its complete lists of materials, clearly written instructions, detailed drawings and photographs of the finished products, the book will commend itself to woodworkers though the dust jacket is rather too lurid for this reviewer's taste.   **G.P.**

Dolly shied and mother's hair came down

Horse-drawn carriages as popular means of conveyance survived longer than is sometimes realised. This reviewer well remembers in the late 1920s that pub yards on market days in the Welsh Marches were thronged with gigs, traps, dogcarts, phaetons belonging to farmers and dealers. Now and again, too, one or two of the local magnates or their ladies would be seen in a victoria or landau driven by a coachman in livery. Then, so it seemed at this stage in time, the horses and the vehicles suddenly vanished and motor cars filled up the pub yards.

As John Thompson explains in his fascinating book *Horse-drawn Carriages* (recently published from 1 Fieldway, Calthorpe Park, Fleet, Hampshire), at the beginning of this century the carriage trade had to supply vehicles for long-distance transport and for the social and leisure pursuits of the aristocracy. By the end of the carriage era the emphasis had changed to short journeys on much better roads, and a much wider section of society was catered for ... the greatest concentration of carriages would no longer be found at the houses of the nobility but, rather, waiting at the railway station.

It is not so many years ago that one of the older residents of Abinger Hammer in Surrey, recalled the long line of carriages waiting at nearby Gomshall station on the outer fringe of the London commuter area. 'But after war started (and he was referring to 1914) we never saw another carriage at Gomshall.'

Gigs and dogcarts remained the most numerous vehicles on the road and John Thompson cites the carriage auctions held at Reading by Thimbleby & Shorland. Over a period of three years from 1976 some 400 carriages were listed and of these 25% were described as gigs, 16% as ralli cars, 15% governess cars, 12% dogcarts, 12% phaetons and 5% waggonettes. The remaining 15% included around 1% each of victorias, landaus, broughams, drags and breaks. The ralli and governess cars appear in greatest numbers because they were the vehicles in fashion at the end of the carriage era.

The book runs to 100 pages in soft covers but does not deal with construction or technicalities as this aspect is the subject of a further volume *Horse-drawn Carriage Construction*. Nevertheless it is a most useful collection of illustrations (in line and halftone), together with descriptions from old trade publications and books on the subject. Though most of the vehicles described are British — and there is an illustration of Queen Victoria starting off on her daily drive at Windsor in the 'donkey chair', with apparently John Brown in attendance — the author has included references to the Concord coach and other American carriages. He makes the point that the Americans built huge numbers on a mass-production basis, and the prices came down accordingly. The idea of standard parts being fitted together on an assembly line was not born with Henry Ford's model T but with the buggy.

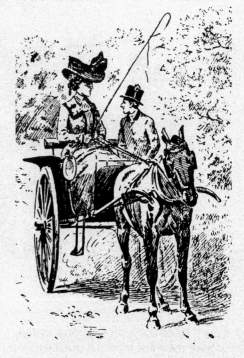

The Americans also developed a whole range of woodworking machines to make spokes and naves and other components for horse-drawn vehicles and by the turn of the century these were capable of very high rates of production. Probably this was why they were not used to such a great extent in Britain where the tradition of hand work persisted and where, of course, demand did not approach that of the American market.

One of the illustrations in the book — a Punch drawing of two Edwardian beauties in a ralli car is a reminder that the fair sex has occupied the driving seat for very many years! Around 1910 this reviewer's mother, who was a keen 'whip' took her father out for an afternoon drive primarily to show off her handling of a new and frisky mare. It was a beautiful summer's afternoon and all went well until they trotted beneath a grove of chestnuts. The light and shadows across the road startled the mare who shied up the bank. The jolt brought mother's hair down and her father's derby went over the hedge. Fortunately the groom had been taken and he got off the back seat (or was pitched off) to restore dignity and order.

But for ever after when passing that spot — in a car by this time — mother's words were the same: 'That's where Dolly shied and my hair came down. Goodness gracious, what a fright I must have looked!'

Horse-drawn Carriages is no. 7 in the series of source books and costs £2.80 plus 30p postage from the author. It is also available through Argus Books Ltd, Argus House, 14 St James Road, Watford, Herts, at £2.80. Together with the carriage construction book now in preparation it will not only encourage model makers to try their skills in building elegant vehicles but stimulate interest in carriage building as at present carried on by a number of craftsmen in this country. **G.P.**

Lurem, make it so easy

It is a jointer, thicknesser/planer, mortiser, drill, shaper, circular saw, tenoner/crosscut, and also, if optional attachments are used, a grinder, sander, woodturner and bandsaw. You can have this combined facility or a simplified version with less operations. Either way, you get real value for money.

If you look closer, the features are even more impressive. Solidly built for reliability intended for hard and continuous work with minimum maintenance. Rugged castings are extensively used yet it is highly manoeuvreable. Individual components are easily accessible. Adjustments are positive and effective. In fact, the C210B is both functional and practical. And safe.

Fortunately, it is inexpensive too. So for your home workshop, professional business or for schools and technical training, it is a sound and safe investment with twelve months guarantee.

Whether you are a DIY enthusiast or a professional with your own commercial business, there are ten good reasons for investing in the Lurem C210B.

lurem For Reliability and Service

For full details write to:
Lurem Machines
9 Biggin Hill Road, Evington,
Leicester, LE5 6HQ.
Telephone: (0533) 735554.

TOOL SALES

190 Nevill Road, Hove, Sussex
Telephone: Brighton 501911

WOODWORKING MACHINES
INSTORE DEMONSTRATIONS

WOODWORKING RANGE

Bosch POF 50 Router
Price £49.50
(inc. VAT at 15%) + P&P

Bosch P10 Jigsaw
Price £36.75
(inc. VAT at 15%) + P&P.

Bosch PKS46 6" Circular
Saw. Price £52.50
(inc. VAT at 15%) + P&P

Black & Decker

ELECTRIC TOOLS

★ *LARGE DISCOUNTS AVAILABLE ON ALL POWER TOOLS* ★

PLEASE SEND FOR CATALOGUE

**190 NEVILL ROAD,
HOVE, SUSSEX**
Telephone: 0273 501911/502360

EASY PARKING
ACCESSORIES AVAILABLE
LARGE STOCKS
DELIVERY SERVICE

Delivery within 28 days

ALAN HOLTHAM

WOODTURNER, WOODTURNERS SUPPLIER, LIGHT WOODWORKING MACHINERY SPECIALISTS

CORONET

An a main stockist for the complete CORONET range we are able to supply most machines, accessories and spares from stock at competitive prices.

CORONET ELF LATHE

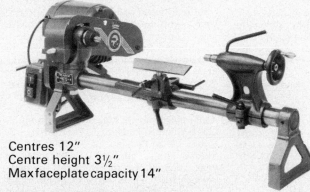

Centres 12"
Centre height 3½"
Max faceplate capacity 14"

Motor ½hp 1425rpm 4 speed

Complete as illustrated for only
£163.00 + VAT
Extra bed lengths from stock at
£5.00 + VAT per foot

CONSORT UNIVERSAL

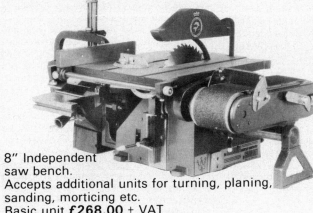

8" Independent saw bench.
Accepts additional units for turning, planing, sanding, morticing etc.
Basic unit **£268.00** + VAT
As illustrated **£520.15** + VAT

ALAN HOLTHAM

HOURS
9.00 – 5.30
Tues. - Sat.

The Old Stores Turnery,
Wistaston Rd., Willaston,
Nantwich, Cheshire.
Tel: Crewe (0270) 67010

We accept Barclaycard or can arrange Terms.

---

workpieces

Seeing for yourself

Woodmen, the appropriately named and rapidly expanding woodworking machinery and equipment dealer, has opened another showroom and warehouse. This is a two-storey building at 104 Churchill Road (off Launton Road) Bicester, Oxon. 'We are well-placed here to service the midlands and northern home counties,' Nigel Voisey and his partner Ashley Phillips told WOODWORKER on 6 March during the official opening week.

The firm had staged an exhibition and demonstrations in the 6,000sq ft showroom which is on two floors. It was well supported by a large number of manufacturers and suppliers and attracted a big attendance from a wide area. One manufacturer told WOODWORKER that he had been amazed at the amount of business placed; he had also received good enquiries for larger machines.

Woodmen, which is based in Cardiff, opened a northern showroom and warehouse at Barnard Castle, Co Durham, earlier this year. Plans are in hand for further expansion in the south east and Scotland where Mr Voisey says business is very encouraging.

The Bicester premises feature a permanent demonstration facility covering machines for home workshops and commercial production. There is also a video installation and the intention is to build up a library of films. As Mr Phillips explained: 'This will allow prospective buyers of, for example, universals to see in about 20 minutes the main features of a particular machine, whereas a full-scale working demonstration could take something like 2hr. Of course, we shall be delighted to stage working demonstrations, but not every would-be buyer can spare the time on a working demonstration of every machine that we have in the showroom.'

Woodmen operates a weekly delivery service to every part of the UK mainland by its own transport (subject to stock availability). In Mr Voisey's opinion delivery of heavy machinery which also requires expert handling, is not satisfactory. 'With our own transport and staff we can ensure that machines which have been test-run before leaving our warehouses are delivered to the customer in working condition. It is expensive but it does mean we save time and money in dealing with complaints and we retain goodwill. But if any machine is not satisfactory we replace it, or give the customer his money back plus the delivery charge.'

Among the ranges demonstrated at the Bicester premises were: Arundel (lathes); Burgess (bandsaws); Coronet (lathes, planers, bandsaws, universals); DeWalt (band and radial arm saws, mitre saw and extractors); Electra (sawbench, planer/thicknesser, grinder, extractor); Elu (portable power tools, sawbenches); Harrison (lathe); Kity (saws, spindles, planer/thicknessers, lathes, universal, extractor); Lurem (saws, planer/thicknessers, spindles, universals, surface planer, thicknesser, chisel mortiser); McCulloch (chainsaws); Multico (saws, surface planers, thicknesser, chisel mortiser, single ended tenoner, spindle, bandsaws); Myford (lathes); Modern (planer/thicknesser, chisel mortiser, mitre guillotine); Morsφ (mitre guillotine); Picador (disc

sander); Sacme (router stand); Sedgwick (planer/thicknesser, sawbench); Shopmate (radial arm saw); Stanley (routers); Startrite (saws, spindle moulder, bench drill, extractor); Wadkin (portable power tools); Warco (bench and pedestal drills, saws, lathe); Willow (bandsaw); Woodmen (K5 universal, workbenches)-

Manager of the Woodmen showroom and warehouse at Bicester is Mike Boden who will be pleased to deal with enquiries and meet those who want to gather new ideas and make the most of their capital and workshop space.

Hotel accommodation at Woodworker Show

For the period of the Woodworker Show (4-9 November 1980), Grand Metropolitan Hotels Ltd offers special booking facilities and rates at its hotels in London in the £20-£25, £25-£30 and £30-£35 ranges for single room with bath. The company's hotel nearest to the Show venue at the RHS New Hall, is St Ermin's (just off Victoria Street, SW1), where a single room with bath is £23 a night.

Reservations can be made either by telephoning 01-629 6611 and asking for central reservations office, or writing to the office at:

Grand Metropolitan Hotels
Freepost 32
London W1E 3YZ

There is no need to use a stamp if the envelope is addressed as above. Grand Metropolitan cannot guarantee first choice of hotel but will reserve the nearest alternative.

Grand Metropolitan Hotels Ltd also has a package accommodation and travel arrangement with British Rail whereby up to 50% of the standard return journey may be saved. Details can be had from Grand Metropolitan at the above address.

Courses

Full-time one year vocational design courses in traditional cabinet making are offered by Shrewsbury Technical College. Details and application forms from the Principal, Shrewsbury Technical College, London Road, Shrewsbury SY2 6PR (Phone: (0743) 51544).

City and Guilds of London Art School offer courses as follows: Three year diploma course in wood and stone restoration: two year certificate course in wood and gesso carving, oil and water gilding and decorative techniques: two year certificate course in lacquer work, gilding, painting furniture, faux marbre, faux bois, frescoes etc. Sae to the Secretary, 124 Kennington Park Road, London SE11 4DJ (01-735 2306).

Musical Instrument Making course from 30 June-4 July at Pudsey F.E. Centre, Richardshaw Lane, Pudsey, Leeds. Fee £14. A week's course offering an opportunity to make one of the following folk or early musical instruments: Appalachian mountain dulcimer, hammer dulcimer, plucked psaltery, rebec, bodhran, tabors and side drums, cittern, bowed psaltery. Details from head of centre A. Coulthard at the above address.

Full-time courses in musical instrument making and repair. Applications are invited for the September 1980 entry to follow a three year full-time course in violin making and repairing at Ystrad Mynach College of Further Education. Details from the Principal, School of Musical Instrument Making and Repairing, Thomas Street, Abertridwr, Caerphilly, Mid Glamorgan (Phone: Senghenydd 830154). Also available at the college is a two year course in piano tuning and repair.

Courses at West Dean

These are a varied mixture and comprise weekend, one and four day courses, five, six and seven day courses plus a 10 day course. Details should be obtained from the college at West Dean, Chichester, West Sussex PO18 0QZ but a brief summary follows to whet the appetite: The 9th to 15th August has been set aside as a family week with a combination of tutors and crafts including clay, sculpture, spinning and weaving, drawing and painting, making simple musical instruments and music making. Experienced workers in wood might be interested in the Cottage Furniture stage 2 course in June (15-20) which will include drawing, solid geometry, setting out, chair design and anthropometrics, drilling aids, steam bending, design and making of formers.

Steenwise Ltd.

TOOLS FOR CRAFTSMEN

GORDON STOKES INVITES YOU TO VISIT HIS NEW STEENWISE WORKSHOP IN BATH

Centrally placed to service Wiltshire, Gloucestershire and South Wales, this new Workshop is equipped with a large range of woodworking machinery, ready for immediate demonstration by specialist craftsmen. Each demonstrator will give you impartial advice on the choice and price of machinery, and help with any technical problems you may have.
The Workshop is open from Tuesday to Saturday – 9.30am to 6.0pm. We are not offering a beautiful showroom, but a real woodworking environment, so come and see for yourself, if the machine of your choice will really do what you want.

Gordon Stokes (Steenwise) Ltd., 110A Mount Road, Whiteway, Bath. Tel: Bath (0225) 22617.

Steenwise policy is to supply machines produced in the U.K. and Europe, by well-known manufacturers, at the best possible prices. Our pricing policy is fair to both customer and manufacturer, we buy at the best possible prices, add a small fixed percentage to cover our costs, we then sell to you at this price, which is often less than the manufacturers recommended price.

We normally despatch direct to your door within seven days from receiving your order. Payment can be made cash with order, cash on delivery or credit card. A confidential hire purchase scheme with attractive rates of interest is also available. Leasing is possible if you are V.A.T. registered. A full cash refund is guaranteed if your goods prove to be defective.

Gordon Stokes says,

"I have always tried to maintain the highest possible standards in this wonderful craft. My training courses offer the woodworker instruction in techniques, intended to develop the individual's ability to the absolute maximum. I decided to become a Steenwise operator because it offers the best of both worlds to my customers – a broad selection of demonstration machinery, some of the finest manufactured in the U.K. and Europe. Together with a mail order system that allows the customer to buy at the best possible price. By selling through Steenwise, I can aid the craftsman in his choice of machinery, knowing that he will have excellent value for money".

We will be pleased to quote for any machine or accessories, and we are sure you will be surprised at the prices we can offer. Trade enquiries will be most welcome. Below are some examples of our current price lists.

Planer Thicknesser
● 10" × 6" Scheppach HM1 2 H.P. Motor, Floor Standing – £399.00.
● 10" × 6" Kity 7136 1½ H.P. Motor, Floor Standing – £564.00.
● 6" × 4" Kity 7139 1½ H.P. Motor, Floor Standing – £347.00.

Band Saws
● Kity 7212 – £299.00.

Circular Saws
● Kity 5017 2¼" depth of cut ¾ H.P. – £169.00.
● Elektra Site Saw 3½" depth of cut 2.3 H.P. (Galvanised) – £159.00.

Special Offer
● Kity 5020 Combination – consisting of a planer thickness or spindle moulder and slot mortiser. Recommended man. price £662.40, Steenwise price £500 including free double ended 5" bench grinder.
● Kity 6646 variable speed lathe, floor standing, recommended man. price £517.50 Steenwise price £469.00 including a free 5" double end bench grinder and six Sorby wood turning tools.
● Kity 10" × 6" planer thicknesser 7136 and dust extractor 695, recommended man. price £1,018.57, Steenwise price £647.50 including hose and attachments.
All prices include VAT at 15%.

For further information about Steenwise stocks and prices, return the coupon to our Head Office in Bingley, West Yorkshire, or telephone us direct on Bradford (0274) 560699 or Bingley (09766) 69136.

Please send me more information about Steenwise stocks and prices

Name . . . .

Address . . . .

. . . .

Showroom and warehouse Limefield Mills, Woods Street, Crossflats, Bingley, West Yorkshire.

THE EMCOSTAR
More Craft . . . Less Space!!

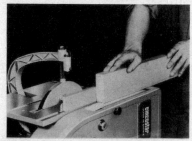
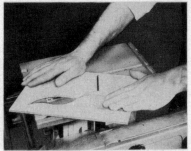
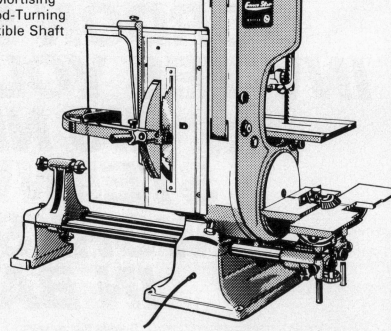
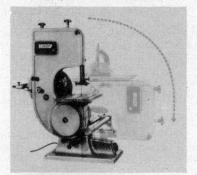

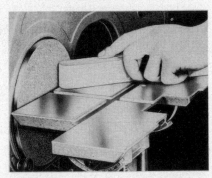

Mr White's treadle lathe. The photograph was taken in the grounds of Lathbury House near Newport Pagnell, during an arts and crafts exhibition. The bottom photograph is a close-up of the workpiece. With rising costs of energy treadle lathes may well be heading for a come-back.

Dennis White still uses a treadle lathe

laminated teak. In the last year of his apprenticeship he turned the four columns supporting a dome over a shop in Thames Street at Kingston. This is still something of a landmark in the town and can be seen from Kingston bridge over the Thames.

In his spare time he specialised in turning four-poster bed posts as well as hand spiral turning. At the end of his apprenticeship his boss gave Mr White the treadle lathe. He still uses it for turning four-poster bed posts though it is more than 100 years old. The wooden beds have been replaced but the treadle parts and headstock are the same as when Mr White first used the lathe nearly 60 years ago.

Always keen to pass on his knowledge to those willing to learn, he gives lessons in turning to selected students. One reader who recently spent three days with Mr White says he is 'an excellent tutor, a gentleman in the truest sense of the word; he inspires confidence in his students and has the patience of a saint. His description of the approach to the task of turning that 22ft length of laminated teak and the working of the block over a period of two weeks is fascinating.'

Many visitors to last year's Woodworker Show saw Mr White demonstrating an Arundel lathe on the stand of Roger's, the Hitchin (Herts) distributor of woodworking tools and materials.

At 73 Dennis White is still an active and dedicated woodturner. Turning is the love of his life and he intends to carry on until he is 'forced to give it up.' This is unlikely as Mr White is turning instructor to five apprentices at Park Green & Co Ltd, in Uxbridge, a company with an international reputation for quality hand-turned peppermills. It was started more than 30 years ago by the present managing director Alan Adgey-Edgar and Mr White has been with Park Green as hand woodturning instructor the whole of that time.

He was indentured to the sum of £25 at the age of 14 to wood turner A. McCrerie of Hampton Wick near Kingston on Thames and started his apprenticeship on a treadle lathe at 5s a week rising by annual increments of 2s 6d a week. In 1929 he turned his biggest job — a 22ft (by 2ft hollow square) length of

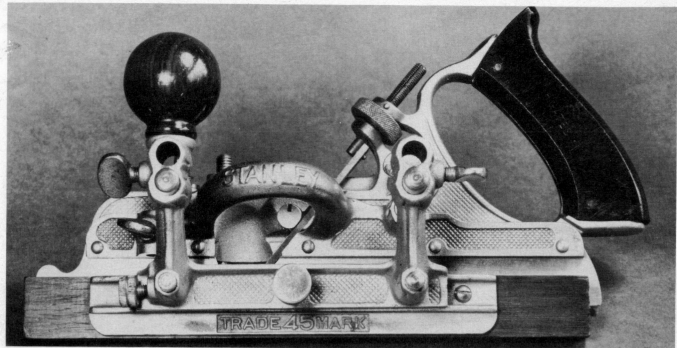

HINTS ON TOOL USE

Guild member Bill Gates of Orpington, contributes the following notes on using the Stanley 45 (which he has had for many years) and the Record 405. 'These are basically identical planes though the Record 405 has some minor modifications in cutter design,' he says. The drawings (taken from his Stanley 45 made in the US) and the pictures are by Mr Gates.

General (Figs. 7, 8 and 9): Work from the front and within limits of comfortable reach, moving backwards as each part is completed. There are three reasons for this: 1 a cleaner cut is made; 2 control of the tool is better; 3 this method is more efficient and should be adopted with all tools of a similar type.

Top: Author's Stanley 45 still in excellent condition. Right: Length of cut approx. 150mm, short fairly fast movement when the use of the plane has been mastered gives best results (see Fig. 9). Below: Left hand bead degraded by flat after finishing face of work (see Fig. 3).

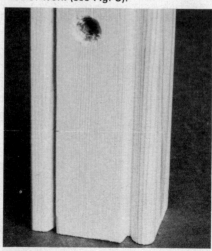

Starting at the rear end and working forward increases risk of grain tearing, particularly when working against the grain. It is also a slow method with long lengths of timber and tends towards unbalanced control over the tool.

In Figs. 7 and 8 the cutter setting is shown. The groove which receives the cutter in the body of the plane must be kept clean and free of dust. Press the cutter fully home when tightening the wing nut. This will set the cutter in its correct position. Additional cutters are available to form hollows and rounds.

Grooving Fig. 1: This shows the plane set up for grooving using a 5mm cutter (C). This is held in the body (B) by a cotter-pin and a wing-nut. The distance of the groove from the edge is controlled by fence (F). Gauge (G) regulates the depth of the groove. The sliding section supporting the cutter, and contributing the shaving thickness on the free edge of the cutter, should be used with all cutters over 5mm in width.

Matching or tonguing Fig. 2: This is a special cutter (C) that cuts the tongue in one operation. Fence (F) controls the position of the tongue on the edge of the board. Gauge (G) is replaced by an adjustable gauge (G/3) on the cutter.

Beading matched boards Fig. 3: A gauge (G/2) is used for this named a beading gauge.

This replaces fence (F). It is attached to the sliding section and sets the position of the bead. Fence (F) is set tight against G/2 to prevent this moving at the rear end. Gauge (G) regulates the depth of the cut. It is important to work the bead below the surface of the work (about 1.5mm), so that when finishing (planing and sanding) the shape of the bead is not spoilt.

Rebating Fig. 4: Fence (F) is attached to the upper holes so that it slides under the cutter (C). The cutter should be wider than the rebate to form a clean edge. The sliding section must be moved under the cutter so that it rests on the timber to prevent the cutter digging-in.

Dado or grooving across the grain Fig. 5: When the distance from the edge exceeds the length of the long arms a batten is used (as shown) to form the guide. Two spurs are now brought into action, one is attached to the body (B) the other to the sliding section. The spurs cut through the fibres in advance of the cutter to provide a clean cut. Both depth gauges (G) and (G1) can be used to set the depth of the groove.

Bead or astragal moulding Fig. 6: The sliding section is adjusted so that it bears on the timber by moving it under the cutter (C). The fence (F) gauges the distance from the edge and depth gauge (G) the depth of the cut.

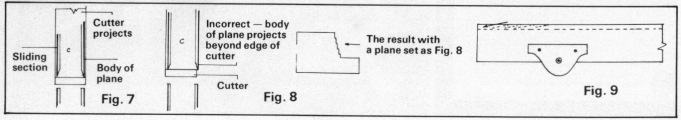

Fig. 7 — Sliding section / Cutter projects / Body of plane / c

Fig. 8 — Incorrect — body of plane projects beyond edge of cutter / Cutter / c

The result with a plane set as Fig. 8

Fig. 9

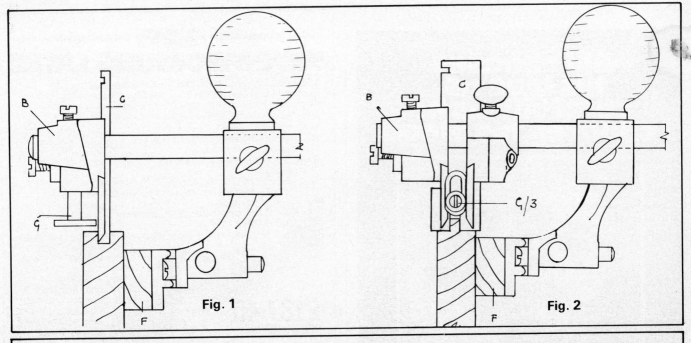

Fig. 1

Fig. 2

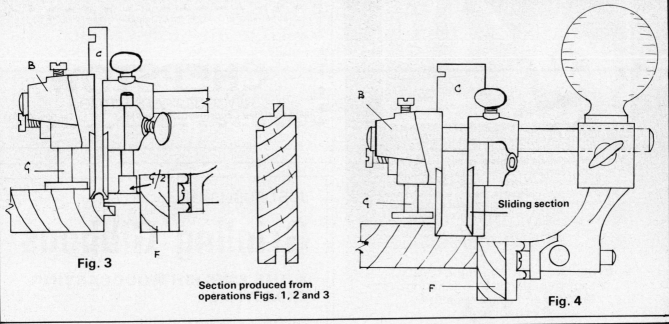

Fig. 3

Section produced from
operations Figs. 1, 2 and 3

Sliding section

Fig. 4

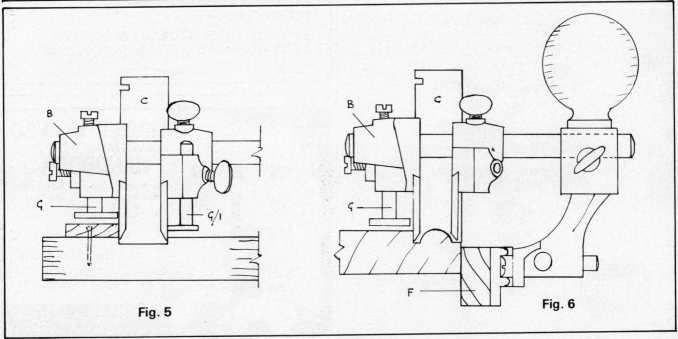

Fig. 5

Fig. 6

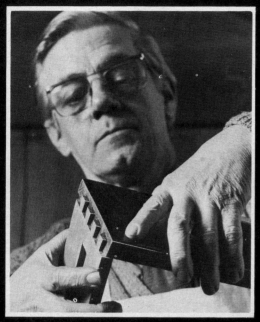

R. W. Shillitoe describes the making of

NEEDLE AND CROCHET HOOK CASES IN VENEER

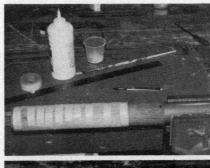

I, like all craftsmen, take a pride in my tools and insist that they are stored in the best conditions. This was the point made by my wife, a skilled needle worker, arguing that the tools of her trade — her knitting needles and crochet hooks in particular — deserved better than a battered cardboard tube sealed at one end with adhesive tape.

A tube plugged at each end and with some means of access was the basic requirement, although as most of her other equipment is housed in a Victorian workbox, something with a period flavour seemed appropriate.

Eventually we decided that the tube would be laminated with veneer, providing a strong and lightweight construction, and the ends would be stopped with pieces cut from the solid and decoratively shaped. The top and bottom of the case would be a simple push fit together, a shoulder formed by reducing the length of the outer laminations of the body, thereby making the joint flush. Sufficient mahogany veneer and solid stuff was available for the manufacture of two containers, one for crochet hooks, the other for knitting needles.

Construction Preparation begins with the selection of a suitable former around which the laminations may be glued. Providing it is straight and of uniform diameter, any material may be used, although it is advantageous for it to be hollow. For the crochet hook case a length of aluminium TV aerial with O.D. 2.5cm was used; some plastics drain piping, O.D. 5.5cm served for the needle holder. The outside of the former needs to be smooth and, if of wood, should be well waxed or varnished to prevent glue from adhering. The length of the former should be appreciably greater than the planned length of the case to enable one end to be held in the vice while work proceeds.

Construction is shown in Fig. 1. Each lamination should be cut slightly oversize in terms of width, remembering that outside layers will need to be cut significantly wider as the diameter of the tube increases. Mahogany veneer is fairly flexible, but danger of splitting during bending may be minimised if the laminations are soaked in warm water for about 20min until pliable and immediately wrapped around the former to dry. It is essential that the veneer is *thoroughly* dry (I used an electric hair dryer) before trimming and gluing.

The body When cut to length and the ends squared, the first lamination is wrapped tightly around the former and cut to width with sharp knife and straight edge. Trial and error removal of very thin slivers may be necessary until a tight butt joint is achieved. The joint is glued, held with veneer tape or pressure sensitive tape, and put aside to dry. When dry check that the tube will slide up and down the former before proceeding further. If the former is warped or the veneer even slightly damp before gluing, you will have made a very nice but very useless veneered former!

The second lamination is cut to width over the first, taking care not to exert too much knife pressure. After final trimming coat the inside thinly but totally with glue, place in position staggering the joints and hold with tape until dry, as before. Contact adhesive is not recommended as some adjustment is usually needed. For the smaller diameter crochet hook case two laminations were felt to be sufficient for this stage, and the needle case required three. The shoulder for the top to butt against is now formed by two (or three) further laminations, cutting these the required amount shorter than the previous layers.

Assembly proceeds as before (Fig.2). If the cutting of the veneer has been done accurately and squarely, trimming of the ends of the body will have been kept to a minimum. This completes the manufacture of the body except for the closure of one end. This will be dealt with after construction of the top has been considered.

The top The top is, in effect, a sleeve and should have a fairly tight push fit over the projecting core of the body. The diameter of the former has therefore to be increased by the thickness of the core. This is most easily achieved by veneering an appropriate length of it with the same number of laminations as the body core. The top is built up on this (Fig. 3). The top should be tried on to the body for goodness of fit after the first lamination. A slightly over-tight fit may be left and eased after completion by gentle sanding, but a loose fit should be tightened by 'sweating on' subsequent laminations.

This is best done by cutting the veneer to the required width when slightly damp and immediately gluing. Providing it is well secured by tape while drying, the end result will be a slight reduction in the diameter of the whole rather than the opening of the butt joint, and has shown itself to be stable. A refinement is to cut the final lamination for top and bottom from the same length of veneer so that the grain runs through the joint.

The ends The end pieces demand squareness and accuracy in cutting the shoulders if a thick unsightly glue line is to be avoided. It is easier to cut the shoulders while the ends are slightly oversize and glue them in position before paring to the correct diameter. Ends may be left plain or shaped according to preference. When shaping, the work is best supported by slipping it back on to the former.

It is here that a hollow former becomes an asset as the build up of air pressure will prevent the insertion of a solid former, once one end has been sealed. This is also an important point to remember when designing the length of the sleeve, as air pressure will tend to prevent the top being pushed fully home.

Finishing is a matter of individual choice. My cases were given the traditional sequence of papering, staining, grain filling, and a full bodied french polish. Once again, handling is facilitated by supporting the parts on the former. The final stage is to glue a roundel of felt inside each end to deaden the sounds of the contents rattling.

The method described is cheap and simple, demands few tools and produces a strong, light and attractive article. It is open to adaptations and modifications. For example, inlay work such as a monogram, could have been worked into the final lamination. The use of contrasting veneers, cone-shaped or oval formers could be considered. Anyone with a homeless telescope, scrolls or certificates need look no further!

Top: The finished articles.
Below: Fig. 2 shows assembly.
Bottom: Fig. 3 construction details.

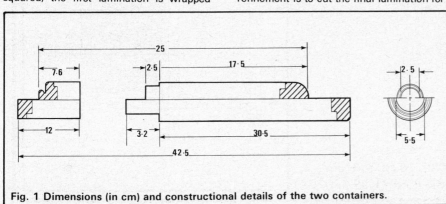

Fig. 1 Dimensions (in cm) and constructional details of the two containers.

CLOCKS

For Everyman Exhibition

sponsored by CLOCKS magazine An exhibition for clock lovers

"We've been waiting for this for 30 years"

"Nothing like it has ever been staged before"

"What a marvellous show"

Comments from last year's visitors

Well it's coming again – Bigger – Better – Longer

If you – Buy – Make – Restore – Collect – Read about or just like looking at or "Talking" clocks, come along to the comfort of the modern Kensington Town Hall – Enjoy the atmosphere of beautiful clocks.

You can even park your car if you come early!

KENSINGTON TOWN HALL,
Hornton St. Kensington, London W8.
Thursday to Sunday 3rd to 6th July 1980. 10 am to 6 pm.
Refreshments are available. Tickets at the door £1.25.

Access to the hall

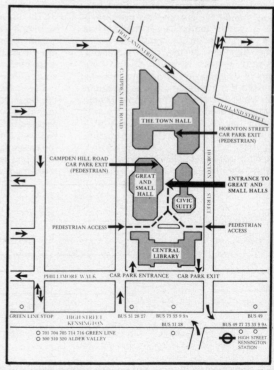

REPLACING A SASH WINDOW

Gordon Warr had occasion to replace a window at a friend's house. It was a small window for a boxroom but the principles shown described here are basically the same for all flat window frames of the domestic type. Those who have not tackled a piece of joinery before should not find a window of this type too difficult either in the making or the fixing, says Gordon Warr.

Most windows of houses are built-in as the walls are erected. This means a new frame must be made slightly smaller than the original to allow it to be manoeuvred into place. The height is less critical, as the sill is bedded onto mortar which allows a little latitude. My experience with replacement windows is to make them around 4mm (3/16in.) smaller than the original.

Because this was a replacement window there were minor modifications as compared with a window bought from a supplier. The joints between the stile and head were of the open mortise and tenon type because the joggle (or horn) would be completely removed when the window was fixed. Normally on new work, the joggle is partly removed by sawing it on the splay; the part remaining is then built

Below left: 1. Setting out frame members. Below right: 2. Gauging mortise in sill. Centre left: 3. Boring out waste from joints. Centre right: 4. Completing mortise with chisel. Bottom left: 5. Cutting shoulder to tenon. Bottom right: 6. Sawing the cheek.

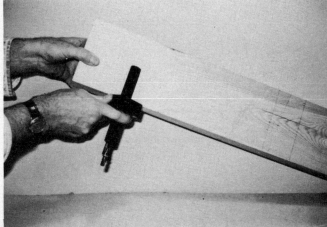

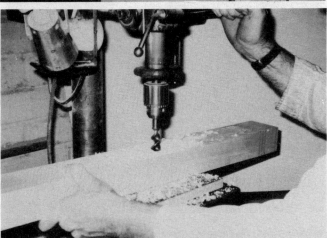

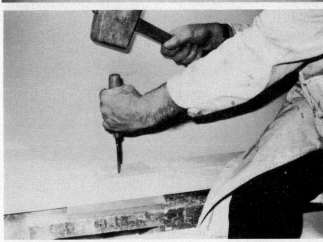

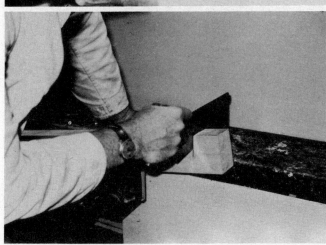

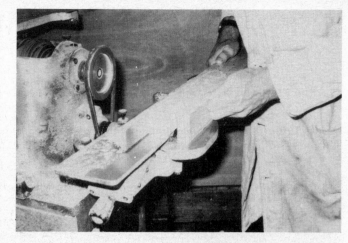
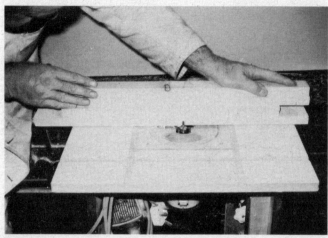
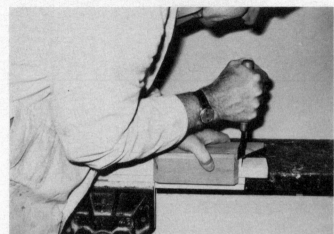
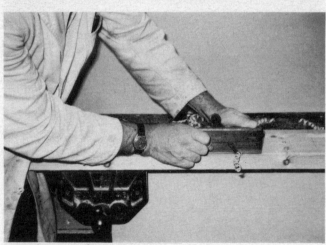
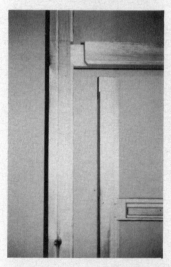

into the brickwork to provide a very firm anchorage. The sill of a window is normally cut so as to fit around the wall. This also applies to a replacement window. Partly because of machining methods used when frames are mass-produced, heads and stiles have the same cross-section, and this includes a groove on the outer edges in line with the one on the underside of the sill (as shown in the drawings). The purpose of this groove is to accommodate the mortar and thus help to hold the window as it is built-in.

While many joinery stockists supply window members ready-machined to the appropriate section, it is not always easy to match new material to an old frame. This is because although window members are normally fairly similar, there are variations in actual cross-sections.

Top left: 7. Forming bevel to the sill. Top right: 8. Rebating on small planer. Centre left: 9. Using router as spindle. Centre right: 10. Using the mitre template. Above left: 11. Forming throating or drip groove. Above centre: 12. The completed joints. Above right: 13. Driving in the wedges. Right: 14. Cramped up and test applied.

There's no easy substitute for an Elu Router

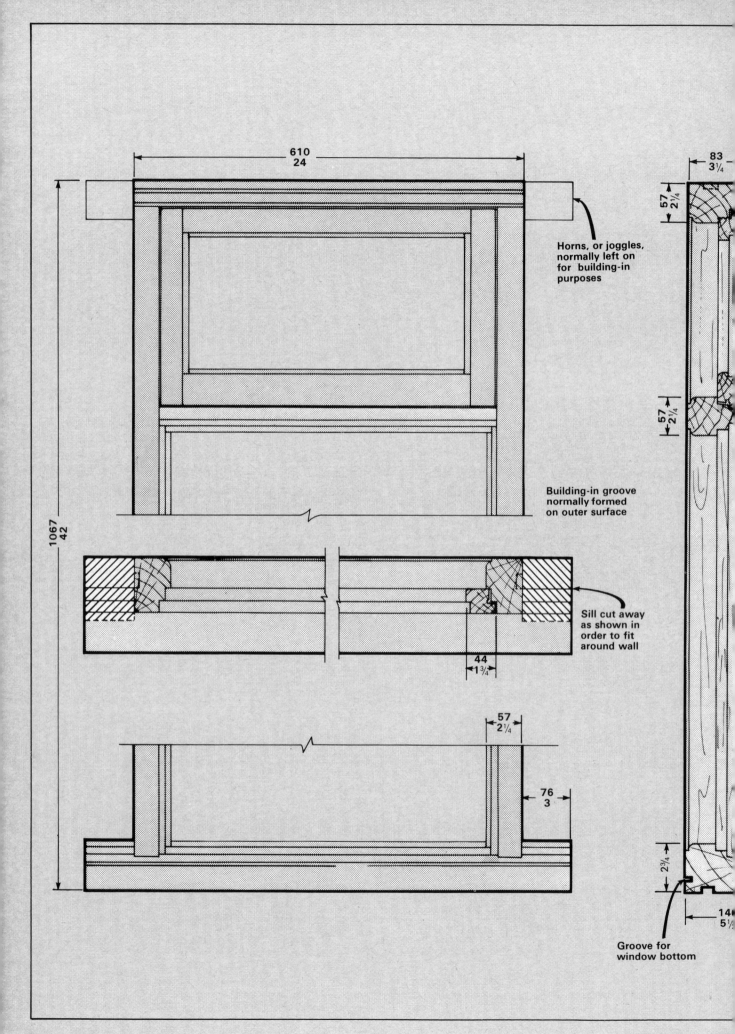

610
24

Horns, or joggles,
normally left on
for building-in
purposes

83
3¼

57
2¼

57
2¼

1067
42

Building-in groove
normally formed
on outer surface

Sill cut away
as shown in
order to fit
around wall

44
1¾

57
2¼

76
3

2¾

14●
5½

Groove for
window bottom

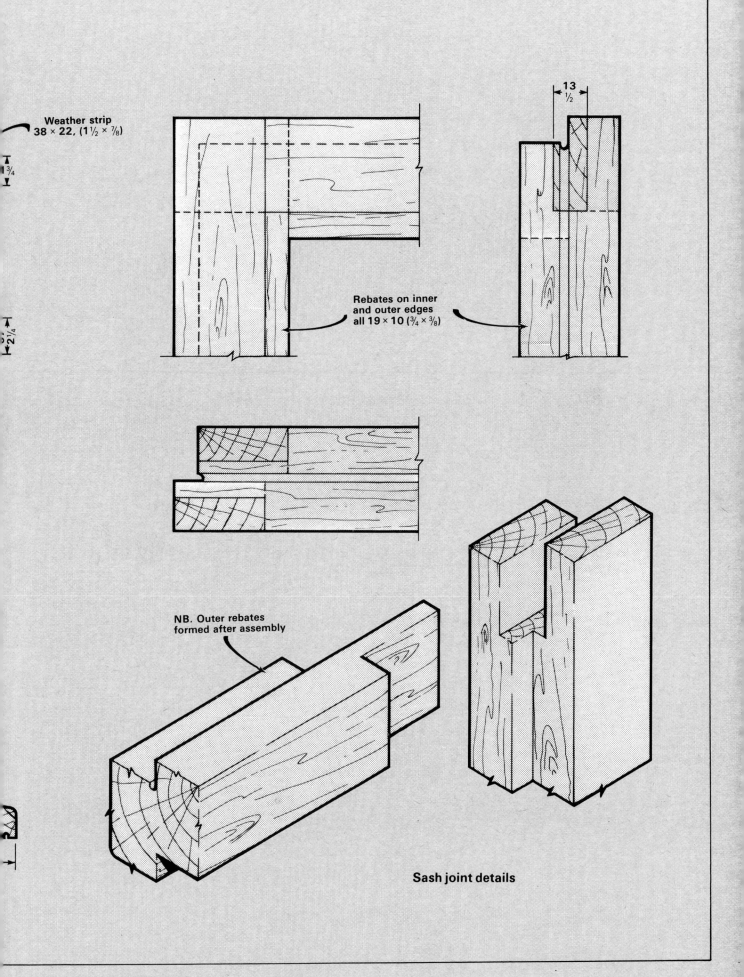

Weather strip
38 × 22, (1½ × ⅞)

13
½

**Rebates on inner
and outer edges
all 19 × 10 (¾ × ⅜)**

**NB. Outer rebates
formed after assembly**

Sash joint details

AmerSaw

A special introduction to the
ROUTER & JIG
SAW TABLE

Free*

FREE
WITH***

HITACHI TR8 ROUTER.................**£97.75**
or
ELU MOF 96 ROUTER.................**£98.90**
or
METABO 4380 ROUTER............**£121.32**
or
METABO 561 JIG SAW.............**£104.65**
or
HITACHI 60A JIG SAW...............**£86.00**

*Other models on application
All inc. VAT. Carriage paid*

**And an invitation to our Woodworking Machinery
Exhibition on May 31/June 1**

USE IT AS A ROUTER TABLE!

USE IT AS A JIG SAW TABLE

This versatile table converts the portable router of Jig saw into "stationary" power tools, in minutes. Frees both hands for better control of work piece. Allows operations otherwise impossible with portable power tools. Increases speed and accuracy. Can be mounted to almost any work surface.

ACS DISTRIBUTION

PARK FARM INDUSTRIAL ESTATE ● STUDLEY ROAD ● REDDITCH ● WORCESTER
Telephone: Redditch 27058, 27083, 26983 or 27541

SASH WINDOW

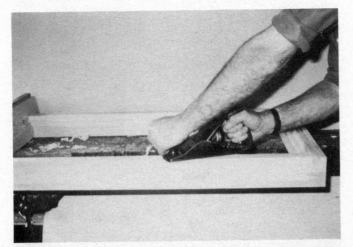

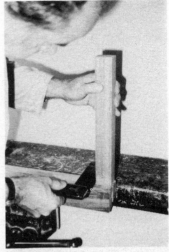

Far left: 15. Levelling off the face. Left: 16. Starting the sash. Below left: 17. Cutting the open mortise. Below right: 18. Checking sash for squareness. Centre left: 19. Awaiting glue to set. Centre right: 20. Sanding face of sash. Bottom left: 21. Levelling off the joints. Bottom right: 22. Rebating edges of sash.

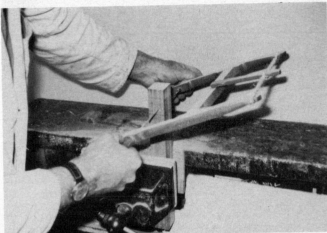

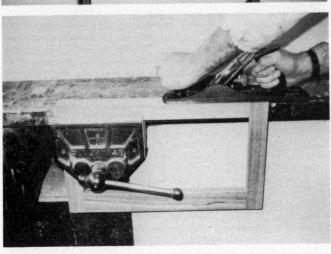

Top from left: 23. Screwing sash to frame; 24. The completed frame; 25. Removing old sash; 26. Sash and transom removed. Far left: 27. Plugging the walls. Centre: 28. Plugs driven into brickwork. Above: 29. Preparing for window bottom.

Timber for a window frame should be selected with care. Joinery redwood is the accepted timber. It should be dry with the minimum of sapwood present. Any stock with annual growth rings wider than 5mm, or approximately five rings/in. should be rejected. Hardwood is sometimes used for the sill, a popular species being keruing.

My window frame started as a plank. The first task was to saw and plane up the various pieces and the next stage was marking out. Head, transome and sill were held in the vice and initially the overall width squared in. Next the thickness of the stiles is marked in (photo 1). In joinery work of this type the joints are kept in line with the rebates wherever possible, and the building-in groove in the sill (and head and stiles), is kept in line with the joints. The stiles are marked in a similar way while held as a pair, and the setting-out is completed by using the mortise gauge (photo 2).

I use a drilling machine to bore out the bulk of the waste from the mortises (photo 3), then a chisel to complete the cutting (photo 4). On the through mortises, the outer side of the mortise is made rather wider, around 3mm (⅛in.); this is known as wedge room. The basic cutting of the tenon is straight-forward sawing (photos 5 and 6), but care is needed to ensure that correct position of the shoulders is established.

My tilting arbor sawbench proved its worth when shaping the sill. Photo 7 shows it in use making the main cut, the waste piece being completely removed by a second cut from the upper surface. The rebate on the sill and the double rebates on the other members were carried out on my small planer (photo 8).

The moulding to the inner edge was done in two stages. The small rebate at the edge of the moulding was formed — this is referred to as a quirk. For the rounding-over I used an electric router set up like a small spindle (photo 9). As I was using a rounding-over cutter which has a guide pin it was unnecessary to use a fence to guide the wood. It simplifies matters if the depth of the moulding is made level with one of the double rebates.

The moulded edges of the shoulders on the tenoned members were cut at 45° as the first stage of forming the mitres needed at these internal corners. This cutting was carried out with a chisel and mitre template (photo 10).

Rather more work is needed in forming the mitres on the mortised members. Reference to the drawings will show that it is first necessary to cut away part of the wood on both sides of the mortise. There are two points here: First, when cutting away the moulding due allowance must be made for forming the 45° cut; second, where the rebate has been formed slightly on the slope, as with the upper edge of the transom, the cut-away part of the stile must be made with a corresponding slope. The mitre to the mortise is formed as for the tenon shoulder.

Various grooves had to be formed. The building-in groove on the sill was cut by making several passes over the circular saw blade; this method was also used for the groove in the sill needed for the tongue of the window bottom. The head was grooved to receive a weather strip.

The drip groove, or throating to the underside of the sill was done with a small plane I made many years ago (photo 11), but

this can be done by circular saw or router. With all the parts thus formed the joints were checked for correct fit (photo 12).

Joinery is always better for some cleaning-up, so I tackled all parts which could not easily be planed or glasspapered after assembly. Wedges were cut ready for cramping-up and a quantity of Cascamite One-Shot prepared.

Photos 13 and 14 show the assembly (checking of which is the same as for any other piece of woodwork). A couple of nails were driven into the open joints at the head as an additional means of securing. Excess adhesive was cleaned-off while still wet. Once the adhesive had set all projecting ends, except the sill, were removed and levelled. Cleaning-up the faces and levelling the joints completed the main frame.

These days the standard way of making sashes is with open mortise and tenon joints; photo 16 shows the start of the marking out. Because the mortises are open the waste can be sawn away (photo 17) and a chisel used for the final trimming to the line. Because of the small section of the sash members the edges were not moulded but rounded-over after assembly. Only the rebates on the inner edges were formed before assembly, and with these cut the sash could be assembled (photos 18 and 19). I rely entirely on adhesive when assembling sashes but apply the G-cramps (seen in the photos) to make sure the joints do not spring, even slightly, open.

With the adhesive set, the surfaces were cleaned-up (photo 20), and rounding over of the inner edges completed with chisel, bullnose plane and glasspaper. Outer edges were levelled-off (photo 21) and the rebates to these edges formed. For this I find the

386

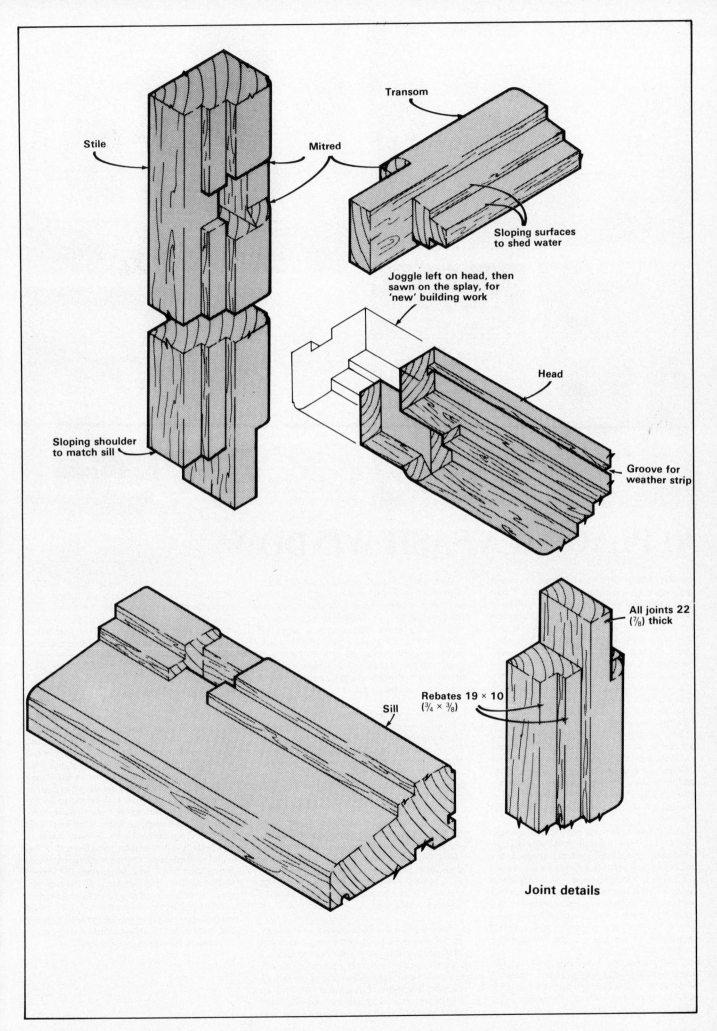

Stile

Mitred

Transom

Sloping surfaces
to shed water

Joggle left on head, then
sawn on the splay, for
'new' building work

Head

Sloping shoulder
to match sill

Groove for
weather strip

All joints 22
(⅞) thick

Rebates 19 × 10
(¾ × ⅜)

Sill

Joint details

Top left: 30. Window bottom fixed in place. Centre: 31. Restoring the plasterwork. Top right: 32. The old cement surround. Far left: 33. Making good cement surround. Left: 34. Complete from the outside. 35. Right: Complete except for decorating.

REPLACING A SASH WINDOW

rebating attachment ideal. It does not cause splitting at the corners (photo 22). When fitting the sashes to the frame I aim for a clearance all round of 2mm (3/32in.). The throating to the sashes as seen in the drawings was carried out with the small plane. Purpose of these grooves is to improve weather-resistance of the sash by reducing the capillary action of rainwater between two fairly close surfaces. Photo 23 shows the sash being hinged. For this type of rebated sash it is necessary to use a pair of cranked sash hinges having a sheradised finish.

The weather strip was prepared to the section shown, glued and nailed and the nails punched well in. A sash stay was fitted. The whole frame was given a thorough application of Cuprinol preservative. This left the surface slightly oily, but after a few days this disappeared and a priming coat of paint was then applied.

The frame that mine was to replace had been built-in in the traditional way though there was no evidence of it having been nailed to plugs in the wall. The old frame was eased outwards at the lower end. This enabled the glass to be removed intact (photo 25), after which the sash was unscrewed and the transome sawn away (photo 26). I used the saw to cut through the head — some sawing was necessary here as the joggles penetrated into the walls for 2-3in.

When fitting new window frames I use the traditional wall plugging and nails. Photo 27 shows the walls being plugged, two on each side being sufficient. Photo 28 shows the four plugs in position, all longer than needed.

Wall plugs should not be sawn-off flush with the walls, but cut to suit the size of whatever is being fixed. This eliminates the need for 'packing' between frame and wall. In this case the frame was a snug fit between the plugs, with a negligible gap at the edges. With the frame positioned, a tommy-bar was used below the sill to lift it and make a tight fit at the head. After checking for being plumb it was nailed to the plugs.

Two plugs were inserted into the vertical joints of the brickwork immediately inside the frame to provide fixing for the window bottom. These needed careful sawing after being driven home to ensure they supported the window bottom horizontally and without packing. The plugs can just be seen in photo 29.

The window bottom had been prepared at the same time as the frame, tongued along one edge and rounded at the other. This now had to be cut to be a loose fit against the brickwork, with the projecting ends and corners also rounded. Nailing to the plugs was all the fixing required, Photo 30 shows the work at this stage.

Making good the plasterwork came next. For small areas sand and cement make a convenient 'backing coat'. A mix of around six of sand to one of cement is adequate. There is no need to wait for the backing to dry before applying the skimming; once it has had an hour or two to set work can proceed. Hardwall skimming plaster should be used for the final

coat, this being no more than 1/16in. (1.5mm) thick, applied fairly wet and brought to a smooth surface with a float (trowel) used in conjunction with a large brush to keep the surface very moist. Too stiff a plaster mix is difficult to spread and get level; it also sets too quickly.

A cement surround, or collar had been added to the outside brickwork of the original frame. Parts of the collar were missing (photo 32). It was necessary to point around the frame and for the pointing to be blended-in to the collar. Photo 33 shows how I went about it. Battens of wood, with an edge bevelled at approximately 60°, were G-cramped to the frame. The thickness of these pieces was such that their outer surfaces were level with the existing cement. By forcing cement mortar between the batten and the collar, the collar was made good, the small gap between frame and wall was filled and the frame sealed against the elements. At the top, the weather strip served as a guide for the sealing operation, the gap below the sill being filled with mortar. Glazing the window completed the installation. Outside painting and inside decorating was done by my friend.

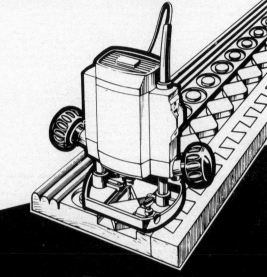

390

Prices quoted are those prevailing at press date and are subject to alteration due to economic conditions.

Woodworker, June 1980

FEEDING TABLE FOR THE BIRDS

**Tom Pettit puts forward an individual project for the older student.
He contends that by the wise choice of problems the student's craft ability will be developed.**

Man's inroads into the natural environment have often caused restrictions in the natural habitat of wild birds forcing them to adapt to change in much the same way as we ourselves are obliged to in our modern society. Cities and towns now boast almost as big a variety of birds as the countryside, and this is leading to an ever-increasing interest in their well-being by society at large, as well as by dedicated bodies such as the Royal Society for the Protection of Birds. The winter of 1978-79 was particularly disastrous for small birds, and it is occurances such as this coupled with our natural fondness for them which leads many people to feed birds daily. This may be a few household scraps thrown onto the lawn, but how much nicer if food can be put on a bird table where it is easier to observe the birds feeding.

The designing and making of a bird table could be a worthwhile experience and is in line with the theme of the article on bird boxes (April issue). The best design problems are those capable of a number of solutions all of which function efficiently. The design poblem or brief should be so worded to produce this variety whether children are working in groups or as individuals.

Design brief A bird table is required and is to be positioned outside the breakfast room window so that the family can readily observe the birds using it. In preparing your design you should pay particular attention to the following:

1 Will the table be on a pole; be suspended from a pole; hang from a tree branch; or fit on the window sill?
2 How big will the platform be?
3 What precautions can you take to prevent food from being blown away?
4 How will it be drained?
5 Will the table be covered by a roof?
6 At what height will the table be above the ground?
7 Will you make special provision for a supply of water?
8 Will there be facilities for providing special foods, nuts and fats?
9 If glue, nails and screws are to be used are there any special precautions to take?
10 The choice of materials and finish are particularly important because of its use. What do you suggest?

Most answers to these questions can be many and varied, each being correct in its own way and each helping to ensure a satisfactory design solution. If each is examined in detail the very many design possibilities become apparent, the construction being as simple or complex as you wish within the ability of the student.

1 Answers to this will be governed by the immediate surroundings to the house. Can a post be set in the ground conveniently? Is there a path directly in front of the window? Will the post disturb a lawn, or can it go into a flower bed? Might it be necessary to suspend the bird table from a horizontal arm on a post in order to put it in full view of the window? (A rockery, dividing wall or some other obstruction may make this necessary). If there is a nearby tree does it have a suitable branch from which to suspend a bird table? (The means by which this could be done is quite a design problem in itself). Failing all else can the bird table be fitted onto the window sill? Is the sill wide enough? Will some form of brackets be necessary to support the table and if so how will they be fixed?

Sketches to illustrate the solutions to these questions — and others which may arise depending upon individual circumstances — should be made. For example, how the post would be concreted into the ground — a hole dug, a flat stone put into the bottom to stand the post on and an infill of rubble and concrete tamped down around it, the surface being trowelled-off with a suitable fall away from the post to shed water. Finding out a suitable mix for the concrete is a good piece of research for the student, who will also have to learn how to mix it; as well as the simple use of a trowel and a spiritlevel to ensure the post is vertical and the table level.

If for some reason concrete cannot be used would inclined braces be necessary and if so how would they be fitted? Methods of fitting a horizontal arm to a post, of suspending a table, or fitting it to a window sill or nearby wall are numerous and should be sketched as appropriate. So too are the means by which the platform can be fixed to the top of a post.

2 The size of the platform may be governed by the space available. For example if it overhangs a path; the type of timber considered suitable and the width obtainable; and even the number and size of birds you wish to attract.

3 Crumbs and dry foods will be blown away or be scattered by the birds. A raised edge or, perhaps, a groove around the table will go some way to prevent this. How tall the edging strip would be and how it would be fixed; or how deep a groove and what section it would be, should be sketched. Sectional sketches would be particularly appropriate.

4 Drainage may be by drilling holes at strategic points or by cut-aways at the corners. Again proposals should be sketched.

5 If a roof is considered desirable this presents further constructional problems. How will it be supported? From the middle of each end of the table, or from each corner? Might this affect the proposals for drainage? Will the roof be single pitched or ridged? What will it be made of and how will it be weather-proofed?

6 Being able to observe the birds feeding will be one factor determining its height, the ease with which food can be put on it will be a further consideration, as will the difficulty it presents to cats should they try to jump up to it.

7 The need to provide water would be during periods of drought and severe frost. Birds will soon knock over small dishes, and freezing water will crack those of glass or pot. Careful thought is therefore necessary in solving this particular problem.

8 It is usual to put nuts in small net bags and mixtures of fat, nuts and meal in coconut shells. How and from where could these be hung?

9 Water in the form of dew, rain and snow, and atmospheric pollution are the hazards to be overcome when work is to be sited out-of-doors. Dampness would soon cause glues other than the modern resins to break down. Similarly, nails and screws should be rust-proofed or of brass.

10 Paint may be an obvious solution, but it is not of a very permanent nature and has to be renewed frequently. Once the surface has broken, and this may be at joints, or because of expansion and contraction of the wood as climatic conditions change, water can enter. This causes peeling of the paint and rotting of the timber. Modern preservatives are suitable, particularly as many are available in a range of attractive colours, the bird table then proving an asset to the garden and in turn enhancing the home.

These considerations, and probably many more arising as the design is developed, indicate the complexity of what at first may be considered a quite elementary piece of work as it could involve almost any kind of woodworking joint. They also illustrate how problem-solving is such a complete educational experience, as each boy or girl can work to the limit of their ability. It will be found in practice that success will build on success as the course proceeds; and by the wise choice of problems the student's craft ability will be developed.

HOW TO MAKE THE MOST OF YOUR PUBLIC LIBRARY

Here Ron Fox gives a brief guide to the classification system adopted by public libraries with particular reference to books on woodworking. He reminds seekers after knowledge that Dr Johnson made the appropriate remark: Knowledge is of two kinds, we know a subject ourselves, or we know where we can find information upon it.

To judge from correspondence in the woodworking press (and from personal contacts) many readers are not perhaps fully aware of the part the local library can play in expanding their knowledge of the craft. Nor is the problem confined to woodworkers; it is estimated that only about one third of the total adult population belongs to a public library.

Most important function of a library is to allow you to become acquainted with the literature of the subject. In addition, of course, the library provides the means to 'try before you buy', a useful facility for the newcomer and also of value to the more experienced. For example, the woodturner might be interested in comparing the two recent offerings: *The Manual of Woodturning* (Gordon Stokes) 1979, Pelham Books (£6.50) 684.08; and *The Craft of Woodturning* (John Sainsbury) 1980, McGraw-Hill (£4.55) Q684.083.

The basis of a library is the classification system. In public libraries non-fiction books are arranged on the shelves so that all books on the same subject are found together. The almost universal system used to achieve this is the Dewey decimal system, named after its inventor. The principle of this system is that all non-fiction books are divided into 10 main categories each of which is divided into 10 divisions each being further divided into 10 sub-divisions, and so on.

By these means any particular sub-division can be further sub-divided as its subject matter becomes more specialised, and any new subject can be slotted into the existing system. The main categories, divisions and sub-divisions are numbered in a hierarchical way and each book has its subject number lettered on the spine. For example, main category 6 (or 600) is Technology (Applied Sciences) within which 684 is Furnishings and Home Workshops within which 684.08 is Woodworking (although books on woodworking will be found under several other subject numbers).

The key to getting the most out of the library is knowing how to use the catalogue. In most public libraries this consists of three main sections: (1) subject index; (2) author catalogue; (3) subject catalogue.

Subject index lists alphabetically all subjects with their subject numbers. The index is kept in the form of a book, card index or, increasingly, a computer listing. Examples of entries from my local library include: cabinet making 684.16; carpentry 694; wood carving 736.4; wooden toys 745.51.

Subject index is used to locate a general area of interest. For more specific enquiries, the author catalogue and/or the subject catalogue provide the necessary information. The author catalogue is arranged alphabetically by author's name, giving information on edition, publication details, subject number etc. The subject catalogue also contains an entry for each book in stock,

this time arranged numerically by subject number, with books under a given number listed in alphabetical order of author's name. The subject catalogue is thus a representation in card index or list form of the books on the shelves. An increasing number of libraries produce rather more ambitious versions in which are shown all books in the entire stock of the county or city, with an indication against each entry of the branch libraries in which the book can be found.

Our approach to the catalogue varies according to what we already know about the required book. To locate a book whose author and title are known we refer to the author catalogue, check that the branch stocks a copy, note the subject number and go to that area of the shelves. If we are not sure of the title but know the author we follow the same process, this time looking at all the titles listed under the particular author. If we know the title but not the author the procedure is slightly more tedious. The best approach is to go to the subject index, check the subject number and scan all entries under that subject number in the subject catalogue. (We can, of course, go straight to the shelves but the advantage of using the catalogue is that we have a positive check that the book is stocked by the branch).

When the required book is out on loan a reservation can usually be made on payment of a fee (usually from 10p to 15p). If the book is not stocked at the branch — or in the entire county — it is still often possible for the librarian to obtain it through the inter-library loan scheme. This in effect gives you access to all books in the entire national system. If the reason for non-inclusion is that the book has only just been published, your own library may already have it on order or might well decide to acquire a copy, in which case you will have 'first go' of it. Never hesitate to seek advice from the library staff. Librarians are the most helpful of people and perform daily miracles of book location.

Pursuit of a given book or subject will sometimes show up anomalies in classification. For example, nearly all books on woodturning are classified to 684.08 but a recent book by Anders Thorlin titled *Ideas for Woodturning* is found under 736.4, which is Wood Carving, while in the local branch of my county library a number of standard books on the subject are classified to 674.

There are two reasons for such oddities: first, a number of specialist sub-divisions of woodwork fall into other classifications such as 745 Handicrafts or are borderline cases; secondly, subject numbers have to be assigned to books by (probably non-woodworker) librarians on the basis of title and brief perusal of contents.

The occasional anomaly inevitably occurs and it pays, therefore, to check the author catalogue for subject number if a particular book is not found where you would expect it to be. It also pays to cast the net fairly wide when using the subject index. You will find

for example: Timber Seasoning 674.38; Wood Finishes 674.43; Veneering 694.69; Furniture Restoration 749. Once familiar with the index a number of peripheral subjects will suggest themselves, eg: Trees and Woodlands 582.16; Woodland Crafts 674.8; Upholstery 684.3.

Surprisingly, in the two major libraries of which I am a member the subject index does not list Woodturning (or Turning). Nor does it include Pyrography, although Marquetry is listed. To find books on these and other unlisted subjects you have to cast about under more general headings in the subject index. If the title and author of one book on the required subject is known, the best plan is to look up that book in the catalogue and note the subject number under which it is shelved, in the hope that all similar books will be catalogued under the same number.

An important point to bear in mind when using the subject index is that separate shelf space (often in a different part of the library) is provided for 'Oversize' books, ie books of large page size; these would be wasteful of space if all the shelves had to be arranged to accomodate them. In the subject catalogue oversize books are denoted by a letter, usually Q in front of the subject number. Their importance for our purpose is that it is quite common for books on woodwork and allied subjects to be in large page size — not least among them the bound volumes of WOODWORKER in the form of *Woodworker Annual*. Other examples include: *The Book of Furniture Making* (Alf Martensson) 1979, Collins, Q684.1; *The Construction of Period Country Furniture* (V. J. Taylor) 1978, Stobart & Son, Q684.1; *The Fine Art of Cabinet Making* (J. Krenov) 1977, Studio Vista, Q684.16; *Illustrated Interior Carpentry* (G. Blackburn) 1978, Evans, Q694; *The Woodburning Stove Book* (G. Harrington) 1977, Collier MacMillan, Q697.2; *Creative Woodturning* (Dale L. Nish) 1976, Stobart and Son, Q745.51; *The Art of Making Wooden Toys* (P. Stevenson) 1971, Nelson, Q745.592.

All the foregoing relates to lending libraries but it should not be forgotten that most local authorities also have a reference library. This is likely to include books not available in the lending section because they are rare, valuable, highly specialised etc. An example is H. L. Edlin's *What Wood is That?* which is unusual for containing small samples of 40 different kinds of wood. This could present obvious problems if available to borrowers and is therefore kept in the reference section of my local library.

A further aspect of the reference library is that it often includes trade newspapers and publications, eg *Timber Trades Journal, Cabinet Maker, Woodworking Industry,* official reports, trade directories and yearbooks, many of which make interesting reading and provide a source of specialist suppliers.

Having mentioned woodturning several times already, I append a short bibliography. This is by no means exhaustive but the books are worth looking at and all have been found on the shelves of my local library.

Information given against each title includes author, date of publication, publisher, price at December 1979 and subject number under which found in the public library. The comments, of course, express my personal views.

The Craftsman Woodturner (Peter Child) 1971, Bell & Hyman, 238 pp. (£8.95) 684.08. A highly regarded book which takes the beginner through all phases of turning and finishing. The approach is via bowl turning as the best way of learning the craft, a valid but not entirely unanimous viewpoint. Techniques are clearly described and superbly illustrated with professionally lit photographs, the action being stopped at the point best illustrating the operation under discussion. The second half of the book covers a number of practical projects illustrated at the same high standard of photography. Highly recommended.

Creative Woodturning (Dale L. Nish) 1976, Stobart & Sons, 284pp (£10.85 hard, £7.95 paper), Q745.51. This is a book about scraping and as such must be the most comprehensive guide we are ever likely to see. The author avers that cutting techniques with gouge and chisel are only to be mastered by the dedicated few, and pushes the beginner firmly in the direction of scraper and abrasive paper. The profusion of excellent photographs which illustrate his words show up with crystal clarity the results of this approach, and could be studied to advantage by all turners and would-be turners.

The Practical Wood Turner (F. Pain) 1958, Evans, 167pp, index, (£4.25) 684.08. A classic which many established woodturners reckon among the best one or two ever written on the subject. Short on finishing techniques but full of the sort of advice and tips that only come from many years in the trade. Full too of the late author's humour and homespun philosophy which can often irritate in a book but in this case doesn't. A very individual book.

The Craft of Woodturning (John Sainsbury) 1980, McGraw-Hill, 208pp (£4.55) Q684.083.

Modern Woodturning (Gordon Stokes) 1973, Evans, 128pp, index (£4.75) 684.08; *Woodturning for Pleasure* (Gordon Stokes) 1976, Evans, 167pp, index (£4.75) 684.083; *The Manual of Woodturning* (Gordon Stokes) 1979, Pelham Books, 210pp, index (£6.50) 684.08. The first two titles are good, clear concise introductions to woodturning techniques and designs. They are complementary although there is a certain amount of repetition of techniques in the second. Both are well illustrated with numerous photographs by the author and can be recommended to the beginner.

The third is rather different being the latest and most ambitious offering by the author on the subject. The stated aim is 'to bring the enthusiast up to the intermediate stage'. While encompassing in somewhat greater detail (and with rather a lot of repetition, some of which is intentional) most of the topics covered in the earlier works, it goes considerably further in several aspects of the craft. Particularly interesting is the distinction drawn between spindle-turning chuck-work and disc-turning, a much more relevant division than the usual spindle *v.* faceplate dichotomy. Illustration is mainly by line drawings provided by V. J. Taylor. Not a book to be read uncritically but an important one.

Ideas for Woodturning (Anders Thorlin) 1977, Evans, 110pp, index (£4.50) 736.4. This is a book of things to make, not how to make them. The designs are Scandinavian in style, making much use of fir and birch with some interesting ideas on how to use partly rotted wood for such things as candle-holders and table lamps. The ideas are very individual and not all will be to everyone's taste. Nevertheless their success may be gauged by the number of examples to be seen at craft fairs and exhibitions.

Letters

Sharpening blades

From: R. R. Gillies, Weybridge, Surrey
Dear Sir,

Has anyone found the secret of sharpening the blades used in trimming knives? New they have a razor's edge but my success in re-sharpening them has been limited. The method I use is honing on an oilstone followed by stropping on an Elu grinder but the end result never quite compares with the original edge. Suggestions would be welcome.

What kind of steel is used nowadays in plane and chisel blades? And why are they still not made with the cast steel that seems to take and hold a better edge? The old blades that I possess are easier to grind than the modern 'tough' type of steel.

What is the best way to sharpen the hollows in the reeding cutters used in combination planes? The smaller blades, in particular, are a problem because no oilstone is small enough to fit into the hollows. My method is to take a small diameter piece of dowel or steel rod round which I wrap a piece of oiled emery cloth. Is there a better way?

As to the time-consuming business of grinding a new bevel on plane blades, the drawing (Fig. 1) from an old book offers a solution. A steel cutter about the thickness of a scraper blade is sandwiched between the two irons. This is the cutting edge. No grinding is necessary, merely a honing on the oilstone. A bonus is that replacement blades (Fig. 2) would be cheaper than conventional blades.

The book gives a tip for users of scrapers. It says that scrapers as supplied by the makers are wrongly shaped, or at least could be improved by gradually rounding-off the edges at A and B in Fig. 3, thus preventing the edges from catching in the surface of the wood. Fig. 3 also shows how the corners C and D can be rounded to different radii for use on mouldings.

Lastly is a tip for resurfacing oilstones which have become hollow or lost their bite. Sprinkle fairly fine 'sharp' sand (you can get it at gardening centres but sieve it to remove the large particles) on a sheet of ¼ in. plate glass (or equivalent). The sand is lightly watered and the face of the oilstone firmly rubbed over it with a circular movement.

Five minutes of this treatment should remedy most defects. Do not worry about the grating sound heard at the beginning because the size of the sand particles soon reduces and also the grating sound; there is no risk of spoiling the stone. When used for the first time the glass is too smooth but after a few minutes it acquires a frosted finish which takes a firm grip on sand.

Reverting to the first paragraph of this letter, I offer a suggestion for cutting dowel rods to length. I used to saw them but this left a ragged edge which needed a clean-up. Now I cut them off with a trimming knife. I lay the dowel rod on the bench and rotate it to and fro under the blade which is pressed down hard. This almost cuts through the rod so that it can easily be snapped off to the required length leaving a clean and slightly bevelled edge ready for immediate use.

Yours faithfully, **R. R. Gillies**

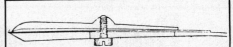

Fig. 1 Plane irons with thin cutter between.

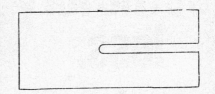

Fig. 2 Steel cutter for improved plane iron.

Fig. 3 Correctly shaped steel scraper.

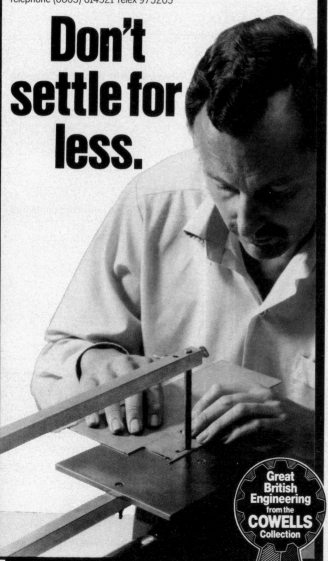

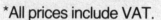

394

Prices quoted are those prevailing at press date and are subject to alteration due to economic conditions.

Woodworker, June 1980

Guild of Woodworkers

Measured music

The Victoria and Albert museum, South Kensington, London SW7, inform WOODWORKER that for personal shoppers it is able to offer measured drawings of musical instruments. These drawings are full-size and complete with photographs. The drawings are of keyboard and non-keyboard instruments and the staff of the museum prepare a pack on request to a size convenient for the personal shopper rather than having ready made-up kits to send out to mail order requests.

Keyboard at £34.50 inc VAT 1. Queen Elizabeth's virginals, late 16th century. 2. Single manual harpsichord, Giovanni Baffo, Venice 1574. 3. Single manual harpsichord, Jerome of Bologna, Rome 1521. 4. Double manual harpsichord, Vaudry, Paris 1681. 5. Clavichord, Barthhold Fritz, Brunswick 1751. 6. Virginals, Thomas White, London 1642. 7. Double manual harpsichord, Thomas Hitchcock, London 1725.

Non-keyboard at £17.25 inc VAT 1. Theorbo, 1637 Venice. 2. Oboe, 18th century Milan. 3. Flute, 1710 London. 4. Bass viol, 1600 London. 5. Alto Viol, 1667 London. 6. Ivory lute, 17th century, Italian.

Safety check

Annual report of the Health & Safety Commission and Executive for financial year 1978-9 points out that the factory inspectorate has begun visiting makers and suppliers to discuss various aspects of safety in relation to articles for use at work.

The commission realises that well-conceived health and safety requirements can be costly, so is to take greater account of the commercial and technical implications.

Some lack of awareness of duties under the Health & Safety at Work Act is shown by smaller businesses, states the report, and there were activities which caused concern. Employers were sometimes reluctant to accept that the duties under the Act applied to them. In 'new entrant' premises employers and employees were generally unaware of their duties in matters of safety, although willing to comply when the requirements were brought to their attention.

The report (ISBN 0 11 883257 3) is published by HMSO at £1.75 plus postage.

Guild tie available

Many members have asked for a guild tie. We have adopted a green tie with two gold-coloured 'bandings' between which is a reproduction of the guild badge also in gold colour. The tie is of a material that should be resistant to creasing and slipping and the cost is £3.25 inclusive of VAT, packing and postage. Cheques or crossed postal orders should be made out to Guild of Woodworkers and sent to David Whitehouse at the guild office, quoting membership number. The address is: PO Box 35, Bridge Street, Hemel Hempstead.

Product liability

Under proposed EEC legislation manufacturers would be strictly liable for any injury caused by faulty products. The Confederation of British Industry has written to the consumer affairs minister (Mrs Sally Oppenheim) saying this is wrong in principle and likely to be damaging in practice to the interests of consumers and producers alike. CBI believes the EEC should follow the new 'model' US legislation which holds manufacturers liable for product injuries only if they can be proved to be at fault.

'This "as-you-were" move has been designed by the Americans to escape from the trap they have fallen into through earlier legislation providing for liability irrespective of fault,' says CBI.

Cash-flow

Cash-flow problems face many firms in the timber and furniture industries but these problems are related to productivity, according to *Management Ratios*. This is an annual publication of business ratios produced by Dunn & Bradstreet Ltd, 6-8 Bonhill Street, London EC2A 4BU.

For some firms a 20% improvement in employee productivity would double the acid-test ratio and bring the cover of liquid assets against current liabilities on to a 1 for 1 basis. Performance varies widely among furniture manufacturing firms, as shown by a 50% variation in material utilisation and a 30% range in employee productivity, according to the Dunn & Bradstreet publication which costs £20.

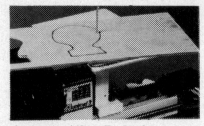

Prices quoted are those prevailing at press date and
are subject to alteration due to economic conditions.

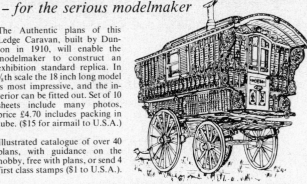

Rotherham scaledown association

The Association will hold its 1980 exhibition at Rotherham Central Library and Arts Centre on Friday, Saturday and Sunday 3, 4, 5 October. The exhibition comprises all types of modelling, entry is free and both junior and senior modellers are invited to participate. Full details from the secretary, C. Grice, 5 Squirrel Croft, Rockingham, Rotherham, South Yorks. Please send sae.

Art in action

The Festival of Art is to be held at Waterperry House, near Wheatley, Oxford, on the 3-6 July. There will be about 50 artists and craftsmen participating: work will be on sale and can also be commissioned. A diy workshop will enable visitors to try their hand at some of the arts and crafts. Waterperry House is situated at the end of Waterperry village 3½ miles from the termination of the M40 and is about an hour's drive from London. It is about eight miles NE of Oxford. Admission charges : adults £2.00, children (6-16) and OAPs £1.00; students with valid cards £1.20. Party rates are available for parties of 15 or more; opening times 10.00am-5.00pm. Diy workshops admission charge 50p each. Further information from Barbara Nash, Augustine Studios, Augustine Road, Brook Green, London W14.

Canadian spring boat show

May 26-30 at the International Centre, Toronto.

Indian miniatures

April 4-June 1 at the National Gallery of Canada, Ottawa, the first of a series of exhibitions which will highlight the many gifts received by the gallery from donors during the past 10 years.

Marquetry national exhibition

The Rt honourable The Lord Mayor of Bristol, Councillor Tom Clarke, will officially open the National Exhibition of the Marquetry Society on Saturday 10th May at 10 am at St Martin's Church Hall, Knowle and it will be open daily (including Sundays) from 10am-8pm until 19 May.

Lectures at the Victoria and Albert museum

Tuesdays in the lecture theatre at 13.15. May 27: The present state of theatre design in Britain by John Bury. June 24: Into the '90s — designing for children by Imogen Stewart. Saturday gallery lectures at 15.00 (assemble in the Main Entrance). May 31: Prince Albert and the V&A by Geoffrey Opie. June 21: Seventeenth-century cabinets by Philippa Barton. Saturday gallery lectures at 15.30 (assemble in the Main Entrance). May 31: French furniture by Frances Buckland. June 7: The High Victorian interior by Imogen Stewart. Thursday in the lecture theatre at 18.30. May 22: Furniture and the National Trust by Martin Drury an annual lecture arranged in association with the Furniture History Society. Sundays in the lecture theatre at 15.30. June 22: The Great Exhibition of 1851 by Geoffrey Opie.

Design Council awards

Scottish Design Centre, 72 St Vincent Street, Glasgow from 8 June-9 August.

Japan season

Japan style at the V&A until 20 July planned by the architect Kiyoshi Seike and the designer Ikko Tanaka provides a representative selection of Japanese artefacts ranging from traditional to ultra modern; from masterpieces in wood, bamboo and lacquer to neon signs, motorbikes and calculators. Admission £1.35, with students, pensioners and children at half price. 24-30 May, London Convention 1980 — Netsuke in Japanese Art, Quaglino's, St James's, London. 26 May-6 June, Exhibition of Japanese Art and Netsuke, S. L. Moss, 51 Brook Street, London W1. 27 May-6 June, Exhibition of Netsuke and other Japanese Works of Art, Eskenazi Ltd, 166 Piccadilly, London W1. 27-31 May, Exhibition of Netsuke, Spink and Son, 5 King Street, London SW1. 29 May, Sale of important Netsuke, Inro and Kiseruzutsu at Sotherby's.

Furniture projects

The summer exhibition this year at the Crafts Council Gallery, 12 Waterloo Place, Lower Regent Street, London SW1 (nearest underground Piccadilly Circus) will examine the work of three craftsmen who make few concessions to existing conventions in the design and making of furniture. All three furniture makers studied at the Royal College of Art.
11 June-5 July, Floris van den Broecke. Geometric areas of pure colour make the work like abstract sculpture, visual impact is often made by intersecting planes of different colours. New pieces use more traditional methods. Pieces on show include a lounging chair and gout stool and a desk of painted wood which opens on hinges to reveal drawers and shelves.
12 July-2 August, Erik de Graaf. Here is a starker approach to design using only painted beech wood and plywood in quiet grey tones. Seats can be adjusted to different positions based on the proportions of the human body.
9-30 August, David Colwell. Working in Wales David Colwell has been perfecting a steam-bent ash folding chair. The original form combines steam-bent ash with rattan but leather and upholstery variations are also available.

Interbuild 81

Following the success of the 38th exhibition the dates of Interbuild 81 have been announced as 29 November to 5 December 1981. Details are available from Christopher John, 11 Manchester Square, London W1M 5AB (phone 01-486 1951).

BBC programme

The Story of English Furniture, BBC TV (BBC1) Sundays 1.25-2.50 pm 25 May-27 July. A repeat of the earlier screened programme introduced by Arthur Negus and Hugh Scully, who trace the evolution of English furniture from medieval times to the 20th century.

International seminar

For woodturners; organised by the Parnham Trust at Parnham House, Beaminster, Dorset, 14 and 15 June, full details from Brian James, at the above address or phone (0308) 862204.

Safe as houses?

Design Centre, Haymarket, London, until Saturday 7 June.

Workshop open week

At Hambledon House, Hambledon, Godalming, Surrey, David Gregson is opening his workshop from 18-24 May from 10.00am to 7.00pm each day. He makes furniture, inlaid boxes, puzzles and other items to commission and for sale. His telephone number is Wormley 3088 or 4620.

Modern Swedish design

At the Victoria and Albert Museum, South Kensington, London SW7 from 9 July to 14 September.

Texprint 80

Britain's textile design trade show is to have a new venue. It will be held at the Royal College of Art, Kensington Gore, SW7 from Wednesday October 1 to Friday October 3 inclusive. Texprint is organised by the Design Council in association with the SIAD. Space is available for 50 top free-lance designers and design groups plus 30 of the best graduate designers of 1980 to present designs suitable for furnishings, fashions and flooring.

Guitar '80

Billed as the first workshop and exhibition exclusively for guitar makers and guitarists to be held from 4-6 June at Kensington Town Hall, High Street, Kensington, London. Called Guitar '80 the exhibition is sponsored by *Musicians Only* and will provide a forum for luthiers and players where visitors will be able to see and discuss traditional and modern methods and materials used by the guitar maker. There will be both established craftsmen and beginners' work to see in assembled and semi-assembled stages. Prominent guitarists will demonstrate playing skills. Admission (valid for three days) £1.00. This includes the catalogue, exhibition guide and entrance to guitar demonstrations.

Dorset exhibition

Dorset County Arts and Crafts Association exhibition is to be held at the High School, Bath Road, Sturminster Newton on 5, 6, 7 and 8 August from 11am to 6pm; demonstrations of various forms of woodworking are also planned.

Devon exhibition

Devon Guild of Craftsmen are holding their summer exhibition at Totnes Community College, Totnes, from 3-22 August inclusive open 10am to 5.30 weekdays and 2pm to 5.30 Sundays, admission is free.

Home improvement

This year the International Home Improvement Exhibition is being opened to the public on the last three days — the 3-5 October. Earls Court is the venue. The exhibition is organised by the Building Trades Exhibition Ltd, the National Home Improvement Council and the Builders Merchants Federation.

Exhibition

15-18 May at Shoreditch College, Egham, Surrey. 'End of an era' theme featuring work of students of CDT and commercial displays. From 1 August Shoreditch becomes a department of Brunel University but remains on the same campus.

QUESTION BOX

Pine furniture treatment

From: Charles Bartley, Spilsby, Lincs

I am experimenting with an 'aged' look to pine furniture. I am using strong caustic soda, washing down with water and reapplying until I reach the desired colour. But after thoroughly washing down a white film keeps reappearing in small areas through the final wax polish. Also I use Resin W to glue most joints. Will caustic soda have any adverse long-term effect and could you recommend an alternative adhesive that can be bought ready mixed? By the way, is there a critical strength of caustic soda to use?

The root cause of your problem is the caustic soda which, while bleaching the wood, is not being properly neutralised by the washing process. The white bloom is no doubt efflorescence caused by crystals left on the wood surface. The alkalinity of the soda is very likely to have a detrimental affect on the glue line by reducing the efficiency of the acid hardener in the adhesive.

Another aspect is that strong alkaline solutions applied to wood, even at room temperatures, commence to break down the hemi-cellulose and lignin of the wood; after all, the meaning of the word caustic is burns or corrodes organic tissue; biting etc. What is happening is that with each application of the fluid the wood surface is being progressively penetrated. This is being aided by hosing-down so that by the time you have secured the right appearance of the wood, it is practically impossible to neutralise the bleaching agent fully.

You could try washing-down the wood with vinegar but this is not likely to be really successful. Our advice is to drop the idea of using caustic soda. In the context of 'stripped' pine furniture the emphasis is really on age; old furniture has become bleached and aged because of long exposure to light, especially to the ultra-violet rays of the spectrum (in some instances ultra-violet lamps are used to hasten bleaching of fabrics).

It would probably be impractical to do this with your wood, while exposing machined piece parts to light by storing them in a greenhouse would not serve any useful purpose generally because the corresponding heat source would tend to split and distort the wood.

In the absence of time bleaching, chemical bleaching must be resorted to or the wood must be stained in order to subdue its natural colour. The use of oxalic acid for bleaching would be better than caustic soda. It can be very successful but it can be tricky on large areas. To make up a solution dissolve 8oz oxalic acid crystals in 4pt of hot water. Apply to the wood using as many applications as necessary; wipe over with vinegar and finally wash down with clear water. It is essential to wear rubber gloves since the chemical is a poison.

We are a little averse to recommending chemical bleaches for wood except for fairly localised removal of stains, for example, because of the difficulty in neutralising the chemical completely. With pine the generally high proportion of sapwood is much more absorbent that the darker-coloured heartwood. Accordingly, it would help if more bleach was applied to the latter and less to the former in order to make neutralising easier. The use of a sanding sealer will not help if crystals are left in, or on, the wood since ultimately they will show through the finish.

In answer to your query as to what represents a critical strength of caustic soda; this depends upon its concentration and its temperature. Caustic soda is strongly alkaline with a pH of about 14 while pure water, neither alkaline nor acidic, has a pH of 7.

Even at room temperature a strong solution at pH 11 will cause breakdown of wood. So if the concentration of caustic is reduced to a level where, at room temperature, it will not harm wood, eg pH of 9, then would it be strong enough to bleach the wood and, if so, why not use ordinary soda whose pH would be nearer the value of 9 or 11? It is not possible to give an emphatic answer. We can only suggest you experiment with the oxalic acid treatment or, alternatively, with a proprietary bleach; or with ordinary soda.

Finishing sculpture

From: F. R. Nunn, Sheffield, Yorkshire

I attempt to carve a variety of woods — from teak to apple, mahogany to lignum vitae, oak to elm. Could you please advise on a finish that will seal the wood against greasy fingerprints etc; retain as nearly as possible the natural colour and bring out the grain; produce a matt, or at least, satin finish.

In general my work is in smooth flowing lines, not intricate detail. Is a matt polyurethane varnish best or is there something better?

Polish invariably tends to darken wood and the end grain being more absorbent will darken most. With mahogany or lignum vitae this darkening will be immaterial but with light-coloured woods the clearest possible finish is used. Oak and elm being open grained require sealing, and two thin coats of transparent polish should be brushed on in a warm dry dust-free room. The sculpture is then ready for waxing with white beeswax. Scrub the beeswax with a stiff nailbrush and briskly brush the carving so as to apply wax evenly all over the work. Several applications of wax will be needed to bring up a mellow glow. With the closer grained woods it is not necessary to seal with polish.

This finish is preferable to using a polyurethane finish which could have a yellowing effect.

Card table restoration

From: C. Green, Rustington, Sussex

Can you please advise on restoring a Victorian single-pedestal card table which swings out at right angles and then unfolds to reveal a green baize surface.

The top when folded is badly marked though there are no deep scratches. The sides, pedestal and base could do with repolishing. The baize is faded and moth - eaten. Can you advise what adhesive should be used to put down a fresh baize and how to do so?

Before repolishing can start it is necessary to correctly identify what finish was used and the diagnosis should be made on an inconspicuous part of the table. Moisten a rag with methylated spirits and try it on the polish which will soften if french polish has been used. If the finish is unaffected try scraping it with the edge of a sharp chisel and if yellow shavings come off then varnish has been used. If light coloured dust comes off it was cellulosed, but in view of the table's age such a finish is most unlikely.

Smooth out the imperfections on the top, pedestal and base with 0000 wire wool and try not to cut through the original polish. If, however, the marks on the table top are very severe it may be necessary to remove all the polish with a steel scraper, glasspaper with fine garnet paper and restore the colour with a weak spirit stain.

It would seem that removal of the entire polish film is not necessary so after using the wire wool, thoroughly dust off and start repolishing with thinned garnet polish. Thinned polish helps the new polish to take more readily to the old and when the rubber needs recharging it can be replenished with normal strength polish. Bodying-up should be followed by spriting-off. The pedestal and base are similarly finished.

It will probably be quite easy to pull off the old green baize and any that is left still adhering to the table can be washed off with warm water. This will dissolve all the old paste which can be entirely removed by scraping. It is recommended that the top should again be covered in green baize and it should be stuck down with paperhanger's paste made up a little thicker than normal.

The baize is generously pasted and the adhesive well worked in with a brush. When the cloth is good and sticky lay it on the table with the surplus hanging over the edges. Use a piece of softwood about 2 or 3in. long and having a rounded edge to lay the baize as though laying veneer with a hammer. Work from the centre outwards. Use the block to work the baize into the recess at the edge of the table and press it well down with the tip of a table knife (not a sharp one).

When the baize is firmly bedded down and before the paste has completely dried, the surplus is trimmed off using a very sharp knife held against a steel straight-edge.

It is understood that baize can be obtained from Bonners Ltd, 35 Upper Wickham Lane, Welling, Kent, or Blands, Oldbury-on-Severn, Glos.

QUESTION BOX

Timber identification

From: F. E. Bell, Kings Heath, Birmingham
Can you please identify the timber sample sent with my letter. It was part of a chair leg from a teak dining suite though the timber appears too light in weight for teak proper. I repaired the chair by making another back leg, the original having broken in the middle where the grain was short. I cut the replacement from a board of the mahogany species called, I think, agba. This stained and polished to match very well.

The owner insists that the suite is teak. I have not examined the complete suite but the chair on close inspection looked like African mahogany.

We have examined the sample of wood and would say quite categorically that this is neither true teak (*Tectona grandis*) nor one of the usual substitutes, ie afrormosia or iroko. We would say that your opinion that the sample is in fact African mahogany (*Khaya* spp.) is correct since microscopic examination confirms this. We would comment that in the old days it was common practice for the back sweeps of mahogany chairs to be bandsawn from something else — birch was a popular choice. The reason for this was the weak point at the junction of the sweep with the straight part of the leg where the grain would be crossed. Birch is much stronger and can be stained to match. Not all mahogany would break easily. Good interlocked grain would resist but mildly interlocked grain, generally preferred because it machined more cleanly, was always suspect; and if your chair leg was made from wood similar to the sample we are not surprised that it failed.

The agba you have used is a good alternative to mahogany and matches-up well; to some extent is stronger than mahogany, at least in toughness, but as stated, the type of grain present is the best criterion on which to judge suitability. If the owner of the furniture feels he needs an official diagnosis of the wood in the suite he should be recommended to send a further sample of the wood to either TRADA at High Wycombe, Bucks, or Timberlab at Princes Risborough, Bucks, requesting microscopic identification.

A small charge would be levied for this but should there be any suggestion of misrepresentation in the original description of the furniture, then he will need an official letter confirming just what has been used.

Timber identification

From: J. F. Robinson, Handsworth Wood, Birmingham
I would be very pleased if you could identify a sample of timber. You will note some hard thin bands in it which have the appearance of limestone.

The sample is typical of iroko (*Chlorophora excelsa*) from tropical Africa. The features you mention are also typical of the species but your description needs clarification.

The thin hard bands are actually thin-walled parenchyma cells which appear on the end grain surrounding one or two large pores and in narrow bands. On side grain the parenchyma makes, or tends to make, a type of partridge wing figure yellowish in colour against the warm brown of the wood proper.

There occurs in iroko 'stone' deposits whose true composition is somewhat conjectural but generally calcareous. Some authorities say they consist of calcium carbonate, others say they are chiefly a phosphate of calcium or apatite. But since some salt of calcium is found in all vegetable tissue its compounds in a given instance presumably could be anything, so the loose term 'stone' seems most appropriate. Indeed, very large 'stones' occurring in iroko logs have been known to break large bandsaw blades. Some evidence of their presence in a log is often noticeable in the wood being rather darker in colour around the enclosed stone.

From the point of view of the use of the converted timber, the deposits are generally minute and are found in the pores of the wood. These can be seen quite clearly in the sample on all faces. Your reference to 'hard' in respect of the parenchyma bands can be explained by saying that cutting edges tend to blunt very quickly due to the deposits and this tends to crush the thin walls of the parenchyma cells, compacting them and making smooth finishing difficult.

The whole position is exaggerated further by interlocking grain. Generally speaking cutting edges must not only be kept sharp when machining iroko but the cutting angle should be reduced from 30 to 15°.

A teak table

From: N. J. Hall, Beccles, Suffolk
I was asked to refurbish the top of a 10-year-old teak dining table and enquired of the original supplier what the finish would be and how best to restore it. I was told that it was teak oil only (which is as I expected) and that I should clean the surface with white spirit to remove any wax, scrape out the scratches and marks, sand all over, then apply four or five coats of teak oil allowing each to become touch-dry before applying the next.

All this I did except that the whole surface was scraped so that the treatment was even all over. But the surface has not come up to the lustre finish that it had before work began and in several places the oil soaks right in and leaves 'dead' patches. Will the lustre appear as the surface matures or is there something I can do to hasten this; and what can I do about the 'dead' patches?

Having completely removed the original finish with scraper and glasspaper we are now in the position of polishing a new piece of wood. There are no previous polishes or varnishes to contend with and polishing with oil should proceed without difficulty. Having applied the teak oil to the table top, it is usual to allow it to sink in for 10min or so and then rub off any surplus with clean cloths.

After several applications a satisfactory polish should appear but occasionally you can come across a patch of wood which refuses to take polish. This can be caused by a spongy area which absorbs oil before a 'body' can be built up. To overcome this 'hungriness' it is suggested that the top in. or so of liquid from a bottle of transparent white polish be poured in to a clean dish and brushed on to the affected area. The clear 'toppings' is in preference to white polish for if the latter were used a noticeable mark would be left.

When the polish is dry it should be smoothed down with worn garnetpaper and re-oiled. If after several applications of oil the surface still lacks lustre, a brisk rubbing with good wax polish should make all the difference.

It is assumed that the table top is solid teak and not teak veneer. Using a scraper on a thin knife-cut veneer could reduce the veneer to paper thinness which might allow the oil to pass through and into the substrate which could be highly absorbent. However, a brushful of 'toppings' should be an effective sealer.

Fungus on elm

From: A. G. Warner, Windsor, Berks
I have purchased 40 cuft of wych elm. The elm has been sawn through-and-through into 2¼in. slabs. It is very wet and has been laid down in-stick for air-drying with a ½in. gap between each board.

Owing to the situation of my workshop the elm is stored in my timber shed which is an enclosed building. It is not draught-proof and during the day the doors are left open. There is little natural light.

The elm has been in the shed for eight weeks. During the fifth week I noticed that some of the boards had a white fungus growing on them. It seems to be concentrated along the line where the sapwood joins the heartwood. On examination the fungus looks like cottonwool but with a harder skin in contact with the wood. When scraped away it leaves a black line.

Is there anything I can do to eliminate the growth? Cost apart, the timber has a beautiful grain and texture, with the usual green cast. It would be a shame to see it go to waste.

The short answer to your problem is to remove the planks to the open air and stack them so that a good current of air can get all round each piece. The best method, if practicable, is to stand each piece on end with the bottom resting on a couple of sticks for example and the piece resting at an angle against a wall. Do not worry about rain; this will not harm the wood although, of course, if persistent it would slow down the drying which really should be aimed at getting the m.c. of the wood, and particularly the sapwood, down below the danger level (for fungi) of 20%.

Wych elm tends to dry rapidly in the right conditions and in this case it means out of doors; the March winds should have hurried along the drying process. Reverting to your timber storage area; this is unsuitable for really wet timber unless it is economic to install a dehumidifier to encourage drying.

A slatted-sided shed is better for wettish wood because of the increased air circulation, but even under such conditions (and for thick wet wood) ½in. sticks are only suitable for timber like oak which is prone to surface checking and where the drying needs slowing down slightly. For the elm, so long as the sticks are aligned properly so as to avoid or restrict distortion, thicker sticks even of 1in. can be tolerated. It is possible that because of the poor air circulation all that has happened is that a surface mould has developed on the wood. These are harmless and when brushed off the wood leave no deep seated discolouration. They do prevent air getting uniformly to the boards however.

Generally, mould fungi are bluish or greyish in colour although like cotton wool. It might be that a more pernicious fungus had attacked the wood and now, under the sluggish air conditions prevailing, has started to develop further.

We would not really expect this to be the case because of the time of year and the presumed lack of heat in the stores, but your reference to the harder skin in contact with the wood suggests a fruiting body, especially in conjunction with the black lines also mentioned. This could mean a fungus such as *Polystictus versicolor* which had attacked the tree. However it would seem the wood looked all right initially, otherwise you would not have bought it. The need now is to get it dry quickly. That will arrest the fungus which could only reassert itself under very wet use conditions.

Polishing a piano

From: John Smith, Lochwinnoch, Renfrewshire

I would like to reproduce on the small articles that I make the same high-quality polish finish to be seen on grand pianos and other instruments. Can such polish be purchased in small quantities? Can it be applied by brush?

If Mr Smith wishes to achieve a finish comparable to a quality grand piano he cannot do better than to use french polish.

As he does not say what woods are used in his small articles the type of polish can only be discussed in general terms. For light woods such as oak or ash, white polish made from bleached shellac is advised. For mahogany, brown polish made from orange shellac is most suitable. Button polish has a yellowish tinge whereas garnet is a darker polish.

To be sure of getting a good quality it is advisable to buy the polish from a trade house which will be able to supply the necessary abrasive papers, stains, grain-fillers, wadding etc. Having stained the work to the desired colour it is necessary to fill the pores of open grained woods with a suitably coloured grainfiller. This is well rubbed in across the grain and after hardening it is rubbed along the grain with a clean rag to remove the surplus. Leave to harden for a day then dust off and wipe over with a rag moistened with raw linseed oil. This gives the filler a clear appearance and after allowing the oil 24hr to dry polishing can begin.

For a piano finish it is recommended that the polish be applied with a rubber rather than with a brush. The rubber is made from white wadding folded in half with three of the corners folded in so that its final shape resembles half a pear. This is covered with a clean soft lint-free rag such as a well-washed handkerchief. The rubber is charged with polish, the rag covering put on and the rubber dabbed in the palm of the hand to evenly distribute the polish which should just ooze through the covering.

Using straight strokes work the rubber across the grain followed by straight strokes along the grain. This is followed by overlapping circular movements. At first pressure on the rubber is light but is increased as the rubber dries out. Should there be a tendency for the rubber to stick a touch of raw linseed oil on its face will act as a lubricant.

Keep charging the rubber and oiling if required until the grain is full and then put the work aside for a day. The polish will sink slightly and the surface should be carefully smoothed with worn 5/0 garnet paper. Dust-off and recommence polishing until the grain is filled. Now charge the rubber with half polish and half meths and work in straight sweeps along the grain. Hardly any oil should be used at this stage.

This is followed by the process of spiriting-off whereby the oil is removed and the polish is brought up to that beautiful finish seen on top-quality furniture. A new rubber is made up, charged with 'half and half' and using long strokes is swept along the grain. As the rubber dries out a little meths is applied to its face and the light straight strokes continued. The rubber must not be allowed to drag. If it tends to do so add a small quantity of meths and glide on. It is essential that the spirit rubber should not be too wet or it will wash away the polished surface. The rubber should just feel cold when touched to the cheek.

Although most polish houses do not sell polish in smaller quantities than 2½litre, there are some who sell quarts and occasionally you meet a friendly polisher who will help out an amateur by letting him have a lesser quantity.

End checking of wood discs

From: Roy H. Mansfield, Basildon, Essex

I purchased 12 × 3in. thick turning discs from a reliable source and these have a coating around the edge which appears to be wax. Where can I purchase it or can it be made up? The discs are elm, ash and sycamore and in good condition and extremely dry having been in my workshop since purchase. Subsequently I bought some walnut from a sawmill in bulk but when I cut it into 12 × 3in. discs and put these under the workbench they split in quite large shakes in places and hair cracks inside which appear when turned. I feel that if wax had been applied around the edges this may not have happened.

We must comment in a general way on your problem because despite the results of laboratory experiments on the drying of wood discs, which seek to prove that by adopting this or that technique or procedure splitting and checking will be avoided, much depends upon circumstances of given air conditions at a given time with a given piece of wood.

We have been commenting recently on some of these methods in the Timber Topics series (and will continue the theme). The difficulty in drying this type of wood section is that the shrinkage force is concentrated round the growth rings or tangentially. It means that if the force overcomes the resistance of the wood then it will split. The objective in trying to reduce this shrinkage force is to prevent the ends of the piece drying out too quickly. If the wood is in the form of a small log, provided the ends can be sealed, then the shrinkage force is restrained by the bulk of the piece, but obviously uniform drying is going to take a very long time.

If discs are cut from wet wood it becomes very difficult to control the tendency for the wood to split. Probably the best method is by the use of polyethylene glycol 1000 (PEG) as Brian Howarth demonstrated in his article in WOODWORKER for November last year; but the wood must be very wet for this to be anyway successful and is not the thing to experiment with on partially dry wood. We would refer to the wax-like material you say appears to have been applied only to the outside edge of the wood, presumably on the sapwood. This may have been deliberate or the coating may have been applied all over the end grain with some of it peeling off, which is not unknown.

Actually, if wax is applied to the centre area (the heartwood) with the sapwood uncovered, this normally would be better than the system you appear to have for the reason that the sapwood holds more moisture than the heartwood; and if this can be balanced out by removing the surplus from the sapwood then the drying is likely to be more uniform.

Reverting to your question as to where you can buy suitable wax for end coating the wood: years ago it was the practice in the timber trade for the ends of valuable timber to be end sealed, the idea being to prevent end splitting by providing an impermeable seal. With that in mind it was quite usual to apply anything from tar to the dregs of paint tins. In more recent years Danish shippers, as a case in point, invariably dip the end of beech squares in hot paraffin wax.

A few years ago the Timber Research & Development Association (TRADA) carried out extensive tests on various compounds intended for the end sealing of wood in plank and log form. The tests included air-drying and kiln-drying phases. While the various wax types all did well in the air-drying stage, most broke down in kiln-drying due to wax melting and running off the wood, so really the materials had to be impervious to moisture and have good adhesion.

The material which came out top was Mobilcir C, a thin, white wax emulsion which dries to a hard elastic film. This was supplied by the Mobile Oil Co, 21 Soho Square, London W1. Another wax compound which did well was Mystox SPL100 supplied by Catomance Ltd, 94, Bridge Road East, Welwyn Garden City, Herts.

You could use bituminous paints or aluminium primer, but adhesion to wet wood is not always satisfactory. In principle, you should seal the end grain; refrain from storing really wet sections in your workshop initially (since this appears to be too warm for the purpose, at least in the winter time); allow the pieces to remain in log form as long as is practicable; and if you have some pieces in your workshop showing minor end checking, remove these to the open and well soak them with water to slow down the drying.

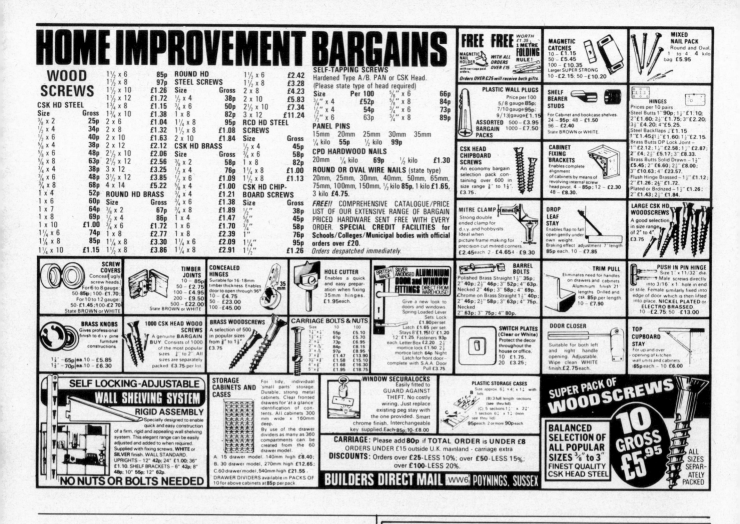

Prices quoted are those prevailing at press date and are subject to alteration due to economic conditions.

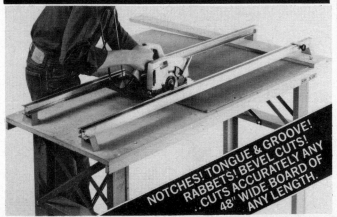

QUESTION BOX

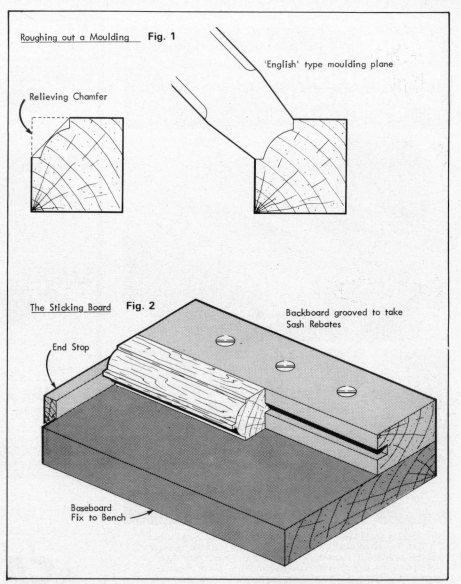

Roughing out a Moulding   Fig. 1

Relieving Chamfer

'English' type moulding plane

The Sticking Board   Fig. 2

End Stop

Backboard grooved to take
Sash Rebates

Baseboard
Fix to Bench

Using old planes

From: R. Horrocks, Tiverton, Devon
I have acquired a collection of Victorian moulding planes in beech and would appreciate advice on the following: 1 is it usual to remove waste to the rough section (particularly the larger ones) prior to using the moulding plane? 2 is there a book which names, dates and describes the applications of the various sections? 3 what method was used to firmly hold small but long pieces during moulding, eg a 75 x 25mm door architrave 2.5m long?

I might add that I have read Michael Dunbar's *Antique Woodworking Tools.* I find it useful although it is essentially concerned with American tools.

We recommend two publications in respect of your query concerning books referring to mouldings: (i) *The Woodworkers' Pocket Book* by C. H. Hayward (Evans Bros Ltd). This contains sectional views of the mouldings employed throughout the various ages of period furniture in UK. (ii) *History of the English House* by Nathaniel Lloyd, reprinted by the Architectural Press 1975. The scope of this book, recognised as a classic on the evolution of the English home, covers much authoritative detail in all aspects of construction and decoration and, of course, includes joinery and its associated mouldings.

As to the workings of the mouldings themselves, it was usual practice with hand moulding planes to rough-out the mould first by removing as much waste as possible with bench planes. As an example, the accompanying sketch (Fig. 1) shows a relieving chamfer worked with a jack plane before the moulding is struck with the ovolo plane. English-style planes are held at an angle to the work, while continental patterns are held upright.

Mouldings being fashioned are held in a sticking board made up for the purpose in hand. The one illustrated (Fig. 2) is suitable for working an ovolo sash bar. The pressure of the moulding plane keeps the stock in place while the jig prevents the workpiece from whipping.

Arnold & Walker's catalogue No. 6 *Traditional Tools of the Carpenter and other Craftsmen,* contains much interesting information on moulding planes and how they are used. Copies (£1.50) each from Roy Arnold, 77 High Street, Needham Market IP6 8AN.

Planing angles

From: R. M. Foden, Southport, Merseyside
Working with certain hardwoods I find that my small block plane with blade set at 20° tends to tear-out when interlocked grain is present. I have obtained a low-angle block plane (cutter at 12°) but find that it tears out much more than the 20° blade. By experimenting I have found that a blade set at approximately 45° is less likely to tear-out than a low-angle plane.

Has the grinding angle of the blade something to do with this? and is it possible to obtain a good-quality small plane, say 6in., with a normally set blade (45°)?

Problems with planing interlocked grain are common with various imported species of timber and may be due to several factors.

In the worst cases the cutting action of edge tools will not suffice and scraping followed by sanding has to be resorted to. Less difficult grain that will respond to planing may often contain deposits of silica and other minerals which will blunt the keen edges of tools and the enterprise is doomed almost before it is started. It is also true that some parcels of timber have been subjected to degrade during the drying process and with the cell structure thus damaged there is no possibility of obtaining a good surface. Pieces so affected should be discarded.

With less fractious woods two variations on normal planing practice should be adopted:

(i) the mouth of the plane should be closed to reduce the escapement gap to almost nil. This will ensure that the sole of the plane holds down the wood fibres to the last possible instant before the cutter starts its work (good-quality metal planes have adjustable mouths) and thereby prevent the fibres from lifting too far in front of the wedge-like action of the cutting iron, breaking off to produce tearing.

(ii) the plane should be held at an angle to the direction of travel, roughly 45°, thus producing a skew or slicing action. Although this effectively reduces the width of the cut at each pass it produces less resistance and the fibres are not so inclined to tear out.

We believe that several of the specialist tool suppliers regularly advertising in WOODWORKER may be able to help you in your search for a small 6in. hand plane. There remains however the interesting possibility of producing your own custom-made plane. A full description of how to do just this will be found in James Krenov's admirable book *The Fine Art of Cabinetmaking.*

Can you help?

From Welling, Kent, D. S. Cotter writes: 'One of the most difficult jobs I am faced with is laying leather on desktops. It is not the actual sticking-down of the leather but obtaining a uniform 'stretch' as any errors are glaringly obvious from the wavering line of gold tooling. If I obtain plain leather is it possible to tool after laying? Or is it a specialist's job?

Any advice would be appreciated and passed to Mr Cotter.

Question Box

Individual replies can now be given to readers' queries. But please enclose s.a.e.

The London Craft Fair

KENSINGTON TOWN HALL
September 26th-28th, 1980

OPENS FRIDAY 26th SEPTEMBER
1.00 p.m. to 9.00 p.m.
SATURDAY AND SUNDAY
10.00 a.m. to 6.00 p.m.

Amazing range of crafts
★ New ideas
★ Gems ★ Minerals ★ Silver
★ Jewellery ★ Enamelling ★ Basketry
★ Glass ★ Weaving ★ Marquetry
★ Pottery ★ Toys ★ Shells ★ Spinning
and many other crafts

plus . . .
Many ideas for creative and profitable hobbies

Admission:
Adults £1, Children and Senior Citizens 50p

Further Details:
Exhibitions Department, MAP Limited
PO Box 35, Hemel Hempstead, Herts HP1 1EE
Telephone: 0442 41221 Extension 276

For those coming by car, there is a car park underneath the Hall

The London
Craft Fair
KENSINGTON TOWN HALL
September 26th-28th, 1980

LIGHTING UP TIME!

FLIP-TOP LIGHTER WITH QUARTZ TIMEPIECE

Our special price

£24.95

including V.A.T. postage and packing anywhere in the U.K.

This is where technological excellence and craftsmen designed elegance meet. Made in a decorative gold coloured chunky casting, this refillable gas lighter also possesses a minute by minute, hour by hour quartz crystal timepiece. It is battery operated, the liquid crystal display clearly registering the time — but that's not all. Press a button on the side of the lighter and instantly the day and month are featured; press it twice and the seconds count is shown. The display can be illuminated at night and it comes with full operating instructions and a six month's guarantee.

N.B. (i) Please make cheques, etc., payable to Model & Allied Publications Ltd.
(ii) Allow 21 days for delivery.
(iii) Goods found to be faulty will be replaced immediately.
(iv) Please add 20% to our Special Prices if outside the U.K. Delivery could be up to 8 weeks.

Model & Allied Publications Ltd.,
P.O. Box 35, Bridge St., Hemel Hempstead, Herts. HP1 1EE.

To: Dept. EO
Model & Allied Publications Ltd.
P.O. Box 35, Bridge St., Hemel Hempstead, Herts.
Please supply .... Flip-Top Lighter(s) with Quartz Timepiece for which I enclose cheque/postal order value ....
Name ....
Address ....
....
....
Barclaycard ☐☐☐☐☐☐☐☐☐☐☐☐☐☐☐☐
Signature .... WW

Woodworking system

Described as the 5-in-1 wood-working system, Shopsmith Mk V from the US is distributed by Sumaco Machinery & Tools, Suma House, Huddersfield Road, Elland HX 9AA (0422 75491). It is a 34in. lathe, horizontal boring machine, 10in. sawbench, 12in. disc sander and 16½in. vertical drill press plus various accessories. The 13.5A motor and rotating parts are contained in the enclosed headstock which locks in any position along the tubular way, while speeds from 700 to 5200rpm are selected by means of a dial. Another feature is the rip fence lock handle which squares and locks the fence to the table. The extension table mounts are either end of the machine to provide extra capacity when sawing, drilling, sanding; it can be used as an auxiliary table for the upper auxiliary spindle.

Leaflet from the manufacturer states that the Shopsmith system can serve as the operating stand and power source for bandsaw, jointer, jigsaw and belt sander attachments.

Electric chainsaw

Further addition to the range of Partner chainsaws from C. D. Monninger Ltd, Overbury Road, London N15 6RJ (01-800 5435), is model 1601H 10in. guide bar (and its 12in. version designated 1602H), both with 1200W motor for 240V mains supply and weighing 5kg. Either a 12 or 14in. sprocket-nosed guide bar can be supplied. Ball and needle roller bearings are provided at all points of rotation. Safety features include double insulated casing and centrifugal clutch while the design of the chain is intended to minimise risk of kick-back. (The A100 electric chainsaw from Monninger was described on page 126 of WOODWORKER for February 1980).

Carving chisels

Six basic-shaped chisels with hardwood handles, also available in sets of six and as a set of six complete with mallet, slipstone, cramps and carving board are among the introductions by CeKa Works Ltd, Pwllheli, Gwynedd, North Wales (0758 2254). This company offers the well-known Ulmia precision mitre saws and accessories in several versions with either backsaw or frame-saw. Angles of 45, 60, 67½, 90, 67½, 60 and 45° can be set to give four, six and eight-sides frames and square ends at 90°.

Drills and attachments

Power tools by Robert Bosch of Germany (distribution in this country is through Robert Bosch Ltd, PO Box 166, Rhodes Way, Watford WD2 4LB (92-44233)), comprise eight hammer drills with either two-speed or variable speed facility, plunging router, jigsaw, circular saw, grinder and orbital sander. There is a range of attachments such as milling stand, drill stand, saw table, router, jigsaw, horizontal bench stand, lathe (190mm diameter, centre height 95mm and maximum distance between centres 960mm), bench grinder, drillsharpener, circular saw, orbital sander, machine vices and angle drive.

Drill model 620-2E with 620W motor is suitable for operating the lathe attachment as it provides a variety of speeds. A drive nut fitted to the spindle after the chuck has been removed is claimed to protect the spindle from damage and to give better power transfer by making a positive connection between drive unit and attachment. All Bosh drills have this feature.

An illustrated leaflet is available.

Allen keys

An 11-piece socket set of Allen keys in a metal case is produced by the Jacobs Manufacturing Co Ltd (incorporating Frank Guylee & Son Ltd), Archer Road, Millhouses, Sheffield (0742 57481). Each set includes 10

heavy-duty sockets with Allen key shanks and a standard Allen key for removing and repositioning the shanks. Another introduction is an 11-piece set comprising nine long-shafted Allen wrenches and extension shaft which fit into an easy-to-grip handle.

Other new items from Jacobs include six designs of rotary cutters and an additional range of miniature rotary cutters, all for use with standard power tools or with the Jacobs flexible shaft extension. In sanding and cutting discs there is a 5in. diameter open-mesh version as well as reinforced cutter in silicon carbide, another in aluminium oxide and a 7in. diameter cutting

Above: CK woodcarving tools. Below: Jacobs' Allen keys.

and sanding disc. Leaflet describing and illustrating Jacobs' products is available.

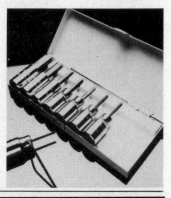

Chisel mortiser

The Perifra Alternax horizontal chisel mortiser made in France is handled in UK by the company known as Machinery Plus Ltd, 9 Biggin Hill Road, Evington, Leicester LE5 6HQ (0533 735554). Model 100 has lever-operated travelling head and fixed table 47 × 9in. (1200 × 230mm) and either automatic pneumatic or mechanical eccentric clamping systems. The head can be canted 20° to either side for slanted mortising and vertical adjustment on the table is 6in. (150mm). Mortise sizes are: width ⅛ — 1⅛in. (3 — 28mm); length 15/16 — 3 3/16in. (24 — 80mm); depth to 3½in. (to 85mm).

According to a leaflet available from the firm, setting-up the machine can be done in a few minutes and simplicity of design and robust construction give smooth and uninterrupted production. An eccentric shaft, belt-driven by 1.5hp electric motor running at 1450rpm, operates three tools (two side tools and one centre cutter) mounted in the head. The side chisels reciprocate on their own axes and the double-edged centre tool oscillates between them. Lubrication of moving parts is by pump.

The machine is supplied with one set of cutting tools, service tools, instruction manual and spare parts list.

Medium-density fibreboard

Medium-density fibreboard (MDF) deserves a close look from woodworkers, especially with the news that £6m is to be spent this year on building the first plant in Britain, writes Arthur Jones. The Caberboard Chipboard Co will be constructing the new factory alongside its existing chipboard mill in Scotland.

One of the main attractions of MDF will be its replacement value in a world where clear qualities of timber are becoming ever more scarce and certainly very expensive. And when the need is for a large clear piece of timber the requirement can rarely be met.

While it is true that MDF has been used commercially in this country for a couple of years, it has had a far larger market in America for some 12 years with the consumption growing year by year. Britain's import (we currently import all our MDF supplies) last year amounted to over 10,000 tonnes.

MDF is made from wood fibres and bonded with resin, but differs considerably from hardboard or chipboard, and is quite a costly sheet material if compared with chipboard. It does not have a layered construction but has fibres of the same size and type distributed throughout the panel. This means that intricate machining or carving operations can be carried out on the faces and edges without exposing any core void or any need for lipping.

The smooth surface permits a high degree of finish. Screws hold well and wear on cutters is low.

A great advantage is the size of panel obtainable, and this can be as much as 3620 x 1220mm and the thickness from 7-32mm. Obviously this offers great scope, and according to the limited market research done into the uses of MDF in this country it would appear that the main users have been the furniture and cabinet manufacturers, with some quite appreciable sales to woodworkers.

This is a material which can be worked to produce intricate patterns without disturbing the homogeneity of the panel and so give a fine finish; and this means it is ideal for those who use hand tools.

There are quite substantial variations between the various brands on the market. This remark is necessary to avoid outright rejection if the initial choice is unfortunate. However, standards are fast improving and we can be fairly sure that inferior panels will be eliminated as competition increases.

Stockists of MDF include: James Latham Ltd, Leeside Wharf, Clapton, London E5 9NG; and Nevill Long & Co Ltd, North Hyde Wharf, Hayes Road, Southall UB2 5NL.

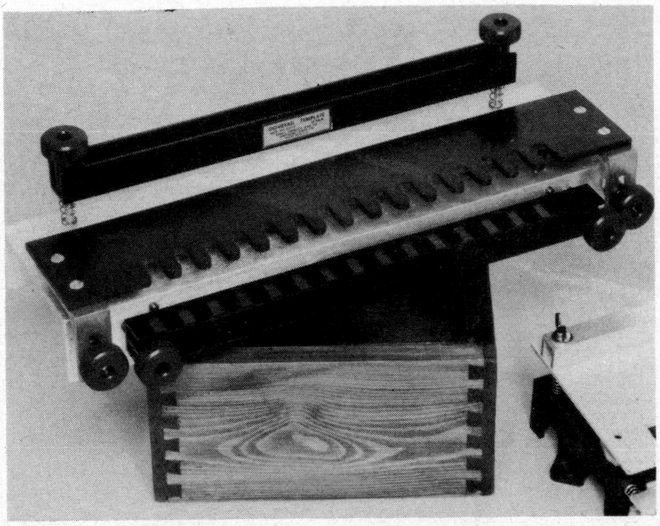

Below: the Perifra Alternax horizontal chisel mortiser made in France.

Model buildings

Since the market cross at Wymondham, Norfolk, was pictured on the cover of WOODWORKER for July 1979, a good deal of interest has been shown in this picturesque half-timbered building. As announced in our December issue last year, Tudor Models Ltd, 10 Spencer Road, Belper DE5 1JY (077382 4484), has introduced to its model kits (1/12th scale) the Wymondham market cross and also a Tudor house. The main structure is of externally-painted plywood panels and Malaysian oak timbers all pre-cut to length and section, according to a leaflet issued by Tudor Models.

In conjunction with students of the London Business School the company is developing its long-term marketing strategy, which involves moving to a purpose-built factory unit provided by the Council for Small Industries in Rural Areas (CoSIRA).

Footnote: Reader Charles A. Knapp of Akron, Ohio, made a model of the Wymondham market cross solely from the picture on the cover of last July's issue and description in the October issue (see page 247 of WOODWORKER for April 1980).

Woodfiller

A woodfiller two-part paste based on polyester resin is suitable for interior and exterior applications including marine work, according to Sylglas Co, Denso House, Chapel Road, London SE27 0TR (01-670 7511). Once the paste is mixed it can be worked into position immediately and curing is complete within 30-40min of mixing, states Sylglas.

Above: Craftsman dovetailing attachment 2571 from Hagemeyer.

Jigsaw and table

Model 072-2 manual scrolling jigsaw can be used in conjunction with model 25444 router/saw table, both items being in the Craftsman range of tools from Hagemeyer (London) Ltd, 25-33 Southwark Street, London SE1 1RQ (01-403 0680). The saw powered by a 240V ¼hp motor with an input of 290W and double insulated, has ⅝in. stroke blade with variable no-load speeds from 0-3600 strokes/min. This is controlled by a trigger movement. The blade is guided by means of the direction knob on top of the housing. Built-in dust blower keeps the cutting line clear and accessories include blade, circle-cutting and edge guide attachment; a selection of 10 different blades is available. RRP is approximately £52.13 exclusive of VAT.

The saw table has grooved die-cast aluminium top 18 × 13¼in., sliding mitre gauge and hinged cutter guard and is supplied complete with fittings to suit Craftsman routers, jigsaws and most other makes of jigsaw, all being fitted underneath the table, states Hagemeyer. RRP is given as £43.43 exclusive of VAT.

Other introductions include the Trim-A-Form model 26269 for controlled routing on stock of any length up to 2 × 8in. wide and supplied with fittings etc said to suit most makes of ¼in. routers — RRP is £37.35 excluding VAT. There is also a dovetailing attachment in two versions: model 2571 suitable for workpieces up to 12 × ⁷⁄₁₆-1½in, thick — RRP £45.65 excluding VAT; and model 2576 for workpieces up to 8 × ¼-½in. thick — RRP £22.57 excluding VAT. Another item is the Rout-A-Form pantograph model 25783 which attaches to unit which is suitable for Craftsman ¼in. routers and most other makes — RRP £19.93 excluding VAT.

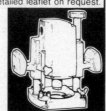
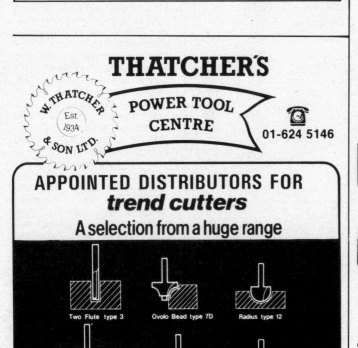

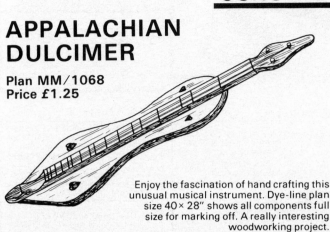

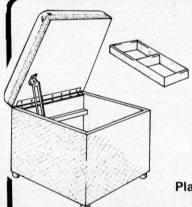
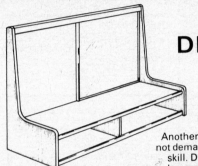

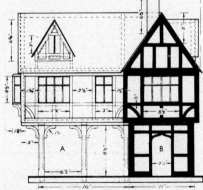
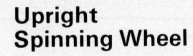

SHOP GUIDE

The quickest and easiest method of reaching all Woodworkers is to advertise in SHOP GUIDE.
Telephone Gill Dedman (0442) 41221 Ex. 241.
Rate: £5.00 per unit. Minimum of 6 months.
★ Mail Order

LEICESTERSHIRE

GLENFIELD   Tel: (0533) 871238
          & (06077) 5288
POOLE WOOD MACHINERY
SERVICES LIMITED
UNIT 3A MILL INDUSTRIAL ESTATE
Open: Mon.-Sat. 8.00am-5.00pm

LEICESTER   Tel. 0455-43254
ROY STARTIN LTD.
134 WOOD STREET   ★
EARL SHILTON
Open: Mon.-Fri. 8.00 a.m.-5.30 p.m.
Saturday 8.00 a.m.-1.30 p.m.

AVON

BATH   Tel. Bath 64513
JOHN HALL TOOLS   ★
RAILWAY STREET
Open: Monday-Saturday
9.00 a.m.-5.30 p.m.

BATH   Tel. Bath 22617
GORDON STOKES (office anytime)
WOODCRAFT SUPPLY   ★
110 MOUNT ROAD, WHITEWAY
Open: 9.30 a.m.-5.00 p.m.
Wednesday and Saturdays only

BRISTOL   Tel. (0272) 311510
JOHN HALL TOOLS LIMITED   ★
CLIFFTON DOWN SHOPPING
CENTRE, WHITELADIES ROAD
Open: Monday-Saturday
9.00 a.m.-5.30 p.m.

BRISTOL   Tel. 0272-629092
TRYMWOOD SERVICES   ★
2a DOWNS PARK EAST,
(off North View) WESTBURY PARK
Open: 9.00 a.m.-5.30 p.m.
Monday to Friday

BRISTOL   Tel. 0272-667013
V. H. WILLIS & CO. LTD.   ★
190-192 WEST STREET
BEDMINSTER
Open: 8.30 a.m.-5.00 p.m. Mon-Fri.
Saturday 9.00 a.m.-1.00 p.m.

BERKSHIRE

READING   Tel. (0734) 586522)
SARJENT'S TOOL STORES   ★
LTD.
44-52 OXFORD ROAD
Open: 8.30 a.m.-5.30 p.m.
Monday-Saturday

BUCKINGHAMSHIRE

MILTON KEYNES   Tel:
A. POLLARD & SON 0908-75221
LTD.   ★
51 QUEENSWAY, BLETCHLEY
Open: 8.30 a.m.-5.30 p.m.
Monday-Saturday

CAMBRIDGESHIRE

CAMBRIDGE   Tel: 0223-353091
H.B. WOODWORKING
69 LENSFIELD ROAD
Open: 8.30 a.m.-5.30 p.m.
Monday-Friday
8.30 a.m.-1.00 p.m. Saturday

PETERBOROUGH   Tel:
PETERBOROUGH   0733-62800
TOOL CENTRE
16 WESTGATE
Open: Mon.-Sat. 9.00am-5.30pm
Thursday 9.00 am-1.00 pm

CHESHIRE

CHEADLE   Tel. 061-491-1726
ERIC TOMKINSON   ★
86 STOCKPORT ROAD
Open: 9.00 a.m.-4.00 p.m.
Wednesday-Saturday
Closed all day Monday & Tuesday

CHESHIRE

CHESTER   Tel: Chester 42082
ROBERT KELLY
19 NEWGATE ROAD
Open: Mon.-Sat.
9.00 a.m.-5.30 p.m.

STOCKPORT   Tel.
M.W. EQUIPMENT 061-480-8481
LIMITED
SHAWCROSS STREET
Monday-Friday
9.00 a.m.-4.45 p.m.

CLEVELAND

MIDDLESBOROUGH   Tel.
REM ELECTRIC   0642-248460
POWER TOOLS
89 PARLIMENT ROAD
Open: 8.30 a.m.-5.00 p.m.
Monday-Saturday

MIDDLESBROUGH   Tel. 0642-
WINTZ   460035/83650
INDUSTRIAL SUPPLIES   ★
2 BESSEMER COURT,
GRANGETOWN
Open: Mon.-Fri. 8.30 a.m.-5.00 p.m.

CORNWALL

HELSTON   Tel.03265-4961
SOUTHWEST POWER TOOLS   ★
MONUMENT ROAD
Open: 8.00 a.m.-5.00 p.m.
Monday-Friday
Saturday 8.00 a.m.-12.30 p.m.

LAUNCESTON   Tel. 0566-3555
SOUTHWEST POWER TOOLS   ★
6 WESTERN ROAD
Open: 8.00 a.m.-5.00 p.m.
Monday-Friday
Saturday 8.00 a.m.-12.30 p.m.

DERBYSHIRE

BUXTON   Tel. 0298-871636
CRAFT SUPPLIES   ★
THE MILL
MILLERSDALE
Open: Monday-Saturday
9.00 a.m.-5.00 p.m.

DEVON

AXMINSTER   Tel. 0297-33656
POWER TOOL CENTRE   ★
STYLES & BROWN
CHARD STREET
Open: 9.00 a.m.-5.30 p.m.
Monday-Saturday

BIDEFORD   Tel. 023-72-3513
NORTH DEVON TOOLS   ★
7-9 MEDDON STREET
Open: Monday-Friday
8.00 a.m.-6.00 p.m.
Saturday 8.30 a.m.-5.00 p.m.

EXETER   Tel. 0392-73936
WRIDES TOOL CENTRE
147 FORE STREET
Open: 9.00 a.m.-5.30 p.m.
Monday-Saturday
Wednesday 9.00 a.m.-1.00 p.m.

CO. DURHAM

DARLINGTON   Tel. 0325-53511
PERCY W. STEPHENSON & SON
171/179 NORTHGATE
Open: 8.30 a.m.-5.30 p.m.
Monday to Saturday

ESSEX

SOUTHEND ON SEA   Tel.
MARSHALL &   0702-710404
PARSONS LIMITED
1111 LONDON RD., LEIGH ON SEA
Open: 8.30 a.m.-5.30 p.m. Mon.-Fri.
Open: 9.00 a.m.-5.00 p.m. Sat.

WESTCLIFFE-ON-SEA   Tel:
CLASSIC   0702-354055
BRASS COMPANY
429/431 LONDON ROAD
Open: 9.00 a.m.-5.30 p.m.
Mon.-Sat.

GLOUCESTERSHIRE

TEWKESBURY   Tel. 0684-
TEWKESBURY SAW CO.   293092
LIMITED   ★
TRADING ESTATE, NEWTOWN
Open: 8.00 a.m.-5.00 p.m.
Monday-Friday

HAMPSHIRE

ALDERSHOT   Tel. 0252-28088
BURCH & HILLS LTD.   ★
BLACKWATER WAY TRADING
ESTATE
Open: 8.30 a.m.-5.30 p.m. Mon.-Fri.
8.30 a.m.-12.00 Saturday

SOUTHAMPTON   Tel.
HAMPSHIRE   0703 776222
WOODWORKING MACHINERY   ★
297 SHIRLEY ROAD, SHIRLEY
Open: Tuesday-Saturday
9.30 a.m.-6.00 p.m.

HERTFORDSHIRE

HITCHIN   Tel. 0462-4177
ROGER'S
47 WALSWORTH ROAD
Open: 9.00 a.m.-6.00 p.m.
Monday-Saturday
Closed all day Wednesday

WATFORD   Tel. 0923-26052
J. SIMBLE & SONS LTD   ★
76 QUEENS ROAD
Open: 8.30 a.m.-5.30 p.m.
Mon.-Sat. Closed Wednesday

WATFORD   Tel. (0923) 49911
TREND MACHINERY & CUTTING
TOOLS LTD.
UNIT N, PENFOLD WORKS,
IMPERIAL WAY
Open: 9.00 a.m.-5.00 p.m. Mon.-Fri.

LANCASHIRE

LANCASTER   Tel. 0524-2886
LILE TOOL SHOP
43/45 NORTH ROAD
Open: 9.00 a.m.-5.30 p.m.
Monday-Saturday
Wednesday 9.00 a.m.-12.30 p.m.

LINCOLNSHIRE

LINCOLN   Tel. 0522-30199/
WOODWISE LIMITED   39871 or
121 HIGH STREET   0522-68428
          & 06077-5777/5288
          (after hours) ★
Open: Mon.-Sat. 9.00am-5.30pm

LONDON

          Tel. 01-624-5146
W. THATCHER & SONS LTD.
221A KILBURN HIGH ROAD NW6
(1st floor above travel agency)
Open Monday-Saturday 9.00-5.30
Closed Wednesday

          Tel. 01-739-7126
CECIL W. TYZACK   ★
79-81 KINGSLAND ROAD
SHOREDITCH E2
Open: 8.45 a.m.-5.15 p.m.
Monday-Friday — Closed Saturday

          Tel.
GENERAL   01-254-6052
WOODWORK SUPPLIES   ★
76-80 STOKE NEWINGTON
HIGH STREET, N16
Mon-Sat 9.00-6.00. Thur 9.00-1.00

GREATER MANCHESTER

MANCHESTER   Tel.
ROBERT KELLY   061-832-9920
UNIT 143, UPPER MALL
ARNDALE CENTRE
Open: Mon.-Sat.
9.00 a.m.-5.00 p.m.

ST. HELENS   Tel. St. Helens
ROBERT KELLY   58672
5 BRIDGE STREET
Open: Mon.-Sat.
9.00-5.30 p.m.

MERSEYSIDE

LIVERPOOL   Tel: 051-709-5341
ROBERT KELLY
28/32 RENSHAW STREET
Open: Mon.-Sat.
9.00 a.m.-5.30 p.m.

LIVERPOOL   Tel. 051-263-1359
TAYLOR BROS. (LIVERPOOL) LTD.
5/9 PRESCOTT STREET
Open: 8.30 a.m.-5.30 p.m.
Monday-Friday

NORFOLK

NORWICH   Tel. 0603 898695
NORFOLK SAW SERVICES
DOG LANE, HORSFORD
Open: 8.00 a.m.-5.00 p.m.
Monday-Friday
Saturday 8.00 a.m.-12.00 p.m.

NORTHAMPTONSHIRE

RUSHDEN   Tel. 093-34-56424
PETER CRISP LIMITED   ★
7 HIGH STREET
Open: 8.30 a.m.-5.30 p.m.
Monday-Saturday
Thursday 8.30 a.m.-1.00 p.m.

Classified Advertisements

FOR SALE

TOOLS TO TREASURE

CARPENTER'S ADZES by Gilpins with 3¾" cutting edge and 36" drop on handle **£24.21.**
WOODCARVER'S ADZES by Henry Taylor with 2" cutting edges and 10" ash handle.
Chisel Blade **£15.71;** Gouge Blade **£20.31**
All prices include P&P in the U.K. Export enquiries welcome.
Drawknives, Inshaves and other tools for the Craftsman Woodworker send large S.A.E. for details:
CORBETT TOOLS. Dept. WW/5
224 Puxton Drive, Kidderminster, Worcs.

YEW PLANKS AND SLABS

Huge selection of English Yew from trees felled 10 years ago, which took 500 years to grow. Unsurpassed for colour and grain £10 to £30 cube.

Tel: Yarpole 236 any time

WALL CLOCKS

Quartz battery movements **£5.95**
Pendulum movements **£5.75**
Clock hands — Black 55p; Brass 75p pair
Colourful ceramic clockfaces **£1.25**
Assorted plastic clockfaces 55p
Prices including post. Full guarantee.
SAE - WOODCRAFT SUPPLY (U.K.) LTD.
38 Summercourt Way, Brixham
TQ5 0DY

WELSH SLATE sharpening stones for sale at very competitive prices. Send SAE for details: Inigo Jones and Co. Limited, Groeslon, Caernarfon, Gwynedd. Tel: 0286-830242.   O-U

NORRIS adjustable panel and smoothing plane. Howkins plough plane. Six small brass-faced planes. Twenty carving chisels. Forty various wooden planes etc. Tel: Lincoln 38902.   Q

Fine Period Furniture
for you to make by hand at home

Large selection of 17th C copies in solid oak or elm for simple home assembly without special tools.

- All materials supplied
- All parts cut, planed and jointed
- Simple instructions
- Save up to 60% on retail prices

Send large SAE for brochure and price list

JACOBUS WORKSHOP
DEPT. W1, South Road, KIRKBY STEPHEN, Cumbria

LARGE collection of presentation mortice gauges to be sold. Brass tube stems. Brass faced fence with exotic woods. 67 Conway Road, Hounslow, Middlesex. Tel: 01-570-5909.   Q

EXCITING IDEAS IN FURNITURE-MAKING FOR NEWLYWEDS, D.I.Y. AND UNSKILLED

ALL you need are a few SIMPLE tools to make your own RE-PRODUCTION, MODERN AND GARDEN FURNITURE etc., from our EASY TO COPY PLANS and SIMPLE CLEARLY MARKED assembly instructions. EACH PLAN is FULL-SIZED. Just trace the plan on wood etc., similar to a dressmaking pattern. SO SIMPLE over 60 plans to choose from. FREE plumbing hints leaflet with each catalogue. Many satisfied customers who re-order once they try the plans. Send 60 p&p inc. TODAY for catalogue to Hamlyn Dept. D.W. 57 Lyneham, Wilts, SN15 4PH.

Chair illus. made in less than a day from plan No. 35 price only £1.99.

Brass or aluminium plates for your project. Letters block or script, example 3" x 1" brass plate with 20 block letter £1.10p, plus post, plus VAT. Also engraved badges, name plates, numbers, labels, etc. in coloured plastic. Trade enquiries welcome.

BRIAN J. BOWMAN TROPHIES LTD.
"Anela" Lower North Street, Cheddar, Somerset. Tel. Cheddar 742774

ROUTERS

If you are thinking of buying a Router, we offer Bosch/Elu range at unbelievable prices.
If you already own a Router Send for our Free Cutter Wall Chart.

BARRIE IRONS MACHINERY
106A Aldenham Road, Bushey, Herts.
Tel. Watford (0923) 30422

BRASS ELECTRICAL FITTINGS. Switches, Power Points, Dimmers, T.V. and Telephone Outlets, etc. Choice of three different designs on all models. Produced in heavy gauge solid brass. Polished, and treated with transparent lacquer to preserve high finish indefinitely. Also French Gilt, Wrought Iron, and a nine difference decorator colour range. All designed for simple replacement of existing plastic models. Full compliance with British Safety Standards. Illustrated colour catalogue FREE from the Classic Brass Co., Dept. WE, 429/431 London Road, Westcliff, Essex. Personal Shoppers welcome.   OPQ

MINIATURE carving tools for the finest detail in sets or singles. Designed and made by woodcarvers (work and tools exhibited WOODWORKER, November 1978). Also retempering, sharpening service. J. Mitchell, 65 Parkhurst Road, Norris Green, Liverpool L11 1DZ.   PQR

LUREM 6" planer/thicknesser (Compact 7) on stand. Excellent condition. £140.00 Tel: 01-949-1015 (anytime).   Q

BRANDING IRONS

Made from solid steel with 15" handle, to last a lifetime. Now you can permanently identify your tools and production pieces. We can quote for special styles for a professional look. Price guide — 3 x ⅜" characters **£6.95p.**

SAE details - Woodcraft Supply (U.K.) Ltd., 38 Summercourt Way, Brixham, TQ5 0DY

BANDSAWS

The BIRCH 2-speed BANDSAW, SANDER and LINISHER 16" throat, 6" depth, tilt. ½ h.p. single phase. Ready to plug in. Stamp illustrated details. Prices.

HAB ENGINEERING (Unit C)
Fardons Ind. Est., 113 Glover Street, Bordesley, Birmingham 9.
Tel: 021 772 2699

CORONET consort with saw table, thicknesser, planer, disc sander with tilting table, stand mounted. List price £614.00 accept £400.00. Also B&D HD1000 circular saw £35.00, vertical drill stand with shaper table £10.00. Tel: Bath 832926. 64 Entry Hill, Bath, BA2 5NA.   Q

MATERIALS

G. K. HADFIELD

Immediate despatch from stock, of materials for clock restoration. Finials, hands, keys, pendulums, suspensions, weights, pulleys and hundreds of other items.

Write, phone or call. Peaceful parking!

Send large SAE 16p for free lists of materials and new/old horological books.

Blackbrook Hill House, Tickow Lane, SHEPSHED, Loughborough LE12 9EY. Phone: Shepshed (05095) 3014.

CRAFTSMEN

Titebond was originally developed in the U.S.A. for the furniture trade and was brought into the U.K. to meet the high standard demanded by makers of fine musical instruments. We now make it available to all discerning craftsmen.
Titebond Aliphatic Resin is: Fast setting, twice as strong, sandable, non-toxic, easy spreading.
8oz container £1.99 plus postage 45p
12oz container £2.80 plus postage 65p
(please add 20p p&p for each additional container).
STRINGS N' THINGS, 63 Far Gosford St., Coventry (0203) 24406 *Trade prices on request.*

MINIATURE 1" to 1' Scale Chippendale drawer pulls, Butts, and H, Hinges, all in Brass. Send £2.00 for samples. Bailey, 131 Centre Drive, Newmarket CB8 8AP. Suffolk.   L-Q

MUSICAL INSTRUMENT MAKERS

Send for *Free Catalogue* of imported tonewood for Lute, Guitar, Violin and Keyboard.

A. HIGHFIELD & COMPANY
Rosewood House, Bridge Road, Downham Market, Norfolk, PE38 0AE

HAMPSHIRE WOODWORKING MACHINERY

297 SHIRLEY ROAD, SHIRLEY, SOUTHAMPTON
Telephone: 0703-776222

Open: Tuesday - Saturday 9.30 a.m. - 6.00 p.m.

Stockists for:
Wadkin, Elu, Startrite, Coronet, Kity, Arundel, Henry Taylor & Sorby.

Everything for the carpenter, joiner, turner and carver.

Ask for price for tools, polishes, finishes, books, etc. *(S.A.E. Please).*

Demonstrations, personal service, mail order (14 days delivery).

Access, Barclaycard and Mercantile Credit.

Answering service day and night.

MULTICUT-2

The world's first universal precision saw, cuts 50mm wood, 10mm metals, plastics, rubber, etc. High performance, safe in use. Do not compare with standard fretsaws. Details, 10p stamp.

HEGNER UNIVERSAL SAWS (U.K.) LTD.
36 Gt. Eastern Road, Hockley, Essex. Tel: Hockley 5669

Demonstrations by arrangement and at suitable exhibitions throughout the year.

FIRST QUALITY 8-day weight driven grandfather clock movements, break arch dials, battery grandfather clock movements 24" and 28" pendulum, battery clock movements from £3.70. All clock accessories, SAE please: Timecraft, 164 Park Road, Formby, Liverpool.   T/C

ENGLISH and Foreign hard and softwoods, Walnut — English, African, American and Brazilian. Oak, Ash, S. Chestnut, Beech, Elm, etc. Large or small quantities supplied. Also veneers stocked. Frank Aldridge, Eccles, Quidenham, Norwich, Norfolk NR16 2PD. Tel: Quidenham 415 and 297.   Q

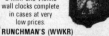

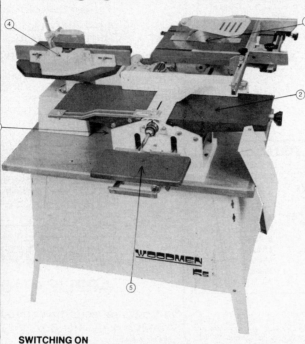

416

Prices quoted are those prevailing at press date and are subject to alteration due to economic conditions.

Woodworker, June 1980

Woodworker

THE MAGAZINE FOR THE CRAFTSMAN IN WOOD

JULY 1980   VOL. 84   No. 1040   ISSN0043-776X

Front Cover: Oak doors at the west end of the parish church of St Andrew, Alfriston, Sussex, see also page 424 *(photo: W. H. Gates).*

Editor	Geoffrey Pratt
Production Editor	Polly Curds
Advertisement Manager	Terence M. Healy
Group Advertisement Manager	Michael Merrifield
Managing Director	Gavin Doyle

ABC
MEMBER OF THE AUDIT
BUREAU OF CIRCULATIONS

SUBSCRIPTION DEPARTMENT: Remittances to MODEL AND ALLIED PUBLICATIONS, PO Box 35, Hemel Hempstead, Herts HP1 1EE. Price per copy 75p includes p&p. Subscription queries: Tel: Hemel Hempstead 51740. Subscription rate, including index, £9.00 per annum; overseas sterling £9.00; $20.00 US for overseas dollar subscribers. Application to mail in the US is pending at Milwaukee, Wisconsin, and at additional offices. Distribution to N. American hobby and craft shops by Kalmback Publishing Co., 1027 N. Seventh Street, Milwaukee, W153233, USA (Tel: 414-272-2060). Distribution to news stand sales by Eastern News Distributors Inc, 111 Eighth Avenue, New York NY1011, USA (Tel: 212-255-5620). Distribution to museums and bookshops by Bill Dean Books Ltd, 166-41 Powells Cove Boulevard, Whitestone, New York 11357 (Tel: 212-767-6632).

WOODWORKER is printed by New Avenue Press Ltd, Pasadena Close, Pump Lane, Hayes, Middlesex. (Mono origination by Multiform Photosetting Ltd, Cardiff), for the proprietors and publishers, Model & Allied Publications Ltd (a member of the Argus Press Group). Trade sales by Argus Distribution Ltd, 12-18 Paul Street, London EC2A 4JS. WOODWORKER (ISSN 0043-776X) is published on the 3rd Friday of the month.

Model & Allied Publications Ltd

PO Box 35, Bridge Street, Hemel Hempstead, Herts HP1 1EE. Telephone: Hemel Hempstead (0442) 41221.

'SINCE TIME IMMEMORIAL'

In recent issues of WOODWORKER there has been discussion of the problems faced by small businesses and by those wishing to establish craft workshops.

Peter Fischer who specialises in furniture making and restoration, as well as veneering and inlaying and joinery at Market Overton near Oakham, Rutland, has sent a copy of a letter he has addressed to the secretary of state for the environment proposing a change in the planning regulations to assist the formation of small businesses. In his covering note to WOODWORKER Mr Fischer writes: 'D. S. Cotter of Welling, Kent (February 1980) has drawn attention to the problem that we have been grappling with for two years now and we are still awaiting a decision on our own application from the department of the environment. I hope that our proposal goes some way towards meeting the problem and I urge readers to write to their MPs, or the secretary of state in support of the proposal.'

Mr Fischer reviews his difficulty over the application for planning permission to change the use of part of his residential property to light industrial use in order to continue his small craft workshop. He explains that neighbours are concerned that future development of his business should not take place to the detriment of the rural environment. 'They are fearful that a grant of light industrial use permission would contain insufficient safeguards for the future. We fully sympathise with their fears and have discovered from our researches that this is a widespread problem.'

His letter to the secretary of state concludes that some provision should be made for the establishment of small business in residential property. Mr Fischer notes that the DOE policy note no. 2 of 1969 makes provision for this in section B clauses 19-22, but points out that it does not go far enough and 'is all too often interpreted very narrowly and results in some cases in quite unnecessary restriction . . .'

He proposes that a new use class of 'cottage industry' be created and defined as follows: The use of residential premises for any business purpose would not require planning permission provided that: 1 not more than 50% of the floor area of the residential property, subject to a maximum area of 1000 sq ft, be used for business purpose; 2 not less than 50% of the labour employed in the business, including directors normally reside in the associated residential premises; 3 no change in the external appearance of the premises is involved.

It is to be hoped that the DOE will favourably consider Mr Fischer's proposals for 'restoring that right enjoyed by our forebears since time immemorial to work in their own homes.'

Timber shortage

Forecasts of a world timber shortage could be self-defeating, said Robin Howard (president of the Timber Trade Federation) recently. Referring to the report prepared by the Centre for Agricultural Strategy at Reading university (WOODWORKER for May 1980), he said there were many good reasons for increasing afforestation in Britain, but to base a case on some hypothetical shortage of timber threatened in 20 years could be self-defeating. It was discouraging to customers to suggest there would be no timber for them to use.

CLOCKS

For Everyman Exhibition

sponsored by CLOCKS magazine An exhibition for clock lovers

"We've been waiting for this for 30 years"

"Nothing like it has ever been staged before"

"What a marvellous show"

Comments from last year's visitors

Well it's coming again — Bigger — Better — Longer

If you — Buy — Make — Restore — Collect — Read about or just like looking at or "Talking" clocks, come along to the comfort of the modern Kensington Town Hall — Enjoy the atmosphere of beautiful clocks.

You can even park your car if you come early!

Access to the hall

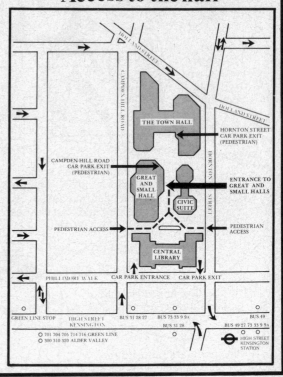

KENSINGTON TOWN HALL,
Hornton St. Kensington, London W8.
Thursday to Sunday 3rd to 6th July 1980. 10 am to 6 pm.
Refreshments are available. Tickets at the door £1.25.

Craftsmen of the Cotswolds

Gimson and the Barnsleys
'Wonderful furniture of a commonplace kind'

Mary Comino
Deputy Director of Cheltenham Museum

The first comprehensive account of the development and work of the two Barnsley brothers and their friend and fellow craftsman Ernest Gimson.

The three men, trained architects and followers of William Morris and the Arts and Crafts Movement, left London to set up workshops in the Cotswolds. There they turned their attention to furniture design, intent on revitalising traditional handicrafts. This book traces the important influence of these remarkable men on the development of early twentieth century furniture design.

Fully illustrated with over 100 photographs of their furniture, architecture and designs, together with many of the original plans and working drawings.

£13.50

 Evans Montague House, Russell Square, London WC1B 5BX

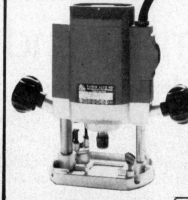

422

Prices quoted are those prevailing at press date and are subject to alteration due to economic conditions.

Woodworker, July 1980

Do you ever wonder what they say about you after six months have passed?

A beautiful piece of wood! That's what you thought. There was no way of knowing it wasn't properly seasoned.

Then all the work you put into it came to nothing. Cracking and warping followed as central heating took its toll. So much for your reputation. And if that hasn't happened to you...you're lucky.

Ever thought of rounding off your craftsmanship by drying your own timber. The Ebac Mini timber seasoner makes it more than practical - it's actually profitable. Takes up very little room. Costs about £350. Running costs: a little over 1p an hour! And it pays for itself through the reduction in cost of buying unseasoned timber. A simple dial setting is all that is needed for precise seasoning of different kinds of wood. No noise. No mess. No fuss.

The Ebac Mini, one of a big range, is the only timber seasoner designed for even the smallest business. Send in the coupon and we'll let you have a leaflet about it. And if any problems come to mind about how suitable it is for your individual business, tell us about them. We'll be glad to give you all the answers - and help - we can.

Dry your own timber - economically
(and keep your reputation)

CHURCH DOORS IN SUSSEX

W. H. Gates on tour in Sussex took these pictures of the parish church of St Andrew, Alfriston. The oak doors at the west end form the subject of this month's cover picture. Details of the construction are shown here. The doors were installed in 1959 and Mr. Gates comments: 'The dovetails although adequate for the purpose have a weakness in the area of the square cut because of the short grain. Undoubtedly the design was copied from the original pair that the replacement doors had to match.'

The picture of the east end of the church is interesting. Note the two wands or staves at left and right; these are the churchwardens' badges of office. Note also the bell ropes. The ringers stand at the foot of the chancel steps and in bellringing terms this is referred to as a 'ground-floor pull'. It is more usual for bells to be rung from a ringing chamber in the tower. It is sometimes said that unseemingly behaviour on the part of ringers in past days resulted in incumbents having ringing chamber floors removed and 'ground-floor pull' substituted. It is not suggested that Alfriston ringers have ever been guilty of unseemly behaviour. In fact, the position of the tower dictates that their bells must be rung from the nave or crossing.

Right: A pair of attractive and beautifully made oak doors in the west end of the church, these are not original and were installed in 1959. **Below right:** View down the nave to the east window. **Below left:** Door detail showing dovetails.

TIMBER TOPICS 9

In the June 1980 issue W. H. Brown FIWSc discussed the use of polyethylene glycol (PEG) for improving the dimensional stability of wood, with particular reference to one of the earliest field tests on the use of PEG for stabilising walnut gunstocks. Here the author explains how the chemical works on wood.

Polyethylene glycol is related to permanent anti-freeze but it must be recognised that this cannot be used as a substitute since its characteristics are quite different. Anti-freeze as used in car radiators is ethylene glycol (a monomer) whereas polyethylene glycol is a polymer. There is an important difference between the two. A monomer (Greek, monos, alone; meros, part) is a simple substance of identical molecules; a polymer is a compound formed of many monomer units linked together to form larger molecules.

In the truest sense of stabilising a hygroscopic substance like wood, by soaking a thin veneer in polymerous chemicals, these replace the water content of the veneer and by applying heat and pressure the chemicals polymerise and the veneer now has become more or less inert in changes of atmosphere. The character of the wood has also changed to a hardened material like plastics.

Thicker wood can also be stabilised by irradiation, ie by the use of gamma rays and polymers whose molecules become fused, so to speak, to the carbon molecules in the wood; but again, the wood is altered in many ways from the original although the treated wood is literally inert.

The use of polyethylene glycol on wood does not render that wood inert but it improves the stability of the wood by 'bulking' it. We have already mentioned that suitable treatment with PEG will reduce potential movement in black walnut by at least half of normal.

In the issue of June 1980 we referred to polyethylene glycol 1000; this value is the preferred molecular weight for all stabilising treatment involving wood generally, but various grades from 200 to 4000 or more are available to industry. We said that Stamm in America was working on the uses of PEG in 1934 and we mentioned that it was only in about 1959 that the first account of one of his field tests was published. The World War II years placed certain restrictions on the American work, but it is only fair to say that in 1946 the Swedish company Mo och Domsjö Ab started research into the use of PEG in treating cellulose fibres. This led to a patent application filed in Sweden in 1952 with the first external patent being published in South Africa in 1954. The latter containing seven claims and 20 examples.

This patent can briefly be summarised as a method of preserving objects or materials apt to be subject to decay, moulding or fermenting processes; or attack by insects or the like; or to change due to fluctuations in atmospheric humidity, which is characterised by using as the impregnating agent and/or preservative a condensation product of an alkylene oxide such as ethylene oxide, for example a polyethylene glycol or a derivative of this. The 20 examples include the impregnation of wood with PEG alone or combined with fungicides; the impregnation of wood with PEG under alternating pressure conditions; treatment of wood for furniture;

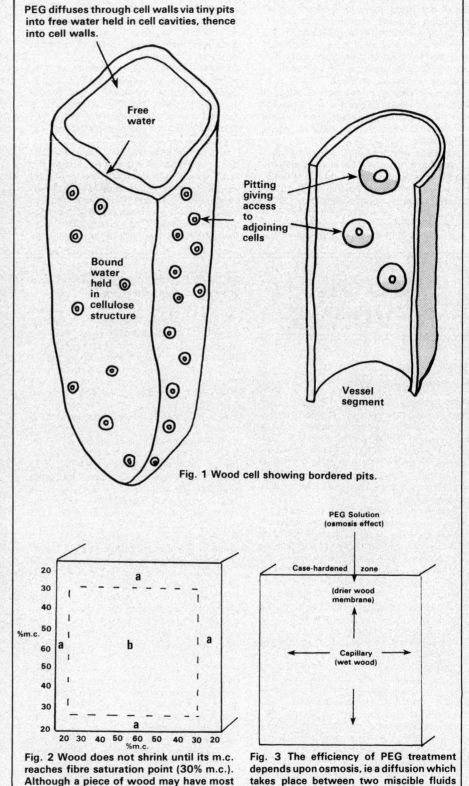

PEG diffuses through cell walls via tiny pits into free water held in cell cavities, thence into cell walls.

Free water

Bound water held in cellulose structure

Pitting giving access to adjoining cells

Vessel segment

Fig. 1 Wood cell showing bordered pits.

Fig. 2 Wood does not shrink until its m.c. reaches fibre saturation point (30% m.c.). Although a piece of wood may have most of its bulk above FSP(b) the outer skin (a) may already try to shrink but because of wet core is restrained and can become case hardened.

PEG Solution (osmosis effect)

Case-hardened zone

(drier wood membrane)

Capillary (wet wood)

Fig. 3 The efficiency of PEG treatment depends upon osmosis, ie a diffusion which takes place between two miscible fluids through a permeable membrane. If the surface of the wood dries out its permeability is reduced and will hamper osmotic impulse.

ingredient in primer paints; and preservation of water-logged fibre products or wood of archaeological value.

It will be noted that whereas Dr Stamm was essentially concerned with timber stabilisation, Mo och Domsjö Ab (a huge timber, paper pulp and chemical organisation), saw much wider implications which is reflected in its research and subsequent promotion of PEG for various purposes. Generally speaking its work in recent years had been concerned with finding better methods of incorporating PEG as a dimensional stabilising agent for the commercial production of wood, veneer, plywood, chipboard and fibreboard, particularly in the fields of impregnation of green veneer with PEG; surface treatment of freshly cut wood with PEG; and pressure impregnation of shipping dry wood with PEG.

We have referred to the bulking effect of PEG which really means that the chemical tends to keep green wood in a swollen state by diffusing into the cell walls as water diffuses out.

We have mentioned in previous Timber Topics that in a green piece of wood water is held in it in two ways: first, as free water in the cell cavities; and second, as bound or imbibed water in the cell walls. In this latter form the water molecules are held between the chains of molecules forming the cellulose content and as drying proceeds below the saturation point, ie when all the free water has been removed from the cell cavities, water removal now causes the cellulose chains to draw closer together and the wood shrinks.

When polyethylene glycol enters a piece of green wood it diffuses into the free water. Later, as the wood is dried and the free water is removed, a concentration of the chemical now diffuses into the cell walls (Fig. 1). The extent of the bulking attained depends upon a number of factors such as the molecular weight of the bulking agent; its solubility in water; the initial concentration of the chemical; its viscosity; the time allowed for diffusion and for holding under non-drying conditions; and the temperature and rate at which drying occurs.

In early American experiments on test pieces of Englemann spruce 50 × 50 × 3mm these were pre-saturated with water; soaked in PEG for 20hr; held under non-drying conditions for a day; and dried slowly for 12 days in a desiccator followed by oven-drying to constant weight at 110°C.

Arising out of these tests* it was suggested that when optimum bulking was sought the wood should take up about 35% of its dry weight of chemical, this stage being followed by storage under non-drying conditions so that the chemical can equalise in concentration throughout the wood structure. However, for maximum dimensional stability PEG must be diffused into the wood in amounts of 25 to 30% of the dry weight of the wood, an appropriate concentration of chemical being in the form of a 30 to 50% (by weight) solution.

If treatment is adequate the maximum potential shrinking and swelling of the wood is reduced to about 80%, at least in theory. The criterion by which the efficiency of the treatment is judged is the degree of diffusion of PEG into the microscopic structure of the cell and fibre walls; and this depends very much on high m.c. of the wood initially. It is not always realised that a freshly-sawn piece of wood, ostensibly soaking wet, may be relatively dry in a thin zone of outer wood (Fig. 2). This can occur in a single warm day's delay before treatment with PEG, resulting in a mild casehardening of the wood surface sufficient to reduce the almost osmosis effect of the treatment. In other words, while capillary action is tending to bring moisture out of the wood osmosis is attempting the reverse, but its thrust, so to speak, is hampered by the hardened surface (Fig. 3). There are, however, suitable means of getting round this. In a future Timber Topic we will explain what these are.

*Factors affecting the bulking and dimensional stabilisation of wood with polyethylene glycols: Paper No. 1751 by Alfred J. Stamm presented at 18th annual meeting of Forest Products Research Scociety, Chicago, 22 June 1964.

BOOK REVIEWS

Tools of the woodworking trades

Philip Walker who is well-known to many readers as a specialist in old woodworking tools, has written an interesting booklet of 32 pages which appears as no. 50 in the Shire Album series by Shire Publications Ltd, Cromwell House, Church Street, Princes Risborough, Aylesbury HP17 9AJ. It is modestly priced at 75p and titled *Woodworking Tools*.

There are numerous drawings, reproductions from old trade catalogues and interesting photographs by John Melville showing that the basic equipment has changed little; and though a woodworker of today would find himself severely limited in a workshop of ancient Egypt, he might manage quite well in a Roman one. Indeed, the Romans appear to have had everything but an efficient tool to bore large holes and they, surprisingly, did not think of the brace and bit.

The author shows how some of the tools of the specialist tradesmen — the cooper, wheelwright and carpenter — were adapted for their needs and how extensive ranges of tools were developed to meet the cabinetmakers' requirement for precision and finish. For example, two tool chests from the 18th century are illustrated together with some of the tools they contained; and there would also have been between 50 and 100 moulding planes in the bottom compartment.

This admirable booklet includes a further reading list and remarks on the comprehensive collections of tools at St Albans city museum in Hertfordshire, the Science museum in London and at museums in the US, W Germany and France. **G.P.**

Back to a golden age of American furniture manufacture

In 1972 Thos Moser, cabinet maker of New Gloucester, Maine, US, began producing furniture in the Shaker style which achieved its golden age of design between 1820 and 1850. Though short-lived this period produced a collection of remarkable furniture which has been discussed in WOODWORKER during the recent past (October 1979, March 1980).

Now Mr Moser has written *How to Build Shaker Furniture* and included detailed measured drawings for 50 pieces which he has designed and made. Each is capable of being built with hand tools, with a few basic power tools or with a completely equipped workshop. He emphasises that the designs are not copies of antiques but, rather, an attempt at perpetuating one small aspect of a vision which fell prey to economic and stylistic pressures 125 years ago.

The book contains five chapters and is well illustrated with drawings and photographs in its 200-plus pages. The first chapter deals with the Shaker sect and its commitment to functionalism which preceded by nearly a century the unadorned forms of the Bauhaus and the international school. This sets the scene for chapter 2 which discusses the materials: wood (with a section on handling and conditioning), adhesives, abrasives, hardware. There is a timely reminder about quality. '. . . use only the very best. Since labour represents three-quarters of the cost of production, it seems to me to be a fundamental absurdity to try to cut corners by using cheap materials . . .'

Chapter 3 is devoted to tools, hand and power, and to shop layout based on the 'ideal' one-man workshop. Mr Moser has some interesting comments on power tools and the use of reconditioned ones: 'a well-worn heavy-duty old tool, well calibrated and with good bearings, is better than a new lightweight model . . .' His remarks on layout are also pertinent.

Chapter 5 comprises the measured drawings with photographs of the finished pieces and notes on material quantities. The drawings are more in the nature of sketches but the dimensions and detail are plain enough to follow. There is a wide range of items here such as shelves, stands, chests, cupboards, tables, chairs, stools, beds, settee, desks, clocks, breadboard; and even bathroom and kitchen cupboard adaptions. In constructing from the drawings the builder is encouraged to change details to suit his individual taste and need. 'Only proportion should hold more or less constant,' says Mr Moser.

Building processes make up chapter 4 which contains sketches of joints and pictures showing various constructional details. There is a useful section on finishing techniques ('in working with Shaker forms it is unwise to overfinish'); and a comment on the art of living with these creations: 'If your carefully-finished table shows the marks of use do not despair. A wear mark here, a slight burn there, a dent . . . surface scratches . . . all these emboss a table top giving it warmth and charm and attesting to the life cycle of a family.'

Published by Sterling in the US and distributed here through the Oak Tree Press Ward Lock Ltd, 116 Baker Street, London W1M 2BB, it costs £3.95 and is a paperback. Mr Moser has written for the builder and, for good measure, he offers what he describes as a short course on tools and woodworking methods. The drawings are by Chris Becksvoort, a cabinet maker and artist.

This book, together with *How to make Colonial Furniture* (reviewed in the June 1980 issue) gives woodworkers a good range of measured drawings for pieces that would not be out of place in British homes. **G.P.**

RACK FOR COOKERY BOOKS

'I made this book rack to hold my wife's cookery books and also to show her what she had missed in the days before I acquired a lathe, writes Richard Large. 'It was also an exercise in turning; leaving part of the wood square in section and part round. This is something which furniture often demands yet writers on turning do not always deal with it.

'The process is quite simple. Maybe this is why no one bothers to explain it. To produce a sharp shoulder between the square and the round (as with the tenon joints on the bottom of the front uprights), I gently offered the parting tool up to the wood until it cut it round. To make a more elegant and rounded shoulder, as on the top of the front uprights, I used a skew chisel, though it may help to make the first cuts with the parting tool.

'Dimensions and construction of the rack will be evident from Fig. 1. I found it was important to ensure that the back rail was low enough to prevent small books slipping through: a cascade of literature into the pudding mix should the rack have to be moved would hardly please the cook!

'Ideally the tenons of the side rails should fit through those of the back rail. One thing I

**Rack for cookery books.
The material is pine.**

Fig. 1

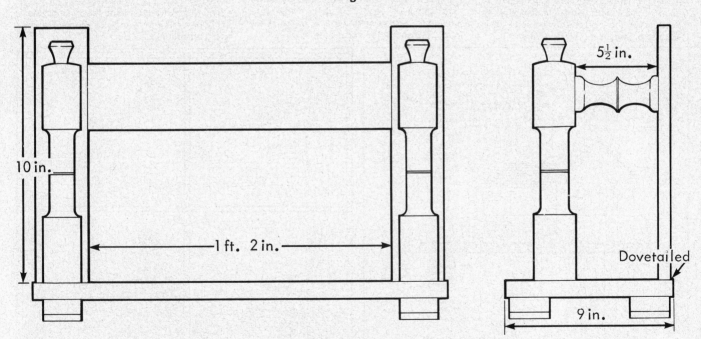

overlooked in making the rack is that when glued joints dry-out (as they did) the shrinkage of the glue may pull the joints out of true so that carefully set right-angles disappear. This should not happen of course with accurate, tight joints but it pays to cramp them nevertheless. The front uprights, being unsupported by other joints, are prone to movement and can be held as in Fig. 2.

'The back uprights are dovetailed into the base but all other joints are mortise and tenon. The feet are turned, drilled through and screwed on. I used pine for the rack though it might have looked better in beech.'

Front uprights $1\frac{1}{4}$ in. square
Back uprights 2×1 in.

Fig. 2

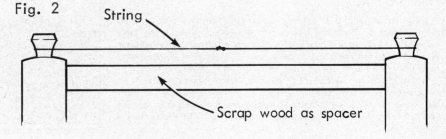

workpieces

Catalogue

A 20-page pocket-size user catalogue has been issued by Rabone Chesterman Ltd, Whitmore Street, Birmingham B18 5BD, and copies are freely available from the company's home sales department. The publication lists and illustrates in full colour product ranges such as measuring tapes; tape rules; spirit levels; steel rules; gauges; carpenters tools; and hole saws.

Treatment for roofs

Has the workshop roof developed a leak? BP Aquaseal Ltd, Hoo, Rochester, suggests that provided the roof is in good overall condition a waterproofing treatment can solve the problem. It recommends a three-stage operation: 1 sweep down the roof surface thoroughly with a stiff brush and remove moss or lichen. Treat the surface with a fungicide (household bleach is ideal but let it dry before the next stage); 2 seal cracks, holes and joints with Aquaseal 88 mastic using a knife or trowel; 3 brush on Aquaseal 5 or 40 (the latter is for flat roofs) with a dampened soft brush or broom. Two coats are recommended, the first being allowed to dry before the second is applied.

The cost? The firm states a can of the 88 mastic (1 litre) is around £2.60; 5 litre of Aquaseal 5 is about £6 and is sufficient to treat 40-50sq ft with two coats; 5 litre of the 40 product is about £8 and covers some 20sq ft with two coats *(see sketch below)*.

New showroom

Mail order supplier of machinery Steenwise Ltd has opened a new showroom at Limefield Mills, Wood Street, Crossflatts, Bingley, Yorks. Customers now have the opportunity of evaluating machines and 'enjoying the benefit of purchasing at mail-order discount prices,' states Steenwise managing director M. Bates.

Horse-drawn vehicles

Around 1904 a Beverley firm known as The East Yorkshire & Crosskills' Cart & Waggon Co Ltd, issued a catalogue of its extensive range of horse-drawn carts as well as hand trolleys and trucks. The illustrations were detailed and excellently done as engravings in perspective, rather than elevations.

The catalogue is available as a facsimile edition running to 159 pages from John Thompson, 1 Fieldway, Fleet, Hampshire, at £1.80 plus 30p postage, or from Argus Books Ltd, Argus House, 14 St James Road, Watford, Herts, at £1.80.

John Thompson in his introduction suggests that the information given in the catalogue provides a very useful basis for model making.

Our spellings!

Readers may wish to note that the word 'harnstone' on page 330 of the May issue should be hornstone and that 'corendum' on page 333 should be corundum.

Black as your hat

In the letter from Hugh Blogg of Broadstairs (WOODWORKER for March, page 187), mention was made of Mozambique mahogany. In fact the reference should have been to Mozambique ebony. Mr Blogg says: 'This is reckoned to be the blackest, incidentally; dirty stuff, like working with soot!'

Drilling holes in glass?

'Don't use an ordinary twist drill. These slip on glazed surfaces and even if you do succeed in starting a hole the chances are that the material will crack in a matter of seconds'. This advice is given by Neepsend Ltd, Lancaster Street, Sheffield S3 8AQ, and the firm goes on to say that the correct type is one such as the Cintride Spearpoint glass drill which comes in sizes from $\frac{1}{8}$ to $\frac{1}{2}$in. diameter at prices from, for example, £1.95 (excluding VAT) for the $\frac{1}{4}$in. diameter drill.

Neepsend points out that the drilling technique for glass is not difficult but it does call for slow speed and therefore a hand-drill should be used. The other essential is lubrication of the tip of the drill. Some people use turps, others find it is just as effective to use milk or water as a substitute.

When starting the hole it is often easiest to turn the handle of the drill half a turn forward and then half a turn back. This makes a tiny depression in the material which keeps the drill on-course. Continue by drilling steadily in the normal way until the tip reaches the other side. Then apply more lubricant to both the top and bottom surfaces. Finally relax the pressure slightly and carry on carefully until a hole with parallel sides is produced.

The method can be used for making holes in mirrors, glass shelves, glass-topped tables and glass bottles.

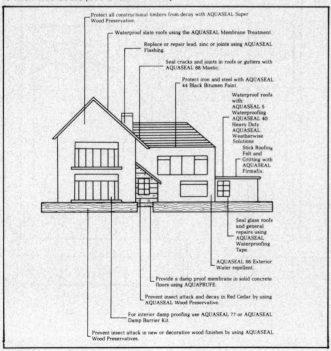

One in the hand

John Parkinson of Belfast has been teaching woodwork at schools and colleges in Northern Ireland for 40 years. Recently he was introducing a group of 12-13 year-olds to their first job in edge planing and duly warned them not to go below the gauge-measured lines. 'Don't finish up with one shaving in your hand', he said.

In the group was Adrian Thompson who likes drawing as well as woodwork. Taking his teacher's humorous remark to heart, Adrian subsequently set to work with his pencil and produced this cartoon which, as Mr Parkinson says in his letter to WOODWORKER, 'has a point'.

THE WORLD'S TIMBER TREES

In the April issue C. W. Bond FIWSc discussed agba as the 11th part of his series. Here he describes merbau and its uses in joinery, turnery and the making of stringed musical instruments.

MERBAU: 12

Intsia spp. *Intsia* — from *Intsi,* a native name in Madagascar. Leguminosae (Caesalpiniaceae).

This is a hard heavy timber very similar to African afzelia, rich golden-brown in colour when freshly cut, darkening slightly on exposure. It gives a general impression of strength and dignity. The vessels are large, giving a coarse texture, berlinia and merbau being similar in this respect but very different

Intsia bakeri
Drawn from material in the Forest Herbarium, University of Oxford (ack. curator).

in character owing to the marked difference in colour. Some of the vessels in merbau contain a yellowish deposit but this does not appear to affect a fully-polished surface.

Although the timber is generally used for heavy construction work such as sills and outdoor structural members, it has a certain refinement when suitably finished for such work as parquet flooring, counter-tops and indoor decorative joinery. It is also effective for ornamental turnery.

Intsia bakeri
Cross section × 10 lineal

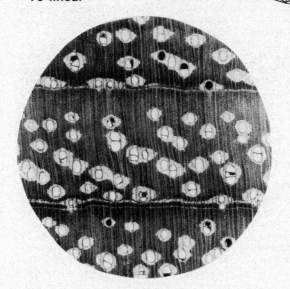

5cm

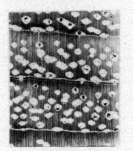

Cross section × 3.3 as seen with a × 10 hand lens

The writer noticed a pronounced resonant quality when working with merbau many years ago. This prompted the making of three violins as an alternative to the traditional maple and sycamore. Merbau, however, is some 40% heavier than sycamore and this has to be borne in mind in such a substitution. And for refined work such as violin scrolls and bent ribs, not to mention purfling, the hardness and coarse texture did not add to ease of working.

The photomicrograph shows conspicuous vasicentric parenchyma, also well-marked 'terminal' parenchyma. Many of the groups surrounding the vessels are wing-like and would be described technically as 'aliform'.

The flower of merbau, like that of berlinia, has one petal and this illustrates one type of flower characteristic of the Caesalpiniaceae.

RECORDER

'The design given here,' says the author, Peter Tomlin, 'is simply a reproduction of the Stanesby recorder of 1700 and should prove perfectly adequate . . . exceedingly cheap and, properly played, a very beautiful instrument . . .'

The recorder is an instrument of the flute family, having the acoustic qualities of a tube open at both ends. Thus it overblows at the octave, unlike the clarinet which overblows at the twelfth. It differs from the transverse flute mainly in that the player's breath is channelled down a wind-way so that it cannot fail to strike the edge of the aperture at the correct angle. It is this which makes the instrument so easy to play — or rather sound. Playing as distinct from just blowing the recorder is quite exacting. This characteristic of easy blowing, unfortunately, also reduces the flexibility of the instrument in the matter of intonation.

In the baroque flute the intonation is under the control of the player to a very large degree. By altering the angle at which the stream of air strikes the far side of the embouchure hole; by slackening the throat muscles; or by altering the size of the mouth cavity the intonation and quality of the note can be infinitely varied. The way the player secures exact intonation, however, depends entirely upon the speed at which the breath strikes the edge of the slot.

Consequently, much recorder playing is out of tune. Moreover, instruments by different makers are often not in tune with each other, while imported instruments have different fingerings from British-made recorders. Of course this is largely due to the fact that the revival of the recorder was school-oriented, where cheapness is all, and there is no great worry beyond actually getting the children to perform something recognisable as music.

Essentially then we see the recorder in a state of arrested development. The modern instrument is exactly what it was in the early 18th century: doubtful intonation, low volume of sound and all; but nevertheless, exceedingly cheap and when properly played a very beautiful instrument. Perhaps some modern Boehm will do for the baroque recorder what was done for the baroque flute. The design given here is simply a reproduction of the Stanesby recorder of 1700 and should prove perfectly adequate.

Making this instrument begins by taking a block of hardwood, preferably box or maple and turned to a length of 180mm with a diameter of 50mm. One end is deeply drilled with a pilot drill, followed by a 25mm flat bit, to a depth of 25mm. This is for the socket of the middle joint. The flat bit is then replaced by a 19mm or ¾ in. twist bit and the head joint is bored right through concentric with the socket.

To strengthen the rim of the socket an ivory or bone ring can be made and fitted. Ivory is more easily worked than bone and is superior in appearance. Personally I prefer not to have ivory as its use means another elephant has come to an untimely end. So of course does bone; but the cow is not facing extinction as is the elephant.

The exterior contour can be turned largely as a matter of taste. A restrained baroque outline, using the characteristic reversed curve, and perhaps a pair of balanced ornamental rings seems about right. I do not recommend incised rings which are a source of weakness in the swelling round the socket; raised rings are much superior.

Next comes the really difficult part: cutting the slot and chiselling the wind channel. The slot is situated 65mm from the top end of the mouthpiece and is 14mm in width and 4mm across; its edges must be sharp and clean cut. Size seems to be important; in practice it makes the recorder harder to blow if the slot is made wider, possibly because a wider slot dissipates the wind pressure. When chiselling the slot it is well to put a spare piece of ¾ in. dowel under the slot to prevent any ragged edges occurring, and to act as a temporary support to the bore of the mouthpiece.

With the slot cut the next thing to be worked is the wind channel. Recorders are classed as fipple flutes, the fipple being the piece of dowel which blocks up the top end of the mouthpiece. This is 65mm in length and should be a tight fit in the bore. On the top of the block (before it is inserted in the mouthpiece) is planed a flat surface 14mm in width to form one side of the wind channel. In section this is rectangular being 3mm by 14mm wide. The other three sides are chiselled out of the solid, from the rounded surface of the bore, in line with the slot already cut. It is useful to insert a slip of wood into the slot in case the chisel should slip and damage the lip of the slot.

Some instruments have a wind channel larger at the outer end and having a slight taper down towards the slot. The purpose of this is to concentrate the stream of air as it passes down the windway, thus increasing its pressure as it strikes the edge of the slot. However, the recorder seems to blow quite easily without it so perhaps it is not so necessary.

Next to be made is the lip which causes the air stream to divide (and vibrate in dividing) causing the air column in the tube of the instrument to vibrate also. The top surface must be chiselled down towards the slot to form a sloping surface. This sloping surface fans out from the edge of the slot and makes an angle of 15° with the centre line of the mouthpiece. The wood is pared carefully away leaving a pair of vertical edges to the left and right of the fan-shaped slope. These two little vertical edges also help concentrate the flow of air where it is needed.

When this has been done the lip of the edge is still curved on its underside where it faces the windway. It should now be undercut at about 60°, the actual edge being blunt (about 1mm in thickness). This is best carried out with a small flat file so that the central blunt portion comes immediately opposite the centre of the wind channel. The undercutting is necessary to convert the interior rounded surface of the bore into a flat surface to match that of the windway.

The fipple is then glued into the mouthpiece so that the inner end comes level with the beginning of the lateral slot. You should now have a windway leading down to a blunt edge and be able to blow a note, rather like a whistle. Shape the mouthpiece and cut away the waste with a coping saw to make a comfortable shape for the mouth.

When the mouthpiece is completed, the next part to be made is the foot joint. Like the mouthpiece, it has a socket for the middle joint, and as it is easier to fit tenons to sockets than the other way round, it is better to make these first. A piece of timber is turned to 100 × 35mm and the ends squared. This is then held in a three-jaw chuck centre-drilled and pilot-drilled from end to end. This is important because it is so easy for a drill to wander off-centre. At least three diameters have to be concentric with every joint made: the bore itself; the sockets for the tenons; and the external contours.

As the flat bit to be used for boring the socket hole has a triangular point about 5mm across the base, a pilot drill smaller than this should be used. When drilling deep holes I find that overheating can be prevented by using the slowest speed of the lathe and rubbing candlegrease on the drill from time to time.

After the pilot drill has been used, a 20mm flat bit is put in the three-jaw tailstock chuck and the socket hole bored to a depth of 20mm. The flat bit is removed and replaced by a 15mm drill and again the foot joint is bored right through. This completes the interior of the foot joint.

The exterior contour consists of the bone ring for the socket, a swelling around the socket to prevent cracks and the traditional flared end, plus any decoration in the form of raised (not incised) rings. The Sunday joint will probably provide a bone ring about 25mm internal diameter. I usually cut a slice of bone off, put it in the three-jaw chuck, turn the interior to the largest size the piece of bone will take and turn its seating round the socket to match its diameter. It is fixed in place with Araldite or similar glue. When set the irregular surface of the bone ring can be turned to a smooth finish.

The foot joint has one hole in it, for right little finger. Its centre is 20mm from the rim of the socket. If it is drilled at right-angles to the bore of the recorder it will break into the socket hole. Therefore it has to be angled towards the bottom end of the foot joint so that it enters the bore farther down than its exterior position. A similar idea is found in the bassoon and also in the clarinet. The purpose is to make the holes suit the spread of the fingers, and prevent the necessity of fitting a key at this place.

If the swelling around the socket is left at 35mm diameter and the 6mm finger hole drilled at an angle of 60°, the hole will just miss the socket for the middle joint and enter the bore at the correct acoustical point. The exterior can be turned by mounting the foot joint on a mandrel.

When the mouthpiece and foot joint are complete, the middle joint with its two tenons can be started. It has seven tone holes; six on the front and one on the back for the left thumb. The finished length is 265mm. A piece of hardwood is turned to a diameter of about 35mm and bored through from end to end with a 15mm drill. This parallel bore has to be converted to a diminished taper, as in the baroque flute. If a flute has already been attempted, the reamer for that can be used for both the recorder and the bassoon.

Two pieces of 20 × 10mm flat steel and 400mm in length are soft-soldered together (making in effect a piece of 20mm square bar 400mm long). This is then turned to a cylindrical section. The drawback is that to do the job a large lathe is required, one with a headstock spindle bore of 30mm and a large four-jaw chuck. If you can get half-round steel it is

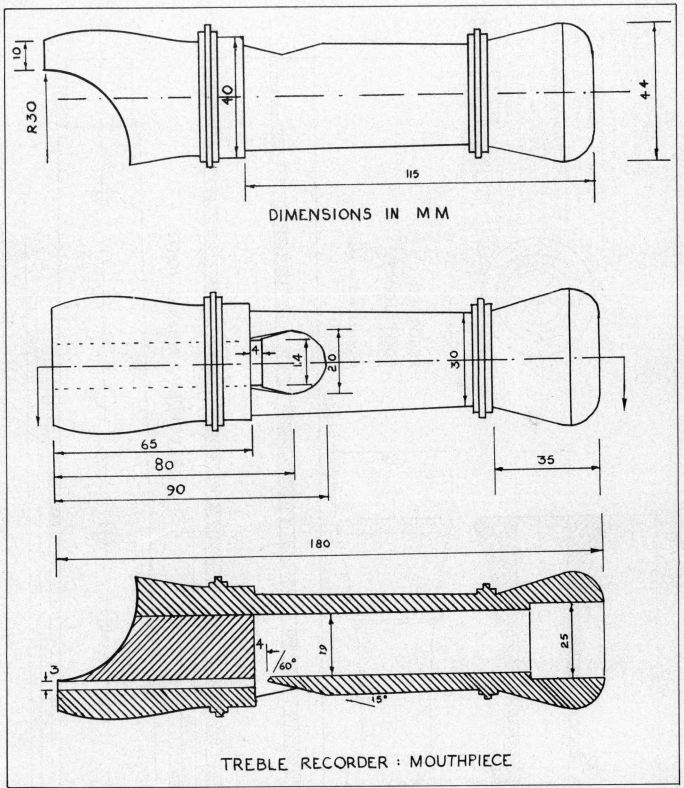

DIMENSIONS IN MM

TREBLE RECORDER : MOUTHPIECE

obviously better but nobody seems to stock it in my county, so I laboriously turn a square section to round section. Fortunately it is a one-off job.

The end of the bar is faced-up to 90° and centre drilled. One end is held in a three-jaw chuck and the other end supported by the tailstock centre which must be set over 2mm, thus turning the steel bar to a taper 19mm at the top and 15mm at the bottom. If the tapered bar is now heated, it will separate into two D-section reamers. The solder can be cleaned-off and the bar hardened if it is cast steel. I have found that mild steel will do the job quite well, though it does not hold its edge very long.

In use the reamer can be held either in the tailstock chuck or in a tap wrench held in the hands. The lathe is set to run at its slowest speed and the bored piece of timber is held in the three-jaw chuck. Then the reamer is fed slowly into the hole. It should be withdrawn at frequent intervals as it gets hot. It will produce a clean, tapered bore if the cutting edge is kept sharp. Rubbing candlegrease on the reamer prevents overheating and the grease gives the bore something of a polish, which is all to the good.

Once the bore has been reamed the wider end is turned down to a good tight fit in the mouthpiece socket and the lower end turned down to fit the socket of the foot joint. The three parts can then be assembled and the first note blown. With the little finger covering the hole already drilled the note should be middle F, slightly flat. Blowing a little harder will produce F an octave higher and blowing harder still the F above that slightly sharp.

The foot joint can be reamed to match the taper of the middle joint, though in practice I have found that it does not seem to make much difference. Perhaps this is because the foot is too short to exercise much influence on the rest of the recorder. The reamer will be found to be longer than is strictly required to ream a tapered bore for a recorder, but this is because it has to be used for other instruments. It should be put into the bore of the recorder as far as it will go; there must be no 'steps' to break the continuity of the bore.

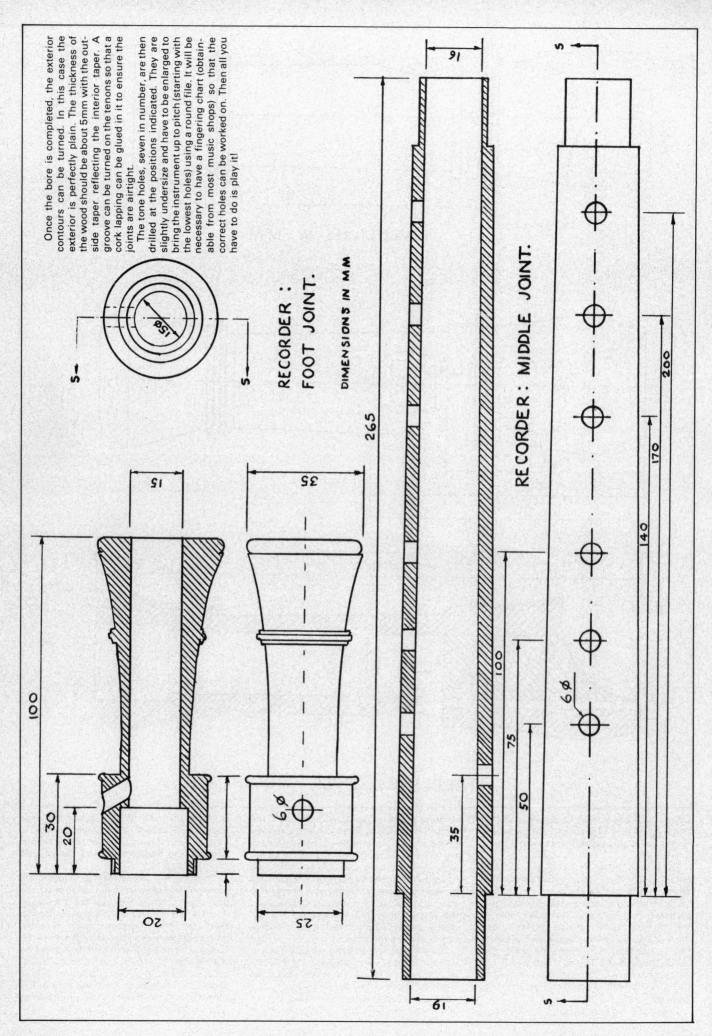

Once the bore is completed, the exterior contours can be turned. In this case the exterior is perfectly plain. The thickness of the wood should be about 5mm with the outside taper reflecting the interior taper. A groove can be turned on the tenons so that a cork lapping can be glued in to ensure the joints are airtight.

The tone holes, seven in number, are then drilled at the positions indicated. They are slightly undersize and have to be enlarged to bring the instrument up to pitch (starting with the lowest holes) using a round file. It will be necessary to have a fingering chart (obtainable from most music shops) so that the correct holes can be worked on. Then all you have to do is play it!

RECORDER : FOOT JOINT.

DIMENSIONS IN MM

RECORDER : MIDDLE JOINT.

THE EMCOSTAR
More Craft . . . Less Space!!

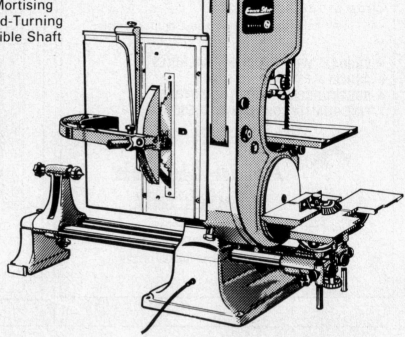
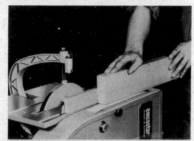

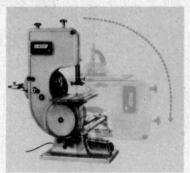
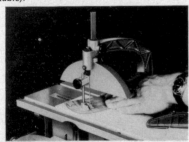

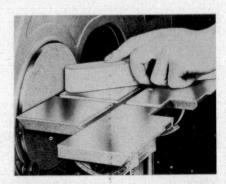

Woodworker Show

Royal Horticultural Society's New Hall
4-9 November, 1980

Full details of the competitive classes at this year's Woodworker Show were given on pages 320-21 of the May issue but readers may like to be reminded that there are nine classes as follows: WA — Cabinet making; WB — Woodcarving; WC — Woodturning; WD — Musical instruments; WE — Marquetry and inlay; WF — Toys; WG — Model horse-drawn vehicles; WH — Junior (under 18) section; WJ — Clocks.

Closing date for entries is Friday 5 September 1980, and all items must be delivered to Royal Horticultural Society's New Hall, Greycoat Street, Westminster, London SW1 (near Victoria station) on Sunday 2 November between 10.30am and 4.00pm. Exhibitors must take away all empty cases, packing materials etc.

Items exhibited can only be reclaimed on the presentation of a control card, and this cannot be done before the end of the Show. The items may be removed from the New Hall between 7.00 and 9.00pm on Sunday 9 November or between 10.00am and 4.00pm on Monday 10 November.

Competitors will be issued with free non-transferable competitors' pass to the Show on presentation of their exhibit to the organisers. Entry forms are available on application to: Exhibition Manager, Woodworker Show, PO Box 35, Bridge Street, Hemel Hempstead HP1 1EE. Entry fee for each item is £1.25 (juniors 75p). Enquiries relating to the Woodworker Show and competitive classes should be addressed to the Exhibition Manager (telephone Hemel Hempstead 41221).

Woodworker/Ashley Iles carving competition

The Woodworker/Ashley Iles international carving competition this year is The Dance. There is one section only, namely figure carving. Closing date is Friday 24 October 1980 and entries should be sent to WOODWORKER office, PO Box 35, Bridge Street, Hemel Hempstead HP1 1EE. Entries must not be submitted before Monday 22 September 1980. Judging will take place at the Woodworker Show.

Below: Some of last year's CLOWNS line up for judging.

Entry is open to professional and amateur craftsmen. There is no entry fee. Pieces entered in this competition are not eligible for entry in the woodcarving classes of the Woodworker Show. Maximum dimensions of figure carvings are $8 \times 4\frac{1}{2} \times 4\frac{1}{2}$ in.

Attention is drawn to the conditions of entry and other details given on page 289 of WOODWORKER for May 1980; a copy of these conditions is available on application to the editor of WOODWORKER, PO Box 35 Bridge Street, Hemel Hempstead HP1 1EE.

There are particular requirements as to the packaging etc. of carvings and entrants are advised to obtain from head postmasters a copy of the leaflet *Wrap up well* which tells how parcels should be packed to minimise damage during transit.

Hotel accommodation at Woodworker Show

For the period of the Woodworker Show (4-9 November 1980), Grand Metropolitan Hotels Ltd offers special booking facilities and rates at its hotels in London in the £20-£25, £25-£30 and £30-£35 ranges for single room with bath. The company's hotel nearest to the Show venue at the RHS New Hall, is St Ermin's (just off Victoria Street, SW1), where a single room with bath is £23 a night.

Reservations can be made either by telephoning 01-629 6611 and asking for central reservations office, or writing to the office at:
Grand Metropolitan Hotels
Freepost 32
London W1E 3YZ

There is no need to use a stamp if the envelope is addressed as above. Grand Metropolitan cannot guarantee first choice of hotel but will reserve the nearest alternative.

Grand Metropolitan Hotels Ltd also has a package accommodation and travel arrangement with British Rail whereby up to 50% of the standard return journey may be saved. Details can be had from Grand Metropolitan at the above address.

ENTER NOW FOR THE WOODWORKER SHOW AND THE WOODWORKER/ASHLEY ILES INTERNATIONAL CARVING COMPETITION.

In January this year W. H. Brown FIWSc discussed gymnosperms (softwoods) versus angiosperms (hardwoods). Here he explains parenchyma and sclerenchyma, both important elements of tree growth and in the economic utilisation of wood.

LOOKING AT WOOD

Wood is a heterogenous tissue composed of several types of cells some of which have the function of mechanical support and others that of conduction. In the softwoods (gymnosperms) both these functions are normally carried on during the growth of the tree in cells known as tracheids. In the hardwoods (angiosperms) a division of labour usually occurs. Mechanical support is furnished by several types of wood fibres which make up a large part of the woody tissue, while conduction of water is carried on in tubular cell fusions known as vessels.

Tracheids also may occasionally be present. A third function of the wood elements, the distribution and storage of carbohydrate food, is carried on in thin-walled parenchyma cells. These are the only components of wood which can be said to be alive and which contain protoplasm, a highly complex food substance. They may be wood parenchyma cells which have a vertical arrangement in the stem of the tree, or ray parenchyma cells which are horizontally arranged.

The word parenchyma is derived from the Greek para, beside; and engchyma, infusion; meaning the ground-work tissue of organs, or the soft, succulent tissue commonest in plants. It is therefore completely distinct from sclerenchyma since the Greek skleros means hard; accordingly sclerenchyma is the term used for the thickened plant tissue of the hard cells of wood, more commonly called fibres.

The vertical or longitudinal parenchyma cells as individuals are usually too minute to be clearly visible at low magnification. But when reasonably abundant and variously grouped in lines or banked about the pores they present features of taxonomic value, especially in the identification of hardwood timbers. Because these cells are thin-walled, an abundance can affect the machining properties of a wood by tending to crumble under the influence of cutting edge force, thus demanding the use of sharp tools with which to produce a smooth surface.

The recognition of a particular pattern of parenchyma may serve to identify an unknown wood or help to place it in a particular category. But as a rule paren-

chyma needs to be used in conjunction with other features when a positive identification is required, although in a few cases parenchyma alone is sufficient. A good example of this is seen in ash (*Fraxinus excelsior*) and hickory (*Carya* spp.) both very similar in appearance and used for similar purposes, although for some uses hickory is superior, eg for pick shafts because of its greater resistance to shock loading.

Examination of end grain under low magnification with a hand lens (Fig. 1) that is, on a small area cleanly cut with a sharp tool such as lino knife, scalpel or half razor blade (double-edged, split lengthwise while still in its wrapper to save cut fingers), will disclose light-coloured, fine, short lines of parenchyma making a reticulate, ladder-like pattern with the rays if the wood is hickory. This is entirely absent in ash. There are other distinguishing features in either timber but if this is comparatively slowly grown, with the annual rings close together, the presence or absence of this form of parenchyma is sufficient for identification purposes.

This can be carried even further. The genus *Carya* produces various species of hickory and a few of pecan although the wood of either is sold as hickory. The pattern of parenchyma referred to occurs in both hickory and pecan, but in true hickory the first lines appear beyond the large, early-wood pores whereas in pecan wood they start between them.

Parenchyma is particularly profuse in many timbers belonging to the Leguminosae family. The rosewoods, blackwood, kingwood, tulipwood and cocobolo possess distinctive banded parenchyma, while berlinia, okwen, white and yellow siris, koko, albizia and afzelia have lozenge-shaped parenchyma surrounding the pores. Observation in these cases must be taken in conjunction with a number of other features, more often than not under microscopic examination.

Sclerenchyma tissues consist mainly of fibres (Fig. 2a): these are long, pointed cells with very thick walls and correspondingly small cavities. They tend to interlace and are capable of contracting and stretching. Some fibres, such as the hairs on cotton seeds, have walls that are almost pure cellulose. In other cases, as in the inner bark (bast) of trees, these fibres contain some lignin in the walls, while in the shorter wood fibres their walls are almost completely lignified.

With the unaided eye, or even with a hand lens, individual fibres in hardwood cannot be seen. They merely represent the background mass. Under the microscope they can be seen quite clearly and by macerating small chips of wood with certain strong oxidising agents, individual fibres may be isolated, studied and measured.

The proportion of fibres present in a hardwood (Fig. 3) will determine its density, its strength and hardness and according to how the fibres are aligned its grain, eg straight, sloping, interlocked, wavy, spiral etc. Several types of hardwood fibre are recognised: libriform (juvenile, undivided); septate (divided by delicate partitions) and gelatinous, where the walls are very thick but contain little lignin; these usually are found in abnormal growth wood.

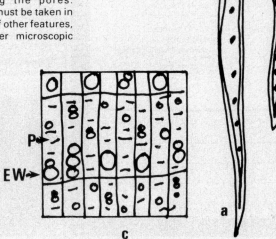

Fig. 2 (a) fibre
(b) tracheid.

Fig. 1 End grain of (a) ash, (b) hickory and (c) pecan as seen with a hand lens. Note distinguishing features of parenchyma especially between b and c. (P = parenchyma; EW = early-wood).

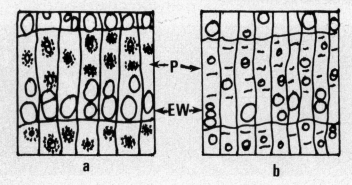

a   b   c

a

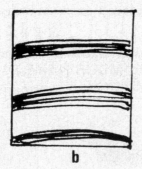

b

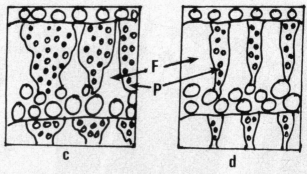

c   d

In the less sophisticated structure of soft-woods, mechanical strength is associated with the proportion of thick-walled tracheids and their deposition (Fig. 3). In each growth ring the early-wood tracheids have thin walls but toward the end of the growing ring the late-wood tracheids become more thicker-walled, and appear somewhat flattened. Since growth conditions each year govern the rate at which the tree grows this may be rapid or slow, with a corresponding variation in the width of each ring and in the proportion of thick-walled tracheids present.

The vertical tracheids (Fig. 2b) of softwoods are often very long; seldom under 1mm in length while extremes of 11mm have been recorded for hoop pine (*Araucaria cunning-* *hamii*) and for one of the coarse-textured pines of India (*Pinus merkusii*). Generally, they run from about 1.5mm to about 5mm or slightly more but 3 to 4mm is a fair average for coniferous woods in general.

Apart from their contribution to timber as a material, wood fibres furnish the pulp from which paper is made. Many wood species are used for this purpose but spruce (*Picea* spp.) is one of the most important. The fibres of spruce are long, strong and high in cellulose content; there is practically no resin, gum and tannin and the wood is light-coloured; therefore little bleaching is required.

Both parenchyma and sclerenchyma are important elements of tree growth and in the economic utilisation of wood.

Fig. 3 Caricature sketches of end grain of softwood (a and b) and oak (c and d). (a) is potentially weak because of its high proportion of thin-walled early-wood tracheids but (b) is potentially stronger because of its higher amount of thick-walled late-wood tracheids. The high proportion of fibres in (d) makes for stronger oak than (c) which has a higher proportion of parenchyma in the late-wood. Note: rays have been omitted from c and d for clarity. (LW = late-wood; EW = early-wood; F = fibres; P = parenchyma).

438

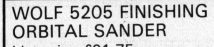

PINE DRESSER TO

C. J. Colston DLC explains how he made a pine dresser. For easier
fitting into an alcove the piece was constructed in two parts

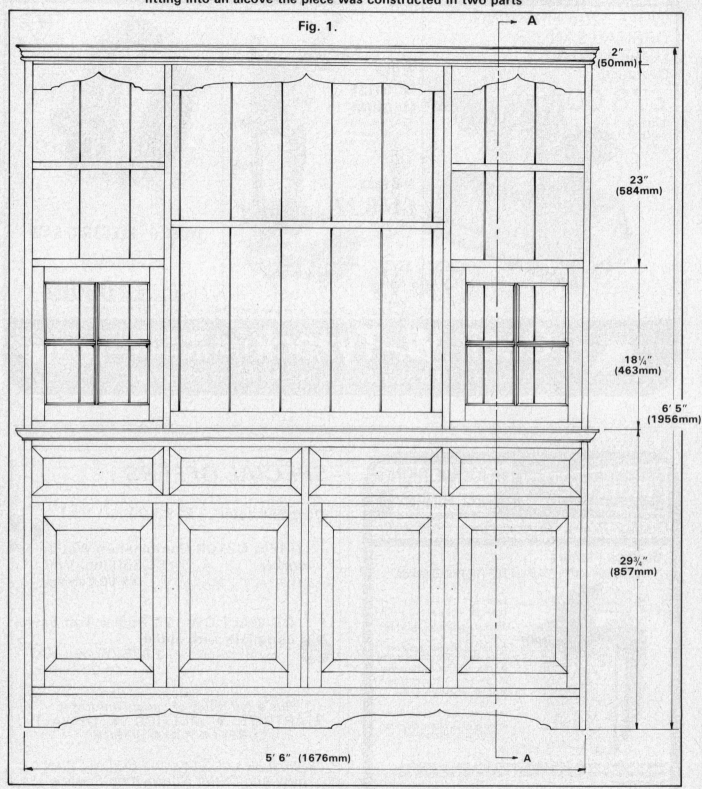

Fig. 1.

2" (50mm)

23" (584mm)

18¼" (463mm)

6' 5" (1956mm)

29¾" (857mm)

5' 6" (1676mm)

A

This dresser was designed to fit into an alcove so the size of the alcove was an important factor in determining the dimensions of the piece. To make it easier to put in I built it in two parts. This also had the advantage of dispensing with some difficult fitting of the top and allowed the top of the base to project so that the edge could be moulded. The high position of the centre shelf was chosen so that a large vase of flowers could be displayed without masking the shelf behind.

In making the bottom section the first thing was to rub-joint the timbers together to produce the sides, bottom, top and centre division. This was done using 6in. wide boards for all but the top where 7in. boards were used. This allowed ample for the jointing and after the glue had set they were planed to size. The timber was bought planed to 21mm thick but after rub-jointing this was reduced to 19mm.

Having planed the timber to size it was

marked out and the joints for the bottom and sides cut. These are stopped, housed, twin mortise and tenon joints. After they were cut and fitted the grooves for the back panels were ploughed as were those for the plinth. The sides were cut 32½in. long and all the other timbers were planed to size. They are all 19mm thick. Fig. 2 shows the constructions that I used.

Lap dovetails for the top rails were cut and

FIT AN ALCOVE

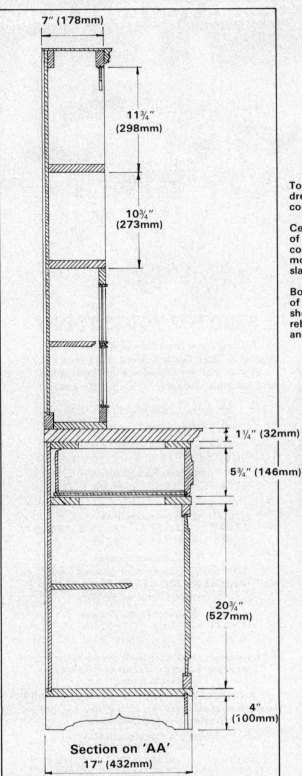

7" (178mm)

11¾" (298mm)

10¾" (273mm)

1¼" (32mm)

5¾" (146mm)

20¾" (527mm)

4" (100mm)

Section on 'AA'
17" (432mm)

Top: Pine dresser completed.

Centre: Detail of top left hand corner showing moulding and slatted back.

Bottom: Detail of pine cabinet showing rebated drawer and handles.

fitted using stopped, housed, twin mortise and tenon joints. The centre division, together with the drawer rails, was fitted next. The basic cabinet was now almost complete with just the division for the drawers and the centre drawer runner to fit. These were fitted with mortise and tenon joints. The mortises for the drawer stops were cut next; if they are not cut before the cabinet is glued together it is difficult to cut them. Indeed, they could not be cut without a drawer-lock chisel and these

(continued p.443).

Steenwise Ltd.
TOOLS FOR CRAFTSMEN

We offer high quality woodworking machinery by most major manufacturers such as De-Walt, Elektra, Arundel Scheppach, Coronet, Kity, Lurem, Sedgewick and Startrite at the best possible price. Below are some examples of our prices.

Post the coupon today for our current price list and find out more about our special summer bargains — don't delay, bargain stocks are limited.

Payment may be by credit card, cash with order, cash on delivery or higher purchase. We will deliver to your door or you may call and collect direct from one of our workshops.

STEENWISE LTD. HEAD OFFICE
Limefield Mills, Wood Street, Crossflatts, Bingley, W. Yorkshire.
Tel. Bingley (09766) 60699 or 69137.

GORDON STOKES (STEENWISE) LTD.
110a Mount Road, Whiteway, Bath. Tel. Bath (0225) 22617.

ERIC TOMKINSON
86 Stockport Road, Cheadle, Cheshire SK8 2AJ.
Tel. Manchester (061) 491 1726 or 428 3740.

RADIAL ARM SAW
- De-Walt DW125 a versatile small workshop machine   **£335.00**

BAND SAWS
- Startrite 352 a professional 2 speed machine with an 11¾" depth of cut and 13⅝" throat – ideal for deep cutting or woodturning blanks   **£575.00**
- De-Walt BS1310 ideal hobbyist saw, 6" depth of cut, 12" throat, 2 speed   **£260.00**
- Inca without motor, 6" depth of cut, 11" throat   **£115.00**
- Inca with motor, 6" depth of cut, 11" throat   **£199.00**
- Kity 7217 all steel professional machine, 5½" depth of cut, 11½" throat   **£299.00**

CIRCULAR SAWS
- Startrite TASP175 10" tilt arbor saw bench, a professional machine in cast iron with 3⅛" depth of cut   **£740.00**
- Startrite TASP275 12" tilt arbor saw bench, with 4" depth of cut   **£785.00**
- Kity 7217 2 speed, 3" depth of cut may be added to and become combination machine   **£270.00**
- Elektra-Combi galvanised steel, 2 H.P. motor, 3⅛" depth of cut   **£149.00**

PLANER THICKNESSER
- Kity 7136 10" × 6"   **£564.00**

COMBINATION
- Kity 7042 the ideal workshop combination with saw capable of 3" depth of cut, 10" × 6" planer thicknesser, 627 spindle moulder and 652 mortiser   **£1250.00**

BENCH GRINDER
- Elektra 7" double wheeled, white grit machine ideal for sharpening woodturning tools   **£89.50**

SPECIAL SUMMER BARGAINS (LIMITED STOCKS)
SPINDLE MOULDERS
- Kity 7227 The "Fantastic spindle moulder" offer including a set of cutters with moulding block as offered by Kity for £432.32 but including a free Kity 206 tennoning carriage, recommended selling price £95.45, an amazing bargain from Steenwise at   **£425.00**

DUST EXTRACTOR
- Kity 695 suitable for all band saws, saw benches and planer thicknessers up to 12" × 8", airflow 720 C.F.M.   **£199.00**

- -

Please send me more Steenwise summer bargains and your current price list.

Name ....

Address ....
....

Please return this coupon to our head office at
Limefield Mills, Wood Street, Crossflatts, Bingley, W. Yorkshire.

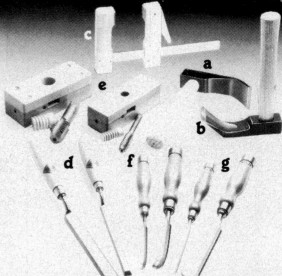

ROGER'S NEW MAIL ORDER CATALOGUE OFFERS YOU EVEN MORE

SEND FOR YOURS TODAY

Turning Tools, Gluepots and Woodscrew Sets, Hammers, Vices, Cramps, Books, Band Saws and lots more in this new catalogue worth looking into!
Just some of the great Tools are listed below.

a)   **Adze** (Chisel) Flat End £14.95

b)   **Adze** (Gouge) Curve £19.55

c)   **Quick Cam Cramp** (Wood)
200mm £4.60   400mm £5.57   600mm £6.55

d)   **Bent Paring Chisels**
¼" £6.33   ½" £6.48   ¾" £6.99   1" £8.35
1¼" £10.97

e)   **Woodscrew Boxes**
½" £21.27   ⅝" £21.27   ¾" £21.27   1" £24.15
1¼" £33.59   2" £40.25

f)   **Heavy Bent Gouges**
6mm £5.59   10mm £5.59   12mm £5.59
16mm £5.59   20mm £5.90   26mm £6.59
Complete Set of 6 £33.00

g)   **Sculptors Firmer Gouges**
¼" £5.09   ⅜" £5.09   ⅝" £5.32   ¾" £5.75
1" £5.98   1¼" £7.25   Complete Set of 7 £37.50

All this and more in one catalogue offering the widest range of tools at your fingertips, by internationally known manufacturers.

For U.K. and Eire £1.10 inc. p&p. Overseas £2.15 in Sterling

We also stock at our shop Power Tools by Kity, Elu, Startrite, Craftsman, De Walt, Surmaco etc.

POSTAGE & CARRIAGE CHARGES
for Orders up to the Value of

£20 ADD 90p	£38 ADD £1.75	£65 ADD £2.75
£25 ADD £1.05	£48 ADD £2.00	£75 ADD £3.00
£30 ADD £1.35	£55 ADD £2.30	£85 ADD £3.20
	£100 ADD £3.40	

**Dept. W.1.,
47, Walsworth Road,
Hitchin,
Herts. SG4 9SU
Telephone: Hitchin 4177**

EVERYTHING FOR THE WOODWORKER

442

Prices quoted are those prevailing at press date and are subject to alteration due to economic conditions.

Woodworker, July 1980

PINE DRESSER

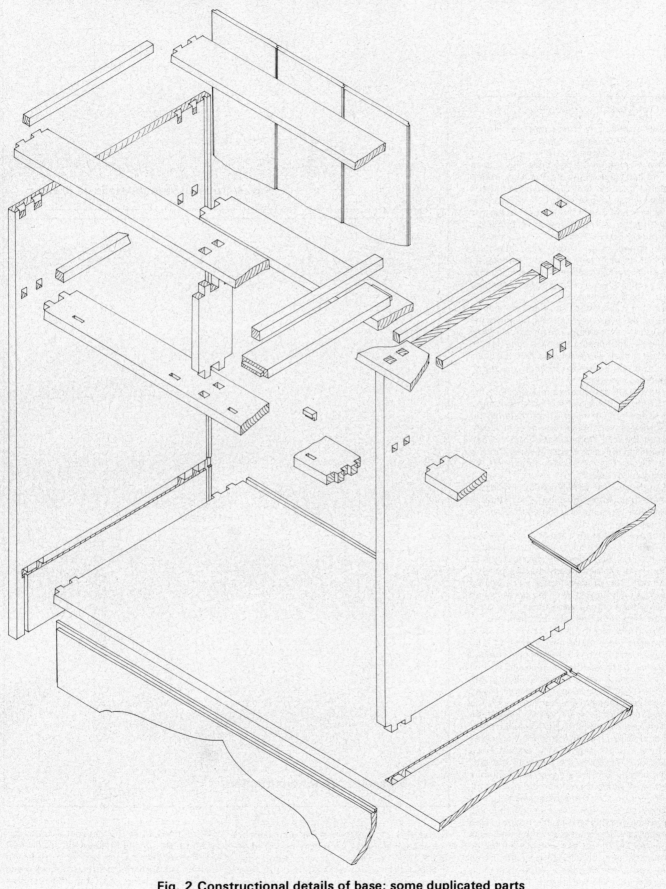

Fig. 2 Constructional details of base; some duplicated parts omitted for clarity.

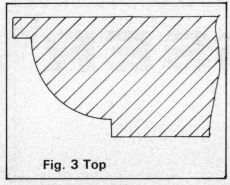

Fig. 3 Top

(text continued from page 441)

are difficult to buy. These mortises are cut with their front edge 25mm back from the front edge of the drawer rail.

The shaping on the two ends (Fig. 1) was cut. At this stage all the inside surfaces were cleaned-up and sealed with polyurethane gloss varnish diluted with 10% white spirit. After this had dried I flatted the surface and glued-up the cabinet. When the glue had set the plinth, drawer runners, kickers and the back panels were fitted. The latter are rebated on each long edge and the bottom edge with a small chamfer cut on the edges to give a relief effect. The top edges are secured with ¾ in. No. 6 screws.

The top was planed to size and the mouldings on the edges were cut. Fig. 3 shows the details of this moulding. The top was screwed to the cabinet making the back edge tight to the rail. I used slot screws to hold the sides and front edge in place to allow the top to expand or contract.

The top was fitted before making the doors and drawers. Fitting it afterwards can disturb the fit and hang of these. All the materials for the drawers were prepared and the lap dovetails at the front, together with the through dovetails at the back, of the drawers were cut and fitted. Fig. 4 shows details of the construction I used.

I prefer to use drawer slips to hold the bottom in place as this allows the bottom to move and in addition it allowed me to use 9mm timber for the sides. The drawer bottoms are 4mm plywood and they are slid into grooves in the slips, which are glued to the inside of the sides and the front before being held into place by two screws in the back rail. The drawer fronts were fielded before gluing-up and after the drawers had set and the bottoms were fitted, they were cleaned-up and fitted into the openings.

Construction of the doors is shown in Fig. 5 and these were made next and fitted. The grooves were fitted with a 9mm panel fielded to match the drawer fronts. The sides and top of the door frames are 1½ in. wide but the bottom rail is 1¾ in. wide. The doors were cut square and hinged from the sides. I set the hinges into the doors so that the line of the cabinet side was unbroken. A rebated overlap could be worked on the door but I decided to fit the doors side-by-side and screw a retaining strip down the inside of the left-hand door to form a dust seal. Two flat bolts hold these doors square and the right-hand doors are held with magnetic catches.

Shelf studs of ¼ in. were used to support the shelves as this enables them to be moved if necessary. The front edge of the shelves is moulded (Fig. 9) and, as for all the mouldings on this cabinet, a Victorian moulding plane was used. Alternatively, a series of scratch stocks could have been used.

Handles and fittings for the drawers and the doors (bought from Martin Bros, Camden

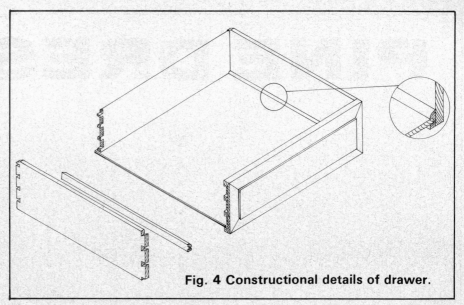

Fig. 4 Constructional details of drawer.

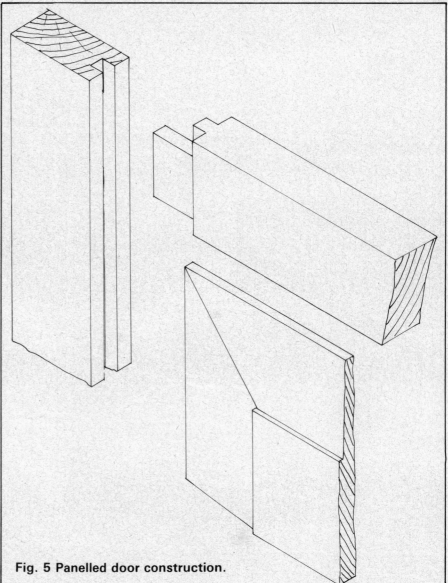

Fig. 5 Panelled door construction.

Street, Birmingham, which has an excellent selection of architectural ironmongery) were fitted. The drawer stops were fitted, the shapes on the plinth were cut and this was glued in position and the cabinet cleaned-up. Three coats of polyurethane varnish produced a good finish. The first gloss coat was thinned while the last coat was an eggshell finish. Having finished the bottom half of the cabinet, the top part was made. All timber was prepared to size with the two end uprights ½ in. wider than the other uprights to allow them to be grooved for the back panels. *(continued p.446)*

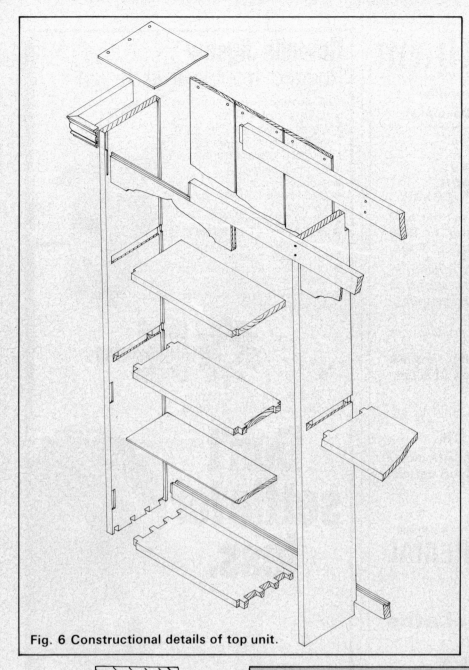

Fig. 6 Constructional details of top unit.

The uprights are lap-dovetailed to the bottom pieces. Fig. 6 shows that the pins are on these bottom pieces and not on the uprights to allow for easy cramping. The bottom is 18mm narrower than the end uprights to allow the back bottom rails to pass.

Once these dovetails were cut the two top rails were mortised and tenoned into the uprights and the shelves were cut into position. Fig. 6 shows the construction used. The top back rail is set-in 12mm to allow the back to be screwed to it and this amount of set-in has to be allowed on both the shelves and the centre uprights. The grooves for the back panels were cut into the end uprights and into the top of the bottom rail.

The frieze was fitted next. This was rebated and fitted into grooves ploughed in the underside of the front top rail, with the ends of the frieze locking into shallow mortises in the sides. Templates were cut in paper for the shaping of this frieze and the shapes were cut with a fine chamfer on the front edge. The inside surfaces were cleaned-up and finished and the carcase was glued-up. The back panels were then cut to size and fitted in the same way as for the bottom of the cabinet and the top board was screwed into place on top of the two rails. The top moulding was cut to the shape shown in Fig. 7, mitred and pinned into place.

The top carcase was now screwed through its bottom shelf into the top of the base before the doors were made. Fig. 8 shows the construction for the doors. I chose this method to avoid cutting long and short shouldered mortise and tenons, which would have been necessary had I worked rebates to accept the glass. I also wanted a moulding to protrude on the face of the doors and by planting the moulding I achieved both requirements. The doors were glued-up and then fitted in place. They were hinged with solid drawn brass butt hinges 2in. long and as on the lower cabinet the hinges were set into the door edge. The glass was 3mm held against the moulding with a bead.

Shelves were fitted on shelf studs so that they lined up behind the horizontal bar in the door and the handles were fitted. Fig. 9 shows the shape of the moulding on the edge of these shelves. Finally, the cabinet was cleaned-up and varnished to match the base.

Fig. 7 Frieze moulding.

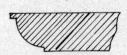

Fig. 9 Shelf.

CUTTING

Bottom cabinet

2	Sides	2ft 8½in. (825mm) × 17in. (432mm) × 19mm
1	Division	28½in. (725mm) × 16½in. (420mm) × 19mm
1	Bottom	5ft 5½in. (1665mm) × 17in. (432mm) × 19mm
1	Top	5ft 9in. (1755mm) × 18in. (460mm) × 32mm
2	Top rails	5ft 5½in. (1665mm) × 3in. (75mm) × 19mm
1	Plinth	5ft 5in. (1650mm) × 4in. (100mm) × 9mm
2	Centre drawer runners	10½in. (267mm) × 3in. (75mm) × 19mm
6	Drawer runners	10½in. (267mm) × ¾in. (19mm) × 19mm
2	Drawer uprights	7½in. (190mm) × 3in. (19mm) × 19mm
8	Drawer stops	1in. (25mm) × 1in. (25mm) × 12mm
11	Back panels	28in. (710mm) × 5¾in. (145mm) × 6mm
4	Drawer kickers	10½in. (267mm) × ¾in. (19mm) × 19mm
2	Shelves	29in. (735mm) × 9in. (230mm) × 15mm
8	Door stiles	21½in. (545mm) × 1½in. (38mm) × 19mm
4	Top rails	16in. (406mm) × 1½in. (38mm) × 19mm
4	Bottom rails	16in. (406mm) × 1¾in. (45mm) × 19mm
4	Door panels	18¼in. (465mm) × 13¼in. (335mm) × 9mm
2	Door rebate strips	21½in. (545mm) × 1in. (25mm) × 6mm
4	Drawer fronts	15½in. (395mm) × 5½in. (140mm) × 21mm
8	Drawer sides	15½in. (395mm) × 5½in. (140mm) × 9mm
4	Drawer backs	15½in. (395mm) × 4¾in. (120mm) × 9mm
8	Drawer slips	15½in. (395mm) × ⅝in. (15mm) × 9mm
4	Drawer bottoms	14½in. (370mm) × 15½in. (395mm) × 4mm ply

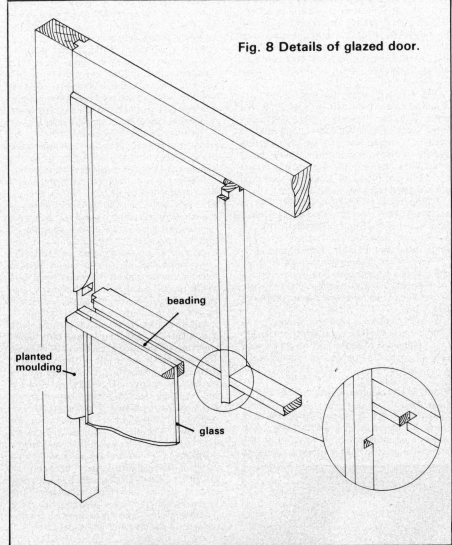

Fig. 8 Details of glazed door.

beading

planted moulding

glass

PINE DRESSER

LIST

Top cabinet

2	Uprights	3ft 6½in. (1080mm) × 7in. (180mm) × 19mm
2	Uprights	3ft 6½in. (1080mm) × 6½in. (165mm) × 19mm
2	Bottom shelves	17in. (432mm) × 6¼in. (160mm) × 19mm
4	Side shelves	17in. (432mm) × 6½in. (165mm) × 19mm
1	Centre shelf	2ft 9in. (840mm) × 6½in. (165mm) × 19mm
2	Top rails	5ft 5½in. (1665mm) × 2¼in. (57mm) × 19mm
1	Bottom rail	5ft 5½in. (1665mm) × 1¾in. (45mm) × 19mm
1	Top	5ft 5½in. (1665mm) × 7in. (180mm) × 9mm
1	Frieze	5ft 5½in. (1665mm) × 3in. (75mm) × 9mm
1	Moulding	5ft 7½in. (1715mm) × 1¾in. (45mm) × 21mm
2	Mouldings	8in. (200mm) × 1¾in. (45mm) × 21mm
11	Back panels	3ft 5in. (1040mm) × 5¾in. (145mm) × 6mm
2	Shelves	15½in. (395mm) × 5½in. (140mm) × 12mm
4	Door stiles	18in. (460mm) × 1½in. (38mm) × 19mm
2	Top stiles	15in. (380mm) × 1½in. (38mm) × 19mm
2	Bottom rails	15in. (380mm) × 1¾in. (45mm) × 19mm
2	Uprights	14½in. (370mm) × ⅞in. (21mm) × 6mm
2	Crossbars	13in. (330mm) × ⅞in. 21mm) × 6mm
1	Moulding	18ft (5.48m) × ½in. (12mm) × 6mm
1	Beading	18ft (5.48m) × ⅜in. (9mm) × 6mm

60 YEARS OF UPHOLSTERY

On turning the title page of *Practical Upholstery and the Cutting of Loose Covers* (Frederick Palmer) published by Ernest Benn Ltd, 25 New Street Square, London EC4A 3JA, you read 'First edition 1921. Second impression 1980.' This speaks for itself. There are those who would consider such a repeat to be a disregard for the progress of the last 60 years. Others might state convincingly that well-tried and tested methods have a reliability which is lacking in many spheres today.

How often do you hear the remark: 'Things are not made like that these days'? But 'that', of course, can mean almost anything; It can refer to methods or to materials.

Regarding methods, this is a personal aspect and is portrayed by the picture on the jacket of the book. This is of an old-time upholsterer working on a period chair. It tells a story. The man is obviously strong, highly skilled and (less obviously) proud of his work. The methods and the lasting qualities which long tradition engenders create the reason for the writing of the book, stated in the author's preface of 1921: 'Practical Upholstery' was written for the love of the thing.'

I was working on a crossword recently to pass the time on a train journey and one of the clues was 'reviewer'; the solution was 'critic.' (It might have been the other way round. I forget.) Those of us who can remember World War I might look at the advertisements which adorn the front and back endpapers of Palmer's book with a certain nostalgia; and I find myself asking 'Who am I to review (still less criticise) so noble and comprehensive a work?' Are pride in one's skill and love of one's job less in evidence today?

It is not for me to say. But I agree with the publisher; so far as these sentiments are concerned the decision to print a second impression must be a wise one.

Referring to progress over the last 60 years, however, the development of so many new materials makes this a subject much more practical and perhaps less sentimental. Surely we must hand it to the chemists — and others — who have done so much for us all in providing a vast array of new materials which in themselves create new processes and methods of working. One great advantage of man-made products is in the fact that they can be varied by the addition of ingredients to render them fire-proof or rot-proof or insect-proof; and recent calamities have shown the importance of these additives. Palmer's book must be read with this in mind.

Though this is a handsome facsimile of the 1921 production the price — £12.95 — might appear high. But there are 38 chapters on practical upholstery and seven on the cutting of loose covers, each one packed with the knowledge and practical experience of the author, to say nothing of 413 drawings illustrating the text. When you consider all this you have second thoughts about the price.   **C.B.**

Letters

From: Peter Walmsley, Preston, Lancs
Dear Sir,
I am reading with interest Jack Hill's series on chairmaking and I think there are one or two points in the article on pages 241-45 of the April 1980 issue that should be clarified. I hope Mr Hill will not take offence.

1 The reference to 'the back sticks may either pass through or be socketed into the bow': you can only socket sticks into the arm bow if there is a back bow as well. Otherwise the crest rail would fall off together with the upper sticks above arm bow.

2 In the text and sketches the author shows the sticks taken right through the back bow with the ends sawn-off on top. To my knowledge this method of construction has never been used on English Windsor chairs, or not as traditional construction. It was used extensively in American chairs and, in fact, I am having correspondence with Michael Dunbar (the American chairmaker) on this very subject.

3 If the sticks are just fitted into drilled through holes then the back has no strength and even if wedges are driven in there is still a tendency for the wedges to work loose as the back flexes with the sitter's weight.

Could I now refer to another subject. As a self-employed man I am in favour of free enterprise but the range of prices for the same machines in advertisements in magazines makes me wonder how large a profit is being made. For example, in the April issue of WOODWORKER a lathe is offered for sale at £195 and list price given of £235.25, a saving of £40.25. Within two pages the same lathe is offered at £187.45, a saving of £47.80. In the same issue a workbench is offered by one firm at £85 and by another at £72.50.

Companies advertise products in order to sell them but I am beginning to think that they are ruining their market as it would seem sensible to wait for the prices to come down rather than buy immediately.

As a case in point, in September 1978 I purchased a particular make of router for £90.56 and yet, two year's later, firms are offering this machine at £78. If you allow for increase in VAT and inflation, then the price I would theoretically have to pay would be approximately £127 which means that this machine is now available at about 60% less than I paid for it — a strong feeling of 'being had'.

The moral would seem to be: don't buy when a product is first advertised, but wait if you can for a year and then 'shop-around.'
Yours faithfully, **Peter Walmsley**

Jack Hill replies: Peter Walmsley's remarks on Windsor chairmaking are appreciated and they are in no way seen as offensive. Indeed, I believe such comment to be valuable in acquiring and spreading knowledge of our craft and above all in 'getting it right.' It is correct, of course, to say that back sticks must go right through the arm bow to carry a comb or crest rail. The line referred to would have been more correct had it come after the paragraph on the double bow back. Sorry about that!

The fixing of back sticks into holes drilled right through the back bow may, perhaps, be more common in early Windsors than Mr

Walmsley appreciates. I possess such a chair and have repaired at least one other similarly constructed. Certainly, this method was used in colonial America and although distinctive styles were later developed over there, I think it is worth remembering that methods of construction travelled across the Atlantic from Europe.

The similarity with the way spokes are fitted into a wooden wheel is an important point here, too. Wheels were being made long, long before Windsor chairs and to utilise a known method of construction seems logical. Incidentally, very early wheelback chairs really did have a wheel complete with central hub and radiating spokes fitted into seat and bow.

Fitting back sticks through the bow is relatively easier than using blind holes drilled from inside the bow. For this reason, presumably, it was (and still is) used. Properly done using sound, cleft material and well-fitting joints it undoubtedly works. The old chair which I have now has a loose back I must admit, but as it has to my sure knowledge been in use for over 70 years that's not bad is it?

In spite of all this, however, I tend to use blind joints in the bow backs which I make as, yes, I believe it to make a stronger back as well as giving a much neater appearance.

From: Bruce Boulter, London SE9 4RP
Dear Sir,
In Question Box on page 263 of the April issue the advice given to G. Roche is, I feel, wrong and misleading in relation to the spindle gouge. I enclose photograph showing

the turning of a bowl with a spindle and I assure you there is little special about me other than the fact that I served a professional apprenticeship.

I have a copy of an American publication in which there is a write-up of Bob Stocksdale, probably the leading bowl turner in the world today. He remarks that he always finishes off with a spindle gouge.
Yours faithfully, **Bruce Boulter**

From: M. Kenning, Middle Littleton, Evesham, Worcs
Dear Sir,
I would like to remark upon two replies in Question Box of the April issue. The first relates to J. C. Delvoir's understairs cupboard (page 261). I think the keyholes are the wrong way round and if used in this manner gaps of around ¼in. will be left when the stile is pushed to the right, while if sufficient length of screw to master the top and bottom rail is left projecting the stile will 'float' when pushed back.

Much better I think if the slots are reversed so that the stile is away from the top and bottom rail and slid towards them to lock. I suggest that keyhole-slotted mirror plates (obtainable from most diy shops) recessed

flush will make a much sounder job than just cutting into the wood. My preference would be to put the plate into the stile and the screws into the door panel.

Having said this I would still not advocate the method outlined on page 261 as a solution, since the 2in. gap either side will make it obvious to the most casual observer that this is not a fixed partition. In my opinion a better way would be to utilise the modern concealed hinge which allows a door to open in its own width. This entails making the hanging stile about 4in. wide to allow for the hinge recess and the thickness to be the same as the overall thickness of the door.

Hiding the lock hole can be done with a false frame, as suggested, but as keyhole slots cannot be used due to the door taking up the whole of the width, I would recommend ⅜in. dowels spaced about 18in. apart, glued into the stile and projecting some ¾in. The ends should be nicely tapered and lubricated with candlewax to fit into corresponding holes in the door panel. This would need to be gently tapped home with the hand and, provided the cupboard is not damp, would not be difficult to remove when required.

But even this would look too much like a door to be really effective so may I offer what I consider to be almost a complete answer: This is to cover the whole of the door panel with t & g matchlining, glued and pinned through the tongues. The end piece covering the lock hole has the tongue cut off and is dowelled on as above. The minimum ⅛in. needed at the bottom of the door for clearance will allow a finger or tool be inserted for the removal of this cover piece.

An added refinement would be to insert a piece of skirting to fit snugly between the walls (not fixed of course). I would defy anyone not 'in the know' to discover the secret. This method could also be used where the distance between the walls is too great to permit the use of a full-width door.

My second remark relates to H. B. Forster's query, also on page 261. The advice given to Mr Forster is sound up to the point where dabbing (presumably localised dirty parts) with oxalic acid is advocated and then staining the bleached parts to match to surrounding areas. This cure will leave the panel just as — if not more — patchy and dirty.

Oxalic acid in the proportion of roughly a heaped teaspoonful to a cupful of warm water will do a very good job of cleaning without undue bleaching but the whole of the panel must be done whether or not it needs it. While the panel is still wet it is alright to apply a little more of the acid on the stubborn parts. When dry and if not completely clean the process can be repeated but, again, not on isolated parts.

Work a little longer on the bad spots but finish up by going over the whole panel. If after two, or at most, three applications a cure is not effected the stains are permanent and only then should bleaching be considered. Indeed, for me that is where the process would stop as it requires skill and knowledge and should not be attempted by a novice who could do more harm than good. Incidentally, oxalic acid does a splendid job of cleaning blue stain on oak.

A word of warning about oxalic acid which is a poison. Items or receptacles used for mixing the acid must not be used thereafter in connection with food or drink. This is important to remember.
I am a member of Guild of Woodworkers.
Yours faithfully, **M. Kenning**

There's no easy substitute for an Elu Router

Price Inc. VAT
ONLY £98.90

Although an electric drill is probably the most popular powered tool to-day for the woodworker, drilling timber is one of the easiest operations using only a hand drill, but consider for a moment how difficult it is to replace the Elu Router with hand tools. It makes sense to buy an Elu Router as your first powered tool.

Versatility. The Elu Plunging Router is without doubt the woodworkers' most versatile powered tool with the capability of grooving, moulding, rabbetting, veining, profiling all types and shapes. Routing to template, contour-router, cutting circles or free — hand working — all present no problem to this machine.

Quality. The MOF 96 is of the highest quality with the side fence manufactured from machined die-cast aluminium and a precision made collet which ensures that the cutter shank does not jam when released.

Safety. The plunging action of the MOF 96 not only makes operation easy but adds to the safety factor as the router can stand in an upright position when not being used with the cutter unexposed.

If you require further information simply write to us requesting details of the MOF 96 with your name and address

Technical Data:

Order No	MOF 96/10
Power	600 watt/0.8hp
Speed	24,000 r.p.m.
Standard collet	¼'' capacity
Max. Cutter dia.	30mm
Depth stop	3 turret positions
Weight	2.7kg (5½ lb)
Standard Equipment	Side fence, guide bush, spanners, "Routing Techniques" booklet, 2-HSS cutters.

Accessory Set:

Order No	96/20
Comprising of	Routing table, Set of legs with clamping plates, Pressure guard with wood block, Pr. 'G' clamps for side mounting, Routing table, Fine adjuster for depth, Fine adjuster for side fence or routing table, Circle cutting guide, Copy follower devise.

Only £60.38 Inc. VAT

If you purchase a MOF 96 Router before 31st July, 1980 you will receive a voucher valid for 12 months, worth £5.75 when you buy the accessory set or any other Elu machine

Elu Machinery Limited, Stirling Way, Stirling Corner, Borehamwood, Herts

♔ CORONET

complete Home Workshop
— comprising:-

 1 **ELF WOODTURNING LATHE**
4 speeds
12" between centres
14" Bowl Turning (as illustrated)

 2 **IMP BANDSAW**
3 speeds
12" throat
5" (approx.) Depth of cut
Table tilts to 45°

 3 **SOVEREIGN 4½" PLANER**
½" rebate
Fence tilts 45°

 4 **CONSORT
SAW/SPINDLE MOULDER**
4 speeds
2¼" depth of cut
Table tilts to 45°
Spindle Moulding (See separate leaflet)

Each unit comes complete with its own motor,
press button starter and cabinet stand.

*Each unit can be purchased separately —
if required for bench mounting
(without cabinets)*

Illustration shows:-
1. 14" plaque being turned
2. Preparing disc for turning
3. 4½" surface planing
4. Spindle moulding shelf mould

 **MAJOR CMB 500**

 **MAJOR CMB 600**

 **MINOR MB 6**

 **7" PLANER CAP 300**

IT'S PLANE TO SEE

During building operations at his home in Steyning, Sussex, 4 year-old Timothy Riseborough tries his hand with a plane. It's one thing for a small boy to get started (left) but quite another to carry through without a knock-kneed stance (right). Perhaps Timothy should have waited for the carpenter to come back from lunch. Fortunately the plane suffered no damage!

TURNING TOOL FORMS FOR EXOTIC HARDWOODS

Tubal Cain has contributed many articles to WOODWORKER in the past and we are pleased to welcome him back. He hopes this article will interest 'plain' turners as many 'have no idea of the real difference between their tools and our tools. It may also help any who have tried to turn their exotic woods with gouge and chisel.' The difference between plain and ornamental turning was referred to by Gordon Stokes in his article on page 94 of the February 1980 issue.

The author's cabinet of smaller ivory-turning tools.

The majority of turners use a softwood or a conventional hardwood as basic materials, with the gouge and chisel as their normal tools. Any reference to a scraper is usually met with derision or, where its use is unavoidable, with the warning that subsequent finishing will be essential. Even experienced professionals seem to have little knowledge of the 'blunt nosed' tools used for turning ivory and the rarer hardwoods. Readers may recall that this caused some rather odd misconceptions in the correspondence columns a few years ago when I did a piece on the sharpening of such tools. I hope this article may spread a little light on the subject.

It is necessary to examine the cutting process in a little detail. With the exception of a few cleaving tools, such as the woodman's wedge and the firewood axe, all cutting tools perform their office by inducing a shear stress in the workpiece; and this is true whether the work be softwood or hard steel.

It is possible to remove material by other means but not if you require dimensional accuracy and reasonable surface finish. When the induced shear stress exceeds the strength of the material, the chip will part from the parent material. With a metal like cast iron the chips are almost like dust, but with softwood (or even mild steel) they are in a continuous ribbon. In many materials, however, the chip may be both ribbon-like and discontinuous — a series of ribbons, in fact.

But it must not be thought that the absence of a ribbon indicates that the material is not 'being cut as it likes to be cut', to quote a well-known authority. (In fact no material *likes* to be cut — the good turner can only do his best to make the process as painless as possible!)

At first sight it would appear that an acute-angled cutting edge is bound to be the most effective as this, surely, will impose the highest shear force on the material. This is not necessarily the case. Indeed in many metal cutting process the tools have cutting angles greater than 90°. These are the so-called negative rake tools. There must, of course, be a clearance on the front face so that the top or rake surface (Fig. 1 shows the nomenclature) actually slopes upwards. Yet the tool still cuts and, indeed, the surface finish is superior. Even conventional metal-working tools may have cutting angles lying between 75° and 85°.

However, the penalty paid for using large cutting angles is that the forces on both tool and work (and hence the power needed to remove a given quantity of material) are considerably increased. So in turning softwood, where a much lower shear force is needed to cut the material, very small cutting angles can be used.

There is another factor to be taken into account as well, neglect of which may result in a lower overall rate of material removal due to the need for more frequent tool sharpening: Work is done at the tool edge and this work appears as heat. In all woodturning the workpiece itself is a very poor conductor of heat, so most heat must flow through the tool; and as the tool edge is very thin its temperature will rise rapidly. This reduces the hardness and increases the rate of blunting. In severe cases the edge may lose its temper completely, calling for drastic re-grinding.

Thus the final decision of the cutting angle to be used must be a compromise between rate of stock removal while cutting; the force on the tool and machine (in most cases in woodturning the force on the hands); and the maintenance of a cutting edge for reasonable periods. In general it can be said that the harder the material the larger ought to be the cutting angle, though this is not universally true. The characteristics of the material must be taken into account as well, eg brass is cut better with a larger cutting angle than steel.

This leads us directly to consideration of the nature of the workpiece. Wood stands in a category of its own, for its strength is different in each of the three planes. It is a fibrous material and the strength along the fibres is vastly greater than across them. Note the difference between planing plankways and across the end grain! This circumstance does, in fact, dictate the tool form when dealing with softwood and fibrous hardwood like oak and so on.

The problem appears in a number of ways. When planing, for example, the blade exerts a shear stress in the material offered to it and if all is well a good clean chip will flow. With some timbers this shear stress may be greater than the cleavage strength of the material. Then the wood will pick-up ahead of the blade and you get a rough surface. To avoid this, most books tell me (I am no expert planer) to reduce the width of the mouth of the plane, so that the flat sole of the body in front of the blade can 'hold the fibres down'.

Similarly in turning with gouge and chisel. Here you are (in spindle turning) cutting across the grain — partly end grain and partly across the plank. The shear force needed is higher than when planing and the risk of exceeding the inter-fibre strength much

greater. So you let the bevel rub and, by putting the fibres under initial compression, prevent the material from failing in this mode.

Most of my own work is done with slide rest tools. It happens that I do have both a gouge and chisel cutter which can be held in the traversing rest and which cannot, therefore, be offered to the work with a rubbing bevel. A very high rate of material removal is thus possible, with close control of dimension and parallelity but the surface finish leaves much to be desired. It is, in fact, only the rubbing of the bevel which permits some timbers to be cut with a good finish — a finish which is enhanced by the burnishing effect of the back of the tool.

With ivory and the more exotic hardwoods there are several differences. The difference in strength in the three planes is not so great and the absolute strength is often higher. They are far less grainy. Indeed, African blackwood turns almost like metal and I can (and do) machine it using conventional metal-cutting tools in an engineer's milling machine. So the need for a rubbing bevel is very much reduced and in many cases totally absent. This is fortunate because the greater shear strength means that you need a much more robust cutting edge. You *can* cut these woods with a gouge, but the edge disappears in seconds, and more time is spent in sharpening than in cutting.

The greater strength also means that more heat is generated, an additional reason for using a large cutting angle. Even then speeds must be reduced or loss of temper will result. In a few cases you are faced with another problem — silex inclusions in the timber. These cause rapid abrasive wear no matter what shape of tool is employed, though this is more tolerable with an obtuse tool than with a gouge or chisel.

Fig. 2 shows a typical tool-face section as used on these materials. The exact angles are not critical. Those shown are taken from a tool used on ivory, blackwood and boxwood. The tool is presented to the work with the top face radial to the work. For convenience most of my finer quality tools are the same thickness; the rest is set so that the top of the tool is at centre height and thus normally

Fig. 1 Cutting edge nomenclature

Work centre

Cutting or wedge angle

Rake angle

Clearance angle

Tool

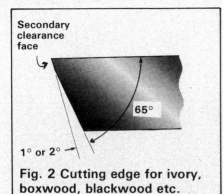

Fig. 2 Cutting edge for ivory, boxwood, blackwood etc.

Secondary clearance face

65°

1° or 2°

horizontal. Slight changes in angle regulate the rate of cutting. It will be observed that this shape is far removed from the conventional scraping tool described in most popular books on turning. The use of a feather or ticketed edge would be impossible. It would not last more than a revolution or two and the finish is atrocious.

Now a few words on the subject of tool finish as it affects the sharpening methods: With few exceptions in ornamental turning no abrasive finishing is possible. Even if it were the skilled practitioner prides himself on having the work finished from the tool (Fig. 3). In my own work where a pattern may have to be cut in the finished surface

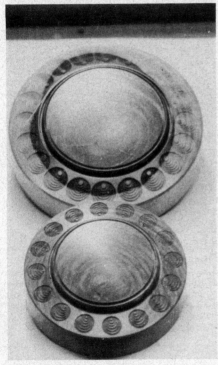

Fig. 3
A pair of gavel blocks in lignum vitae. Note the reflective surface obtained direct from the tool.

abrasive finishing would be fatal, as I must be able to rely on the dimensional accuracy of the work — sometimes to a matter of a few thousandths of an inch. (Ivory can be turned down so thin as to be almost transparent, when it may be only 0.005in. thick).

The abrasive finishing of any workpiece is necessitated partly by the nature of the material; even with a sharp rubbing chisel on softwood some of the fibres are pulled out of the surface, or in hardwood by the finish of the tool cutting edge. Just as a notch in a plane iron will leave a ridge so the grinding marks on a tool will leave ridges on the

surface of boxwood or blackwood. Very small, it is true, but if you are aiming at the truly reflective surface which is typical of ornamental — or any other — turning in these materials, such ridges must rank as defects.

If you examine the cutting edge of the classical scraping tool under a magnifying glass you will find not just a series of grinding marks but a profile which resembles nothing less than the peaks of the Himalayas. It is not surprising that much work with garnet paper is needed after using such a brutal instrument! And as the finest paper cannot produce the desired surface; wire wool, then woodshavings must follow. And perhaps the final indignity of encapsulation within a coffin of polyurethane!

What I have written so far relates to hand-held tools but there is no difference if you are using slide rest tools. The same considerations apply, as indeed they do to the small tool bits employed in ornamental cutting-frames. There is, however, an added complication in some cases in that the plan form of the tool may be of importance; not because some of these tools may be 'form tools' (a not uncommon circumstance), but rather because a V-tool, for example, may be required to cut intersecting grooves where the form produced by one side of the V must meet and match exactly the form produced by the other side (Fig. 4). This calls for specialised equipment both in the grinding and subsequent resharpening, and I do not propose to deal with these matters here.

As regards the preparation and sharpening of these tools, carbon steel is always used. This takes a high polish, better than high-speed steel. (Though I do use a carbide tip when roughing down from the log to the stock cylinders). After roughing to shape by any convenient manner — and remembering that if any forging is needed always 'forge large and grind small'; the forging operation will inevitably lead to some decarburisation of the surface — the tool is hardened using a water quench to obtain the highest figure.

Fig. 4

An ivory box lid, 66mm diameter. The patterns demand extreme accuracy in setting and very precise tool angles. Such a pattern could never be polished, so that the tool edge must be lapped to ensure a high finish.

In the case of tools made from old files all the teeth are first ground off and the file thoroughly annealed before rehardening. For small tool bits — which are about 1/8 x 7/32 x 3/4in. long — tempering is done by boiling in water, with a little salt added, for 10min. For others the shank is heated till the palest of pale straw reaches no closer than 1/8in. of the business end. That is for finishing tools. Roughing tools are tempered to pale straw for about 1in. of length at the cutting end, as you expect to have to regrind these more frequently, and a reasonable life is required.

If much grinding is required the first part is done on a high-speed grinder with an A36Q5V30W wheel and frequent recourse to the waterpot, but the normal wet grinding on a slow wheel is preferred. For those fortunate enough to have one, the top and front faces — or sides of a side-cutting tool — are got up on a 400-grit wheel loaded with paraffin but I generally use a (relatively) rough Arkansas wheel.

For normal hand turning tools the final polish is bought up by rubbing on a very fine and hard Arkansas with neatsfoot oil. At this stage I put a secondary bevel, about 2° different from the original, on the clearance face. Concave tools — form tools — are rather different, because as a rule it is not

TURNING TOOL FORMS

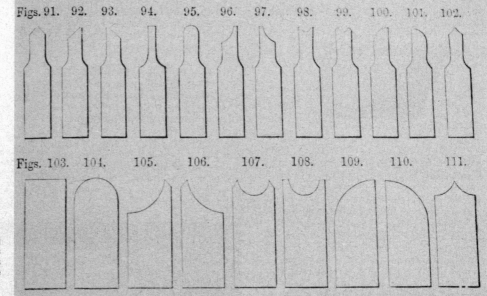

Figs. 91. 92. 93. 94. 95. 96. 97. 98. 99. 100. 101. 102.

Figs. 103. 104. 105. 106. 107. 108. 109. 110. 111.

Fig. 5

Plan forms of cutting-frame tools used in ornamental turning. Slide rest tools are similar but larger. The figures correspond to Holtzapffel catalogue numbers.

possible to grind the concave surface accurately. This means that the shape has to be formed very nearly to size before hardening. To prevent decarburisation and scaling I use several methods: (a) with a large tool, wind with iron wire and 'clart' it over with a paste made from water and ground-up chalk (whitening); (b) for smaller tools paint with anti-scale paint as used by enamellers; or (c) put a blob of toothpaste on the end. The tool must then be very gently heated from the shank till this stops rolling about (the 'flavour' may even catch fire), after which it may be heated normally. The covered end may discolour blue but is usually free of loose scale.

The top and side surfaces are ground as described above and the concavity treated with first a medium and then with a fine India stone (oiled) either cylindrical or conical, held in a drill or lathe chuck and slowly rotated. A similar Arkansas stone is used in the same fashion to finish though I frequently do this part of the work 'offhand'.

The surface finish achieved is normally quite satisfactory but for the cutting-frame tools where superfinish is essential, and in extreme cases for slide rest tools, two further processes are brought into play. The tool is first lapped with finely ground Arkansas stone powder on a brass lap (for concave

tools a brass cone is used held in a chuck) on the clearance face, and then lightly rubbed on the top or rake face to remove any burr. The work is brought to perfection by lapping a secondary angle using jeweller's rouge on an iron lap.

These tiny cutting-frame cutters (Fig. 5) are almost always finished using an angle-controlling jig or 'goniostat' (WOODWORKER for March 1974 *et seq*) to ensure that both the plan form angles and the clearance angles are held to close limits. Fig. 5 shows a few standard shapes for these tools.

These tools do cut despite the considerably greater cutting angle than the softwood turner is accustomed to. Fig. 6 shows a piece of quartered Brazilian rosewood being rough-turned with a tool of No. 93 shape (Fig. 5, but larger). Note the curled-up ribbons — and reflective surface. I have had ribbons 5-6ft long when turning box or similar woods, even longer when turning ivory. Though the rate of material removal may seem pitifully slow to the plain turner, whether spindle or bowl turning, it must be remembered that not only are the materials used more expensive, but so is the finished artifact. The work done is more complex so more attention must be paid to the tooling. Horses for courses, in turning as in everything else!

Fig. 6

Rough-turning a cavity in quartered Brazilian rosewood. This is a relatively 'grainy' species, but ribbon chips are formed. Note the finish obtained even here — the tool is cutting full depth, facing inwards.

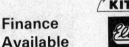

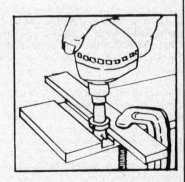
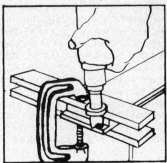

COUNTRY CHAIRS AND CHAIRMAKING

A number of country chair types incorporate curved or bent parts in their construction and it would seen helpful, therefore, to describe how these parts are formed. Much modern furniture uses curved wooden components, of course, but these are mass-produced in hydraulic or vacuum presses and frequently are of glued multiple-laminal construction and not of solid section. Traditionally, chair makers bent their wood by hand methods (although simple machines were later introduced) using solid timber. It is these methods which will be discussed here.

All the timbers commonly used in making country chairs have good bending properties. Ash, beech, oak, yew, the various fruit woods and elm, in spite of common claims and personal preferences, exhibit no great differences in tests carried out at Princes Risborough Laboratory, although some appear to have certain disadvantages in practice. Ash for example, although an excellent bending wood and the preferred choice of many

the wood to distort or split during this period. The more usual way is to use seasoned timber (air-dried and not kilned) having a moisture content (m.c.) of about 25%. (Kiln-dried stuff at 12 to 15% is too brittle for most bending work of this kind). Although greater physical strength is required when bending air-dried wood, in all other respects it appears to have similar bending properties to green material. Moreover, bends of seasoned wood can be ready for use sooner and distortion problems are much reduced.

Wood bends best when it is heated right through to the boiling point temperature (100°C). This softens the fibres of the wood rendering them more pliable and therefore less likely to fracture under the stresses and strains of bending. It is the peculiarities of these stresses which are responsible for most bending failure, for in the process of bending wood is subjected to two induced stresses which cause the fibres on the convex face of a bend to be stretched under tension while those on the concave face

bows etc a bending table is required. Heavy iron plates such as the one shown in Fig. 2 were to be found in most chairmakers workshops but one stongly made in hardwood makes a good substitute.

The traditional method of bending Windsor back bows was to steam green wood and then to bend it quickly round a former on the bending table. Secured first at the top centre by means of a peg and wedge, the workpiece was pulled into place and held tight against the former with more pegs and wedges. A tough piece might have to be levered into place as shown. After a while the two ends would be tied with cord and the piece hung up to set to shape. This relatively simple method served generations of chairmakers once the knack was learned. Many now much admired old chairs had their backs bent in this way.

For improved results, ie fewer fibre failures on the convex face, it has been found beneficial to limit the strain on this face by means of a steel supporting strap in close contact

4: deals with # STEAM BENDING OF WOODEN COMPONENTS

craftsmen, has a tendency to lift or feather if the grain runs out on the convex side of a bend. Both beech and oak, especially if on the dry side before steaming, are prone to surface fractures. On the other hand elm, considered by some to be unsuitable, bends extremely well.

The wood chosen for bending should be selected, straight grained and free from even the tiniest of knots or other defect. Ideally it should be cleft and not sawn; this was how the old chairmakers prepared their material. Experience has shown, however, that straight grained sawn timber can be bent with equal success. Old timber or wood from old trees or from trees grown either very quickly or very slowly is to be avoided where possible. Wood from towards the outside of the tree tends to bend better than true heartwood.

Most wood can be bent green, that is, quite soon after felling and without being seasoned. Many old chairmakers bent all their wood in the green state (in the cold as it was known) without the need for the heat treatment described later. They simply pulled the piece, sometimes a freshly cut ash or yew coppice pole of the right diameter, round a former of the required shape where it was kept in place by means of some simple clamping device. This method works quite well but better results are obtainable if the wood is first softened by the application of moist heat. The disadvantages of using green wood, however, are that a longer period is required for setting and drying after bending and there is the added tendency for

shorten under compression. In bending chair parts it is the first of these which is most often the limiting factor.

The required heat is most easily provided by placing the wood to be bent in saturated steam at atmospheric pressure inside a steam box or tube, such as one of those illustrated in the diagrams (Fig. 1). Such a steamer is easy enough to make. Its essential requirement is that sufficient steam is made available to subject the wood to the correct temperature for the requisite length of time. For all practical purposes this is 100°C for approximately 1hr for each in. (25mm) of thickness. It may be found necessary to lag the steamer to maintain this temperature.

There appears to be little advantage in steaming wood for prolonged periods or using steam at high-pressure — the main purpose of steaming is to heat the wood and not to saturate it with steam. Immersing wood in boiling water, which is done as an alternative to steaming, achieves the same objective but with the disadvantage that the over-wet wood takes much longer to dry after being bent. Wood with 25% m.c. or slightly above is already sufficiently wet for bending purposes when heated; steam at normal pressure provides a satisfactorily moist heat with little further wetting, or drying, effect.

The second piece of equipment required is a bending table or frame to which are fixed the formers or jigs on which various shapes can be bent. Some formers, those for bending the back uprights and rails for ladderback and spindleback chairs, for example, may be held in a vice. For Windsor back bows and arm

with it. In its simplest form this strap consists of a flexible steel band fitted at each end with wooden blocks to form end-stops. Steel of about 18SWG is suitable, cut a little wider than the wood being bent and with the end-stops arranged so that they bear closely on its end. A strip of thin aluminium, or plywood, attached to the inside surface protects those timbers prone to staining when in contact with steel in moist conditions.

A simple supporting strap, with or without end-stops, used with the traditional peg and wedge method of bending works quite well providing the strap is kept in close contact with the convex surface throughout the bend. The more elaborate support shown in the diagram results in fewer failures still and is well worth the extra effort involved in making it. In principle the close fitting end-stops restrict the stretching movement of the fibres of the convex face thus reducing the stresses set up by tension, while in practice the back plates help support the end-stops and prevent any tendency for them to swivel under pressure. The removable handles provide the extra leverage which make the physical task of bending that bit easier.

Before placing wood to be bent into a back or arm bow in the steamer it should be measured to length and its two ends cut square to fit nicely to the end-stops of the supporting strap. The centre point is clearly marked at this stage, too, so that it can be located after steaming without delay.

In the steamer, pieces for bending should not be in contact with each other or with the sides of the steamer as this sometimes

STEAMERS & FORMERS

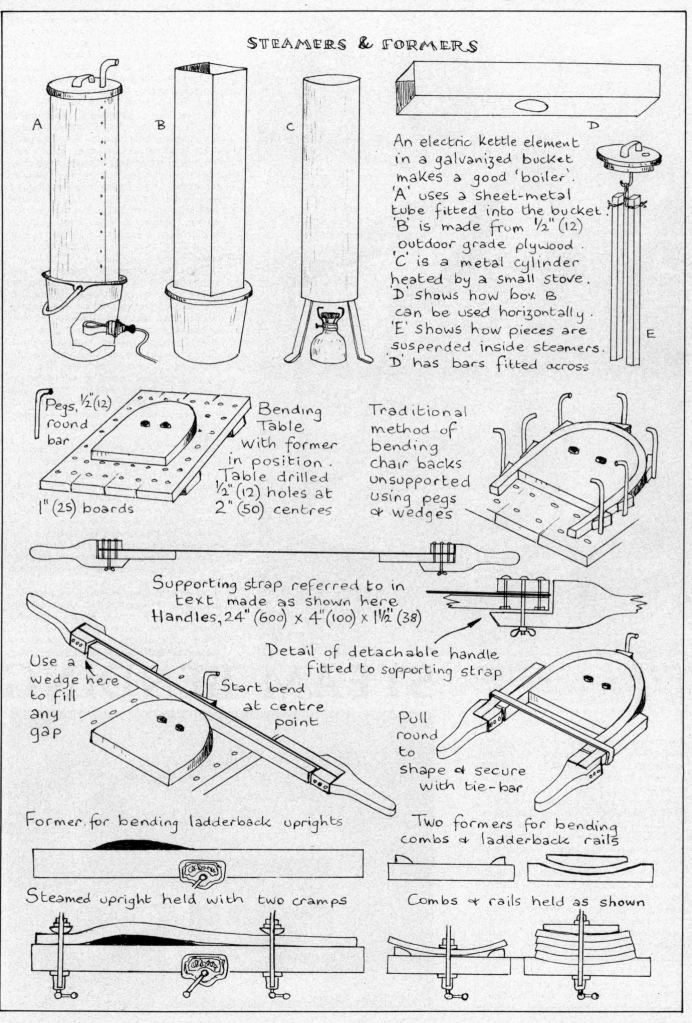

An electric kettle element in a galvanized bucket makes a good 'boiler'. 'A' uses a sheet-metal tube fitted into the bucket. 'B' is made from ½" (12) outdoor grade plywood. 'C' is a metal cylinder heated by a small stove. 'D' shows how box B can be used horizontally. 'E' shows how pieces are suspended inside steamers. 'D' has bars fitted across

Pegs, ½"(12) round bar

Bending Table with former in position. Table drilled ½"(12) holes at 2"(50) centres

1"(25) boards

Traditional method of bending chair backs unsupported using pegs & wedges

Supporting strap referred to in text made as shown here Handles, 24"(600) x 4"(100) x 1½"(38)

Detail of detachable handle fitted to supporting strap

Use a wedge here to fill any gap

Start bend at centre point

Pull round to shape & secure with tie-bar

Former for bending ladderback uprights

Two formers for bending combs & ladderback rails

Steamed upright held with two cramps

Combs & rails held as shown

Opinions vary about the time required for bends to set and the conditions under which this process should take place. The time varies according to the species; its m.c. before steaming; its cross section; radius of the bend; and the ambient temperature of the workshop. Some like to keep the piece in place on the former. However drying, and thus setting, is hastened if the bend is removed from the former soon after bending, providing it is held to shape by the tie-bar.

To avoid tension fractures, which can occur even at this stage, the supporting strap should be left in place during the whole or at least most of the setting time. For air-dried ash back-bows of 1¼in. (32mm) square section, a general rule is overnight on the former followed by several days off the former in an average room temperature of about 60°C, with the strap and tie-bar in place.

The back uprights of ladderback and spindleback chairs are bent in pairs over the simple former shown in the diagram and held in place with cramps until set. The uprights are rounded, and shaped where required, before steaming and bending. A supporting strap is not essential here as the curvature is quite small but one may be used if thought necessary. It should be noted that the bending process tends to flatten round surfaces in contact with the former and clamps; consequently some cleaning-up of these surfaces will be required. A scraper followed by glasspaper is a good way to do this.

A former for bending combs and ladder-back rails is shown (Fig. 3). Combs of up to ⅞in. (21mm) may be bent in this way after steaming for about an hour. Ladderback rails of, say, ⅜in. (9mm) should be steamed for about 30min and several may be bent simultaneously one inside the other as shown. Uprights, combs and rails are best left held on the former until set. Testing the tightness of the cramps at intervals until they feel loose gives an indication of when a bend has set.

It does not follow, however, that because a piece is set to shape that it is ready to be built into a chair. A further period is usually necessary for drying purpose. Although some old chairmakers were known to incorporate backbows into chairs before they

Above: Fig. 2 Pulling a bowback to shape on an old type, outdoor bending table. *(Courtesy Museum of English Rural Life).*
Right: Fig. 3 Bending table with chair back bent after steaming, using simple supporting strap with pegs and wedges.

STEAM BENDING

results in staining. Have everything ready at the bending table — pegs, wedges, a mallet, clamps etc. No time should be wasted once the wood is taken from the steamer as loss of heat will spoil the bend. For this reason it helps if the supporting strap is at the same temperature as the piece to be bent. This can be done by placing the strap in the steamer for several minutes before it is needed. Wear gloves to protect the hands — and an extra pair of hands are often helpful too.

With the supporting strap in place the workpiece is secured at the centre point and the two halves pulled simultaneously round the former with one smooth steady motion. Once there it is held in place with some form of clamp or tie-bar and left to cool and set to shape.

Jack Hill's previous articles on country chairs and chairmaking appeared in the March, April and May issues this year.

Below: Fig. 4 These components all steam bent. Two back uprights for a ladderback; various bow-backs and a rocker for a rocking chair.

were properly dry, a few extra days in a warm room is recommended. During this time bows should be held to shape by having cord tied across their open ends; there is some tendency for bends to straighten out when freed from restraint even when apparently dry. This is particularly so in conditions of high humidity. A method frequently employed to counter this is to bend the piece to a slightly smaller radius than the required one and so allow for any change in curvature.

Some final points for emphasis: wood for bending must be straight in the grain and free from defects; it is hot moist fibres which bend most easily so the steamer must reach and remain at boiling point for the requisite time; the piece must be bent onto the former quickly before it has time to cool; until set bends must be held to shape and this may be done either on the former or off.

Failures are not uncommon when bending wood and, like so much else, experience is the best teacher and the surest way to success.

Above: Fig. 5 'Jack' Goodchild, one of the last of the old chairmakers (he died in 1950) working on the final stage of assembly; the back of a single bow-back Windsor chair. *(Courtesy Museum of English Rural Life)* 'Jack' Goodchild (in model form) was the subject of WOODWORKER cover picture in January.

WHAT'S ON

College exhibition

7 — 10 July annual exhibition of work of full-time students completing three-year course at Buckinghamshire College of Higher Education, Queen Alexandra Road, High Wycombe. Majority of the work will have been produced on the following courses: MA furniture design & technology; BA three-dimensional design specialising in furniture etc; BSc timber technology; diploma in furniture production.

Finger-jointing seminar

Seminar to examine the economical and technical factors of finger-jointing sawn-wood will be held at Hamar, Norway, from 16-19 September. The programme includes visits to plants and a research institute. Details from Timber section, ECE/FAO Agriculture & Timber Division, Palais des Nations, CH-1211, Geneva 10, Switzerland; or Export Council of Norway, Norway Trade Centre, 20 Pall Mall, London SW1Y 5NE.

Art in action

The Festival of Art is to be held at Waterperry House, near Wheatley, Oxford, on the 3-6 July. There will be about 50 artists and craftsmen participating: work will be on sale and can also be commissioned. A diy workshop will enable visitors to try their hand at some of the arts and crafts. Waterperry House is situated at the end of Waterperry village 3½ miles from the termination of the M40 and is about an hour's drive from London. It is about eight miles NE of Oxford. Admission charges : adults £2.00, children (6-16) and OAPs £1.00; students with valid cards £1.20. Party rates are available for parties of 15 or more; opening times 10.00am-5.00pm. Diy workshops admission charge 50p each. Further information from Barbara Nash, Augustine Studios, Augustine Road, Brook Green, London W14.

Furniture projects

The summer exhibition this year at the Crafts Council Gallery, 12 Waterloo Place, Lower Regent Street, London SW1 (nearest underground Piccadilly Circus) will examine the work of three craftsmen who make few concessions to existing conventions in the design and making of furniture. All three furniture makers studied at the Royal College of Art.

11 June-5 July, Floris van den Broecke. Geometric areas of pure colour make the work like abstract sculpture, visual impact is often made by intersecting planes of different colours. New pieces use more traditional methods. Pieces on show include a lounging chair and gout stool and a desk of painted wood which opens on hinges to reveal drawers and shelves.

12 July-2 August, Erik de Graaf. Here is a starker approach to design using only painted beech wood and plywood in quiet grey tones. Seats can be adjusted to different positions based on the proportions of the human body.

9-30 August, David Colwell. Working in Wales David Colwell has been perfecting a steam-bent ash folding chair. The original form combines steam-bent ash with rattan but leather and upholstery variations are also available.

A -- Z OF HAND TOOLS

In the May issue John Sainsbury dealt with the draw knife (sometimes called drawing knife or draw shave) and the hand drill. This article is about dowel jigs which are increasingly popular these days.

Wherever possible in this series references have been made in general terms as regards manufacturers' products.

Dowelling of timber has been an accepted practice for many years but the present-day popularity of the dowel jig can be attributed largely to the increasing use of man-made sheet materials, particularly particleboard, and the difficulty experienced in joining these materials with traditional timber joints.

For many years beech framework in upholstered furniture was dowelled, as also were butt-jointed boards. The earliest form of dowel jig, called a dowel centre, was simply a cylinder available in various sizes from ¼-½in. with a small spike in the centre of one end. When butt-jointing, one length of board was pre-drilled and the small cylinder inserted into each hole (a flange prevented the cylinder from dropping completely into the hole). The boards were then held together in position, and struck with a mallet so that the spike indented the timber in the exact position for the matching hole to be drilled.

Above:
Record 148 jig

Below: four pictures showing the 148 Dowel jig in use.

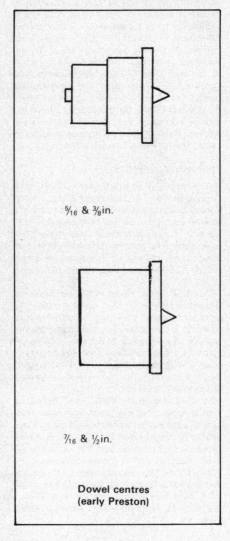

⁵⁄₁₆ & ⅜in.

⁷⁄₁₆ & ½in.

Dowel centres
(early Preston)

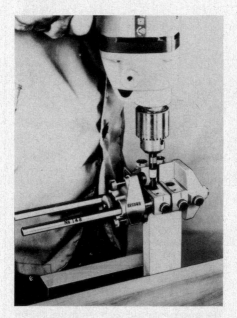

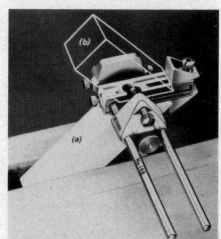

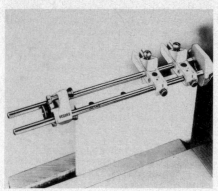

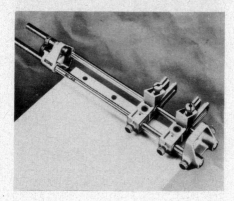

Dowels in those days were accurately made by punching long straight-grained beech or birch through a steel dowel plate. (These were made by Marples up to the 1960s).

One of the earliest dowelling jigs was produced by Stanley USA. This consisted of a number of interchangeable drill bushes or guides which could be fixed in a frame. The frame was fitted with a screw clamp enabling it to be clamped to the wood to be jointed. All joints were possible but each hole required a movement of the jig to a previously marked position.

Woden improved upon this design with a pair of bushes which could be accurately set side by side and placed centrally or in any position in relation to the timber thickness. As with the Stanley, great care had to be exercised in marking-out to ensure exact placement of the matching hole, since boring could not be carried out from both ends of the drill bushes.

The most significant advance came with the introduction of the Record 148 jig. This was designed to meet every possible application in both frame and carcase construction. Only a minimum of marking-out is required on the timber and once the jig is set up no further adjustment of bushes is required throughout a particular project. Since boring can take place from both ends of the bushes extreme accuracy is assured. No other jig gives this type of facility. A range of metric and imperial bushes ¼-⅜in. are provided.

Another useful jig is the Dowlitt manufactured by Pelidon (Engineering) Co. This consists of a jig bar with adjustable width position gauges. Two sizes are available with three sizes of drill bushes to cover all applications.

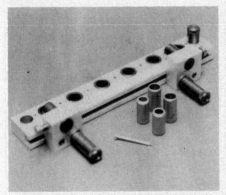

Dowelmate produced by E. P. Barrus Ltd is another jig with pairs of drill bushes enabling holes in each component of the joint to be bored at one setting.

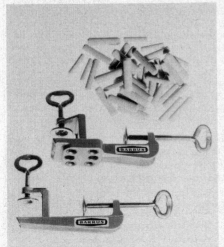

Guild of Woodworkers

Where's it made?

In *Dealer Link no. 3,* a publication issued to stockists of Stanley tools, an interesting point is made on the issue of country of origin. The publication says that country of origin marking is essential information which enables the consumer to make his decision. The denial of it could be considered interference with his (or her) freedom to purchase.

It continues: 'According to the National Consumer Council, if products were to be marked with the country of origin, this would mean much wider origin marking than exists at present and it could only be achieved by an extension of the law. The council does not feel that this is among consumers' most urgent needs, or that they would necessarily make a great deal of use of more information if it were provided . . .

'Fair competition demands that products are marked with their country of origin. Without these markings fair competition becomes distorted and misleading — and eventually the consumer, who apparently should be protected, by being denied origin markings is the one who suffers and pays.

Of course, other things influence a shopper: price, what a product is made of, how long is it likely to last, how much will it cost to run, availability of spares and service facilities. But we like to know where a thing is made, particularly when spares and service are considerations.

Writing a safety policy

When five or more are employed the law says that a policy statement about health and safety organisation must be drawn up by the employer and 'brought to the notice of employees'. While it is not possible to offer 'model' safety policies applicable to all places of work, a report *Effective Policies for Health & Safety,* will be useful to those having to write such a policy. It suggests ways and means and points out pitfalls and emphasises that 'the essential tone of the policy must be established by the company (or employer) which writes it . . . The document cannot be bought or borrowed, nor can it be written by outside consultants or inspectors . . .'

The report has been prepared by the accident prevention advisory unit of HM factory inspectorate following examination during the past five years of the organisation and arrangements for health and safety in a range of undertakings. It is published by HMSO as ISBN 0 11 8832549 and costs £1 plus postage.

The craft achievement

'Within the realm of the contemporary visual arts the greatest achievement of the last decade must surely lie with the crafts,' wrote Dr Roy Strong, director of the Victoria & Albert museum in the *Financial Times* of 15 January. 'For many people this has passed by almost unnoticed but others, from the mainland of Europe and the United States, have been keenly aware that Britain during the 1970s underwent a creative renaissance in the crafts unparalled elsewhere,' he added.

'This has embraced everything . . . It has also been achieved in the face of much indifference, particularly from the printed media who either ignore craftsmen or wave them a hand from the columns of the woman's page. To read the arts pages of the major dailies for the decade will produce little evidence for posterity on this amazing movement.

'The problem now lies in its direction during the 1980s, the danger that success brings of over-institutionalisation and how its fecundity of invention can influence and lift the low standard of taste prevalent in most areas of mass production.'

In his article, Dr Strong considered education and the arts. 'The education bandwagon, which was the justification for much of the vast expansion in arts activities for a period, now looks like a dead duck. The revival in theatre must owe much to the fact that drama is a part of Eng Lit in schools, our full opera houses and concert halls have a similar debt to the introduction of music-making in education, but there is no comparable achievement in the field of the visual arts. Habitat has probably done more to raise the average level of British day-to-day living than any school.'

' . . . use your talents'

The Society of Ornamental Turners *Bulletin* always contains much of interest and the March issue (no. 62) is no exception. It is edited by A. Mayor, Kenilworth, Hayesfield Park, Bath BA2 4QE. One article that is likely to be read by other than ornamental turners explains the making of a spinning wheel having a driving wheel of 24in. diameter with rosewood hub and yew felloes or segments. The wheel has 12 spokes and 12 half-spokes. Author Ian C. Audsley says he has been able to produce a perfectly true running wheel.

Another topical article in the March issue is written by Frank M. Knox on the market for ornamental turnery. About design he says: Design is primarily a matter of shape and decoration. The shape should be pleasing and the decoration should not kill the shape . . . the design should relate to a real problem . . . Then comes the matter of workmanship, ie ornamental turnery. There are many competent woodworkers and hand turners today who put commendable items on the market for the discerning buyer but they don't have ornamental turnery and therein lies the secret. Combine good design with beautiful woods and ornamental turnery and you have a saleable item which collectors will buy at good prices simply because there is nothing else like it on the market . . . Buyers of collectables want exclusiveness above all else.

And who is Frank Knox? He is American and to quote his article: ' . . . a retired business executive who never had even a high school course in shop practice, who took up cabinet making as a potential retirement hobby at the age of 40, discovered ornamental turning 16 years ago and has now made the Bergdorf Goodman *Christmas Gift Catalog.*' The moral? Find and use your talents.

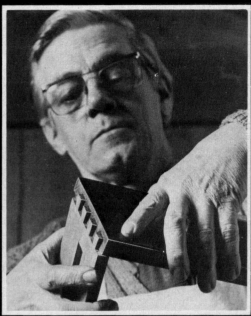

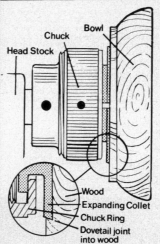

GET TO KNOW THE TIMBERLITE LINE-UP

Get to know the real value of Timberlite savings and service

DW125 RADIAL ARM SAW BY DEWALT. The pro-standard saw that really earns its keep. Thanks to a full specification line-up including: Radial Arm Versatility. All-angle Cross-Cut. Rip/Bevel/Mitre Facility. Accessory Range for greater work scope — Groove Cuts/ Housings/ Rebates/ Mouldings/ Sanding/ Boring/ Grinding/ Jig Saw. It's easy to see why this versatile machine is classed as a complete workshop. Order now and take advantage of our Free Stand offer (worth £42.55). This DeWalt DW125 Radial Arm Saw is only £337.00 plus £9.00 carriage.

DEWALT BANDSAW (BS1310 12"). The ultimate 2 speed compact — fully motorised for bench use. Timberlite price £238.00 plus £9.00 carriage.

Elektra HC260 Combined Planer and Thicknesser only £379.00 plus £9.00 carriage from Timberlite. Superb value Cash and labour saving benefits combined. 10" x 6" capacity surface and auto-feed thickness planer with rigid-cast frame and finely machine ground tables and bed. Powerful 2HP integral induction motor (suited to domestic supply). Top working performance/specification: HSS steel knives. Auto feed, Easy Change over from thicknessing to planing. Infinite thicknessing bed adjustment.

SITE CIRCULAR SAW BENCH. ELEKTRA COMBI 4000 with die-cast aluminium mitrefence with 45° scale. Rise and fall of blade/fitting arbor up to 45°. Single phase 2.2kw (3.1HP) Black Dia: 315mm.
Timberlite price now only £159.00 plus £9.00 carriage.

WHEEL MOUNTED ELEKTRA COMPRESSOR FROM TIMBERLITE now only £274.80 plus £15.00 for carriage. This unit offers a capacity of 7 cubic feet per minute and a maximum pressure of 140 p.s.i. This unit complies with B.S. Regulations.
Full kit includes spray gun, tyre gauge and oil gun, blow gun and hose for £89.00 extra.

ELEKTRA GRINDER TN150W for only £125.50 plus £5.00 carriage. This special Timberlite offer gives superb value for woodturners. Elektra TN150W combination dry and wet-stone grinder. Offers all the speed advantages of dry grinding PLUS efficient slow revving wet stone razor edging for your tools.

The unbeatable **ATLAS WELDER 130 BY TECHNIKA** — available from Timberlite at only £53.90 plus £4.00 carriage. Tested by Bradford University as being ideal for small jobs. (Full assessment available). Built in stamped plate, completely plasticized, highly insulating — Thermostatic protection against possible overloads. Power supply warning light — Continuous welding current regulations by magnetic shunter with external handwheel operation. Winding protection by special oven treated resins.

Dust extraction perfection from Elektra. The **ELEKTRA SPA 1100** is the ideal attachment for planer/thicknesser and spindle moulders. Keeps your workshop clean. Protects your machinery — complete with castors/air filter bag/PVC chip bag and heavy duty textile chip bag 2.5m flexi-spiral hose. Only £169.00 from Timberlite plus £9.00 carriage.

The hardworking **ELEKTRA DB800 LATHE** at only £198.00 plus £9.00 carriage. Built on a robust square tube frame this compact unit offers 4 speed V Belt Drive on a maximum turning diameter of 320mm together with revolving centres. Accessories available.

Get this superb orbital sander into your workshop. The powerful high speed **ELU MVS93 SANDER.** With more than 20,000 sanding strokes per minute (which ensures absolutely smooth running) and the large-area sanding pad any surface will be sanded rapidly and cleanly.
Old paint, wood, veneers or marquetry, and even metal surfaces, form the ideal applications for this "lightweight" model. Timberlite price only £53.05 plus £4.00 carriage.

NEWLY INTRODUCED: The **ELU MH155 and MH182 SILENT PORTABLE SAWS.** Heavy-duty, compact and functional. These new portable circular saws are fitted with the incredible carbide tipped blade and riving knife. Buy now at the unbeatable Timberlite price of £69.00 for the Elu MH155 and £93.00 for the Elu MH182 (£4.00 carriage in each case).
Elu portable circular saws — powerful and universal in their application, but extremely light-weight and convenient to use. Fitted with a robust Universal a.c./d.c. motor rated for continuous service. Infinitely variable depth-of-cut adjustment and bevel angle adjustment up to 45°. Thanks to the new "three-point suspension" these saws are extremely stable when making all straight and bevel cuts. The fence and the large allround base enable these saws to be guided accurately. These saws are, of course, fitted with a slipping clutch and with Elu's well-known pivoting safety guard and riving knife.

THE PROFESSIONAL **PLUNGE ROUTER MOF96 AND SPARES KIT.** This machine is made to measure for the advanced do-it-yourself enthusiast.
It's small, handy, powerful and exceptionally versatile. For example. It copes with grooving, moulding, rabbetting, veining, profiling of all types and shapes. Routing to templates, contour-routing, cutting circles or free-hand working — all present no problem with this machine.
All for the unbeatable Timberlite price of £80.35 plus £4.00 carriage.
Spares kit for the above is now offered at £56.00.

Delivery 21-28 days subject to availability of stock

Stockists of DeWalt, Elu, Elektra, Apollo and Atlas

Barclaycard/Access Welcome

ALL PRICES INCLUSIVE OF VAT.

Timberlite

Timberlite Limited, Victoria Buildings, Luddenden Foot, Halifax. HX2 6AA Tel: Halifax (0422) 884075 884788/33575 (24 hour service)

GUILD OF WOODWORKERS

Guild necktie in green with two narrow gold-coloured 'bandings' between which is the guild badge also gold-coloured, is now available at £3.25 inclusive of VAT, postage and packing. Members requiring a tie should send cheque or crossed postal order together with their guild number and address to:

David Whitehouse, Administrator, Guild of Woodworkers, PO Box 35, Bridge Street, Hemel Hempstead HP1 1EE

Prices quoted are those prevailing at press date and are subject to alteration due to economic conditions.

Fine woodworking demands a fine bench

- Danish made woodwork benches of superb quality, chosen by craftsmen woodworkers and craft teachers the world over.
- Made from solid kiln dried Danish beech. Precision machined and sanded tops are oiled and sealed against warping etc.
- Unique multiple vice holds for secure, comfortable and accurate working at all angles. On principal models this includes exclusive Lervad double row bench dog clamping system running full length of bench top.
- Varied choice of models to suit every woodworkers need. Built in cupboards or moveable cupboards and tool racks available.

Lervad are also leading school workshop suppliers of both wood and metalwork benches and storage units.
If you are involved in teaching please ask for School Workshop catalogue.

A) Lervad bench No. 610CU with two integral vices, double row bench dog system and built-in cupboard. B) Carving between single row bench dog system on Lervad bench No. 600. C) Commodious shoulder vice, one of the three ways of work holding on models 610 and 611. D) Exclusive Lervad pattern tail vice which also operates with bench dog clamping system running full length of top (Models 610 & 611)

LERVAD *Made by craftsmen for craftsmen*

LERVAD (UK) LTD, 18, CRENDON STREET, HIGH WYCOMBE BUCKINGHAMSHIRE HP13 6LS. TEL: (0494) 32561
Please send me full details of Lervad work benches.

Name _____

Address _____

_____ W.7.0

Prices quoted are those prevailing at press date and are subject to alteration due to economic conditions.

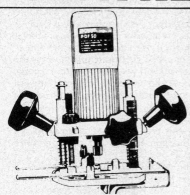

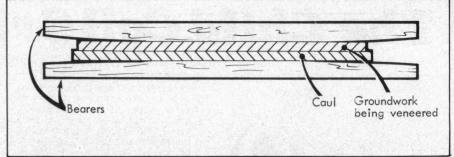

Fig. 1. Method of laying veneer by cauls

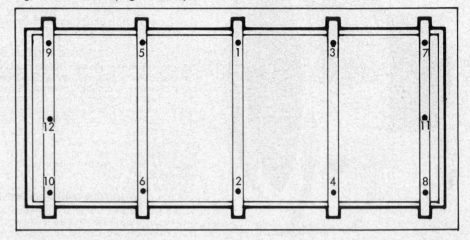

Fig. 2. Bearers in position: dots give positions for G-clamps and numbers indicate tightening order.

Matching veneer

From: N. Goddard, Hyde Heath, Amersham, Bucks

I want to match the style of some veneering and find that this involves cutting a centre panel or rather area of burr grain with a surround of straight grain. How do you achieve a really super butt of the joints of the veneer? I have done veneering before but it was uncomplicated by the above considerations.

I have seen a craftsman working and seem to recall peaflour being brought to the rescue when things were not quite perfect!

Our experience of laying veneer is confined to replacing missing and broken pieces but we believe that the theory following is sound and if the suggestions are followed there should be no difficulty in obtaining close joints. Cutting the centre panel of burr veneer has to be done carefully to prevent corners and pieces of short grain from breaking off. Because the grain is curly these veneers do not remain flat but are inclined to cockle. If a straight edge was placed on the veneer and the edge cut with a sharp knife, as soon as the straight edge was removed the veneer would buckle and throw the edge crooked. To flatten the veneer, both sides should be damped with thin glue size. When the veneer has softened it is placed between two flat boards and weighted down; after a few hours the veneer will have dried out quite flat and can be trimmed to shape.

This is done by placing it on a piece of flat board, pressing a straight edge on the veneer and cutting it with a very sharp knife. To prevent inaccuracies, it is advisable to secure the straight edge at both ends with G-clamps.

If the surround is to be crossbanded it should be cut to width with a sharp cutting gauge. The veneer is placed on a flat board with its edge overhanging about ⅛in. A batten is cramped across the veneer just far enough from the edge to clear the end of the gauge. Use sufficient pressure on the gauge to cut half way through then reverse the veneer and complete the cut. If the cut edge is not perfect it can be shot true on a shooting board. Let the strip overhang the shooting board by ¹⁄₁₆in., clamp it flat with a batten and trim it with a sharp plane set fine. The corners are cut using a mitre square.

Laying straight grained veneer with a hammer is quite straightforward but this method is not recommended for burrs as the moisture in the glue causes the veneer to swell and cockle up.

Laying will be facilitated if the veneers are fitted and glued on to a sheet of stout paper. The groundwork is toothed with a toothing plane, first diagonally and secondly with the grain. Brush on glue size, allow it to dry before coating both veneer and groundwork with hot glue. This glue is allowed to chill; that is the hand can be laid flat on it and taken off without sticking.

To lay the veneer hot cauls are used. These are pieces of flat, straight grained pine about ¾in. thick and slightly larger than the piece to be veneered. Sufficient 2 × 2in. bearers should be prepared to go across the work in pairs at intervals of 6 — 8in. Fig. 1 shows the arrangement, the bearers being planed convex so that pressure on the handscrews at the bearer ends will squeeze the glue from the centre outwards. Have sufficient handscrews ready and opened out to the correct distance. Heat the caul all over until a hand cannot comfortably be placed on it, set the veneer in place, put two bearers in position at the middle of the caul and handscrew down to force the glue out at the sides. Clamp a second and third pair of bearers about 6in. from the first and screw down. Continue placing further bearers and screwing down until the end of the work is reached (Fig. 2) and leave the glue to dry for 24hr. The paper on which the veneer was glued can then be scraped off.

For gluing veneer scotch glue is used. This used to be sold in cake form but is now more generally available as pearl glue. It can be bought from most polish houses. It should be used fresh as frequent re-heating diminishes its holding power.

If, despite all precautions, the veneers do not butt together perfectly, any small gaps can be filled with beaumontage of the correct colour.

Seasoning laburnum and damson

From: Frank Gorse, Deniolen, Caernarfon

I have cut down two small and slightly rotten laburnum trees from which I hope to salvage some oyster veneers. Could you please give me information on seasoning and conversion? I also have the offer of a small damson tree which I should like to use for turning at some time in the future. Should I cut the trunk into suitable lengths to speed drying or would this increase wastage due to splitting?

Very great care is needed to dry laburnum because of its distinct tendency to split. Years ago the craftsmen had an advantage in that the service conditions for furniture and cabinets were much less dry and warm than in present times. Accordingly, they could cut their oyster veneers from the ends of laburnum logs when these were only part dry which made it easier for cutting, drying and laying.

We would suggest you crosscut your material to lengths suitable for eventual handling on the saw bench and stand them on end, with the bottoms resting on some dunnage or bricks to lift them off the ground (in the open air) in a spot that remains shaded during hot sunny weather. The bark should be left on the wood and by about June there should be a need for the pieces to be well wetted by means of hose, watercan or bucket in order to allow the centre thickness to dry while the outside remains moist.

Any fine checking on the ends should be discouraged by the application of more water. When the bark begins to peel, or can be removed easily by hand, the wood is virtually as dry as can be expected and could be brought into the workshop to condition. The problem however is that really dry wood is not ideal for sawing into veneer because apart from its relative hardness it has become fairly brittle.

We suggest therefore that by the early summer (assuming the wood is piled as suggested), you start experimenting by cutting a few veneers and drying these indoors. In the normal way a piece of wood crosscut from the end of a log gives an angle of 90° between the plane of the cut and the axis of the tree. If, however, the wood is offered to the saw so as to make a sloping cut, the angle is reduced to about 70° and it has been found that this relieves the growth stresses in the wood and reduces the chances of the wood splitting; it also produces a more attractive type of grain by concentric cutting. The resulting veneers could then be stacked with very thin sticks between for final drying.

Damson logs should be stood on end and treated as already mentioned. Provided they are not allowed to dry too rapidly, they will benefit by being cut to shorter lengths because drying through each piece can more easily be rendered uniform.

Seasoning elm

From: Richard Stanford, Brixham, Devon
Please can you advise me on putting elm in-stick to season. I have bought some elm and sawn it into ½, 1 and 2in. boards. I want to make sure I season it correctly so that in a few years I can use it to make furniture.

Elm dries fairly rapidly but with a very marked tendency to distort. There is little tendency to check and split (apart from a few checks across the grain) but there is some liability for collapse to occur. With your thicknesses, distortion could be more likely in the ½in. and 1in. boards while collapse, if it did occur, would be in the 2in. pieces. Collapse is caused when surface-drying of wood is too far advanced from the wetter core and is created by what is known as liquid tension force. In effect the wood behaves somewhat like a cycle tyre inner tube that has its air withdrawn — it collapses. Collapsed wood usually has a slightly corrugated surface (wash-boarding) and when crosscut has some internal checking.

Suitable seasoning involves piling your wood outdoors on bearers sufficiently thick to lift the pile off the ground by at least 7 or 8in. at the front and 4in. or so at the back (to give a fall); and (and this is important) placing the bearers at about 12in. centres. The sticks which must be used to separate each layer of boards should be not less than ⅝ nor more than ¾in. thick; and must be placed in perfect alignment with the bearers.

Failure to do this will contribute to distortion as the wood dries. If, for instance, the sticks are set between the bearers, as the wood tends to sag this will transmit itself to the wood above and the same thing will happen if the sticks tend to wander. The top of the pile should have some protection from hot sun. This can be any old dunnage but if sheeting such as tarpaulin is used it should not be draped down the sides since this prevents suitable air flow over the boards.

If it is possible to weight down the top of the pile with bricks or hardcore, this will help to hold down distortion. The 2in. pieces should be at the bottom, the ½in. next and the 1in. at the top for these reasons: in drying, moisture-laden air tends to fall to the bottom of a pile of wood and be evaporated from there. By having the 2in. boards at the bottom they will dry more slowly and the tendency to collapse will be reduced to a minimum, especially in your case where some salt in the air is liable. Salt being hygroscopic will tend to hold the surfaces of the boards moist while the centres dry out. The weight of the 1in.

boards will reduce the distortion tendencies in the ½in. boards.

You do not say what quantity of wood you have so we have framed our reply on the basis of a reasonable amount. Any modification due to there being only a few boards must take the reasons for the technique mentioned into account.

There are one or two other aspects you should recognise: if your elm is ex a tree killed by Dutch elm disease it is probable any bark still adhering to the wood will be riddled with the holes of the elm bark beetle; these cause no damage to the wood but if there is some bark left on it ought to be removed and burnt to avoid any spread to elm trees in the area. It is possible that your supplier has already attended to this.

Elm is also liable to attack by *Lyctus* (powder-post) beetle during air seasoning. This would be confined to the sapwood. We suggest you keep your eye on the edges of the boards during the summer months and if tiny piles of yellow powder do appear, then either the sapwood should be sawn off each board or it should be brushed with a clear preservative. It is quite probable, however, that it will never happen.

As a rule of thumb keep your wood in the open air until a couple of months before you want to work on it when it could be brought indoors to adjust to room temperatures and humidity. Starting from now, and given a reasonable year, your thin boards will be reasonably air dry in six months, your 1in. in nine to 12 months and your 2in. in a couple of years. After that their moisture content will fluctuate according to time of year.

'Chinese Chippendale' style

From: Eric Wright, Cottingham, Humberside
I have been asked to make a small china cabinet modelled on an original of mahogany with pagoda-shaped top and fret borders on a stand. Could you say if the frets on the legs and doors were implanted or carved? I am at a loss to know how this was done in days of old. Could it be a single layer of veneer stuck on paper and cut out?

The cabinet appears to be of the 'Chinese Chippendale' style; intricate oriental fretwork patterns obviously fascinated craftsmen and patrons at this date and abound on all sorts of mid-18th century furniture.

Three basic methods were employed at the time: 1 When chair legs or other supports liable to receive knocks or wear and tear were enriched, the fretwork was invariably carved into the solid timber. 2 If the area to be decorated was less vulnerable — say a frieze or the fall front of a secretaire and the pattern was larger, then the fret was sawn out of a thin strip of wood and glued to the surface. 3 Open frets such as the gallery around a tea table were always of three-ply construction to make this delicate feature stronger.

We are certain the legs of the cabinet you refer to would receive the standard treatment described above. It is less easy to say whether the rails also exhibit the same technique. However, if close examination of the original shows that elements of the fret are missing then it is safe to assume that it was cut and applied. The frets surrounding the glazed panels were most probably sawn out and glued to the frame.

Elm mantleshelf

From: Keith Tierney, Dyserth, Rhyl, North Wales
Towards the end of last year I topped a new brick fireplace with an elm mantleshelf 2in. thick. To date I have not varnished it. The problem is that there is slight warping of ½ to ¾in. at one end only. Is there any way of correcting this before I apply the varnish? Dimensions of the mantleshelf are: width 35in., depth 14½in. and there is a 13×9in. piece taken out of the centre leaving 11in. either side.

There is certain information missing in your letter so we can only discuss this in a general way by drawing attention to factors which might apply. Elm is a wood which releases its moisture fairly rapidly in drying but with a marked tendency to distort. It is certainly not a wood that takes kindly to: (a) being subjected in use to more warmth on one side than on the other; (b) being fixed to new brickwork whose excess moisture could be absorbed by the wood; and (c) being used in these situations in a single piece as wide as 14½in.

We note the wood was placed in position about three months ago but since slight warping is beginning to show, this could suggest that during this period the fire has not been in use which, if correct, further suggests that later this year when drying is more complete your distortion problem might be greater.

Much depends upon how the wood is fixed; warping could be restrained by adequate fixing. Strictly speaking, your new brickwork ought to have been dried-out gently before any wood was introduced into the room and, in turn, the wood should have been dried properly before being planed. It would also have been better to have used a jointed top, say, from two or three pieces, but this could have been impractical in your case.

If you can remove the mantle without undue difficulty you could wait until the summer when drying ought to be complete and then true-up the wood. Otherwise, we suggest you place as many heavy objects on the mantle as is convenient in order to restrain the wood against further distortion over the next two or three months. If, of course, your fire has been regularly lit since you fitted the mantle, it would appear your fixing is sufficient to reduce distortion of the wood considerably.

Billiard cue

From: John Baines, Blackwood, Gwent
Could you please identify a sample of wood. It was the tip of a very old billiard cue.

The specimen is of pear wood *(Pyrus communis)*. This wood was, and probably still is, used occasionally for billiard cue shafts although ash and hornbeam are more usual. The trouble with pear was its high cost and the disadvantage at times of a ripple figure and the presence of flecks which weakened the piece.

In the sample the wood has fractured due to cross grain, which is usually more easily avoided in ash purchased in tapering squares to ensure straight grain. Incidentally, pear wood used for this purpose was generally known as alisier.

Individual replies can now be given to readers' queries. But please enclose s.a.e.

WHAT'S NEW IN EQUIPMENT

Extraction system

For the Elu DS140 grooving and jointing machine an extraction system for removal of dust and chips at source has been developed by Trend Machinery & Cutting Tools Ltd, Unit N, Penfold Works, Imperial Way, Watford WD2 4YY (0923 49911). This facility is valuable when Melamine-faced chipboard is being worked, states Trend. The extraction system costs £125 plus VAT.

Two-speed jigsaw

With choice of two operating speeds (2150 or 2800 strokes/min) and four 'swing' settings from 0 to 3 (maximum), model ST142/01 from Elu Machinery Ltd, Stirling Way, Stirling Corner, Borehamwood WD6 2AG (01-953 0711), is provided with side fence, tilting base for cutting at angles up to 45° and blade holder to accept most makes of jigsaw blade.

The two-speed facility combined with the adjustable pendulum (swing) action of the blade allows the most suitable operating characteristics to be selected for a range of materials including timber and particleboard, states Elu. To facilitate the accurate cutting of circles a trammel bar is offered as an

ELU D140 with Trend dust extraction system.

optional extra and the machine can be used for making plunge cuts into wood without the need to drill a pilot hole.

Model ST142/01 has a rated 450W motor for 220V a.c./d.c. supply fitted with safety switch and catch to prevent accidental operation. The maker states that the carbon brushes should be changed after 400-500hr of operation; this is a simple operation. Bearings are grease-packed for life and grease in the gearbox is sufficient for some 500hr of operation. Price is given as £99 plus VAT.

Also from Elu is a modified version of the MHB90/10 hand sanding machine available with belts as fine as 150 grit and fitted as standard with extraction system. A frame which surrounds the sanding area of the machine is said to ensure a square-on approach when sanding flat pieces. The machine can be used without the frame and also used as a static sander by means of an inversion stand which is available as an optional extra. Price is £162 plus VAT.

Rotary sanding

Maximum operating speed of the Rotosand is given as 3000rpm and the device can be used with high-speed portable electric drills, states the Rawlplug Co Ltd, Rawlplug House, London Road, Kingston upon Thames KT2 6NR (01-546 2191). Rotosand is a solid plastics wheel 4½in. diameter impregnated throughout with aluminium oxide grit which gives a mild but very effective abrasive action, states Rawlplug. It will not clog or glaze in use and a fresh abrasive surface is always presented to the workpiece. It does not have to be mounted on a backing pad. Goggles should always be worn when abrading. RRP of Rotosand is £2 exclusive of VAT.

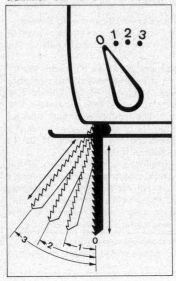

Swing settings of Elu jigsaw blade from 0-3.

Clock kits and clocks

With reference to the announcement relating to the Emperor regulator clock kit (page 259 of WOODWORKER for April), Emperor Clock Co Ltd, 3 The Parade, Trumps Green Road, Virginia Water, Surrey (09904 3813), has sent further details of the long-case clock kits and finished clocks available from the American company of the same name. All the wood in the case kits as well as finished clocks is worked from 1in. hardwood stock planed to ¾in.

Kits can be had without movement for assembly, or as assembled unfinished case without movement or completely assembled and finished with movement. An illustrated leaflet gives details and prices. A range of finished clocks can be seen at the Virginia Water premises.

The company is also marketing some 11 items of Queen Anne style reproductions in kit form. Director P. F. Trimming says: 'We have a small supply of furniture kits in stock which we offer to customers who, having built a clock, may wish to progress further.'

Flexible shaft kit

Addition to the range of accessories from Garryson Abrasives Ltd, Spring Road, Ibstock LE6 1LR (0530 61145), is No. 1250 Utiliflex flexible shaft kit complete with three adaptors (to enable the shaft to be driven from a variety of power sources) and also a spare inner core. Length is 1110mm (38in.), chuck 0-6.3mm (¼in.), maximum speed 6000rpm. Garryson states that the core can be changed as necessary in a few seconds. Price is given as £17.83 plus VAT. Leaflets illustrating and describing the various flexible shafts and the 50, 60 and 80mm flapwheels are available.

Drill and grinder

From Wolf Electric Tools Ltd, Pioneer Works, Hanger Lane, London W5 1DS (01-998 2911), comes details of model 3977 general-purpose 13mm variable-speed rotary percussion drill and model 8313 light industrial 125mm bench grinder. These have recommended list prices respectively of £69.50 and £57.50.

The drill is powered by a 420W motor and the percussive action (up to 35,000 blows/min on full load) can be switched off by means of a finger-tip selector ring when rotary drilling is

required. Maximum capacity in hardwood is given as 22mm. Varying pressure on the trigger switch gives speeds between zero and full-load maximum of 1750rpm but speeds can be pre-set via a speed setting dial.

Bench grinder is fitted with one coarse and one fine wheel driven by a 200W motor producing no-load speed of 3000rpm. It is said to comply with the current safety regulations and standard features include eyeshields, adjustable spark guards and adjustable tool rests to take up wheel wear.

Descriptive leaflets of both products are available.

Pin nail punch and holder

From Millturn Engineering, Unit 32, Klondike Estate, Rushenden Road, Queenborough, Kent, comes a pin nail punch and holder for use with standard pin nails (.040in. diameter) up to 1¼in. long. Mail order price is £2.99 inclusive of postage, packing and VAT together with full instructions. Millturn states that the tool is precision-made in hardened steel and is particularly useful when pins have to be put in tight corners and awkward positions. It eliminates marked workpieces and hammered fingers and supports the nail as it is hammered home.

Prices for quantities and other details can be had from Millturn Engineering at the address given above.

Automatic stacking

The Perifra 850 and 851 stacking machines to handle panels and solid timber of 3 × 2m size on to pallets are available through Machinery Plus Ltd, 9 Biggin Hill Road, Evington, Leicester LE5 6HQ (0533 735554). The former is a front stacker which could be used behind a double end tenoner; the latter stacks laterally behind a moulder or automatic mortiser. Both are adjustable for length, width adjustment being by means of an articulated arm with electric release. Model 851 is loaded by a pneumatic push rod from the conveyor belt. Separators are available to protect coated panels from damage.

These stackers do not have to be bolted to the floor and can be used as production demands on a variety of machines thus saving on manpower, time and money, states Machinery Plus. The Perifra is made in France.

Woodworker PLANS SERVICE

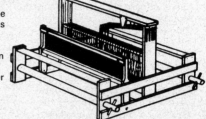

Power drill and screwdriver

Model D-1015 power drill and screwdriver is an addition to the range of portable power tools by Wadkin Ltd, Trent Lane, Castle Donington, Derby DE7 2PU. Weighing 1.6kg (3½lb) it is double insulated and available for 110 or 240V, 380W operation. Featuring a trigger-grip control for stepless speed variation from 0-2600rpm it has direction of rotation controlled by a switch in the handle to provide reversing action for tapping and screwing.

Efficiency as a screwdriver is said to be enhanced by a slipping clutch operated by a prominent nose ring. Drilling capacity is given as 15mm in wood (maximum), tapping capacity in aluminium 10mm (maximum) and screwing capacity 6mm. List price is approximately £83.

Kite-Mark for tools

BSI has assigned its Kite-Mark to three of the portable power tools from Wadkin. The models are: L-1512 hand planer 92mm; R-500 plunge router 60mm; and PD-1920 dual action impact drill 13mm. These are industrial tools available for 110 and 240V supplies and listed at £73, £128 and £84 respectively.

Dremel No. 738 disc/belt sander has 6 x 3in. tilting table and is 15in. high, 10in. wide and 12in. deep.

Routing table with extraction

Spindle routing machine table with extraction facilities is designed to accept an Elu 1¾hp router motor mounted in an inverted position on the underside of the table with the spindle protruding through a hole in the working surface. The adjustable side fence on the table is vented at the point where dust is created and when used in conjunction with a 75cfm extraction system 98% of dust particles are said to be removed.

Price of the table, side fence, extraction hood and pressure guard is £95 plus VAT. Extractors, hose and routing motor sets are also available. For details apply to Trend Machinery & Cutting Tools Ltd, Unit N, Penfold Works, Imperial Way, Watford WD2 4YY (0923 49911).

Holesaws

There are 15 sizes from 19mm (¾in.) to 76mm (3in.) in the range of holesaws from the professional products division of Black & Decker Ltd, Bath Road, Harmondsworth, Middx (01-759 2411). These are said to be suitable for use in all power tools with chucks and to have impact-resistant alloy steel bodies welded to HSS teeth.

The long barrels give up to twice the depth of cut possible with the previous all-HSS holesaws, states B & D. The saws are designed to fit existing 8, 10 or 13mm mandrels, according to their size, but they have the advantage of a longer pilot drill and an improved clamping arrangement.

Prices are between £2.20 and £6 (list) excluding VAT.

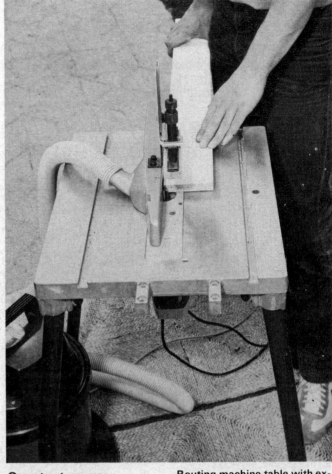

Routing machine table with extraction on side fence.

Constant power

Another two-speed drill with switch-controlled hammer action is available from Black & Decker Ltd, Maidenhead, Berks. It is model 400H having ½in. chuck and 400W motor driving through a mechanical gearbox giving either 2400 or 900rpm. The mechanically geared reduction keeps the power constant. There is no diode or electronic speed reduction which effectively slows the drill speed by cutting the power supply and hence reducing performance, states B & D.

Drilling capacity is given as ½in. diameter in steel, ¾in. in masonry and 1in. in wood. Recommended retail price of the 400H is £33.95 including VAT and plastics carrying case.

Disc/belt sander

No. 738 is the Dremel disc/belt sander powered by a 1.0A series-wound 220V motor giving disc speed of 4400rpm and belt speed of 2700 surface ft/min, RRP is given as approximately £70.64 including VAT. The machine incorporates a simplified tracking adjustment for true running of the 1 × 30in. belt and has a 6 × 3in. tilting work table; the base has holes for bench-mounting.

Dimensions are: 15in. high, 10in. wide and 12in. deep; weight is approximately 11 lb. The machine is supplied with two sanding belts and one 5in. diameter sanding disc; and six grit sizes in belts and three in discs are available.

For more details contact Microflame (UK) Ltd, Vinces Road, Diss IP22 3HQ (0379 4813).

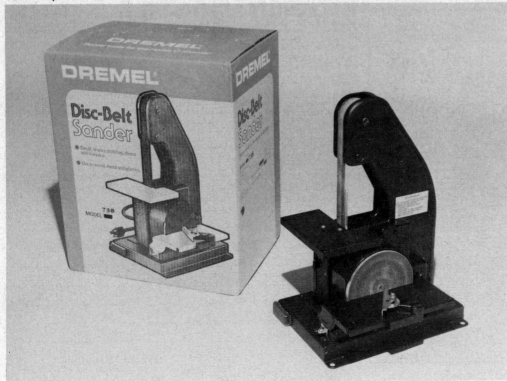

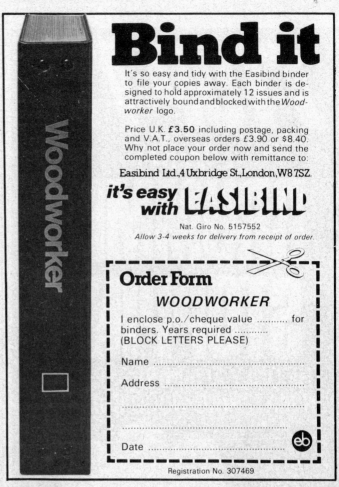

STOP IT!
with
BRUMMER STOPPING

THE ONLY ALL-PURPOSE FILLER IN MATCHING WOOD COLOURS!

FILLS CRACKS, GAPS & HOLES IN WOOD, METAL, GLASS, FIBREGLASS, PLASTER ETC.

STANDARD • LIGHT OAK • MEDIUM OAK • LIGHT MAHOGANY • LIGHT WALNUT • CEDAR • NATURAL OAK • DARK OAK • MEDIUM MAHOGANY • MEDIUM WALNUT • TEAK

Also in CREAM and WHITE

* Won't shrink or expand.
* Contains built-in adhesive.
* Gives a smooth, hard surface — ideal for all finishes.
* Can be sanded just like wood.

BRUMMER STOPPING — INTERIOR HEATPROOF MADE IN ALL COLOURS

TWO GRADES —
YELLOW LABEL — for interior use
GREEN LABEL — waterproof, for outside use

BRUMMER for the Professional finish

From D.I.Y. and Hardware shops

Further information from:
CLAM-BRUMMER LTD.,
Maxwell Road, Borehamwood, Herts.
Tel. 01-953 2992

APPLIED STRAIGHT FROM THE TIN!

Prices quoted are those prevailing at press date and are subject to alteration due to economic conditions.

SHOP GUIDE

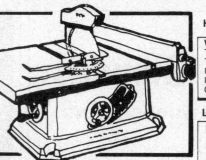

The quickest and easiest method of reaching all Woodworkers is to advertise in SHOP GUIDE. Telephone Gill Dedman (0442) 41221 Ex. 241.
Rate: £5.00 per unit. Minimum of 6 months.
★ Mail Order

100 up at Doncaster: the modellers' pageant

Pageant of the Horse at Doncaster racecourse, held this year on 20 April, has over the past six years become a premier one-day horse show, attracting many of the 'big names' in jumping, driving and other events in which the horse reigns supreme.

It is also a major occasion for the makers of model horse-drawn vehicles whose numbers and enthusiasm have increased during the same period. Indeed, John Thompson in his *Model Wheelwright 1980 Yearbook* writes: 'Six years ago when I first published plans of horse-drawn vehicles I little realised how quickly the hobby would grow ... models were hardly ever seen at exhibitions.'

But not now. More than 100 models had been assembled in the vast lower area of the main grandstand and many, very many, of the estimated 60,000 attendance thronged the two long lines of tables on which almost every type of vehicle (and farm implement, too,) was to be seen.

Entries came from all over the country much to the pleasure of John Pearce, hon secretary of the Model Horse-Drawn Vehicle Club, who assisted in staging the impressive display. Also pleased was Barrie Voisey, Stoke on Trent-based supplier of model making equipment, whose stand was permanently awash in a sea of heads! A lot of visitors were evidently determined to become modellers.

The Doncaster event is not a competition but each exhibitor received a commemorative plaque from Councillor J. C. Cornwell, chairman of the recreation, culture & health committee of South Yorkshire CC which organises the Pageant in co-operation with Doncaster borough council.

Right: Royal Mail coach and gipsy caravan formed part of the entry by R. H. Orgill.

When it comes to saws, we know how to cut.

In the 130 years we've been in business, we've built up the widest range of top quality woodworking machinery in Britain.

Furthermore, we have also earned a reputation for cutting prices to a very reasonable level indeed.

So come along and talk to one of our branch managers. You'll find he demonstrates more than a little generosity, and a lot of very expert knowledge.

Price cut to only £369.50 inc VAT (MRP £471.50)
The DeWalt DW 125 10″ radial arm saw
This radial arm saw cross-cuts at any angle. It also bevels, mitres and rips. With the right accessory, it can cut grooves, housings, rebates and mouldings, or sand, grind, bore or jigsaw.

Price cut to only £41.40 inc VAT
Sarjents 10″ circular saw kit
Specially designed for us, which means a lower price for you. All the metal parts are supplied and it requires no special tools to assemble. Motor extra — price on application. Detailed step-by-step plans and instructions to build a saw giving over 3″ depth of cut, rise and fall and tilting table.

Cut price natural Arkansas oilstones
Some beautifully set in wooden cases, these are the finest sharpening stones around. Available in over 25 sizes, for example:
Natural Arkansas, Slip No. 416 £7.26 inc VAT
Natural Arkansas, in box 4″ × 1½″ × ⅜″ £6.96 inc VAT
Natural Arkansas, in box 8″ × 2″ × ¾″ £16.96 inc VAT
Natural Arkansas, Square 4″ × ½″ £4.02 inc VAT
Natural Arkansas, Triangle 4″ × ⅜″ £3.91 inc VAT
Natural Arkansas, Round 4″ × ⁵⁄₁₆″ £4.83 inc VAT
Natural Arkansas, ½ Round 4″ × ¼″ £4.02 inc VAT
Prices liable to change without notice.

SARJENTS TOOLS

Absolutely everything for the craftsman.

62-64 Fleet Street, Swindon, Wiltshire. Tel: 0793 31361 Telex: 449485
44-52 Oxford Road, Reading, Berkshire. Tel: 0734 586522 Telex: 848695
150 Cowley Road, Oxford. Tel: 0865 45118
EXPORT: Thorn Street, Reading, Berkshire. Tel: 0734 586522 Telex: 848695

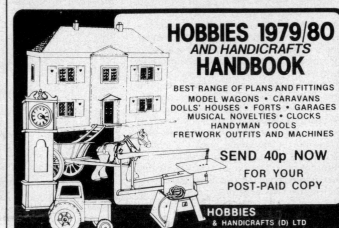
480

Prices quoted are those prevailing at press date and are subject to alteration due to economic conditions.

Woodworker, July 1980

Classified Advertisements

Telephone Gill Dedman (0442) 41221 Ex.241

All classified Advertisements must be pre-paid.
Private and trade rate 14p per word (minimum £2.40). Box Numbers £1.00 extra. Display box rates s.c.c. £3.00 (min. £7.50). All advertisements are inserted in the first available issue.
Box replies to be sent care of Advertisement Department, P.O. Box 35, Bridge Street, Hemel Hempstead, Herts, England HP1 1EE. There are no reimbursements for cancellations.

FOR SALE

Fine Period Furniture
for you to make by hand at home

Large selection of 17thC copies in solid oak or elm for simple home assembly without special tools.

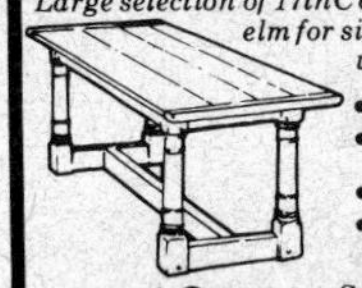

- All materials supplied
- All parts cut, planed and jointed
- Simple instructions
- Save up to 60% on retail prices

Send large SAE for brochure and price list

JACOBUS WORKSHOP
DEPT. W1, South Road, KIRKBY STEPHEN, Cumbria

MINIATURE carving tools for the finest detail in sets or singles. Designed and made by woodcarvers (work and tools exhibited WOODWORKER, November 1978). Also retempering, sharpening service. J. Mitchell, 65 Parkhurst Road, Norris Green, Liverpool L11 1DZ. PQR

ROUTERS

If you are thinking of buying a Router, we offer Bosch/Elu range at unbelievable prices.
If you already own a Router Send for our Free Cutter Wall Chart.

BARRIE IRONS MACHINERY
106A Aldenham Road,
Bushey, Herts.
Tel. Watford (0923) 30422

CORONET MAJOR, saw, planer, thicknesser, morticer, 6" belt sander, combination table, wobble saw, box combing jig, gearbox, large diameter turning etc. Very good condition. Today's list price £1,250. Want £750.00. No offers. Tel: Keighley 67000. Buyer collects. R

MYFORD ML8 lathe, brand new, never been installed or unpacked, £200.00. Tel: Leatherhead 74717. R

TOOLS TO TREASURE

CARPENTER'S ADZES by Gilpins with 3¾" cutting edge and 36" drop on handle £24.21.
WOODCARVER'S ADZES by Henry Taylor with 2" cutting edges and 10" ash handle.
Chisel Blade £15.71; Gouge Blade £20.31

All prices include P&P in the U.K. Export enquiries welcome.

Drawknives, Inshaves and other tools for the Craftsman Woodworker send large S.A.E. for details:
CORBETT TOOLS. Dept. WW/5 224 Puxton Drive, Kidderminster, Worcs.

MARQUETRY veneers 150 × 6" × 4, 50 × 8" × 6", 60 × 12" × 6", 20 × 18" × 8, 12 × 18" × 12" approx., extensive selection, £20. 25 woodcarving tools in case, little used, £35. Peters, 76 Harlyn Drive, Pinner. Tel: 01-866-0863. R

EXCITING IDEAS IN FURNITURE-MAKING FOR NEWLYWEDS, D.I.Y. AND UNSKILLED

ALL you need are a few SIMPLE tools to make your own RE-PRODUCTION, MODERN AND GARDEN FURNITURE etc., from our EASY TO COPY PLANS and SIMPLE CLEARLY MARKED assembly instructions. EACH PLAN is FULL-SIZED. Just trace the plan on wood etc., similar to a dressmaking pattern. SO SIMPLE even our 60 plans to choose from. FREE plumbing hints leaflet with each catalogue. Many satisfied customers who re-order once they try the plans. Send 60 p&p inc. TODAY for catalogue to Hamlyn Dept. D.W. 57 Lyneham, Wilts, SN15 4PH.

Chair illus. made in less than a day from plan No. 35 price only £1.99.

BOUND WOODWORKERS, "offers invited. 1933 minus 2 pages. 1937, 1938 used. Others as new. 1939, 40, 41, 48, 50, 52-55, 55-59, 47 minus October. 51 minus May, June. 56 minus July. 9" × ⅝" sole steel shoulder plane. 3" wide flexicramp. Goscut 200. All as new. Irving, 9 Halton Road, Lancaster. R

CORONET blue series imp bandsaw £185. Sovereign planer/thicknesser £160. Shopmate r/arm saw £175. Tel: 0280-703191. R

MINIATURE carving tools for the finest detail in sets or singles. Designed and made by woodcarvers (work and tools exhibited WOODWORKER, November 1978). Also retempering, sharpening service. J. Mitchell, 65 Parkhurst Road, Norris Green, Liverpool L11 1DZ. PQR

BRANDING IRONS

Made from solid steel with 15" handle, to last a lifetime. Now you can permanently identify your tools and production pieces. We can quote for special styles for a professional look. Price guide — 3 x ⅜" characters **£6.95p.**

SAE details - Woodcraft Supply (U.K.) Ltd., 38 Summercourt Way, Brixham, TQ5 0DY

WELSH SLATE sharpening stones for sale at very competitive prices. Send SAE for details: Inigo Jones and Co. Limited, Groeslon, Caernarfon, Gwynedd. Tel: 0286-830242. O-U

LATHE, woodturning, 24" centres, 4" swing, cast bed, 4 speed, inner and outer faceplate. Complete with motor. £65. Bench sander, heavy-duty 6" excellent condition £65. Electric motor, Brooks, 1 HP, capacitor start, single phase, 2,800 revs. As new £35. Tel: Slough 43376. R

CARPENTER'S and cabinet maker's tools, complete set available through death of owner who used them for many years. Offers at £250.00 ono. For details Tel: 01-373-2444. inspection by arrangement at Mortlake. R

FARNWORTH DIY bench plane/rebater 4½ blade £65. Tel: 01-361-1685 (North London). R

SAWBENCHES, tungsten blades, spindles, planers, lathes. Send 48p for technical catalogues. Beverley, Alford, Lincs. RST

LARGE industrial type jig-saw by Crossland 2' 9" throat. ½ HP motor will drive. Buyer collects. Offers? Tel: Glossop 62056. R

EMCO STAR as new, most accessories plus many spare bandsaw blades, slot-boring turning, spindle moulding etc. Emco-Rex Planer/Thicknesser. To buy new £1,200+. All for £800. Wills 01-445-8581. R

WALL CLOCKS
Quartz battery movements	£5.95
Pendulum movements	£5.75
Clock hands — Black 55p; Brass 75p pair	
Colourful ceramic clockfaces	£1.25
Assorted plastic clockfaces	55p

Prices including post. Full guarantee.
SAE - WOODCRAFT SUPPLY (U.K.) LTD.
38 Summercourt Way, Brixham
TQ5 0DY

MEDDINGS 25" throat jigsaws on floor stand with spare vice type blade holders. Single phase £250. Tel: Maidstone (0622) 51974. R

LATHE SP 800 Luna 3 speed 240v 32" turning. Brand new cost £370 accept £290. Tel: 0202-427781, 43 Watcombe Road, Southbourne, Bournemouth. R

THATCHER'S

POWER TOOL CENTRE
01-624 5146

THIS MONTHS SPECIAL OFFER ON ELU PLUNGE ROUTERS

MOF 96 ROUTER (600 watt) PLUS ROUTER ACCESSORY SET

MRP £159.28
Our Price £109

Both items are available separately.

1200 watt/1.7HP Our Price **£125.00** MRP £156.40
1600 watt/2.2HP Our Price **£151.00** MRP £188.60
Above prices include VAT. P&P £3 on each machine. Discounts/special offers always available from
W. Thatcher & Son Ltd. 221A Kilburn High Rd. London NW6 7JL (First floor above Travel Agents)

WORKSHOP EQUIPMENT

WOODCARVING tools

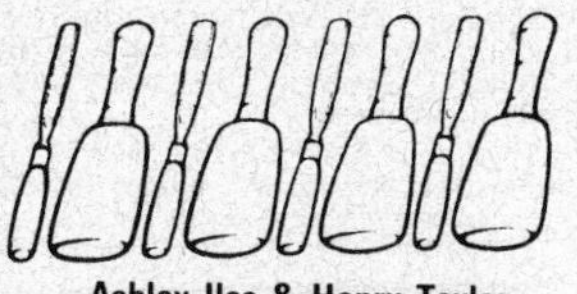

Ashley Iles & Henry Taylor Arkansas Bench and Slip Stones, Bench Screws, Carvers, Vices, Professional Turning Tools.

send 20p in stamps for illustrated catalogue

Alec Tiranti Ltd
70 High St., Theale, Reading, Berks.
21 Goodge Place, London W1

ROUTER CUTTERS

We are specialist stockists of all types of H.S.S. and T.C.T. Router Cutters, in all shank sizes to fit all makes of Portable Routers and large industrial machines. Send for illustrated catalogue. — Small orders welcomed. We also offer a 24 hour resharpening service for all router cutters. Marlow Zenith Cutters, P.O. Box 32, Marlow, Bucks. Tel. (06284) 3247

CIRCULAR and band saw blades for all applications from: A. A. Smith of Lancing Ltd, Churchill Industrial Estate, Lancing, Sussex. Tel. 09063-4474. L-R

LEISURECRAFT IN WOOD WITH CORONET

The full range of these universal and independent machines on show.
Demonstrations and lessons.
Full back-up of tools and accessories for Turning, Carving and Marquetry.

KENTERPRISE LTD.
122 & 124 Camden Road,
Tunbridge Wells
Tel. Tunbridge Wells 23475

BUILD your own circular sawbench 9" floor model. Also 12" bandsaw or 6" planer using plywood and easily obtainable/inexpensive parts. Comprehensive plans £4 each machine cwo (or sae further details). Miraplans Thornfield, Warthill, York. R

MULTICO cutter blocks 3½"d and 4½"d. ⅝" bore ideal for DeWalt. With 20 pairs of cutters and 2 setting tools. Tel: 01-904-0484. R

WASHITA & ARKANSAS whetstones now readily available from importer. Large selection. S.A.E. for lists. C. Rufino, Manor House, South Clifton, Newark, Notts. T/C

1980 COLOUR BROCHURE NOW AVAILABLE

The Complete Works

We supply all you need to build your own clock — Grandfather/ Mother, traditional or modern. Yes, Charles Greville & Co. offer you from stock the most comprehensive range of Europe's finest clock movements and dials. Plus British plans and kits. Easy to follow — simple instructions and prompt attention from a long established family business. We supply the movements and the choices.
A satisfying hobby — a D.I.Y. project — build an heirloom. Send today for full colour brochure on our comprehensive service showing a vast range of clock movements and accessories for antique, long case, bracket, cuckoo, battery clocks, barometers, etc. 50p *(money refunded with first purchase).*

Charles Greville & Co.

Dept (WW7), Unit 5, Rear Airport House,
Purley Way, Croydon, Surrey. Tel: 01-686 2972
Ample car park. Personal callers most welcome.
Open 9.30-5.30 Mon.-Fri. Open Sat. 9-12.30

Woodworker

THE MAGAZINE FOR THE CRAFTSMAN IN WOOD

AUGUST 1980 VOL. 84 No. 1041 ISSN0043-776X

Front Cover: The interior of Stoneywell Cottage, Leicestershire, originally designed by Ernest Gimson. This view shows the room and its contents today. *(Photo: courtesy Evans Bros.).* See also feature on Edward Barnsley p.508.

Editor	Geoffrey Pratt
Production Editor	Polly Curds
Advertisement Manager	Terence M. Healy
Advertisement director	Michael Merrifield
Managing Director	Gavin Doyle

MEMBER OF THE AUDIT BUREAU OF CIRCULATIONS

SUBSCRIPTION DEPARTMENT: Remittances to MODEL AND ALLIED PUBLICATIONS, PO Box 35, Hemel Hempstead, Herts HP1 1EE. Price per copy 75p includes p&p. Subscription queries: Tel: Hemel Hempstead 51740. Subscription rate, including index, £9.00 per annum; overseas sterling £9.00; $20.00 US for overseas dollar subscribers. Application to mail in the US is pending at Milwaukee, Wisconsin, and at additional offices. Distribution to N. American hobby and craft shops by Kalmbach Publishing Co., 1027 N. Seventh Street, Milwaukee, W153233, USA (Tel: 414-272-2060). Distribution to news stand sales by Eastern News Distributors Inc, 111 Eighth Avenue, New York NY1011, USA (Tel: 212-255-5620). Distribution to museums and bookshops by Bill Dean Books Ltd, 166-41 Powells Cove Boulevard, Whitestone, New York 11357 (Tel: 212-767-6632).

MAP

Model & Allied Publications Ltd

PO Box 35, Bridge Street, Hemel Hempstead, Herts HP1 1EE. Telephone: Hemel Hempstead (0442) 41221.

CRAFTSMEN IN SCHOOL

An article in the *Times Educational Supplement* for 2 May discusses 'craftsmen in residence' which 'are dotted around the country in schools and community colleges . . . Usually funded three ways by the school or education authority, the Crafts Council and the regional Arts Association, they bring a taste of excellence and a breath of fresh air to the art departments . . .' The Crafts Council (12 Waterloo Place, London SW1Y 4AU), which has helped to arrange most of the introductions, is described as the major source of information.

The article suggests that young craftsmen, particularly woodworkers, find it hard to survive alone. They require a lot of space to set up their equipment and often need, but cannot afford to buy, the sort of equipment that many schools have in their crafts workshops. Craftsmen of all sorts have a great deal to contribute to education but their presence in schools is heavily dependent on official funding. The *Times Educational Supplement* hopes that the government will continue to recognise the value of the craftsmen in residence scheme by supporting it and perhaps enterprising schools will approach local firms for subsidies.

Sevenoaks school, two comprehensives in S Wales, Burleigh community college in Leicestershire are among the educational establishments said to have craftsmen in residence. The SW Arts Association has a woodworkers roadshow touring the region and bringing a toymaker, model maker and a woodturner into schools for two days.

This is, of course, a two-way process leading to a better appreciation of what craftsmanship involves in practical terms and what pupils themselves can achieve. Indeed, as Jack Hill pointed out in WOODWORKER for July last year there could be more involvement with the community outside school. 'It might be possible,' he wrote, 'to invite more craftsmen into the school, for these men have more to teach than many teachers.'

Mr Hill also explained how a craftsman had helped in a project at his school (restoration of a horse-drawn vehicle). The wheels were repaired by 'an old but very professional wheelwright . . . and we had gained much from the experience,' he wrote.

Overseas readers get copies more quickly

The publisher of WOODWORKER has concluded arrangements to despatch all subscription copies to countries outside UK by accelerated surface post (ASP) or bulk airmail post (BAP). This will have the effect of greatly speeding delivery of WOODWORKER to postal subscribers. Indeed, subscribers in N America, Australasia, the Far East and African countries should receive their copy within 10 to 14 days of despatch from here. Subscribers in Europe should receive their copy in two to five days.

Please let the subscriptions manager know if the new service is effective but do not be surprised if this issue of WOODWORKER reaches you before the previous month's edition which was, of course, sent under the existing postal arrangements.

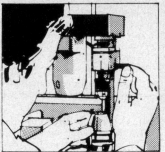

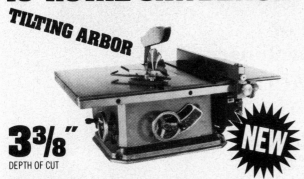

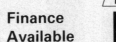

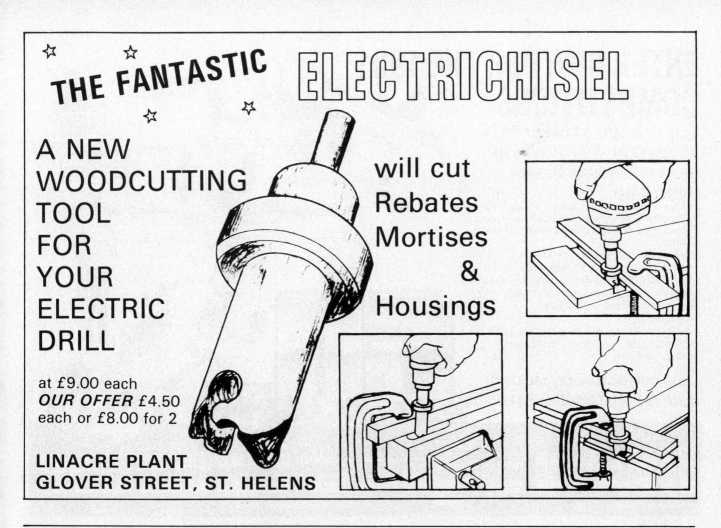

ENTER NOW FOR THE 1981 COMPETITIONS

Cups, Special Awards, Medals and Prizes to be won in classes to suit everyone.

40 Classes to Enter including:- ● Loco ● Marine ● Aircraft ● Military ● Steam Traction ● General Engineering ● Road Vehicles ● Horse Drawn Vehicles

Whatever your interest or age — previous winners have ranged from 5 to 89 years — show your model to over 70,000 appreciative enthusiasts in the world's leading exhibition of its type.

Send now for full contest details and entry forms to:-

Exhibition Manager, M.E. 1981, Model & Allied Publications Ltd., 13/35 Bridge Street, Hemel Hempstead, Herts.

Competition entry closing date is 24th October 1980

50TH Golden Jubilee Model Engineer Exhibition

1st - 10th JANUARY 1981   **WEMBLEY CONFERENCE CENTRE**

**Visit our showroom Tuesday to Saturday 9.30 a.m.-6.00 p.m.
Machines displayed, demonstrated and stocked.**
Stockists for: **Startrite, Kity, Coronet, Arundel, Elu and Wadkin**
Competitive prices

LEITZ T.C.T. CIRCULAR SAWS

These are good quality general purpose Tungsten Tipped Carbide Saws.
Here are some examples of saw prices.
If the size you require is not shown, ring or write for a quote.

Diameter	No. of Teeth	Price
200mm	34	£31.05
200mm	42	£33.35
225mm	40	£39.39
225mm	60	£44.28
250mm	40	£36.23
250mm	60	£40.25
300mm	48	£43.13
300mm	60	£46.86

We offer a sharpening service for all your blades and cutters.

Elu SPECIAL OFFER!

Hand Planer MFF 80 with Carbide Tipped Blades **£82.00** (incl. VAT)
PLUS *FREE* Metal Case with Plastic liner, dust bag and extra set of carbide tipped blades.
Total Value **£102.35** (p&p £2.00)

STARTRITE

MACHINES FOR QUALITY AND VALUE

Startrite Bandsaw Model 352, dual-speed for sawing wood, timber products, Laminates, plastics and light alloys, etc. 13¾" throat **£531.00** (+ VAT)

Tilt Saw bench. Model SP175 with table extension giving area of 28"×60" for panel sawing, 10" diameter saw blade, 3⅛" rise and tilt up to 45°. **£909.00** (+ VAT)

Delivery Extra.

KITY BANDSAW 7212 *£336.38* incl. VAT.
with a *FREE* additional bandsaw blade
Independent Bandsaw on small stand
Cutting depth up to 140mm; Cutting Width (throat) 290mm

MACHINES FROM CORONET

In stock: Major 500 Universal
Major 600 Lathe
Elf Woodturning Lathe
Imp Bandsaws — Consort
Universal Range

HAMPSHIRE WOODWORKING MACHINERY
297 Shirley Road, Shirley, Southampton SO1 3HU Tel. (0703) 776222

SAE for catalogue   *Mail order*   *Answering service*   *Credit facilities*

---

490   Prices quoted are those prevailing at press date and are subject to alteration due to economic conditions.   Woodworker, August 1980

Alan Holtham

Woodturner   Woodturners' Supplier

Light Woodworking Machinery Specialist

As a major supplier of woodworking machinery we are Main Stockists for:

CORONET, ARUNDEL, ELU, AJAX, STANLEY, STARTRITE, ZINKEN, SCHEPPACH, SHOPSMITH, MAFELL, DEWALT, BOSCH, TREND, AMERSAW, EUMENIA, MAFELL.

Visit our combined workshop/showroom to discuss your requirements or to take advantage of our demonstration facilities.

FOR ALL TURNING AND CARVING ENTHUSIASTS— we have recently been appointed main stockist in the North of England for the superb Henry Taylor range

of DIAMIC woodturning and ACORN woodcarving tools

WOODTURNING is our speciality, and we also stock a comprehensive range of accessories and fittings.

TRY our improved
WOODTURNERS SMOCK
Following the success of our first smock we have now introduced an improved version with zip up neck.

Sizes S, M, L & XL all **£7.50**   inc. V.A.T. & carriage

THIS MONTH'S SPECIAL OFFERS!

WOODTURNING & WOODCARVING BEGINNERS' PACKS

Everything you need to get started with these fascinating hobbies:

1. WOODTURNING Consisting of CORONET ELF lathe, chuck, set of 8 DIAMIC brand tools, garnet paper, polish, sealer, wax, smock and pack of selected hardwood turning blanks.
Normal Price £290.00.
Special Offer Price £255.00 inc. VAT & Carr.

2. WOODCARVING Set of 12 ACORN brand professional carving tools in canvas roll, slipstones, carvers screw, 4 rifflers, smock, pack of selected Lime carving blanks, booklet: "How to make a start in Woodcarving".
Normal Price £93.00.
Special Offer Price £73.50 inc. VAT & Carriage.

THE OLD STORES TURNERY
WISTASTON ROAD
WILLASTON
NANTWICH
CHESHIRE Tel: CREWE 67010

Hours:
Tues-Sat
9.00-5.30

We cordially invite you to our
WOODCARVING & WOODTURNING SPECTACULAR

AT THE OLD STORES TURNERY, WISTASTON ROAD, WILLASTON, NANTWICH, CHESHIRE

on Friday, Aug. 8th & Saturday, Aug. 9th 9.30 a.m.-5.30 p.m.

Continuous displays of carving and turning by both professional and amateur craftsmen. Exhibition of finished work.

Examine the superb range of DIAMIC Brand woodturning tools, and ACORN brand carving tools and accessories manufactured by HENRY TAYLOR LTD. OF SHEFFIELD.

HENRY TAYLOR PERSONELL will be on hand to discuss your requirements.

£100 of tools to be won in a FREE to enter competition.

M6 Motorway Junction 17, 8 miles. The Old Stores Turnery is situated just off the A534, 3 miles from Crewe and 1 mile from Nantwich.

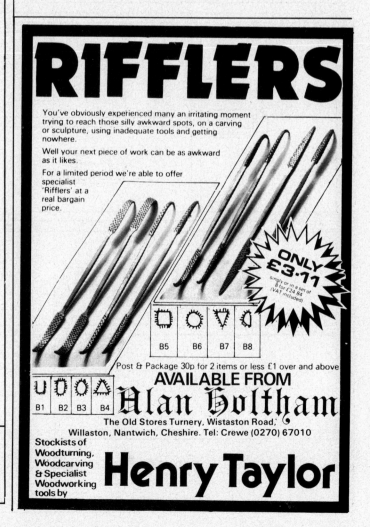

RIFFLERS

You've obviously experienced many an irritating moment trying to reach those silly awkward spots, on a carving or sculpture, using inadequate tools and getting nowhere.

Well your next piece of work can be as awkward as it likes.

For a limited period we're able to offer specialist 'Rifflers' at a real bargain price.

ONLY £3·11
singly or in a set of 8 for £24.84 (VAT included)

B5   B6   B7   B8

Post & Package 30p for 2 items or less £1 over and above

AVAILABLE FROM
Alan Holtham
The Old Stores Turnery, Wistaston Road, Willaston, Nantwich, Cheshire. Tel: Crewe (0270) 67010

B1   B2   B3   B4

Stockists of Woodturning, Woodcarving & Specialist Woodworking tools by

Henry Taylor

REPORTING FOR

Whether in the front line or the drawing room A. Yarwood's military chests are both functional and decorative. He has based his design on the chests used by officers of the British armies campaigning during the Napoleonic wars. Shades of Salamanca, Vitoria and Waterloo!

The pair of military chests described here were based on originals seen in museums. Chests of this type were made for the use of officers of the British armies campaigning during the Napoleonic wars and intended to hold clothes, equipment and personal belongings. The chests were carried by the officers' batmen from the baggage wagons to the tents. The chests were usually made in pairs so that one could stand on top of the other. Most of the chests contain only drawers, but I have seen them made as in the lower drawing of Fig. 1, with a writing flap incorporated.

Each chest was fairly large — up to 42in. long and 20in. high and deep (Fig. 2). An interesting feature is the fitting of brasses to protect the corners of the chests as they were transported. This brasswork is coming back into some modern furniture designed on lines similar to the original military chests.

Early chests were cabinet-made pieces, often displaying a high degree of craftsmanship. Honduras mahogany was commonly

Right: Fig. 1. Two types of military chests as used in the Napoleonic wars.

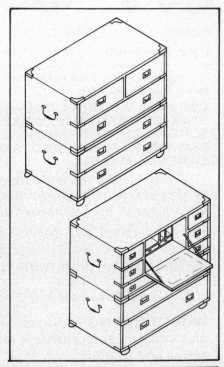

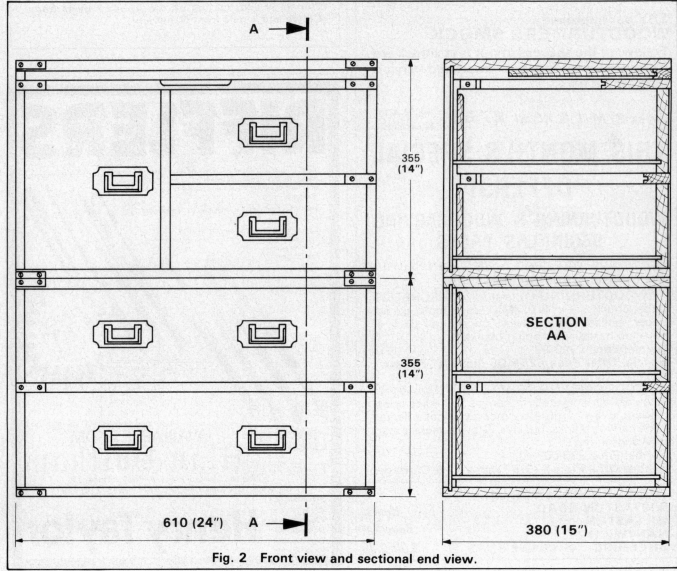

Fig. 2   Front view and sectional end view.

ACTIVE SERVICE

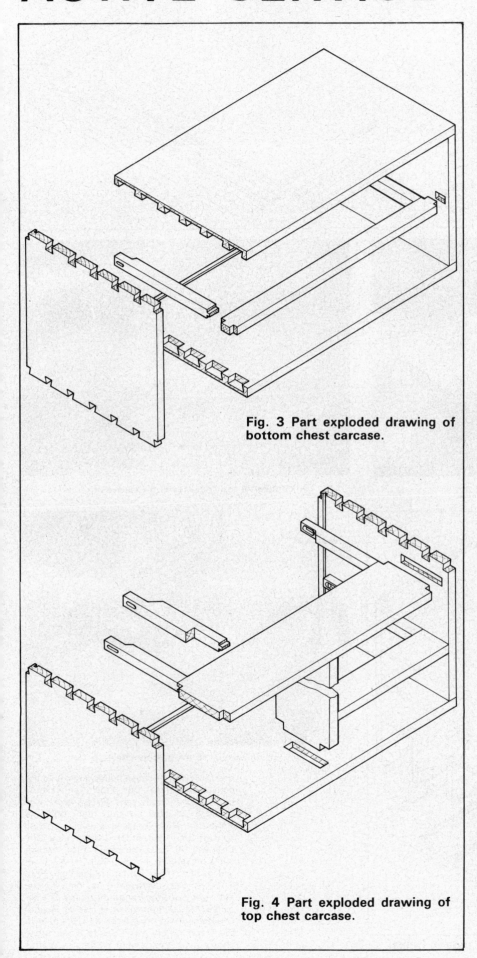

Fig. 3 Part exploded drawing of bottom chest carcase.

Fig. 4 Part exploded drawing of top chest carcase.

Gluing and cramping one of the carcases.

Testing the fit of the pigeon hole assembly.

Drawer sides a sliding fit in carcases.

Screwing a corner brass in place.

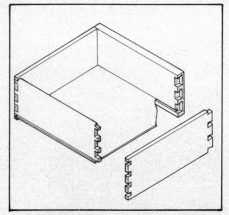

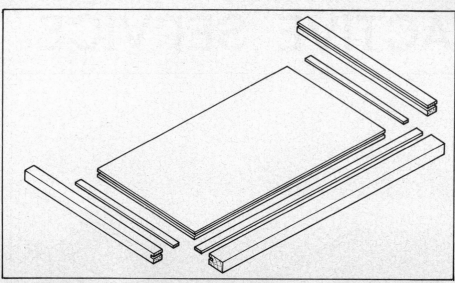

Above: Fig. 5 Part exploded drawing of one of the drawers. Right: Fig. 6 Exploded drawing of writing leaf.

Fitting one of the lifting handles.

The completed top chest ready for varnishing.

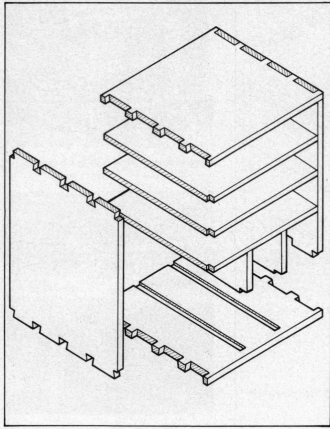

Fig. 7 Part exploded drawing of the pigeon holes.

Fitting castors to the bottom chest.

used. My pair of chests follow closely to the constructional methods of the originals, but I used African mahogany (*Khaya ivorensis*) because of the present high price of Honduras. All the brasswork was purchased by post from Woodfit Ltd, Whittle Low Mill, Chorley PR6 7HB. Another firm from which such brasswork is obtainable is World of Wood, Industrial Estate, Mildenhall IP28 7AY. African mahogany is not a true mahogany as is the Honduras variety. The so-called African mahogany is one of several varieties within the species *Khaya*. I believe the wood which was used to make these chests was the variety *ivorensis*, mainly because its colour was a deep reddish-brown. Other varieties of the species tend to be somewhat lighter in colour. The trees grow in W Africa — the Ivory Coast to Gabon.

Full grown trees are large producing boles up to as much as 6ft in diameter, and sometimes producing good clean logs up to 60 or even 70ft long. The timber produced from these logs is a mahogany-coloured hardwood, more the colour of Spanish or Cuban mahogany which is darker than Honduras. Cuban mahogany is a different variety of the species *Swietenia* than Honduras. African mahogany tends to be rather cross grained and, as a result, is sometimes difficult to work to a clean finish. The wood is tough but, apart from its tendency to cross grain, works quite well with hand tools. On the whole it is a good furniture hardwood.

In order to obtain the 15in. (380mm) wide boards for the boxes of the carcases, I had to edge-join pieces from $\frac{3}{4}$in. (19mm) boards 8in. (205mm) wide (Fig. 3). Edge jointing was carried out by shooting the edges to be joined, grooving them with $\frac{1}{8}$in. (3mm) grooves ploughed to a depth of $\frac{3}{8}$in. (10mm) and then gluing two 8in. boards to each other edge to edge with a $\frac{3}{4}$in. (19mm) wide plywood tongue between.

When these jointed boards had been

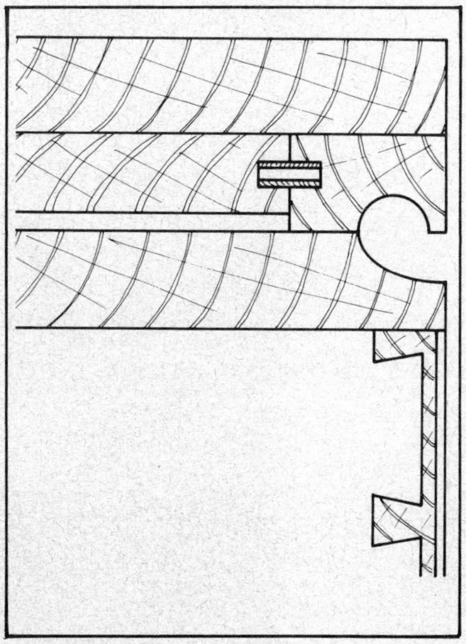

Above: Fig. 8 Sectional drawing through writing leaf to show fingertip details.

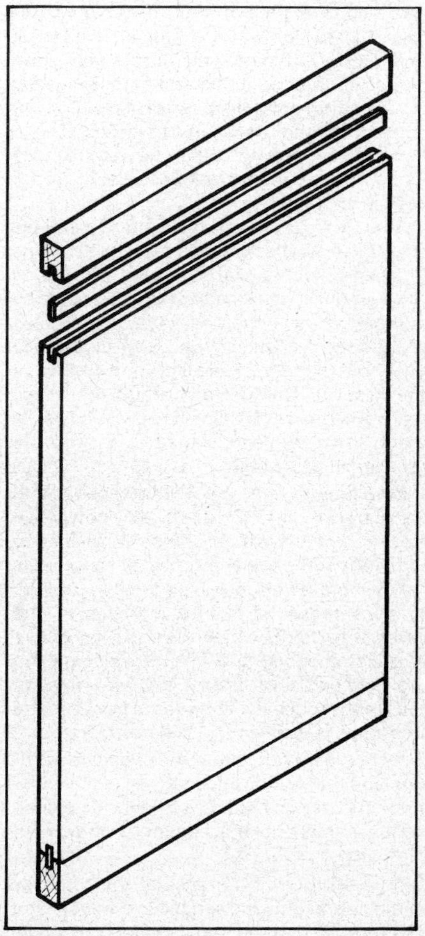

Above: Fig. 9 Part exploded drawing of door for upper chest.
Below: Fig. 10 The corner brasses.

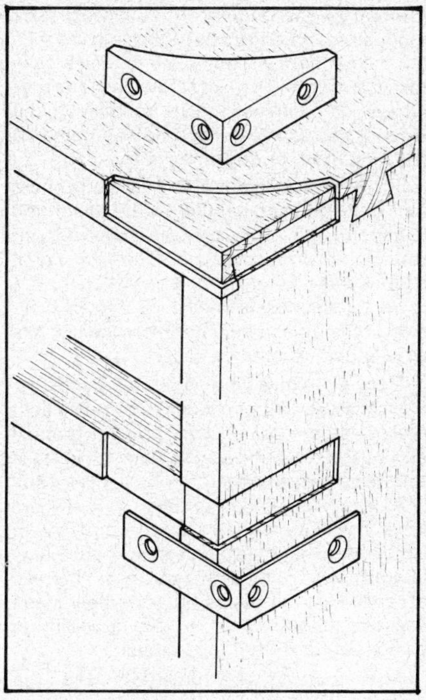

CUTTING LIST

Sizes are in in. and mm. No allowances have been made for any waste. Most mm dimensions have been rounded to the nearest 5mm.

Carcases		
4 ends	$13\frac{1}{2} \times 15 \times \frac{5}{8}$	(345 × 380 × 16)
4 tops or bottoms	$24 \times 15 \times \frac{5}{8}$	(610 × 380 × 16)
2 backs	$23\frac{1}{4} \times 14\frac{1}{4} \times \frac{1}{8}$	(590 × 360 × 3)
1 slide rail	$23\frac{1}{4} \times 5 \times \frac{5}{8}$	(590 × 125 × 16)
1 door partition	$10 \times 5 \times \frac{5}{8}$	(255 × 125 × 16)
1 drawer rail	$13\frac{3}{8} \times 2 \times \frac{5}{8}$	(340 × 50 × 16)
1 drawer rail	$23\frac{1}{4} \times 2 \times \frac{5}{8}$	(590 × 50 × 16)
2 drawer runners	$9 \times 1\frac{1}{4} \times \frac{5}{8}$	(230 × 30 × 16)
4 drawer runners	$12 \times 1\frac{1}{4} \times \frac{5}{8}$	(305 × 30 × 16)
Pigeon hole box		
2 ends	$11\frac{1}{2} \times 9 \times \frac{5}{16}$	(290 × 230 × 8)
2 tops or bottoms	$9\frac{1}{2} \times 9 \times \frac{5}{16}$	(240 × 230 × 8)
2 shelves	$11 \times 9 \times \frac{5}{16}$	(280 × 230 × 8)
2 uprights	$4 \times 9 \times \frac{5}{16}$	(100 × 230 × 8)
Writing slide		
1 front lipping	$22\frac{3}{4} \times 1\frac{1}{4} \times \frac{5}{8}$	(580 × 30 × 16)
2 end lippings	$13 \times 2 \times \frac{5}{8}$	(330 × 50 × 16)
1 writing surface	$20\frac{1}{4} \times 10 \times \frac{1}{2}$	(515 × 255 × 13)
Drawers		
2 fronts	$22\frac{3}{4} \times 6\frac{1}{16} \times \frac{3}{4}$	(580 × 155 × 19)
2 fronts	$12\frac{5}{8} \times 5\frac{7}{16} \times \frac{3}{4}$	(320 × 140 × 19)
4 sides	$13\frac{3}{4} \times 6\frac{1}{16} \times \frac{1}{2}$	(350 × 155 × 13)
4 sides	$13\frac{3}{4} \times 6\frac{1}{16} \times \frac{1}{2}$	(350 × 140 × 13)
2 backs	$22\frac{3}{4} \times 5\frac{5}{16} \times \frac{1}{2}$	(580 × 135 × 13)
2 backs	$12\frac{5}{8} \times 4\frac{11}{16} \times \frac{1}{2}$	(320 × 120 × 13)
2 bottoms	$22\frac{1}{4} \times 13\frac{3}{4} \times \frac{1}{8}$	(565 × 350 × 3)
2 bottoms	$13\frac{3}{4} \times 12\frac{1}{8} \times \frac{1}{8}$	(350 × 310 × 3)
Door		
2 lippings	$9\frac{1}{2} \times 1 \times \frac{1}{2}$	(240 × 25 × 13)
1 panel	$9\frac{1}{2} \times 9\frac{1}{2} \times \frac{1}{2}$	(240 × 2 × 13)

Also required
8 corner brasses
5 rail brasses
4 carrying handles
7 drawer or door handles
$\frac{1}{2}$in. (13mm) brass CS screws

FOR ACTIVE SERVICE

removed from their cramps, they were carefully planed flat to finish ⅝ in. (16mm) thick and 15in. (380mm) wide. They were then planed to their exact finished lengths ready for the cutting of the lap dovetails joining the corners of the two carcase boxes. These dovetails were quite straightforward to make using traditional techniques. Each corner carries six tails (Fig. 4).

The two carcase boxes were assembled dry and their back edges planed flat. This enabled accurate ploughing of ⅛ in. (3mm) wide grooves inside each of the box sides top and bottom near their back edges to receive plywood backs. These grooves are cut so as to be within the rear tail of each joint; otherwise the grooves would show when the boxes were glued together. The two plywood backs were sawn out and planed to fit into the grooves at this stage.

Both drawer rails, the writing slide rail and the cupboard partition piece were now sawn from ¾ in. (19mm) thick board, than planed to finished widths and thicknesses. These sizes can be obtained from the cutting list. Tenons to joint these parts into mortises in the carcase parts were sawn and the respective mortises chopped. Grooves were ploughed in the rear edges of drawer and writing slide rails ready to receive tongues to be cut on the front end of drawer and slide runners.

It should be noted that the cupboard partition and the writing slide rail are much wider than the drawer rails. This allows the pigeon hole assembly to be accommodated without difficulty.

Now all interior surfaces of the carcases could be scraped and sanded to a smooth and clean finish and the two carcases glued and cramped. The plywood backs had to be fitted before cramping. While the glue was setting and with the carcases still in their cramps, the drawer and slide runners were fitted. Tongues were sawn in their front ends to fit in the previously cut grooves in the rails. The back of each runner is reduced from 1¼ in. (32mm) to ¾ in. (19mm) to allow slots to be cut for 1¼ in. (32mm) gauge 8 screws to hold the rear of each runner to the carcase. The tongues are glued into the grooves in the rails but the runners are not glued to the carcase inside surfaces. The slot screwing at the rear allows the carcase sides to shrink and expand (as they will being solid wood) against the long grain of the runners.

It is essential to place and fit the runners into their grooves parallel to the upper and lower surfaces of the carcase if good drawer running is to be possible. One final detail about these runners is that the one on the left of the upper chest is fitted and screwed to the side of the pigeon hole box after the box has been glued into the carcase.

The pigeon hole box (Fig. 7) was made from agba (another African wood) which is a light pinkish-brown colour, very straight grained and very clean and easy working. All parts of this box were made from pieces 9in. (230mm) wide planed to finish ⁵⁄₁₆ in. (8mm) thick. The corners of this box are jointed with common through dovetails and all partitions jointed with stopped housings. It was essential for the box to be accurately made because it was later to be fitted in its compartment in the upper chest.

After cutting the dovetails and the housings the box was assembled dry to test for joint fit, all interior surfaces were sanded and the assembly glued and cramped. When the glue was set quite firmly the box was planed to fit into its compartment into which it was glued. The drawer runner along its

One view of the completed chests.

right hand side could then be glued to the drawer rail and screwed to the side of the pigeon hole box.

The drawer parts were now planed to size; side pieces planed to fit into their respective compartments; drawer fronts planed to fit in place; and backs planed ¾ in. (19mm) narrower and about ¹⁄₃₂ in. (less than 1mm) shorter than the fronts (Fig. 5). The resulting very slight taper towards the rear of a drawer assists its free running when the drawer is fitted. The lap dovetails of the fronts and the through dovetails of the rear of the drawers were then cut. Grooves for the drawer bottoms were ploughed on the insides of the fronts and sides; the insides cleaned by sanding and the drawer boxes glued up. Once the glue had set plywood bottoms were cut to size and planed to fit into the grooves.

After sanding the upper surfaces of the bottoms they were glued into their grooves and pinned up under the bottom edges of the drawer backs. The drawers were then ready to be planed and sanded to a smooth sliding fit in the carcase. When the running of the drawers was satisfactory they were given a liberal coating of candlewax to ensure continued smooth running.

Now the writing slide could be made. It should be noted that the end lippings of the slide are longer than the width of the writing surface (Fig. 6). Dowels let into the underside of each of these lippings at the rear prevent the slide from being pulled out too far. These dowels can only be fitted after the slide has been completed, so accurate and smooth running of the slide in its compartment was necessary. The top surface of the slide was coated with a piece of imitation leather pvc cloth-backed material stuck to the board of the slide with a pva glue (Evo-Stik Resin W). The front of the lipping and the upper surface of the slide rail are shaped with a gouge to form a finger-grip to enable the slide to be pulled out from its resting position in the chest (Fig. 8).

The cupboard door is a single piece of solid wood ½ in. (13mm) thick fitted at both ends with a narrow lipping edge jointed with loose tongues (Fig. 9). This door could now be made and hung in place with a pair of 1½ in. (38mm) brass butts after carefully fitting the door in its compartment. The door is held in position with a tiny nylon door catch fitted at its rear. This is the only truly modern fitting used in making these chests.

It was probably an unnecessary precaution that all the brasswork was fitted before a final cleaning-up of the wooden surfaces. This meant that all the brasses were screwed in place then taken off again before the final light planing, scraping and sanding could take place. However, the extra work involved seemed to me at the time to be worthwhile, although some may have their doubts about this.

Each corner of the chests was marked-out to receive the corner brasses as were the places where drawer and slide rails meet the carcase ends (Fig. 10). Recesses were cut with a fine saw and a sharp chisel and the brasses screwed in place with ½ in. (13mm) gauge 4 brass CS screws. The carrying handles were screwed centrally at each end with ¾ in. (19mm) gauge 6 brass CS screws. Recesses for the brass drawer and door handles were cut and the handles fitted and screwed in place.

All brasses were removed and all outer surfaces thoroughly scraped and sanded. The finish chosen for this piece of work was Furniglas polyurethane french polish. This is applied in a manner very similar to traditional french polishing. It is my opinion that this polyurethane finish is superior to the traditional french polish finish in that the lustre is equal but the resulting surface is much harder and also reasonably heat-proof — at least against such things as hot water which can seriously damage a shellac finish.

Finally, castors were screwed at each corner of the underside of the bottom carcase to complete the two chests.

MULTI-TOOLS
OF HARROGATE

SPECIALISTS IN SUPPLY AND DISTRIBUTION OF ALL TYPES OF WOODWORKING AND ENGINEERING HAND AND MACHINE TOOLS STOCKISTS OF DUST EXTRACTORS FOR LIGHT INDUSTRIAL USE. *NOW IN STOCK:* 'ELU & CRAFTSMAN' PORTABLE POWER TOOLS

SERVICE AND TECHNICAL BACK-UP WITH ALL SALES.

Permanent Demonstration Machines on Display.

JUST QUOTE YOUR ACCESS AND BARCLAYCARD NOS.

 WOODWORKING MACHINES

Black & Decker
INDUSTRIAL
LIGHT MACHINE TOOLS AND WOODWORKING MACHINE SPECIALISTS

158 KINGS ROAD, HARROGATE, N. YORKS. HG1 5JQ TELEPHONE: HARROGATE (0423) 55328 66245

CARPENTRY WORKBENCHES

The Rawdon range of Carpentry Workbenches are manufactured from a high quality kiln-dried African hardwood. Both models have front and tail vices with dog clamps and the de-luxe model has five drawers and a tool cupboard.
Standard model £85 + VAT De-luxe £125 + VAT

For comprehensive details and a complete list of stockists, complete this coupon and send it to Rawdon Machines Sales Ltd., Sizers Court, Henshaw Lane, Yeadon, Leeds LS19 7DP.

RAWDON MACHINE SALES LTD

Name _____

Address _____

WW8

Cowells Jigsaw
Rugged, trouble-free design

Widely accepted by educational authorities for use in schools, this jigsaw is indispensable for the modelmaker and handyman who are looking for a no-nonsense, hard working machine.

- One piece body casting
- Balanced crankshaft to minimise vibration
- Built-in safety features
- Large diameter spindles and bearings for long, continuous trouble-free work
- A price anyone can afford
- Cuts wood, plastics, metal, slate, bone etc.
- Continuously rated motor

Write to us **now** for details, and address of your nearest stockist

Cowell Engineering Limited

Oak Street Norwich NR3 3BP England
Telephone (0603) 614521 Telex 975205

Don't settle for less.

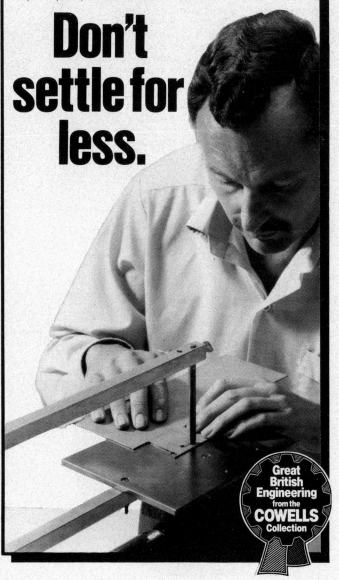

Great British Engineering from the COWELLS Collection

THE WORLD'S TIMBER TREES

Here C. W. Bond, FIWSc describes Australian blackwood. The famous mulga wood used for boomerangs is also a species of *Acacia*. In July the author discussed merbau.

AUSTRALIAN BLACKWOOD 13

Acacia melanoxylon — *Acacia* from *akakia*, the name used by Dioscorides (a 1st century Greek botanist who wrote on medicinal plants), probably so called from *akazo* — to sharpen, a reference to the lanceolate leaves; *melanoxylon* — Greek for black wood. Leguminosae (Mimosaceae).

There are some 350 species of *Acacia*, 300 occurring in and characteristic of the flora of Australia, some of them being specially adapted to very dry climatic conditions.

The famous mulga wood used for boomerangs is a species of *Acacia* from Australia and is perhaps the hardest wood in the world. Australian blackwood is not hard nor is it black, in spite of the specific name. It is soft enough for excellent working qualities and while it cannot be compared with African blackwood or the ebonies, it is dark and dignified enough to take its place among the highest class of the world's decorative timbers. The base colour is golden-brown and this is enhanced with darker or blackish markings.

The tree is common in S Australia and Tasmania and the wood has in the past been exported to this country both in the solid and as highly-figured veneer. There is some connection between the colour and seasonal variation in growth.

The photomicrograph shows vessels chiefly solitary, fairly small to moderate in size and rather sparsely distributed. Parenchyma cells are by no means so conspicuous as in some other woods of the family, being less numerous but they follow the family pattern in being definitely vasicentric. The rays, although very fine, show up quite plainly in cross-section as dark lines, the ray cells being full of deposits. Gum arabic is produced by *Acacia senegal*.

5 cm

Acacia melanoxylon
Drawn from material in the Forest Herbarium, University of Oxford. With acknowledgements to the curator.

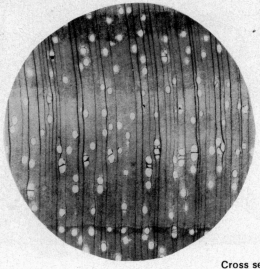

Cross section × 10 lineal.

Cross-section × 3.3 as seen with a × 10 hand lens.

Time & Motion

GBC1

GB3

GMC1G

GFC2

Join the move to Woodhouse Marketing for the finest range of wall, bracket and long case clocks available. Georgian bracket clocks, Vienna wall clocks, Grandmother and Grandfather clocks available in kit form, as full size plans, or as individual components to order.

Woodhouse Marketing (Clocks) Ltd

Spence St, Leicester
Tel (0533) 763579

Cases of selected woods cut from solid, combine with superb solid brass fittings to produce truly elegant timepieces. Choice of Westminster or battery movements complete with dial and hands. Send 25p for brochure.

ACCESS BARCLAYCARD VISA

WEBB'S FOR WOODWORKING

BANDSAWS

BK1 ONLY **£75.50**
List Price £110.13
BK2 ONLY **£79.50**
List Price £118.78
Carr £3.50

BURGESS
These British made bandsaws are market leaders for small workshop use. 12" throat, table tilt to 45° for angle cuts and max. cut 3" wood or 1" metal. BK2 has 2-speed facility for cutting wide range of materials. Sanding belts can be fitted. Superb quality superb prices. Spare blades now only £1.50 each.

ROUTERS

3600B
Collett 2 h.p. Plunge Router
List Price £166.75
OUR PRICE £132.95
inc. Carr.

MAKITA
The ultimate in value — uses all imperial shank router cutters. Just look at the accessories you get with this machine. Straight fence. Trimmer fence for laminates. TCT Cutter. Collett sleeves for ¼" & ⅜" cutters. Tool kit & template guide plus a Makita hat! Top quality steel router table only £29.95 — turns your router into a mini spindle — moulder.

SANDERS

9900B 3"
List Price £123.05
OUR PRICE £98.25
inc. Carr.
9401 4" (illustrated)
List Price £166.75
OUR PRICE £132.95
inc. Carr.

MAKITA
Makita Belt Sanders are robust and powerful to do a professional job. Both incorporate belt tracking, quick release belt change and dust bag.

BLACK & DECKER
DN330 with 13" throat and table tilt to 45°. List Price £107.00.
OUR PRICE £79.95 + Carr. £3.50.

BIRCH
Big 2-speed bandsaw. Big 16" throat. Big 6" cutting depth. Big ½ h.p. motor. Sanding attachment, 2 sanding discs and adjustable fence supplied. Big value from Webb's **£165** + Carr. £3.50

OTHER BARGAINS
DEWALT BS1310 **£247.50**. CORONET IMP **£287.50**. EMCO BS2 **£256.50**. KITY 612 (unmotorised) **£185.00** all + Carr. £6.00.

BLACK & DECKER
The famous HD1250 with 1 h.p. motor and ¾" collett size. Ideal general purpose router. List Price £131.10. **OUR PRICE £94.95** + Carr. £2.50.

MAKITA
3601B 1½" Collett 1½" h.p. Router List Price £123.05. **OUR PRICE £98.50** inc. Carr. Smaller version of the 3600B but same superb range of accessories — will also fit the router table.

ZINKEN GAMMA ROUTER KITS
The small router unit is precision made for intricate work — supplied with 2 kits. No. 7 includes template guides and accessories for internal-external shaping. No 8 incorporates a flexible drive — ideal for woodcarving and trimming and finished decoration work.
Kit No. 7. List Price £86.25. **OUR PRICE £76.25** + Carr. £2.50.
Kit No. 8. List Price £113.27. **OUR PRICE £99.65** + Carr. £2.50.

SKIL SANDCAT
A great new lightweight mini belt sander with maxi Skil power behind it. Ideal for one-hand operation and for tight jobs where the larger machines won't go.
List Price £60.83. **OUR PRICE £49.95** + Carr. £2.00.

MAKITA PALM SANDER
A superb single-handed orbital sander. Industrial quality at DIY price. Ideal for motor trade or wood work shop. Simply cut standard sanding sheets in half.
List Price £44.85. **OUR PRICE £35.50** inc. Carr.

Black & Decker
ORS Industrial Orbital Sander List Price £92.00. **OUR PRICE £68.95** + Carr. £2.50. Heavy duty power from B & D for all those tough woodworking jobs.

OTHER BARGAINS
SKIL 400H 4" Belt Sander. List Price £166.75. **OUR PRICE £132.95** inc Carr.
MAKITA 9045N Heavy Duty Orbital Sander. List Price £98.90. **OUR PRICE £78.95** inc. Carr.
B & D TRADESMAN GD47 Sander. List Price £52.90. **OUR PRICE £39.50** inc. Carr.

RADIAL ARM SAWS

DEWALT 10" DW125
List Price £471.50.
OUR PRICE £355.00 + Carr. £8.00.
The most versatile of machines — ideal for small workshops. Made by specialists. It rips, crosscuts, mitres, bevel cuts and lots of other functions.

SHOPMATE 10" 5200A This famous saw offers similar facilities to the DeWalt DW125 — super versatility at a great price.
ONLY **£319.50** + Carr. £8.00. **ALSO SUSEMIHL 8"**
List Price £258.75. **OUR PRICE £219.50** + Carr. £5.00.
DEWALT 12" 1370 List Price £598.00.
OUR PRICE £462.00 + Carr. £8.00. **ALL RADIAL ARM SAW ACCESSORIES ARE AVAILABLE AT COMPETITIVE PRICES.**

Send cheque/PO or write for details (with 10p stamp)

WEBB'S POWER TOOLS LTD,
1750/1760 Pershore Rd. Kings Norton,
Birmingham B30 3BH Tel. 021-459 1561.

ALL PRICES INC. VAT.
MOST ORDERS SECURICOR DELIVERED
QUOTED CARR. U.K. MAINLAND ONLY.
ALL PRODUCTS CARRY
FULL MAKER'S GUARANTEE.

WE WELCOME ACCESS AND BARCLAY CARD SIMPLY QUOTE CARD NUMBER BY TELEPHONE OR LETTER

DO-IT-YOURSELF GRANDFATHER CLOCK KITS IN SOLID HARDWOODS

FROM **£221.33** (INC. VAT).

INCLUDING WEST GERMAN MOVEMENT

* Antique quality.
* Solid ¾" hardwoods. Black Walnut; Pennsylvania Cherry, and American Oak.
* Easy to assemble, parts pre-cut and pre-mitred.
* Solid Brass West German triple and single chiming movements, with pendulum and weights. Guaranteed for 20 years. Fully assembled Clocks are available.
* Money back guarantee.   * Prompt delivery.

For full details just write to us for our FREE 6 page colour leaflet with order form.
(Price shown does not include postage & packing)

CREDIT FACILITIES
NOW AVAILABLE
DETAILS ON REQUEST

EMPEROR® CLOCK COMPANY

Emperor House, (Dept. WW)
3 The Parade, Trumps Green Rd, Virginia Water
Surrey GU25 4EH Tel: Wentworth 3813/3834

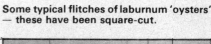
Some typical flitches of laburnum 'oysters' — these have been square-cut.

THE

V. J. Taylor, a former editor of WOODWORKER describes recent acquisitions at Longleat

Longleat house near Warminster, Wilts, celebrates its 400th anniversary this year. It must be well known to many readers both as the home of the 6th Marquis of Bath and as a treasure-house containing priceless pieces of furniture and other works of art.

To mark the anniversary, which he has called Longleat 400, the Marquis commissioned two more magnificent examples of craftsmanship: the Makepeace table and the Longleat wallhanging. Both were unveiled on 18 March by Sir Hugh Casson.

The table was designed by John Makepeace (whose work has often been shown in WOODWORKER) and made in his workshops at Parnham House, Beaminster, Dorset, by head cabinet maker Andrew Whateley. Some four months were needed for the work. The result certainly justifies the time taken as the design harmonises superbly with the white marble fireplace, coffered ceiling and book-lined walls of the red library at Longleat.

Most striking feature of the table is the pure white top composed of 22 segmented petal-like shapes faced with feathered and matched holly saw-cut veneer; the 'petals' are centred on a circular motif formed by laburnum oysters. These oysters are, in fact, thin slices cut transversely across the branch of a laburnum tree; slices cut at right-angles give a roughly circular design while a cut made diagonally will yield an elliptical shape.

Consciously or not, the undersurface of the table (perhaps stand would be a better word) is reminiscent of a peer's coronet, and the wood used for it is an unusual one, namely *Robinia pseudoacacia*. The three timbers used for the table — holly, laburnum and robinia — all came from trees grown on the estate. Conservation-minded readers will be pleased to know that replacement trees will be planted and, in fact, the saplings were on show alongside the table.

Top: John Makepeace (left) and Andrew Whateley cast their expert eyes over the finished product.
Centre: Cramping a pair of ribs to an interspacing block. Note the shaped cramping blocks.
Left: Clearly shows the method of assembly of the stand. Notice how heavily over-size the parts are at this stage.
(Photographs in this article are by P. E. and M. E. Payne, Bridport, copyright John Makepeace).

The 'ribs' laid on a plank as if for marking out. Note that the run of the grain has to be chosen so that each rib will match reasonably well with the others.

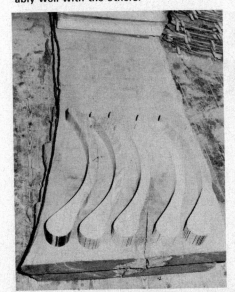

LONGLEAT 400

Technically the most difficult problem must have been the setting-out and the assembling of the stand. The ribs had to be selected very carefully so that when finished the configuration of the grain on each one was similar to that of its fellow. Both the ribs and the interspacing blocks had to be cut heavily oversize before dowelling and glued together. Cramping the assembly must have been a problem, too, as shaped blocks had to be used in conjunction with the cramps.

Benching the stand to its final sculptured appearance could not have been easy either, as the amounts of wood which had to be cut away had largely to be determined by eye. One could truthfully say that benching on this scale merits the description of carving as the graceful lines of the finished stand are a far cry from those of the original parts.

The top, which is veneered on both sides of a plywood core, must also have entailed meticulous setting-out; and laying down the veneers even more so as there would have been no way of estimating the size of the central motif of oysters until they had been cut and matched-up.

Each 'petal' had its outer curved edge covered with a curved lipping of holly steambent to shape and cramped and glued in place, while the holly veneer or both the top and the underside were carried over it to conceal it. Finally, the whole job was given a clear satin finish which shows off the grain patterns to perfection.

The table is a beautiful addition to the wealth of art treasures at Longleat, and as a piece representative of the 20th century proudly holds its own with the furniture of other centuries.

Although not strictly within the limits of our interest it would be churlish not to mention the other acquisition — the superb wallhanging. Based on the concept of a stylised Longleat tree. Amanda Richardson, a young Cornish needlewoman, has developed the Marchioness of Bath's original idea into a glowing panel of fabrics and applique. The intricate border of vines and flowers was worked by the Royal School of Needlework.

Top: Marking out for insetting the 'oysters' into the holly veneer.
Right: Cramping up one of the curved pieces of the lipping — another piece lies on the top of the core. The cramp itself is unusual but highly useful, being a twinned-edition of a sash cramp.
Below: The finished table — a beautiful design plus immaculate workmanship have produced a piece which is worthy to stand as a specimen of 20th century craftsmanship.

The Longleat table in holly, laburnum and robinia commissioned by the 6th Marquess of Bath to celebrate the 400th anniversary of Longleat House.

THE FINISH OF FURNITURE NEEDS CAREFUL THOUGHT

Charles Cliffe gives some timely reminders on finishing furniture. 'There are several distinct and necessary processes to be gone through,' he says

The first woodfinisher was Noah. Having completed the Ark he pitched it within and without with pitch: a protective finish rather than a decorative one.

In exterior work the emphasis is on protection, although decoration such as colour as well as brand of paint has to be considered. Interior woodwork must also be protected, not from the elements but rather from human handling, dust and everyday household use. Decoration is of great importance and the choice of the most suitable finish needs careful thought.

Most pieces of furniture are stained uniformly to the desired shade and then polished but before arriving at the required finish there are several distinct and necessary processes to be gone through.

The surface of the wood must be thoroughly prepared so as to be free from all blemishes. Whereas a coat of paint may cover imperfections, any inequalities or tool marks will be revealed in all their nakedness when the wood is polished. Marks left by the smoothing plane are removed by a cabinet scraper, a flat piece of steel whose edges are sharpened to form a burr. When the scraper is properly sharpened and used it removes the finest of shavings (not dust) and leaves the wood perfectly prepared for glasspapering.

Wrap the glasspaper around a cork block and rub only in the direction of the grain and not across it. Start with a medium grade paper such as F2 and finish off with 5/0 garnet. Abrasive paper usually ceases to cut, not because its cutting particles are blunt but because the paper is clogged with dust. It will help, therefore, if at intervals the paper is tapped against the edge of the bench to dislodge accumulated dust.

Having smoothed all surfaces and dusted them off, staining has to be considered. Wood is stained for several reasons. Stain can enrich the appearance and reveal the full beauty of the grain and figuring. Less expensive woods such as baywood can be made to resemble Cuban mahogany, and furniture made from beech is frequently finished to match either oak or mahogany. Stain is used to give all the different woods in the one piece of furniture a uniform colour and to match all the furniture in one room.

Stains fall into two main categories: water stains and spirit stains. Water stains are probably easier to use but their disadvantage is that they raise the grain. To a certain extent glasspaper bruises the wood fibres which tend to swell when water is applied. This is overcome by sponging the surface with clean water immediately after glasspapering and thereby raising the grain. As soon as the wood is dry the rough fibres are glasspapered smooth and the stain is then applied. This time the grain will rise to a much lesser extent and will require very little papering to smooth it.

Spirit stains have the advantage of not raising the grain. However, they dry rapidly and unless the sequence of application is planned so that the work is completed quickly and all the edges kept 'live', overlapping may occur. Some parts will consequently be stained twice and will show up when polished.

Water stains are usually brushed on and the surface rubbed dry with a rag when staining is complete. Spirit stains are often put on with a rag and similarly rubbed in. Whichever type of stain is used, let it dry for about 24hr before going on to the next stage.

Having completed the staining, consideration has to be given to the finish required. Is a full gloss the most suitable or would a dull finish look better? This depends not only on the wood being used but also the finish of other pieces in the same room. Another factor is the use to which the furniture will be put. Will hot dishes or spilt drinks be likely to endanger the polish? Whatever the finish it is advisable to apply it as soon as possible before the recently stained surface becomes marked or dirty.

Generally speaking a dull finish suits oak better than a brilliant polish, especially if an antique appearance is required. The grain is open and would absorb great quantities of polish if left unfilled. A grain filler of whiting and turpentine coloured with Vandyke brown is rubbed across the grain with coarse rag. When all surfaces have been covered wipe off clean along the grain and allow the filler until the next day to set. So that the filler does not show up white in the grain, rub a little raw linseed oil all over and when dry brush on two coats of transparent white polish. Smooth down with fine worn glasspaper after which the work should be wax polished.

Cuban mahogany was imported in the late 18th century. Its red colour was enhanced by rubbing it with red oil made by dissolving $\frac{1}{4}$lb alkanet root in 1pt of raw linseed oil. The work was subsequently varnished. When at the end of the century Honduras mahogany came into use, it seems to have been polished with raw linseed oil only and this has produced an attractive honey colour. Although mahogany may be oiled, waxed, varnished or french polished its beautiful colouring and fine figuring are shown at their best when brilliantly polished with french polish.

There are several polishes made by dissolving different shellacs in methylated spirits. Brown polish comprising 6oz orange shellac dissolved in 1pt of meths is considered the most suitable finish for mahogany. When repolishing mahogany the appearance can be 'warmed up' by using garnet polish which has a dark brown colour. The polish is applied by means of a rubber made of wadding folded to the shape of half a pear and enclosed in a clean piece of cotton or linen. The polish is poured on to the face of the wadding which is then covered with the cotton rag whose ends are twisted together on the upper side of the rubber. When the ends are twisted the rubber should be dabbed in the palm of the hand to evenly distribute the polish. The face of the rubber must be free from wrinkles and should be moist with polish but by no means wet. Without pressing too hard, wipe over the whole surface first with the grain and then across the grain. After this the rubber's path over the work consists of small overlapping circles.

When the rubber dries out it is re-charged with polish, care being taken not to overdo it. If the rubber tends to drag a spot of raw linseed oil is applied to its face to act as a lubricant. Very little oil is needed. Use only raw oil not the boiled variety.

The action of the rubber is twofold: It distributes an even amount of polish over the work and it burnishes the shellac to produce a brilliant finish. Were it not for this burnishing action, a thicker polish could be used and applied with a brush to achieve the same result with less time and effort.

Apart from the skill required to french polish successfully, this finish does have some snages. It cannot withstand hot dishes being rested on it, neither will it tolerate wet flower vases. Spilled alcoholic drinks will dissolve the lac and wreck the finish. For this reason table tops are sometimes given the more durable linseed oil finish while the legs and framework are french polished. Alkanet root may no longer be available but a trade house may be able to supply red oil.

Other durable finishes for table tops are the polyurethane varnishes. These are heat and water-resistant and if care is taken with their application, very good results are obtained. Some of these finishes have to have a catalyst added whereas others come ready for use. It is a matter of reading the manufacturer's instructions and following them.

In all cases it is necessary to work in a warm, dry and dust-free atmosphere. The work must also be warm and dry. It cannot be brought from a cold damp atmosphere into a warm room and then varnished. It must be given time to dry and warm up. Similarly, the varnish must be at room temperature otherwise it will not flow properly. Finally the brush used must be absolutely clean and free from dust. Flick the bristles back and forth between the fingers to clear any dust which may be there before dipping into the varnish. Carefully apply a good flowing coat and a first-class finish should result.

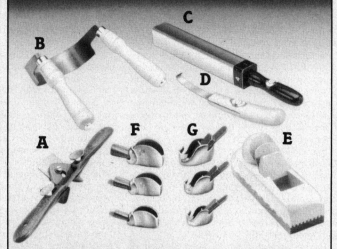

TIMBER TOPICS 10

W. H. Brown FIWSc concludes his discussion of polyethylene glycol (PEG). He says that if time is at a premium then the use of green wood treated with PEG is the answer. And the chemical could also be used to advantage where a carver, working only at odd times on a block of wood not as dry as it might be, has to leave the work for a day or more in a warm room.

In Timber Topics 8 (June 1980); 9 (July 1980) we have been discussing the use of polyethylene glycol (PEG) for improving the dimensional stability of wood. It is now important to consider how much benefit the average woodworker could expect to derive from occasional or regular use of the chemical.

In the widest sense of dimensional stability this is mainly important in industrial applications where fluctuating air conditions in storage or service could lead to unwanted shrinkage or swelling of wood items. Two good examples are in plywood manufacture and for gunstocks, both of which have benefited from PEG treatment.

In the context of what could be termed domestic wood use dimensional stability more generally means freedom from excessive shrinkage, not swelling, because the primary requirement for good woodworking is the use of dry material which is what everyone strives for. Since the occasions when the wood is thought to be too dry are few the tendency for swelling to become part of the stability problem is small.

This does not mean there is little use for

Fig. 1. The large area of end grain in tree discs helps the diffusion of PEG since this is 9 to 15 times as fast in the fibre direction as in the transverse direction. Treated wood resists the formation of V-shaped splits.

PEG treatment in craft woodworking; there could be but the need should be considered carefully. One direction in which the chemical has shown promise has been in relation to the difficult problem of trying to reduce the occurrence of V-shaped splits developing in tree discs cut from green logs. Tests have shown that in green wood PEG diffuses nine to 15 times as fast in the fibre direction as in the transverse direction. So since the wide surface of tree discs are all end grain it ought to be possible to rapidly bulk the fibres by soaking the pieces in the chemical thereby improving the drying quality of the wood (Fig. 1).

To get down to practicalities, however, let us consider a block of hardwood 12 × 12 × 6in. (300 × 300 × 150mm) intended to be used for turning a bowl. If the wood is to be treated with PEG in order to prevent splits and checks occurring it must be really wet, either naturally so (green) or induced by soaking in water. There are two aspects here which require thought: one, what would be the point in treating the wood in the bulk form and then discarding much of it in roughing-out; and two, really wet wood with a moisture content (m.c.) perhaps higher than 100% and

probably at least 60%, does not split or check because it cannot shrink until its moisture has been removed down to the fibre saturation point of about 30%.

From this stage down to final equilibrium of 10% room condition, the amount of shrinkage liable to cause splits to develop is controlled by factors such as the bulk of the wood which would restrain shrinkage; the amount of the bulk above the saturation point (the centre thickness); and the type and the species of wood. In other words, a piece of hardwood of the size mentioned could be at risk from splitting while it was drying; but how significant is this in practical terms for the purpose mentioned?

Taking the approximate size of a finished turned bowl that could be produced from our hypothetical block, this might be something like 10in. (250mm) diameter, 5in. (125mm) deep, with sides maximum 1in. (25mm), and the wood itself would be a mixture of tangential and radial wood (Fig. 2). In effect the majority if not all of the wood is around the 1in. (25mm) thickness; but we are discussing where the greatest benefit of PEG treatment might lie were we to use it.

Suppose we treated the original block with PEG. As mentioned the wood must be really wet if it is to accept a suitable diffusion of the chemical, and since polyethylene glycol is

FIBRE DIRECTION

water-soluble the treated wood must be stored under cover for drying to a suitable m.c. for turning which, for the size of the block mentioned, could be two or three years. This does not seem an attractive proposition so supposing the wet block is rough turned and then treated with PEG in order to reduce the chances of splitting later on, would this offer much advantage?

In a publication of the US Department of Agriculture Forest Products Laboratory *How PEG helps the hobbyist who works with Wood: 1972* (by H. L. Mitchell), the author states: 'PEG is not recommended for the routine processing of 1in. lumber destined for use in furniture, cabinets and other indoor uses: it is not normally needed. Simply follow the suggestions for drying and conditioning to the proper moisture content and no serious problems should result'.

It must be understood that in the context of proper m.c. mentioned by Mitchell, in America due to the high degree of air conditioning prevailing there, room atmosphere of 73° F + with relative humidity (RH) commonly at 30%, equilibrium m.c. for wood is around 6%, somewhat lower than our average level of 10% m.c. This suggests that since American room conditions do not appear to merit timber at 1in. (25mm) being treated with PEG, why bother to treat our similar wood which will not generally dry down as low?

There is a subtle difference, however, between flat boards of this thickness where each board has an individual growth pattern, and a rough turned bowl of similar thickness

but which invariably contains a mixture of tangential and radial wood. In the former the wide surfaces are either sawn tangentially, radially or mid-way between the two; in the latter various parts of the turnery will present surfaces in many varying planes. That is the reason for turning: it displays the various changing facets of wood character to best advantage.

The presence of pith in a piece of turnery wood must be avoided and invariably is because, as with tree discs, the greater shrinkage potential around the growth rings (tangentially) than across them (radially) is the principal factor contributing to splitting; if the pith is discarded then splitting tendencies are reduced.

Reverting now to potential shrinkage, this will vary with the species. But starting from about 30% m.c. as the wood dries, at least half of its probable shrinkage will have occurred when the wood has dried to around 18% m.c. The remainder of the shrinkage that is likely to occur will be at a lower rate and this rate will be approximately the same for all species. To give an example: English oak, according to test results, has a shrinkage value of 7.5% tangentially and 4.0% radially in drying from the green (30% m.c.) to 12% m.c., or ¹⁵/₁₆in. (23.8mm) and ½in. (12.7mm) in 12in. (300mm).

If the above is considered it will be seen that for each 1% m.c. change (ie 30% to 12% is a m.c. change of 18), shrinkage for English oak is 1.3mm tangentially and 0.7mm radially. However, when wood dries down to an air-dry level below about 18% m.c. we have to think in terms of possible movement by swelling as well as by shrinkage. Since as we have said there is now a slowing down of moisture out of any wood, the value is approximately 1.0mm in 300mm tangentially for each 1.0% m.c. change and 0.65mm in a radial direction.

Referring again to our hypothetical block of wood, if it were dried slowly and carefully splitting and checking should be minimal and

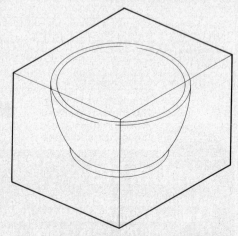

Fig. 2. None of the surfaces of a turned bowl will be in a true tangential or radial plane; therefore shrinkage values will be between the two.

Woodworker Show

Royal Horticultural Society's New Hall
4-9 November, 1980

All correspondence and entry forms: Exhibitions Manager, Model and Allied Publications Ltd, PO Box 35, Bridge Street, Hemel Hempstead HP1 1EE.

GENERAL CONDITIONS OF ENTRY

1. Each entry shall be made separately on the official form and every question must be answered. Be sure to include the estimated value of your model. LAST DAY OF ENTRY WILL BE FRIDAY, 5 SEPTEMBER 1980.
2. All entry forms must be accompanied by a remittance for the appropriate entry fee(s).
3. The competition entry fee will be £1.25 for seniors, 75p for juniors.
4. A junior shall mean a person under 18 years of age on 1 November 1980.
5. No exhibit which has previously won a bronze medal, rosette or higher award at any of the exhibitions promoted by this company shall be accepted for these competitions. The organisers reserve the right to transfer an entry to a more appropriate class.
6. Entries may be submitted by amateur or professional workers.
7. The decision of the judges shall be final.
8. Competitors shall state on the entry form:
   (a) that the exhibit is their own work and property;

(b) any parts or kits which were purchased or were not the outcome of their own work.
(c) the origin of the design.

9. Exhibits will be insured for the period during which they will be at the exhibition. Insurance of exhibits in transit to and from the exhibition is the responsibility of the competitor.
10. Model and Allied Publications Ltd reserves the right to refuse any entry or exhibit on arrival at the exhibition and shall not be required to furnish any reason for doing so.
11. Model and Allied Publications Ltd reserves the exclusive rights to describe and photograph any exhibits entered for competition or display and to make use of of any such photograph or descriptions in any way the company may think fit.
12. Competitors will be issued with a free non-transferable competitors pass to the exhibition on presentation of their exhibit to the organisers.

Location & parking

Many readers will be familiar with the Royal Horticultural Society's exhibition halls in London. For those who are not the New Hall is situated in Greycoat Street (off Vincent Square), Westminster SW1. It is roughly five minutes' walk from Victoria station (BR and London underground) in the direction of Westminster Abbey. St James's Park station on the underground is also within a few minutes' walk. Bus services along Victoria Street are frequent with stops at Broadway and Strutton Ground, both quite near the New Hall.

Woodworker/Ashley Iles carving competition

The Woodworker/Ashley Iles international carving competition this year is The Dance. There is one section only, namely figure carving. Closing date is Friday 24 October 1980 and entries should be sent to WOODWORKER office, PO Box 35, Bridge Street, Hemel Hempstead HP1 1EE. Entries must not be submitted before Monday 22 September 1980. Judging will take place at the Woodworker Show.

Entry is open to professional and amateur craftsmen. There is no entry fee. Pieces entered in this competition are not eligible for entry in the woodcarving classes of the Woodworker Show. Maximum dimensions of figure carvings are 8 × 4½ × 4½in.

Attention is drawn to the conditions of entry and other details given on page 289 of WOODWORKER for May 1980; a copy of these conditions is available on application to the editor of WOODWORKER, PO Box 35 Bridge Street, Hemel Hempstead HP1 1EE.

There are particular requirements as to the packaging etc. of carvings and entrants are advised to obtain from head postmasters a copy of the leaflet *Wrap up well* which tells how parcels should be packed to minimise damage during transit.

ENTER NOW FOR THE WOODWORKER SHOW AND THE WOODWORKER/ASHLEY ILES INTERNATIONAL CARVING COMPETITION.

Judging at last year's show.

Timber Topics 10 ... *continued from page 504*

the initial rough turning could eliminate some of this, but drying of thick hardwood takes time. If this is no problem there would seem little point in using PEG. Taking a rough turned bowl, say 10in. (250mm) in diameter, well air-dried with a m.c. at this stage of 15% in oak, and expected to dry eventually to 10% m.c. and using the shrinkage guidance

already mentioned, the expected 'pull' due to shrinkage across the diameter would be equal to a change of 5% m.c. or 4mm ($\frac{5}{32}$in.) across 250mm (10in.); and that small amount is for all tangential wood which is very unlikely; the shrinkage could be less.

If, however, time is at a premium then the use of green wood treated with PEG is the

answer. And the chemical could also be used to advantage where a carver, working only at odd times on a block of wood not as dry as it might be, has to leave the work for a day or more in a warm room. Liberal brushing of the wood with a PEG solution each time the wood is left could help reduce splits and checks to a minimum.

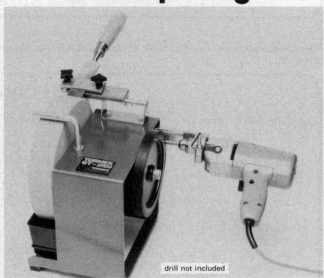
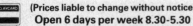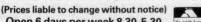

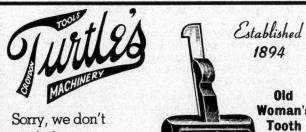

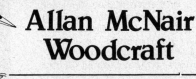

'WONDERFUL FURNITURE

R. W. Grant DLC FRSA MSIAD reviews *Gimson and the Barnsleys*, Mary Comino's account of the development and work of the two Barnsley brothers and their friend and fellow-craftsman Ernest Gimson. The book is published by Evans Brothers Ltd, Montague House, Russell Square, London WC1B 5BX, at £13.50. The jacket illustration is reproduced on the front cover of this issue of WOODWORKER.

There are uncounted hosts of books on woodworking in all of its many aspects and of these the world's most eminent library has some 450 on the specific subject of the craft itself. It would be a fair guess that comparatively few of this number deal with historical development and even fewer with the arts and crafts movement which originated in this country and which has since exerted a powerful and world-wide influence on designers and makers.

Over half a century has elapsed since the last major work on this subject was published (*Ernest Gimson – his Life and Work* (1924)) and Miss Comino's book is timely on two counts: first, a major exhibition of the work of Ernest Gimson and the Barnsley brothers was held at Cheltenham museum in 1976; the exhibition generated much interest and placed into proper perspective the importance of these three men; second, as announced in WOODWORKER for April (and discussed in detail elsewhere in this issue), the launching of the Edward Barnsley Educational Trust will hopefully secure the continuance of this magnificent heritage.

It is a curious fact of publishing life that book reviewers as often as not remain anonymous. Thus their credentials are not open to inspection. Yet we have to accept their respectability and authority. However, this reviewer has practised the tenets of the arts and crafts movement for many years and first came under the influence of Edward Barnsley (the son of Sidney) in the late 1950s, since when he has maintained a close contact with this doyen of designer-craftsmen who has assumed a position of mentor to a privileged pupil. He has also received direct instruction from one who himself was taught by Ernest Gimson's foreman Peter Waals. With a father who had met William Morris's daughter, May, on many occasions; and as a dancer with the famous Headington Quarry morris team (whose dances Gimson and his group performed and enjoyed so much along with folk dances in their Cotswold village as part of their total involvement in rural life), this reviewer feels a curious affinity with these men at many points.

Mary Comino's book is a fascinating and riveting story of unique men who left no formal writings on their art though their work bears silent witness to their modesty and genius. She has carried out an impressive piece of research and is confident in handling her material. To trace the whole life of these men must have been a formidable task.

Early chapters sketch the influences attendant upon Gimson and the Barnsleys; they were all trained as architects which may be the key to their later success in furniture designing. Architecture has been described as the mistress of the arts and that eminent first Elizabethan, Thomas Wootten, defined it as having three conditions: commodity, firmness and delight. Pugin, Ruskin and Morris at the close of the last century in orchestrating the Gothic revival and the arts and crafts movement, were all to take up this theme and this had a direct bearing on the thinking of Ernest Gimson and the two Barnsley brothers. Later chapters deal with their furniture making and designing with such thoroughness that even the methods of costing the items are considered.

While the book naturally focuses upon the three men, others who were associated with their enterprise are given due attention. Illustrations show what superb draughtsmen the three were, yet the contribution of F. L. Griggs (well-known for his brilliant illustrations in the Highways & Byways series of books published in the 1900s) is recorded, as is the work of Norman Jewson (whose own book *By Chance I did Rove*, is absorbing reading on the life of these Cotswold craftsmen).

It is pleasant also to read of those worthies who actually carried out the designs. Their names are given prominence and what a marvellous team they must have been. Too often works are ascribed to the initiator of a design, whether it be a chair or a church, and the name of the craftsman directly responsible for the realisation of the product is ignored. It has been a pleasure often to watch Edward Barnsley's own men exercising their exquisite woodworking skills. The hope is that their record may be set down at some time.

Readers will be pleased to know that Mr Barnsley has consented to some of his designs being published in future issues of WOODWORKER and thus we can all share in contemporary furniture design *par*

The jubilee cabinet *(photo Srdja Djukanovic, Daily Telegraph).*

Interior of the jubilee cabinet in figured English walnut inlaid with ebony and sycamore. Designed by Edward Barnsley and made in the Froxfield workshop by George Taylor and Herbert Upton *(photo: B. G. Burrough).*

THE EDWARD BARNSLEY EDUCATIONAL TRUST

excellence. In the development and practice of the craft Mr Barnsley has quite recently said that the past exists for the present and the present exists for the future. No doubt this sentiment would have been heartily endorsed by his father and uncle, and it gives the lie to those who claim to be making a fresh approach that owes nothing to the past; what then will future generations make of this rather absurd posture?

At £13.50 *Gimson and the Barnsleys* may be considered over-priced, but it is a rare book that will become in its time much sought after. Written from impeccable sources there are a few errors: The reader for instance will search in vain for Swaithland in Leicestershire but should be directed to Swithland as the home of the durable roofing slates mentioned in the text. The sepia reproduction (there are over 100 large photographs of designs and actual pieces of furniture) obscures something of the subtle selection of grain which was one of the hallmarks of the work of these men. And curiously there is no reference in an otherwise excellent bibliography to J. W. Mackail's standard biography of William Morris, the progenitor of many of the ideals set out in this book.

Training craftsmen to high standards

By I. G. Cleaver

The last direct link with the arts and crafts movement and the Cotswold school of furniture making, which was in serious danger of being broken, will not now be severed. The workshop of Edward Barnsley, at Froxfield, Petersfield, Hampshire, which has been producing high-quality hand-made furniture since 1923, has for some time been threatened with closure.

Edward Barnsley is 80 (WOODWORKER for April). Although he is still extremely active and vigorous, with a continuing youthful enthusiasm for producing furniture, inflation has made survival of his workshop difficult. In addition, the competition of high wages which may be earned elsewhere has made the recruitment of young apprentices almost impossible, resulting in the present workforce being reduced to one full-time craftsman who has not long finished his apprenticeship, and two part-time craftsmen (one of whom is 65 years of age).

Twenty years ago there were as many as eight craftsmen producing highly individual pieces of furniture, while in its heyday the workshop employed some 13 craftsmen including apprentices, each being responsible for making a piece of furniture from start to finish. Today these are in great demand as collectors' pieces and change hands from time to time at greatly increased prices. Although orders continue to be placed, and are sufficient for the next two years or so, the prospect of closure had become a serious possibility.

Edward Barnsley (centre left) and George Taylor discuss the jubilee cabinet in the Froxfield workshop. Far left is Oskar Dawson (65) and far right Mark Nicholas (23) the other craftsmen involved in making the cabinet *(photo: Donald C. Eades).*

Fortunately a few prominent clients and friends realising that the workshop was in jeopardy (and with Mr Barnsley's concurrence), approached the charity commissioners with a view to forming an educational trust to continue to train young craftsmen to the high standards of the workshop; and to ensure that the golden link of the chain originated by William Morris, and so faithfully carried on by his disciples Ernest Gimson and the brothers Ernest and Sidney Barnsley in their Cotswold workshops, should not be severed and perhaps lost for ever. That trust has been formed but there is still much to do before the first apprentices will be taken on.

The aims of the trust will be, broadly, to train young apprentices to a high standard of skills and design, but with a greater regard for financial parity with their skilled counterparts in industry and elsewhere; and to continue to take on pupil-apprentices who after suitable training would then set up their own small workshops, similar to the dozen or so already in existence in the country, and most of whom were former pupils of Edward Barnsley.

Mr Barnsley emphasises that the trust intends to select apprentices and pupil apprentices who are not able to pay high premiums or fees for training. He visualises that some apprentices will join his firm and so build up the number of craftsmen in Froxfield.

The latest and possibly best-known of these is Alan Peters, at present working with three assistants in Cullompton, Devon. Mr Peters was apprenticed to Barnsley for seven years before entering Shoreditch college and then the London school of arts and crafts. After a short spell of teaching, he decided that teaching was not for him so he set up his own workshop, first at Midhurst and subsequently in Cullompton. In 1979, after a year's study tour in the Far East, he won the Winsor & Newton craft award, presented in association with the Guild of Master Craftsmen, and whose outstanding ebony desk was illustrated in WOODWORKER for March 1979.

When making this award to Mr Peters, the director of the Victoria and Albert museum (Dr Roy Strong) said: . . . there is no dearth of designers, but in many skills craftsmen are in danger of becoming a dying race.' He reiterated that the demand for commissioned furniture was as great as ever. So there is no doubt at all that if the terms of the Edward Barnsley education trust are right, the future

supply of quality furniture and skilled craftsmen are assured.

As is to be expected, many of Barnsley's former pupil-apprentices have moved away from the Gimson/Barnsley tradition and have developed their own characteristic styles while still maintaining the highest standards of integrity in workmanship and materials. Barnsley himself, through force of circumstances and by drawing on his 50 years' experience as a craftsman/designer, has developed a highly-successful, individual style based on the Cotswold style. By the intelligent and controlled use of powered tools and new materials; by the introduction of curves and the fining down of wood sizes, and fusing these into his experience of the present to meet contemporary needs, he has established his reputation as the greatest living furniture designer/craftsman.

The need for the training of craftsmen and the demand for commissioned furniture in the US, has resulted in at least two schools of furniture design being established there. Two of Edward Barnsley's former pupil/apprentices, quite unknown to each other and yet only a few hours' ride apart, have founded schools of furniture design. There are Ian Kirby who has opened in Bennington, and David Powell in Easthampton. Although both were educated in design studies in British universities they received their practical training with Edward Barnsley, where they achieved high standards in craftsmanship and design, before setting up their own workshops in this country and subsequently emigrating to the US.

Both schools have been most successful and both have long waiting lists. Pupils are taken for varying periods of training from 15 weeks to three or four years according to their woodworking experience. The emphasis in both schools is on good design and meticulous craftsmanship, using the best available materials. Thus they closely follow the Barnsley concept. It is expected that pupils will, on completion of training, set up on their own or take posts as designers in industry. Those who prefer to remain in the workshops will produce commissioned furniture for Kirby and Powell, who can still find time to carry out their own commissions in addition to their teaching commitments.

On a recent visit to the Barnsley workshop at Froxfield it was apparent that while the designs have changed little basically, except that they have become much more refined and sophisticated, ingenious modifications in construction methods have been devised. Shortage of quality timbers and the effects of central heating have almost eliminated the use of solid timber today. Legs and rails of tables and chairs are now often built up of maple cores and faced with rosewood, ebony or other choice wood strips about ⅛-¼in. thick, and put together with synthetic glue in the same sequence as they are cut from the board.

Central heating has necessitated the increased use of blockboard, laminboard and chipboard, with veneers for table tops and carcase sides and ends. Bow or serpentine drawer fronts and curved stretcher rails are made up of laminations sawn out of solid wood, and glued together in the order which they were sawn out of the wood. Drawer sides and backs are often built up of plywood edged with oak or other wood.

On show in the Barnsley workshop during the trust appeal will be the jubilee cabinet (made to celebrate the 25th anniversary of the Queen's coronation). This is a writing cabinet in specially-selected English walnut with ebony and sycamore herring bone inlay.

Contrary to general practice, where one craftsman usually saw the job through from start to finish, this cabinet was the combined work of all four craftsmen who were in the workshop at the time. Barnsley considers it to be one of his most successful pieces. Because it was made for a special occasion cost was not a factor in the making; neither was it to a client's specifications. Thus Barnsley was free to use his imaginative genius without conditions. It took 900hr to make and was sold long before completion.

As always, Bert Upton, the foreman who was apprenticed with Barnsley in 1924 (and has since retired), was responsible for the selection of the walnut and the oak. As I know from personal experience Mr Upton knew exactly what to look for and where to find the highly-figured walnut used for the 13 or so panels required for the cabinet. Most of this was walnut which he had stored away for just this sort of job for upwards of 30 years.

Most of the work was carried out by Bert Upton and George Taylor who joined Barnsley as an apprentice in 1937, with Oskar Dawson turning the ivory handles and newcomer Mark Nicholas helping with the internal fittings.

Mark Nicholas (23) who began with Edward Barnsley some five years ago *(photo: Donald C. Eades).*

It is hoped that the appeal will raise £200,000. Then a teacher/manager will be appointed who will be responsible for the training of the apprentices. At the same time, the remaining full and part-time craftsmen will continue to execute the orders already commissioned. Edward Barnsley will exercise overall control and act as design consultant for the trust, a post which his 27 years as design consultant at Loughborough teachers training college from 1938-65 makes him ideally suited.

Reference has been made to George Taylor who was apprenticed to Edward Barnsley in 1937.

Ever since George Taylor started working in wood he became fascinated with it, and soon began to experiment in shaping wood as well as constructing with it. This, together with a life-long interest in wild life, led naturally to the carving of wild animals as a hobby. His work attracted the attention of a Selborne bookseller who was organising an exhibition to celebrate the 250th anniversary of the birth of the naturalist Gilbert White.

Mr Taylor supplied several carvings for that exhibition. His work attracted so much attention that he has not looked back. Orders for wild life carvings poured in and about 10 years ago he gave up working full-time for Edward Barnsley, and henceforth devoted half his time to furniture making and the other half to woodcarving.

He has extended his experience to carving in stone with great success, but still considers wood to be above all the other materials for carving. However, he enjoys making furniture so much that he does not contemplate giving it up to devote himself to full-time woodcarving.

Details of the Edward Barnsley Educational Trust (registered as a charity No. 279514) have now been issued. Patrons are Viscount Eccles, Sir Emmanuel Kaye, Sir George Trevelyan, John Barnfield, Donald Gimson, David Helling, John Minoprio and James Noel White. The trustees are Jon Barnsley, Nigel Grimwood, Gerry Jenkins and Mary Medd. Secretary to the trust is Karin Antonini, The Bee House, Cockshott Lane, Froxfield, Petersfield, Hants, from whom forms can be obtained by those wishing to contribute to the trust.

The initial target is £200,000 which would enable the trustees to embark upon the training programme. In his appeal letter Mr Jenkins also points out that Mr and Mrs Barnsley will participate in the work of the trust and will guide and influence the policy of its training programme.

Contributions may be made as donations, bankers orders or deed of covenant.

Barn owl landing. In ash about 14in. high.

Tree creeper in yew approximately 11in. high.

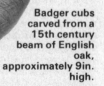

Badger cubs carved from a 15th century beam of English oak, approximately 9in. high.

Top right: George Taylor with the cabinet for the city of Portsmouth freedom scroll presented to the late Earl Mountbatten of Burma *(photo: Donald C. Eades).* All four carvings on this page are examples of George's work *(photos: Bill Wills).*

Right: Badger cleaning itself. In walnut approximately 7in. high.

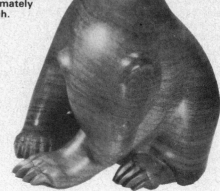

Fox in yew approximately 14in. high.

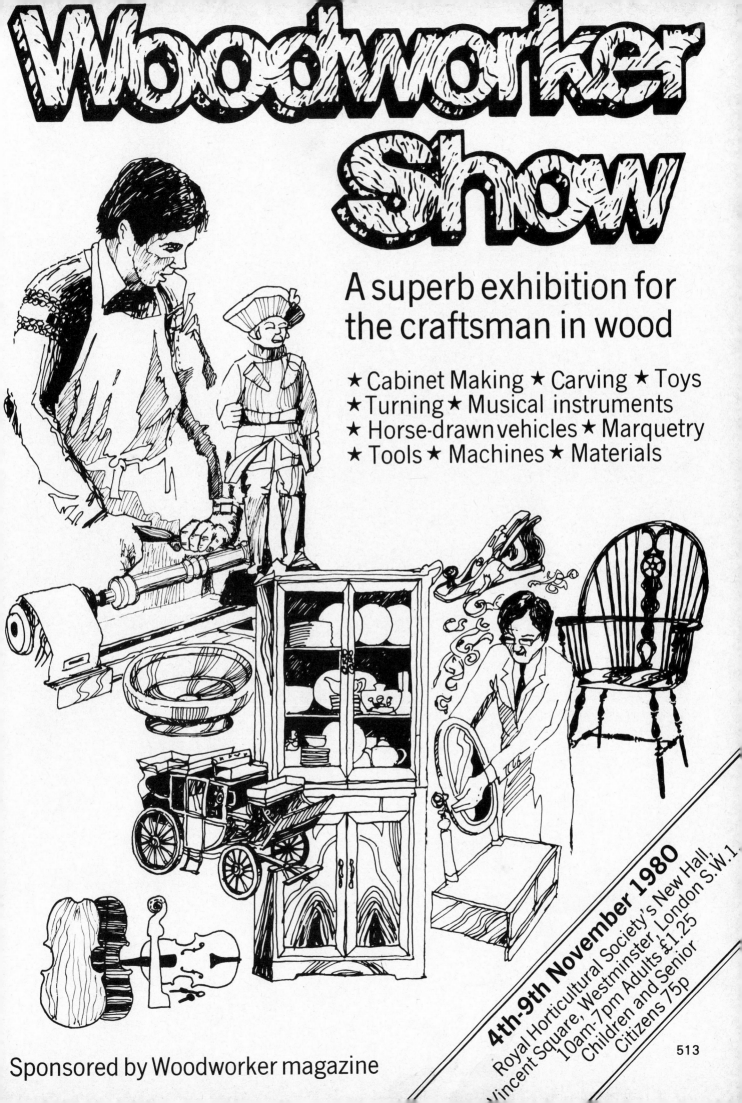

Woodworker Show

A superb exhibition for the craftsman in wood

★ Cabinet Making ★ Carving ★ Toys
★ Turning ★ Musical instruments
★ Horse-drawn vehicles ★ Marquetry
★ Tools ★ Machines ★ Materials

4th–9th November 1980
Royal Horticultural Society's New Hall,
Vincent Square, Westminster, London S.W.1
10am–7pm Adults £1.25
Children and Senior
Citizens 75p

Sponsored by Woodworker magazine

513

CORONET
WOODWORKING MACHINES

Universal & Independent models for Woodworking & Woodturning

SAWING ● BOX COMBING ● WOBBLE SAWING ● SPINDLE MOULDING ● PLANING
THICKNESSING ● REBATING ● MORTICING ● SLOTTING & GROOVING ● DISC SANDING
BELT SANDING ● GRINDING & POLISHING ● TURNING ● LONG HOLE BORING

Bench mounted
& Cabinet models
ideal for . . .
PROFESSIONALS
AND D-I-Y
ENTHUSIASTS

*Whatever woodworking
operation you need —
Coronet have the ideal machine.*

Since 1946 Coronet have achieved a world wide reputation as
leading designers and manufacturers of Quality woodworking
machines with production of castings, machining and
assembly being carried out in our modern factory — to
achieve essential standards of accuracy.
Today our extensive range includes universal machines with
fitments and attachments which can be purchased as and
when required. — to suit your particular needs.

Send Now for
BROCHURE
on all models

CORONET
TOOL CO LTD
Alfreton Road
Derby DE2 4AH

see the Coronet Range in action

—at Coronet Works and
Learn-a-Craft Training
Centre in Derby
—by arrangement
Telephone: 0332-362141

—at Stockists. Coronet
Demonstrators visit
main Stockists
throughout the year.
Send for details.

Please send me brochure, price
list & my local stockists address.
I enclose stamps, value 15p for p & p.

NAME _____

ADDRESS _____

_____

C/W 8.80

CORONET WOODWORKING MACHINES

WITH OR WITHOUT *ATTRACTIVE* **CABINET STANDS**

MAJOR Universal CMB 500

CONSORT Universal CON 403

MAJOR LATHE CMB 600

MINOR LATHE MB 6

NEW

ELF TURNING LATHE

IMP BANDSAW IMP 100

7" PLANER CAP 300

4½"
SOVEREIGN PLANER SOV 200

SOME OF OUR MAIN STOCKISTS
~full list available on application

BALLYMENA
G. Gardiner & Co. Ltd.,
49 Ballymoney Street, Ballymena,
Co. Antrim.
Tel. 0266 6384

MANCHESTER
Jos. Gleaves & Son Ltd.,
Gateway House, Piccadilly Station
Approach, Manchester.
Tel. 061 236 1840

BIGGIN HILL
Parry & Sons Ltd, 186 Main Road,
Biggin Hill, Kent.
Tel. 095 94 73777

NANTWICH
Alan Holtham,
The Old Stores Turnery, Wistaston
Road, Willaston, Nantwich.
Tel. 0270 67010

CARDIFF
Woodmen,
43b Crwys Road,
Cathays, Cardiff.
Tel. 0222 36519

PETERBOROUGH
Williams Distributors,
108-110 Burghley Road, Peterb
Tel. 0733 64252

DUBLIN
J. J. McQuillan & Son Ltd.,
35-36 Capel Street,
Dublin, Eire.
Tel. 0001 746745

READING
Sarjents Tool Stores,
44-52 Oxford Road, Reading.
Tel. 0734 586522

EXETER
John Wride & Co. Ltd.,
147 Fore Street,
Exeter, Devon.
Tel. 0392 73936

SOUTHAMPTON
Hampshire Woodworking
Machinery, Hoe Farm House,
Hoe Lane, Bishop Waltham,
Hants.
Tel. (04893) 2275

HARROGATE
Multi-Tools of Harrogate
158 Kings Road,
Harrogate, NTH, Yorks.
Tel. 0423 66245

WATFORD
J. Simble & Sons Ltd.,
76 Queen's Road, Watford,
Herts.
Tel. 0923 26052

PRACTICAL COURSES
in WOODMACHINING AND WOODTURNING
for owners or intending purchasers of

Universal WOODWORKING MACHINES & LATHES

GAIN PRACTICAL EXPERIENCE UNDER EXPERT GUIDANCE

The Courses, in our modern, fully equipped Training School offer tuition in the use of Woodworking machines — for owners, stockists, instructors and trainee tradesmen. Regular (½ / 1 / 1 ½ and 2 day) courses cover a wide range of woodworking operations, with individual tuition in woodmachining & woodturning on universal & independent machines. Courses are for day visitors or residential.

Send coupon or phone for details
LEARN-A-CRAFT LTD.
Monk St., Derby. Tel: 0332-364384

LEARN A CRAFT

NAME _____
ADDRESS _____
_____
_____

LEARN A CRAFT

LC/W 8.80

Join the Professionals with an EMCO woodworking machine

Letters

From: Peter Child, The Olde Hyde, Little Yeldham, Halstead CO9 4QT
Dear Sir,

Referring to Roy H. Mansfield's enquiry in Question Box (page 401 of the June 1980 issue), we have been selling hardwood discs coated with wax for many years and it could be that we are his 'reliable source.'

The coating is paraffin wax (which we also supply) and our method is to melt a quantity in a shallow metal rectangular trough 24 × 10in. heated by a Calor gas burner underneath. The level of melted wax is kept topped-up to between ½ and 1in. deep. Precautions are, of course, taken to prevent the wax catching fire.

Discs are rolled in the wax to coat the whole edge. Not too quickly or the wax will not have time to soak into the grain; and too thin a coat will flake off later. The circular faces are left exposed (Fig. 1).

rosewood, lignum vitae and other valuable hardwood. Up to now we have been fully successful. The wax must be applied *immediately* after cutting. If small checks have already developed the wax stops them from spreading.

Frequently we are asked how to season small logs of fruitwood etc. for turning. These should be cut with a chainsaw into just over the finished dimensions required and the ends waxed immediately. The centre of the pith must not be contained within any piece but is permitted if it appears on the surface (Fig. 2).

Yours faithfully, **Peter Child**

From: W. E. Whitehead, Bedford
Dear Sir

Re R. R. Gillies' enquiry on sharpening the blades used in trimming knives (WOOD-WORKER for June, page 393), if you can get a yellow razor stone it is simple. If the knife is bad a few rubs on a finishing stone as used for chisels, then a rub on the razor stone — and you are there. I use this way to sharpen surgeons' scalpels and it works on most edge tools (razors great!)

Yours faithfully, **W. E. Whitehead**

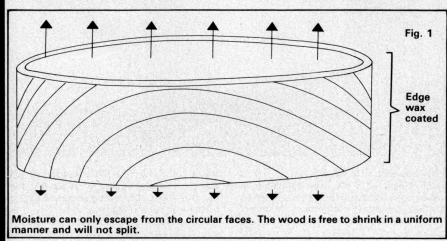

Fig. 1

Edge wax coated

Moisture can only escape from the circular faces. The wood is free to shrink in a uniform manner and will not split.

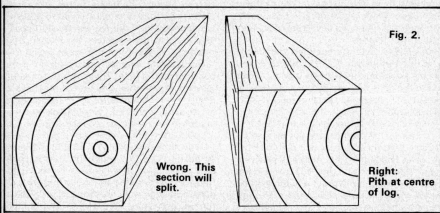

Fig. 2.

Wrong. This section will split.

Right: Pith at centre of log.

Since the wax prevents moisture leaving the edges the disc loses it evenly from all parts of the faces so shakes do not develop from the centre. The discs can be cut from the wettest of timber but will season to perfection with only a negligible risk of splits developing. We cut many hundreds and lose less than 1% due to checking.

We treat the end grain of square-section timber similarly. Because the wood is cut to relatively small dimensions before seasoning we get less wastage due to internal building stresses than if we seasoned in-plank in the conventional way. Seasoning square-section timber is also much quicker. We treat all our timber including our growing stocks of ebony,

From: F. T. Kettle, Northolt, Middlesex
Dear Sir,

I am a very new reader (and also a member of Guild of Woodworkers) and have made use of the services of advertiser Brian J. Bowman, the engraver of Cheddar, Somerset. It was only a small order but the thought and attention given to it pleased me very much — as did the finished article.

If the rest of the advertisers in WOOD-WORKER are up to the same standard, the magazine is to be congratulated.

Yours faithfully, **F. T. Kettle**

course at an establishment like Rycotewood or similar college, evening classes leading to a certificate, courses like the City and Guilds courses; would all he feels he a great help when trying for a Crafts Advisory Council, Area Arts Association or some other form of grant or loan. Without any formal qualification it seems to be a very hard task to convice any committee that has funds available. The chance of being a supervisor at an evening class might also be easier and this would provide a regular further source of income.

Promotion of one's self is difficult, the confidence to know that if the work really is good it will sell sooner or later is important.

Current pressures on galleries and shops to buy work suggests an insecurity on the part of the craftsman regarding its saleability. David and Jean have none of this insecurity, they know their work is good. They do not feel the embarrassment about pricing that many craftsmen feel. A realistic price is charged that reflects the work involved and the quality of that work without overpricing. Embarrassment only leads to apologetic prices guaranteeing the impossibility of earning a living. Why should the words 'craft' and 'homemade' or 'handmade' immediately make some people think of cheapness or inferior workmanship. That because it is 'crafty' it can therefore be obtained at a ridiculously low price. Many of the callers at David's workshop almost expect him to give

Left: Church pew in English oak, stained and wax polished. Below: English oak corner cabinet with linseed oil finish. *(Photos: P. A. L. Brunney).*

An odd sort of quote perhaps to start a short review of a furniture exhibition in Cambridge and a business which is based on the Essex border. The 3rd floor of the central library in Lion Yard, Cambridge, was the spacious, neutral setting for 'Wood and ceramics' an exhibition held in May by David and Jean Whitaker (furniture and woodturning) and Alan Foxley (ceramics, porcelain, stoneware).

David and Jean started their handmade furniture business in 1977. When David left school he wanted to become a boat builder but in the early 50s met parental opposition. Freelance enterprise at this period was looked upon as 'dropping out'. However, David managed to combine making racing dinghies for his friends, for his own satisfaction, with the business world of the P&O group in London, for his mother's peace of mind. Changes within the P&O group in the early '70s brought threats of redundancy and when these materialised David and Jean decided after a lot of soul searching and very hard thinking to translate 'if only' into reality and 'go it alone'.

Jean soon became a competent woodturner quite a necessity since requests for tables with turned legs started to come in. She modestly claims that pottery evening classes gave her the feel of turning 'in the round' so it wasn't too difficult to learn. A pupil of Fred Pain's gave her the benefit of his advice and instruction and Jean admits to still returning for advice on the odd occasion. She uses a Myford ML8 lathe and produces turnery in elm and oak. She makes all the knobs, door handles and fittings for her husband's cabinet work. With two small children she was more or less housebound anyway and so has been able to work during the odd 'free'

hours for some time. A measure of the success she is achieving is reflected in the fact that she is now talking of concentrating full time on her turning.

Her contribution to the exhibition included elm table-ware (salad bowls, side bowls, cheese platters, barbecue plates and small platters finished with paraffin oil to prevent contamination), three-legged stools (in oak, ash and elm), table lighters, barometers and maritime clocks plus the most delightful Victorian-style circular foot-stools in wax-polished oak or elm. These 13in. diameter foot-stools with their tiny turned feet have a domed centre suitable for one's own design of tapestry work, but would look equally attractive with velvet or regency striped tops.

David and Jean started their business in a garage-workshop adjacent to their cottage. At present this has expanded to workshop and woodstore. David hopes in the near future to combine the workshop and store to make one large work area; he will then add a further woodstore at the rear. The double doors of his garage have been removed and replaced with a very attractive display window.

His philosophy is, buy as you need, expand when necessary; as a cabinetmaking friend of his in the Lake District, Peter Hall, wisely counselled him at the start of his venture: *'You* can go without food, your bank manager *cannot* go without money.' David started small with a loan from a sympathetic bank manager, since he was unable to get support elsewhere due to the fact that he would not be able to expand fast or support apprentices.

If he was thinking of starting now, in the light of his experiences over the past three years, he would approach things differently. Formal qualifications, such as a two-year

comfortable'

his work away because it has been made 'at home' so to speak.

Craftsmen have to be realistic business-men. Motivation leads to money: producing quickly enough to eat while concentrating on enjoying the challenge and the problem can often be self-defeating.

Breaking into the woodturning market is hard; there are many, many wood turners. Cultivation of a warm responsive relation-ship with timber merchants is very important. David often travels miles to find just the right piece of timber, often calls in on his suppliers when he is passing just to chat in the hope that when they have what he requires they will take the initiative and phone him. Timber prices vary considerably, generally being cheaper as one moves away from London, quality also varies. A con-tinuing regular supply and stock of sound timber is the life blood of a cabinetmaker.

David turns his precious 'spare' capital into timber stocks — a wise precaution with rising and fluctuating supplies. He prefers his wood air-dried if he can obtain it, air-dried oak is excellent for the style of chairs he makes, no movement occurs at the joints; some kiln-dried wood can be very hard on bandsaw blades, he says. But for tables there is no alternative but to use kiln-dried timber.

Believing in only adding machinery when necessary, David's power tool collection may seem modest when one appreciates what he achieves with it, but each piece has been chosen mainly from H.B. Woodworking, Cambridge with extreme care and a lot of homework. He has a Kity spindle moulder, Kity planer, DeWalt bandsaw, Elu bench grinder, Myford ML8 lathe, and latest and at present favourite addition, a mortiser from Modern Woodworking Machinery of Lutter-worth. This has cut out the slog of hand mor-tising which previously took up a lot of time.

David describes his furniture as 20th century styled traditional. All furniture is an evolution of earlier styles, no piece can be said to have evolved independently — his slat back and rush seated chairs are obvious extensions of the country styles so ably described in earlier issues of WOOD-WORKER by Jack Hill; but they have a modern, clean, streamlined feel about them while still possessing a timeless quality.

The exhibition featured among other things an English oak refectory table, corner cabinet and many chairs both rush seated, upholstered and in hide. Unfortunately due to the lack of service lift some of the more beautiful larger pieces, like a circular table (the design of which was recently approved by one of England's well-known furniture-makers) could not be displayed and David had to rely on scale models to show more of his range. A great pity.

He had sold a coffee table in oak to a customer in a wheelchair since it was slightly higher than the conventional coffee table but lower than a dining table. A case of unintentional customising. The quote at the start of this article came from a local reverend gentleman who ordered chairs for the parish council rooms. After sitting in one of David's chairs and wriggling about he declared 'Yes, just right, it's not too comfort-able — they won't fall asleep but on the other hand they will be well enough seated to con-tribute to the meeting.' This resulted in an order for four more chairs. More ecclesias-tical commissions have followed including the small pew featured here (p.518). All David's furniture in oak and ash, other than chairs, is priced on an individual commission basis, details available on request.

All furniture is made from solid timber so grain and colour variation do occur but pieces ordered together are matched as nearly as possible. Most work is undertaken in elm, ash or oak but prices for other timbers can be given on request. Sizes of any table, refectory, trestle, circular, can be altered to suit individual requirements. Other pieces are made to commission and enquiries are welcome, delivery is dependent on a number of factors but the normal period is 10-16 weeks, 25% deposit is needed to confirm orders and charges do have to be made for delivery.

Rush seated elm dining chair.
(Photo: P. A. L. Brunney).

Above: Slat back dining chair in elm (Photo: P. A. L. Brunney). **Below: David cramping dresser door frame in his workshop.** (Photo: Ciba-Geigy).

All enquiries should be addressed to either David or Jean Whitaker, Frogge Cottage, 48 Frogge Street, Ickleton, Saffron Walden, Essex (phone Great Chesterford 304).

LIVING CRAFTS '80

The sixth in the series of annual 'Living Crafts' exhibitions took place in the beautiful grounds of Hatfield house, Herts, in early May. Some 200 specialised and professional craftsmen, from many English counties were demonstrating more than 80 different craft skills, some of which date back to Anglo-Saxon times. One such ancient and now rarely practised craft, the weaving of willow basketry was shown by a Cambridgeshire lady Jane Greening. Her busy workshop is an old barn close to fen country and the special types of willows she uses — almond willow (*Salix triandra*) and purple osier (*Salix purpurea*) are purpose-grown on Somerset marshland between the rivers Parrett, Yeo and Tone (WOODWORKER for July 1979). Her strong, withy, many-patterned basketry — in white, buff or brown — is much sought after for cribs and hampers, baskets for cats, fishing, fruit and vegetables.

Among this year's exhibitors was Hampshire wood sculptor Derek George, who specialises in bird sculpture. His Dartford Warbler in New Forest oak was presented to HM the Queen when she visited the New Forest last year. He had on show a swan which won the approval of Peter Scott and which was to be auctioned at Slimbridge to raise funds. Mr. George says that as a wood sculptor, it is the life rings of the tree with their varying patterns that inspire his work. Many hours, sometimes days, are spent searching forest land for wood, followed by endless sawing to discover that unique marking in the grain that will harmonise with his next subject. It is rather like searching for the pearl in the oyster; this anticipation of discovery is exciting. Most of Mr George's sculpting is carried out with a knife, followed by hours of sanding and polishing to bring out the grain. He has a studio in Stubbington, Hants.

George York & Son, Long Buckby, were making high-class bespoke footwear; they supply boots to members of the Pytchley Hunt and also still make thatcher's leggings.

Joiner and carpenter H. Wakefield of Fishtoft, Boston, has added a new skill to his repertoire: he now makes traditional-style rocking horses carved from solid timber and finished with leather saddles and harness. The traditional style rockers are in ash and painted to match the horse. Mr Wakefield started work as an apprentice wheelwright near Boston, 'though I never made a complete carriage, and rubber tyres and modern wheels meant that wheelwrighting could no longer supply a living', he said. In 1977 he diversified and started making rocking horses to commission . . . they take about 80-100 hours to complete.

Mr Wakefield likes to use lime or jelutong for the head and makes the body from either pine or jelutong. His manes are very realistically set into the arch of the neck: made from real horsehair they are individually glued into place, tails are often a cow's tail and again authentic. Though a sturdy product capable of providing a family heirloom with 'years of nursery riding', his horses have a delicate quality about them which is instantly appealing.

Next to Mr Wakefield enchanting Victorian action toys were being made by husband and wife team Neil and Lorraine Chapman of Houghton. Basil Kassanis of Harpenden, Herts, was sculpturing bas-reliefs in elm and chestnut, and next to him in the Old Palace stables John Halford of Stubbington, Hants, was making his scale models of antique farm implements, farm waggons, carts and ploughs some of which are only seen today in museums.

Mr Fox of Fowlmere Joinery, had a drop front bureau and cupboard/bookcase on display. His workshop is at Fowlmere, near Royston. Mr Wilde of Benson, Oxford, was exhibiting his beautiful marquetry again;

Ralph Hentall, a regular to Hatfield, was carving his traditional lovespoons and Ralph Bridgeman was again showing his ability as cabinet maker and joiner. He now has a display of his work and other crafts at The Craft Centre, 1 New Road, Ware.

In the solar room we found Robert Longstaff from Woking, making and showing his many types of ancient musical instruments. Included in his catalogue are various harps, three styles of hurdy gurdy, a lute, cittern, medieval fiddle, rebec, appalachian dulcimer in triangular or waisted design, two styles of plucked psaltery, two versions of bowed psaltery, hammered dulcimer, tamborin, several seizes and types of tabor, a bodhran and a kantele which is loosely based on the Finnish kantele with 15 strings. Many of these instruments are available in kit form only requiring diy tools to assemble them plus glue and varnish. Materials, parts and accessories are available from the extensive workshops at Southill Park Arts Centre, Bracknell.

We were pleased to meet Robert Turner of Sandon, near Buntingford, who was introducing his new range of reproduction furniture, veneered in mahogany, all drawers being made from solid mahogany dovetailed together and designed for use in lounge, hall or bedroom. At present Mr Turner employs two apprentices who left school after 'O' levels and now at 17+ and 18 attend day-release courses at the London College of Furniture. They have embarked on the traditional four year apprenticeship as yet not joined by Mr Turner's 10-year-old son, but who knows? Besides the range of furniture

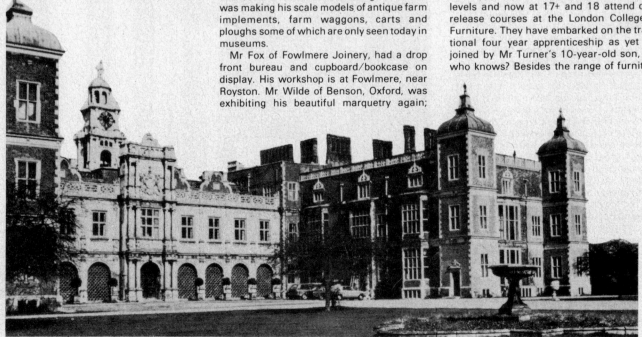

mentioned above he also makes typical fine English clocks of the style fashionable between 1700 and 1750, in oak, mahogany or walnut into which he can fit a selection of movements, dials and chimes. Each clock is marked and dated individually and retails at around £1,700. Restoration work is also covered by this enterprising small firm.

We were delighted to make the acquaintance of Brian Bostock. He won a prize in last year's Woodworker Show in the cabinetmaking class and now runs his own workshop, just off Green Lanes (five minutes from the Wood Green shopping centre in London N8). Mr Bostock produces a variety of furniture using hand-making methods and specialises in designing to individual client's requirements for the home, for presentation and for churches. He will undertake complete schemes of interior design, picture framing and antique furniture restoration. Smaller items of woodcraft and turnery are in regular production in his workshop where visitors are very welcome (a telephone call is appreciated 01-341 2511).

A new venture for Mr Bostock is the holding of one-day cabinetmaking teach-ins in his workshop. The aim being to provide a group of similarly interested people with the opportunity to learn traditional methods of hand cabinetmaking. Each course is self-contained but all are arranged to complement each other.

20 September: Table and frame making; 27 September: Carcase construction; 4 October: Drawer making; 11 October: Chair making.

Full details of the courses can be obtained from Brian Bostock, Bostock Woodcraft Ltd, 5 Fairfax Mews, Fairfax Road, London N8 0NH (01-341 2511). Lunch is provided, courses are limited to six persons and costs are in the order of £25. Individual assistance will be attempted if people wish it on specific personal woodworking problems.

Many of Hatfield's regular exhibitors were also present and we were pleased to see Alan Duncan, (woodcarving); John Hill (brushes); Martin Hazelwood (sculpture); Absalom Cottrell (besoms); David Gratch (woodturnery and furniture); and many others again. As always the fine weather brought out the crowds and the queues! It all seems to have been good for business. See you again next year.

Top: Basket making by Periwinkle Crafts from Dry Drayton, Cambs. Above: Robert Longstaff from Woking with some of his range of ancient musical instruments including bowed psaltery (front) and pochette (top right). Below: Robert Turner of Sandon gets on with drawing his reproduction furniture plans oblivious of the visitors to his stand.

Craftsman at work

Charles Johnston, of Wrea Green will be making and repairing violins, cellos, viols and lutes in the Craftsman at work series at Samlesbury Hall, Preston, Lancs, 11.30 to 5p.m. from July 22 to 27. Musical instrument making materials will also be on sale.

Carving and turning

8-9 August Woodcarving and woodturning spectacular at the Old Stores Turnery, Wistaston Road, Willaston, Nantwich, Cheshire, 9.30am to 5.30pm each day. Alan Holtham, proprietor of the Old Stores Turnery, in conjunction with Henry Taylor (Tools) Ltd of Sheffield, is holding demonstrations and exhibitions of work. Several professional carvers and turners will show their skills and there will be special displays of Taylor tools. The company's representatives will be present to discuss visitors' requirements and to advise on selection.

Design Council awards

Until 9 August at the Scottish Design Centre, 72 St Vincent Street, Glasgow.

Furniture projects

Summer exhibitions this year at the Crafts Council Gallery, 12 Waterloo Place, Lower Regent Street, London SW1 (nearest underground Piccadilly Circus) include: until 2 August Erik de Graaf, and from 9 to 30 August David Colwell, both furniture makers who studied at the Royal College of Art.

Craftsmanship 1980

Until the 31 August organised by the Cornwall Crafts Association at Trelowarren, Mawgan-in-Meneage, Cornwall.

Svensk Form

Continuing its series of contemporary design exhibitions the Victoria and Albert museum is presenting Svensk Form, an exhibition of craft and design, organised by the Swedish Society of Industrial Design for the Swedish Institute. The exhibition will focus on the caring aspects of design and there will also be a small mixed display of items of Swedish design from the '30s to the '70s drawn from the museum's own collections on show during the exhibition (outside the lecture theatre, room 66.) Location of main exhibition, 48E, admission 50p, children, OAPs and students 25p, party rate 25p each; family Saturdays, adults 30p, children, students and OAPs 25p. Open until 14 September.

Southern Counties Craft Market

The seventh exhibition and craft market will take place at the Maltings, Farnham, Surrey, from 10-12 October.

Eastern Counties Craft Market

The ninth craft market will be held at the Rhodes Centre, Bishops Stortford, Herts; from 14-16 November. Further details from Patricia Beswick, Thele, Great Amwell, Ware SG12 9RT.

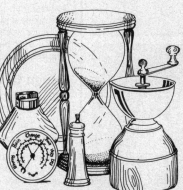

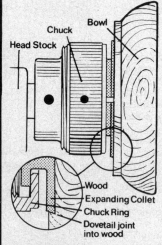

522   Prices quoted are those prevailing at press date and are subject to alteration due to economic conditions.

GETTING BACK THE PROFILE

Fig. 1 Rounded profile of a neglected chisel.

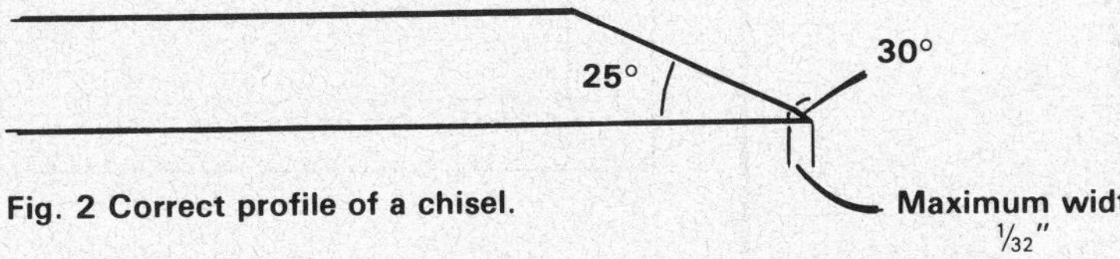

Ian Thwaites tells how he hand-ground a set of chisels

I inherited a set of six chisels which had been wrongly sharpened and had the rounded profile shown in Fig. 1. I made enquiries about the cost of grinding, sharpening and honing the set but as this was considerable I decided to try and do the job myself.

I would need a grinder but decided the expense of this did not justify my requirement. Instead I chucked a grinding wheel in my power drill mounted on a bench stand of the horizontal variety. Then came a hitch. I do not have a permanent workshop. The weather was cold so I would have to do the work indoors but my family could not be expected to put up with the noise of the drill running for long periods.

So I went to hand-working. I removed the breast-piece from a breast drill and secured the drill in my Workmate (see photo). The drill has a high-ratio gear and although the work took longer and was spread over a period of time the arrangement worked well — and avoided domestic discord! There was another plus-point: the grinding wheel revolved more slowly than if it had been chucked in the power drill, so less heat was generated in the tool being sharpened. (More about this later).

In WOODWORKER for July 1975 on pages 205-6 there was an article setting out the correct profile and angles for a chisel (Fig. 2) which also described a rather unusual sharpening action developed by Walter Holland to help maintain the correct chisel profile more easily than the conventional grip. I tried this method and found it suited me very well.

The basic bevel angle of a chisel should be 25° while the cutting angle should be 30°. For best results and a long-lasting sharp edge the cutting bevel should not exceed 1/32 in. To achieve these angles accurately a carpenter's bevel gauge is used. This can be set to the required angles by using a protractor but to make it easier and facilitate quicker setting in the future I cut the jig shown in Fig. 3 from strip wood, making sure that the long sides were parallel and cutting one short side to 25° and the other short side to 30°.

The jig doubled as a honing guide when held against the oilstone (Fig. 4). Once the correct angle had been set at the beginning of the sharpening action it was not difficult to maintain throughout the entire action. With experience the correct angle can be found on the oilstone without using the jig, though I checked back from time to time. I placed the jig on the stone, held the chisel up against it and removed the jig. Sharpening could then begin as usual.

To grind to the correct 25° took a long time. I soon discovered that a good light was necessary, especially when checking against the gauge. I also wore eye protection against metal particles and sparks.

Earlier I mentioned heat generated in the tool being sharpened. If the tip gets too hot the temper is 'drawn' with the result that it will not be so easy to sharpen and will not hold a keen edge for very long. As soon as a chisel became slightly warm I took it from the wheel and allowed it to cool off. I kept three

Fig. 2 Correct profile of a chisel.

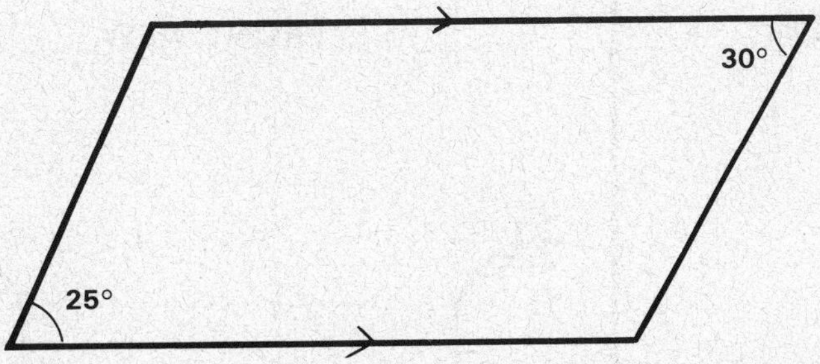

Fig. 3 Simple jig cut from stripwood

Maximum width 1/32"

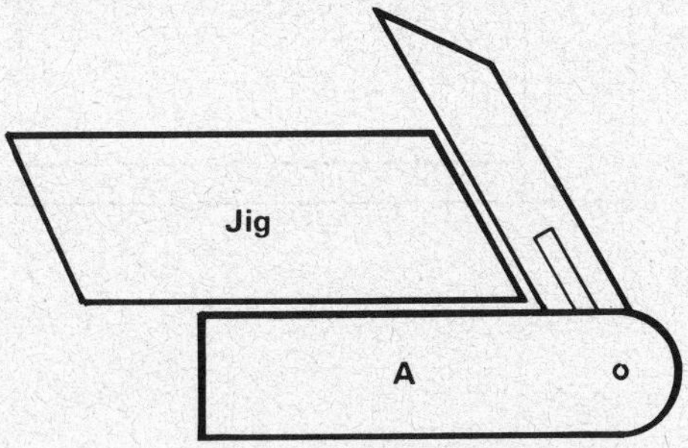

Fig. 4 Using jig (A) to set bevel gauge (B) as honing guide

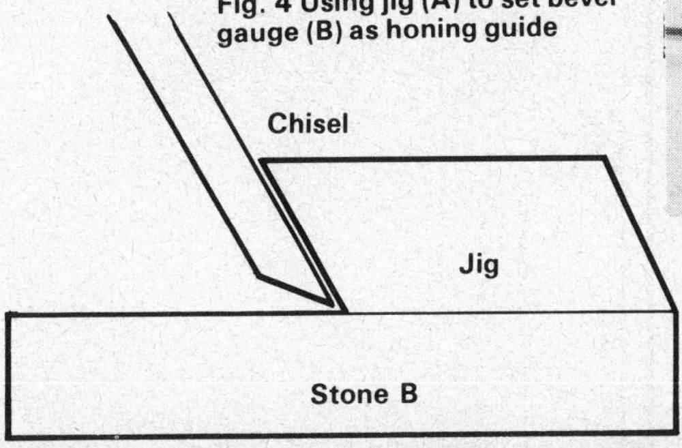

Jig

Chisel

Jig

Stone B

Above: checking chisel against carpenter's bevel gauge set to correct angle. Below: breast drill with grinding wheel in chuck.

chisels on the go: I ground the first a little then put it down and went on to the second and then the third, doing a little at a time and constantly checking. When nearing the correct profile I worked even more slowly and carefully. I checked each chisel not only against the bevel but against a small square to ensure that the working edge was not running off at an angle.

I shaped the final cutting edge by having a brief go on the wheel then honing on the oilstone. It took longer than just 'topping-up' in the normal way but it achieved a keen edge. I kept a piece of scrap wood handy to try out the chisels from time to time.

All in all I found the job worthwhile though time-consuming. It was not as difficult as I had anticipated and it taught me one thing at least: never to let a chisel of mine develop a rounded profile!

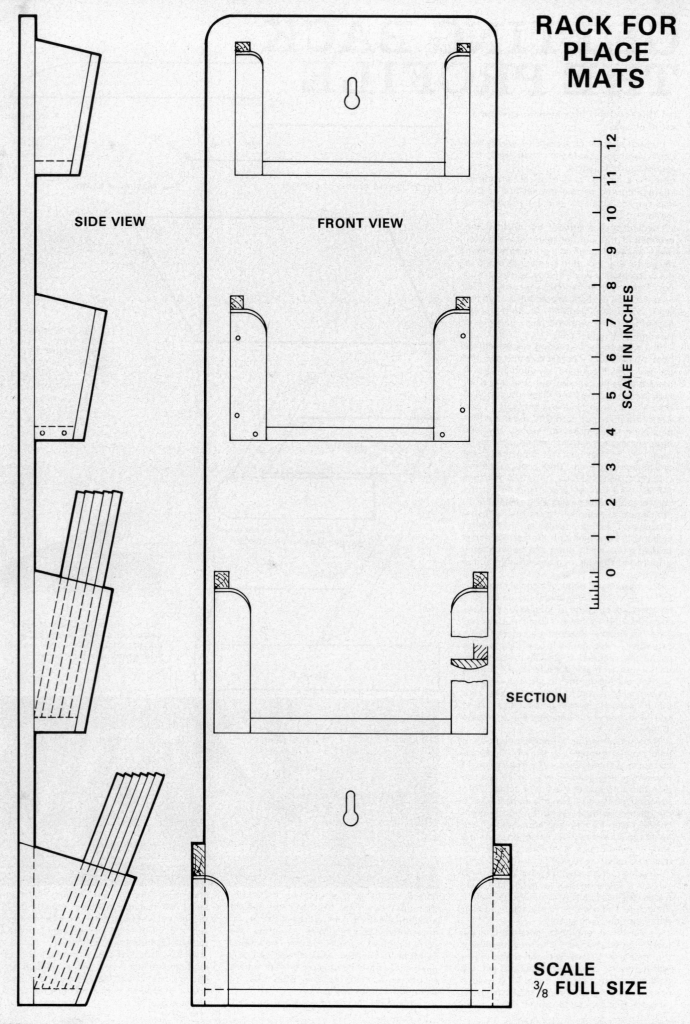

RACK FOR PLACE MATS

SIDE VIEW

FRONT VIEW

SCALE IN INCHES

SECTION

SCALE
⅜ FULL SIZE

RACK FOR MATS

Hugh Blogg makes a rack for place mats and tells about Dorothy Forster's ghost

'Many place mats are adorned with pictures of charm and beauty and it seems a shame to hide them away in a drawer', writes Hugh Blogg, Kingsgate, Broadstairs.

'An idea and design of mine is the rack for place mats (or whatever you like to call them). The construction of the rack is elementary — made from short ends or small offcuts, with simple butt joints glued and pinned'.

Mr Blogg suggests the rack is not only convenient but it provides a colourful and decorative addition to the kitchen, as well as a reminder of scenes and places visited. 'As the eye catches such a picture, the burden of washing-up can be illumined by a happy recollection', he writes, adding that Mrs Blogg almost invariably will have her favourite mat showing the historic Lord Crewe Arms at Blanchland in her native north.

'There is little point in giving all the detailed measurements because these will be determined by the sizes of mats used in makers' households. It is the sort of job easily made by any woodworker of moderate skill, who is termed in the US a 'Sunday carpenter'!

'The back is from a piece of yellow pine reclaimed from the drawer bottom of old furniture. Other parts are from oddments of waste. The front pieces that retain the mats in the pockets are from a spare length of flattish ovolo moulding.

'Every joint is a butt joint and so long as the facing surfaces are planed square and true, glued with Resin W and pinned (using panel or veneer pins), the job will remain strong and sound for long service.

'The pinheads were set down with a fine pin punch and the holes stopped with plaster-of-Paris coloured in accordance with the intended finished colour, which in this case was Vandyke brown.

'It pays to set out the profile or side view of the job in pencil, exactly as a cabinet maker will lay out his design on what is known as a "rod", full-size.

'This can be done on plywood, hardboard or a sheet of newspaper. Parcel the mats together in their respective sizes and stand the parcel on the rod to give the sizes and slopes of the various pockets, leaving ample space for easy removal and replacement of the mats.

'Make the complete pockets first, checking for winding before fixing them to the back. The slotted screw holes provide for the hanging on the wall, using a couple of gauge 10 countersink or roundhead screws.

'Painting or staining is needed to finish the rack to a uniform colour if it is made from a variety of woods.

'I first wet the whole job with hot water. When it was dry I cut down, using fine glass-paper, all the surface fibres that had stood up for a drink! I made up one of the most commonly-used stains by french polishers (an aqueous solution of Vandyke brown powder) which I again applied hot. After another light cutting down when the job was thoroughly dry, I gave it several coats of thin shellac brushed on, cutting down between coats with spent fine glasspaper.'

Footnote: The Lord Crewe Arms hotel is named after Nathaniel, Lord Crewe who was a prince-bishop of Durham in the 18th century. The building is an ancient one and is reputed to have a priest's hole hiding place used as a sanctuary during the border raids. The hotel is said to have a ghost — that of Dorothy Forster whose family had owned the property from the 16th century. During the 1715 rising her brother Thomas supported the Jacobite cause but was captured by the Hanoverian faction and taken to Newgate jail in London to await trial.

Dorothy with the aid of a local blacksmith managed to make a key to her brother's cell which she took to London and cleverly arranged his escape, brought him back and hid him in the priest's hole when danger threatened until he was able to escape to France. She married the blacksmith, heard no more of her brother but after her death her ghost sought word of him from guests occupying her old room, drawing attention by tugging at the counterpane of the bed!

Lord Crewe married into the Forster family. His bride was another Dorothy Forster and according to a local guide book there is some confusion as to which Dorothy it is who haunts the place.

When the editor stayed at the hotel some years ago he was not awakened by a tugging at the counterpane but was somewhat taken aback on going into one of the very long corridors to see a figure emerging from what appeared to be a solid wall at the far end. The figure had a familiar look. It was the editor's reflection in a very large mirror which at first glance could be taken for a window. This happened before breakfast, not after dinner!

Woodworker, August 1980

Musical instrument course

From September an all-year round course on a two-day basis covering the design and construction of musical instruments is being organised in Norfolk. A. C. Highfield, principal of A. Highfield & Co, Rosewood House, Bridge Road, Downham Market PE38 0AE, tells WOODWORKER that the subjects covered will include: types and properties of timbers; soundboards and resonance; finger-board design and fretting; bending timbers; assembly methods using moulds, clamps and specialist adhesives.

Intended primarily for beginners the course is on a practical level with special attention being given to instruments such as dulcimers, harps, mandolins etc. Mr Highfield says there will be a maximum of two students on any one course so tuition will be very much 'on a one-to-one basis. At the end of a course the students will be in possession of a hand-made instrument of good appearance and tonal quality.'

For further details write to Mr Highfield at the address given above.

Craftsmen you can see

More than 800 different craft workshops and retail shops are listed in the second impression of the 18th edition of *Craft Workshops in the English Countryside* published by the Council for Small Industries in Rural Areas (CoSIRA) at £1.25 plus 30p postage and packing. The guide has an index of products; and the workshops and retail shops, with information about the items made and sold, are listed in ABC order by counties.

Copies of the guide can be had from CoSIRA publications department at 141 Castle Street, Salisbury SP1 3TP.

Getting down at Brass Tacks

Brass Tacks, described as London's first multi-purpose community workshop, collects unwanted furniture (and domestic electrical appliances) to 'recycle' and sell in its own shop. For the time being collection is limited to east London. Brass Tacks provides work for 20 long-term unemployed people in the 19-24 age group who are being instructed by skilled supervisors. Practical experience is supplemented by day-release schemes to colleges where possible.

The project has been initiated by the Mutual Aid Centre, 18 Victoria Park Square, London E2 9PF. Manager is Brian Dean with Huw Roberts and John Pratt as furniture restoration supervisors and Norman Bright supervising upholstery work.

It is hoped that Brass Tacks will hold open evenings when people from the Dalston area of east London can use the workshop's tools and facilities to do their own restoration under expert supervision. For more details telephone Mr Dean on 01-249 9461.

Craft teaching

Readers have enquired about the publications mentioned in the article on page 238 of the April 1980 issue (Nesting box for wild birds). Author Tom Pettit says that these are: *Teaching Craft, Design & Technology* and *Design Education at Secondary Level*. The former is available free of charge from Room 2/11 Elizabeth House, Department of Education & Science, York Road, London SE1 7PH. The latter is issued by The Design Council Education Service, 28 Haymarket, London SW1Y 4SU. At the time of writing the article the latter was a consultative document only. The final paper is due during this year.

'AS MUCH AS NECESSARY'

This is always the aim in storekeeping and as production costs continue to rise guesswork has to be eliminated. Eugen Lutz GmbH makes extensive use of computers in many operations

Almost in the shadow of the Schwarzwald the main factory of Eugen Lutz is at Mülacker-Lomersheim in the state of Baden-Württemberg. From such a thickly-wooded area it is appropriate that a wide range of portable power tools for woodworking (and also metalworking, plastics and catering) should be produced to be marketed through the Elu international chain of 12 subsidiaries and 40 general agencies.

Recently WOODWORKER visited the Mülacker factory which was set up in 1928 to make light alloy castings. After the war production was extended to portable circular saws, routers and other tools and today Elu has a highly sophisticated organisation in which computers are widely used for the numerical control of machining functions and for monitoring and calculating stock levels. At the main works the central stores has no less than 20,000 storage spaces serviced by robots controlled by computer. This, says the management, helps to realise the aim in storekeeping which is 'as much as necessary but as little as possible.'

Computer links co-ordinate the work of the various manufacturing plants in Europe into a common production programme and there is a network integrating the nine European subsidiaries. Book-keeping and management functions, sales and administration are also computerised. All this, says Elu, 'helps to maintain a satisfactory cost structure — much to the advantage of our customers.'

In addition to the Mülacker factory there are plants at Dornhan (Germany), Betschdorf in France and Twinsburg in Ohio. A new factory for diecastings is now being commissioned at West Berlin.

Below left:
Automatic stock system at the central stores; there are 20,000 storage spaces serviced by this computer-controlled carriage.
Below right:
This machine presses stators and armatures from steel strip.
Bottom left:
Diecasting aluminium and zinc for baseplates and other components.
Bottom right:
Stators and armatures are wound on this machine.

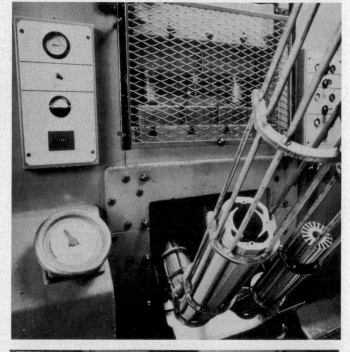

Above:
Assembling the MOF96 router motor and base-plate.

In this operation armatures for the MOF96 router are built into the bearing housing.

Below:
Every Elu product is subjected to rigorous testing. Here the MOF96 is undergoing high-voltage tests for electrical safety.

Right:
Another step in producing the MOF96: stator and armature are put into the motor housing.

After all checks and tests have been carried out the MOF96 goes to the packing department for delivery by company-owned road vehicles to European subsidiaries.

How to get the most from your advertisement in . . .

Woodworker

Give a full description of the product or service you want to sell.

Book a series of advertisements to ensure that you reach the whole potential market. Remember your customer could quite easily miss the issue which contains your advertisement.

If you want to cancel your advertisement then simnply pick up the 'phone and tell us. You will only be charged for the ones which have appeared.

Lastly, to get the most from your advertisement consult us first. We are here to help you . . .

Turning parana 'pine'

From: A. G. Helyer, Canton, Cardiff

Would it be advisable to attempt to turn parana 'pine' and what standard of finish could be attained? Due to its unpopularity in other forms of joinery I am prompted to enquire if it can be used with any degree of success.

Parana 'pine' *(Araucaria angustifolia)* is closely related to the monkey puzzle tree *(Araucaria araucana)* and as such its growth characteristics differ considerably from the true pines *(Pinus spp.)*. Largely it is compressive stress built up in the tree which results in a tendency for the wood to distort and/or to shrink in its length during seasoning, or afterwards, when the residual stresses are relieved by machining. Because of this parana 'pine' is regarded principally as a joinery and flooring timber.

It was used a few years ago for turning into broom handles until ramin took its place. It does produce good mouldings from a six-cutter or spindle moulder due to its uniform texture, but logically if long, clean mouldings distort when coming off the machine, at least they stand a very good chance of being pulled back when used or straightened by crosscutting, while slight distortion in a cheap broom handle is often accepted.

The same cannot be said of a cut-to-length table lamp or table leg which would be rejected; and a bowl turned from the wood could be a more critical example because of the extra wood removed from the inner side of the blank as opposed to the outer side, since cutting relieves stress. Although we would not recommend parana 'pine' for special turnery we must say that if the wood finished well off the lathe and remained so for a few days, it would then remain remarkably stable in service: a rather uncertain principle to adopt though.

Seasoning oak for carving

From: Phil Rain, Yearby, Co Cleveland

I want to season oak for carving. When I collect pieces of oak they seem to split at the end of the branches. Could you please tell me why this happens?

To understand why your oak tends to split at the ends while it is drying (seasoning), look at the sawn end of a branch: here you will see annual rings composed of several rows of large pores and radiating out from the centre (pith), rays which in oak are quite wide. Your wood is wet and since the watery sap is more easily removed through end grain in drying, the ends of the piece tend to dry out well in advance of the rest of the length.

When wood dries it tries to shrink and English oak has a shrinkage potential of 7.5% tangentially (along the annual rings) and 4.0% radially (across the rings). The structure of the rays tends to restrain the radial shrinkage; but they encourage splits to form by a cleaving action when the wood begins to shrink along the rings.

If you have a piece of split wood you will see from the end that the wood has shrunk away from certain rays which have behaved like wedges to part the wood. This is a natural tendency of all wood but is more pronounced in some especially where there is a wide differential shrinkage potential tangentially and radially. It is extremely difficult to reduce this tendency but, in effect, what is required is that all moisture removal must be slowed down, especially in the early stages of drying.

The wood should be stored in the open air with the bark left on and with shading from direct sun, ie with tarpaulin, polythene sheeting or old plywood lying on top (but not corrugated iron since this may cause black staining of the wood); or the wood could be stored in a shady spot. The ends of the pieces should be protected by applying something waterproof to slow down drying from the ends: bituminous paint, paraffin wax, tar paper for example.

In warm weather do not hesitate to wet the pieces with a can or hose or a few buckets of water thrown over the wood. The object must be to keep the outsides of the wood wet while the insides are drying and that can mean two years or more in the open air before any attempt is made to bring the wood indoors. There are various methods of trying to avoid end splitting and we use the word 'trying' advisedly since, as we have said, it is not easy to accomplish.

We have been discussing the use of polyethylene glycol (PEG) in this respect in the Timber Topics series in recent issues and this will be completed before we go on to other matters.

Cleaning cedar cladding

From: Dr A. Duff, Salisbury, Wilts

I would like your advice on cleaning a section of cedar cladding which has been covered with Timba-drua for a number of years. I want to replace this finish with Cuprinol, having already done so with a garage door. I used a proprietary stripper and scraped and sanded, but for a large, fixed vertical surface this same method would be too laborious. Timba-dura is a good protective but it covers the grain and behaves like tar in the removal process.

Both Timba-dura and Cuprinol come under the general description of water-repellent preservative finishes and as such are formulated to give lasting protection in every sense. In other words, once applied to wood they bond to the fibres, resist peeling off and the pigments are colourfast. Accordingly it is almost impossible to remove them short of sanding and even this is usually not very satisfactory.

We are not quite clear how much pigment is on your wood; the orginal Timba-dura formulation for cedar was so-called natural, that is it was lightly pigmented so that when applied to new cedar it enhanced its natural colour and slowed down its eventual fading. Clear or transparent Cuprinol serves the same purpose.

Since the natural colour of wood is fugitive and rapidly lost on weathering, the idea with all these finishes is to refurbish with a more heavily pigmented version once the original colour of the wood fades. Timba-dura was also produced in a heavily pigmented black formulation to meet the demands of architects. Since you speak of the finish covering the grain and behaving like tar, we wonder whether this is what has been applied to your wood. If this is the case, then lighter-coloured formulation applied over the old finish would obviously appear much darker.

However you could consider the following: All these finishes are compatible one with the other so there is no problem changing from one colour to another, except in the sense of obscuring what is underneath. Fortunately, the more coats applied provides greater water-repellency to the surface and a better build-up of colour.

We suggest you wash down the wood using a domestic detergent and stiff brush or broom and then review the appearance in the light of the colour you now want, trying out the new finish on a fairly obscure part of the cladding. A two- or three-coat finish now may give you what you want, but a further single coat each year will improve the situation.

Burning with a circular saw

From: F.T. Key, Shavington, Crewe, Cheshire

As a comparatively new owner of an 8in. saw bench not now in production I would appreciate advice on the types of blades to be used. The saw supplied with the machine is 8in. diameter with gullet teeth, on a ⅝in. spindle and is powered by a ¾hp enclosed motor having capacitor start.

When sawing a few lengths of semi-hardwood 1in. thick and some softwood up to 2in. thick I have experienced smoke coming from the bench. It seems to be burning the wood. (I do not think I have pushed the workpiece too hard — on the contrary I am inclined to be on the slow side). Is this the result of a dull blade which needs sharpening? Yet the blade has not yet had a large amount of use.

It would appear desirable to consider purchasing a tungsten carbide-tipped blade

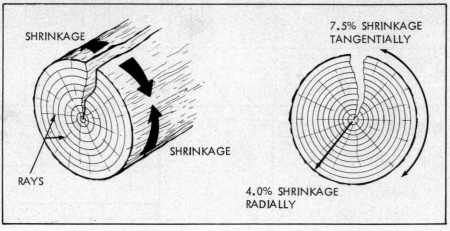

SHRINKAGE

RAYS

SHRINKAGE

7.5% SHRINKAGE TANGENTIALLY

4.0% SHRINKAGE RADIALLY

though I understand these take up a fairly wide cut. I am not particularly keen on the use of laminated board but would a TCT blade be suitable for this type of work, also bearing in mind the possibility of easily chipping the surface?

In addition I would appreciate your view on hollow-ground blades.

In our experience the commonest cause of burning on a circular saw is a blunt blade. Close inspection of the tips of the teeth should be carried out to establish whether there are any dull tops or 'shiners' on them (so called from the reflected points of light on a blunt tooth). Note also that after much resharpening the blade will need to be 'stoned' to ensure the concentricity of the rim and the teeth will need to be regulleted.

For this the blade should receive the attention of a professional saw doctor or be returned to the maker for servicing. A related cause of burning could be too little set on the teeth to provide adequate clearance (technically known as the saw kerf) and this would normally be done when the blade is regulleted and sharpened.

Having made these observations it must be stressed that no saw blade, however sharp, can be expected to perform tasks for which it is not intended. The commonest operations performed on a circular saw are those of ripsawing and crosscutting. The tooth design for each operation is different due to the fibrous nature of wood and the configuration of the timber cells across and along the grain. The sketches here show the commoner types of tooth design for these operations. The correct type must be employed for the job in hand.

If, however, the foregoing has been properly attended to and the problem is still evident there are further factors to be considered:

1 An 8in. diameter saw blade should theoretically run at 4,500rpm to achieve optimum efficiency. In practice such saws are often run at something like 2,500rpm to reduce bearing wear — and still function well at this speed.

2 The riving knife at the back of the saw should be at least as thick as the saw blade (20 gauge is usual for an 8in. diameter saw) but no thicker than the kerf that the saw produces. It should be set back from saw rim no more than ½in.

3 Imperfectly seasoned and resinous woods are likely to cause burning as the gullets of the saw quickly become clogged and overheating then occurs. This can be reduced somewhat by increasing the set of the teeth and clearing the gullets by brushing paraffin into the gullets with the saw stationary. We note that you say the saw seems to be burning the wood — the scorch marks on the cut piece will be immediately visible. If there are none then the smoke is likely to be from a slipping belt drive or an over-loaded electric motor.

It is commonly appreciated that tungsten carbide-tipped (TCT) saw blades have a much longer cutting life than carbon steel blades but their eventual maintenance normally means that the blade must be returned to the manufacturer or a firm specialising in that sort of work. While it is true that TCT blades produce a wider kerf, their longer running time between sharpening makes them attractive to many

Saw teeth types

Rip-saw teeth lean forward and are said to have a positive hook or rake. Sharpened on the tops only.

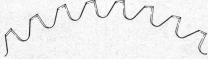

Cross-cut teeth lean back and are said to have a negative hook. They are bevelled on the leading edge as well as the top.

Saw for laminated boards and plywood. Numerous small teeth avoid whiskered and chipped edges.

sawyers. They are certainly very effective when used for cutting man-made boards (particleboard), though the manufacturer's advice should be sought on the actual tooth type for specific materials.

Hollow-ground saw blades are generally used for dimension (crosscutting) sawing and on certain types of blade designed to leave a planed finish to the stock. It would be useful to possess such a blade for special jobs, but in the general nature of home workshop use it would be better to invest in standard rip and crosscut blades.

It is yew

From: D. R. Sage, Pinner, Middlesex
I have enclosed sample of timber and wonder if you can identify it please. It is from a small plank I purchased with a lot of other timber from a local mill. Unfortunately it was the only piece and is 48 × 8 × 2in. and quite heavy. It turns and finishes very well and has a good grain pattern. I paid 50p for the plank and I think it is possibly yew.

We have examined the sample and confirm your belief that the wood is yew (Taxus baccata). Although hard and compact as a rule, sometimes irregular grain makes clean finishing difficult. If you find this happening in turning try altering the angle of cut. In shaping yew through moulding machines the cutting angle is reduced from 30° to 15° to give a smoother finish. In other words the cutting edges scrape rather than cut. The small sample you sent in is remarkably good and if the whole piece is similar, then for the price you paid you seem to have a bargain.

Charcoal burning

From: Kenyon Jew, Witherley, Atherstone, Warwickshire
Could you please advise if it is possible to make small quantities of charcoal that would be suitable for burning on a barbecue fire. I have a poplar and two 'crack' willows cut into noggins about 8-10in. for use on an open fire. In total this amounts to more than a ton of wood.

I have plenty of bricks, sand, soil and space for making a kiln and could chop the noggins into pieces 1-2in. square if necessary.
Charcoal as you probably know is an amorphous form of carbon prepared by charring wood. In other words, ordinary wood (molecules of carbon, oxygen and hydrogen) is decomposed by burning so that the carbon element is left more or less intact and available as a source of heat. Good charcoal accordingly should consist of at least 90% of carbon and little more than 3% of ash, with any remaining constituents being oxygen and hydrogen.

The old method of preparing charcoal, still practised, is to build a large conical heap of wood logs on a plan which allows channels for the ingress of air; and spaces by which the products of combustion are carried away, ie smoke (oxygen, hydrogen) and ash by clearing at the base. The heap is covered with turf or clay, with openings to regulate the air supply.

Production of good charcoal depends upon the air supply being as low as possible and the temperature high. The time required for carbonisation to be completed would obviously depend on the size of the pile, but something like 24 to 48hr of continuous burning would be necessary, and there might be difficulties in this in the sense that a large pile would need attention during the night.

It is highly probable that the Forestry Commission could give you further information on charcoal burning. Today, of course, charcoal is produced in special retorts and is even shaped into brickettes, but since you have some bricks available to you it would be possible to build a small charcoal kiln following the lines mentioned above, ie air spaces which could be blocked off as necessary; ash clearing space ditto; top vent to take off smoke etc.

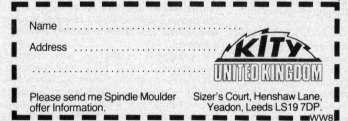

WHAT'S NEW IN EQUIPMENT

Nineteen-piece high speed steel twist drill selector available from tool shops, hardware shops and engineers' merchants.

Work benches and looms

Emir brand work benches in the No. 1500 (budget) series have bonded well tops presenting a beech edge 70mm deep for stiffness and 140mm working width, with planing stop 35 × 18mm; the well is provided with sweep-out chutes each end. The benches have legs from 50 × 50mm beech with drawbolted rails for KD assembly and tops laminated from 25mm beech on 15mm 700D pine chipboard. A shelf is provided on the bottom rails (reversible to form a tray). Finish is one coat of clear sealer.

No. 1502 is described as a single place bench 1250 × 460 × 800mm high fitted with one 150mm vice. No. 1512 junior bench is 940 × 610 × 700mm high fitted with two 150mm vices. No. 1512 middle bench is 1250 × 610 × 800mm high fitted with two 175mm vices.

Details of these and other benches for the woodworking and metal working trades are available from Emmerich (Berlon) Ltd, Wotton Road, Ashford TN23 2JY (Ashford — Kent — 22684). The company also makes wooden tools including mitre blocks and boxes; sawing trestles; square and mitre shooting boards; bench hooks; clipping boards; oilstone boxes; bench vices in beech; carvers and carpenters mallets; gauges.

Emmerich produces the Harris looms — floor looms 36 and 42in. widths; counterbalance four shafts and six treadles; countermarch four to eight or 12 shafts and six to 12 treadles; table looms four, eight and 16 shafts; folding loom 34in. with four shafts and eight treadles; rug (vertical) loom 36in. two shafts; and accessories such as vertical and horizontal warping mills; warping board; bobbin rack; wool rice/floor swift; loom benches; shuttles; raddle; temple in range of sizes; warp sticks threading and reeding hooks; and fork beater.

Leaflets and price lists for all products are available on application.

Personal safety products

A wide vision goggle in pvc which can be worn over the widest spectacle frames and is ventilated to keep the lense free of mist is one of several personal safety products from James North & Sons Ltd, PO Box No. 3, Hyde SK14 1RL (061-368 5811). Another is the Vega dust mask having a light aluminium frame with cotton wool filter pads and described as efficient against nuisance dusts. For protection against noise of drills, hammers and lathes etc there is the Saturn ear defender said to be light and comfortable to wear.

These products are distributed through hardware and diy wholesalers; for more details get in touch with James North marketing services department at the address given above.

Byproduct collectors

Mobile collectors for wood byproduct (made in Italy under the Coral name) are handled by Extracta Engineering Ltd, Holder Road, Aldershot, Hants (0252 316661). There are various types which can be supplied as single mobiles for connection to as many as three woodworking machines or installed in a ducted system. Capacities range from 600-5000cfm in single to four-bag filters with motors from 1-7.5hp operating at 2800rpm off three-phase supply, though there is an optional single-phase on the smaller models.

Needlefelt filter bags are fitted as standard and cotton waste collection sacks can be supplied instead of plastics sacks. It is understood that Coral equipment can be lease-purchased through Extracta and the company is interested in hearing from distributors throughout UK.

Selecting the drill

The RUKO drill selector holds up to 19 metric or fractional size HSS twist drills. The drill is selected by rotating the top until the required size appears in the aperture and by inclining the selector the drill is released. Twisting the top prevents the drills falling out. Marketed by RCF Tools Ltd, Townend House, Walsall WS1 1NS (0922 612336), the selector is available through tool shops, hardware stores at a suggested retail selling price of £9.95 exclusive of VAT.

Four jigsaws

Four models (nos. 561-564) of Metabo jigsaws at prices from £91 to £109 are announced by B. Draper & Son Ltd, Hursley Road, Chandlers Ford, Hants (04215 66355). Model 561 is described as a one-speed saw while no. 564 has infinitely variable speed and orbital blade movement adjustable to four settings and creating a pendulum effect.

Motors fitted are 500V controlled by a slide switch for one-hand operation. For bevel cuts the soleplate can be tilted left or right and locked at angular settings of 15, 30 and 45°. Other features include ribbed pads either side of the gearbox housing to allow the tool to be clamped in a vice for stationary use, and air blast to point of cut so that guideline remains visible.

It is said that wood can be plunge-cut without need for pilot holes and that 18 types of blade and three wood rasps are available.

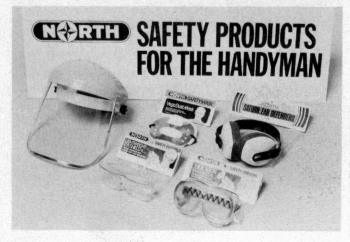

Left: Safety products from James North. Above: CMS series bag filter from Extracta Engineering.

Prices quoted are those prevailing at press date and are subject to alteration due to economic conditions.

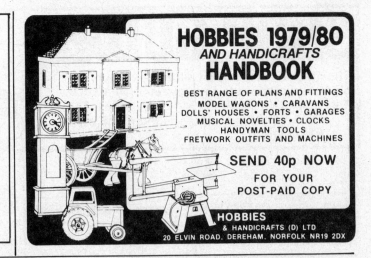

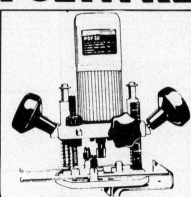

SHOP GUIDE

The quickest and easiest method of reaching all Woodworkers is to advertise in SHOP GUIDE.
Telephone Gill Dedman (0442) 41221 Ex. 241.
Rate: £5.00 per unit. Minimum of 6 months.
★ Mail Order

HERTFORDSHIRE

WATFORD Tel: (0923) 49911
TREND MACHINERY & CUTTING TOOLS LTD.
UNIT N, PENFOLD WORKS, IMPERIAL WAY
Open: 9.00 a.m.-5.00 p.m. Mon.-Fri.

LANCASHIRE

LANCASTER Tel: 0524-2886
LILE TOOL SHOP
43/45 NORTH ROAD
Open: 9.00 a.m.-5.30 p.m.
Monday-Saturday
Wednesday 9.00 a.m.-12.30 p.m.

AVON

BATH Tel: Bath 64513
JOHN HALL TOOLS ★
RAILWAY STREET
Open: Monday-Saturday
9.00 a.m.-5.30 p.m.

BATH Tel: Bath 22617
GORDON STOKES (office anytime)
WOODCRAFT SUPPLY ★
110 MOUNT ROAD, WHITEWAY
Open: 9.30 a.m.-5.00 p.m.
Wednesday and Saturdays only

BRISTOL Tel: (0272) 311510
JOHN HALL TOOLS LIMITED ★
CLIFFTON DOWN SHOPPING
CENTRE, WHITELADIES ROAD
Open: Monday-Saturday
9.00 a.m.-5.30 p.m.

BRISTOL Tel: 0272-629092
TRYMWOOD SERVICES ★
2a DOWNS PARK EAST,
(off North View) WESTBURY PARK
Open: 9.00 a.m.-5.30 p.m.
Monday to Friday

BRISTOL Tel: 0272-667013
V. H. WILLIS & CO. LTD. ★
190-192 WEST STREET
BEDMINSTER
Open: 8.30 a.m.-5.00 p.m. Mon-Fri.
Saturday 9.00 a.m.-1.00 p.m.

BERKSHIRE

READING Tel: (0734) 586522)
SARJENT'S TOOL STORES ★
LTD.
44-52 OXFORD ROAD
Open: 8.30 a.m.-5.30 p.m.
Monday-Saturday

BUCKINGHAMSHIRE

MILTON KEYNES Tel:
A. POLLARD & SON 0908-75221
LTD. ★
51 QUEENSWAY, BLETCHLEY
Open: 8.30 a.m.-5.30 p.m.
Monday-Saturday

CAMBRIDGESHIRE

CAMBRIDGE Tel: 0223-353091
H.B. WOODWORKING
69 LENSFIELD ROAD
Open: 8.30 a.m.-5.30 p.m.
Monday-Friday
8.30 a.m.-1.00 p.m. Saturday

PETERBOROUGH Tel:
PETERBOROUGH 0733-62800
TOOL CENTRE
16 WESTGATE
Open: Mon.-Sat. 9.00am-5.30pm
Thursday 9.00 am-1.00 pm

CHESHIRE

CHEADLE Tel: 061-491-1726
ERIC TOMKINSON ★
86 STOCKPORT ROAD
Open: 9.00 a.m.-4.00 p.m.
Wednesday-Saturday
Closed all day Monday & Tuesday

CHESHIRE

CHESTER Tel: Chester 42082
ROBERT KELLY
19 NEWGATE ROAD
Open: Mon.-Sat.
9.00 a.m.-5.30 p.m.

STOCKPORT Tel:
M.W. EQUIPMENT 061-480-8481
LIMITED
SHAWCROSS STREET
Monday-Friday
9.00 a.m.-4.45 p.m.

CLEVELAND

MIDDLESBOROUGH Tel:
REM ELECTRIC 0642-248460
POWER TOOLS
89 PARLIMENT ROAD
Open: 8.30 a.m.-5.00 p.m.
Monday-Saturday

MIDDLESBROUGH Tel: 0642-
WINTZ 460035/83650
INDUSTRIAL SUPPLIES
2 BESSEMER COURT,
GRANGETOWN
Open: Mon.-Fri. 8.30 a.m.-5.00 p.m.

CORNWALL

HELSTON Tel.03265-4961
SOUTHWEST POWER TOOLS ★
MONUMENT ROAD
Open: 8.00 a.m.-5.00 p.m.
Monday-Friday
Saturday 8.00 a.m.-12.30 p.m.

LAUNCESTON Tel. 0566-3555
SOUTHWEST POWER TOOLS ★
6 WESTERN ROAD
Open: 8.00 a.m.-5.00 p.m.
Monday-Friday
Saturday 8.00 a.m.-12.30 p.m.

DERBYSHIRE

BUXTON Tel. 0298-871636
CRAFT SUPPLIES ★
THE MILL
MILLERSDALE
Open: Monday-Saturday
9.00 a.m.-5.00 p.m.

DEVON

AXMINSTER Tel. 0297-33656
POWER TOOL CENTRE ★
STYLES & BROWN
CHARD STREET
Open: 9.00 a.m.-5.00 p.m.
Monday-Saturday

BIDEFORD Tel. 023-72-3513
NORTH DEVON TOOLS ★
7-9 MEDDON STREET
Open: Monday-Friday
8.00 a.m.-6.00 p.m.
Saturday 8.30 a.m.-5.00 p.m.

EXETER Tel. 0392-73936
WRIDES TOOL CENTRE
147 FORE STREET
Open: 9.00 a.m.-5.30 p.m.
Monday-Saturday
Wednesday 9.00 a.m.-1.00 p.m.

DEVON

PLYMOUTH Tel. 0752-330303
WESTWARD BUILDING SERVICES
Lister Close, LTD.
Newnham Industrial Estate, Plympton
Open: Mon.-Fri. 8.00 a.m.-5.30 p.m.
Sat. 8.30 a.m.-12.30 p.m.

CO. DURHAM

DARLINGTON Tel. 0325-53511
PERCY W. STEPHENSON & SON
171/179 NORTHGATE
Open: 8.30 a.m.-5.30 p.m.
Monday to Saturday

ESSEX

SOUTHEND ON SEA Tel.
MARSHALL & 0702-710404
PARSONS LIMITED
1111 LONDON RD., LEIGH ON SEA
Open: 8.30 a.m.-5.30 p.m. Mon.-Fri.
Open: 9.00 a.m.-5.00 p.m. Sat.

WESTCLIFFE-ON-SEA Tel:
CLASSIC 0702-354055
BRASS COMPANY
429/431 LONDON ROAD
Open: 9.00 a.m.-5.30 p.m.
Mon.-Sat.

GLOUCESTERSHIRE

TEWKESBURY Tel. 0684-
TEWKESBURY SAW CO. 293092
LIMITED ★
TRADING ESTATE, NEWTOWN
Open: 8.00 a.m.-5.00 p.m.
Monday-Friday

HAMPSHIRE

ALDERSHOT Tel. 0252-28088
BURCH & HILLS LTD. ★
BLACKWATER WAY TRADING
ESTATE
Open: 8.30 a.m.-5.30 p.m. Mon.-Fri.
8.30 a.m.-12.00 Saturday

SOUTHAMPTON Tel.
HAMPSHIRE 0703 776222
WOODWORKING MACHINERY
297 SHIRLEY ROAD, SHIRLEY
Open: Tuesday-Saturday
9.30 a.m.-6.00 p.m.

PORTSMOUTH Tel. 0705-
EURO PRECISION TOOLS 697823
LTD ★
235 London Road, North End.
Open: Mon.-Fri. 9.00a.m.-5.30 p.m.
Sat. 9.00 a.m.-1.00 p.m.

HERTFORDSHIRE

HITCHIN Tel. 0462-4177
ROGER'S ★
47 WALSWORTH ROAD
Open: 9.00 a.m.-6.00 p.m.
Monday-Saturday
Closed all day Wednesday

WATFORD Tel. 0923-26052
J. SIMBLE & SONS LTD ★
76 QUEENS ROAD
Open: 8.30 a.m.-5.30 p.m.
Mon.-Sat. Closed Wednesday

LEICESTERSHIRE

GLENFIELD Tel. (0533) 871238
& (06077) 5288
POOLE WOOD MACHINERY
SERVICES LIMITED
UNIT 3A MILL INDUSTRIAL ESTATE
Open: Mon.-Sat. 8.00am-5.00pm

LEICESTER Tel. 0533-394841
EQUIPMENT FACTORS
Unit 3A Mill Lane Ind. Est., Glenfield
Open: Mon.-Fri.
8.00 a.m.-5.00 p.m.
Sat. 9.00 a.m.-12.00 noon

LEICESTER Tel. 0455-43254
ROY STARTIN LTD.
134 WOOD STREET
EARL SHILTON ★
Open: Mon.-Fri. 8.00 a.m.-5.30 p.m.
Saturday 8.00 a.m.-1.30 p.m.

LINCOLNSHIRE

LINCOLN Tel. 0522-30199/
WOODWISE LIMITED 39871 or
121 HIGH STREET 0522-68428
& 06077-5777/5288
(after hours) ★
Open: Mon.-Sat. 9.00am-5.30pm

LONDON

GENERAL Tel. 01-254-6052
WOODWORK SUPPLIES ★
76-80 STOKE NEWINGTON
HIGH STREET, N16
Mon-Sat 9.00-6.00. Thur 9.00-1.00

HANWELL Tel: 01-567-2922
G. D. CLEGG & SONS
83 Uxbridge Road, W7 3ST
Open: 9.00 a.m.-6.00 p.m.
Mon. to Fri.
9.00 a.m.-5.30 p.m. Saturday

Tel. 01-624-5146
W. THATCHER & SONS LTD. ★
221A KILBURN HIGH ROAD NW6
(1st floor above travel agency)
Open Monday-Saturday 9.00-5.30
Closed Wednesday

Tel. 01-739-7126
CECIL W. TYZACK ★
79-81 KINGSLAND ROAD
SHOREDITCH E2
Open: 8.45 a.m.-5.15 p.m.
Monday-Friday — Closed Saturday

GREATER MANCHESTER

MANCHESTER Tel.
ROBERT KELLY 061-832-9920
UNIT 143, UPPER MALL
ARNDALE CENTRE
Open: Mon.-Sat.
9.00 a.m.-5.00 p.m.

ST. HELENS Tel. St. Helens
ROBERT KELLY 58672
5 BRIDGE STREET
Open: Mon.-Sat.
9.00-5.30 p.m.

Prices quoted are those prevailing at press date and are subject to alteration due to economic conditions.

MERSEYSIDE

LIVERPOOL Tel: 051-709-5341
ROBERT KELLY ★
28/32 RENSHAW STREET
Open: Mon.-Sat.
9.00 a.m.-5.30 p.m.

LIVERPOOL Tel. 051-263-1359
TAYLOR BROS. (LIVERPOOL) LTD.
5/9 PRESCOTT STREET
Open: 8.30 a.m.-5.30 p.m.
Monday-Friday

NORFOLK

NORWICH Tel. 0603 898695
NORFOLK SAW SERVICES
DOG LANE, HORSFORD
Open: 8.00 a.m.-5.00 p.m.
Monday-Friday
Saturday 8.00 a.m.-12.00 p.m.

NORTHAMPTONSHIRE

RUSHDEN Tel. 093-34-56424
PETER CRISP LIMITED ★
7 HIGH STREET
Open: 8.30 a.m.-5.30 p.m.
Monday-Saturday
Thursday 8.30 a.m.-1.00 p.m.

NORTHUMBERLAND

BLYTH Tel. 06706-69279
ALAN McNAIR WOODCRAFT
69/71 Plessey Road
Open: 9.30 a.m.-5.30 p.m.
Mon.-Sat.

NOTTINGHAMSHIRE

KEYWORTH Tel. 06077-
POOLE WOOD 2421/5288
EQUIPMENT LIMITED
141 BROWNS LANE,
STANTON ON THE WOLDS
Open: Mon.-Sat. 9.00am-5.30pm

NOTTINGHAM Tel. 0602-811889
THE WOODCUTTER ★
5 TUDOR SQUARE,
WEST BRIDGEFORD
Open: Tues.-Sat. 9.00 am-5.30 pm
Fri. 9.00 am-7.30 pm. Closed Mon.

OXFORDSHIRE

OXFORD Tel. (0865-45118/9)
SARJENT'S TOOL STORES LTD. ★
150 COWLEY ROAD
Open: 8.30 a.m.-5.30 p.m.
Monday-Saturday

STAFFORDSHIRE

TAMWORTH Tel: 0827-56188
MATTHEWS BROTHERS. LTD
KETTLEBROOK ROAD
Open: Mon.-Sat.
8.30 a.m.-6.00 p.m.
Demonstrations Sunday mornings

SUFFOLK

BURY ST. EDMUNDS Tel:
TOOLS & THINGS 0284-62022
21 CHURCHGATE ★
Open: 9.00 a.m.-5.30 p.m.
Monday-Saturday

SURREY

CROYDON Tel. 01-688-5513
L.H. TURTLE ★
6-12 PARK STREET
Open: 8.30 a.m.-5.30 p.m.
Monday-Saturday

SUSSEX

GUILDFORD Tel. 0483-61125
MESSINGERS FOR TOOLS
14-18 CHERTSEY STREET
Open: 8.30 a.m.-5.30 p.m.
Closed all day Monday

CHICHESTER Tel: 0243-528142
THE WOOD SHOP ★
LAVANT
Open: 8.00 a.m.-7.00 p.m.
Mon.-Sat.

HASTINGS Tel. 0424-423072
THORCROFT ★
181/182 QUEENS ROAD
Open: 8.30 a.m.-5.30 p.m.
Monday-Saturday
Closed all day Wednesday

WORTHING Tel. 0903-38739
W. HOSKING (TOOLS & ★
MACHINERY)
96a MONTAGUE STREET
Open: 8.30 a.m.-5.30 p.m. Mon-Sat
Wednesday 8.30 a.m.-1.00 p.m.

WEST MIDLANDS

WEST BROMWICH Tel: 021-
CONWAY SAW & 533-5461/2
SUPPLY LTD
SWAN LANE
Open: 8 am-6 pm Mon.-Fri.
9 am-1 pm Saturday

WILTSHIRE

SWINDON Tel. (0793-31361)
SARJENT'S TOOL STORES LTD. ★
64 FLEET STREET
Open: 8.30 a.m.-5.30 p.m.
Monday-Saturday

YORKSHIRE

BINGLEY Tel. 0274-560699
STEENWISE LIMITED ★
LIMEFIELD MILLS,
WOOD STREET, CROSSFLATS
Open: Monday-Friday
9.00 a.m.-5.00 p.m.

YORKSHIRE

HALIFAX Tel. 0422-884075/
TIMBERLITE LTD 884788/33575
VICTORIA BUILDINGS ★
LUDDENDEN FOOT
Open: Mon.-Fri.
9.00 a.m.-5.00 p.m.

HARROGATE Tel.
0423-66245/55328
MULTI-TOOLS ★
158 KINGS ROAD
Open: 8.30 a.m.-6.00 p.m.
Monday-Saturday

LEEDS Tel. 0532 790507
GEORGE SPENCE & SONS LTD.
WELLINGTON ROAD ★
Open: Monday-Friday
8.30 a.m.-5.30 p.m.
Saturday 9.00 a.m.-5.00 p.m.

SHEFFIELD Tel. 0742-441012
GREGORY & TAYLOR LTD
WORKSOP ROAD
Open: 8.30 a.m.-5.30 p.m.
Mon.-Fri.
8.30 a.m.-12.30 p.m. Sat.

SCOTLAND

ABERDEEN Tel. 0224-630300
ROSS MACHINE TOOLS ★
18a DEE PLACE
Open: 8.00 a.m.-5.00 p.m.
Mon.-Fri.

SCOTLAND

DUMFRIES Tel. 3413
JOHN KELLY (answerphone)
60 FRIARS VENNEL ★
Open 9.00 a.m.-5.00 p.m. Mon.-Sat.
Closed Thursday

EDINBURGH Tel. 031-337-
SCOTSPAN 7788/665-3121
195 BALGREEN ROAD
Open: Mon.-Fri.
9.00 a.m.-3.00 p.m.

PERTH Tel: 0738-26173
WM. HUME & Co. LTD
8 ST. JOHN'S PLACE
Open: 8.00 a.m.-5.30
Mon.-Sat.
8.00 a.m.-1.00 p.m. Wed.

N. IRELAND

CO. ANTRIM Tel: 0266-6384
GEORGE GARDINER
49 BALLYMONEY STREET
BALLYMENA
Open: 8.30 am-5.30 pm Mon.-Sat.,
8.30 am-1.00 pm Wednesday

WALES

CARDIFF Tel. (0222) 372561
JOHN HALL TOOLS LIMITED ★
22 CHURCHILL WAY
Open: Monday-Saturday
9.00 a.m.-5.30 p.m.

CARMARTHEN Tel. 0267-7219
DO-IT-YOURSELF SUPPLY,
BLUE STREET, DYFED
Open: 9.00 a.m.-5.30 p.m.
Monday-Saturday
Thursday 9.00 a.m.-1.00 p.m.

NEWPORT Tel. 0633-842996
REUTER MACHINE TOOLS
100a ALEXANDRA ROAD ★
Open: 9.30 a.m.-5.30 p.m.
Monday-Saturday
Closed 1.00 p.m. Thursday

You can buy with confidence from the shops in this Shop Guide.

★ Shops offering a mail order service are denoted by an asterisk

---

Shop Guide Advertisements

£5.00 per Unit

Minimum of SIX insertions.

I Enclose remittance of £30.00 ☐

I wish to be invoiced. ☐

Please tick as appropriate.

COUNTY ....

TOWN ....

NAME OF COMPANY/SHOP ....

....

ADDRESS ....

....

To: Gill Dedman
WOODWORKER MAGAZINE
P.O. Box 35,
13 Bridge Street, Hemel Hempstead,
HP1 1EE.

TELEPHONE No. ....

DAYS AND HOURS OF BUSINESS

....

....

*TO DENOTE MAIL ORDER SERVICE
AVAILABLE ☐

ADVERTISEMENTS WILL BE INSERTED IN THE FIRST AVAILABLE ISSUE

Woodturning Courses

four days with
MIKE LAW
(Thos Harrison & Sons)

Relax into a four-day long woodturning course in the informal atmosphere of our farmhouse home. We offer comfortable accommodation, good food, and professional tuition in the heart of this beautiful countryside.
Please write or telephone for details: Mike Law, The Longhouse, Maxworthy Cross, North Petherwin, Launceston, North Cornwall. Tel: STD (056685) 322.

Classified Advertisements

540

Prices quoted are those prevailing at press date and are subject to alteration due to economic conditions.

Woodworker, August 1980

FOR ALL SUPPLIES FOR THE

Craft of Enamelling

ON METAL

Including
LEAD-FREE ENAMELS

PLEASE SEND STAMP FOR FREE CATALOGUE, PRICE LIST AND WORKING INSTRUCTIONS

W. G. BALL LTD.

ENAMEL MANUFACTURERS

Dept. W. LONGTON
STOKE-ON-TRENT
ST3 1JW

SITUATIONS VACANT

We are an Isleworth based Antique Dealers/Decorators seeking skilled joiners. The work involved is the adaptation of panelled rooms and the construction of architectural features, for example, doorways, chimney-pieces, etc. Our work is effected in clean, modern workshops, and travelling to Europe and America for periods of approximately 14 days to erect panelled rooms could be involved. Our current rate is £2.50 p.h. and there is plenty of overtime available at time and a half.

Please call our
Mr. Bernard Westwood on
01-560 7978 to discuss the job.

Experienced Joiners

Permanent job in clean, warm and modern workshop in West London. £2.50 ph + overtime. Please call 01-560 7978.

PARTIALLY trained cabinet maker seeks job in a small workshop, (preferably rural). Interested in restoration work, carving and traditional methods of cabinet making. Please reply to: Box No. 268 (Cumbria), c/o Woodworker, MAP Ltd., 13-35 Bridge Street, Hemel Hempstead, Herts. HP1 1EE.   S

GENERAL

BUILD CLOCKS FOR HOBBY OR FOR SALE
DIY full size plans. Free brochure and price list of movements and dials with order. Send large SAE with £2.45 for G'mother Clock Plan, 6' 3" tall, or £1.45 for Vienna Wall Clock Plan 4' high, or 30p and SAE for brochure and price list only.
We also sell G'fthr, G'mthr and Vienna wall clocks complete in cases at very low prices.
RUNCHMAN'S (WWKR)
4 Walford's Close, Harlow, Essex. HARLOW 29937

MAKE YOUR OWN CLAVICHORD — full size plans and instruction manual. Write for details to: Early Keyboard Instruments, Morley Farm, Brancepeth, Durham DH7 8DS.   S/X

CLASSIFIED

Telephone Gill Dedman
(0442) 41221 Ext. 241

HARPSICHORD — maker specializes in producing jacks of traditional woods. To your own measurements if necessary. Top quality work only. Tel: (0873) 831117.   S

HARP PLANS

Full size plans and instructions sheets for Celtic, Gothic and Knee harps as well as full range of gut and brass strings, hardware and tonewood for home constructions. Please send s.a.e. for full details and price list.
Also available – full size plans for Bowed psaltery — £2.50.
Complete Bowed psaltery kit £18.50. Hammered dulcimer kit (51 string) £61.40
Appalachian dulcimer kit (4 string) £24.90 (Bowed psaltery kits in cherry or walnut, dulcimer kits in mahogany).

Michael Saunders (Luthier)
1 Waterloo Cottages, Letton,
Hereford, HR3 6DN
Tel: Eardisley 352

GUITAR MAKERS AND REPAIRMEN

Whether you build or repair guitars we feel sure that our 36-page catalogue will be of interest to you. It includes everything for the amateur and professional instrument maker.
Spruce, Pine & Cedar Soundboards, Rosewood, Maple, Mahogany, Ebony, S pecialist Glues & Finishes. Pearl and Abalone, Bindings, Necks & Bodies. Pick-Ups, Tails & Bridges. Construction Books & Plans.
Send 55p to: **Strings n' Things, 63 Far Gosford St., Coventry.**

CRAFT DESIGN PLANS

CRAFT EQUIP ● TOYS ● FURNITURE
A new project or hobby? Lots of ideas packed inside my latest catalogue listing detailed plans of spinning, weaving, art, tapestry, needlework, toys and furniture designs. Get the satisfaction of building it yourself and save £'s on shop prices. Send 18p stamps for catalogue to:
DAVID BRYANT
4 Grassfield Way, Knutsford, Cheshire.

CRAFT AND ANTIQUE TOOLS

WOODSCREW BOXES

complete with taps, ½, ⅝, ¾, 1" —
£17.50 each.
CRATEX RUBBERISED SHARPENING STICKS AND GRINDER WHEELS FOR FINEST EDGES, FLAP WHEELS FOR FINISHING CARVINGS, ETC.
Stamp for details:
CRAFT SUPPLIES OF WORKSOP,
12 Brandsmere Drive, Woodsetts, Worksop, S81 8QN.

"Arrow" Swiss made woodcarving tools supplied, highest quality.
Details from:
Massy Wykeham Ltd.,
5th Floor,
26 Cross Street,
Manchester M2 7AW
Tel: 061 834 5022

MARTIN ANTIQUES, always have an interesting selection of old woodworking tools. Callers only at 36 St. Stephen Street, Edinburgh. Tel: 556-3527.   O-Z

1980 COLOUR BROCHURE NOW AVAILABLE

The Complete Works

We supply all you need to build your own clock – Grandfather/Mother, traditional or modern. Yes, Charles Greville & Co., offer you from stock the most comprehensive range of Europe's finest clock movements and dials. Plus British plans and kits. Easy to follow — simple instructions and prompt attention from a long established family business. We supply the movements and the choices. A satisfying hobby — a D.I.Y. project – build an heirloom. Send today for full colour brochure on our comprehensive service showing a vast range of clock movements and accessories for antique, long case, bracket, cuckoo, battery clocks, barometers, etc. 50p *(money refunded with first purchase).*

Charles Greville & Co.

Dept (WW8), Unit 5, Rear Airport House,
Purley Way, Croydon, Surrey. Tel: 01-686 2972
Ample car park. Personal callers most welcome.
Open 9.30-5.30 Mon.-Fri. Open Sat. 9-12.30

CLASSIFIED

Telephone Gill Dedman
(0442) 41221 Ext. 241

MATERIALS

CRAFTSMEN

Titebond was originally developed in the U.S.A. for the furniture trade and was brought into the U.K. to meet the high standard demanded by makers of fine musical instruments. We now make it available to all discerning craftsmen.
Titebond Aliphatic Resin is: Fast setting, twice as strong, sandable, non-toxic, easy spreading.
8oz container £1.99 plus postage 45p
12oz container £2.80 plus postage 65p
(please add 20p p&p for each additional container).
STRINGS N' THINGS, 63 Far Gosford St., Coventry (0203) 24406 *Trade prices on request.*

MINIATURE 1/12 scale Chippendale drawer pulls, Butts, Hinges all brass. Send £2.00 for samples. Bailey, 131 Centre Drive, Newmarket, CB8 8AP.   S/X

MODELMAKER reducing stock offers Pear, Holly, Box, Ebony etc. All at realistic prices. S.A.E. for sizes, prices. Box No. 470 (Surrey), c/o Woodworker, MAP Ltd., 13-35 Bridge Street, Hemel Hempstead, Herts. HP1 1EE.   S

trym timber

THE WEST COUNTRY'S FIRST SPECIALIST WOOD SHOP

High quality planed Hardwoods and Softwoods always in stock for immediate collection. Mouldings, sheet materials and doors a speciality. A wide range of fixings, fittings, adhesives. Fiddes finishes and a rare selection of every type of woodworking tool is available for all the enthusiast's needs.

Come and see the haven we have created for lovers of fine timber at:
29 Canford Lane, Westbury-on-Trym, BRISTOL.

Our parent company carries one of the largest ranges of timber species, plywoods and veneers in the country; it also specialises in timber, plywood and fixings for boatbuilders. A comprehensive price list is available for £1.00 immediately refundable on the first purchase of £25 +. Please note the minimum mail order value for timber products is £25 and for fixings etc. £5.

Write now to:
ROBBINS LTD., Cumberland Road, Bristol.
A full description of the company's activities appeared in the Dec. 1979 issue of the 'Woodworker')

G. K. HADFIELD

Immediate despatch from stock, of materials for clock restoration. Finials, hands, keys, pendulums, suspensions, weights, pulleys and hundreds of other items.

Write, phone or call. Peaceful parking!

Send large SAE 16p for free lists of materials and new/old horological books.

Blackbrook Hill House, Tickow Lane, SHEPSHED, Loughborough LE12 9EY. Phone: Shepshed (05095) 3014.

SEASONED TIMBER for Woodcarvers, Turners, Woodworkers. 10 years in own stock. Bubinga (French Cameroons) golden brown with darker featherings, hard, close grained, up to 96" × 24" × 2". Padauk blood red, 100" × 24" × 1" maximum. Maple (Canadian) (144" × 8" × 2" max.) pure white, straight, close grained, any sizes cut to telephone order. 2p to 3p per cubic inch, or £20 cube for full width boards. 25p stamps for sample. Archery Shop, 21 Wastdale Road, S.E.23. Tel: 01-699-1107. S

Materials for the Amateur and Professional
VIOLIN & GUITAR MAKER

Send S.A.E. 12p
plus 50p for either cat.
50p deductable
from purchase £5.00 or over

SYDNEY EVANS LTD.
45 Regent Place,
Birmingham, B1 3BN
Tel: (021) 233-1741

MULTICUT-2

The world's first universal precision saw, cuts 50mm wood, 10mm metals, plastics, rubber, etc. High performance, safe in use. Do not compare with standard fretsaws. Details, 10p stamp.

HEGNER UNIVERSAL SAWS (U.K.) LTD.
36 Gt. Eastern Road, Hockley, Essex.
Tel: Hockley 5669

See us in August at "Recro '80", Stoneleigh, Coventry 1-10th and Craft Show, Wembley 21-23rd.

542

Prices quoted are those prevailing at press date and are subject to alteration due to economic conditions.

Woodworker, August 1980

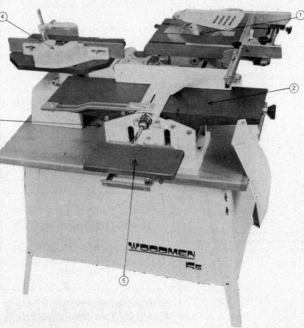

THE MAGAZINE FOR THE CRAFTSMAN IN WOOD

SEPTEMBER 1980   VOL. 84   NO. 1042   ISSN0043-776X

Front cover: Master woodcarver A. Hunstone of Tideswell, Derbyshire, at work in his studio *(courtesy of British Steel Corporation and Henry Taylor (Tools) Ltd, The Forge Lowther Road, Sheffield S6 2DR).*

Editor	Geoffrey Pratt
Production Editor	Polly Curds
Advertisement Manager	Terence M. Healy
Advertisement director	Michael Merrifield
Managing Director	Gavin Doyle

ABC MEMBER OF THE AUDIT BUREAU OF CIRCULATIONS

SUBSCRIPTION DEPARTMENT: Remittances to MODEL AND ALLIED PUBLICATIONS, PO Box 35, Hemel Hempstead, Herts HP1 1EE. Price per copy 75p includes p&p. Subscription queries: Tel: Hemel Hempstead 51740. Subscription rate, including index, £9.00 per annum; overseas sterling £9.00; $20.00 US for overseas dollar subscribers. Application to mail in the US is pending at Milwaukee, Wisconsin, and at additional offices. Distribution to N. American hobby and craft shops by Kalmbach Publishing Co, 1027 N. Seventh Street, Milwaukee, W153233, USA (Tel: 414-272-2060). Distribution to news stand sales by Eastern News Distributors Inc, 111 Eighth Avenue, New York NY1011, USA (Tel: 212-255-5620). Distribution to museums and bookshops by Bill Dean Books Ltd, 166-41 Powells Cove Boulevard, Whitestone, New York 11357 (Tel: 212-767-6632).

WOODWORKER is printed by New Avenue Press Ltd, Pasadena Close, Pump Lane, Hayes, Middlesex. (Mono origination by Multiform Photosetting Ltd, Cardiff), for the proprietor and publisher, Model & Allied Publications Ltd (a member of the Argus Press Group). Trade sales by Argus Distribution Ltd, 12-18 Paul Street, London EC2A 4JS. WOODWORKER (ISSN 0043-776X) is published on the 3rd Friday of the month.

Model & Allied Publications Ltd

PO Box 35, Bridge Street, Hemel Hempstead, Herts HP1 1EE. Telephone: Hemel Hempstead (0442) 41221.

'PARADOXICAL BLOCKAGES'

It is probably no coincidence that readers have the same thought as boffins in the government 'think tank'. Numerous enquiries have come to WOODWORKER recently on the subject of training; the report by the 'think tank' (officially the Central Policy Review Staff) titled *Educational Training & Industrial Performance* (HMSO price £4.25), appeared around the same time.

Critical of all the parties involved: educational and training establishments as well as schools; employers, trade unions; the government, the report proposes reforms to clear what it calls the 'paradoxical blockages between education and employment'. One, relating to young people, proposes that apart from introducing training and further education the content and duration of courses should be determined by what is required to enable trainees to reach set standards.

Evidence of the 'paradoxical blockages' comes from David Wallis, president of the British Woodworking Federation. He told the BWF annual general meeting in May: 'A good supply of competent craftsmen is absolutely vital for our industry. Now is the time — however financially difficult — when we should be training more of them.' Mr Wallis went on to say that there was a danger of training courses, not only for woodworking machinists but for craftsmen generally, being closed due to insufficient number of trainees at technical colleges throughout the country. 'This would be highly damaging to our industry and we cannot afford to lose these courses', and he urged BWF members to investigate the situation for themselves and play their part locally in the training field.

But whatever is done to provide more and better training facilities the real push will have to come from the people. And this means a change in attitude. H. N. Raine, chairman of the Technical Education Council, put this succinctly in the *Financial Times* on 2 June: 'While much has been done we have yet to deliver the full potential of technical education. I return to the point that a change is needed in the regard given by the community to vocational careers . . .'

Fine art craftmanship

The Made in Yorkshire exhibition at the stable court galleries adjacent to Temple Newsam house near Leeds, in May and June showed something of the rich store of craftsmanship exisiting in that 'county of broad acres'. However, not all would agree with the exclusion of traditional crafts such as clogmaking on the grounds that although skill is required no creative design innovation has taken place.

Overall impression of the display was of art rather than craft. Indeed the organiser — Yorkshire Arts Association — defined it as 'fine art craftsmanship'.

Wood useage was represented by musical instruments, furniture and three-dimensional jigsaws. In the first category John Cousen of Huddersfield and Carl Hanson of Hipperholme, Halifax, had various renaissance (wind) instruments including recorders, sorduns, flutes and cornamuse, while John Barrett of Bradford had string instruments. Furniture was represented by work from John Hardy, Shelley, Huddersfield, who is also an adviser to the Indian government on KD furniture manufacture for export. The jigsaws were by Peter Stocken of Doncaster.

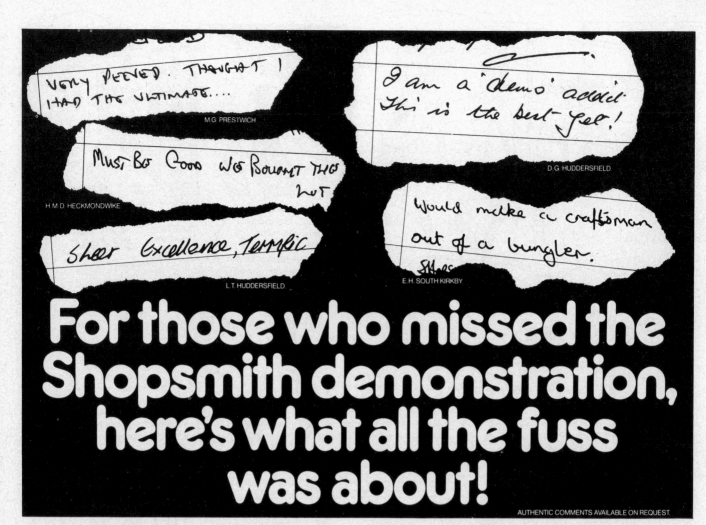

VERY PEEVED. THOUGHT I HAD THE ULTIMATE....
M.G. PRESTWICH

I am a 'demo' addict. This is the best yet!
D.G. HUDDERSFIELD

MUST BE GOOD WE BOUGHT THIS LOT
H.M.D. HECKMONDWIKE

Would make a craftsman out of a bungler.
S.H.RS.
E.H. SOUTH KIRKBY

Sheer Excellence, Terrific
L.T. HUDDERSFIELD.

For those who missed the Shopsmith demonstration, here's what all the fuss was about!

AUTHENTIC COMMENTS AVAILABLE ON REQUEST.

In June, Sumaco held the opening of their new showrooms in Elland. The centre of attraction was the American Shopsmith Mark V Workshop System. As you can see from the above comments it made quite an impression. In fact, 35 customers decided on the spot that it was the machine for them!

But if you missed the demonstration you will naturally be feeling a little in the dark about the remarkable capabilities of the Shopsmith Wood-working System. You probably won't even know that in a single compact unit no bigger than an ordinary bicycle is a woodworking system giving five machine operations in the basic package with a total of 16 or more available.

Virtually any woodworking machinery operation you wish to carry out, the Shopsmith can do it with a degree of accuracy seldom found elsewhere. Fortunately though R.J. De Cristoforo, one of Americas foremost woodworkers published a book with over 150 different woodworking operations – every one being carried out on the Shopsmith Mark V. Whether you are contemplating your first machine or have a complete workshop, De Cristoforo's book is a book for every serious woodworker. It is simply bursting with photographs and illustrations.

And if you missed the showroom opening we will always be happy to show you what the fuss was all about.

Just complete the coupon and we will do the rest.

The Shopsmith Mark V is available from SUMACO and selected dealers. Suma House, Huddersfield Road, Elland, West Yorkshire.

To SUMACO Machinery & Tools, Suma House, Huddersfield Road, Elland, West Yorkshire.

I enclose 25p for full Shopsmith Catalogue ☐
I enclose £9 for Power Tool Woodworking for Everyone ☐

Name_____

Address_____
_____
_____

Telephone_____

SUMACO Showroom Open Monday – Saturday 9 am – 5 pm
Thursday and Friday 9 am – 7.30 pm.
ww/9

Prices quoted are those prevailing at press date and are subject to alteration due to economic conditions.

Timberlite

Get to know the real value of Timberlite savings and service

DW125 RADIAL ARM SAW BY DEWALT. The pro-standard 10″ saw that really earns its keep. Thanks to a full specification line-up including: Radial Arm Versatility. All-angle Cross-Cut. Rip/Bevel/Mitre Facility. Accessory Range for greater work scope — Groove Cuts/ Housings/ Rebates/ Mouldings/ Sanding/ Boring/ Grinding/ Jig Saw. It's easy to see why this versatile machine is classed as a complete workshop. Order now and take advantage of our Free Stand offer (worth £42.55). This DeWalt DW125 Radial Arm Saw is only £317.00 plus £9.00 carriage.

DEWALT DW1370 12″ Radial Arm Saw. Superb versatility with a full accessory range. More power with an industrial product at a D.I.Y. price of only £411.00 plus £15.00 carriage.

DEWALT BANDSAW (BS1310 12″). The ultimate 2 speed compact — fully motorised for bench use. Timberlite price £225.00 plus £9.00 carriage.

Elektra HC260 Combined Planer and Thicknesser only £365.00 plus £9.00 carriage from Timberlite. Superb value Cash and labour saving benefits combined. 10″ x 6″ capacity surface and auto-feed thickness planer with rigid-cast frame and finely machine ground tables and bed. Powerful 2HP integral induction motor (suited to domestic supply). Top working performance/specification: HSS steel knives. Auto feed, Easy Change over from thicknessing to planing. Infinite thicknessing bed adjustment.

SITE CIRCULAR SAW BENCH. ELEKTRA COMBI 4000 with die-cast aluminium mitrefence with 45° scale. Rise and fall of blade/fitting arbor up to 45°. Single phase 2.2kw (3.1HP) Black Dia: 315mm.
Timberlite price now only £130 plus £9.00 carriage.

WHEEL MOUNTED ELEKTRA COMPRESSOR FROM TIMBERLITE now only £273.80 plus £15.00 for carriage. This unit offers a capacity of 7 cubic feet per minute and a maximum pressure of 140 p.s.i. This unit complies with B.S. Regulations.
Full kit includes spray gun, tyre gauge and oil gun, blow gun and hose for £89.00 extra.

ELEKTRA GRINDER TN150W for only £125.50 plus £5.00 carriage. This special Timberlite offer gives superb value for woodturners. Elektra TN150W combination dry and wet-stone grinder. Offers all the speed advantages of dry grinding PLUS efficient slow revving wet stone razor edging for your tools.

The unbeatable ATLAS WELDER 130 BY TECHNIKA — available from Timberlite at only £40.00 plus £4.00 carriage. Tested by Bradford University as being ideal for small jobs. (Full assessment available). Built in stamped plate, completely plasticized, highly insulating — Thermostatic protection against possible overloads. Power supply warning light — Continuous welding current regulations by magnetic shunter with external handwheel operation. Winding protection by special oven treated resins.

Dust extraction perfection from Elektra. The ELEKTRA SPA 1100 is the ideal attachment for planer/thicknesser and spindle moulders. Keeps your workshop clean. Protects your machinery — complete with castors/air filter bag/PVC chip bag and heavy duty textile chip bag 2.5m flexi-spiral hose. Only £165.00 from Timberlite plus £9.00 carriage.

The hardworking ELEKTRA DB800 LATHE at only £165.00 plus £9.00 carriage. Built on a robust square tube frame this compact unit offers 4 speed V Belt Drive on a maximum turning diameter of 320mm together with revolving centres. Accessories available.

Get this superb orbital sander into your workshop. The powerful high speed ELU MVS93 SANDER. With more than 20,000 sanding strokes per minute (which ensures absolutely smooth running) and the large-area sanding pad any surface will be sanded rapidly and cleanly.
Old paint, wood, veneers or marquetry, and even metal surfaces, form the ideal applications for this "lightweight" model. Timberlite price only £53.05 plus £4.00 carriage.

ELEKTRA CONCRETE MIXERS: The Hobby-Mix 120 mains operated 240-volt AC 50 Hz for professional and D.I.Y. Robust, Powerful and Reliable with an amazing capacity and incredible speed of operation, easily transportable in the average estate. Timberlite price £138.00 plus £4 carriage.

THE PROFESSIONAL PLUNGE ROUTER MOF96 AND SPARES KIT. This machine is made to measure for the advanced do-it-yourself enthusiast.
It's small, handy, powerful and exceptionally versatile. For example. It copes with grooving, moulding, rabbetting, veining, profiling of all types and shapes. Routing to templates, contour-routing, cutting circles or free-hand working — all present no problem with this machine.
All for the unbeatable Timberlite price of £80.35 plus £4.00 carriage.
Spares kit for the above is now offered at £56.00.

Full cash refund guaranteed on any machine supplied if you are not completely satisfied.	Cheques, P/O, C.O.D., Credit arranged. Access/ Barclaycard welcome.

imberlite

ALL PRICES INCLUSIVE OF VAT.

Timberlite Limited, Victoria Buildings, Luddenden Foot, Halifax.
HX26AA Tel: Halifax (0422) 884075/884788/33575
(24 hour personal service)
Please allow 14-21 days for delivery

Prices quoted are those prevailing at press date and
are subject to alteration due to economic conditions.

549

Once you've bought the books you'll be able to make the shelves

FINE WOODWORKING

Anyone who enjoys making beautiful things out of wood will be simply over-whelmed with contents of 'Fine Woodworking', a richly detailed bi-monthly publication for serious woodworkers. Here you will find the kind of information that is timeless and hard to find anywhere else. That is why all back issues are kept in print, forming a graphic woodworking encyclo-paedia. And why, within five years, a stag-gering 250,000 woodworkers subscribe to this magazine. Now regularly available from the SUMACO Library. Annual subscrip-tion **£12.00.** Single copies **£2.00** each.

TAGE FRID TEACHES WOODWORKING

206 pages in which Tage Frid details everything about joinery that he has found necessary and useful in 50 years as a master craftsman. Frid, a native of Denmark and currently professor of woodworking and furniture design at Rhode Island School of Design, shows in complete step by step photo sequence concise details which are of equal benefit to professional woodworkers, amateurs and schools. **£11.00** each.

POWER TOOL WOODWORKING FOR EVERYONE by R. J. De Cristoforo.

Over 150 woodworking machinery operations superbly photographed and illustrated in 324 pages of useful hints and ideas on getting the maximum results from your workshop equipment. Although all operations are carried out on the Shop-smith Mark V woodworker, this book is a must for anyone thinking of buying or already using woodworking machines. **£9.00** each.

WOODTURNING

A small but very useful publication showing the lathe, the equipment, the wood

and how woodturning is done. 25 pages with 54 photographs and illustrations. **90p** each.

HOME WORKSHOP GUIDE TO SHARPENING

160 pages showing how to sharpen practically any type of tool. Achieve pro-fessional results every time with this comprehensive volume as a guide. **£2.90** each.

PROJECT PLANS

A selection of plans to make your wood-working more interesting and enjoyable. New plans are being continually added. **85p** each or 6 as illustrated for **£4.50.**

SUMACO
Woodworking Library

Showroom open Monday to Saturday 9 a.m. to 5 p.m. on Thursday and Friday until 7.30 p.m.

Sumaco Machinery & Tools. Suma House, Huddersfield Road, Elland, West Yorkshire, HX5 9AA. Telephone Elland (0422) 75491. Telex 51182 Sumaco.

Post to:
Sumaco Woodworking Library, Suma House, Huddersfield Road, Elland, West Yorkshire, HX5 9AA.

Complete the coupon by ticking which publications you require and how many at the prices indicated. Your cheque/postal order should be made payable to "Sumaco Woodworking Library." Please note that all items are VAT Zero Rated and that prices include postage and packing.

√ required items	Publication	Quantity	Cost
	Fine Woodworking. Annual Subscription	6	£12.00
	Fine Woodworking. Single copy		£ 2.00
	Tage Frid Teaches Woodworking		£11.00
	Power Tool Wood-working for everyone		£ 9.00
	Woodturning		90p
	Home Workshop Guide to Sharpening		£ 2.90
	Project Plans		85p
	Project Plans Set	6	£ 4.50

Please allow 21-28 days delivery.

Block capitals please.

Name ....

Address ....

....

Project Plans Title(s) ....

WW/9

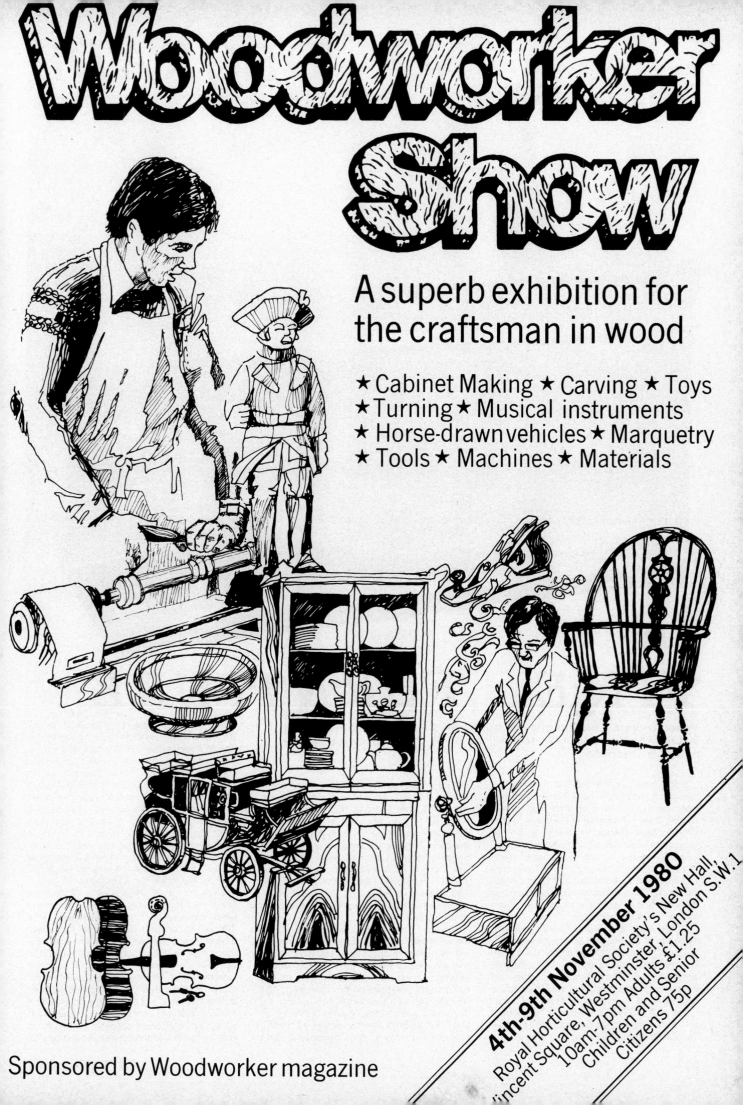

Woodworker Show

A superb exhibition for the craftsman in wood

★ Cabinet Making ★ Carving ★ Toys
★ Turning ★ Musical instruments
★ Horse-drawn vehicles ★ Marquetry
★ Tools ★ Machines ★ Materials

4th-9th November 1980
Royal Horticultural Society's New Hall,
Vincent Square, Westminster, London S.W.1
10am-7pm Adults £1.25
Children and Senior
Citizens 75p

Sponsored by Woodworker magazine

NO DEGRADE

IN FINE FURNITURE

Vacuum drying system ensures continuous supplies of timber with virtually no degrade. How technology helps the craftsmen at Titchmarsh & Goodwin

Sixty years ago Gordon Goodwin made a reproduction buffet in English oak. This piece was the forerunner of the high-quality ranges from Titchmarsh & Goodwin, Trinity Works, Back Hamlet, Ipswich, in home-grown timbers such as oak, walnut, ash and yew. Today that buffet has pride of place in the company's boardroom and is witness to a successful combination of good timber, making by hand in the old-fashioned sense of the word and running a business in anything but the old-fashioned way.

Order book and production records are evidence of the success of this combination. Only once in the past 20 years has there been no overtime worked by the 95 craftsmen employed by Titchmarsh & Goodwin. Of course, at the top end of the market sales are less affected by cyclical demand but hand-made by T & G is in the nature of a hallmark for discerning buyers at home and abroad. Thus it is that something like 50% of the

pieces go for export with the Netherlands and Germany being major buyers of the English oak styles from Tudor to 18th century.

But while there are thousands of designs in the drawing office covering these ranges, the customer wanting something special can be fairly certain that the Ipswich craftsmen will make it, be it a painted, lacquered and gilded Chinoiserie cabinet taking around 1000 hours of skill, or Chippendale-style chairs in mahogany hand-made in the mode of the master.

Though there may well be an old-fashioned sense of craftsmanship nothing is old-fashioned about a business which uses modern aids to further the skills of cabinet maker, carver, turner, polisher, gilder, upholsterer, leatherworker. Moreover, the founder continues as president and day-to-day matters are in the capable hands of his sons Peter and Jeremy whose responsibilities also cover the company's own

sawmill on the outskirts of Ipswich, where there is in addition a chairmaking workshop. The Witnesham mill converts home-grown timber bought standing to meet production requirements at Trinity works which amounts to some 30000cu ft of East Anglian oak a year. An unusual feature of the mill is that break-down is carried out by two horizontal framesaws to give a fine saw finish to each board. These French-made machines also have the advantage of one-man operation and a relative slow cutting speed which reduces the amount of down-time for doctoring the sawblades.

Sawn timber is put in-stick at Witnesham to air-dry over a period of many years. In the past, however, it has sometimes been difficult to ensure supplies of fully-dried timber throughout wet winter months. Now the company has installed a Bollmann HTV 30-1 vacuum system at the mill, and Mr Goodwin says: 'We are able to undertake far more complicated jobs than originally anticipated. A recent example was some 4 × 4 × 96in. long oak posts for four-poster beds which were dried to absolute perfection in about a quarter of the conventional time. We are planning to dry fresh-sawn walnut and other difficult timbers and I have no reason to believe that the system will produce anything other than perfect timber in the shortest possible time.'

Five months' experience of the Bollman has convinced Mr Goodwin that it is ideal for a furniture manufacturer (and for a timber merchant) who needs to dry timber with minimum of degrade (because it operates at low temperature). The drier is 6m long and 1.6m in diameter and even with its ancillary equipment does not take up a large area. 'It can be used by unskilled labour and with careful planning can produce a very useful throughput,' says Mr Goodwin. It is also capable of drying green timber.

The Bollman system uses the method of lowering the air pressure in the drier at low temperature to achieve a higher evaporation rate, ie faster drying accompanied by gentle treatment of the timber. The energy needed to heat up the material is fed in via heating panels which are placed between the individual board layers of the stack of sawn timber.

The moisture escaping from the timber is passed as steam over condensing surfaces and changed into water. This is drained out of the vessel without interruption of the drying cycle and results in shorter drying times. The circuits for heating, creating a vacuum, cooling and water extraction are automatically controlled. Only daily checks are necessary. The process is best suited to square-edged timber so Titchmarsh & Goodwin is doing the second conversion on a bandsaw at Witnesham mill. This means that bark, sapwood and defective wood is removed early on and not sent to congest the storage at Trinity works.

At Witnesham the heating boiler is oil-fired (gas-fired versions are available). The boiler is coupled to a simple pumped and pressurised water system for providing warm water to the heating panels in the vacuum chamber. An alternative would be to use a steam-to-water calorifier instead of a boiler, taking the heat required from an existing steam heating system. To meet site requirements loading and unloading of the vessel is done using a set of portable rails, though in a tandem or larger installation a gantry hoist could be used.

Importer of Bollmann equipment is Cubbage-Bollmann Ltd, Harrem House, Ogilvie Road, High Wycombe, Bucks, that at Witnesham being supplied by Poole Wood Equipment Ltd, 141 Browns Lane, Stanton-on-the-Wolds, Keyworth, Notts.

Left: Coffer with Jacobean-style carving. Top: Gateleg table. Above: Horizontal frame-saw gives fine saw finish to each board. Below: Bollmann HTV30-1 vacuum system.

POWERED WOODCARVING

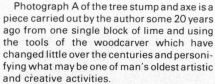

Robert Grant tries out the Dremel Moto-tool — and does some incised leaf decoration as an encore. Pictures are by John Peacock.

Developments in woodcarving are comparatively rare and like so many other branches of woodworking when they do occur they are often linked to the introduction of powered tools to replace human muscle.

Recently the Dremel Moto-tool has become available in this country, introduced from the US, where already it has caused something of a renaissance in woodcarving.

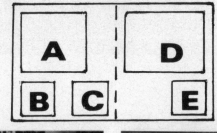

Photograph A of the tree stump and axe is a piece carried out by the author some 20 years ago from one single block of lime and using the tools of the woodcarver which have changed little over the centuries and personifying what may be one of man's oldest artistic and creative activities.

By comparison photograph B shows one piece carried out by the author, this time using the Dremel Moto-tool with its range of rotary burrs and sanding heads in a fraction of the time taken by traditional methods but with comparable results. No time has to be lost sharpening edge tools and wielding a mallet — it is simply a matter of selecting the right burr and guiding the light and slim Moto-tool with almost the same free expression with which one uses a pencil. Knots and 'difficult' grain are no problem and one can whittle, incise or sculpt at will.

The heron was made in under three hours from an odd length of Parana pine newel post, marked-out and bandsawn to rough shape in the conventional way (photograph C). With the block held in the vice (photograph D), the Dremel Moto-tool was put through its paces. At 25,000rpm it rapidly sliced away the waste producing a form that only needed a change to a sanding head to bring the piece to a fine finish.

The incised leaf decoration (photograph E) on the pine chopping board was carried out in a flush of enthusiasm and as an encore. A simple pencil outline only was drawn on the board and the tool whirled away in an ecstasy of free expression. Easy enough for a responsible youngster to use (there are certain fundamental safety precautions to be observed, such as working against the rotation of the bit and wearing goggles) yet capable of such results as to recommend it to the serious amateur and professional user.

A whole range of accessories to the basic power unit are available: flexible drive, jigsaw and router base with wide applications in many hobbies and crafts from model to pattern making.

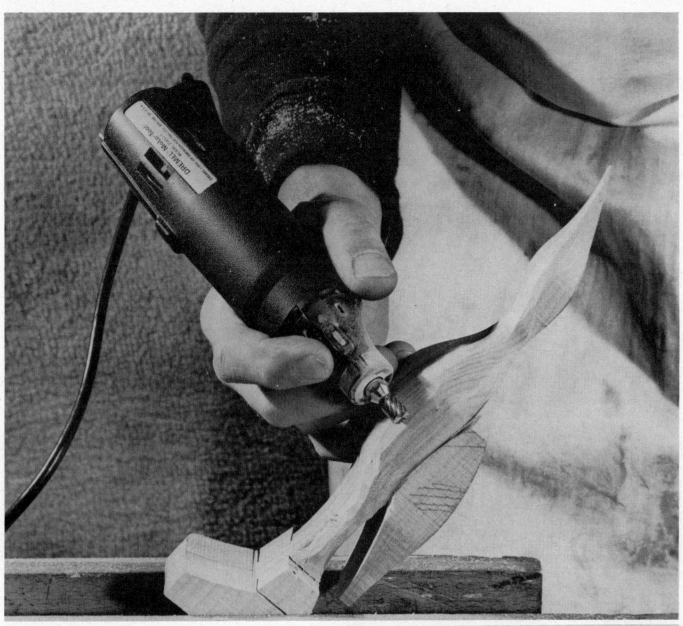

Leaflets are available and Microflame also forwarded copies of two US publications: *A Beginner's Look at Woodcarving with Creative Power Tools* (Willard Bondhus); and *The Wonderful World of Power Hand Tool Woodcarving* (E. S. Boyd). The first is one of a series of booklets for 'the beginning artist, craftsman or hobbyist' sponsored by Dremel and the author is a well-known carver and associate editor of the *Mallet* (National Carvers Museum of the US). The second carries the price of $4 and is published by the author from 1325 E 100th Terrace, Kansas City, Missouri 64131.

Both publications give directions for power carving and contain patterns and projects, with sketches and photographic reproductions.

Dremel Moto-tool is available in Britain via Microflame (UK) Ltd, Vinces Road, Diss IP22 3HQ.

WOODEN MALLET

**'I make mine,' says
Michael Ashcroft**

I find mallets are quite easy to make. They can be in a variety of sizes to suit individual preference or the type of work in hand. The mallet described would be suitable for light benchwork or for use by a youngster and weighs about 1lb (400gr) depending on the wood used.

A tough hardwood is required: beech or elm, the latter being very tough when seasoned naturally; maple is often considered ideal. Although ash might be considered the best timber for the handle, the mallet looks best if the same timber is used throughout.

I prepare the timber to the chosen width and thickness as shown in the drawings and then mark out and cut the tapered rectangular hole through the mallet head, using an electric drill to remove the waste. I then clean-up with the chisel.

Having shaped the handle to fit the hole cut in the head, application of linseed oil helps in fitting the handle to the head. When this is done (and it is really the most difficult part of the whole job), I complete the shaping of the head and handle. The angle of slope of the faces is such that each face comes flat on the work when the mallet is rotated from the elbow.

Faces are end grain. End grain can be planed with a sharp plane but it is sometimes easier to saw the faces to a line and sand the surface smooth and true. The corners of the head are taken off with glasspaper.

That part of the handle which forms the grip needs to be a comfortable fit in the hand, round and, of course, smooth. Obviously, the handle should be thicker at the end so that it will not slip through the hand when being used.

Finally I give the mallet a generous coating of linseed oil.

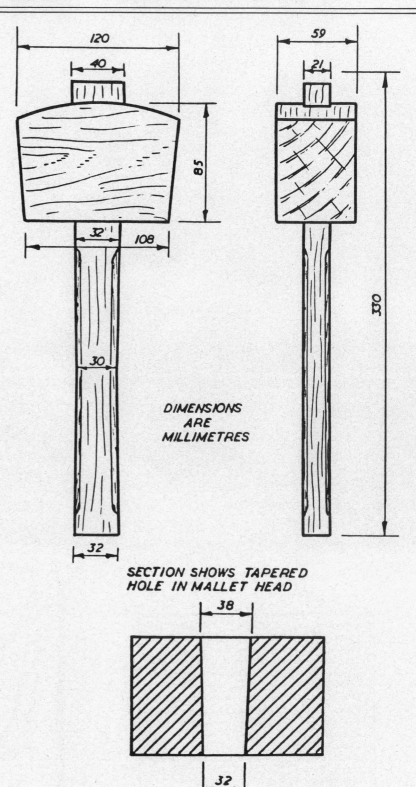

DIMENSIONS
ARE
MILLIMETRES

SECTION SHOWS TAPERED
HOLE IN MALLET HEAD

DETAIL SHOWS TAPER
ON MALLET HANDLE

POINT OF
ROTATION

SLOPING FACE COMES
FLAT ON WORK

OK, so the Elu TGS 171 is a very appealing machine, but it is also versatile and has many new safety features.

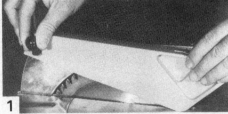

SAFE AND VERSATILE

The TGS171 is like no other saw and combines accurate cross cutting and safe ripping of wood, plastics and even aluminium.

The snip-off action eliminates the problem of the saw trying to climb the material. This controlled action improves the quality of cut essential for picture framing, aluminium window sections, architraves, in addition to cutting table legs all the same length using the stop. The spring return ensures the head goes back to its locked position and the guard re-shields the blade completely (4).

It is simple to change from a mitring saw to sawbench, as no tools are required. The riving knife is permanently fitted to the machine and swung into position, the adjuster is located at the rear and the whole table is turned over, the guard with the quick release button (1) is quick to fit. The no-volt release switch (2) adds to the safety, the switch turns itself off when the power is taken away.

The legs are quick release and adjustable for an uneven floor surface, and the whole machine can be easily stored in the boot of a car (3) for complete portability.

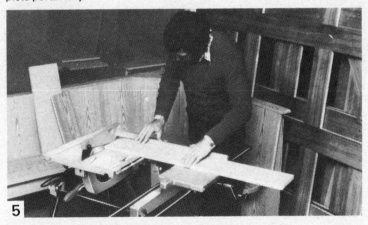

TABLES LEFT AND RIGHT

With the extension table on the right, large boards and panels can be cut easily. The sliding table (5) on the left ensures accurate cutting square 90° panels, essential when cabinet making.

BACK-UP THROUGHOUT THE U.K.

Elu have established a network of Authorised Dealers throughout the U.K. All Elu machines have a full 12 months guarantee covering free parts and labour. Although from our experience the induction type motor fitted to this machine is both reliable and quiet.

MAXIMUM PRICES YOU WILL PAY (INC. VAT)

TGS Sawbench/Mitre Saw, including riving knife and guard.	£322.00
171 20 22 00 Woodworking Set (TCT Sawblade, rip fence and mitre fence).	£ 52.90
171 20 22 03 Set of legs	£ 24.72

Send the coupon below for your FREE colour brochure, accessories list and prices.

Elu Machinery Limited
Stirling Way
Stirling Corner
Borehamwood, Herts
Tel: 01-953 0711 Telex: 926144

Please send the TGS 171 colour brochure

Name _____

Address _____

_____ Tel: _____

New

The Shoreditch Achievement

Shoreditch college was founded in 1907 to train teachers in handicraft. In 1951 it moved from Pitfield Street, London, to Coopers Hill, Englefield Green, Egham, Surrey, where it occupied a site and buildings that had originally been the Royal Indian engineering college. From August this year Shoreditch merges with Brunel university though remaining on the Englefield Green site.

The exhibition of students' work held during May and therefore the last to be staged under the old regime was formally opened by Avigdor ('Vic') Cannon, the retiring head of design technology at Shoreditch. Mr Cannon commented that at a time when the national interest demands a strong practical involvement 'our subject is fast becoming another abstract study.'

He went on to say: 'The educational implication of design as expressed in design technology is that of a complete experience.

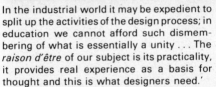

In the industrial world it may be expedient to split up the activities of the design process; in education we cannot afford such dismembering of what is essentially a unity . . . The *raison d'être* of our subject is its practicality, it provides real experience as a basis for thought and this is what designers need.'

Earlier Mr Cannon pointed out that schools made the mistake of thinking of design as something on its own, a closed system ending with a proposal for somebody else to make and prove. It was a superficial imitation of industry, long wedded to this division between thinkers and doers. 'The Shoreditch achievement', he said, 'is to have maintained a great tradition in the face of the vicissitudes of the recent past and to have emerged as a college in good heart. It is our hope that the exhibition embodies these aspirations and this tradition — long may they continue.'

P.558 top: Laminated dining table in rosewood and yew by Simon J. Quarmby. Bottom: Designer's desk in elm by David Waller. (Both 3rd yr B.Ed.)
P.559 top left: Loveseat in ash by Chris G. Sturgeon (3rd yr B.Ed.), top right: Cabinet in ash by Gerald R. Harrison (3rd yr Certificate), right: Corner unit in ash by H. F. James (3rd yr Certificate), below: Laminated dining table in ash by Paul D. Gully (3rd yr B.Ed).

HUSBAND & WIFE in a WORLD OF MINIATURES

Ten years ago John Davenport was working for a Sussex cabinet maker restoring antiques. He developed an interest in miniatures and decided he would like to collect them. But apprentice pieces, or travellers pieces were very expensive. 'I was disappointed at many sales and outbid by other collectors', says John who realised that his chances of making a collection of any merit were practically nil.

So he started making his own miniatures. It was not easy to get information on apprentice pieces but after a lot of research he found the right scales and the most popular pieces to make.

At first he had no intention of selling but rather to make a collection. Then he was persuaded into accepting commissions and now the majority of his work goes to America. Fixing a price is difficult. He says he makes the piece first and does not think about the price until the work is finished. 'Otherwise it takes a lot of the pleasure out of making it.'

He makes the cabinet furniture — handles and locks — by hand as it is almost impossible to buy what he wants. He also makes some of the smaller hinges though he does buy in the larger ones.

'One of my biggest problems is finding suitable timber. It has to be reduced so thin for miniature work. And it must be old, seasoned stuff and very carefully selected. The right veneers have to be used to match the period of the particular piece. I french polish and ''dull'' the finish to get the true antique look. I learnt this from my father who was a french polisher,' says John.

He photographs each piece to ensure that there is no exact repetition; each is signed and dated. Individuality of each piece is his aim.

For the Davenports making miniatures is very much a family affair. Mrs Davenport, Julie, has been helping John with the paper work for some years but she has started making and polishing miniature furniture for the cheaper end of the market. She also runs an arts and crafts stall at the Old Granary in Bishops Waltham, Hants, where her husband exhibits during the summer months.

Now the Davenports, who live at Swaythling near Southampton, are exhibiting and selling at miniature fairs. They get a lot of enjoyment in meeting people with similar interests.

Top: secretaire and davenport, scale 1" to 1', standing on Victorian side table, scale 2" to 1'.
Above: Julie Davenport's stall at the Old Granary.
Below: left, another view of the davenport and right, Georgian bachelor's chest in walnut, scale 1" to 1'.

by
SYLVIA
HAYES

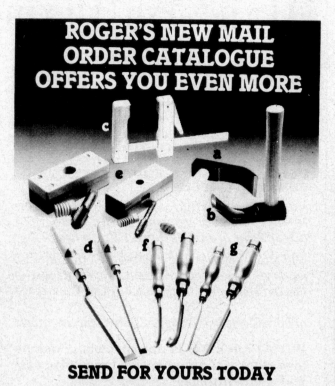

562

Prices quoted are those prevailing at press date and
are subject to alteration due to economic conditions.

Woodworker, September 1980

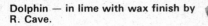
Dolphin — in lime with wax finish by R. Cave.

CARVING IN
GUERNSEY

Fireside bellows carved by A. Brehaut to a design originating from tapestry worked by his wife.

Bowl in utile by Mrs I. Pouteaux.

Armorial achievement of the Carey family carved by Miss M. Cleal in jelutong and freijo.

Celtic beast — relief carving in jelutong is the work of Miss Strugnell and was inspired by a card design.

In Guernsey Eric Grimsley runs evening courses for adults. The venue is St Peter Port Secondary School and the subject is carving. Mr Grimsley says: 'I start beginners with a design of a Tudor rose relief carving. This gives them the basic techniques of setting-in and handling gouges and afterwards the class member decides what to make or carve, or in some instances both. Resource material on design and ideas is supplied and use of clay is encouraged for three-dimensional work. Sketches are the starting point and sometimes full-size details are essential before the class member attempts the work.

'I try to demonstrate basic techniques to the class as a group, but work on an individual basis with each member. I encourage them to attempt a variety of work inspired by book illustrations, though sometimes a piece of wood will give a starting point'.

Mr Grimsley adds that Guernsey with an area of 25 sq ml has a scarcity of natural timber and most of what is used by the class comes from local timber yards — or from his school supply. Occasionally someone brings in driftwood which after it is dried can be suitable for carving.

Work by some of Mr Grimsley's class members is shown above.

R. W. Grant DLC FRSA MSIAD has designed and illustrated this

WRITING DESK

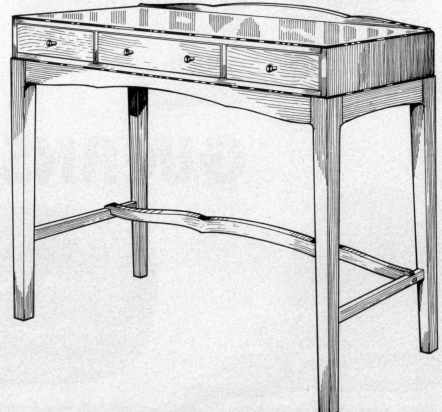

WITH UNDERFRAME RAILS OF 'GUNSTOCK` SHAPING

This elegant piece has been designed with the less spacious home in mind and features delicate ovolo mouldings on the carcass and drawer fronts.

The underframe rails display the interesting 'gunstock' shaping (Fig. 1). The correct height for a writing surface has been borne in mind when using a conventional chair and allowance made for knee and leg space as well.

The construction (Fig. 2) employs standard cabinet making joints although the traditional panelled back and solid drawer bottoms have been replaced by mahogany-faced plywood to simplify the work. The piece was originally made in Honduras mahogany and the board with the most interesting grain was selected and set aside for the drawer fronts to ensure visual continuity.

The whole job was finished with two coats of sanding sealer and then wax polished. The drawer pulls were satin-finished aluminium but mahogany turned pulls could be substituted if desired, in which case they should be fitted with their end grain lining up with the direction of the drawer front grain. The 1/4 in. ovolo moulds were worked with a small powered router and ovolo bit but they could be struck with either a moulding plane or scratchstock.

For those who wish to attempt this piece the order of making should be: carcass, underframe and drawers. Fig. 2 also shows the joints used and it is assumed that the maker will be competent in cutting single and double lapped dovetails. As is usual on wide

boards the outer dovetails are made smaller to increase the gluing area (see p164 of March 1980 issue of WOODWORKER), and an allowance must be made at the back edges for the working of the rebate to take the plywood back.

The inside of the carcass should be finished before gluing-up; but note that the drawer running surfaces should not be wax polished as this will result in the sticking of the drawer later on. The little drawer stops should be glued into their mortises with the grain upright. They should be so positioned that the drawer front will project beyond the carcase front by 1/4 in., this being the ovolo size which will give the drawers their 'proud' effect.

The back retaining strip will have to be fixed either by dowelling or by screwing up through the back rebate lip before the plywood back is fitted and screwed into place. In the event of a drawer becoming hopelessly jammed, access can then be gained via the back panel. For this reason it is not considered wise practise to glue a back in.

With the carcass completed the underframe can be prepared. It should be noted that it is bigger overall than the carcass by the width of the ovolo moulding which is worked around the top of the underframe. This not only helps the visual stability of the design but overcomes the difficulty of making a carcass and underframe fitting exactly flush. Curvature of the 'gunstock' shaping is given in Fig. 3, and Fig. 4 shows how the curve at the top of each leg is achieved. This should be of no more than 1/4 in. radius. The

taper on the legs will have to be worked before the side stretcher rails can be temporarily cramped to the end frames in order to scribe the tenon shoulder lines. The central stretcher rail has the same 'gunstock' shaping as the top rail and it is joined to the side stretcher rails with an overlapped tenon. The top of this rail is rounded over to help shed the dust. It will be observed that it is set well back from the front to allow the user plenty of leg room.

The carcass should be attached to the finished underframe before the drawer stock is prepared and planed to fit the openings. Wooden buttons or, alternatively, slotted metal plates may be used to hold the carcass firmly down. With both due allowance must be made for the possible movement in width of the carcass.

It is for this reason also that the drawers are not made to touch the back of the carcass, being left short by some 1/4 in. or so. Fig. 5 shows the construction of the drawers with the plywood bottom glued into grooves in the front and sides, but running underneath the back and fixed with countersunk screws. The grain of these bottoms may be arranged to run parallel with the drawer fronts, as would have to be the case if solid drawer bottoms were employed.

The drawer back is made some 1/8 in. or so lower than the drawer sides and rounded over on its top edge. This is to prevent the possible jamming of the drawer by sheets of writing paper bunching up. The favoured drawer side stock of the cabinet maker was always quarter sawn oak because of its

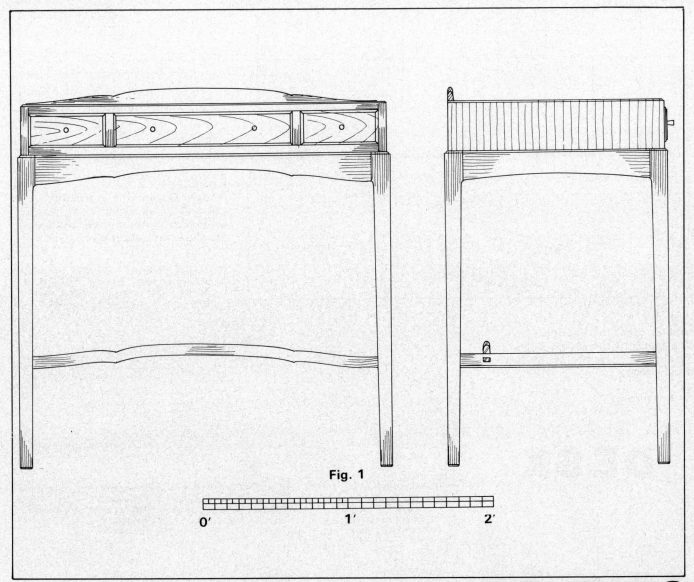

Fig. 1

0'   1'   2'

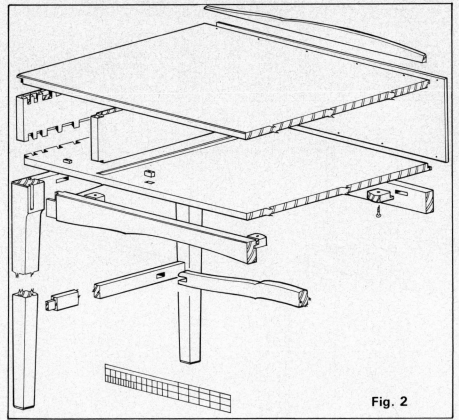

Fig. 2

WRITING DESK

dimensional stability and hardness, thus ensuring trouble-free running. Many, incidentally, would fit cedar of Lebanon drawer bottoms because of its slight scent in an otherwise stale volume of air.

Another idea employed from the 18th century onwards was to line the drawer with blue paper (it can still be obtained) to protect the contents. It should be noted that the outer sides of the drawers should not be sealed or waxed as this will inevitably cause the drawer to stick. A little candlegrease may be rubbed on as a lubricant if desired.

The drawer pulls are fixed at the points shown on the scaled elevation drawing (Fig. 1). They are positioned slightly above the centre line of the drawer front by some $\frac{3}{32}$ in. This is to counteract the visual discrepancy apparent if they are fixed exactly on the centre line, whereupon they will appear to be too low.

With the job completed the final task is to level the legs and to work a small $\frac{1}{8}$ in. chamfer at the bottom of each leg with a block plane. This has a twofold purpose: it will prevent the possible splintering of the bottom of the legs if the piece is suddenly moved; and will obviate the shearing action of a sharp arris on the pile of a carpet.

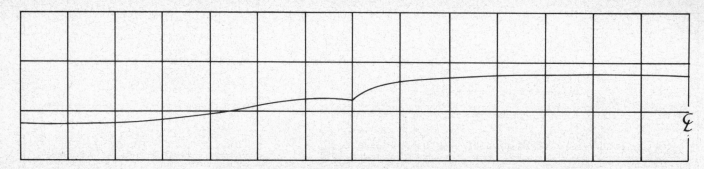

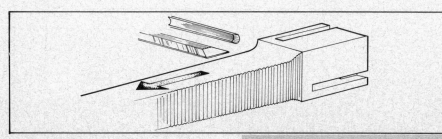

Fig. 3.
Above: Curves for 'gunstock'
stiles (1 in. squares).
Underframe rail shown, others
are the same curvature.

Fig. 4.
Above: Sketch showing how
the blend of the radius and
straight is achieved at the top
of the legs.

DESK

Fig. 5.
Below: Sketch showing drawer
construction.

Cutting list

(Net sizes shown)

Item	No.	Length	Width	Thickness	Material
Carcass					
Top	1	2ft 6in.	1ft 6in.	$^{11}/_{16}$in.	Mahogany
Bottom	1	2ft 5½in.	1ft 6in.	$^{11}/_{16}$in.	Mahogany
Ends	2	4in.	1ft 6in.	$^{11}/_{16}$in.	Mahogany
Dividers	2	3¼in.	1ft 5¾in.	$^{11}/_{16}$in.	Mahogany
Retaining strip	1	2ft 6in.	1¼in.	⅜in.	Mahogany
Back (grain vertical)	1	2ft 5½in.	3½in.	¼in.	Mahogany-faced plywood
Fixing buttons	10	1¼in.	1in.	¾in.	Mahogany
Drawers					
Side drawer fronts	2	6¼in.	2⅞in.	¾in.	Mahogany
Side drawer backs	2	6¼in.	2¼in.	⅜in.	Mahogany
Side drawer bottoms	2	1ft 4½in.	5¾in.	¼in.	Mahogany-faced plywood
Central drawer front	1	14¾in.	2⅞in.	¾in.	Mahogany
Central drawer back	1	14¾in.	2¼in.	⅜in.	Mahogany
Central drawer bottom	1	1ft 4½in.	14¼in.	¼in.	Mahogany-faced plywood
Drawer sides	6	1ft 5in.	2⅞in.	⅜in.	Mahogany or quartered oak
Drawer stops	4	½in.	½in.	¼in.	Mahogany
Drawer pulls	4	¾in. dia			Brass or aluminium
Underframe					
Legs	4	2ft 1⅛in.	1¼in.	1¼in.	Mahogany
Front rail	1	2ft 6in.	2⅜in.	¾in.	Mahogany
Back rail	1	2ft 6in.	2⅜in.	¾in.	Mahogany
End rails	2	1ft 6in.	2⅜in.	¾in.	Mahogany
Side stretcher rails	2	1ft 5in.	1⅛in.	⅝in.	Mahogany
Central stretcher rail	1	2ft 6in.	2in.	⅝in.	Mahogany

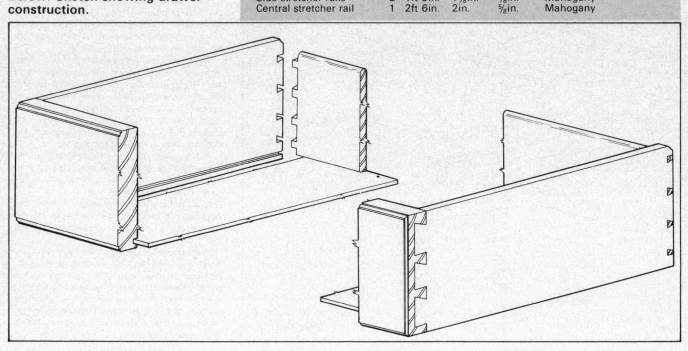

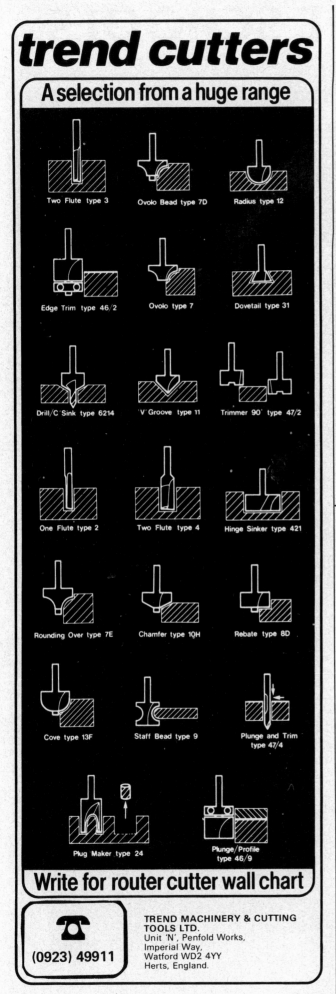

WORK BY THE SCHOOLS

Here are some of the pieces made by fifth year pupils of Lord William's Upper School at Thame, Oxon. Anthony J. Lord of the craft department tells WOODWORKER that William Edwards, who made the coffee table, has now got an apprenticeship as a carpenter with the National Trust.

An example of work by pupils at Lord William's was illustrated on page 571 of the October 1979 issue.

(All photographs by N. S. Lilley)

Right: Telephone seat by Simon Baker in teak veneered chipboard and afrormosia.
Below: Coffee table by William Edwards made from locally felled elm.
Below centre: Tripod table by Andrew Groves has a utile base with pivoting sapele top.
Below right: Folding cake stand by Maxwell Reid in maple and Brazilian mahogany.

Below: Audio cabinet by Philip Nixey in mahogany veneered chipboard and utile.

Below: Record cabinet by Robert Nicholls in utile and mahogany veneered chipboard.

Space saver

MY PROBLEM IS I NEED 5 DIFFERENT MACHINES BUT I ONLY HAVE THE SPACE FOR ONE, NOT THAT I COULD AFFORD 5 ANYWAY

WHY DON'T YOU INSTALL A STARTRITE ROBLAND UNIVERSAL WOODWORKER? IT DOES ALL THE JOBS YOU NEED AND TAKES UP LESS SPACE THAN AN OFFICE DESK

BUT DON'T UNIVERSALS LACK THE POWER OF INDIVIDUAL MACHINES?

NONSENSE! THE ROBLAND HAS 3 MOTORS TO GIVE YOU PEAK POWER FOR EVERY SINGLE JOB

ROBLAND K210 UNIVERSAL

- 3" rise and fall tilt arbor circular saw with sliding table.
- 8¼" wide surface planer, 48" tables.
- 5 7/8" x 8¼" thicknesser with power feed.
- 1¼" spindle moulder with rise and fall spindle.
- 5" x 5/8" mortiser with length and depth stop.

- Available in single or three phase electrics.

STARTRITE
MACHINE TOOL CO LTD
69-71 Newington Causeway, London, SE1 6BH
Telephone 01-407 7356

LET YOUR WOOD GET A BREATH OF FRESH AIR

says W. H. Brown FIWSc

When preparing your wood for carving remember that exposing the wood to air must extract unwanted moisture uniformly and at a rate that will not cause splits and shakes to develop. Various woods and their drying rates are given below as well as hints on what to look for when buying partially-dry wood.

Conditioning of wood in order to prepare it for carving involves exposing it to air which will extract the unwanted moisture uniformly, and at a rate that will not cause splits and shakes to develop. A few years ago I visited the famous Bavarian state carving school at Oberammergau where, because of the local associations with the Passion Play, large quantities of wood carvings are produced for the tourist trade. The carvings range from sacred statues and Last Supper groups of all sizes to more typically national character studies. A notable feature of the school is the excellent condition of the wood used: this is principally oak and lime in thick planks which are simply placed in-stick in low piles, with a little top protection, and are left to dry for several years.

There is nothing special in the technique which is the same elsewhere. The difference between one area and another is in the air conditions which govern wood drying, ie temperature, humidity and air circulation. In the Bavarian alps air conditions are generally ideal for slowly drying refractory woods like thick oak. During the winter, despite heavy falls of snow, the air is dry and crisp most of the time and air circulation is good so that some drying of piled wood can take place. The winter sun can be quite hot in sheltered spots but, again, snow melting on the wood can reduce any tendency for fine surface checks to occur.

When spring begins to give way to warmer weather these alpine regions are under the influence of the warm, southern föhn winds which pick up humidity from the melting snow at high altitude and bring the well-known, lethargic humid atmosphere to the valleys, an atmosphere which discourages rapid evaporation of moisture from the surfaces of seasoning wood, and by so doing reduces splitting and checking tendencies.

In the artificial drying of wood, ie in a drying kiln, one of the basic principles is to ensure the outer zones of wood are kept moist so as to encourage continuous capillary action of the interior moisture, decreasing the humidity and increasing the temperature as the wood dries. It can be seen that to a great extent this happens naturally in the alpine region mentioned. It can also be noted in the Swiss alps in the drying of softwood intended for cuckoo clocks. In countries like Britain with its variable and unpredictable climate, much greater control over the elements is needed. This can be done in a number of ways. For example, air circulation can be increased or decreased over the surface of drying wood by changing the thickness of the sticks used to separate the pieces, and/or by stacking the wood sideways-on, or head-on, to the prevailing wind.

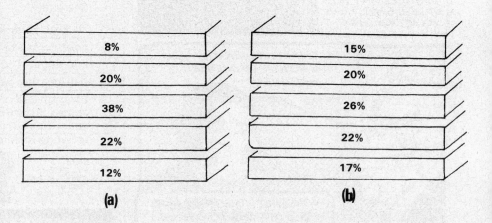

(a) (b)

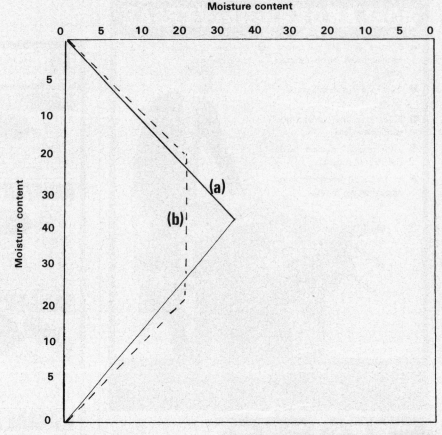

Fig. 1 Moisture distribution through thickness of wood. Both samples have an average moisture content of 20%, but in sample (a) the gradient is steeper thus rendering the wood more liable to split and check. Sample (a) is drying too rapidly at the surface, whereas in sample (b) movement of moisture is reasonable.

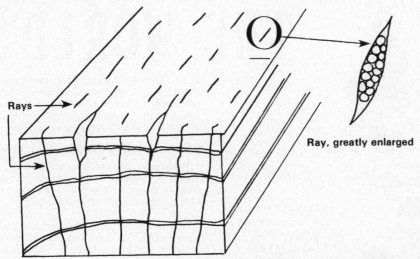

Rays →

Ray, greatly enlarged

Fig. 2 Wood rays are boat-shaped; when large, as in beech, oak and plane tree their pointed ends tend to act like wedges, forcing the wood apart as it shrinks and encouraging end splitting and surface checking to occur.

Wet wood cuts more easily than dry wood because as it dries, so its hardness and strength properties increase. Furthermore, drying stresses tend to exaggerate directional strength and may increase hardness, eg by casehardening. It is not practical to carve wet wood so the aim should be to remove surplus moisture from it in such a way as to obtain a fairly uniform distribution of the remaining moisture throughout the thickness, thereby reducing stress and casehardening tendencies; in other words by levelling out the moisture gradient as far as possible.

For example, two pieces of wood each with an average moisture content (m.c.) of 20% have a sample taken from each and these are sawn into five strips through the thickness. The m.c. of each is assessed and in one this reads as follows: core, 38%; intermediate, 20 and 22%; outside 12 and 8%. The corresponding strips in the second sample read, 26; 22 and 20; 15 and 17%. The former sample has a fairly steep gradient, the latter a relatively flat one. Steep moisture gradients encourage splitting and checking of wood. (Fig. 1).

Suitable time must be allowed for drying to take place in step with the wood's ability to give up its moisture. This is not the same for all species. Particular care is also needed when drying species with large rays which tend to act as tiny wedges intent on forcing the wood's fibres apart. (Fig. 2).

Timbers which dry slowly. Apple; black bean; European boxwood (very slow); sweet chestnut; ekki (very); greenheart (very); jacareuba/Santa Maria (very); lignum vitae (very); all true oaks and Australian silky 'oak' (very); okan; E African olive; pear and wallaba. Sticks used for separating planks should be no thicker than ½in. (12mm) for wood 1½in. (38mm) thick or more.

Timbers which dry fairly rapidly. African 'walnut'; agba; alder; European ash; beech and birch; C American 'cedar'; elm; guarea; iroko; jelutong; European lime; mahogany; makoré; meranti; plane tree; purpleheart; sapele; sycamore and willow. Sticks of about ⅝in. (16mm) are suitable.

Timbers which dry rapidly. Abura; afara/limba; alstonia; idigbo; obeche (very rapid). Sticks of ¾in. (19mm) are suitable.

Timbers needing special care. Beech (distortion and surface checking due to large rays); oak and plane tree (large rays); sweet chestnut (surface checking and splitting along the growth rings, ie ring shakes); ash (tends to split at ends); elm (distortion); birch (tends to distort).

The above categories are mostly applicable to wood being dried from the fresh-sawn (green) state. If wood is partially dry at the time it is acquired the technique to follow to complete the drying will depend firstly on the condition of the wood, and secondly on time of year. In Britain we can anticipate that timber piled to dry in the open air will begin to do so slowly in March and continue at around the same pace until June to September when it will obtain the benefit of higher temperatures to evaporate unwanted moisture quite rapidly from the wood. It is during these summer months that humidity adjacent to the surfaces of the wood needs to be relatively high in slow-drying species; therefore wetting the piled wood is often necessary.

It is helpful to know how long the wood has been cut and how long it has been lying about prior to purchase. While I am never keen on logs being left lying in, say, long grass for lengthy periods (because this encourages sap stain of sapwood), nevertheless during the warmer parts of the year this can retard drying which is not always a bad thing. Keeping the bark on round logs is useful as this also tends to slow down the drying and cracking; peeling bark does give an indication of drying progress. Even under ideal conditions it can take a long time for dense hardwoods of 2in. (50mm) thickness, for example, to dry in the open air; and very thick pieces, say 6in. (150mm), may still be wet at the centre after many years' exposure to external air.

Many woodcarvers use a purpose-built box type of bench with a top which can be tilted to facilitate the work and beneath the racks and drawers holding tools there is space for storing the odd thick chunks of wood which the carver loves to hoard. It is essential first to ensure these pieces are really dry before being stored, and second to remove them for examination during the summer. This is to make sure no beetle damage is developing and to let the wood get a breath of fresh air, so to speak.

WHAT'S ON

Craftsmanship 1980
Until 31 August organised by the Cornwall Crafts Association at Trelowarren, Mawgan-in-Meneage, Cornwall.

Southern Counties Craft Market
The seventh exhibition and craft market will take place at the Maltings, Farnham, Surrey, from 10-12 October.

Svensk Form
Continuing its series of contemporary design exhibitions the Victoria and Albert museum is presenting Svensk Form, an exhibition of craft and design, organised by the Swedish Society of Industrial Design for the Swedish Institute. The exhibition will focus on the caring aspects of design and there will also be a small mixed display of items of Swedish design from the '30s to the '70s drawn from the museum's own collections on show during the exhibition (outside the lecture theatre, room 66.) Location of main exhibition, 48E, admission 50p, children, OAPs and students 25p, party rate 25p each; family Saturdays, adults 30p, children, students and OAPs 25p. Open until 14 September.

Finger-jointing seminar
Seminar to examine the economic and technical factors of finger-jointing sawnwood will be held at Hamar, Norway, from 16-19 September. The programme includes visits to plants and a research institute. Details from timber section, ECE/FAO Agriculture & Timber Division, Palais des Nations, CH-1211, Geneva 10, Switzerland; or Export Council of Norway, Norway Trade Centre, 20 Pall Mall, London SW1Y 5NE.

Interbuild 81
Following the success of the 38th exhibition the dates of Interbuild 81 have been announced as 29 November to 5 December 1981. Details are available from Christopher John, 11 Manchester Square, London WI 5AB (phone 01-486 1951).

Marquetry in New York
1980 annual exposition — work by members of the Marquetry Society of America, 2-26 September. Open to the public on weekdays only, 9am-5pm No. 6 Plaza Level, World Trade Centre, New York NY.

Eastern Counties Craft Market
The ninth craft market will be held at the Rhodes Centre, Bishops Stortford, Herts; from 14-16 November. Further details from Patricia Beswick, Thele, Great Amwell, Ware SG12 9RT.

Salisbury Festival of Arts
Those interested in music, arts and crafts should make a note to visit Salisbury in September when the city holds its annual festival of the arts. Running from 4-17 September the festival includes a lavish programme of concerts in the cathedral and other musical and theatrical events in other venues in the city. From 7-11 September in Salisbury's city hall there is to be a major craft exhibition called Craft Plus '80 which will include demonstrations by craftsmen and women, plus stalls. Further information may be obtained by sending a sae to the Publicity Officer, Crafts Plus '80, 12 Fieldside, East Hagbourne, Oxfordshire.

THE WORLD'S

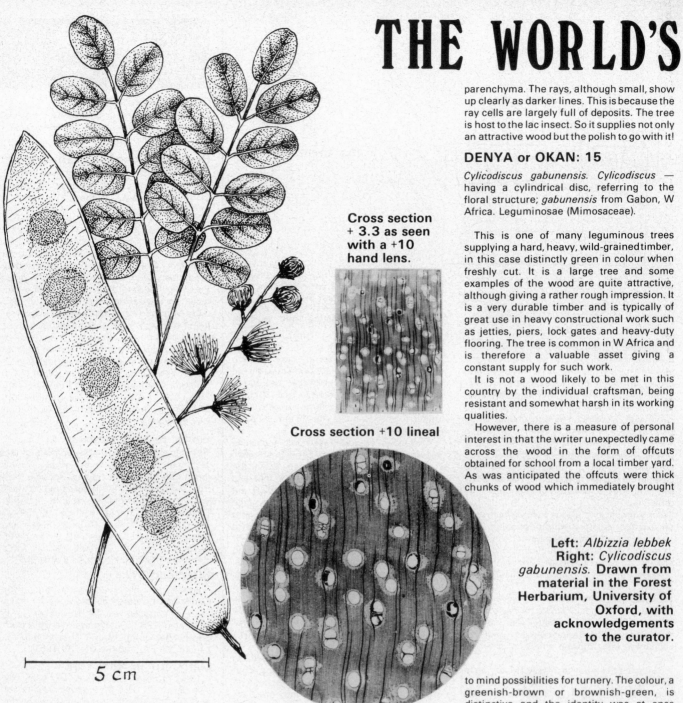

Cross section + 3.3 as seen with a +10 hand lens.

Cross section +10 lineal

Left: *Albizzia lebbek*
Right: *Cylicodiscus gabunensis.* **Drawn from material in the Forest Herbarium, University of Oxford, with acknowledgements to the curator.**

5 cm

---

parenchyma. The rays, although small, show up clearly as darker lines. This is because the ray cells are largely full of deposits. The tree is host to the lac insect. So it supplies not only an attractive wood but the polish to go with it!

DENYA or OKAN: 15

Cylicodiscus gabunensis. Cylicodiscus — having a cylindrical disc, referring to the floral structure; *gabunensis* from Gabon, W Africa. Leguminosae (Mimosaceae).

This is one of many leguminous trees supplying a hard, heavy, wild-grained timber, in this case distinctly green in colour when freshly cut. It is a large tree and some examples of the wood are quite attractive, although giving a rather rough impression. It is a very durable timber and is typically of great use in heavy constructional work such as jetties, piers, lock gates and heavy-duty flooring. The tree is common in W Africa and is therefore a valuable asset giving a constant supply for such work.

It is not a wood likely to be met in this country by the individual craftsman, being resistant and somewhat harsh in its working qualities.

However, there is a measure of personal interest in that the writer unexpectedly came across the wood in the form of offcuts obtained for school from a local timber yard. As was anticipated the offcuts were thick chunks of wood which immediately brought

to mind possibilities for turnery. The colour, a greenish-brown or brownish-green, is distinctive and the identity was at once apparent. The resulting trial bowl was a handsome example, but there was quite a dramatic change in appearance after a year or so in the sunlight: the colour changed to a deep rich brown, almost unique and very different from the original.

The photomicrographs show the large vessels evenly distributed with a suggestion of oblique arrangement and the well-marked vasicentric arrangement of parenchyma cells. The rays are not large but are dark and conspicuous; and the ray cells are seen under higher magnification to be full of deposits in numerous globules.

So much for certain woods from the Leguminosae, a family which gives a host of commercial timbers. A few (and it is a few) of the most important are afzelia, angelin, brazilwood, bubinga, cabbage-bark, cocobolo, cocus, copalwood, kempas, kingwood, mora, panga-panga, pernambuco, purpleheart, pyinkado, sabicu, sissoo, tulipwood, vinhatico, wallaba, zebrano — the list of trade and local names seems almost endless.

In the 13th part of his series (August issue) C. W. Bond FIWSc described Australian blackwood and its uses. Here he discusses kokko, a common species in India and sometimes referred to as East Indian walnut. He also deals with denya or okan which is a very durable timber though somewhat harsh in its working qualities.

KOKKO: 14

Albizzia lebbek. Albizzia — in honour of Albizzi, a famous Italian naturalist; *lebbek —* probably from an old Arabic name. Leguminosae (Mimosaceae).

This is a common species in India and is probably in various ways one of the most useful of trees. It is extensively cultivated elsewhere in the tropics and sub-tropical regions, often as a roadside or avenue tree. The ripe pods are flat and more or less transparent and light enough to be borne along on the wind.

The wood is distinctly open and coarse in texture but it is, nevertheless, very attractive with its varying brown colour. It is sometimes referred to as East Indian walnut, though there is little resemblance, being so much coarser than either the home-grown walnut (*Juglans regia*) or the American black species (*Juglans nigra*). The colour might be similar.

Although common in India, export is limited but it may be met in veneer form. It is somewhat similar to elm in hardness and weight and in its working qualities: not a particularly easy wood to work having an unpleasant scent and rather wild grain. In addition it produces an irritating dust in abrasive operations. Despite these criticisms anyone going to India is likely to find kokko in general use for a variety of work.

The photomicrographs clearly show the reason for the open texture. The very large vessels, almost perfectly circular in cross section, are conspicuous and the wood shows another classic example of vasicentric

TIMBER TREES

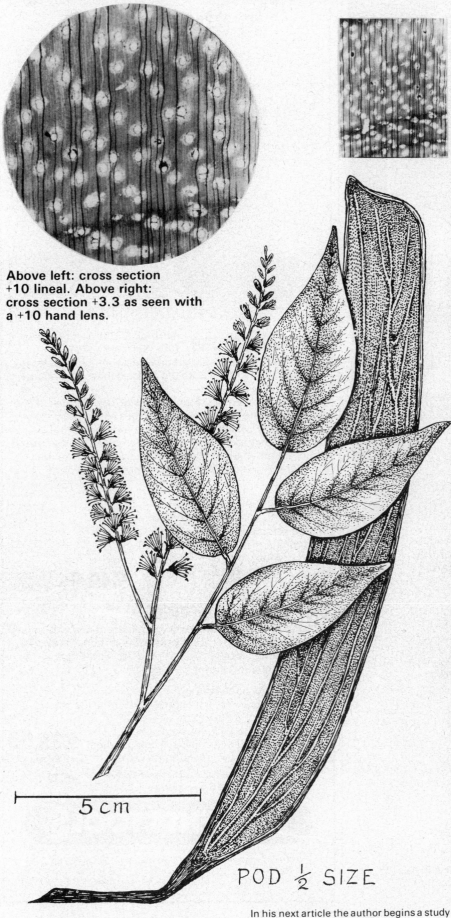

Above left: cross section +10 lineal. Above right: cross section +3.3 as seen with a +10 hand lens.

5 cm

POD ½ SIZE

In his next article the author begins a study of Meliaceae (the mahoganies).

Woodworker, September 1980

573

You're making wicker furniture

'The only limit on the production of wicker furniture is one's own imagination,' says John Bausert in his book *Wicker & Cane Furniture Making*. His designs are pleasing and in every instance the guide-lines, in more or less tabular form, are concise and easy to follow. The 18 full-page pictures give an indication of the range of design and they certainly bear out his assertion.

This American production is soft bound but the colour photograph on the front cover is pleasing in itself and worth protecting. The instructions in this specialised branch of furniture making are written in an encouraging and personal style. A page with just the simple words 'Dedication. To my father — who never pushed' seems to sum up the character of the whole book. (It made me think. When I was young I needed rather a lot of pushing!)

Reproduced from hand-written script the book has over 100 drawings and photographs which illustrate the procedures very clearly. There is an introduction followed by seven chapters and a short summary.

Introduction: This refers briefly to history in the use of rattan (a climbing palm), a description of the plant with methods of extraction, sizes and market conversion. Six UK sources of supply are listed.

Hand caning: Tools and suitable sizes are listed together with step-by-step instructions, seven in all, and notes on finish.

Pre-woven or machine caning: Similarly, five stages in the use of pre-woven cane for chair seats are treated in a concise manner.

Fiber *(sic)* rush: There is a brief description of this material followed by a list of tools for its use. Again, the text is divided into five processes each one described in detail.

Splint: This follows precisely the same order beginning with a description of the material. Four sections are included here and the foregoing chapters would be particularly useful in repair work, referring as they do to pre-constructed frames.

Weaving: This brief chapter deals with the use of wider and thicker cane for stool seats.

Wicker: This chapter deals with heavier material in the complete construction of (1) a basket plantstand; (2) the making of a complete chair. The required sizes of rattan vary in this work from flat binding widths of 6mm to solid pieces 1½in. in diameter. The mixture of metric and imperial measurements does not appear to be important. Tools and dimensioned materials are listed for both items.

Combination wicker and machine caning: Fully described for a cocktail table.

The book comes from Sterling Publishing Co Inc, 2 Park Avenue, New York NY 10016, at $6.95 (£3.50). **C.B.**

Marquetry

Published as a hardback in 1971, *The Art and Practice of Marquetry* (William Alexander Lincoln) is now available as a paperback of 304 pages at £3.95. Publisher is Thames & Hudson Ltd, 30 Bloomsbury Street, London WC1B 3QP. Apart from the omission of a few illustrations the paperback appears to have the same text as the 1971 edition.

Catalogue

Twelve-page booklet in colour describing and illustrating the Unimat 3 system (basically lathe with attachments for wood and metal working), has been received from E.M.E. Ltd (E.M. Equipment Ltd), B.E.C. House, Victoria Road, London NW10 6NY.

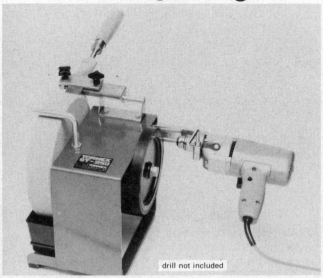

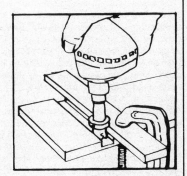
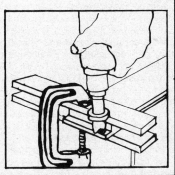

RESTORING ANTIQUE FURNITURE

Charles Cliffe offers some hints

Wherever you travel these days you see antique shops and posters advertising antique fairs. There is a growing interest in antiques and when we look at some of the furniture displayed it is not hard to see why. The design is good, the workmanship is top-class and the wood used is invariably superior to that obtainable today.

Much of this furniture when acquired by the dealer is in need of restoration and the work put in by the cabinetmaker and polisher is necessarily reflected in the asking price. Many pieces require so much attention that they are uneconomical to repair and will be added to the repairer's stock of old wood which he uses to restore less damaged items. Very often there are several such dilapidated pieces poked away in the corners of the auctioneer's sale room and after a word in the right ear these can be had quite cheaply.

Don't be carried away by an excess of enthusiasm and find that you have bought a worm-riddled heap which is only fit for the bonfire. Make a critical examination so that you know precisely what work lies ahead. If you feel you have the ability and the time then make your purchase.

Having brought your piece home it will have to be cleaned of all dirt, grease, wax and old furniture polish. This is best done with warm water and toilet soap. Brass handles and fittings should be removed and put away in a safe place, but not so safe that you can't find them again! If there are mouldings or decorative pieces which unscrew, remove them and label them so that they can be replaced in their original position.

Missing or broken pieces have to be replaced or repaired. If the replacement is made from a piece of old wood of a similar type to the original the repair will blend in all the better. Over the years the rails mortised into chair and table legs get more than their share of abuse. If the rail is broken in the middle the cure is usually to make a new rail using the old one as a pattern. Should one of the tenons have been broken, then a false tenon can be fitted (Fig. 1) and the rail glued back in position.

This may not be as straightforward as it sounds for it may mean splaying the legs to permit the tenons to enter the mortises. If splaying the legs is likely to force further joints apart it may be preferable to have a false tenon at one end of the rail and having first inserted the opposite end into its mortise you then slide the false end into position. Having fitted your new rail, emulate any wear marks which might have been caused by heels resting where they should not! (Fig. 2).

Fig. 2. Wear marks on chair rail.

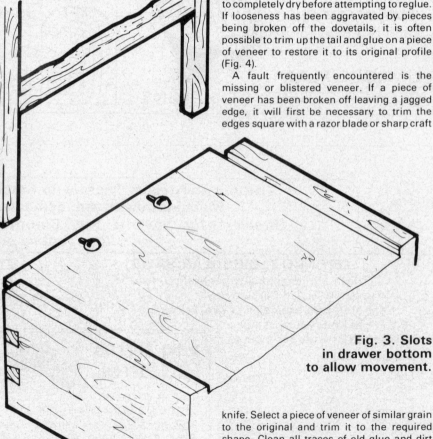

Drawers often show their age by splitting at the bottom or suffering from looseness of the dovetails. The bottoms were usually made from thin wood with the grain running from side to side. The front edge was glued into the slot ploughed into the drawer front while the rear edge was tacked to the back of the drawer. As the bottom dries out over the years and shrinks it splits on account of being secured at both ends.

The cure is to remove the pins at the back, clean the edges of the split, glue together and when set re-fix with screws and cut slots in the drawer bottom to allow for further movement (Fig. 3). If the dovetail joints are loose they should be carefully tapped apart and all traces of old glue removed. Sometimes it is necessary to soften the old scotch glue with hot damp cloths before the joints can be parted. If you have to do so give the wood time to completely dry before attempting to reglue. If looseness has been aggravated by pieces being broken off the dovetails, it is often possible to trim up the tail and glue on a piece of veneer to restore it to its original profile (Fig. 4).

A fault frequently encountered is the missing or blistered veneer. If a piece of veneer has been broken off leaving a jagged edge, it will first be necessary to trim the edges square with a razor blade or sharp craft

Fig. 3. Slots in drawer bottom to allow movement.

knife. Select a piece of veneer of similar grain to the original and trim it to the required shape. Clean all traces of old glue and dirt from the groundwork and using hot scotch glue lay the new veneer in position. Place a piece of waxed paper over the patch and weight it down with heavy weights until the glue has set.

It can happen that the glue fails and the veneer rises in the form of a blister. If it is small cut it along the grain with a razor blade and lift one half of the blister just sufficiently to work some hot glue underneath. Do the same with the other half, wipe off the surplus glue with a damp rag and weight down until dry. A bird's wing feather is useful for inserting hot glue under blisters. If the blister happens to be a large one it will help if a second cut is made across the blister at right

Fig. 1. Fitting false tenon.

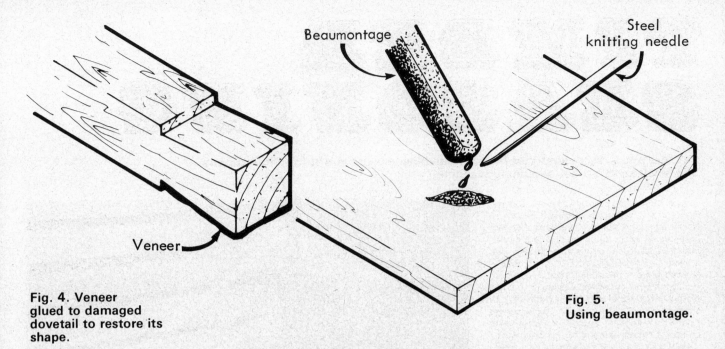

Beaumontage

Steel knitting needle

Veneer

Fig. 4. Veneer glued to damaged dovetail to restore its shape.

Fig. 5. Using beaumontage.

angles to the first so that the glue can be more easily worked right in.

If a small piece of veneer is missing it may be easier and just as effective to use hard stopping or beaumontage. This is made from beeswax and resin and is coloured to match mahogany, walnut and various shades of oak. It is bought in sticks like sealing wax from polish suppliers. Hold the stopping above the blemish to be filled and touch the end of it with a hot steel knitting needle (Fig. 5). When sufficient stopping has dripped off to slightly overfill the blemish, allow it to go hard and then level it off flush with a wide chisel.

Another frequently encountered defect is the bruise which occurs when something heavy has dropped on the wood and compressed its fibres. Here are ways of swelling the fibres and thereby levelling the bruises:

If the polish remaining on the surface is to be stripped off the bruise can be filled with methylated spirits and the meths set alight. Blow out the flame just before the spirit is burnt away. If the bruise is not brought level the first time the process can be repeated.

It may be that the area around the bruise is well-polished and it is inadvisable to risk damaging by having blazing meths in close proximity. In this case steam can be used.

If the film of polish over the dent is unbroken take a needle and prick through it a few times. Fill the dent with water and let it soak into the wood for about 10min. Place a piece of wet wadding over the bruise and raise steam by applying a hot domestic iron or a hot poker to the wadding. Here again more than one application may be needed.

Allow the treated area to dry completely before glasspapering smooth prior to staining. Spirit stains are used in preference to water stains as the latter could swell the fibres further and cause a bump to appear where previously there has been a hollow.

If the antique is french polished and the polish has not cracked at all it can be eased-down with fine glasspaper or steel wool. Dust off and start polishing with thinned polish. This will help the new polish to take more readily to the old.

A badly cracked or scarred finish has to

come off and can be removed with a chemical stripper. These are particularly useful on moulded or carved surfaces. But follow the maker's instructions. If the surface is a plain one, such as a table top or a drawer front, the old polish can be burnt off by placing the surface in a vertical position and sweeping a meths-soaked rag over the area and setting alight to it from the bottom. The wood will be left clean and dry, ready for repolishing. Do not use this method in a wooden shed where the floor is covered with shavings or other combustible materials.

If the old finish has been completely removed the choice of what new finish to use is entirely in the restorer's hands. Where the greater part of the original polish is in good order and only a small area needs repolishing we have to identify the old finish so that we can restore with the same kind of polish. If french polish is suspected moisten an inconspicuous piece with meths and if the polish softens your suspicions are well-founded. If it does not soften then the surface is scraped with a sharp chisel and if yellow shavings are produced the finish is varnish. Should white powder be scraped away the piece has been cellulosed.

A cellulose film can sometimes be rejuvenated by brushing it with cellulose thinners to soften the cellulose and redistribute it over the work to form a new surface. Antiques should not, of course, be cellulosed; but it is as well to know how to deal with those that have been so treated.

There is no way of rejuvenating varnish by softening it. Smooth it with 000 steel wool and then dust it absolutely clean. With a perfectly clean brush apply a flowing coat of clear varnish in a warm, dry, dust-free room. If the brush is not really clean disfiguring streaks will result. If the atmosphere is damp the finish will be cloudy. If dust is present the finish will be rough to the touch. Avoid these simple pitfalls and the resulting finish should be perfectly satisfactory.

If your antique is made from oak it has almost certainly been wax polished. This gives a duller finish than french polish and seems to suit oak better.

Traditionally the polish was made from beeswax and pure turpentine but if a harder finish is required carnauba wax may be added. Shred the carnauba wax and cover it

with about four times its volume of turpentine or white spirit. Dissolve the mixture in a double boiler similar to a glue kettle and add shredded beeswax equal in amount to the carnauba. Stir well togehter. When cool the mixture should be of the consistency of soft butter.

With a piece of rag rub the polish well into the wood and try to spread it evenly. If a large table top is being polished it helps if the rag is wrapped around a brick as the additional weight lessens the physical effort of the polisher. Surplus polish is rubbed off with a second cloth which brings up a gloss, while a third cloth is used to impart the final polish. Several applications of polish should be given to bring up a deep mellow glow. In fact, as with oil polishing, waxing can go on for as long as the polisher wishes.

BOOKS

Further reading on the subject:

1. Antique Furniture Repairs by Charles Hayward. £5.50.

2. Staining and Polishing by Charles Hayward. £5.50.

3. Wood Finish and Refinish by S. W. Gibbia. £5.20 (paperback).

4. Golden Homes Book of Basic Furniture Renovation. £1.75.

5. Care and Repair of Furniture by Desmond Gaston. £4.95.

6. Repairing and Restoring Antique Furniture by John Rodd. £6.95.

7. The Finishing and Refinishing of Wood by F. Oughton. £2.95.

8. Furniture Doctoring and French Polishing by C. Harding. £1.95.

9. The Practical Handbook of Furniture Refinishing by John H. Savage. Approximately £2.50.

These titles are available from Stobart & Son Ltd, 67-73 Worship Street, London EC2A 2EL.

TIMBER SEASONING

Pat Sharp has discovered that his one-man business can profit from investment in a small-scale timber seasoning machine.

When Pat Sharp formed Haydon Design Products, Ratcliffe Road, Haydon, Northumberland, about 10 years ago he had little capital but a lot of talent and a determination to succeed on his own. He says: 'As a reader of WOODWORKER ... I probably learned some of my skills from it. I have had no training in furniture design or manufacture.' Nevertheless, the extent of his success can be gauged by the growing number of regular customers who have created a steady demand for his products.

He works in a variety of woods: pine, yew, elm, ash, oak, beech, lime. He makes chairs, benches, tables and dressers, fruit bowls, inlaid chess tables and hand-turned chessmen. He designs everything himself and most of his products are made to order, such as specially robust tables for the S Tyneside education authority. Another regular order is lids for earthenware storage jars made by nearby Barden Mill Pottery.

For some years pine furniture has been popular. Booming sales have, however, attracted an increasing number of suppliers and the market is now heavily saturated. Mainly for this reason Pat Sharp began to use mostly home-grown hardwood.

He also invested in an Ebac Mini dryer as he found that purchase of properly seasoned hardwood was costly and quality was variable. It would do his reputation no good if after six months or so a customer came back to complain of defects in the timber.

All timber contains water, some species more so than others. Indeed the weight of water in a newly-sawn piece can exceed that of the timber itself. When the water in the timber starts to dry out the timber's weight is reduced and shrinkage takes place. If the drying process is not properly controlled the shrinkage can manifest itself in stresses within the timber which lead to defects such as splits.

It is essential that the timber is dried to a humidity level which is in equilibrium with the environment in which the finished item will be used. (These factors have been discussed in detail in the Timber Topics series during recent months).

Though the fastest drying is achieved at high temperature the risk of degrade in the timber, particularly hardwood, increases at high temperature and the general rule is that the lower the temperature the better the quality. Some commercially available seasoners such as Ebac dryers are designed to operate in the temperature range which is the best compromise between speed and quality — about 60°C (140°F). This is higher than most dehumidifiers but lower than steam-heated kilns.

Rate of evaporation is dependant on the difference between the vapour pressure exerted by the wet timber and the vapour pressure of air. One way of increasing this difference in favour of the timber, so encouraging rapid drying, is to heat the timber and

The Ebac Mini positioned in the chamber. *(All photos in this article by Malcolm Halliman Photography).*

increase its vapour pressure. Another way is to lower the vapour pressure of the air. This method is adopted in Ebac dehumidifiers: encouraging evaporation by removing moisture from the air surrounding the timber.

As damp air is drawn into the machine the moisture is condensed on to a refrigerated coil, the condensate runs off to drain and the dry, cold air is re-warmed with the heat extracted from it as it passes through the refrigerated coil. It is re-circulated through the timber stacked in the associated kiln chamber, encouraging more evaporation. Moisture-laden hot air is not vented into the atmosphere; this saves in operating costs.

Kiln chambers can be simple and inexpensive, using conventional building materials. There are, however, two important factors: 1 the chamber should be well insulated against heat loss; 2 it should be vapour-proof. It is also useful to incorporate a small inspection door in the chamber so that the operator can enter the kiln to monitor performance. (A small door is necessary so as to minimise loss of heat. For drying cycles of less than seven days a twice-daily check is advisable; for longer cycles a check once a day should suffice. Checking the drying cycles indicates whether any improvements could be made. It is essential that the timber is dried down to a humidity level which is in equilibrium with the environment in which the finished item will be used.

The Mini at Haydon cost about £350 and has been installed about 10 months; it can dry up to 50cu ft at a time. Pat Sharp now buys all his timber green and he can dry 1in. thick softwood (mostly pine) in about 20 days and 2in. thick hardwood (generally oak) in around 80 days (operating on 24hr cycles).

TO CONTROL COSTS

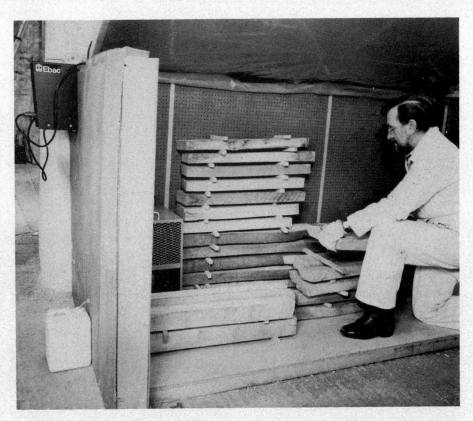

Pat Sharp with some of his products. The inlaid chess table and hand-turned chessmen are all in elm, and the fruit bowl is yew. Right: He is loading wood into the chamber, which has had the top and front removed. The control box can be seen mounted on the outside of the chamber, with the water collector below.

He uses a moisture meter as a check for dryness, though operation of the Mini is controlled by means of a dial which regulates the rate of water extracted from the atmosphere.

Pat Sharp says it is too early to make a full assessment of the costing but he has achieved substantial savings on the purchase of timber. He also points out that efficient insulation of the kiln chamber is important in reducing the running costs.

There are Ebac machines which can dry up to 1000cu ft in one load and at varying rates. All are designed around five basic principles:

1 simplicity of installation and operation; 2 low capital and running costs; 3 high quality without degrade should result; 4 the process should have a high efficiency level and be power-conserving; 5 the equipment should be able to withstand relatively demanding conditions in the kiln chamber.

Woodworker Show

Royal Horticultural Society's New Hall
4-9 November, 1980

All correspondence and entry forms: Exhibitions Manager, Model and Allied Publications Ltd, PO Box 35, Bridge Street, Hemel Hempstead HP1 1EE.

GENERAL CONDITIONS OF ENTRY

1. Each entry shall be made separately on the official form and every question must be answered. Be sure to include the estimated value of your model. LAST DAY OF ENTRY WILL BE FRIDAY, 5 SEPTEMBER 1980.
2. All entry forms must be accompanied by a remittance for the appropriate entry fee(s).
3. The competition entry fee will be £1.25 for seniors, 75p for juniors.
4. A junior shall mean a person under 18 years of age on 1 November 1980.
5. No exhibit which has previously won a bronze medal, rosette or higher award at any of the exhibitions promoted by this company shall be accepted for these competitions. The organisers reserve the right to transfer an entry to a more appropriate class.
6. Entries may be submitted by amateur or professional workers.
7. The decision of the judges shall be final.
8. Competitors shall state on the entry form:
   (a) that the exhibit is their own work and property;

   (b) any parts or kits which were purchased or were not the outcome of their own work.
   (c) the origin of the design.

9. Exhibits will be insured for the period during which they will be at the exhibition. Insurance of exhibits in transit to and from the exhibition is the responsibility of the competitor.
10. Model and Allied Publications Ltd reserves the right to refuse any entry or exhibit on arrival at the exhibition and shall not be required to furnish any reason for doing so.
11. Model and Allied Publications Ltd reserves the exclusive rights to describe and photograph any exhibits entered for competition or display and to make use of of any such photographs or descriptions in any way the company may think fit.
12. Competitors will be issued with a free non-transferable competitors' pass to the exhibition on presentation of their exhibit to the organisers.

1 2 3 4
complete
Home Workshop

CORONET
WOODWORKING MACHINES

Universal & Independent models for
Woodworking & Woodturning ♛

**SAWING ● BOX COMBING ● WOBBLE SAWING ● SPINDLE MOULDING ● PLANING
THICKNESSING ● REBATING ● MORTICING ● SLOTTING & GROOVING ● DISC SANDING
BELT SANDING ● GRINDING & POLISHING ● TURNING ● LONG HOLE BORING**

Bench mounted
& Cabinet models
ideal for . . .
PROFESSIONALS
AND D-I-Y
ENTHUSIASTS

*Whatever woodworking
operation you need —
Coronet have the ideal machine.*

Since 1946 Coronet have achieved a world wide reputation as
leading designers and manufacturers of Quality woodworking
machines with production of castings, machining and
assembly being carried out in our modern factory — to
achieve essential standards of accuracy.
Today our extensive range includes universal machines with
fitments and attachments which can be purchased as and
when required. — to suit your particular needs.

Send Now for
BROCHURE
on all models

CORONET
TOOL CO LTD
Alfreton Road
Derby DE2 4AH

*Please send me brochure, price
list & my local stockists address.
I enclose stamps, value 15p for p & p.*

NAME _____

ADDRESS _____

_____

_____ C/W 9.80

see the Coronet Range in action

—at Coronet Works and
Learn-a-Craft Training
Centre in Derby
—by arrangement
Telephone: 0332-362141

—at Stockists. Coronet
Demonstrators visit
main Stockists
throughout the year.
Send for details.

Prices quoted are those prevailing at press date and
are subject to alteration due to economic conditions.

CORONET
complete Home Workshop
— comprising:-

1 **ELF WOODTURNING LATHE**
4 speeds
12″ between centres
14″ Bowl Turning (as illustrated)

2 **IMP BANDSAW**
3 speeds
12″ throat
5″ (approx.) Depth of cut
Table tilts to 45°

3 **SOVEREIGN 4½″ PLANER**
½″ rebate
Fence tilts 45°

4 **CONSORT SAW/SPINDLE MOULDER**
4 speeds
2¼″ depth of cut
Table tilts to 45°
Spindle Moulding (See separate leaflet)

Each unit comes complete with its own motor, press button starter and cabinet stand.

Each unit can be purchased separately — if required for bench mounting (without cabinets)

Illustration shows:-
1. 14″ plaque being turned
2. Preparing disc for turning
3. 4½″ surface planing
4. Spindle moulding shelf mould

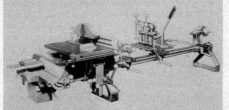

MAJOR CMB 500

MAJOR CMB 600

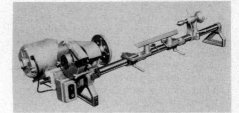

MINOR MB 6

7″ PLANER CAP 300

Jack Hill concludes his series on

COUNTRY CHAIRS AND CHAIRMAKING

5: ## RUSH SEATING OF LADDERBACKS AND SPINDLEBACKS

Traditionally, country-made ladderback and spindleback chairs had seats of woven rush. This semi-aquatic plant once grew in great profusion throughout most of Britain and was therefore readily and cheaply available. Most seat weavers, or matters as they were known in earlier days, were women and children who often worked as outworkers in their own homes. In some areas itinerant rush weavers were once a familiar sight, often sitting at the roadside to re-rush old chairs collected from nearby cottages (Fig. 1).

The rushes normally used to make chair seats are the English green rush (*Scirpus lacustris*) — the true bulrush. (Those tall plants with the brown velvety tops often called bulrushes are not rushes at all but reeds in fact). Drainage schemes and river pollution have together greatly reduced the number of rushes growing in this country and a great many are imported, mainly from Holland. These are a salt water variety of rush and are usually shorter in length than the English rush.

Rushes are sold by the bolt, a large bundle measuring approximately 40in. (1m) around its base and weighing between 5 and 6lb. (2.3-2.7kg). Each rush tapers along its length the thick end being known as the butt, the thin end as the tip. In store they should be kept dry but for use must be dampened to make them pliable enough to manipulate without breaking. This is done by placing them in a bath of cold or tepid water for 2-3min after which they should be wrapped in a damp sack or piece of old blanket and left overnight to mellow.

Damp only what can be used at one time. An average sized seat, say, 14 × 14in. (355 × 355mm) requires approximately 1½lb (0.7kg) of dry rush. As it is usual to do the work in stages, it will be found that about three dozen (that's 36 for those who don't know what a dozen is!) rushes is sufficient for each stage. As each damp and mellowed rush is used it is wiped clean with a cloth squeezed between finger and thumb. This also presses out surplus air and should always be done from tip to butt to avoid splitting the rush. Any brittle tips are broken off at this stage too.

Basically, rush bottoming or matting is done by taking two rushes of similar size, placing them alongside each other (butt to tip) and twisting them together to form a strong smooth coil of·even thickness. This rush coil is woven over and round the frame of the chair. The twisting or coiling, which is all-important, takes place as the work proceeds and is done only on the top of the seat and around the framework where it will show; underneath the rush is not twisted.

Fig. 1 A rush matter or bottomer re-seating chairs by the roadside early this century. (ack. *Museum of English Rural Life, University of Reading*).

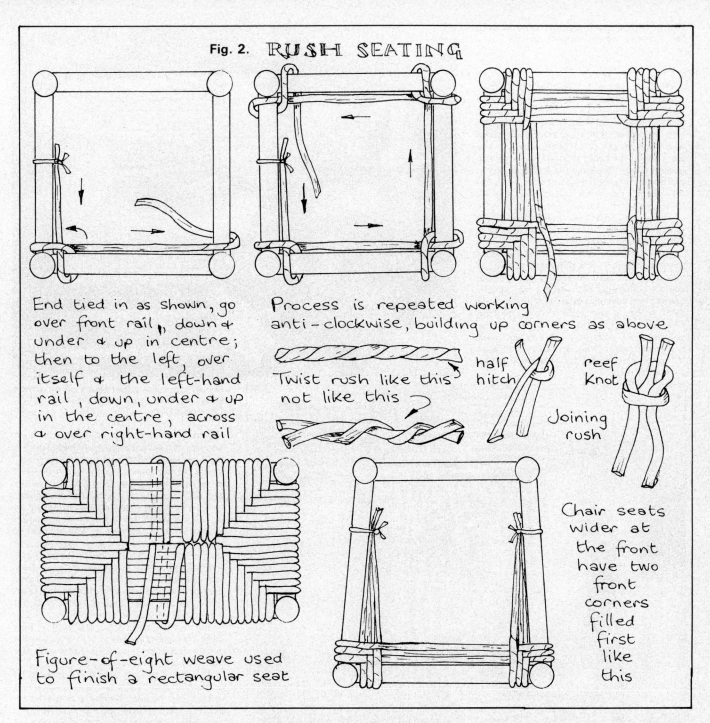

Fig. 2. RUSH SEATING

End tied in as shown, go over front rail, down & under & up in centre; then to the left, over itself & the left-hand rail, down, under & up in the centre, across & over right-hand rail

Process is repeated working anti-clockwise, building up corners as above

Twist rush like this not like this

half hitch

reef knot

Joining rush

Figure-of-eight weave used to finish a rectangular seat

Chair seats wider at the front have two front corners filled first like this

Good work is characterised by having coils of even thickness throughout, worked to a covering of five or six coils to the in. (25mm). A single rush is used if thick enough or three or even four can be used together if they are very thin. The rushes should be twisted together between finger and thumb and not coiled loosely around each other. It is a good idea to practise twisting coils before beginning an actual job in order to get the feel of the correct movement.

The start is made by tying the first ends of rush tightly together with string. For a square or rectangular seat the string is then tied to the inside of the left-hand rail of the chair frame about halfway along. The rushes, brought over the top of the front rail, are held in the left hand (of a right-handed person) while the right hand begins the twisting, the twist being made away from the corner. The coil goes below the front rail, up behind it on the inside of the frame and, twisted again, to

the left, over itself and over and under the left-hand rail. Then without twisting it comes up on the inside again and goes across to the opposite front corner where, twisted again, it goes over the right-hand rail and the whole process is repeated. (See Fig. 2 for weaving sequence.) The rush is pulled quite tightly across. Care has to be taken to ensure that the cross-over which forms at the corners as the work proceeds is kept 'square' (Fig. 3).

New rushes are joined on as old ones run out by tying-in with a reef knot, or an extra can be added to one that has become too thin by means of a half hitch. Joins are made underneath and clear of the corners. Some professional bottomers work with pairs of rushes of uneven length and simply twist in a new length of rush as necessary. Coils must be well-made for this; and knotting, although it takes a little longer, is recommended to begin with.

Rush seats are padded in order to firm the centre and raise it slightly above the edges of

the chair frame. Padding also tightens up the weaving and makes the seat stronger and therefore more hard-wearing. Short ends and broken pieces of rush can be used for this but they must be thoroughly dry (Fig. 4). Clean straw is also suitable for use as a padding material. The padding is built up gradually, usually working from the underside of the seat, by using the fingers to push handfuls of material into the pockets of rush which form at the corners. This is done after every 10 or 11 rounds of weaving. A packing stick is used to push the padding firmly in as the pockets get deeper and the space between them smaller.

The coiled rushes shrink a little as they dry out. For this reason a seat is best made in two or three stages leaving it at least overnight between each stage. After this the coils can be pushed closer together, resulting ultimately in a much firmer finish. The final coils should be worked as close together as possible.

When a seat is rectangular rather than square the corners are woven as described and the remaining centre portion is completed with what is known as the figure-of-eight weave. In this the rush coil is worked over the front rail, underneath and up in the centre, over the back rail, underneath and up in the centre, then over the front rail again, and so on. This weave is worked right across the space; but from the centre line — measured and marked before the work begins — the coiling is reversed so that it matches up with the coils already worked at the corners on the other side.

Chair seats are often wider at the front than at the back. The difference is usually only a few in. but it is enough to require a slightly different technique, for square corners are essential when rushing and the extra space on the front rail must first be filled and squared-off (Fig. 5). After this the sequence for square or rectangular seats can be followed. There are several ways of filling the extra space but only one need be described here:

Fig. 5 (Opposite page) Close-up of corner being worked. Note twist put into rush.
(Jack Hill).

First the length of the back rail is measured and this distance is marked in pencil on the front rail leaving an equal space at each end. These are the spaces which have to be filled to square-off the seat. The weaving rushes are tied into the left-hand rail as before, worked normally over the first corner, taken across to the opposite front corner and again worked over in the normal way. Instead of continuing to the back corner, however, the rushes are cut and tied-in to the right-hand rail halfway along, as shown in Fig. 2. New rushes are tied in each time and worked over the front two corners only until the marks on the front rail are reached. After this the weaving is continued round all four corners in the normal way. Again the work is best done in stages and padded as it proceeds. If a centre space remains it is filled with the figure-of-eight weave.

All seats are completed by tying the final end of the rush to the last coil opposite to it underneath the seat. Neatness on the underside is a mark of good craftsmanship. All loose ends and knots should be tucked away out of sight and the rushes bedded-in close to one another as the work progresses.

Some chairs have wooden edging pieces fitted after the rushing is completed — thin fillets of wood pinned on to the edge of the seat, partly to protect the rush but mostly for the sake of appearance. These are not really essential and are now rarely fitted. If you are renovating an old chair which has them it is perhaps as well to replace them so that the chair remains authentic. A rush seat requires no further finish and with normal use and wear should last 10 to 15 years; many last much longer.

Jack Hill's previous articles in this series appeared in the March, April, May and July issues this year.

Fig. 4 (Left) Chair seating. Stuffing the corner pockets underneath the seat.
(Jack Hill).

Carving Tools at 7s9p

Reader F. D. Armitage of Sandwich, Kent, has kindly lent us a copy of the *R.D. Scheme of Woodcarving – elementary course* by Henry Rogers and J. W. Darnbrough. It was published in 1897 by E. J. Arnold & Son of Leeds and Simpkin, Marshall, Kent & Co of London, at a cost of 2s 6d. A companion volume dealt with advanced carving and both publications contained 12 'exercises' accompanied by pull-out 'schemes' or drawings.

On the reverse of the title page is an advertisement for the R.D. No. 1 set of six carving tools 'delivered free to any address in the United Kingdom on receipt of 7/9.' These were all sharpened and ready for use and one Washita slip and one strop was included!

After the manner of the time — Queen Victoria's diamond jubilee year — Rogers and Darnbrough dedicated their work to 'that illustrious patron of all useful arts and crafts, the most hon the Marquis of Ripon . . .' We do not know if Lord Ripon had a set of the carving tools at 7/9!

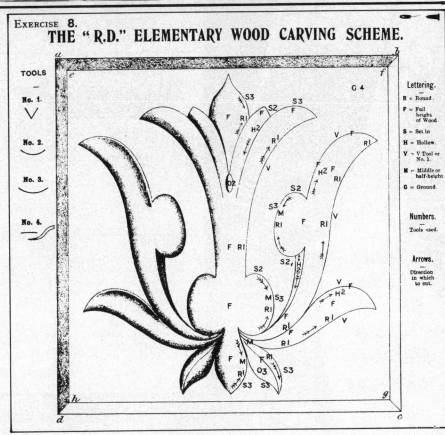

EXERCISE 8.

THE "R.D." ELEMENTARY WOOD CARVING SCHEME.

TOOLS

No. 1.

No. 2.

No. 3.

No. 4.

Lettering.

R = Round.

F = Full height of Wood.

S = Set in

H = Hollow.

V = V Tool or No. 1.

M = Middle or half-height

G = Ground.

Numbers.

Tools used.

Arrows.

Direction in which to cut.

Carving Medieval and Modern

Top left:
One place offering sanctuary to criminals in bygone days was Beverley. In St Mary's church is a misericord, believed to depict an embezzler. The carver depicted the criminal as a monkey suggesting, perhaps, that he thought money made a monkey of men!

Left centre:
A medieval batman is depicted in this misericord carving which is to be found in Ripon cathedral, Yorkshire.

Left below centre:
Novel bench end is a carved representation of the Stockton & Darlington Railway Locomotion No. 1 which can be seen in Stockton church.

Above:
Dominating a Forestry Commission picnic area at Wark, Northumberland, are these totem poles carved in traditional style by three forestry workers. Each pole is about 20ft high.

Far left:
The famous walker of Swaffham, Norfolk, is commemorated in this carving in the church there.

Left:
Commemorating William Strickland who introduced turkeys into Britain is a carved lectern at East Boynton church, Yorkshire.

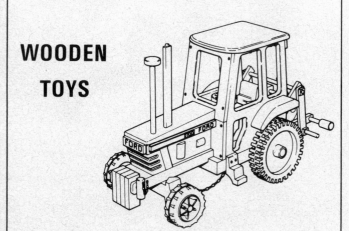
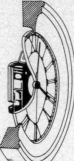

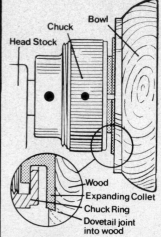

588

Prices quoted are those prevailing at press date and are subject to alteration due to economic conditions.

Woodworker, September 1980

From: A. Mackay, Edinburgh EH7 4LX
Dear Sir,

Readers may be interested to know how I solved a problem of accurately drilling and mortising round legs. I bought a solid-type transparent 6in. plastics protractor of 360°, drilled a hole through its centre into which I fitted a rubber grommet.

Then with the leg secured in a suitable V-jig with the first hole or mortise cut, I fit the protractor snugly over the leg and zero by eye to the vertical. I then turn the leg, together with the protractor, until the desired angle lines up with the drill.

I find this cheap and easily-made gadget works a treat.

Yours faithfully, **Andy Mackay**

From: Robert Griffiths, Ottery St Mary, Devon
Dear Sir,

I was interested in the article about Dennis White's treadle lathe on page 373 of the June issue. Over the years I have seen in use treadle lathes for both wood and metal turning. In fact as an apprentice we had an old treadle lathe in the carpenter's shop which I was able to use at odd times.

A lot of us have to work in a shed-cum-workshop which has no power and is often a fair distance from the house and here a treadle lathe would be a real asset. I have yet to be convinced that the modern sophisticated lathe has any edge over the old-style treadle, though someone could perhaps design a treadle that is a little more efficient than the old machines. However, with a large flywheel these were no trouble to operate.

The modern factory may need high-speed production but the craftsman in his home workshop does not. There is also the consideration of noise. I live in a modern house on an estate and any noise whatsoever is resented by neighbours whose only interest appears to be peering at the TV. So anything that allows us to pursue our craft in peace and quiet would be more than welcome.

Yours faithfully, **Robert Griffiths**

From: Samuel E. Schwartz, Jackson Heights, NY 11372
Dear Sir,

As an overseas reader WOODWORKER comes to me about a month late so I have only just seen the query by G. Roche (April issue, page 263) on the matter of turning small bowls on a drill-powered lathe.

This can be done quite well. I have been doing this on a Black & Decker lathe attachment purchased by mail from B & D in the UK some 10 years ago. The attachment is powered by a ⅜in. commercial-duty drill made in the US; it fits the drill holder well.

The lathe attachment is supplied with a 6in. faceplate; maximum swing over bed is 6in. and I find that by following these procedures I can turn out a very decent bowl of that size:

1 The platform on which the lathe bed is attached is cramped to the workbench so as to reduce vibration.
2 A speed reducer is interposed between the power line and the drill. These reducers are electronic and work with universal motors and the speed can be varied from 0-2200rpm (the speed of the drill). Roughing-down is started at about 750rpm, as on the big lathes. Once the block is reduced to a true disc the speed is increased to 1500-2200rpm. Note that this is a small bowl and well attached to the faceplate; there is no vibration at all.
3 I use standard strength turning gouges ¼ and ⅜in. sizes, square end and not necessarily deep-fluted. The main effect is to take light cuts and be patient. With light cuts there is no strain on the drill motor whose torque has been increased with the reduced speed. The light cuts produce a smooth surface even on end grain and little glasspapering is needed.
4 The papering should be done very lightly without straining the motor of the drill.

I trust these notes may help Mr Roche in his use of the drill-powered lathe. I have found the speed reducer (made in US by the Heath Co in kit form) very helpful and I am sure something similar will be available in Britain.

Yours faithfully, **Samuel E. Schwartz**

From: P. D. Cazaly, Banstead, Surrey
Dear Sir,

In response to letter from H. Nichols (page 337, May issue) regarding the difficulties he is experiencing with a hand mirror, I may be able to help.

Although the mirror in the photograph looks round I think upon examination it will be found to be slightly elliptical in which case the way to insert the glass is as follows:

Find a small piece of thick velvet and cut a shape to match the mirror shape, but about 1in. smaller all round, and lightly glue it to the inside of the back of the frame, pile facing away from the handle. A little packing may be needed behind the velvet. Now, ensuring that there are no obstructions inside the frame and the back of the mirror itself is clean, insert one end of the glass sideways at right angles to the case from the direction of the handle. Gradually rotate the glass under the edge, at the same time pushing down on the velvet. Ensure that the glass is kept as flat as possible on to the frame.

The glass, which should have thin ground edges, should then slide in and around under the rim and seal itself on the velvet which holds the glass tight against the rim.

Finally with damp fingers twist the glass inside the rim until it is tight.

Yours faithfully, **P. D. Cazaly**

From: Group-captain P. G. Thomson RAF (retd), Gairloch, Ross-shire
Dear Sir,

With reference to the problem faced by H. Nichols of Wymondham on the repair of an ebony hand mirror (page 337 of the May issue), the short answer would be to refer to that admirable book *Repairing and Restoring Antique Furniture* (John Rodd) published by David & Charles. On page 135 the author devotes one or two paragraphs to the repair of such oval hand mirrors.

I had to deal with the repair of an ebony looking-glass before I had access to John Rodd's book but fortunately I did not have to remove the glass. I did, as it turns out, make an accurate guess at the original technique and perhaps I may summarise it here: It depends upon the glass having a fairly steep bevel and upon a resilient backing, usually of felt. It is essential that the glass be oval and although the one in the photograph on page 337 of the May issue appears to be circular I do not think that it can be.

The lip and groove were, of course, integral with the rest of the ebony frame and the groove was cut rather more deeply at the handle end. The glass was 'fiddled' into the groove towards the handle, then fed into its proper place where it was held quite firmly by the 'spring' in the backing and the bevel of the glass.

I suppose the making of hand mirrors like this was something of a cabinetmaker's trick. The lip of the groove was, of course, very vulnerable at the end grain where most of the trouble happens.

Yours faithfully, **P. G. Thomson**

The book mentioned in this letter is available from Stobart & Son Ltd, 67-73 Worship Street, London EC2A 2EL, at £6.95.

From: Alan Cowie, ACL Home Repairs, Hull
Dear Sir,

The other week I was some distance from home and workshop facilities and was called upon to replace a casement sash. After some thought I proceeded as follows: 1 out of some 35 × 25mm PSE I made a dry frame to fit the window opening (Fig. 1). I chamfered the outer edge all round and this chamfer serves as a rough capillary grove (Fig. 2). 2. I made a second dry frame out of 40 × 15mm PSE so that when placed on top of the first frame it formed the section shown in Fig. 3.

A liberal coat of primer was applied and both frames screwed together and the outer edge of the second (outer) frame was chamfered all round. The assembled twin frame was hung and glazed in the usual way. I should add that all joints were painted then butted. I hope these notes will help other readers who may be 'put on the spot.'

Yours faithfully, **Alan Cowie**

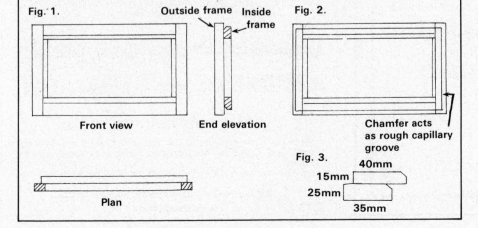

Fig. 1.

Front view   Outside frame   Inside frame

End elevation

Fig. 2.

Chamfer acts as rough capillary groove

Plan

Fig. 3.

40mm
15mm
25mm
35mm

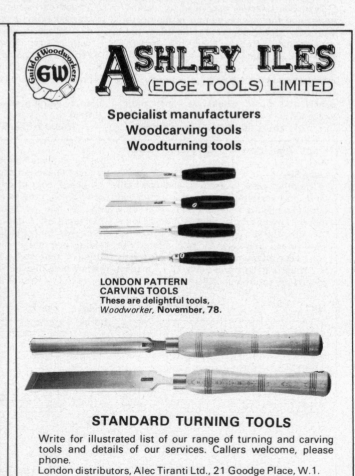
---

workpieces

Drum to the front!

Modellers of horse-drawn vehicles are reminded that the Rotunda museum at Woolwich, London, houses several army wagons, a mobile kitchen, mobile workshop and a drum cart. This vehicle mounted a huge kettle drum and has a high seat for the drummer and, according to Model Horse-Drawn Vehicle Club *Newsletter No. 44* (March-April 1980), the drummer must have felt very isolated indeed. His 'was not a job to be envied,' writes the club's hon secretary John Pearce adding, 'this cart has a very deep dish to the wheels and with the spokes having a recurve to them. There is a very nice model of this cart inside the museum, plus a great many other models, field guns etc. There are also brass guns (and limbers) presented to Queen Victoria by Napoleon III. The museum is housed in a huge tent erected for the 1851 exhibition and the tent itself is housed in the building.'

With the *Newsletter* Mr Pearce encloses drawings of a 1925 ice cart as used in Massachusetts. This was usually driven as a pair-horse vehicle.

MH-DVC hon secretary's address is 4 Brentlea Crescent, Higher Heysham LA3 2BT.

Air-dried hardwood

Major Goulden of Horam Manor Farm, Heathfield, East Sussex (phone 04353 2597) has 1976 air-dried home-grown timber available. Major Goulden tells WOODWORKER that the timber is available in squares, boards or slabs and bowl blanks in oak, ash, wild cherry, hornbeam and elm. Some holly, hawthorn and sycamore is also available plus a small supply of 4in. round ivy, though this latter is not yet ready for use. Major Goulden has been laying down increasing stocks of hardwood over the last five years and will be able to assure regular customers of a continuing supply.

Evenings and weekends are the best times to contact him at the above address and telephone number.

Chair for the kirk

New chair for the moderator (president) of the general assembly of the church of Scotland has been made by the well-known firm of A. H. McIntosh & Co Ltd, Mitchelston Drive, Kirkcaldy, and given to the church along with two side, or conveners' chairs and 12 companion chairs for ex-moderators. The pieces replace furniture stolen from the church of Scotland assembly hall at Edinburgh more than a year ago.

Designed by Thomas Robertson, the firm's design consultant, the chairs have been made by James Allison and John Graham, two senior craftsmen at Kirkcaldy factory. Six apprentices were also involved as it was an opportunity for them to do work not in the usual line of McIntosh business.

Timber used was mainly home-grown oak with blue upholstery arranged in four panels on the chair backs to form a cross. The carved decoration was carried out by Brian Robertson, upholstery by Finlay Thain and the polishing by Balfour McGrory.

Each arm of the moderator's chair has a

built-in and recessed writing surface.

Mr Robertson says: 'I have tried to design chairs which are in keeping with the fabric of the assembly hall and modern in style but not necessarily tied to the last quarter of the 20th century.'

Money-box church

In the church of St Laurence at Foxton, Cambs, there is a model of the building which also serves as a money-box: lift the steeple and pop in a coin! Though a craftsman might be critical of the workmanship, most people are prepared to make allowances for the circumstances under which the model was made.

Indeed, most of the work was done with a pocket knife about a century ago by Charles Impey, who was a local farmhand. He died in 1885 at the age of 38. He had no drawings and apparently memorised each part of the building and then went home and completed the appropriate section of his model. He also carved the collection plates for the Methodist chapel at Foxton.

Although Impey's model might not win many competition prizes, says a correspondent, it is interesting to speculate on how many coins have been popped through the

slot beneath the steeple. Imprey's legacy to the parish of Foxton has been much appreciated throughout the years.

Moderator's chair for the church of Scotland general assembly in Edinburgh has a carved panel featuring the burning bush designed as three branches of olive bearing fruit with flames shooting from the bush and the St Andrew saltire (cross). A dove with outstretched wings crests the panel. The back pillars of the chair are capped with entwined thistles. A Celtic motif on the front legs terminates in the symbols of bread and wine.

Join the Professionals with an EMCO woodworking machine

SIX FANTASTIC MACHINES FOR THE EIGHTIES

EMCO DB5 Woodturning-lathe
Perfection in all details. Modern in concept. Safe in function. Renowned for its capacity and light but robust construction.

Emcostar
Requiring a minimum amount of space, this machine is capable of no less than sixteen separate operations. No other woodworking machine can offer you so many possibilities. Without doubt, one of the most versatile general purpose machines on the market.

Emcostar Super
The universal woodworking machine with 13 different operations. An absolute must for the professional or the more ambitious amateur. No workshop can be without one.

EMCO Rex B20 Planer Thicknesser
Powerful, sturdy and safe. This machine will solve all your problems. Easy to operate and accuracy second to none.

EMCO BS2 Bandsaw
Three-speed band saw for wood, metal or plastic. Unique in its price class. Safe, accurate and amazingly versatile.

EMCO TS5 Table Saw
The robust table saw for both the amateur and professional. A cost saver in every sense of the word and unbeatable for its manoeuvrability.

You don't have to earn a lot to own an EMCO woodworking machine; but you do have to be able to recognise a range of machines which are outstanding for their versatility and quality.

Built to give you years of reliability, service and pleasure.

A machine to suit everybody's needs.

Emco the name that spells energy, eminence and efficiency.

Decide now to invest in an EMCO machine. Fill in the coupon, or better still call in at your nearest stockist and see for yourself. You won't be disappointed.

BEC THE B ELLIOTT GROUP

Coupon
Please send me further details of the EMCO Woodworking machines

Name _____

Address _____

To: E.M. Equipment Ltd., BEC House, Victoria Road, London NW10 6NY
Tel: 01-965 4050 Telex: 922832

Guild of Woodworkers

Oakleaf carvers came to Sussex

Guild of Woodworkers pioneer course in woodcarving was held at West Dean college, Chichester, Sussex, from 24-25 May, with Philip Bentham and John Sainsbury as tutors.

Numbers were limited so that members could have the full benefit of individual tuition and the discussion sessions which covered a wide variety of topics such as conditioning and seasoning of wood, choice of tools, sharpening, care and maintenance, finishing and cleaning of carvings.

Perhaps in honour of the approaching Oak Apple Day (29 May) the course was offered a weekend project 'carve an oakleaf' though members who wished to do so were able to work on their own subjects. Tools and materials were available to those who had not brought their own.

Members were welcomed to West Dean by guild administrator David Whitehouse who was accompanied by the editor of WOOD-WORKER (Geoffrey Pratt), Mrs Pratt and the tutors. The following attended: E. R. Swain, Sittingbourne; E. W. Huggins, Alcester; E. C. Allen, Romford; C. J. Piper, Pinner; G. S. Limb, Dunholme; J. P. G. Webb, Tenby; R. J. Sibley, Weymouth; W. H. Strutton, Capel; G. F. Effrem, Minneapolis, USA; J. Harrap, Ludgershall; and M. W. Abrahamson, Dublin.

The tuition and workshop facilities as well as the high standard of accommodation at West Dean were greatly appreciated and members expressed pleasure at the opportunities presented by the course for an exchange of views and experiences not only on carving but on matters of mutual interest to woodworkers. Hints, tips, names of suppliers were passed round the workshop — and the bar which is conveniently (and strategically) placed in the great oak hall of West Dean house, the mansion built entirely of flint in 1804 for the 1st Lord Selsey and adapted in 1971 to form a college for arts and crafts recognised by the DES and administered by the Edward James Foundation.

For those who could bear to leave the workbench the gardens and park of the 6000 acre estate provided much of beauty and interest. Many of the existing mature beeches, limes, horse chestnuts, planes and cedars were planted around 1810 though considerable planting has been carried out by the James family since acquiring the estate in 1891. The gardens of some 30 acres are informal and have retained a 19th century character which reflects the style and scale of the house.

Within the park are the buildings erected by the Weald & Downland open air museum, an independent charitable organisation established in 1968 to rescue and rebuild traditional buildings which would otherwise be demolished. The site is leased by the museum from the Edward James Foundation.

It is interesting to note the new central heating system being installed at West Dean to service the house, workshops, studios and other buildings is to be fired on wood chips and byproduct largely provided by the estate's own forest resources.

Encouraged by the success of this first residential course for woodcarvers the guild is extending its crafts programme to locations in the north and, subsequently, to the midlands. Already requests have been received for residential courses (weekends) covering such subjects as gilding, marquetry and cane seating and the administrator will be glad to hear from members about other subjects on which they would welcome expert tuition and the opportunity of exchanging experiences. While no guarantee can be given of the inclusion of any subject in the GoW crafts programme every attempt will be made to meet members' wishes.

Simplification

There is to be some simplification (and also extension) of the law relating to notification of accidents when SI 1980 no. 804 *(The notification of accidents and dangerous occurrences regulations)* comes into force on 1 January 1981. Guidance notes are due from the Health & Safety Executive later this year.

G. M. Gray

Member (No. 0979) G. M. Gray died on 15 April. He was 49 and lived at Harborne, Birmingham. Guild of Woodworkers offers condolences to Mrs Gray who says her husband took much pleasure in working with wood, an activity completely different from his daily routine.

594

Prices quoted are those prevailing at press date and are subject to alteration due to economic conditions.

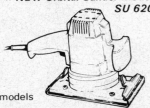

596   Prices quoted are those prevailing at press date and are subject to alteration due to economic conditions.   Woodworker, September 1980

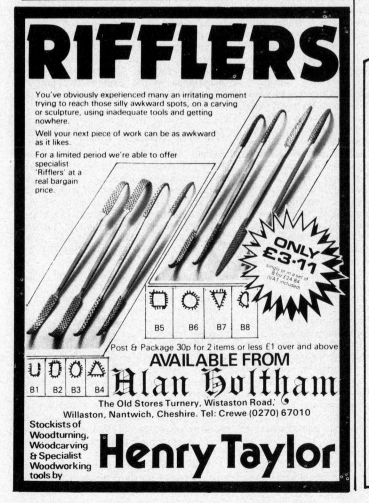

BOOK REVIEWS

Bridge that gap

Orbis Publishing has produced a new diy series of books (four in all) printed in Czechoslovakia, two of which have come into the WOODWORKER office for review. *Making Furniture* edited by David Thomas is value for money in laminated board covers at £3.95, but we have reservations about some of the statements claimed in the introduction: The editor maintains that 'making your own furniture is not only cheaper and more satisfying than buying ready-made items, it also gives you complete control over the quality of materials used'.

We are not convinced about the claim that it is cheaper to diy particularly with chipboard — when contemplating building two wardrobes some four years ago it was £10 cheaper than the ready-made equivalent available from a well-known chain store. With their firm's power tool machinery facilities obviously they could produce a better product with no time factor involved. We agree, of course, that diy is satisfying and you can control quality to some extent.

Economy is certainly the theme of this practical book which has a very clear, concise layout with instructions given in simple step-by step stages and colour illustrations, plus full colour photographs of each design.

These stage-by-stage instructions for every project accompanied by detailed drawings and exploded diagrams enable you to see clearly how each piece fits together. Cutting lists to finished sizes are given for each project worked out from standard timber sizes which in their turn have been averaged out from those listed by timber yards. You may need to adjust these sizes if your local timber yard stocks something slightly different. If a great deal of timber or boards are required for a project there are useful cutting plans showing the easiest and most economical way to cut them.

The projects are totally metric but conversion charts are included as some timber merchants still deal in imperial sizes. The book is an odd mixture of traditional cabinetmaking using well-known joints and hardwood or softwood plus typical diy projects using laminated chipboard and plastics joints. Clear instructions and illustrations covering all the traditional joinery techniques used in the projects are included at the end of the book.

The editor states that 'with a little experience anyone can tackle the projects in the book. All you need is a basic tool kit and plenty of spare time. Start with some of the easier projects and as you gain confidence in your ability, try some of the larger more difficult designs.'

Some of the projects, eg corner cupboard (p45) require a high quality of craftsmanship and are certainly not a typical diy exercise. With the techniques needed to complete most projects I would have hoped for better designs — the *Stanley Book of Furniture* published some years ago — required the same degree of expertise but contained infinitely better designs for the era.

However, the projects are mainly basic (tables, seating and storage units) and would therefore appear to be suitable for someone in the stage of transition from diy to cabinetmaking where skills are still being learnt and improved but more demanding tasks are being sought. The range is wide and the scope for conversion of the projects is certainly there. Most woodworkers will find something to make in this book even if it is only a simple window box for the beginner or a screen or corner cabinet for the more skilled.

The chapter on techniques alone, is probably the most important in the book and makes it a good buy for someone starting to learn the finer points of construction.

Making Furniture, attractive easy-to-make furniture designs for every room in the house, edited by David Thomas, £3.95. Orbis Publishing Ltd, Orbis House, 20-22 Bedford-bury, London WC2N 4BL. **C.R.C.**

Choose, use and care

The second of the books from Orbis Publishing is *Diy Tool Guide* edited by Rick Ball, also in laminated board covers and priced at £3.95, again in full colour with clear diagrams and exploded drawings, excellent step-by-step instructions and full cutting lists.

The supplementary title to this book is *How to choose, use and care for your tools and equipment* and this is exactly what the book does. The five chapters cover the basic tool kit, tools one by one, power tools, tools to make yourself, fixing and fastening and tool care. Appendices deal with tool hire and metric conversion charts. There is no point in trying to skimp on a tool kit. The old saying 'you get what you pay for' is nowhere truer than in the tool shop. Cheap tools may be adequate for those limiting their achievements to diy, fixing the odd shelf or similar project, but their working life is invariably brief.

The high cost of good tools means very few can buy an instant kit; most of us slowly build up a good range of versatile tools as each one becomes crucial for the next project. Which brings us to the problem of which tool to buy first. Clearly, there are certain indispensable tools: hammer, screwdriver and saw — but which hammer, which saw . . .?

The Diy Tool Guide has been devised to answer these questions impartially after analysing the current tools on the market. To try and prevent costly mistakes, the elements of a versatile basic kit are explained.

Although the book deals mainly with woodworking there are smaller sections on tools for bricklaying and laying concrete; also included are sections on ladders, scaffold towers, spanners and wrenches, obviously intended for the diy man.

Some may be surprised that the electric drill is given such a prominent place, a judgement which may not meet with approval among traditional craftsmen; but time, effort and frustration can be saved by using this tool. The value of choosing good names is stressed — an after-sales service from a reputable manufacturer amply repays the extra money spent on the tool. The advice is buy the best you can afford and maintain it well.

Tools one-by-one illustrates the right tool for a particular job and how to care for that tool. As a traditionalist I find the section on power tools and power finishing particularly useful. I was pleased to see 'safety first' stressed — 'the best way to handle tools is also the safest'. Careless handling of hand tools is dangerous but careful handling becomes even more essential where power tools are concerned. Twin threats of electricity and a rapidly spinning circular saw blade must breed caution. In use and in storage elementary precautions avoid accidents with cutting tools.

In chapter 4 (Tools to make yourself) sash-cramp, jig, workbench, tool-belt and mounting a vice are included as money savers, but are very good and useful extensions of the basic range. The jig used as a guide for cutting timber at an angle in a power sawbench is a useful tool to construct and the sash-cramps are a real money saver. The modern woodworker's bench, the major project in this section, is an excellent design able to be dismantled should you wish to move it. Equipped with both front and end vices, movable bench-stop, tool-well, cupboard, drawers and peg rails to enable various shaped constructioned items to be firmly held while being also gripped in the vice, it would be found invaluable by many.

Screws and nails are covered in another chapter dealing with all aspects of fixing and fastening. A short section on tool care includes the care of electric drills, sharpening planes, chisels, gouges and saws. The appendices on tool hire and on metric conversion factors are useful additions.

In an emergency most households can muster a collection of basic tools accumulated over the years and scattered throughout the house but I would thoroughly recommend this book to the young person who has just begun to look after his own property and who has only had a little experience in the past in selecting and choosing his personal range of tools. **C.R.C.**

Carving then and now

Reader Norman Place of Broxbourne who has a particular interest in carving comments that the *Manual of Traditional Wood Carving* originally published by American Dover Publications Inc in 1911, is a must for amateur woodcarvers. It is still available in facsimile being distributed by publisher Constable & Co Ltd, 10 Orange Street, Leicester Square, London WC2H 7EG. The price is £5.

Mr Place says: 'Apart from a short spell at the London School of Furniture, most of my carving experience has been gained in my own workshop and that has meant learning by mistakes. This book, I think, limits that prospect in the future.

'The contents cover all aspects of wood carving. There are chapters on the woods, tools — and clay modelling — and much space is devoted to the history of the craft and to design (a subject I find difficult and somewhat irksome). With over 1,000 working drawings and photographic examples you need no longer stare at blank sheets of paper. It is squared tracing paper for me in the future.

'The author mentions firms who specialised in carving. He says that while some men would be better at carving hands others would make a better job of faces and, as a result, work would be passed from one to another. He maintains that of all the carvers in the country only about 100 would be capable of turning out a decent job in-the-round — and that after seven years' apprenticeship. A sobering thought.

'Some excellent work is illustrated: German, Italian, French, Scandinavian as well as our own Grinling Gibbons. The author comments on the finer qualities of the work and how he thinks the carver approached the subject.

'It appears that the craftsman of the day would work to drawings prepared by the designer who must have had some experience of the carver's capabilities and problems. The craftsmen could only interpret the design to the best of their ability which accounts for the individuality that exists in all their work.

'Reservations I have about the book: it was of course written nearly 70 years ago; the pieces you can reproduce (there are detailed instructions) are old fashioned — most readers would perhaps not wish to get to grips with carved photo-frames or ornate coalboxes; the layout and design may seem charming to some — and irritating to others; the writing is at times in ponderous style. But this is to complain about the very essence of the book. It really comes down to whether a reader is prepared to overlook these small points so as to gain from the superb information contained in the 568 pages (plus index).

'I suppose my only real criticism is that the author mentions architectural terms and expressions of which I was unaware. Only by patient reference to the illustrations did such terms and expressions become clearer.

'Nothing can ever replace the hard slog of experience but close study of the manual provides many worthwhile tips and reveals fascinating examples of the way it *was* done.'

Manual of Traditional Woodcarving (edited by Paul N. Hasluck) was originally entitled *Cassell's Wood Carving* and is a republication of the 1911 edition. It is paperbound and opens flat for easy reference.

Woodturning: surprise and delight

John Sainsbury's *The Craft of Woodturning* is arguably the best on the subject since F. J. Pain's classic *Practical Wood Turner*. Those of us who have followed the tenets of Pain's earlier publication will need Sainsbury's book because of its important inclusions containing advances in machines and equipment, such as expanding collet chucks.

With a craft that has only three basic movements to master: those of cutting either straight, convex or concave lines, it is a continual surprise and delight to discover what can be achieved with this most pliable of the woodworking arts; and John Sainsbury has explored virtually every facet between the covers of his well-produced book. He has made a thorough job of it, too, writing from years of experience and observation. The diagrams and photographs are excellent and the work is thus highly-illustrated. The text is concise and unequivocal.

There are but a few minor observations and criticisms that can be made. For instance, clean softwood stickers are to be preferred to the hardwood recommended by the author when sticking planks to be air-dried. The risks attendant upon hardwood stickers staining and impacting local areas of the boards can easily spoil valuable timbers.

Readers should beware that polyethylene glycol (PEG) — see WOODWORKER for November 1979 and June 1980 — mentioned in the book, and being increasingly used to stabilise timber, can lead to difficulties later on when attempting to polish turned items. This is on account of the waxy residue of PEG. There is no reference to spiral turning, often regarded as a challenging part of the woodturner's art (but perhaps unfashionable?) and no projects for toymaking are included.

Nevertheless, it is an outstandingly comprehensive book on the subject and can be recommended to both tyro and expert. The cost is £4.55 and publisher is McGraw-Hill Book Co (UK) Ltd, Shoppenhangers Road, Maidenhead SL6 2QL.   **R.W.G.**

Veneering and marquetry explained

In *Veneering Simplified* Harry Jason Hobbs sets out to encourage his readers to try veneering. He has outlined simple methods to achieve quick results. These include, in addition to normal work, the use of ready-cut assemblies mounted on paper and rolls of very thin flexible veneers with paper or foil backing. No mention is made of the difficulties of finishing the latter material.

Before getting down to veneering the history of the craft and details of how veneers are made are treated at length. A third of the book is thus occupied before the chapters on tools, materials and equipment and deciding what to tackle.

However, when at last the author begins on the techniques involved in veneering he explains these fully and eruditely, covering knife and saw cutting and laying. The diagrams and step-by-step photographs are excellent and with the detailed text everything is made clear. It is unfortunate that the photographs of specimens of veneer are in monochrome, particularly as the descriptions in the text are somewhat confusing. For example birch is listed as 'tan with light-brown wavy grain'. The projects offered are relatively simple and most of them are pleasing.

The author suggests that his readers should buy ready-made whitewood boxes from a craft shop on which to lay veneers. One of these illustrated is comb jointed and the other butt jointed, both showing end grain. No balancing or cross-band veneer is used but the problems likely to arise are ignored.

Information on adhesives will be confusing to English readers. Animal glue is written off as being old-fashioned and not suitable. The alternatives offered are white glue, yellow glue and veneering glue, all of which would be outside the experience of all but American readers. The third one is evidently contact adhesive which would be difficult to spread sufficiently evenly for veneering.

In one chapter ideas are given for home-made tools and apparatus which are a great saving of expense, but the veneer press is described as having flat chipboard cauls instead of the more usual slightly curved ones. Another idea is the use of bricks wrapped in polythene bags as weights on newly-laid veneer. These do not promise very even pressure. Although emphasising the need to protect veneer surfaces from damage the author suggests the use of a 12in. hacksaw blade as a straight edge. Damage from the teeth would seem inevitable.

In spite of its faults the book should give the beginner a start on the craft and enable him

or her to produce some worthwhile work. This is particularly so if veneering is restricted to small areas for which the methods described are more appropriate.

Publisher is Thames & Hudson Ltd, 30 Bloomsbury Street, London WC1B 3QP, and the price is £5.50.

There is a convincing air of authority about the Marquetry Society of America's *Modern Marquetry Handbook*. The examples of work by members, shown in photographs, demonstrate what can be done and should act as a spur to readers to try the craft. The diagrams and step-by-step photographs are excellent and, together with the carefully written text, explain the methods very clearly. As in the companion book the photographs of veneers would have been more informative had they been in colour.

Practically all aspects of marquetry have a place in the volume. Every method of cutting veneers is discussed and the pros and cons of each given. Simple knife cutting is followed by fretsaw methods including bevel cutting by hand and machine. The 'window' scheme and multi-layer work are dealt with fully.

The laying of veneers has a section to itself but the matter of adhesives is confusing, largely because of the American terms used. However, more information about the characteristics of the glues is given than in the companion book. A whole chapter is devoted to finishing the work where the reader has the choice of several methods. He or she is left in no doubt as to what to use and how to proceed for each, but is left to decide by experiment which one to adopt for the work in hand.

In addition to normal marquetry with wood veneers, a chapter deals with the use of bone, plastics, and mosaics built up from fragmented veneers. The special effects obtained and the various possibilities are illustrated by photographs. The author explains how photographs can be converted into marquetry designs; the enlargement and reduction of pictures for the same purpose is also covered.

The valuable technique of sand shading is the theme of another part; here again the instructions are lucid and leave nothing to chance. Ample warnings are given to avoid the snares of this process.

The old bogey of veneering end grain crops up in the suggestion that ready-made whitewood boxes are suitable for veneering. These are comb or butt jointed, showing end grain; but no mention is made as to the likely hazards.

Among the interesting and valuable chapters are two of particular merit, both based on experiences of members of Marquetry Society of America. One 'Useful inventions and innovations', is what we would call 'Hints and Tips' and is a mine of information on a wide range of ideas, including the sharpening of steel scrapers and the making of cutting jigs. The other is a question-and-answer chapter giving advice on problems that are almost sure to beset beginners and advanced workers alike.

It would be difficult to find any gaps in the vast amount of expertise which has gone into the compiling of this book which costs £6.50 and is also published by Thames & Hudson.
                                                                H.C.K.

QUESTION BOX

Seasoning round timber

From: P. J. Firth, Warboys Fen, Cambs

Some months ago I came across a small log of apple in a dry woodshed. Bark still on; 18 × 5in. diameter; very dry. I turned a bottle shape from part of it which very quickly split radially in semi-outdoor workshop conditions. After taking the thing indoors the crack widened to ¼in. extending the full length and almost to the heart.

I have now been given a much larger log, a piece of which has behaved in much the same way. I understand the lot lay in the open for six years after felling. This splitting is presumably due to internal stresses set up by haphazard seasoning. Is there any way they can be relieved. I am familiar with normal air-drying procedure.

All small diameter logs are difficult to season without some degrade occuring. This is on account of the problem of trying to get a uniform rate of drying throughout the bulk of the piece which will not create excessive stress, bearing in mind that potential shrinkage follows along the lines of growth and that this is compressed into a relatively small area.

To understand what must be done it is essential to grasp the fact that no matter how many years a piece of wood has been exposed to a certain atmosphere, it will never have a moisture content (m.c.) that is out of step with that atmosphere; and atmosphere in this context means its general average of relative humidity (R.H.) In the average warm atmosphere of a living room the R.H. varies from winter (when the heating is on) from 50-55%, giving an equilibrium moisture content (EMC) for wood of roughly 10%, to the summer when the R.H. may get a little higher, say, 60%.

In the open air the R.H. will seldom average less than 70% for any reasonable drying period equalling 13-14% m.c. for wood. But for most of the year the R.H. is at 80% or so, or 16%-plus m.c. for wood.

From the type and intensity of the splitting you have encountered with the small log it sounds rather that it did not dry much, if at all, in the so-called dry woodshed, possibly because it was buried under other wood or was denied reasonable air circulation. It is possible that initially it was exposed to hot sun so that the outside zone of wood became dry and casehardened thus preventing easy removal of moisture from the centre.

This may be a logical explanation why, once the outer zone was relieved by the cutting and the inner zone began to dry a little in the slightly warmer atmosphere of the workshop, the wood started to split and this was encouraged to extend further when the wood was moved to the drier indoor atmosphere.

Your larger log is behaving in similar fashion for similar reasons. You say the log was lying in the open for six years after felling. If this was in grass or weeds then no essential drying would take place despite the time element. Apple is a wood that dries slowly and to keep logs in good trim, while a current of air over all faces of the wood is necessary, this must not encour-

age the wood to dry rapidly in the early stages. In warm weather wetting the wood helps keep the outside moist.

The idea is to slowly dry the wood in such a way that moisture at the surface links up with that in the core. In other words liquid moisture is being drawn towards the surface where, by evaporation, it is removed as vapour. If the continuity of capillary action of the moisture droplets is broken by too rapid surface drying, then the wood begins to develop the wrong type of stress and trouble starts. Painting the ends of the log with a water-proof substance such as bitumen helps to slow down drying from the ends.

Seasoning pine

From: Dr C. A. J. Brightman, Hampton Wick, Surrey

I have cleaned some old pine floorboards which I intend to use for making a cupboard. The wood seems to be of much better quality than most pine you can buy today. Would it be practical for me to buy unseasoned pine and season it at home? An alternative would be to 're-season' the pine that I buy.

There are two places where I could conveniently season wood: 1 the loft in which there is a reasonable circulation of air; 2 the garage where there is relatively little air circulating. I would be grateful for your advice.

Pine (European redwood), enters this country with a moisture content (m.c.) of around 15 or 16% and after discharge from the vessel much depends upon how the wood is stored. Generally speaking, this is in the form of closely-piled boards stacked in open-sided sheds so that even after many months of storage, the m.c. is virtually the same. If by chance the boards are placed in-stick in the open (an unusual practice) they would not dry out much more, but they could pick up moisture during the winter and if purchased then might have a m.c. of 17 or 18%. In the average warm living room, the equilibrium m.c. that flooring would attain is around 10%. This means that if old dry floor boards are removed from such an environment, they should not shrink or warp if used for other work to be placed in similar surroundings.

If, however, new wood is purchased with a m.c. of, say, 16% and is then placed in that environment, it will gradually adjust its m.c. to equilibrium with its surroundings.

As a rule of thumb assessment, plain sawn (tangentially sawn) wood (and your flooring is probably of this type) can be expected to shrink by 1mm in 300mm for each m.c. change. In other words, wood at 16% m.c. drying to 10% m.c. would tend to shrink by 6mm in 300mm or, as an example, a floor board 4½in. (113mm) wide would shrink by about ³⁄₃₂in. (2.3mm) under these conditions. This is relatively small but if the wood cupped in drying then the shrinkage would be exaggerated.

Storing wood in a loft is no different from a merchant's covered store; generally speaking, the relative humidity (R.H.) of the air in a roof void is too high to reduce the m.c. of wood below an air-dried figure although in some circumstances the wood might come down to 13 or 14% m.c. in high summer. A garage is seldom of use in drying wood because of the sluggish atmosphere.

The best way to handle wood of this type is to break it down into over-size piece parts

and store them in the environment of use for a few weeks. This, of course, is not always convenient, but unless you can duplicate warm room conditions elsewhere with a R.H. of 50 or 55% and air changes that do not reduce temperature nor increase R.H. unduly, there is not much alternative. Many timber merchants have a moisture meter on the premises and if requested can give an instant m.c. reading.

Trouble with a plane

From: Ian Lambert, 79 Delbury Court, Deercote, Telford, Salop

I have a 22in. Mathieson plane with 2½in. iron bought in good condition for £5. I am now in the process of trueing the plane and have trued-up the sole, re-mouthed the plane and hollow-ground the iron using a hand wheel and toolrest. I fitted the iron and opened-up the mouth to about ¹⁄₆₄in. as I wanted to produce a fine shaving.

The plane produces a thin shaving but after two or three passes clogs up between the iron and the mouth. Do I need to open the mouth still further? Is my grinding and honing wrong (I have made sure the breaker iron is a good fit)? The angle I use, which on a Stanley jack plane seems to work well, is about 33°.

I would also be pleased to hear from others in Salop (Shropshire) who are interested in woodworking.

There are a number of factors which singly, or in combination, can produce the phenomenon of choking in a plane. At the outset it may appear obvious to state that the regulation or set of the plane iron will affect the outcome. Thus an iron projecting, say, ¹⁄₆₄in. through the sole of a plane will require an escapement for the shaving at the mouth of at least ¹⁄₆₄in. In practice this will have to be a fraction more to provide the necessary clearance.

The commonest cause of the problem is due to the back iron not seating exactly on the plane iron, causing the shavings to pack at this point. The front edge of the back iron must bear truly on the back of the plane iron (for fine work it should be positioned as close to the edge as possible with the two irons screwed securely together) not only in section but also across the whole of the iron.

Experts will give a mirror-finish to the back iron to further assist the passage of the shaving. It is not unknown for the actual plane irons to be twisted or curved and it is recommended that this be checked. Meticulous attention should be paid to the backing-off of the iron to ensure a perfectly flat and smooth surface to mate with the back iron.

You do not say what kind of timber you are planing but it should be observed that resinous timbers are obviously prone to jamming in the plane while interlocked grain may only produce a friable dust. Similar results are obtained with over-dried or 'carroty' timbers.

It is suggested that you check and rectify any of the faults mentioned above and then test the plane by regulating the blade to a very fine setting and trying it out on a true surface of any straight-grained piece of mild-working hardwood. If the problem is still there then it may be taken that the mouth size is too fine and must be opened by degrees until the plane can be made to run smoothly. It is not thought that the method and angles that you have adopted in honing the plane iron have any bearing on the matter.

Finishing plaques

From: G. W. Gilbank, Sheffield

I carve wood plaques and for a finish apply two coats of teak oil. I leave for 24hr to soak in and then apply beeswax and plenty of elbow grease! Is this the correct method for a lasting finish and how often should it be polished after the finish has been applied? Is there any difference in using teak or linseed oils and is there any way in which I could age or darken the hardwood plaques to make them look older?

It is a little difficult to advise on the most suitable finish without seeing a plaque but two applications of teak oil followed by beeswax vigorously rubbed in should produce a pleasing gloss. The teak oil will help to seal the grain and assist the build-up of a good wax shine. Raw linseed oil will bring up the figure of the grain to a remarkable degree if applied not too liberally and then well rubbed in until quite dry. It will also help with the ageing and darkening effect which you are aiming for.

Carved work can be polished with white french polish applied with a bear hair mop to seal the grain. It can be finished by wiping with a rubber charged fairly full with glaze (made from 6oz gum benzoin dissolved in 1pt of meths). Apply the glaze with a light touch and be careful not to go over the same place twice until the previous coat is dry.

An alternative method is to brush on a mixture of equal parts of french polish and glaze.

If the plaques are of oak they can be attractively aged by fuming with .880 (point eight eighty) ammonia. Alternatively they can be wiped over with a solution of bichromate of potash, common soda or lime water. These will also age mahogany.

A mellow finish can be achieved with several applications of wax polishing but waxing, like oil polishing, can go on indefinitely. French polishing and glazing will give a lasting finish with less effort.

Colour of wood

From: Bernard Thompson, Oakmere, Cheshire

A cherry tree about 15in. diameter had a very attractive pink colour in the heartwood when fresh felled and a wych elm of about 30in. diameter was bright red in the heartwood when fresh felled. The colour in the cherry disappeared entirely when the wood was cut and turned and the wych elm logs now in the garden have lost their colour in the exposed ends. Is there any way of retaining the colours in these timbers?

I have cut up an oak log. There were a lot of big burrs which I cut off separately and the rest into 2, 3, 4 and 5in. slabs. I have waxed the ends. What is the best way of seasoning the slabs to avoid cracking? At present they are stacked up (with spacers between) in the garden with protection from rain and sun. Could you also please say what is the best way of treating the burrs so that I may be able to use them for turning. They are now in a heap, bark uppermost, with a sheet over them.

I have an Ebac Mini dehumidifier and use PEG and have adequate space in the garden for storage but limited space inside the workshop. I have pieces of laburnum, apple, pear, damson and plum stacked outside in the round. Can you offer general advice about seasoning these?

Years ago a favourite catch-question put to young timber students was: What white wood is pink when it is green? The answer: American white oak whose heartwood is pink to red when freshly sawn. This characteristic, however, applies to the heartwood of all timber species in the sense that the original colour is transient once the cut surfaces are exposed to light and, in general, the wood darkens to an extent governed by the amount and type of pigments in the wood. For example, western red 'cedar' tends to turn silver-grey; light-coloured woods like sycamore and satinwood and softwoods like pine and spruce take on a yellowish cast; many tropical hardwoods progressively darken in a matter of days or a few weeks.

Sometimes the finish applied to wood will delay colour change for a time by filtering down, so to speak, the ultra-violet light responsible. Pine furniture in a 'natural' finish is a good example, but gradually the wood starts to 'yellow'. This is much less than, say, the darkening of afrormosia or iroko because the pigments are lower in pine heartwood.

There is nothing really that can be done to preserve the natural colour of wood as seen originally. Oddly enough although your wych elm will become more uniformly brown with exposure, if there are any green streaks present in the wood (and there frequently are in this species) these are of mineral origin and usually are retained even after exposure of the wood. They can add character to the wood.

With regard to your thick oak, good seasoning methods demand that the drying rate be slowed down and this can be done by using thin spacing sticks about ½in (12mm) thick. Much of the included moisture is removed from wood by capillary action, ie by the attraction of water particles one to the other. You will, therefore, appreciate that for capillary action to be continuous the surfaces of the wood must be kept moist. If there is a lag then the surface of the wood attempts to shrink but is held by the wetter zones lower down, the wood becomes stressed in consequence and now is liable to split and check.

It is important to keep some top and end protection on the wood against the drying action of the sun but not against rain because, as you can see, this is important too. Top cover should, therefore, be raised slightly above the wood and during dry spells it does no harm, and usually a lot of good, to wet the wood with a hose or by other means. Left to dry like this oak will take several years but you must realise that very thick oak may never achieve a uniformity of drying in the open air. In other words, if the centre thickness is at or above 30% m.c. (fibre saturation point, when wood starts to shrink) it is still green, although the outer zones may be at 16 or 18% m.c.

The use of polythelene glycol (PEG) and of the dehumidifier must be considered carefully. PEG used to treat green wood will allow more drastic drying conditions to be used (see articles in recent issues of WOODWORKER) and in this category we could place the dehumidifier. But we would not recommend a dehumidifier to dry really wet oak because of the resistance to moisture movement through the wood created by the presence of tyloses which block the pores. This does not mean you cannot use the equipment to dry oak but it ought to be used for oak with a m.c. below 20%

uniformly. To achieve this sort of uniformity in oak the wood usually needs to be broken down to smaller dimensions in order to facilitate deeper drying.

You appear to possess some very good equipment but we would suggest you augmented this by acquiring a moisture meter (Protim Ltd, Fieldhouse Lane, Marlow, produces several reliable types at a reasonable price). Such an instrument will give a direct reading of m.c. and this would help guide your seasoning technique which could be built around slow air drying, the use of PEG and final drying by dehumidifier.

Reverting to the oak burrs: these are not ideal subjects either for seasoning in the solid or for turning because of the irregular structure of the wood. Normally a burr would be steamed in order to soften it prior to cutting it into veneers which would then be dried. We suggest you break down the pieces into suitable sizes and allow them to dry in-stick. With regard to your other logs, these are a little more tolerant of rapid drying than your oak. Nevertheless they must be allowed to dry down slowly, stacked in the open with a good current of air over and around each piece. Bark left on not only helps slow down the drying but is a good indicator of drying progress as it begins to crack and peel.

Black locust

From: J. D. Wildridge, Workington, Cumbria

Could you please identify a specimen of timber. It is from a tree originally in the grounds of a house in Norwich and was about 40ft high. The specimen appears to be false acacia, according to the book *Trees of Britain and Europe* but the book does not describe the timber.

You are quite right in your diagnosis that the tree was a robinia or false acacia, otherwise known as black locust *(Robinia pseudoacacia)*. The heartwood is greenish in colour when freshly cut turning a golden-brown after seasoning. The texture is rather coarse and the grain usually straight. Robina compares favourably with oak in general strength but is tough like ash. In fact, on the continent (in France and Belgium particularly) the wood is used extensively for wheels for wine carts, barrows, wagon bottoms etc and for planking in boats.

Since you were acquainted with the tree you probably remember the general shape and form of the leaves. These are in pairs, rounded or notched at the base; the bark is characterised by deep, interlacing fissures. The wood, structurally, if viewed on end grain with a pocket lens after a clean cut has been made with a sharp knife, will be seen to be ring porous with all the pores appearing blocked with tyloses and the pores in the early wood tending to undulate somewhat in their formation, not unlike those in elm. Light-coloured parenchyma tissue joins up a few of the small pores and appears wing-like. The wood is rather difficult to work due to the hard, horny nature of the latewood bands in each ring.

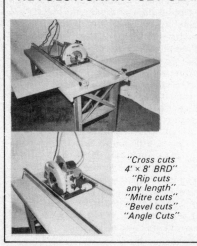

602

Prices quoted are those prevailing at press date and are subject to alteration due to economic conditions.

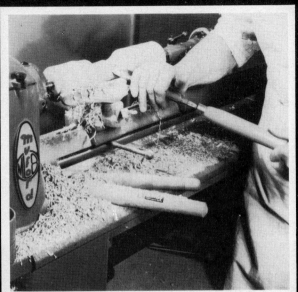

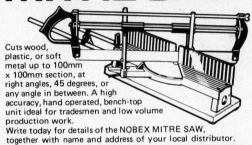

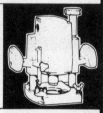

604

Prices quoted are those prevailing at press date and are subject to alteration due to economic conditions.

Woodworker, September 1980

KD system

The Titus KD system 3 is described as basically a two-part fitting comprising a dowel screw and 25mm diameter cup fitting with locking piece which can be either hand or machine placed. It has been developed as a fastening for knock-down furniture having particleboard components. Over the next six months up to 12 compatible and interchangeable items are to be introduced as part of the system by Titus Tool Co Ltd, 32 St Mary's Road, London W5 5EU (01-597 7497). The new fitting is available in face and edge boring versions and comes in white, brown or pine colour.

Drill stand

Power tool accessories branded Wolfcraft include the Hobby Mate dowel jointing jig; dovetailer and combjointer; Supershaper shaping and routing attachment which can be hand-held or bench-mounted; and a drill stand 450mm high and having 240mm stroke. The column is of hexagonal section and there is an adjustable depth scale and depth stop for repetition drilling.

The stand is said to be suitable for use with power drills of British and European manufacture. It has a 150 × 170mm table and drill feed is controlled by a lever via rack and pinion mechanism. A vice (no. 4920) is available as an extra; this vice can be fitted to the table. RRP of the stand is given as £18.50 approximately. Wolfcraft products are distributed by PTS Tool Specialists Ltd, PO Box 24, Henley Street, Camp Hill, Birmingham (021-773 7364).

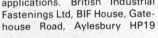

Craftsman model 2310-90 10in. radial arm saw from Hagemeyer.

Application of hot-melt

Hot-melt technology has been developed for a wide variety of fastening, filling and sealing applications. British Industrial Fastenings Ltd, BIF House, Gatehouse Road, Aylesbury HP19

10in. radial arm saw

Model 2310-90 10in. radial arm saw from the US comes in the Craftsman range through Hagemeyer (London) Ltd, 25-33 Southwark Street, London SE1 1RQ (01-403 0680). Retail price is given as £477.39 exclusive of VAT; this figure includes box-frame base and four legs. The worktable is 40 × 30in. and setting instructions are given in a work function chart located on top of the radial arm.

The saw carriage has permanently lubricated ball bearings running on replaceable tracks and an adjustable key is incorporated in the column support to compensate for wear. The sawblade can be moved up or down in $\frac{1}{8}$in. increments.

The 10in. diameter blade is directly mounted to the 1.5hp motor which has automatic brake and double-ended shaft to allow for mounting of accessories. There is automatic overload protection and in addition to the on-push-off switch a no-volt release switch mechanism is provided.

★   ★   ★

3DS (0296 81341), has introduced two hot-melt applicators which operate off standard 13A socket outlets. Model HM23 uses 8mm stick-form adhesive and carries SRP of £15.60. Model HM112 takes 12mm diameter sticks, can apply 600gr of adhesive/hr and is fitted with thermostat to pre-regulate the operating temperature; SRP is given as £21.60. Both prices are exclusive of VAT.

For further details and names of local stockists get in touch with BIF at the address given above.

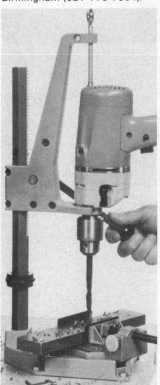

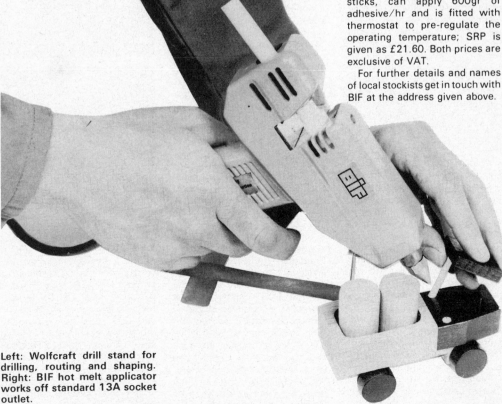

Left: Wolfcraft drill stand for drilling, routing and shaping. Right: BIF hot melt applicator works off standard 13A socket outlet.

High technology in woodworking machinery

Five years of research and development by Wadkin Ltd has culminated in the introduction of the FDR router moulder. The machine provides high-speed moulding (up to 40m/min) with superb single-knife finish; quick, easy and safe setting-up; safe working environment; minimum utilisation of floor space, segmented tooling; and hydrogrip sleeves.

The FDR is offered as a 'package' comprising the machine itself; integral close-fitting sound enclosure (which reduces the noise level to well below the 90dB(A) requirement); with segmented cutters; and Autoform NX grinder to profile TCT cutters at the same speed as HSS cutters. Profiling of TCT cutters at such a fast rate is in itself a significant development. Indeed, Wadkin is the only manufacturer able to offer this facility.

To meet the current safety requirements of different countries, the sound enclosure is fully interlocked and is linked to an automatic d.c. electrical braking system on all cutter heads. Main adjustments can be made from outside the enclosure. Extraction is contained within the enclosure the number of outlets depending on the head make-up of the machine.

Of modular design, the FDR can be assembled to suit the requirements of individual customers though the model demonstrated recently can be described as a push/through-feed type with infeed and outfeed rollers to ensure positive feeding of softwood or hardwood. The infeed rollers are followed by a 6000rpm belt-driven roughing head or predressing head, then two high-frequency (HF) side heads, tilting from 0 to 45° and operating at 15000rpm or at 3000rpm for setting-up. There is also a bottom head prior to the outfeed rollers. Slitting or deep-grooving heads (belt-driven) can be added if so desired.

Wadkin states that the high spindle speeds of the HF heads, together with the extreme accuracy of the hydrogrip sleeves guarantee a very high-quality single-knife finish and eliminate the need for jointing.

A further interesting development is that the close-fitting type of sound enclosure will be offered on all future Wadkin moulders. Not only will this incorporate all the safety features mentioned previously, but it will improve efficiency by making communication easier between the operator at the infeed and the operator at the outfeed.

Wadkin Ltd is at Green Lane Works, Leicester LE5 4PF (0533 769111).

WHAT'S NEW

Right top: FDR router moulder with sound enclosure in the raised position. The machine cannot be fully operational unless the front is closed down and locked. Infeed is at right. Overall the machine is height 1.58m, width 1.89m; overall length depends on number of heads and is from 3.14 to 4.44m. Right: Model NX Autoform profile grinder to grind cutters from either TCT or HSS blanks at fast speed. The profile is transmitted to the blank from the template in centre foreground. The abrasive wheel, which is a key factor in the operation, is distributed in UK exclusively by Wadkin.

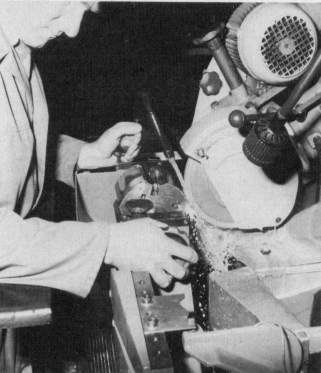

After-sales service

A service division has been formed by Wadkin Ltd and centralised at Green Lane Works, Leicester, with David Reynolds as general manager. There is a 'red sheet' service for emergencies and breakdowns; this is actioned the same day and additional costs of priority shipments are borne by the customer. Normal 'green sheet' service for ex-stock items covers despatch within three days. Service calls are generally responded to within 24hr by the 16 service engineers throughout the country who are directed from Leicester.

The company has also reviewed its service policy and a guide to this and the spare parts replacement programme is available from the service division at Green Lane Works, Green Lane Road, Leicester LE5 4PF (0533 762541).

Portable power tools division of Wadkin (Trent Lane, Castle Donington, Derby DE7 2PU), has added model TR-30 trimmer to the range. For 240V supply the tool has a 430W motor giving a no-load cutting speed of 29000 rpm. As standard it is fitted with 6mm collet but an alternative collet can be supplied for ¼in. shank cutters. The trimmer can be adapted as a portable router for chamfering, flushing and grooving operations, states Wadkin, and the list price is £62.

Angle grinders

The SMEA822 and SMEA622 are 2200W angle grinders of 180mm and 230mm diameter respectively in the industrial power tool range from Black & Decker Ltd, Bath Road, Harmondsworth UB7 0BX (01-759 2411). In the Tradesman range the company introduces the 230mm GD3115 1600W angle grinder. All machines are available for either 115V a.c./d.c. or 240V a.c. supplies. Prices respectively are stated as £129, £132 and £74 ex VAT.

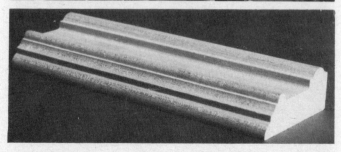

Section of mahogany moulded in one pass on the FDR router moulder at 30m/min. This picture shows the complex profile, but only the moulding itself reveals the high standard of finish.

Snip-off saw and sawbench

As briefly noted in WOOD-WORKER for June 1980 Elu Machinery Ltd, Stirling Way, Stirling Corner, Borehamwood WD6 2AG (01-953 0711), has introduced the TGS171 tilting snip-off saw and sawbench with a range of accessories for wood and metal working. By means of the sliding table attachment the saw can be used for panel cutting. Other features include three-point extraction; accuracy by means of positive locking device for cutting angles at 45° or 90°; blade guarded throughout the cutting operation; simple changing from snip-off to saw-bench; automatic reset to off when plug switch is disconnected; bench mounting or free-standing on four turbular steel legs. The 1.5hp motor is for 220V supply and blade size is 250mm (10in.) diameter operating at 2750rpm.

The Elu MFF80 power plane weighing 8lb previously offered in kit form complete with carrying case is now available at £73 plus VAT, as an independent machine but with side fence and reversible TCT blade which is replaceable at a cost of £4.80. The plane complete with carrying case, dust bag and bevelling fence continues to be available at £89 plus VAT.

Drill for modellers

Model makers may be interested in the Titan electric drill with a 3mm chuck and drill body 114 × 44mm diameter. It is supplied with a tool kit including collets, eight twist drills and 12 assorted tools including wire brushes, grinding discs and burrs. Additional accessories, including a drill stand, are available as optional extras. The drill

High quality dovetail saw (dozuki), appropriate for fine tenon and mitre cuts, is among new professional woodworking tools imported exclusively by the Japan Woodworker Trading Company.

operates off a 12V d.c. supply. Price with carrying case is given as £19.50 excluding VAT and a converter whereby the drill can operate off mains supply costs £13.50 excluding VAT. For further details get in touch with West Hyde Developments Ltd, Unit 9, Park Street Industrial Estate, Aylesbury, Bucks (0296 20441).

Portable power tools

Power drills and stand; impact drills; grinders; circular saws and bench table and bench system; jigsaws; power planer and hand and bench plane; orbital sanders; chainsaw, together with accessories are described and illustrated in the AEG electric power tools catalogue issued through AEG-Telefunken (UK) Ltd, 217 Bath Road, Slough SL1 4AW (Slough 872101).

Among the jigsaws is STPE60 with pendulum motion and electric speed control. Orbital sander VSS260 is provided with extraction to a bag attached and has a 2mm oscillation at 25000 a minute. Power planer EH822 has a working width of 82mm and depth adjustable from 0-2mm with rabeting depth to 22.5mm and no-load speed of 11000 rpm.

The catalogue is available from distributors or AEG at the address given above.

Hand tools from Japan

Hand tools such as saws, rasps and chisels and water stones are imported from Japan by Japan Woodworker Trading Co, 1004 Central Avenue, Alameda, California 95401. The saws — dovetail, keyhole, mortise and double-edged carpenter's style — cut on the pull stroke. Chisels are from ¼ to 1½in. wide and have handles of Japanese oak hooped to reduce risk of splitting. The water stones are said to incorporate extremely sharp abrasive surfaces that cut faster; the stones are 2½in. wide. Further information and catalogues can be had from the company at the address given above.

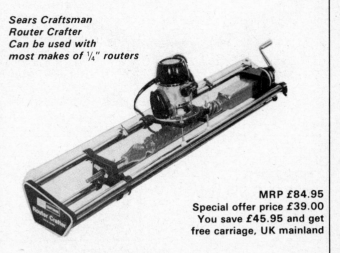

Prices quoted are those prevailing at press date and are subject to alteration due to economic conditions.

SHOP GUIDE

The quickest and easiest method of reaching all Woodworkers is to advertise in SHOP GUIDE.
Telephone Gill Wynn (0442) 41221 Ex. 241.
Rate: £5.00 per unit. Minimum of 6 months.
★ Mail Order

610
Prices quoted are those prevailing at press date and
are subject to alteration due to economic conditions.
Woodworker, September 1980

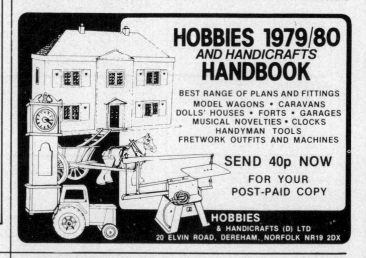

Classified Advertisements

Telephone Gillian Wynn

(0442) 41221 Ex.241

All classified Advertisements must be pre-paid.
Private and trade rate 14p per word (minimum £2.40). Box Numbers £1.00
extra. Display box rates s.c.c. £3.00 (min. £7.50). All advertisements are inserted in the first available issue.
Box replies to be sent care of Advertisement Department, P.O. Box 35,
Bridge Street, Hemel Hempstead, Herts, England HP1 1EE. There are no
reimbursements for cancellations.

FOR SALE

BUSINESS OPPORTUNITY

Make Slate or Chipboard Tables for you to Sell

Example: We supply 7ft × ½" Slate, Cloth, Rubber, Balls, Plan etc. for around £200. You provide Timber. (7ft Slate Tables sell commercially at £400 or more).

INTERESTED?
Then Phone (0253) 883426 OR
Send £2 + S.A.E. for plan and Lists, etc. Stating size required. Quantity discounts available.

SNOOKER ADVICE CENTRE

HIGH POINT, GARSTANG RD. EAST, SINGLETON, BLACKPOOL, LANCS.

FOR SALE: Complete set of hand and machine tools including 6" Myblo circular saw, Burgess powerline bandsaw, 4" Linisher, Black and Decker drill, stand, jigsaw, sander attachments, 17 sash molding planes. Offers about £450.00. Tel: Oxford 49575. T

BRANDING IRONS

Made from solid steel with 15" handle, to last a lifetime. Now you can permanently identify your tools and production pieces. We can quote for special styles for a professional look. Price guide — 3 x ⅜" characters £6.95p.

SAE details - Woodcraft Supply (U.K.) Ltd., 38 Summercourt Way, Brixham, TQ5 0DY

APPROX. 7,000 sq. ft. 2m.m. Sapele veneer full leaves 9½ft. long for sale of deal for universal woodworking M/C single phase. E. Ford, 16 Beckett Avenue, Market Bosworth, Near Nuneaton.

GLOUCESTERSHIRE Area Health Authority have for sale by tender — Multico bandsaw machine model D1, single phase motor. Metal Clad Ltd. combined surface planing/thickness machine 16" cutters, 5.8 amps 4HP. Multico Hollow chisel motorising machine model K1 ¾ HP motor, 4.5 amps. Single phase, some chisels/augers countersinking tools. Metal Clad Ltd circular saw 10.7 amps, 7.5 HP 3 phase. Some saw blades. All in good condition but requiring modification to comply with 1974 Woodworking Machinery Regulations. Purchaser responsible for removal costs. Tender documents/further details from: Gloucestershire Area Health Authority Supplies Service, 2 Montpellier, Gloucester. Tel: Gloucester 418571 Ext. 220. T

THATCHER'S

POWER TOOL CENTRE ☎ 01-624 5146

BIG DISCOUNTS ON ELU/BOSCH POWER TOOLS ALSO ROUTER CUTTERS

Please send 40p Stamps for full Brochure & Price Lists
221A Kilburn High Rd. London NW6
1st floor above Travel Agency

QUEEN ANNE & REGENCY LEGS

IN SOLID GRADE I TEAK

REGENCY

15" × 1¾"	SET OF 4	£ 10 – 50 inc P + P
18" × 1¾"	,, ,,	£ 11 – 50	,,
28" × 2"	,, ,,	£ 15 – 00	,,

QUEEN ANNE

15" × 3"	SET OF 4	£ 18 – 00 inc P + P
18" × 3"	,, ,,	£ 19 – 00	,,
28" × 4"	,, ,,	£ 25 – 00	,,

3 OR 4 LEG PEDASTALS ALSO AVAILABLE ON REQUEST

(TRADE ENQUIRIES INVITED)

Sheraton Furniture & Fine Art

67 Popes Avenue, Strawberry Hill, Twickenham, Middlesex, U.K.
Phone: 01-898 6263

ROSEWOOD, BURR WALNUT, figured mahogany, other assorted veneers. Exceptional. Half price. Tel: 0203-69501. S/W

WALL CLOCKS

Quartz battery movements	£5.95
Pendulum movements	£5.75
Clock hands — Black 55p; Brass 75p pair	
Colourful ceramic clockfaces	£1.25
Assorted plastic clockfaces	55p

Prices including post. Full guarantee.
SAE - **WOODCRAFT SUPPLY (U.K.) LTD.**
38 Summercourt Way, Brixham
TQ5 0DY

SUMMER SALE OFFER (stocks permitting) Lurem 210B universal woodworker complete on stand £1,288 inclusive of VAT (MRP £1,779 inclusive of VAT). Trymwood Services, 2A Downs Park East, Bristol, Tel: 629092. T

MYFORD ML8 lathe on heavy wooden stand with grinding wheel attachment. Child coil grip chuck, revolving centre face plates etc. Little used £200.00. Buyer collects. Tel: 01-311-9165. T

CLAVICHORD, SPINET, Virginal, Harpsichord + Guitar kit as well as finished producers for 10 years. 4 × 12p stamps: Classical Harpsichords, 79 Hull Road, York. STU

CHARIOT PLANE FOR SALE: Rosewood, German silver and steel. Unique. R. Kell, 1 Allison Place, Alnwick, Northumberland. Tel: 602823. T

OVER 300 copies "Woodworker" for sale. — 1938-1978 Offers? Morrison, Tel: Kinross 0577-62544. T

WELSH SLATE sharpening stones for sale at very competitive prices. Send SAE for details: Inigo Jones and Co. Limited, Groeslon, Caernarfon, Gwynedd. Tel: 0286-830242. O-U

R & S TOOLS LINCOLN LTD., BEEVOR STREET, LINCOLN.
Telephone: Lincoln 0522 36168/9
Why pay more when you can get up to 25% discount off most leading makes of power tools and hand tools

STOCKISTS OF:
ELECTRIC POWER TOOLS:
 AEG — ELU — BOSCH — MAKITA — SUPER STORK — SKIL
 WOLF — METABO — WADKIN — KANGO

WOODWORKING MACHINES:
 DEWALT — MULTICO — SEDGWICK — WADKIN — START-TITE

ABRASIVES:
 ENGLISH — TEX — KLINGSPOR — UNIVERSAL GRINDING WHEELS

SAWBLADES:
 SANDVIK — TEX — MICOR — FIRTH BROWN

HAND TOOLS:
 ALL LEADING MAKES OF BUILDING AND ENGINEERING TOOLS

SOLE AGENTS FOR: SWIFTSURE CUTTING & GRINDING DISCS

**FOR YOUR QUOTATION — PLEASE TELEPHONE BETWEEN
8.30 a.m. and 5 p.m.**

CLASSIFIED

**Telephone Gillian Wynn
(0442) 41221 Ext. 241**

EXCITING IDEAS IN FURNITURE-MAKING FOR NEWLYWEDS, D.I.Y. AND UNSKILLED

ALL you need are a few SIMPLE tools to make your own REPRODUCTION, MODERN AND GARDEN FURNITURE etc., from our EASY TO COPY PLANS and SIMPLE CLEARLY MARKED assembly instructions. EACH PLAN is FULL-SIZED. Just trace the plan on wood etc., similar to a dressmaking pattern. SO SIMPLE over 60 plans to choose from. FREE plumbing hints leaflet with each catalogue. Many satisfied customers who re-order once they try the plans. Send 60p p&p inc. TODAY for catalogue to Hamlyn Dept. D.W. 57 Lyneham, Wilts, SN15 4PH.

Chair illus. made in less than a day from plan No. 35 price only £1.99.

SAE FOR LIST of surplus tools many unused including Unimat 3, Stanley No. 50, universal wood moulding plans Yankee spiral screwdrivers etc. Cotton, Hillcrest, Balloch, Inverness IV1 2HP or Culloden Moor 336. T

SAWBENCHES, tungsten blades, spindles, planers, bandsaws, lathes. Send 48p for technical catalogues. Beverley, Alford, Lincs. RST

WOODCARVING

BEGINNERS START HERE

Complete set comprises:
The highly acclaimed "Book of Woodcarving" by Charles Marshall Sayers.
Set of four Ashley Iles Tools as recommended by the author, in a canvas roll and two India sharpening slips.
Complete set £26.90 including P&P in the U.K. or send for further details and lists of Woodcraftsmans Tools.

EXPORT ENQUIRIES WELCOME

CORBETT TOOLS (Dept. WW/9),
224 Puxton Drive, Kidderminster,
Worcestershire

SUPER PACK OF WOODSCREWS

BALANCED SELECTION OF ALL POPULAR SIZES ⅜" to 3" FINEST QUALITY CSK HEAD STEEL

10 GROSS £5.95 + 95p CARR & VAT

ALL SIZES SEPARATELY PACKED

Save £££s now on those DIY jobs with this **giant superpack bargain** containing every popular sized screw. Also 4 kilo nail pack assortment of round and oval 1" to 4" Save 25p and carriage when buying with woodscrews (above). Normally £5.95, now reduced to £5.70 carr. pd.

HANDIMAIL ww 9 **POYNINGS, SUSSEX**

BOOKS AND PUBLICATIONS

HOBBY'S ANNUAL

No.11 55p POST FREE

PLUS FREE PLAN OF MILK FLOAT

Worth 70p **100 PAGES**

Over 100 plans including four novelty doll's houses, clocks, forts, hand and power tools. The hobby annual.

Hobbys, (Dept. W) Knight's Hill Square, London SE27 0HH. 01-761 4244

WANTED

WOODWORKING TOOLS WANTED — unusual or quality items, ebony/brass, braces by Marples, wooden Norris plans, Spiers or Norris plans in gunmetal or over 20" long, anything by Holtzapffel, ploughs with pantent adjustments, miniature plans, Stanley tools numbers 10¼, 51/52, 71, 196, 444 plans in ebony or boxwood. Reg. Eaton, 35 High Street, Heacham, Kings Lynn, Norfolk. Tel: (0485) 70067. T-Z

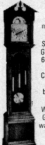

616   KINDLY MENTION 'WOODWORKER' WHEN REPLYING TO ADVERTISEMENTS   Woodworker, September 1980

THE MAGAZINE FOR THE CRAFTSMAN IN WOOD

OCTOBER 1980 VOL. 84 No. 1043 ISSN0043-776X

Front cover: At Manningtree, Essex, Ian Tucker builds closely accurate copies of early harpsichords. Except for drawing the wire for the strings, and the bridgepins which are ready-made, all parts for the instruments are made by hand. See also articles on pp. 648-9. (Photo: Peter Craig).

Editor	Geoffrey Pratt
Production Editor	Polly Curds
Advertisement Manager	Terence M. Healy
Advertisement director	Michael Merrifield
Managing Director	Gavin Doyle

MEMBER OF THE AUDIT
BUREAU OF CIRCULATIONS

SUBSCRIPTION DEPARTMENT: Remittances to MODEL AND ALLIED PUBLICATIONS, PO Box 35, Hemel Hempstead, Herts HP1 1EE. Price per copy 85p includes p&p. Subscription queries: Tel: Hemel Hempstead 51740. Subscription rate, including index, £10.20 per annum; overseas sterling £10.20; $23.00 US for overseas dollar subscribers. Application to mail in the US is pending at Milwaukee, Wisconsin, and at additional offices. Distribution to N. American hobby and craft shops by Kalmbach Publishing Co, 1027 N. Seventh Street, Milwaukee, W153233, USA (Tel: 414-272-2060). Distribution to news stand sales by Eastern News Distributors Inc, 111 Eighth Avenue, New York NY1011, USA (Tel: 212-255-5620). Distribution to museums and bookshops by Bill Dean Books Ltd, 166-41 Powells Cove Boulevard, Whitestone, New York 11357 (Tel: 212-767-6632).

WOODWORKER is printed by New Avenue Press Ltd, Pasadena Close, Pump Lane, Hayes, Middlesex. (Mono origination by Multiform Photosetting Ltd, Cardiff), for the proprietor and publisher, Model & Allied Publications Ltd (a member of the Argus Press Group). Trade sales by Argus Press Sales and Distribution Ltd, 12-18 Paul Street, London EC2A 4JS. WOODWORKER (ISSN 0043-776X) is published on the 3rd Friday of the month.

Model & Allied Publications Ltd

PO Box 35, Bridge Street, Hemel Hempstead, Herts HP1 1EE. Telephone: Hemel Hempstead (0442) 41221.

THE SIMPLE WAY

One hundred years ago John Williams Benn (later Sir John Benn Bt) launched *Cabinet Maker* which is now the weekly newspaper of the furniture and furnishing trades. As part of the CM centenary celebrations Benn Brothers Ltd has issued a special magazine in which there is a review of British furniture design and development since 1880.

Author Molly Harrison says it is doubtful whether the work of the arts and crafts movement (WOODWORKER for August 1980) has ever been fully appreciated. 'Here were educated men and women working with their hands, caring passionately about the use of good materials, about honest craftsmanship and modern design.'

Among the many craftsmen who were inspired by the movement were four who made simple, dignified furniture during the last decade of the 19th century: Ernest Gimson, C. F. A. Voysey and Sidney and Ernest Barnsley. They abhorred show and over-decoration and their furniture was slowly and beautifully made, simple and distinguished.

However, the followers of the arts and crafts movement had felt themselves to be missionaries. For them, the design of furniture and other domestic objects had a political and sociological significance. But they had failed to deal at all with the fundamental problem of 20th century manufacture — how to use the machine in the best way for the work needed. They did not realise that machine-production had come to stay.

Molly Harrison says it was Sir Ambrose Heal who first designed and sold machine-made pieces of good design. Heal & Sons had been producing Victorian furniture until Ambrose joined the family firm and began to design pieces in fumed or waxed unstained oak.

The best-designed furniture in the 20s and 30s was produced by Sir Gordon Russell, much of whose work has to this day retained a certain rural flavour which is very much in the English tradition: natural woods, fine craftsmanship and understated elegance. There is no doubt that many of the pieces designed by him then, and still now, will be sought after by collectors in years to come.

However, the British public remained little interested in new design and leadership in furniture-making between the wars came from the German Bauhaus, though there was a slow, gradual trend towards simpler furniture. During the war the utility furniture scheme was establised and primarily because of the shortage of timber a simple design was evolved. As a result the furniture available was an enormous improvement on what most people had had before. Utility furniture will certainly go down as a milestone in the history of English furniture.

Furniture today is increasingly informal and adaptable and the science of ergonomics is enabling designers to avoid some of the inhuman proportions of pre-war chairs. Nearly all furniture is lighter to look at and to use. Is this the trend for the 80s and 90s?

Price increased

WOODWORKER has increased its cover price from 50p to 60p with effect from the October 1980 issue. USA and Canada rate rises from $2.25 to $2.75. Single copies by post are 85p. The home subscription rate is increased to £10.20 and the overseas sterling rate likewise to £10.20. For overseas dollar subscribers the rate goes to $23.

KITY SERVICE

A new concept in after sales back-up

Like other manufacturers, Kity guarantee their machines, provide spares and a maintenance service, but Kity plan sheets go one step further, they help you exploit the full potential of your machines.

Kity plan sheets give detailed specification about materials, design, cutting and machining for all kinds of woodworking projects. Fill in the coupon and we will send you a free 44 page book all about this invaluable and unique Kity service.

KITY UNITED KINGDOM Kity U.K., Sizers Court, Henshaw Lane, Yeadon, Leeds LS19 7DP. West Yorkshire.

WW10

618

Prices quoted are those prevailing at press date and are subject to alteration due to economic conditions.

Woodworker, October 1980

Invitation to Willis

ON SHOW WILL BE:
Bench Saws
Radial Arm Saws
Surface Planers
Thicknessers
Cross-cut Saws
Spindle Moulders
Surfacers
Mortisers
Circular Saws
Bandsaws
Grinders
Routers
Lathes
Drills

MANUFACTURERS:
Wadkin Bursgreen
De Walt
Kity
Black & Decker
Chepstow
Bosch
Coronet
Elu
Startrite
Wadkin
Mafell
Wolf
Multico
Stanley

Woodworking Machinery Exhibition

September 23rd to 27th, 1980 at 190-192 West Street, Bedminster, Bristol.
Open every day between 9.00 a.m. and 6.00 p.m. — Refreshments available.
SAVE £££'S on our SPECIAL EXHIBITION DISCOUNTS* . . . . . .
From the smallest D.I.Y. electric hand tools to Wadkin Industrial Machinery — everything under one roof.
V.H. WILLIS & CO. LTD., 190-2 West Street, Bristol BS3 3NB. Tel: Bristol 667013/4.
*If you can't visit our exhibition in September you could still qualify for our special discount during that period. Ring 0272-667013 for details.

The ELU 'MOF 96' Router

D.I.Y Power Tool of the Eighties....

The MOF 96 hand router is compact, simple to operate and gives a professional finish to your work. Its plunging action and powerful 600 watts motor with 24,000 r.p.m. ensure long cutter life, and even the biggest cuts are handled with ease.

Grooving, moulding, rebating, trimming laminates, cutting patterns to templates, forming contour work and cutting circles can be performed with only a little practice.

Kit A — Router with standard equipment
MOF 96 routing machine, 2 guide rods, side fence, guide bush for template work, 2 spanners, illustrated instruction manual, 2 cutters included plus 4 extra cutters FREE from Willis.

OUR PRICE . . . . ONLY £86.00
incl. VAT & CARRIAGE

Kit B — Router accessory set
This converts your portable plunging router into a most useful stationary machine. Kit comprises: Router table, 4 legs, fence plates and fine adjustment for table; SUVA guard & pressure guide; depth adjuster; copying follower device; circle trammel bar and SUVA protection guard.

OUR PRICE . . . . . . ONLY £51.50
incl. VAT & CARRIAGE

Full money-back guarantee on all machines sold by Willis.
Credit card holders are welcome to order by phone: Ring Bristol 667013 and quote your Access or Barclaycard numbers.

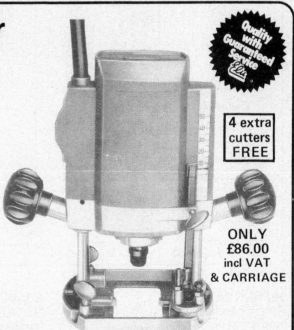

4 extra cutters FREE

ONLY £86.00 incl VAT & CARRIAGE

V. H. WILLIS & CO. LTD.
190-192 West Street,
Bedminster,
Bristol BS3 3NB.
Tel: Bristol (0272) 667013/4

Please send me . . . . . MOF 96 router/s Kit A and/or
. . . . . Kit B. Method of payment: CHEQUE ☐
Access/Barclaycard ☐ (delete as appropriate)
Credit Card No.
Name
Address
Signature

620

Prices quoted are those prevailing at press date and are subject to alteration due to economic conditions.

Woodworker, October 1980

Once you've bought the books you'll be able to make the shelves

FINE WOODWORKING

Anyone who enjoys making beautiful things out of wood will be simply overwhelmed with contents of 'Fine Woodworking', a richly detailed bi-monthly publication for serious woodworkers. Here you will find the kind of information that is timeless and hard to find anywhere else. That is why all back issues are kept in print, forming a graphic woodworking encyclopaedia. And why, within five years, a staggering 250,000 woodworkers subscribe to this magazine. Now regularly available from the SUMACO Library. Annual subscription £12.00. Single copies £2.00 each.

TAGE FRID TEACHES WOODWORKING

206 pages in which Tage Frid details everything about joinery that he has found necessary and useful in 50 years as a master craftsman. Frid, a native of Denmark and currently professor of woodworking and furniture design at Rhode Island School of Design, shows in complete step by step photo sequence concise details which are of equal benefit to professional woodworkers, amateurs and schools. **£11.00** each.

POWER TOOL WOODWORKING FOR EVERYONE by R. J. De Cristoforo.

Over 150 woodworking machinery operations superbly photographed and illustrated in 324 pages of useful hints and ideas on getting the maximum results from your workshop equipment. Although all operations are carried out on the Shopsmith Mark V woodworker, this book is a must for anyone thinking of buying or already using woodworking machines. **£9.00** each.

WOODTURNING

A small but very useful publication showing the lathe, the equipment, the wood and how woodturning is done. 25 pages with 54 photographs and illustrations. **90p** each.

HOME WORKSHOP GUIDE TO SHARPENING

160 pages showing how to sharpen practically any type of tool. Achieve professional results every time with this comprehensive volume as a guide. **£2.90** each.

PROJECT PLANS

A selection of plans to make your woodworking more interesting and enjoyable. New plans are being continually added. **85p** each or 6 as illustrated for **£4.50**.

SUMACO
Woodworking Library

Showroom open Monday to Saturday 9 a.m. to 5 p.m. on Thursday and Friday until 7.30 p.m.

Sumaco Machinery & Tools. Suma House, Huddersfield Road, Elland, West Yorkshire, HX5 9AA. Telephone Elland (0422) 75491. Telex 51182 Sumaco.

Post to:
Sumaco Woodworking Library, Suma House, Huddersfield Road, Elland, West Yorkshire, HX5 9AA.
Complete the coupon by ticking which publications you require and how many at the prices indicated. Your cheque/postal order should be made payable to "Sumaco Woodworking Library". Please note that all items are VAT Zero Rated and that prices include postage and packing.

✓ required items	Publication	Quantity	Cost	Block capitals please.
	Fine Woodworking. Annual Subscription	6	£12.00	
	Fine Woodworking. Single copy		£ 2.00	Name ....
	Tage Frid Teaches Woodworking		£11.00	Address ....
	Power Tool Woodworking for everyone		£ 9.00	
	Woodturning		90p	
	Home Workshop Guide to Sharpening		£ 2.90	Project Plans Title(s) ....
	Project Plans		85p	
	Project Plans Set	6	£ 4.50	

Please allow 21-28 days delivery.   WW 10

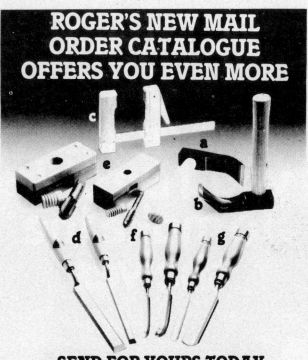

SHAVINGS FROM A VILLAGE WHEELWRIGHT'S SHOP

'It was just shillings and pence'

This was the comment by a retired wheelwright to Jocelyn Bailey's husband. But there was a measure of compensation as she explains in these notes on the subject of broad wheels

Hind broad wheel 5ft. high.

During the past few years we have been pleased to have had visits to our old village wheelwright's shop by groups of children from primary schools in the area. My husband, a fourth-generation wheelwright, explains all that he can in the time allocated for these visits. However, we felt conscious of the need to have rather more 'props' on display to help further parties to understand more about the wheelwright's craft. With this in mind we acquired a broad wheel such as would have been on a Kent or Sussex four-horse waggon. It is a hind wheel standing 5ft high and is big and exciting enough to attract the children's attention. We ourselves find considerable interest in noting the features peculiar to these old broad wheels.

It was amusing to see my husband roll the wheel along the road after collecting it from its home farm to take it to a pick-up point for lorry transport. He walked and ran quite rapidly with it and did not stop when someone called out a greeting. When he did eventually stop he said: 'There you are, anyone else would have soon had it flat on the ground. You have to keep it rolling fast!'

Since its arrival customers and callers seem fascinated by this worm-eaten relic. I feel the same myself when I think that the making and repairing of wheels like this was once commonplace in our old shop.

The felloes of our broad wheel are 6in. wide and it is shod with two rows of strakes. The spoke tongues for a straked wheel are square, while a hoop-tyred wheel usually has round tongues. The felloe joints of a broad wheel have two dowels instead of the single one that is sufficient in the later average build of wheel. We still have the gauge for marking the dowel holes in the felloe ends of a broad wheel.

We could not resist placing our old samson over the wheel for a photograph as a reminder of the hectic job of 'shoeing' a wheel with red-hot strakes. The first few of

the felloe joints were forced together for the nailing on of each strake by inserting wooden wedges into the joints either side, but after several alternate strakes were on it was necessary for the samson to be applied over the strake nail heads and the samson screws tightened to bring the felloe ends close enough for the application of each remaining strake.

Each strake covered a felloe joint and the ends of a double row of strakes were slightly staggered. The wheel was supported in a vertical position for straking by a wooden frame over the shoeing pit, and the wheel quickly turned to let each newly applied

View of the 15 × 15in. nave and the 6in. wide felloes.

Old wooden gauge for marking the twin dowel holes in ends of 6in. felloes for broad wheel. Pencil marks made at the two right angle corners. Note hole for hanging up the gauge.

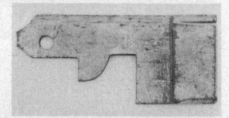

Youngster takes notes during a school visit to the workshop. Teacher in background is tape-recording the visit.

strake dip into the water in the pit to cool. The conditions would be quite dramatic; some smoke and flame from the wood of the wheel, plenty of hammering of the strake nails into the hard well-seasoned wood, and a lot of steam as a hot strake quenched noisily in the water — plus the creaking sound of the wheel joints tightening up as the metal contracted.

The nave of our broad wheel is 15in. diameter and 15in. long and has two separate iron bearings or 'boxes' in the centre. These massive wheels ran on axles made entirely of wood (beech for choice but

Samson placed over wheel as for application of red-hot strakes.

oak sometimes used); the axle arms had iron plates nailed on to take the wear. Later waggons had iron axle arms which had equal strength in much smaller bulk and so allowed the use of lighter wheels with smaller naves which were fully lined with a one-piece cast-iron bearing.

When we have visitors to our workshop we always bring out a copy of Harold Philpot's plan of the *Broad Wheeled Sussex Waggon*. One section of this shows details of a double-straked broad wheel. We note in the *1980 Model Wheelwright Yearbook* that John Thompson offers Harold Philpot's plan and says that seeing this drawing at the Science museum in London was a factor which led him to taking up the recording of horse-drawn vehicles.

One point to remember, of course, is that wheelwrights themselves did not have drawings; their data evolved from generations of workshop practice together with patterns cut out in thin wood and parts from old vehicles that were saved for reference.

The growing interest in horse-drawn vehicles is gratifying to families like my husband's who have a direct working link with such vehicles when they were in everyday use. One retired wheelwright said to my husband: 'It was just shillings and pence in wheelwrighting, wasn't it Bert?'. Maybe so, but there was a measure of compensation in the satisfaction derived from learning (and applying) special skills and using seasoned English timber in the making of useful things for your fellow men. Bert says I will never be able to fully describe that factor in my writings on the craft!

Axle arm of old one-piece wooden axle. Note the iron wear plates underneath and the linch pin still intact.

Two rows of strakes have the joins staggered as seen here.

Seminar for woodturners

Woodturning is ubiquitous and standards of design and workmanship are generally abysmal, writes Richard Raffan who is a woodturner at Sandford, Crediton, Devonshire. He attended the international seminar for woodturners held at Parnham house, Beaminster, Dorset, on 14 and 15 June. 'Such a gathering was not before time,' he writes.

Nearly 130 came from this country, North America, Australia and Europe to hear eight speakers, take part in discussion groups and generally exchange ideas. On the second day it was open to the public to see demonstrations on pole, ornamental and standard modern lathes and to visit the trade exhibition and the exhibition of turnery which ran throughout June.

The lecturers generally avoided technical aspects of the craft being concerned more with the quality of the end product than how it was achieved. The concern was best put by David Ellsworth (USA): 'There is always craft in being an artist but not always art in craft.' Frank Knox (USA) speaking on ornamental turning lamented the fact that so many using the Holtzapffel lathe could not resist decorating every surface and by showing such lack of sympathy for the material and overall design tended to ruin the end result. (For more about Mr Knox see WOODWORKER for July 1980, page 463). Similarly, Richard Raffan felt turners could be so carried away displaying technical skills and grain that form and function tended to be forgotten.

Contemporary turning in the concurrent exhibition exemplified the approach in which the object is free of turnery gimmicks. This could be seen in Neville Neal's chairs; Stephen Hogbin's (Canada) segmental forms; or the bowls of Bob Stocksdale (USA), Jim Partridge or Richard Raffan.

Speakers who fired the imagination were Stephen Hogbin and David Ellsworth. The former showed the development of his segmental forms where the cross-section of a turned form assumes major importance. Turned shapes are cut, reassembled differently and, perhaps, turned again. The possiblities are immense. The latter uses wood most people might regard as useless. With great imagination and skill he creates fragile bowl-like forms from burrs split or full of holes and rot.

With few industrial or ornamental turners present the accent was on hand turning in small workshops. Those attending the seminar undoubtedly found it stimulating and it will be interesting to see what effect it has on future work.

Ornamental turners

Following the retirement of A. Mayor from the editorship of the *Ornamental Turners Bulletin* (the journal of the Society of Ornamental Turners), J. F. R. Ince has taken up the appointment. His address is: Wangfield House, Curdridge, Hampshire. Correspondence relating to the *Bulletin* should be sent to Mr Ince at the address given.

Not enough!

For 1980-81 the government grant to the Crafts Council is £1 200 000. The council says that it will be unable to maintain activities at their present level and there will therefore be no craftsmens' tours and funds for other activities will be reduced.

So far as the woodworker's needs are concerned the Meliaceae might be considered the most valuable of plant families. This is because of the range of high-quality timbers it supplies, famed for their appearance in the choicest decorative schemes and their excellent working qualities.

Most of the woods mentioned in this series are well-known to every craftsman in wood and need little in the way of description; but in collecting information one is impressed by the family characteristics: large, heavy, woody seed capsules produced from flowers which are very small. These capsules contain winged seeds or, in some genera, fleshy fruits; but there are close morphological similarities between these two types.

A note on the shortcomings of drawing from herbarium specimens is perhaps necessary here. There are some 40 genera and 600 species in the Meliaceae and this gives rise to a greater than usual diversity of floral forms, most of the flowers being numerous but very small; others are over 10cm long.

The only way to do anything like justice to such magnificence, even for the few timbers mentioned here, would be to travel to the tropics and draw, or better still, photograph the flowers in colour from life. But this is hardly a practical proposal and the next best is to do what one can with the desiccated, poisoned, discoloured and fragile herbarium specimens. However, the relationship between different timbers and the basic family characteristics are illustrated by these portrayals, limited though they be.

What these flowers lack in size they make up in number, the much branched thyrses of some species being 2-3ft. long. (It is generally known that a racemose inflorescence is like a foxglove, the lowest flower opening first. In a cymose inflorescence the terminal flower opens first. A thyrsus, strictly speaking, shows both, the primary axis being racemose, the secondary axes cymose. The term is also applied to any closely branched inflorescence with many flowers.

All woods vary to some extent owing to rate of growth and other environmental influences. But in general those of this family are similar in texture and hardness and in their working qualities, which made Chippendale, Hepplewhite and others the famous names they still are.

The woods to be included in this series are: crabwood or andiroba; cedar; sapele; utile (with reference to heavy sapele or heavy mahogany); guarea; African mahogany; African walnut; Honduras or central American mahogany or baywood; Cuban or 'Spanish' mahogany; and avodire. They are placed in this order which from their generic names is alphabetical.

Cross section × 3.3 as seen with a ×10 hand lens.

Right: Cross section × 10 lineal

The family consists of trees and shrubs and is confined to the tropics and the warm temperate regions of both hemispheres. It takes its name from the genus *Melia,* from an old name for the ash, the leaves of some species ('Spanish' mahogany for instance) having a strong resemblance to those of our familiar ash tree.

There is one feature of the Meliaceae over which woodworkers may rejoice: most species can be successfully raised in plantations.

CRABWOOD (ANDIROBA): 16

Carapa guianensis. Carapa — from a native name in the Carribean; *guianensis* — from Guyana.

There are 10 species of *Carapa* the seeds of which are fleshy, in a heavy capsule, and those of the crabwood tree yield an oil. Some species grow in swamps in association with the mangroves.

The tree is fairly large and occurs over a considerable area from Brazil northwards to Honduras and through the West Indian islands, and so is important in supplying a mahogany substitute for furniture and general structural purposes. The wood may be considered as a second-rate mahogany, not likely to be encountered frequently although figured logs do occur and it might possibly be met as veneer.

Known as andiroba in Brazil it has also been referred to as Demerara mahogany and Surinam mahogany but it has not been accepted as a mahogany by international trade. It is plainer, less attractive, darker and duller in colour than its better-known relatives; also somewhat denser, less easy to work with hand tools and less stable.

The photomicrograph shows a texture and structure similar to the mahoganies. Characteristic black deposits are seen in some of the vessels which have a tendency to a radial arrangement. Rays are very small and parenchyma cells are inconspicuous, but a tangential line of them can be seen quite clearly. 'Paratracheal' parenchyma (that is in association with the vessels) is also present but not conspicuous.

In this family both the frequency and the arrangement of parenchyma cells are very variable.

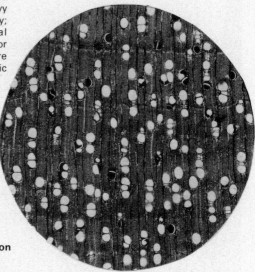

THE WORLD'S TIMBER TREES

C. W. Bond FIWSc has now completed descriptions of certain timbers from the Leguminosae, the last one being okan: 15 in the September issue. This month he begins a survey of 10 woods from the mahogany family, the Meliaceae. This could be regarded as the craftsman's family since it has supplied woods which have been universal favourites for almost 300 years.

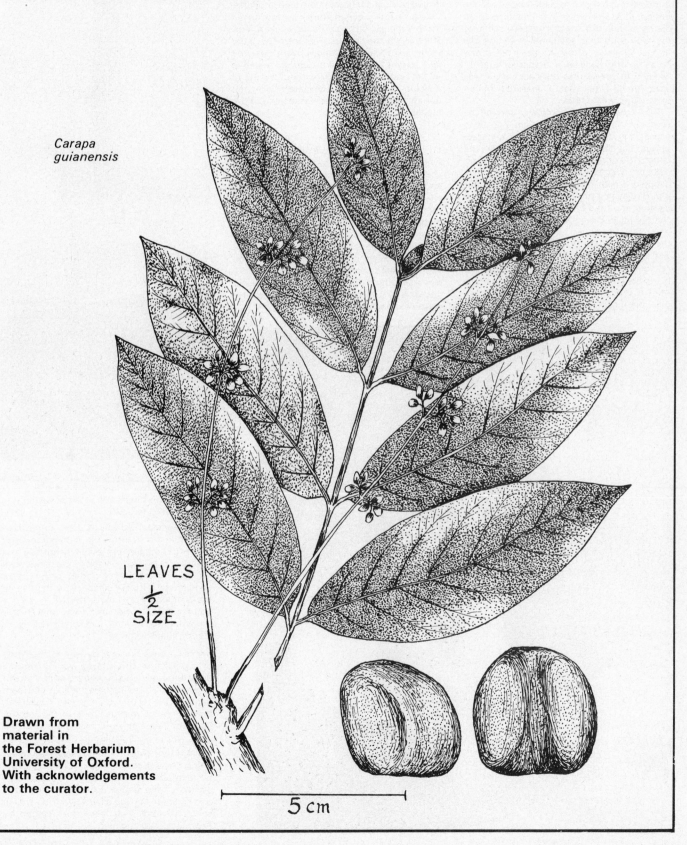

Carapa guianensis

LEAVES $\frac{1}{2}$ SIZE

Drawn from material in the Forest Herbarium University of Oxford. With acknowledgements to the curator.

5 cm

A PAGE FOR SMOKERS

Richard Large tells how he made a bowl to hold pipes; and a pedestal ashtray.

I turned the bowl in two pieces: the bowl itself and the upright, leaving the centre of the bowl in so that it formed the base of the upright. The bowl was small enough (overall diameter 6in.) to be held on a screw chuck of the type with two additional holes on the flange. Whether or not to leave the screw holes in the base is a matter of pride. I decided to saw across the base and it was after doing this that I invested in an expanding collet chuck.

When the bowl was completed I drilled the centre of the upright section with a ½in. bit to accept the tenon turned on the separate upright but did not remove the bowl from the chuck. The upright is also short enough to be held on a screw chuck. If this method is adopted a neat finial can be turned on the top. However, I turned my upright between centres and then fitted a separate finial of contrasting wood (mahogony) — the bowl and upright were ash. Of course, I should have realised and wishing to use this for the bowl and (for reasons which will become apparent) not being able to remove the bowl from the chuck until it was completed, the upright should have been turned first.

With the two pieces completed I did some preliminary finishing before joining them. I drilled the top section for the pipe supports, taking care to place the holes evenly. I used three supports but it could have taken four. The upright can be glued into the bowl. If the wood is sufficiently strong you can make the joint a tight fit and drive the upright in with a mallet and carry on work without having to wait for the glue to dry. A delicate finial on the upright will, however, restrict the use of the mallet.

I had a 'step' between the two pieces so the whole thing went back in the lathe for final shaping with a sharp, round nosed scraper. I ended up with a flowing shape and a sudden change in grain direction. This is an effect that is either liked or disliked! The support pieces were turned on the screw chuck. The flange of the support is outermost and it is surprisingly easy to cut across this with the point of a skew chisel. The flanges of the supports had to be big enough to prevent the pipes slipping but elaborate shapes are not necessarily a good idea. Finally the supports were polished and glued in.

Smokers particularly will know that pipes have deceptive shapes and therefore it is important to check the internal shape and diameter of the bowl.

The pedestal ashtray is 22in. high, base 7in. diameter and tray 5¾in. diameter with the three components joined by mortise and tenons. I preferred to keep to the same style for the components rather than have completely different shapes. By increasing the diameter of the bottom third of the stem a greater degree of stability was imparted to the job. When turning the stem use of a back steady is advisable.

The base would not fit between the centres of my lathe but the ashtray would. The tray and stem were glued together and put back in the lathe for final finishing but base and stem joint is pulled tight with a screw. Thus it can be dismantled and put back in the lathe if burns or stains make repolishing necessary.

As the bottom of the ashtray had to be polished and free of blemishes such as screw holes, I used a screw chuck (again) removing the central screw and relying on two small screws in the flange. I carefully measured and shaped the top of the stem so that it covered the holes left by the screws when the two pieces were joined.

OK, so the Elu TGS 171 is a very appealing machine, but it is also versatile and has many new safety features.

SAFE AND VERSATILE

The TGS171 is like no other saw and combines accurate cross cutting and safe ripping of wood, plastics and even aluminium.

The snip-off action eliminates the problem of the saw trying to climb the material. This controlled action improves the quality of cut essential for picture framing, aluminium window sections, architraves, in addition to cutting table legs all the same length using the stop. The spring return ensures the head goes back to its locked position and the guard re-shields the blade completely (4).

It is simple to change from a mitring saw to sawbench, as no tools are required. The riving knife is permanently fitted to the machine and swung into position, the adjuster is located at the rear and the whole table is turned over, the guard with the quick release button (1) is quick to fit. The no-volt release switch (2) adds to the safety, the switch turns itself off when the power is taken away.

The legs are quick release and adjustable for an uneven floor surface, and the whole machine can be easily stored in the boot of a car (3) for complete portability.

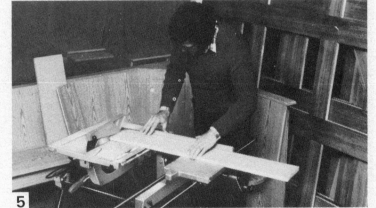

Send the coupon below for your FREE colour brochure, accessories list and prices.

TABLES LEFT AND RIGHT

With the extension table on the right, large boards and panels can be cut easily. The sliding table (5) on the left ensures accurate cutting square 90° panels, essential when cabinet making.

BACK-UP THROUGHOUT THE U.K.

Elu have established a network of Authorised Dealers throughout the U.K. All Elu machines have a full 12 months guarantee covering free parts and labour. Although from our experience the induction type motor fitted to this machine is both reliable and quiet.

MAXIMUM PRICES YOU WILL PAY (INC. VAT)

TGS Sawbench/Mitre Saw, including riving knife and guard.	£322.00
171 20 22 00 Woodworking Set (TCT Sawblade, rip fence and mitre fence).	£ 52.90
171 20 22 03 Set of legs	£ 24.72

Ledge

Caravan

by John Thompson

It is said that Dunton of Reading built only three of his superb Ledge caravans. Now after 60 years a replica is being constructed by a farmer at Calgary in South Africa

Only the best materials and workmanship will suffice when slender wheels like these have to carry such a large vehicle.

The living waggons built for travellers and showmen in late Victorian and Edwardian times were a triumph of design both in their decorative and functional qualities. It is the traditional style of carving and paintwork on the exterior which is the most obvious feature of the caravans. But just as important a characteristic is the internal layout. The arrangement of the furnishings was common to all five types of caravan (the Reading, Ledge, Showman, Bow top, and Open lot) and for comfort and convenience in a confined space it would be difficult to surpass it.

Dunton of Reading was perhaps the best-known builder. His work represents a peak of achievement in caravan construction, equivalent to Chippendale or Grinling Gibbons in their particular fields. During the 50 years prior to 1920 the Dunton family arrived at a characteristic style of under-works, carving and painting which was used on their famous Reading vans.

They also built a very small number of Ledge caravans (perhaps only three) which were superb specimens. One of these is owned by Reading borough museum and a start has been made on restoration work. Mervyn Jones of Holywell in North Wales, owns the twin of this van and he tells me that he purchased it as a wreck. The wheels and some carving had been removed to replace parts on the other van before the museum

Left: Mrs Wells with some freehand carving work.

acquired it. I wonder if the third Dunton Ledge still exists.

Now after a lapse of 60 years a Ledge to the Dunton pattern is being built. But not in the brick-walled yard at Crane Wharf, Reading. The work is being done on a farm at Calgary near East London, South Africa, where Robin Wells rears beef cattle and also finds time to collect and restore horse-drawn vehicles.

I had drawn scale plans of the Ledge van at Reading in 1975, spending many hours on, in and under the vehicle measuring it and sketching. Probably a few hundred models have been built from these plans since the first appeared in WOODWORKER for January 1976. But to the best of my knowledge Mr Wells is the first person to tackle a replica.

He is well qualified to take on the task having been a C & G finalist in carpentry and joinery in 1944. He ran his own business until 1971 doing some work for motor body builders and wheelwrights, as well as marine, church and shopfitting jobs. On the farm at Calgary he has set up a blacksmith's and wheelwright's shop, so the lack of facilities for ironwork (which deter many people from vehicle building) is no problem.

The caravan was started about a year ago and Mr Wells estimates that during that period the equivalent of six months' full-time has been spent on it. The construction is very similar to the original though it has been necessary to make some substitution of materials. For example, the usual roof covering was layers of canvas put on with white lead paint and varnished over. As the South African climate would cause this form of covering to dry and crack, three layers of glassfibre have been substituted.

The forecarriage or cradle is subjected to a lot of stress and for both functional and aesthetic reasons it needs to be light and to have the members curved. On the Dunton vehicles the forecarriages were made of home-grown ash. On the replica the curved parts have been formed by laminating ¼in. thick sapele, cold-glued over formers. The shafts have been made in the same way using locally-grown knobwood which, Mr Wells maintains, bends nearly as well as ash.

Underframing is mostly of oak and sapele. The wheels have felloes of red pear, cut to shape on a bandsaw. Spokes are of oak or assegai and the stocks (or hubs) are of yellow wood, once a common timber in South Africa and used for the Boer trek waggons of pioneer days; now it is scarce and expensive. The superstructure of the caravan is all of South African pine, selected for its lightness and freedom from knots.

The timber has been machine-planed and the moulding on the matchboarding machine-prepared. Otherwise, all joints, chamfering, mouldings and carvings have been worked by hand. Mrs Wells — Cynthia — undertook much of the freehand carving and has been very enthusiastic over the whole project. Work is now going ahead with fitting-out the interior and putting on the finishing coats of paintwork.

Visitors are welcomed at Calgary where they can see not only the blacksmith's and wheelwright's shop but a collection of 30 different carriages and carts, with many more awaiting restoration. They are also able to take rides in some of the old vehicles.

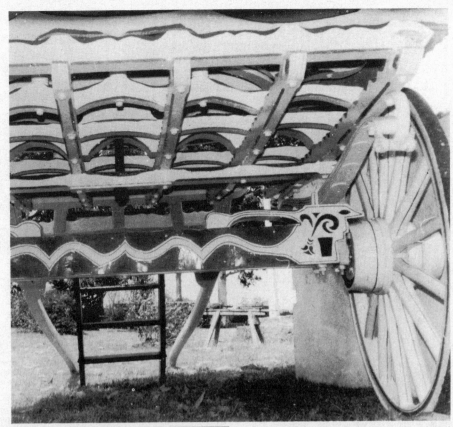

Those wishing to emulate Mr Wells — or to model the Denton Ledge — are reminded that a set of ⅛in. scale plans (10 sheets) can be had from M.A.P. Plans Service, PO Box 35, Bridge Street, Hemel Hempstead HP1 1EE, at £4.70 plus 35p for postage and packing.

Above: The intricately carved and painted forecarriage.

Below: The partially complete caravan at Calgary. Mr Wells is assisting the blacksmith to tyre a wheel on the platform.

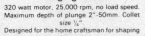

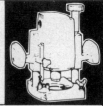

632

Prices quoted are those prevailing at press date and are subject to alteration due to economic conditions.

Woodworker, October 1980

BOOK REVIEWS

The task of the spinster

Eliza Leadbeater who is a collector of spinning wheels and a handspinner of international repute, has written a book in the Shire Album series on *Spinning and Spinning Wheels,* published by Shire Publications Ltd, Cromwell House, Church Street, Princes Risborough, Aylesbury HP17 9AJ, priced 60p.

The spinning wheel is one of the most familiar of bygones, the epitome of an unhurried yet industrious way of life that seems so refreshingly different from our own. But if we think of a spinning wheel as a picturesque item providing a talking point in the corner we should not forget the hours of toil the cottage dwellers spent working at it.

With some types of wheel the spinner had to walk to perform her task and the floor around the wheel often showed the marks of wear. Handspinning is a slow and laborious process and only part of the task of converting fleeces, flax or other fibres into a thread suitable for weaving.

Spinning as a craft is enjoying a revival. This little book traces the development of the spinning wheel, the principles of the spindle and the origins of the craft of spinning. It explains how the fibres are prepared for spinning and lists the many tools used. The process of spinning with a wheel is detailed and many photographs of wheels from Britain, Europe and N America are included to illustrate the different types used in flax and wool spinning.

The mechanics and variations of the U-flyer system are discussed and spinster's accessories such as the niddy-noddy and click reel are illustrated.

The book concludes with a list of places to visit for those interested in seeing the craft for themselves and a list of books for further reading on the subject. These latter include the author's own book *Handspinning* (published by Cassell, 1976), a recognised instruction book. With her husband, Christopher, she is known as a manufacturer and supplier of equipment for handspinning, weaving and dyeing. Her interest in the origin of wheels and spinning was fostered by the gift from her husband of a Canadian Saxony wheel. Since then they have together researched the development of textile hand tools and the early inventions of the industrial revolution.

They are striving towards the permanent display of their personal collection of spinning wheels and tools in the barn of their early 17th century timber-framed Cheshire cottage. **P.C.**

'quaking tarts and quivering custards'

Not perhaps the title one would expect to head a review of *English Domestic Furniture 1100-1837,* but such a homely statement conjures up the laden Welsh dresser of my youth and the stone flagged pantry floor groaning with home-made produce in the pre-refrigerator days when bead-hung muslin covers kept the flies out of milk, preserves and wines alike; and the wooden shelves were filled as fast as they emptied with lovingly produced country fare.

This is Ivan Sparkes' third book on the history of English furniture and to my mind is not only an enlightening and informative source but a real pleasure to read. The book covers English domestic furniture from the early medieval period, just after the Norman conquest, to the end of the Regency period in the early 19th century. It is a broad period for a single book and Ivan Sparkes has wisely concentrated on the popular furniture of the period — tables, beds, chests, cupboards, writing furniture, nursery furniture and chairs with some details on cabinetmakers, their designs and trade, upholstery, craftsmen, tools and timber.

Almost all the pieces illustrated are in the Victoria and Albert museum, though some are in the Wycombe chair museum (of which Mr Sparkes is curator) and a few other sources are also acknowleged.

The book traces the growth in development and design of furniture and reflects the changing shape of society. From the medieval sturdy plank chest to the sophisticated veneered and inlaid Regency commode is a big step. The author says he has attempted to present this development in the form of a story containing answers to problems which he has experienced in recognising the basic differences between styles and pieces of English furniture and in the way in which they have developed. He has succeeded.

Many experts have strong views, and often differing views, on the evolution of national styles and the influence played by various craftsmen in the furniture of their period; others highlight regional and social factors which govern the introduction of a particular style. Ivan Sparkes 'treads warily' between these views but gives a bibliography of source books for the reader to pursue his or her own chosen field of study and research.

The many quotations within the book are fascinating, from those relating to apprentices' behaviour and wages to timber prices (sawing one walnut tree and hewing cost 3s 6d in 1491). An early example quoted of the use of a medieval Trades Description Act was the fining of two carpenters 6d and damage to the value of 2s being awarded to Roger de Multon who in 1317 brought an action to court against the two carpenters whom he employed to build a house of oak. He had detected some of the out-of-sight timbers were alder and willow!

When the feasts of early years are detailed it is not surprising that tables in the 15-17th centuries were solid affairs with heavy, turned legs linked by stretchers to give rigidity. Table cloths of 6yd were not uncommon. When communal living in the hall began to pall, dining of the family in smaller rooms became the vogue and so consequently the furniture became scaled-down to fit. The draw-top table came into being in 1550-1650 to overcome the problems of additional places when occasionally necessary, followed by folding tables and gate-leg tables 'a little table of wainescott with two fallinge leaves'. When an inventory was made of the goods and furnishings of Cardinal Wolsey at Hampton Court palace in the 16th century, the building contained 280 beds!

The author says that the only item of medieval furnishing to survive in any quantity was the chest. He goes on to describe the coffer, dug-out chest, boarded chest, joined chest, framed or panelled chest, mule chest, tallboys, chests and drawers of the 17th century, the commode and the 18th century dressing table.

Changing names of furniture over the centuries cause confusion. The situation is readily illustrated by the early types of cupboard. Leading authorities frequently differ over nomenclature. We know the cupboard was in use in the time of Queen Elizabeth I but the form was a board or shelf for the display and service of cups and plates. The easiest description of this type of cupboard is given in Sir Thomas Kyton's inventory of 1603 'Item, a thing like stayres to set plate on'. Ivan Sparkes details the armoire and aumbry, court cupboard, court cupboard with aumbry, food cupboard, press cupboard, press and wardrobes, sideboard and dresser.

It is always a source of surprise to me that something I grew up with and very much took for granted has a proper name and is a special design in its own right. The dresser which our Cardiganshire and Pembrokeshire corgis lived in is actually a West Wales dresser — the kneehole with arched cove is *really* known as the dog kennel. As a child I spent a lot of my time in that 'dog kennel' — it was nice and warm and safe, also the main space in front of the black-lead range was taken up by the cats: there was, too, always the possibility that the kettle would suddenly boil over and splashes of scalding water would necessitate a fast retreat — much more the cats' forte.

The chapter on writing furniture, bookcases and cabinets is particularly interesting. I always wondered where the term *loafer* originated. The chapter on nursery furniture does, as the author says, conjure up Victorian nurseries; and Peter Pan — suitably sized furniture is a lovely phrase. It came as a complete surprise to read that baby cages, baby trotters or go-carts were known in the Middle Ages and appear in 17th century paintings. These frameworks of wood on casters, leather or wooden rollers support the child but leave the arms free and are supposed to encourage him/her to walk. A quote from Loudon, writing in 1839, conveys a stern admonition: 'the table is made lower than a chair in order that the nurse may have the more power over the child when she is washing it'. Help!

Chairs are no longer restricted to persons of rank, and Ivan Sparkes gets fully into his stride in the chapters on chairs and seating furniture (his earlier books in this series have been on *The English Country Chair* and *The Windsor Chair*). I like the caquetoire — the conversation chair, designed 'primarily for women' (caquetoire means to chatter)! The reading chair introduced about 1720 would find four willing occupants in my house today; what a practical shape (if one is in trousers) for support of both book and elbows. The Regency chair in beech circa 1810 (illustrated on page 131) is so graceful it seems a pity its fine lines were ever obscured when 'someone sat in it'; and the late 18th century sofa of Grecian couch shape on page 153 cries out for an elegant lady to recline gracefully on it in a beautiful Empire line dress.

This is a book with a new fact or surprise on every page. It may detail domestic furniture but it is royally written. It will become a well-thumbed treasure on my bookcase (bookstand? chiffonier? beaufait?).

An Illustrated History of English Domestic Furniture (1100-1837). The Age of the Craftsman (Ivan Sparkes), is published by Spur Books Ltd, 6 Parade Court, Bourne End, Bucks, at £6.95. **P.C.**

IF YOU ARE ON THE TILES

Take Heed

Alan Holtham offers tips to woodturners who favour circular ceramic tiles set into wooden frames as cheeseboards, ashtrays, teapot stands and so forth. But select your timber carefully and choose a tile that complements the grain pattern and colour.

Probably one of the most popular accessories used by the woodturner today is the circular ceramic tile. With well over 200 designs to choose from there is a fascinating variety which can be incorporated into a suitable piece of timber. The majority of tiles currently available are either 6in. or 3½in. diameter and these are usually set into appropriate wooden frames as cheeseboards, teapot stands, wall plaques, coasters, ashtrays and so forth.

However, there is a danger with this type of work of trying to use up odd scraps of timber, just slapping in any old tile and leaving the final product looking like those other mass-produced 'gifty' items seen in tourist shops. These items not only look poor but devalue the timber from which they are made. On the other hand, if you select your timber carefully and choose a tile that complements the grain pattern and colour, then the results can be attractive and make very acceptable presents.

The procedure when using tiles is fairly straightforward, though there are one or two points to note if you want to save expensive mistakes in terms of timber and cracked tiles. Selection of the most suitable blank is of paramount importance. It must be bone dry. If there is any movement or shrinkage after the tile is fixed there is a real danger of the tile cracking. Believe me, once the tile is inset it is very difficult to remove.

Let me take as an example the making of a cheese and biscuits platter with an inset 6in. tile. The material needed is a disc 12-14in. diameter and 1¼-1½in. thick. I have a theory that warped pieces are not necessarily to be discarded since if they have already warped (Fig. 1), then the internal stress has been relieved and they should not move much further when worked. This has yet to be scientifically proved but it seems to work! When working with warped pieces use the largest possible faceplate (Fig. 2) and pack out any large gaps between the plate and the timber to minimise vibration during the roughing-out phase. With the lathe revolving at between 500 and 700rpm clean up the edge of the disc using a ⅜in. deep fluted roughing gouge (Fig. 3). With this completed now start work on the face which in this case, since I shall be using an expanding chuck, will become the base of the platter.

At this stage with the disc running more evenly the speed can usually be put up a notch to around the 1000 mark; but do not overdo it if there is still vibration.

I start by rounding over the underside towards the rim (Fig. 4), using the bowl gouge, handle well down to keep the bevel rubbing. This bevel contact business is very important on these larger discs; otherwise you finish up with the two characteristic patches of roughness on the end grain areas which can never be removed no matter how many sheets of garnet paper you use. I feel there is a tendency to over-emphasise the 'correct' tool technique but this is one occasion where the correct technique matters.

With the edge completed flatten-off the base, working from the outside towards the centre (Fig. 5). With this nice and level mark out a 3½in. diameter circle (Fig. 6) and cut out a recess to take the expanding chuck (a depth of about ⅛in. should be plenty for a 12in. diameter disc); slightly dovetailing the periphery of the recess with the corner of a small skew (Fig. 7). With all this completed to your satisfaction (Fig. 8) the whole of the underside of the platter must now be finished, so carry out any necessary papering and apply your choice of polish. For items that are going to be subject to a lot of handling, or come into contact with food, I prefer a couple of coats of quick-drying Melamine finish applied with a cloth (Fig. 9) and burnished hard, possibly with a touch of friction polish if a high gloss is required.

With the underside completed the platter can be reversed onto the chuck (Fig. 10) and

the front tackled. Incidentally, these chucks give a firm hold for this sort of work — I have yet to lose a bowl off one. As a point of interest, though, I did once make the mistake of leaving a large platter on one of these chucks on the outboard end while turning on the inboard.

Of course this had to happen when I was at a prestigious exhibition surrounded by a critical audience of craft teachers. In trying to dazzle them with a display of virtuoso (?) turning techniques I applied a rather heavy cut on the piece between centres (more like a controlled dig-in really); the piece on the outboard end rapidly detached itself from all contact with the lathe, bounced on the floor between two of the nearest spectators, then taking on the appearance of a UFO disappeared over the top of the stand across the aisle. Try explaining that away as standard procedure! I didn't sell many chucks that day. I mention this only to emphasise that the obvious potential danger can be overlooked if you are not concentrating. Woodturning should be relaxing but do not treat it with too much familiarity.

To get back to the platter, do make sure that the recess for the tile is really flat so that it sits firmly (Fig. 11), and if necessary use a flat scraper to finish off (Fig. 12). Similarly do not make the recess so tight that the tile is a 'heavy drive push fit' since this allows no room for timber movement; leave a gap of at least 1/16in. all round the tile. The method of fixing the tile is important. Tile cements should never be used since they set rigid and cannot therefore flex under changing conditions. I use a flexible adhesive such as Clam, Evo-stik Contact or Copydex.

Fig. 13 shows a couple of examples of the finished item, the left-hand one being a nicely marked piece of olive ash, the right-hand one being elm.

Teapot and casserole stands are just a variation on the same theme using different sized tiles but all being let in from the front (Fig. 14). Another popular use of the tile is in wall plaques. I always feel these look better if the tile is put in from the back thus hiding the rim. (Fig. 15). In this case the back rebate is turned first and then reversed onto the chuck as before for shaping of the front (Fig. 16). The tile is glued-in from the back. To finish off I usually stick a small piece of brown paper over the whole back and trim round with small scissors. A small ring hanger is all that is needed to complete the job.

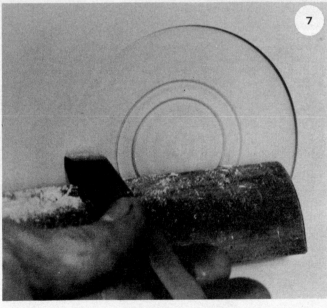

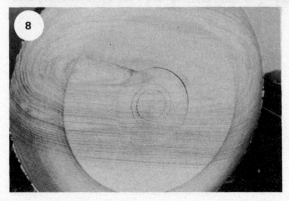

1. Already warped piece. 2. Use the largest possible faceplate when working with warped pieces. 3. Clean up the disc edge with a ⅜in. deep fluted roughing gouge. 4. Rounding over the underside towards the rim. 5. With the edge completed flatten off the base working from the outside towards the centre. 6. Mark out a 3½in. diameter circle. 7. Dovetail the periphery of the recess with the corner of a small skew. 8. Underside of the platter ready for finishing.

ON THE TILES

9. Melamine finish applied with a cloth. 10. Platter reversed onto the chuck. 11. Make sure the recess for the tile is flat to give a firm seating. 12. Use a flat scraper to finish off if necessary. 13. Left-hand tile set in olive ash, right-hand in elm. 14. Variations on a theme. 15. Put the tile in from the back to hide the rim as in this wall plaque. 16 Reversed on the chuck for shaping the front.

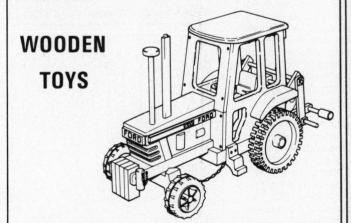

Development of AMERICAN COLONIAL FURNITURE

Bow-back Windsor. Circa 1780.

In the March issue (pages 172-3) Jane Pullen told of her visit to the US to study Shaker and early American colonial furniture. Here Mrs Pullen explains how — and why — the American colonists developed distinctive new styles and made changes in methods of manufacturing. 'Nails and screws were hard to come by at first and there was no glue so accurate joints, pegs and wedged keys were a vital part of the construction of any wooden item.'

The first settlers on the North American continent found a land inhabited by a relatively few native tribes living in harmony with nature. They hunted and fished but made little impact on the environment. Immense stands of some hitherto unknown timber species covered the land. The settlers were fully occupied in clearing areas to grow crops and in providing shelter for themselves of a very basic nature.

Their first furniture was little more than tree stumps; roughly-hewn planks; three-legged stools for the uneven earth floors of their dwellings; and slab-sided chests and trunks for storage purposes. Whereas in Britain oak had been the primary source of timber, with a long tradition in manor and monastery, the settlers — mainly of rural stock — were unhampered by tradition. Moreover, the species were easier to convert than oak; giant white pine, maple, hickory, birch, red oak, cherry, ash and butternut were readily to hand. The broad axe, adze and pitsaw made the conversion and working of all this timber conducive to lighter, less cumbersome furniture.

Pieces did not have to be of solid construction; wood was abundant for replacement of items that broke. More durable timbers such as walnut were reserved for furniture subjected to tougher wear, or for the sophisticated centres of colonial government.

The settlers — or American colonists as they came to be called — lived in isolated communities, retaining attitudes and skills at first that they had learned in their countries of origin. This made regional styles identifiable and dateable. Being thus influenced,

early American colonial furniture was in some respects almost identical to 17th and 18th century British and European furniture.

Gradually distinctive new styles appeared engendered by the different timbers and the isolation of the communities. Nails and screws were hard to come by at first and there was no glue so accurate joints, pegs and wedged keys were a vital part of the construction of any wooden item.

Over the years there evolved the need in growing communities for a specialist in working wood. The person who assumed this position would have been an all-round craftsman. Besides supplying items of hardware and cordage he would repair broken items of general usage — and probably run his own small farm as well. But primarily he would serve the community by making furniture and woodware suited to particular needs and circumstances; and using the materials in his locality.

An example of this adaptability is the American waggon seat or bench. This could be used in the waggon, then removed and used in the home. A Windsor settle probably evolved from this, a purely American design. The Windsor settle was a light, long board with sticks for a back, making it a more flexible and lighter item altogether.

Wealthier colonists tended to import fashionable furniture from Europe and these pieces were copied by cabinet makers working in more densely populated areas. Even then the different timbers available resulted in an 'Americanisation' of the designs and eventually became the Federal period furniture. These items were too fragile for everyday use and country style — or what came to be known as colonial style — predominated.

Governor Patrick Gordon of Philadelphia is credited with bringing the first Windsor into the North American continent. He died in 1736 and it is recorded that five Windsor chairs were among his effects. Be that as it may, the American Windsor as such first appeared in Philadelphia around 1750. This city was the cultural capital of the colonies and it is fair to assume that Gordon's chairs were close copies of Windsors imported from England. For nearly 100 years Windsors were America's favourite type of seating in every situation from tavern to kitchen, from courtroom to bedroom. They were light, strong, comfortable and inexpensive, all qualities applicable to the market of the time. They were accepted throughout the strata of American society and for this reason were allowed to develop from the comb-back chair into a variety of lighter and more graceful styles.

There were three types distinguished as stick-chairs: Windsors, slat-backs and 'fancies'. The basic construction was the same: parts were either turned or whittled and drilled sockets were used to assemble them. This distinguished them from the cabinet maker's chairs which were shaped with saws, planes and joints. Stick-chairs were more akin to the craft of wheelwright and cooper. Roughly the same tools were used in their construction — the adze, froe, scorpe, spokeshave, drawknife and shaving horse.

It was never a primitive folk art. It was also far from crude rustic furniture, so this implies some sort of standardised skill. Small country shops produced a variety of items required by a growing population. Work was made to order, there being little capital available to finance large stocks.

Reference to such a small workshop can be found in the records of Samuel Stickney Jr of Beverly, Mass. He worked during the late 18th and early 19th centuries and his records indicate he sold scores of small items and repaired and manufactured an assortment of wooden articles, including the chair illustrated in this article. Urban workshops could, of

Continuous arm Windsor. Circa 1790.

course, operate on a different basis. Excess items could be made and stocked or sold in job lots, for instance to a ship's captain to make up his trading cargo; also to merchants to be shipped in waggon lots to other centres.

The development of the English Windsor and American Windsor chair serves to illustrate in one particular field all the divergent factors. In England the history of the Windsor is couched in a vocabulary that evokes all the trades employed in assembling the article: bodger, benchman, bottomers, benders, framers, finishers and so on. The various categories of craftsmen produced one part of the whole. For example, the bodger working in beech plantations made turned legs and stretchers on a pole lathe from green timber, stacking them to season and moving on to the next plantation. The seasoned timber was then transported to the place of assembly for the next stage.

The American chairmaker tended to work from the beginning to the end of his product. This, coupled with the divergence in timbers, influenced the emergence of differing styles and finishes. White pine and chestnut were used for seats (although there is now no chestnut in America, it having been wiped out by a virus similar to dutch elm disease). The legs were usually of maple, the stretchers could be red oak, the back sticks maple or ash and the bent or steamed components black ash; hickory could be used in any or all of these functions. Cherry, butternut and birch were also used.

To make the conformity of the whole they were usually painted with one coat of flat dark paint. Oddly enough the paint served to enhance the finished product to a marked degree. Later in the 19th century the vogue for decoration emerged with stencil, banded and gilded designs.

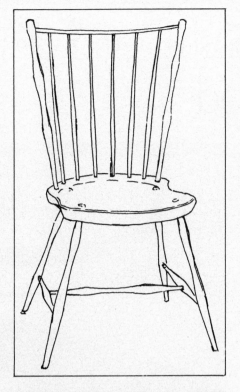

Rod-back Windsor. Samuel Stickney jr. Circa 1810.

American stick-furniture used green wood at the outset. This was easier to convert, stronger and more supple in function being cleft rather than sawn and leading to a lighter, slimmer product. The legs were assembled with a more exaggerated splay to give more stability to a lighter piece and, as previously mentioned, the whole was assembled by one man resulting in a distinctive custom-made item. The best examples to indicate the divergence in style from English Windsor chairs are the two illustrated.

The bowback Windsor has the seat an oval shape wider but narrower front to back, slim tapering sticks and heavily scrolled legs and stretchers, all reducing the overall weight. The continuous-arm Windsor has a more conventional shield-shaped seat but all the stick-work, back and legs are set at greater angles and shaved down where possible. The long continuous double curve of arm utilises the strength and suppleness of hickory or ash in the green state. The pinnacle of basic essentials in chair construction came with the Shakers.

Early in the 19th century Lambert Hitchcock began making chair parts in Connecticut (and then complete chairs) on a mass-production basis. Factory production came to supply a booming population; the westward-moving pioneers sent back east for furniture; and factory items began to be produced for this developing market. The individual drilling and assembly was mechanised; tooling and machinery promoted the means of manufacturing identical items in the quantity demanded and the country style of colonial furniture came to an end.

Michael Dunbar of Portsmouth in New Hampshire, has brought about something of a revival of the traditional American Windsor. After collecting original examples he studied the constructional process and became a chairmaker in his own right. His book *Windsor Chairmaking* (available through Stobart & Son Ltd) gives instructions for making examples.

Fine craftsmanship and design at Rycotewood

More Rycotewood pictures on page 652.

At Rycotewood college, Priest End, Thame, Oxon, City & Guilds courses are being replaced progressively by Technical Education Council courses. The new prospectus indicates the probability that all fine craftsmanship courses at Rycotewood will be offered under Design & Art Technical Council arrangements as from September this year.

In addition to the two-year course the college is offering a one-year full-time advanced course to allow for specialisation in one of the areas covered by the department of fine craftsmanship & design. Emphasis will also be given to commercial subjects associated with the establishment and operation of small businesses. Purpose of this higher certificate course is to give students who have a good grounding in craft skills an opportunity to specialise in one subject and reinforce this work by relevant supporting studies. 'Management and business studies,' states the college prospectus, 'play a large part in this course which makes it particularly suitable for those who intend to become self-employed.'

The arrangements for mature students will continue and the prospectus points out that though local education authority grants are not always available for such students, the training services division of the Manpower Services Commission provides assistance under the training opportunities scheme (TOPS). Particulars are available from local job centres.

Above: card table (G. Dowell).
Below right: chair in ash (J. Higson).

Left: Reproduction of a Charles Rennie Mackintosh table by R. Wilson. Mackintosh works were in demand at a recent auction of the decorative arts by Sotheby in London during July.

Opposite right: tools, mitre block (A. Boor), cramps, (G. Dowell), chamfer plane (G. Dowell), shoulder plane (T. Milson).

Left: miniatures, left to right: ladderback chair (G. Wilke), side table (M. Westgate), shieldback chair (A. Boor).
Above: Oak blanket chest (J. Dale). Below left: miniature of cabinet by Ernest Goodwin (A. J. Smith). Below right: bedside cabinets by D. Paton and chair by Miss Louise Bryan.

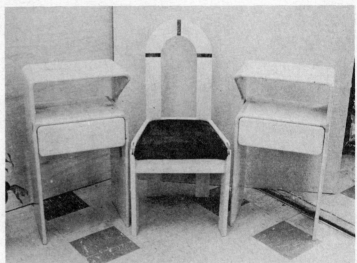

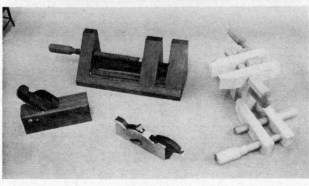

Above right: yew table with tilting top (R. Lewin), left: sofa table (S. Field).

Prices quoted are those prevailing at press date and
are subject to alteration due to economic conditions.

CORONET WOODWORKING MACHINES

WITH OR WITHOUT *ATTRACTIVE* CABINET STANDS

 **MAJOR Universal CMB 500**	 **CONSORT Universal CON 403**	 **MAJOR LATHE CMB 600**	 **MINOR LATHE MB 6**
NEW  **ELF TURNING LATHE**	 **IMP BANDSAW IMP 100**	 **7" PLANER CAP 300**	4½"  **SOVEREIGN PLANER SOV 200**

SOME OF OUR MAIN STOCKISTS
~full list available on application

BATH
Gordon Stokes (Woodcraft Supply) Ltd.,
202 The Hollow, and 110 Mount Road, South Down, Avon, Bath.
Tel. 0225 22617

BRITON FERRY
Woodmen,
49/51 Neath Road, Briton Ferry, West Glam.
Tel. (0639) 820803

CHESTER
Robert Kelly & Sons Ltd.,
19 Newgate Row, Chester.
Tel. 0244 42082

GUILDFORD
V. Messinger & Sons Ltd.,
14-16 Chertsey Street, Guildford, Surrey.
Tel. 0483 61125

LONDON
Parry & Sons Ltd.,
329-333 Old Street, Shoreditch, London.
Tel. 01 739 9422

PERTH
William Hume & Co.,
St. Johns Place, Perth, Scotland.
Tel. 0738 26173

PRESTON
Speedwell Tool Co.,
62 Meadow Street, Preston, Lancs.
Tel. 0772 52951

SOUTHEND
Marshall & Parsons Ltd.,
1111 London Road, Leigh-on-Sea, Essex.
Tel. 0702 710404

SUTTON
Glossop, Simmonds & Co. Ltd.,
300 High Street, Sutton, Surrey.
Tel. 01 643 6311

SWINDON
Sarjents Tool Stores,
64 Fleet Street, Swindon.
Tel. 0793 31362

TUNBRIDGE WELLS
Kenterprise Ltd.,
122 and 124 Camden Road, Tunbridge Wells, Kent.
Tel. 0892 23475

UXBRIDGE
Mahjacks Builders and Suppliers Ltd.,
27 Windsor Street, Uxbridge.
Tel. 0895 32625

PRACTICAL COURSES
in WOODMACHINING AND WOODTURNING

for owners or intending purchasers of

Universal WOODWORKING MACHINES & LATHES

GAIN PRACTICAL EXPERIENCE UNDER EXPERT GUIDANCE

The Courses, in our modern, fully equipped Training School offer tuition in the use of Woodworking machines — for owners, stockists, instructors and trainee tradesmen. Regular (½/1/1½ and 2 day) courses cover a wide range of woodworking operations, with individual tuition in woodmachining & woodturning on universal & independent machines. Courses are for day visitors or residential.

Send coupon or phone for details
LEARN-A-CRAFT LTD.
Monk St., Derby. Tel: 0332-364384

LEARN A CRAFT

NAME _____
ADDRESS _____
_____

LC/W10/80

HINTS ON TOOL USE

In the June issue Guild of Woodworkers member Bill Gates of Orpington, Kent, contributed hints on using the Stanley 45 plane. Here he gives some notes on routing techniques together with his drawings and photographs.

When a small quantity of mouldings are required and a machine table is not available the following method can be used: A wide piece of timber is planed to the finished thickness (A) as shown in Fig. 1.

This is held in a vice and moulded on each edge. The mouldings are then cut off neatly to size on a sawbench using a hollow-ground blade.

The process is repeated until the timber is too narrow to be held in a vice. (Photo A).

Preparation of a panel Fig. 2: A jig made to hold the work during machining operations. Jigs can be simple arrangements such as blocks attached to the bench with a clamp to hold the work securely, or elaborate in design when the number of workpieces justifies this.

Jig in Fig. 2 is adjustable and designed so that a minimum of alteration is required to change the setting quickly. When the work is placed in the position as shown by the dotted lines, it is necessary to add a distance block between the work and the eccentric lever clamp.

The work should be machined across the grain first, any slight breakage that may occur at the edge will then be removed when cutting down length of the timber (Photo B).

Staircase A template made from 6mm hardboard can be prepared to route the housings in the stair string, this template being held in place with panel pins. Blocks fastened to the bench (or clamps) will be required to hold the work securely during machining. The router operation is controlled with a guide bush.

Accuracy in setting-out and cutting templates is important because they regulate the finished result. The other operations for the stair are also performed with the router. These operations include tongues, grooves, rebates and moulding (Fig. 3 and Photo C).

Louvred ventilating frame Fig. 4: This requires a template to route the housings in the frame. Templates of this type are reversible and can be used on right-and-left hand jambs. The louvres are nosed with a radius cutter that matches the end of the housing (Photo D).

A similar template to route the housings in the sides of a step ladder is shown in Fig. 5. A wider template is required as the housings are taken right through.

Stopped rebates Machined with a double fluted cutter. The distance from the edge is controlled by the fence. The waste is removed from the inner part of the rebate first by dropping-in. This leaves the full width of the face to support the tool until the last operation (Photo E).

A

B

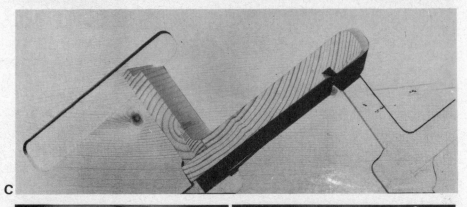

C

D   E

A. Small moulding sections, work held in a vice, a piece of timber to support the base of the router is essential. (a) Finished moulding (b) timber held in vice while being moulded (c) support batten for router base fixed to bench. B. Preparation of a panel showing jig. C. Tread and riser wedged into string of staircase. D. Louvred ventilating frame. E. Stopped rebates machined with a double fluted cutter.

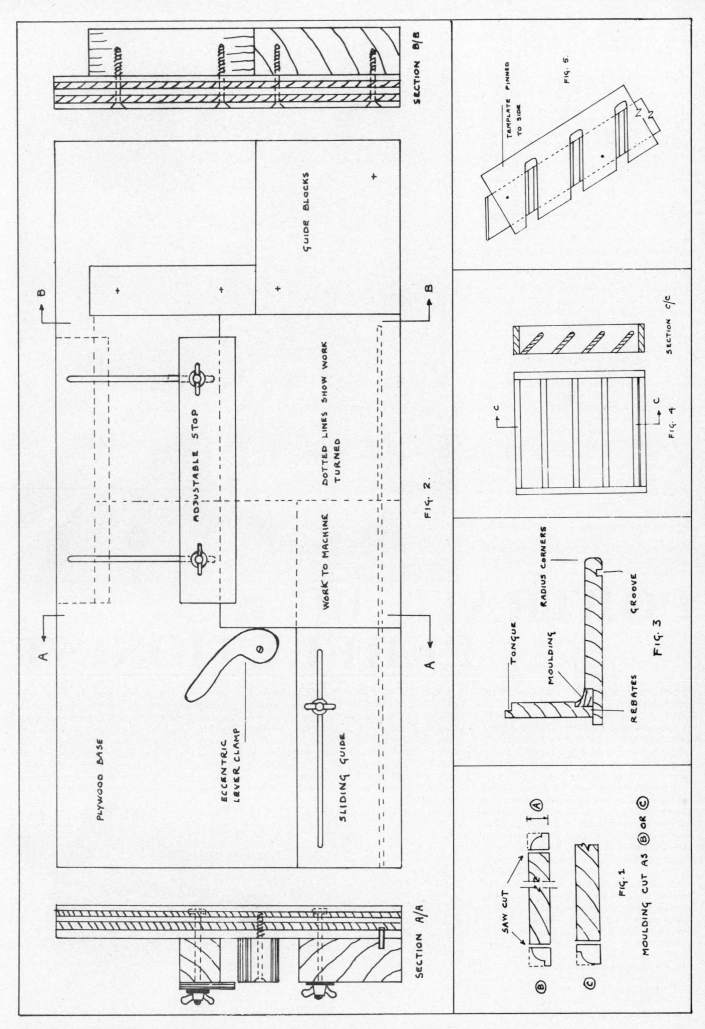

SECTION B/B

GUIDE BLOCKS

B

B

+

+

+

+

A

ADJUSTABLE STOP

DOTTED LINES SHOW WORK TURNED

FIG. 2.

WORK TO MACHINE

A

A

PLYWOOD BASE

ECCENTRIC LEVER CLAMP

SLIDING GUIDE

SECTION A/A

TEMPLATE PINNED TO SIDE

FIG. 5.

SECTION C/C

C

C

FIG. 4

RADIUS CORNERS

GROOVE

TONGUE

MOULDING

REBATES

FIG. 3

SAW CUT

A

B

C

FIG. 1

MOULDING CUT AS B OR C

A. J. Lown at work. In the foreground is the John Thompson trophy awarded to Mr Lown at the 1979 WOODWORKER show.

Making a piece of furniture is usually to satisfy a need for such an item. Another branch of woodwork is based on the sheer joy of attaining perfection to the smallest detail. Projects start with a good deal of research and the selection of a very small amount of materials followed by many hours of meticulous work on tiny joints in small section members of the job. Light metalwork is involved too, demanding extra techniques.

Scale model horse-drawn vehicle making is this specialist craft, and a foremost exponent is A. J. Lown. On a recent visit to his Croydon home he showed me his collection of waggons, every one of which has won a prize or prizes. He has reached such a high standard that anything better seems impossible, yet he does it consistently.

A boyhood in a small Cambridgeshire fen village brought him in contact with a variety of farm waggons and carts but he regrets that he did not take as much notice of their features as he could have done. Later in life, he came to the London area to work in a flour mill as a maintenance man, using both woodwork and metalwork skills. He is still remarkably fit after nine years' retirement and enjoys his hobby in a garden workshop which he built himself. Model making started after he wrote to the well-known expert David Wray, who sent him the plans of a Northamptonshire waggon which he made as his first project. To his surprise it won first prize in a competitive show.

After visiting A. J. Lown who works for the pleasure and satisfaction of producing perfect models, H. C. King presents this

PORTRAIT of a PERFECTIONIST

Authenticity is Mr Lown's watchword. He will use only the same woods as those of which the originals were built. One problem is finding materials with fine enough grain to look realistic. This applies particularly to elm and ash. Some modellers, to his disgust, use ramin but not Mr Lown who complains that 'it looks wrong and splits if you look at it'.

Although most of the originals are painted in bright colours, and some model makers do the same, he prefers to leave his unadorned except for clear matt polyurethane. The choice of woods and their beauty are there for all to admire and there is no possibility of faulty workmanship being masked with filler.

The tyres of wheels are another bone of contention. The originals were iron so he refuses to follow the trend and use brass as many modellers do. The nearest he can get is mild steel which he uses for these and other fittings, including tiny straps and linch pins.

Heading photo of A. J. Lown acknowledgements to Croydon Advertiser. Waggon photos and line drawing by H. C. King.

In addition to a lathe and a comprehensive kit of hand tools, Mr Lown has devised several aids to his work. One is a jig for producing spokes of uniform section. The marking out of the nave mortises to take the spoke tenons is a difficulty overcome by making a jig for the job. A strip of thin metal is cut to a length equal to the circumference of the nave. The mortises are spread out along

its length and cut out carefully. When butt jointed and trued-up, it is a tight push-fit on the nave and the mortises can be marked out on the wood. Its use relies, of course, on precise turning of the naves.

Mr Lown averages one model a year but in addition he corresponds with other enthusiasts in Britain and America. He works for the pleasure and satisfaction of producing

Glamorganshire waggon.

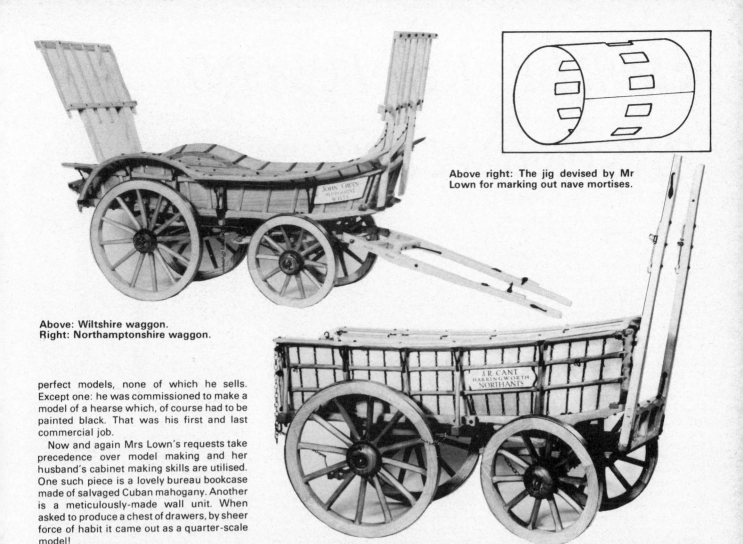

Above right: The jig devised by Mr Lown for marking out nave mortises.

Above: Wiltshire waggon.
Right: Northamptonshire waggon.

perfect models, none of which he sells. Except one: he was commissioned to make a model of a hearse which, of course had to be painted black. That was his first and last commercial job.

Now and again Mrs Lown's requests take precedence over model making and her husband's cabinet making skills are utilised. One such piece is a lovely bureau bookcase made of salvaged Cuban mahogany. Another is a meticulously-made wall unit. When asked to produce a chest of drawers, by sheer force of habit it came out as a quarter-scale model!

BOOK REVIEWS

'Get yourself some catalogs'

Thomas H. Jones' *Furniture Fix and Finish Guide,* is a real diy guide written 'for the home craftsman' and the style throughout is peculiarly direct and, at the same time, homely. Attention is drawn to the difference between repairing and restoring. The work consists of 11 sections: 1 Getting Started in which valuable antiques and fakes are both described together with advice on tools. 2 Furniture Styles. The characteristics of period furniture (with dates) are noted and American, French and English styles from the 17th century to the present time are all illustrated. There is also a period finish summary and drawings and photographs of metal knobs and handles from various periods.

Section 3 is devoted to Adhesives and Gluing. It offers sound advice on a range of adhesives with practical reference to ungluing and clamping. Section 4 bears the simple heading Wood. Wood identification is treated in modest detail and there are over 40 photographs of samples of various woods. These are of good quality but would, of course, be more effective in colour. It is difficult to portray wood for purposes of identification but these photographs have been carefully selected and are quite instructive.

Section 5 is on Chair Repairs. There are several valuable hints on this rather specialised subject and the numerous illustrations are good. Cane and rush seatings are dealt with. Likewise, section 6 Basic Upholstery is fully illustrated and it is emphasised that only the basics are included. Materials and tools are well depicted.

Section 7 is devoted to Other Repairs. This is comprehensive although quite brief and it stresses the variety of repairs, particularly the design and making of dowel joints and repairs to veneered work.

Section 8 is styled The Original Finish — Rejuvenate or Remove? This is self-explanatory, dealing with finish reviving and removal and concludes with major distressing or out and out fakery.

Three final sections: Spot Surface Repairs and Spot Refinishing; Clear Finishes; and Opaque Finishes round off a very homely treatise as indicated in the title and the brief preface. I can hardly agree with a note on the jacket — 'Discover the satisfaction of recycling . . . with fast, easy and inexpensive techniques!' Inexpensive maybe, but fast and easy — well, doubtful.

A brief bibliography is included, also a list of sources of supply of the materials mentioned. This is hardly applicable in this country and in reaching the end of an instructive book I could only refer back to section 1: 'The first step is to get yourself some catalogs.'

This American book comes from Reston Publishing Co Inc, Reston, Virginia and costs $13.95. UK distributor is Prentice-Hall International, 66 Wood Lane End, Hemel Hempstead HP2 4RG, and the price is given as £9.05. **C.B.**

What about solar kilning?

In some ways perhaps *Fine Woodworking Techniques* is like *Woodworker Annual,* though the former is a selection of articles from the American magazine of that name whereas the latter contains all the pages, less covers, of the British publication.

The American book is published by the Taunton Press, 52 Church Hill Road, Box 355, Newtown CT 06470, and is available in this country through Stobart & Son Ltd, 67-73 Worship Street, London EC2A 2EL, at £8.95. It is excellently produced with illustrations of high definition. There are five sections: wood; tools; joinery; finishing; turning and marquetry; and shaping and carving; and an index. Each article is reprinted in full as it originally appeared in the magazine but the grouping into sections is done to allow readers to compare articles that would have been separated in a strictly chronological presentation. Footnotes have been added where a reference is made to an article that is also reprinted in the book.

A useful inclusion is the selection from the Methods of Work column of the magazine. As we know in Britain, readers' tips so often complement the specialist article and give valuable guidance on techniques and tools that make the task easier.

The 50 articles represent the contribution of 34 craftsmen one of whom is Peter Child from Essex. His subject is bowl turning. An article of interest by Paul Bois (an appropriate name) gives plans for building a solar drying kiln. If solar energy in direct form becomes truly cost-effective in this country woodworkers will have a head start. **G.P.**

EARLY KEYBOARD INSTRUMENTS

In a well equipped workshop near Chichester, John Storrs makes a variety of early keyboard instruments, based on historic harpsichords, spinets and clavichords. They are finished to a high standard and available as complete articles or in kit form for home assembly or educational projects. John Storrs seasons and selects his own timbers. He uses poplar and walnut for casework, lids and stands, quarter-sawn and framed where required for stability. Both these timbers polish well (traditionally the poplar was painted). Lime is used for the keyboards and any small mouldings where it is a suitable wood for delicate carving. Beech is used for wrestplanks and jacks, the jack tongues being of holly. Soundboards are quarter-sawn European spruce. Normally ebony (with bone slips for the sharp tops) is used for key coverings, arcades and sharps.

Mr Storrs says that little further cutting or drilling is required to assemble one of his kits. All parts are accurately shaped and drilled. A special feature of all the kits is that soundboards are ready mounted on the liner framework, with bridges and bars attached and bridge pin holes drilled. Assembling a kit, says John Storrs, is basically a matter of gluing together the pre-shaped parts using only a few simple hand tools and materials.

He has based the design of his single and double manual harpsichords on the standard small harpsichord made by the Ruckers workshop in Antwerp, enlarging it in both compass and registration as was the practice of many Flemish and French makers of the late 17th and early 18th centuries. Handstops have been substituted for the earlier projecting registers. Mr. Storrs produces three versions of the basic design . . . plain poplar, walnut or poplar casework with Flemish decoration. The compass, of these instruments is GG to e³, 4¾ octaves. There are three registers, two 8ft and one 4ft, and a buff stop. The double manual has a sliding coupler mechanism. Dimensions are 80×34 × 9½in. (203 × 86 × 24cm) for the single and 85 × 34 × 9½in. (216 × 86 × 24cm) for the double.

His bentside spinet is based on popular 18th century domestic keyboard examples. It has a single 8ft register and a buff stop, and a five octave compass from FF to f³. Some octave spinets with a triangular form have survived from the 17th and 18th centuries though none at normal pitch. Mr Storr's triangular spinet is derived from the bentside form and despite the limited compass permitted by the short bass strings it is a very versatile instrument with a resonant tone quite out of proportion to its modest size. The compass is C to f³, 4½ octaves and the case measures 43 × 25 × 6in. (109 × 61 × 15cm) overall. Mr Storrs says many of his spinets are used in schools and by groups playing renaissance and baroque music.

Of all the keyboard instruments he regards the clavichord as the simplest and most expressive, with its extremely direct mechanism. The volume of sound can be controlled by changing the speed of attack. By varying the pressure on a key while the note is sounding a vibrato effect can be obtained. Historic clavichords still in existence today tend to be either very small fretted instruments with a compass of four octaves or less or large five octave unfretted instruments. The one produced by John Storrs is an intermediate type, small and unfretted, double strung with a 4¾ octave compass from GG to e³, making it suitable for nearly all the baroque keyboard repertoire. Being an unfretted instrument expressive playing of chromatic passages is possible and the individual player can tune the instrument to suit his or her personal tastes.

Another facet of this interesting business is reflected in the residential courses that John Storrs runs several times a year in Chichester and which are usually advertised in the What's On columns and classified section of WOODWORKER. Courses are of two lengths: 10 days for spinet and clavichord making and 17 days for harpsichord making. Courses are limited to 10 participants. Details of these and the kits and finished instruments can be obtained from John Storrs, Hunston, Chichester, Sussex PO20 6NR (phone 0243 789605).

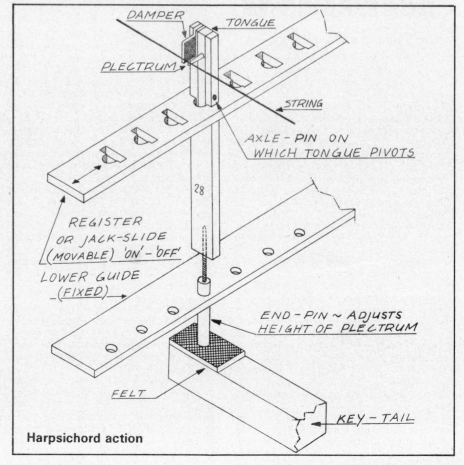

DAMPER
TONGUE
PLECTRUM
STRING
AXLE - PIN ON WHICH TONGUE PIVOTS
28
REGISTER OR JACK-SLIDE (MOVABLE) 'ON' - 'OFF'
LOWER GUIDE (FIXED)
END - PIN ~ ADJUSTS HEIGHT OF PLECTRUM
FELT
KEY - TAIL

Harpsichord action

AT MANNINGTREE THERE'S MUSIC IN THE MAKING

At Manningtree in Essex, where the river Stour estuary narrows to form the border with Suffolk, Ian Tucker and his wife make what he describes as 'closely accurate copies of early harpsichords.' At present four instruments are under construction: a French double manual by Sebastian Garnier of 1747; an English anonymous, also a double (1623); a single manual Ruckers of 1635; and a spinet by Marcus Siculus (1540).

Mr and Mrs Tucker make the whole of the instruments excepting the drawing of the wire for the strings and the bridgepins which are ready-made. 'Otherwise, all parts are hand-made. We try to copy the materials used on the originals and only change the design if some element has failed or if the compass of the original instrument is too limiting. In such a case we might increase the compass by a split note or two in the bass and perhaps a note or two in the treble.'

Glues are generally either rabbit or hide though on rare occasions a proprietary adhesive has been substituted. A great variety of woods are used such as poplar, lime, spruce, yellow pine, Italian cypress, cedar of Lebanon, pear, apple, holly, ebony, box, brown and white oak, blue and red plum, wild cherry, greengage, sycamore, beech, tulipwood, lignum vitae and Cuban mahogany, the last mostly as veneer.

Decoration of soundboards is carried out using egg tempera over a sealing coat of glair (beaten egg white). Case decoration is either natural finish or painted. Sometimes gesso is used as a ground to paint on, especially in panelled work. Water gilding is the most common method of applying gold but occasionally he resorts to a mordant such as glair or short oil gold size.

Mr Tucker adds that the Flemish instruments normally have a lot of printed paper decoration. Originally this was woodblock printed. 'Eventually we hope to produce some woodblocks but currently we have silk-screen printed our paper.' The outside of these instruments is painted, either marbled or plain, with some foliate design as a border.

The action is made from pear for the registers and jack bodies with holly tongues and a brass or phosphor bronze axle, hog bristle spring and either brown turkey, raven or condor quills. Strings are of steel, soft iron, phosphor bronze and soft-drawn brass.

MAKING JACKS

Donald Garrod wrote a series of articles on making harpsichords which were published in WOODWORKER during 1973-4. These prompted William Groom of Gilwern to follow in his footsteps and he has been successfully making them ever since. In September 1979 WOODWORKER published an article by Mr Groom on a method of keyboard construction for readers who wished to make their own individual keys but lacked the necessary machinery used by the trade for positioning and manufacture of such keys.

WOODWORKER has recently heard from Mr Groom that in addition to keyboards he has been specialising in producing jacks. With an emphasis on quality that has been clearly demonstrated he is supplying several professional makers with his product. The specimen jack which he sent to the office was of beech with holly tongue and hog's bristle spring. Mr Groom says that some makers prefer pear, walnut or yew all of which are also traditional species. When one considers that a harpsichord may have four ranks of jacks with about 60 in each rank Mr Groom's offer of a supply of jacks at competitive prices seems very tempting.

The sketch on page 648 of harpsichord action was sent by Mr Groom, who says the action has existed in a virtually unchanged form for five centuries. It shows how the upward movement of the jack causes the plectrum to pluck the string, then, on descent, the simple escapement allows the plectrum to miss the string. The light spring traditionally of hog's bristle returns the tongue. (This spring is not shown in the sketch). On sounding the string sustains its tone while the key is depressed but on the key's release the damper kills the vibrations.

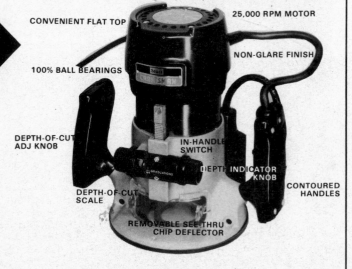
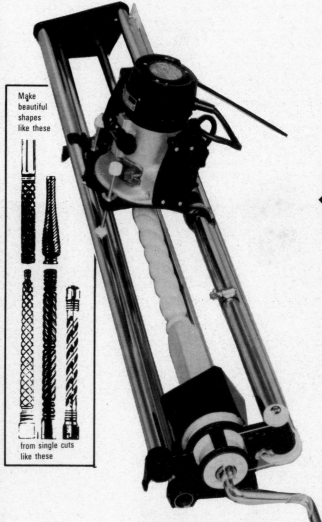
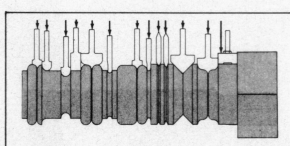

Woodworker Show

A superb exhibition for the craftsman in wood

★ Cabinet Making ★ Carving ★ Toys
★ Turning ★ Musical instruments
★ Horse-drawn vehicles ★ Marquetry
★ Tools ★ Machines ★ Materials

4th-9th November 1980
Royal Horticultural Society's New Hall,
Vincent Square, Westminster, London S.W.1.
10am-7pm Adults £1.25
Children and Senior
Citizens 75p

Sponsored by Woodworker magazine

Above: Reproduction card table in mahogany made by Eric Grimsley. Construction details are featured elsewhere in this issue.

Examples of work by students by Rycotewood college, Thame, Oxon, include left: storage box in yew by J. Cropper and tantalus by D. Paton. Below left: four foot diameter dining table in burr elm veneer with ash underframe by Rupert Andrews. Below: chair in stained plywood by Miss S. J. Oakland. Further examples of students' work can be seen in this issue under the heading 'Fine craftsmanship and design at Rycotewood.'

'...the screw may twist...'

'Screwdrivers are for taking screws out hammers are for putting them in', so an old joiner told me when I was a boy; but my father soon corrected any wrong ideas which I might have picked up. 'Birmingham screwdrivers' were strictly taboo as far as we were concerned.

A screwdriver is really a lever for turning screws. Once the screw threads have taken hold of the wood fibres the screw causes it to worm its way into the timber. Its progress is helped by the gimlet action of the screw point.

The power of a screwdriver's lever action is shown in Fig. 1. The broader the handle and the longer the blade the more powerful is the turning action. In practice it is not turning the screw which causes the difficulty but holding the end of the screwdriver in the slot of the screw. When a screw has been driven fully home the slot in the head should be as good as it was before use. A torn screw slot is the trade mark of a learner. Once a screwdriver has slipped off the screw head the screw is not only more difficult to drive but it is infinitely more difficult to unscrew.

To prevent the screwdriver from slipping off the head of the screw it is essential to hold the screwdriver tightly against the screw. Concentrate more on this aspect rather than turning the screwdriver. It is also essential that the edge of the screwdriver should fit the screw as in A in Fig. 2. The edge should not be too narrow as at B, not too wide as at C. If the edge is too wide it will tear up the face of the wood unless the screwdriver is held at an angle as in D. This is bad practice as holding the screwdriver out of the upright will tend to cause it to slip out of the slot.

Another reason for the screwdriver slipping is that the edge has been incorrectly ground. The properly ground screwdriver has flat faces and a flat point as in Fig. 3. Rounded edges or convex faces will cause the tool to ride out of the slot. When grinding a screwdriver use the side of the grindstone as in photo 2. By grinding across the blade you will ensure flat faces and the cross-grinding will give the blade a better grip in the slot.

Photo 1 shows an assortment of screwdrivers. Starting at the 'Birmingham screwdriver' and going clockwise we have a cabinet-maker's London pattern followed by an oval shaped boxwood-handled tool. Then a spiral rachet driver with interchangeable bits. Next two rachet screwdrivers, one for slotted screws and the other for Pozidriv screws. After these is a Pozidriver and a Phillips screwdriver. The long tool is an electrician's screwdriver while the 'stubby' is a mechanic's tool. Finally there is a screwdriver bit which fits into a woodworker's brace. Tremendous leverage can be obtained from a brace but it is not always easy to keep the bit in the slot. Whenever you can keep the whole weight of your body on the brace and, if the brace has a rachet, sweep the handle backwards and forwards through a quarter of a turn.

By making the handles oval or with flat faces a better grip and more leverage can be obtained. The spiral rachet drives screws by pressure being applied to the handle. This is a useful tool for running in a large number of small screws. It is not quite so good with large screws as the driver tends to slip out of the slot.

Leverage

Fig. 1.

Left: power of screwdriver. Right: grinding screwdriver on face of emery wheel.

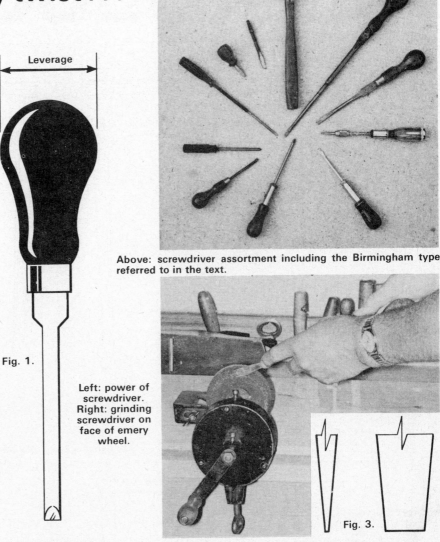

Above: screwdriver assortment including the Birmingham type referred to in the text.

Fig. 3.

W. S. Gilbert had in mind an unpleasant type of screw when he wrote *The Yeoman of the Guard*, but here Charles Cliffe writes about the screws we use — and the screwdrivers we should use to drive them

Fig. 2. Width of screwdriver in relation to screw head.

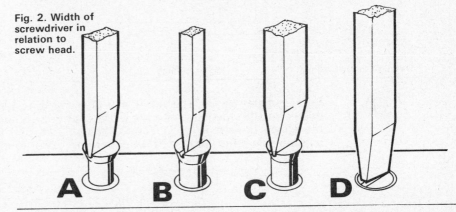

A   B   C   D

Those who have difficulty in rotating the screwdriver and at the same time keeping pressure on the screw will appreciate the rachet too. Pressure on the screw can be maintained while the hand turns backwards and forwards through a quarter of a turn.

Withdrawing screws is usually more difficult than putting them in. Sometimes the screws rust or are held fast because the wood fibres have set around the threads. In outdoor work it is advisable to grease the screw before driving it home as this will facilitate withdrawal later on. Frequently the slot is filled with paint. To free a difficult

screw place the screwdriver in the slot and give the handle a smart tap with a mallet. This will loosen the rust on the fibres and force the screwdriver well into the slot. Do not let the screwdriver slip out of the slot because it will slip out easier next time.

Sometimes an obstinate screw can be freed by screwing it in for a quarter turn to release the grip of the fibres. A few drops of paraffin on the screw may help to loosen the rust. If this fails a red hot poker applied to the head of the screw will expand the screw and shrink the wood fibres. Withdrawal should then not be too difficult.

REPRODUCTION

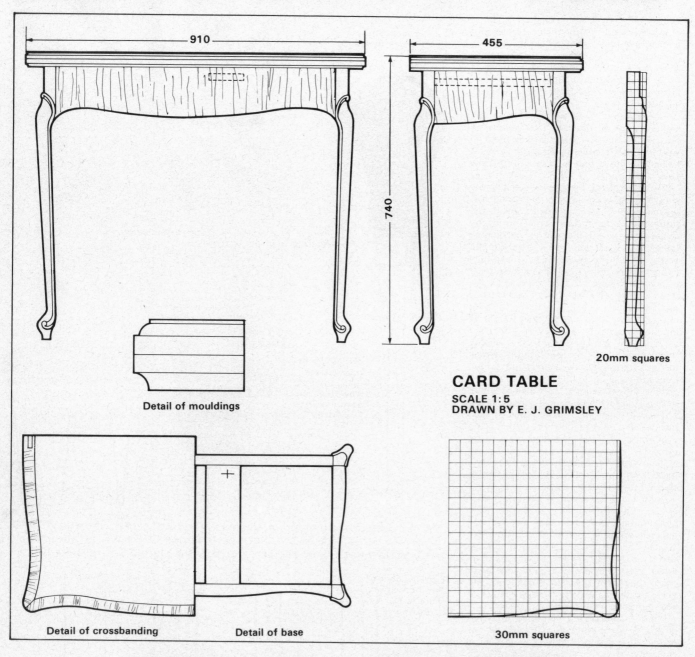

910

455

740

20mm squares

CARD TABLE

SCALE 1:5
DRAWN BY E. J. GRIMSLEY

Detail of mouldings

Detail of crossbanding

Detail of base

30mm squares

Eric Grimsley says: 'The table size was made to suit my particular needs but the measurements can be changed providing, of course, the shape is kept in proportion. The table is, perhaps, not for the beginner as a fair degree of woodcarving experience is required.'

CUTTING LIST
(dimensions in mm)

No.	Item	L	W	T	Material
4	legs	700	50	50	Mahogany
1	front rail	800	130	30	,,
1	back rail	800	130	25	,,
2	end rails	380	130	30	,,
2	top lipping	910	50	18	,,
4	top lipping sides	455	50	18	,,
2	top end lippings	840	50	18	,,
1	cross-rail centre	360	100	25	Softwood or mahogany
2	tops	810	355	18	Blockboard

CARDTABLE by E. J. Grimsley

Frame construction The traditional method would have been stopped haunched mortise and tenon joints but dowels or a combination of dowel and mortise and tenon can be used. Before shaping is undertaken the joints should be marked out and cut. When marking-out depth I allowed for shaping at the top of the leg — not too deep. Final fitting can be left until later. Once the basic frame joints are cut the centre cross-rail can be positioned, setting it out off-centre and about 26mm below the top of the rail. This joint can be dowelled or stopped mortise and tenon.

Shaping legs First I accurately marked and cut out a template to the proportion given in the drawings. The legs could then be cut out on the bandsaw and shaped to the sections with a spokeshave (Fig. 1), allowing for carving on the knee and toe (Figs. 3 and 5). I shaped the side of the legs first (Fig. 1). Although the grain is not always the same, as a general guide the timber is worked with a spokeshave in the direction of the arrows (Fig. 2). A tracing is made of the scrolls for the carving on the knee and the toe.

Woodcarving detail The scrolls are best marked out with carbon paper and I made sure the carving was in the centre of the leg (Fig. 3). Starting with the knee, I used a parting tool to go around the design roughly. I next set-in the scrolls using gouges that fit the curves. I found ⅜ in. Nos. 8 or 10 and ½ in. No. 6 suitable. I then set-in to the lines both sides of the arch shape using a shallow gouge 1 in. Nos. 2 or 3 (not too deep) and finished the carving of the knee using gouges and scrapers. I carved the scroll using a ½ in. No. 6.

I marked the position of the shoulder on all the joints so that the top of the leg pummel could be carved. I cut across the grain but not too close to the line as this must be finished when the joint is glued-up (Fig. 4).

The toe could then be carved but it was necessary to ensure that both sides were the same shape and the tracing was at the same height and would flow into the flat 'ribbon' (Fig. 5). Before the toe is carved a flute is carved down the leg linking up the carving on the knee and toe. I marked out a parallel line to the back edge with a pencil gauge and using a fluter carved the flute down the leg (Fig. 6) working with the grain and finishing just short of the toe. Once the flute was carved flatter gouges (Nos. 2 or 3) removed waste and I worked into the section (Fig. 6) using the same techniques as on the knee. (Files or rifflers and scrapers are useful on difficult grain). Cleaning-up of the legs was done with garnet or aluminium oxide paper working through the grades.

Shaping rails These were cut on the bandsaw (marked out using a template) and shaped using a spokeshave and scrapers. With this completed the veneering could be started. I used Scotch glue but a contact adhesive can be used. After the rails had been veneered they could be marked out for the shape at the bottom; this is best done using cardboard cut to the shape required.

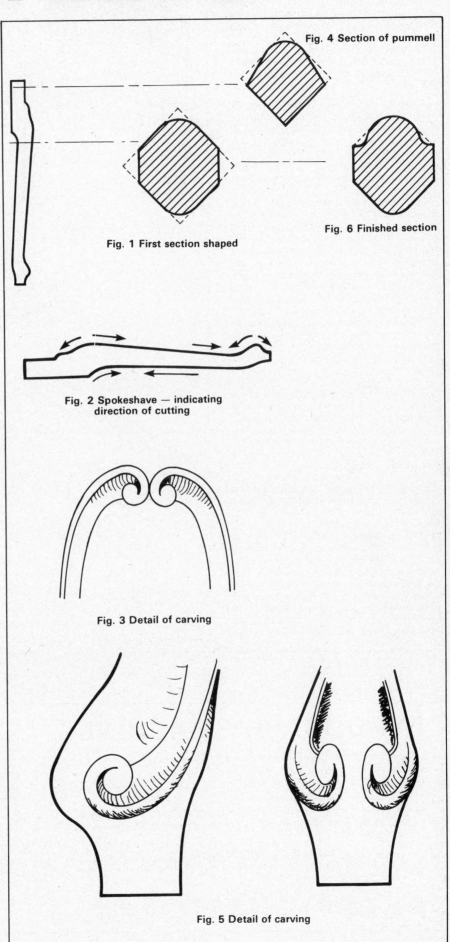

Fig. 4 Section of pummell

Fig. 6 Finished section

Fig. 1 First section shaped

Fig. 2 Spokeshave — indicating direction of cutting

Fig. 3 Detail of carving

Fig. 5 Detail of carving

(Continued from page 655)

Because of the short grain I left a thicker piece by the shoulders and after it was glued together it was shaped to the curve. Care has to be taken once the rail has been veneered because it is easy to 'lift up' the veneer and repairs will then be required.

The back rails are not veneered or shaped. Before gluing-up special cramping blocks were required to fit over the pummel and carving (Fig. 7).

Gluing-up I glued-up the front and back rails first and when dry finished-off the shaping of the rails. I cross-framed the ends not forgetting to glue and cramp the centre cross-rail. When gluing-up it is well to see that the legs do not kick in or out and to measure the diagonals to ensure the legs are square.

Top The top can be made from solid timber though I used blockboard lipped at the edges and the corners mitred (Fig. 8). I used a loose tongue and groove joint. Once the top was glued-up the shape was transferred to a template. I used a router with template follower after removing the bulk of the waste by bandsawing. I veneered the top using Scotch glue and when this was dry I routed the moulding round the edges.

The playing surface was then crossbanded around the edge and very carefully parallel to the edge with a scratchstock (Fig. 9). The two tops were joined together using a card table hinge.

Finishing I applied a grain filler, stained the timber to a medium mahogany colour and finished with french polish. The baize was cut out roughly to shape in one piece. The surfaces were then sized and I used PVA to glue down the baize before trimming the baize using a craft knife.

Fitting the top to the base This method allows the top to swing through 90° and open out while supported by the base. A little geometry is required to locate the pivot point. A block is shaped to the dimensions and a bolt fitted into the block. A corresponding hole is drilled in the centre cross-rail. The block (Fig. 10) is screwed to the underside of the top, a washer placed between the block and the cross centre-rail and a washer and nut placed on, but not tightened up too much. Little pads of baize can be applied to the frame to prevent marking the top.

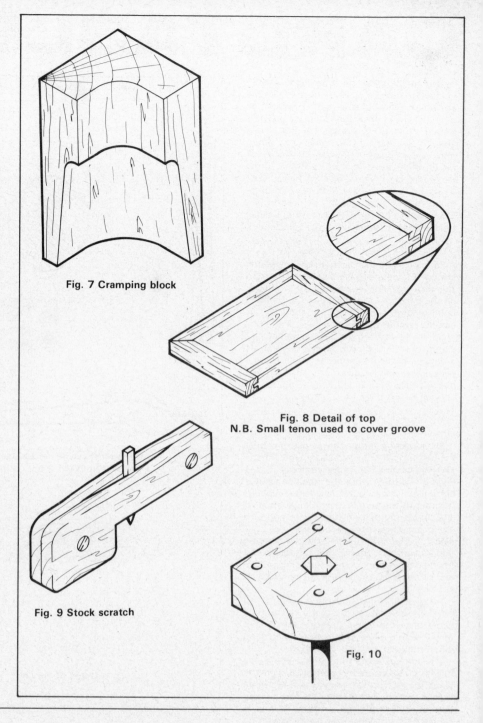

Fig. 7 Cramping block

Fig. 8 Detail of top
N.B. Small tenon used to cover groove

Fig. 9 Stock scratch

Fig. 10

Ligna

27 May to 2 June 1981. Ligna Hanover International trade fair for woodworking machinery and equipment. Further details can be had from the organiser at Messegelände, D-3000 Hanover 82, West Germany, or from the fair office at PO Box 283, Braeside, Sanderstead Road, Sanderstead, South Croydon CR2 0AJ.

British dolls

The members of the British Doll Artists Association are professional artists who make original dolls and figures in a wide variety of media. Although many work with the aid of assistants many more work alone. The majority of the figures are made to order for foreign customers so this exhibition is a rare opportunity for the general public in this country to see this interesting aspect of modern English craftwork. The exhibition also includes examples of book designs and illustrations by Gwen White on the subject of toys and dolls. Open until 28 September at the Museum of Childhood, Bethnal Green, admission free, closed Fridays.

Home improvement exhibition

To be held at Earls Court 30 September — 5 October, organised by the Building Trades Exhibition Ltd, National Home Improvement Council and the Builders Merchants Federation. Further information from Jenny King, 11 Manchester Square, London W1M 5AB (01-486 1951).

Princely magnificence

An exhibition of the court jewels of the Renaissance 1500-1630 including rare and important pieces borrowed from 13 different countries, including Italy and the Imperial collections in Vienna, an addition to private collections and the National Trust. Portraits including records of the lost jewels of the Renaissance. The portraits have been assembled especially for the jewels worn by the rulers and courtiers of the Tudor, Valois and Hapsburg courts. Jewellery designs by such artists as Holbein, Jacob Mores and Guilio Romano are on show. Jewels as an integral part of the Renaissance revival of magic and occult sciences are included and also jewels in politics as the costly gifts formally exchanged between princes, ambassadors and courtiers. Also to be seen are rings and jewels given to commemorate betrothal, marriage and death, tokens of love and friendship. Another section deals with jewels produced as replicas or re-creations and fakes. Open from 15 October to 1 February 1981, weekdays 10.00 to 5.30 Sundays 2.30 to 5.30. Closed every Friday and 24, 25, 26 December and 1 January. Admission adults £1.50, children, OAPs and students 50p, parties of 12 or more 50p each.

Dial an exhibition

If you want to be sure not to miss a major exhibition, or if you are looking for something to do in London, Dial an Exhibition will give you plenty of ideas. 01-730 0977 is the number to ring.

Svensk Form

At the Victoria and Albert museum until 14 September, admission 50p adults, children OAPs and students 25p, party rates 25p each. Remember the museum is closed every Friday.

Salisbury festival of arts

Running from 4-17 September the festival includes a programme of concerts and musical and theatrical events. From 7-11 September the Craft Plus exhibition will be held in the city hall. This will include demonstrations and stalls of craft material. Further information may be obtained from the publicity officer, Crafts Plus '80, 12 Fieldside, East Hagbourne, Oxon.

Marquetry in New York

1980 annual exposition — work by members of the Marquetry Society of America, 2-26 September. Open to the public on weekdays only, 9-5pm No. 6 Plaza Level, World Trade Centre, New York, NY.

Woodworker Show

Sponsored by WOODWORKER this year's Woodworker Show will take place from 4-9 November inclusive at the Royal Horticultural Society's New Hall, Vincent Square, Westminster, London SW1. Open from 10 am — 7 pm, admission charges are adults £1.25 children and senior citizens 75p. The exhibition includes cabinet-making, carving, toys, turning, musical instruments, horse-drawn vehicles, marquetry, tools, machinery, materials; opportunities to talk to experts on all aspects of woodworking; and displays and working demonstrations by some of the well-known colleges of further education who are respected in the field of woodwork.

Arts competition

Friary, Guildford (Surrey) celebrations. Artistic representation of the Friary from earliest history to present day. Three-dimensional forms are elegible. Details and entry forms from: Walter Williams, 100 Woodbridge Road, Guildford. Entries close 10 October, 1980.

BOOK REVIEW

Plans for plywood construction

When I was a small boy, I had an ancient aunt who held the opinion that it was dangerous to go into the water until you could swim. It would be easy to adopt the same rule to woodwork by insisting that no job should be attempted until the making of the full range of joints has been mastered.

The compilers of *Plywood Planbook* think otherwise. They believe that beginners should be encouraged to have a go by producing something worthwhile by using easy methods, thus having a useful item of which to be proud. The attractively-produced volume is a collection of plans which have already appeared in various American magazines.

One or two of them are a little unusual by British standards. The rest are cleverly designed to enable the tyro to use the simple methods described. A 26-page introductory section deals with the selection of the materials including adhesives and finishes for indoor and outdoor work, followed by hints on construction, assembling and finishing.

Although simplicity is the keynote of the book, it has been carried to the extreme. A number of the plans show glued and nailed butt joints, some with strengthening fillets. These could be adapted easily to the use of more orthodox methods and joints.

The book is produced by the American Plywood Association and all the projects are intended to be made of plywood. Clever layout plans to use an 8 × 4ft or 4 × 4ft sheet are given for each job, making economical use of the whole panel. The American terms for the grading of different types and qualities of material could be confusing for British readers. However, there should be no difficulty in choosing suitable plywood for any of the many projects in the book.

This also applies to nails and screws specified in American sizes. Obtaining supplies of ¾in. plywood could be difficult in this country and the cost very high but other material could be used. In 34 of the 40 plans, the edges of the plywood are not masked although self-adhesive veneer edging is mentioned in the introduction. One design shows half-round moulding for the purpose.

The profusion of photographs, monochrome and colour, and the drawings are very good technically and give the necessary information clearly and in an easily understood way. In addition to the introduction and plans the book contains a number of useful tables, one of which grades the projects as being 'easy, medium and hard'. Although essentially a beginners' book, the more advanced worker would find ideas in many of the designs. These he could adapt easily to his more ambitious constructional methods.

It is published in America by H. P. Books and distributed here by Argus Books Ltd, Argus House, 14 St James Road, Watford WD1 5PN, and priced at £3.95.   **H.C.K.**

Letters

From: Hugh Blogg, Kingsgate, Kent
Dear Sir,

R. M. Foden of Southport (WOODWORKER for June, page 404) tells of the failure of his low-angle plane to clean-up difficult grained wood. There was no improvement in the use of one having a lower angle. This is not surprising for such planes are not designed to do so, no matter how accurately made. Mr Foden should invest in a good-quality smoothing plane, learning the intricacies of its adjustment to bring out the beauty of figured woods.

I have yet to come across a timber that has beaten me in this respect, except on one occasion when I discarded a maverick wood containing silica.

This is how I suggest his low-angle plane can be modified in a simple way to do what he requires: Remove the blade and resharpen it, but make the sharpening angle around 60° (which is a steep angle of course) on the oilstone. This need be done with only very few strokes on the stone. To prove the effectiveness of the technique I did the same with my own low-angle plane, which I seldom use, but I resharpened by using the flat side of a gouge sharpening slip, in the manner in which I sharpen turning tools.

Now assuming the angle of slope of the blade, relative to the sole of the plane, to be 20°, the resultant and virtual cutting angle will be around 80°, ie 60 + 20°. With the cutting edge superlatively sharp and set very fine the plane will remove very fine crinkled shavings and the most difficult grain can be smoothed.

This advice is borne of much study and experience of the technology concerning the theory of cutting and cutting angles for both wood and metal. It may not be generally known that the same problem occurs in metalworking where a smooth, lustrous finish is needed without the aid of abrasive cloths.

Yours faithfully, **Hugh Blogg**

From: M. Kenning, Evesham, Hereford & Worcs
Dear Sir,

N. Goddard of Hyde Heath, Bucks, inquires on page 470 of the July issue about matching veneer. I would in all sincerity advise him to get some practical tuition without which (in my opinion at any rate) it is virtually impossible to reach any degree of proficiency. I would advise him to forget the peaflour he mentions and the beaumontage referred to in the reply, or stopping or fillers of any kind.

In the situation where a cross grain frieze is joined to a main veneer and the join is ragged and open, even partially, no amount of filling is going to put it right; and the fault is going to be magnified out of all proportion when the panel is polished, particularly on horizontal surfaces. These joins must be 100% true and hairline. They are not at all difficult to achieve once you have learned to handle the hammer and knife with confidence.

To acquire this confidence three things are needed after you have been taught the basics: practice, more practice and still more practice!

There is a time-honoured method of laying by hand friezes of any kind. And as far as I am aware this method has never been improved. It is to cut the main veneers on the panel, after laying, to the required distance in. This can be done with a gauge provided the edges of the panel are perfectly true and unbroken. The crossbands (which are seldom more than about 12in. long and often shorter) are then cut with the knife and straightedge, on a waste piece of wood, and after testing dry for fit, veneering to the main veneer, always working the hammer towards the join.

Where the crossbands have to be joined to make up length these can be done individually or overlapped, as can the mitres. My preference is for the overlapping method. Care must be taken when cutting the veneers for the friezes that sufficient is left on so that it overhangs the panel. The overhang is trimmed off later.

These remarks apply only to straight uncomplicated edges. Circles, ovals, ogees and broken edges straight or curved need a slightly different technique but the principle is the same. However, the subject is extensive and beyond coverage in a letter.

Another point I would like to make is that when flatting veneers, particularly expensive burrs, do not use size no matter how weak — the danger of the veneers sticking together and breaking when being prised apart is too great. Plain, cold (or warm) water is sufficient at the flatting stage. If worried by the small amount of moisture left in the veneers use a slightly thicker glue. In my 50 or so years working as a cabinet maker and laying all types of veneers from the cheap balancers to the expensive saw-cut curls, I have never found it necessary or desirable to glue-size veneers at the flatting stage. Nor have I ever seen this carried out by any cabinet maker with whom I have worked.

A further point is the laying of burrs by hand. The reply to Mr Goddard's query states 'this method is not recommended for burrs as the moisture in the glue causes the veneer to swell and cockle up.' Since synthetic glues are not mentioned is it believed there will be less moisture in the glue if the caul method is used as against the hammer method?

Before the introduction of sophisticated presses, thermo-setting adhesives; and before veneer preparing and pressing became a specialised trade (not all that long ago), each 'maker' made the article himself from start to finish, including all the veneering and cleaning-up. Dining table tops, 'robe doors and such like in burrs and all types of exotic veneers were done with the hammer. In most 'hand shops' there was neither space, time nor facilities for heating cauls easily. Only work involving marquetry or the most difficult of saw-cut veneers was laid by cauls, though not in the way outlined in the reply to Mr Goddard.

Yours faithfully, **M. Kenning**

Merger

We are informed that Craft Supplies of Worksop has merged with Woodcraft Supply (UK) Ltd, 38 Summercourt Way Brixham TQ5 0DY, which distributes quality woodworking products. Director John Sainsbury asks that all correspondence should be sent to Woodcraft Supply at the Brixham address.

660

Prices quoted are those prevailing at press date and are subject to alteration due to economic conditions.

Woodworker, October 1980

THE FANTASTIC ELECTRICHISEL

A NEW WOODCUTTING TOOL FOR YOUR ELECTRIC DRILL

will cut Rebates Mortises & Housings

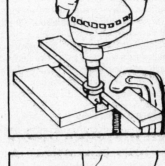

at £9.00 each
OUR OFFER £4.50
each or £8.00 for 2

**LINACRE PLANT
GLOVER STREET, ST. HELENS**

**Visit our showroom Tuesday to Saturday 9.30 a.m.-6.00 p.m.
Machines displayed, demonstrated and stocked.
Stockists for: Startrite, Kity, Coronet, Arundel, Elu and Wadkin
*Competitive prices***

Elu for the man who wants more from his machines. The NEW TGS171 - Two machines in one. Use it as a CUT OFF SAW or SAW BENCH. It will cut aluminium, wood, plastic. Price **£258** incl. VAT *Save £64 off MRP.*
Plus FREE set of legs, value £24.
See it at our demonstration. Carriage extra.

Band saw 612
£178 (incl. VAT)
(MRP £215.00)

Save & EARN MONEY with brilliant KITY machinery. But now! Beat the price rises.

Circular saw 617
£153 (incl. VAT)
(MRP £187.45)

Spindle moulder 627
£243 (incl. VAT)
(MRP £299.00)

FOR THE WOOODTURNER
A choice of lathes for you to see and try.
Only at H.W.M. can you browse & find the lathe to suit your needs and pocket.

The CORONET ELF
£160 + VAT

The ELF 30"
between centres
£170 + VAT

Major 500 Universal lathe   **£400** + VAT
Major 600 Lathe   **£435** + VAT
KITY Unique Variable Speed (large capacity)   **£370** + VAT
Arundel lathes from **£75** to **£400** + VAT
J3 J4 and M230
Carriage extra by quotation.

2 DAY DEMONSTRATION
28th & 29th October 1980
Tuesday 10 a.m. — 8.00 p.m.
Wednesday 10 a.m. — 5.00 p.m.

Come and see the technical representatives demonstrate their machines. Ask their advice. Let them sort our your problems. See routers / grinders / bandsaws / saw-benches / planers / spindle moulder etc.

Bring this 'ad' with you when you come to the demonstration and we will give you a FREE gift.

WOODWORKERS
Please send for details of courses of instruction in woodmachining and turning. Head you inquiry 'Wood-workers'.

VOUCHER
Send for a free price list & we will include a voucher worth £1 towards your first order over £10.

SPECIAL SAW OFFER — To pruchasers of this saw a T.C.T. general purpose 180mm blade for **£25** (incl. VAT) (You can pay up to £40 for a similar blade.) *Carriage extra.*

WOOD TURNING ACCESSORIES
Special low heat grinding wheels:
5" × ¾ wheel   **£4.90** + VAT
6" × ¾" wheel   **£5.90** + VAT
Safety Specs.   **£3.50** + VAT
Universal chuck —
The famous 6 in 1   **£29.50** + VAT
Rustin's clear plastic
coating outfit   **£3.40** + VAT
Rustin's black plastic coating **£2.30**+ VAT
— Sorby Tools — wide range —
— handled or unhandled —

HAMPSHIRE WOODWORKING MACHINERY
297 Shirley Road, Shirley, Southampton SO1 3HU Tel. (0703) 776222

SAE for catalogue   Mail order   Answering service   Credit facilities

---

workpieces

End checking of wood discs

The white wax emulsion known as Mobilcer C which was subject to tests carried out by TRADA in connection with the end sealing of wood in plank and log form (page 401 of WOODWORKER for June 1980) is supplied as stated by the Mobil Oil Co Ltd. Mobilcer C is available in drums and the smallest quantity supplied is understood to be 22.5 kilo which costs about £9 plus VAT and carriage.

To speed delivery the company suggests that orders should be sent to its Central Order Board, Wallasey Bridge Road, Birkenhead L41 11EF, Merseyside, rather than to the special products division in London.

Training courses

Machine woodcraft courses for beginners, intermediate and advanced craftsmen are offered by Peter Clark Woodcraft Ltd (trading as Rawdon Woodturners) at the former Quaker school house, Low Green, Rawdon, Leeds. The courses are of two and three-day duration and residential facilities are available locally.

Peter Clark, who is in charge, has now made an arrangement with Kity UK, Yeadon, Leeds, whereby he will give instruction to purchasers or intending purchasers of that firm's machines.

Additional distributors appointed by Kity UK are: Woodmen, Newgate, Barnard Castle, Co Durham; Woodmen, Churchill Road, Bicester; John Hall Tools Ltd, Clifton Down Shopping Centre, Bristol; Delfmine Ltd, Fairy Street, Bury; Guernsey Woodcarvers, St Saviour, Guernsey; Electrical Breakdown Services, Conway Street, Hove, Brighton; Walker & Anderson (Kings Lynn) Ltd, Windsor Road, Kings Lynn; Woodwise, High Street, Lincoln; J.N. Tool Sales, High Street, Ramsgate; and James McMahon Ltd, Collooney, Co Sligo, Ireland.

Fine American William and Mary walnut upholstered stool with Spanish foot from New England, circa 1710-1720 exhibited by Church Street Galleries at the recent Fine Art and Antiques Fair.

Wood preservatives

British Standards Institution has published in two parts BS5761 *Wood preservatives – accelerated ageing of treated wood prior to biological testing.* The standard implements CEN (European Committee for Standardisation) agreements. The procedures described are intended to simulate more closely the exposure of treated wood to climatic and other conditions encountered in service. Part 1 is titled *Evaporative ageing procedure* and part 2 *Leaching procedure.* Each part costs £2.60 (£1.56 to BSI subscribing members) from BSI sales department, 101 Pentonville Road, London N1 9ND.

Industry helps schools

The Confederation of British Industry (CBI) has set up a section called Understanding British Industry (UBI) to help schools in their contact with industry. Details of the project together with other sources of information available to schools are given in the Stanley *Link Bulletin – summer 1980* which is published by the educational service of Stanley Tools Ltd, Woodside, Sheffield S3 9PD. The UBI project is based at the Resource Centre, Sun Alliance House, New Inn Hall Street, Oxford OX1 2QU.

From the autumn of this year *Link Bulletin* will be published twice yearly. Full-colour issues will relate to a chosen theme and in addition a colour pull-out chart will give the teacher practical help to interpret the theme in a school situation.

Sales outlet

At the end of this year woodcarver and turner Ian Norbury is opening a gallery at his workshops at 28 Painswick Road, Cheltenham, for display and sale of fine woodwork. He says: 'I do not intend to live off the proceeds so I see it as being a permanent exhibition place for woodwork of the highest quality.' Readers who may be interested in an outlet for their work can get in touch with Mr Norbury at the address given.

Finishes for model vehicles

Another interesting communication from John Pearce, hon secretary of the Model Horse-Drawn Vehicles Club, is *Newsletter no. 45* (May-June). Among its contents are hints on painting and lining models contributed by a member (Mr Wallwork) who says that when a nice warm deep brown colour is required, mix Furniglas light oak as base colour adding Furniglas brown mahogany to colour required. This makes an excellent shade for panels of any vehicle.

For lighter finish and for a finish that will enhance the finer points of a model rather than leaving it dark and uninteresting, and will also blend well with the Furniglas on panels etc, dissolve ½oz permanganate of potash in ½pt of hot water and allow to cool. Dilute the shade required ½, ⅓, ¼, ⅛. Remember to label bottle 'full strength' etc. The stain is cheap to make and diluted as required will last a long time, gives a nice brown tint to oak or mahogany and enhances the grain, especially of oak, the ¼ or ⅛ dilution being preferable. Being a water stain it raises the grain a little and so requires a light rub down before finishing.

Another useful tip when a varnish finish is required: After final sanding (this of course depends on the individual) apply two or three coats of Furniglas no. 1 home french polish with a soft brush. It is quick-drying and three coats takes only a short time. Wash brush out in meths. The polish has a slight colouring effect and after three coats is a light brown. Very lightly rub with very fine glasspaper and then apply one coat of clear gloss finish Ronseal polyurethane Hardglaze.

The *Newsletter* mentions the scale model kits produced by Remploy Ltd. One of these is a well-bottomed gig popular towards the end of last century. Price is given as £20.25 plus postage and packing and the sole agent is Carson Toy Co, Priorslee Castle Works, Holyhead Road, Oakengates, Telford, Salop. Each kit contains all the components needed for construction as well as instructions and scale drawings.

John Pearce's address is: 4 Brentlea Crescent, Higher Heysham LA3 2BT.

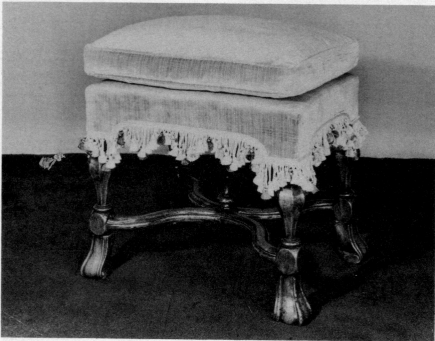

Workshop training films

A selection of 16mm films on workshop practice for apprentices and students appears on a free reference guide just issued by the Central Film Library. Subtitled *Classic Workshop Training Films* the film guide will be mailed out to the relevant departments of secondary schools, further education and technical colleges and polytechnics, mechanical engineers, manufacturers of machinery and machine tools, timber and metal products, MSC skill centres, trade unions and employers' associations.

The guide lists 100 titles on health and safety at work and workshop practice; some are basic training films while others demonstrate specific techniques used in woodworking, metalworking and machine tool operation. Many of the films are classic black and white made some years ago but still relevant and in popular demand. Some are on free loan and some are available for purchase. Copies of the guide are available from CFL Marketing Unit, COI, Hercules Road, London SE1 7DU (01-928 2345 × 424). All hire and sale enquiries should be directed to the CFL at Bromyard Avenue, Acton, London W3 7JB (01-743 5555).

Musical instrument repair

Work done by students attending the musical instrument repair courses at Merton Technical College, Morden, was shown at an open evening during June. The exhibits were working ones and set pieces mainly by students completing two years of full-time study. The aim was to show prospective employers, careers officers and craft teachers something of the range of instruction offered by Merton which covers string, brass and wind instruments as well as a limited amount of organ building.

Musical instrument technology will be a feature of the college display at this year's Woodworker Show, RHS New Hall, Westminster, London SW1, from 4-9 November. This will also be of interest to careers and craft teachers having pupils who may wish to take a course in repairing musical instruments after completion of school education.

Cross-legged carvers

Recently Ashley Iles, director of Ashley Iles (Edge Tools) Ltd, East Kirkly, Lincs, has been on business to the Far East. He tells WOOD-WORKER: 'I spent a lot of time with the carvers in Bali. It was quite beyond anything I could have dreamed of. Some of the carvers, particularly Talem of Mas, are world-famous. The carvers work seated cross-legged under just a rough shelter. They use solid steel tools with mallet.'

Mr Iles has brought back from the Far East some interesting carvings. One he describes as an ivory concentric ball on a stand composed of three elephants. It has 15 balls inside each other about 3in. diameter.

Sheraton period mahogany Pembroke table crossbanded with tulipwood on four tapered legs mounted on brass castors, circa 1790, exhibited at the Fine Art and Antiques Fair by Millers Antiques, Kelvedon.

Wood windows

Wood windows and energy saving will become the major issue of the 80s, according to the British Woodworking Federation, 82 New Cavendish Street, London W1M 8AD, which points out that windows are the most critical part of the building envelope in terms of energy conservation.

The federation has published a number of leaflets on the subject of windows: *Wood Windows & Energy Saving; Specifications Tests & Performance; Installation & Adaptability; The Wood Window in Architecture.*

Wood windows are further discussed in *Outlook No. 5* (spring 1980). This publication is issued jointly by the federation and the Timber Research & Development Association (TRADA), the latter having its office at Stocking Lane, Hughenden Valley, High Wycombe HP14 4ND. One of the articles in *Outlook* explains why Nordic timber has been the natural choice for the manufacture of windows in many countries and goes on to discuss the design factors considered by Nordic makers and specifiers. (It would be to advantage if these factors were more widely considered in this country).

Bandsaw safety

Two safety modifications have been incorporated in current models of the Volant, Rapier and 216/316 series of vertical bandsaws by Startrite Machine Tool Co Ltd, 69-71 Newington Causeway, London SE1 6BH (01-407 7356). The first is a telescopic guard which fits between the adjustable upper blade guide and the head of the machine. The guard wraps completely round the blade with a $\frac{3}{16}$ in. gap for inserting new blades. The second involves electrical cut-out interlocks to the bandwheel and transmission doors. The doors are interlocked with a single microswitch so that the machine can only be re-started by operating the main start push button after doors have been closed.

Timber research

Ways in which the timber-based industries and Princes Risborough Laboratory as a government financed research establishment could achieve still closer links were discussed by Dr Eric Gibson, head of PRL, at the annual general meeting of the British Woodworking Federation in London on 21 May. Over the past 18 months, said Dr Gibson, PRL had held a series of mini open-days and these had been valuable in encouraging a flow of information between the timber-based industries and the laboratory. He hoped to see this 'two-way traffic' extended.

Reminding the meeting that research takes a long time to carry out and even longer to bring into effect, Dr Gibson commented that the PRL programme was wide-ranging. Currently there were three very topical areas of study: decay in softwood joinery; suitability and maintenance of joinery hardware; and construction and behaviour of timber beams used in building construction.

Over the years the laboratory had accumulated information on all aspects of timber technology and this was continually being added to. 'We have the research facilities, the expertise and the in-depth knowledge. We can provide guidance through the codes of practice and through the medium of our own publications,' added Dr Gibson.

All that glasspaper

Conservationists will be pleased to know that English Abrasives Ltd uses 1500 tonnes of waste glass every year in the manufacture of glasspaper and similar abrasives. Overall some 100000 different types of abrasive sheets, discs and belts are supplied for home and export markets.

The business began in 1830 when Thomas Goldsworthy in Manchester sold emery powder imported from Greece. (It would be nice to know if it came in via the port of Liverpool and the Liverpool & Manchester railway whose 150th anniversary is being celebrated along with that of English Abrasives). In 1842 the first technological advance was made by producing coated abrasive sheets. As other companies joined the organisation, brands like Britannia, John Bull, Atlas, Oakey (remember the Duke of Wellington's head on all those sheets?) and Fascut came under the English Abrasives banner.

With factories at Manchester and Tottenham, London, the company is in its 150th anniversary year starting a £250000 extension at Tottenham and increasing its wide abrasive belt manufacturing capacity. Among new products launched this year are self-adhesive sanding discs and sheets known as Super-Stik and a new range of aluminium oxide wheels for bench grinders.

Electric guitars

At Guardbridge near St Andrews, Fife, Ian Watt (trading as Watt-Halley) makes and repairs electric guitars. His leaflet showing his location at The White House, 7 River Terrace, Guardbridge (just off the Dundee-St Andrews road and near the Guardbridge paper mill), also points out that he offers fret stoning and setting-up, refretting, fitting pick-ups, hardware and electronics, respraying, new necks and bodies as well as various designs for guitar making and such extras as inlay work, exotic woods and electronics. The workshop is open from Monday to Saturday 9.00am to 6.00pm.

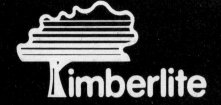

Get to know the real value of Timberlite savings and service

DW125 RADIAL ARM SAW BY DEWALT. The pro-standard 10″ saw that really earns its keep. Thanks to a full specification line-up including: Radial Arm Versatility. All-angle Cross-Cut. Rip/Bevel/Mitre Facility. Accessory Range for greater work scope — Groove Cuts/ Housings/ Rebates/ Mouldings/ Sanding/ Boring/ Grinding/ Jig Saw. It's easy to see why this versatile machine is classed as a complete workshop. Order now and take advantage of our Free Stand offer (worth £42.55). This DeWalt DW125 Radial Arm Saw is only £337.00 plus £9.00 carriage.

DEWALT DW1370 12″ Radial Arm Saw. Superb versatility with a full accessory range. More power with an industrial product at a D.I.Y. price of only £411.00 plus £15.00 carriage.

DEWALT BANDSAW (BS1310 12″). The ultimate 2 speed compact — fully motorised for bench use. Timberlite price £238.00 plus £9.00 carriage.

Elektra HC260 Combined Planer and Thicknesser only £375.00 plus £9.00 carriage from Timberlite. Superb value Cash and labour saving benefits combined. 10″ x 6″ capacity surface and auto-feed thickness planer with rigid-cast frame and finely machine ground tables and bed. Powerful 2HP integral induction motor (suited to domestic supply). Top working performance/specification: HSS steel knives. Auto feed, Easy Change over from thicknessing to planing. Infinite thicknessing bed adjustment.

SITE CIRCULAR SAW BENCH. ELEKTRA COMBI 4000 with die-cast aluminium mitrefence with 45° scale. Rise and fall of blade/fitting arbor up to 45°. Single phase 2.2kw (3.1HP) Black Dia: 315mm.
Timber price now only £149.00 plus £9.00 carriage.

WHEEL MOUNTED ELEKTRA COMPRESSOR FROM TIMBERLITE now only £274.00 plus £15.00 for carriage. This unit offers a capacity of 7 cubic feet per minute and a maximum pressure of 140 p.s.i. This unit complies with B.S. Regulations.
Full kit includes spray gun, tyre gauge and oil gun, blow gun and hose for £89.00 extra.

ELEKTRA GRINDER TN150W for only £125.50 plus £5.00 carriage. This special Timberlite offer gives superb value for woodturners. Elektra TN150W combination dry and wet-stone grinder. Offers all the speed advantages of dry grinding PLUS efficient slow revving wet stone razor edging for your tools.

The unbeatable ATLAS WELDER 130 BY TECHNIKA — available from Timberlite at only £40.00 plus £4.00 carriage. Tested by Bradford University as being ideal for small jobs. (Full assessment available). Built in stamped plate, completely plasticized, highly insulating — Thermostatic protection against possible overloads. Power supply warning light — Continuous welding current regulations by magnetic shunter with external handwheel operation. Winding protection by special oven treated resins.

Dust extraction perfection from Elektra. The ELEKTRA SPA 1100 is the ideal attachment for planer/thicknesser and spindle moulders. Keeps your workshop clean. Protects your machinery — complete with castors/air filter bag/PVC chip bag and heavy duty textile chip bag 2.5m flexi-spiral hose. Only £165.00 from Timberlite plus £9.00 carriage.

The hardworking ELEKTRA DB800 LATHE at only £165.00 plus £9.00 carriage. Built on a robust square tube frame this compact unit offers 4 speed V Belt Drive on a maximum turning diameter of 320mm together with revolving centres. Accessories available.

Get this superb orbital sander into your workshop. The powerful high speed ELU MVS93 SANDER. With more than 20,000 sanding strokes per minute (which ensures absolutely smooth running) and the large-area sanding pad any surface will be sanded rapidly and cleanly.
Old paint, wood, veneers or marquetry, and even metal surfaces, form the ideal applications for this "lightweight" model. Timberlite price only £53.05 plus £4.00 carriage.

ELEKTRA CONCRETE MIXERS: The Hobby-Mix 120 mains operated 240-volt AC 50 Hz for professional and D.I.Y. Robust, Powerful and Reliable with an amazing capacity and incredible speed of operation, easily transportable in the average estate. Timberlite price £135.00 plus £4.00 carriage.

THE PROFESSIONAL PLUNGE ROUTER MOF96 AND SPARES KIT. This machine is made to measure for the advanced do-it-yourself enthusiast.
It's small, handy, powerful and exceptionally versatile. For example. It copes with grooving, moulding, rabbetting, veining, profiling of all types and shapes. Routing to templates, contour-routing, cutting circles or free-hand working — all present no problem with this machine.
All for the unbeatable Timberlite price of £80.35 plus £4.00 carriage.
Spares kit for the above is now offered at £56.00.

Full cash refund guaranteed on any machine supplied if you are not completely satisfied.

Cheques, P/O, C.O.D., Credit arranged. Access/ Barclaycard welcome.

ALL PRICES INCLUSIVE OF VAT.

Timberlite Limited, Victoria Buildings, Luddenden Foot, Halifax.
HX26AA Tel: Halifax (0422) 884075/884788/33575
(24 hour personal service)
Please allow 14-21 days for delivery

TOOLS FOR CRAFTSMEN

We offer high quality woodworking machinery by most major manufacturers such as De-Walt, Elektra, Arundel Scheppach, Coronet, Kity, Lurem, Sedgewick and Startrite at the best possible price. Below are some examples of our prices.

Post the coupon today for our current price list and find out more about our special summer bargains — don't delay, bargain stocks are limited.

Payment may be by credit card, cash with order, cash on delivery or higher purchase. We will deliver to your door or you may call and collect direct from one of our workshops.

STEENWISE LTD. HEAD OFFICE
Limefield Mills, Wood Street, Crossflatts, Bingley, W. Yorkshire.
Tel. Bingley (09766) 60699 or 69137.

GORDON STOKES (STEENWISE) LTD.
110a Mount Road, Whiteway, Bath. Tel. Bath (0225) 22617.

ERIC TOMKINSON
86 Stockport Road, Cheadle, Cheshire SK8 2AJ.
Tel. Manchester (061) 491 1726 or 428 3740.

RADIAL ARM SAW
● De-Walt DW125 a versatile small workshop machine **£335.00**

BAND SAWS
● Startrite 352 a professional 2 speed machine with an 11¾″ depth of cut and 13⅝″ throat – ideal for deep cutting or woodturning blanks **£575.00**
● De-Walt BS1310 ideal hobbyist saw, 6″ depth of cut, 12″ throat, 2 speed **£260.00**
● Inca without motor, 6″ depth of cut, 11″ throat **£115.00**
● Inca with motor, 6″ depth of cut, 11″ throat **£199.00**
● Kity 7217 all steel professional machine, 5½″ depth of cut, 11½″ throat **£299.00**

CIRCULAR SAWS
● Startrite TASP175 10″ tilt arbor saw bench, a professional machine in cast iron with 3⅛″ depth of cut **£740.00**
● Startrite TASP275 12″ tilt arbor saw bench, with 4″ depth of cut **£785.00**
● Kity 7217 2 speed, 3″ depth of cut may be added to and become combination machine **£270.00**
● Elektra-Combi galvanised steel, 2 H.P. motor, 3⅛″ depth of cut **£149.00**

PLANER THICKNESSER
● Kity 7136 10″ × 6″ **£564.00**

COMBINATION
● Kity 7042 the ideal workshop combination with saw capable of 3″ depth of cut, 10″ × 6″ planer thicknesser, 627 spindle moulder and 652 mortiser **£1250.00**

BENCH GRINDER
● Elektra 7″ double wheeled, white grit machine ideal for sharpening woodturning tools **£89.50**

SPECIAL SUMMER BARGAINS (LIMITED STOCKS)
SPINDLE MOULDERS
● Kity 7227 The "Fantastic spindle moulder" offer including a set of cutters with moulding block as offered by Kity for £432.32 but including a free Kity 206 tennoning carriage, recommended selling price £95.45, an amazing bargain from Steenwise at **£425.00**

DUST EXTRACTOR
● Kity 695 suitable for all band saws, saw benches and planer thicknessers up to 12″ × 8″, airflow 720 C.F.M. **£199.00**

- -

Please send me more Steenwise summer bargains and your current price list.

Name ....

Address ....

....

Please return this coupon to our head office at
Limefield Mills, Wood Street, Crossflatts, Bingley, W. Yorkshire.

WW/10

Charles D. Cliffe offers some hints on

GLUE AND GLUING

STILL TRUE

Victorian tradesmen used to say: 'If glue's too cold it will not hold; if glue's too thick it will not stick.' This is still true. Whatever joints are being glued it is essential to have the glue hot and of the right consistency.

There are many different adhesives used these days to join one piece of wood to another. Some are applied straight from the container and form an excellent bond within a few minutes. Others are mixed with cold water and have gap filling properties. But for many repair jobs such as re-gluing loose joints in old furniture and for gluing veneer to its groundwork we cannot do better than to use time-honoured Scotch glue.

This is made by boiling the hides, hooves and bones of animals and straining the product into coolers where it stiffens into a jelly. The jelly is cut into thin sheets and dried on frames of netting. The imprint of the netting can be seen on the cakes of glue. At the present time it may not be easy to buy cakes of Scotch glue but there is usually no difficulty in obtaining it in pearl form. If you do buy it in cake form the glue should have a clear amber appearance. If it is cloudy the quality is likely to be poor. In a dry atmosphere the cake will probably be hard and brittle whereas if damp gets to it, the cake will become pliable. It should never be really brittle but should possess a fair amount of toughness. Just how tough it is we shall find out when we break it into small pieces.

To break the cake, first wrap it in a cloth and with a hammer smash it into small pieces. The cake is wrapped to prevent the pieces flying about as the hammer breaks it up. If the glue is tough and requires quite an effort to break it into small pieces, it can be assumed to be good stuff. If the edges of the pieces have a rough appearance the glue will be stronger than if the edges are smooth. If the glue is dark coloured or has an unpleasant smell it has gone bad and should be thrown away.

The glue is made in and used from a glue pot consisting of an inner container for the glue suspended in an outer container (Fig. 1). The old-style glue pots were made of cast iron and provided they are not burned dry or cracked will last almost indefinitely. The inside of the glue container should be tinned, otherwise the iron will act on the glue with the result that when gluing light woods the joints will show up as black lines. If over the course of time the tinning burns off, the pot should have all the glue washed off and then be cleaned with acid. Using tallow as a flux, the pot should be heated with a blowlamp and plumbers' solder melted on the bottom and sides.

To prepare a pot of glue, fill the inner container about three quarters full with small pieces from the broken cake. Cover the pieces with cold water and allow to stand for about 12hr. The pieces will then have softened into a jelly form. The outer vessel is three-quarters filled with clean water and with the glue pot placed inside it the glue is boiled up on the stove.

Keep stirring the glue with a stick until it is completely dissolved. Within half an hour the liquid should be rather like a thin golden syrup. If it is too thick it can be thinned by adding a little hot water. Although it is common practice to use the hot water from the outer container, this is not recommended because the water in the outer container soon becomes rusty. Clean water is far better.

When the glue has boiled a white scum appears on the top. This is an impurity and should be removed with a stick and thrown away. Repeated boiling causes glue to lose strength. For this reason it is inadvisable to prepare larger quantities than can be used in a short space of time.

A well-made joint in seasoned wood properly glued will last a lifetime and the joint will be stronger than the wood from which it was made. This can be demonstrated by gluing together two boards. After the glue has set try to break the joint. Invariably the joint will remain firm while the boards will split.

Before starting to glue joints together it is essential to assemble all the required equipment. Any cramps should be ready to hand and the glue brush and glue sticks should be near the pot. The sticks are used to stir the glue and to apply it. Some suggested shapes are shown in Fig. 2. The pointed stick is used for working glue into dowel holes as well as for stirring the glue. A flat stick is useful for applying glue to the sides of mortises, while the brush is needed for gluing the edges of boards in rubbed joints. If the glue brush is mislaid a short piece of cane can be hammered out at one end to form fibre 'bristles' (Fig. 3).

When gluing dowelled joints assembly will be facilitated if the ends of the dowels are slightly pointed and the holes just eased with a countersink (Fig. 4). A groove should be cut down the length of each dowel to allow air to escape from the bottom of the hole.

Not only must the glue be hot but the wood must be warm as well, particularly if the workshop is on the chilly side. Make sure that the wood is thoroughly warm. Don't just scorch the outer fibres or the joint will be likely to fail.

A certain amount of judgement is required to tell whether the glue is of the correct consistency. Test by dipping the brush into the glue, then lift the brush several inches above the level of the glue. There should be a slight kink in the flow of the glue and the hot stream should hit the glue in the pot with a distinct rattle. If the glue flows from the brush without kinking it is too thin (but after a further short period of boiling it will soon stouten). If the kink is pronounced the glue is too thick and will need to be thinned by adding a small quantity of clean hot water.

Glue holds wood together by adhesion and also by excluding air from the joints. The glue penetrates the fibres of both pieces of wood being joined with the result that the joint is, in fact, united by numerous dowels of glue. It is for this reason that joints held together with Scotch glue must fit closely. Scotch glue does not possess gap-filling properties. Having glued the joints the work must quickly be cramped-up and left overnight to allow the glue to set.

Fig. 1. Section through glue pot.

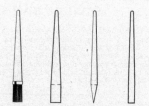

Fig. 2. Glue brush and sticks

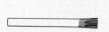

Fig. 3. Cane glue brush.

Fig. 4.
Dowels grooved and ends rounded for entry into countersunk holes.

When gluing soft or open-grained wood which absorbs the glue more readily, it helps to have the glue slightly thicker. If the wood is very close-grained, use glue a trifle on the thin side to enable it to penetrate the fibres. A fairly thin glue, strained through muslin should be used for veneered work. Apply the glue with a large brush so that an even spread can be achieved quickly.

Some woodworkers dip the brush into the glue and then remove the surplus by pressing the brush against the side of the pot. Eventually a thick crust of glue accumulates around the rim. A better method is to stretch a wire 'regulator' across the top of the pot. The full brush is drawn across the wire and the surplus glue drops back into the hot glue. The pot remains clean and waste is avoided.

At some time or another we have all overfilled the outer water container with the result that the kettle has boiled over, made a horrible mess and probably excessively thinned the glue. Boiling over can be avoided by placing a match under the flanged rim of the glue container and thereby allowing the steam to escape. Another way is to file a small V in the rim of the water container. This has the advantage of permanency whereas the match can fall out.

Finally when the work is glued-up, take a rag, dip it in hot water and wipe away all surplus glue. If the surplus is allowed to go hard it will have to be cut away with a chisel and the surface of the joint will probably be marked.

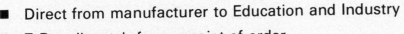

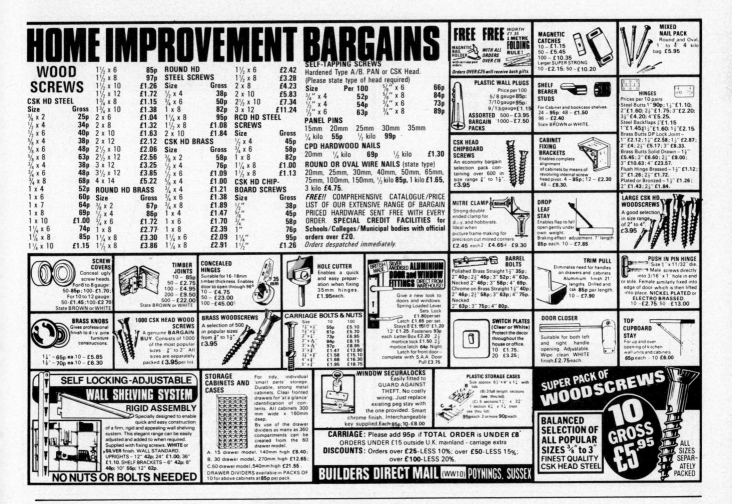

Guild of Woodworkers

Modelling a canal boat

Boat building in miniature is one activity of John Hankin (no. 0236) who lives at Lathom near Ormskirk. His latest model is of a horse-drawn boat as used on the Leeds & Liverpool canal. Mr Hankin says it is timber-built with transom stern and adds that as the L & L is a broad canal, boats were built to a beam of 14ft 3in. (as opposed to the 7ft beam of the narrow boat) with a length of 60ft. This gives a nicely proportioned vessel.

'So, to ½in. scale my model is 7¼in. wide amidships and 30in. stem to stern. The details were obtained from photographs, books and from my memory of these boats in use and being built or repaired in the yard I passed on my way to school.'

Mr Hankin continues: 'After preparing drawings the keel stem and stern posts were made from oak and fitted together. The ribs which followed next were bridle jointed together and bowsawn to shape; they were fitted to the keel by means of folding wedges and glue, the positioning being checked from the drawings and a piece of cotton stretched from stem to stern posts as a centre line.

'The planking is, in the main, veneer and pinned and glued to the ribs. However, ⅜in screws were used on some of the stern pinned and glued to the ribs. However, ⅜in. in shape to the transom. When the glue had set the screws could be removed and replaced with pins; and where the appearance was of benefit this was done.

'On the full-size boat the "bends" at the bow were steamed to shape. I tried this without success on the model but the problem was solved by bowsawing to shape. I borrowed a gadget known as a flexible curve from my daughter's school equipment. This is a plastics strip that can be bent in curves and remains in shape and with this the bend of the bow planks was obtained. Each plank had to be individually made and fitted, trial and error being the only way of getting results. The upward sweep to the bow has to match on port and starboard sides or the boat will look unbalanced.

'Once the hull was built (this took about six

months) the rest was relatively easy. Fore and after decks and the cargo space are all planked. The water casks fore and aft are each made with 12 staves. They are made in one parallel length then sawn in two to make two casks, the curved barrel shape being worked afterwards. The smaller details: cabin chimneys, bilge pump, scuttle covers, provender box, rudder and tiller and ropework completed the building.

'Painting follows the style used on the L & L which favoured decorative scrolls and fancy lettering.'

Mr Hankin is now making a glass case to house his model.

Canal note: Woodwork on the canals was the subject of an illustrated article in the March 1980 issue.

French polishing

Courses in french polishing tailored to an individual's needs are offered by member C. D. Cliffe (no. 0443) at 3 South Close, Bexleyheath DA6 8HH, Kent (01-303 3976). He will take one student at a time, provide all materials needed and arrange the course where possible on days to suit. The hours are approximately 10.00 am to 4.30 pm and transport to railway station can be arranged.

Mr Cliffe regrets he is unable to offer accommodation but has a nearby address available for anyone requiring an overnight stay. He says that although tuition will be tailored to an individual's needs, he will work over a broad outline which will include: Preparation of wood to be polished; varieties of french polish and stains; grain filling; bodying-up and spiriting-off; repolishing and restoration.

The fee is £30 for two days' tuition and this includes lunches and refreshments.

Prices quoted are those prevailing at press date and are subject to alteration due to economic conditions.

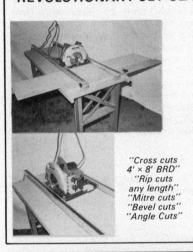

Refinishing a double bass

From: J. S. Ansett, Maidstone, Kent
I have acquired a very old double bass which a previous owner had thought to 'improve' with a thick application of varnish (probably a polyurethane) poorly applied and quite unsuitable. Could you please advise on the removal of this varnish? If at all possible I should like to leave some of the original varnish intact.

It is difficult to answer this query without seeing the instrument. We would hesitate to use a solvent and our personal answer would be to procure a flexible scraper and scrape the whole surface. A cabinet scraper can be ground to whatever shape is required and a thin blade tends to minimise force.

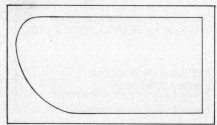

This would be a time-consuming process but when complete the instrument could be finished with the finest grade abrasive and re-varnished with violin varnish suitably coloured. We would recommend a piece of a fine bandsaw blade, say 4 × 2in. with the end ground to the profile shown in the sketch. The scraper should be used with one hand.

This idea could well leave the initial varnish more or less untouched.

Making good a damaged top

From: F. G. Greer MRCVS, Leigh, Lancs
I have an old walnut chest; the top is 3ft × 1ft 7in. Paint remover was accidently spilt on to it and although wiped off within about one minute it was not thoroughly wiped off and, in fact, was smeared over a greater area than the original spill.

There is now an irregular light area on about one-fifth of the top. Whatever the original finish it has been merely waxed occasionally for the last 100 years. Could you please suggest remedial measures. I expect some artistry will be required and I hope to rise to the occasion!

It is never easy to say what treatment to apply without actually seeing the piece. However if the suggestions are followed Mr Greer should make a satisfactory restoration and be all-set for the next 100 years!

The extent to which the top is damaged will determine what steps need to be taken to put matters right. If in addition to the stripped area there are blemishes and scratches on the remaining four-fifths it will probably be better to strip the complete top.

After stripping neutralise the stripper in accordance with the manufacturer's

instructions. Smooth the surface with 000 wirewool and wipe off all traces of dust. The top will need colouring to match the rest of the piece and a spirit stain is advised. A water stain might soften the animal glue and cause the veneer to lift. Spirit stain is made by dissolving 1oz of spirit-soluble dye in 1pt of meths. A mixture of red and yellow dyes with a little black added should be suitable.

The top can be french polished using white polish, or two coats of white polish can be brushed on, eased down when hard with fine, worn glasspaper and then waxed.

Should the polish on the top be in good condition, apart from the damaged area, the patina should be preserved as far as possible and stripping avoided. Remove the old wax polish by washing it with white spirit. If a meths-dampened rag softens the underlying polish, then the piece was originally french polished; otherwise it was probably varnished. The damaged area will have to be coloured to match and, as Mr Greer says, this is where the artistry comes in. It may help if the spirit stain is weakened by the addition of more meths. More than one application of stain will then be needed and by a careful adjustment of the colours a good match should result.

If the top is to be french polished it is advisable to begin by using thinned polish as this will help the new to take more readily to the old. Having gone over the surface two or three times, the rubber should be charged with normal-strength white polish and the top bodied-up and spirited-off in the usual manner. Should the newly-stained area show up lighter than its surroundings some polish may be coloured by adding some spirit stain. The coloured polish can be carefully brushed on to the light patch. When dry some clear polish should be brushed over the coloured area. When this is hard bodying with the rubber can continue.

Sodium hydroxide

From: Dr C. A. J. Brightman, Hampton Wick, Kingston upon Thames
I recently had a painted table top (in pine) stripped by a commercial firm. Could you please tell me whether sodium hydroxide damages pine and if it does how does it damage the wood? Would any useful purpose be served by applying a dilute acid such as 5% acetic to neutralise the sodium hydroxide? Cracks have appeared in the end grain of the boards that compose the top. Would application of linseed oil help prevent the cracks spreading? Would a polyurethane varnish be suitable for the table top? There is no purpose in applying a fine finish as I intend using the table in the garage.
Sodium hydroxide (caustic soda) is corrosive and alkaline. In contact with wood, and particularly coniferous wood, it tends to break down the molecular structure particularly the lignin element.

Much depends upon the concentration of the chemical and the temperature of the solution as to its corrosiveness, and in respect of damage to wood on the time element; thus long-term scrubbing of a softwood floor using warm soapy water, perhaps with a detergent added, does more damage to wood than the short-term application of a strong caustic soda solution designed to strip paint from wood.

In this latter use one would only expect a minor roughening of the wood surface to occur, attributed as much to scraping as to chemical breakdown, with a slight loss of natural colour in the wood.

There is not much point in applying a dilute acid to the wood because all alkalis are soluble in water. If the firm doing the stripping finished-off the job properly it would have neutralised the chemical effect most probably by washing down with water. This may well be the reason for the cracks appearing in the wood: these would be caused by the wood drying down from a high m.c. to a lower one. Linseed oil will not help reduce cracking and may well encourage the wood to pick up dirt particles from the air in the garage.

We suggest you leave the table unfinished for a few weeks, in the garage to adjust its m.c. to the environment. Any cracks could then be filled with hard stopping and the top varnished. We feel that one of the Ronseal range would be better than a straightforward polyurethane varnish since the modifications to the polyurethane oils in Ronseal make them less likely to fail under the changing atmospheres liable in the average garage. Much depends on how you intend using the table; if it is only going to serve as a bench it might be better to leave it bare.

Pitch pine

From: P. Hollingsworth, Hibaldstow, S Humberside
I have acquired a piece of pitch pine that I would like ripped into planks to make tables etc. It is very resinous. Is there any way to get rid of the resin or failing this what is the best finish to apply?

There is no satisfactory way in which to remove resin from pitch pine because of the preponderance of canals and ducts which hold it. True resins are insoluble in water, but they dissolve in alcohol and other solvents and they have the capacity to harden on exposure to air. Accordingly, it is only possible to use these characteristics as far as is practicable, eg if a very resinous piece of wood is brushed liberally with white spirit prior to painting this will soften the resin, tend to force it into the wood and, when the primer is applied, this will increase this tendency so that the undercoat and top coat now seal the wood against subsequent bleed through of resin.

Normally pitch pine is used structurally (where resin is of little consequence) and apart from this other uses have mainly been confined to ecclesiastical work such as church pews and screens. For this purpose an ordinary alkyd or phenolic varnish was used and, bearing in mind that several coats were required to give a satisfactory finish, the softening effect of the first coats on the resin and the light sanding down between coats had the effect of producing a hard seal to the wood.

If you look at the difference between the density of the early-wood and late-wood in the annual rings of pitch pine you will note the relative softness of the former and the hardness of the latter. In effect the first one or two coats of paint or ordinary varnish tend to be absorbed irregularly by the wood so that multiple coats are essential to obtain a good smooth finish by either media.

If, however, a varnish based on synthetic resin, eg polyurethane, is used on this type of wood then polymerisation of the chemicals on the surface of the wood could, and probably would, be adversely affected by the presence of resin and/or the difference in absorbency of the wood. You could of course experiment with a finish such as Ronseal on a spare piece of the wood, sanding between coats and gradually building up a finish, but as mentioned it remains to be seen whether this would be as good as ordinary varnish.

What wood is it?

From: M. Hughes, Scarborough 6th Form College, Scarborough, Yorks

I would be most grateful if you could identify a timber sample. The plank from which it was taken came in a job-lot of assorted hardwood. The whole plank was peppered with dozens of small knots. Our guess is doussié but we have never previously seen such a heavily-knotted piece.

The sample is indeed typical of *Afzelia* spp. a small group of trees of the Leguminosae family occuring throughout W. Africa and part of E. Africa. As you probably know, three species produce timber brought into Europe under the names of afzelia (British Standards Institution recommended name): apa and aligna (Nigeria); and doussié (Cameroons and France). You may well be right that the wood did originate from W Africa but, academically, we would say it would be impracticable to go beyond an identification of *Afzelia* spp. because while the structure of your sample holds up generally to that of afzelia/doussié *(A. africana, A. bipindensis and A. pachyloba)*, it lacks storied rays which are usually present.

There is, however, a further species, *Afzelia quanzensis,* which grows in Uganda, Tanzania and Mozambique and produces a timber sold as mbembakofi, mkora, chamfuta or mussacossa, literally indistinguishable from afzelia/doussié by appearance but generally without storied rays.

It is, therefore, conjectural as to the exact identification of your sample. It must be said that the disturbed grain due to knots could also have affected the normal forming of the rays in storeys. With regard to the multiple-knot formation, this is probably due to beetle damage to the cambium resulting in the formation of what are called adventitious shoots: these are small, twig-like branches which spring from the cambium (ordinary knots start from the pith).

Afzelia trees grow in the transition area between the open savannah and the closed, moist forest and, accordingly, are not always straight and tall but may be irregular due to natural causes or because of damage to the outside of the bole. The adventitious shoot normally makes only a small diameter before being pruned by a natural process known as cladoptosis, a word derived from the Greek klados, sprout; ptosis; falling; an annual shedding of twigs.

Timber measure

From: J. A. Abraham, Plymouth, Devonshire

Could you explain the buying of timber at auctions? I am interested to know how the price is worked out, eg £6/cube. Does this mean that the price is £6/cu ft and is this the same as 12 × 12 × 12in. or 1728cu in? If so am I correct in saying that 10ft of 4 × 2in. = 960cu in. or a little more than ½ cube or £3 in value? In my experience this is not so.

The price quoted for a commodity like wood ought to be qualified. In other words 'per cube' without qualification is meaningless since it could refer to cu ft or to cu m. Ostensibly the UK timber trade has gone metric but there is still much business, especially in a small way, conducted on the basis of imperial dimensions and quantities; accordingly a price quoted as 'per cube' is invariably construed as meaning 'per cu ft'.

Your assumptions regarding volume of wood are correct but the matter will be clearer if you appreciate that basically all timber mensuration (except for logs) is based on board measure, ie surface measure, ignoring thickness. Cubic volume is then assessed by computing the total surface measure, adjusting this value according to thickness and finally dividing this total by 12 in the case of cu ft.

Obviously, in trade terms, one is dealing with many pieces but the same method is applied to a single piece if one is to be accurate. Take your hypothetical piece of wood: 10ft × 4 × 2in. board measure would be taken by multiplying the length in ft by the width in in. and then dividing by 12, ie 10 × 4 = 40; divided by 12 = 3.333 superficial ft, board or surface measure. To obtain cu ft this figure must be adjusted according to thickness and then divided by 12, ie 3.333 × 2 = 6.666; divided by 12 = 0.555 cu ft.

Naturally, odd pieces are invariably marked-up or rounded-up but your assumption is correct, a piece of wood of the size mentioned is only slightly more than half a cu ft. When viewing a piece of wood try to mentally assess the volume by the use of 12 or parts of 12. For example 2 × 4in. multiplied together = 8 or ⅔ of 12 (a ft): ⅔ of 10 = 6.666 and divided by 12 again gives the right answer.

This amounts to mental aerobatics but try a few exercises based on 1½ 4 6in., 3 × 4in., 2 × 1in. etc. A cu ft of wood contains 12 board ft 1in. thick, while a cu m contains 423,802 board ft 25.4mm thick. In effect, wood at £6/cu ft would equal approximately £212/cu m.

Matching black finish

From: Howard K. Watkins, Goring-on-Thames, Oxon.

Could you please tell me how I could match the finish on the sample sent with my letter? I need to match oak and oak veneer (which is what I presume the sample to be) and also to get a near match on parana 'pine.'

The small sample sent us appears to be part of a specially prepared panel intended for a specific but unspecified purpose, with the jet black finish having been applied by machine. The construction of the plywood substrate is unusual, being composed of seven cross-banded veneers to which a further constructional veneer has been bonded, plus a face veneer. These latter veneers have been applied with their grain running in the same direction. This tends to give an unbalanced panel, further exaggerated by the fact that only the face veneer is finished. There is no balancing finish to the reverse of the panel. We mention this because it seems to suggest the construction of the outer veneers was intended to give support when the finish was flowed on and cured in the machine.

Whatever the object the black finish seems only to have penetrated the outer veneer which appears to be oak and was heavily pigmented in the sense that while a hard semi-gloss finish has resulted, it has allowed the open pores of the wood to show through, ie the paint has not entirely filled the pores.

It would seem that only by experimenting with different media will you approach this finish. For example, with black vinyl paint as a base, finishing off with a wax polish or semi-gloss paint rubbed down between coats and buffed with fine steel wool.

You do not say what you want to make or give any details as to size; accordingly it is difficult to advise a suitable method. Small items can be ebonised by using a series of dips but you speak of oak veneer so this would probably be out.

You would be well advised to have care in using a black dye; aniline dye does not raise the grain of the wood but it does tend to dry quickly and when applied to wood by brush may take patchily. A black pigmented dye can be made up from 1lb carbon black to 1 gal raw linseed oil plus 2 gal drying japan, (or pro rata). But you might find it expedient to enquire from one of the firms specialising in furniture finishes as to whether any of their products would meet your requirements.

Identification

From: J. R. Caulder, Emsworth, Hants

Could you please identify the sample of timber sent with my letter? And could you recommend a suitable box (sic) for the identification of timbers.

Your small sample is characteristic of *afzelia* spp., a hardwood originating in tropical Africa. It usually arrives in UK under the trade name of afzelia or doussiè when shipped from W Africa, or as chamfuta or mbembakofi when originating in E Africa. It is not possible to be more specific than this without further information. The wood is very durable and strong and is used in construction, dock and harbour work, furniture, window and door frames, laboratory benches, veneer, etc.

With regard to your request for a suggestion for a suitable box we are rather puzzled; any box is suitable to hold wood samples, all conditions of size and strength being met. We suspect that word 'box' should have read 'book'. Even if this is correct assumption on our part, no single book will provide all the answers to identification of timber since the subject is a very complex one.

If you want to think more deeply around the subject we suggest you try to obtain from HM Stationery Office (through a local bookseller) a copy of Forest Products Research *Bulletin No. 25; Identification of Hardwoods; a Lens Key* (2nd edition 1960). This will provide much basic data, but like all books allied to the subject of identification of wood it assumes the reader has some knowledge, however small, of wood anatomy. The identification, or attempted identification, of an unknown piece of wood calls for much scrutiny, and often recourse to a microscope in order to study the intimate structure of the wood; softwoods generally require microscopic examination. However, much can be done with the aid of a hand lens of × 8 or × 10 magnification.

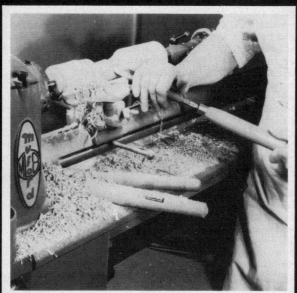

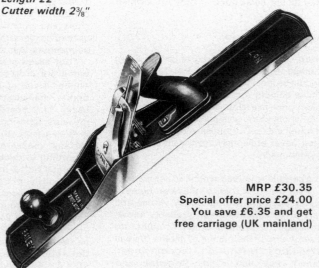

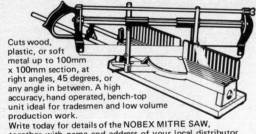

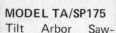
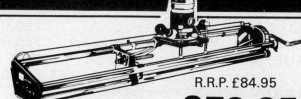

Art in Action

A bright opening day for Art in Action on 3 July at Waterperry House, Wheatley near Oxford, enhanced the garden party atmosphere of this four-day craft show. Long dresses for the ladies helping with the organisation appeared to be *de rigueur;* only the large hats were not in evidence. What was in evidence — and welcome — on a 1980 summer's day was a coal fire burning in the elegant 18th century fireplace of a ground-floor salon of Waterperry house where the press office had been set up.

The gardens and grounds of the house with its graceful Queen Anne-style frontage lend themselves to Art in Action. Marquees had been placed conveniently to supplement the craft displays in various outbuildings. An excellently produced guide included a 'what to see — where to find it' feature so it was easy to arrange one's tour.

Judging by the attendance at Stewart Linford's 'workshop' the making of Windsor chairs has considerable appeal. He and his helper had a steamer going; it was wood-fired and they showed how yew, trimmed on the spot with drawknife, could be bent round formers. Readers who have followed Jack Hill's articles in recent issues will be familiar with the process and the tools used. Stewart Linford makes chairs in a variety of patterns, all with elm seats, and uses different timbers for backs, legs and rails. His address is Little Aufrics Lodge, Watchet Lane, Little Kingshill, Great Missenden, Bucks. This is, of course, the traditional country for Windsor chair making.

Woodworkers, including furniture and instrument makers, were together in one of the outbuildings. Here Martin Grierson from 10 Barley Mow Passage, London W4, was honing plane irons. He was then going on to lay veneer on a plywood substrate forming part of a cabinet. He teaches design at several colleges and feels strongly that the current plight of the furniture industry is closely linked with an insufficient appreciation of good design. Nearby, Philip Koomen who lives at Beansheaf Terrace, Wallingford, Oxon, was using a cabinet scraper to great effect on an oak panel. He studied at High Wycombe college and now specialises in cabinet making by traditional methods. Another former student of High Wycombe, Peter Blomfield, designs and makes traditional furniture to specific requirements using machine and hand techniques. He specialises in Regency styles and had one of his elegant small tables on display. His address is Willow Wood, Bit Lane, Ludgershall, Aylesbury, Bucks.

Two craftsmen from farther afield were Cecil Jordan, Throstles, Haresfield Lane, Brookthorpe, Gloucester, and Adam Paul, Crabbe Studio, Parham hall, Woodbridge, Suffolk. Cecil Jordan is a woodturner specialising in exotics. He produces boxes, bowls and spillikins and showed how effective burr can be in bowl turning. His work has been purchased by the Victoria & Albert museum for its permanent collection.

Adam Paul was making a violin. He spent four years at the International School of Violin Making, Cremona, and returns to the continent to buy his raw materials. 'The way prices are going frightens me,' he said. He thinks this must make it very difficult for anyone starting up in instrument making today. The search for alternative timbers has

not yet produced anything that is wholly acceptable in place of the traditional woods. Like others following the same craft Adam Paul makes many of the specialist tools he uses and finds that the best steel comes from the continent. British steel does not hold its edge. On the other hand he praised British-made woodworking machines. 'Well-made and well-engineered' was his comment.

In addition to violins Adam Paul makes violas and violincellos, all on the original Stradivari system and in the true Italian style, though each instrument has an individual character in the finishing of the scroll, sound holes, purfling, arching and edges. He operates a repair service and offers a limited number of instruments for sale and hire.

Village Woodwork is a small firm making dining furniture in solid English oak. Refectory tables and sideboards in traditional styles are a speciality and sets of matching ladderback chairs with rush seating can be supplied to order. Despite its name the firm is at 14A Vicars Road, London NW5. The recession has not so far affected business which seems to indicate that people are pre-prepared to invest in well-made furniture.

Handturned box of spillikins in various exotic woods.

In the carving section of Art in Action it was interesting to meet Raymond Stevenson who lives at Brownleaf Road, South Wooding-

dean, Brighton. He trained with Jaycee, the well-known maker of repro furniture, and is now the firm's chief carver. He travels a lot at home and overseas to demonstrate his skills and has become in a sense a salesman-extraordinary for his firm. Now he has taken up wood sculpture in his spare time though like other busy people his 'spare time' is in limited supply.

The marquee devoted to country crafts was a temporary home for Roger Coltman who makes spinning and weaving equipment which attracted a lot of attention. His address is Netting Cottage, Netting Street, Hook Norton, Banbury, Oxon. Nearby the Basketmakers Association was demonstrating various types of basketwork including cane and rush seating. The association is compiling an index of craftsmen and also arranges classes, courses and demonstrations. Chairman of the association is Mrs Barbara Maynard, Saxon House, Ickleton, Saffron Walden, Essex.

A popular place was the craft market marquee. Among the small workshops and galleries were those of Joan Barnett, The Old House, Park Road, North Leigh, Oxford (pokerwork decoration and designs); Crowdys Wood Products Ltd, The Old Bakery, Clanfield, Oxford (furniture, spinning wheels, lamps, tableware, kitchen utensils, toys); Rita Fathers Pokerwork Craft, Rose Cottage, Chapel Lane, North Leigh, Oxford (pokerwork on decorative turned bowls, pictures, boxes and domestic ware); Caroline Ford Toymakers, Manor Farm, West Ashby, Horncastle, Lincs (wooden games and toys and jigsaw puzzles); R. C. Griffiths (Woodwear) Ltd, Poplars Barn, Manor Road, Brize Norton, Oxon (hand-made giftware in English yew); Geoffrey Heywood, 6 St Helens Crescent, Benson, Oxford (woodturner in hardwoods specialising in clocks and barometers).

Another highly-skilled branch of woodwork is wood engraving on box or holly or other close grained and stable hardwood. Sarah van Neikerk who teaches at the Royal Academy schools and the C & G art school, was showing the work involved. It calls for good eyesight and a steady hand as well as artistic skill and mastery of very small tools. Sarah van Niekerk, who lives at Wilcote Grange, Finstock, Oxon, also had an interesting display of old wood blocks which were widely used for illustrating before the development of metal halftones; there were some of the large wooden type which printers favoured in the old days very often for posters.

A number of sculptors were at work; John Jennings, 23 Kingswood Court, Brewery Road, Horsell, Woking, Surrey, was originally a cabinet maker who took up woodcarving and inscription work and then studied sculpture. He lectures at Guildford. John Roberts, 89 Mantua Street, London SW11, who is currently employed restoring the north front of Westminster abbey holds the C & G certificate in carving and gilding and was a prize winner in woodcarving. Now his medium tends to be stone.

Art in Action is sponsored by the art department of the fellowship of the School of Economic Science. It is now in its fourth year and is held at Waterperry house which belongs to the school and provides accommodation for residential courses. Part of any profit from Art in Action will be used to help finance restoration of the house. The organiser's office is at Augustine Studios, Augustine Road, London W14 0HZ, from which details can be obtained.

Miniature turning tools

At Woodworker Show last year Ashley Iles (Edge Tools) Ltd, East Kirkby, Spilsby, Lincs (East Kirkby 372), showed a prototype set of six miniature turning tools suitable for small, intricate work (bobbins for example) where standard tools would be clumsy. So much interest was expressed by visitors that a production programme was planned and the high carbon manganese steel tools are now available from stock at £17.93 plus VAT for the set of six in box. Individual tools are available at £2.98 each plus VAT.

The set comprises $\frac{3}{16}$ in. round nose chisel; $\frac{3}{16}$ in. square end chisel; $\frac{1}{4}$ in. skew chisel; $\frac{1}{8}$ in. diamond point chisel; $\frac{1}{4}$ in. shallow gouge; and $\frac{3}{16}$ in. half-round gouge. All have beech handles.

The chisels, supplied ready for sharpening on oilstone, are British-made throughout.

Ashley Iles boxed set of miniature turning tools.

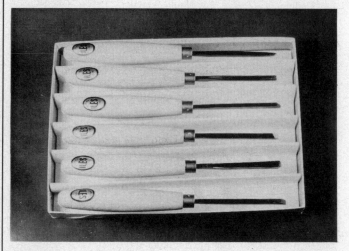

Screwdriver adaptors

Screwmaster brand screwdrivers now include adaptors with ratchet mechanism and sleeve at the end of the drive shaft to hold all types of standard $\frac{1}{4}$ in. A/F screwdriver bits. The bit holder is available in 3in. and 8$\frac{1}{4}$ in. lengths and both come with either a magnet or retaining clip at the base of the sleeve to hold the bit in place. The magnet will also attract a screw.

Adaptors and bits are available separately or in kit form comprising adaptor, together with no. 1 Pozidriv, no. 2 Pozidriv, $\frac{3}{16}$ in. and $\frac{1}{4}$ in. flat bits. Retail prices are given as from £3.35 to £4.90 for the bit holders and £5.95 to £7.50 for the kit form (all prices exclusive of VAT).

Screwmaster drivers are products of J. Stead & Co Ltd, Greenland Road, Sheffield (0742 445472).

Power drills

More drills are introduced by the Portable Power Tool Division of Wadkin Ltd, Trent lane, Castle Donington, Derby DE7 2PU. Both have 750W motors and two speeds. Model D-1320 is a 13mm rotary drill developing 700 or 1400rpm and available for 110V and 240V supplies. It weighs 3kg (6½lb) and the list price is £73. Model PD-1930 is the heavy-duty companion to the PD-1920 impact drill already in the Wadkin range. It weighs 3.2kg (7lb) and the speed change (700 and 1400rpm) and percussion mechanism are operated by separate controls on the nose casting. It is fitted with 13mm chuck and the list price is £84. Capacity of both models in wood is 30mm.

Measuring tape

Supaline is a steel measuring tape 30m length and 10mm wide in a choice of graduations: combined inch-metric; SI metric; and standard continental metric. The graduations are printed on a yellow background and the tape is housed in a moulded plastics case. Produced by Rabone Chesterman Ltd, Whitmore Street, Birmingham B18 5BD (021-554 5431), Superline carries a suggested retail list price of £9.96 plus VAT.

Tool range

Portable power tools made in US are introduced to the British market by WEN Products Ltd, Marshall House, 468-72 Purley Way, Croydon CR9 4BL (01-681 2600). The range includes cordless drill; five power drills for mains supply; chain, reciprocating, sabre, jig and circular saws as well as a power plane, belt and orbital sanders and a router kit. There is also the Task Force kit of four miniature power tools.

Illustrated leaflet is available on application.

SHOP GUIDE

The quickest and easiest method of reaching all Woodworkers is to advertise in SHOP GUIDE.
Telephone Gillian Wynn (0442) 41221 Ex. 241.
Rate: £5.00 per unit. Minimum of 6 months.
★ Mail Order

Prices quoted are those prevailing at press date and
are subject to alteration due to economic conditions.

Classified Advertisements

Prices quoted are those prevailing at press date and
are subject to alteration due to economic conditions.

Woodworker, October 1980   KINDLY MENTION 'WOODWORKER' WHEN REPLYING TO ADVERTISEMENTS

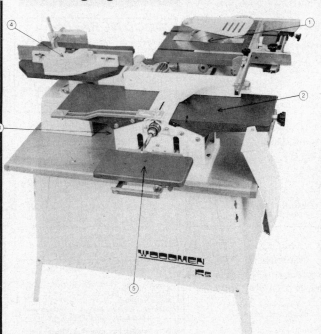

THE MAGAZINE FOR THE CRAFTSMAN IN WOOD
NOVEMBER 1980 VOL. 84 No. 1044 ISSN0043-776X

FRONT COVER: This impressive four-poster in mahogany, beech and pine was made about 1825, probably by Gillow of Lancaster, for Clifton castle, Yorkshire. The printed cotton hangings date from the 1880s. The bed was given to Leeds corporation by Mrs J. H. Curzon-Herrick in 1963 and is shown at Temple Newsam House, near Leeds, the magnificent mansion which is now one of the three art museums adminstered by Leeds city council. *(Photograph reproduced by courtesy of Leeds art galleries).*

Editor	Geoffrey Pratt
Production Editor	Polly Curds
Advertisement Manager	Terence M. Healy
Advertisement Director	Michael Merrifield
Managing Director	Gavin Doyle

SUBSCRIPTION DEPARTMENT: Remittances to MODEL AND ALLIED PUBLICATIONS, PO Box 35, Hemel Hempstead, Herts HP1 1EE. Price per copy 85p includes p&p. Subscription queries: Tel: Hemel Hempstead 51740. Subscription rate, including index, £10.20 per annum; overseas sterling £10.20; $23.00 US for overseas dollar subscribers. Application to mail in the US is pending at Milwaukee, Wisconsin, and at additional offices. Distribution to N. American hobby and craft shops by Kalmbach Publishing Co., 1027 N. Seventh Street, Milwaukee, W153233, USA (Tel: 414-272-2060). Distribution to news stand sales by Eastern News Distributors Inc, 111 Eighth Avenue, New York NY1011, USA (Tel: 212-255-5620). Distribution to museums and bookshops by Bill Dean Books Ltd, 166-41 Powells Cove Boulevard, Whitestone, New York 11357 (Tel: 212-767-6632).

WOODWORKER is printed in Great Britain by H. E. Warne Ltd., East Hill, St. Austell, Cornwall, PL25 4TN for the proprietor and publisher, Model & Allied Publications Ltd (a member of the Argus Press Group). Trade sales by Argus Press Sales & Distribution Ltd, 12-18 Paul Street, London EC2A 4JS. WOODWORKER (ISSN 0043-776X) is published on the 3rd Friday of the month.

 Model & Allied Publications Ltd

PO Box 35, Bridge Street, Hemel Hempstead, Herts HP1 1EE. Telephone: Hemel Hempstead (0442) 41221.

Responsible yet cost-conscious approach to safety

HM Chief Inspector of Factories Jim Hammer in a report *Health & Safety: Manufacturing and Service Industries 1978* (HMSO £3.50 +pp) said recently that 1979 saw the beginnings of a more overt questioning of the costs and benefits of health and safety legislation. The report concerns the work of the factory inspectorate (and incorporates the annual report of HM Inspector of Explosives); it deals with the events of 1978 but the extended foreword 'written from the perspective of 1979' discusses 'cost-benefit' considerations within this context.

Mr Hammer believes that managements can develop a responsible yet cost-conscious approach to health and safety obligations by specifying the objectives and making clear to every employee, through managements' safety policy that there is a clear commitment. And it should be accepted that safe working is simply an aspect of efficient working.

Each area of the factory inspectorate is responsible for a national industry group (NIG). These groups have been set up to meet the need for increasing specialisation in technology and local industry. They provide a focal point for data pooling about practises, precautions and standards; a stimulus to guidance; to develop contacts with similarly interested bodies and maintain consistency of enforcement nationally on an industry basis.

The furniture and woodworking NIG is responsible for all aspects of furniture making and woodworking (*NIG Report 1977*, HMSO £1.50). Three main categories from this report are pinpointed in Mr Hammer's survey, namely dust, noise and safeguarding of woodworking machines. Càse history 289 deals with sampling to determine wood-dust-in-air levels and finds that in addition to the high readings for some machinery certain assembly work, eg hand-sanding, produces dust concentrations well above threshold limit value (TLV) for non-allergenic wood dust of $5mg/m^3$. The conclusions drawn therefore indicate local exhaust ventilation is necessary and increasing attention should be devoted to this problem.

In too many cases where firms have already fitted ventilation systems basic faults have been noted. . . such as insufficient enclosure of the dust-producing part; poor ducting reducing air flow; and wrongly situated hoods so that capture of dust is totally ineffective.

Under the noise category, particular attention has been paid to the problem of suppressing noise at multi-cutter moulding machines. Attention has also been devoted to the possibilities of using a flexible material suspended on a suitable framework, rather than dense, solid enclosures, to cut down noise in some band resaw areas.

Discussions continue with many employers on problems of guarding machines. A common approach is being formulated to bring about greater awareness and sharing of knowledge to solve particular problems. The policy for safety in individual workshops and on factory floors must be an expression of individual will, at the highest level, to create and maintain a safe and healthy place of work.

POWERLINE give you no more excuses for not

HANDY ENGRAVER
An invaluable tool for marking valuables, toys, camping and sports equipment, jewellery and many other items in the home and workshop.

GLASS ENGRAVER
With this kit anyone can create their own designs on glass, personalise a gift or add a distinctive touch to their favourite piece of glassware. Complete with 3 points for a variety of effects.

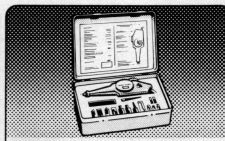

HOBBYIST KIT
A great two speed engraver kit complete with 15 different tools for work on glass, wood, metal and leather.

BK1 BANDSAW
The popular single speed bandsaw that's the ideal DIY tool. Cuts almost any material quickly, cleanly and easily.

BK2 BANDSAW
Two speeds and sanding belt make this our most versatile bandsaw for cutting a wide range of materials faster and neater.

MINI BANDSAW
Designed for beginner and experienced do-it-yourselfer alike this lightweight 'table-top' bandsaw will be a must for every home workshop.

969 AIRLESS SPRAYER
The most economical airless sprayer for all those jobs around the home and garden. Many optional accessories.

500 AIRLESS SPRAYER
A high performance model giving pressure of 2,300 p.s.i. and capable of spraying cellulose, emulsion, varnish etc.

700 AIRLESS SPRAYER KIT
This powerful sprayer kit comes complete with all the accessories for a really professional finish to all those spraying jobs around the home and garden.

SR122 COMPRESSOR SPRAYER
Unique, all-in-one portable package. Compact, light weight, simple to operate. Spray almost anything from roses to car bodies. Pressure of 14 p.s.i. at 1 cfm.

WOB.L COMPRESSOR SPRAYERS
1008 piston compressor complete with high quality gun and interval/external mix nozzles – ½ h.p. 3.0 c.f.m. at 40 p.s.i. Also available 808 ⅓ h.p. 2.5 c.f.m. at 35 p.s.i. 708 ¼ h.p. 2.0 c.f.m. at 30 p.s.i.

EM254 COMPRESSOR SPRAYER
High performance from ⅓ h.p. motor. Complete with gun and hose, delivers 30 p.s.i. at 2 c.f.m. Also available without motor.

aving the right tools!

PROFESSIONAL ENGRAVER
Superior performance, heavy duty, continuously rated power unit for really professional results on glass, metal, plastics and ceramics. Complete with 4 points, inc. 1 diamond and 1 solid carbide tips for a variety of effects.

SOLDERING IRON KIT
Light, easy to use and comes complete with solder, rest, tweezers and quick change tip for intricate electrical work.

SCREWDRIVER KIT
Pistol grip gives pounds more leverage. Complete with 2 Phillips and 2 slotted bits plus extension with 6 metric sockets. A must for motorists and motorcyclists.

CIRCULAR SAW BLADES
Extra hard chromium finish means they last up to 5 times longer than ordinary blades. Range from 149mm (5⅞") to 254mm (10"). Bore sizes to suit most popular saws.

VAC PACS
Sawdust, shavings, gritty dirt, even cold embers – Powerline Vac Pacs get to grips with them all. Light, mobile, easy to use. Choose 5 or 10 gallon model. Plus WAD 50 which sucks up spills, blocked sinks, wet leaves etc.

CABLE REEL
Mini Reel with twin sockets and overload cut-out for complete safety. 26ft of cable for all occasions an extension is needed.

SAND A DISC
Tough, non-clog, open mesh lets you see the surface you're preparing through the disc itself. Fine or coarse, kit includes pad and arbor.

Powerline tools are specifically designed to help you get the most out of your hobby, greater enjoyment from doing it yourself and, above all, they make the job easier to tackle. From soldering to spraying, engraving to sawing it always pays to have the right tools for the job — it pays to choose Powerline. See them at your local DIY/ Hardware counter or send for list of stockists and FREE colour brochure.

All products covered by our 500 day guarantee.

500 DAY Guarantee

POWERLINE

For the professional amateur

**Burgess Power Tools Limited
Free Post,
Sapcote, Leicester LE9 6JZ.**

Once you've bought the books you'll be able to make the shelves

FINE WOODWORKING

Anyone who enjoys making beautiful things out of wood will be simply overwhelmed with contents of 'Fine Woodworking', a richly detailed bi-monthly publication for serious woodworkers. Here you will find the kind of information that is timeless and hard to find anywhere else. That is why all back issues are kept in print, forming a graphic woodworking encyclopaedia. And why, within five years, a staggering 250,000 woodworkers subscribe to this magazine. Now regularly available from the SUMACO Library. Annual subscription **£12.00**. Single copies **£2.00** each.

TAGE FRID TEACHES WOODWORKING

206 pages in which Tage Frid details everything about joinery that he has found necessary and useful in 50 years as a master craftsman. Frid, a native of Denmark and currently professor of woodworking and furniture design at Rhode Island School of Design, shows in complete step by step photo sequence concise details which are of equal benefit to professional woodworkers, amateurs and schools. **£11.00** each.

POWER TOOL WOODWORKING FOR EVERYONE by R. J. De Cristoforo.

Over 150 woodworking machinery operations superbly photographed and illustrated in 324 pages of useful hints and ideas on getting the maximum results from your workshop equipment. Although all operations are carried out on the Shopsmith Mark V woodworker, this book is a must for anyone thinking of buying or already using woodworking machines. **£9.00** each.

WOODTURNING

A small but very useful publication showing the lathe, the equipment, the wood and how woodturning is done. 25 pages with 54 photographs and illustrations. **90p** each.

HOME WORKSHOP GUIDE TO SHARPENING

160 pages showing how to sharpen practically any type of tool. Achieve professional results every time with this comprehensive volume as a guide. **£2.90** each.

PROJECT PLANS

A selection of plans to make your woodworking more interesting and enjoyable. New plans are being continually added. **85p** each or 6 as illustrated for **£4.50**.

SUMACO
Woodworking Library

Showroom open Monday to Saturday 9 a.m. to 5 p.m. on Thursday and Friday until 7.30 p.m.

Sumaco Machinery & Tools. Suma House, Huddersfield Road, Elland, West Yorkshire, HX5 9AA. Telephone Elland (0422) 75491. Telex 51182 Sumaco.

Post to:
Sumaco Woodworking Library, Suma House, Huddersfield Road, Elland, West Yorkshire, HX5 9AA.
Complete the coupon by ticking which publications you require and how many at the prices indicated. Your cheque/postal order should be made payable to "Sumaco Woodworking Library." Please note that all items are VAT Zero Rated and that prices include postage and packing.

√ required items	Publication	Quantity	Cost	Block capitals please.
	Fine Woodworking. Annual Subscription	6	£12.00	
	Fine Woodworking. Single copy		£ 2.00	Name ....
	Tage Frid Teaches Woodworking		£11.00	Address ....
	Power Tool Woodworking for everyone		£ 9.00	....
	Woodturning		90p	....
	Home Workshop Guide to Sharpening		£ 2.90	Project Plans Title(s) ....
	Project Plans		85p	
	Project Plans Set	6	£ 4.50	

Please allow 21-28 days delivery.

WW11

NOT PRETTY
very BUT
PRACTICAL

Most designers of woodworking machines are engineers, whose prime concern is the simple and economical manufacture of their product. They will go to great lengths to improve the design of their machines, shaving a few pence off the cost and yet increasing the strength of a particular component. This is all very well, but frequently the manufacturer misses the point altogether, making his well engineered machines beautiful to look at, but extremely difficult to use.

The Kity combination is very practical. Kity's first thoughts are to the woodworker. Let me give you an example. In most mono block combinations the Circular Saw and the Spindle Moulder use the same work table. The manufacturer's demonstrator will slickly gloss over this point, side stepping the issue or even

using two machines (one demonstrating the Circular Saw and the other the Spindle Moulder). Can you imagine the time and work required to make a cross cut on the saw, and immediately after produce a rebate on the Spindle Moulder. You have to remove all the guarding and tooling, but what is more to the point, when you want to reproduce the same rebate you have to completely re-set the Spindle Moulder again. This could be good engineering but not much thought has been given to the user. The Kity combination offers you Independent Machines all driven from one motor, a saw, planer thicknesser and spindle moulder – to move from one to another and back again simply slip a belt – **no other adjustment is necessary**, simple but very practical.

Cross cutting with the mitre guide, and tungsten carbide saw blade on the 617 Saw.

Details of the kick back washers, serated feed roller and twin cutter block. (Note this area would normally be guarded). On the 636 Machine.

The Kity concept simple but very practical

Kity offers you Circular Saws, Bandsaws, Planer Thicknessers, Spindle Moulders and Slot Mortisers, along with a complete range of accessories, motors and floor stands.
Each machine can be independent or part of a combination for example:
You can start your work-shop with a circular saw, motor and stand. After a few months you can mount your saw on the large table, and drive any other machine from your existing motor. You can then continue to add machines until you have a fully equipped work-shop. This is a unique flexibility, that will benefit the professional and the amateur woodworker alike. Using a mixture of Kity independent and combination machines, you can build a work-shop that exactly suits your requirements. You do not have to purchase one complete unit that costs a lot of money and may be a compromise in size, or difficult to use. With Kity you do not have a lot of complicated attachments, nor do you have to swing the machine into different positions or use a special tool. Simply slip the belt from one machine to the next.

The Circular Saw 617
This is the heart of most workshops. The Kity machine has a cast and machined, tilting work table, a rise/fall arbor with hand wheel control, it accepts blades up to 9″ in diameter giving a 3⅛″ depth of cut, and is capable of running at two speeds, 3400 rpm and 7000 rpm. It is

powered by a 1½ H.P. motor with No Volt Thermal Overload Starter. You will have no difficulty in cutting any wood based material, from melamine faced chipboard to African hardwoods.
Accessories included in the price are the mitre-guide with repeat cut stop, and wobble washers for grooving. The machine is guarded to comply with international standards.

The Planer Thicknessers 535, 635, 636
Kity manufacture three 'under and over' planer/thicknessers, a 10″ × 6″, 8″ × 6″ and a 6″ × 4″.
Each machine is available with stand and motor and can be used as an independent unit or will fit as part of the 700 combination.
Each machine has cast tables and a twin knife cutter block and is of the 'under and over type'. The thicknesser is power fed with an adjustable thicknessing table giving true results along with the whole length of the timber, this is usually difficult to achieve with the 'over fed' clamp type thicknesser. The 636 and 635 both have unusual long (40″) surfacing tables ideal for straightening a twist in a plank of timber.

Spindle Moulders 626/627
The Spindle Moulder is a versatile and powerful tool. It does a totally different job to a router, although the system is similar. For example:
The 626 & 627 are capable of making large rebates 1¼″ × 1¼″ in hundreds of feet of timber. They will also produce moulding, deep grooves, tongue and groove joints, V-joints, tenons, profiles and counter profiles, all with effortless power.
The 626 has a standard adjustable fence with the capability of positioning the cutting tools over a 4″ vertical range. The 627 has the same specifications but with individual micro

adjustable fences. Both machines have cutting speeds of 7000 rpm, and are guarded to full international standards.

The 625 Slot Mortiser
The only machine in the whole range that is *not* available as an independent machine. Working from the 700 table it will provide a ½″ slot, up to 5″ long and 4″ deep. An excellent machine for mortice joint production.

The 612 Bandsaw
Kity make an all steel, two wheel, Bandsaw with a 5½″ depth of cut and an 11½″ throat, it will accept blades from ¼″ for tight turns to ⅞″ for deep cutting and planking of timber. Unlike 'Plastic' Bandsaws the steel construction of the Kity machine allows you to set a high blade tension. This enables you to cut fast and in a straight line through hardwood and knots with a maximum depth of 6″, 'Like a hot knife through butter'.

Service and Support
All manufacturers claim to provide a service. We can demonstrate ours BEFORE you purchase your machine.

Kity Information
As Kity user, every few months you will receive an 'in house' newsletter printed exclusively for you. It includes other Kity users' practical ideas as to how to make more use of your Kity machines, plus information on new accessories, competitions and many other interesting ideas.

Kity Plan Sheets
Titles are issued for a nominal charge exclusively to Kity users and include, 'basic joints', 'carpentry work bench' and 'fitted kitchens'. These practical plan sheets include cutting lists and complete manufacturing instructions on the relevant subject, and a new title is issued every 3 to 4 months.

 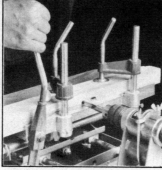 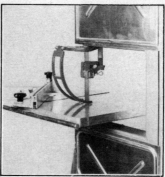 

A rebate being cut in a piece of moulded timber. Producing a Mortice. The Bandsaw with mitre guide. Simply slipping the belt.

Stockist Training
Most manufacturers ask for a large order when appointing a new stockist plus a continual minimum yearly quota. This is not the case with Kity. We expect all our stockists to attend our product training courses, which enables the stockist to offer the best technical advice when you make your purchase, without the pressure to 'sell' minimum quantities. In the long term we will have far less service problems if you have chosen the right machine for the job, through correct advice.

Instructions on machines
Many service problems arise because machines are incorrectly assembled or adjusted, or are used far beyond their capabilities.
Each Kity machine has a comprehensive instruction book to ensure you have the knowledge to use the machine correctly.

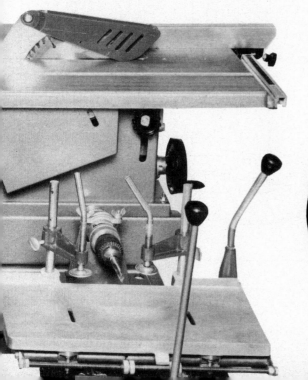

Two Year Guarantee
Should there be a problem with your machine we will make every effort to repair or replace as necessary at no cost to yourself, during the first two years of use.

For more information about this, and many more Kity products, please fill in this coupon and return

NAME ....
ADDRESS ....
....
.... TEL. ....

BASIC MARQUETRY · 1

Marquetry is an ancient craft which seems to be having a revival. It is popular with both sexes. Indeed many of the top exponents of the craft are women, writes Ernie Ives who contributes this new series. His first article deals with the essential tools and materials; the former are few in number and inexpensive. The second article will cover preparation and cutting of the picture. The third will consider borders, back and edges and the fourth will be devoted to completing the picture.

The author is well-known as an exponent of marquetry and prize winner at the Woodworker Show and is editor of the craft's own journal *The Marquetarian*.

Fig. 1 (Below) Selection of equipment. Fig. 2 (bottom left) blades. Fig. 3 (middle) three types of blades. Fig. 4 (bottom) sharpening a blade.

Marquetry is an ancient craft which seems to be having a revival at the present time not only in this country but in North America and other countries too. WOODWORKER has therefore asked me to write a series on basic marquetry. If this is well received the intention is to offer further articles on more advanced techniques. Basic Marquetry will be a practical series where step-by-step instructions are given to produce a simple picture with the limited equipment that a beginner at the craft might have.

The usual definition of marquetry is the art and craft of making pictures and decorative designs in wood veneer. These pictures may be simple or complex according to your skill or artistic fancy. Do not believe those who say: 'You must have patience to do that!' Once you get started and see the work building up before your eyes, the interest will carry you through to the end.

Tools Like most other crafts marquetry needs tools but these are few in number and inexpensive. Indeed, many will of necessity have to be made by you. In this part of the series we will look at the essential tools and materials required as well as some of the more desirable ones and show how many can be made. A selection of the equipment is shown in Fig. 1.

Craft knives Some craftsmen make their own from ground-up hacksaw blades but I think it is better to buy, or make, a holder which will take a fine pointed scalpel blade (Fig. 2). Visit your local art, craft and model shops and choose one that feels comfortable in your hand remembering that once the marquetry bug bites you could be using it for many hours at a time. Don't forget to check on the availability and price of spare blades.

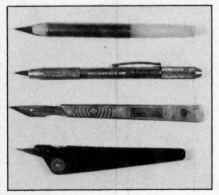

Blades I use three types of blade, all by Swann-Morton, (Fig. 3). No.11 is for almost all the cutting in a picture; the slightly shorter and stiffer No. 10a in a scalpel holder is for straight lines and parquetry; and the round-bladed No. 20 is for scraping off surplus glue and tape. These are available at most large chemists as well as art, craft and office supplies shops.

Obviously with use the blade will get blunt. The rich will no doubt throw it away and use another but the canny will want to restore the edge. While the edge can be resharpened on a stone and stropped, it is easier to grind the back away and shorten the blade as, with normal use, only the tip gets blunt (Fig. 4).

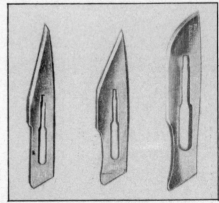

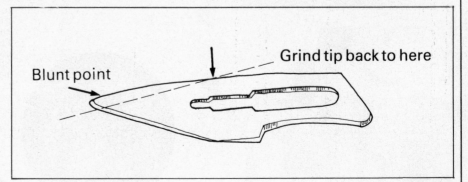

Blunt point — Grind tip back to here

Sandpaper files No grinder? Make yourself a sandpaper file (Fig. 5). In fact make several as they have many other uses. The sizes given in the drawing are only approximate and the material can be almost any wood or ply about ⅜in. thick. Cover one side with a fairly coarse (say 80 grit) abrasive paper and the other with fine (about 180 grit). I find aluminium oxide sander belt paper ideal but garnet, silicon carbide and emery paper will do; glass paper is not of very much use.

To sharpen the blade, extend it as far as practical out of the holder. With some models the blade may have to be turned over to prevent it jack-knifing into your finger when the pressure is applied to the back. Keep the back at a low angle and draw it towards you in long steady strokes (Fig. 6), first on the coarse side and finishing on the fine. Any burrs that are formed can be rubbed off on this side too.

Cutting board This can be improvised from a piece of plywood or hardboard but it will be kinder on the knife, more pleasing to use and last longer if the surface is covered with linoleum or vinyl floor tiles. Alternatively, if you have a table which can be set aside for marquetry cover the surface of the table with the lino.

Steel straightedges Bought steel straightedges with ground surfaces and bevelled edges are nice to have but expensive. For shorter work a 12in. steel rule is ideal, longer lengths can be improvised by buying 1½-2in. wide ¹⁄₁₆ or ⅛in. bright mild steel strip. I have also found an old, large machine hacksaw blade to be most useful. All these straightedges (including the steel rule) can be made non-slip by gluing fine garnet paper to the undersides. Wooden straightedges are not suitable as the knife quickly chips the edge. Beware also of buying the pressed steel 'safety' rules. The edges of these are not always straight and the indentations marking the divisions tend to catch the knife.

Veneer saw Although for many years I did without a veneer saw (Fig. 7), since I bought one I have found it so useful that I would not be without and recommend you to get one as soon as possible. They can usually be

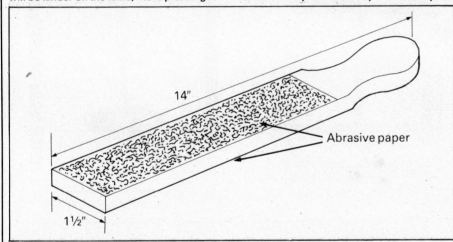

14"

Abrasive paper

1½"

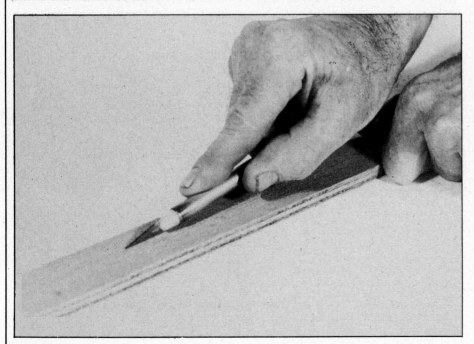

Fig. 5 (Left) Sandpaper file. Fig. 6 (bottom) another stage in sharpening a blade. Fig. 7 (above) veneer saw.

obtained from one of the veneer suppliers advertising in WOODWORKER.

A fair substitute can be made from an old table knife (Fig. 8) by filing teeth on the rounded end and putting a slight bend in the blade so that the cutting end can lie flat against the work without catching the handle. In both saws the teeth point *towards* the handle so that they cut on the pull stroke. They also seem to cut better if the teeth are bevelled to cut like a series of knife edges.

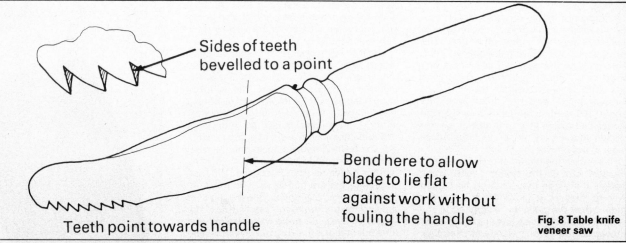

Sides of teeth bevelled to a point

Bend here to allow blade to lie flat against work without fouling the handle

Teeth point towards handle

Fig. 8 Table knife veneer saw

Lighting Little fine work can be done without a good light and for me one of the Anglepoise-type fitted with a spot lamp is essential (Fig. 9). Spotlamps are more expensive than the ordinary lamp but give a concentrated light beam which can be further away from the work for the same amount of light. The built-in aluminium reflector keeps the heat from the shade so that your forehead is less likely to get burned every time you peer closely at the work.

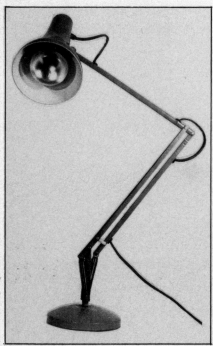

Presses An old letterpress or bookbinder's press (Fig. 10) is excellent for laying the picture to the baseboard but a wooden caul press can be made. The one illustrated in Figs. 11 and 12 was made by a 15-year old girl at school. Make the bearers of hardwood of substantial depth, say 2in. for a 16in. width. Slightly curve the edge of each bearer that touches the cauls. To find the correct amount of curve first make the bearers straight and assemble the press with a piece of board in place of a picture.

Tighten the nuts and note how much curve this has put on the top edge of each one. This is the amount of curve to be planed on the bottom edge. The bottom bearers are curved in the same way as the top. Without this curvature the centre of the picture would not get pressed.

Fig. 9 (Left) Anglepoise-type light fitting. Fig. 10 (centre) Presses for laying the picture. Fig. 11 (bottom) caul press.

Fig. 12 (Above) Components of caul press.

A number of books which illustrate this type of press show ordinary wing nuts for applying the pressure. No way will you get sufficient pressure on these with your fingers and if you have to use a spanner then it is better and cheaper to buy hexagon nuts. A box spanner with a tommy bar is often easier to use than an open-ended spanner for this purpose.

For small pictures a press can be improvised from two boards and four cramps (Fig. 13).

Veneer Some veneers will no doubt be obtainable locally. These may be suitable for a few parts of the picture and for the borders, back and edges. Most will have to be obtained from one of the specialist marquetry suppliers. None of the veneers recommended for the design will be particularly hard to cut but some of the burrs may be buckled and bumpy. The treatment of these will be given when the time comes to use them. A cutting list for the design is given in the last paragraph of this article.

Baseboards The veneer picture will have to be mounted on a board. Plywood (birch or mahogany) and chipboard ⅜-⅝in. thick is most suitable. Choose a high-density chipboard not one with a very fibrous centre. Laminated board is also very good but not so readily available. Blockboard should generally be avoided as the core tends to shrink irregularly and produce a slightly uneven surface which will show when the picture is highly polished.

Glue Two types will be needed: (i) a white PVA for the butt jointing of the pieces and for laying the picture to the baseboard; and (ii) a contact adhesive for edging the baseboard and for laying the picture if a press is not available. A small container with a

Fig. 14 (Right) For dampening gummed paper.

pointed spout is useful for applying the PVA glue when making the picture but as the spout quickly seems to get blocked a small jar and a strip of veneer will do the job just as well. Some prefer to use balsa cement for this as it dries quickly but you have to be careful to remove the surplus as the PVA glue used for laying the picture will not stick to it properly.

Gummed paper tape While the picture is being made certain parts will have to be held together with gummed paper tape — the sort that has to be licked or dampened before use. Easiest to obtain is the brown although industry uses a translucent white through which the joint can be seen while it

is wet. This is the type that will be seen in the photos of the making of the picture. Neither of them are very pleasant to lick so fill a small pot with a foam sponge (Fig. 14), dampen it and use by first drawing the back (the un-gummed) side of the tape across the sponge and then the gummed side.

The tape will curl up but after a few seconds it will uncurl again ready for use. Gummed tape has three advantages over self-adhesive tapes: (i) it can easily be removed by damping; (ii) as it dries it

Fig. 13 (Below) Improvised press.

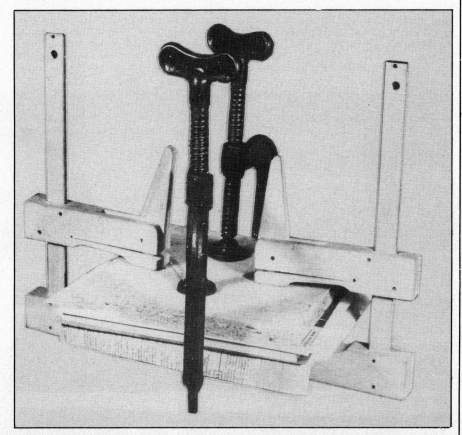

shrinks which tends to pull the join together; and (iii) it does not cling so tightly to the wood that the fibres are pulled out when it is removed. Sellotape is prone to do this if it is left on soft woods when the picture is being pressed.

Sellotape and masking tape Despite what I have just said, Sellotape does have its uses in marquetry if it is carefully scraped off after its work is done and not left on when the work is pressed. Some woods are very brittle; some shapes will have some short grain. Sellotape placed on the surface of these before they are cut will help to hold the piece together until it is glued in place. It is also useful when cutting through on to a dark veneer where the knife mark is difficult to see unless the Sellotape is stuck on the surface first.

Masking tape is stronger than the other two tapes and can be used to reinforce the edges of the picture while it is being made and to hinge the tracing to the work, but the remarks made about Sellotape apply to this too.

Carbon paper Black carbon paper is used to transfer the design to the veneer. Do not use blue. It can make an incredible amount of mess on the work when it gets mixed with the dirt and the glue. Yellow and white carbon paper (from dressmaking shops) have their use when marking on to dark veneers. Use an empty ball point pen, hard pencil or stylus to transfer the lines on to the work.

Wax pot Certain woods are hard and tend to cling to the knife. To overcome this to some extent the blade can be stabbed at intervals into a candle stump but it is safer to have this, or beeswax, melted into a small pot. A lead fishing weight put into the bottom of the pot before melting the wax will give it weight enough to hold itself down on the table when the knife is stabbed into the wax.

Sanding, sealing and polishing materials will be dealt with later.

The picture I intend to use for this series is shown in Fig. 15. If you would like to get the veneer ready you will need the following pieces in 12 × 6in. size which is standard for some veneer suppliers (the burrs can be smaller): 1 piece each of aspen, Nigerian walnut, ayan, sycamore, sap walnut, European walnut, black walnut, lacewood and oak; 4 pieces of sapele; and a selection of burrs as available from walnut (various), myrtle, maple, lacewood, elm and ash. Minimum of three types is required.

The next article will deal with preparing and cutting the picture.

Fig. 15. Picture prepared with the equipment described in this article.

For CDT Departments

Tom Pettit makes some proposals on how design and problem solving can be the basis of woodwork courses in junior forms. He says: 'I am well aware that circumstances vary from school to school and that the content of this article may only serve as discussion'.

The form of many present-day timetables severely limits the time available for craftwork. This is particularly so in lower school, where it may be as little as two periods a week for a term or so; or perhaps four periods a week over a considerably shorter period. Almost invariably group sizes are in the region of 20, almost certainly of mixed ability and frequently of boys and girls.

In these circumstances the professional skill of the teacher of craft, design and technology is vitally important and he could very understandably feel over-awed by the task with which he is faced. Even though these restrictions may be eased a little in middle school there is no more than the minimum of time during years one, two and three to prepare children for entry into an examination course in year four. Teachers in middle schools have the added responsibility of protecting the autonomy of their own establishment and at the same time preparing the children for the work to be done on transfer to senior school.

It is essential that the basic requirements of the subject are not overlooked in the multiplicity of what must be taught, including some form of sketching and technical drawing which often has to be accomplished within the workshop periods. Although I vividly remember as a child having to prepare all materials from rough

joints — butt, halvings, housings, bridle, mortise and tenon (and possible variations) single dovetail, common dovetail, dowel. This leads to box, flat frame and carcase constructions.

The suggested sequence of graded design problems which follows would be suitable for first, second and third year children and indicates how the basic woodworking techniques may be taught by problem solving. Initially the design problem may be put to the group as a whole, the proposed work being chosen to teach particular techniques. Later on variations to a basic problem may be given to smaller groups within the class to lend variety to the work; or to individual children once the teacher has built up a 'library' of design problems each of which he knows will require the children to acquire certain techniques and skills.

By this approach boys and girls can learn basic woodwork in a more purposeful way than by the previous more formal methods, with the additional benefit of designing individual pieces. At all times there must be insistence on correct use of tools and of methods. If basic techniques such as setting-out, use of saws and chisels, gluing and nailing and such like, can be repeated the more beneficial the course becomes.

The following design briefs will provide

wooden letter opener from the European beech provided; this measures 250 × 35 × 10mm. Make several sketches of suitable shapes, each drawn around a centre line making provision for a handle and a blade with a sturdy rounded point. How will you decide on the length of the handle? How will you make it comfortable to hold? What will be the section of the blade? Using the techniques employed in the previous design briefs transfer the shape to the wood, saw and smooth to shape. This work is to be finished with cellulose sanding sealer and chilled wax. (Alternatives to the letter opener are plant labels; garden pegs for a line band; kitchen spatula; wooden spoons; or salad servers.)

Wooden toy Make 2-dimensional or 3-dimensional sketches of a wooden toy suitable for a younger sister or brother. These can be in the form of motor vehicles, boats, aeroplanes and such like. Each part must be shaped accurately before being assembled with a PVA glue and panel pins. If wheels are necessary how will you fit them? Bright colours are always attractive to children — which will you use? What kind of paint might be best? From the experience of your previous work what kind of wood do you think will be suitable?

Wooden mallet You are to design a small wooden mallet to be used as a toy or for

TEACHING WOODWORK BY PROBLEM SOLVING

sawn boards, the use of machine-planed timber has been readily accepted for many years. This avoids many initial mistakes and is a great time-saver. The choice of easily worked timbers adequate to give the required results is also a sensible recommendation.

It is appropriate to outline under headings what the content of the three-year course might be. The time and extent to which topics are studied will, of course, be a variable factor.

Timber technology Properties and characteristics of softwoods and hardwoods; world distribution of timber; growth of the tree; grain, longitudinal and end; defects, decay and insect attack; manufactured boards.

Techniques and method Measurement, use of steel rule; setting-out, use of try square, marking knife, sliding bevel, single marking gauge (and later the mortise gauge) marking-off waste; making templates; cleaning-up with smoothing plane and glasspaper before and after assembly; assembling, use of G- and sash cramps; finishes and finishing.

Tool skills The above plus the use of rasps, Surform and files; sawing across and with the grain with tenon, coping, panel and rip saws; chiselling, horizontal and vertical paring, cutting mortises and variations; planing with the grain and across end grain; drilling holes, pedestal drill, wheel brace and joiners' brace; within limits use of special planes for rebating and making grooves.

Construction Single piece items in animal, mechanical or human form; simple

the student with the basic experience to embark on an examination course commencing in the fourth year. It is not intended that craft teachers should adopt these proposals. They are offered for consideration when devising a series suitable for their own situation.

1st YEAR Wooden mouse From the wedge of hardwood provided (70 × 20 × 30mm reducing to 10mm) you are to make the body of a mouse using rasps, files and glasspaper to produce the shape. Indicate on your design sheet what you propose to bring from home to use as the tail, ears, eyes, whiskers and, possibly, the nose. Make sketches and notes to show how these will be fitted and fixed (tactiles and paper-weights are alternatives).

Simple profile carving You have been provided with a short end of redwood from a board 95mm wide and 20mm thick. Draw round this on your design sheet and within the shape draw an animal, mechanical or human form to be cut out with the coping saw. Repeat this several times until you have decided on the most suitable shape. Will it be better to have the grain of the wood running horizontally or vertically?

From your chosen shape and using carbon paper draw and cut out a card template. With this template transfer the shape to the wood and saw to shape. How will you smooth the various surfaces? To keep the wood clean and to beautify the grain you are to finish the work with a clear varnish. Will the final piece stand on its edge, have a base attached or hang on the wall? How will you achieve this?

Letter opener You are required to make a

light woodworking. For something like this the wood will need to have special properties. What do you think these should be? How big and what shape will you make the head and the handle? How will you join these together? The finished work could be varnished or rubbed with linseed oil; which do you think will be best and why?

2nd YEAR. Work requiring more precision, further tool skills and continued insistence on use of correct methods.

Plant label/rod rest You have been provided with a piece of resin-bonded plywood (WBP) of 100 × 60 × 6mm and a length of redwood square section 18 × 18mm. From these you are to design and make either a plant label or a fishing rod rest. The two pieces can be glued and nailed or glued and screwed together. Which do you think will be best and why? Can you devise a simple joint which will give added strength to the work? Draw sketches to show the shape of the end to be pushed into the ground. Find out why WBP has been specified; and how you would mark out its shape for a rod rest. What do you think would be a suitable overall finish for the work; and what must you do to the work before the finish can be applied?

Candle holder Study the length of African hardwood you have been given and measure its length, width and thickness carefully. Then decide how it can be cut up and by the use of butt or simple halving joints fitted together to form the base in which to hold two table candles. Make sketches of as many ideas as you can showing where the candles would be fitted and how the ends of each part would be shaped. How would you make the holes for the candles? What do you consider would be a suitable finish? If you are going to glue felt to the underside to protect the table top should this be done before or after the finish is applied?

Lamp base Select no more than six of the short random lengths of hardwood which have been provided and by gluing them together make the base for table lamp. You should avoid gluing to end grain and it will be necessary for the ends of each piece to be carefully finished before and, perhaps again, after the work has been assembled. How will you do this? How will you arrange for the flex to reach the lamp? How will you complete the underside of the base? What do you consider will be a suitable finish?

Money box Design a simple box to be made of redwood and 3mm plywood in which to save small coins. What do you think are suitable dimensions for length, width, height? How thick should the sides be? How will the box corners be jointed? And pinned? Can they be butt jointed or might you use a simple lap joint and panel pins? What kind of glue would be suitable to strengthen these joints? How will the top and bottom be fixed? What provision will you make for putting in the coins and for retrieving them? Will the finished box be painted or varnished? (A pencil box or small tray are alternatives.)

Kitchen chopping boards What are the foodstuffs you are likely to chop on these boards? Why are such boards desirable? What do you consider to be the minimum overall size adequate for this purpose? Find out what hardwoods are suitable for such a piece of work. Sketch as many suitable shapes and forms of edge decoration as you can. How could you make a circular board? Do you consider a handle to be necessary and if so what shape might it be and how would you fix it? If glue is to be used must it be a special kind? Many kitchen worktops are covered with hardwearing laminated plastics which are hygienic; could your board be covered with such a laminate and if so how would it be fixed? For such a piece of work which is going to be washed frequently what do you consider to be a suitable finish? (A sawing board with provision for cutting angles at 45° and 90° may appeal to some students).

3rd YEAR More demanding work of greater complexity, further emphasis on design, correct use of materials, tool use and constructions, more advanced assembly work. It is also at this time, that modifications to the timetable may result in reduced group sizes and work can progress at students' own speed with a view to completely individual work in the fourth and fifth years.

Racks As an addition to your kitchen facilities you are to make a rack to hold six eggs. The construction should involve housing joints by which ends or supports are jointed to the platform. You should pay particular attention to the overall appearance but at the same time keep the size to a workable minimum. The size of hole will be most important and it is suggested that the positions of the holes are determined by first making a card template. (Racks for books, magazines, letters and toast — small open shelves).

Flat frame racks for fixing to walls From the lengths of redwood provided which are 34 × 18mm in section, you are to make a flat frame jointed together by bridle or mortise and tenon joints. Using suitable dowel rod,

make provision for hanging spice jars, or hats and coats to the frame. How will the frame be fixed to the wall? Do you need to shape the edges to improve it aesthetically? What kind of finish would you apply? (Mirror stands and domestic milk bottle crates offer similar constructions).

Stools Use the experience of the previous exercise to design a low stool with a wooden top. This should be of veneered chipboard or plywood. Use reference material (books, posters and such like) to find out how to modify the joints. How will you fit and fix the top; how will you treat the edges? Will the finished stool be varnished or painted? Assembling this work will be more difficult than any done previously and accuracy is most important. You must check with the try square, winding strips and, diagonally, with a lath; be sure that you know what these methods are.

Boxes for specific items You are asked to design a box with lid for your personal use. The corners must be jointed and you should consider use of lap joints, housing joints or dovetails. Give particular thought to how the bottom and lid are to be fitted; any necessary partitions; the most suitable type of wood; and the finish to be applied. Obviously the overall sizes will be determined by what the box is intended to hold. For example collectors' equipment (say for philately); fishing tackle; playing cards; jewellery or other items. For jewellery a lining of flock would be appropriate.

Small cabinets Where might you use a cabinet? How would you determine its size? Would it have a shelf (or shelves); and how would you house them into the carcass? Might there be other divisions? By means of simple sketches show how the back would be fitted and fixed. Would you have hinged doors or sliding? What would they be made of; and might there be a mirror? How will the cabinet be fixed to the wall? A cutting list should be added to your design sketches and this should also state the finish to be employed.

I am well aware that circumstances vary from school to school and that the content of this article may only serve as discussion. Those problems which allow for a number of different solutions, depending upon the child's natural ability and educational progress, and at the same time teach the required skills are most likely to prove successful. There must be ready access to suitable resource material at all times.

The aesthetics of good design should always be emphasised, although what constitutes good or bad design is often a personal decision. Choice of construction, shape, materials, function, finish, efficiency and cost are part of design and are bound up with the aesthetics of what is made. Enthusiasm and self-motivation should also increase if the work is found to be emotionally satisfying. Validation of the completed work by children and staff is important. At this stage it has been found worthwhile to make a further three-dimensional sketch (in colour) of the completed work. This further strengthens the student's confidence in his or her ability to sketch and design.

By the end of the third year it is expected that the child can reasonably, in consultation with the teacher, embark on a further two years of problem solving in preparation for external examinations. It is anticipated that during this period many of the design briefs would be the original work of the student.

BOOK REVIEW
More about the material

Preliminary perusal of *Trees, Timber and Woodworking* by Alfred Crane, left a strong impression that the publisher had done a great disservice to the author. The reproduction of the photographs is very poor indeed, due to a combination of the method of printing and the inferior quality of the paper on which they are printed. Surely the price-tag of £4.25 for a 147-page book justifies far better quality.

Mr Crane believes, as most woodworkers would agree, that the more a craftsman knows about the material on which he works, the better his results will be. He therefore sets out to give a great deal of information on wood and its uses with some history and botany thrown in, all in an interesting way. Although the book is aimed at senior schoolboy readers there is much of interest for adults.

Forestry with its history and the conversion of timber in the mill are dealt with at length, while materials such as veneers, plywood and chipboard have a chapter to themselves. A good section on the seasoning of timber includes details on the structure of wood of various kinds. The text is augmented by a profusion of line drawings. These are rather crude and many are poorly reproduced. In a number of cases they are not supported by any related text.

Chapter 3 on Applications and Use starts with the Tudor period on the building of ships and the growing of timber with 'knees' for this purpose. Descriptions and diagrams show how timber-frame houses were built in the same period. Special characteristics of some timbers are listed as being suitable for such work. Here again, 11 pages of sketches and wretched photographs have no explanatory text, a notable example being a 'crucked' house.

Another chapter gives a good account of the development of furniture through the ages. The rest of the chapter is concerned with the activities of some of the famous cabinet makers and designers of the 17th and 18th centuries. A list of locations at which some of their work can be seen is particularly useful. In a further section several of the surviving country crafts are described. These include the use of coppice wood for basket and hurdle making; the wheelwright's skills; and pole lathe turners of chair parts. Rather strangely, carving by Grinling Gibbons is cheek-by-jowl with farm wagon construction. Following immediately after this is a section of wood finishing, starting with early methods including oriental lacquer work. Later, the author deals with the production and use of shellac and some of the modern productions such as polyurethane and catalyst lacquers.

The book ends with a glossary of terms used in connection with wood. A list of timbers used in building, joinery and cabinet making gives full details of their characteristics and appearance. Lists of books for further study, places to visit and useful publications is also appended.

Mr Crane has fulfilled his intended purpose of interesting his schoolboy readers in his subject. In addition, he has given them an incentive to continue to study it by reading other books, by visiting some of the locations he lists and by research.

Publisher is New Horizon, Horizon House, 5 Victoria Drive, Bognor Regis, West Sussex.
H.C.K.

workpieces

Grading American plywood

Some of the characteristics of American plywood have been discussed by Jack Gianni, senior representative of the American Plywood Association, the trade organisation representing 85% of plywood manufacturers in the US.

Speaking at a seminar organised by James Davies (Timber) Ltd, the Swindon-based timber merchant and importer of panel products, Mr Gianni said there were two main types of ply: exterior with 100% waterproof glueline; and interior which differs from exterior only in that either the glueline is not completely waterproof, or the type of veneer used for the back or inner panels of the board could possibly affect the performance of the bond.

The APA has devised a definitive reference and grading system based on the performance and/or the appearance of the board. This tells the customer which particular type of plywood should suit his needs, as well as detailing support requirements when the board is used structurally.

Criteria governing the grading and referencing system include: type of adhesive used to bond the veneers making up the board; type of timber used to make up the different layers, particularly the front and back veneers — there are 72 different species, split into five groups, used by APA member-manufacturers; and finish of the front and back veneers which can make the difference between the board being classified for engineering or appearance purposes.

'The different grades combined with the choice of wood types means there are about 3500 different plywood variations available to meet the needs of our customers,' said Mr Gianni. 'That is why we stamp the easy-to-understand grading and reference on every sheet of plywood along with our ASP stamp.'

Memorial tablet in Co. Durham.

What the carver missed

Readers who have visited Cragside at Rothbury in Northumberland will find much of interest in the mansion built for the first Lord Armstrong by the well-known architect of Victorian days, Norman Shaw. Armstrong was the celebrated engineer and scientist who made a fortune out of armaments and was also a pioneer of electrical energy. In fact, Cragside had its own hydro-electrical installation from the 1880s.

Much of the furniture was probably designed by Shaw specially for the house and there are pieces by Gillow in the collection that is still being catalogued by the National Trust to which the property was transferred some years ago by the present peer in satisfaction of death duties.

Hugh Blogg, who never misses an opportunity for close study of woodwork in stately homes, castles and churches, spotted something unusual when going round Cragside a few months ago. He writes: 'The carved wainscot has a small area not completed by the craftsman. Only about 30 min work I would say. But why? It is an interesting speculation.'

He has another poser from the north. This is a World War 1 memorial tablet in Quebec parish church, Co Durham. 'Do you notice anything curious or odd about it? (See illustration above.) The answer is given on page 724.

Above: Jack Gianni (right) answers questions during the seminar.

Catalogues

From Donarte Reproductions Ltd, 170 Scudamore Road, Leicester LE3 1UQ, come full-colour leaflets describing and illustrating movements for the Donarte collection. There are German Black Forest movements and two types of English movement for longcase clocks. Other leaflets cover the Victoria Vienna double-weight regulator clock and also the Albert design, the Elizabeth and the Edward, the last being described as split column design. Other leaflets deal with clock cases design and production services and with longcase clocks.

Woodhouse Marketing (Clocks) Ltd, Spence Street, Leicester (a member of the Donarte group), has issued a loose-leaf folder comprising pricelist of movements and plans and pricelists for the clocks mentioned in the previous paragraph as well as other models. There are separate sheets for mouldings, trunk bunn feet, turned knobs in sycamore and also for tables and dining chairs.

Cabinetware supplier

With the object of supplying specialist items that are difficult to buy locally, Stuart Sykes Cabinetware is established at Leas End, Underbarrow, Kendal LA8 8HB (Kendal 27101). Its catalogue (price 40p) lists cabinet furniture as well as router bits, picture framing kits, mouldings and carvings, door furniture, finishes. There is a separate section for hand tools.

The separate price list also gives quantity rates on many of the items. Stuart Sykes says: 'We welcome suggestions for goods which customers think we should stock. If customers have had difficulty in obtaining any particular piece of cabinetware we will do our best to search it out.'

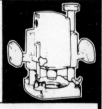

NEW! from EME

EMCO-REX 2000

WOOD MACHINING CENTRE

The new EMCO-REX 2000 is an amazing combined planing and thicknessing machine with automatic feed. Used by professionals and in home workshops. The basic machine is very versatile and can easily be adapted with the custom built circular saw, mortising and spindle moulding attachments.

The New EMCO-REX is one of the finest made machines on the market and without doubt the finest value.

★ 2 YEAR GUARANTEE
★ MADE BY THE LARGEST MANUFACTURER OF SMALL MACHINE TOOLS IN THE WORLD!

£395.00 SPECIAL INTRODUCTORY PRICE INCLUDES FREE STAND VAT EXTRA

250mm x 150mm thicknessing capacity

See us on stand 6/7/8/9 at the Woodworker Show

250mm circular saw

mortising

spindle moulding

FREE!

SEND TODAY FOR LITERATURE
E. M. EQUIPMENT LTD,
B. E. C. HOUSE,
VICTORIA ROAD,
LONDON NW10 6NY.
Telephone: 01-965 4050
Telex: 262750

EME
BEC

For full details of this equipment and a list of stockists in your area send for our FREE catalogue.

NAME _____

ADDRESS _____

_____

_____ W

THE WORLD'S TIMBER TREES

In October C. W. Bond FIWSc dealt with crabwood, no. 16, one of the lesser-known members of the mahogany family. This month he comments on cedar of which two principal species are in common use. The wood generally is very easy to work provided tools are kept really sharp.

CEDAR: 17

Cedrela spp. Meliaceae

There are seven species of *Cedrela* (a variation of *Cedrus*) softwood cedar of Lebanon, named from Kedron, both woods having a pronounced odour. In Havana the fragrance of tobacco and that of cedar wood are blended and well-known in the packing of cigars. Two principal species are in common use: *C. odorata* and *C. mexicana,* the names being self-explanatory. The trees occur from southern Mexico throughout central America and the West Indies and the wood is in constant demand for furniture, boat building and for characteristic native carvings.

Cedar is similar in colour to the mahoganies but is coarser in texture, softer and lighter in weight. It is a delightful timber to work with hand tools, some of it being rather dull in character, while some material is deeply coloured and very lustrous. There may be varying degrees of exudation of a sticky substance on the surface which might cause some inconvenience in working, but the wood generally is very easy to work provided tools are kept really sharp. It is useful for lining wardrobes and chests, the chemical nature making it resistant to fungal and insect attack.

Below: cross section × 3.3 as seen with a × 10 hand lens

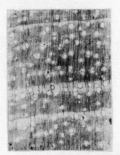

Below: cross section × 10 lineal

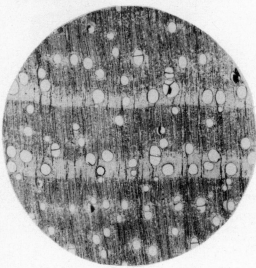

The photomicrograph shows a feature unusual in tropical woods, namely a strong tendency to being ring-porous. The growth rings are plainly marked with larger vessels and there are bands of terminal parenchyma showing up as lighter cells. Parenchyma cells are numerous in this case and could be described as terminal, vasicentric and diffuse, all three types being present.

In 1948, during the shortage of wood for educational purposes I was amazed to receive a consignment of lustrous cedar. This material was the most outstanding I ever had for school and after all these years I hope the boys remember it. I certainly do!

Cedrela odorata

Drawn from material in the Forest Herbarium University of Oxford. With acknowledgements to the curator.

5 cm

704

Woodworker, November 1980

complete Home Workshop

CORONET
WOODWORKING MACHINES

Universal & Independent models for Woodworking & Woodturning

SAWING • BOX COMBING • WOBBLE SAWING • SPINDLE MOULDING • PLANING
THICKNESSING • REBATING • MORTICING • SLOTTING & GROOVING • DISC SANDING
BELT SANDING • GRINDING & POLISHING • TURNING • LONG HOLE BORING

Bench mounted
& Cabinet models
ideal for . . .
PROFESSIONALS
AND D-I-Y
ENTHUSIASTS

*Whatever woodworking
operation you need —
Coronet have the ideal machine.*

Since 1946 Coronet have achieved a world wide reputation as
leading designers and manufacturers of Quality woodworking
machines with production of castings, machining and
assembly being carried out in our modern factory — to
achieve essential standards of accuracy.
Today our extensive range includes universal machines with
fitments and attachments which can be purchased as and
when required. — to suit your particular needs.

Send Now for
BROCHURE
on all models

CORONET
TOOL CO LTD
Alfreton Road
Derby DE2 4AH

see the Coronet Range in action

—at Coronet Works and
Learn-a-Craft Training
Centre in Derby
—by arrangement
Telephone: 0332-362141

—at Stockists. Coronet
Demonstrators visit
main Stockists
throughout the year.
Send for details.

Please send me brochure, price
list & my local stockists address.
I enclose stamps, value 15p for p & p.

NAME _____

ADDRESS _____

_____

_____ C/W 11.80

CORONET
complete Home Workshop
— comprising:-

1 ELF WOODTURNING LATHE
4 speeds
12" between centres
14" Bowl Turning (as illustrated)

2 IMP BANDSAW
3 speeds
12" throat
5" (approx.) Depth of cut
Table tilts to 45°

3 SOVEREIGN 4½" PLANER
½" rebate
Fence tilts 45°

**4 CONSORT
SAW/SPINDLE MOULDER**
4 speeds
2¼" depth of cut
Table tilts to 45°
Spindle Moulding (See separate leaflet)

Each unit comes complete with its own motor, press button starter and cabinet stand.

Each unit can be purchased separately — if required for bench mounting (without cabinets)

Illustration shows:-
1. 14" plaque being turned
2. Preparing disc for turning
3. 4½" surface planing
4. Spindle moulding shelf mould

MAJOR CMB 500

MAJOR CMB 600

MINOR MB 6

7" PLANER CAP 300

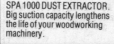
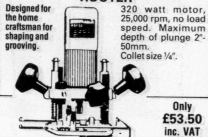

4 GREAT OFFERS FROM CECIL W. TYZACK

AVAILABLE IMMEDIATELY BY POST OR DIRECT FROM OUR STAND 55/56 & 63/64 – DEMONSTRATIONS THROUGHOUT THE DAY.

Complete MFF80 ELECTRIC HAND PLANER in carrying case

£76.36
(post & VAT included)

the "small" Plane with the large capacity

Its compact, impact-resistant casing and powerful motor plus its ability to rebate to a depth of 22mm (⅞") makes the MFF80 Planer the ideal machine for use by craftsmen, both professional and amateur, on the building site, and in the joinery shop.

Complete with carrying case with dust bag and Tungsten carbide blades, and side fence.

MOF 96 ELU PORTABLE ROUTER AND KIT

£78.00
(post & V.A.T. included)

KIT COMPRISING HAND ROUTER MOF 96

With ¼ Collet and Nut; Adjustable Side Fence and Guide; Guide Bush; 1-1¼" H.S.S. Router Cutter ¼ Shank; 1-1½" H.S.S. Router Cutter ¼ Shank; Two spanners.

Elu ®

5" & 6" double-ended Bench Grinders

Prices include post & V.A.T.

Tools such as scissors, chisels, drills, plane irons, or cold chisels, or garden implements such as lawnmower blades, secateurs or garden shears can be sharpened without effort on this machine.
Despite their small dimensions the double-ended bench grinders have an optimum performance. The diecast aluminium body and the robust motor ensure a long life. Spark arresters are of course, fitted to both sides.
An accessory that is highly recommended is the tool holder and grinding attachment.

MWS 146 — with 2-5" wheels £35.00
MWS 147 — with 2-6" wheels £45.00
MWS 148 — with 2-7" wheels £55.00

THE NEW 2-SPEED ORBITAL PORTABLE JIGSAW

£80.00
(post & V.A.T. included)

The 2-speed and 4 position pendulum action jigsaw with canting base to 45° is suitable for cutting wood, plastics and metal. The speed and orbit can be selected for all these materials.
Capacity:
Wood maximum 60 mm
Aluminium and non-ferrous metals 20 mm.
Mild steel maximum 6 mm.

Technical Data:	ST 142/01	Pendulum	
Voltage	220/250V	Adjustment	4 position
Input	450 Watt	Nett Weight	2.6 kg.
Output	280 Watt 0.38 HP	Standard	Steel carrying
Angles	Up to 45°	Accessories	case, 3 jigsaw
Length of stroke	26mm		blades, side fence
Stroke speed	1. Speed 2150/min.		spanner 8mm
	2. Speed 2800/min.		Allen key 6mm

CANE TABLE WITH GLASS TOP

Bamboo, cane and rattan are good looking and relatively inexpensive; they can be put with almost any style. Popular as a pretty framework for upholstery, they also make an interesting combination with glass.

Furniture in this style is flourishing in north London. The Cane Store run by Andrew Basham can be easily found if you walk from Finsbury Park with its well-kept lawns and colourful flowerbeds along Seven Sisters Road, over the canal and down the hill. Here with a display area/shop above and a cellar which enjoys a constant summer and winter temperature below, the canes, bamboos, rushes, seatings and wrappings of the chair caner's art are stored like precious wine bottles laid down under the pavement arches.

WOODWORKER visited Andrew Basham in his store to learn a little about the craft of caning, rushing, basketry and furniture making.

Andrew sells rattan canes which are used principally in furniture making. Manau cane from Indonesia is the strongest of these and comes in 9-10ft sticks; it bends least well of the rattans, usually comes in sizes 10-70mm but above 45mm is not really a feasible proposition. Tahiti cane is more supple than manau, not as knotty to look at since the joints are usually scraped; although flexible it can crease when bent. It is available in 12-13ft sticks, the most popular size being 30mm thick.

Kooboo cane has been washed and sulphured and especially after soaking bends very easily; it is usually used as a decorative cane since it nails well and unlike bamboo does not shatter. It comes in 4mm-14mm sizes up to 18ft lengths and can be coiled quite successfully.

Lapping or wrapping is used to bind over joints in cane furniture and this is first quality half glossy, rattan peel which Andrew sells in addition to a natural centre cane more suitable for basketry. It is usually soaked for about 2hr before use.

Indonesian cane is used for plant stands and picture frames. Batu rattan is similar to Tahiti in texture but has better jointing and therefore a better aesthetic appearance. Bamboo is straighter and more rigid than cane; it is hollow and can therefore be easily split lengthways into two for edging wooden furniture. It is more brittle and different techniques have to be employed when working with it.

The Cane Store also stocks centre cane (basket cane), polished beads and basket bases, plus basketry tools and books on the subject. Chair seating cane and the tools for recaning are available; so too is French cane (manufactured cane chair seating sold by the ft from a roll). Willow, rush and seagrass are sometimes available though this last year's crop of east European rush

has been disastrous and little is being imported: 1200 bolts as opposed to the normal 5000 intake.

Miscellaneous items include mirrors, pictures, bamboo and bead curtains, doormats in seacord, trellis and rush mats. WOODWORKER watched Andrew make a glass-topped cane table similar to the one in the heading shot; although this is a more 'chunky' version.

Cutting list and hints

Two-and-a-half — 3 sticks of 30-35mm manau cane is the minimum requisite for a coffee table of this type, but the sizes chosen are optional and vary according to the taste of the individual maker and his/her own personal needs.

This table needed four legs each 15in. long, four sides each 17in. long and four lengths each 22in. long (all finished sizes), plus a piece of glass for the top. *Important:* If you are a beginner buy your glass first and make your table to fit the glass not *vice versa*. The top does not, of course, have to be glass, though this we feel is the most attractive material. An alternative is bamboo ply over chipboard.

The table constructed here incorporates a roughly woven shelf for magazines made from Kooboo cane. Try to match your cane for appearance — figure and knots. Remember in assembly to try and avoid screwing into or joining at a knot. It is important also to drill holes to the correct depth for the width of cane chosen; if they are too shallow, joints will tend to 'pop out'.

The cane chosen *must* be straight. It can be straightened at all of the earlier stages of construction in the hardwood jig shown in Fig. 1.

Holes are drilled with a 37mm round cutter (in 30-35mm cane) mounted in a portable power drill held on a drill stand, or with a centre bit (Fig. 2). Assembly is easiest if pieces are held in a vice particularly when drilling end holes (see Figs. 3-5). Drill pilot end holes first through leg uprights, then place 2½in. × 12 screws and screw up. Andrew uses a Taurus brand wooden handled screwdriver as he needs to get a good grip to screw into the cane end grain. The two sides are constructed first and then the long pieces added between (Fig. 6), after checking the legs are parallel (by eye) and straightening if necessary by hands and feet.

Before the lower bars are inserted they should be drilled to take the canes of the magazine rack (five holes per bar in this table). There is often a lot of taper in cane so always keep looking at the cane. Try to put the blemishes and poorer marked pieces where the eye will not see them. Put them underneath if possible and if you do find taper try not to put two thick or two thin parts together. Always work on the side nearest you and keep turning the work in the vice. This helps to keep the work true and parallel.

Drill both the leg tops to take the long pieces with a ⁷⁄₃₂in. HSS drill bit, follow with a countersink to produce a circular hole. Then repeat the procedure for the lower bars. Check for squareness before assembly. Drill pilot holes in length end grain and assemble tapering off the side pieces with a Surform tool to produce a better join. Countersink all screws.

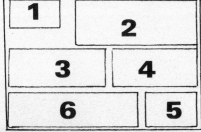

1	
	2
3	4
6	5

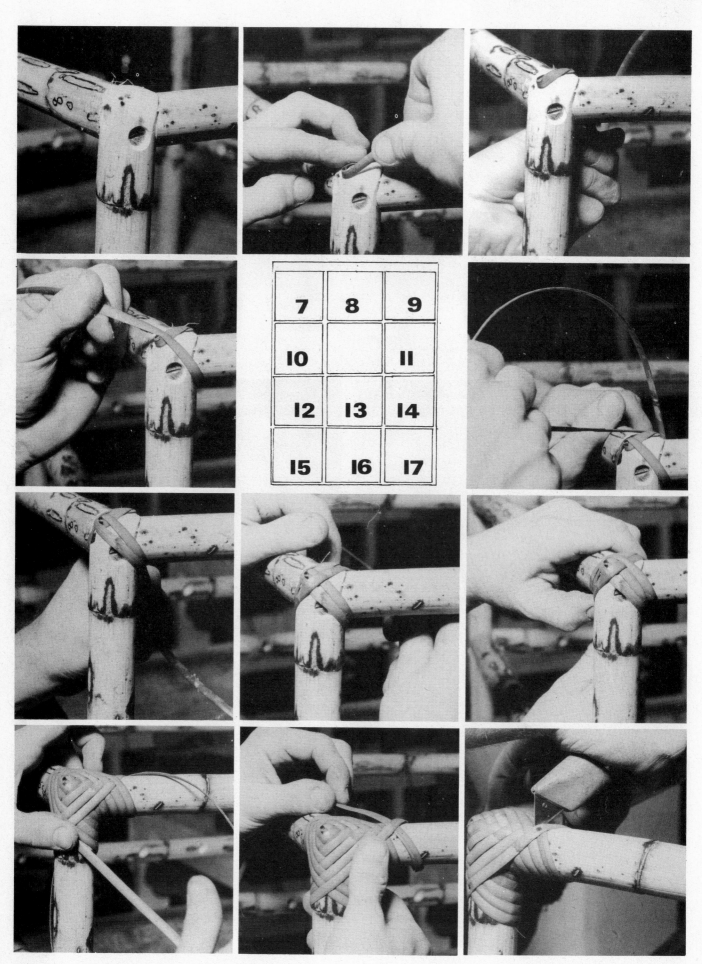

LAPPING

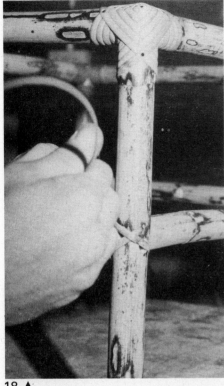

18 ▲

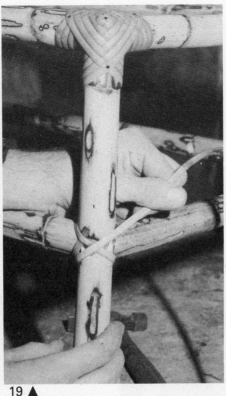

19 ▲

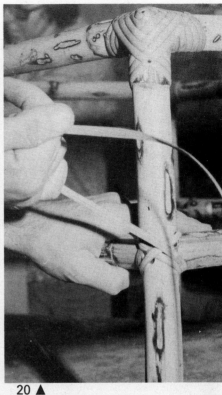

20 ▲

21 ▼

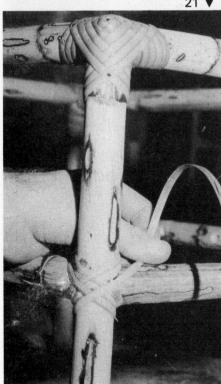

22 ▼

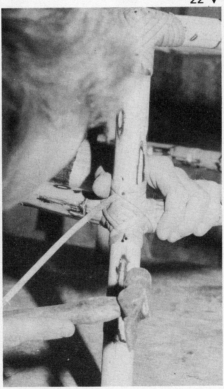

23 ▼

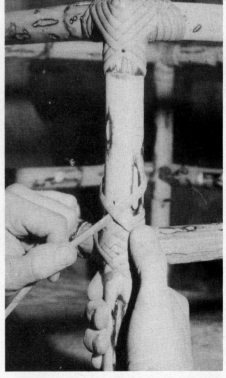

Andrew always drills pilot holes to take a size 12 screw and then tightens up all the way round the table. He experimented with dowel jointing but found it hard to guide the drill into the end grain. It would, however, be an ideal joint if this problem could be overcome. If preferred Pozidriv screws can be used.

Lapping Soak the lapping cane for 2-3hr. Surform the tops of the legs to follow the curves of the cane on the sides and ends. Here if preferred a rasp can be used instead of a Surform tool. The table should be held in the vice for steadiness and strength. The stages of lapping are illustrated (Figs. 7-17) from stage 1, placing a tack (Fig. 7) on the point of the corner and binding around following three points to make a centre triangle. It is important to keep one hand

always at the back of the work and both hands working together feeding the cane around. When the binding is finished the end loops back upon itself (Fig. 16).

A tack or tacks are put in to finish off for safety and a Stanley knife used to cut off the spare cane (Fig. 17). The cross of the side bindings must be central otherwise a lop-sided appearance is achieved. It is also important to bind tightly, firmly and evenly (Figs. 18-23).

CANE TABLE

Magazine shelf This is made of wetted pieces of cane; it is not necessary to soak Kooboo cane as it is sufficiently pliable. Place the long pieces first (Fig. 24), weave in the rest and cut to suit (Figs. 25, 26). (Andrew uses garden secateurs to cut his cane), push fit into the previously drilled holes (five in the long pieces, four in the ends), bend as necessary to achieve a good fit; a few gentle hammer taps may be needed to ensure a tight arrangement.

24 ▶

▼ 25

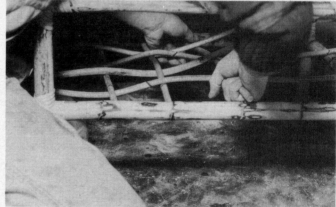

◀ 27

26 ▲

Kooboo bending

28 ▼

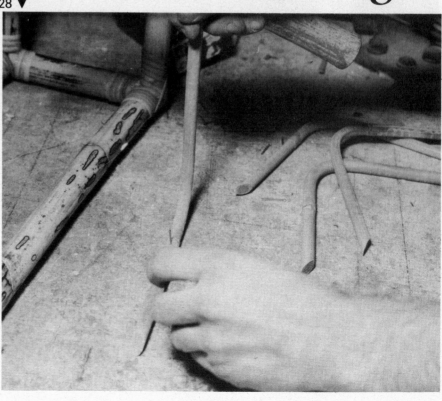

Cane decoration Fig. 27 shows the bending by hand of the Kooboo cane to fit the top and act as a support for the glass. It is often a good idea to use one piece as a template, cut the ends on a mitre block with ordinary roll cut secateurs. Oval pins (or wire nails or panel pins) are used to fix the cane (25mm pins on 8-10mm cane) into place (Figs. 28, 29). Check by eye at all times for squareness and use as many nails as necessary to secure centres and corners of cane.

Finish the underframe in the same way (Fig. 30); mitre the ends after fitting (Fig. 31). The glass is arrised and 'sits' on the top. Bevel the base of the legs. Seal with polyurethane, one coat of spray lacquer can be used; wood stains are also a possibility for finishing. These should be brushed well on and in and allowed to soak into the cane. In the light of experience Rustins' wood stains seem to be the most penetrating.

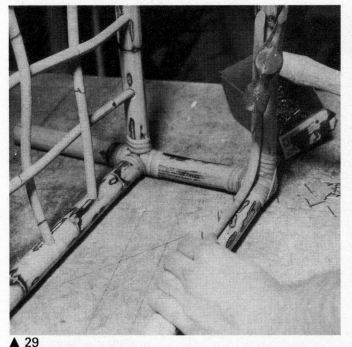

▲ 29

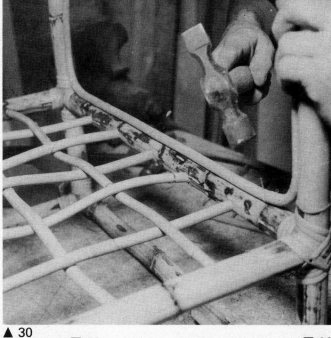

▲ 30

▼ 31

▼ 32

Some books: *Cane and Raffia,* Search Press, London 1969; *Canework for the Dolls House,* by Winifred Garrett and Mary Thornton, Dryad Press; *Cane and Rush Seating* by Margery Brown, B. T. Batsford 1976.

BOOK REVIEW

Making toys for Christmas?

Well thought out and well laid out are justifiable terms to introduce *Rodney Peppé's Moving Toys,* though soft covers rather than hard-back would perhaps have been more suitable binding for a book that will get a lot of use on and around the bench.

The book is divided into sections on balancing toys, string toys, models, slot-together toys and decorative toys and for easy reference the contents pages carry small illustrations of the toys: a useful idea. In addition to the illustrations (a number in colour) and diagrams there are material lists and detailed instructions for preparing the component parts and assembling them.

In his introduction the author points out that although the toys were all made with the aid of a fretsaw machine it is possible to make them with a hand fretsaw. He says the

book is not intended for 'raw beginners who would be entitled to a step-by-step analysis of each stage of construction. It is aimed, rather, at those who are fairly skilled but perhaps lack the designing ability to put their ideas into practice.' He goes on to say that it is a source book of toy ideas from the past, re-designed for the present.

On techniques and tools there is straightforward advice while the materials section is useful particularly in its references to adhesives, paints and lacquers.

The various toy mechanisms are interesting. The climbing monkey for example and the sand-toy leotard (J. Leotard invented the flying trapeze in 1859), the latter being worked by a sand motor. Another ingenious operation is that of the Tivoli acrobats in which a ball provides the motive power, counterbalancing the three figures and finishing up on the board to score as in a game of bagatelle.

Of the decorative toys, the bird-tree (based on a Japanese idea) is a nice combination of decorative piece and puzzle,

though there could be criticism of the decorative alphabet which as the author points out is too sophisticated for teaching the ABC. 'But they (the letters) do make attractive and unusual building blocks.' Maybe, but somewhat less sophistication would serve better in a 'look and learn' situation.

Price of *Moving Toys* is rather high at £6.95. However, it is an attractive book as well as a useful one, so to that extent the price-tag is justified, even more so if toys for Christmas is a workshop activity. Publisher is Evans Brothers Ltd, Montague House, Russell Square, London WC1B 5BX. **G.P.**

FURTHER READING
Selected reading list
for toymakers:
WOODWORKER December
1979 p755 and Toy
making WOODWORKER December
1978 pp556-563

TIMBER TOPICS II

Here W. H. Brown FIWSc tells how to measure wood cubic content. Though the timber trade has officially gone metric the selling of small quantities of boards is frequently based on imperial measure, simply because it is more convenient to do so and because of the unwieldiness of the metric unit by comparison

In buying small quantities of timber there can sometimes be confusion over the manner in which the price has been struck. This is usually because of uncertainty as to the method of measurement involved. Since 1970-1 the timber trade has officially gone metric; but in the absence of legislation the selling of small quantities of boards is frequently based on imperial measure, simply because it is more convenient to do so and because of the unwieldiness of the metric unit by comparison, the cubic metre (cu m) being some 35 times larger than the cubic foot (cu ft).

Dimension stock, ie boards with the same width and thickness, especially softwood, offered at so much a lineal ft or lineal m is straightforward enough. But it is the random-width hardwood, either square-edged or unedged (waney edged), which usually gives rise to conjecture as to content.

In commercial practice, clearly defined methods of measuring wood and rounding up or down those measurements not quite exact, invariably result in totals which are within economic limits. However, when this is applied to one or two boards of unequal dimensions, the non-trade purchaser may not readily reconcile price with volume.

Take a single piece of square-edged hardwood, say 6ft 2in. long × 8⅞in. × 1½in. For convenience sake a seller would probably call this 6ft × 9in. × 1½in. There is very little difference either way; on the original dimensions the board contains 4.56 super ft surface measure and 4.5 super ft when rounded off.

Ignoring metrication for the moment it should be noted that two phrases have crept into the discussion, ie super ft and surface measure. The simplest method of measuring a quantity of planks of varying width but of the same thickness is to measure and calculate the content of the surface area (called board measure) on the basis of length and width, add all together, adjust this value according to thickness and, finally, divide this total by an appropriate divisor to obtain the cubic contents.

Thus (with imperial measure) length in ft multiplied by width in in. and divided by 12 gives surface or board measure, expressed as 'super ft as thickness'. When this figure is adjusted to suit the thickness the expression is 'super ft as 1in.'

A super ft is the same as a sq ft, ie it contains 144sq in. Therefore if so many super ft 'as 1in.' is divided by 12 the result is cu ft. Reverting to our hypothetical board, which we said contained 4·5 super ft on rounded-off dimensions, we ignored the thickness which was 1½in.; accordingly, to adjust the surface measure to 'as 1in.' we

must add a further half of the surface measure to the total, ie 4·5 + 2·25 = 6·75 super ft. If this is now divided by 12 the answer is 0·5625 cu ft.

In this example, by no means uncommon, we are talking of simple arithmetic involving decimals. In practice this does not really apply, except in the sense that measurements must be taken on length, width and thickness in order to price the goods. What happens is that the measurer, by long practice, makes a rapid mental calculation based on what his rule has shown; and generally a board of the sizes mentioned would be assumed to equal half a cube.

However let us look at the same piece of wood, this time measured in metric: 1 cu ft is equal to 0·0283cu m, therefore 0·5cu ft equals 0·0142cu m. It would seem to suggest that it is simpler to measure single boards or a few boards in imperial measure provided rounding up or down is carried out fairly, although in these days of pocket calculators either method ought to be reasonable.

The official recommendations regarding the metric measuring of normal specification (6ft & up long; 6in. & up wide) hardwood is that lengths must be taken from 1·80m (6ft approx), rising in increments of 10cm (4in. approx); and widths to be measured from 150mm (6in.) and up in

In effect rounding down the width slightly since the metric equivalent of 8⅞in. is 225·4mm. On this hypothesis, 1·8 × 0·22m = 0·426m as thickness add 0·213m (to make up for thickness of 38mm) = 0·639sq m. Using the conversion factor of 10·764 (sq m to sq ft), 0·639sq m = 6·88sq ft, which compares very favourably with the 6·75 super ft we obtained by imperial measure.

By any method of measurement unedged (waney edged) boards should be measured across the narrowest face at points mid-way through the wane. If the boards are very irregular or tapering in shape, then an average of three measurements taken across the face of the board should be used to assess surface measure.

The following figures should prove useful: 1sq ft surface measure equals 0·0929sq m, and 1sq m surface measure equals 10·764sq ft. Similarly 1cu ft equals 0·0283cu m, and 1cu m equals 35·315cu ft.

Round logs are measured very differently if their cubic content is the basis of sale. Generally speaking, however, small logs are priced individually at so much each, or by lineal ft or m. In the trade round logs are sold on what is called Hoppus measure, metric calculations being simplified by the use of log tables where cu m can be called off according to the girth of the log in mm and the length of the log in 300mm steps.

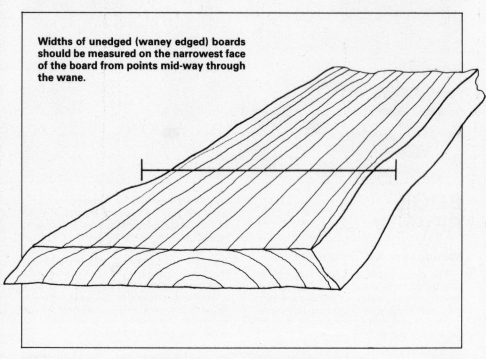

Widths of unedged (waney edged) boards should be measured on the narrowest face of the board from points mid-way through the wane.

increments of 10mm (⅜in. full). Short lengths and narrow strips are those falling from 1·70m in length in decrements of 10mm, with widths going from 50mm and up in increments of 10mm.

In our example (6ft 2in. × 8⅞in. × 1½in.), if measured in metric ought to be called 1·80m long, dropping the 2in., while the width would be called 220mm (ie 150mm (6in); 50mm (2in.); 20mm for 22mm (⅞in.).

Lengths are measured in steps of 100mm and girths in steps of 20mm but once these dimensions are known, the log contents can be simply assessed.

There are other ways of calculating the cubic contents of a log, one official method being to square the quarter girth of the log in m and multiply by the length in m ($\frac{1}{4} G^2$ (m) × L (m) = Hoppus m cu (Hm^3).

Ever thought of drying your own timber?

Even if it's as little as 10 cubic feet, Ebac has a machine that's simple to operate and economical to run. The Ebac Mini timber seasoner costs about £360 and will give you exactly the kind of timber quality you want. And it pays for itself through the reduction in cost of buying undried timber. A simple dial setting is all that is needed for precise seasoning of different kinds of wood. No noise. No mess. No fuss. Over a hundred units have been installed in the last two years.

See Ebac small-scale timber dryers at the Woodworker Show.

Ebac Ltd Stand 35

Ebac Limited
Greenfields Industrial Estate
Bishop Auckland, County Durham
Telephone 0388 5061

Upholstered stool by Edward Barnsley

The description and drawings of this piece have been prepared by R. W. Grant DLC FRSA MSIAD. It is the first of Mr Barnsley's designs for furniture to be made available to WOODWORKER and is reproduced from the full-size working drawings by his permission. Other pieces originating in Mr Barnsley's celebrated workshops at Froxfield, Hants, will be detailed in subsequent issues of WOODWORKER.

The stool has a drop-in type seat and as can be seen from the perspective drawing the piece exemplifies the economy of materials and overall simplicity which are hallmarks of any successful design. Further study will reveal the subtlety of line and the pleasing relationship of one part to another.

The original, made in the Froxfield workshops, was constructed in blackbean and the seat was covered with a tapestry. Those making this stool would do well to obtain, if not blackbean, a timber with similar characteristics and a seat-covering material that will not by colour or texture detract from the delicacy of the piece.

However, the construction of the stool is robust and should present no special difficulties to the practised woodworker. As the joints are principally mortises and tenons no detailed description of the manufacture of the piece need be given, except to point out one or two particular intricacies.

To avoid excessive short grain where the curve of the legs meets the rails a variation on the standard shoulder of the tenon has been adopted which, in effect, mitres the two pieces. Readers may prefer to make a template to mark out these shoulders (the angles can be obtained from the drawing) and perhaps make a wooden jig (on the lines of the standard mitre template) to ensure cutting accuracy. The striking of the curve from leg to rail can then be achieved once the joint is fitted.

It will be noted that the rebated end rails are dowelled to the side rails; and to accommodate the through rebate on the side rails the end rails are 'cogged' over that piece of the rebate to block off what would otherwise be an unsightly gap at each end.

All edges, apart from actual joint areas, are generously rounded over and this should not be attempted until the construction has been completed and a dry fit made. Some final blending will not doubt have to

CUTTING LIST

Net sizes shown. Dimensions in in.

Number	Description	Length	Width	Thickness	Material
4	Legs	12	2¼	1⅛	Blackbean or other hardwood with similar characteristics
2	Stretcher rails	12	1⅝	9/16	
2	Top rails	35¾	2⅜	1⅛	
2	End rails	14	1⅝	1¼	
1	Centre rail	13½	1½	5/8	
1	Seat base	34	14	½	Plywood
1	Foam pad	34	14	1	Medium density
12	Dowels	2	—	5/16 dia	Birch
1	Undercover	Cut to give sufficient overlap all round			Unbleached calico
1	Top cover				To suit

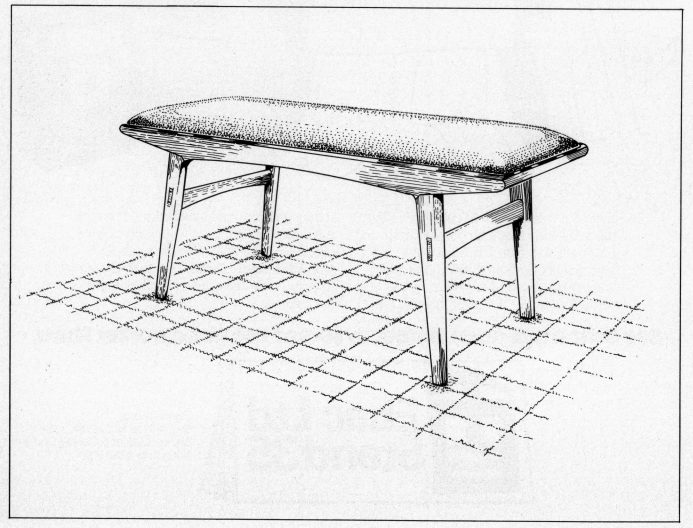

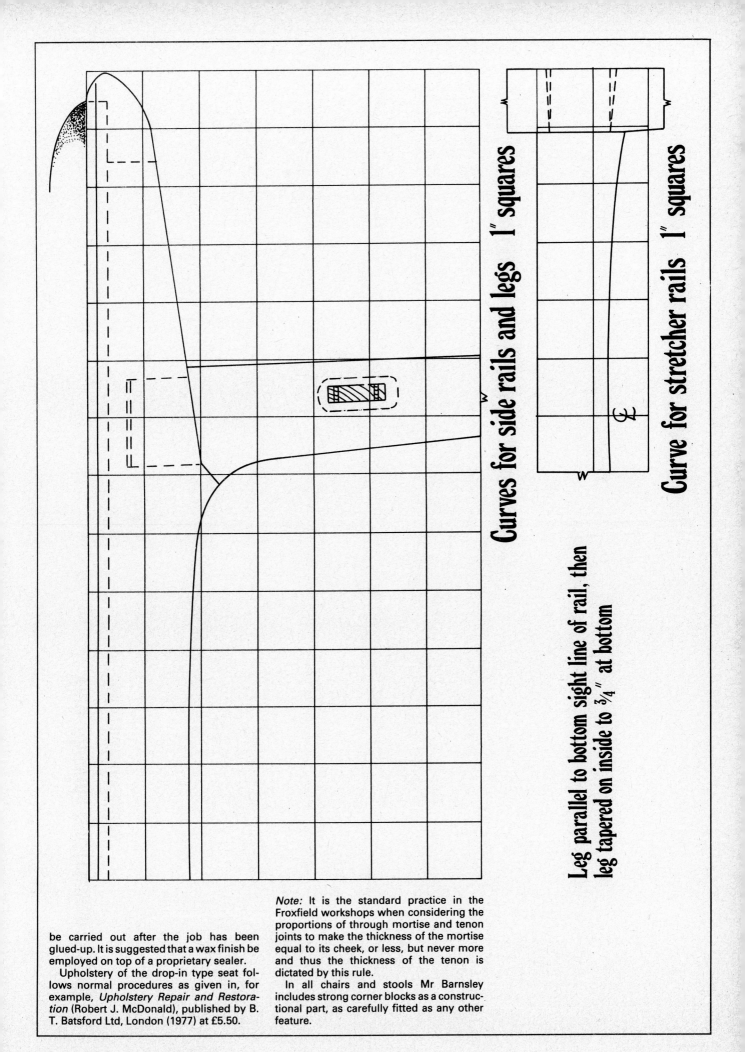

Curves for side rails and legs 1″ squares

Curve for stretcher rails 1″ squares

Leg parallel to bottom sight line of rail, then leg tapered on inside to ¾″ at bottom

be carried out after the job has been glued-up. It is suggested that a wax finish be employed on top of a proprietary sealer.

Upholstery of the drop-in type seat follows normal procedures as given in, for example, *Upholstery Repair and Restoration* (Robert J. McDonald), published by B. T. Batsford Ltd, London (1977) at £5.50.

Note: It is the standard practice in the Froxfield workshops when considering the proportions of through mortise and tenon joints to make the thickness of the mortise equal to its cheek, or less, but never more and thus the thickness of the tenon is dictated by this rule.

In all chairs and stools Mr Barnsley includes strong corner blocks as a constructional part, as carefully fitted as any other feature.

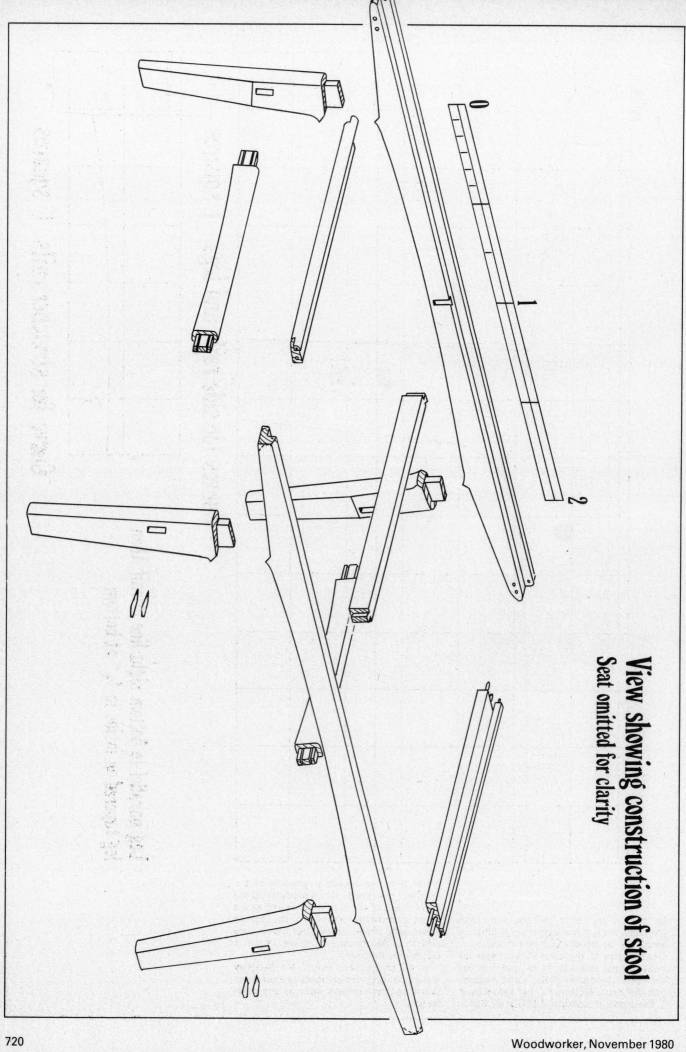

View showing construction of stool

Seat omitted for clarity

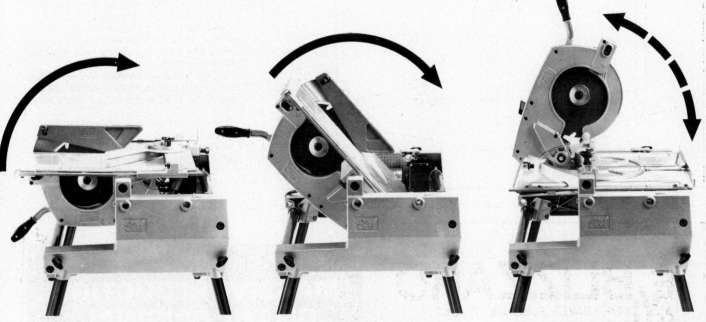

Guild of Woodworkers

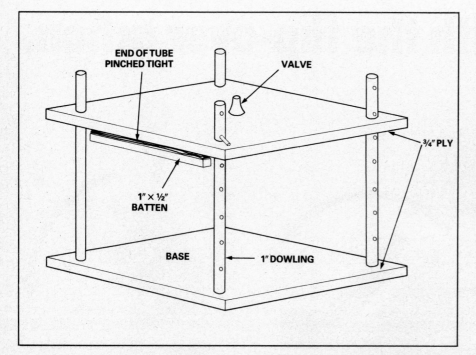

END OF TUBE PINCHED TIGHT

VALVE

¾" PLY

1" × ½" BATTEN

BASE

1" DOWLING

No pressing problems

From the old-world village of Weobley, Hereford & Worcs, Rodney W. Dovaston (no. 0036), gives advice on making a bag press. This follows his reading of the book reviews (p599 of WOODWORKER for September 1980) of *Veneering Simplified* and *Modern Marquetry Handbook.* He writes: 'It seems that some woodworkers may have difficulties in applying even pressure when doing veneering, marquetry etc. I have overcome this by making an air (bag) press using a section of inner tube from a car or lorry tyre.

'As shown in the sketch the top section slides up and down the four uprights. Holes ¼in. diameter are drilled about 1in. apart to retain the top sliding section at different heights by means of pegs. Stick the ends of the inner tube together before clamping with 1in. batten using screws or bolts — and keep the tube stretched tightly.

'To operate the press I slide the top section down the uprights to about 1in. above the work to be pressed and use pegs above and below to retain the section in position. I then inflate the tube (bag) by means of a footpump via the inlet valve to about 15-20lb/sq in.

'A larger press can be made by cutting the tube to give two sections of rubber which have to be glued and clamped all the way round.

'I should add that it is advisable to cover the work with thin paper and to dust the rubber with french chalk so as to stop the rubber pulling as it is inflated.'

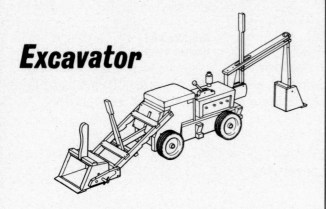

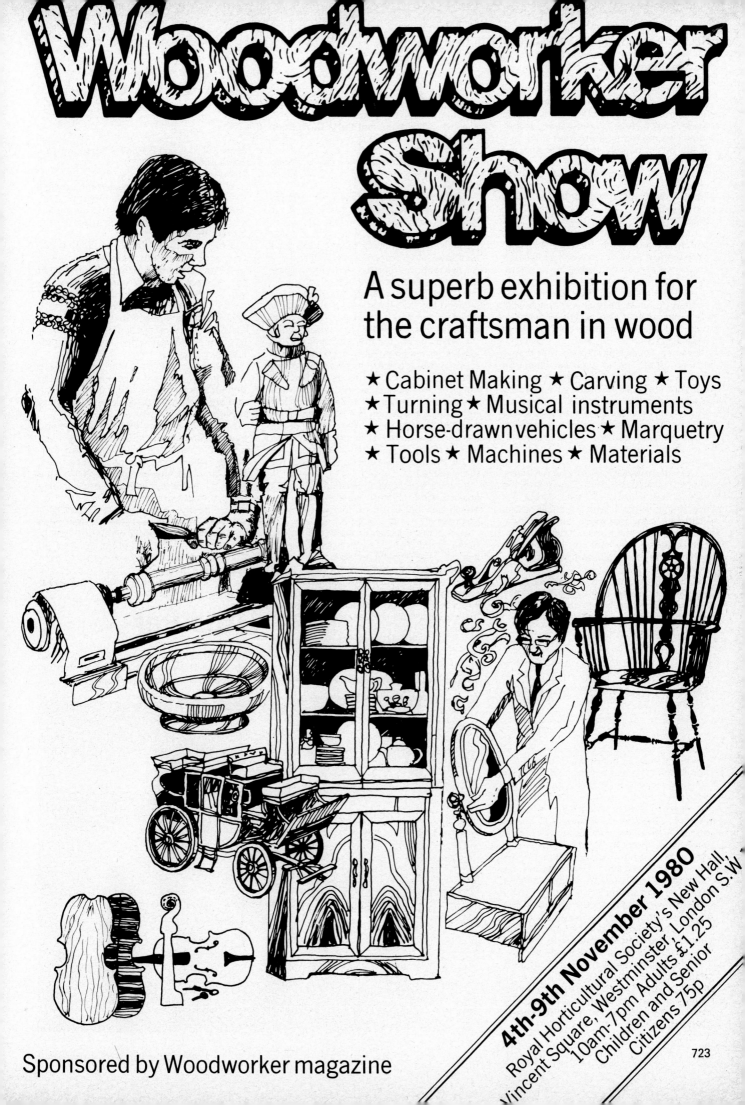

Woodworker Show

A superb exhibition for the craftsman in wood

★ Cabinet Making ★ Carving ★ Toys
★ Turning ★ Musical instruments
★ Horse-drawn vehicles ★ Marquetry
★ Tools ★ Machines ★ Materials

4th-9th November 1980
Royal Horticultural Society's New Hall,
Vincent Square, Westminster, London S.W
10am-7pm Adults £1.25
Children and Senior
Citizens 75p

Sponsored by Woodworker magazine

723

From: R. Sherwin, Turnright Woodworking Co, Aerlec Works, Hanbury Road, Stoke Prior, Bromsgrove B60 4AD

Dear Sir

I have read the appreciation of Frank Pain in the August 1978 issue. The writer (Peter Baylis) mentions some of the 'party pieces' which Frank turned. I wonder if any reader could give me more information about two of the items, namely the soldier and the miniature sundial?

Yours faithfully, **R. Sherwin**

From: C. W. Bond FIWSc MCCEd, Leamington Spa

Dear Sir

To paint woodwork so that it resembles marble is referred to in Ruskin's The Lamp of Truth in his *Seven Lamps of Architecture*; and is heartily condemned — 'gross degradation' and similar expressions. So it could be said about staining a wood to resemble another (for instance ebony) that he would have classed this also as 'gross degradation'. So I stand condemned for this letter at the outset!

Even so, what looks handsomer than a concert grand piano with an ebonised finish? (The piano is handsome in its own right but that is another story.) A uniform, black, highly-polished piece of ebonised woodwork may be satisfactory in every way, but ebony itself is never a featureless black so that an ebonised finish is different and always looks more artificial than the genuine wood.

The feature we call texture in wood is very difficult to analyse. The diameter of the vessels has a lot to do with it, but not everything. Woods with identical vessel diameters may look quite different even though colour also may match closely. Natural lustre, ray size, arrangement of parenchyma cells all contribute to the mystery.

Referring to botanical similarities, floral structure and wood structure are naturally akin. It could hardly be otherwise. Two well-known woods, the subject of this note, are botanically related:

	EBENALES	
	(Natural Order)	
SAPOTACEAE	EBENACEAE	STYRACACEAE
(Family)	(Family)	(Family)
Makoré	Ebony	No commercial woods

For this reason I put forward the suggestion of staining makoré with a dark stain as a substitute for ebony. The two woods are not *very* much alike in texture apart from the arrangement of their parenchyma cells. The vessels of makoré are considerably larger, profusely distributed and clear of contents, while those of ebony are smaller, sparsely distributed and full of dark gum in the heartwood. Nevertheless, the botanical relationship is fairly obvious however difficult it may be to describe.

Respective weights would give the game away, but there may be occasions when such 'deception' would be permissible provided, of course, that the article in question was not said to be, or labelled, 'ebony'.

There may be readers of WOODWORKER who would like to try it out. Makoré is an irritating wood to work with especially on a lathe; but perhaps respiratory irritation is part of the fine to be paid for 'gross degradation'!

Anyhow, there is 'life' in ebonised makoré which makes it very attractive.

Yours faithfully, **C. W. Bond**

From: William Sinnott, Coatbridge, Lanarkshire

Dear Sir

I am indebted to the readers who replied (April 1980 p248) to the query by A. C. Weller (December 1979 p739). However, they all omitted to say that there are two fences with this Miller's patent plane: one for use with the fillester/rabbet bed and one for use with the matching and plow irons. Mr Weller seems to have both.

It is apparent that my plane is a Stanley 41 and perhaps the photograph of it may be of interest to readers. I sharpened up the irons and gave its face a wipe with a drop of oil.

I also have in my possession an adjustable beading plane. I hope that one of these knowledgeable gentlemen will tell me something about it. It has seven beading irons: ⅛, ³⁄₁₆, ¼, ⁵⁄₁₆, ⅜, ⁷⁄₁₆ and ½in. and marked on the fence is 'Pat Sept 11 88.' The iron is held in position in the same way as with the Stanley 45 and Record 050 and it has the same type of depth gauge. The thumbscrews are exactly the same as those on the Stanley 41, so it is possibly from the same stable.

It seems likely that the additional irons I got with the Stanley 41 were made for the previous owner by his brother who was an engineer fitter and turner.

In WOODWORKER for April 1980 p236, Henry Taylor (Tools) Ltd, advises owners of lignum vitae mallets to keep them in a plastics bag when not in use. One of these mallets will stay in perfect condition if it stood on a pad which has been dampened with raw linseed oil. It would not do beech mallets any harm to receive the same treatment.

Yours faithfully, **Wm Sinnott**

Below: Wm Sinnott's Stanley 41 plane.

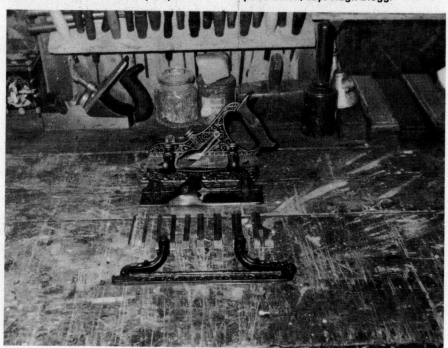

From: W. T. Baker & Sons (Aberkenfig) Ltd, Aberkenfig CF32 9AB

Dear Sir

With reference to the paragraph on page 428 and the letter on page 448 of the July 1980 issue, both of which are on the subject of discount prices, I am disturbed by the current trend.

If this continues I think that in 10 years' time or so this country's tool trade could be in the hands of about 50 mailorder firms. At the moment shops like ours selling woodworking machinery are kept open merely to show people what machines and tools look like. Some mailorder firms are offering up to 30% or more, off prices. If they are buying at normal trade price they are working for less than 5%.

I feel this is rather like someone trying to take away the job you are doing by offering to do it as well as you do for 30% less than you are getting. And succeeding in getting the job.

My view has been that in business you have to consider the future and not just the present. This is the basis on which individual traders have kept going in the past. But I now ask myself why don't I do the same thing as the mailorder firms and play them at their own game.

Incidentally, I have been reading WOODWORKER for 60 years. I started when I was an apprentice carpenter with a firm still in production — A. Gaylard & Son of Bridgend. And I still look forward to each copy of the magazine.

Yours faithfully, **W. T. Baker**

Answer

The curious tablet (page 700). What is odd about it? The entablature or oak mount is upside down, says Hugh Blogg.

If you want a professional finish to your furniture, use a pair of scissors.

When you own a DeWalt Power Shop, you can do as much with your wood as any professional.

You can cut at any angle, lengthways or crossways.

You can bevel and mitre.

And, with the right attachments, you can power through the boring, grinding, routing, sanding and jointing.

So, whatever you want made, you can make it yourself, paying only for the materials.

And you get professional performance without having to call in the professionals.

No circular saw, let alone a handsaw, can give you such precision and versatility.

And you slash the time taken because of the powerful motor that also acts as a general power source for the full range of DeWalt attachments.

You don't risk an inch of precious wood. And DeWalt's rigorous attention to safety features stops you risking your precious hands.

Your DeWalt Power Shop is precision made and solidly engineered for a lifetime's use.

But what if you don't want to use it for a lifetime?

Just sell it.

You'll find plenty of people keen to own the best saw on the market. And it depreciates very, very slowly.

So buy the saw you always promised yourself and give your wife the furniture you always promised her.

You'll save money on every joint.

And here's the first cut.

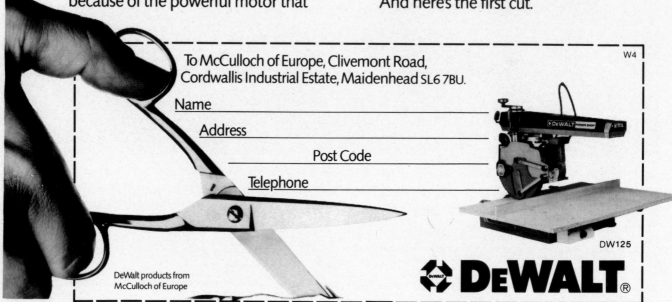

To McCulloch of Europe, Clivemont Road, Cordwallis Industrial Estate, Maidenhead SL6 7BU.

W4

Name

Address

Post Code

Telephone

DW125

DeWalt products from McCulloch of Europe

DeWALT ®

JEMCO TOOLS LIMITED

THE AMAZING SAW & ROUTER GUIDE

Very robust construction gives performance suitable for trade or DIY applications. Will out-perform most radial and table saws giving very accurate mitre cuts, groove and straight cuts up to 50″ when used as cross cut. Particularly suitable for kitchen and bedroom furniture making, staircases and general building carpentry.

Both guides are supplied without saws if own saw or router is to be used.

Also now available, SAW MATE, very similar to the SAW GUIDE but supplied without legs, braces and supports, to use in conjunction with your own bench, saw horses, or may even be used on the floor.

SAW MATE & Skil 574 Saw £99 incl. VAT & P&P.

Complete range of SKIL, HITACHI, SHOPMATE, VILLAGE BLACKSMITH, TOOLKRAFT AND THE REVOLUTIONARY JET CLAMP, ALL AT TRADE DISCOUNT PRICES.

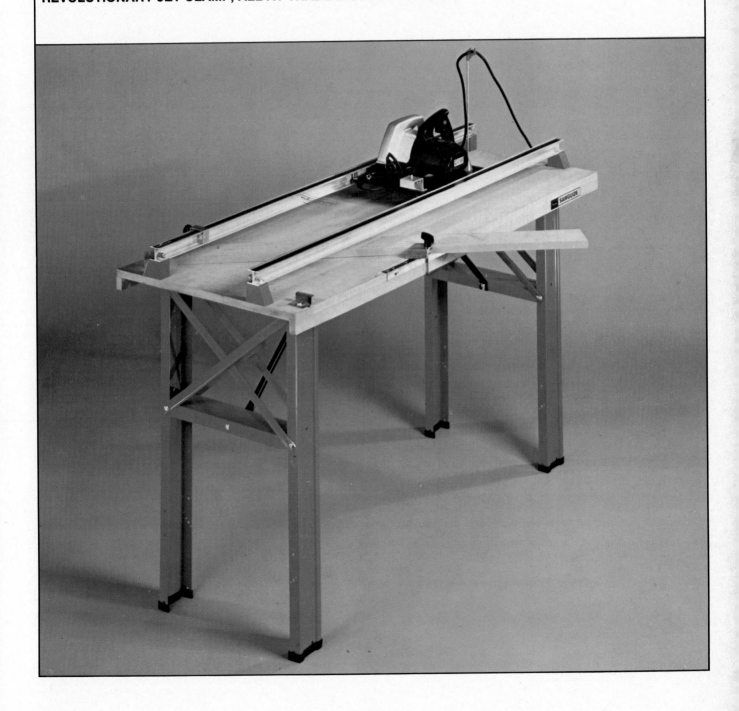

trend cutters with 1/4" shanks

One Flute Cutters

At the high speed of the router, the one flute cutters will perform very well. They are ideal for engraving and shallow pattern work. The TCT version needs careful handling to avoid breakage.

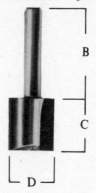

D INCH	D MM	C mm	B mm	ORDER REF	HSS	TCT
1/16 "	1.6	5	25	2/1	■	
1/8 "	3.2	8	25	2/2	■	□
1/8 "	3.2	13	37	2/20	■	□
5/32 "	4	9.5	25	2/3	■	□
3/16 "	4.8	11	25	2/4	■	□
3/16 "	4.8	19	37	2/40	■	
7/32 "	5.5	19	25	2/5	■	
1/4 "	6.3	19	32	2/6	■	□

Two Flute Cutters

Two flute cutters should give a cleaner finish than their one flute counterparts, and at the right feed speed will give clean cut edges to the work. If the material is abrasive however, use a TCT version.

* These cutters, only available in tungsten carbide, are designed for use by the amateur when grooving, rebating and trimming.

S Prefix means cutter is made from solid Tungsten.

	D INCH	D MM	C mm	B mm	ORDER REF	HSS	TCT
	13/64 "	5	16	25	3/1	■	□
	15/64 "	6	16	25	3/2	■	□
*	1/4 "	6.3	16	25	T14		□
	1/4 "	6.3	16	25	3/20	■	□
	1/4 "	6.3	28	32	3/21	■	□
	1/4 "	6.3	25	25	S3/22		□
	9/32 "	7	16	37	3/3		□
	5/16 "	8	19	25	3/4	■	□
	23/64 "	9	19	25	3/5	■	□
*	3/8 "	9.5	16	25	T38		□
	3/8 "	9.5	25	32	3/50	■	□
	25/64 "	10	19	25	3/6	■	□
	15/32 "	12	19	25	3/8	■	□
*	1/2 "	12.7	16	25	T12		□
	1/2 "	12.7	19	25	3/80	■	□
	33/64 "	13	17	25	3/9	■	□
*	5/8 "	16	16	25	T58		□
	5/8 "	16	19	25	4/2	■	□
	23/32 "	18.2	21	25	4/4	■	□
	3/4 "	19	25	37	4/5	■	□

Edge Trimmers

90° Trimmer

Bevel Trimmers

Combination Trimmers

Pierce and Trim Cutters

Ovolo (Beading) Cutters

Rounding Over Cutters

Rebate Cutters

Chamfer Cutters

Cove Cutters

All dimensions given in

A	C mm	D mm	ORDER REF
90°	12	18	46/2 □
90°	25	18	46/20 □

A	C mm	D mm	ORDER REF
90°	12	18	47/1
90°	12	18	47/2

A	C mm	D mm	ORDER REF
80°	14	20	47/3
60°	10	24	47/6A
45°	10	24	47/6B
30°	10	24	47/6C

A1 A2	C1 C2	D mm	ORDER REF
45° and 90°	6 and 6	21	47/5 □
60° and 90°	3 and 9	12	47/7 □

C mm	D mm	ORDER REF
18	7.5	47/4 □
20	6.35	47/8 ■

D mm	R mm	C mm	ORDER REF
15.1	3.2	10.2	7D/1 ■ □
21.3	6.3	13.3	7D/2 ■ □
27.7	9.5	16.5	7D/3 ■ □

D mm	R mm	C mm	ORDER REF
17.6	4.8	11.8	7E/1 ■ □
21.6	6.3	12.6	7E/2 ■ □
25.0	8	14.3	7E/3 ■ □
28.0	9.5	15.8	7E/4 ■ □
34.4	12.7	19.0	7E/5 ■ □

D mm	C mm	ORDER REF
6.35	11	8D/1 ■ □
9.5	14	8D/2 ■ □

C mm	A	ORDER REF
13.0	45°	10H/1 ■ □
11.0	30°	10H/2 ■ □

D mm	R mm	C mm	ORDER REF
4.8	4.8	12.8	13F/1 ■ □
6.4	6.4	14.4	13F/2 ■ □
9.5	9.5	17.5	13F/3 ■ □

Roman Ogee

D mm	R mm	C mm	ORDER REF
25	4	13.5	8E/1 ■ □
30	6.3	20	8E/2 ■ □

Ovolo Cutters

D mm	R mm	C mm	ORDER REF
17	5	10	7/2 ■ □
23	8	13	7/4 ■ □
28	10	15	7/5 ■ □
32	12	17	7/6 ■ □

Staff Bead Cutters

D mm	R mm	ORDER REF
20	5	9/1 ■ □
22	6	9/2 ■ □

Dovetail Cutters

C mm	D1 mm	HSS	TC	ORDER REF
9	10	15°	10°	31/1 ■ □
9.5	12			31/2 ■ □
11	14			31/3 ■ □

'V' Groove Cutters

A	C mm	D mm	ORDER REF
30°	12	20	11/1 ■ □
45°	12	15	11/3 ■ □
60°	12	13	11/5 ■ □

Radius Cutters

D mm	R mm	C mm	ORDER REF
6	3	15	12/3 ■ □
10	5	18	12/5 ■ □
14	7	18	12/7 ■ □
16	8	18	13/1 ■ □
18	9	18	13/2 ■ □

Light Duty Trimmers

These trimmers are available complete with arbor and bearing, and is available as a substitute for the one-piece trimming cutters with bearings fitted as an integral unit.

B mm	C mm	A	ORDER REF
Arbor with Bearing			33/6 ■
16	10	90°	34/6 □
Replacement Bearing			B33/6B ■

Light Duty Edge Slotters

Range of slotting blades to fit an arbor. Designed for recessing edge and weather strips, into board edges. Slotters available in various sizes to suit application.

47/7A-D

A	C mm	ORDER REF
Arbor		33/9 ■
1.5	9	47/7A □
2.0	9	47/7B □
2.5	9	47/7C □
3.0	9	47/7D □

Plunge Drill/Counterbore/Sink

WOOD SCREW REF	d	D mm	C mm	ORDER REF
No8	3/16"	9.5	20	62/80 □
No10	7/32"	12	20	62/10 □
No12	1/4"	16	20	62/12 □

Plug Maker

WOOD SCREW REF	D mm	d mm	ORDER REF
No8	9.5	16	24/80 □
No10	12	16	24/10 □
No12	16	16	24/12 □

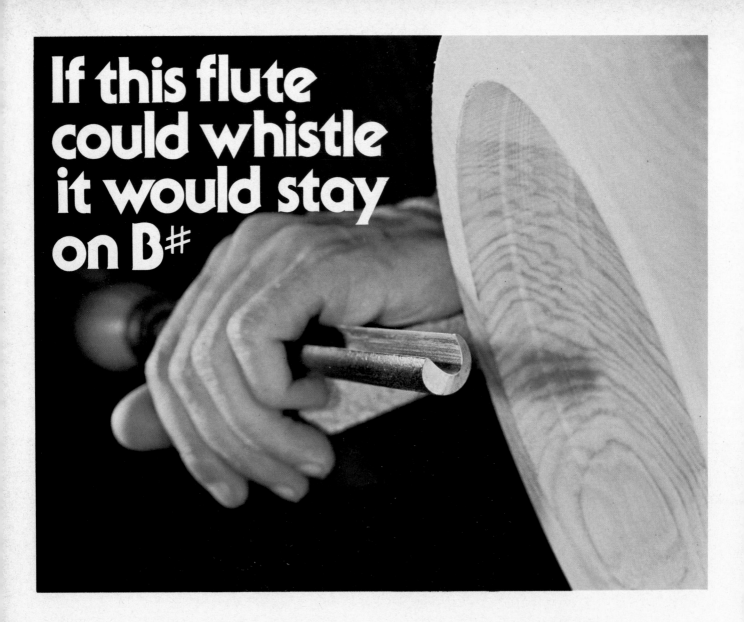

If this flute could whistle it would stay on B#

But it's not just a tone deaf flute, it's a new woodturning tool with a difference and it's from the specialists, Henry Taylor Tools.

It's been cleverly designed by Roy Child and very carefully made in High Speed steel, balanced with a comfortable handle.

It's unique, multi purpose flute shape gives fast freecutting, roughing out plus effortless control of fine finishing cuts. It slices away those rough grain patches, outperforming a full set of four bowl turning gouges, what's more it costs much less at £18.50 plus V.A.T.

That's why we call it Superflute .... it works like magic.

THIS NEW **SUPERFLUTE**

DIAMIC

Will be available at the WOODWORKER SHOW, Royal Horticultural Society's New Hall, Westminster, London. 4th — 9th November. and all main stockists of Henry Taylor Tools.

Henry Taylor Tools

The Forge. Lowther Road. Sheffield S6 2DR.
Telephone 0742 340282. Telex 547381.
Cable and Grams "Screw Sheffield".

Elektra Beckum
the
other craftsman

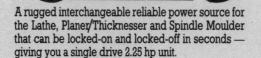
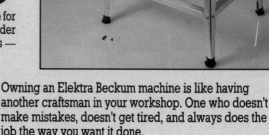

Charles Cliffe explains how to make the

SLOTTED-SCREW JOINT

The slot-screw joint, comprising hidden screws driven into keyhole slots, is a strong method of butt jointing two boards together. Screws are run at intervals along the edge of one board so that the heads project about ½in. Holes are bored in the edge of the other board to allow the screw heads to fit into them and slots of sufficient size to accommodate the shanks are cut at one side (Fig. 1).

Plane the joint absolutely true, or possibly very slightly hollow. With the face sides outwards and board X ½in. to the right of board Y, the two pieces are gripped in the vice preparatory to marking-out (Fig. 2).

incline slightly to the left. This will help to draw the joint together. Board Y is gripped in the vice and X is placed on top so that the screw heads are in the holes. With a mallet tap the top board to the left when the heads of the screws will dovetail themselves into the slots. The joint should be taken apart, the screws tightened half a turn, the joint glued and finally assembled.

If the joint has been planed slightly hollow it is as well to cramp the centres of the boards together and incline the cramp ½in. to the right so that when the joint is driven home the cramp will be at right angles to the edge.

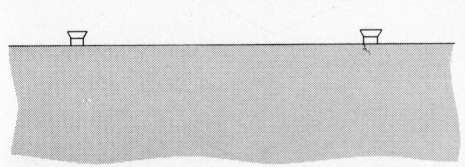

With the marking gauge set to half the thickness and working from the face sides gauge both boards.

Select a bit whose diameter is slightly larger than the head of the screw and bore holes in piece X deep enough to house the screw. With a narrow chisel cut slots slightly wider than the shank diameter to the right of these holes. The length of these slots should be between ½ and ⅝in.

Drive the screws into board Y so that they

Fig. 1 Details of slotted-screw joint

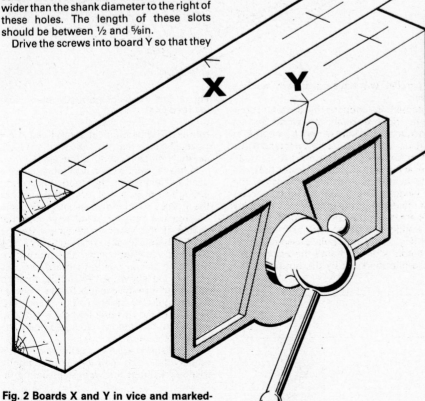

Fig. 2 Boards X and Y in vice and marked-out

Name changed

Pye Thermal Bonders Ltd, of Cambridge, which produces radio frequency (RF) generators and presses for curing timber laminations etc, is now known as Pye RF Systems Ltd. The address remains Nuffield Road, Cambridge CB4 1TW, and the company states that no other changes in policy are visualised.

Expansion at Ebac

Manufacturer of air conditioning and timber drying equipment Ebac Ltd, Greenfields Industrial Estate, Bishop Auckland, Co Durham, has extended its factory floor space from 10,000 to 14,000 sq ft. The extension will accommodate the fabrication department and allow for growth in the company's business during the next year or two.

Machinery move

Leicester Wood Technique Ltd, which handles Oppold and Howema tooling for joinery and furniture, together with its associated company Machinery Plus Ltd, the UK main agent for Lurem woodworking machinery, have moved from Biggin Hill Road, Evington, Leicester, to Hothorpe House, Main Street, Theddingworth, Lutterworth LE17 6QY. Telephone number is 0858 880643 and telex 342484.

Restoring 'junk' furniture

A 12-page guide to restoring old furniture is published by Sterling Roncraft Ltd, Chapeltown, Sheffield S30 4YP, under the title of *Junk Genius*. The projects illustrated in the booklet have been chosen to represent 'junk' rather than pieces on the fringe of the antique market and the text covers use of the company's products for stripping, filling, colouring and finishing. There are notes on cabinet furniture, mouldings and drawers and a description of the processes used in restoring tables, chairs, small cabinet, mirror and chest-of-drawers.

Limited numbers of these booklets are available. Please send sae (8½ × 6in. approximately) to Sterling Roncraft Ltd at the address given above.

Machines from Germany

Second edition of *German Woodworking Machinery* is a catalogue of products made by firms in the VDMA (the trade association of woodworking machinery manufacturers), with text in German, English, French, Spanish and Italian languages. It runs to more than 500 pages and carries some 550 illustrations of principal products as well as brief details. There is a classified index of products.

The overall format and arrangement of the publication is similar to the Ligna Hanover catalogue so many users of woodworking machinery will find themselves on 'home ground' when going through the classified index. All types of machines are included from the standard classic ones to production line equipment.

Copies of *German Woodworking Machinery* are available free of charge from the general secretary of VDMA e V, Lyoner Strasse 18, PO Box 71 01 09, D-6000 Frankfurt-Niederrad 71, West Germany.

WEDGING

**Charles D. Cliffe says:
Wedging supplements good
joinery; it does not rescue bad
work.**

In joinery wedges are frequently used to
prevent the mortise and tenon joint from
pulling apart. Common examples are window frames and framed doors. For maximum holding power the wedges must be
correctly shaped and fitted properly. Equally important the joint must fit together well.

When I was about 15, I hoped to wedge-
up an ill-fitting mortise and tenon before my
father spotted it. I was too late, of course,
and he commented sadly:

*'If it weren't for putty, paint and glue,
What would we poor joiners do?'*

Wedging supplements good joinery. It
does not rescue bad work.

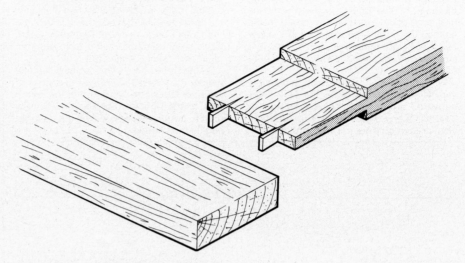

**Fig. 3 Tenon fox-wedged ready for
assembly.**

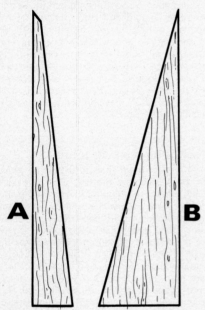

**Fig. 1 Correct and incorrect forms of
wedges.**

Two forms of wedge are shown in Fig. 1.
The correct shape is at A; the angle of slope
is acute but the point is made stronger by
being trimmed to an obtuse angle. The
wedge B is cut at too obtuse an angle which
reduces its holding power.

Having cut the mortises and tenons the
'wedging' has to be cutout to enable the
wedges to be inserted and driven home.
Fig. 2 shows one correct and two incorrect
examples. At C the wedging has been
correctly done, the slope is at an easy angle
and reaches almost through the wood. The
angles of the wedging at D are too steep and
of insufficient depth so the wedges will not
be secure. The wedging at E, having been

cut parallel, will have hardly any holding
power.

It sometimes happens that the tenon does
not go right through the wood and in
consequence the joint cannot be wedged in
the usual way. In these circumstances the
joint is fox-wedged. The mortise is made
wider at the bottom than at the top, the extra
width being equal to the thickness of the
two wedges. The tenon is slightly shorter
than the depth of the mortise and two saw
kerfs are cut in the end. The joint is glued,
the wedges are glued and inserted in the
kerfs (Fig. 3) and the whole is assembled. As
the tenon is driven home the wedges are
forced into the kerfs by the bottom of the

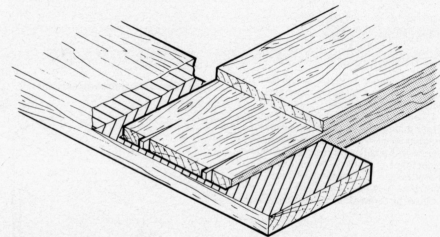

**Fig. 4 Cut away of correctly made fox-
wedged joint.**

mortise. The tenon is thus expanded into a
dovetail shape (Fig. 4). If the joint has been
carefully made it cannot come apart.

In heavy framework a tusk tenon is often
used and in this joint the tenon is made long
enough to project well beyond the end of
the mortise. The tenon is usually ½th of the
depth of the framework and is set out in the
centre of the work. In consequence the
mortise hardly weakens the wood at all. The
tenon is recessed below the mortise to
provide a strong bearing surface and it is
also sloped above. A rectangular tapered
hole is cut through the tusk to take a wedge
which holds the assembled joint securely.
The end of the rectangular hole is cut ⅛in.
nearer to the tenon shoulders than the
width of the mortised piece.

Thus if shrinkage reduces the width of the
timber the joint can be drawn tightly
together without the wedge becoming in-

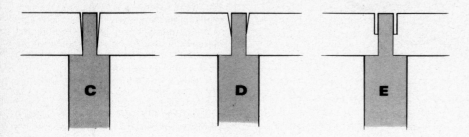

**Fig. 2 Correct and incorrect wedgings cut
out.**

Fig. 5 (Right) Tusk tenon with hole for peg and mortise. Fig. 6 (Above) Joint assembled and wedged.

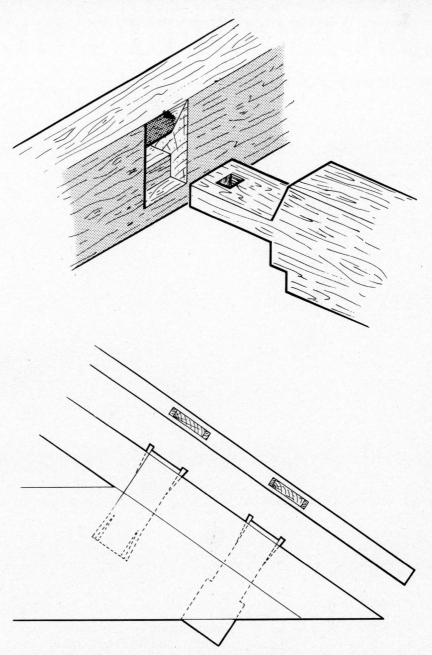

operative through 'bottoming' on the end of the rectangular hole. Figs. 5 and 6 show the joint prior to fitting and the action of the wedge when assembled. In cabinet work this joint is often used to secure the framework of refectory tables.

In some joinery work the joints are held securely together by means of folding wedges. Examples are transom rails in door and window frames where the uprights go from top to bottom in one piece and the rails are tenoned into them. The tenons are cut and fitted in the usual way and are sawn and bevelled to fit each other as shown by the dotted lines in Fig. 7, thereby forming a locked joint. To allow the bevelled tenons to pass each other the mortise is made wider than the rail, in fact twice the width of the two hooks. The extra width of the mortise is filled with a pair of folding wedges which are glued before being driven home.

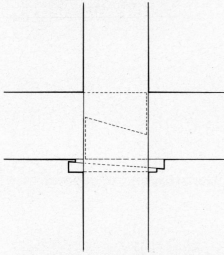

Fig. 7 (Left) Locked tenons and folding wedges. Fig. 8 (Above) Fox-wedged and loose tenon joints.

An interesting example of fox-wedged and wedged tenon joints may sometimes be seen in triangular frames such as are found under staircases. If the tenons had to be cut out of the solid rail parallel to the bottom the mortises would have to be cut at such an acute angle as to be useless. The difficulty is overcome by using two loose tenons. One is fox-wedged, the other is shouldered and inserted from the lower edge. The complete joint is glued and cramped together to make a very strong job (Fig. 8).

When a number of light window or door frames have to be glued and wedged-up there may be insufficient pairs of sash cramps available. In these circumstances a pair of wooden cramps (Fig. 9) may be made. Provided the angle of the back of the mortise and the splayed end of the cleat are the same a very good cramping effect will result.

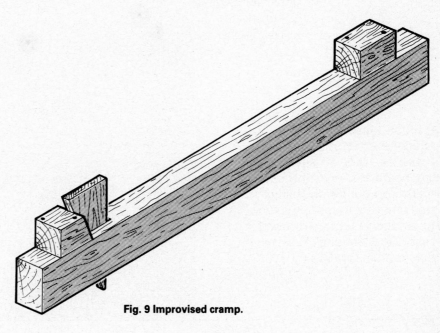

Fig. 9 Improvised cramp.

WORKSHEET 1 NEW SERIES

Record storage unit

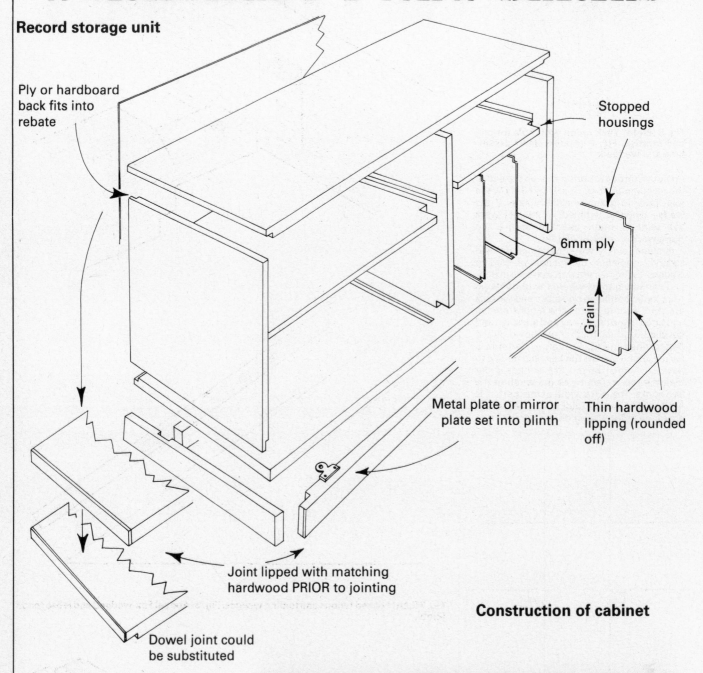

Ply or hardboard back fits into rebate

Stopped housings

6mm ply

Grain

Metal plate or mirror plate set into plinth

Thin hardwood lipping (rounded off)

Joint lipped with matching hardwood PRIOR to jointing

Construction of cabinet

Dowel joint could be substituted

A simple unit to hold audio equipment, records and cassettes. Made of veneered chipboard as shown but could be made from solid wood using traditional methods for jointing up wooden boards. A drawer for cassettes is optional. Finish with polyurethane and wax.

Cutting list Part	No.	(net sizes shown in mm and in.) Length	Width	Depth	Material
Top	1	1080(42½)	460(18)	16(⅝)	Veneered chipboard
Base	1	1080(42½)	460(18)	16(⅝)	Veneered chipboard
Ends	2	610(24)	460(18)	16(⅝)	Veneered chipboard
Vertical division	1	600(23⅝)	460(18)	16(⅝)	Veneered chipboard
Horizontal division	1	500(19¾)	460(18)	16(⅝)	Veneered chipboard
Horizontal division	1	560(22)	460(18)	16(⅝)	Veneered chipboard
Record divisions	2	430(17)	440(17¼)	6(¼)	Veneered ply
Plinth ends	2	450(17¾)	75(3)	16(⅝)	Veneered chipboard
Front	1	1050(41⅜)	75(3)	16(⅝)	Veneered chipboard
Cross member	1	1035(40¾)	75(3)	22(⅞)	Softwood
Back	1	1080(42½)	610(24)	4(³⁄₁₆)	Ply or hardboard
Fittings	6	Mirror plates			

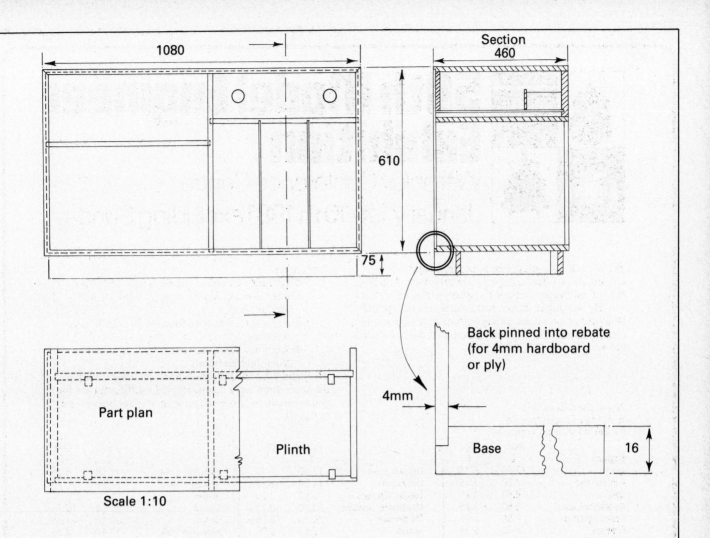

1080

Section
460

610

75

Part plan

Plinth

Scale 1:10

Back pinned into rebate
(for 4mm hardboard
or ply)

4mm

Base

16

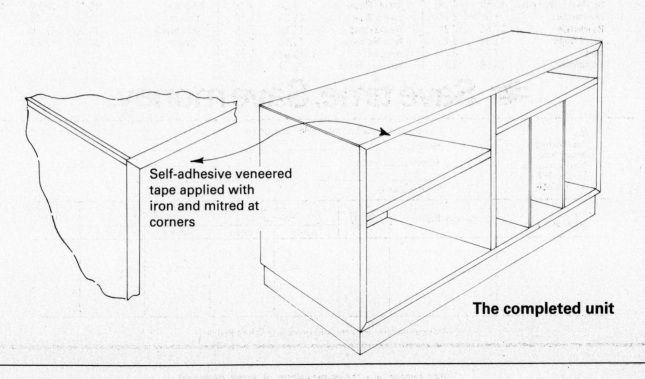

Self-adhesive veneered
tape applied with
iron and mitred at
corners

The completed unit

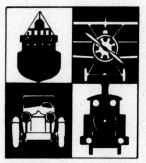

50th Model Engineer Exhibition

Wembley Conference Centre
January 1st - 10th 1981 excluding Sunday

British Rail, in conjunction with the Exhibition Organisers, is offering a special country wide inclusive rail and admission package to visitors to this exhibition.

By booking in advance you can obtain the special Rail/Admission prices, available from anywhere in the country through to Wembley Complex station, detailed below.

Remember—
* Wembley Complex station is just 10 minutes from London Marylebone by 'Quick-Link' train services.
* Regular train service from 06.00—23.30 every weekday.
* Wembley Complex station is three minutes walk from the Exhibition.

To obtain your special Rail/Admission tickets complete the application form below, allowing sufficient time for your order to be processed (at least 14 days before date of travel).

Second Class Return fares
To Wembley Complex from B.R. stations in the County/Region of—

	Adult £	Child £		Adult £	Child £		Adult £	Child £
England			Leicestershire	11.50	5.75	Yorkshire (South)	17.50	8.75
Avon	13.50	6.75	Lincolnshire	14.50	7.25	Yorkshire (West)	21.50	10.75
Bedfordshire	7.50	3.75	London (Greater)	2.50	1.25	**Wales**		
Berkshire	6.50	3.25	Manchester (Greater)	20.50	10.25	Clwyd	21.50	10.75
Buckinghamshire	6.50	3.25	Merseyside	20.50	10.25	Dyfed	23.50	11.75
Cambridgeshire	7.50	3.75	Norfolk	12.50	6.25	Glamorgan (Mid)	16.50	8.25
Cheshire	18.50	9.25	Northamptonshire	7.50	3.75	Glamorgan (South)	16.50	8.25
Cleveland	27.50	13.75	Northumberland	31.50	15.75	Glamorgan (West)	19.50	9.75
Cornwall	25.50	12.75	Nottinghamshire	13.50	6.75	Gwent	14.50	7.25
Cumbria	27.50	13.75	Oxfordshire	7.50	3.75	Gwynedd	23.50	11.75
Derbyshire	13.50	6.75	Shropshire	16.50	8.25	Powys	19.50	9.75
Devon	20.50	10.25	Somerset	14.50	7.25	**Scotland**		
Dorset	14.50	7.25	Staffordshire	15.50	7.75	Central	31.50	15.75
Durham	27.50	13.75	Suffolk	8.50	4.25	Dumfries & Galloway	31.50	15.75
Essex	5.50	2.75	Surrey	5.50	2.75	Fife	34.50	17.25
Gloucestershire	12.50	6.25	Sussex (East)	7.50	3.75	Grampian	37.50	18.75
Hampshire	9.50	4.75	Sussex (West)	7.50	3.75	Highland	40.50	20.25
Hereford & Worcester	12.50	6.25	Tyne & Wear	29.50	14.75	Lothian	31.50	15.75
Hertfordshire	4.50	2.25	Warwickshire	11.50	5.75	Strathclyde	31.50	15.75
Humberside	20.50	10.25	West Midlands	13.50	6.75	Tayside	34.50	17.25
Isle of Wight	11.50	5.75	Wiltshire	10.50	5.25			
Kent	7.50	3.75	Yorkshire (North)	23.50	11.75			
Lancashire	23.50	11.75						

≷ Save time. Save money.

To:
Area Manager,
British Rail,
Marylebone Station,
London NW1.
ref: MT/ME

Please supply the tickets listed below and send to

Name _____

Address _____

_____ Tel No. _____

S.A.E. enclosed.

From Name of Station	County/Region	Date of Travel	No. of Passengers		Fares		Total £
			Adult	Child	Adult £	Child £	

A cheque/postal order is enclosed (payable to British Rail) for £

Prices quoted are those prevailing at press date and are subject to alteration due to economic conditions.

50th Model Engineer Exhibition

Wembley Conference Centre
1st — 10th January, 1981
(Except Sunday 4th)

PLAN YOUR VISIT NOW

The Exhibition will open at 10.00 a.m. each day (not open Sunday 4th) and will close at 7.00 p.m. except on Thursday 8th, when the Exhibition will remain open until 9.00 p.m.

ADVANCE TICKETS

Advance tickets at the normal rate and advance party tickets at more favourable prices are available on all days direct from the Exhibition Manager, Model Engineer Exhibition, at the following rates:

	ADULT	CHILDREN/OAP's
AT DOOR OR ADVANCE: for small parties less than **10**	£1.50 each	£1.00 each
ADVANCE: for parties greater than **10**	£1.25 each	75p each

Teachers/Leaders of parties greater than **10**: free in ratio one per **10** in party
Teachers/leaders must remain with their parties while they are at the Exhibition

These tickets are designed to help regular visitors from waiting in long queues that often form on both the Saturdays and other well attended days. While it is not possible to guarantee that even those with advance tickets may not have to wait at the special 'Advance Ticket' position at the main entrance for a short while, these tickets will take precedence over non-ticket holders. Please use the coupon below.

Please also note the special cheaper British Rail fare rates being advertised in this magazine for those booking to come by rail in advance and that trains to and from Marylebone on the Princes Risborough line stop regularly at Wembley Complex Station, three minutes walk from the Conference Centre. Car Parking at 80p for the day is available for thousands of cars between the Wembley Stadium and the Conference Centre.

PARTY & ADVANCE BOOKINGS APPLICATION FORM

Please complete and return to:
The Exhibition Manager, Model Engineer Exhibition, Model & Allied Publications Ltd., 13/35 Bridge Street, Hemel Hempstead, Herts HP1 1EE, England.

.........................Adults at £1.50 each or at £1.25 each............
............Children/OAP's at £1.00 each or at 75p each.........
(All admission charges include VAT)   TOTAL ....

I enclose cheque/PO for amount stated above, made out to Model & Allied Publications Limited. Final date for receipt of applications for advance tickets, 1st December 1980. All aplication must be accompanied by a stamped addressed envelope.

Please forward tickets to: *BLOCK CAPITALS PLEASE*

Name ....

Address ....

....

....

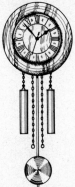

740

Prices quoted are those prevailing at press date and are subject to alteration due to economic conditions.

Woodworker, November 1980

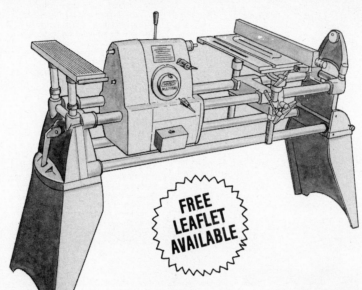

Woodworker PLANS SERVICE

Weaving, Spinning from the DAVID

TABLET LOOM

A frame developed for weaving ties, braids and belts etc., and which frees the weaver of restraints usually associated with card weaving. Designed to accommodate up to 24 cards but can double up. A most intriguing form of weaving for the beginner to commence with and even the advanced will find the frame a useful asset. Illustrated leaflet included describing how to card weave a number of patterns. Plan on one sheet.
Plan DB1 Price £2.50

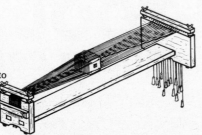

TABBY LOOM

A simple tabby loom having rollers, warp and cloth beams and fitted with a rigid heddle. Weaving widths 228mm (9"), 380mm (15"), and 508mm (20"). Canvas aprons. Ideal for beginners but it is surprising what can be achieved with warp and what colour variations, tufting etc. Plan on one sheet.
Plan DB2 Price £2.50

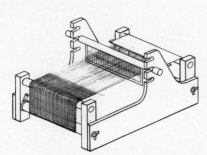

610mm (24") TABLE LOOM

A lever operated four shaft table loom. Weaving width 610mm (24"). Solid frame design uses only two mortise and tenons on the whole job. Designed for either string or wire heddles, complete with rollers, warp and cloth beams. This loom opens up the scope for a wide range of patterns. Make cushion covers, shoulder bags, scarfs etc. Plan on two sheets.
Plan DB3 Price £4.25

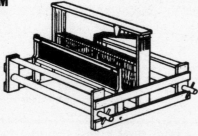

INKLE LOOM

An interesting loom designed for weaving narrow braids. Plan sheet includes three designs. A floor standing inkle which can double up as a warping frame, and two table inkles, open and closed sided. Latter will weave up to 300mm wide warp lengths 2-2.5m. Parts list and full instructions for mounting a warp on the loom. Texture produced is firm and close.
Plan DB4 Price £2.50

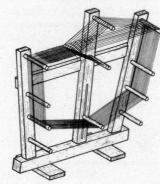

1070mm (42") FOOT POWER LOOM

A floor standing four shaft foot power counterbalance loom. Weaving width up to 1070mm (42"), but could make wider/narrower to suit if this is not the width you want. Overall height 1475mm (58"). Rugged frame design with treble roller heddle suspension assuring horizontal frame at all times. String heddles, canvas aprons, foot pedals and lamms. A design for the enthusiast on which a multitude of patterns can be woven. Make skirt lengths or weave yourself material for a suit. Plan on three sheets.
Plan DB5 Price £4.95

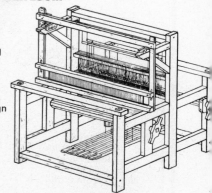

WARPING MILL

This warping mill design consists of a vertical revolving drum supported within a floor standing frame. The drum is fitted with pegs for securing the warp to, and the frame is complete with heck block for spreading warps up to 15-20 metres (15-20 yards). Plan on two sheets.
Plan DB9 Price £2.50.

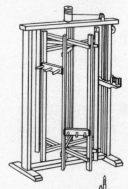

UPRIGHT SPINNING WHEEL

In this vertical style spinning wheel the mother-of-all arrangment is situated above the main wheel. The latter is 470mm (18½") diameter and the rim is of segmented design. Simpler lines than the sloping wheel above but nevertheless graceful in appearance and of course functional. Plan on three sheets.
Plan DB13 Price £4.25.

SLOPING SPINNING WHEEL

This design is a replica of an authentic spinning wheel from olden days, having a 486mm (19") diameter wheel with bent wood rim. Plan is complete with mother-of-all, distaff, treadle operation etc. A feature of this wheel is its attractive turnings which make it a most decorative piece besides being functional. A design for the enthusiast woodturner. Plan on two sheets.
Plan DB/12 — Price £4.25

SPINNING STOOL & CHUNKY STOOLS

A stool specially suited for spinning using the wheel. Solid four legged seat and upright back having a wheel motif. Complements spinning wheel design plan 12, above. Plan on one sheet.
Two stools, one 520mm (20½") high, the other 700mm (27½") high. Chunky style design, ideal for making in pine. Use as kitchen stools, bar stools, etc. The smaller one would suit the 1070mm (42") foot power loom. Ideal to have around the house. Plan on one sheet.
Plan DB20/21 — £2.50

nd Toy plans
BRYANT collection

GREAT WHEEL

The great wheel is thought to have its origins in China and introduced to this country via India and Europe. Sometimes known as walking, muckle or spindle wheels, many were used in the Wool Mills of the 17th century. At the time the invention was a significant step forward from the simple spinning spindle. The wheel shown here is a measured drawing of a hoop-rimmed wheel on display at the National Trust property Quarry Bank Mill, Styal. **Plan DB47 Price £2.50.**

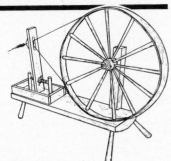

NOVELTY TOYS

Plan DB32 Price £2.50

Exciting, amusing toys for children. Five plans on one drawing, pirouetting ballerina, tumbling man, waddling duck, mystery money box, and climber. All drawn full size on a big sheet plan.

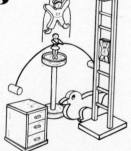

Plan DB33 Price £2.50

Six more exciting, amusing toys. Zig-Zag man, Swinging acrobat, Woodpecker-up-a-post, Wobbly wheel dog, Whip and tops, and scissor toy. All drawn full size on a big sheet plan.

Plan DB36 Price £2.50

A collection of toy cars including, saloon, sports, coupe, estate, mini, pickup truck, police patrol, racing car, dormobile and a trailer. Simple construction based on 32mm (1¼") diameter wheel size. Children will love playing with these. All drawn full size, dimensioned, parts list etc. on a big sheet plan.

Plan DB48 Price £2.50

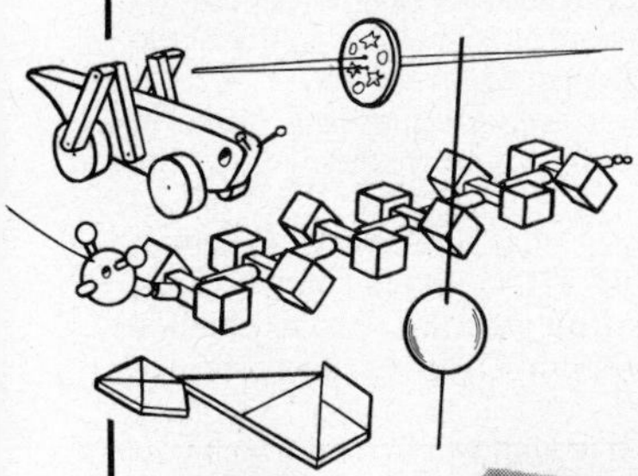

6 fascinating, easily made toys. A clunky Caterpillar pull-along is ideal for toddlers. The Grasshopper clacks its rear legs as it is pushed, a Spinning Top shows how colours can be mixed and blended, the Magic Ball can be made to slide on string giving the appearance of defying gravity, the Tangram Puzzle tests the young mind with shapes that fit together, and a Spinning Satellite completes an experimental range of very simple novelties which will give endless hours of amusement coupled with a degree of education.

PACK AWAY DOLLS HOUSE!

Plan DB46 Price £2.50

A really easy-to-assemble, open plan dolls house which several children can play with together — they can each have their own room! For parents, this dolls house offers the advantage that it can be quickly disassembled and conveniently packed away as the illustration below shows. A real space saver!

BARGAINS from BENMAIL
HURRY! LIMITED OFFERS

Here's your chance to get the big Sears Craftsman circular saw at a real bargain price

Check These Features:- 7½" Blade. Safety "lock off" button to prevent accidental starting. Push button spindle lock for easy blade changing. Rear dust exhaust. Graduated rip fence. Die cast aluminium blade guard. Precision helical gearing. Speed 5400 rpm. Cutting depth 2⅜" at 90° — 2⅛" at 45°.

MODEL No. 096-2 2⅛ HORSE POWER

MRP £89.95
Special Offer Price £62.00
You save £27.95 AND get FREE CARRIAGE (UK Mainland)

POWER TOOLS

Cat. No.		MRP	Our price
259	Dremel Moto Tool with 30 accessories	£41.80	£36.00
748-2	Craftsman 1hp heavy duty router	£89.95	£67.00
736-2	Craftsman ⅞hp router	£79.95	£59.00
721-2	Craftsman variable speed sabre saw	£42.50	£31.00
163-2	Craftsman dual action orbital sander	£45.00	£34.00
172-2	Craftsman 3" belt sander	£92.50	£68.00
320RLE	Bosch ⅜" Reversing drill with screw/drill kit	£45.50	£38.50
400-E	Bosch ½" hammer drill, 400 watt	£49.00	£42.00
620-2E	Bosch ½" hammer drill, 620 watt	£82.50	£70.00
P10	Bosch jigsaw	£37.25	£31.00
PST50E	Bosch variable speed jigsaw	£45.50	£38.50
PSS230	Bosch orbital sander	£43.50	£37.00
PWS115	Bosch 4½" grinder	£67.50	£57.25
PSP250	Bosch spray gun set	£48.50	£41.50
PKS46	Bosch 6" circular saw	£57.50	£49.00
PKS65	Bosch 7½" circular saw	£89.50	£76.00
POF50	Bosch plunging router	£55.00	£47.00
S7	Bosch milling stand	£44.50	£38.00
S8	Bosch routing bench for above	£19.95	£16.95
S2	Bosch drill stand	£19.95	£16.95
S18	Bosch lathe kit	£56.25	£47.80
1130	Barrus universal drill stand	£39.96	£31.00
1120	Barrus shaper table for above	£18.11	£14.40
1050-5	Barrus shaper att. with five cutters	£18.40	£14.60

HAND TOOLS

04	Record 2" smoothing plane	£18.98	£14.50
311	Record 3 in 1 plane	£26.11	£22.00
050C	Record combination plane, 18 blades	£52.67	£44.00
020C	Record circular plane	£43.93	£37.00
405	Record multi plane, 24 blades	£126.50	£101.50
52E	Record QR woodwork vice 7"	£36.80	£30.00
No. 1	Record metalwork vice, 3"	£21.85	£17.50
130	Record cramp heads	£8.63	£7.25
148	Record dowelling jig	£23.52	£18.50
M1160	Marples draw knife	£13.80	£11.75
M2410	Marples 12" bow saw	£13.80	£11.75
M1002	Marples set of eight turning tools	£39.68	£33.00
M60	Marples set of 12 carving tools	£58.65	£49.00
73	Stanley 10" ratchet brace	£18.80	£15.00
M444/S5	Marples set of 5 blue chip chisels	£19.09	£15.25
130	Stanley Yankee screwdriver	£15.99	£13.00
13-030	Stanley plough plane, 3 blade	£16.10	£13.00
13-052	Stanley plough plane, 10 blade	£32.99	£27.00
13-050	Stanley combination plane, 18 blades	£50.45	£42.00
D8	Disston 26" × 6pt handsaw	£21.97	£17.50

All prices include VAT
Carriage **FREE** on order over £20 (UK mainland).

Free bargain tools lists with each order. Wide range of Henry Taylor and Marples woodcarving and woodturning tools in stock.

BENMAIL, 48 Station Road, St. Georges, Weston-super-Mare, Avon BS22 0XL.

Tel: 0934 24385   *We close Thursdays*

That's the machine for me Or is it...?

Here John Mercer considers some of the reasons for buying machines and offers several useful checklists. But he says: 'The whole field of woodworking is personal experience between you, the wood and your tools. My remarks are based on my own experience; there will no doubt be others who have their own valid opinions'

Some of the processes in working a piece of wood are not always enjoyable: cutting a large piece of timber into the smaller pieces required for the project, then truing these with a plane or hand-sanding the assembled object (though most workers possess some sort of orbital sander, albeit a drill attachment). And then some of us are frustrated by our attempts to produce that really professional-looking joint; or we fail to achieve the subtle and elusive shape of an edge-mould.

For whatever reason we desire some sort of machinery to aid us. To some of us machines will always be just a way of taking the sweat out of woodwork. To professionals machines are necessary for efficiency or as the means of producing works of special quality and design that could only be dreamt of with hand tools.

As far as the amateur is concerned, it would seem a shame to spend, say, £1000 on sophisticated machinery merely to save time and sweat. I feel that with machinery we can afford to be more ambitious in the projects we carry out. Using the machines for re-sawing and truing timber we find that half the work is done. With more machines the shaping, jointing and final sanding can be done. So where has all the skill gone? Mostly it has gone into designing, thinking and jig-building and finally producing an article of greater complexity with neater joints and better overall finish. The skills required in machine woodworking are different but no less exacting than in hand processes and have to be learnt thoroughly to give greater rewards.

Having decided that a machine is what you want the next step is to get some idea of the range available. You are reading WOODWORKER and will have seen all the advertisements for machines. You can learn a lot from these about machinery specifications and prices. It is a good idea to define in your own mind what you are going to use the machine for. I find that most projects can be carried out on a machine that handles 10 × 3in. though this can vary if your interests are as diverse as toy building and bridge building. One thing to remember is that times and needs inevitably change.

When you have an idea of the type you want it is best to see it in operation. A really good opportunity to see nearly all the common makes of machines at one time is the Woodworker Show where the stands are staffed by people who know about the machines and are pleased to demonstrate them. If you do not go to the Show then you will most likely go to your nearest stockist. He should be able to show you a range of machines and demonstrate at least some of them. It may not be possible to see all the machines operating as it can be difficult to keep 50 or so models on permanent demonstration.

Here is a short checklist:

1 Is the machine the one you want?

2 Is a good manual supplied with the machine?

3 Is the manual in English? (It is your right to have one).

4 Does the stockist know what he is talking about?

5 Can you go to him later with your problems?

6 Are cutters widely available for the machine?

7 Are spares freely available?

8 Read the instruction manual. You may save yourself a lot of trouble later.

9 Are there any hidden extras you will need?

10 When you get the machine home check that you have all the pieces. If not, ring the stockist immediately.

On the subject of guarantees you will find there are no real problems with machinery. Manufacturers are extremely reasonable and will usually make exchanges without question. And, of course, your rights are protected by legislation.

Safety is an important factor in choosing a woodworking machine and, to be fair, most manufacturers are versed in the requirements of safe design of their products. But be wary of practices recommended in some manuals. I think it advisable to conform with the safety requirements of industry and though, for example, the Woodworking Machines Regulations 1974 are not enforced for home users, you can be sure that practices deemed dangerous for industry will be no safer for you. Stockists like their customers to count the notes out with 10 fingers! So do remember safety all the time. It is easy to cut a new piece of wood if you make an error. Sewing fingers back on (I am reliably informed) is neither pleasant nor always successful!

The subject of electric motors is complicated. It seems absurd that buyers get so concerned with horse power that they fail to ask the important questions:

1 Will the motor power the machine comfortably at the maximum capacity?

2 Can it be used non-stop or only intermittently?

3 Will it last a long time?

These are the really relevant questions. Knowing the horse power can only, at best, give a rough idea of the power the machine has for cutting wood. There are, for instance, bandsaws with 1hp motors which will cut 5in. solid wood. It is also possible to buy one with a 1hp motor that will cut 10in. in oak, though it costs more. The best way of judging the power of a machine is to see it running.

Castiron tops and frames are lovely to have and are probably best. But the cost is high so unless you are very serious or have a lot of money, you may have to lower your sights. There is nothing so bad about cast alloy or pressed steel that cannot be overcome: Castiron is hard-wearing and resilient but pressed steel frames can be as strong as castiron and should not be rejected on the grounds that they look flimsy.

As a simple test of the strength of the machine you have only to press gently on the table to see if it gives. A slight push on the fence will test for rigidity there.

It is not possible here to fully discuss every type of machine available so I shall deal only with the main points of the most common machines. For example the circular sawbench, radial arm saw, bandsaw, planer/thicknesser, jointer, spindle moulder and combination machines. Finding a machine having all the features listed here would either be impossible or very expensive. My remarks are intended as guidelines, you, as the buyer will have to select those you feel are most relevant to your needs.

Circular sawbench. Available as floor or bench-mounted types. The bench is always regarded as the mainstay of the workshop and therefore it is not a good idea to skimp. You will do much work on this machine so consider the following carefully:

1 What is the maximum depth of cut with the largest blade?

2 What is the maximum rip width that the fence will accommodate?

3 Can extension arms for panel ripping be fitted?

4 Can a sliding crosscut table be fitted?

5 Is a mitre slide supplied with the machine?

6 Does the table or blade tilt for bevel ripping (tilting blade is preferable).

7 Will it take a wobble saw for grooving?

8 Are there stops for returning the blade to the vertical accurately?

9 Is it guarded adequately? (40% of accidents happen on saws).

I recommend that you fit a tungsten carbide tipped (TCT) blade as soon as possible. It is true that they are expensive but they last very much longer and produce a fine finish.

Bandsaws. It is well worth deciding if you would be better off with a bandsaw or a circularsaw. The bandsaw has the advantage of large depth of cut and simplicity of use. It lacks the accuracy of a sawbench but to some users this does not matter. In the main, larger bandsaws have two wheels and the smaller versions have three wheels. Three wheels give a larger throat to the saw. Two wheel versions tend to be better for large ripping — and the blades last longer. Ask:

1 What is the maximum depth of cut?

2 What is throat size?

3 Is a rip fence and a mitre fence supplied?

4 Does it have a tilting table?

5 How many speeds does it have? (Two are preferable).

6 What are the maximum and minimum widths of blades that can be fitted?

(The wider the blade the straighter the cut).

7 Will it cut other materials such as plastics, metal, etc.
8 Has it got two wheels or three?

Radial arm saw. Probably the most accurate of power saws. The ability to keep the wood still and pull the blade through it on a track is a boon if you are using a lot of jigs to hold the work. The pre-set angles on the tilt are accurate enough for picture framing as well as crosscutting to a high degree of accuracy. But first check on the following:

1 Are attachments available?
2 What is the maximum crosscut width?
3 What is the maximum rip width?
4 Maximum depth of cut?
5 Is it easy to adjust and take up wear in the machine?
6 Can the arm be set absolutely rigid in one position?

The radial arm saw is more expensive than a sawbench but the higher cost is justified by the accuracy of operation.

Planer/thicknesser. The planer/thicknesser has largely taken over from the combination of thicknesser and separate surfacer. The thicknesser is power-fed which makes life easy and gives a consistent finish. The advantage of the thicknesser is that a number of boards can be planed to the same thickness easily; also timber can have any warp taken out in a few passes. The surfacer is hand-fed and is used to get one flat edge and one square edge before going through the thicknesser. It is also used as a jointer to give a good edge joint. Consider these points:

1 What are the capacities of the machine?
2 Is there a tilting fence on the surfacer?
3 An adjustable outfeed table can be an advantage.
4 Is a knife-setting gauge available?
5 Long tables on the surfacer are an advantage.
6 Are there two feed speeds on the power feed unit?

Planers are extremely useful but the knives must be kept sharp and accurately set up. TC knives give finer finish on the harder woods and last a long time, though they are very expensive.

Surfacer. If you cannot justify investing in a planer/thicknesser, you may decide on a surfacer only. One advantage is that the surfacer is usually capable of rebating. Your checklist is:

1 What is the width of cut?
2 Is there a thicknesser attachment available? (Usually hand-fed).
3 Are extension rollers available for longer timber?
4 Are there guards for rebating?
5 A tilting fence is a useful addition.

Spindle moulder. The spindle moulder is often the last machine to be purchased, and commonly one that you wish you had bought earlier. Though many are wary of the spindle moulder there is no reason why this machine cannot be used safely if the correct procedures are carried out in accordance with makers' instructions and all safety checks run through before starting up. The spindle moulder is much more flexible and useful than people realise.

You should check on:

1 Size of table.
2 Rise and fall of spindle.
3 Diameter of spindle — is it standard? (30mm is preferred).
4 Is a shaw guard or roller guard supplied?
5 Is a good range of cutters available?
6 Are there two speeds on the machine?
7 Is a sliding tenoning carriage available for it?
8 A drum sander is a useful attachment if available.

Combination machines. There is no list of features as each separate part of the machine can be treated as a whole. There are two main types: the separate unit with a common motor and the one-piece. With the separate machine driven by one motor there are two things to consider:

1 It can be broken down later to form the separate machines if you purchase the stands and motors.
2 It can be built up slowly.

With the monobloc types which have to be bought as one unit and cannot be split later there are some advantages:

1 Compactness for smaller workshops.
2 Usually a lower initial cost.

It is unusual to find a combination machine that can run two parts at the same time, so if two of you are using the machine you would be better off with separates. Ensure that the machine you are buying is fitted with a no-volt release switch which will prevent start-up as soon as you plug in.

No shortages on the timber side

Markets correspondent Arthur Jones reports that it is a good time to buy timber and plywood while these are plentiful and attractively priced

Woodworking craftsmen are basically concerned with two aspects of the timber trade: supply of the materials they use and the price. Most will have heard about falling prices in the timber trade and will have welcomed such a trend, especially after the very steep increases which took place in 1978 and 1979.

However, there are dangers ahead in such trends. Prices fall because there is too much wood chasing too few orders. The timber importers quickly try to correct this situation by buying less wood to match the lower sales and this means that, when demand increases after the recession, we quickly enter a phase of shortages and rising prices.

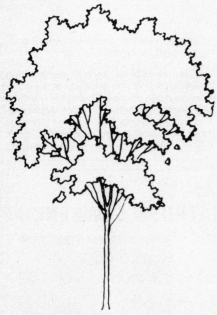

At the moment there are no shortages to worry craftsmen on the timber side. Stocks of softwood, hardwood and plywood are excellent. If anything they are still too high and forcing timber firms to make attractive offers to get quicker turnover at a time of high interest rates. Many prices, especially in hardwood and plywood, have taken a tumble this year.

Looking first at the softwood market, it must be remembered that the importers are now receiving wood which they bought at peak prices at the end of last year and the start of 1980. They have been selling 1979 wood at the lower rates. They need to push up prices if they are to make any profit on the new wood. In the present state of the market their chances are far from good.

But craftsmen normally buy top-quality joinery specifications to meet their needs, and the sharpest price falls have occurred in carcassing grades. Do not expect to see softwood prices in the right grades fall too much. They will firm faster than any other grade.

With other countries also facing the problems of inflation the Scandinavian joinery producers will be facing a real drop in earnings if they can do no more than hold present prices. There could be a small limit to the present period of low-cost offers in softwood. It could be a mistake to anticipate a continuing falling price list, and there might well be some supply problems in contrast to the present plentiful stock situation.

In the hardwood sector there are currently few difficulties in obtaining the species required; what shortages there are can usually be attributed to regional variations. Buyers near to the main importing centres of London, Liverpool and Avonmouth are best placed.

Many American hardwood species are popular and here we are reaping the benefit of a low dollar rate to the £. American oak is especially favoured and it is now selling at a cheaper price than has been seen for a long time.

Continuing to be among the most popular hardwood is Brazilian mahogany. This is still cheaper (in spite of some appreciable increases in price) than comparable W African hardwood. It is a sad truth that the volume of hardwood coming from W Africa these days is comparatively small. This means that many timbers — such as maho-

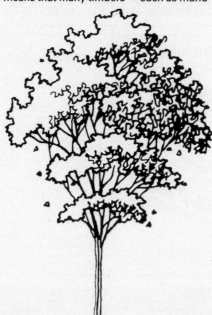

gany, afrormosia, utile — are now less plentiful and much more costly. There is unlikely to be any quick change in the African scene.

Nowadays the principal area for tropical hardwood is the Far East, and we continue to receive substantial supplies. Prices have taken a tumble this year. Countries like Malaysia and the Philippines, where all the talk was of export controls and prices were rising monthly, have seen a world slump in demand and have had to drop their prices quite dramatically. Red meranti, which rose by no less than 35% in price in a spell of six months, lost most of that gain in three months. Many Far Eastern sawmills could

not remain in operation in the face of this decline in demand.

Pricing arrangements among countries to hold up hardwood prices have come unstuck. While this helps craftsmen initially, giving them cheaper hardwood, there is little doubt that in due course the trading cycle will move on to the stage where shortages will occur and prices return to their upward movement.

Furniture manufacturers are going through a recession in Britain. They are the big hardwood users so stocks in the country should remain high, perhaps until the end of the year. Just so long as there is a lot of hardwood in stock and industrial buyers are few, then craftsmen will be able to get an exceptionally good deal from the timber stockist. But this happy state could be short-lived.

The plywood market is varied. Cut sizes provided by the Finnish market make birch plywood popular. This plywood has not been subject to the price falls of other species because of the control exercised by the Finnish producers over their production so that it does not run ahead of market demand. There has even been a small price increase this summer, in contrast to the big falls in the price of Far Eastern plywood.

Most of the Far Eastern producers are in the Komasi association. This is designed to fix the quantities available for export of the redwood plywood from the Far East, and to agree prices. They have been steadily increasing their prices for a long time but this year found that nobody would buy at their last increased price list. Sales were being made during the summer at anything up to 30% below the proposed list price, such was the collapse of the market.

American and Canadian softwood plywood has been attractively priced, helped by a slump in N American housebuilding, competition between the mills and the low dollar rate in Britain.

STAND NO. 59 — *Where you're really talking turning.*

ON THE STAND — Self selection from the tool bar — Unhandled or handled professional turning tools. Spindle Gouges ⅛″ to 1½″. Skew Chisels ⅛″ to 1½″. All Scrapers ⅛″ to 1½″. Roughing out Gouges ¾″-1″-1¼″. Bowl Turning Gouges ¼″, ⅜″, ½″, ¾″. Parting Tools ⅛″ to ½″. Beading Tools ¼″ and ⅜″. Sets of 3-5-8 in Presentation Boxes. Long and strong Chisels and Gouges. *Place your Order now and collect at the Show. Write of phone anytime.*

LONDON KIT

For your new Lathe. See our "LONDON" set of eight including ROUGHING OUT GOUGE and BOWL TURNING GOUGE.

"These are delightful tools" — WOODWORKER NOV. 78.

ON THE STAND — 600 different **CARVING TOOLS**. With or without handles. **SETS** of 6-12-18-24-30 in presentation boxes. SENEX black LIGNUM VITAE MALLETS and all sundries.

Write or phone for details of our tools and services 12 page colour catalogue 60p. No waiting. Delivery from stock.

Better buy...

British Tools

(EDGE TOOLS) LTD.
EAST KIRBBY,
SPILSBY, LINCS
Phone 07903-372

BOOK BARGAINS

While Stocks Last

Half Price!

(Returned Stock From U.S. Distributor)
(SLIGHTLY SOILED)

Clocks
10003 Electric Clocks and Chimes	£2.50	**£1.25**
10029 Electric Clocks and How to Make Them	£2.50	**£1.25**
10004 How to Make an Electric Clock	£1.50	**75p**

Do It Yourself
10037 Toyshop Steam	£4.95	**£2.47**
16005 Know Your Materials—Balsa	£1.00	**50p**
16006 Know Your Materials—Doping & Finishing	£1.00	**50p**
16007 Know Your Materials—Hardwoods	£1.00	**50p**
16008 Know Your Materials—Metals	£1.25	**62p**
16009 Know Your Materials—Plastics	£1.00	**50p**
16010 Know Your Materials—Plywoods	£1.25	**62p**

Woodworking:(including Musical Instruments)
16037 Chips from the Woodworker	£4.95	**£2.47**
16034 Door Making for Carpenters and Joiners	£1.50	**75p**
16033 Elementary Staircasing for Carpenters and Joiners	£1.50	**75p**
16003 Folk Harps	£3.00	**£1.50**
16038 Windowmaking for Carpenters & Joiners	£1.50	**75p**
16029 Woodworker Vol. 1 (1901)	£7.50	**£3.75**
16025 Woodworker Annual Vol. 81	£5.95	**£2.97**
16026 Woodworker Annual Vol. 82	£6.50	**£3.25**

To: ARGUS BOOKS LTD., Dept C, 14, St. James Rd, Watford, Herts.

Please send the Following

Code No .... Title .... £ ....
Code No .... Title .... £ ....
Code No .... Title .... £ ....
Code No .... Title .... £ ....
Code No .... Title .... £ ....
Code No .... Title .... £ ....
Code No .... Title .... £ ....

Please Add 50p for purchases up to £5
£1 up to £10 AND £1.50 thereafter to cover p&p

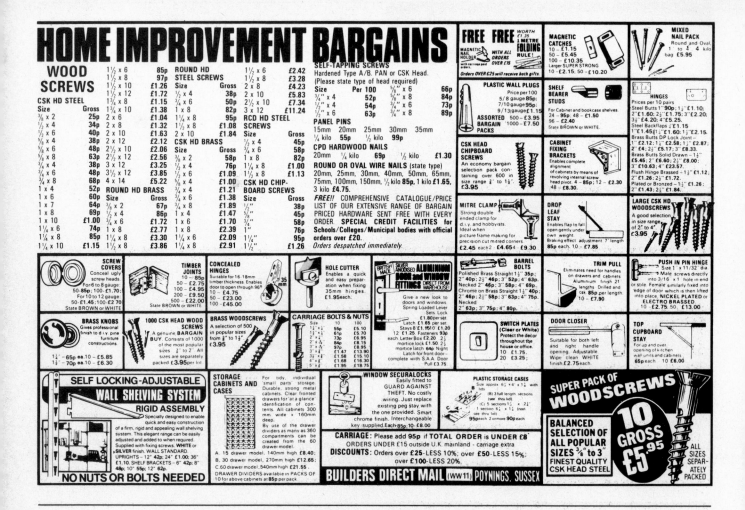

EMCO-REX 2000

Craftools are pleased to be able to offer you the amazing Emco-Rex 2000 combined planing and thicknessing machine with automatic feed.

After extensive tests by ourselves we are confident to offer you one of the finest machines on the market which is a truly attractive and economical proposition for every demanding do-it-yourselfer.

The basic machine is a very versatile 10″ × 6″ planer thicknesser, having features normally associated with more expensive machines, which can be quickly customised to your workshop requirements by the addition of the easily interchangeable accessories of a circular saw, slot mortiser and spindle moulder.

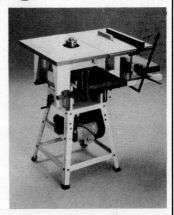

SPECIFICATION: SURFACE PLANER: 34″ × 10″ bed enabling accurate finishing of long timbers. Tilting fence to 45° and traverse to allow for natural wear of cutters. Two knife cutter block housed in high precision bearing, important for high quality planing results.
THICKNESSER: Fully automatic feed of timber up to 10″ × 6″. Fitted with serrated steel feed roller and finely ribbed discharge roller with anti-kickback teeth for your personal safety. Sensitive and easy adjustment of table by handwheel positioned within easy reach complete with calibrated scale.
CIRCULAR SAW: Depth of cut 3¼″, cants to 45°. Choice of 2 speeds, 2800/4300 rpm. giving finest cuts on all materials. Rip and mitre fence.
SPINDLE MOULDER: 26″ × 17″ table. 2″ vertical adjustment with robust 30 mm spindle. 2 speeds 6000/4000 rpm. accepting a wide range of cutters for all moulding and rebating work.
SLOT MORTISER: 5¾″ rise and fall of table. Chuck accepts bits up to 13 mm. 2 speeds 2800/4300 rpm.

CRAFTOOLS

100A ALEXANDRA ROAD, NEWPORT, GWENT.

Tel: 0633 842996

Contact us today for full details of our special offers

SPECIAL INTRODUCTORY OFFER

10″×6″ PLANER THICKNESSER COMPLETE WITH 2½ hp MOTOR & STAND	£408.00
WOOD MACHINING CENTRE AS ABOVE BUT INCLUDING SAW, MORTISER & SPINDLE	£760.00
DELIVERY	£10.00

SIMPLY POST OR TELEPHONE YOUR ORDER TODAY 10 DAYS DELIVERY

Roy Startin Limited

134 Wood Street, Earl Shilton, Leicestershire.

Tel: 0455-43254 (Office); 0455 47174 (Nightime).

HAND TOOLS
Craftsman Router Recreator (3 dimensional reproducer)	**£119.00**
1 H.P. H/D Router (Craftsman)	**£63.70**
⅞ H.P. Router (Craftsman)	**£56.22**
7½″ Circular Saw (Craftsman)	**£67.47**
3″ Belt Sander (Craftsman)	**£65.50**

BAND SAWS
De-walt BS1310, 2 speed	**£259.00**
Kity 7212, on stand 1.5 H.P. motor	**£299.00**
Burgess Mini Bandsaw	**£59.00**

CIRCULAR SAWS
Kity 7037, 2 speed, 3″ cut, on baseplate with double-ended motor, ideal starter pack for your Kity combination	**£268.00**
Mafell saw bench, 92mm cut, tilt blade, 3 H.P. motor	**£135.00**

PLANER THICKNESS MACHINES
Kity 7136 (10″ × 6″)	**£575.00**
Electra HC260 (10″ × 6″)	**£379.00**
Emco REX2000 (10″ × 6″)	**£430.00**

DISTRIBUTORS IN LEICESTERSHIRE FOR:
KITY, ELECTRA, DEWALT, ZINKEN, CRAFTSMAN, BOSCH, BLACK & DECKER, SUMACO, EMCO.

SPINDLE MOULDERS
Kity 7227	**£380.00**
Electra TF100K (less motor)	**£281.45**
Electra TF100K (with motor)	**£368.00**
Set of 12 cutters and block for Electra	**£85.00**

COMBINATIONS
Kity 7042, including 617 saw, 636 planer, 627 spindle, 652 slot borer, 700 table D/E motor	**£1,260.00**
Zinken compact, including industrial guards	**£1,250.00**
International K5, 2″ saw, 6″ × 4″ planer thickness, spindle moulder and slot borer	**£590.00**

DUST EXTRACTORS
Kity 695	**£199.00**
Electra (complete with hose)	**£170.00**

GRINDERS
Electra TN150W wet and dry grindstone	**£124.00**

ALL PRICES INCLUDE V.A.T., PAYMENT BY C.O.D. OR CASH WITH ORDER, ACCESS CARDS ACCEPTED.

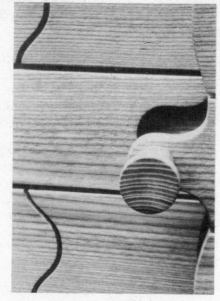

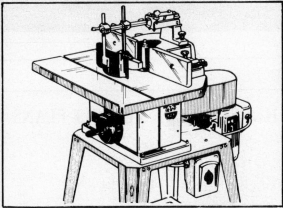

PHOTOCOPY SERVICE

We are able to supply photocopies of articles from many past issues of WOODWORKER at a nominal cost of 10p a page (minimum 50p) plus postage. Readers are asked to give month and year of the issue required to Mrs Anne Duncan at WOODWORKER office which is PO Box 35, Bridge Street, Hemel Hempstead HP1 1EE (0442 41221).

We cannot guarantee to supply photocopies from all past issues as unfortunately the office files of back-numbers are not complete.

Woodworker, November 1980

Prices quoted are those prevailing at press date and are subject to alteration due to economic conditions.

751

Cowells Jigsaw
Rugged, trouble-free design

Widely accepted by educational
authorities for use in schools,
this jigsaw is indispensable for
the modelmaker and handyman
who are looking for a no-nonsense,
hard working machine.

- One piece body casting
- Balanced crankshaft to minimise vibration
- Built-in safety features
- Large diameter spindles and bearings for long, continuous trouble-free work
- A price anyone can afford
- Cuts wood, plastics, metal, slate, bone etc.
- Continuously rated motor

Write to us **now** for details, and address
of your nearest stockist

Cowell Engineering Limited

Oak Street Norwich NR3 3BP England
Telephone (0603) 614521 Telex 975205

Don't settle for less.

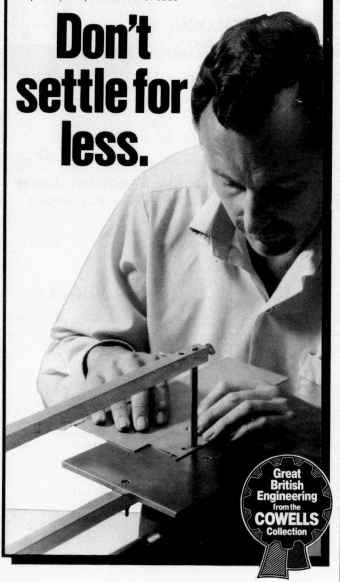

Great British Engineering from the COWELLS Collection

QUESTION BOX

Limed oak suite
From: A. F. Codling, Wallington, Surrey

I have bought a solid oak dining suite which is 40 years old, light in colour and with a limed oak finish. I recall the former owner 20 years ago rubbing a white powder into the grain and then applying wax polish.

The table extends to 7ft 6in. and the two leaves are in perfect condition but the centre is marked and the grain very open and dirty. I have tried brushing with no effect. The sideboard is slightly marked (a ring where a glass has stood) and the grain dirty. Also this piece has darkened in comparison with the table and chairs.

Can you advise please?

The usual difficulty is to know just what has been applied to the wood over 40 years. Mostly, either a liming paste or one made from unslaked lime and water would have been rubbed into the bare wood across the grain, and after drying rubbed down lightly with glasspaper, then sealed with a coat of white french polish and finally finished with a white wax polish in which was incorporated zinc white powder to help to increase the white deposit.

There were slight variations on the theme, but the final finish was either white french polish or wax on top. Too much wax applied over the years without being rubbed out and burnished would tend to collect dirt. This might account for the difference in colour of the various items.

To restore the whole suite, it would seem that it ought to be stripped right down, resanded and refinished but this is not the sort of thing to be attempted if there are restrictions on space and expertise.

We suggest you tackle the centre leaf of the table first: clean this up by sanding and use of white spirit. That is to say, white spirit and a nylon washing-up pad will remove dirt and surplus wax, and sanding (by hand or portable machine) will get you back to bare wood. On no account must water be used to clean the wood; and metal cabinet scrapers for smoothing must be avoided like the plague unless everything is absolutely dry. Moisture and iron salts combine with tannin in oak to make an ink-type stain that is difficult to remove. Even perspiration on the hands can provide that moisture.

When the wood is properly sanded and brushed lightly to remove sander dust from the pores, complete by wiping over with a clean cloth dampened with white spirit. Obtain a proprietary liming paste, or mix whiting with water to form a thick paste and rub this well into the grain (remember moisture/metal already referred to). When this is dry brush off surplus whiting paste across the grain, then with a clean rag rub well with the grain. Finish with a white wax polish made from paraffin wax, turps and zinc white. Although you will be restoring the centre top, if properly done it will appear lighter than the extension leaves; this will gradually adjust as the centre top is exposed to light.

Be careful in attempting to clean the extension leaves; white spirit will do the job if used sparingly. The same remarks apply to the legs and under frame. Use your experience with the table eventually to tackle the other items; but with large areas such as top, sides and front of a sideboard, the treatment meted out to one part must be followed exactly for the others. One of your local merchants could no doubt supply the liming material and white wax.

Colour change in wood
From: J. D. Ralphs, Milton Keynes, Bucks

I carve mainly small figures and abstracts in locally-obtained hardwood such as elm, beech, holly and box. My normal method of finishing is to fill the grain with home-made button polish, rub down with fine steel wool and polish with beeswax.

This invariably darkens the wood to a strong yellow or brown whereas I prefer to keep as light a shade as possible. I have tried filling with white french polish and using the whitest beeswax I can obtain, but there is little improvement.

I have noticed some professional carvings in elm and beech finished to a pale colour — almost a silvery creamy-grey. I was told the carver used no filler but a Renaissance wax developed by the British museum for preserving vellum. Have you any information about this?

I find that most of my carvings in box darken to a deep yellow within a year or so and that the rate of darkening is very variable and unpredictable to the extent that an insert or addition, even if carried out at the time of the original carving with wood from the same block, remains distinguishable almost indefinitely. Is there anything I can do to prevent or control the darkening process; and what is the explanation?

The natural colour of wood is progressively lost on exposure to light, the type and degree of colour change depending on various factors directly related to the wood and associated with the time element which, in turn, is related to the type of exposure. All wood contains various colouring pigments together with various substances and compounds like tannin, acids and so on. And all wood contains some moisture. Even your carvings probably contain at least 6% of moisture, ie considered as weight of water to weight of wood.

Exposure to light causes a chemical reaction to occur in the pigments of the wood causing these to darken, eg the freshly-sawn yellow colour of iroko will very quickly begin to take on a warm, 'teak' brown colour, while the whiteness of freshly-sawn holly, sycamore and box-wood will tend to yellow. Freshly-sawn beech is whitish in colour but progressively takes on a light-brown cast. If, however, the freshly-sawn wood is placed in a drying kiln and subjected to heat in order to dry it rapidly, the warmth and humidity created in the wood will turn its colour to quite a dark reddish-brown, not just at the surface but throughout the thickness. This colour is relatively fast if the wood is used indoors but if left in the open air will gradually turn greyish.

Any substance applied to wood will, in itself, cause a colour change however slight; and although 'clear' finishes tend to slow down the action of light on the pigments, there is a limit as to how much darkening they can reduce.

With your boxwood the yellowing would be progressive so that were a piece of the same original piece of wood to be inserted, while this would also yellow it would do so at a different rate in the first place and, as an insert, would no doubt be smaller than the original and accordingly contain slightly less chemical pigmentation. Hydrolysis, ie decomposition of a chemical compound by the addition of water, enters into the reasons for colour changes in wood, as occurs in the red beech mentioned and in western red cedar used externally (which eventually goes silver-grey if left untreated). We know of no way short of introducing a bleach into the finishing of very light-coloured woods which will be successful in the long term. We suggest you ask the British museum if it will disclose the recipe or formula of the Renaissance wax you mention.

Making pine furniture
From: S. C. Clark, London SE23

I wish to make a set of kitchen furniture in pine in the traditional English farmhouse-style. Can you please tell me how I can get an antique finish rather than a bright, clear finish? Also is there a particular kind and grade of timber that I should specify to the merchant for this kind of furniture?

Part of the answer to your inquiry lies in the choosing of a good design since, suitably traditional, it will tend to emphasise the almost antique appearance of what might be termed old-fashioned English farmhouse furniture as opposed to modern contemporary styles.

If your design is in line with what you want to achieve then, really you cannot do better than use a modified polyurethane for finishing, for example one of the proprietary brands which has no shine and is resistant to hot plates, dilute acids and so on. The various types of this particular brand are compatible one with another. It is therefore possible to mix, say, matt with semi-gloss or gloss to produce the right appearance.

We would not especially recommend you to try bleaching your wood to obtain a dull antiquated appearance, or to wash the wood down with a strong soda solution. We are sure this would not give the right appearance and the wood could become patchy in some circumstances.

As for the pine itself, this is known in the trade as European or Russian redwood. The best grade you will probably find will be 'unsorted', ie it is a composite grade incorporating 1st, 2nd, 3rd and 4th quality. If it is practicable to shop around and select the timber yourself, then this is desirable but suppliers will select for you against your specification.

Reverting to the finish, the only way to get the right type would be to experiment on some spare wood of the same species. And on the subject of designs you may well find much useful information in a book such as V. J. Taylor's *The Construction of Period Country Furniture*, published by Stobart & Sons Ltd, London.

HAMILTON

57-59 Regent Street, Plymouth PL4 8HD

NEW

scheppach

HMO RANGE

Come and see this exciting range of machines from Scheppach being demonstrated on Stand No. 65.

Planer Thicknesser, Circular Saw, Band Saw, Slot Mortiser and a clever combination based on the Planer Thicknesser.

They'll all be there and they're all new!

NAME ....

ADDRESS ....

....

.... TEL. ....

Send now for more information to 57-59 Regent Street, Plymouth PL4 8HD

QUESTION BOX

Sawblades

From: J.K.A. Latko, New Ash Green, Kent

In cutting the segments for built-up turning I use a radial saw but cannot obtain a clean crosscut. I have three blades for the saw: HSS universal having 72 teeth and supplied with the machine; a TCT universal blade with 32 teeth; and a TCT precision blade having 64 teeth (mentioned in the instructions supplied with the machine).

The first two blades have been professionally sharpened recently. The third blade is new. The HSS blade opens a wide gap on entering the wood. The universal TCT blade does not give a clean cut. The precision blade seems to groove the wood (on the engine side) when leaving the cut, as shown on the specimen.

Can you please advise what kind of blade I should use?

You do not say what type of saw tooth you are using for this operation and we advise you to study the reference to saws on pp 530-1 of WOODWORKER for August 1980 to obtain the correct type.

However there are various other factors which we feel should be checked as well, not least the correct speed for the saw and again the reference in August mentions this. The specimen you sent indicates that the poor results obtained are evidence of what is known as saw wobble.

This can be attributed to a variety of causes such as play in the radial arm mechanism; slackness in the saw spindle bearings; poor fit and tightness of the saw collars and retaining nut. All these should be carefully checked and rectified as necessary.

Condition of the machinery apart, the most likely cause of the trouble is to be found in the nature of the operation being carried out. The oblique cut being attempted will cause the saw plate (which is usually of a light gauge as fitted to these machines) to deflect and set up a wobble which results in a poor finish.

On a conventional table circular saw this can be eradicated by packing the saw with felt guide pieces, but this is not possible on a radial arm saw. You might try taking a series of light cuts gradually increasing the depth until the piece is severed; or alternatively obtain a heavier gauge saw blade. We suggest that you refer to the saw manufacturers for advice on this aspect.

Another approach would be to saw the segments slightly oversize, poor finish and all, and use a planing jig to accurately shoot the pieces to finish size. This jig can easily be made by adapting a conventional shooting board by the addition of a wedge-shaped piece placed against the stop bar to bring the segment face parallel to the running edge of the board. Such a planed finish will be superior to any sawn fit.

Decorating a chair

From: A. J. Swain, Bromham, Bedford

I wish to make in mahogany, an elbow dining chair of the Regency period. The design involves inlay work and painted floral sprays. Must the inlay be inset into the groundwork or is it permissible to veneer the field, effectively employing marquetry? I ask this because the member to be inlaid is the top back rail which will be bowed in plan and I do not have mahogany of sufficient section. I can only improvise by using softwood veneered on all four surfaces.

Regarding the painted floral decoration: how is the wood treated before painting so as to control absorption? Is the painting fixed before application of finish? Which type of finish is recommended and is any special treatment involved?

Is the wood of the fig tree of any use in furniture and cabinet making?

The first part of your query illustrates the perpetual challenge faced by woodworkers in dealing with their materials. The tax on one's adaptability and ingenuity to successfully employ a right technique for a particular situation brings with it much of the fun of the craft. If you feel that veneering the rail is right then you have no problem. It is certainly a solution that has been used many times before.

As to the painted floral decoration you do not say whether you propose using stencils or free-hand techniques, but the general method of procedure is the same.

The wood to be decorated should be given a coat of clear size, such as white french polish, to provide a substrate. This should be lightly flatted when dry using the finest grade of glasspaper (rubbing two pieces of 00 glasspaper together to reduce their cut will do the trick).

The actual painting may be undertaken with poster colours, which are brilliant and opaque but do tend to lie thickly on the surface, and artists' oil colours are to be preferred. While some of the pigments in these colours are dense and need only one application, others are so thin that two or more applications may be necessary. The addition of zinc white usually overcomes this transparency with the net result that the tone of the colour is altered. Thus it is advisable that a trial run be carried out before attempting the final job.

When thoroughly dry the painting may be fixed with a coat of brush polish, after which it may be wax polished; here again a slight toning down of the colours will be observed.

It is interesting to note that many of the practitioners of the renewed interest in traditional canal boat painted ware, which include numerous wooden items, use the modern enamel or cellulose-based paints for their effects.

Finally, the wood of the common fig tree has little to commend it for cabinet making purposes. It is a white somewhat 'fleshy' wood with little durability.

Can you help?

Until recently C. H. Collier of Bexhill on Sea, Sussex, was able to buy garden rakes made of cane. But not now, so Mr. Collier wonders if he could make one. 'The snag so far as I am concerned is in bending the cane and maintaining its rigidity. Can you assist by providing any information as to the bending,' he asks?

If readers are able to help their letters will be passed to Mr Collier who, incidentally, describes cane rakes as 'very useful because of their lightness and surprising strength.'

In the reference to saws in the August issue the drawings of saw teeth types may be somewhat confusing. We therefore give here simplified diagrams.

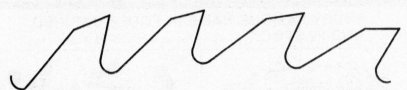

No 1:
Ripsaw teeth lean forward and are said to have a positive hook or rake. Sharpened on the tops only.

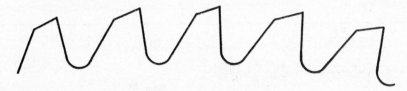

No 2:
Crosscut teeth lean back and are said to have a negative hook. They are bevelled on the leading edge as well as the top.

No 3:
Saw for laminated boards and plywood. Numerous small teeth avoid whiskered and chipped edges.

PROTECTIVE GARMENTS

A COMPLETE RANGE FOR ALL PRACTICAL PURPOSES

- Direct from manufacturer to Education and Industry
- 7 Day dispatch from receipt of order
- All garments fully guaranteed
- Prices firm for 12 months from January 1st
- The best value for money

for Brochure and Price List contact:

MOORFIELD
of LANCASHIRE

**PERSEVERENCE MILL
OLIVE LANE DARWEN
LANCASHIRE BB3 3DS
TEL. 0254 - 74131-2-3**

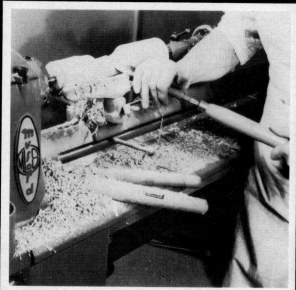

Below: Emco-Rex 2000 multi-purpose machine with attachments fitted. For photo purposes guard to spindle moulder not shown.

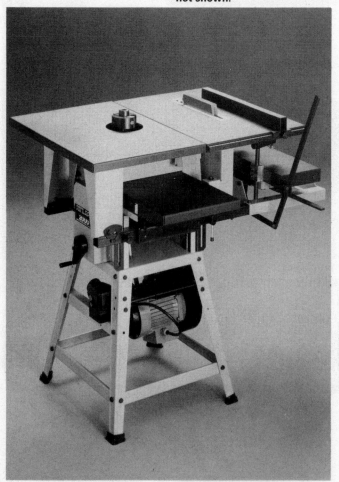

Multi-purpose

Though basically a planer/thicknesser with feedworks, the Emco-Rex 2000 can perform other operations by means of attachments, namely saw, mortiser and spindle moulder. These are locked to the thicknessing table as desired, though it is said that once assembled the saw and mortising attachments need not be removed. This permits planing and thicknessing to be continued without conversion and resetting.

The basic machine has planing table 850mm long and thicknessing table 450mm long with respective widths of 260 and 250mm and 3mm maximum depth of cut. Feed is given as 5m/min and cutter speed 6000rpm. Power comes from a single-phase or three-phase a.c. motor of 2·5-2·8hp input capacity. Covered drive is provided along with safety features such as anti-kickback guard, chip clearance hood etc.

Saw attachment has 250mm diameter blade giving 82mm depth of cut at speeds of 2800 or 4300rpm. The 650 × 430mm table can be tilted to 45°. The

Above: Emco-Rex 2000 multi-purpose machine shown as basic planer/thicknesser.

mortiser has a 450 × 200mm table with 110mm clamping height and is adjustable. Chuck capacity is 0-13mm and operating speeds are 2800 or 4300rpm. Spindle moulder table is 650 ×

430mm with height adjustment of 50mm. Cutter spindle is 30mm diameter and speeds are 6000 or 4000rpm. The milling cutterhead is 100mm diameter and approximately 40mm wide with 30mm bore.

Emco-Rex 2000 is made in Austria and introduced here by E.M.E. Ltd, B.E.C. House, Victoria Road, London NW10 6NY (01-965 4050), from which leaflets, prices and other details may be obtained.

Portable sawmill

An improved version of the Philip Cole portable sawmill is being marketed. Mr Cole tells WOODWORKER: 'It has greater capacity, stronger chain, protective guards, is cheaper and British-made.' Price for a 36in. machine with chain, guards, extension pieces and washers for lap boarding and with two Stihl 075AVE (111cc) engines is £899 ex VAT and delivery charges. There is a range of optional accessories. Mr Cole is at 16 Kings Lane, Flore, Northampton NN7 4LQ (0327 40337 — evenings and weekends).

The mill consists of a double-ended guide bar with attached verticals and side rollers. A roller frame is rigidly clamped to the verticals but this can be adjusted up or down by undoing two knobs. Two conventional chain-saw engines power the specially ground chain and wooden barriers are fixed between the power units and the verticals as a safety measure.

Maximum width of cut is 36in. but it is said that larger butts can often be dealt with by doing a slab cut, rotating 180° and repeating this on the other side to bring the width within 36in. The butt is then rotated a further 90° and milling starts in the normal way. Maximum thickness of cut is 15in. or 26in. with extensions. Under average conditions cutting rate is said to be 6-7sq ft/min.

For further details, price list and leaflet write to Philip Cole at the address given above.

Double mitre saws

Haffner double mitre saws which can simultaneously mitre both ends of windowframe sections are available from C. D. Monninger Ltd, Overbury Road, London N15 6RJ (01-800 5435). Machines of special length can be supplied to order and versions with one saw head for single-ended operation are available on request.

Wood, plastics or metal sections up to 3.5m may be mitred depending on which model is selected: DGS180, DGS181 or DGS182. Minimum cutting length varies from 100 to 500mm according to model and whether the cutting heads are perpendicular or tilted through 45°. Maximum cutting width and depth range up to 200 and 110mm respectively.

All models are pneumatically operated and automatic and two independent 3-phase motors (2200W for the 180 and 182 and 2900W for the 181) run the saw blades at 3800 and 3200rpm respectively. Extraction channels are built into the machines.

Leaflets and further details can be had from Monninger.

Routing ropes and spirals

Router Crafter (model 2525) takes advantage of the router's versatility by providing a means of mounting a workpiece and guiding the router for a number of precise shaping operations, states Hagemeyer (London) Ltd, 25-33 Southwark Street, London SE1. It will handle square or round workpieces 1-3in. thick and up to 36in. long to produce straight or tapered parts with beads, coves, flutes and also right or left-hand ropes or spirals. Hollow centre parts can also be made.

The machine is supplied with mounting clamps for fixing to bench or other surface. Construction is of diecast aluminium with chromed metal tubes and the weight is approximately 12lb. Further details and leaflet can be had from Hegemeyer.

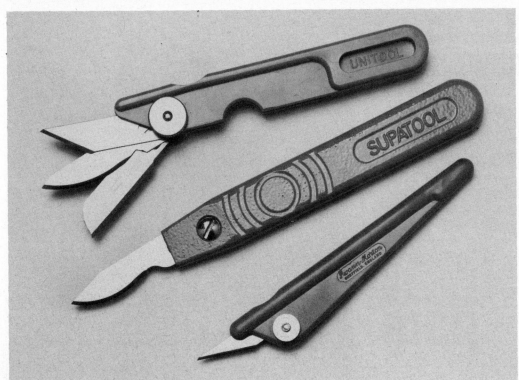

Knives for marquetry

The Craft Tool from Swann-Morton Ltd, Penn Works, Owlerton Green, Sheffield S6 2BJ, comes with three blades, each one shaped for a specific purpose. These are held in the handle by pressure exerted by a knurled screw — when this is loosened the blades can be moved in and out as required.

The company states that the blades have surgical-style cutting edge and are produced from the same steel as scalpel blades. The Craft Tool (available through most craft shops and stationeres) is said to be useful for marquetry.

Other items from Swann-Morton include the Unitool comprising three heavy-duty scalpel blades fitting into a handle; and Supatool, the handle of which can accommodate a choice of five heavy-duty blades.

Left top: Unitool; centre Supatool; bottom Craft Tool supplied with three blades each shaped for a specific purpose.

Machines from Multico

Two interesting machines are introduced by Multico Co Ltd, Brighton Road, Salfords, Redhill RH1 5ER (Horley 2444). These are SM160 spindle moulder and RA630 14in. radial arm crosscut saw. The spindle moulder has castiron table 900 × 760mm (35½ × 30in.) with parallel T-slot machined across the table length to permit use of cast mitre fence and slide supplied with the machine. Raising and lowering of the spindle assembly is controlled by a large balanced handwheel operating through a vertical lead screw and spiral gear movement. Three-phase versions of the machine have 4/5hp two-speed motor giving cutter head spindle speeds of 3600 and 7200rpm; single-phase versions have 3hp single-speed motor giving spindle speed of 7200rpm.

Both single and three-phase versions have reversing switch for reverse rotation machining and the latter have rotary switch for easy speed change. The electrics are controlled by mushroom-head no-volt release starter switch and electro magnetic and mechanical foot brake provides instant stop on the cutter head.

Vertical stroke of spindle is 160mm (6¼in.) and weight of the machine is approximately 300kg. Horizontal chip extraction shute is available for 125mm hose as an accessory.

Left: Craftsman model 2525 Router-Crafter with a 1hp Craftsman router mounted thereon, c/w example work pieces.

The radial arm crosscut has maximum depth of cut of 115mm (4¼in.) and the 355mm (14in.) diameter blade is powered by a 3hp motor secured in a cast cradle bearing-mounted on the main overarm. Crosscut capacity is 630mm (24¾in.) and ripping capacity 930mm (36⅝in.) with standard table and 1m with table modification. The motor unit may be locked in any position along the overarm and revolved in a horizontal plane through 360° with positive stops at prime angles and tilted in a vertical plane through 90° with positive stops at prime angles.

The motor is controlled overall by a thermal no-volt overload release starter wired into a trigger switch on the main control switch on the main control handle. An 80mm extraction outlet (adjustable vertically for ripping) is fitted to the main guard with anti-kickback fingers; extraction hood for crosscutting is an optional accessory.

Main worktable is made up of two sections of HD chipboard. The main section is bolted to a sub-frame which in turn is bolted to the main base. The sub-frame has two clamp screws on the top side which secure the right-angle wood fence, together with a distance piece.

Specifications and leaflets relating to the machines and their accessories are available on application to Multico.

Right: Multico SM160 spindle moulder comes in single and three-phase versions.

For pokerwork

Plaques, boxes, gift and kitchenware articles in sycamore, lime, beech and box are now supplemented by several sizes of square and rectangular boxes in lime. The items are from Janik Wood Crafts, Brickfield Lane, Ruthin, Clwyd LL15 2TN (08242 2096), which states that these and pokerwork tools etc are available from craft shops or direct from the Ruthin address. Prices and other details can be had on application.

762   **Prices quoted are those prevailing at press date and are subject to alteration due to economic conditions.**   Woodworker, November 1980

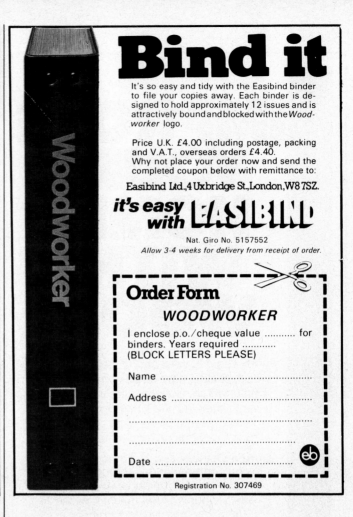

IMPROVE YOUR HOME WITH WOOD

Have you given up in disgust because your projects didn't work out? Instead of feeling proud, could it have all been much better? Don't give up, working with wood can be very satisfying. We'll help you achieve professional results you'll be proud of and save you pounds on home improvements.

During October and November we'll be giving demonstrations throughout the country. We can show you how easily woodworking machinery can help you improve your home – come and see for yourself.

Return the coupon and we'll send you a list of demonstration venues and a free extra-long carpentry pencil.

FREE CARPENTRY PENCIL

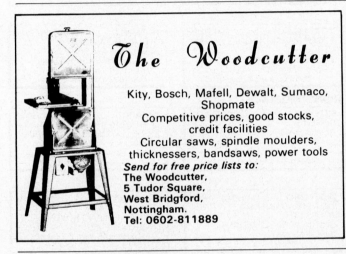

Classified Advertisements

From:

....

....

....

I enclose remittance value.......................to cover ....

Insertions under the heading:

WORKSHOP EQUIPMENT	☐	BOOKS, PUBLICATIONS, ETC	☐	
COURSES	☐	GENERAL	☐	
CRAFT AND ANTIQUE TOOLS	☐	MATERIALS	☐	
WANTED	☐	FOR SALE		

To: **WOODWORKER**
CLASSIFIED ADVERTISEMENT DEPT.
P.O. BOX 35, 13 BRIDGE STREET,
HEMEL HEMPSTEAD, HERTS. HP1 1EE

★ Lineage rate 14p a word. Minimum charge £2.40

✦ Semi display single column cm= £3.00 (Minimum £7.50 which is 2.5 cm. Maximum 5 cm)

★ Box number 50p extra

Name and address if to appear must be paid for

BLOCK CAPITALS PLEASE

Classified Advertisements

Telephone Gillian Wynn

(0442) 41221 Ex.241

All classified Advertisements must be pre-paid.
Private and trade rate 14p per word (minimum £2.40). Box Numbers £1.00
extra. Display box rates s.c.c. £3.00 (min. £7.50). All advertisements are inserted in the first available issue.
Box replies to be sent care of Advertisement Department, P.O. Box 35,
Bridge Street, Hemel Hempstead, Herts, England HP1 1EE. There are no
reimbursements for cancellations.

FOR SALE

EXCITING IDEAS IN FURNITURE-MAKING FOR NEWLYWEDS, D.I.Y. AND UNSKILLED

ALL you need are a few SIMPLE tools to make your own RE-PRODUCTION, MODERN AND GARDEN FURNITURE etc., from our EASY TO COPY PLANS and SIMPLE CLEARLY MARKED assembly instructions. EACH PLAN is FULL-SIZED. Just trace the plan on wood etc., similar to a dressmaking pattern. SO SIMPLE over 60 plans to choose from. FREE plumbing hints leaflet with each catalogue. Many satisfied customers who re-order once they try the plans. Send 60 p&p inc. TODAY for catalogue to Hamlyn Dept. D.W. 57 Lyneham, Wilts, SN15 4PH.

Chair illus. made in less than a day from plan No. 35 price only £1.99.

CORONET CONSORT (blue), extra long lathe attachment and cabinet stand. Excellent condition £350.00 ono. Tel: Stonehouse (045-382) 2445.

MYFORD, CORONET, B & D., Arcoy attachments, accessories. SAE details. Pyatt, 'Melfort', Park Lane, Cheadle, ST10 1PD. Tel: (053-84) 3361. UV

WELSH SLATE sharpening stones for sale at very competitive prices. Send SAE for details:- INIGO JONES AND CO., LIMITED, Groelon, Caernarfon, Gwynedd. Tel: 0286 830242. V-B

ATTACHMENTS FOR CORONET MAJOR universal namely saw table and planer/thicknesser. Complete with bed bar guards etc. £185 ono. Tel: 061-439-4171. V

ANTIQUE pit saw with handles and 7' blade. Offers. P. Butler, Holt Laith, Holt Head, Slaithwaite, Huddersfield, W. Yorks. Tel: Huddersfield 843832. V

WOLF 4" belt sander, immaculate condition. Used twice £85.00 Tel: Royston 45211. V

ROUTERS

If you are thinking of buying a Router, we offer Bosch/Elu range at unbelievable prices.
If you already own a Router Send for our Free Cutter Wall Chart.

BARRIE IRONS MACHINERY
106A Aldenham Road,
Bushey, Herts.
Tel. Watford (0923) 30422

ROSEWOOD, BURR WALNUT, figured mahogany, other assorted veneers. Exceptional Half price. Tel: 0203-69501. S/W

RECORD 45 moulding plane, complete boxed, 37 cutters. £55.00. Tel: Week St. Mary 414 (Devon). V

THATCHER'S POWER TOOL CENTRE ☎ 01-624 5146

BIG DISCOUNTS ON ELU/BOSCH/KITY POWER TOOLS
ALSO ROUTER CUTTERS

Please send 40p Stamps for full Brochure & Price Lists
221A Kilburn High Rd. London NW6
1st floor above Travel Agency

CORONET 4½" PLANER attachment and thicknesser Poly V Drive. Rarely used £135.00. Tel: Ottery St. Mary 3111. V

WOODCARVERS— *The Design Stage is always difficult why not try mine?*

8" in the round – figure or animal drawn in detail.
Front view, rear view and both profiles £5
14" × 10" design for alto-relievo work £5
Two 14" × 10" designs for bas-relief £5
Guaranteed 'one-off' designs to your requirements in above sizes £25
Larger Designs — Price on application — All Prices inclusive.

R. J. DENNIS, 119 Moira Road, Donisthorpe, Nr. Burton-on-Trent, Staffs

ATTACHMENT FOR CORONET MAJOR including planer and thicknesser, saw table, wobble saw and box combing jig, new moulding block, mortiser and chuck, £400.00 one lot. Box No. 447 (Notts.), c/o Woodworker, MAP Ltd., 13-35 Bridge Street, Hemel Hempstead, Herts. HP1 1EE. V

DREMEL woodcarving tool, new, cutters etc. Half price. Highly figured Brazilian Rosewood veneer — cheap. 14 Peel Street, Southport, Merseyside. Tel: 41005. V

COLONIAL FURNITURE DESIGNS:- Detailed 8" × 10" sheet plans 55p each. A distinctive and challenging style for both amateur and professional. Send S.A.E. for full range to:- D. Warne, Timbercraft, End Cottage, Holbeach St. Marks, Spalding, Lincs. PE12 8DX. V

TOOLS TO TREASURE

Cabinetmaker's pattern Screwdrivers with solid polished Boxwood handles by Marples of Sheffield.
3" – £2.85   5" – £3.57   8" – £5.27
Set of 3 – £11.00
Prices include P & P in the U.K.
EXPORT ENQUIRIES WELCOME.
Send S.A.E. for details of Adzes, Drawknives and other tools for the craftsman woodworker.
CORBETT TOOLS Dept., WW/11
224 Puxton Drive, Kidderminster, Worcs.

WORKSHOP EQUIPMENT

CL T-PRICE WAR — Elu and De Walt machines at considerably reduced prices. Send or telephone for brochures and prices. MACHINE SALES & SERVICES (BOURNEMOUTH) LIMITED, 56 Strouden Road, Bournemouth. Tel: 0202-527781. VWX

STANLEY NO. 45 all gun-metal, 20 cutters. Not in Stanley planes book, by Elvin Fellens. Very Rare. Offers? Tel: 01-570-5909. V

A. POLLARD & SON

De-Walt, Shopmate,
Kity, Elu,
Susemihl
We offer good service, good stocks and low prices
Dust extractors
A. Pollard & Son,
51 Queensway,
Bletchley, Milton
Keynes.
Tel: 0908-75221

ACCESS —
BARCLAYCARD

Business established over 50 years.

Equipping a Workshop?
TRYMWOOD SERVICES
Supply quality light and heavy duty woodworking machinery: Lurem, Bursgreen, Sedgwick, De Walt, Elektra, Kity, Elu and Arundel and Myford lathes (free turnery tuition for buyers). Call at:
2A Downs Park East (Nr. the Downs), Bristol 629092
9 a.m.-5.30 p.m. Mon. to Fri.

CIRCULAR AND BAND SAW BLADES for all applications from A. A. Smith of Lancing Limited, Churchill Industrial Estate, Lancing, Sussex. Tel: 09063-4474 (24 hrs). T/Z

SHERWOOD TURNING LATHES

All cast iron constructed. 3¾" CH 24" or 36" B.C. 3 or 4 speed, bowl turning up to 14" dia. ball-bearing spindle c/w face plate, centres etc. Prices from **£58.92** inc.VAT.

Send stamp for leaflets and details of above and other low-priced machines and motors.

**JAMES INNS (Engs),
Main St., Bulwell, Nottingham.**

ROUTER CUTTERS

We are specialist stockists of all types of H.S.S. and T.C.T. Router Cutters, in all shank sizes to fit all makes of Portable Routers and large industrial machines. Send for illustrated catalogue. — Small orders welcomed. We also offer a 24 hour resharpening service for all router cutters.
Marlow Zenith Cutters, P.O. Box 32, Marlow, Bucks.   Tel. (06284) 3247

WASHITA & ARKANSAS whetstones now readily available from importer. Large selection. SAE for lists. C. Rufino, Manor House, South Clifton, Newark, Notts. T/C

WOODTURNERS SUPPLIES

Woodturning tools, Peppermills, Salt mills, Barometers, Thermometers, Lighters, Hourglasses, Eggtimers, Ceramic tiles and clock faces, Clock movements, Spinning wheel plans, Sealers & Polishes, etc. Fast and efficient mail order service + competitive prices. S.A.E. for lists.

ERIC TOMKINSON
86 Stockport Road, Cheadle, Cheshire, SK8 2AJ. Tel. 061-491-1726
Shop open Weds., Thurs., Fri. & Sat.

PETER CRISP OF RUSHDEN
THE CARPENTER'S SHOP

Hand Tools by leading makers. Stockists of:
● Craftsmen, Coronet, Elu, Kity
   Woodworking Machinery
● Sorby Turning Chisels
● Taylor Carving Chisels
● Gomex T/Carbide Circular Saws

Stock list 25p
Illustrated Catalogue — £1.00
(Refundable on first order over £10)

High Street, Rushden, Northants.
Telephone:
093 34 56424-7

CLASSIFIED
Telephone Gillian Wynn
(0442) 41221 Ext. 241

CONVERT TIMBER YOURSELF

With a portable chain saw mill. Cuts a 36" width. 200 sq.ft. per hour. Keenest prices. Brochure, demonstration, PHILIP COLE, 16 Kings lane, Flore, Northampton. Tel: Weedon 0327-40337 (evenings).

BOOKS AND PUBLICATIONS

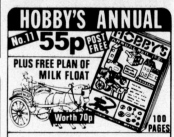

HOBBY'S ANNUAL
No.11   **55p** POST FREE
PLUS FREE PLAN OF MILK FLOAT
Worth 70p
100 PAGES

Over 100 plans including four novelty doll's houses, clocks, forts, hand and power tools. The hobby annual.

From W. H. SMITH & SON or direct from
Hobbys (Dept. W) Knight's Hill Square, London SE27 0HH. 01-761 4244.

POPULAR Crafts

The monthly hobby magazine that's packed with creative ideas for pleasure and profit. **60p**

TWO-DAY Woodturning Course for beginners in mid-Norfolk village. Two students only. Accommodation available. SAE for details please. Doug Kneeling, Church Lane, Beetley, Norfolk. NR20 4AB. T/C

How to get the most from your advertisement in . . .
Woodworker

Give a full description of the product or service you want to sell.

Book a series of advertisements to ensure that you reach the whole potential market. Remember your customer could quite easily miss the issue which contains your advertisement.

If you want to cancel your advertisement then simply pick up the 'phone and tell us. You will only be charged for the ones which have appeared.

Lastly, to get the most from your advertisement consult us first. We are here to help you. . .

THE MAGAZINE FOR THE CRAFTSMAN IN WOOD

DECEMBER 1980 VOL. 84 No. 1045 ISSN0043-776X

FRONT COVER: Hollowing out a sycamore blank during the first stage of making a large salad bowl. Feature pp780-783 *(Photograph W. David Askham).*

Editor	Geoffrey Pratt
Production Editor	Polly Curds
Advertisement Manager	Terence M. Healy
Advertisement Director } MAP Leisure	Michael Merrifield
Managing Director } Division	Gavin Doyle

SUBSCRIPTION DEPARTMENT: Remittances to MODEL AND ALLIED PUBLICATIONS, PO Box 35, Hemel Hempstead, Herts HP1 1EE. Price per copy 85p includes p&p. Subscription queries: Tel: Hemel Hempstead 51740. Subscription rate, including index, £10.20 per annum; overseas sterling £10.20; $23.00 US for overseas dollar subscribers. Second-class postage paid in US at Milwaukee, Wisconsin, and additional offices. Change of address. US Postmaster: Send address changes to Model & Allied Publications Ltd, PO Box 35, Bridge Street, Hemel Hempstead HP1 1EE, United Kingdom. Distribution to N American hobby and craft shops by Kalmbach Publishing Co, 1027 N. Seventh Street, Milwaukee, W153233, USA (Tel: 414-272-2060). Distribution to news stand sales by Eastern News Distributors Inc, 111 Eighth Avenue, New York NY1011, USA (Tel: 212-255-5620). Distribution to museums and bookshops by Bill Dean Books Ltd, 166-41 Powells Cove Boulevard, Whitestone, New York 11357 (Tel: 212-767-6632).

WOODWORKER is printed in Great Britain by H. E. Warne Ltd, East Hill, St Austell, Cornwall PL25 4TN for the proprietor and publisher, Model & Allied Publications Ltd (a member of the Argus Press Group). Trade sales by Argus Press Sales & Distribution Ltd, 12-18 Paul Street, London EC2A 4JS. WOODWORKER (ISSN 0043-776X) is published on the 3rd Friday of the month.

Model & Allied Publications Ltd

PO Box 35, Bridge Street, Hemel Hempstead, Herts HP1 1EE. Telephone: Hemel Hempstead (0442) 41221.

'To give greater rewards'

We are frequently asked for guidance on the purchase of machine tools but as a contributor wrote in the November issue: 'The whole field of woodworking is a personal experience between you, the wood and your tools.' The advice we give is: Study as many catalogues as possible, then go and see the actual machines under demonstration, or better still, working conditions.

Individual users are no different from industrial users when it comes to the purchase of capital equipment; and of course this applies to woodworking machines just as much as, say, a washing machine or a motor car.

It is not always easy to see different types or makes under demonstration or working conditions and this is one reason why the Woodworker Show in London last month has become an event of the greatest importance to craftsmen. The Show is one place where it is possible to see a wide variety of machines and associated equipment under demonstration conditions and to discuss individual requirements with manufacturers, distributors and — just as important — with fellow craftsmen.

For those who were unable to visit the Woodworker Show the advice which our contributor gives is worth repeating: Go to your nearest stockist (this is where the Shop Guide feature in each issue of WOODWORKER is so useful). He should be able to show you a range of machines and demonstrate at least some of them. Of course it may not be possible to see all the machines operating as it can be difficult to keep 50 or so models on permanent demonstration.

In addition to manufacturers' catalogues and our regular 'signpost' feature on newly-introduced machines and other products, there are numerous books covering the subject. One newly published is *Machines for Better Woodwork* from Evans Bros Ltd of London (and which will be reviewed in our columns). Author Gordon Stokes explains that the ever-increasing range of specialised machinery makes the choice between models bewildering — and mistakes are expensive.

He sets out to describe the differences between models so that the individual can choose the machine best suited to his needs, whether it be the home workshop or small commercial business. Inevitably, the book is somewhat limited in that because of the number of machines by different makers only one in each class can be considered. However, it provides a great deal of useful information as well as sound advice on workshop layout in regard to basic principles because, again, layouts vary so much according to individual needs and the amount of money that can be spent.

Another factor to be considered when purchasing machine tools was put by our contributor in November: 'It would seem a shame to spend, say, £1000 on sophisticated machinery merely to save time and sweat. I feel that with machinery we can afford to be more ambitious in the projects we carry out... The skills required in machine woodworking are different but no less exacting than in hand processes and have to be learnt thoroughly to give greater rewards.

Introducing the
WARCO
MULTI-TOOL
the 5-in-1 woodworking centre

● Versatile tool combining circular saw, disc sander, lathe, drill press and horizontal drill

● Simple to use – converts quickly and easily

● Powerful 1½HP heavy duty motor, single phase, with variable speed (700/5200 rpm)

● All components lock for maximum accuracy and stability

● Built-in safety features, overload circuit breaker, enclosed pulleys, etc.

● Adjustable work-table height for extra versatility

FREE LEAFLET AVAILABLE

● Complete with 14 useful accessories – at no extra cost

● A sturdy and compact tool thoughtfully designed for all precision woodwork in workshop or hobby room

And for the model engineer: Other top-quality tools from Warco include: Bench Grinders, Tool Trolleys, Hobby Bench Drills, Universal Bandsaws. Send for details.

CIRCULAR SAW
★ 9″ diameter blade
★ 14″ x 18½″ table extending to 18⅜″ x 56″
★ 0°-60° mitre gauge
★ 0°-45° table tilt

LATHE
★ 34″ between centres
★ Hard-chrome plated tubular steel ways
★ 360° tool rest swing

DRILL PRESS
★ Drill to centre of 16½″ circle
★ 14″ x 18½″ table
★ Chuck to table 26″
★ Chuck to floor 58″

HORIZONTAL DRILL
★ Unlimited length capacity
★ 4¼″ quill feed
★ 0°-90° table tilt
★ Sealed bearings

DISC SANDER
★ 12″ diameter
★ 113 sq ins sanding surface
★ 0°-45° table tilt
★ 0°-60° mitre gauge

ONLY £500
Plus VAT & Carriage

INCLUDING FREE ACCESSORIES:
Mitre Gauge, Rip Fence, Lathe Tool Rest, Cup Centre, 1¼″ Saw Blade Arbor, Arbor Wrench, Sanding Disc, Sandpaper, Chuck & Key, Allen Wrench, Tailstock, Extension Table, Upper Saw Guard, Lower Saw Guard.

SOLE U.K. AGENTS
WARREN MACHINE TOOLS LTD.,
MIDDLE STREET, SHERE, SURREY GU5 9HF.
Tel. Shere (048641) 3434. Telex 859455.

Prices quoted are those prevailing at press date and are subject to alteration due to economic conditions.

If you want a professional finish to your furniture, use a pair of scissors.

When you own a DeWalt Power Shop, you can do as much with your wood as any professional.

You can cut at any angle, lengthways or crossways.

You can bevel and mitre.

And, with the right attachments, you can power through the boring, grinding, routing, sanding and jointing.

So, whatever you want made, you can make it yourself, paying only for the materials.

And you get professional performance without having to call in the professionals.

No circular saw, let alone a handsaw, can give you such precision and versatility.

And you slash the time taken because of the powerful motor that also acts as a general power source for the full range of DeWalt attachments.

You don't risk an inch of precious wood. And DeWalt's rigorous attention to safety features stops you risking your precious hands.

Your DeWalt Power Shop is precision made and solidly engineered for a lifetime's use.

But what if you don't want to use it for a lifetime?

Just sell it.

You'll find plenty of people keen to own the best saw on the market. And it depreciates very, very slowly.

So buy the saw you always promised yourself and give your wife the furniture you always promised her.

You'll save money on every joint. And here's the first cut.

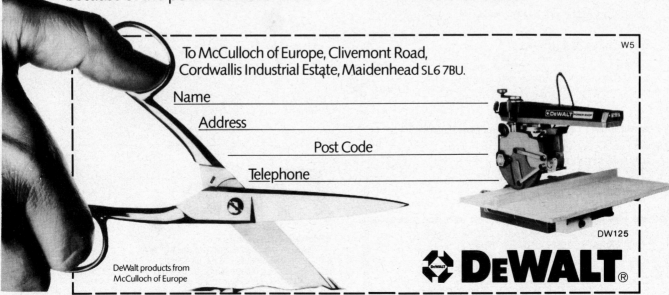

W5

To McCulloch of Europe, Clivemont Road, Cordwallis Industrial Estate, Maidenhead SL6 7BU.

Name

Address

Post Code

Telephone

DeWalt products from McCulloch of Europe

DW125

DeWALT ®

SARJENTS TOOLS for a fine range of sharpening stones

In addition to a comprehensive range of woodworking machinery we also stock a huge selection of hand tools. Listed is a selection of sharpening equipment offered to help keep your tools in top condition.

INDIA — Use India stones where a fast, sharp edge is required. Made from aluminium oxide, they are a rapid cutting abrasive and are used as a preliminary final honing stone. Our India stones are oil filled at the factory, but use of a fine honing oil is recommended.

ARKANSAS — Used after an India stone, natural Arkansas will produce the ultimate in cutting tool edges. Use ample thin oil to help cutting, prevent clogging and disperse chips. Stored carefully, Arkansas stones will produce a fine polished sharp edge year in, year out.

		INDIA				ARKANSAS
Shape	Size	coarse £ p	medium £ p	fine £ p	comb. £ p	£ p
rectangular	8″ × 2″ × 1″	5.75	5.75	5.75	6.75	—
	8″ × 2″ × ¾″	—	—	—	—	17.75
	6″ × 2″ × 1″	4.25	4.25	4.25	5.25	—
	6″ × 2″ × ¾″	—	—	—	—	13.75
	4″ × 1½″ × ½″	—	—	—	—	7.75
	4″ × 1″ × ½″	—	3.50	3.50	3.50	—
	3″ × ⅞″ × ⅜″	—	—	1.30	—	—
square	4″ × ½″	1.75	1.75	1.75	—	4.30
	4″ × ⅜″	1.75	1.75	1.75	—	4.25
	4″ × 5/16″	—	—	—	—	3.50
	4″ × ¼″	1.75	1.75	1.75	—	3.25
triangular	4″ × ½″	2.10	2.10	2.10	—	4.30
	4″ × ⅜″	2.10	2.10	2.10	—	4.25
	4″ × 5/16″	—	—	—	—	3.50
	4″ × ¼″	2.10	2.10	2.10	—	3.25
round	4″ × ½″	2.50	2.50	2.50	—	6.60
	4″ × ⅜″	2.50	2.50	2.50	—	5.50
	4″ × 5/16″	—	—	—	—	5.25
	4″ × ¼″	2.50	2.50	2.50	—	4.25
half-round	4″ × ½″	2.10	2.10	2.10	—	6.50
	4″ × ⅜″	—	—	—	—	5.50
	4″ × 5/16″	—	—	—	—	4.50
	4″ × ¼″	—	—	—	—	4.25
round-edge slip	4½″ × 1¾″ × ½″ × 3/16″	—	2.75	2.75	—	—
	4½″ × 1¾″ × ¼″ × 1/16″	—	2.60	—	—	—
	4½″ × 1⅞″ × ⅜″ × ⅛″	—	—	—	—	8.25
	3¼″ × 1¾″ × ¼″ × 1/16″	—	—	—	—	7.50

Also available (in medium India only)

point	knife	reamer	silversmith	sewing machine feed
3″ × 5/16″ base £3.00	4″ × 1″ × ⅛″ £2.50	5″ × 1″ × 3/16″ £2.00	4″ × ½″ × 3/32″ £2.50	4″ × ⅝″ × 3/16″ £2.75

Sizes quoted are approximate

HONING OIL
½ litre best quality fine grade honing oil
£3.90

HONING GUIDE
No. 36 honing guide helps maintain the correct angle on chisels and plane irons
£4.60

STONE BOX
A sturdy beech box in which to keep 8″ × 2″ stone
£2.75

All these prices **include** postage, packing and VAT

(Prices liable to change without notice)
Open 6 days per week 8.30 - 5.30

SARJENTS TOOLS

44-52 Oxford Rd., READING (0734) 586522
62-64 Fleet St., SWINDON (0793) 31361
150 Cowley Rd., OXFORD (0865) 45118

FROM THE QUIRKS OF NATURE

Story and pictures by W. David Askham

David Gratch has a workshop near Royston in Hertfordshire. He is an accomplished craftsman who in recent years has built an enviable reputation as a woodturner and furniture maker. David Askham visited him at his home and workshop – both skilfully converted from an old maltings – to find out about his craft interests and techniques

Above:
Dining table in larch. The aim was to give the impression that the top is floating.

Although David Gratch has been a full-time professional for only six years he was working part-time before that. However, his interest can be traced back to his school days when he realised he was good with his hands and had a deep love of woodwork. After a career culminating in a managerial position with a large timber company his constant yearning to be creative with timber eventually led him to learn how to turn wood.

Although his designs constantly evolved, basically his idea was to provide a wide range of woodware that would be practical to use in a house. Possibly domestic woodware would be the best description of his product range.

He retains a relatively open mind on what he will make, provided the best medium for the purpose is wood. A good example of his attitude is not to turn wooden goblets. Although he admits that at one time people drank beer or mead from wooden mugs, he rules them out on hygiene grounds. Utensils should be easily and safely washed and therefore need some sort of finishing treatment to make them impervious to liquids. But he is firmly opposed to chemical treatment of his eating utensils.

He says: 'I don't know how it will affect my health or anybody else's. So in essence, I'll use wood with a finish that is not harmful; the finish that I use is edible oil or pure beeswax and nothing else'. A natural, hygienically safe finish is applied to his platters, bowls, rolling pins, chopping boards, cheese boards, sugar bowls, spoons, mortars and pestles; basically items that can be turned.

Home-grown timber is used almost exclusively for a very simple reason. He buys it in large quantities and in log form from mills where he has it cut to his own requirements and in his presence.

He dries his timber and can follow the history of each log almost from the beginning. 'I know the history of a particular log, what it can do, what it can't do and what it should be used for and what it shouldn't be used for. One particular log of ash is not necessarily identical to another log of ash. It depends on where it grew, on what type of soil. And was it near to water and how fast did it grow? The hardness and stability of the timber will vary according to its growing conditions'. Thus he is able to judge, from this period of observation and conditioning, to what purpose he should put a particular piece of timber.

The species he uses are generally ash, brown oak, sycamore, yew, a little normal oak, burr oak if it is obtainable; and wych elm to a large extent. 'I also use some apple for particular purposes where I need very close grain timber like, for example, in rolling pins where I get the weight of the apple and the close grain effect. It is a very dense wood and it also turns extremely well'.

Ash is one of his favoured woods both for aesthetic and practical reasons. When considering turned platters or salad bowls, for example, it is most important that they wash well repeatedly. Ash, in his experience, is ideal, unlike oak which goes black with washing or beech which if washed too frequently will split. Another benefit is the resilience ash has to sharp cutting edges; so chopping boards or platters do not show cutting marks like teak or other darker woods do. Another timber that is tolerant of washing is wych elm. The ancients recognised this and used elm wood as pipes for water systems.

David Gratch has a marked preference for timbers that reveal the quirks of nature. He does not like using the timber that industry is looking for – which is usually free of knots and twists and with long, even grain.

Basically industry uses timber that can be machined well and finished by mechanical means. So the extraction of the most beautiful pieces of a particular log can only be undertaken, essentially, by the individual craftsman at some cost, because of the high wastage of material.

He talks vividly and with enthusiasm about the part nature plays in preparing his raw material. 'If you are looking for those quirks of nature,' he says, 'you have got to accept wastage of up to 50%; but at the same time what you are left with is a piece of art on its own because nature has made it, not man. But when you talk of quirks of nature you can take it even further and say, in the case of those old sycamore trees for example, something happened during their growth that changed the colour from white to a wonderful array of grey – black – green, sometimes even red. The same applies to beech. These are the sorts of woods I am looking for; anything that is out of the ordinary, anything that cannot be machined but can only be worked by hand. That justifies, in my view, the existence of a hand craftsman'.

Right:
10 in. diameter turned salad bowl in ash.

We had already touched on the finish of his tableware as I asked him how he finished his furniture. 'I use mainly polyurethene or similar. I try to keep as natural an appearance as possible so that anybody running his fingers over my products feels the wood and not a heavy film of either french polish or whatever the finish is. But at the same time it gives protection so that spillage or dirt can be wiped off, or washed so that at the end of the day it will look as good as when it came out of my workshop'.

About his furniture-making and his philosophy for a small workshop he explains: 'The biggest justification for a small workshop is that people come in all different sizes, have different wishes and different tastes. Quite often they are not likely to find the type of furniture they have in mind or will fit in with the scheme they desire for their particular homes'.

What factors influence David Gratch's furniture design? 'Furniture design must meet practical requirements. When I tackle a commission the most important considerations are: what is the function of the particular piece? How do you solve the problems you are faced with? Once the practical solution has been reached the next consideration is that it has to look right; but not the other way round. I don't sculpt a piece and try to make it as practical as I can. My priority is practicality first and visual appearance second'.

For example, in making a coffee table for a married couple with young children, he would avoid an oblong or square shape with sharp corners which could be damaging to children, especially toddlers. He would make a round table. 'If you sum up my style', he says, 'it is more the cottage style, though I try to be as original as I can within my ability'.

Below:
David Gratch demonstrating his 'left-handed' workbench.

Above left: Pile of sycamore blanks awaiting first-phase turning. Above right: A selection of David Gratch's turned tableware. Below: A pile of roughly-turned blanks slowly drying out before the bowls are finally finished. It takes time to produce a quality product.

David also likes making fitted kitchen units, especially those to the exact requirements of the housewife. Making kitchen units is time-consuming and at present he is trying to concentrate more on occasional furniture, dining tables and chairs. 'We do our own caning or rushing, and at the moment I have got a few coffee tables to make, a bookcase and hi-fi housing. In other words furniture to house all those weird and wonderful things you buy but do not necessarily know how to accommodate'.

On the subject of tools for his kind of work David Gratch considers that suppliers tend to overlook the fact that though many small workshops have progressively disappeared, many are coming back. And manufacturers are not catching on to this new requirement. They are introducing equipment that is supposed to do a particular job of work for the professional small workshop. 'In quite a few cases I find products are inadequately tried and tested. For example, people put on to the market tools that don't do the jobs they are supposed to do'.

His knowledge of wood cutting tools has been put to good account in designing a range of HS steel long and strong deep gouges for bowl turning. His new tools absorb the harsh treatment they receive when shaping hardwoods such as wych elm, teak or certain types of sycamore. He has also developed a skew chisel which instead of being made from an oblong-shaped bar is made from a round-sectioned bar in HS steel.

David Gratch is a left-handed craftsman. He had difficulty in finding a left-handed bench of suitable quality so designed and made his own taking all the best features of benches made in this country and in America. He is not intending to market his bench but is willing to help anyone faced with similar problems.

As it is no easy matter to find the most suitable timber for specialised craftwork, David Gratch has set up a timber purchasing pool. He buys logs basically for economic reasons and has built up a good stock of certain hardwoods from which he can satisfy other people's needs as well as his own.

Every two or three months he sends out a stocklist of his timber and those 'in the pool' have first refusal of the material. They can visit his workshop and select whatever they want, either small or large quantities.

He explains: 'If I do not have their particular requirements in stock they tell me what sort of timber and quantity they need; then when I go and buy my future timber they have the advantage of my bulk-buying prices. The only thing pool members have to do is just send me six self-addressed envelopes and £1 and I send out the stocklist with any news I have regarding timber. I do not turn people away that are looking, for example, for small pieces for lace bobbin making, or a big hospital that uses a tremendous quantity. As long as they are members of the pool they can come, look and pick up the type of thing they want and I will help them as much as I can'.

At present there are about 45 members and he thinks the pool has a promising future.

A visit to David Gratch's workshop is informative and enjoyable. You are left in no doubt of his feeling for the raw material of his craft and of his critical approach to the tools of his craft. He sees scope for improvement and is keen to contribute to tool design.

You will also learn some interesting things about turning, for example deep bowls, as well as furniture – like a small table in Brazilian walnut which is a piece made by a turner rather than a cabinetmaker; and the dining table in larch with a 6 × 3ft top that gives the impression of 'floating'. Then there is his workbench with its underparts, legs and stretchers in Scots pine for stability and top of London plane for close grain and stability.

It all makes you realise that there is much more to selecting timber than you think.

Left:
Circular occasional table in Brazilian walnut made entirely by turning.

Below:
David Gratch turning a sycamore blank.

The hang of hinges

BY C. D. CLIFFE

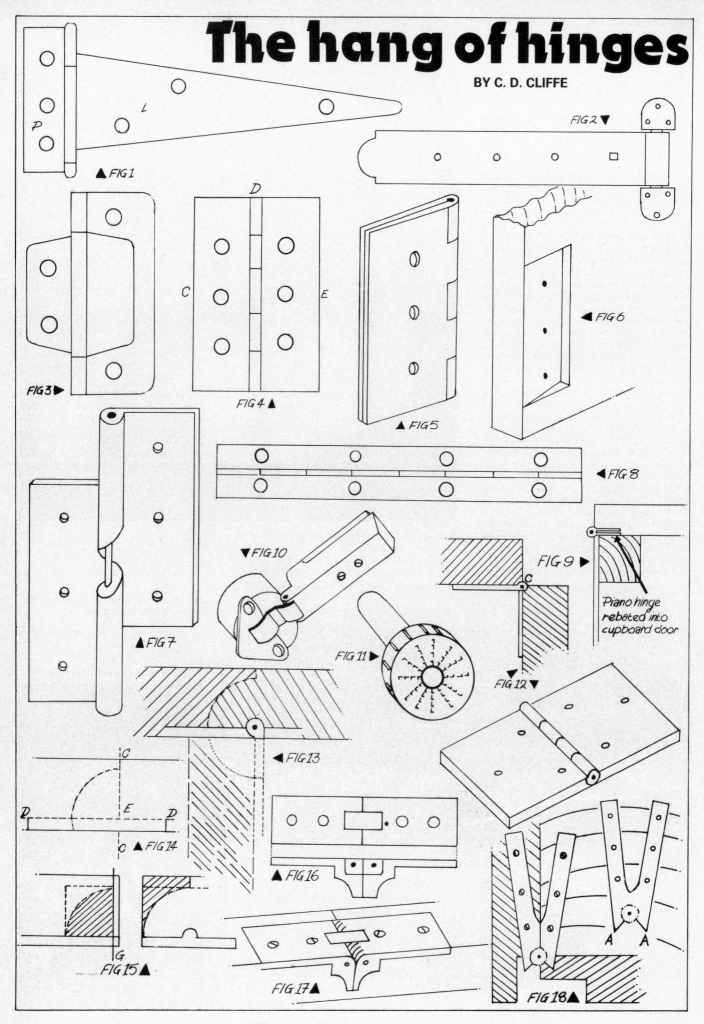

Piano hinge rebated into cupboard door

In order to fit hinges so that they operate correctly it is necessary to appreciate how they work. It is true to say that everything hangs on the position of the pivot and the sinkings are therefore cut so as to site this correctly. Butt hinges are common to both joinery and cabinet makers whereas rising butts, gate hinges and cross garnets are used principally by joiners. On the other hand dolphin hinges, link-plates and flap hinges are used almost exclusively in the cabinet trade.

One of the simplest hinges to fit is the cross garnet or tee hinge (Fig. 1). The plate P is screwed to the door frame so that the pivot is in the centre of the clearance gap between the door and its frame. To prevent the pull of the screws from splitting the frame it is usual in the larger hinges to stagger the screw holes in the plate rather than have them in a straight line. The leaf L is screwed to the door and if the door is of ledged construction the screws should be long enough to pass through the door and into the ledges.

For heavy gates and garage doors the reversible gate hinge (Fig. 2) is used. The straps are screwed through the doors and into the rails. A coach bolt with a square shank fits into the square hole near the pivot and passes through the centre of the stile. The castiron cups are screwed to the frame, the lower cup of the bottom hinge is forced towards the door and the lower cup of the upper hinge is forced away from the door. This takes up any looseness in the hinges and ensures an equal gap between door and frame when the door is swinging freely. When all is correct the upper cups are screwed to the frame.

The hurl hinge (Fig. 3) is used by joiners for hinging light doors and window frames. The larger leaf is cut away to enable the smaller leaf to fold into the cut-out; thus the hinge when closed is only the thickness of one leaf. The advantage is that the hinge does not have to be let into the door and the leaf thickness provides sufficient clearance when the work is painted. The leaf where the screw holes are closer together is fixed to the stouter member, usually the frame, while the other leaf is screwed to the lighter member where the wider spaced holes distribute the pull of the screws over a greater area.

The butt hinge (Fig. 4) is one of the most widely-used and may be of castiron, pressed steel or brass. The hinge is usually fitted in pairs but for large wardrobe doors and heavy entrance doors it is fitted in threes. The thickness of the hinge when closed is sunk entirely into the door to save time and give improved appearance.

Position the hinge on the door stile, mark the ends with a steel marker, close the hinge as in Fig. 5 and with the marking gauge set to the bare thickness of the knuckle B, gauge a line on the face of the door stile. With the hinge open set the gauge from the side of the hinge C to the centre of the knuckle D and mark the edge of the door stile. Cut away the wood for the hinge and fix with screws. In good-class work the slots of the screws should be parallel with the hinge pin. Having screwed all hinges to the stile gauge a line on the frame to mark the inner limit of the hinge and in common work screw the hinge in position on the frame.

For a better job cut a tapering recess to house the back part of the hinge (Fig. 6). The recess allows the weight of the door to be taken by the hinges rather than the screws.

A form of hinge frequently encountered in joinery is the skew hinge or rising butt (Fig. 7). The hinges are made with a spiral joint rotating round a central pin and come in pairs, either left or right-hand. The illustration depicts a left-hand hinge. As the door is opened from the outside if the hinges are on the right then the door is right-handed and vice versa.

Fitting is similar to ordinary butts except that the inside of the knuckle should stand out 1/16in. beyond the edge of the door and frame. The corners of the frame above the hinges require cutting away to accommodate the knuckle which rises when the door opens. The action of the hinge is twofold: it helps the door to rise over a fitted carpet and it causes the door to close automatically.

Another type of butt is the piano hinge (Fig. 8). This is a long narrow hinge which as its name suggests is used on piano falls. It is made of brass and the one hinge runs the entire length of the fall. Similar hinges, usually of alloy, are often used to hinge the doors of kitchen cabinets. In these cases it is usual to rebate the inner face of the door sufficiently to house both leaves of the hinge (Fig. 9).

Frequently the concealed cabinet hinge (Fig. 10) is used for hanging kitchen furniture doors, particularly where the carcase is of chipboard. A special cutter (Fig. 11) used in an electric drill bores the sinking for the hinge which has the advantage of allowing the door to open within the width of the cabinet. Thus it clears adjacent walls or furniture.

The backflap hinge (Fig. 12) is used mainly by joiners. This hinge is found on wooden folding tables and on the leaves of kitchen tables. Sometimes the holes for the screws are countersunk on the opposite sides to an ordinary butt hinge. The flanges do not then have to be let-in to the top or leaf but the knuckle has to be recessed so that its centre C is level with the under face of the top. Consequently there is no gap showing between the top and leaf when the leaf is down.

In cabinet work where a better appearance is desired the rule joint is customary. Whether the table leaf is up or down the hinges cannot be seen and when the leaf is down only the moulded edge and rebate of the top is visible. The hinges are of the back flap pattern except that one leaf is longer than the other. Use only the best-quality hinges to ensure the joint works smoothly.

The joint is shown in both open and closed positions in Fig. 13. To set out the joint so that it works sweetly it must be appreciated that the centre from which the arcs are struck defines the shape of the moulding. Fig. 14 is a section of the joint. The dotted lines CC and DD indicate at intersection E the centre of the hinge pin which is the centre from which the quarter circle must be struck. CC is the joint line which determines the edge of the rebate and DD is the depth to which the hinge is let in.

Fig. 15 shows how the work is gauged. The hinge flaps are of unequal length and it is advisable to check before buying that the hinges are all of identical thickness and position of centre pin.

The joint is made by first working the rebate and then forming the mouldings with a pair of rounds and hollows or a universal plane. The arcs are first marked on the sides with compasses. There is no difficulty in marking the table top or fixed part and there will be no trouble in marking the flap if it is left a trifle full at G in Fig. 15, and the rule joint marked out before planing the joint true.

To set out the fixed part square lines across the top, underside and both edges. Then the thickness line of the hinge should be marked on the edges and this will give the centre for the arc. The radius can be the thickness of the table top minus two and a half to three times the thickness of the hinge flange. The line on the underneath side will give the centre of the recess for the knuckles of the hinges. The recesses can be cut with a chisel and a small gouge. When letting in the hinge flaps to the fixed part use short stout screws and run them in straight taking care to keep the pins of the hinges dead in line.

Another hinge used by cabinet makers and restorers is the link joint hinge found on card tables. There are several patterns to suit different kinds of table but the main idea is that there is no knuckle standing up above the surface of the table when open for playing. Fig. 16 shows a plan and elevation of one kind of hinge and Fig. 17 how the hinge is fitted to the table. A marking gauge is used to set out the width of the top plate. For marking the sides it is usually better to draw the shape with paper templates and compasses, taking care to keep within the lines when cutting away the wood.

The dolphin hinge (Fig. 18) is used by cabinet makers in secretaire bookcases. What appears to be a drawer front is in fact a fall-down flap with a fitted writing compartment. The bevelled ends A of the hinge restrict the amount by which the hinge opens and support the fall horizontally for writing. The diagram shows the hinge fitted to the fall and the side of the writing compartment. The fall and the bottom of the sliding compartment are rebated as shown.

Lay the fall perfectly level with the bottom. Open the hinge fully and position it so that the pivotting centre of the hinge is exactly where the surfaces of the fall and bottom meet. Having marked round the edge of the hinge with a steel marker let in the hinge flush so that it can slide smoothly into the carcase of the bookcase. When the fall is raised in the vertical position it engages with a catch which prevents it from falling when pulled out like a drawer.

Fig. 1. Cross garnet hinge
Fig. 2. Reversible gate hinge
Fig. 3. Hurl hinge
Fig. 4. Butt hinge
Fig. 5. Butt hinge (closed)
Fig. 6. Tapering recess to house backpart of hinge
Fig. 7. Rising butt hinge (left-hand)
Fig. 8. Piano hinge
Fig. 9. Inner face of door rebated to house both leaves of hinge
Fig. 10. Concealed cabinet hinge
Fig. 11. Cutter for sinking concealed cabinet hinge
Fig. 12. Backflap hinge and elevation showing hinge fitted
Fig. 13. Rule joint open and closed
Fig. 14. Section of joint
Fig. 15. Gauging the joint
Fig. 16. Plan and elevation of link plate hinge
Fig. 17. Link plate hinge fitted to table
Fig. 18. Dolphin hinge and hinge fitted to secretaire

Guild of Woodworkers

Programme for 1981

Following the appointment of Albert L. Beezem as administrator of the guild in succession to David Whitehouse, the programme of activities for 1981 is now being finalised.

Already the special insurance scheme for members' woodworking tools and equipment arranged with the Iron Trades Mutual Insurance Co Ltd has attracted a good response. For an annual premium of only £5 members are insured against all risks of physical loss or damage with but three exceptions: the first £10 of each and every loss; wear and tear, electrical and mechanical breakdown, gradual deterioration; and losses due to climatic conditions. The sum insured is £500.

Further details and application forms are available from Mr Beezem.

For 1981 the administrator is arranging a programme which will take account of the wide interests of members. There will be practical courses (for smaller numbers so that everyone can have the benefit of personalised tuition) and courses for less restricted numbers. In this latter category will come visits to houses and museums where the collections are of particular significance to woodworkers.

It is anticipated that at least one course will be of topical interest: namely starting in business. Other probable subjects are conditioning of timber; working with lesser-known species; and insects and fungicides and methods of control. Full details will be announced in WOODWORKER but members wishing to have specific information can write to Mr Beezem, Guild of Woodworkers, P.O. Box 35, Bridge Street, Hemel Hempstead HP1 1EE (Hemel Hempstead 41221 ext. 293/4/5).

Guide to craftsmen

Kent Guild of Craftsmen is hoping to publish next spring a booklet *Craftsmen of Kent*. This is intended for distribution through tourist information centres, craft and book shops and other suitable outlets in the county.

It will contain entries saying where each craftsman may be contacted and where his products can be seen and bought. Those living and working in Kent wishing to publicise their work through the medium of the booklet can get further information from Gill Cannon who is secretary of Kent Guild of Craftsmen. Her address is The Studio, 329 High Street, Rochester.

Chainsaw hazards

In March issue last year we drew attention to the risks associated with use of chainsaws and in particular to vibration-induced white finger (vwf) or Raynaud's phenomenon. Injuries due to vibration have been studied by Dr M. J. Griffen of Southampton university on behalf of the Health & Safety Executive, and the results are published as research paper no. 9 *Vibration injuries of the hand and arm: their occurrence and the evolution of standards and limits*, HMSO (ISBN 011 883271 9), £1.50 plus postage.

Dr Griffin points out that use of anti-vibration (A-V) chainsaws over the last few years suggests that they are less likely to cause vwf. However, the period of vibration exposure and the number of studies are not yet sufficient to be sure that the vibration characteristics of all A-V saws in good condition are sufficiently low to prevent any new cases of vwf. A-V saws have been introduced into this country on a wide scale largely due to the decision of the Forestry Commission to insist on vibration limits on chainsaws.

British vibration limits and standards are discussed in detail on pp13-15 of the report, which suggests that the type, model and condition of the tool or machine involved and its operating speed are prime factors. Posture and hand-grip also affect the transmission of vibration to the hand.

Protection against dust

Hazards associated with wood dust were referred to in the November issue (report of HM Chief Inspector of Factories). Ian D. G. Full of Chippenham (no. 0380) has sent a note about the Airstream helmet which he says 'provides me with personal dust protection as well as face and eye protection. I did not have extraction in my workshop. I used a conventional facemask which was not very comfortable nor 100% effective. It caused difficulty in breathing and misting of the safety spectacles which I always wear.'

Mr Full says the Airstream helmet is a product of Racal Safety Ltd, no. 1 Building, Beresford Avenue, Wembley HA0 1RU. Racal will supply descriptive leaflets and a list of distributors from whom the helmet can be obtained.

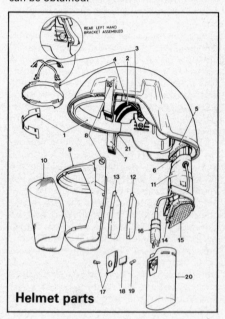

Helmet parts

Marquetry notes

The latest issue of the quarterly magazine *The Marquetarian* (official journal of the Marquetry Society) has arrived on the office desk. Particularly appropriate, at this time since WOODWORKER is running a series of articles on basic marquetry by the editor of *The Marquetarian,* Ernie Ives. We were pleased too, to have some of the members of the society enter the marquetry classes at this year's Woodworker Show. It is good to see that this hobby/craft is growing in popularity throughout the country. Both Ernie Ives and Mrs G. M. Walker (hon. gen. sec. of the society) are busy people but both spend a large percentage of their precious time helping beginners and talking about their art.

WOODWORKER was privileged to attend the AGM of the St Albans branch of the society in the spring and hear Mrs (Johnny) Walker who was guest speaker on that occasion. She spoke (as requested) on finishing and also judged the competition entries submitted by the society members. 13 entries were submitted in the 'Open'

section and 9 in the 'Beginners' section; a very creditable turnout for a small group. Winners were: Open, first: Standing in the corner by Geoff Barnett, second: Market place in St Albans by Frank Taylor and third: Suffolk village by Arthur Tissington.

Beginners, first: Man's best friend by Pat Aldridge, second: Leo by Pat Aldridge and third: Andalucia by Arthur Tissington. Geoff Barnett in his introduction said they were honoured to have as guest speaker, a lady who is a life member of the society (there are only 10) and who has been hon. gen. sec. since 1968. Mrs Walker was born in Cambridge and became at 18 an LCC nursery teacher; she has a keen interest in drama, is a skilful oil and watercolour artist and a marvellous marquetarian. She never loses an opportunity to preach the marquetry gospel, teach and demonstrate. Mrs Walker, modestly replied that once the marquetry bug bites you cannot stop. Practice makes perfect.

In 1981 the National Exhibition, the high-spot of the marquetry year, will be held in St Albans, arranged and hosted by the local society. The 1980 National was held at Bristol and two St Albans members were among the prize winners. Audrey Canton and Arthur Tissington both received third prizes for their respective entries.

Full details and reports on the National plus several pictures are included in the autumn issue of *The Marquetarian* (No. 112). The issue also contains a profile of E. G. Robins (rosebowl winner 1980), focus on marquetry groups throughout the country, readers' letters, suppliers, details of booklets and designs for autumn as well as more in the series 'Marquetry for beginners'. The editorial and publishing office is 63 Church Lane, Sproughton, Ipswich, Suffolk IP8 3AY and any enquiries should be addressed to E. Ives. A sae would be appreciated in any matters requiring a personal reply.

Sawbench and Mitre Saw combined: ELU TGS 171 the saw with the flip-over action.

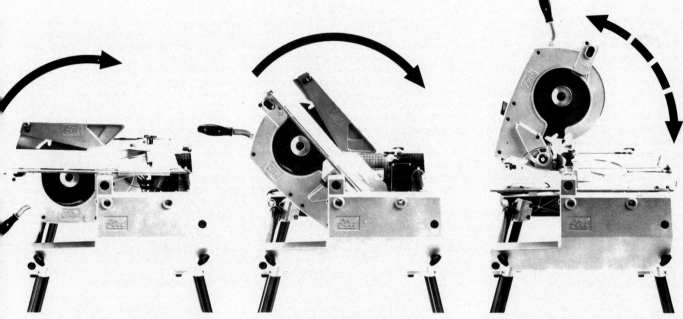

A circular sawbench . . . . . just flip-over . . . . . a perfect mitre saw.

Sawbench for fast, reliable working. Cut depth adjustable up to 60 mm. For wood, plastics and even aluminium. Also large panels can be sawn with the optional sliding table.

This flip-over action avoids the need for two machines. Operates from normal electricity supply and available in 110 V for building sites. Quiet and reliable induction type motor.
Quick release legs enable the saw to be carried anywhere.

Accurate and precise mitering for snip-off and mitre sawing. Spring loaded pin provides positive locking at 90° and 45° left and right. Other angles set by graduated scale.

You can flip over the TGS 171 Call in and see your ELU Dealer and flip it over yourself. Or fill in and post the coupon today.

ELU Machinery Ltd.,
Stirling Corner
Boreham Wood, Herts. WD6 2AG.

Please send more information of the TGS 171 saw with the flip over action to:

Name _____

Company _____

Adress _____

_____ Tel. _____

Charles D. Cliffe offers some tips on FINISHING OAK FURNITURE

Oak for furniture is becoming increasingly popular and some of the ways in which this attractive wood can be finished are described.

Fumed oak Stable fittings of oak which are subjected to ammonia fumes darken to a rich brown colour and by copying this natural process we can impart fairly quickly a similar appearance to our work. Using ammonia has two advantages: The grain is not raised and the colour does not fade. Full strength ammonia is used. It is known as 'point eight eighty' because its specific gravity is 0.880. And beware of inhaling the fumes.

Before starting to fume make sure the work is clean and free of dust and greasy fingermarks. Leave cupboard doors and drawers open so that all edges may be darkened. If the work is very large a small, almost airtight room will be needed. For small pieces a cupboard or large box will make a fuming cabinet. Depending on the type of oak used and the depth of colour desired fuming will take between four and 12hr.

Place the work to be fumed in the centre of the cabinet so that the fumes can reach all round it and seal up all cracks and holes to prevent fumes escaping. Pour ammonia into shallow dishes or saucers placed on the floor around the work. This allows the fumes to circulate. Close the cabinet door securely. If a large number of pieces are to be fumed it may be worthwhile fitting a glass panel in the cabinet so that progress can be watched.

Another method is to bore a hole in the side of the cabinet and push through it a tight fitting stick of the same oak as the piece being fumed. The stick is withdrawn at intervals to check the colour.

During the course of examination some parts of the work may have darkened sufficiently while others are still too light. Remove the work from the cabinet and give the dark parts a couple of applications of white polish or wax and continue fuming. The polished surfaces will not be affected by subsequent fuming but the untreated places will darken to match. When the required tone is obtained take the work out of the cabinet and leave it in the fresh air for a few hours to 'air off'.

Finally brush on two coats of white polish with a camel hair mop and when hard smooth down with fine glasspaper. Dust off and wax polish.

Brown oak Dissolve 2oz of bichromate of potash in 1pt water and brush it on letting light and air get to the work. This helps with the colouring. If the wood assumes an orange tinge this can be toned down by adding a little Vandyke brown or walnut stain.

Alternatively, a rich brown colour can be had from a fairly strong solution of permanganate of potash (1oz to 1qt water). This is bright crimson when applied but soon turns brown. Use a sponge (not a brush) and apply it speedily over the work to keep the edges 'live'; otherwise the sponge marks will show. This stain will ruin a brush by rotting the bristles.

Dark oak Mix 2oz Vandyke brown in 1pt ammonia and add 1oz bichromate of potash. The addition of a little spirit red to the polish may improve the tone.

Limed oak This finish was frequently used 30 or 40 years ago but is not so popular at the present time. Ordinary slaked lime is mixed with water to the consistency of thin cream. Using a canvas pad apply the lime by rubbing across the grain until the pores are filled. If a brush is used make sure it is not a bristle brush because the lime will ruin it. Wear rubber gloves to protect the hands. Let the lime dry completely before removing surplus lime by glasspapering along the grain with fine paper. Carefully dust-off and with a mop apply two coats of transparent white polish. When hard, smooth with worn glasspaper. Finally wax polish.

Spirit stains These can be made by dissolving 1oz of spirit-soluble powder in 1pt of methylated spirits. When the stain is made up allow any sediment to settle and pour the clear stain into a clean bottle. If you make up black, red, green and yellow stains you should be able to produce any shade you need. For light oak equal parts of black and red with a touch of green will be satisfactory.

For a medium finish roughly equal parts of red and black are used; for a Jacobean finish rather more black than red is needed. As these proportions of stain are approximate, it is advisable first to try the various combinations on a piece of waste wood of the same kind as the work in hand. When the stain is completely dry lightly rub down with worn glasspaper prior to applying two coats of transparent white polish. Finally wax polish.

A real mellow finish requires the wax polish to be applied evenly and well rubbed in over a period of weeks.

American method Because of climatic conditions American organs, desks and sewing machine cabinets are not usually french polished. Long spells of hot dry weather can cause a shellac film to soften and lose its brilliance. Should you wish to restore or match such a piece of furniture this is the usual method: Brush on a coat of elastic varnish and when dry grind down the surface with pumice powder and water. Dry off thoroughly, remove all traces of the powder and apply another coat of varnish. This procedure may be repeated three or four times. Having built up a sufficiently good body the final brightness is brought up by vigorous rubbing. To restore furniture polished in this manner it is usually only necessary to ease-down with fine glasspaper, dust off and apply a flowing coat of clear varnish.

BOOK REVIEWS

'Schlock' or 'borax'

For those who like the challenge of mending furniture, or perhaps, are driven to it by economic necessity, a book by an American author should prove a useful source of ideas, for no two breakages and subsequent repairs are ever alike. Mel Marshall has written *How to Repair, Upholster and Refinish Furniture* which is distributed through Harper & Row Ltd, 28 Tavistock Street, London WC2E 7PN, at £6.95.

This is confessedly not a book on the restoration of quality antique furniture but rather a householder's practical guide to the reinstatement of second-hand furniture. As such it covers the treatment of broken and damaged pieces by resorting to a variety of artifices that range from dowels to distilled water. The book faithfully follows the three major elements of its title, with supplementary chapters on tools, materials and supplies. The last are named all from American sources which is not surprising as this is yet another book from across the Atlantic; and of course the reader has to cope with American terminology.

The author's introductory review of the development of American furniture is interesting from an historical point of view; and the early introduction of mass-production techniques may account for the high mortality rate among the pieces that the book ingeniously suggests how to revive. But when you have to cope with classes of furniture labelled 'schlock' or 'borax' you are immediately confronted with the wide differences in language that can exist in 'English-speaking' countries. Hopefully you can resort to some expatriate American neighbour (as I had to do) to be told that these terms generally mean shoddy workmanship. **R.W.G.**

'This is your bible'

Alf Martensson's *The Woodworker's Bible* is appropriately named. At the outset of my teaching career I was sent into a school for teaching practice at the proverbial deep end. The board of education at that time issued a 'Handbook of Suggestions for Teachers' and the headmaster thrust a copy into my hands with the stern remark: 'This is your bible'. My first thought was that he was taking the name in vain. Perhaps life was sterner in those days.

The Oxford dictionary refers to a bible as an 'authoritative book'. By way of introduction in *The Woodworker's Bible* there is an excellent dictionary of tools and devices; and as there are no less than 350 small but clear illustrations in this dictionary alone, this in itself merits the adjective 'authoritative'.

Even so, in the first column of the first chapter (The Workshop), the author states: 'You need very few tools to do good quality work'; and almost before you begin to read you see the words 'to love wood, to love furniture, to enjoy making things. It might sound corny, but ...' Corny or not this must be a clear reflection of the author's character. (I read in the paper not very long ago how Mr Mugabe referred to Lord Soames using the word 'love'. Who would say that love is not the surest of all foundations?) The whole section is a mass of sound advice for anyone setting up a workshop for the first time. I wish that such concentrated advice had been available half a century ago!

The next chapter is devoted to Portable Power Tools. Circular saws, jigsaws, drills, jointers and groovers, planers, sanders, routers, are all described together with jigs and templates. The comprehensive and sound advice on choosing, purchasing and maintenance is part of the general theme. Accent is on safety.

A chapter on Woodworking Machines follows. This includes circular saws of all types, bandsaws, jigsaws. All are fully described with methods of operation and maintenance; again with repeated emphasis on safety. This leads to surface planers and thicknessers, both machines being thoroughly described with complete advice on adjustment and maintenance. Planing faults are tabulated together with their causes. Also there are comprehensive descriptions of spindle moulders, drills, mortise and tenon cutting, lathes, sanders and grinders; and there are expert comments on combination machines.

There follows a complete chapter on Woodworking Joints and this includes joints for sheet materials. There is no point whatever in trying to list the various types of wood jointing. It is sufficient to say that every possible joint and combination of joints are expertly described and beautifully illustrated. Hand and machine joints are dealt with and it is impossible to criticise any detail of these excellent guiding principles.

The next chapter (Furniture Construction) opens with reference to strength. The author points out the difficulty of analysing the stresses to which furniture is subjected by 'people sitting or standing on it, pushing it, turning it on end, dropping it and so on'. A number of small drawings illustrate these forces very well and here again tabulated information appears specially useful. As a basis for design, surely, strength is essential.

A section on glues follows which is comprehensive, and wood reinforced with carbon fibre is mentioned, together with an insight into its future use in furniture design and construction.

As to the designs illustrated for tables, chairs and cabinets — work by various individuals — I can only take off my hat as a token of admiration.

The chapter on Wood as a Material is authoritative and well illustrated and leads to conversion of the standing tree, a description of air and kiln seasoning and methods of measuring moisture content. Practical advice on the purchase of timber is included, together with notes on storage.

A brief chapter on Finishing — filling, staining, oil finishes, shellac, wax, varnish, lacquers, bleaching and spraying — completes a handsome publication into which a great deal of effort and experience has been incorporated. I am certain that my old headmaster would have had the greatest admiration for The Woodworker's Bible.

It is published by Pitman Publishing Ltd, 39 Parker Street, London WC2B 5PB, at £7.95. **C.B.**

Attraction of woodworking tools

Writing in the Financial Times for 28 June under the heading 'Before Black and Decker', Janet Marsh stated that it is little more than a year since Christie's, South Kensington, held their first major auction devoted entirely to the tools of the carpenter and allied trades. (See WOODWORKER for July 1979, p394.)

Since then such sales have become a regular feature of the London and provincial saleroom, so it is not a surprise to see a revival of interest in the basic books on the subject – R. A. Salaman's Dictionary of Tools, W. L. Goodman's British Planemakers and lately Philip Walker's Woodworking Tools. Neither, therefore, was it a surprise to receive for review Antique Woodworking Tools, a guide to the purchase, restoration and use of old tools for today's shop by Michael Dunbar, published by Stobart & Son Ltd, 67-73 Worship Street, London EC2, at £7.50.

Michael Dunbar is the author of Windsor Chairmaking also published by Stobart, and many magazine articles on antiques. He is a chairmaker and specialist in antiques, furniture care and old woodworking tools. He is also one of the few contemporary craftsmen in America producing Windsor chairs by hand, using 18th century methods and original tools.

This latest book brings together information on tools of the 18th and 19th centuries for amateurs, professionals and collectors. Using antique tools is a matter of personal preference – it gives a more contemplative approach to the craft of woodworking and the medium of wood. To understand antique tools properly Michael Dunbar considers that they should be studied within their original context so his explanation covers three main points: the medium, the men and the products.

This is a very readable book, it maintains variety and does resist the very real temptation to ramble which the author admits was strong when he tried to decide what not to include.

Michael Dunbar says he has not produced a final word but rather a personal introduction to a viable alternative to modern tools that the modern craftsman may not have previously considered. Obviously the chapters on how and where to buy old tools are of a transatlantic bias but the practical information contained in what not to buy and the detailed chapters on bench planes, moulding planes, special purpose planes, saws and boring tools are worth reading for their advice and wealth of information. The book ends with a short bibliography and a comprehensive index. **P.C.**

The faith to leave the doors open: God is at home to visitors.

Church furnishing and decoration in England and Wales by Gerald Randall is a historical introduction to English church furniture. The author stresses that the book has been written partly with students in mind, the numerous notes and excellent index bear this out; it is also designed for the increasing number of people who are interested in the history of their local church and the even larger number of people for whom looking round churches is a natural part of a holiday or a Sunday afternoon drive.

Since I belong to the latter group and regularly visit churches both in the British Isles and on the continent with great interest and usually great pleasure I found this book a delight particularly as it contains illustrations spanning half a century of collection.

Some of the oldest and even a few of the more recent, therefore show arrangements that have since been altered but many have been chosen deliberately for just this fact. Recent restoration has brought to light previously invisible details of paintings but also, alas, many important pieces have been destroyed.

As the author so rightly points out by far the largest repository of English and Welsh furniture and decoration are the churches, abbeys and cathedrals, both Anglican and Catholic. The gap that has existed up until now concerning the subject is ably filled by Gerald Randall's fully illustrated book (240 pages contain 262 photographs). The scope of the work is wide and the chapters each deal with a different aspect following the natural progression through the church from porch to memorials via the font, seating and other nave furniture, screens, chancel seating, eucharistic furniture, wall painting, glass and mosaics.

A fascinating range of miscellanea is also discussed such as armour, biers, clocks, commandment boards, dole cupboards, organ cases, lights, carvings, shrines, sword rests and tiles and obscure subjects like acoustic jars, wig stands, pax, dog tongs, hudds and gotches.

It is always a pleasure to pick up a book, open it at random and find a well-loved piece or memory on the page. . . on page 35 of this book I was delighted to see a photograph of the north door knocker from the porch of Durham cathedral which my husband made in pottery for our wall. It is a magnificent mask of a bronze lion, and a source of great personal delight every time it is viewed.

Also pleasurably viewed is the inclusion of recent artists like Henry Moore, John Piper and Graham Sutherland, to mention just a few. Their work should be seen next to that of the earlier craftsmen if a proper historical survey of any weight or meaning is to be attempted.

WOODWORKER readers may perhaps find much in the book that is not woodwork and therefore feel that to spend £15 on a book which is not just 'their subject' is a luxury. I feel that it is a luxury to indulge. Anything viewed out of context can very soon become meaningless. A church viewed just for its ornate pulpit or its pews without an appreciation of the other wonderful trappings present is a mockery.

Many of my favourite churches have been included, so perhaps I am biased but they are so obviously favourites of the author, too, since he has personal knowledge of more than a thousand of those considered in this book.

The designer of the book rarely gets acknowledged; this book shows that designer and author both think on clear, uncluttered lines and do justice therefore to the clean simple lines of the early material in the book and also to more ornate fittings of the baroque. The first Norman abbot of St Albans (Paul de Caen) described the inadequate efforts of his people as 'rudes et idiotas' but much of the early Anglo-Saxon work (and workers) was far from this description.

This book is dedicated to 'those incumbents who lock their churches and hide the key, thus proclaiming that God is not at home to visitors' in the hope that it may help to persuade them to change their minds. . .I hope so too.

Church Furnishing and Decoration in England and Wales by Gerald Randall, published by B. T. Batsford Ltd, 4 Fitzhardinge St, London W1H 0AH, at £15. **P.C**

Change of pace for a Quaker School

Peter Clark teaches machine usage on the fringe of the Yorkshire dales. He does not promise to turn you into an expert craftsman but there are many techniques that can be taught during the training period. 'The quality of your work will increase enormously,' he says

On the fringe of the Yorkshire dales at Rawdon near Leeds, Peter Clark and his wife have converted a former Quaker school into a machine woodcraft training establishment. Here, Rawdon Woodturners (the trade name for Peter Clark Woodcraft Ltd) offers courses for up to three people at a time at beginner, intermediate and advanced levels.

Mr Clark, a Lancastrian who 'strayed' into Yorkshire for his education, subsequent apprenticeship in joinery and shopfitting, and studies leading to an HNC in building and finally a teacher-training course at Leeds college of education, became increasingly aware of the importance of training for those who buy woodworking machinery.

After four months searching a wide area he and his wife found the derelict Old Friends school at Rawdon. Much hard work was necessary to get the premises ready but Mr Clark says: 'I felt it would be a challenge to set-up courses not offered through educational establishments except for those training to be craftsmen. My idea, too, was that amateur and professional craftsmen buying woodworking machinery, some of which is fairly sophisticated, would also benefit from training.'

He believed that having the right type of equipment was important and that it should be suitable for those using it, ie the amateur and professional craftsman. He chose Kity combination machines and Coronet, Arundel and Kity variable speed lathes.

To advertise the courses Mr Clark prepared a descriptive leaflet for mailing to those who responded to his advertisements in WOODWORKER and other publications. The first course got off the ground in May. Since then others have followed in quick succession. Three types are offered: woodturning; general machine woodworking; and woodturning and general machine woodworking. The first two occupy two days each and the third takes up three days.

The woodturning course covers use of Arundel J4, Coronet major and Kity 664 machines with general principles of turning and setting-up. Spindle work is dealt with such as marking-out, setting-up, roughing-out, smoothing-off, cutting beads and coves, rounding-over and trimming-off. Bowl turning, including faceplate work such as screw chuck, cup chuck, finishing and polishing, is included as well as long hole boring, copying and, of course, the use of gouges, chisels, the parting tool and other tools.

The general machine woodworking course takes in circular, band and crosscut saws, planer/thicknesser, spindle moulder and mortiser and involves the use of two large Kity combinations, a Kity bandsaw, Woodmen K5 combination and De Walt DW125 saw. Particular emphasis is placed on safe working practices.

The woodturning and general machine woodworking course combines the main elements of the other two courses with emphasis on either turning or machining depending on individual requirements. Recently Mr Clark has introduced courses specifically for users, and would-be users, of Kity machines.

A two-day course is £35 a day for each person and this includes tuition, provision of tools, equipment etc, lunch and refreshments. Accommodation can be arranged locally to suit a person's needs.

And who are those who have been to Rawdon Woodturners? A solicitor, lecturer, farmer, clerical worker, to mention just a few. Some had already bought machines and wanted to know how best to use them. Others contemplated purchase but first sought knowledge of how the machines should be operated. Apprentices from a nearby firm of woodturners have also been pupils, with the approval of the training board.

Mr Clark keeps in touch with his course members. 'We are happy to help them at any time,' he says. 'And we always aim to make the courses very personal affairs.'

For the future he hopes to increase the number and variety of courses. His aim is to organise at least two a week with occasional weekend ones, and to enlarge the scope using a wider variety of machines. But he intends to maintain individual tuition. Thus all courses will continue to be for not more than two or three persons at a time.

The old Quaker school (right) at Rawdon near Leeds

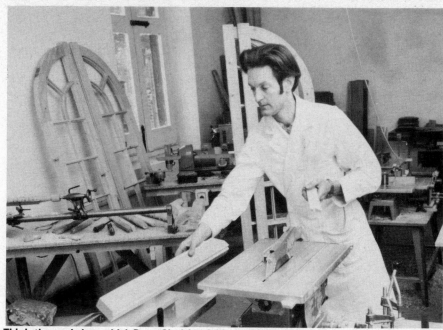

This is the workshop which Peter Clark has laid out in the building shown above

50th Model Engineer Exhibition, Wembley.

VISITORS CANNOT AFFORD TO MISS THIS.

To mark the Golden Anniversary of the Model Engineer Exhibition we are offering, for a limited period only, all the machines in the Cowell Collection at special prices.

<u>See Exhibition Guide for full details.</u>

If you are thinking about buying a machine tool for a home workshop, you must see the very comprehensive range which we have to offer.

You may not know for instance, that the popular Cowells 90 Lathe is available to four specifications, or that our new Wetstone Grinder is available in motorised or unmotorised versions. Have you heard about our precision Roller Filing Rest ?

As usual we will have new products on display and we are looking forward to discussing these with you, so please make a point of calling on us.

Cowell Engineering Limited

See us on Stand 24

BASIC MARQUETRY · 2

In his first article (WOODWORKER for November) Ernie Ives discussed the essential tools and materials for marquetry. Here he goes on to explain the preparation and cutting of the picture which is a country cottage scene: 'It is rather simplified but should give you an insight into many of the techniques involved and some practice in the use of the knife and in using the veneers'.

The design (Fig. 1) I have drawn for you is of an attractive country cottage scene. It is rather simplified but should give you an insight into many of the techniques involved, some practice in the use of the knife and in using the veneers. Treat the drawing as a guide only. Impose on it your own ideas. Alter the shapes if you wish. Change the veneers if you think you can improve the effect. Remember that no two pieces of veneer are exactly alike and yours could be considerably different from mine. I have not put in every shadow on a simple picture like this but assume that the sun is shining from the top right-hand corner so that the front of the building is brightly lit and the ends in shade.

As a beginner at marquetry you will quickly realise that the palette of colour available in natural wood is limited. There are no blues, bright reds or greens. Dyed woods can be obtained but in most pictures these do not blend in well with the natural veneers. You can overcome this lack of colour by using the tone, grain and figure of the wood to produce the required effect. In making up the design I have refrained from using 'freak' veneers or veneers that are no longer available. Therefore, you should be able to produce a picture as good as the one illustrated.

The first job is to make a tracing of the design. Use a sharp hard pencil or, preferably, a drawing pen. If you can scale-up the design slightly (the original measured 8½ × 10in. some parts could be less fiddly but you should not have any real problems in making it to the size printed.

The window method. Most marquetarians nowadays use what is known as the window method to cut their pictures. This involves hinging the design to the background veneer or, if no background, to a waste veneer or cardboard. Parts of the design are then transferred on to this using carbon paper and one of these parts is cut from the background leaving a hole or 'window'. By placing a veneer under this window you can see its likely effect in the picture. If it is suitable the piece can be cut in using the edge of the window as a template to guide the knife and the piece is glued in place. All the rest of the pieces are done in the same way.

After this the picture is trimmed square, stringers and borders added and the assembly glued to a baseboard. This is edged, cleaned-up and polished. Sounds simple? Well it is, really, but before we go through it step-by-step you will have to make a decision. Do you want to see the finished picture the same way round as the design or as a mirror image of it?

Fig. 1 (left) The country cottage. . . 1. Aspen 2. various burrs 3. Nigerian walnut 4. ayan 5. sycamore 6. sap walnut 7. European walnut 8. black walnut 9. lacewood 10. sapele 11. afara 12. oak.

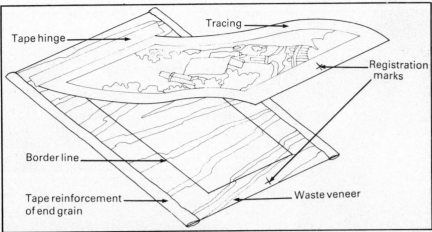

2▲

Fig. 2 Preparation of the waste veneer.
Fig. 3 The sky and road veneer taped together.
Fig. 4 Holding the knife to cut straightish shapes.
Fig. 5 The roof cut out.

3

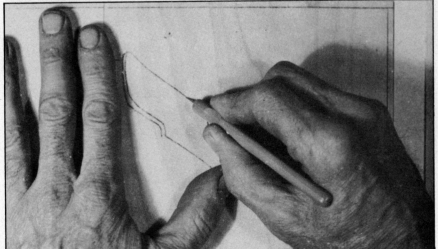

▲
4

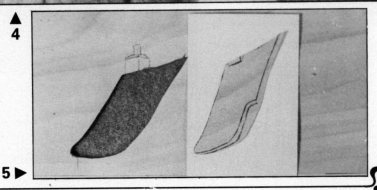

5 ▶

7

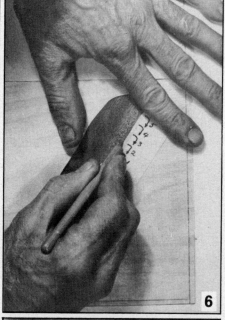

6

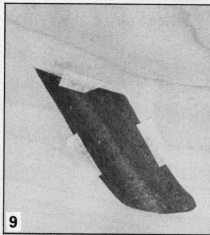

9

Reason for asking is that we shall cut the picture from the back (the side that will be glued to the baseboard). This is because the knife is wedge-shaped and thus gives a closer join on the face side but it does mean that the picture ends up the reverse of the design. All that is necessary to correct this is to turn the tracing over. I will assume that you want the picture to end up the same way as drawn.

Waste veneer. As there is no real background to this picture you can either use a waste veneer (any piece of softish, light veneer such as sycamore or obeche, about 1in. bigger all round than the design), or a piece of thin card of similar size. The latter is the method that I used. On to the top edge of this hinge the tracing with masking or gummed paper tape (Fig. 2). If veneer is used reinforce the ends by folding the tape over them to prevent splitting. Alternatively, as the sky forms the bulk of the upper part of the picture and the walnut road the lower, the two woods for these can be taped together to make up the background (Fig. 3). The joint line should be below the bottom level of the sky and above the top line of the road.

Using the cardboard-waste veneer method, mark-out the border line and the lower limit of the sky. As you will see as we go along it is a waste of time to mark out the whole picture. Add a registration mark to

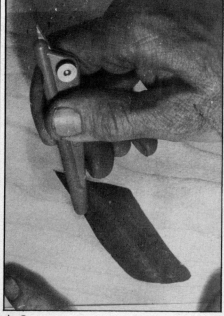

▲ 8

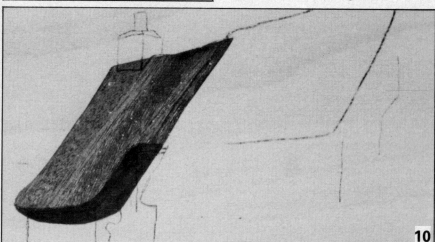

10

Fig. 6 The stepping cut technique.
Fig. 7 Run a little glue round the hole.
Fig. 8 Rub the piece in place with the knife handle.
Fig. 9 Slightly buckled pieces can be held in place with tape.
Fig. 10 The shadow area overcut.
Fig. 11 Continuation of work on walls and roofs.

11 ▶

NEW! from EME

EMCO-REX 2000
WOODWORKING CENTRE

The New EMCO-REX 2000 is an amazing combined planing and thicknessing machine with automatic feed. Used by professionals and in home workshops. The basic machine is very versatile and can easily be adapted with the custom built circular saw, mortising and spindle moulding attachments.

The New EMCO-REX is one of the finest made machines on the market and without doubt the finest value.

★ 2 YEAR GUARANTEE
★ MADE BY THE LARGEST MANUFACTURER OF SMALL MACHINE TOOLS IN THE WORLD!

250mm x 150mm thicknessing capacity

£395.00 SPECIAL INTRODUCTORY PRICE INCLUDES FREE STAND VAT EXTRA

250mm circular saw

mortising

spindle moulding

FREE!
SEND TODAY FOR LITERATURE
E. M. EQUIPMENT LTD,
B. E. C. HOUSE,
VICTORIA ROAD,
LONDON NW10 6NY.
Telephone: 01-965 4050
Telex: 262750

For full details of this equipment and a list of stockists in your area send for our FREE catalogue.

NAME _____

ADDRESS _____

_____ W.

the bottom of the tracing outside the picture area and mark this through on to the waste veneer. This registration mark must be kept in alignment when all the subsequent marking-out is done.

Cut out a rectangular shape from the waste about ⅛in. outside the border line and below the sky limit mark. Pieces which come up to the border line will all be cut that much over so the finished picture can be trimmed back to the right size later. Place the sky veneer under the opening, adjust it for the best grain effect and then cut it into the hole. If part of your veneer is darker than the rest, keep this towards the top of the picture as the sky always appears lightest at the horizon. It does not matter if this piece does not fit tightly — just keep it in place with gummed tape.

Where to start cutting. As general rule start from the background and work to the foreground. Anything that is behind anything else is put in first. We already have the sky in but we also want some fairly simple shapes for you to start with. Try the roof on the extension to the house. Mark this and the area around it on to the sky veneer.

The overcutting technique. We shall use this technique a lot so I will explain why. We used it where the sky ran into the borders to allow for later trimming to size, though overcutting in other places can simplify the shape of the piece and make it less fragile.

More importantly if the piece is cut and glued exactly to the right shape and when the adjacent piece is cut up to it, it is easy to leave a tiny sliver of the background or waste veneer in the joint unnoticed in the glue and dirt until the picture is cleaned-up and polished. Then it will show badly. Overcutting the line will prevent this and will give a fresh, clean join for the glue to adhere to. Mastery of this technique can make the cutting of a picture so much easier as I hope to show as we go along.

Looking at the roof piece, note that it must fit exactly where it touches the sky but everywhere else it can be cut over the line.

Using the knife. Insert the blade so that only about ⅜in. projects from the handle. With the straighter shapes hold the knife at a low angle to the direction of the cut but square across it (Fig. 4). Cut out the roof as shown in Fig. 5 which also shows inset the piece that was removed to give you an idea of the amount of overcutting. Select a piece of Nigerian walnut, place it under the window, adjust for the best grain effect and hold it in place with a couple of pieces of masking tape or paper clips. Once experience has been gained finger pressure alone will be sufficient to prevent the piece from moving while it is being cut.

Stepping cut technique. Using the window as a template, cut round the edge and score a line into the piece below with the knife tip. Instead of starting at the end farthest away from you and pulling the knife round the edge in one long sweep as would seem to be the most natural way, start at the nearest end and work along in about ⅜in. steps. This way you should be able to accurately follow the edge and get a good tight fit. The arrows in Fig. 6 give some idea of the method.

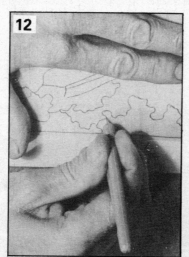

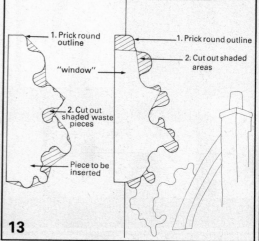

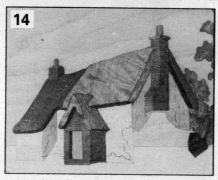

Having marked all the way round remove the lower piece. With the softer woods this marking cut will have almost cut through the veneer but the harder woods will have to be gone over again, still using the stepping cut, until the piece is free.

Run a little glue round the hole (Fig. 7) or round the piece, insert it from the face side (here again the wedge shape of the blade makes it easier for the piece to go in from the face side) and rub it in place with the end of the knife handle (Fig. 8). Scrape off any surplus glue with a round blade or a razor blade. If the wood is a little buckled it may be necessary to use a few small pieces of gummed tape to hold it in place (Fig. 9). Make sure that all the tape is kept on the face side of the picture. Very little should be needed for this picture if the pieces fit properly.

Below the roof is a narrow curved piece. With this we will see the advantage of overcutting in strengthening the piece. Whichever way the grain is put some parts will be short and fragile. Mark-out the piece on to the roof, cut on the line around the top edge and where it touches the sky. I then go well over the line to make the piece about ⅜in. wide. Fit and glue in the darkest piece of walnut you can find (Fig. 10). Allow the glue to dry before cutting in the adjacent walls; meanwhile the chimney and the other roof can be fitted.

Work can continue in a similar way on the house up to the stage shown in Fig. 11. All the pieces are fairly straightforward so you will have a chance to perfect this cutting technique before trying the more curly shapes. Some specimens of ayan may be hard and brittle. If yours is like this use the stepping cut technique with much shorter

steps. If it keeps breaking put some Sellotape on the surface first and cut through that. Oak could be substituted. Do not be tempted to use a rule for the straight lines; they will appear unnaturally straight in the picture. Do them as straight as possible freehand.

Cutting in the foliage. Before the end wall of the house is done it would be better to cut in the tree behind it and some of the foliage on that side of the picture too. The problem here can be twofold: (i) to cut round the curly shape; and (ii) to fit in the rather fragile and buckled burr veneers.

To cut round these tight curves the knife must be kept more upright (Fig. 12) and used with a pricking action, the steps being very short. This brings us to the next marquetry rule: The sharper the curves and the harder the wood so the length of the steps is decreased and the more upright the knife is held.

This is not the end however. Many pieces are broken by trying to lift them out whole from the surrounding veneer when one or two fibres of wood are still bridging the cut. The answer to this is shown in Fig. 13. When cutting out the window, cut across the peninsula-like areas and remove them first; when cutting the insert, cut across the 'bays' and remove the surrounding waste veneer.

Fig. 12 Hold knife more upright to cut curly shapes.
Fig. 13 Cutting and fitting curly-shaped pieces to prevent breakages.
Fig. 14 The house ready for the windows.
Fig. 15 Sketch of simplified windows.

Fig. 16 The roadway cut in.
Fig. 17 The banks and lawns fitted.
Fig. 18 Bushes cut in.
Fig. 19 Now the fence is put in.
Fig. 20 The cutting complete from the face side.

The problem of buckled veneer can be solved in several ways. If you know that a piece will be required, a few days before the whole piece can be soaked in water for about 5min until it is soft and pliable, then placed between two pieces of chipboard and put under heavy weights or in a press. After 24hr the chipboard is turned over (so that the dry outer faces are against the veneer) and put-back under pressure for a further two days. If it is kept in a dry atmosphere the veneer will often go back to its buckled state. With care it should be satisfactory for some weeks — longer if kept weighted down.

If the buckling is not too severe mark round the window on to the veneer with a pencil and cut out the piece about ⅜in. larger all round. This will often relieve the tension in the wood sufficiently to enable it to be fitted in. If this is not enough rub some dilute PVA glue (say 3 parts glue to 1 water) into the surface and place the veneer between two vinyl tiles or in a plastics bag and weight it down. After about 20min the glue will have dried sufficiently to keep the wood flat while it is being cut. The wood will also be nice and soft. If it is left until the glue is really dry the wood becomes hard again and the surface gritty. Although it will be flat it may still be difficult to cut.

Windows. When the picture has reached the stage shown in Fig. 14 we can consider doing the windows; or they can be left until last. An enlarged picture of a window is given in Fig. 15, together with the order in which to cut the pieces. The diagonal line across the panes is not for two separate pieces of wood but the change in colour from the heartwood to the sapwood of a piece of walnut. This looks more realistic than a plain piece of hardwood which is often recommended. If you wish you can add curtains and pot plants!

Cut the slots for the framework freehand and, using a steel rule to guide the knife, cut slivers from the edge of a short piece of walnut veneer. The combination of freehand-cut slot and rule-cut pieces still seems to give a natural looking effect. A piece 2-3in. long will be easier to cut straight than a large piece; and the width can be estimated.

Try the sliver in the slot, snip it to length and glue it in. It is not so practical to overcut these simple rectangular shapes. But if you only glue the edge of the piece that does not have to be re-cut and take care not to leave any background in the joint when the adjacent piece is cut out, there should be no problem. Special care will have to be taken as the windows are dark and tiny slivers of the white sycamore wall left in the join will show badly.

Roadway. Cut out the whole road including the dark walnut shadow area and try to find a piece that will have this shadow in the figure in the veneer (Fig. 16). If you can use it, it will normally look better than using two separate pieces. However, if your search for such a piece is unsuccessful, put the waste piece back in place and cut the pieces in one at a time. It is here that those with a good stock of veneers have the advantage. Do not forget to cut right over the fence posts as the road can be seen between them.

Fit the brick wall banks next as by overcutting on to the lawns the short grained pieces can be strengthened. Large areas of lawn are difficult to reproduce well in wood. This is why I have broken them down into several pieces (Fig. 17) and why I have planted a number of trees. Afara, oak and ayan are suggested but use any other veneer if it has more suitable figuring. Now complete the rest of the bushes (Fig. 18). I added the large bush in the lawn after the design was completed as it looked bare there — you can add it now.

The latch and horeshoe on the door can be omitted but it is good practice to try and cut them in. Keep the knife upright, take very short steps and remove some of the waste wood round each piece in the manner described for the foliage. These pieces will probably be too fragile to pick up on the point of the knife like normal-sized pieces, unless the tip of the blade is first touched into a spot of white glue and the piece picked up by the glue.

Tackle the fence next. Cut in the top of each post oversize then the aspen piece, cutting right across the rail. Finally fit the sap walnut side. When all the posts are done cut in the rail. The picture should now be at the stage shown in Fig. 19.

Tree. Cut in the foliage. Save the waste from the sky as part of it will be fitted back in where it can be seen through the leaves. Try and find a nice piece of walnut for the trunk and a knot for the sawn-off bough. Fig. 20 shows the face side of the picture with all the cutting completed. Note how little tape has been used to hold the pieces together.

The next article will deal with borders, back and edges.

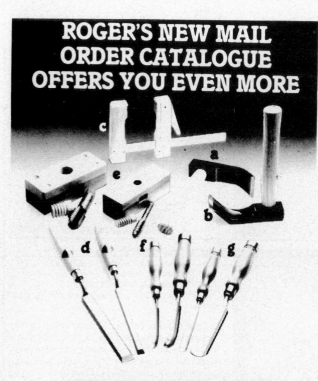

THIS FANTASTIC PRIZE

Winner of last year's Sjöberg family crafts competition was Nicholas Bott of Kingston upon Hull (WOODWORKER for December 1979). His prize: a holiday for two in Sweden. Nicholas and his brother flew from Gatwick on 17 August for Copenhagen and thence to Jönköping where they arrived 'in glorious sunshine' to be met by a representative of Ab Bröderna Sjöberg. They were taken to the Esso hotel at Jönköping and on the following day visited the company's factory at Stockaryd accompanied by managing director Bo-E. Sjöberg.

Nicholas writes: 'The tour of the factory was very interesting and afterwards we were taken on a trip of the surrounding countryside. The views were fantastic and the air so fresh. Mr Sjöberg took us to lunch at a home for the disabled from where his firm employs a percentage of its workforce. Later he entertained us to dinner at a very lovely restaurant.

'On the Wednesday we went by train to Göteborg. The weather wasn't too kind to us at first and we spent half the day getting wet! However the sun did show itself in the afternoon and we took a sight-seeing trip round the city.'

Thursday was spent in Jönköping and on the following day there was a 330km train trip to Stockholm. 'We rose early, had a quick breakfast and caught the train at Jönköping changing at Näsyö. We then spent about 4½hr on the train to Stockholm though we hadn't long in the city as we had to catch the 18.38 back to Fälköping. The next train was the 23.08! However, we took a two-hour boat trip round Stockholm and also did some shopping before catching the train. We duly changed at Fälköping and arrived at Jönköping at about 22.50, tired!'

Saturday turned out to be eventful for Nicholas and his brother. 'We decided to do some shopping in Jönköping. The shops close at 1.15pm on Saturdays but we weren't aware of this and in fact we were looking round a shop that had actually closed while we were in it.

'When we came to buy some cut glass there was nobody to take the money and we couldn't get out because the doors were locked! We managed to find a caretaker who unlocked the doors and let us out. Quite an experience.

'Alas,' wrote Nicholas, 'the holiday finished too soon and on Sunday morning we were up early to catch the plane at Jönköping airport, on to Copenhagen, and then back to England. A very pleasant holiday and I would like to thank Mr Sjöberg once again for his great hospitality and friendship and, of course, WOODWORKER for its part in this fantastic prize.'

Nicholas and his brother were accompanied to Sweden by their parents.

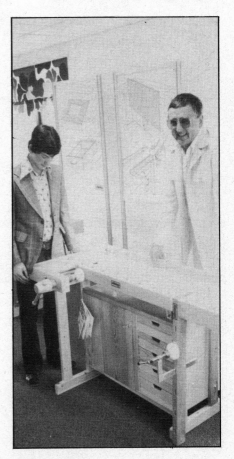

Bo-E. Sjöberg (right) and Nicholas Bott with the most popular workbench in the Sjöberg range — the BS122/142.

SPECIAL OFFER

Furniture at Temple Newsam House and Lotherton Hall

by Christopher Gilbert MA FMA FSA

One way in which the National Art-Collections Fund marked its 75th anniversary in 1978 was by sponsoring this large and important two volume catalogue of the celebrated furniture collection at Temple Newsam and Lotherton Hall, the two country house museums run by Leeds city council.

The main strength of the collection lies in elite English 18th century furniture, much of which was commissioned for great houses now destroyed. Leeds also possesses many excellent Tudor and Stuart pieces including an important holding of regional oak furniture, while the 19th century is represented by an impressive array of well documented masterpieces (several with royal connections) displayed at Lotherton Hall.

This is the first complete catalogue of a public collection of English furniture to appear for 50 years and it has been enthusiastically welcomed by reviewers, scholars and collectors.

The work is in two volumes (12 × 9¾in.), 522pp, 14 col. plates, 680 b & w illustrations, and describes 662 individual pieces or suites of furniture.

Normally priced at £60 the work is available as a special offer to readers of WOODWORKER until 31 December 1980 at £39, if ordered directly from the Keeper, Temple Newsam House, Leeds LS15 0AE. Cheques payable please to 'NACF Leeds Furniture Catalogue'. Orders will be promptly dealt with.

The author, in addition to being Principal Keeper of Temple Newsam, is hon curator of the Chippendale Society, editor of the *Furniture History Society Journal* and one of the most distinguished furniture historians of his generation.

Alan Holtham

Woodturner   Woodturners' Supplier

Light Woodworking Machinery Specialist

As a major supplier of woodworking machinery we are Main Stockists for:

CORONET, ARUNDEL, ELU, AJAX, STANLEY, STARTRITE, ZINKEN, SCHEPPACH, SHOPSMITH, MAFELL, DEWALT, BOSCH, TREND, AMERSAW, EUMENIA, MAFELL.

Visit our combined workshop/showroom to discuss your requirements or to take advantage of our demonstration facilities.

FOR ALL TURNING AND CARVING ENTHUSIASTS— we have recently been appointed main stockist in the North of England for the superb Henry Taylor range

of DIAMIC woodturning and ACORN woodcarving tools

WOODTURNING is our speciality, and we also stock a comprehensive range of accessories and fittings.

SEE US AT THE INTERNATIONAL WOODTURNERS AND CARVERS EXHIBITION.

New Bingley Hall, Stafford.
13th & 14th December.

THIS MONTH'S SPECIAL OFFERS!

ORIGINAL FLEXICLAMPS

For glueing up laminated turnery. Heavy duty steel band 3″ wide with handled tensioner. Five sizes opening to:

18″	£14.23
15″	£12.87
12″	£12.04
10″	£11.36
7″	£10.99

All prices include VAT and carriage

THE OLD STORES TURNERY
WISTASTON ROAD
WILLASTON
NANTWICH
CHESHIRE Tel: CREWE 67010

Hours:
Tues-Sat
9.00 - 5.30

EMCO MACHINES for Hobby & Trade

EMCO BS2

3-SPEED BANDSAW

For: Wood, Metal, Plastic.
Cutting Height: 5½″
Throat: 14″
Table Size: 15¾″x15¾″
LIST PRICE £284 inc. VAT

OUR PRICE:
£255 inc. VAT
Available Ex-Stock

EMCO TS5

TABLE SAW

Motor Capacity 1.2 hp
Table Size: 19½″ x 15¾″
Saw Blade Size: 8″
LIST PRICE £201 inc. VAT

OUR PRICE:
£181 inc. VAT
Available Ex-Stock

COMPLETE RANGE OF WOODWORKING MACHINES AND ACCESSORIES AVAILABLE.
PHONE OR WRITE FOR FREE ILLUSTRATED CATALOGUE & PRICE LIST.

EURO PRECISION TOOLS LTD.

235 London Road, North End, Portsmouth. PO2 9HA
TELEPHONE: 0705-697 823

EMCO IN CLEVELAND

See the new EMCO REX 2000 machining centre starting with a combined surface planer thicknesser 10″×6″ together with a 10″ circular saw attachment giving 3¼″ depth of cut, and two cutting speeds, 2800/4000 rpm. Other attachments include the spindle moulder with 2 speeds at 6000/4300 rpm, 30 mm, spindle diameter and 2″ adjustment in height. Finally the mortising attachment with ½″ chuck with 4½″ height and 7½″ width.

EMCO REX 2000 Planer thicknesser
complete with motor ....£395 & £59.25 VAT
Mortising attachment ....£77.00 & £11.55 VAT
Circular saw attachment ....£70.00 & £10.50 VAT
Spindle moulder ....£107.00 & £16.05 VAT
Above prices include carriage.

AN IDEAL COMBINATION MACHINE WHERE MONEY AND ROOM ARE AT A PREMIUM

ASK ABOUT THE other machinery in the EMCO RANGE, also LUREM, KITY ELEKTRA.
WOODTURNING LATHES BY ARUNDEL with HENRY TAYLOR Turning chisels BENCH GRINDERS 5″, 6″ and 8″ also POLISHERS, linishers with 5 year guarantee by KEF.
WADKIN PORTABLE POWER TOOLS — Quality machines at keen prices.
WAGNER AIRLESS SPRAY GUNS — BOTH DIY AND INDUSTRIAL.
MICOR CARBIDE TIPPED BLADES in range of qualities.
NOB EX MITRE SAWS   H AND TOOLS AND ABRASIVES

Drop us a line or give us a call about your interest in the above products at
WINTZ INDUSTRIAL SUPPLIES
2 Bessemer Court, Grangetown, Middlesbrough, Cleveland TS6 7EB
Eston Grange 460035   **Mon-Fri**

NOT PRETTY BUT *very* PRACTICAL

Most designers of woodworking machines are engineers, whose prime concern is the simple and economical manufacture of their product. They will go to great lengths to improve the design of their machines, shaving a few pence off the cost and yet increasing the strength of a particular component. This is all very well, but frequently the manufacturer misses the point altogether, making his well engineered machines beautiful to look at, but extremely difficult to use.

The Kity combination is very practical. Kity's first thoughts are to the woodworker. Let me give you an example. In most mono block combinations the Circular Saw and the Spindle Moulder use the same work table. The manufacturer's demonstrator will slickly gloss over this point, side stepping the issue or even using two machines (one demonstrating the Circular Saw and the other the Spindle Moulder). Can you imagine the time and work required to make a cross cut on the saw, and immediately after produce a rebate on the Spindle Moulder. You have to remove all the guarding and tooling, but what is more to the point, when you want to reproduce the same rebate you have to completely re-set the Spindle Moulder again. This could be good engineering but not much thought has been given to the user. The Kity combination offers you Independent Machines all driven from one motor, a saw, planer thicknesser and spindle moulder — to move from one to another and back again simply slip a belt — **no other adjustment is necessary**, simple but very practical.

Cross cutting with the mitre guide, and tungsten carbide saw blade on the 617 Saw.

Details of the kick back washers, serated feed roller and twin cutter block. (Note this area would normally be guarded). On the 636 Machine.

The Kity concept simple but very practical

Kity offers you Circular Saws, Bandsaws, Planer Thicknessers, Spindle Moulders and Slot Mortisers, along with a complete range of accessories, motors and floor stands.
Each machine can be independent or part of a combination for example:
You can start your work-shop with a circular saw, motor and stand. After a few months you can mount your saw on the large table, and drive any other machine from your existing motor. You can then continue to add machines until you have a fully equipped work-shop. This is a unique flexibility, that will benefit the professional and the amateur woodworker alike. Using a mixture of Kity independent and combination machines, you can build a work-shop that exactly suits your requirements. You do not have to purchase one complete unit that costs a lot of money and may be a compromise in size, or difficult to use. With Kity you do not have a lot of complicated attachments, nor do you have to swing the machine into different positions or use a special tool. Simply slip the belt from one machine to the next.

The Circular Saw 617
This is the heart of most workshops. The Kity machine has a cast and machined, tilting work table, a rise/fall arbor with hand wheel control, it accepts blades up to 9″ in diameter giving a 3⅛″ depth of cut, and is capable of running at two speeds, 3400 rpm and 7000 rpm. It is powered by a 1½ H.P. motor with No Volt Thermal Overload Starter. You will have no difficulty in cutting any wood based material, from melamine faced chipboard to African hardwoods.
Accessories included in the price are the mitre-guide with repeat cut stop, and wobble washers for grooving. The machine is guarded to comply with international standards.

The Planer Thicknessers 535, 635, 636
Kity manufacture three 'under and over' planer/thicknessers, a 10″ × 6″, 8″ × 6″ and a 6″ × 4″.
Each machine is available with stand and motor and can be used as an independent unit or will fit as part of the 700 combination. Each machine has cast tables and a twin knife cutter block and is of the 'under and over type'. The thicknesser is power fed with an adjustable thicknessing table giving true results along with the whole length of the timber, this is usually difficult to achieve with the 'over fed' clamp type thicknesser. The 636 and 635 both have unusual long (40″) surfacing tables ideal for straightening a twist in a plank of timber.

Spindle Moulders 626/627
The Spindle Moulder is a versatile and powerful tool. It does a totally different job to a router, although the system is similar. For example:
The 626 & 627 are capable of making large rebates 1¼″ × 1¼″ in hundreds of feet of timber. They will also produce moulding, deep grooves, tongue and groove joints, V-joints, tenons, profiles and counter profiles, all with effortless power.
The 626 has a standard adjustable fence with the capability of positioning the cutting tools over a 4″ vertical range. The 627 has the same specifications but with individual micro adjustable fences. Both machines have cutting speeds of 7000 rpm, and are guarded to full international standards.

The 625 Slot Mortiser
The only machine in the whole range that is *not* available as an independent machine. Working from the 700 table it will provide a ½″ slot, up to 5″ long and 4″ deep. An excellent machine for mortice joint production.

The 612 Bandsaw
Kity make an all steel, two wheel, Bandsaw with a 5½″ depth of cut and an 11½″ throat, it will accept blades from ¼″ for tight turns to ⅞″ for deep cutting and planking of timber. Unlike 'Plastic' Bandsaws the steel construction of the Kity machine allows you to set a high blade tension. This enables you to cut fast and in a straight line through hardwood and knots with a maximum depth of 6″, 'Like a hot knife through butter.'

Service and Support
All manufacturers claim to provide a service. We can demonstrate ours BEFORE you purchase your machine.

Kity Information
As Kity user, every few months you will receive an 'in house' newsletter printed exclusively for you. It includes other Kity users' practical ideas as to how to make more use of your Kity machines, plus information on new accessories, competitions and many other interesting ideas.

Kity Plan Sheets
Titles are issued for a nominal charge exclusively to Kity users and include, 'basic joints,' 'carpentry work bench' and 'fitted kitchens'. These practical plan sheets include cutting lists and complete manufacturing instructions on the relevant subject, and a new title is issued every 3 to 4 months.

A rebate being cut in a piece of moulded timber.

Producing a Mortice.

The Bandsaw with mitre guide.

Simply slipping the belt.

Stockist Training
Most manufacturers ask for a large order when appointing a new stockist plus a continual minimum yearly quota. This is not the case with Kity. We expect all our stockists to attend our product training courses, which enables the stockist to offer the best technical advice when you make your purchase, without the pressure to 'sell' minimum quantities. In the long term we will have far less service problems if you have chosen the right machine for the job, through correct advice.

Instructions on machines
Many service problems arise because machines are incorrectly assembled or adjusted, or are used far beyond their capabilities.
Each Kity machine has a comprehensive instruction book to ensure you have the knowledge to use the machine correctly.

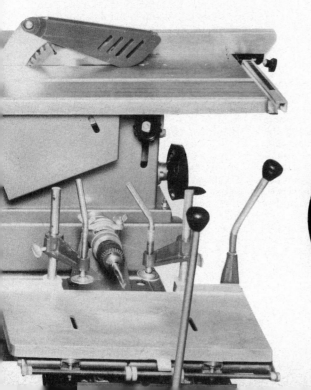

Two Year Guarantee
Should there be a problem with your machine we will make every effort to repair or replace as necessary at no cost to yourself, during the first two years of use.

For more information about this, and many more Kity products, please fill in this coupon and return

NAME . . . .

ADDRESS . . . .

. . . .

. . . . TEL. ww12

KITY
UNITED KINGDOM
Kity U.K. Sizers Court, Henshaw Lane, Yeadon, Nr. Leeds
Tel:(0532)509110

workpieces

Enthusiasts at Nantwich

'More like a supermarket at times!' This is how Alan Holtham describes the woodcarving and turning spectacular at his Willaston, Nantwich, premises on 8 and 9 August. He estimates that 600 people saw displays of finished carving and turning and talked with the two carvers and several turners who were demonstrating their skills.

Henry Taylor (Tools) Ltd, D. Arundel & Co Ltd and Coronet Tool Co Ltd, had products on show with representatives in attendance to discuss visitors' requirements.

A competition to judge how long it takes to make a carving tool from the steel blank was won by A. Wilkie from Maghull, Merseyside. He was presented with a set of 12 woodcarving tools made by Henry Taylor and a beech mallet. W. E. Maddock (Staffs) and D. P. Hemington (Leicester) were joint runners-up. The time taken for the manufacture of the gouge on display was in fact 9.6 min!

Mr Holtham says: 'We had visitors from England, Scotland and Wales. The event was a chance for keen woodworkers to meet each other and discuss their various difficulties and at the same time be able to consult the experts who were on hand. All in all it was a great success and we hope the spectacular will be repeated on an annual basis.'

Right wood

In the article on the mallet (p556 of WOODWORKER for September 1980) it was said that maple is often considered an ideal wood. In fact the wood named by the author of the article is apple, not maple as printed.

Insurance for models

In Model Horse-Drawn Vehicles Club *Newsletter No. 46* (July-August), hon secretary John Pearce reports on 'a fantastic collection' of models at chateau Chambord in NW France. These are of a train of seige artillery and associated equipment and other military engineering items, in all about 30 models.

The *Newsletter* contains useful hints on making chains for model vehicles and mentions *Discovering Horse-Drawn Carriages* (D.J. Smith) which has appeared as a second edition from Shire Publications Ltd, Cromwell House, Princes Risborough, Aylesbury HP17 9AJ, at 95p. Several other books of interest to modellers are also referred to.

Mr Pearce says he has been asked about insurance for models in transit from show to show and while on display. He would be glad to hear what members who regularly attend shows do about insurance. His address is: 4 Brentlea Crescent, Higher Heysham LA3 2BT.

Apples and pears!

Well not quite. Apples and doors would be more accurate — and another chapter in the saga of Franco-British trade relations. The British Woodworking Federation reports that doors by a manufacturer in this country failed to pass the French standard test. The manufacturer then had its doors retested alongside French-made doors which had successfully passed the French tests.

The work was done by Timber Research & Development Association (TRADA) near High Wycombe. Peter Shapcott, director of the BWF, has welcomed the initiative of the manufacturer in challenging what amounted to an 'export block' because of the 'ferocity of the tests carried out on British doors by the French CTB performance testing unit. It remains a mystery why the British doors in this particular case did not receive approval for entry into France,' adds Mr Shapcott.

Over to you M Valery Giscard d'Estaing!

Exporting

A batch of Mainframe timber seasoners has been ordered from Ebac Ltd of Bishop Auckland, Co Durham, by Carstens, the woodworking machinery specialist of Sweden. The machines have been modified to meet Swedish requirements. Ebac is also modifying its Mini, Minor, Mainframe models as well as the master control box to comply with German regulations.

Demand for timber drying machines in SE Asia, Australia and New Zealand is such that Ebac has opened an office in Singapore.

Cream on the order

Following on the announcement in the October issue (page 659) we have now had a copy of the first issue catalogue issued by Woodcraft Supply (UK) Ltd, St Peter's Hill, Brixham TQ5 9TE. Director A. J. Davey says the catalogue is free to readers of WOODWORKER, though a stamp will be appreciated.

Mr Davey writes: 'I am UK representative for Woodcraft Supply Corporation of Woburn, Mass, but I wish to make clear that in a trading sense we have no connection. Our catalogue has been produced jointly by fellow-director John Sainsbury and myself for the UK market.'

The catalogue runs to 16 pages covering accessories, clock kits and movements, instruments, wheels and pegs, workshop safety products and abrasives, tools, woodturning accessories, miniature woodturning items, marking punches and books, and many other items.

Details are included of the courses in woodturning run by John Sainsbury and the order form in the catalogue carries a promotion offer of a ¼lb carton of Devonshire cream (minimum order of £30). 'We have made the Woodcraft guarantee as strong as we possibly can and have combined VAT into all prices,' adds Mr Davey.

Balance sheet of safety

The balance sheet of health and safety at work cannot easily be quantified, states the Health & Safety Commission in its report for 1979-80. But it is important to ensure that costs are justified by improved health and safety, bearing in mind the benefit not only to industry but to the community from a reduction in accidents and ill-health at work.

Thus HSC makes a practice of full consultation and discussion with those concerned and prepares appraisals of costs and benefits of new safety requirements.

As part of the consultation process HSC recognises that use can be made of standards drafted by other organisations such as the British Standards Institution, industry's own committees and the commission's industry advisory committees. Whatever the source of the standard, HSC considers it should be prepared on a basis of consensus between the major interests, or subject to wide consultation, before being incorporated in the framework of control.

The report (ISBN 0 11 883275 1) is published by HMSO at £3.25 plus postage.

Timber preservation

Rentokil library of 12 titles covering pests and timber preservation now includes *Decay of Timber in Buildings* (C. R. Coggins). Leaflet giving prices and details of all titles can be had from Rentokil Ltd (Advice Centre), Freepost, East Grinstead, Sussex.

Birthday celebration

At Victoria Buildings, Luddenden Foot, Halifax, Yorks, Timberlite Ltd is celebrating its first year of trading as a distributor of woodworking machinery and tools. 'We are having a bonanza on the leading brand names,' says Mrs Val Criddle who is manager of the business, adding that the small buyer as well as the industrial user stands to benefit.

'We pride ourselves on giving a first-class service no matter how small the order. Staff help and advise on all aspects of Timberlite products and collection outside normal working hours is no problem. Indeed, customers have collected even on Boxing day,' comments Mrs Criddle.

She suggests that customers can make their craftwork more effective with the best brandname products and 'although demand is growing and Timberlite is expanding, the wide choice of products offered and the service will be staying the same. "Satisfied customers" is our motto and we intend to live up to it.'

The house of the mouse

On a late summer holiday in the north of England, Anne Duncan of WOODWORKER and her husband, Gordon, visited Kilburn, York, where 'mouse man' Robert Thompson established his workshop. Born in 1876 the son of the village joiner, his ambition was to create in English oak work to compare with that of the great craftsmen of mediaeval times. He achieved this desire both in his ecclesiastical and domestic woodwork. He adopted his mouse mark for no apparent reason – and it has become one of the best-known trade marks.

Thompson's tradition of craftsmanship continues in the village. His cottage is now a showroom for furniture, clocks and many other articles made in the enlarged workshops by Robert Thompson's Craftsmen Ltd, the business carried on by his two grandsons.

Two things impressed Mrs Duncan, apart from the high standard of the furniture: the large amount of timber in-stick adjacent to the workshops; and the number of people visiting the house of the mouse.

Rush for seating

Following publication of Jack Hill's series of articles on country chairs and chairmaking in the March, April, May, July and September issues this year, readers have asked for suppliers of rush for seating.

We understand that rush can be obtained from the following: I. & J. L. Brown, 58 Commercial Road, Hereford HR1 2BP; Robert J. Hill, Hollin House, Strawberry Lee Lane, Totley Bents, Sheffield S17 3BA; and Deben Craftsmen, 9 St Peter's Street, Ipswich, Suffolk.

The author of the articles points out that prices vary and carriage is extra so it is advisable to ask for quotations.

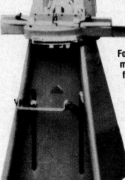

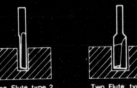

CORONET WOODWORKING MACHINES

Universal & Independent models for Woodworking & Woodturning 👑

CORONET
WOODWORKING MACHINES

MAJOR Universal CMB 500

CONSORT Universal CON 403

MAJOR LATHE CMB 600

MINOR LATHE MB 6

NEW

ELF TURNING LATHE

IMP BANDSAW IMP 100

7" PLANER CAP 300

4½" SOVEREIGN PLANER SOV 200

SOME OF OUR MAIN STOCKISTS
~full list available on application

BALLYMENA
G. Gardiner & Co. Ltd.,
49 Ballymoney Street, Ballymena,
Co. Antrim.
Tel. 0266 6384

MANCHESTER
Jos. Gleaves & Son Ltd.,
Gateway House, Piccadilly Station
Approach, Manchester.
Tel. 061 236 1840

BIGGIN HILL
Parry & Sons Ltd, 186 Main Road,
Biggin Hill, Kent.
Tel. 095 94 73777

NANTWICH
Alan Holtham,
The Old Stores Turnery, Wistaston
Road, Willaston, Nantwich.
Tel. 0270 67010

CARDIFF
Woodmen,
43b Crwys Road,
Cathays, Cardiff.
Tel. 0222 36519

PETERBOROUGH
Williams Distributors,
108-110 Burghley Road, Peterb
Tel. 0733 64252

DUBLIN
J. J. McQuillan & Son Ltd.,
35-36 Capel Street,
Dublin, Eire.
Tel. 0001 746745

READING
Sarjents Tool Stores,
44-52 Oxford Road, Reading.
Tel. 0734 586522

EXETER
John Wride & Co. Ltd.,
147 Fore Street,
Exeter, Devon.
Tel. 0392 73936

SOUTHAMPTON
Hampshire Woodworking
Machinery, Hoe Farm House,
Hoe Lane, Bishop Waltham,
Hants.
Tel. (04893) 2275

HARROGATE
Multi-Tools of Harrogate
158 Kings Road,
Harrogate, NTH, Yorks.
Tel. 0423 66245

WATFORD
J. Simble & Sons Ltd.,
76 Queen's Road, Watford,
Herts.
Tel. 0923 26052

Can you help?

Until recently C. H. Collier of Bexhill on Sea, Sussex, was able to buy garden rakes made of cane. But not now, so Mr. Collier wonders if he could make one. 'The snag so far as I am concerned is in bending the cane and maintaining its rigidity. Can you assist by providing any information as to the bending?' he asks.

If readers are able to help their letters will be passed to Mr. Collier who, incidentally, describes cane rakes as 'very useful because of their lightness and surprising strength'.

From: M. G. H. Dickinson, Bath, Co Avon
Dear Sir

I have been lent a Stanley plane no. 55 with the request that I find out how to assemble and use it. It is very similar to the Stanley 45 owned by Bill Gates and illustrated in his article on pp374-5 of WOODWORKER for June 1980, but possibly with more parts.

It has four boxes of cutters with it, giving 55 cutters in all. The label on the boxes says it was made by The Stanley Rule & Level Plant, The Stanley Works, New Britain, Conn, USA.

Ideally, I would like to get hold of the instruction book that presumably went with it originally but if you have any information that would be of help or interest I would be most grateful.

Incidentally, the plane belongs to a school workshop and so the information should be put to good use, especially as some excellent work is produced there.
Yours faithfully, **Michael Dickinson**

This letter was referred to Mr Gates who kindly undertook to investigate. With the co-operation of Stanley Tools he was able to obtain a copy of the 55 plane handbook together with notes on the uses of the 55 which originally appeared in Woodworker Annual *for 1929. Copies of these documents have been sent to Mr Dickinson.*

From: J.K.W. Wheatley, Minister Lovell, Oxford
Dear Sir

I refer to The World's Timber Trees article on page 436 of the August 1979 issue which deals with *Afrormosia elata*. In northern parts of Rhodesia (we have now returned after 30 years farming there), a fairly common tree is *Afrormosia argolensis* since renamed *Pericopsis angolensis*.

I presume the species name refers to Angola, W Africa, from whence comes the afrormosia timber sometimes available in Britain. Is not this the afrormosia sold here as *elata* and not the *angolensis* which I know? The latter is very hard, beautiful to work, very heavy, of middle brown colour which fairly quickly darkens on exposure to light, sometimes almost reaching a purple-black. After cutting a white bloom appears on the surface and continues to do so for months. Is there any explanation for this?
Yours faithfully, **Jack K.W. Wheatley**

C.W. Bond FIWSc, author of the series The World's Timber Trees, comments: There are four, if not six, species of Afrormosia (Pericopsis) occurring in tropical Africa and the afrormosia of commerce probably includes more than one species. My reference to the specific name elata was based on the fact that the slide for the photomicrograph and the herbarium specimen were both identified as that species. Afrormosia angolensis was first recorded in the 1906-

1910 supplement of the Index Kewensis.

I was particularly interested to learn that the genus Afrormosia has recently (a few years ago) been changed to Pericopsis. This name was first recorded in 1864 by a botanist named Thwaites and is therefore the earlier name. Research occasionally causes botanical alterations to be necessary, when the first name is substituted. (As if the names of timbers are not confusing enough as it is!)

The colour of afrormosia (Pericopsis) is extremely variable. As to the bloom you mention, I cannot explain this except that I have noticed a peculiar lustre on some pieces. It is quite likely that I have never seen a specimen of the species angolensis. I understand that elata is the largest tree and therefore the principal one commercially.

From: P. Pledger, Selsey, West Sussex
Dear Sir

With reference to the article on page 653 of the October 1980 issue ('... the screw may twist...' by Charles Cliffe), I would suggest that screwdrivers be ground concave so that the blades fit the slots.
Yours faithfully, **P. Pledger**

From: A. Fisher, Itchingfield, Sussex
Dear Sir

Most of us who are amateurs do not have enough cramps, especially of the larger variety. I have always managed with folding wedges but these are not very convenient to use. Recently I needed a pair of sashcramps and thought of buying some loose heads but hesitated when I saw the price.

Instead I bought two plain G-cramps of the largest bent variety, not the cast pattern. I cut off the side opposite the screw and drilled a ¼in. hole in the back and countersunk this on the inner side. I did not have a metal countersink bit but found that an old woodworking one was hard enough for the job.

I then cut a groove in the narrow edge of a 2 × 1in. batten in which the back of the cramp would slide, and bored ½in. holes at intervals in the batten and fixed a substantial stop at one end.

The cramp slides in the groove and is secured where required by a ¼in. countersunk bolt with a wingnut and washer underneath. This makes a light but quite serviceable long adjustable cramp for about £1. (see sketch below).
Yours faithfully, **A. Fisher**

Letters

From: Mrs Jean Fox, Southwater, Horsham, Sussex
Dear Sir

With reference to Alan Holtham's article on turning for tiles in the October issue p634, I would like to make one point. As a woodturner I agree that to allow for wood movement you cannot have a tight-fitting tile, but as a housewife I would not buy a cheeseboard with a 1/16in gap round the tile as this would act as a dirt and germ trap.

To overcome this problem I fix my tiles in with a flexible water-proof bath sealant such as Dow Corning which will fill the gap completely and will move with the wood if necessary.
Yours faithfully, **Jean Fox**

From: N. M. A. Evelegh FCA, clerk to the Worshipful Co of Turners, 1 Serjeant's Inn, Fleet Street, London EC4Y 1JD
Dear Sir

For the last two years the Worshipful Company of Turners has held a meeting of practical turners to discuss all aspects of their business. These meetings, in London, have been well attended and appear to have been useful.

Last year the meeting heard a talk about the work being carried out on the training of young people and this was followed by a general discussion about training in general. There was then a buffet lunch at which people were able to meet and chat with fellow turners from all round the country. After lunch there was a further discussion on matters, including the holding of exhibitions for the sale of turners' goods, the setting up of a registry and directory of turners and the quality of modern tools.

Another of these functions will be held in March 1981 and anyone who might like to attend and who is not already on our mailing list should write to me at the address given above. Even if they are unlikely to be able to attend, I would be pleased to hear from them if they would like their name to be added to the list of turners which I am preparing for circulation to anyone who is interested in the craft.
Yours faithfully, **Nigel M. A. Evelegh**

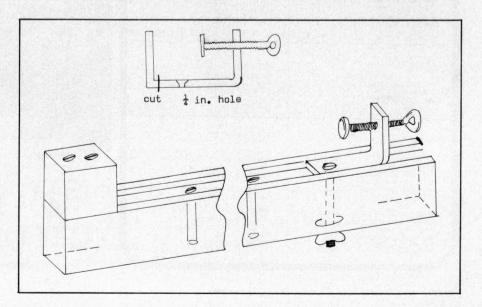

cut ¼ in. hole

BARGAINS from BENMAIL

HURRY! LIMITED OFFERS

Here's your chance to get this Super Skil power plane at a real bargain price

Check These Features:- Double edged carbide blades 75mm wide. Combined rip and mitre guide. V groove for making 45° bevels and 90° corners. Safety switch. Adjustable chip deflector. Speed 12,500 r.p.m. Input watts 1,030.

MODEL No. 98H

MRP £103.39
Special Offer Price £80.00
You save £23.39 AND get FREE CARRIAGE (UK Mainland)

POWER TOOLS, ETC.

Cat. No.		MRP	Our price
259	Dremel Moto Tool with 30 accessories	£41.80	£36.00
292	Dremel Engraver	£11.75	£10.00
2525	Craftsman router crafter	£84.95	£39.00
748-2	Craftsman 1hp heavy duty router	£89.95	£67.00
736-2	Craftsman ⅞hp router	£79.95	£59.00
163-2	Craftsman dual action orbital sander	£45.00	£34.00
172-2	Craftsman 3" belt sander 1hp	£92.50	£68.00
25189	Craftsman router recreator	£159.95	£115.00
593-U	Skil sandcat belt sander, 300 watt	£60.84	£49.95
96H	Skil power plane, 480 watt	£80.39	£67.00
1474H	Skil ½" reversing hammer drill, 500 watt	£65.44	£55.00
574U	Skil 7¼" circular saw, 1,000 watt	£62.10	£52.00
1490H	Skil 4½" bench grinder, 36 & 60 grit stones	£50.03	£41.50
320RLE	Bosch ⅜" Reversing drill with screw/drill kit	£45.50	£38.50
400-E	Bosch ½" variable speed hammer drill, 400 watt	£49.00	£42.00
450-ZE	Bosch ½" variable speed hammer drill, 450 watt	£68.50	£58.00
620-ZE	Bosch ½" variable speed hammer drill, 620 watt	£82.50	£70.00
P10	Bosch jigsaw	£37.25	£31.00
PST50E	Bosch variable speed jigsaw	£45.50	£38.50
PSS230	Bosch orbital sander	£43.50	£37.00
PWS115	Bosch 4½" angle grinder	£67.50	£57.25
PSP250	Bosch spray gun set	£48.50	£41.50
PKS46	Bosch 6" circular saw	£57.50	£49.00
S9	Bosch saw table for PKS46 saw	£39.95	£33.50
PKS65	Bosch 7½" circular saw	£89.50	£76.00
S10	Bosch saw table for PKS65 saw	£49.95	£42.00
POF50	Bosch plunging router	£55.50	£47.00
S7	Bosch milling stand	£44.50	£38.00
S8	Bosch routing bench for above	£19.95	£16.95
S2	Bosch drill stand	£19.95	£16.95
S18	Bosch lathe kit	£56.25	£47.80
S40	Bosch twist drill sharpener attachment	£19.95	£16.95
1130	Barrus universal drill stand	£39.96	£31.00
1120	Barrus shaper table for above	£18.11	£14.40

HAND TOOLS

04	Record 2" blade smoothing plane	£18.98	£14.50
311	Record 3 in 1 plane	£26.11	£22.00
050C	Record combination plane, 18 blades	£52.67	£44.00
020C	Record circular plane	£43.93	£37.00
405	Record multi plane, 24 blade	£126.50	£101.50
52E	Record QR woodwork vice 7"	£36.80	£30.00
No. 1	Record metalwork vice, 3"	£21.85	£17.50
130	Record cramp heads	£8.63	£7.25
145	Record bench holdfast, 6⅞" opening	£14.38	£12.00
146	Record bench holdfast, 7⅝" opening	£19.55	£16.50
135/2	Record sash cramp, 24" capacity	£14.38	£12.00
135/4	Record sash cramp, 36" capacity	£15.53	£13.00
140	Record corner cramp, 2" capacity	£6.33	£5.25
141	Record corner cramp, 4¼" capacity	£14.95	£11.90
148	Record dowelling jig	£23.52	£18.50
M1160	Marples draw knife	£13.80	£11.75
M2410	Marples 12" bow saw	£13.80	£11.75
M1002	Marples set of eight turning tools	£39.68	£33.00
M60	Marples set of 12 carving tools	£58.65	£49.00
M60A	Marples set of 6 carving tools	£31.63	£26.00
M444/S5	Marples set of 5 blue chip chisels	£19.09	£15.25
RB10	Stanley replaceable blade plane	£15.35	£11.50
13-030	Stanley plough plane, 3 blade	£16.10	£13.00
13-052	Stanley plough plane, 10 blade	£32.99	£27.00
13-050	Stanley combination plane, 18 blade	£50.45	£42.00
71	Stanley hand router, 3 blade	£19.75	£16.00

All prices include VAT
Carriage **FREE** on order over £20 (UK mainland).

Henry Taylor and Marples Woodcarving and woodturning tools in stock.

BENMAIL, 48 Station Road, St. Georges, Weston-super-Mare, Avon BS22 0XL.

Tel: 0934 24385   *We close Thursdays*

"CRAFTOOLS SELECTED"

Each month **CRAFTOOLS** will offer you a superb high quality woodworking machine by a well known UK or European manufacturer at a very competitive price. We are able to do this by careful planning and purchasing on our part.

But at the same time we do not neglect that all important guarantee and back up service that you the customer has a right to expect. We will even give a full cash refund if you are not entirely satisfied within 7 days of purchase.

So each month look for "**CRAFTOOLS** Selected". It may be the machine you are looking for.

MVS 93 ORBITAL SANDER

CRAFTOOLS are pleased to offer this powerful high speed sander with more than 20,000 sanding strokes per minute ensuring smooth vibration free running. Together with its large area sanding pad any surface will be sanded rapidly and cleanly.

Old paint, wood, veneers, marquetry and even metal surfaces provide no obstacles for this quality machine.

Handy and light, this machine is a must for all woodworkers and comes complete with an assortment of sandpaper sheets.

Normally: £55.00 inc. VAT.

"**CRAFTOOLS** Selected" price: **£40.00 inc. VAT & Carriage.**

ST 142/01 ORBIT JIGSAW

Elu's reputation as manufacturers of high quality woodworking machines are further enhanced by this superb, powerful jigsaw. Together with its rotary action, providing excellent balance and quiet running, orbit adjuster, with four positions to suit the material to be cut and a second gear for cutting aluminium, non-ferrous metal and steel, it makes this the most versatile jigsaw on the market today.

Further features include a tilting base to the left or right (45°) and a side fence as standard. Facility to take any make of blade. Safety on/off switch needing only thumb action to operate which cuts out when the grip is released. Blower fan for keeping the cutting area clear of swarf and dust. Coming to you complete in a metal carrying case this machine would normally cost: £113.85 inc. VAT.

"**CRAFTOOLS** Selected" price: **£75.00 inc. VAT & Carriage.**

Remember we carry all leading makes of machines and accessories so why not write or telephone today for a quote and our catalogue.

Please send me your catalogue of woodworking machines and accessories.

Name ....

Address ....

....

CRAFTOOLS 12 Turner St., Newport, Gwent. Tel: 0633 842996.

Prices quoted are those prevailing at press date and are subject to alteration due to economic conditions.

WORKSHEET 2 NEW SERIES

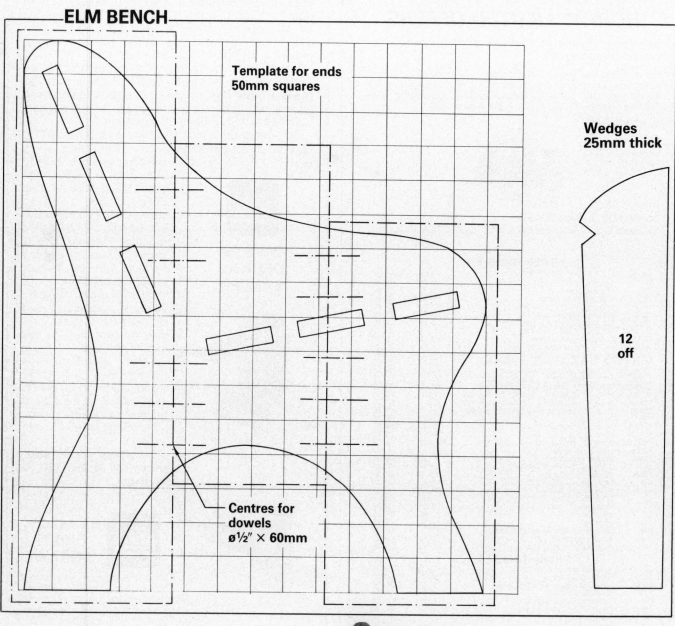

ELM BENCH

Template for ends
50mm squares

Wedges
25mm thick

12 off

Centres for
dowels
ø½" × 60mm

This design of garden bench is both attractive and very comfortable. It can be made from any suitable hardwood in a series of simple stages. The ends are made from three pieces dowelled together before the end shape is cut. A waterproof glue such as Cascamite is essential. The large mortice holes should be marked from both sides and bored out with a large bit first. The photograph shows a bench 5ft (1152mm) long but this can be adjusted to suit. A suitable exterior finish is vital.

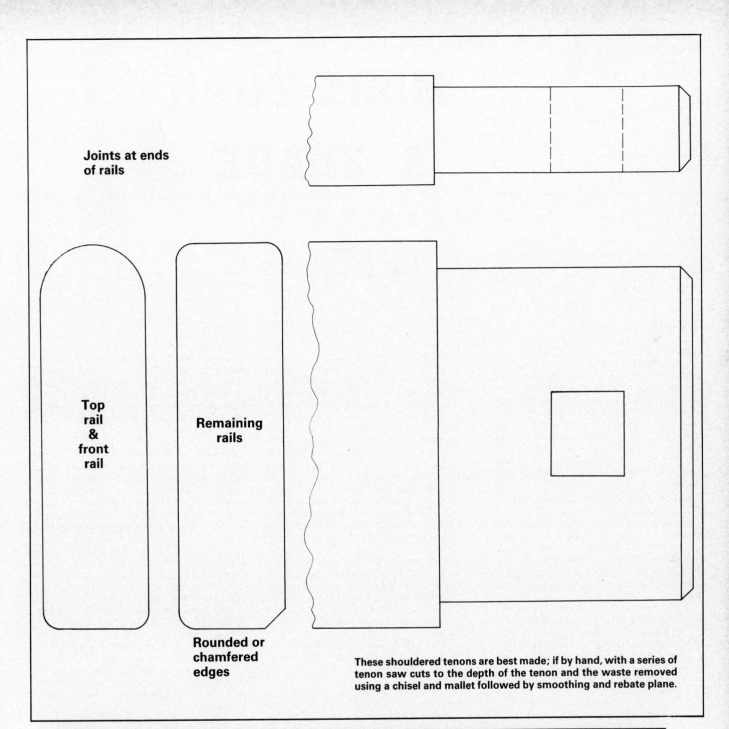

**Joints at ends
of rails**

**Top
rail
&
front
rail**

**Remaining
rails**

**Rounded or
chamfered
edges**

These shouldered tenons are best made; if by hand, with a series of
tenon saw cuts to the depth of the tenon and the waste removed
using a chisel and mallet followed by smoothing and rebate plane.

PARTS LIST					
PART	NO.	LONG	WIDE	THICK	MATERIAL
ENDS	2	820/32¼"	240/9½"	35/1⅜"	HARDWOOD
ENDS	2	550/22"	,,	,,	,,
ENDS	2	500/20"	,,	,,	,,
RAILS	6	1152/60"	115/4½"	32/1¼"	,,
WEDGES	12	120/5"	25/1"	25/1"	,,
DOWELS	20	60/2½"	ø½"	ø½"	,,

Welsh harps

A touring exhibition organised by the Welsh Arts Council with the support of the Crafts Council, is at the Crafts Council Gallery, 12 Waterloo Place, London SW1Y 4AU, until 17 January 1981. A collection of instruments, photographs and documents traces the harp's evolution from the simple stringed form of bardic tradition to the concert instrument of today. Posters, letters and concert programmes tell the stories of the colourful and varied careers of the Welsh harpers and the story of the Eisteddfodau. Much of the exhibition material from the Welsh Folk Museum, St Fagans, Cardiff, and from Robert Morley & Co Ltd, 4 Belmont Hill, London SE13 (01-852 6151), has never been shown in public before. To demonstrate the continuing tradition, the craft department of the Welsh Arts Council has commissioned a contemporary harp maker, Merlin Maddock, to make a harp specifically for the exhibition.

Christmas shopping?

This year why not try the craft shop at the Victoria and Albert museum, South Kensington, London SW7, for your presents? The craft shop is managed by the Crafts Council (open 10.00 am-5.30 pm Monday to Thursday, Saturday; 2.30-5.30 pm, Sunday; closed Fridays) and offers individual craftsman-made pieces in a wide price range. Domestic pottery, blown glass, turned wooden boxes, silk scarves, hand woven silk, toys and original jewellery plus a great many craft books are only a small sample of the range.

Autumn and winter courses at West Dean

Once again we have a list of courses at West Dean College, on our office desk, and once again a pleasing mix and infinite variety seems to be available for the October to March period that the pamphlet covers. A few we have particularly noted are:

Soft furnishing — loose covers for chairs. A course in two parts, a weekend (30 January-1 February) giving advice on selecting fabrics, measuring chairs, cutting plans, estimating material, making piping and a cushion, and five days (22-27 February) to complete the cover/covers of your choice.

A new working with wood course — whittled spoons, bowls and toys (30 January-1 February).

Symposium on gilding

Conservation department of the Victoria and Albert museum is holding a one-day exhibition and symposium on gilding on 4 December from 10.00am to 5.50pm. Applications for tickets (£10 each to include buffet lunch) should be made to Malcolm Green of the V & A conservation department, South Kensington, London SW. The symposium is organised on behalf of the United Kingdom Institute for Conservation.

Canadian Indian art

To 30 November the Cliffe Castle museum, Spring Gardens Lane, Keighley, Yorks, has an exhibition of the work of artist-craftsmen of the Indian tribes of British Columbia. There are some 100 pieces of carving (including wood) as well as weaving and basketwork. The exhibition is mounted by Bradford art galleries and museums department in association with the provincial museum of British Columbia and the Canadian high commission in London.

MORE THAN A SHADE

Once a jolly swagman camped by a billabong, under the shade of a coolibah tree. . .

Now the coolibah, sometimes cooba or coobah, has a distinction beyond that of giving shade to jovial swagmen. It is authoritatively stated to be the hardest wood known, writes Hugh Blogg, Kingsgate, Broadstairs: With an SG of 1.3, and comparative workability (CW) number of six or more, one would expect the only person to be able to make anything from it to be a metalworking fitter and turner. It is reckoned to be superior to lignum vitae for underwater bearings, bushes, pulleys etc.

Following an article I wrote on the hardest woods, including coolibah, I was pleased to hear from Neville Sanders of Gawler, S Australia, who promises to send me a piece of coolibah to try. His information about some of the eucalypts and acacias growing down-under is interesting and I will pass on some of what he writes:

'Regarding the tree or timber coolibah, this is the common name for three varieties of eucalypts: *Eucalyptus microtheca, E. coolibah* and *E. raveretiana*. The first is reported to be the hardest and although I have not tried this timber myself, I have turned some very hard local woods seasoned at home. I am currently trying to obtain some coolibah, and if successful I would certainly be prepared to send you a bit. I must mention that it could take some time to obtain.

'Although it grows in all states except Victoria and Tasmania, it is only to be found in the dry country in the centre of Australia.

'One timber which I have just received from the dry country is gidgee (*Acacia cambagei*) and I am awaiting its drying-out ready to turn. It seems to have a similar appearance to mulga (*Acacia aneura*) which is probably better known to you.

'If you have not tried mulga, I would be willing and able to send you a piece as I recently obtained a trunk about 6in. in diameter and about 7ft long. I intend making myself a set of small goblets from this piece. The wood has been seasoning for four to five years and is ready for use.

'Regarding ironwood, which was mentioned by you, this is the common name for some Australian timbers including *Backhousia myrtifolia* and *Erythrophleum chlorostachys* (red ironwood), *Choricarpia sub-argentea* (ironwood box) and *Acacia estrophiolata* (ironwood wattle).'

Mr Sanders also mentioned that he was attempting to put together a collection of bud vases made from as many different timbers, both local and imported, that he can obtain. I am not quite certain what is meant by a bud vase, but I have asked him

what size rough-turned blanks he needs for these. I can then reciprocate by sending some of our timbers. It would be appropriate for him to have a piece of sanders wood. It is red sanders I believe.

It is interesting to note that Australians use the common-or-garden term wattle as the name for any of the *Acacia* species. The name comes from the early settlers who used the wood to make their wattles or hurdles. The long, pliable branches were split in much the same way as our sweet or Spanish chestnut; and hazel is used for the same purpose.

Footnote: W. H. Brown FIWSc points out that over the years the classification of many Australian woods was confused mainly because of the many different local names pertaining to a single species which, in itself was very similar both in tree form and as timber to a host of others of the same genus.

Since the bulk of the indigenous trees are eucalypts or acacias this was not surprising. The fact that commercial names like ash and oak were given to many of the trees did not help either.

In fairly recent years, and encouraged by our own British Standard nomenclature for timber, CSIRO has made strenuous efforts to standardise Australian timbers both by botanical classification and by preferred common name. Australian Standard ASO2; 1970: *Nomenclature of Australian Timbers* is the document for reference and gives the following:

Coolibah *Eucalyptus microtheca, E. coolabah, E. raveretiana*

Black ironbox *Eucalyptus raveretiana*. The wood of *E. raveretiana* is accordingly known either as coolibah or as black ironbox

Gidgee *Acacia cambagei*

Mulga *Acacia aneura*

Cooktown ironwood. This is the Australian standard name for *Erythrophleum chlorostachys* (alternative name red ironwood)

Backhousia myrtifolia now has the standard name of ironwood with alternative names of carrol ironwood and grey myrtle

Ironwood box *Choricarpia subargentea*

Ironwood wattle *Acacia estrophiolata* or *A. excelsa* depending on State.

From the point of view of descriptions of Australian timbers, with a few exceptions like jarrah, karri and silky 'oak', the woods of that area have never been of much interest to the UK timber market. Accordingly, very few of our books even touch on them. Howard in *Timbers of the World* does give a brief mention to coolibah and a few more.

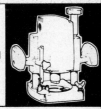

814
Prices quoted are those prevailing at press date and
are subject to alteration due to economic conditions.
Woodworker, December 1980

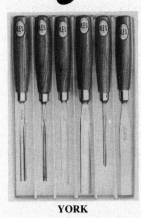

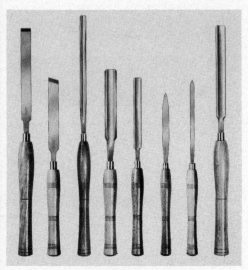

TIMBER TOPICS 12

Here W.H. Brown FIWSc explains why European ash and N American hickory are the premier woods for making special tool handles. He also advises on how to select wood handles: 'The most reliable indication of the strength of a handle is its density... examine the end grain...'

European ash (Fraxinus excelsior) and N America hickory (Carya spp.) are, when specially selected, two of the toughest woods obtainable and for that reason are the premier woods for making special tool handles. These can be classified by use into three types: cutting tools such as axes, hatchets and adzes; digging tools such as picks and hoes; and driving tools like various hammers and mauls.

Compared with European ash, hickory is much tougher, stronger in bending, stiffer and more resistant to shock loads. Accordingly it is preferred for the longer type of handle likely to be associated with heavy work such as felling trees or picking up the road. Toughness, the ability of wood to absorb a large amount of energy and so resist repeated sudden sharp blows or shocks, in non-technical terms means 'flexibility without brittleness'.

Under certain use conditions such as pulling nails with a claw hammer, excessive loads may be applied to the wood, or through accident the handle itself may hit an object instead of the tool head. When this happens the expected does not occur — the handle does not snap and let the tool head fly off. Or does it?

Where a misplaced blow or excessive force causes a hickory or ash tool handle to break it should do so with a splintering action (Fig. 1a) in which the tough fibres of the wood act as individual strands. Each resisting one is torn apart and thus creates a relatively slow, 'safe' break rather than a sharp or brash fracture which could be dangerous to anyone standing near. With this latter type of wood failure there are valid reasons why the wood is behaving out of character. Usually the principal one is carelessness on the part of the user; not necessarily in the manner of use of the tool but of its care when not in use.

Neither ash nor hickory have very good natural resistance to decay. If a handle made from either wood is persistently allowed to get wet and remain so for long periods, there will be a definite tendency for decay organisms to develop which, even in incipient form, will begin to severely deplete the toughness and strength of the wood; its resilience will be lost and the wood will become 'carroty'.

In the context of natural durability, this is assessed according to the results of graveyard tests where all heartwood sections of different woods 30in. long × 2 × 2in. are driven in the ground as posts and thereafter are periodically checked for decay development. Ash by this means is classified as perishable, ie less than five years' potential life in that dimension when in contact with the ground. Hickory is ranked as non-durable, ie five to 10 years.

The sizes of these test pieces are not much different from those sawn as blanks, say, for axe handles. And while the classifi-

cation is for wood in contact with the ground, there is perhaps a parallel because the normal and safe way of standing a heavy axe when not in use is with the head resting on the ground. In circumstances where an axe is left like this but with the head in wet grass and the handle resting against a fence or tree, its potential life may not be much different from those shown by the tests.

It is not easy to avoid periods of prolonged wetness in some tool handles, either because a tool is in more or less continuous use in all weathers, or because intermittent use has produced a very dry shaft and a loose head and the tendency now is to encourage the wood to swell by wetting it. This is perhaps reflected in the American contention that some 75% of hickory axe handles are sold for replacement purposes. In other words, 25% of production goes into complete tool sales and for each one sold the user purchases three replacement handles.

The industrial use of felling axes in America is high by comparison with the general use in this country but there are many owners of axes, hatchets and choppers who rely on their periodic use to carry out rough felling, lopping and topping of smallish trees wanted for their wood. Where for one reason or another an ash or hickory handle fails and a replacement is sought there are one or two points worth noting.

A common fault when the average person selects a wood handle is to choose on the basis of eye appeal, the assumption being that an attractive appearance means quality. This is an entirely erroneous conclusion since a good-looking handle might be the poorest in terms of toughness, stiffness, hardness, shock-resistance and resilience. In effect, it means that there is a definite leaning on the part of the purchaser on 'an all-white' handle. But a hickory tree while it produces a wide, white-coloured sapwood, also contains a reddish heart. Similarly, the heartwood of ash is frequently almost black, referred to in the trade as red or brown 'kern'. Tests have shown that weight for weight, sound hickory and ash have the same strength, toughness and resistance to shock regardless of whether the wood is all-white, all-red/brown/black, or a mixture of white and coloured wood (Fig. 2).

The most reliable indication of the strength of a handle is its density. That is to say, of two pieces of the same size and dryness the heavier will be found to have the better strength qualities. A fairly reliable guide is to examine the end grain for rate of growth and proportion of dense summer-wood to porous spring-wood in each annual ring. Spring-wood is easily recognised by the rows of large open pores.

A growth rate of five to 10 rings to 1in. (25mm) with a proportion of summer-wood

of at least 50% of each ring will indicate good strength. Finally, long axe handles and pick shafts when dropped on end on a hard surface such as a concrete floor should emit a clear ringing tone: a dull sound is associated with inferior quality.

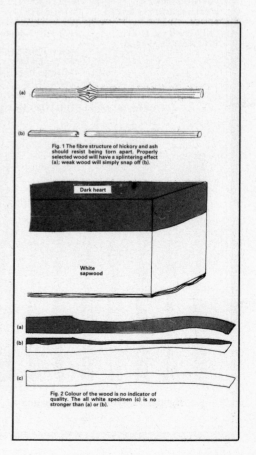

Fig. 1 The fibre structure of hickory and ash should resist being torn apart. Properly selected wood will have a splintering effect (a); weak wood will simply snap off (b).

Dark heart

White sapwood

Fig. 2 Colour of the wood is no indicator of quality. The all white specimen (c) is no stronger than (a) or (b).

LAMPSHADES FROM

From Dartford West Secondary Boys' School, J. S. Jackson reports on using scrap veneers for lampshades. 'The project has proved quite popular with my woodworking groups with 2nd and 4th year pupils showing interest in the designs,' he says.

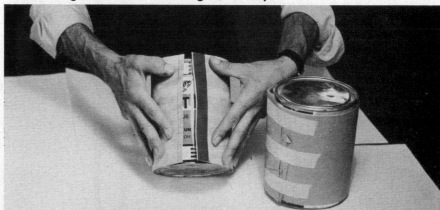

Years ago I inherited a large roll of assorted veneers ranging from the pale sycamore and oak to the colourful rosewood and zebrano. None of the individual parts were large enough for a major piece of work and as the roll accompanied me to various parts of the country, the veneers became decidedly tatty. I had visions of them all ending as firewood spills, and eventually I was spurred into designing something that would use them up.

I had noticed that today's trend in lighting is towards a decorative hue, so I decided to use up the roll of veneers as lamp shades. This would also serve as an exercise for my pupils.

Plain shade. If more than one shade is to be made or, as in my case, young boys are making many shades, it will be convenient if a former is prepared to assist in bending the veneer to shape. I used an old glue tin with a diameter of just over 140mm. This tin had raised edges to make it straight. Brown paper wrapped around the tin and secured with Sellotape sufficed here (Photo 1).

At this stage it might be convenient to explain how the length of the veneer — the circumference of the shade — is determined. I decided to increase the diameter to 145mm to give ample clearance over the tin. This 145mm is multiplied by 22/7 (circumference = dia. × 22/7) giving a figure of 455.7mm. Adding 15mm for the lapping of the joint and dropping the 0.7mm for convenience gives a figure of 470mm. The formula being: dia. × 22/7 + 15.

The shade is made first. The mahogany veneer that is to form the shade is cut to a size of 470 × 180mm with the ends of the veneer perfectly square. The veneer is best cut on a cutting board and for this I used a piece of 18mm birch plywood with the face edge planed true.

A sharp 25mm bevel-edge chisel is adequate for cutting the veneer but I found that a straightedge G-cramped to the cutting board guaranteed the veneer would be of equal width (Photo 2).

Having a cutting guide that would not move minimised risk of an accident.

A pencil line, 15mm from the end, is squared across at one end of the veneer. The veneer is turned over and a similar line 15mm from the end, is squared across the opposite end. These areas at each end are to be bonded together and it assists if these areas are shaded in with a pencil.

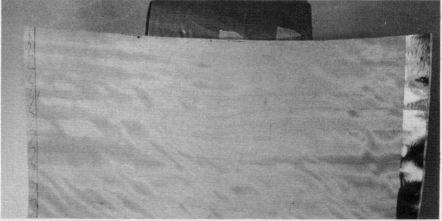

I find this useful as more often than not it can be a week or more between lessons; anything that will help pupils to remember what happened in previous lessons is always an asset.

The veneer is taped on the opposite sides to the shaded areas; this prevents the veneer splitting. I used Sellotape but any tape will do as long as it can be easily removed afterwards (Photo 3). The veneer can be dampened to assist the bending.

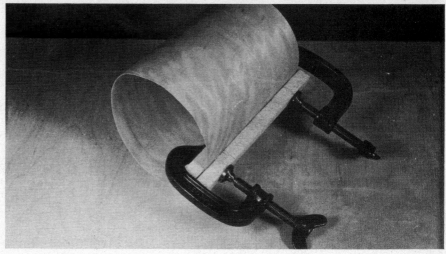

Top to bottom: 1. Old glue tin used to bend veneer. 2. Cutting veneer strips. 3. Taping and marking veneer ends. 4. G-cramping the joint.

SCRAP VENEERS

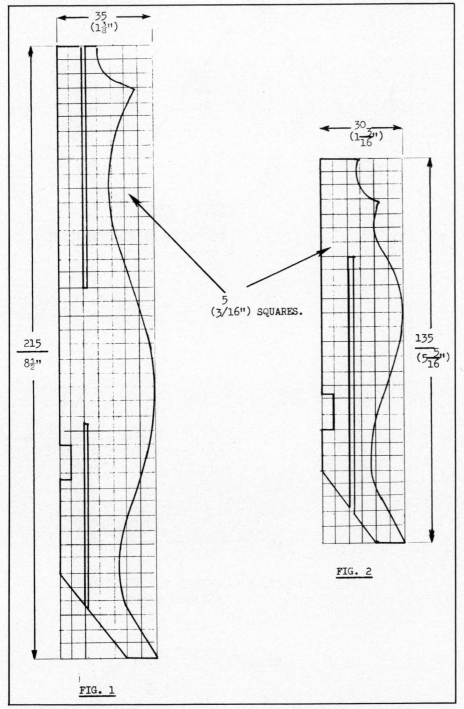

35
(1⅜")

30
(1³⁄₁₆")

5
(3/16") SQUARES.

215
8½"

135
(5⁵⁄₁₆")

FIG. 1

FIG. 2

prevents splitting and is also heat-resistant.

After experimenting I found that nails driven into lengths of timber (and the nails filed to a point) were ideal for burning patterns in the shade. I have three tools so that while one is being used the other two are heating up.

I always find willing helpers when this job is in progress but if you are without assistance, blocks of angled timber arranged about the gas ring can safely prop up the burning tools while they are heating (Photo 6). (But beware of the timber catching fire.)

The variety of patterns that can be burnt on the shade is limitless; however, I have found that the impromptu attempt — following the grain for instance — can produce some remarkably good results (Photo 7). The shade is given light glasspapering to remove rough edges caused by burning the pattern before the final coats of polyurethane are applied.

For the base I mounted a piece of mahogany on the lathe and turned it to a diameter of 170mm. I turned a couple of V-shaped grooves on the edge of the base to break the straightness of the shape. The base was cleaned-off and the centre clearly marked. Before moving to the next stage the diameter of the finished shade should be measured and the size noted.

The three feet are made and their position marked on the bottom of the base (Photo 8). The three feet can now be fixed on the base. The base is turned over and the six points that form the positions for the dowels marked (Fig. 5).

With a pair of compasses set at the radius of the shade and from the centre a circle is drawn on the base. A line is drawn through the centre so that it touches the circle at A and B. With the compasses set at the same radius and from point A two arcs are drawn to cut the circle at A^1 and A^2. This is repeated from position B to give the other two points B^1 and B^2. These six points form the centres for the six dowels, 10mm dowelling being used.

The positions of the six holes are marked with a bradawl and the holes drilled to an even depth. A useful jig for achieving this is shown (Photo 9). The 10mm drill is used to make a hole through a length of 25mm square timber. The timber is cut so that the drill exposed equals the required depth of the hole.

Six pieces of dowel, 40mm in length, are cut and glued into the base. The notches to secure the shade are cut into the dowel and the outside of these dowels shaped.

The hole for the cable is drilled in the centre of the base and the brass collar to hold the light fitting is screwed into the base.

Lattice shade. The sycamore and rosewood veneers are cut into strips 35mm wide. I found that a 35mm wide straightedge G-cramped level to the face edge of the cutting board ensured that all veneer bands were of equal width. The inner sycamore bands are cut to the required 470mm lengths and the outer rosewood bands to a length of 460mm. The circumference length of the inner band is longer than the outer band because the inner band overlaps onto itself.

The vertical sycamore and rosewood bands are cut to a length of 180mm. When the vertical and horizontal lengths have been cut to length it is advisable to clean-off the face sides and edges of the strips with fine glasspaper.

Keeping the shaded areas dry, the veneer can be held under a running tap and when wet can be immediately bent around the former. No special precautions are needed. The edges of the veneer are overlapped and the weight of the tin is sufficient to keep the shape until the veneer dries (Photo 1).

Though most glues will bond the edges of the veneer, I found an impact adhesive best. There are impact adhesives that do allow repositioning before the final bonding; any discrepancy in alignment can then be adjusted before the final bonding. Coat both shaded areas of the veneer with the impact adhesive. When the adhesive is touch-dry the veneer is bent around the former and the ends brought together and pressed down to form the shade. Though contact adhesive provides a quick and waterproof joint I prefer to apply pressure to the joint

for a short period of time afterwards — this is best done with two suitable pieces of timber placed over the joint and nipped together with small G-cramps (Photo 4).

The sycamore strips to form the surround about the top and bottom of the shade are now cut, a straightedge G-cramped to a cutting board being preferable.

The sycamore strips are placed around the shade and the gluing area checked and marked. Paper clips are ideal for holding these strips in position (Photo 5). Impact adhesive is applied to both gluing areas and when touch-dry the sycamore strips are bonded around the top and bottom of the shade.

Any ragged edges on the shade can be cleaned off with fine glasspaper and polyurethane applied to the inside and outside of the shade. This seals the grain,

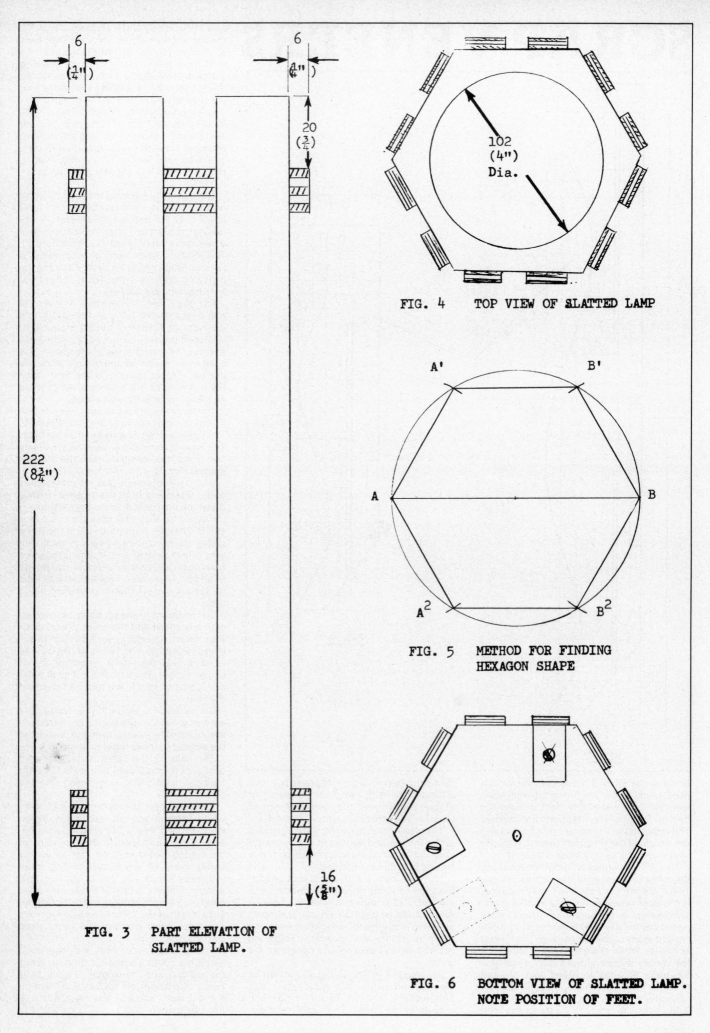

6
($\frac{1}{4}$")

6
($\frac{1}{4}$")

20
($\frac{3}{4}$)

222
($8\frac{3}{4}$")

16
($\frac{5}{8}$")

FIG. 3   PART ELEVATION OF
SLATTED LAMP.

102
(4")
Dia.

FIG. 4   TOP VIEW OF SLATTED LAMP

A'   B'

A   B

A^2 B^2

FIG. 5   METHOD FOR FINDING
HEXAGON SHAPE

FIG. 6   BOTTOM VIEW OF SLATTED LAMP.
NOTE POSITION OF FEET.

The gluing area is marked on the bands (Photo 10). It is useful if the bands are held down with Sellotape to prevent movement. After marking these positions the bands are separated and the ends of the horizontal bands that are to overlap on to each other marked. A pencil line is squared across the band 15mm from the end. The band is turned over and another pencil line is squared across the opposite end, again 15mm from the end. This is repeated on the other three sycamore bands and the gluing area shaded. These gluing areas are coated with impact adhesive and when touch-dry the inner bands are bent to form a circle and the two 15mm glued ends pressed firmly together.

The outer rosewood bands are placed on the outside of the sycamore band and the positioning and the gluing area checked and marked. Paper clips are ideal at this stage (Photo 5). The outside of the sycamore veneer band is coated with impact adhesive and the corresponding gluing area on the inside of the outer rosewood band coated. When the adhesive is touch-dry the outer rosewood veneer is pressed firmly onto the inner band to form one band; sycamore on the inside and rosewood on the outside.

This operation is repeated on the other three bands and the vertical bands are also glued together. The vertical veneer strips are now woven through the circular horizontal bands and the positions of the gluing areas checked where the bands criss-cross. Paper clips are helpful in holding the bands in position. When all the gluing areas have been checked and marked they can be coated with impact adhesive and after a suitable time lapse, pressed firmly together.

Surplus adhesive and fingermarks are carefully cleaned-off with fine glasspaper and the shade treated with polyurethane.

Woven shade. The procedure described above is followed in making the woven shade with its five horizontal bands.

Reading lamp. The 9mm plywood forming the base is marked and cut to the shape of a triangle with sides 130mm long. To find the shape of the triangle a line is drawn 130mm long. Compasses are set at the same 130mm and from each end of the line an arc is drawn. Where these two arcs intersect is the apex of the triangle. The three points are joined to form the triangle.

At this stage the triangular base can be drilled for the cable and the brass collar for the lamp holder fixed.

The uprights are now made. The three pieces of timber are left longer at each end so that a panel pin can be driven into the waste timber. This allows the three pieces to be cut and cleaned-off at the same time, ensuring identically-shaped uprights. Fig. 1 shows the shape of the uprights. The position of the housings to hold the triangular base is marked on the uprights and the housings sawn across and chiselled out. The triangular base is then tried into the housings and checked for a tight fit.

The uprights are cut with a coping saw and cleaned-off, the waste ends removed and the uprights separated. The slots in the uprights (Fig. 1) are marked and sawn. For this job I use a fine tenon saw cutting both sides at an angle and, if necessary, completing the cut with a coping saw. Any ragged edges inside the saw cuts are removed by sliding a piece of glasspaper down the slots and rubbing sideways.

The base and the three uprights are glued together making sure the inside of the

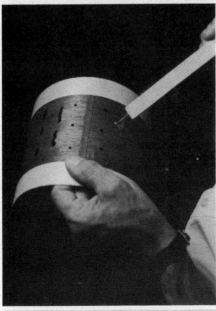

Top: 5. Using paper clips to hold strips in place. Above: 6. Using angled blocks to prop up burning tools. Left: 7. Burning holes in shade. Below left: 8. Feet screwed to base. Below: 9. Using the jig to get holes to equal depth.

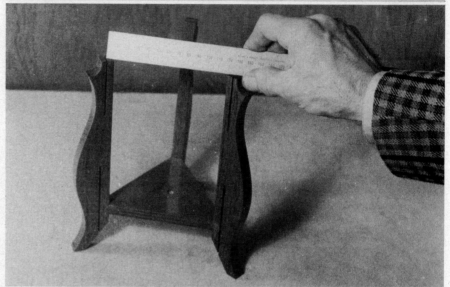

uprights are 90° to the base. When the glue has set the uprights can be cleaned-off and polished.

Length of the two veneer bands that are to form the top and bottom of the shade can now be determined. The distance from the centre of one upright to the centre of the other upright is measured (Photo 11). If the triangle has equal sides and the uprights are glued square to the base, the distance between the slots should be the same. A triangle can now be drawn out on paper with the length of the sides equal to the distance between the slots. In my case it was 130mm.

Two of the sides are marked in the centre and a line drawn between the two marks and the triangular points opposite. Where these two lines intersect is the centre of the circle. The circumference of this circle, plus 10mm allowance for lapping, will be the length of the veneer band. For example:

Length of veneer = (twice radius × 22/7 + 10mm.

In my case length = (twice 75 × 22/7) + 10mm.

length = (470.8) + 10mm.

length = 481mm (to the nearest decimal).

Alternatively, or if the triangular base sides are not all equal, another method can be adopted. A length of veneer is cut longer than the approximate circumference length, formed into a circle and held together with paper clips. It is then slid down the slots and adjusted to make the shape required.

If all is well, the 10mm lines are marked on the veneer bands — opposite ends and opposite sides — coated with impact adhesive and after a suitable time lapse firmly pressed together.

The band can be slid down the three slots and the overlap of the veneer joint butted-up against one of the uprights so that the joint is hidden. There should be no need to glue these bands in position, the final coat of polyurethane being sufficient to hold the bands in place.

Plant pot holder. Photo 12 shows a plant pot holder based on the same idea as the reading lamp described. Fig. 2 shows the shape of the leg uprights.

Slatted shade. This is easily made and does not involve the used of veneers (Figs. 3, 4).

The 15 and 12mm ply making up the base and top ring are cut square with sides 140mm long. The 12mm piece that is to make the top ring is marked out (Fig. 5).

First the centre is found and then a circle drawn with radius of 70mm. A line is drawn through the centre so that it touches the circle at A and B. From A, and with the compasses set at 70mm, two arcs are drawn to cut the circle at A^1 and A^2. This is repeated from position B to give the other two points B^1 and B^2. Lines are drawn between these points to give the required hexagonal shape. A circle is drawn on the top with compasses set at a radius of 51mm. Later this circle will be cut out.

The 12mm ply square with the marking out showing on the top is placed over the 15mm ply and the two pieces nailed together with a single nail driven through the centre. This ensures that both shapes will be identical. The two shapes are sawn

CUTTING LIST WITH SUGGESTED CHOICE OF VENEERS
Sizes in mm and in. No allowance for waste

PLAIN SHADE	mm	in.	
1 Shade	470 × 180	18½ × 7³⁄₁₆	mahogany
2 Horizontal bands	460 × 35	18¼ × 1⅜	sycamore
1 Base	170 × 170 × 22	6¾ × 6¾ × ⅞	mahogany
6 Pegs	30 × 10 dia dowel	1³⁄₁₆ × ⅝ dowel	dowel
3 Feet	30 × 22 × 12	1³⁄₁₆ × ⅞ × ½	mahogany
LATTICE SHADE			
4 Horizontal bands	470 × 35	18½ × 1⅜	sycamore
4 Horizontal bands	460 × 35	18¼ × 1⅜	rosewood
6 Vertical bands	180 × 35	7³⁄₁₆ × 1⅜	sycamore
6 Vertical bands	180 × 35	7³⁄₁₆ × 1⅜	rosewood
1 Base	170 × 170 × 22	6¾ × 6¾ × ⅞	mahogany
6 Pegs	30 × 10 dia dowel	1³⁄₁₆ × ⅝ dowel	dowel
3 Feet	30 × 22 × 12	1³⁄₁₆ × ⅞ × ½	mahogany
WOVEN SHADE			
5 Horizontal bands	455 × 35	17⅞ × 1⅜	rosewood
6 Vertical bands	195 × 35	7¹¹⁄₁₆ × 1⅜	rosewood
1 Base	170 × 170 × 22	6¾ × 6¾ × ⅞	mahogany
6 Pegs	30 × 10 dia dowel	1³⁄₁₆ × ⅝ dowel	dowel
3 Feet	30 × 22 × 12	1³⁄₁₆ × ⅞ × ½	mahogany
READING LAMP			
1 Horizontal band	481 × 85	18¹⁵⁄₁₆ × 3⅜	zebrano
1 Horizontal band	481 × 60	18¹⁵⁄₁₆ × 2⅜	zebrano
3 Uprights	215 × 35 × 12	8⁷⁄₁₆ × 1⅜ × ½	mahogany
1 Base	130 × 130 × 12	5⅛ × 5⅛ × ½	mahogany ply
PLANT HOLDER			
1 Horizontal band	481 × 90	18¹⁵⁄₁₆ × 3⁹⁄₁₆	zebrano
3 Uprights	135 × 30 × 12	5⁵⁄₁₆ × 1⅜ × ½	mahogany
1 Base	130 × 130 × 12	5⅛ × 5⅛ × ½	mahogany ply
SLATTED LAMP			
1 Top	127 × 127 × 12	5 × 5 × ½	mahogany ply
1 Base	127 × 127 × 15	5 × 5 × ¹¹⁄₁₆	mahogany ply
12 Slats	222 × 22 × 6	8¾ × ⅞ × ¼	mahogany ply
3 Feet	30 × 22 × 16	1³⁄₁₆ × ⅞ × ⅝	mahogany

Left: 12. Plant pot holder. Above: 13. Slatted shade. Below: 15. General view of slatted, woven and lattice shades with base.

Above: 14. Using aid for nailing slats. Below: 16. Lattice shade. Right: 17. Plain shade. Far right: 18. Reading lamp.

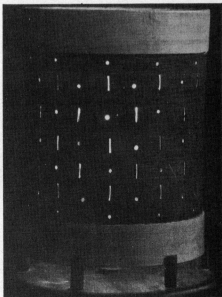

and cleaned-off. Before separating them two corresponding edges are marked on the two pieces of plywood; this assists later when they are assembled.

The three feet are made then glued and fitted to the base. Fig. 6 shows how they are positioned behind a slat so as to be hidden from view. The hole for the cable can also be drilled and the fitting for the lamp holder screwed to the base.

The circle in the top is now cut out with a coping saw and a rasp, half-round file and glasspaper used to clean the inside of the circle, care being taken as the edges will easily break.

The 12 slats are sawn, planed and cleaned-off prior to assembly. If the shade is to be stained it is best to do this before assembly. The slats are glued and nailed to the base first. The position on the slats is marked and the nails slightly driven into the 12 slats.

As an alternative to punching the nails down, I find that nipping-off the heads prior to driving them home is satisfactory. The slats can be screwed but when a number of shades are being made it can be an expensive method of fastening.

When all the slats have been fixed to the base the top is fixed, Photo 14 shows a simple aid for making the top rigid to assist nailing. A heavy piece of timber is G-cramped to the bench and the top ring fed over it. When all the slats have been fixed cleaning-off can be done before the final coat of polyurethane is applied.

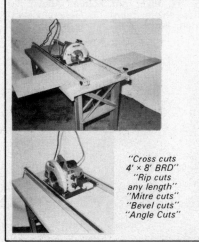

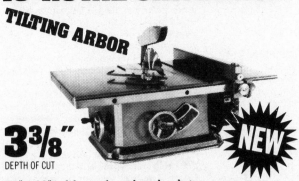

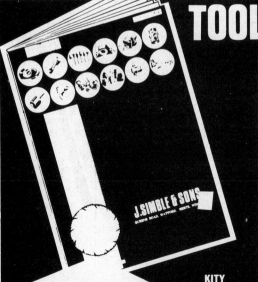

Eucalyptus wood
From: J. Smith, Bideford, Devon

A friend has to cut down a eucalyptus tree and says I can have it. The trunk is about 35ft. long tapering from 15in. down to 3in. My main interests are turning and carving so can you please tell me if this wood is suitable for this work? Also what is the best way to cut and store the wood? If eucalyptus is unsuitable for turning and carving can you suggest other uses for it?

We cannot be specific in our reply since there are several hundred separate species of eucalyptus in existence and a number of these Australian species have been planted in many countries including UK.

Accordingly we will generalise on the wood obtained from the trees. All species produce highly refractory timber, that is to say in seasoning the wood takes on serious stresses. These are liable to cause it to split, warp and 'collapse', a state whereby the surface of the wood becomes corrugated and there are internal checks.

In Australia this is recognised and it is usual for the wood to be kiln-dried in the normal way when, at the end of the drying run, it is re-conditioned by steaming at high temperature, when the wood regains much of its original shape. The problem is this: if the wood can be used in its originally prepared dimensions it can be excellent, but any serious departure from this and the wood may distort badly.

To give an example: Tasmanian 'oak' is imported here in 1in. thick dimension stock for strip flooring. It is machined and laid and makes a very fine floor; and literally every piece imported is usable. However, should that same stock be deep-cut so as to make two nominal ½in. thick boards then trouble is likely. The pieces would tend to cup and the saw would tend to wander, due to the inherent stress built up in the wood. Tasmanian 'oak' is actually the product of several species of eucalyptus lumped together for commercial purposes.

We see no reason why you should not be able to use the wood for turnery and carving provided care is taken in seasoning and general handling. Air-drying must be slow and it would help if the log was broken down into rough piece-part dimensions, although this might not be satisfactory to you. Bear in mind what we have said about resawing and apply this thinking to carving. In other words, some deep carving might be detrimental if a lot more wood is being taken off one side. This would be different from turning where the removal of wood is balanced.

So far as we know only a few species of eucalyptus have been successful in the west country, but they have been of the ornamental variety not favoured in Australia for timber, so there is not much information about their liability to produce gum lines in the wood. Their occurrence in some timber species does sometimes detract from their ease of working.

We feel you should take advantage of the opportunity to acquire the wood. Many species of eucalyptus are now grown in Africa and among the recommended uses for the wood is turnery, but of 42 species listed only three are suggested for carving, probably for the reason we have given.

Parana 'pine'
From: R. Scott, Hounslow, Middlesex

I have acquired some 6-8 × ¾in. planks (planed) of parana which because of its lack of knots I had intended using for making a grandmother clockcase. Having read the reply to the query about turning this timber (WOODWORKER for August p530) I am wondering if this would be wise. If this timber is not suitable for the clockcase what could I use it for?

Problems associated with the potential use of refractory timbers like parana 'pine' are usually individual. For that reason it is not practicable to try to relate one use to another except in the sense of awareness of the nature of the wood.

One of the most successful uses for parana 'pine' has been for staircase construction. Yet if you consider the preparation of the long stringers for this use it would seem to suggest that by routing or trenching out on one face of a fairly wide board so as to take the treads and risers, the wood was now badly unbalanced and likely to cup. This would be the definite tendency but by piling the machined pieces to await assembly, cupping is restrained by the weight of the pieces, while final assembly holds everything in place.

There is no reason why you should not make up your clockcase from this wood, but it would be advisable to store the boards in the environment of eventual use for as long as possible to enable the moisture content (m.c.) to adjust. Breaking down the wood to oversize piece parts helps in this.

There is one final word of warning, and it applies to any wood and not just parana 'pine': if the finished clock is to be positioned near to a heating appliance, the wood must be dried down much lower than would be normal. In other words, to 6% m.c. at least instead of the 9 to 11% m.c. more generally applicable.

Limed oak panelling
From: R. C. Krincks, South Woodford, London E18

The entrance hall of my house is panelled in oak and to make the wood appear lighter it has been treated with lime. The lime is lying in the grain and gives the panelling a peculiar white finish. Could you please advise me how best to remove this lime without causing too much damage to the wood?

It is difficult to advise you for several reasons. Basically, if the whole surface of the panels are washed down, say, with white spirit and after drying are sanded mechanically, in theory this would be about the most one could expect in trying to restore the oak to something like its original appearance. In practice, however, quite apart from the fire risk in employing relatively large amounts of spirit, if the deposits in the grain are lime, then cold water is about the only liquid which, given time, would soften the deposits and allow them to be brushed out. Firstly, though, you have vertical surfaces which would not accept or absorb much water; and secondly, water would be the last thing to apply since if the panels are oak veneered these could swell and lift, and if solid oak, water could get behind the framing with detrimental results.

The 'lime' that was used may not be true lime but a liming paste made up from a wax base to which zinc white was added; if this has been used then it has probably bonded itself tightly to the walls of the open pores. In other words, doubtless whoever was responsible for liming the wood would not anticipate its ultimate removal and would have ensured that not only was the filling of the grain adequate, but that the ultimate finish — polish, varnish or wax — was a suitable seal.

It seems to us that while you might well clean up each panel working carefully with white spirit and a nylon pad, it is extremely doubtful if you could do much with the liming short of sanding; and even this could fail if the oak is veneer because of its thinness.

Sticking table top covering
From: J. K. W. Wheatley, Minster Lovell, Oxford

I have been asked to repair a mahogany cabriole leg table the top of which has an inset of velvet or plush. This must be renewed. What adhesive would you advise? Copydex has been suggested but is there a solvent for this should the cloth ever have to be renewed? If I use scotch glue in a thin layer is it likely to stain through?

If you use Copydex as you suggest the material should stick down without staining. I would not think there is need to worry about a solvent for if you make a good job of covering the table top you are hardly likely to have to take if off again!

It is probable that the original covering was stuck down with paperhangers' paste in the same way that green baize or billiard cloth is stuck to cardtable tops. The paste is made up quite thick, about half the usual quantity of water being used; it is well brushed into the cloth and then left until it is very sticky before it is laid on the table top.

Using the rounded edge of a flat piece of wood in the manner of a veneering hammer, start from the centre of the cloth and work towards the edges. This will press out any air bubbles and ensure that the cloth is firmly stuck down all over.

With the tip of a blunt table knife the cloth is pressed well down into the recess at the table edge. Having firmly bedded down the cloth the surplus is trimmed off with a sharp knife held against a steel straightedge.

If Copydex is used as an adhesive it is advisable to apply it sparingly to both surfaces to be joined and let it dry thoroughly. Correctly position the cloth and place it on the table when it will immediately stick. A Copydex remover is obtainable from the maker of the adhesive at 1 Torquay Street, Harrow Road, London W1.

Scotch glue is not advised as it is likely to penetrate the cloth and show through in patches.

Almond wood
From: Mrs E. W. Norris, West Bridgford, Nottingham

We have been offered two stumps of almond and would like to know whether or not this wood is of any use for carving.

The wood of the European almond (*Amygdalus communis*) is a yellowish to dull light reddish-brown colour, frequently relieved by lighter or darker-coloured streaks. It is an excellent carving wood as a rule but much depends upon its condition. If for example, the stumps have been left lying around in, say, wet grass for several months then there might be soft patches of decay present. But even this contingency would not necessarily spoil the wood if the proposed carvings were to be relatively small. The wood should be stored with a reasonable air circulation around the pieces.

Renovating an oak table
From: J. Fortune, Hartlepool, Co Cleveland

I have a solid oak table which I believe was made in the 1920s. It has one piece as the top and two sliding leaves and spiral legs and cross-bars. The table appears to have been stained and french polished dark oak and top and legs are now badly faded.

Is it possible for the staining to be removed? It would in my view be impracticable to use any form of sanding or scraping on the spiral legs and I wonder if there is any other method; or a firm that would undertake the work for me?

I wish to match the table to other pieces in light oak that I have made for the dining room.

The short answer is that the stain used on the table cannot be removed in the sense that the item can be renovated to match your other light oak furniture. It is essential to say this because cleaning-off the top finish, whether this is french polish or cellulose, demands the use either of patent strippers or strong soda solutions. These have a definite tendency to bleach the wood irrespective of the stain which is fixed in the surface fibres of the wood.

In the case of the solid top, after stripping machine sanding no doubt would restore the surface to somewhere near a natural finish, but there would probably still be much darker zones in the joints between the frame and the panels. And as you rightly suggest there would be some difficulty in cleaning up the twisted or spiral legs.

There is also the vexed question of where to do the cleaning-up, using relatively large quantities of caustic material; in many instances this aspect alone is fairly daunting. We feel it would be best to have a talk with one of your local furniture restorers with a view to finding out the type of finish he could obtain and, of course, the cost of doing so. You will probably find the most natural look will be one approximating to stripped pine. Furniture restorers are generally listed in the Yellow Page directory.

Refurbishing a dressing table
From: Michael Gamble, Sandringham, Victoria, Australia

I have bought a Victorian-style dressing table in either satinwood or amboyna mahogany on which something has been spilt. This has stripped the french polish in patches leaving whitish pale wood; underneath the piece is a soft fawn yellow colour.

What stains, fillers and colour of french polish will I have to use to bring the piece back to original?

From the description I would think that the piece is satinwood veneered. Amboyna was used mainly for friezes and decorative work and is dark salmon-pink in colour with an exotic wild burr.

The dressing table could be valuable as only good-class work was made in satinwood. I hesitate to advise on repolishing the top without sight of the piece but, obviously, this is impossible.

From the description of the amount of damage to the polish I would guess that it will need stripping. Mr Gamble does not say what condition the veneers are in. From my experience, a piece so abused has been damaged in other ways. I suspect there may be blisters, cracks, bits of veneer missing or broken and so on. If this is so (and it is not unusual) then all these should be repaired before any repolishing is undertaken.

I suggest that if at all possible Mr Gamble should seek a qualified restorer who would be better able to advise him. If the piece is valuable it would pay to have professional restoration work done.

But should everything otherwise be normal and Mr Gamble still wishes to go ahead, the procedure is stripping with a good-quality stripper to the maker's instructions; neutralising; lightly scraping and sandpapering (taking care not to go through the veneers which may be thin in parts). The normal french polishing method is used. Filling the grain should not be necessary as this would have been done by the original polishers. No colouring should be needed and I suggest he starts with transparent polish and if any darkening is needed to continue with button.

It must be realised that while this method of polishing, if done correctly will give a beautiful, flat and mirror-like finish, almost impossible to obtain with the modern brush-on finishes, it is nevertheless relatively soft and non-resistant to heat, spirit splashes and heavy articles such as flowers vases and suchlike. I advise that when the dressing table is put to rights Mr Gamble has a glass top made to fit, with polished edges all round. This will protect the top and enhance the appearance of the piece.

It may be necessary to raise the glass top above the surface using small transparent buttons obtainable at any good cabinet ironmonger. Any patina will, of course, be lost and the top will look new as compared to the front, but only time can cure this unless the same treatment is given to the front and sides of the dressing table.

Warping of oak
From: J. C. Ghest, Merrow, Surrey

About 12 years ago I bought several pieces of oak 1 × 9½in. wide and 4ft long. Three of the pieces I have kept lying flat on each other in the garage loft but I now find that two are slightly warped. If I had them planed again on one side I would lose an ⅛in. thickness and if both sides were planed I would lose a ¼in.

Would the boards warp again after I had used them with both sides planed, or is it possible to take out the warp so that I could use the full thickness? If I did this would the timber remain flat afterwards?

It is difficult to give a positive answer to these questions as so much depends on the original drying process.

We assume the boards are flat-sawn and cupped away from the heart, which is almost inevitable. A period of 12 years in fairly dry conditions would result in a slight advantage, but boards should never be kept lying flat against each other.

If the outsides of the boards were 'set' in a state of tension (case-hardened) through too rapid drying in the first place, the stresses are probably permanent.

It might be possible to remove the warp by warming the convex side and damping the concave side. If you did this and then stacked the boards with stickers in a warm place well weighted down for a few weeks it might help, but we would not like to say that the distortion would not return.

Planing would partially remove any possibly case-hardened tissue, but we note that you do not wish to do this. Try the above suggestion first if you are not in a hurry.

Polishing marquetry
From: R. Richardson, Chelmsford, Essex

On taking up pictorial marquetry I decided to use white transparent polish with white oil as a lubricant rather than linseed oil since there is less chance of darkening the veneers when using white oil. However, despite apparently successfully spiriting-off at the final stage the polish does not fully harden and any pressure on the pictures causes the polish to sweat. Repeated spiriting-off has not effected a cure.

I use materials and polish from a reputable supplier and should emphasise that I have had this problem when using linseed oil. Am I using too much? Should there be a different process to eradicate the oil at the final stage, other than spiriting-off? Does it really make that much difference using white oil as against linseed oil?

I understand white oil is a mineral oil, a non-drying oil.

Having used the brand of polish that you mention I can rule out the polish as being at fault. That leaves the oil and the technique.

White mineral oil is a non-drying, petroleum derivative, whereas linseed oil (either raw or boiled) is a drying oil obtained from a plant. The white oil is slightly miscible with the polish and will act as a plasticiser. This will make the polish film more elastic and therefore softer. Excess white oil will cause the surface to sweat under pressure (or heat) as you describe.

Linseed oil is not miscible with the polish but will tend to get buried in the film as the polish is built-up and in effect toughen it slightly as it dries. Used in excess it can cause the surface to crack or craze. Properly used both types of oil are equally good and none of these problems should arise if only a minute quantity is used and is spirited-off in the usual way.

The traditional way of applying the oil is to dip the finger in the oil but now I use an eye dropper bottle which gives a definite and repeatable amount each time. Use two drops for a picture area of about 1½sq ft. Do not use any oil until the surface has been sealed either with a sanding sealer or with polish.

If only small quantities of the linseed oil are used (and it is not put on to the bare wood) there should be no darkening of the light veneers, although I usually do use the white oil to guard against this possibility.

THE ONLY WAY TO BE SURE OF YOUR ISSUE EACH MONTH

Is to order it NOW through your local Newsagent

Simply fill in the form and hand it to him

...or if you would prefer to become a subscriber, complete the coupon opposite enclosing the appropriate remittance.

Return to: Model & Allied Publications Ltd
Subscription Department, P O Box 35
Hemel Hempstead, Herts,
HP1 1EE England.

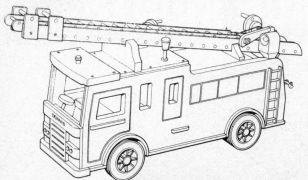

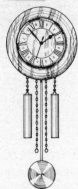

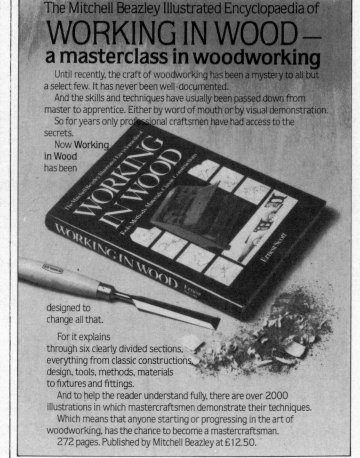

Power plane

With reversible cutters belt-driven by 710W motor the Metabo Expert 4382 plane has die-cast aluminium body and loop handle in which is the on-off switch. Provision is made for connection to an extraction system and a bench-mounted stand is available so that the tool can be used as a fixed planer.

For edge chamfering a V-groove on the front of the bed-plane provides a firm guide and while the guide fence can be locked at any angle, there are quick setting locators at 15, 30 and 45°. Rebates can be cut to depth of 22.5mm and width of 82mm, states B. Draper & Son Ltd, Hursley Road, Chandlers Ford, Eastleigh SO5 5YF (04215 66355), from which further details can be obtained. Priced at £108.95 plus VAT the Expert 4382 is available for either 110 or 240V supply.

Trestle-dogs

For making up trestles or saw-horses, trestle-dogs are introduced by Newfield International Co Ltd, Hall Lane, Elton, Sandbach, Cheshire (09367 2331) in packs of two (to make up one trestle). The hinged brackets come in either zinc plate or orange stove enamel finish and utilise 3 × 2in. PAR timber section. Holes are provided in the dogs for nailing or screwing to the timber. Srp is given as £5.95 for a pack of two dogs; the price includes VAT.

Storage equipment and drill press

Multi-drawer storage cabinets and storage boxes under the Raaco brandname from Denmark have been added to the range of products distributed by Microflame (UK) Ltd, Vinces Road, Diss IP22 3HQ (0379 4813). In enamelled steel the cabinets include combinations of 15, 25, 35 and 45 plastics drawers with dividers. The moulded plastics storage boxes have divided trays for small parts and accessories. Srp for the cabinets is from £9.66 (15-drawer model) and the boxes are from £4.96 (both prices include VAT).

Microflame has also introduced the Dremel model 210 drill press (12in. high) enabling the Moto-Tool to be used as a bench-mounted pillar drill. The rising table permits a Dremel vice head to be fitted for holding small components. Another attachment converts the Moto-Tool into a router. Price of the drill press is given as £18.80 and the drill press vice is £11.39 (both prices include VAT).

For other information and names of local stockists write to Microflame at the above address.

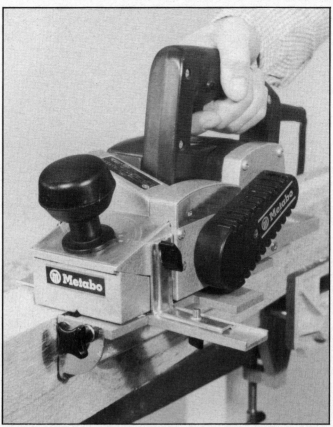

Metabo Expert 4382 plane has extraction facility and is available for either 110 or 240V supply

Dowel jointing

A dowel jointing jig for edges or faces is the Wolfcraft Hobby-mate in 6, 8 or 10mm sizes (approximately ¼, ⁵⁄₁₆, ³⁄₈in.). Supporting accessories include matched dowel drills with depth stops and selection of dowels in the three sizes available in two different pack sizes.

The 8mm size is also offered in kit form comprising dowelling jig, drill and quantity of 8mm dowels; this retails at about £8.97 including VAT. Individual jigs are about £4.49 each including VAT.

Wolfcraft products are distributed by PTS Tool Specialists Ltd, PO Box 242, Henley Street, Camp Hill, Birmingham (021-272 4370).

Parts for staircases

Spindles, newels, rails and fittings for staircases are made by H. Burbidge & Son Ltd, Whittington Road, Oswestry SY11 1HZ (0691 5131), in hemlock or Brazilian mahogany. A leaflet from the company illustrates and describes the items and the various styles and types available. It also gives staircase configurations showing how the individual parts could be used and includes hints on construction.

Copies of the leaflet can be had on application to Burbidge which specialises in repetitition woodturning and machining of components.

Routing ropes and spirals

Router Crafter (model 2525) takes advantage of the router's versatility by providing a means of mounting a workpiece and guiding the router for a number of precise shaping operations, states Hagemeyer (London) Ltd, 25-33 Southwark Street, London SE1. It will handle square or round workpieces 1-3in. thick and up to 36in. long to produce straight or tapered parts with beads, coves, flutes and also right or left-hand ropes or spirals. Hollow centre parts can also be made.

The machine is supplied with mounting clamps for fixing to bench or other surface. Construction is of diecast aluminium with chromed metal tubes and the weight is approximately 12lb. Further details and leaflet can be had from Hegemeyer.

Copycat

A copying device designed to fit the 663 and 664 woodturning lathes produced by Kity UK, Sizers Court, Henshaw Lane, Yeadon, Leeds LS19 7DP (0532 504456), is available through Kity distributors. It is accompanied by a range of standard profiles and the company claims regular and accurate copies of balustrades, fencing, table legs etc can be produced. A useful addition is the availability of blank profiles to allow the woodturner ease of repetition for his own designs.

To trim laminates

Self-guiding trimming cutter having a roller bearing mounted on the cutter base so that it follows the edge of the substrate, is for use on laminates. Known as model 46/2SG, the machine has a 90° cutting edge but other cutters operating on the same principle can be supplied with cutting edges at 80, 60, 45 and 30° angles. Shank diameters of 6 and 8mm, ¼ and ³⁄₈in. are available.

Model 46/2SG is introduced by Trend Machinery & Cutting Tools Ltd, Unit N, Penfold Works, Imperial Way, Watford WD2 4YY (0923 49911).

Grinding TCT cutters

In the September 1980 issue (p606) details were given of the Autoform NX grinder to profile TCT cutters at the same speed as HSS cutters. Wadkin Tooling division of Wadkin Ltd, Green Lane Works, Leicester LE5 4PF, has now issued a leaflet (*Five Star Tooling*) describing the special abrasive wheels used on the NX grinder. The advantages of these are said to include rapid stock removal, saving in cost, low wheel wear, grinding of TC and backing material together and quality of the ground finish.

The abrasive wheels are 230mm diameter and seven standard sections are offered as well as TCT cutter blanks from 60 to 150mm long.

Bench-mounted drill

With choice of 12 spindle speeds, ⅝in. capacity chuck, rack and pinion table height adjustment and rotating and swivelling table, the Rexon model RDM150A bench-mounted drill is described as ideal for all workshop situations.

It is introduced by Calder Woodworking Machinery Ltd, Station Road, Sowerby Bridge, HX6 3LA (0422 31861), at £149 plus VAT. Parts are said to be interchangeable and the heavy-duty construction ensures precision operation.

Tool bags

Things to hold tools — bags, rolls, basses, pouches, cases, holdalls, are made by H. Fine & Son Ltd, Woodside Place, Woodside Avenue, Alperton, Wembley HA0 1XB (01-903 7155), in leather, canvas and plastics. More than 300 versions are produced as well as tarpaulins and industrial covers. Leaflets describing and illustrating the ranges are available.

Sawing machines

Four bandsaws: B400 16in. throat; B500 20in.; B600 24in.; B700 28in. (approximate diameter of the band wheels in mm is indicated by the model number) are announced by Multico Company Ltd, Brighton Road, Salfords, Redhill, Surrey RH1 5ER (Horley 2444). All are available for both single and three-phase supply and all are vertical floor-standing models. A selection of blades is available to cover applications from straight ripping to intricate cutting and profiling.

Main frames are of heavy gauge sheet steel with tilting cast work tables having mitre slot machined parallel to the table edge for the fence and slide provided. Castiron adjustable rip fence for right and left-hand use is also provided.

Upper and lower bandwheels are cast, precision-machined, balanced and rubber tyred and run in sealed bearings. The upper wheel is adjustable for tensioning and tracking. Upper and lower blade guide assemblies are provided and there is an adjustable upper blade guard as well as guarding below the table. Motor is controlled by thermal no-volt release starter with an instant stop footbrake on the lower drive wheel.

An extraction outlet is provided for 80mm hose fitting.

Multico has also added to its range mitre and crosscut saws, model numbers being MS/TCT300; MS/T300 and MS/N250. MS/TCT300 is a combined bench circular saw and swivel table mitre saw having a 300mm (12in.) blade giving up to 53mm depth of cut and powered by 1.3hp single-phase motor. No-volt release starter is available as an accessory.

MS/T300 is described as a single operation machine similar in specification to the TCT but without the circular saw operation. The blade is guarded by an automatically retracting guard and extraction is contained in the main guard assembly. The machine may also be set-up for bench mounting on the Multico ODE extractor cabinet stand.

MS/N250 is a single operation machine having 250mm (10in.) blade but not the swivel table feature other than fixed main cast base incorporating the rear fence. The power unit may be adjusted to right or left through a push-down front handle with positive stops at prime angles and a side lever lock for intermediate stops. MS/N250 may be mounted on a cabinet stand.

Prices and further details can be had from Multico which states that its machines are for wood and aluminium cutting and are readily transportable.

Cabinetmaker's glue

Woodweld is the latest product from the household division of Holt Lloyd Ltd, Lloyds House, Alderley Road, Wilmslow SK9 1QT (0625 526838). Claimed by the company to be ideal for all woodworking jobs (in particular for repairing damaged furniture) the glue is applied direct, without prior mixing, to the surfaces needing to be bonded. It dries in 10min, the excess can be removed while still wet by using a damp cloth; and though overnight is recommended as the period necessary to obtain maximum bonding a good strength is claimed for one hour's wait. There are no harmful fumes, ordinary washing removes the glue from hands and tools and once dry it is resistant to heat, water, lacquers, paints, varnishes etc, states Holt Lloyd. Available in 225ml plastics containers at rrp 99p + VAT.

Cut with Superflute

A multi-purpose professional tool designed to replace a full set of four bowl turning gouges, has been developed by Henry Taylor (Tools) Ltd. Superflute was the brainchild of woodturner Roy Child, and has been produced to give fast free-cutting for roughing-out with effortless control for fine finishing-cutting. The manufacturer claims the cutting edge stays sharp longer than most conventional carbon-steel tools so it slices through rough grain patches and is suitable for most abrasive timbers. Superflute is tangless and the special handle combines rigidity and leverage with balance and precision. Superflute made its debut at this year's Woodworker Show in November and is available from all main stockists at £18.50 + VAT.

Springs for rockers

Springs fashioned from Scotchply material are suitable for use on upholstered rocking chairs and on chairs that are made to recline or swivel. It is claimed that the springs are noiseless. No cams or rocker blocks are necessary, nor are steel springs and brackets.

Scotchply is distributed by 3M United Kingdom Ltd, 3M House, PO Box 1, Bracknell RG12 1JU (0344 26726), which states that a spring 3in. wide, 6-7in. long and 0.26in. thick mounted with a 3⁄8in. diameter bolt has been found to give excellent results. For more information and names of stockists of Scotchply springs get in touch with 3M Industrial Specialties at the address given above.

Portable sawbenches

The Gjerde portable saw bench designed and developed in Norway primarily for the building trade and small volume users, is a widely used piece of equipment. Indeed some 100 000 have been sold in Norway. Now the saw is introduced to the UK market as Nor-Saw models 1202 and 1602 through Norcem UK Ltd, Old Bath Road, Twyford RG10 9PQ (0734 340223), which is appointing stockists having the necessary back-up facilities for spares, service and demonstration, according to sales manager G. J. Billett.

Both models are of similar configuration. The 1202 without feed table occupies a floor area of 520 × 780mm, has a working height of 520mm and weighs 80kg. Power is provided by a 1.5kW single-phase TEFC motor driving through a V-belt. 240 and 110V versions are available so that the 1202 can be operated off a 13A socket outlet, or a small generator on site work. The 20mm diameter saw arbor in sealed-for-life bearings runs at 2800rpm. When fitted with 300mm diameter sawblade cutting capacity is said to be 104mm or 65mm when the blade is at tilt angle of 45°. A detachable stand provides the correct working height.

Model 1602 has a one-piece frame, is heavier and has greater cutting capacity. It occupies a floor area of 640 × 780mm and weighs 130kg, takes a 400mm diameter sawblade on a 25mm diameter arbor to provide maximum cutting depth of 150mm, or 100mm when the blade is tilted through 45°. A 2.2kW motor drives the sawblade through V-belts at 2800rpm.

Each model is supplied with TCT sawblade, feed table with adjustable support trestle legs and adjustable fence for ripping and crosscutting. A range of other accessories is likely to be available in the near future. Guarding conforms to the requirements of the Woodworking Machines Regulations 1974. Bench construction is pressed and welded steel.

Norcem points out that its product, currently made in Norway, derives its versatility from the design of the saw assembly, motor and drive being carried beneath the table in a frame that can be tilted up to 45° and rotated through 90°. With the sawblade at right angles to the feed table crosscutting can be carried out and by turning the blade through 90° ripping is facilitated. The blade elevation mechanism is lever-operated so that an upward feed motion can be employed. For crosscutting and ripping the blade can be set at the required height by lifting the elevating lever and locking it in position by a screw clamp. Clamping of the turntable is effected by use of a screw device and a calibrated scale is fitted.

Norcem is also distributing the Jøtul range of woodburning stoves made in Norway by an associated company. For further details and names of local distributors get in touch with Norcem at the address given above.

On the Nor-Saw a calibrated scale is used for the rapid and accurate setting of the blade angle.

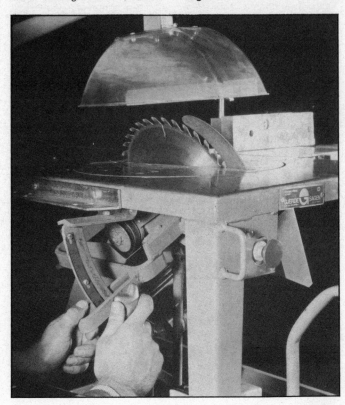

SHOP GUIDE

The quickest and easiest method of reaching all Woodworkers is to advertise in SHOP GUIDE.
Telephone Mary Bell (0442) 41221 Ex. 241.
Rate: £5.00 per unit. Minimum of 6 months.
★ Mail Order

LEICESTERSHIRE

LEICESTER   Tel. 0455 43254
ROY STARTIN LTD
134 WOOD STREET
EARL SHILTON
Open: Mon-Fri 8 a.m.-5.30 p.m.
Saturday 8.00 a.m.-1.30 p.m.

MARKET HARBOROUGH   Tel.
THE MMO SHOP   0858 63502
33-37 ST. MARYS ROAD
Open: Tuesday to Saturday
9.00 a.m.-1.00 p.m.
2.00-5.00 p.m.

AVON

BATH   Tel. Bath 64513
JOHN HALL TOOLS   ★
RAILWAY STREET
Open: Monday-Saturday
9.00 a.m.-5.30 p.m.

BRISTOL   Tel. (0272) 311510
JOHN HALL TOOLS LIMITED   ★
CLIFFTON DOWN SHOPPING
CENTRE, WHITELADIES ROAD
Open: Monday-Saturday
9.00 a.m.-5.30 p.m.

BRISTOL   Tel. 0272-293089
ROBBINS LIMITED
MARINE & CRAFTSMAN DEPT.
CUMBERLAND ROAD
Open: Mon-Fri 8.00 a.m.-5.00 p.m.
Saturday 8.30 a.m.-12.30 p.m.

BRISTOL   Tel. 0272-507966
TRYM TIMBER
29 CANFORD LANE
WESTBURY-ON-TRYM
Open: Mon-Sat 9 a.m.-5.30 p.m.
Wednesday 9 a.m.-1.00 p.m.

BRISTOL   Tel. 0272-629092
TRYMWOOD SERVICES   ★
2a DOWNS PARK EAST, (off
North View) WESTBURY PARK
Open: 9.00 a.m.-5.30 p.m.
Monday to Friday

BRISTOL   Tel. 0272-667013
V. H. WILLIS & CO. LTD   ★
190-192 WEST STREET,
BEDMINSTER
Open: Mon-Fri 8.30 a.m.-5 p.m.
Saturday 9 a.m.-1 p.m.

BERKSHIRE

READING   Tel. (0734) 586522)
SARJENT'S TOOL STORES   ★
LTD.
44-52 OXFORD ROAD
Open: 8.30 a.m.-5.30 p.m.
Monday-Saturday

BUCKINGHAMSHIRE

MILTON KEYNES   Tel. 0908
A. POLLARD & SON   75221
LTD.   ★
51 QUEENSWAY, BLETCHLEY
Open: 8.30 a.m.-5.30 p.m.
Monday-Saturday

CAMBRIDGESHIRE

CAMBRIDGE   Tel. 0223-353091
H. B. WOODWORKING
69 LENSFIELD ROAD
Open: 8.30 a.m.-5.30 p.m.
Monday-Friday
8.30 a.m.-1.00 p.m. Sat

CHESHIRE

NANTWICH   Tel. Crewe 67010
ALAN HOLTHAM   ★
THE OLD STORES TURNERY
WISTASTON ROAD, WISTASTON
Open: Tues-Sat 9a.m.-5.30p.m.
Closed Monday

CLEVELAND

MIDDLESBROUGH   Tel. 0642-
WINTZ   460035/83650
INDUSTRIAL SUPLIES   ★
2 BESSEMER COURT
GRANGETOWN
Open: Mon-Fri 8.30 a.m.-5 p.m.

CORNWALL

NEWQUAY   Tel. 063 73 2516
CONWAY SUPPLIES
(NEWQUAY)
70 FORE STREET
Open: Mon-Fri 9 a.m.-5.30 p.m.

DERBYSHIRE

BUXTON   Tel. 0298-871636
CRAFT SUPPLIES   ★
THE MILL
MILLERSDALE
Open: Mon-Fri 9 a.m.-5 p.m.
Saturday 9 a.m.-1 p.m.

DERBY   Tel. 0332 361575
THE MMO SHOP
33-35 PEARTREE ROAD
Open Tues-Sat 9 a.m.-1 p.m.
2.00 p.m.-5.00 p.m.

DEVON

AXMINSTER   Tel. 0297 33656
POWER TOOL CENTRE   ★
STYLES & BROWN
CHARD STREET
Open: 9.00 a.m.-5.30 p.m.
Monday-Saturday

EXETER   Tel. 0392 73936
WRIDES TOOL CENTRE
147 FORE STREET
Open: 9.00 a.m.-5.30 p.m.
Wednesday 9.00 a.m.-1.00 p.m.

PLYMOUTH   Tel. 0752 330303
WESTWARD BUILDING SERVICES   ★
LTD., Lister Close, Newnham
Industrial Estate, Plympton
Open: Mon-Fri 8 a.m.-5.30 p.m.
Sat 8.30 a.m.-12.30 p.m.

PLYMOUTH   Tel. 0752-266179
JOHN WRIDE & CO (PLYMOUTH) LTD
146 CORNWALL STREET
Open: Monday to Saturday
9.00a.m.-5.30p.m.
Wed 9.00a.m.-1.00p.m.

CO. DURHAM

DARLINGTON   Tel. 0352 53511
PERCY W. STEPHENSON & SON
171/179 NORTHGATE
Open: 8.30 a.m.-5.30 p.m.
Monday to Saturday

ESSEX

SOUTHEND ON SEA   Tel.
MARSHALL &   0702 710404
PARSONS LIMITED   ★
1111 LONDON RD., LEIGH ON SEA
Open: Mon-Fri 8.30 a.m.-5.30 p.m.
Sat. 9.00 a.m.-5.00 p.m.

GLOUCESTERHIRE

TEWKESBURY   Tel. 0684
TEWKESBURY SAW CO.   293092
LIMITED
TRADING ESTATE, NEWTOWN
Open: 8.00 a.m.-5.00 p.m.
Monday-Friday

HAMPSHIRE

ALDERSHOT   Tel. 0252 28088
BURCH & HILLS LTD   ★
BLACKWATER WAY TRADING
ESTATE
Open: Mon-Fri 8.30 a.m.-5.30 p.m.
Saturday 8.30 a.m.-12.00

SOUTHAMPTON   Tel. 0703
HAMPSHIRE   776222
WOODWORKING MACHINERY   ★
297 SHIRLEY ROAD, SHIRLEY
Open: Tuesday-Saturday
9.30 a.m.-6.00 p.m.

PORTSMOUTH   Tel. 0705
EURO PRECISION TOOLS   697823
LTD   ★
235 London Road, North End
Open: Mon-Fri 9 a.m.- 5.30 p.m.
Sat 9.00 a.m.-1.00 p.m.

HERTFORDSHIRE

HITCHIN   Tel. 0462 4177
ROGER'S
47 WALSWORTH ROAD
Open: 9.00 a.m.-6.00 p.m.
Monday-Saturday
Closed all day Wednesday

WATFORD   Tel. (0923) 49911
TREND MACHINERY & CUTTING
TOOLS LTD
UNIT N, PENFOLD WORKS
IMPERIAL WAY
Open: Mon-Fri 9 a.m.-5 p.m.

KENT

TUNBRIDGE WELLS   Tel. 23475
LEISURECRAFT IN WOOD or 2465
124 CAMDEN ROAD   (home ★
TN1 2QZ   workshop)
Open: Mon-Fri 9 a.m.- 5.30 p.m.
Early closing Wednesday

LANCASHIRE

LANCASTER   Tel. 0524 2886
LILE TOOL SHOP
43/45 NORTH ROAD
Open: Monday to Saturday
9.00 a.m.-5.30 p.m.
Wed 9.00 a.m.-12.30 p.m.

LEICESTERSHIRE

GLENFIELD   Tel. (0533) 871238
          & (06077) 5288
POOLE WOOD MACHINERY
SERVICES LIMITED, UNIT 3A,
MILL INDUSTRIAL ESTATE
Open: Mon-Sat 8 a.m.-5 p.m.

LEICESTER   Tel. 0533 877862
EQUIPMENT FACTORS
Unit 3A Mill Lane Ind. Est.,
GLENFIELD
Open: Mon-Fri 8 a.m.-5 p.m.
Sat 9.00 a.m.-12.00 noon

LINCOLNSHIRE

LINCOLN   Tel. 0522 36168/9
R & S TOOLS (LINCOLN)
LIMITED
BEEVOR STREET LN6 7AD
Open: Mon-Fri 8.30 a.m.-5 p.m.
Sat 9.00 p.m.- 12.00 p.m.

LINCOLN   Tel. 0522 30199/
WOODWISE LIMITED   39871 or
121 HIGH STREET   0522 68428
          & 06077 5777/5288
          (after hours) ★
Open: Mon-Sat 9 a.m.-5.30 p.m.

LONDON

LONDON   Tel. 01-636 7475
BUCK & RYAN LIMITED   ★
101 TOTTENHAM COURT ROAD
W1P 0DY
Open: Mon-Fri 8.30 a.m.-5.30 p.m.
Saturday 8.30 a.m.- 1.00 p.m.

HANWELL   Tel. 01-567 2922
G. D. CLEGG & SONS
83 Uxbridge Road, W7 3ST
Open: Monday to Friday
9.00 a.m.-6.00 p.m.
Saturday 9.00 a.m.-5.30 p.m.

KILBURN   Tel. 01-624 5146
W. THATCHER & SONS LTD   ★
221A KILBURN HIGH ROAD NW6
(1st floor above travel agency)
Open: Mon-Sat 9 a.m.-5.30 p.m.
Closed Wednesday

SHOREDITCH   Tel. 01-739 7126
CECIL W. TYZACK   ★
79-81 KINGSLAND ROAD
SHOREDITCH E2
Open: 8.45 a.m.-5.15 p.m.
Mon-Fri — Closed Sat

MERSEYSIDE

LIVERPOOL   Tel. 051-263 1359
TAYLOR BROS (LIVERPOOL) LTD
5/9 PRESCOTT STREET
Open: Monday to Friday
8.30 a.m.-5.30 p.m.

NORFOLK

NORWICH   Tel. 0603 898695
NORFOLK SAW SERVICES
DOG LAND, HORSFORD
Open: Monday to Friday
8.00 a.m.-5.00 p.m.
Saturday 8.00 a.m.-12.00 p.m.

NORTHAMPTONSHIRE

RUSHDEN   Tel. 093-34 56424
PETER CRISP LIMITED   ★
7 HIGH STREET
Open: Monday to Saturday
8.30 a.m.-5.30 p.m.
Thursday 8.30 a.m.-1.00 p.m.

NORTHUMBERLAND

BLYTH   Tel. 06706 69279
ALAN McNAIR WOODCRAFT
69/71 PLESSEY ROAD
Open: Monday to Saturday
9.30 a.m.-5.30 p.m.

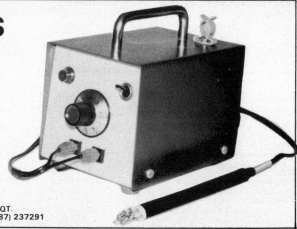

Classified Advertisements

FOR SALE

 **Portable Electric Tools**

SANDERS-240V	Our Spec. Price	Carriage
MVS 93 Orbital Sander	£43.00	£2.00
MVS 94 Orbital Sander	£73.00	£2.00
MVS 47 Orbital Sander	£106.00	£2.00
MHB 90/00 Belt Sander	£127.80	£3.00
MHB 90/10 Belt Sander with Frame	£134.00	£3.00

SAWS

ST 142/01 Jigsaw Orbit Action 2 - Speed 240 Volt	£78.00	£2.00
MH 155 Circular Saw 2 ³⁄₁₆″ Depth of Cut 240 Volt	£67.12	£2.50
MH 182 Circular Saw 3⅛″ Depth of Cut 240V	£85.50	£3.00

COMBINATION SAW TABLES

055 00 34 00 Saw Table	£67.27	£4.00
055 00 34 01 Routing Table complete with Pressure Guard	£77.62	£4.00
055 00 34 05 Saw Table complete with Pivot Arm & Mitre Fence	£105.60	£4.50

SAW BENCH/SNIP-OFF SAW - 240V

TGS 171 Saw Bench/Snip-Off Saw.	£245.71	£6.00
Accessory Set for Wood	£46.57	£2.50
Accessory Set for Alum.	£83.21	£2.50
H.S.S. Saw Blade for Alum.	£21.00	£1.00

PLANER

MFF 80/10 Planer/Rabbeter Set complete with Dust Bag, Side Fence, T.C.T. Blades & Case	£74.00	£2.36

BISCUIT JOINTER/GROOVER SET

DS 140/10 Jointer complete with T.C.T. Grooving Blade & Case	£160.00	£2.00

PLUNGING ROUTERS - 240V

MOF 96 Router Set ¼″ Collet	£68.00	£2.00
Accessory Kit	£45.00	£2.00
MOF 98 Router complete with ½″ Collet	£150.80	£2.30
MOF 31 Router complete with ⅜″ Collet.	£125.00	£2.30

PLASTIC TRIMMER - 240V

MKF 67 Plastic Edge Trimmer with 8mm Collet.	£124.00	£2.00

DOUBLE ENDED GRINDERS - 240V

MWS 146 5″ Dia. Wheels.	£32.25	£2.75
MWS 147 6″ Dia. Wheels.	£42.25	£2.75
MWS 148 7″ Dia. Wheels.	£52.25	£2.75
MWA 149 Grinder/Honer	£90.20	£2.75

ALL PRICES INCLUDING V.A.T.

Barclaycard VISA Accepted

Cecil W. Tyzack LTD TOOLS AND MACHINERY
79/81 Kingsland Rd, Shoreditch, E2 8AG
Tel: 01-739 7126 & 2630

TOOLS TO TREASURE

CARPENTER'S ADZES by Gilpins with 3¾″ cutting edge and 36″ drop on handle — **£24.21.** WOODCARVER'S ADZES by Henry Taylor with 2″ cutting edges and 10″ ash handle. Chisel Blade — **£15.71.** Gouge Blade — **£20.31.** Rosewood handled cabinetmaker's marking Knives — **£1.20.** All prices include P&P in the U.K. EXPORT ENQUIRIES WELCOME. Drawknives, Inshaves and other tools for the Craftsman Woodworker. Send large S.A.E. for details.
CORBETT TOOLS Dept., WW/12, 224 Puxton Drive, Kidderminster, Worcs.

Reproduction Legs in Solid Teak

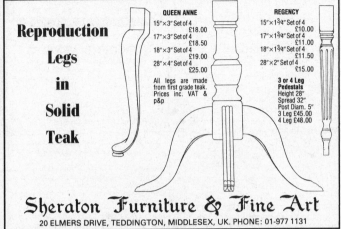

QUEEN ANNE

15″×3″ Set of 4	£18.00
17″×3″ Set of 4	£18.50
18″×3″ Set of 4	£19.00
28″×4″ Set of 4	£25.00

REGENCY

15″×1¾″ Set of 4	£10.00
17″×1¾″ Set of 4	£11.00
18″×1¾″ Set of 4	£11.50
28″×2″ Set of 4	£15.00

All legs are made from first grade teak. Prices inc. VAT & p&p

3 or 4 Leg Pedestals
Height 28″
Spread 32″
Post Diam. 5″
3 Leg £45.00
4 Leg £48.00

Sheraton Furniture & Fine Art
20 ELMERS DRIVE, TEDDINGTON, MIDDLESEX, UK. PHONE: 01-977 1131

EXCITING IDEAS IN FURNITURE-MAKING FOR NEWLYWEDS, D.I.Y. AND UNSKILLED

ALL you need are a few SIMPLE tools to make your own RE-PRODUCTION, MODERN AND GARDEN FURNITURE etc., from our EASY TO COPY PLANS and SIMPLE CLEARLY MARKED assembly instructions. EACH PLAN is FULL-SIZED. Just trace the plan on wood etc., similar to a dressmaking pattern. SO SIMPLE over 60 plans to choose from. FREE plumbing hints leaflet with each catalogue. Many satisfied customers who re-order once they try the plans. Send 60 p&p inc. TODAY for catalogue to Hamlyn Dept. D.W. 57 Lyneham, Wilts, SN15 4PH.

Chair illus. made in less than a day from plan No. 35 price only £1.99.

ARUNDEL E5 bowl Philp headstock, unused without faceplate £35. Picador fig. 300 speedshaft unused £12. Brooks three phase 2hp 1000rpm TEFV motor with forward/reverse starter £120. Tel: Portsmouth 381421. **W**

CORONET IMP bandsaw on stand, Major lathe on stand with saw, two tungsten blades, extension roller, planer, thicknesser, mortiser, grindstone set, sander, tilting table, turning tools, chucks etc. Excellent condition, current cost £1500, £700. Tel: Chester 29397. **W**

SJOBERG WORKBENCH, with Vice Clamp, Deadman and other extras. bought 1978 but unused £95.00. Tel: Glemsford 280456. **W**

FOR SALE Large collection of good quality woodcarving tools, contained in two oak chests, good condition, purchaser collects. (Wrotham Area). Box No. 478, c/o Woodworker, 35 Bridge Street, Hemel Hempstead, Herts.

MEDDINGS MARK 1V bench model Jigsaw. 18″ tilt table 25″ throat. Precision machine for wood plastic or model making. As new £400. 01-947 3202.

SMALL QUANTITIES (minimum 10 cu.ft). Unseasoned English hardwood regularly available e.g. ash, elm; 4 to 6ft lengths 3″ and 2″ thickness in widths 6″ to 15″. Ash, oak; 8ft plus lengths 3″, 2″ and 1″ thickness in 6″ to 15″ widths. Also available yew, cherry, sweet chestnut, etc. Tel: Congleton 71604 or evenings Congleton 4861. **WXY**

ROUTERS

If you are thinking of buying a Router, we offer Bosch/Elu range at unbelievable prices.
If you already own a Router Send for our Free Cutter Wall Chart.

BARRIE IRONS MACHINERY
106A Aldenham Road,
Bushey, Herts.
Tel. Watford (0923) 30422

HARDWOODS, Rosewood, Tulipwood, Partridgewood, Walnut, Cocobolo, Blackwood, Satinwood, Ebony, Noamboana, Purpleheart, Padauk etc. Chart. Reading (0734) 695336 evenings, Saturdays.

CORONET MAJOR Lathe on special bench. 1hp motor, several extras. Chucks etc. Five months old, little used £550. Weston Super Mare 20111. **W**

KITY 7136 10″ surface and thickness planer
with dust extractor as new.
Warranty **£650** ono. **KITY 7227** Spindle moulder/stand with free cutter to the value of £150. As new. Warranty **£380** ono.
Tel: 021 743 5018 or 021-743 0715

STARTRITE BANDSAW 352, 2 years old, little used £450. Buyer collects. Tel: Haslemere (0428) 52428 office hours. **W**

CORONET CONSORT Universal Saw (Blue) with lathe, disc sander, accessories, tools. Virtually unused. Offers. Etwall 2513. **W**

WELSH SLATE sharpening stones for sale at very competitive prices. Send SAE for details:- INIGO JONES AND CO., LIMITED, Groelon, Caernarfon, Gwynedd. Tel: 0286 830242. **V-B**

SEARS CRAFTSMAN Heavy Duty ½hp Sabre Saw. Auto scrolling. 1″ stroke. 12 speed. Special makers stand, spare blades, 155 volt, unused £75 ono. 01-974 3202. **W**

ROSEWOOD, BURR WALNUT, figured mahogany, other assorted veneers. Exceptional Half price. Tel: 0203-69501. **S/W**

COLLECTION OF WOODWORKER MAGAZINES 1950 to May 1980. Incomplete collection 1932 to 1949. Offers? Tel: Middlesborough 89686. **W**

SAWBENCH, planer, sander, workbench, lathe, etc. SAE for details. Pyatt, Melfort, Park Lane, Cheadle, ST10 1PD. Tel: 053-84 3361. **WX**

COURSES

Rawdon Woodturners

I offer comprehensive courses in woodmachining and woodturning on Arundel, Coronet, Kity, and DeWalt Radial Arm machines.
Each course is tailored to suit the individual's requirements. The course includes instruction on ripping, cross-cutting, planing, thicknessing, mortising, tenoning and all aspects of the spindle moulder. On the lathe I cover the correct use of gouges and the setting up of work.
Why not take advantage of my 20 years of industrial and educational experience and realize the full potential of your machinery. My workshop is on the edge of the beautiful Yorkshire dales with ample residential facilities nearby. Write now for more details to

Rawdon Woodturners
Peter Clarke Woodcraft Ltd
Old Friends School Low Green
Rawdon, Nr Leeds, West Yorkshire
Tel: Leeds (0532) 676068

WOODTURNING
Personal Tuition with a Difference

Individual 2 or 4 hour courses to accommodate your personal requirements at times to suit you, including evenings and weekends. I take only one pupil at a time.

Telephone Thanet (0843) 67405 or 01-851-0590 or send SAE for Prospectus.

Write to:

bruce boulter
12 Colview Court,
Mottingham Lane,
London SE9 4RP

TWO-DAY Woodturning Course for beginners in mid-Norfolk village. Two students only. Accommodation available. SAE for details please. Doug Keeling, Church Lane, Beetley, Norfolk. NR20 4AB. **T/C**

WEEKEND COURSE . . .

Make your own APPALACHIAN DULCIMER from a kit under the guidance of an established instrument maker. The large workshops are in a lovely village on the Welsh Borders. Previous woodworking experience not necessary. Fee £40.00 inc. materials. B&B and meals at very reasonable prices. Send SAE for details to:
BERNARD ELLIS, The Coach House, Dilwyn, Herefordshire. HR4 8HW. Telephone: 05445-583.

WOODTURNING TUITION, two days, spindle and bowlwork. No scrappers! Michael F. Norris, Byfield, Northants. Tel: Byfield 61053. **SUWYACE**

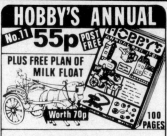

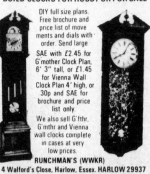

Marilyn Monroe
Unseen Archives

Marilyn Monroe

Unseen Archives

MARIE CLAYTON

p

This is a Parragon Book
This edition published in 2004

Parragon
Queen Street House
4 Queen Street
Bath
BA1 1HE

Text ©Parragon
For details of photographs see pages 382-383

Produced by Atlantic Publishing
Designed by John Dunne

A catalogue record for this book is available from the British Library.
ISBN 1 40541 400 6

Printed in China

Contents

Introduction

Even many years after her death, Marilyn Monroe is still one of the greatest legends of the twentieth century. In her films she projected a unique and fascinating persona - a child-woman who was both innocent and full of sexuality, someone whom men desired, but who women found unthreatening. In real life, she was a beautiful and complex woman who felt deeply insecure, and who just wanted to be loved enough to wipe out her unhappy past.

She was born on the wrong side of the tracks, an illegitimate and unwanted child, who spent most of her early years in a series of foster homes, and became a teenage bride rather than return to the orphanage. A few years later she discovered the one lover who would never let her down, and started an all-consuming affair with the camera. She fought every adversity and setback with determination and humour, and went on to become the most famous movie star of the twentieth century. In her brief film career she appeared in several classic movies, as well as many more that are memorable only for her presence.

Marilyn Monroe: Unseen Archives charts Marilyn's fascinating life, from her unhappy childhood, through her time as a superstar, to her tragic early death. The exciting collection of photographs not only includes movie stills and portraits, but also many other less well known pictures taken during her career. The photographs are accompanied by detailed and perceptive captions, which give a rounded portrait of one of the world's greatest film stars. Marilyn Monroe the person may no longer be with us, but Marilyn Monroe the star is an extraordinary and unforgettable woman whose legend lives on.

Acknowledgements

This book is dedicated to William and Emily Clayton.

The book would not have been possible without the help of
Jonathan Hamston, Matt Smithson, Giovanni D'Angelico, Maria Lopez-Duran,
Zohir Naciri and Scott Kirkham.

Thanks also to Kate Truman, Cliff Salter and Trevor Bunting.

Marilyn Monroe

Unseen Archives

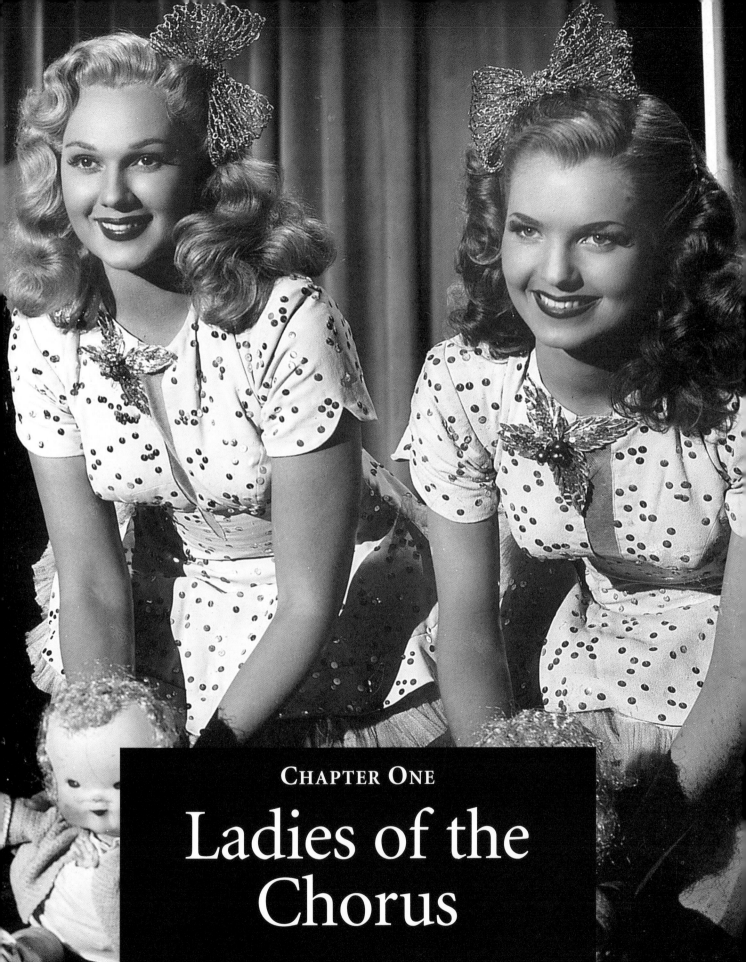

Chapter One
Ladies of the Chorus

After Marilyn Monroe became famous, she told so many different stories about her childhood that it is often not clear where the truth lies. However, she was definitely born on 1 June 1926 in Los Angeles, just a few miles from Hollywood. Her mother, Gladys Pearl, was a film cutter, who worked at Consolidated Film Industries. Gladys had first been married to John Baker, with whom she had two children, Jack and Berniece, but the marriage had ended in divorce in 1923. Afterwards John Baker took the children back to Kentucky, leaving Gladys in California. She wasn't alone for long - in 1924 she met and married Martin Edward Mortensen. This marriage also failed, and Mortensen had long vanished from the scene before Gladys became pregnant with her third child. She never stated who the father was - perhaps she didn't really know - but one of the most likely candidates was Charles Stanley Gifford, foreman of the day shift at Consolidated. Despite this, the new baby was registered as Norma Jeane Mortensen - although during her childhood she was also sometimes known as Norma Jean Baker.

By all accounts, Gladys was not cut out to be a mother. She was still only a teenager when she gave birth to her first two children, and she had often left them with neighbours while she went out to enjoy herself. She was only just 24 when Norma Jeane was born, and was not in a settled relationship. Gladys's mother, Della Monroe, was not willing to offer help or a home, since she was about to leave on a trip round South East Asia with her current beau. Gladys had to manage on her own, with only the help of her close friend, Grace McKee. Not long after the birth she had to return to work to support herself, so she arranged for the baby to be cared for by the Bolender family, who were neighbours of Della, now back from the Far East.

Ida Bolender and her husband, Albert Wayne, were a devoutly religious couple, who looked after various local children as an extra source of income. Although Marilyn later portrayed herself as being unhappy and living in grinding poverty at this time, there is no evidence that her life was really like that. The Bolenders may not have been rich, but they lived comfortably and Norma Jeane was well dressed, had toys to play with and was not neglected. The family even owned a Model A Ford, and Norma Jeane had a pet dog named Tippy. She stayed with the Bolenders for seven years - which was the longest period of stability in her childhood. Nevertheless, it was a confusing situation for a young child - she was neither a temporary visitor, nor a part of the family. Ida Bolender had her own son, and there was a procession of other foster children, none of whom stayed as long as Norma Jeane. She later recalled having once called Ida "Mama", and being told that Ida was not her mother - the lady with the red hair was. Her mother came to visit at weekends, although these visits became less frequent as time went by. Marilyn later said that Gladys never seemed to smile, or offer any affection, so she found it difficult to think of her as "mother".

At the age of seven, Norma Jeane's world changed completely. When a neighbour killed her pet dog she was distraught with grief, and the Bolenders called Gladys. After helping to bury Tippy, Gladys paid the Bolenders to

date and took Norma Jeane away with her. She took out a mortgage on a small house in Arbol Street, near the Hollywood Bowl. To finance the payments, she let the house to an English couple with a grown-up daughter, while renting back a room for herself and Norma Jeane to live in. The couple were actors, and their daughter often worked as a stand-in. Since Gladys, and her close friend Grace McKee, were both still working at Consolidated, the talk at home was naturally full of movies and film stars.

Unfortunately, this interlude did not last long. Early the following year Gladys was taken to hospital, having suffered a severe bout of depression that swiftly descended into some kind of mental breakdown. She was formally pronounced insane at the end of 1934, and was to spend most of her life in various hospitals until 1967,

seemingly having lost her ability to cope with normal day-to-day life for any length of time. Meanwhile, the young Norma Jeane was taken in hand by her mother's friend, Grace. Grace had no children of her own and she apparently came to regard the child almost as her own daughter, particularly after she later became Norma Jeane's legal guardian. Grace was a big fan of Jean Harlow, and she began to instil the belief that one day Norma Jeane would also be a famous movie star. She dressed the child up, showed her how to use makeup and took her to the movies regularly. However, her plans were interrupted when she met Erwin "Doc" Goddard, and he and Grace married after a whirlwind courtship. One month later, Norma Jeane entered an orphanage - perhaps because the newly married couple wanted some privacy, or because money was short and she was one mouth too many to feed. Whatever the reason, yet again Norma Jeane felt let down, unloved and abandoned - feelings that were beginning to shape how she would behave and react in the future.

The orphanage was not as bad as she later sometimes painted it, and the studio publicity machine, anxious to take advantage of any opportunity to publicize their new star, also exaggerated its supposed horrors. Grace came to take her for outings at weekends, when they went to the movies or she treated the child to a makeover at the beauty parlour.

When she left the orphanage, soon after her eleventh birthday, Norma Jeane was placed with a series of foster families, before finally going to live with Grace and her husband. Doc had three children from a previous marriage; one of them, Eleanor - known as Beebe - was around the same age as Norma Jeane and the two of them became great friends. Beebe had had a terrible childhood before this time, coping with a genuinely psychotic mother and a series of abusive foster homes, as well as grinding poverty. Many people believe that Marilyn used some of Beebe's experiences to create the story of her own abused childhood.

Once more, however, this promised stability was interrupted, when Doc was offered a job on the East Coast. Again, Norma Jeane found herself surplus to requirements, as the Goddards decided that they could not afford to take her with them. It also meant that she would lose her first real friend of her own age. However, Grace had a solution - Norma Jean should marry James, the twenty-year-old son of her friend and neighbour, Ethel Dougherty.

Although Norma Jeane and James Dougherty knew each other well, and had even dated on occasion, he was five years older than her and regarded her as still very much a child. But she had a crush on him, and he was flattered by the attention. Grace and Ethel conspired to send them out on regular dates, and soon he came to regard Norma Jeane in a rather different light. However, they probably would not have married - except that for Norma Jeane it was marriage, or return to the orphanage, while Jim could see no real reason not to go along with the idea.

After their wedding, the young couple moved into an apartment. Norma Jeane tried hard to be a good wife, but she hated housework and had no idea about cooking.

Previous Page: One of the first "glamour" publicity poses of Marilyn, for her role in *Ladies of the Chorus*.

Opposite: Even at an early age Norma Jeane Baker was not camera-shy. Here she is as a toddler, sitting on the Bolenders' Model A Ford.

Right: A chorus girl at Columbia...

Like many young husbands, Jim saw nothing wrong with seeing his friends regularly, which his wife perceived as a rejection of her company. He found it difficult to cope with her extreme sensitivity and insecurity. When he was posted to Catalina Island, where he trained new recruits, another complication came into play, as Norma Jeane attracted scores of admirers. She had no thought of being unfaithful, but Jim was still jealous.

Once Jim was posted abroad, Norma Jeane returned to live with his mother, Ethel, who found her a job at her own workplace, the Radio Plane munitions factory. It was here that army photographer David Conover spotted her, featuring her in many of the shots he took of women doing war work. He was so impressed by her ability to look good on camera that he came back to take more photographs, and suggested that she should try a career as a model. Norma Jeane needed little encouragement, and she soon signed up with the Blue Book Agency, based in Sunset Boulevard and run by Miss

Emmeline Snively. The Blue Book not only found modelling assignments, it also ran classes in makeup, grooming, posing and fashion work, the cost of which was deducted from models' fees. Norma Jeane was an apt and willing pupil - although she was still juggling these new commitments with her job at Radio Plane. Miss Snively persuaded her new signing to bleach her hair blonde, to improve her appearance in photographs and increase demand for her services.

As she became successful, Norma Jeane gave up her old job and moved out of her mother-in-law's house and into an apartment - mainly because Ethel disapproved of her new career and growing independence. Inevitably Norma Jeane's new life soon led to the end of her marriage to Jim, although they did not officially divorce until September 1946.

Meanwhile, Norma Jeane was introduced to the National Concert Artists Corporation, who became her agents and arranged her first screen test with Twentieth

Left: The publicity office came up with "interesting" stories to catch the eye of the Press, and one of the first about Marilyn was that she was a babysitter who had been "discovered". To fit this, she is pictured reading to twin babies Eric and Dick.

Below: A few years later it was older boys who were more interested in the young Marilyn...

Century Fox in July 1946. Fox offered her a standard six-month contract, with a salary of $75 per week and an option to renew for another six months at twice this. Grace McKee had to sign on Norma Jeane's behalf, as she was still under age. Ben Lyon, head of talent at the studio, also decided that she had to change her name. Norma Jeane wanted to keep the name Jean, and picked Monroe as her surname, after her grandmother. Lyon then suggested her first name should be Marilyn, after stage actress Marilyn Miller. Norma Jeane went along with this - but years later she said she never liked her new name and wished she had held out for Jean.

Although she now seemed to be on her way to stardom, Marilyn Monroe was to find that the struggle was not over yet. In her first year under contract she had only three bit parts in B-movies, despite having appeared at hundreds of Press calls and photo opportunities. Although Fox had picked up their first option, at the end of the year they declined to renew and Marilyn was out on the Hollywood circuit again, along with thousands of other aspiring starlets. Refusing to give up, she carried on modelling but also cultivated as many film contacts as possible. At one of countless Hollywood parties she was introduced to Joe Schenck, co-founder of Fox and a very influential ally, who soon persuaded Columbia Studios to hire her on a six-month contract in March 1948. At Columbia, she met drama teacher Natasha Lytess, who took her in hand and later became her personal drama coach, and was given her first proper film role. *In Ladies of the Chorus*, she played Peggy Martin, a chorus girl desperate to marry her socialite boyfriend, and also had her first chance to sing. Despite good reviews, this time Marilyn's contract option was not picked up in September.

At this point Marilyn may have despaired, but she soon had a piece of good fortune. At a New Year's Eve Party she met influential agent Johnny Hyde, who was very taken with her and soon invited her out. He not only came to adore Marilyn, he also seemed able to see a star quality in her that others had failed to spot. From this point on, Marilyn's career took a turn for the better. Shortly afterwards she had a small, but significant part in a Marx Brothers' film, *Love Happy*, followed by a role as a chorus girl in *A Ticket to Tomahawk*. By August, Johnny was her agent and had turned his full attention to nurturing her career. A small part in her first high-profile film, *The Asphalt Jungle* directed by John Huston, began to get her noticed and not long after that she landed a good role in *All About Eve*. This film was one of the most successful of 1950, and it brought Marilyn to the attention of Fox studio head Darryl Zanuck, and Johnny Hyde was finally able to get her that elusive long-term contract.

Throughout this period, Johnny Hyde had been urging her to marry him - he had left his wife soon after meeting Marilyn and had introduced her to top Hollywood society, as well as paying for minor cosmetic surgery and a wardrobe of good clothes. Not only was he in love with her, he was suffering from heart disease and was worried about what would happen to her after he was gone. If she had married him Marilyn would have been a rich woman, but she consistently refused. Partly because she didn't want to marry someone she didn't love, partly because she was still devastated that her voice coach, Fred Karger, had refused to marry her, and finally because she feared she would never be taken seriously as an actress if she was Mrs Johnny Hyde. The decision was to cost her dear - that December, Johnny died suddenly of a massive heart attack. Marilyn was heartbroken - although she had not loved Johnny, she had cared very deeply for him. His family immediately repossessed everything he had bought her and they threw her out of his home, then after the funeral his associates at the agency refused to take her calls. Marilyn was left in limbo - she had her contract, but it was coming up for renewal and she had no one to protect her interests.

Once again, she refused to give up, and took matters back into her own hands. After catching the attention of Spyros Skouras, president of Fox, by attending an exhibitors' dinner in a skin-tight cocktail dress, her contract was renewed. During 1951, Marilyn appeared in several rather insignificant movies for Fox, but in August the studio agreed to loan her to RKO, to film *Clash by Night*, directed by Fritz Lang. This was the first proper dramatic part that she had ever been given, with a top director, and although her role was just a supporting part she made the most of it, getting some excellent reviews. It was her performance in this film that finally made Fox sit up and take notice, and decide that perhaps she was ready for a leading role.

Opposite: A demure-looking Marilyn poses in a sexy, strapless gown. At this point in her career she was still one of hundreds of aspiring starlets.

Norma Jeane

Opposite: An early picture of Marilyn at the beach, when she was still a teenager called Norma Jeane Baker. Despite her youth, she already instinctively knew how to pose for the camera.

Above: The young Norma Jean was persuaded to join the Blue Book Agency, after photography David Conover discovered her doing war work in the Radio Plane munitions factory. She was in demand as a model, and it was not long before she was also taken on by National Concert Artists Corporation. A screen test at Fox followed, and a standard six-month contract. It was Ben Lyon at Fox who changed the budding starlet's name to Marilyn Monroe.

A Star is Born...

Right: James Dougherty, Marilyn's first husband. They had married in June 1942, just three weeks after her 16th birthday, but the relationship was short-lived. Marilyn later told reporters that her first marriage had been a mistake, but Jim believed they would have remained together had he not been sent away on active service less than two years after their wedding. Their divorce was made final in September 1946.

Opposite: To create interest in their new starlet, the Fox publicity department concocted a story that Marilyn had been discovered when she had been hired as a babysitter for a casting director and Marilyn was pictured reading a story to three-year-old Joanne Metzler. Stories like these made hundreds of young girls believe that they too could be discovered, if only they were in the right place at the right time.

Below: A publicity photograph released at the same time as Marilyn's first movie - a bit part in *Scudda Hoo, Scudda Hay*, which was filmed during the course of her first year under contract at Twentieth Century Fox. Marilyn's part was mostly cut before the movie was released in April 1948, so she only appears in the distance in one shot.

Smile, please...

Left: The publicity department took an endless series of "cheesecake" photos of all the Fox contract players. Marilyn was always ready to appear for a photographic session, as she knew her future career depended on being noticed by somebody in a position of power. She was successful in this, first becoming one of Joseph M. Schenck's "girls" and then catching the eye of influential agent Johnny Hyde.

Right: Sometimes the publicity pictures took on a more practical aspect, as in this "how to look like a movie-star" beauty session, in which Marilyn is shown applying makeup for the cameras.

Below: Another part of the budding starlet's life was a succession of classes, in which they learned acting, singing and dancing, as well as studying movement and voice culture. In contrast to her screen image, in reality Marilyn was no dizzy blonde and worked hard to improve her acting technique, studying at the Actors' Lab off Sunset Boulevard and seeking to perfect every aspect of her performance.

Ladies of the Chorus

Right: In 1948 Marilyn was briefly under contract to Columbia Studios, and had a part in *Ladies of the Chorus*. She played singer Peggy Martin (third from the right, front row) and Adele Jergens (centre, back row) played her mother, although she was only just over eight years older than Marilyn. This was Marilyn's first co-starring role, but it was only a low-budget "B" movie so it made little impact on her career.

However, the picture was significant in that Columbia Studios' drama coach, Natasha Lytess, was assigned to work with Marilyn on her portrayal of the burlesque singer. Natasha was soon to become Marilyn's personal teacher and her advice and support quickly became indispensable to her insecure pupil.

Love conquers all?

Left : A still from *Ladies of the Chorus*, in which Marilyn receives a corsage from an admirer. The movie gave her a chance to sing for the first time, and she was assigned to voice coach Fred Karger. She fell in love with Karger, but he refused to marry her, later marrying actress Jane Wyman instead.

Right: Marilyn gazes lovingly into the eyes of Rand Brooks, who played her handsome socialite boyfriend, Randy Carroll, in the movie. The plot has the two of them planning to marry, despite the social divide which threatens to keep them apart. In the end love conquers all.

Below: Posing for illustrator Earl Moran. Moran was one of America's most renowned cheesecake artists and Marilyn modelled for him regularly between 1946 and 1949, earning $10 an hour. It was steady work that kept her going as she tried to break into the movie business. Moran produced several charcoal and chalk pictures of her that featured on various calendars.

Johnny's girl

Opposite: Ladies of the Chorus was shot in only ten days. Marilyn told reporters later that when the film was released, she was so excited that she drove past the theatre several times to see her name on the marquee. She wished that it said "Norma Jeane" rather than "Marilyn Monroe", so that all the people who had ignored her in the past could see it.

Above: Unfortunately Columbia Studios chief Harry Cohn was not so impressed with her performance, and Marilyn's option was not picked up. However, Marilyn had been taken under the wing of William Morris agent Johnny Hyde, a well-connected Hollywood player who had managed Rita Hayworth. Johnny introduced Marilyn into his social circle and contributed financially to ensure that his protégée looked the part, paying for some minor cosmetic surgery and for hairdressers to colour her hair.

A ticket to ride...

A Ticket to Tomahawk was Marilyn's first film for Twentieth Century Fox since they had declined to pick up her option two years earlier. The movie was a rather low-key musical Western and did little for her career - but it would have done much better if it had been properly promoted. Unfortunately, Fox had just released a Betty Grable comic Western, *The Beautiful Blonde from Bashful Bend*, which had been badly reviewed and had done rather poorly, so at the time they were not inclined to spend further money on publicity for another Western that could also prove to be a flop.

The Asphalt Jungle

Below: Johnny Hyde was instrumental in getting Marilyn the part of Angela, the mistress of a bent lawyer, in *The Asphalt Jungle*. John Huston's movie was a commerical success but unusual in two ways: it portrayed criminals as ordinary people rather than as gangsters and, more importantly, he had decided not to include any established stars in the cast. Marilyn only had three scenes but she certainly made an impact. Here she is pictured with Sam Jaffe, who played Doc Riedenschneider, the criminal who sets up the jewel heist that the plot hinges on.

Opposite: Louis Calhern played the lawyer, Alonzo D. Emmerich. In the film, Angela gives him a false alibi for the jewel heist, but when she is questioned by the police her loyalty wavers. Her big dramatic scene was shot in only two takes.

Right: Marilyn with her co-star Dan Dailey in *A Ticket to Tomahawk*. She played one of four chorus girls in a story that involved a stage-coach owner trying to stop the new-fangled railroad from ruining his business.

All About Eve...

Johnny Hyde was also instrumental in getting Marilyn cast in *All About Eve*, starring Bette Davis and directed by Joseph L. Mankiewicz. Hyde taught Marilyn that it was better to have a small part in a good movie with an excellent director, than a leading role in a poor movie with a mediocre one. It was this lesson that led to her battle to obtain director and script approval in later years.

Opposite: A publicity shot for Fox's newest star - but despite her growing box-office appeal she was still on a basic salary.

Right: With Thanksgiving approaching in November 1950, the Press office saw an ideal opportunity to talk turkey...

Below: Anne Baxter, Bette Davis, Marilyn and George Sanders in a scene from *All About Eve*. Marilyn played aspiring actress Claudia Caswell, and was introduced by Sanders as "a graduate of the Copacabana school of acting". Although her part was small, it was crucial to highlight the contrasting characters of Eve, played by Anne Baxter, and Margo, played by Bette Davis. The picture went on to receive 14 Academy Award nominations and won Best Movie, while Mankiewicz took Best Director and George Saunders was awarded Best Supporting Actor.

Pin-up

The editors of *Stars and Stripes*, the newspaper for U.S. occupation forces, voted unanimously to award the title of Miss Cheesecake of 1950 to Marilyn. The 1st Marine Division also christened her Miss Morale as they left for Korea. She always felt that her rise to stardom was accelerated by the devotion of soldiers, for whom she was a favourite pin-up.

With a powerful patron behind her and two critically successful movies completed, it seemed that Marilyn was on the way to achieving her ambition. But at the end of 1951 Johnny Hyde died of a heart attack and Marilyn found herself alone and dependent on her own resources again.

Miss Valentine

Opposite: Publicity poses were usually glamour shots, as Fox began to see Marilyn as a replacement for Betty Grable, who was nearing the end of her career. However, Marilyn was still roped in to do her share of opportunistic poses...

Right: For Valentine's Day 1951, she was dressed in a sexy two-piece cowgirl costume and posed with a heart-shaped target.

Below: Although Marilyn only had a small part in *As Young As You Feel*, her name was billed above the title to capitalize on her recent success. It had also convinced studio head Darryl Zanuck to finally offer her a long-term contract. In a scene from the movie, Marilyn, as Harriet, takes dictation from industry boss Louis McKinley, played by Albert Dekker. It was on the set of *As Young As You Feel*, while she was still grieving over the death of Johnny Hyde, that Elia Kazan introduced Marilyn to the playwright Arthur Miller - an encounter that Marilyn did not forget.

Muscle toning...

Marilyn goes through her exercise routine for the benefit of photographers. She told them that you needed to put a lot of effort into the routine, to really exercise most of the muscles in the body, and that she admired the way French women walked. "They don't just plod down streets like so many horses - they jiggle, they bounce, they weave - they come to life."

In her early career she was concerned about a healthy lifestyle and keeping fit and often went running in the morning. In later years this habit slipped as the sleeplessness, drugs and insecurity began to take their toll.

Marilyn was working on *Home Town Story* when she heard that she had secured a seven-year contract with Twentieth Century-Fox. Although this gave her the security of a weekly salary regardless of whether or not she worked, it also meant that the studio had control over her career. She would not be permitted to work on stage, radio or television unless sanctioned by Fox and she could be lent out to another studio if such an arrangement suited studio boss Darryl Zanuck. During the first year her salary was set at $500 a month and was due to rise steadily to $3,500 by the time the contract expired.

Above: When she was voted "the present all GIs would like to find in their Christmas stocking", the Fox Press office swung into action to photograph Marilyn amply filling an oversize stocking.

Opposite: The title of Cheesecake Queen provided the opportunity to feature her plunging a sword into a cheesecake, at a party given by Michael Gaszynski, a former Polish diplomat who was celebrating the passing of his American citizenship exams.

CHAPTER TWO

Gentlemen Prefer Blondes

Although at the end of 1951 Fox did try Marilyn as the lead in a serious drama - *Don't Bother to Knock* - it was not very successful commercially and she was soon back in light comedy roles. The first of these was *Monkey Business*, a screwball comedy in which Marilyn played the only sane character. When it was released, it was a measure of her growing popularity that cinema owners often featured her name to publicize the movie, rather than those of her more famous co-stars, Cary Grant and Ginger Rogers.

Whenever Marilyn worked, her personal drama coach, Natasha Lytess, had to be near by on the set. Marilyn originally met Natasha at Columbia, where she had been the drama coach assigned to help the young starlet prepare for her role in *Ladies of the Chorus*. When Marilyn had signed her new contract with Fox, the only privilege she had asked for was that Natasha should be hired as her personal drama coach, and to work with other contract players when possible. Marilyn's reliance on Natasha often drove her directors and co-stars mad. Rather than looking to the director at the end of a take, she sought Natasha's approval - and if she didn't get it she would ask for a retake. Directors resented a second authority usurping their own, while other actors were put under pressure, as they knew that the take used would be the best one of Marilyn, so they had to be good every time.

While Marilyn was working on *Monkey Business*, a potential disaster loomed. In May 1949, she had posed nude for photographer Tom Kelley, and the picture had been used anonymously on a 1952 calendar - which now adorned gas stations and barbershops across the country. Someone had recognized Marilyn as the blonde stretched out artistically on red velvet, and the story was about to break in the Press. In the moral climate of the early 1950s, the scandal could have ruined her budding career - posing nude was not something a nice girl did, and no Hollywood star had ever been caught out behaving in such a way. Fox executives were all for denying the whole thing, but Marilyn thought she should just tell the truth and admit everything - and for the first time, her view prevailed. An exclusive interview was arranged with journalist Aline Mosby, and the story ran in U.S. newspapers in March. Marilyn confessed that she was the blonde, and explained that she had desperately needed the money to pay off debts and that this had been the only honest way she could earn it quickly. She mentioned that the photographer's wife had been present at the shoot, and said that she felt she had done nothing to be ashamed of. The result was a triumph, instead of a disaster. Public sympathy swung behind her and the calendar was reprinted many times during the early fifties - it is estimated that as many as four million copies were sold.

Two days after the story broke, Marilyn met baseball star Joe DiMaggio for the first time. He had seen a publicity photo of her with two White Sox players, and asked who she was. Later he discovered that one of his drinking buddies knew her and could arrange an introduction. After dinner he called her every night and they were soon a famous couple, with their romance documented in all the newspapers. Marilyn loved the warmth of his Italian family and valued the feeling of security he gave her, and the impression that he was batting on her side.

She certainly needed support, as within a couple of months another potential threat to her career appeared. All the publicity about Marilyn as she became a star had been built around the fact that she was an orphan, who had become successful despite adversity. Now a journalist had tracked down her mother - who was not only still alive, but had just been released from the latest in a series of state mental institutions. Coming just after the "nude calendar" revelations, the timing could not have been worse. Marilyn quickly gave another exclusive interview, this time to Erskine Johnson, saying that she had not known as a child, when she had spent time in an orphanage and in foster homes, that her mother was in hospital. She also said that, having discovered that her mother was still alive, she had been in contact and was offering help as required. The last part at least was true - Marilyn's business manager, Inez Melson, had been visiting Gladys to make sure she had sufficient money since 1951. Again, the explanation was accepted and Marilyn retained her public following.

Meanwhile, she was about to begin work on her next major starring role. In *Niagara*, she played a sultry seductress who plans to murder her husband so she can be with her lover. The scene where Marilyn croons along with a record was so sexually charged that it outraged representatives from the Women's Clubs of America, and had to be hastily modified. Throughout filming, Marilyn pushed the limits of what was acceptable, and she outshone the more experienced actors with whom she was working. When she was on the screen, the audience didn't look at anyone else. After the film was completed, everyone was left in no doubt that Marilyn was truly a star.

In 1952, five films featuring Marilyn were released - *Clash by Night* for RKO and *We're Not Married, Don't Bother to Knock, Monkey Business* and *O Henry's Full House* for Fox. Her next film for Fox was already lined up. The studio had originally bought the rights to *Gentlemen Prefer Blondes* for Betty Grable, but director Howard

Hawks, who had recently worked with Marilyn on *Monkey Business*, was convinced she was perfect for the part of Lorelei Lee. Despite some studio reservations as to whether she was up to the demands of the role, she was paired with Jane Russell and at the beginning of November 1952 work started on costume and makeup tests. In this movie, Marilyn has a far more polished and sophisticated look than she had achieved before - and this is often attributed to the influence of Hawks. For the dance numbers, Marilyn worked hard with choreographer Jack Cole to perfect her technique, because she knew she had no natural ability here, as she did with acting and singing.

By now, Marilyn was beginning to cause problems on set with her chronic lateness. She would arrive at the studio early, but was still locked in her dressing room hours after filming was due to start. It was a habit that often drove her directors and co-workers crazy, because they saw it as evidence of unprofessionalism, laziness or as deliberate rudeness. However, on this film co-star Jane Russell soon realized the cause. It wasn't that Marilyn would not come to the set - she couldn't. She was terrified of going in front of the camera, because she could not bear the thought of failing, of being less than perfect. She spent hours doing and re-doing her makeup, and working herself up to the point at which she could perform. It was this very intensity with which she approached her roles that came over on the screen, and made her such a unique star. Jane provided a simple and fairly effective solution - every morning she would stop by Marilyn's dressing room and collect her. Once on set, Marilyn would work, as long as the atmosphere was conducive, and as long as Natasha was on hand.

The following year, 1953, was one of the high points in Marilyn's career. In January, *Niagara* was released and went on to earn more than five times what it had cost to make, confirming Marilyn as a top box-office draw. In April she began work on another major role, co-starring in *How to Marry a Millionaire*. In this, she was working with two well-established stars, Betty Grable and Lauren Bacall. The studio made much of a supposed feud between

Previous page: Marilyn and Jane Russell strike a pose in *Gentlemen Prefer Blondes*.

Opposite: Although she was the blonde, Marilyn was being paid far less than Jane Russell was, as she was still locked into her studio contract on a weekly salary.

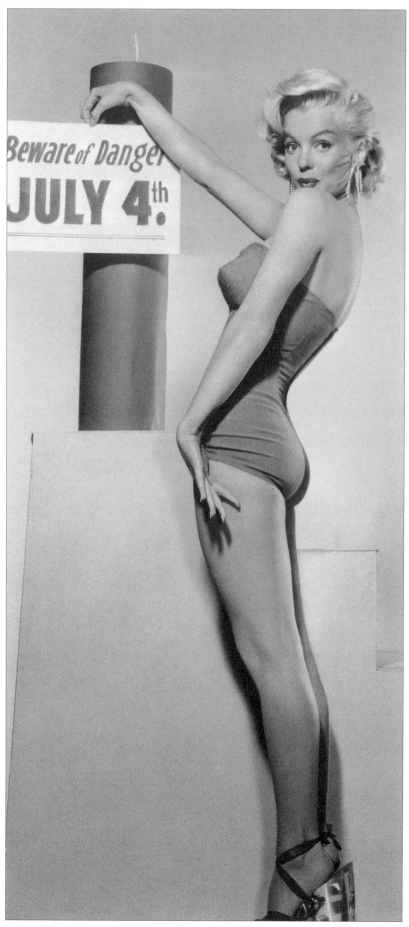

Marilyn and Betty - the incoming star and the outgoing one - but in fact they got on well and became great friends. Although she had been dubious about playing the part of a girl who wore glasses, the "accidents" built round her character's short-sightedness confirmed Marilyn's talent as an actress with a gift for comedy.

In July, *Gentlemen Prefer Blondes* was released, and it quickly became a spectacular success. Both the public and the critics loved it and it brought Marilyn her first awards for her talent, rather than her looks - *Photoplay* magazine's Best Actress of 1953, and Best Friend a Diamond Ever Had award from the Jewelry Academy.

As part of the publicity campaign, Marilyn and Jane Russell were invited to leave their prints outside Grauman's Chinese Theater on Hollywood Boulevard. The tradition had begun when Mary Pickford and Douglas Fairbanks had accidentally stepped into some wet concrete outside the theatre, and Grauman had suggested they add their signatures to the footprints. Marilyn went to the theatre when she was a child, and had tried to fit her feet into the stars' prints as she daydreamed about becoming famous herself. So the occasion really was a dream come true. She had asked for a diamond to dot the "i" in her name, but settled for a rhinestone - which very soon caught the eye of a souvenir hunter and was stolen.

Marilyn had gone straight from *Gentlemen Prefer Blondes* to *How to Marry a Millionaire*, with little rest in between, and now she was about to start on *River of No Return*. Charles Feldman of Famous Artists, who was acting as her agent although she had not signed the contract, was becoming concerned about the effect of continuous working on her health

Left: To publicize the July release of *Gentlemen Prefer Blondes*, Marilyn appeared in a campaign to promote safety during 4th July celebrations.

Opposite: Marilyn shows off some of her assets.

- and was worried that her career might be damaged by overexposure. When the studio informed her that immediately after *River of No Return* they intended to put her in another musical, *The Girl in Pink Tights*, Feldman advised her to turn the project down. He also thought that this would signal to studio executives that he and Marilyn were aware of just how important she had become, as a prelude to renegotiating her contract. On one hand Marilyn was reluctant to turn down an assignment because of her insecurity, and because she had no savings to tide her over if the studio suspended her, but on the other she had her own worries about accepting the film. Firstly, she was annoyed that no one thought it important that she should see the script - she had only been sent a précis of the plot - and from that, it was evident that the character was similar to those she had played in her last two films. This fuelled another worry - she was afraid of being typecast and outliving her usefulness, so she wanted to play a wider range of roles. In addition to the studio choosing all her projects with no reference to her, they were also assigning the director, and Marilyn had learned how important it was to work with directors who could bring out the best in her. Lastly, yet again she was being expected to star in a movie for her usual salary of $1,500 a week - negotiated way back in 1951 before she had become a star - while her co-star, Frank Sinatra, would be paid $5,000 a week. She went off to Canada for location filming on *River of No Return* with these issues still unresolved.

Marilyn had another problem to sort out. Joe DiMaggio had several times asked her to marry him, but she couldn't make up her mind what to do. She loved him and valued the stability and support he offered - but he was not interested in art and books, as she was, and was incredibly jealous of any attention she received from other men. Most of their arguments were to do with her need for public adulation and her habit of dressing provocatively. More importantly, he wanted her to give up the movies and become a beautiful, ex-movie-star housewife, while she was still focused on obtaining the respect and adulation in her career that she felt she deserved. They decided that Joe should join her in Canada, and away from the stresses of Hollywood they would try to come to a decision.

The filming of *River of No Return* was not a happy experience for many of those concerned. Director Otto Preminger made little secret of his lack of enthusiasm for the project and took a great dislike to Natasha Lytess. When Natasha upset child actor Tommy Rettig, causing him to forget his lines, Preminger banned her from the set, although Marilyn quietly made sure that the studio reinstated her. Both Marilyn and co-star Robert Mitchum had physically demanding roles, and part of the plot involved travelling down rapids on a raft, which meant that they had to spend a great deal of time doused in water for continuity.

Marilyn, who usually got on well with children, was surprised that Tommy Rettig avoided her off set. She asked him why, and was devastated to discover that he had been told by his priest that it was fine to work with "a woman like her", but implied that he should not socialize with her. Luckily things improved between them after DiMaggio arrived, as Tommy was impressed that such a famous baseball star obviously respected Marilyn and the three of them even went fishing together.

After filming finished, Joe took Marilyn off to spend a few days with his family in San Francisco, and then they returned to Hollywood. Although he wanted her to give up the movies, he could understand her battles with the studio - particularly over money. Money meant respect - so the more money they were prepared to pay, the more they respected you. On the matter of *The Girl in Pink Tights*, Marilyn was now ready to give in and start work on the movie. Natasha had been pressurizing her to accept it, because she was afraid that if Marilyn didn't, her own position on the Fox payroll would be put in jeopardy, while Feldman didn't think it was that important if Marilyn felt she had to do it. However, at this point DiMaggio proved what an astute businessman he was, by pointing out that if Marilyn refused the film, Fox would have no backlog of Monroe pictures to release, thus putting Feldman in a much stronger bargaining position. When the first day of shooting arrived, Marilyn failed to turn up on set.

Opposite: Marilyn first appeared on *The Jack Benny Show* in September 1953, and afterwards she and Benny became great friends. Marilyn did the show to publicize her films, but since her contract with Fox did not allow her to receive cash for this type of work she was given a black Cadillac convertible with a red interior instead.

Clash by Night

Above: Marilyn poses with actor Keith Andes, who played her love-interest in *Clash by Night*, which was released in 1952. She had been loaned out by Fox to RKO and it was her first major role in which some serious acting was required. Along with Barbara Stanwyck, Marilyn would have her name above the titles. She insisted that her personal drama coach, Natasha Lytess, was present on set, which did not please director Fritz Lang, although eventually a compromise was reached. Determined to impress, she employed acting teacher Michael Chekhov in addition to working on the part with Natasha.

We're Not Married

Actor David Wayne looks stony-faced as Marilyn gives him a peck on the cheek in a scene from *We're Not Married* which had a star-studded cast including Ginger Rogers, Fred Allen and Zsa Zsa Gabor. The movie told the stories of five different couples who find out some time after the wedding that they are not legally married because the judge's licence was not valid. Marilyn plays a housewife who enters the Mrs America beauty pageant. Her role was hastily added to the storyline to cash in on her growing popularity, and scriptwriter Nunnally Johnson later admitted he had deliberately created opportunities for her to appear in two bathing costumes.

Right: One of the bathing costumes from *We're Not Married* was reused for a Fox publicity still, when Marilyn posed for yet another Valentine picture for the U.S. armed forces.

Opposite: Swimsuit glamour girl... : Although the studio had begun to cast her in a steady stream of pictures, Marilyn had not forgotten the importance of publicity and was still prepared to pose for photographers. It would not be long though before she yearned to escape from the "blonde bombshell" image.

Dating Joe DiMaggio

Above: Joe DiMaggio talks to newsmen in the Press room at Yankee Stadium just before a game is due to start. He and Marilyn met on a date in March 1952 at the Villa Nova restaurant, and soon became an item in the Press.

Left: DiMaggio had taken his ten-year-old son, Joe Jr., to meet Marilyn, and they had got on well - Marilyn had an empathy with most children. However, Joe's ex-wife, actress Dorothy Arnold, was furious and told newspapermen that she intended asking the courts to modify her divorce to stop such visits, because Joe Jr. had come home talking of Marilyn's "beautiful legs" and calling her a "doll".

Opposite: Marilyn checks out her appearance. Later she would spend hours in front of the mirror before appearing on set - not because she was vain, but because she couldn't bring herself to appear until she thought everything was absolutely perfect.

A screwball comedy

Opposite: Marilyn appears in a swimsuit and (above) with Cary Grant in publicity stills for *Monkey Business* filmed at the start of 1952. The movie was a screwball comedy starring Cary Grant and Ginger Rogers but shortly before shooting began studio boss Darryl Zanuck asked the scriptwriters to expand both Marilyn's part and that of the monkey!

Marilyn played a dumb blonde secretary, and Grant a scientist who is trying to invent an elixir of youth. One of the laboratory monkeys mixes a formula and puts it in the water cooler - and of course this turns out to be the youth potion that everyone is seeking. Several characters then unknowingly drink the potion and revert to their childhood, providing the writers with plenty of opportunity for comedy.

A visit from Joe

When Joe DiMaggio visited the set he was photographed with Cary Grant and Marilyn - but newspaper editors cropped out Cary Grant and photographs of Joe and Marilyn were sent around the world. Costume designer William Travilla, who worked with Marilyn on many movies, said that of all the outfits that he had created for her this beige jersey dress which she wears in her opening scenes in *Monkey Business* was her least favourite.

A little Monkey Business...

The swimsuit poses were at least related to the plot of the film - after Barnaby Fulton (Cary Grant) drinks the youth potion he rushes out and buys a sports car, and then takes Lois Laurel (Marilyn) for a spin and they end up going swimming.

While she was filming *Monkey Business*, Marilyn developed appendicitis but she refused to go into hospital for an operation until the end of April after she had completed her part. However, although she was prepared to put up with a lot of pain in order to retain her part in the film, she was reputedly regularly late arriving on set, a habit that was to become more pronounced in the years to come. Howard Hawks later said of her that she was "late every day...but she knew all her lines".

Opposite: Marilyn signs an autograph for a fan. Later a group of New York-based fans were known as the Monroe Six, and they were always present when she was due to appear. When she lived in New York they followed her around, tipping each other off as to what she was doing. She valued their devotion, and once invited all of them to a picnic at Roxbury, where she was living with Arthur Miller.

Calm before a storm

Marilyn relaxes in the sun on the terrace of her home in Hollywood. However, just as she had finally realized her childhood ambitions, playing opposite Cary Grant in a Howard Hawks movie, her past came back to haunt her. Marilyn had been recognized as the nude model in a calendar which had been distributed all over the U.S. and the morality clause in her contract allowed the studio to dismiss her should the public react unfavourably to this revelation. Poised on the verge of success, Marilyn was in danger of losing everything she had striven so hard to achieve. However, in contrast to the advice of the studio publicists, Marilyn's instinct was to admit that she had modelled for the pictures, pleading poverty as the motive. The public forgave her and the publicity only increased her profile.

As early as 1952, Marilyn was already being thought of by many as just a dumb blonde. It was a stereotype that infuriated her, as it prevented her being considered for more serious acting roles. Part of this was due to studio head Darryl Zanuck, who considered Marilyn to be "empty-headed", but it is debatable whether Marilyn would have risen so high so fast if her early screen roles had been more varied. As it was, she quickly developed a persona that the public loved - and then spent the rest of her career trying to get away from it.

Miss America...

Since *Monkey Business* opened in Atlantic City, home of the Miss America beauty pageant, Marilyn was invited to be Grand Marshal - the first woman to appear in the honorary role. She took part wearing a low-cut dress that was very revealing, and when the inevitable storm burst a few days later she coyly commented, "People were staring down at me all day long, but I thought they were admiring my Grand Marshal badge." Joe deeply disapproved of Marilyn's selection of such immodest attire and was angered when pictures appeared in the Press.

Niagara Falls

In her second leading role, Marilyn shared star billing only with Niagara Falls. She played Rose Loomis, who plans to murder her husband, played by Joseph Cotten, so she can be with her lover. The plan goes wrong, and both Rose and her lover end up dead. The film featured what was the longest walk in screen history at the time - 116 feet of Marilyn swivelling her hips provocatively as she moved away from the camera, wearing a tight black skirt. It caused a sensation - but Marilyn told readers of *Life* magazine, "I've been walking since I was six months old - I just use it to get me around."

Left: Marilyn proves she really could look good in any old thing...

Opposite: Marilyn with Henry Hathaway, director of *Niagara*. Although he was notorious for shouting at actors, he was concerned about Marilyn, not only looking after her on set but advising her to get a good agent to limit the endless publicity demands on her time.

Gentlemen Prefer Blondes

Above: Marilyn arrives in New York in October 1952 to publicize *Monkey Business.* However, this would be one of the few public appearances she would make for some months. After years of tirelessly seeking publicity to advance her career, the studio signalled a new confidence in her and Marilyn was instructed to concentrate solely on preparing for her new role in Howard Hawks' latest project, *Gentlemen Prefer Blondes,* based on the book by Anita Loos.

Having already directed Marilyn in *Monkey Business*, Howard Hawks understood that comedy, rather than drama was her forte. He persuaded Darryl Zanuck, head of production at Fox, that the combination of established Jane Russell and popular new-comer Marilyn Monroe could be successful at the box office. On her 26th birthday Marilyn was thrilled to be offered the part of Lorelei, created on Broadway by Carol Channing.

Above: Marilyn's drama coach Natasha Lytess explains a point between takes.

Right: Jane Russell with Marilyn on the set of *Gentlemen Prefer Blondes*. The two stars got on very well together - even though Russell was being paid ten times what Marilyn earned for making the movie under her standard studio contract.

Two little girls from Little Rock...

Jane and Marilyn play two showgirls travelling to France on a cruise liner, where Lorelei is to marry her wealthy boyfriend, Gus Esmond. Esmond Sr. is convinced Lorelei is a gold digger, and hires a private detective to prove it. Marilyn was determined not to squander the opportunity offered to her. She worked late into the evenings to perfect Jack Cole's dance routines. Together the girls performed the show's opening number "Two Little Girls from Little Rock" but the best-remembered song in the film is Marilyn's rendition of "Diamonds Are a Girl's Best Friend".

Above: After seeing a diamond tiara belonging to Lady Beekman, Lorelei tries out a napkin ring for effect, commenting that she loves to find new places to wear diamonds.

Left: Newcomer Tommy Noonan played the wealthy playboy, Gus Esmond. His rather naive character stood little chance against the wiles of blonde bombshell Lorelei.

Diamonds are a girl's best friend

Above: Irene Crosby, Marilyn's stand-in on *Gentlemen Prefer Blondes*, poses with the star. On set Marilyn had gathered around her a small group of people with whom she had a strong rapport. Natasha was always present, but loyal makeup man Whitey Snyder and hairdresser Gladys Whitten were also there to encourage and support her.

Opposite: Diamonds are a girl's best friend... Marilyn poses with thousands of dollars' worth of real diamonds to publicize *Gentlemen Prefer Blondes*. In real life, Marilyn did not care much for expensive jewellery and owned very little. The items she wears in her Press photographs are all borrowed from the studio or from jewellers.

Worst-tressed actress

Opposite: Marilyn's looks were not admired by everyone. Hairdressers in America voted her America's "Worst Tressed" actress saying that her hair looked like a "shaggy dog". They suggested she should cut at least three inches off. Elizabeth Taylor was voted "Best Tressed" at the same time, for being "glamorously trim".

Right: Marilyn's hair colour was naturally a rich red-brown and quite curly. During her career as a blonde, she went through every shade from golden to platinum.

Above: Marilyn studies some of theatre-director Max Reinhardt's original manuscripts, which she had recently acquired at auction, paying $1,335. Her interest in the papers no doubt stemmed from the fact that Natasha Lytess had been part of Reinhardt's theatre company in Germany. Marilyn's purchase caused the Press to complain that she had deprived a university library of the chance to have the manuscripts, which would have meant they were available for all students to study. Marilyn replied that she was thinking of donating them. However, Reinhardt's son acquired them from her at cost - and then sold them on at a handsome profit.

Dressed to impress...

Leading Hollywood costume designer William Travilla - known simply as Travilla - designed many of the dresses that Marilyn wore in her films, including the outfits for *Gentlemen Prefer Blondes*. But both Howard Hawks and Travilla could take credit for the slick and sophisticated costumes in the picture which helped change Marilyn's image on screen. Travilla also designed many of the memorable dresses she wore to public events. She had very few formal clothes of her own - whenever she needed to dress up she would borrow something from the studio wardrobe.

Above: No sooner had Marilyn dealt with the crisis over the calendar photographs, when her mother came back to haunt her - the publicity office at Fox had told the Press that Marilyn was an orphan, but a persistent reporter tracked Gladys Baker down and found out she had recently been released from a state mental hospital.

Opposite top: Gossip columnist Walter Winchell, Marilyn and Joe Schenck at a party for Winchell's birthday at Ciro's in Hollywood in May 1953. Winchell was also a friend of Joe DiMaggio.

Opposite bottom: Marilyn and Jane Russell were invited to leave their prints outside Grauman's Chinese Theater as part of the publicity for the release of *Gentlemen Prefer Blondes*. Marilyn jokingly suggested that they should leave imprints of what they were famous for instead - her behind and Russell's chest.

Best rear view

Above: Although this is a publicity photograph for *Gentlemen Prefer Blondes*, Marilyn is wearing a robe that was one of her costumes from *Niagara*. The studio often recycled costumes between different stars and different movies. After four months of filming, *Gentlemen Prefer Blondes* was completed in March 1953. Fox now recognized Marilyn's potential as a box-office draw and scheduled her to commence work on a new picture with only four days' break.

Opposite: According to movie cameraman Frank Powolny, Marilyn had the best rear view of all the movie stars he had photographed during his career.

How to Marry a Millionaire

Opposite and previous pages: Marilyn as Pola Debevoise in *How to Marry a Millionaire*, with co-stars Betty Grable and Lauren Bacall. The movie was designed to capitalize on the success of *Gentlemen Prefer Blondes*, although neither the script nor the direction was as accomplished as that of the Hawks musical. Marilyn was exhausted by having expended so much energy in mastering the routines on her previous film and was further handicapped by her usual nerves in front of the camera.

Marilyn's character was terribly short-sighted but refused to wear her glasses in public, which led to a lot of comic mishaps.

Right: Jack Benny and Marilyn out on the town. After they became friends they often became involved in pranks together. At one point they reportedly visited a nudist beach, with Benny wearing a false beard and Marilyn a black wig.

Below: Spyros Skouras, president of Twentieth Century-Fox, and Darryl Zanuck, co-founder and studio head. Skouras frequently championed Marilyn, while she felt Zanuck was responsible for the long string of "dumb blonde" roles she was forced to play.

On the Jack Benny Show

Opposite: Marilyn gets a hug from comedian Jack Benny in a publicity picture for her guest appearance on his show, transmitted live from the Shrine Auditorium in Los Angeles on 13 September 1953. Marilyn performed a comedy skit with Benny and sang "Bye Bye Baby" before taking the opportunity to mention the release of *How to Marry a Millionaire.* She was thought to have aquitted herself well playing opposite the very experienced Jack Benny and despite the fact that she frequently needed multiple takes when acting in movies, she did not seem unduly worried that the programme was live.

Above: Marilyn being interviewed in Hollywood by United Press reporter Vern Scott.

Marilyn and Joe

Joe and Marilyn continued to date although he preferred to stay out of the limelight. He seldom accompanied her on public appearances, sometimes waiting outside to collect her at the end of the evening. The Press still speculated as to whether, and when, they would marry, but although Marilyn valued Joe's steady devotion and his close-knit family she was not ready to give up her career and all that she had struggled to achieve to be the sort of wife he wanted.

Despite starring in two of the most commercially successful films of 1953, Marilyn was living in a small rented apartment on Doheny Drive near Sunset Strip. Joe would have preferred that Marilyn did not work, but he took considerable interest in the financial and contractual discussions which followed her recent successes. Marilyn had made the leap from starlet to star and she and her advisers decided that it was time to renegotiate her contract with the studio.

Opposite: During the filming of *River of No Return* in Alberta, Canada in August 1953, Marilyn slipped on some wet rocks and damaged her leg. It had to be bandaged and she was forced to hobble around for several days. This was not the only difficulty on set. During the filming of *How to Marry a Millionaire*, director Jean Negulesco had sought to accommodate Marilyn's wishes by tolerating Natasha Lytess's interference. However, on *River of No Return*, Otto Preminger banned Natasha from the set, insisting that she remain in Marilyn's dressing room. The movie over-ran and Marilyn's co-star Robert Mitchum is said to have dubbed it "the picture of no return".

In the film Marilyn plays Kay, a saloon singer, who ends up travelling down a river on a raft with farmer Matt Calder (Robert Mitchum) and his young son (Tommy Rettig). By a strange coincidence, Mitchum had been in the army with Marilyn's first husband, Jim Dougherty.

Below: Yet another swimsuit pose...
All the photographers that Marilyn worked with commented on how professional and dedicated she was.

Left: Trying on different outfits before posing for a photograph to promote safety during the forthcoming Independence Day celebrations.

River of No Return

Joe DiMaggio joined Marilyn in Canada while she was filming *River of No Return*. They had been dating for more than a year, but Marilyn could not make up her mind whether to marry him. He brought his friend, George Solotaire, and they went on fishing trips, sometimes accompanied by Marilyn and young Tommy Rettig.

Opposite above: Jack Benny and Marilyn, in a publicity picture for her TV debut on his show.

Opposite below: Tommy Rettig and Marilyn attending a film. After a shaky start the two of them got on well together.

CHAPTER THREE

There's No Business Like Show Business

Fox's response to Marilyn's failure to start on *The Girl in Pink Tights* was immediate. They couldn't get hold of Marilyn herself, who was lying low protected by Joe, but they contacted both her agents and Natasha. Famous Artists informed the studio that she was not ready to start on the film because she still hadn't seen the script. Marilyn had trusted Natasha to be on her side, come what may, but in this instance - perhaps worried about losing her lucrative job - Natasha criticized Marilyn's behaviour and tried to get her to relent. Marilyn never forgave her for it and although they worked together on two more films, from then on Natasha's days were numbered.

Meanwhile the studio asked Marilyn to report in, to shoot retakes on *River of No Return*. Everyone understood that it was one thing to refuse to start a project, and quite another to fail to finish one, thus preventing its release and costing the studio hundreds of thousands of dollars. Marilyn's first instinct was that it was a ruse to get her onto the lot, so she fled to San Francisco with Joe. However, her agents discovered that the retakes were indeed necessary, and persuaded her to return. As soon as they were completed, Marilyn returned to San Francisco and continued to sit tight. The studio had no option but to suspend her.

But there was an unexpected twist to come. Marilyn appreciated everything Joe was doing for her - far from holding himself aloof from the movie business as he had done before, now he was fully involved in sorting out her problems with the executives at Fox. Perhaps she took this to mean that he was reconciled to her continuing her career, and she finally agreed to be his wife. They were married in San Francisco, and only on the day did Marilyn call the studio to let them know. Despite efforts to keep the wedding quiet, the Press turned up in force and pictures appeared in all the newspapers. Fox had little option but to lift the suspension - to do otherwise would have seemed churlish - and they informed Famous Artists that Marilyn should report to work at the end of January, after the honeymoon.

For more than a week, the newlyweds enjoyed the seclusion of a remote cabin in the mountains, far from civilization. Marilyn said later that it was during this period that she and Joe really got to know one another. However, at the end of January Joe had to be in New York, so they returned to Los Angeles - to find that Fox had finally sent a copy of the script for *The Girl in Pink Tights*. After reading it, Marilyn still did not want to do the movie. Now she was in the position of questioning the studio's ability to select suitable projects and the reaction was predictable. She was put back on suspension and the studio released a Press statement pointing out that her last few movies had been outstandingly successful, which was all the evidence needed that they were the best people to decide what she should work on. In the background to this public furore, Charles Feldman of Famous Artists was quietly renegotiating Marilyn's contract. She wanted more money, and approval of the script, director and cinematographer.

Since she was back on suspension again Marilyn was a free agent, so Joe invited her to come with him to Japan as a continuation of their honeymoon. They were going to Tokyo for the opening of the baseball season, but when they arrived it was Marilyn, not Joe, who was the centre of attention. At a Press conference in their hotel, all the questions were directed at her and she announced that she planned to spend a few days in Korea, entertaining U.S. soldiers. Joe did not approve, but Marilyn had always been a big favourite with the troops and felt she owed much of her early success to their support.

Back in Los Angeles, Marilyn found out that Fox had agreed to drop *The Girl in Pink Tights* and instead offered her a supporting role in *There's No Business Like Show Business*, with the promise of the lead in *The Seven Year Itch* - a successful Broadway play to be directed by Billy Wilder. She was back on salary, but only until August 1954, when a new contract would come into force, giving her an additional fee of $100,000 for *The Seven Year Itch*. However, the studio refused to budge on her last requirement. It was always unlikely that they would - at Fox, Zanuck alone decided what films were going to be made and who was going to make them. If he gave in to Marilyn, who knows what concessions others would demand in future? Marilyn scaled down her demands, asking only for approval of her choreographer and dramatic coach, but the studio would not agree to this either. Finally, however, they conceded that Marilyn should be consulted about the choice of coach and choreographer. It seemed as if matters were settled - but in fact now Marilyn knew that she would not get the creative control she wanted, she was already working on other plans.

Marilyn's character in *There's No Business Like Show Business* was hastily tacked on at the last minute, to create an alternative project she could work on instead of *The Girl in Pink Tights*. The result was not entirely successful, but the main function of the storyline was to provide a framework for the songs of Irving Berlin and the cast included established stars like Ethel Merman and singer Johnnie Ray. Marilyn worked hard on her routines, so as not to be outclassed by her more experienced song-and-dance co-stars. Unfortunately she didn't get on with the director, Walter Lang, and was suffering from the after-effects of a bout of pneumonia, caught entertaining the troops in Korea in below-freezing temperatures. Most critics agree that it is one of her less successful films, and Marilyn was deeply upset at its lukewarm reception. She felt she had caved in to studio assertions that they knew what was best for her, and now she was being panned for it.

Since the schedule on *There's No Business Like Show Business* had overrun, Marilyn was forced to start *The Seven Year Itch* with no break in between. When she left for location filming in New York, Joe put on a good show when seeing her off at the airport, but in fact their marriage was already in trouble. Joe's jealousy had boiled over on more than one occasion - perhaps even into physical violence, according to some reports - and Marilyn was beginning to feel that she had made a big mistake. However, Joe did still love her and a few days later he followed her to New York. Generally he kept out of the way when she was working, but unfortunately he was on hand for the shooting of the famous skirt scene in *The Seven Year Itch*. As Marilyn stood over the subway grating, with her skirt blowing up almost to her waist and thousands of New Yorkers cheering and yelling, he was seen leaving the street with a grim expression on his face. When Marilyn came back to the hotel they had a furious row, and by the next morning their marriage was all but over.

Although her private life now lay in tatters, at least her professional life was coming together. In 1953, photographer Milton Greene had taken a series of pictures of her that she loved, and which seemed to capture a different Marilyn, bringing out aspects of her personality that no one else seemed to see. Since then Greene had listened to her complaints about the studio and, keen to break into film production himself, he had suggested they form their own production company. As soon as it became obvious that Marilyn was not to get the creative control she wanted from Fox, she started talking seriously to Milton Greene about forming Marilyn Monroe Productions. With her own company she would be able to choose the roles she played and would have the control over her career that she so desperately wanted. At the same time, she planned to dispense with Famous Artists as her agents and move over to MCA, as she felt Feldman had failed to achieve even the most basic improvements to her contract.

In December 1954, Marilyn moved to New York, first staying in a hotel and then moving in with Greene and his wife at their house in Weston, Connecticut. Early the following year, Marilyn and Milton Greene held a Press conference to announce the formation of Marilyn Monroe Productions. Fox was not going to give up their biggest star without a fight, and their legal representatives

Previous page: Marilyn and Joe DiMaggio seem wonderfully happy on their wedding day, but unfortunately it was not to last.

Above: Although she was technically still on her honeymoon, in February 1954 Marilyn took some time out to entertain troops in Korea. Here she bends to talk to some of the soldiers who waited in near-freezing temperatures to hear her perform.

quickly pointed out that Marilyn was under exclusive contract to them for the next four years. However, lawyers for Marilyn Monroe Productions had studied the contracts with Fox, and found a number of anomalies and broken promises - including non-payment of the $100,000 additional fee for *The Seven Year Itch* - which they ruled meant the contract was null and void.

The legal battles were to continue throughout 1955, although halfway through the year the emphasis changed. Marilyn Monroe Productions had planned to find a financial backer to enable them to develop their own projects, but as time went by it became apparent that this was not going to happen - and meanwhile Marilyn had a lifestyle to maintain. At first, Fox had *The Seven Year Itch* in the can ready to release, but after it proved astoundingly successful they had no more Monroe films to follow it up with. At the end of December 1955, Marilyn and Fox signed a new contract, which not only gave her a much more lucrative financial deal - including a percentage of the profits - but also the creative controls she craved, with approval of script, director and cinematographer. In addition, she was permitted to undertake one independent film project each year. At the time it was an unprecedented amount of power for an actor to have, and represented the first breach in the traditional studio system.

Marilyn made no films throughout the whole of 1955 - concentrating instead on developing her acting skills by working with Lee Strasberg at his Actors Studio. Strasberg believed that she had great talent and he was a major influence on her future acting style. At first she was too insecure to go to the general sessions at the Actors Studio, so he taught her privately at his home. He also advised her to begin psychoanalysis to release the unresolved tensions from her childhood, and Marilyn rushed to follow his instructions, starting sessions with Dr Margaret Hohenberg. Lee Strasberg also went on to provide the replacement for Natasha, in the form of his wife, Paula, who took over the role of personal drama coach on Marilyn's remaining films.

In New York, Marilyn was able to move around incognito when she wished, by the simple expedient of wearing casual clothes, covering her hair, and wearing dark glasses. Most of the time she found this liberating, but sometimes she couldn't resist slipping back into the Marilyn persona. Several people who witnessed the transformation were fascinated by it. At one moment she would seem like an ordinary person, hardly worthy of a second glance, and then she seemed to throw some kind of inner switch and a magnetism suddenly appeared, turning heads and causing people to flock round her.

During this time, Marilyn also became a part of New York literary life in a way she had never been in Hollywood, introduced to exclusive circles by the Greenes. She appeared at parties and first

Opposite: Marilyn on the set of *The Seven Year Itch* in New York, with director Billy Wilder (left) and co-star Tom Ewell.

Above: Marilyn breaks down in tears in the passenger seat of a Cadillac driven by her attorney, Jerry Giesler, after facing the Press during the announcement of her separation from Joe DiMaggio.

nights, and also donated her services to charity on several occasions. Despite the fact that their divorce was about to be finalized, Joe DiMaggio was also still very much on the scene: he turned up regularly in New York to take Marilyn out or to offer help and support. Reporters sometimes took this as a sign of an imminent reconciliation, but Marilyn always denied that they were anything more than just friends. Joe might have wished for more, but Marilyn in fact had already quietly begun a relationship with playwright Arthur Miller.

She and Arthur Miller had first met in Hollywood back in 1950, and after he returned to New York she had written to him several times. Miller was one of the most celebrated playwrights of the day, and had won the Pulitzer Prize for his 1948 play, *Death of a Salesman*, although he had struggled to repeat its success

subsequently. Now Marilyn was living in New York and moving in literary circles, it was only a matter of time before they would meet again. Miller had been attracted to Marilyn from the first, as she was to him, but he was married, with two young children. He didn't want to divorce his wife, and she didn't want to be a home-wrecker, so nothing further had come of it. Now, however, Miller's marriage was in trouble anyway. As they spent more and more time together - both in private and in public - the Press soon got wind of their unlikely friendship. At the first night of Miller's play, *A View from the Bridge*, Marilyn met his parents for the first time. Not long afterwards, she was invited to their home, and after she left Miller told them that she was the girl he was going to marry. Nobody really took him seriously, but within less than a year he and Marilyn were married.

Opposite: In New York during her battle with Fox for recognition and an improvement in the terms of her contract, Marilyn faced the Press to reveal her "new look".

Above: With Jacques Cemas, Sammy Davis Jr., Milton Greene and Mel Tormé at The Mocambo in 1955, where they were celebrating Davis's return to show business after his accident.

Love birds...

Although it had taken some time to come to a decision, there is no doubting the genuine feelings between Marilyn and Joe as they snuggle up to each other in the judge's chambers on their wedding day in January 1954. The wedding itself was planned as a rather low-key affair; Marilyn wore a neat chocolate-brown suit with an ermine collar and Joe a dark blue suit with the same polka dot tie he had worn on his first date with Marilyn. Joe had wanted to marry in a church, but both he and Marilyn were divorced so it was not possible. During the brief, three-minute ceremony, Marilyn promised to "love, honour and cherish" her husband - but the word "obey" was left out.

At the time of her wedding Marilyn was in dispute and on suspension from Fox, but she called the studio publicists an hour before the wedding to let them know. It was long enough for them to put the word round and - despite the happy couple's desire to keep the ceremony private - hundreds of reporters descended on San Francisco town hall after having been tipped off. The Press were excluded from the actual ceremony, but afterwards Joe and Marilyn smiled for photographers and waved to the fans as they hurried to Joe's blue Cadillac. They spent their honeymoon night at the Clifton Motel in Paso Robles, before vanishing to a hideway cabin in the mountains to spend some tranquil time walking in the woods and fishing.

En route to Tokyo...

Opposite: Joe had been invited to Tokyo to open the 1954 Japanese baseball season, and since she was back on suspension after refusing to appear in *The Girl in Pink Tights*, Marilyn decided to accompany him.

Above: During a brief stopover in Honolulu, Marilyn and Joe, along with San Diego Padre manager Lefty O'Doul, were given traditional flower leis.

Left: At a Press conference in Japan, Marilyn poses happily for photographers. Joe was not happy that his wife seemed to be getting more attention than he was - particularly as the Press call had been arranged for him.

Below: Although this scene appears tranquil, when Joe and Marilyn first landed in Tokyo they were mobbed by fans - to the extent that the couple had to take refuge back in the plane. Joe and Marilyn eventually had to leave via the baggage hatch and hide in the customs hall until the fuss died down a little. However, when they arrived at the Imperial Hotel they were mobbed again and the fans refused to disperse until Marilyn appeared on a balcony to wave.

Opposite: Marilyn arrives at Seoul City Airport by chopper, on her way to entertain the American troops who were still stationed in war-torn Korea. She had been invited by the Far East command of General John E. Hull.

In Korea...

Opposite: Despite the sub-zero temperatures and occasional flurries of snow, Marilyn appeared in a low-cut, skin-tight purple sequinned gown - with no underwear. At the time she did not appear to notice the cold but she was to suffer for it later, coming down with pneumonia after she had returned to Japan. Here her famous wiggle is demonstrated to appreciative troops, who answered with whistles, cat calls and applause.

Above: Sergeant Guy Morgan, from Marion, North Carolina, presents Marilyn with a 25th Division "Wolfhounds" scarf.

Right: During the four-day tour, Marilyn did ten shows, singing such favourites as "Diamonds Are a Girl's Best Friend", "Bye Bye Baby" and "Somebody to Love Me". She also included "Do It Again", but the lyrics had to be toned down to "kiss me again" to avoid inflaming the over-excited audience any further. Here she is on stage at the K-47 airbase in Chunchon, Korea.

Above: Many of the soldiers who had come to see Marilyn had walked for over ten miles and they gave her a rapturous welcome. While she was in Korea, many of her performances were filmed and the footage was later put together to create a documentary, which she narrated.

Opposite above: Pfc. James R. Goggin gets a bit of personal service, as Marilyn helps out in the 2nd Division Mess.

Opposite below: Marilyn samples the food herself. Later soldiers said that her appetite was "Great, she eats everything".

Geisha Girls

Left: After a sukiyaki dinner in Kobe, Japan, Marilyn poses with a group of Geisha girls. The dinner had been given in honour of Joe DiMaggio by the Central League, one of Japan's professional baseball organizations, but as usual it was Marilyn who was the centre of attention. So soon after their honeymoon, the trip had brought home to Joe how difficult it would be to be married to the world's greatest sex-symbol. He was not comfortable with his wife being admired by other men, and more crucially he disliked the fact that Marilyn encouraged them and enjoyed all the attention.

Below: Marilyn tries out her baseball batting skills.

Opposite: On her return to America, Marilyn felt refreshed and ready to resume her battle for better contract terms. During her absence, Charles Feldman, of Famous Artists, had been working tirelessly on her behalf - although she still had not signed a contract with his agency.

No Joe...

At the *Photoplay* magazine awards in Hollywood in March 1954, Marilyn was pictured with actor Alan Ladd (above) and columnist and friend Sidney Skolsky (opposite). She explained to the Press that Joe did not like crowds - but he came to collect her afterwards. Marilyn had been honoured as Most Popular Film Actress of 1953.

Having spent some time with Joe in San Francisco, Marilyn was still under suspension, but had returned to Hollywood for the *Photoplay* awards. The contractual negotiations between the studio and Charles Feldman were protracted but sufficient progress had been made for her to begin work on *There's No Business Like Show Business*. *The Girl in Pink Tights* had been dropped and Fox conceded that Marilyn should not make more than two films each year. However, she had been refused the level of creative control she sought, only being granted approval of the choreographer and dramatic coach.

Starting a family?

Above: Marilyn demonstrates her singing and dancing skills in *There's No Business Like Show Business*. Her part had been written into the script specially, to give her an alternative project to *The Girl in Pink Tights*.

Left: Marilyn with co-star Johnnie Ray, who played Steve Donahue. His character starts as part of the Donahue song and dance act, but he leaves to become ordained as a priest.

Opposite: Due to her lingering illness throughout filming, Marilyn apparently fainted three times on set, which gave rise to rumours that she was pregnant. She told interested newsmen that she and Joe certainly wanted to start a family, but that she was not yet expecting.

There's no business like show business...

Above: A production still from *There's No Business Like Show Business*. Marilyn's character of Vicky was given some of the production numbers written for Ethel Merman - which led to an interesting mixture of styles. Unlike the other lead actors, Marilyn was not a professional singer or dancer, but she worked hard with her coaches so her performance would measure up. Marilyn's routines were choreographed by Jack Cole with whom she had worked on *Gentlemen Prefer Blondes* but the others were created by Robert Alton.

Opposite: Marilyn with her drama coach, Natasha Lytess, during filming. Marilyn was only to do one further movie with her - *The Seven Year Itch* later in 1954. Natasha had tried to pressure Marilyn into doing *The Girl in Pink Tights*, and Joe DiMaggio disliked her intensely, so by 1956 she had been replaced by Paula Strasberg.

"After You Get What You Want...."

Opposite: The dress Marilyn wore for her performance of Irving Berlin's "After You Get What You Want You Don't Want It" in *There's No Business Like Show Business*, consisted of sequinned white net over a flesh-coloured body stocking, with strategically-placed silver and white flowers and a slit high up onto the hip, masked with white fringing. Marilyn had recently signed an exclusive recording contract with RCA, so the film soundtrack featured Broadway star Dolores Gray.

Above: Marilyn takes some time out to visit Merle Oberon on the set of her new film, in which she was playing Napoleon's Josephine, and director Henry Koster entertains them both with a joke.

Left: Lewis K. Gough, past National Commander of the American Legion, presents Marilyn with a trophy and plaque in July 1954, for her morale-building activities on behalf of the armed forces.

Miss Modesty...

Above: Marilyn and Joe having dinner at El Morocco on East 54th Street in New York where Marilyn was on location filming *The Seven Year Itch*. Despite the smiles, Joe was deeply unhappy about his wife's continuing film career. He wanted her to settle down and be a wife - and hopefully a mother - but Marilyn was still totally absorbed in her work.

Joe objected strongly to Marilyn's habit of wearing revealing and low-cut dresses and in deference to him she often wore much more modest outfits during their brief marriage. He also disliked her going without underwear - and once made her wait in the powder room of a restaurant until suitable undergarments could be delivered. Despite these problems Marilyn found him deeply attractive - soon after they met she said of him, "He has the grace and beauty of a Michelangelo. He moves like a living statue."

Right: The strategically-placed fabric rose was no doubt there to appease Joe - and photographers did have a habit of shooting from above when Marilyn wore low-cut dresses.

The Seven Year Itch

Above: Backstage at the Martin Beck Theater, Marilyn has her eyes made up Oriental-style by actor David Wayne, as Joe looks on, amused. The two of them had been to see *The Teahouse of the August Moon*, in which Wayne starred.

Opposite: Marilyn listens to director Billy Wilder outside the apartment on East 61st where some of the exterior sequences of *The Seven Year Itch* were filmed. Wilder had seen George Axelrod's adult comedy after it opened on Broadway in 1952 and had recognized its potential for adaptation for the cinema, although Hollywood's Production Code meant that the screenplay had to be less daring than the original production. While Marilyn had agreed to begin work on *There's No Business Like Show Business*, her agent, Charles Feldman, had been involved in securing the role of "The Girl"- the archetypal dumb blonde without even a name - for Marilyn.

The story is slight: husband Richard Sherman (Tom Ewell) is alone in New York during a sweltering summer, as his wife and young son have left for Maine. Sherman is determined to work, but is distracted by the arrival of "The Girl" (Marilyn), who has sublet one of his neighbour's apartments. Because of the heat, she walks around her apartment scantily dressed and keeps her "undies" in the icebox. He fantasizes about starting a relationship with her but she is more interested in his air-conditioned apartment - and is relieved to find that he is a married man so she feels safe with him!

Left: At the end of the film, Sherman decides on fidelity and goes off, taking his son's canoe paddle, to join his wife and son, leaving Marilyn with the use of both the apartments.

Below: During one of the movie's fantasy sequences "The Girl" gets her toe caught in the tap and has to be freed by a plumber, played by Victor Moore.

Opposite: The heat wave that is an integral part of the plot was also an excuse for Marilyn to wear all kinds of skimpy costumes.

Every male fantasy...

Philip Strassberg of the *New York Daily Mirror* said of *The Seven Year Itch,* "This is the film that every red-blooded American male has been awaiting ever since the publication of the tease photos showing the wind lifting Marilyn Monroe's skirt above her shapely gams. It was worth waiting for."

However, much the footage taken on location on Lexington Avenue and 52nd Street was not used in the film because of the background noise and poor light. The scene was shot again on a soundstage back at the Fox studio in Hollywood. The famous pleated, white halter-neck dress that Marilyn wore was part of a set of costumes designed by William Travilla, who had worked on Marilyn's costumes for *Gentlemen Prefer Blondes.*

The famous skirt sequence

The shooting of the skirt-lifting scene on the street was as much about publicizing the movie as about getting the scene. The studio publicity department had leaked plans to the Press, so by the time filming started there were hundreds of photographers and thousands of cheering onlookers. At least fifteen takes were done, leading Marilyn to comment to director Billy Wilder that she hoped they weren't for his private collection, to be screened at stag shows. The skirt blew up past Marilyn's waist several times - and even though she wore two pairs of panties the final shots were far too revealing to be used in the movie.

Unfortunately, Joe had been persuaded to come and watch the filming by his friend Walter Winchell. The sight of his wife displaying her underwear as thousands of men cheered was too much for him, and he left the scene looking visibly displeased. Back at the hotel that night he and Marilyn argued badly, and the next day he left New York for California.

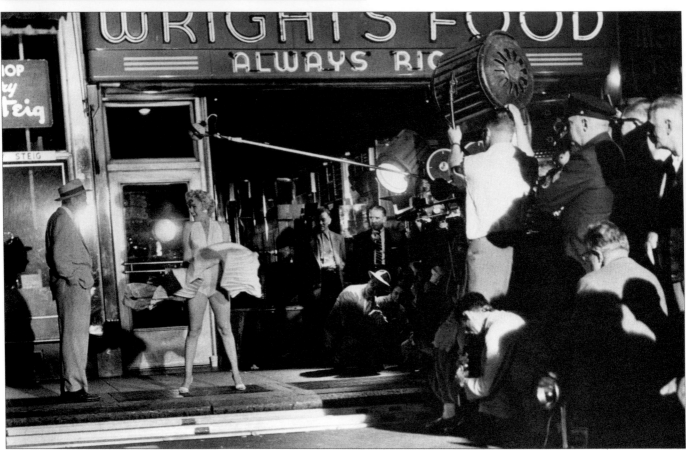

Working with Billy Wilder

Opposite: Marilyn discusses a scene with Billy Wilder on the set of *The Seven Year Itch*. Marilyn had been very keen to work with him - although that didn't stop her arriving late and requiring numerous retakes even when Wilder was happy. Wilder said of her later, "She is a very great actress. Better Marilyn late than most of the others on time." Marilyn often had difficulty remembering her lines so Wilder broke down scenes into smaller sequences to aid her. Despite this, the movie was almost two weeks behind schedule on 4 November when principal photography was finished.

Above: Marilyn with Tom Ewell, in a publicity still for the movie. Although Marilyn had been Wilder's first choice to play "The Girl" the role of Sherman had been more difficult to cast. Wilder had been favourably impressed by Walter Matthau's audition and Gary Cooper had also been seriously considered before the part was given to Tom Ewell who had begun his career in theatre and had played Sherman in the original Broadway play.

Above: Despite Sherman's fantasies, "The Girl" is entirely innocent and has no idea how he feels about her. Marilyn was superb at putting across a sense of sexuality with no apparent awareness of the effect she was having. Co-star Tom Ewell found her to be charming and courteous in real life - she even apologized for the taste of cough medicine on her breath during their kissing scene. She was taking it for a lung infection caught during the skirt-lifting sequence.

The star and the stand-in...

Above: Marilyn with Billy Wilder and Tom Ewell during filming in New York in September 1954.

Right: Gloria Mosolino, who was Marilyn's stand-in during shooting of *The Seven Year Itch* in New York. Before Marilyn came on set, Gloria had done the skirt-lifting scene eight times to test the lighting and the blower system. She was a professional stand-in, but such essential people in the film-making process usually stay in the background since they rarely make it into the final film. Such was Press interest in the sequence, however, that even Gloria was interviewed - and the folks back home in Pottsville, Pennsylvania, were horrified that she had revealed her undies in public for $20 a day and lunch money.

Spot the difference

Opposite: Europe's glamorous screen star Gina Lollobrigida had once said with some emphasis that she and Marilyn were quite different. This prompted Broadway columnist Earl Wilson to bring the two of them together at the Trans-Lux Theater in New York. Despite her view, the resulting picture reveals several similarities...

Above: Back in Hollywood, Marilyn was pictured with her attorney, Jerry Giesler, outside her Beverly Hills home. Newsmen were gathered to hear a statement, as studio publicist Harry Brand had recently announced that Marilyn was filing for divorce from the Yankee Clipper.

Heading for divorce...

Marilyn clings to Jerry Giesler for support as he gives an official statement to the Press on 6 October, 1954, revealing that she had filed a suit for divorce on the grounds of "mental cruelty" against Joe DiMaggio. As Marilyn posed for photographers she was obviously close to tears, and she refused to say a word herself, leaving all the talking to Giesler.

Everyone speculated about what had gone wrong after only nine months of marriage, as to outsiders they had seemed to be such a golden couple. Marilyn later described their marriage as a "sort of crazy, difficult friendship with sexual privileges. Later I learned that's what marriages often are."

Joe moves out

Above: After the Press statement, Marilyn leaves her home in her attorney's car, heading for the studio where she was to complete scenes for *The Seven Year Itch*.

Opposite: Joe had already left the house that morning, moving his possessions out with the help of his friend Reno Barsocchini. He told reporters he was leaving Los Angeles and would not be coming back to the house that he had rented to share with Marilyn, but he refused to discuss the divorce action any further. Privately, he was reluctant to accept the proceedings as final, making several attempts to persuade Marilyn to change her mind.

Divorce granted

Opposite: In court in Santa Monica in California, before Judge Orlando H. Rhodes, Marilyn sat subdued and dressed all in black. She gave ten minutes of tearful testimony, alleging that Joe was "cold and indifferent, would get into moods and wouldn't speak to me for days at a time...if I tried to coax him to talk to me, he wouldn't answer me at all or he would say 'Leave me alone! Stop nagging me!'"

Above: Marilyn puts her signature to her divorce papers. There were tears in her eyes when the judge said, "Divorce granted." However, it was not final until the following year, October 1955.

Marilyn in hospital

Opposite: Marilyn poses for stills at the studio, although she was just about to go into the Cedars of Lebanon Hospital in Los Angeles for surgery to correct her chronic endometriosis.

Right: Although she tried to leave the hospital by the back door on 12 November, 1954, newsmen were lying in wait to catch her looking tired and ill and far from her usual glamorous self. Despite the divorce, Joe practically lived at the hospital during the five days she was there, and visited her constantly at home in the early part of November. This started rumours that a reconciliation was on the cards - but Marilyn denied it.

Above: Newsmen and curious onlookers throng round as Marilyn leaves the Santa Monica Superior Court on 27 October, 1954, followed by her attorney, Jerry Giesler.

What's in the stars?

Above: Marilyn has her palm read by fortune teller Hassan, at the Beverly Hills Hotel. He couldn't have got it more wrong - he said she was an excellent sailor, whereas Marilyn commented that she got seasick just looking at water, and he said she would go on to have two children.

Opposite: Marilyn being interviewed by Maria Romero at the Beverly Hills Hotel, accompanied by photographer Milton Greene who had come to California with ambitions of becoming a movie producer. Marilyn had first met Greene in the spring of 1954 and was delighted to find in him someone who appreciated her talent and supported her desire for more creative control of her material.

Leaving L.A.

For once Marilyn keeps her curves well covered as she chats with Charlie Farrell at the Racquet Club in Palm Springs in December 1954. She was soon to leave for New York, where she was to remain for the whole of the following year - except for a brief trip back in early January 1955 to film additional dialogue for *The Seven Year Itch*.

After consultations with a lawyer over her contract with Fox, Marilyn sacked her agent Charlie Feldman and announced that she and Greene had established their own company, Marilyn Monroe Productions.

New look Marilyn?

At a Press conference to launch Marilyn Monroe Productions in January 1955 in New York, reporters were told to expect a "new and different" Marilyn, so they were rather disappointed when she appeared looking very much like the old model. She had bleached her hair a more platinum blonde and was dressed all in white, with a pure white mink, in an effort to look like Jean Harlow, as the first film the new company intended to produce was Harlow's life story, with Marilyn in the lead role. The effect was rather lost on the assembled members of the Press, who seemed more interested in whether the mink actually belonged to Marilyn; - she replied, "It's mine for the night."

Just visiting

Opposite: Milton Greene and Marilyn had become sidetracked by the idea of portraying her as the ideal person to play Harlow, and the result was disastrous. The newspaper coverage the following day didn't even mention the formation of Marilyn Monroe Productions, instead being full of jokey comments, such as, "The new her didn't show up."

Left and above: Despite her estrangement from Twentieth Century Fox, Marilyn returned to Hollywood to reshoot one scene for *The Seven Year Itch*. Pausing on the staircase of the set, dressed in a nightgown and high-heeled slippers, she only had one line to say: "We can do this all summer." Afterwards she told newsmen that she hoped she could work out her differences with the studio and quipped that she was a changed woman - and might even start wearing underwear.

Above: Marilyn with Joe DiMaggio, Joe's brother Dominic, and Dominic's wife, leaving a restaurant in Boston. Newsmen wanted to know if the meeting was a reconciliation, but Marilyn assured them it was not.

Left: While she was living in New York, Marilyn was involved in several campaigns to raise money for charity. Here she gives the Press advance warning of the date of her appearance on the opening night of the circus, in aid of the New York Arthritis and Rheumatism Foundation.

Opposite: Publicity shot for *The Seven Year Itch*, which was soon to be released. At a party shortly after shooting finished, director Billy Wilder told Marilyn to stay with the character she had created, and to stop trying to move into more serious acting roles. Although she respected Wilder as a director, Marilyn had no intention of taking his advice.

A new career?

Marilyn hands a programme to a rather surprised-looking Milton Berle (above), at the New York première of *East of Eden*, which starred James Dean. She was acting as a celebrity usherette in the Astor Theater, and the proceeds from the occasion were donated to the Actors Studio by director Elia Kazan.

Marilyn had recently become involved with the Actors' Studio, both attending sessions there and privately studying drama with Lee Strasberg at his home. Although Strasberg was not impressed with the world of film, feeling that stage acting was the only true medium, he was quick to use Marilyn's celebrity to earn additional money for the Studio and for himself personally. In Strasberg Marilyn felt she had found someone who understood her needs and could offer her the opportunity to become a serious actress. She had conquered Hollywood but still craved the respect that she had imagined would come with stardom.

A social success

Left: Marilyn takes the floor with Truman Capote at El Morocco in 1955 - but seems rather distracted by something across the room. She and Capote had first met in 1950 and they became friends. He wanted Marilyn to play Holly Golightly in *Breakfast at Tiffany's*, but the part finally went to Audrey Hepburn - who was nominated for an Oscar as Best Actress in the role.

Opposite: At the opening night of Tennessee Williams' play, *Cat on a Hot Tin Roof*, Marilyn caught everyone's attention in a skin-tight sheath dress and a white mink. In New York Marilyn had an opportunity to change her life. She had been taken-up by the literary set and was in great social demand. It was only a matter of time before she was to renew her aquaintance with Arthur Miller.

Below: Milton Berle, acting as the ringmaster of the Barnum & Bailey circus, gets an armful of Monroe charms at a rehearsal for her forthcoming appearance in aid of charity.

Pink elephant...

Left: At the opening of the Ringling Brothers Barnum & Bailey Circus at Madison Square Garden in New York at the end of March 1955, Marilyn led the parade mounted on a pink elephant to portray "The Day After New Year's Eve" or a "Pleasant Hangover". The crowd of 18,000, who had paid $50 per ticket, roared with approval when she appeared

Below: The week-long Bement Centennial celebrations included a beard-growing contest - and Marilyn was invited to test the authenticity of some of the entrants' facial hair.

Although she continued to make some celebrity appearances, Marilyn settled to a routine in New York. She attended the Actors Studio regularly, saw her analyst almost daily and visited the Strasbergs at home frequently. She had also begun to see Arthur Miller, taking great care to avoid the attention of the Press.

Dripping with jewels...

Left: Looking every inch the movie star, Marilyn appears at an event for the Jewelers' Association in New York, dressed in a costume made entirely of jewellery.

The Seven Year Itch

The June 1955 première of *The Seven Year Itch* was a gala affair, with stars such as Grace Kelly, Henry Fonda, Eddie Fisher and Richard Rodgers attending. To mark the occasion, a 52-foot high poster of Marilyn, in the famous skirt-lifting pose, was erected above Loew's State Theater in Times Square in New York. The one shown opposite was the second version - the first had to be replaced as there were complaints that it was too revealing. The image turned Marilyn into a vivid cultural icon, which still endures today. Marilyn was accompanied to the première by Joe, sparking rumours of a reconciliation, but she told reporters they were "just good friends". The movie went on to become the biggest hit of that summer, making a fortune for Fox - but Marilyn was still not paid her bonus as agreed.

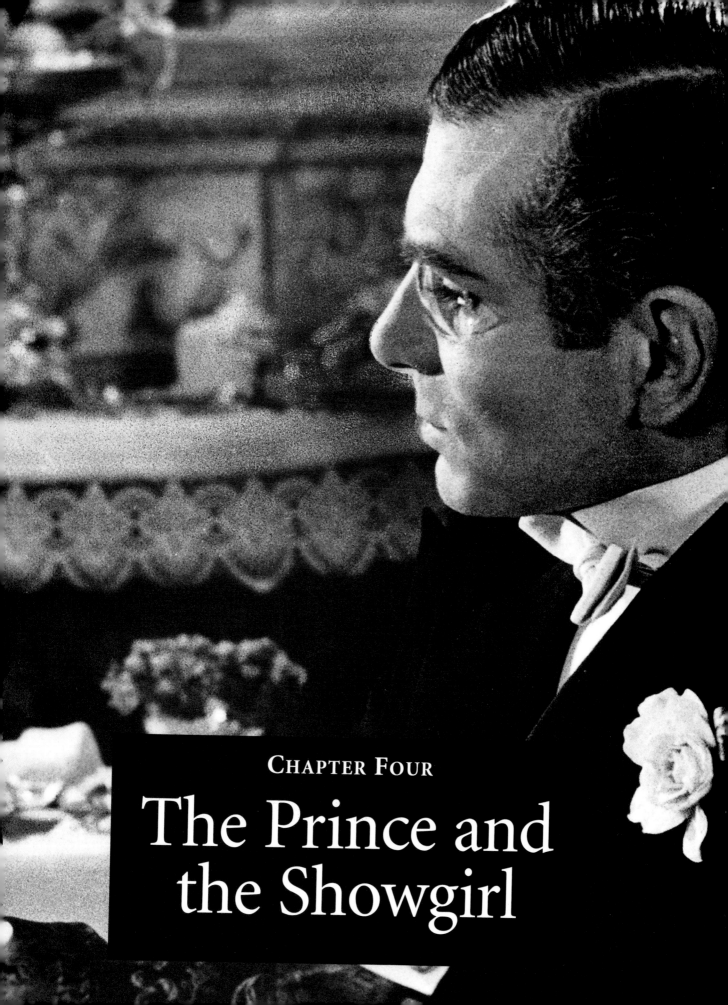

CHAPTER FOUR

The Prince and the Showgirl

At the beginning of 1956, Twentieth Century Fox issued a Press release saying that they and Marilyn had finally come to terms, and that she would soon return to Hollywood. Many people had not really expected her to win and the victory made certain areas of the Press begin to sit up and take notice of the "new" Marilyn - *Time* magazine even called her a "shrewd businesswoman". As if she felt that now she had reached a turning point, soon she legally changed her name to Marilyn Monroe.

Meanwhile, she stayed in New York, continuing her acting classes with Strasberg. Although she had been both studying and attending sessions she was not a member of the Actors Studio, which involved a formal audition and official approval. Once accepted, members were free to perform as little or as much as they liked. However, in February, Marilyn acted at the Studio in front of a proper audience for the first time, after Strasberg convinced her that she was ready. The scene chosen was the introductory one from *Anna Christie*, where Anna appears in a bar on her return home. It had already been made famous by Greta Garbo, since it was the opening scene in the Swedish star's first talking picture, and so became forever linked with the "Garbo talks!" advertisements. Before she went on, Marilyn was almost paralysed with nerves, but once she began she performed perfectly, without forgetting any of her lines. Most people in the audience were astonished at the depth of her interpretation, and at the end they applauded - although it wasn't usual to do so at Studio sessions. Strasberg was delighted and told her she was a great new talent - which

was exactly what she had been working so hard to achieve. Marilyn was euphoric, but as usual - however well she had done - her delight never lasted, and self-doubt would soon gradually and insidiously return.

An important part of the new contract with Fox was that Marilyn would be able to make one independent film a year. She fully intended to take advantage of this concession, and she had already begun talks with playwright Terence Rattigan and Laurence Olivier, with a view to appearing in a film of *The Sleeping Prince*, which Olivier had performed on stage in London with his wife, Vivien Leigh, in 1953. Marilyn wanted to act with Olivier because she felt his reputation as one of the greatest English classical actors would finally make people regard her seriously as a performer. Olivier was keen to do the project because it would give him the opportunity to both co-produce and direct, and he hoped an association with Marilyn would revitalize his career. At a Press conference in New York they announced their plans - but Marilyn upstaged everyone when the narrow strap on her dress broke, threatening to reveal more than was decent. Whether it was by accident or design, it immediately put the old, seductive Marilyn back on centre stage, replacing the new, serious one. Perhaps it was deliberate, since she did not yet have confidence in herself as a serious performer, but she had ample evidence that her sex appeal was a powerful weapon that would bring her what she wanted.

At the end of February, Marilyn returned to Hollywood. There they were to find her very much changed - she had taken on the system and won, she had learned self-possession and she certainly appeared much more self-confident. If she thought the events of the last year would bring her respect in the movie world, however, she soon found she was mistaken. Many saw her actions as evidence that she had tried to turn her back on Hollywood, which had put her where she was, while her interest in serious acting was regarded by her detractors as pretension, and not as a performer beginning to grow.

As soon as she arrived back, Natasha Lytess tried to get in contact. In Marilyn's absence, Natasha had been kept on the payroll at Fox, and she expected to step straight back into her old role. However, Strasberg had sent his wife, Paula, to work with Marilyn instead, so Fox abruptly terminated Natasha's employment. Distraught and angry, she immediately tried to contact her former pupil, but she found that her notes were not answered and phone calls were not taken. Finally, in desperation, Natasha turned up at Marilyn's home. She was turned away at the door, but thought she saw Marilyn at the window above. Soon afterwards, she poured out her heart to the Press, claiming that she had "created" Marilyn, and that she deserved better treatment. Natasha's presence had often caused dissension on set, and on later films others suspected that - rather than helping - she had fed Marilyn's insecurity by demanding retakes when they were not necessary. She had earned a good living for many years as Marilyn's personal coach, not to mention the many times that her pupil had helped her out financially. Marilyn may have needed Natasha, but the reverse was also true. When it came down to it, Marilyn becoming self-confident enough to be able to function without her was not really in Natasha's interest. Unfortunately for her, Marilyn believed that she had been let down, and she had no hesitation in dropping her former coach, now that she had an acceptable alternative.

Marilyn had returned to start work on *Bus Stop*, the film of a Broadway hit. The plot was simple - innocent cowboy comes to town and falls in love with bar room singer, regarding her as an "angel"and refusing to accept her tainted past. Singer does not take him seriously, but is finally won over by his adoration and honest, straightforward character - cue happy ending. This was the first film that Marilyn was to undertake at Fox after achieving her newly won power, and studio bosses were worried about what impossible demands she might make. When she first saw the elaborate costumes that had been designed for her role, she dismissed them as totally unsuitable, and everyone immediately feared the worst. To their surprise, Marilyn suggested that they should look round the costume department, and she picked out a series of shabby, second-hand outfits that she felt were more appropriate for a down-at-heel bar room girl. Director Joshua Logan was delighted - he had been reluctant to take the project initially, as he had believed that Marilyn couldn't act. He was convinced otherwise by speaking to Strasberg, who had given her a glowing testimony, and now here was evidence that Marilyn really was taking her role seriously. Alone of all her directors, he planned alternative shooting schedules to allow for the occasions when Marilyn was late, which cut down tension on the set considerably.

However, this amicable relationship with her director was not mirrored with Marilyn's co-stars, Don Murray and Hope Lange. Marilyn was annoyed that Murray was impervious to her charms, seeming more interested in Lange - whom he later married. As for Lange, Marilyn insisted that her blonde hair be dyed darker, so as not to compete with her own bright tresses; one of the downsides of Marilyn's new-found power was that her ever-present insecurity could be allowed free rein.

Despite this, Marilyn worked hard, first on location in the desert near Phoenix, Arizona, and then in the mountains at Sun Valley, Idaho. The difference in temperature, coupled with the light clothes she wore in character, brought her down with such a severe case of bronchitis that she had to be hospitalized. Marilyn suffered from recurring bronchial problems, and this was not the first time that she had been so ill that she needed medical attention. She was kept in hospital for four days before she was allowed back to work.

Previous page: A rather sleepy-looking Marilyn arrives at New York's Idlewild Airport early on the morning of 2 June, 1956 - the day after her 30th birthday - after flying in from Los Angeles.

Opposite: Reporters waited outside Marilyn's New York apartment to catch a picture of her after Arthur Miller announced that they were to marry, during his testimony to the House UnAmerican Activities Committee in Washington. She had been keeping out of sight until that moment, having been warned by everyone - including Miller himself - to keep out of his passport problems.

On her return, she faced one of the most important scenes of the movie - Cherie's monologue about her life. Marilyn was renowned for being unable to remember lines, and this was a long speech. Logan knew she would not be able to do it in one take, which raised a second problem - the time she needed to psych herself up to perform. He resolved both problems by keeping the camera running, take after take, without ever calling "Cut!". As he had hoped, Marilyn just kept going, and he was able to piece together all the best bits to create a stunning and moving scene. Marilyn was delighted - Miller had convinced her that she would not be able to consider herself a real performer until she could handle complicated dialogue, and she had finally succeeded.

While filming was in progress, Arthur Miller had been staying in Reno, Nevada, establishing residency so he could obtain a divorce. While they were apart Marilyn kept in touch with long phone calls, but the day after his divorce was finalized they met up in New York. Miller had another problem. He had applied for a passport to go to England, partly to accompany Marilyn when she went to film *The Sleeping Prince*, and also because his play, *A View from the Bridge*, was about to be staged there. However, he had been briefly associated with the Communist Party many years before, and had already been turned down for a passport on a previous occasion - and it was now the height of the McCarthy witch-hunts against Communism. He was called to appear before the House UnAmerican Activities Committee to testify, and he co-operated fully - except that he refused to name names. Despite this, he was at first not held in contempt, as many others taking a similar stance had

Opposite: According to studio publicity, Marilyn's vital statistics were 38-23-36 and she was 5'5" tall. She was certainly more voluptuous than many of today's female stars, but curves were much more fashionable in the fifties.

Above: Arthur Miller and Marilyn pose for photographers with Laurence Olivier shortly after their arrival in England.

been - to some extent because everyone was distracted by his announcement that he intended to marry Marilyn.

As the news of the impending nuptials spread, the Press went crazy. Newsmen and photographers camped outside their door, and followed them everywhere they went, even after they left New York for the Miller family home at Roxbury, Connecticut. Marilyn was used to such attention, but Miller was not. He was also not the kind of writer who could work in any surroundings, and in these conditions he found it impossible to produce the rewrites he was under a deadline to complete. Finally they married in secret, in a judge's chambers just over the state line in

White Plains, New York, followed by a Jewish ceremony, also in secret, in New York. After the event was officially announced, Miller hoped that everyone could go back to normal life. Little did he know that his life with Marilyn would never be normal.

Two weeks later, after Miller finally obtained his passport he and Marilyn arrived in England. *The Sleeping Prince* was to be filmed as *The Prince and the Showgirl,* but the project was not a good experience for most of those concerned. The first problem had come up before they even left America - Strasberg demanded that his wife, Paula, be paid a guaranteed salary of $25,000 for ten weeks' work plus expenses - far more than anyone else on the film except Olivier and Marilyn herself. When Milton Greene, Marilyn's business partner, understandably objected to this, Strasberg simply pointed out how fragile Marilyn was, and said that he would accept a percentage of the movie's profits instead. Apart from using her to improve his financial situation, many believe that Strasberg also manipulated her for his own ends. Marilyn was his most high-profile pupil, and he was seemingly determined that he alone would get the credit for her achievements. Far from really supporting her on *The Prince and the Showgirl*, he constantly criticized Olivier - who regarded Method acting with contempt - in long telephone calls from New York, while Olivier's direction of Marilyn was undermined ·by Paula Strasberg on set. However, Strasberg was careful not to get involved personally in the film - so if Marilyn succeeded he could take the credit, while if she failed he could blame Olivier.

As for Olivier himself, apart from his problems with Paula Strasberg he was exasperated by Marilyn's lateness and difficulty in remembering lines, and was frustrated by his inability to get through to her. Marilyn had been excited about working with such a famous and respected actor, but now she was afraid he would ruin her performance. She thought he was condescending much of the time - particularly after he told her before one scene to "be sexy". For her, the film had never been about "being sexy" - it was about being accepted as a serious performer. In this she had misjudged the material, because in fact the role called for exactly the kind of beautiful, uncomplicated and seductive blonde that she had played so well so many times in the past.

On top of· all this, Marilyn and Miller's marriage was already in some trouble - it was the first time the two of them had spent extended time together, and the first time Miller had had to deal at first-hand with her work anxieties, sleeplessness and insecurity. Marilyn the person had turned out to be quite different from Marilyn the fantasy. Miller was in the habit of jotting down stray thoughts for use in later work, and apparently Marilyn read

some of them, which had led her to doubt that Miller really did love her. From that moment on, she never felt quite so safe and secure in Miller's love as she had done before. There was further unhappiness in their marriage when towards the end of August, Marilyn became pregnant with a much-wanted child, but miscarried the baby within a few weeks.

Marilyn had also come to distrust her business partner, Milton Greene. Greene and Miller had always disliked and distrusted one another, each resenting the influence the other had on Marilyn. Greene was not happy that Miller intended to be actively involved in Marilyn Monroe Productions. In turn, Miller had no faith in Greene's abilities, and he tried to convince Marilyn that she didn't need him. As for Marilyn herself, she came to suspect that Greene was working against her, not supporting her in arguments with others on set and going along with cuts of her scenes. All in all, it was a miracle that *The Prince and the Showgirl* came in under budget and more or less on time.

Below: Marilyn and Arthur attend the opening night of *A View from the Bridge* in London.

The Prince and the Showgirl...

At a Press conference at the Plaza Hotel in New York in February 1956, Marilyn and Laurence Olivier announced their intention to make a film version of Terence Rattigan's *The Sleeping Prince*. They planned to film in England, where Olivier had had a hit on the London stage with the original play, in which he had starred with his wife, Vivien Leigh. Marilyn had agreed to pay $125,000 for the movie rights and an additional sum for Rattigan to write the screenplay.

The proposed movie about Jean Harlow's life story had fallen through and so this was to be the first project undertaken by Marilyn Monroe Productions.

Above: Marilyn leans forward to speak to eager reporters, telling them, "I'd like to continue my growth in every way possible."

Opposite: Although she looked quite demure in her outfit, complete with coat, scarf and gloves, during the course of the interview the spaghetti strap of Marilyn's dress broke, instantly drawing everyone's attention. Olivier was convinced it had been done on purpose, but it certainly guaranteed that they were both front-page news the following day.

Right: At the end of February 1956, Marilyn poses for photographers as she boards a plane in New York to return to Hollywood. She had been away from the film capital of America for over a year, as negotiations were carried out to resolve her contract dispute with Fox. Most people had felt she would not win her battle with the studio, but now she was returning in triumph having obtained several concessions that were unique at the time - including a percentage of the profits, and approval of script, director and cinematographer.

Previous page: Marilyn and Susan Strasberg, daughter of Marilyn's mentor Lee Strasberg, seem mesmerized by Laurence Olivier. The three were backstage at the Cort Theater in New York, where Susan was appearing in *The Diary of Anne Frank*.

Left: Despite what reporters might have said, there was no denying that Marilyn looked both seriously smart and glamorous in her new wardrobe of tailored suits and matching gloves.

Above: Both Marilyn and Jack Warner look delighted as it is announced that she is to co-star with Laurence Olivier in the movie of *The Sleeping Prince* for Warner Brothers.

Fined!

Left: Marilyn appears in court in Beverly Hills, charged with driving without a licence. The offence had taken place back in 1954 when she was first becoming famous, but the judge was not impressed and lectured her severely before imposing a $56 fine.

Opposite: In court, awaiting her turn before the bench, with attorney, Irving L. Stein.

Below: Milton Greene, vice-president of Marilyn's independent production company, faces the Press with her just after she returned to Hollywood following her long exile in New York. Marilyn Monroe Productions and Fox had recently come to terms, so Marilyn had returned in triumph.

Top of the world!

Above: Marilyn chats to James Cagney at a cocktail party given by *Look* magazine in Beverly Hills in March 1956. The Hollywood Press was full of stories about her return to the fold and news of her latest project.

Opposite: The first movie she was scheduled to make for Fox was *Bus Stop*, which was based on a Broadway hit written by William Inge. When the play was adapted for the screen, writer George Axelrod bore Marilyn in mind and added details from her own life. Joshua Logan, who was on the list of 16 directors approved by Marilyn, was well-versed in Stanislavsky and The Method and had a reputation as a talented director of sensitive actors.

Bus Stop

Marilyn plays Cherie, a down-at-heel bar room singer, with Don Murray as Bo Decker, her devoted admirer. While singing "That Old Black Magic" badly in a bar, Cherie is spotted by innocent cowboy Bo, who is in town for a rodeo. He decides to marry her, despite her dubious past, and carry her off to his isolated farm in Montana. At first Cherie will not agree, but eventually she warms to his honest intentions and enthusiasm. On set Don Murray did not always find it easy to work with Marilyn. While shooting the scene where Cherie tries to leave Bo, one of Marilyn's improvised gestures cut Murray's eyelid but Marilyn failed to apologize.

Marilyn vetoed the elaborate costumes originally designed for the part, and picked out some tattered clothes from the studio wardrobe instead, which she felt would be more in keeping with her character. Much of the look of the film was designed by Milton Greene, who had a wonderful visual eye for what would work on camera.

Above: Hope Lange, making her debut, appeared with Marilyn in *Bus Stop* as a young girl who Cherie meets on the bus. Marilyn insisted that her co-star's hair was tinted a darker shade, so it would not compete with her own blonde looks. Much of Marilyn's dramatic monologue on the bus, in which she told the story of Cherie's life, was cut when the studio insisted the movie was too long - and Marilyn always believed that this had cost her the chance of an Oscar.

Although Logan was patient and tried to accommodate Marilyn's needs, he had a tough time keeping the production on schedule. As before, she found it difficult to remember her lines and spent hours in her dressing room before being able to face the camera. Paula Strasberg had replaced Natasha Lytess as Marilyn's acting coach but although Logan liked her on a personal level, he was not about to have his authority on set undermined and at first confined her to Marilyn's dressing room.

Opposite: Marilyn with Arthur O'Connell, who played Virgil Blassing, the young cowboy's older and wiser guardian.

Mr President...

Opposite: At a party thrown by Joshua Logan, director of *Bus Stop*, Marilyn was introduced to Indonesian President Sukarno. He had particularly asked to meet her because he was interested in Hollywood and her movies were very popular in his country. The party also marked Marilyn's 30th birthday.

Above: At a Press conference, the journalists may all have their heads down but Marilyn - as usual - knows exactly where the camera is.

Right: A kiss for the photographer. Marilyn was far better with stills photographers than she was on a film set - she didn't feel the same pressure to perform, but was still able to conjure up her star persona for the camera. By the time work on *Bus Stop* had finished at the end of May 1956 she was physically and emotionally exhausted. Marilyn had felt the need to show her year with Strasberg had made a difference to her performance and, in addition to this, filming in the desert of Arizona and the cold in Sun Valley had put a strain on her health.

Happy birthday...

Arriving on 2 June at Idlewild Airport in New York on a flight from the west coast, Marilyn is presented with a birthday cake in her limousine. She had celebrated her 30th birthday the previous day in Hollywood. Reporters wanted to know about her romance with playwright Arthur Miller, but she just smiled mysteriously and blew them a kiss.

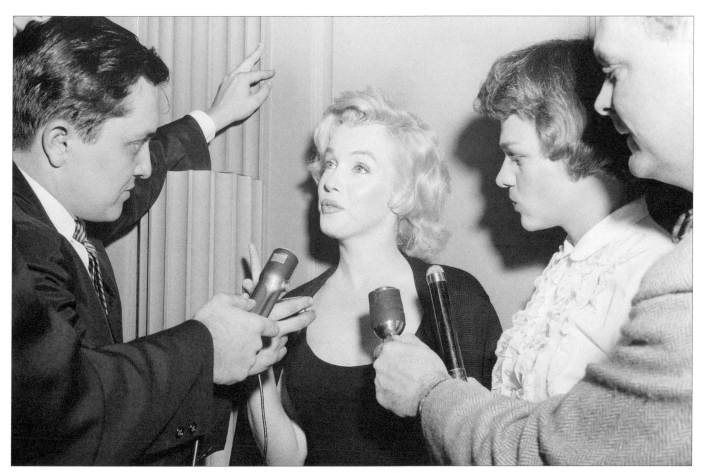

Mrs Arthur Miller

While Marilyn had been filming *Bus Stop*, Miller had spent some six weeks in Nevada in order to obtain his divorce. He had been called to appear before the House UnAmerican Activities Committee to answer questions about his past association with the Communist Party and had revealed to the Committee that he wanted a passport so he could go to England to "be there with the woman who will then be my wife". Washington reporters descended upon him and he told them that he expected to marry Marilyn within "a day or two", adding that whether or not he got his passport, Marilyn would be going to London as Mrs Arthur Miller.

Reporters then rushed to the apartment on Sutton Place, where Marilyn had been keeping out of sight, to ask for her side of the story. Until then she had refused to be interviewed, afraid of saying the wrong thing and damaging Miller's chances, but now she called an impromptu Press conference and told reporters how happy she was to be getting married.

Two lovebirds...

On 22 June, 1956 Marilyn and Arthur Miller appeared before the Press together in front of the Sutton Place apartment, where they were staying in New York, to talk about their forthcoming wedding. They told reporters they planned a simple ceremony, they had not yet set the date, but that it would be "sometime in July". At one point Marilyn hugged Miller so hard that he had to tell her to stop, "or I'll fall over". Following comments by Francis Walter, chairman of the HUAC, reporters asked Miller if he would enjoy his honeymoon in America if he did not get his passport, but Miller pointed out that it would be difficult to do so, as Marilyn was already committed to going to England.

In the country...

It soon became apparent that reporters would give them no peace, so the happy couple left for Miller's home in Roxbury, Connecticut. Unfortunately the Press soon followed them there. To try to keep them at bay, a photocall was arranged and Miller and Marilyn appeared, casually dressed. They told reporters that there would be no wedding for several days, and Miller appealed to them to go away for a short while and allow Marilyn to get some rest. He promised an announcement the following Friday.

Waiting for news

Opposite: Miller and Marilyn with Miller's basset hound, Hugo. Since they were followed everywhere by newsmen, Miller's cousin, Morty, had carried out some of the wedding preparations on their behalf, including arranging for their blood samples to be tested - which had to be done before they could apply for a licence. Details were still secret, but the wedding was planned for 1 July, at the home of Miller's agent, Kay Brown, just over the state border in South Salem, New York and the ceremony was to be performed by Rabbi Robert Goldberg.

Left: While reporters waited for news of the wedding, Miller was waiting for news from the HUAC. Finally, instead of citing Miller for contempt, they gave him until 7 July - six days before Marilyn was scheduled to leave for England - to change his mind and reveal the names of his friends who had attended a Communist-sponsored meeting of authors in the late forties.

A bad omen

Opposite top: Marilyn rushes past reporters, ashen-faced and shaking, after witnessing a terrible car accident nearby. Journalist Mara Scherbatoff had been following them in a car driven by the young brother of her photographer, who had lost control and crashed into a tree. The boy had some injuries, but Scherbatoff was seriously hurt and she later died in hospital. Miller had had enough of the media circus, and he brought the wedding forward to that evening, arranging for the ceremony to be held at the Westchester County Court House in White Plains, New York, with Judge Seymour Robinowitz officiating.

Above and opposite below: The day after the civil ceremony, the newlyweds looked happy and carefree as they left for a romantic picnic together - although Marilyn privately believed that the death on the very day of her wedding was a bad omen.

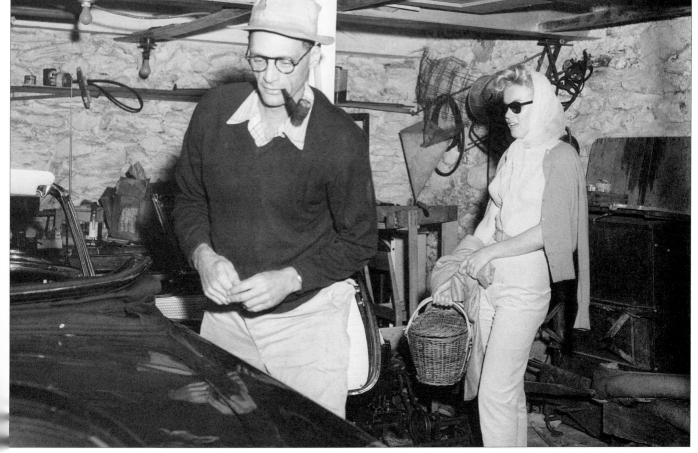

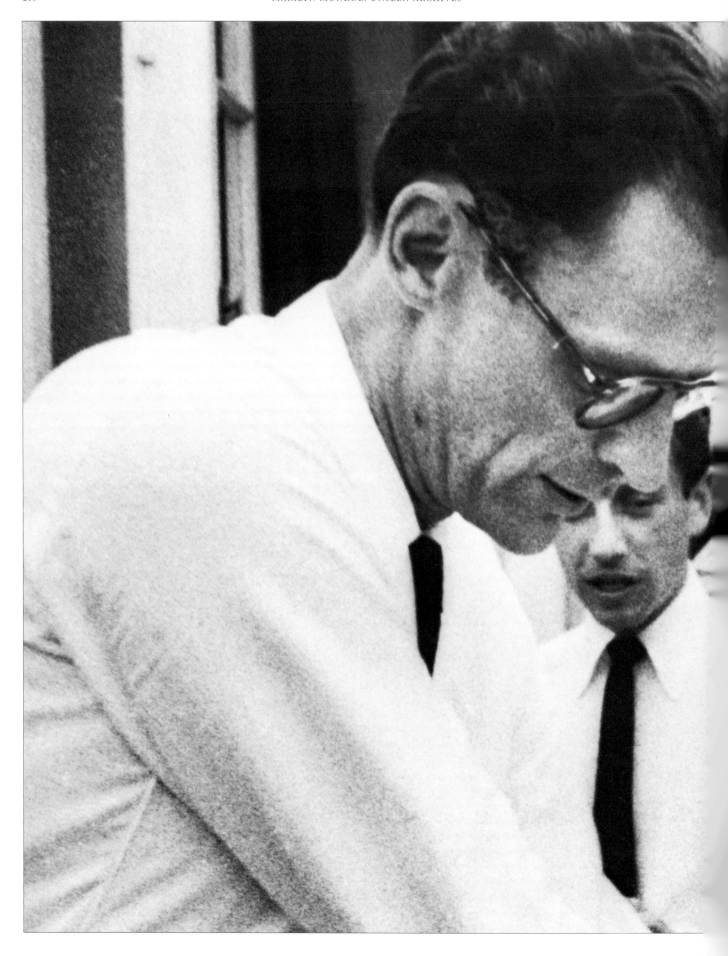

Egghead weds Hourglass

The religious ceremony was held, as planned, in the garden of Kay Brown's farmhouse. The civil ceremony had thrown reporters off guard, so the occasion was only for family and friends. The bride wore a sheath of champagne satin and chiffon, with a scoop neck, and was given away by Lee Strasberg, who she now regarded as a substitute father figure.

London bound

Luckily Miller was granted a passport, and only twelve days after their wedding he and Marilyn were off to London on their honeymoon. Newsmen commented that Marilyn seemed to be a changed woman - for once she was on time for the flight, and she demurely refused to kiss her new husband for the cameras until he patted her on the hand and gave his permission.

Opposite: The long flight from America had left Marilyn looking rather dishevelled, but she and Arthur Miller posed happily for London photographers. A Press conference had been arranged at one of the airport hotels, and Marilyn smiled radiantly, proud to be standing with her new husband, and to be embarking on her first film with her own production company.

Above: Both Laurence Olivier and his wife, Vivien Leigh, had come to the airport to meet the Millers. News had broken in the papers only a couple of days previously that Vivien was pregnant, at the age of forty-two.

Left: Although the trip to England had been organized around Marilyn's filming schedule, it was also the first time the couple had been away together since their marriage and they planned to enjoy some romantic time together.

Next door to the Queen...

A limousine took the Millers to Surrey, along with Milton Greene, while the Oliviers followed in a second car. A grand Georgian mansion, Parkside House, had been rented for Marilyn and Arthur Miller to stay in. It was situated right next to Windsor Great Park - with a private gate into the park itself. A long drive ensured some privacy, but Marilyn insisted that a group of photographers were allowed up to the house immediately, and that they should all pose for a few more pictures - even though a proper Press conference had been scheduled for the following day. Although Vivien Leigh smiled bravely, she was clearly somewhat unhappy at being asked to pose next to a woman twelve years her junior, who was renowned for her attractiveness to men, particularly as the Oliviers' marriage had been going through a rocky patch of late.

Another day, another Press conference

Opposite: Marilyn was delighted that Miller was apparently willing to support her publicly as she geared herself up to begin work. Unfortunately he had never seen this side of her, and it wasn't long before he began to wonder just what he had taken on.

Above and left: Despite a promise to Olivier, Marilyn arrived over an hour late for a Press conference that had been arranged in the Lancaster Room of the Savoy Hotel in London. Olivier had entertained journalists alone while they all waited, and he was not in the best of moods. However, as usual, Marilyn charmed everyone into forgiving her. Previously Olivier had said that he had planned to fall "most shatteringly in love" with Marilyn, but now she was married to Arthur Miller, and he and Vivien were expecting a child together - which might signal a new start in their troubled marriage. He therefore was far more reserved with Marilyn than he had been in New York, which she found very unsettling.

Above: After three Press conferences in three days, Marilyn still managed to look fresh and happy. Photographers were rather disappointed that she was rather conservatively dressed - they had expected someone a bit more like her screen persona. Despite this they enthusiastically snapped her picture, while newsmen screamed questions.

Opposite: To ensure filming went smoothly, Olivier intended to work on a closed set - meaning no Press or outside visitors would be allowed in during shooting - so photographers made the most of every opportunity to take pictures of Marilyn, even catching her with cigarette in hand.

In London...

Above: Interest in Marilyn was at fever pitch in London, and crowds turned out to see her whenever she appeared in public. Despite the fact that this was often very intrusive, she was always aware that she owed her fans a great deal.

Left: For once, Marilyn is not the centre of attention. If she chose not to turn on her Marilyn persona, she could often pass unnoticed in a crowd. Despite this, when she and Arthur Miller went to the theatre - which they did quite often in London - the number of people who turned out to see them was so great that the police had to be called to clear a path for them to enter and leave the building. Marilyn was used to this kind of public furore, but Miller found it very hard to adapt to it.

Opposite: Olivier and Marilyn share a quiet word at yet another Press conference. They apparently got on famously at these affairs, complimenting each other and appearing to enjoy working together, but unfortunately this happy atmosphere was not destined to last long once filming began.

Following pages: Although they were seemingly enjoying a carefree time in London, both Marilyn and her husband were aware that Congress was about to vote on whether to cite Miller for contempt. Although he had his passport, his problems with the HUAC had not gone away by any means.

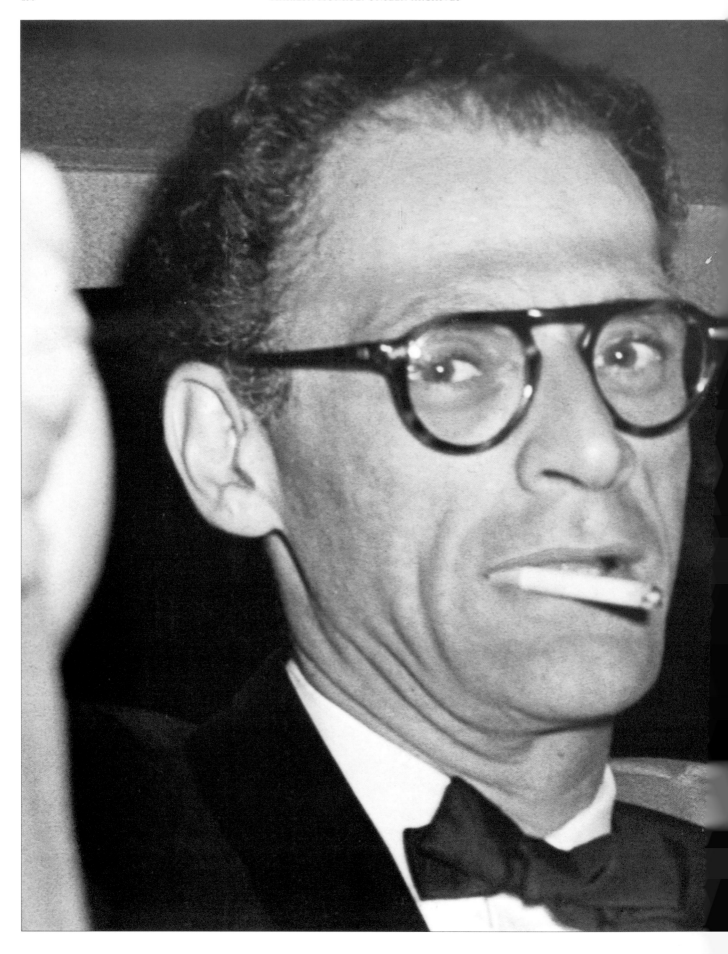

The Prince and the Showgirl

Right: Olivier was not only starring as the Grand Duke who falls in love with a showgirl, he was also directing the film. The working title was still that of the play - *The Sleeping Prince* - but the film was finally released as *The Prince and the Showgirl*, perhaps to reflect Marilyn's equal billing.

Marilyn quickly gained the support of one of her co-stars - Dame Sybil Thorndike, a legendary actress on the London stage. After less than a week on set, she said to Laurence Olivier, who was an old friend of hers, "You did well in that scene, Larry, but with Marilyn up there, nobody will be watching you. Her manner and timing are just too delicious. And don't be too hard about her tardiness, dear boy. We need her desperately. She's really the only one of us who knows how to act in front of a camera!"

Her remarks did not go down well with Olivier, who was convinced that he was a master of his craft.

Tension on set

Right: Problems on the set of *The Prince and the Showgirl* began almost at once. Olivier did not believe in Method acting, and Marilyn came to mistrust him, particularly after he instructed her to "be sexy" for one scene. Although he was not present in person, Marilyn's mentor, Lee Strasberg, had sent his wife Paula as Marilyn's drama coach and she took every opportunity to undermine Olivier's direction.

Opposite: Marilyn was unwell during most of filming: fearful of failure in front of the camera, she was using alcohol and prescription drugs to help her cope with her anxieties. However, even when she arrived on set looking dishevelled after a sleepless night, the combination of Marilyn's ability to sparkle for the camera and the skill of cinematographer Jack Cardiff, who had worked on *The Red Shoes* and *Black Narcissus*, managed to produce a stunning image.

Below: Lee Strasberg, who offered advice and criticism at a distance during filming.

Above: Arthur Miller was not solely in England to accompany Marilyn - he was also there to work. His play, *A View from the Bridge*, was being performed on the London stage. Here he and actress Mary Ure discuss her role.

Left: Marilyn attended the opening night of the play, supporting her husband in his work as he had supported her. They both knew that her presence would guarantee that the Press would also turn out in force.

Opposite: In *The Prince and the Showgirl* Marilyn played Elsie Marina, an American showgirl, who catches the eye of the Prince Regent of Carpathia, who is in London for the coronation of King George V.

At the Comedy...

The opening night of *A View from the Bridge* was held at the Comedy Theatre, but it was performed before the members of a newly-created private theatre club - the New Watergate Theatre Club. The Lord Chamberlain had objected to a scene in which one man kissed another on the lips, and had refused to grant the necessary permit for public performance. Both Marilyn and her husband had to become members of the club before they were allowed inside to see the play - even though he was the author. Marilyn had recently been ill, but she was still determined to appear.

Above: Both the Millers obviously enjoyed the performance. The story was of particular personal significance to Miller at the time, as it involves a man's decision to betray his friends, which leads to his destruction.

Opposite: Marilyn signs her application form for membership.

Out on the town...

Above: Vivien Leigh was appearing in *South Sea Bubble*, and Marilyn and Miller went to the Lyric Theatre to see a performance. After the show they walked hand-in-hand through an excited crowd.

Opposite: Towards the end of August 1956, Miller decided to fly back to America for a few days to see his children. The trip was intended to be a secret - the name on his ticket was Mr Stevenson - as there was always a possibility that his return to America would precipitate more problems with the HUAC.

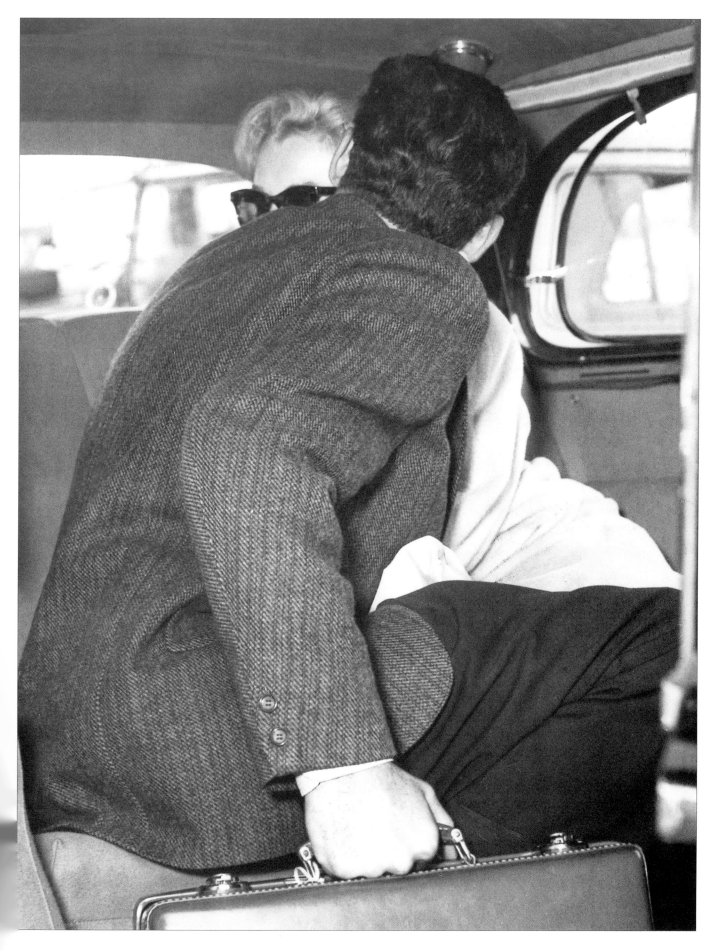

Bad news...

Above: While Miller was away, Marilyn was left alone at Parkside House. Marilyn viewed his departure as another small betrayal, particularly since filming *The Prince and the Showgirl* was not progressing as she had anticipated and the atmosphere on the set was strained. Her intake of barbiturates had increased alarmingly, and she was often not fit to work for days at a time. During this period she discovered she was pregnant, but within a few weeks she had miscarried the baby.

Opposite: The Millers leave the Palace Theatre by the stage door, after seeing Brecht's *Caucasian Chalk Circle* performed in German. This was Marilyn's first night out after recovering from her miscarriage, but it was also the couple's celebration of Miller's return from America. They arrived late and a surprised management ushered them into seats in the stalls.

Opening night...

Opposite: Marilyn and Arthur arrive at the black tie première of *A View from the Bridge*. Marilyn wore a scarlet satin gown so tight around the knees that walking was an achievement. As a result of her attendance the publicity for the play was tremendous, and promoter Binkie Beaumont had signed up over 13,000 members to his hastily formed theatre club - pocketing the small membership fee.

Marilyn felt that she had lost some part of Miller's love, and she was now working hard to win it back. She had miscarried their baby and she had read somes notes he had jotted down which, she felt, showed he regretted having married her. He found her needs hard to cope with, and her constant demands were interfering with his work as a writer and so he had withdrawn somewhat. There were misunderstandings on both sides - he did not appreciate how much she dreaded being abandoned, and she did not understand that a writer may draw on real life, but is not necessarily expressing how he personally feels in his characters' views.

Above: Marilyn arrives at a dressmaker to find an outfit in which to be presented to Queen Elizabeth II at the Royal Command Performance of *The Battle of the River Plate* in London, in October 1956. She went in looking pale and timid, but emerged poised, confident and glittering in a gold dress.

Vivien Leigh, Laurence
Olivier, Marilyn and
Miller take their seats for
the performance. Many
members of the audience
were more interested in
studying Marilyn than
watching the play, but it
proved to be a success
and was well reviewed.

Goodbye London

Opposite: Backstage, Marilyn meets some of the cast of *A View from the Bridge*. At the end of the play she accompanied Miller onto the stage and they took a bow hand in hand.

Above: Goodbye London... Marilyn and her husband were both relieved when filming was over and they were able to return to America. The strain of working had brought out a different side of Marilyn, one that Miller had never had to cope with before. As for Marilyn, she had come to doubt that Miller really loved her. In addition to this, in September Marilyn had been pregnant, but had lost her much-wanted baby within a few weeks.

Kisses

On 20 November, 1956 the
Oliviers saw the Millers off at
London Airport. It was kisses all
round as everyone agreed that
they had to put on a good face in
public for the sake of the film. It
was not only the Millers who
were going home disillusioned -
Olivier was disappointed that he
had apparently missed an
opportunity to revive his
flagging career, while Vivien had
also lost her baby - and as it
turned out, her last chance to
save the marriage. She and
Marilyn had totally failed to
develop any kind of rapport, and
during the time in England they
had only met on formal
occasions.

After his experience on this film,
Olivier considered Marilyn a
"thoroughly ill-mannered and
rude girl", but years later he said,
"Maybe I was tetchy with
Marilyn and with myself,
because I felt my career was in a
rut... I was as good as could be,
and, Marilyn! Marilyn was quite
wonderful, the best of all."

Marilyn visits the Actors
Studio on her return to New
York, telling reporters that
she still longed to do
dramatic roles.

Opposite: Proceeds from
the premiere of Elia Kazan's
Baby Doll, starring Carroll
Baker, were pledged to the
Actors Studio, since many of
its stars were members and
Kazan was the director.
Marilyn was roped in as a
celebrity usherette.

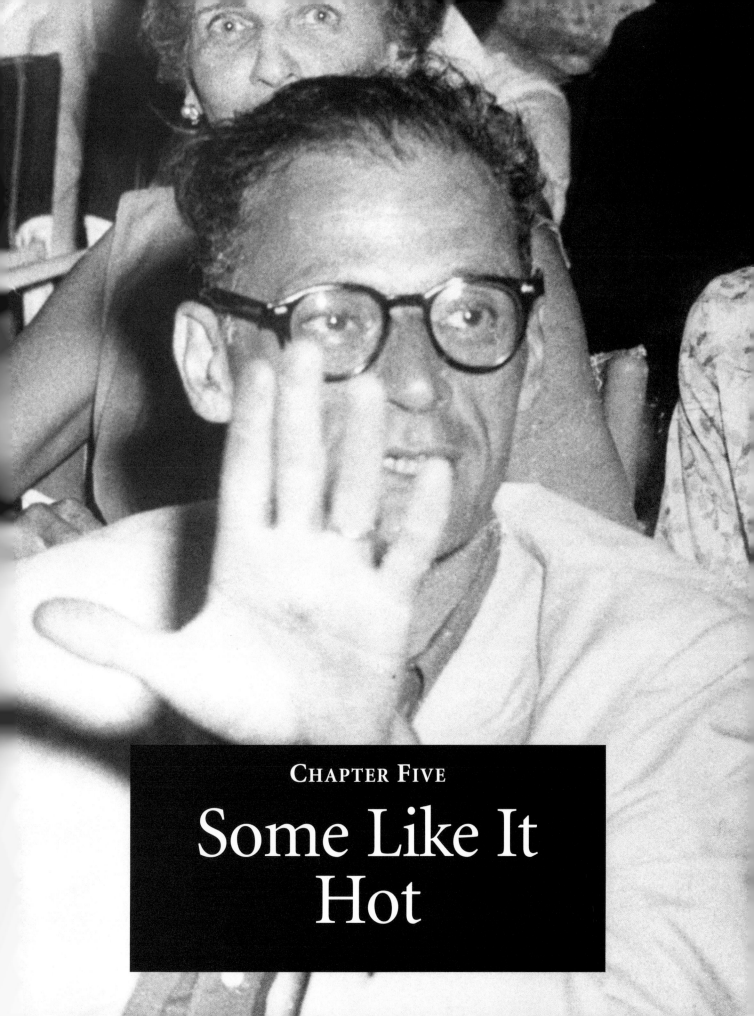

Some Like It Hot

While Marilyn had been away in England, *Bus Stop* had been released. She had seen a rough cut of the film in London, and had been devastated because part of her performance had been cut, and much of the dramatic monologue that she was so proud of had ended up on the cutting-room floor. She had wanted Miller and Strasberg to see her achievement, and now they never would. She also felt that the cuts had ruined her chances of an Oscar nomination - and what was all the more galling was that Don Murray was nominated as Best Supporting Actor, and as Most Promising Newcomer for the British Academy Awards. She turned on director Joshua Logan, berating him for spoiling her performance, but in fact he had fought to keep much of the material and been overruled by studio bosses, who felt the movie was too long. Despite this, the reviews were glowing, with almost every newspaper critic commenting that Marilyn had proved that she really could act.

Back in New York at the beginning of 1957, the rough cut of *The Prince and the Showgirl* did not initially look quite as good, and when it was first released later in the year the reviews were mixed. However, it picked up five nominations for the British Academy Awards, including Best Foreign Actress for Marilyn. In the event, she did not win, but in 1959 it did bring her Italy's most prestigious acting award - the David Di Donatello statuette for Best Actress in a Foreign Film. Many critics now regard it as one of her finest performances, and she easily steals the film from Olivier. However, at the time Marilyn felt that

Milton Greene had let her down with their first independent production, and Miller fuelled this view, finally convincing her that she no longer needed Greene. As a result, Greene was fired from Marilyn Monroe Productions and a new board of directors was appointed. He may have made mistakes, but it was a poor return for a man who had practically given up his own career to help Marilyn, who had supported her financially when she was on suspension throughout the greater part of 1955, and who had helped her achieve her revised contract with Fox. Much later, Marilyn confessed to Greene's wife, Amy, that Milton was the only man she had ever trusted, but that Miller had driven him away and she had felt unable to resist. The truth was that at the time, Marilyn was more concerned with making a success of her shaky marriage.

After all the draining experiences in England, she now wanted to take some time off. Her contract with Fox called for her to make four films for them within seven years, of which she had so far completed one. There were plans for her to appear in a remake of *The Blue Angel*, with Spencer Tracy as co-star, but despite prolonged negotiations on both sides the idea was eventually shelved. Until Fox came up with an acceptable project, she could choose whether to work or not. She decided that what she really wanted to do was to try and be a good wife: to create a proper home for Miller, where he could work in peace, and to have a baby. For the moment she put her own work on hold and concentrated on furnishing their new apartment in New York, complete with a writing room for Miller, while she also began treatment at Doctors Hospital to enable her to carry a baby to term.

Meanwhile, events from the past were coming back to haunt both Miller and Marilyn's ex-husband, Joe DiMaggio. First of all, in February 1957 Miller was finally indicted by a federal grand jury on two counts of contempt of Congress, as a result of his failure to name names at his House UnAmerican Activities Committee hearing in 1956. If he was proved guilty, each count could mean a huge fine and up to a year in prison. His lawyers were confident that he would win, because the questions he had refused to answer were actually nothing to do with what the HUAC was supposed to be investigating, namely the abuse of passports. Despite this, Miller was too stressed to concentrate on his work, partly because of the legal proceedings hanging over him, and also because his defence would run up huge legal fees.

As for DiMaggio, an event that had happened in 1954, just after his divorce from Marilyn had been granted, now suddenly and unexpectedly hit the news. After they separated, DiMaggio had hired a private detective to follow Marilyn, and had come to the conclusion that she was having an affair with her voice coach, Hal Schaefer. In early November, DiMaggio and Frank Sinatra were having a drink together when news came that Marilyn's car had been seen parked outside an apartment building. DiMaggio and Sinatra joined the detective and his associate outside, and the four of them broke into one of the apartments, expecting to catch Marilyn *in flagrante delecto*. However, they had the wrong apartment - they had broken down the door of Florence Kee. The noise had alerted the rest of the building, so Marilyn, who was apparently having dinner with Schaefer and another woman next door, escaped without being seen. At the time, Sinatra managed to keep his and DiMaggio's name out of the newspapers, but many months later the full story of the event which had become known as the "Wrong Door" raid was published in *Confidential* magazine. Kee promptly sued her famous intruders, but the case dragged on for years, so Sinatra was not called to testify until early 1957. The newspapers had a field day, but eventually DiMaggio settled out of court.

Unfortunately, Miller's legal problems were not to be settled so easily. Marilyn came with him to Washington, although by now she was again pregnant. Reporters swarmed over the Federal District Court to see her, but she was keeping out of sight and Miller explained that he thought that everyone should stay focused on the issue at hand. After that, journalists tried to contact Marilyn at the house where the Millers were staying. Finally she appeared to speak to them, clearly stating her support for her husband. At the end of a six-day hearing, the defendant was found guilty on both counts, though soon afterwards the judge revised his verdict to a conviction on only one charge, for which Miller was fined $500 and received a suspended sentence of one month. His lawyers instantly appealed, and in a much more hopeful mood he and Marilyn left to spend the summer on Long Island.

Their happiness was short-lived - just over two months later Marilyn collapsed in terrible pain and was rushed by ambulance to Doctors Hospital in New York. Her much-wanted pregnancy had turned out to be ectopic, and had to be terminated to save her life. Although she was devastated, she managed to put on a good face for reporters as she left the hospital ten days later. However, apart from the natural sadness of losing her baby, she also felt a failure as a wife because she was not able to give Miller a child, and she now seemed convinced that sooner or later he would leave her. Shortly afterwards, she took an overdose of sleeping pills, but Miller found her and called for help. In an attempt to convince her that he still loved her, he started work on turning his short story, *The Misfits*, into a screenplay for her. Unfortunately, Marilyn did not take this gesture in quite the way in which it was intended. Now that Miller was busy working he cut himself off at the very moment when she needed emotional support, and - what was even worse - she began to suspect that he was only staying with her to get his screenplay accepted and revive his flagging writing career.

At the beginning of 1958, Twentieth Century Fox began to panic that they had let a year go by without

Previous page: A classic glamour shot of Marilyn Monroe, swathed in furs and posed with lips half open and eyes half closed. It was used as the cover picture on the July 1954 issue of *Movie Fan* magazine, not long after Marilyn's marriage to Joe DiMaggio, with the words, "All My Glamor Is For Joe!"

Opposite: Marilyn smiles as she leaves the Lennox Hill Hospital in New York after gynaecological surgery in 1959, which was intended to enable her to carry a baby to term.

getting another Marilyn Monroe film. They had no intention of accepting *The Misfits* as a potential project until Miller's conviction was overturned, and there was no sign in the immediate future of that happening. However, they had nothing else that Marilyn was prepared to consider. Meanwhile, director Billy Wilder sent her the script for *Some Like It Hot*. The story was set in 1929, and involves two musicians, who inadvertently witness the St

Valentine's Day Massacre and have to hide from the Mob. They disguise themselves as women and join an all-girl band, led by singer and ukulele player Sugar Kane. Marilyn was initially not interested in the part, because in the film Sugar never realizes that the two "girls" are men, which Marilyn felt was taking the concept of being a "dumb blonde" to a ridiculous extreme. And had she not fought to get away from being cast in dumb blonde roles?

Below: At the première of *The Prince and the Showgirl* at New York's Radio City Music Hall, Marilyn stops to admire one of the elaborately uniformed soldiers on display. Reviews of the film were mixed at the time, but Marilyn's performance later became regarded as one of her finest.

Opposite: Director Billy Wilder chats to Marilyn in a break during filming for *Some Like It Hot*, on location on the beach at San Diego, California. Marilyn had intially been wary about playing another dumb blonde, but husband Arthur Miller had persuaded her that the story was a sure-fire winner.

Miller, however, pointed out that the script was outstanding, and would be a sure-fire winner. Both her agents and Fox agreed. Even though the film was to be made by the Mirisch brothers and distributed by United Artists so they wouldn't make a penny from it, Fox felt it was in their interest to get Marilyn back to work - and if the movie was the success everyone thought it would be, it would enhance her value as a Fox property.

Finally, Marilyn gave in and signed the contract. Again Paula Strasberg was hired as dramatic coach. Billy Wilder, having dealt with Natasha Lytess, knew the score. Renowned for his caustic wit, he soon exerted his authority on set and put Paula firmly in her place, although he welcomed her support of Marilyn. He also admired Marilyn's sense of comedy, and was prepared to listen to her ideas with respect. It was apparently her idea to change Sugar's first appearance to establish her kooky nature from the outset, so the train suddenly lets off a puff of steam as she teeters down the platform on her high heels, making her jump and the audience laugh. Despite these good omens, Marilyn was soon arriving late, demanding retakes and forgetting her lines. As well as her old demons, she now had to cope with an increasing intake of prescribed drugs: sleeping pills to get her to sleep, uppers to wake her up, and tranquillizers to calm her down. Wilder said later that the experience of working on the project brought him to the verge of a breakdown - and although the end result turned out to be worth it, at the time he had not believed there would be a final product.

As an added complication, towards the end of shooting, Marilyn again became pregnant. Luckily the most strenuous parts of the movie had already been filmed, but Marilyn took every opportunity to rest in an attempt to carry the baby to term. However, in December she miscarried this baby too - it was her last attempt to become a mother.

In March 1959, *Some Like It Hot* had its première on Broadway. It was an instant success, both with the critics and at the box office. It not only outgrossed all other films in the first half of 1959, but also established a box office record for any comedy that remained unbroken

for many years. It is fondly regarded as Marilyn's best film by many of her fans, and is still shown regularly after more than four decades.

Despite this massive success, 1959 was to be another year when Marilyn made no films. Fox was aware that, according to her contract, they had to put her in a movie by 14 April, or lose the right to one of the four pictures they were entitled to. She was assigned to *Time and Tide*, a script based on novels by William Bradford, to be directed by Elia Kazan. She was due to start work on 14 April, but when Kazan came on board he demanded extensive rewrites, so Marilyn was instructed to remain in New York until they needed her - although her salary would be paid from the original start date. Meanwhile, Kazan decided he didn't want to cast Marilyn, but preferred Lee Remick. Fox had failed to notice that Marilyn's contract specified that filming had to start ten weeks from her official start date - which was April 14 - so they were totally surprised to receive notification from her lawyer on 25 June that she was no longer obliged to appear in *Time and Tide*. What was worse, she wanted payment for the film, as per the terms of her contract, even though she hadn't worked on it, and was insisting she be released from one of the films she owed. The studio's legal department confirmed that all these demands were in accordance with her contract: Fox should have asked for an extension, and had failed to do so. Although the New York office cast around for an excuse to get out of paying, the Hollywood end wanted to avoid another lawsuit. Marilyn was a really hot property after the success of *Some Like It Hot*, and they now had another project for her. As a result, all her demands were met - yet again Marilyn had taken on the studio and won.

The new film was *The Billionaire*, co-starring Gregory Peck and to be directed by George Cukor. At first Marilyn had been excited and happy about it, and she was scheduled to start work in October rehearsing her musical numbers. However, the film - later renamed *Let's Make Love* - didn't start full filming until early in 1960. By the start date, Gregory Peck had dropped out after the script was altered to build Marilyn's role, and her new co-star was French sex symbol Yves Montand.

Opposite: Marilyn waves to newsmen through the window of the car, as she is driven away. She always made a big effort to be co-operative with the Press and had quickly developed the skill of turning the coverage to her best advantage. She cultivated allies in the Press - notably Sidney Skolsky, who not only wrote favourably about her in his column, but also helped her to write articles that were published under her own name.

Wrong door raid

Right: Frank Sinatra testifies at the 1957 investigation into the famous "Wrong Door" raid, which had been carried out in 1954. He claimed that he had remained in the car while Joe DiMaggio, along with private detective Philip Irwin and his associate, broke down the apartment door to see if Marilyn was inside, but his story was contradicted by Irwin, who said that all four of them had been involved in the break-in.

Below: When Arthur Miller was put on trial for contempt of Congress in Washington, Marilyn accompanied him but stayed out of sight until the trial was over. When she finally did agree to speak to reporters, she told them she had spent the time reading transcripts of the proceedings in court.

Opposite: Marilyn with society hostess Elsa Maxwell at an April in Paris Ball, held in 1957.

A visit from the stork?

Above: In April 1957, Marilyn had found out she was expecting a baby. Her doctor had warned her that it might be an ectopic pregnancy, in which the foetus develops inside a fallopian tube instead of in the uterus, but she had put such thoughts out of her head and was euphoric at the thought of finally becoming a mother.

Opposite above: Onlookers laugh as Marilyn lights a super firecracker to start inaugual ceremonies at the reactivated Rockefeller Center Sidewalk Superintendents Club in New York. The firecracker triggered a dynamite blast in the excavation pit of the new 47-storey Time & Life building nearby.

Opposite below: Marilyn and her husband refuse to be drawn on whether she is pregnant, as they arrive back in New York after a short holiday in Jamaica.

Although she was depressed when the pregnancy did turn out to be ectopic and had to be terminated, Marilyn still managed to put on a brave and happy face for newsmen as she left Doctors Hospital in New York with Arthur Miller in August 1957.

Conversation Piece...

Opposite: Actress Joan Copeland was Arthur Miller's sister, and when she opened in Noel Coward's *Conversation Piece*, Marilyn went to the first night party in the Barbizon Plaza Hotel to congratulate her sister-in-law.

Above and right: At the 1958 March of Dimes Fashion Show, Marilyn appeared as one of the models and was pictured with twins Lindy and Sandy Sue Solomon, who were featured on the March of Dimes poster. The charity helped children with polio, and one of the twins walked with crutches after recovering from the illness. The fashion show was held at the Waldorf-Astoria and it featured designs by members of the couture group of the New York Dress Institute, as well as other designers from New York, California and Italy. Marilyn wore a champagne-coloured silk dress with a fitted jacket designed by John Moore for Talmack.

Signing up...

Above: Harold Mirisch, president of the Mirisch Company, talks to Marilyn about their upcoming production, *Some Like It Hot*, Billy Wilder and I.A.L. Diamond's screenplay based on a German film entitled *Fanfares of Love*. Marilyn's role was supposed to be peripheral to the main action, but the minute she arrives on screen she seems to take over the movie. Despite her misgivings about playing another dumb blonde, she needed a hit when *The Prince and the Showgirl* did not do as well as expected.

Opposite and following pages: When Arthur Miller was inducted as a member of the National Institute of Arts and Letters on 21 May, 1958, Marilyn happily signed autographs for her fans.

Some Like It Hot

Opposite: Marilyn and Arthur Miller leaving New York for Hollywood, where Marilyn was to start work on *Some Like It Hot*.

Above: Co-star Tony Curtis had to spend almost the entire movie in drag, since the plot involved two male musicians who witness the Valentine's Day Massacre in 1920s New York and disguise themselves as women to escape the Mob. Curtis was uncomfortable in costume at first, but with the help of drag artist Barbette, quickly learned how to walk like a woman. Lemmon was not so adept a pupil.

Right: Director Billy Wilder discusses a scene with Marilyn. She had been dismayed to discover the film was being shot in black and white, rather than Technicolor, as per her contract with Fox. Wilder explained that tests had shown that the thick makeup Tony Curtis and Jack Lemmon had to wear in their guise as women turned greenish when filmed in colour, making them look like clowns.

Right: Joe E. Brown, who played millionaire Osgood Fielding III, chats with Marilyn on set. Fielding falls in love with "Daphne" - Jack Lemmon in drag.

Above and opposite: Marilyn as Sugar, the ukelele player in the "all-girl" band. Wilder had considered several actors for the male leads in *Some Like It Hot*, including Frank Sinatra and at an early stage Danny Kaye and Bob Hope, before settling on Curtis and then Lemmon. Despite difficulties on *The Seven Year Itch*, Wilder rated Marilyn's performance highly and cast her in the role of Sugar considering it the weakest role and therefore vital to chose the right actress for the part. Filming began in early September 1958 but Wilder and Diamond continued to work on the script during shooting.

A real artist...

Above: Marilyn shares a joke on the set of *Some Like It Hot*.

Opposite: Director Billy Wilder gives Marilyn some quiet advice. When Joe Hyams of *The New York Herald* interviewed Wilder towards the end of filming, he complained of Marilyn's unpunctuality and inability to remember lines. When asked if he would work with her again, he replied, "I have discussed this with my doctor and my psychiatrist and they tell me I'm too old and too rich to go through this again." However, this was the reaction of the moment and he later said of Marilyn, "Anyone can remember lines, but it takes a real artist to come on the set and not know her lines and yet give the performance she did!"

On the beach

Opposite: Tony Curtis posing as bogus oil baron Mr Shell to attract Sugar's attention. Although set in Florida, the exterior scenes were filmed at the Hotel del Coronado, a Victorian mansion built in the 1880s near San Diego which had been a haunt of the rich and famous over the years and was said to have been where Edward VIII met Mrs Simpson.

Above: Marilyn on location with Paula Strasberg. Most of Marilyn's directors had been angered by Paula's interference on set, but Wilder firmly established who was boss early on.

Marilyn pregnant

Opposite below and left: During the shooting of the bathing scene, Marilyn wore a 1920s bathing suit that was considerably more modest than most of the swimming costumes she had been photographed in previously. On the first attempt at shooting this scene, a shark was believed to have been spotted in the water, so filming had to be stopped three hours earlier than planned.

Opposite above: Marilyn chats to Arthur Miller between takes. Although he was tied up with writing commitments in New York, Miller came to Hollywood to support Marilyn as often as he could. As filming proceeded Marilyn realized she was pregnant again, and in some of her later scenes her costumes had to be let out. Unfortunately by this time she was so hooked on sleeping pills and alcohol that she was unable to give them up. Between takes she asked her assistant to bring a flask of coffee which was said to contain vermouth. By late October Marilyn had missed nearly two weeks of filming because of illness and many more hours by arriving late on set, costing the production some $200,000.

A box-office success

Above: Sugar chats to Josephine, while she takes her bath. Tony Curtis became terribly frustrated at Marilyn's inability to remember her lines, which often led to dozens of takes of simple scenes, and at her habitual lateness. At times Marilyn seemed unable to cope with even the simplest dialogues needing more than 40 takes to say "It's me, Sugar". Curtis famously commented to journalists that kissing Marilyn was "like kissing Hitler", but he later said that it was a throwaway line that had been taken far too seriously. Although Marilyn was upset she always refused to fight her battles in the Press, and merely replied that Curtis had only said it because she wore prettier dresses in the movie.

Despite all the problems during production, and even a disastrous preview, *Some Like It Hot* was a huge success at the box office, becoming one of the three top-earning pictures of 1959. It has become a classic movie, still entertaining audiences 40 years later and is counted amongst Marilyn's best-ever performances.

Opposite: Frenchman Maurice Chevalier admires Marilyn's assets as he tours the set of *Some Like It Hot*. Marilyn's rather revealing dress had been designed by Orry-Kelly who created it specifically for the picture. The movie received six Oscar nominations, including Jack Lemmon for Best Actor and Wilder for Best Director but Orry-Kelly, nominated for Best Costume Design, was the only winner.

Running wild

Opposite: A candid shot of Marilyn, taken on the beach. Her hair had been lightened to almost white for *Some Like It Hot* and it was beginning to show the strain of all those years of bleaching.

Left: Carson McCullers greets Marilyn with a kiss. The two women had known each other since Marilyn's early days in New York in 1955 when she and Marilyn had both been occupants of the Gladstone Hotel on East 52nd Street.

Above: Marilyn meets Danish author Isak Dinesen - otherwise known as Baroness Karen Blixen, author of *Out of Africa* - at the New York home of U.S. writer Carson McCullers. Both she and Arthur Miller had been invited to the event, which took place during Blixen's lecture tour of America in February 1959.

In the public eye...

Above: Arthur Miller and Marilyn attending the première of *Some Like It Hot* at Loew's Capitol Theater on Broadway in New York, on 29 March, 1959. Marilyn had lost her baby early the previous December, and had been staying out of the public eye as she recuperated.

Opposite: A Twentieth Century Fox publicity shot, taken by Frank Powolny. Another shot in this series became the most famous picture in the world of Marilyn, when artist Andy Warhol used it as the basis for his series of silkscreen prints of her.

Opposite: Marilyn braves icy winds at La Guardia Airport as she arrives in Chicago for the release there of *Some Like It Hot*.

Above: Arthur Miller escorts Marilyn away from Lennox Hill Hospital, where she had been having corrective surgery to try to cure her chronic endometriosis. Despite appearances, their marriage was already in deep trouble as Marilyn had become convinced that her failure to give him a child would drive him away.

Exits and entrances

Opposite: Despite her feelings, as usual Marilyn put on a good show for reporters.

Left: Marilyn had always been interested in Russia - all her drama coaches had based their teaching on the work of Russian actor and director Konstantin Stanislavsky. When Soviet Premiere Nikita Khrushchev visited the Fox studios during his tour of America, she flew from New York to attend the lunch in his honour and for once in her life arrived early.

Below: Arthur Miller and Marilyn arrive in New York in November 1959. She was due to begin work within a few days on *The Billionaire*, later called *Let's Make Love*, but in the event did not start on the project until early in 1960. The leading man was to have been Gregory Peck, but by the start of filming he had moved to another project and there were many problems in finding someone to replace him. Miller had spent months working on revisions to his screenplay for *The Misfits* and hoped that Marilyn would be free to begin shooting the movie in April 1960.

Right: Marilyn strikes a pensive pose as she listens to Nikita Krushchev speak.

Opposite: Despite looking luminously beautiful in this publicity picture, by the end of 1959, Marilyn was in a poor state of health, and the start of filming on *Let's Make Love* was delayed as she regularly called in sick. This was not unusual on occasion, but now there were days on end when she did not arrive for work. Apart from her problems with drugs and alcohol, this was also her way of showing that she was not happy with the script, and Arthur Miller was called in to rewrite whole sections of it. His involvement was never credited, as the forthcoming *The Misfits* was to be billed as both his screenwriting debut and the first time he had written anything specifically for Marilyn.

CHAPTER SIX

The Misfits

The plot of *Let's Make Love* is a comedy of mistaken identity and misunderstanding. It involves a show in production in Greenwich Village that is a satirical life history of fictional billionaire Jean-Marc Clément. The billionaire himself hears about the production, turns up at rehearsal, and falls for blonde bombshell Amanda Dell. The director mistakes him for a look-alike come to audition for the part of Jean-Marc Clément in the show - and because of his amazing resemblance he gets the part … Originally, much of the comedy depended on the fact that Jean-Marc Clément was not able to sing or dance, but was required to do so to appear in the show and get the girl - which was why Gregory Peck had originally been cast. After he dropped out, several other stars turned the part down but Miller suggested Yves Montand, who was in America touring with his one-man show. His English was poor and he was a renowned song-and-dance man, which made rather a nonsense of the plot. These drawbacks were instantly overlooked when he agreed to do the movie, because Fox were desperate to get it underway before they lost any more time. Marilyn, Miller, Montand and his wife, Simone Signoret, soon became great friends, sharing adjacent bungalows at the Beverly Hills Hotel. Marilyn went shopping with Simone, Miller coached Montand with his English. That didn't stop Montand and Marilyn starting a passionate affair after Miller left for New York to work on the script of *The Misfits*, and Signoret returned to France.

For Marilyn, the affair was not so much about falling in love as seeking attention and some much-needed affection. Miller had abandoned her again to work on his script, and although *The Misfits* was supposed to be for her, she now firmly believed it was really all about getting his own career back on track. Perhaps Marilyn also began her affair because she wanted to see how Miller would react - would he still care, would he be angry and upset and come running? The answer was no. Grateful that at last Marilyn seemed happy to be working, he decided to leave well alone. As for Montand, he was a stranger in Hollywood and was enticed into an affair with a beautiful woman, far from home. He didn't expect it to lead anywhere - and for that matter neither did Marilyn. Signoret also ignored what was going on - when asked about it later she replied that if Marilyn was in love with her husband it just proved what good taste she had.

Apart from this, the filming of *Let's Make Love* proceeded predictably, with the usual lateness on set, forgotten lines and missed calls. The major difference from Cukor's point of view was that he did not have to deal with Paula Strasberg, Marilyn having temporarily fallen out with her.

Meanwhile, Miller had virtually completed the script of *The Misfits*, which was due to begin filming in July. From the beginning he had an ambiguous and unresolved attitude to the whole project. On the one hand, he was creating a vehicle for Marilyn, and his personal life with her meant that there were themes he could not bring himself to explore. On the other, he was continually striving to repeat the success of *Death of a Salesman*, and hoped that *The Misfits* would prove to be as good, if not better. A further complication was that he took a stance of moral superiority over Hollywood - referring to Marilyn's loyal audience as "the great unwashed" - even while he was trying to tap into the success and riches of the movie business himself. He had partly resolved this to himself by hoping that *The Misfits* would not go on general release, but would be roadshowed in select cinemas, with exclusive and expensive showings. Director John Huston quickly disabused him of this idea - it was apparent to him that what Miller had created was a potentially good and workable movie, but not a masterpiece.

Because *Let's Make Love* had run so late - not solely due to Marilyn but also because of an actors' strike - she had to go almost straight from one project to the other. Given the emotional demands that working made on her, this was always going to be dangerous because she had no time to build up her reserves again. The other problem was the nature of the material. Marilyn had hoped and believed that Miller would create an exciting and different dramatic role for her to play, but instead all he had come up with was just another version of Marilyn. He gave his character, Roslyn, feelings that Marilyn had, put words into her mouth that Marilyn had spoken, made her act just like Marilyn. When he had started he had been in love with Marilyn, so his Roslyn was in many ways an idealized and sanitized version of her. Now the Millers were almost on the point of divorce, held together only by the project, and he had a very different view of his wife. Unfortunately, he had been unable to translate this effectively into the role, so Roslyn was not a rounded person. Marilyn was devastated that he had chosen to portray her as so vulnerable, wounded and helpless, with no depth or complexity and so little to offer. It made her uncomfortable that he both refused to acknowledge her dark side, and that he had revealed so many private moments of her life on screen for all to see.

There were even more tensions and fights than usual during filming - all exacerbated by the fact they were working in the Nevada desert in July, with daytime temperatures often over 100ºF. Halfway through filming, Marilyn's health completely broke down, and she left Nevada for Los Angeles, where she checked into the Westside Hospital for ten days. However, she returned to complete the movie, which finished shooting a month later. Not long afterwards, Marilyn and Miller announced that they had separated, and a couple of days later, her co-star Clark Gable died of a heart attack. The film has become so famous for these events, and for the problems on set, that its quality is often overlooked. Gable gave one of his finest performances, and despite everything Marilyn is superb.

The forthcoming divorce from Miller meant yet another failure for Marilyn, who was still recovering from doing the two films back-to-back and trying to function despite her increasing dependence on drugs. She went back to New York, hoping to find sanctuary with the Strasbergs, but instead of allowing her to rest, Strasberg talked her into agreeing to appear in Somerset Maugham's *Rain*, which he planned to direct. He felt that completing a serious acting role successfully would restore her self-esteem, but he also had no previous film credits, so he needed Marilyn to get the project off the ground.

On Christmas Eve 1960, Marilyn was alone, but suddenly a mass of flowers was delivered. The card with them said, "Best, Joe." As Marilyn said to her assistant, there was only one Joe, and from that moment he began to feature once again in her life.

Marilyn travelled to Mexico to file for divorce on 20 January, 1961, in the hopes that the inauguration of President John F. Kennedy on the same day would keep the Press occupied. A few days later she attended the preview of *The Misfits*, but she and Miller carefully avoided each other. She became even more deeply depressed afterwards, and on the advice of her analyst, Dr Kris, she signed herself into the Payne-Whitney Clinic under the name Faye Miller. In the state she was in, Marilyn probably did not realize that the Payne-Whitney was a psychiatric hospital. She had always been terrified of going mad and being locked away, because she believed her family had a

Previous page: Marilyn strikes a pose during a number for *Let's Make Love*, which went into production at the beginning of 1960. This time the biggest delay to filming was not caused by either Marilyn's lateness or ill health - a strike by actors to preserve residual payments, later joined by The Writers' Guild, shut down production for several months.

Opposite: Marilyn and Yves Montand rehearse on set. At a cocktail party to welcome Montand to Hollywood, Marilyn told reporters that next to her husband and Marlon Brando, Montand was the most attractive man she knew. What she did not mention was that she had told friends in private that he reminded her of Joe DiMaggio.

history of insanity. Her great-grandfather
had committed suicide, her grandfather
had died in hospital suffering from
dementia, and her grandmother, Della, had
been diagnosed as a manic-depressive. In
addition, her mother, Gladys, had spent
years going in and out of various hospitals.
However, the facts may not be quite so
straightforward. Her great-grandfather had
killed himself when his health was failing
and his farm was about to be repossessed -
and many people committed suicide during
the Great Depression of the 1930s. Her
grandfather had suffered dementia, but
later study of his medical records seemed to
show it was almost certainly caused by an
infection that attacked his brain tissue - and
not by an inherited weakness. Her
grandmother, Della, died of heart disease
and had also suffered a stroke, both of
which can lead to erratic behaviour, and
there is no real evidence that she was
psychotic. As for Gladys, she certainly
suffered from depression, but at the time
the illness was often not properly
diagnosed, while the effects of new drugs
were not fully understood. Several of her
friends believed that a temporary inability
to cope became a lifelong incapacity, purely
because of the effect of the drugs she was
prescribed.

However, when Marilyn realized
where she was, she apparently broke a glass
door with a chair and threatened to cut
herself if she was not immediately released.
Attendants subdued her, and carried her to

Right: Marilyn rehearsing a dance number in
Let's Make Love.

Opposite: Clark Gable and Marilyn in a scene
from *The Misfits,* which was filmed during the
summer of 1960 in Nevada. Gable resembled
the picture of the man that Gladys had told
the young Norma Jeane was her father, and
when she was a child Marilyn had often
fantasized that she really was the daughter of
the famous movie star.

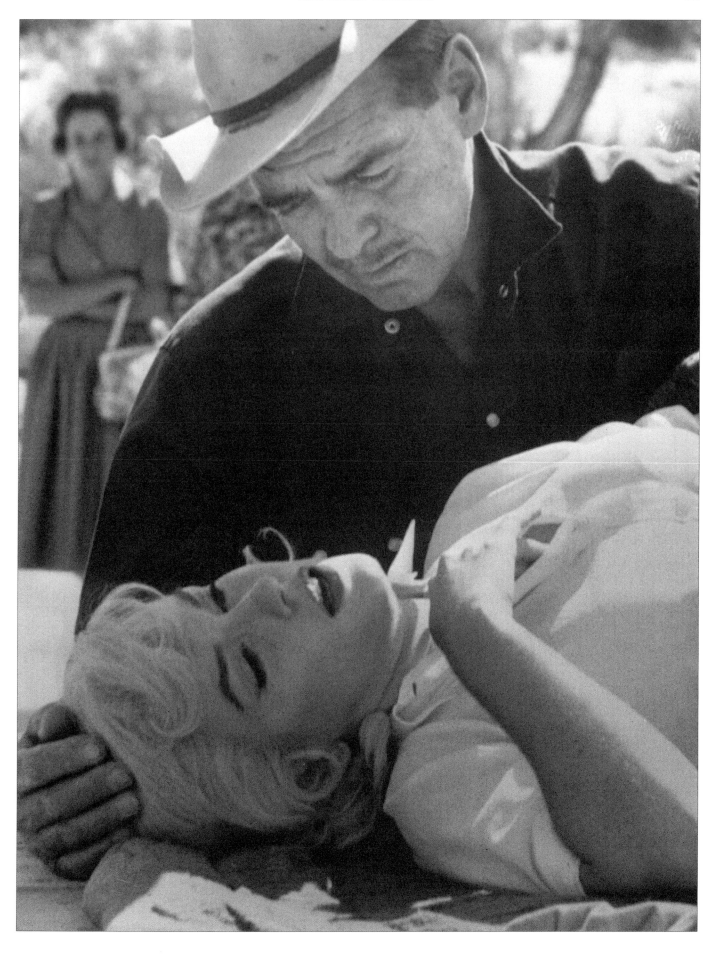

the ward for violent patients, where she was sedated and restrained. She tried to contact the Strasbergs, but it was DiMaggio who finally found her and obtained her release. Although doctors initially said she was not fit to leave, he insisted that she was transferred and took her to the Columbia-Presbyterian Medical Center - another hospital, but at least not a psychiatric one.

Despite all this, Strasberg was still trying to get *Rain* off the ground, and Fox were pushing her to make a comedy film called *Goodbye, Charlie* as the last picture they were owed under her contract. No one seemed to realize that it was largely the way she worked that had put her in hospital in the first place. In the event, Cukor, the approved director for *Goodbye, Charlie*, dropped out of the project and none of the other directors named in her contract could do it - except Lee Strasberg. He suddenly ceased to object to Marilyn making another comedy when he saw the chance to command a fee as her director. In the event, the fee he wanted was too large, and Fox agreed to forgo the project as long as Marilyn agreed that they were still owed a film. Strasberg's own project, *Rain*, also fell through and Marilyn refused to make it without him.

After Marilyn had left the hospital, DiMaggio had taken her off to Florida, where he was working with the Yankees during their spring training. There she sat in the sun, walked on the beach and generally enjoyed DiMaggio's company - although they were now just friends and there was no possibility of a new marriage. It was not the end of her health problems - she was admitted to hospital twice more that year: for an operation to correct an unspecified internal problem, and for surgery to remove her gall bladder.

Back in Hollywood in the summer of 1961, Marilyn was soon involved in the world of endless parties and entertaining, and it was inevitable that she would be invited to Peter Lawford's beach house. She already knew Lawford from her early days in Hollywood, and he was a friend of Sinatra, but Lawford's parties were now the ones to be invited to because he was married to Pat Kennedy. Sooner or later his brothers-in-law, the President and the Attorney-General, would be attending. It was at Lawford's house that Marilyn met both Kennedy brothers, and although she may have had a fling with the President, it was Bobby Kennedy with whom she started a more serious affair.

The dream of a new life in New York was now well and truly over, so Marilyn decided to base herself back in Hollywood, although she still kept her Manhattan apartment. She found a small apartment on Doheny Drive, in the same house in which she had lived when she first became a star nearly seven years earlier. It may have seemed like coming home, but perhaps it was just an attempt to pretend that the last few years had not happened.

Left: Marilyn prepares to film a dance scene from *Let's Make Love*. It was a rehearsal within a rehearsal, as the film was set backstage as a theatre company puts together a satirical play with song and dance routines. She performed several of her routines with famed song-and-dance man Frankie Vaughan.

Welcome to Hollywood!

On 15 January, 1960, Twentieth Century-Fox hosted a cocktail party in Hollywood to welcome Yves Montand - who was to co-star in *Let's Make Love* with Marilyn. He was not the first choice - Gregory Peck had originally been slated for the part, but had to drop out after delays in filming meant the dates would clash with other commitments. Several other well-known actors, including Cary Grant and Jimmy Stewart, had turned the part down, before Arthur Miller suggested Montand. At the time, Miller was working on rewrites of the script of *Let's Make Love* and was desperate to finish the movie so Marilyn could move on to his project, *The Misfits*.

Above: Marilyn flanked by co-stars Frankie Vaughan and Yves Montand at the cocktail party. Part of the reason for the party was also to introduce the cast to the Press. Montand was not well known in America - and his English was far from fluent - but his recent one-man shows in Los Angeles and New York had been a great success.

Left and opposite: Right from the start there was a certain chemistry between Marilyn and Montand - and it was not long before they started a passionate love affair.

Let's Make Love...

Arthur Miller and Yves Montand became great friends even before filming started - Montand had appeared in the French production of Miller's play, *The Crucible*. Montand's wife, Simone Signoret, and Marilyn also got on very well. At the start of filming *Let's Make Love* the two couples rented adjacent bungalows at the Beverly Hills Hotel and spent a great deal of time together. However, in April 1960 Miller returned to New York, leaving Marilyn to finish work on the movie, while Simone Signoret had already returned to France. It was almost inevitable that Marilyn and Montand, left alone together, would begin a relationship.

Right: Director George Cukor discusses a scene with Marilyn. Choreographer Jack Cole had worked out the dance sequences for *Let's Make Love.* Cole had worked on all Marilyn's dance routines since *Gentlemen Prefer Blondes* in 1953. She trusted him implicitly and had specifically requested his services for *Let's Make Love.* Cukor, exasperated at having to deal with Marilyn's constant lateness and insecurities, left much of the direction of the dance scenes to Cole. Marilyn and Cole were firm personal friends, but working on this project strained their relationship to the limit. Marilyn's marriage to Arthur Miller was unravelling fast, and her intake of pills was rising rapidly. Studio executives were also alarmed that she didn't look as good on camera as usual - the daily rushes were often disappointing. Despite all her problems, she had always managed to produce something magical for the camera - but this time it was not to be.

Too many curves?

At the start of filming Marilyn was quite svelte, but during the enforced halt caused by the actors' and writers' strike during March 1960 she put on a considerable amount of weight and in some later scenes - like the one opposite - she looks distinctly chubby. Cukor complained that this meant it took much longer to set up each scene as he had to film Marilyn from the most flattering angle.

My Heart Belongs to Daddy...

Right: Studio head Buddy Adler complained that Marilyn looked so overweight in the first version of this dance sequence that it seemed as if she was pregnant. He also hated the chalky-white makeup that had been developed for her role, similar to that used in *Bus Stop*. In *Bus Stop* it had been appropriate, as her character of Cherie worked nights and slept through the day, but now it made her look even more unhealthy. Producer Jerry Wald tried to assure him that the dance sequence would be so fast-paced in the final edit that the audience would not notice Marilyn's looks.

However, delays in filming had caused the film to be $500,000 over budget, and despite all their concerns about Marilyn's appearance, there were to be no retakes.

Sewn in...

Left: Adler also explained that a major reason for the "bumpy" look round Marilyn's middle was that the sweater she was wearing had been sewn to her leotard, causing it to move strangely and ride up. He claimed that if the stitching was removed, the sweater would move loosely and naturally and the problem would be solved. Marilyn had been working on set on her own, filming all the song and dance sequences, and she had yet to complete the bulk of her scenes with Montand, even though the proposed start date for *The Misfits* was now looming.

Take it from the top...

Left: Marilyn in pensive mood on the set of *Let's Make Love.*

Below: A still from the finished scene, in which Marilyn dances and sings Cole Porter's "My Heart Belongs to Daddy".

Opposite: However bad she was feeling, Marilyn could always raise a smile for the camera. Since early January 1960, she had been seeing a new psychoanalyst, Dr Ralph Greenson, who had been recommended by her analyst in New York. Greenson tried to limit her intake of pills and to help her regain some kind of composure so she could complete the movie. He was to remain her analyst until her death, some two years later.

Celebration!

Opposite: Twentieth Century Fox studio head Buddy Adler welcomes Marilyn as she arrives to complete *Let's Make Love*.

Left: Marilyn proudly displays her Golden Globe award, which had just been presented by members of the Hollywood Foreign Press Association for her performance as the "Best Actress in a Motion Picture Comedy" in *Some Like It Hot*. Many were surprised that she had not also been nominated for a "Best Actress" award at that year's Oscars but Marilyn warmly congratulated Simone Signoret, who had been nominated for her role in *Room at the Top*.

Below: At a party on set, Marilyn celebrates her birthday with the cast and crew of *Let's Make Love* where they gave her a seed pearl necklace. Filming was finished by mid June with only dubbing to complete but even this was subject to endless delays when Marilyn put off returning to work until mid July.

Off to Reno...

Left: Gail Sawyer, daughter of Nevada Governor Grant Sawyer, presents Marilyn with a bouquet of roses as she arrives at Reno Airport to begin work on *The Misfits.* Miller had embarked on writing the script for Marilyn as a way of showing his love for her, but as the relationship disintegrated she viewed it less as a gift of love and more as him using her name to get his first screenplay off the ground.

Opposite: Marilyn poses for photographers with her usual carefree smile intact - despite the fact that Montand had now returned to France and his wife, so her very public affair with him was over.

Below: A scene from *The Misfits,* in which Gay (Clark Gable) and Roslyn (Marilyn) plant lettuces in the garden.

The Misfits

Right: Marilyn poses with some of the cast and crew of *The Misfits*. At the top of the picture is Arthur Miller, with Eli Wallach below him, and at the front are Montgomery Clift, Marilyn and Clark Gable. Director John Huston is standing behind Marilyn.

Below: Arthur Miller and Clark Gable chat on set. The part of Gay Langland had first been offered to Robert Mitchum, but he found the script "incomprehensible".

Opposite: Marilyn played Roslyn Tabor, in Reno to get a divorce from her husband. She drives a seriously dented car, as men are always driving into her to get an introduction. Marilyn felt the character of Roslyn was too sweet and saccharine to be at all believable.

Director John Huston, Marilyn and Arthur Miller confer on set. All the way through shooting Miller was rewriting and adjusting the script and was still unable to decide how the piece would end. Although Huston had at first said it was "magnificent", he still felt it needed serious cuts and revisions. Miller hoped he had written a great American story, something to rival his most successful play, *Death of a Salesman*, but Huston was more realistic and could see that the story was deeply flawed. Miller believed in his creation so much that he was unable to step back and reappraise it. Marilyn was hurt and angry that Roslyn, who was so obviously based on herself, revealed no elements of her own dark side. She felt this was due to Miller's inability to accept this aspect of her life - and took it as a rejection of the person she really was.

Don't shoot!

Above: Roslyn begs Gay not to shoot the rabbits that have eaten their newly-planted lettuces. Marilyn herself was very sentimental about wild animals and hated to see them hurt.

Opposite: Gable gives Marilyn a big hug. Despite the heat and the strain of waiting for Marilyn, he did not turn against her. When he died of a heart attack soon after shooting finished, many people blamed her behaviour for causing him stress, but it was more likely his insistence on doing some of his own stunts or the fact that he was a heavy smoker that had led to the problems with his heart. On set Gable was calm and patient with both Marilyn and Montgomery Clift who was also a troubled personality. However, Marilyn said of Clift that he was "the only person I know who's in worse shape than me".

Following pages: A close-up of Marilyn, in one of the many wigs made for her to wear in the movie, and Gable.

A not so happy couple...

Opposite and above: Arthur Miller and Marilyn on the set of *The Misfits* in 1960, as filming is coming to an end. Although they still kept up the pretence of being together in public, it is noticeable that in these pictures Marilyn does not have her usual bright smile or sparkle, and that there seems to be a certain distance between husband and wife. By the time shooting was nearly over there were rumours that Miller was having an affair with Inge Morath, a young photographer who was visiting the set and Marilyn had moved into Paula Strasberg's suite at the hotel. Only a week after the film wrapped they announced their plans to divorce.

Strange bedfellows?

Left: Strangely prescient of a relationship which was to develop between Marilyn and John and Robert Kennedy, a cinema-owner in Spokane, Washington, advertises a speech by presidential nominee Senator John F. Kennedy, next to Marilyn's name - one of her films is currently showing inside.

Above: During filming of *The Misfits* the cast and crew were often working out in the boiling sun in the desert, and Marilyn was careful to shade her skin.

Opposite: With no Montand and Miller on his way out, Marilyn was ready to give love a miss for a while and concentrate on sorting out her life instead. While making *The Misfits* her health had deteriorated to such a state that she had to be hospitalized for several days. Her dependence on prescription drugs had made it almost impossible for her to work and by the time filming was over Marilyn was at a very low ebb.

Putting on a happy face...

Left: Montgomery Clift and Marilyn arrive at Capitol Theater on Broadway on 31 January 1961, for a preview of *The Misfits.* Miller was also there with his children, but the two of them avoided each other. A typical review from the *New York Daily News* said, "Miss Monroe has seldom looked worse; the camera is unfailingly unflattering. But there is a delicacy about her playing and a tenderness that is affecting."

Below and opposite: Marilyn leaves the Columbia-Presbyterian Medical Center, where she had spent three weeks trying to pull herself out of the depths of depression.

In and out of hospital...

Above: Joe DiMaggio, who was in Florida helping to coach the New York Yankees during their spring training session, invited Marilyn to join him there to recuperate after her release from the Columbia-Presbyterian Hospital. In Florida she spent long periods in the sun relaxing and renewing her friendship with Joe.

Opposite top: Joe arrives to visit Marilyn in the Polyclinic Hospital in New York in June 1961, where she had undergone an operation to have her gall bladder removed. It was the fifth time she had been admitted to hospital in ten months.

Opposite bottom: A frail-looking Marilyn is discharged from hospital nearly two weeks later. As usual, the Press were there in force.

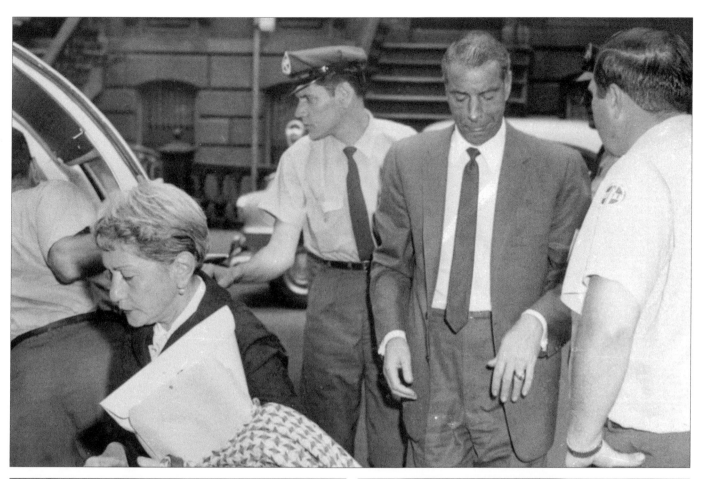

CHAPTER SEVEN

Something's Got To Give

At the beginning of 1962, Marilyn was seeing her analyst, Dr Ralph Greenson, every day. There are mixed views about his treatment of Marilyn. On the one hand, he was undoubtedly totally committed to her, but on the other, many believe that he became far too emotionally involved and had lost any semblance of objective distance. Even more controversially, he involved Marilyn in his home life - as he did to an extent with some other patients - and she often had dinner there after her sessions, sometimes stayed overnight and had even spent her last Christmas with his family. One of the first rules of psychoanalysis is that the analyst should avoid personal involvement, but Greenson appeared to believe that traditional methods had failed with Marilyn, and that what she actually needed was to experience a normal, stable family life. His detractors accuse him of wanting to control Marilyn - as many men had tried to do before - and he certainly attempted to screen who she saw. His friend, Eunice Murray, became her housekeeper, and it was Murray who found the house on Fifth Helena Drive that became Marilyn's last home. Marilyn liked it because it was a Mexican-style building that was reminiscent of Greenson's house.

Excited about having a proper home of her own, Marilyn planned to fly to Mexico to buy furniture, artwork and tiles so she could create the same kind of colourful Mexican décor that she had enjoyed at the Greenson house. By all accounts she hoped the move would mark yet another new beginning, and in an effort to tie up loose ends, she had agreed to do *Something's Got To Give* for Fox, to complete her studio commitment. Unfortunately, in the midst of this positive atmosphere, word came that Miller was to marry again. The news affected Marilyn badly - it brought back all her lost dreams of being a good wife, having a family and creating a home. When she came back from Mexico, she had obviously slipped back into the old cycle of too many pills, mixed with too much champagne.

A few days after her return, Marilyn arrived at the Golden Globe Awards, obviously the worse for drink. When she collected her statuette for World's Favourite Female Star, her acceptance speech was rambling and inconclusive and gossip started in Hollywood that she was finished. Despite this, a couple of weeks later Marilyn had pulled herself together enough to report for costume fitting and makeup tests for her new movie, and the studio breathed a sigh of relief.

The plot of *Something's Got To Give* was based on *My Favourite Wife*, a popular 1940 comedy about a woman who has been shipwrecked on a desert island for many years and is believed dead, but who finally returns home to find her husband is married to another woman. The original script needed work and Marilyn was delighted when Fox appointed Nunnally Johnson to rewrite it. Johnson had written the screenplay for *How to Marry a Millionaire*, and although Marilyn had spent years trying to get away from the kind of dumb blonde character he had created, she now knew she desperately needed a big hit to boost her reputation and silence wagging tongues. Anyway, the role of Ellen Arden would be different, because for the first time she would be playing a wife and mother. Another inducement was her co-star, Dean

Martin, and Fox had also appointed Cukor to direct, with whom Marilyn had worked on *Let's Make Love.*

Johnson created a script that Marilyn was pleased with, and which incorporated many of her ideas, but he left the project before filming began. A series of other scriptwriters then worked on it and Marilyn became increasingly unhappy as the screenplay moved away from Johnson's version. New pages were always sent out to cast and crew on different-coloured paper, so that everyone could be sure they were working from the same sheet, but at one point the studio resorted to sending rewritten pages on white paper to Marilyn, to try to fool her that no changes were being made.

Because of the script problems, shooting was put back until 23 April, but by then Marilyn was ill and Dean Martin also failed to appear as he was still working on another movie. Although Marilyn managed several days' work over the next few weeks, she spent much more time at home with a fever - although she continued to work there with Paula Strasberg, trying to make some sense of the rewrites that continued to arrive daily. She now often went to see Greenson twice a day.

In the middle of all this, Greenson and his wife left for a long-planned trip to Europe. Greenson said later that he had become worried about Marilyn's increasing dependence on him, and that he himself desperately needed a break from the pressures of dealing with her. The week after he left, Marilyn turned up at the studio early and worked hard each day. She had been invited to sing "Happy Birthday" to the President at a gala forty-fifth birthday salute at Madison Square Garden and she was desperate to go. The previous week, there had been a great deal of publicity about the fact that Miller had been an honoured guest at a presidential dinner party for the French Minister of Culture, and Marilyn was determined not to miss the chance to show that she was a presidential favourite too. Nevertheless, the studio was reluctant to let her go, because filming of *Something's Got To Give* was running so far behind.

On Thursday 17 May, Marilyn worked until noon, then flew to New York to prepare for Saturday night. She came on as the finale, singing the simple song in an outrageously sexy way that delighted the entire audience. By Sunday evening she was on her way back to Los Angeles, ready to start work again on Monday morning, and she continued to report for filming the following week. As far as she was concerned she had only missed one day, and that was that. The studio executives at Fox saw it differently. At the time the entire movie industry was going through upheaval, and the old guard at Fox were being criticized for indulging the stars and giving in to their whims at the expense of the stockholders. In Italy *Cleopatra* was being filmed with Elizabeth Taylor and Richard Burton, and although it had already cost millions it was still going over budget; Fox had been forced to sell off part of its back lot to pay for it all. It was the wrong moment for Marilyn to challenge the studio's authority.

Behind the scenes, there was already talk of either closing the movie down or firing Marilyn and replacing her with someone else. Whether or not she was aware of these rumours, Marilyn continued to work intermittently, and relations with Cukor deteriorated. On 1 June she celebrated her thirty-sixth birthday with the cast and crew, and maybe the thought of getting older affected her badly, as it was the last day she appeared on set. The following week, desperate negotiations went on between her agent and Fox, in conjunction with Greenson - who had been hastily called back from his trip. Despite assurances that Marilyn would be back at work after a week's rest, Fox fired her from the movie. They had intended to replace her with Lee Remick, but Dean Martin refused to hear of it, saying he had signed to co-star with Marilyn and if she wasn't part of the deal, then neither was he. For the moment the picture was put on hold, while everyone considered their options.

In Marilyn's camp, they knew they needed some good publicity, and fast, to counteract the rumours that she had finally had a complete breakdown. Just before the movie closed down, Marilyn had done a photo session on set in which she swam in a pool, and had mischievously removed her costume under water. The resulting nudes were sensational, and they were quickly released - one appeared on the cover of *Life* magazine at the end of the month. Another high-profile photography session was organized with Bert Stern, for *Vogue.* The publicity and the groundswell of public opinion, which was sympathetic to Marilyn, did make Fox think again. By mid-July Marilyn was

Previous page: A publicity shot for Marilyn's ill-fated last movie, *Something's Got to Give.*

Opposite: But for the hair that has escaped from under the scarf, Marilyn almost succeeds in disguising herself as she uncharacteristically avoids the camera.

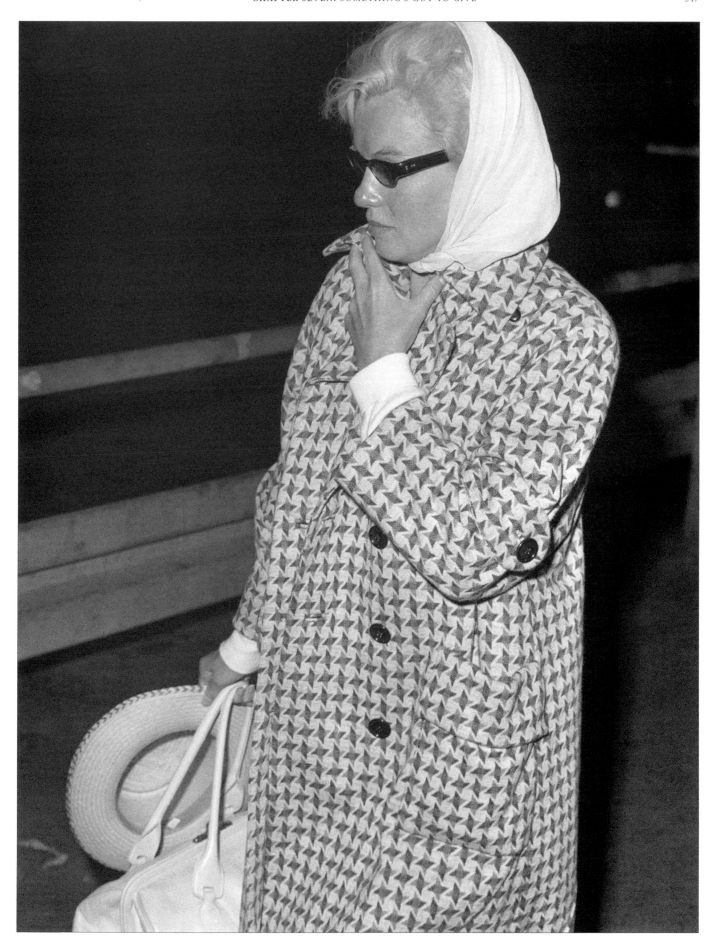

Right: Marilyn rushing out of the Yankee Clipper Hotel in Florida, after visiting the Yankee Clipper himself, Joe DiMaggio. Their marriage had been short-lived but now, as in 1954 when they were first dating, Marilyn appreciated Joe's loyalty and steadying influence.

informed that they had agreed in principle to reinstate her, although final details of the deal were still being worked out and filming could not begin again until early September because Dean Martin was fulfilling other commitments.

It seemed as if, once again, Marilyn would manage to turn disaster into triumph, but in reality those close to her were worried about whether she was currently capable of working. Unlike previous times when she had been down and apparently out, but had come back fighting, this time she seemed to be finding it more difficult.

On 3 August, Marilyn persuaded Dr Engelberg to give her a prescription for twenty-five Nembutal tablets. Engelberg and Greenson had been working together to control her drug intake, but for some reason they did not communicate about this prescription. The following day, Greenson came to Marilyn's house and spent much of the afternoon with her. She had been invited to dinner at Lawford's house, and Greenson was also going out to dinner so he left around 7.00 pm. Nearly an hour later, Lawford called to find out if Marilyn was coming over, and was concerned at her slurred speech. When Marilyn finished the call by telling him goodbye, alarm bells rang and he in turn telephoned Marilyn's lawyer, Milton Rudin, who called her housekeeper. Eunice Murray assured him that Marilyn was fine. It was not until the early hours of 5 August that Murray became concerned that the light was still on in Marilyn's room. Everyone knew she was unable to sleep if there was the slightest chink of light in the room, and her bedroom was always fitted with blackout curtains. Murray called Greenson, and the two of them broke into the room, to find Marilyn sprawled across the bed, the telephone receiver still in her hand. She had been dead for some time, and an autopsy showed large amounts of both Nembutal and chloral hydrate in her system.

The theories about Marilyn's death could - and have - filled many books, and they range from a straightforward suicide to conspiracy and murder. The reality is that no one really knows the truth. She had certainly tried to commit suicide in the past, and she had also taken accidental overdoses. Given her lifestyle, it is also possible that additional medication was obtained from someone unaware of what she had already taken. However, it is highly unlikely that she was murdered, and none of the motives so far proposed hold water under close examination. The real tragedy is that previously she had always been found in time, and this time she wasn't.

Marilyn's funeral was held at Westwood Memorial Park, in Los Angeles, and was arranged by Joe DiMaggio with the help of her half-sister, Berniece Miracle, and her business manager, Inez Melson. DiMaggio refused to allow her Hollywood friends to attend, holding them morally responsible for her death, and Press and photographers were kept at a distance. Her trusted makeup man, Whitey Snyder, did her makeup for her final appearance, fulfilling a promise made as a joke many years previously. DiMaggio also fulfilled an old promise, arranging for a single red rose to be delivered to her grave twice a week.

Even many years after her death, Marilyn Monroe is still one of the greatest legends of the twentieth century. In her films she projected a unique and fascinating persona - a child-woman who was both innocent and full of sexuality, someone whom men desired, but who women found unthreatening. In real life, she was a beautiful and complex woman who felt deeply insecure, and who just wanted to be loved enough to wipe out her unhappy past. In her brief career she appeared in several classic movies, as well as many more that are memorable only for her presence.

It was perhaps inevitable that Marilyn Monroe the person would die young, but Marilyn Monroe the star is an extraordinary and unforgettable woman whose legend still lives on.

Flying down to Mexico...

Above: Joe gives Marilyn a goodbye kiss as she leaves for Mexico City on a short vacation in February 1962. She was travelling there to buy some Mexican-style furnishings for her newly acquired home in Hollywood. She had admired the style in the home of her analyst, Dr Ralph Greenson. Marilyn had not worked since shooting on *The Misfits* had finished towards the end of 1960, but the studio intended that she should begin filming *Something's Got to Give* as soon as rewrites to the script were complete.

Left: Marilyn waves to newsmen on her return from Mexico City in March 1962. However, she was not in good spirits having heard that Arthur Miller had remarried.

Opposite: A small white poodle, called Maf, had been given to Marilyn to keep her company after she had spent some time in a psychiatric hospital the previous year. Like many of her pets it was not properly house-trained. After she died, Maf went to live with Frank Sinatra's secretary, Gloria Lovell. Many people believe it was Sinatra who had given her the dog, but it may also have been her publicist, Pat Newcomb.

Female World Film Favourite 1961

In March 1962, Marilyn was presented with an award as Female World Film Favourite 1961 by the Foreign Press Association at their Annual Award ceremony in Hollywood.

Opposite: Actor Rock Hudson presented the award to Marilyn, and seemed almost as pleased as she was. Her slim and glamorous new look belied the fact that she was both physically and mentally fragile.

Above: Marilyn arrives for the party after the ceremony with Mexican screenwriter José Bolaños. They had met during her recent trip to Mexico City, and after her death he told the world that they had planned to marry. However, the relationship didn't last for long.

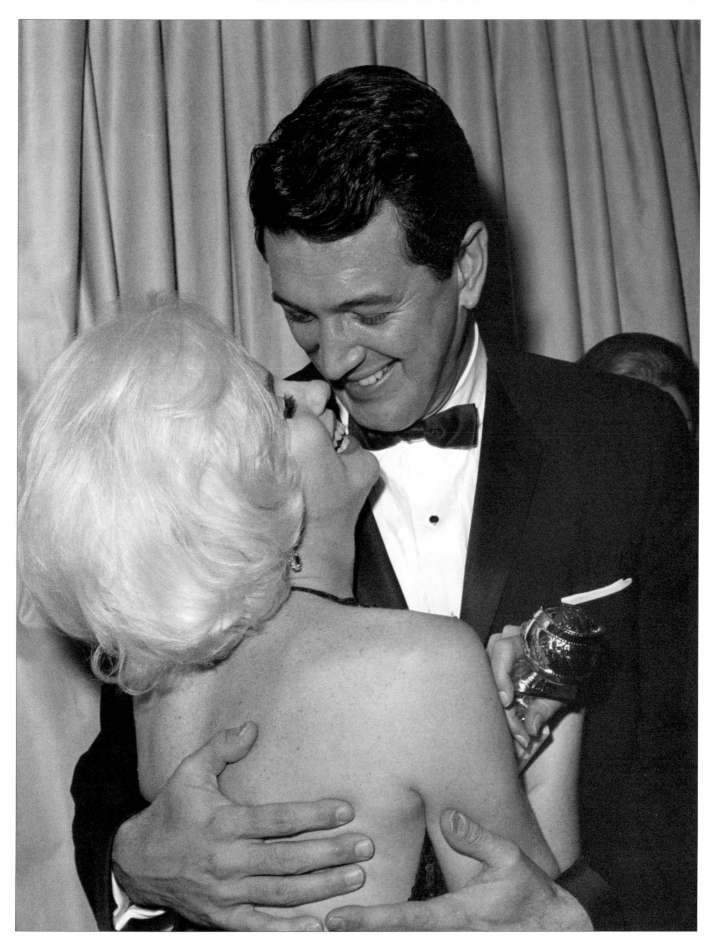

Happy Birthday, Mr President

Opposite: Marilyn sings "Happy Birthday" to President John F. Kennedy at a fund-raising event at Madison Square Garden in May 1962. She was ushered on stage by Peter Lawford, who introduced her as "the late Marilyn Monroe". After she had sung the first verse alone, she invited the audience to join in as a six-foot cake with 45 oversized candles was carried onstage.

Left: During a swimming scene in *Something's Got to Give*, when the Press had been invited on set to take some pictures, Marilyn caused a sensation by removing her swimming costume underwater. Progress on the picture had been painfully slow at a time when the studio could ill-afford to lose money and the atmosphere on set was tense. Although Marilyn looked superficially slimmer and fitter than she had done in several years, she was unable to function without medication and constant support from Dr Greenson, her psychoanalyst.

Skinny-dipping

Above: When she emerged from the pool photographers snapped nude pictures and these stunning images were immediately released for publication. One of them was used on the cover of *Life* magazine in June 1962.

Opposite: Marilyn as Eve Arden in *Something's Got to Give.* Very little of it was completed before Marilyn was fired from the picture on 8 June 1962. The following year the script was revised yet again and the movie was made as *Move Over Darling*, with Doris Day in Marilyn's role, and James Garner taking the Dean Martin part.

Right: On her 36th birthday, and on one of her last public appearances, Marilyn came onto the field at Chavez Ravine Dodger Stadium in Los Angeles, along with outfielder Albie Pearson, before a Yankees v Angels benefit game on 1 June 1962. She was appealing for donations to the Muscular Dystrophy fund.

Day of the dead...

Above: After Marilyn was found dead, on 5 August 1962, the police were called to her home on Fifth Helena Drive. They searched unsuccessfully for a suicide note, and interviewed her analyst, Dr Ralph Greenson, Dr Engelberg, and housekeeper Eunice Murray. Reporters were prevented from approaching, but photographers took pictures of Marilyn's house with the two toy stuffed dogs on the lawn.

Left: Mrs Eunice Murray, Marilyn's housekeeper and companion, leaves the house with handyman Norman Jeffries after the body has been removed to the mortuary. It was Eunice who called Dr Greenson, after apparently becoming concerned that the light was still on in Marilyn's room. When the two of them broke the door down it was too late to rouse her. Eunice had been given her job on the recommendation of Dr Greenson. She had no formal training as a nurse, but he often used her as a companion to patients of his who he felt needed day-to-day support. She did not normally stay overnight at Marilyn's house, but on the night of the star's death she had slept in one of the spare rooms.

An empty home...

Above: The bedroom where Marilyn's body was found. She had still not really settled into the house, and much of the furniture and many of the decorative pieces she had ordered in Mexico had not yet been delivered. There were piles of bags in many corners, as there was no storage. The house was in Spanish-colonial style and was L-shaped with a small guest house. Much of the interior was painted white - like most of the other places Marilyn had lived.

Left: After Marilyn's body was taken away, the police sealed all the rooms in the house. When her estate was released, the house and much of its contents was bought by Mr and Mrs Gilbert Nunez. Many of the items that had once belonged to Marilyn were auctioned off by their children in 1997.

Cause of death?

The autopsy report on Marilyn concluded that she had died of "acute barbiturate poisoning - ingestion of overdose". There were no signs of any external violence, but she had 8mg of chloral hydrate and 4.5mg of Nembutal in her bloodstream. The theories as to how this happened range from suicide, through accidental overdose to murder.

Marilyn's funeral took place at the Westwood Funeral Chapel and was arranged by her old love, Joe DiMaggio. During the service she lay in an open casket, dressed in green. Her makeup man, Whitey Snyder, had done her makeup for the very last time - having been fortified by a large amount of gin. Joe had refused to allow her Hollywood friends to attend. So there were only thirty-one invited mourners including the Strasbergs, the Greenson family and several of Marilyn's employees. Arthur Miller chose not to attend.

Opposite top: A police officer stands guard over the crypt where Marilyn will be laid to rest.

Opposite bottom: Marilyn's casket is carried out of the Westwood Park Chapel, past a line of guards.

Grief stricken

Above: Joe DiMaggio, and his son Joe DiMaggio Jr. - in his U.S. Marine dress uniform - stand shoulder to shoulder at Marilyn's funeral. Joe Jr had been one of the last people to speak to Marilyn on the phone.

Opposite above: Marilyn's psychoanalyst, Dr Ralph Greenson, with his wife and two children, at the funeral.

Opposite below: Joe is overcome by emotion as the casket is taken from the hearse and placed on a stand in front of the crypt. A recent biography of DiMaggio claims that the day of the funeral - 8 August, 1962 - was to have been the day that he and Marilyn were to remarry.

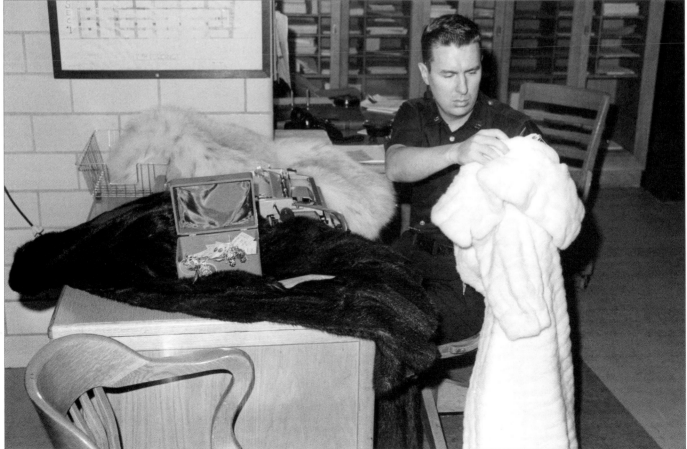

The aftermath...

Opposite top: Sam and Enid Knebelcamp were the only foster parents of Marilyn's to attend the funeral. She lived with them during the late 1930s, when Grace McKee Goddard temporarily was unable to look after her ward.

Opposite bottom: Marilyn's furs and jewellery were still in police safekeeping for some time after her death. The bulk of her estate was left to Lee Strasberg, with part of it going to Dr Kris to further the work of a psychiatric institution. Dr Kris selected the Anna Freud Foundation in London where it has been used to fund the Monroe Young Family Centre. At first most of the money went in taxes, and nothing was paid out to any of the beneficiaries for nearly ten years. Later on, her percentage of the profits from later movies began to flow through - and then royalties from merchandising and licensing. Current income is in millions of dollars.

Left: Mrs Eunice Murray told reporters that Marilyn had not seemed suicidal to her.

Below: Coroner Theodore Curphey (centre) with Dr Norman Farberow on the left and Dr Robert Litman on the right, announce the findings of the psychiatric suicide team and the autopsy test on Marilyn to the Press. Her death is officially ruled as a "Probable Suicide".

Chronology

1926

1 Jun Marilyn is born Norma Jeane Mortensen in Los Angeles, California

13 Jun The new baby is left with the neighbouring Bolender family after her mother returns to work

Dec At her christening, the baby is named Norma Jeane - but she spells her second name with and without the "e" throughout her childhood

1927

July The toddler Norma is nearly suffocated by her grandmother, Della Monroe, who is later admitted to the Metropolitan State Hospital in Norwalk, LA County

23 Aug Della dies of a heart attack in hospital

1933

Jun Norma Jeane leaves the Bolenders to live with her mother, Gladys, in North Hollywood

Aug Gladys obtains a mortgage and they move into a house on Arbol Street, sharing it with an English couple

Oct Gladys hears that her grandfather, Tilford Hogan, has committed suicide

1934

Jan Gladys is admitted to a rest home in Santa Monica, having suffered a mental breakdown

1935

Jan Gladys is committed to the Metropolitan State Hospital in Norwalk, LA County, with a diagnosis of paranoid schizophrenia

Apr Gladys's estate is assessed as she is no longer able to manage her affairs

1 Jun Grace McKee becomes responsible for liquidating Gladys's estate

13 Sept Norma Jeane is placed in the Los Angeles Orphans Home Society

1936

26 Feb Papers are legally filed to allow Grace to become Norma Jeane's legal guardian

1937

Spring Grace becomes Norma Jeane's legal guardian

26 Jun Norma Jeane leaves the orphanage and lives with Grace and her new husband

Nov Norma Jeane goes to live with Ida Martin, a distant relative in Compton, LA

1938

Aug Norma Jeane goes to live with Anna Lower, Grace's aunt

1941

Dec Norma Jeane begins dating Jim Dougherty

1942

19 Jun Norma Jeane marries Jim Dougherty and the newlyweds move into an apartment

1943

Spring Jim and Norma Jeane move back to his parents' home, to look after it while they are away

Autumn The young couple move into their own apartment again

Jim Dougherty is called up and joins the Merchant Marines - he is sent first as an instructor to Catalina Island

1944

Spring Jim is posted to a ship in the South Pacific

Apr Marilyn returns to her mother-in-law's home and starts work at Radio Plane Munitions Factory in Burbank, California

1945

26 Jun At Radio Plane, Marilyn is photographed by David Conover for a feature in *Yank* magazine

2 Aug Marilyn is taken on by the Blue Book Agency

1946

26 Apr First appearance of Norma Jeane on the cover of a national magazine, *Family Circle*

Jun Norma Jeane dyes her brunette hair blonde

Jul Harry Lipton of National Concert Artists Corporation becomes Norma Jeane's agent

16 Jul Norma Jeane has her first interview with Ben Lyon at Twentieth Century Fox

19 Jul At a screen test for Twentieth Century Fox, Norma Jeane comes over very well

29 Jul First mention of Norma Jeane (as Jean Norman) in a Hollywood gossip column

26 Aug The aspiring actress signs her first studio contract, with Twentieth Century Fox, and changes her name to Marilyn Monroe

Sept While in Las Vegas to obtain her divorce, Norma Jeane spends time in Las Vegas General Hospital, first with an acute mouth infection after her wisdom teeth are removed, and then with measles

13 Sept Norma Jeane is granted a divorce from Jim Dougherty in Las Vegas, Nevada

1947

Summer Filming of *Dangerous Years*, with Marilyn's first speaking role

Although Marilyn's first movie role is in *Scudda Hoo, Scudda Hay*, most of her part is later cut

Summer Filming of *Dangerous Years* with Marilyn's first speaking part

26 Jul Marilyn is told that her contract with Twentieth Century Fox is not to be renewed

25 Aug Marilyn's contract with Twentieth Century Fox runs out

4 Dec Marilyn signs a management contract with Lucille Ryman and John Carroll

7 Dec Release of *Dangerous Years*

1948

Feb Marilyn meets Joe Schenck at a Hollywood party

20 Feb Marilyn is crowned Miss California Artichoke Queen

14 Apr *Scudda Hoo, Scudda Hay* is released

9 Mar Marilyn signs a six-month contract with Columbia

Vocal coach Fred Karger works with Marilyn on her songs for *Ladies of the Chorus*, but her devotion to him is not reciprocated

Apr Marilyn meets Natasha Lytess, head drama coach at Columbia, who later becomes her personal drama coach for some years

Filming of *Ladies of the Chorus*

9 Sept Marilyn's contract with Columbia is not renewed

22 Oct   Release of *Ladies of the Chorus*

31 Dec   Marilyn meets agent Johnny Hyde from the William Morris Agency at Sam Spiegel's New Year party

1949

Feb   Marilyn films a part in *Love Happy*, and is mentioned in Louella Parsons' gossip column

27 May   Marilyn poses nude for the famous calendar photograph by Tom Kelley, which is published anonymously

24 Jul   Earl Wilson first interviews Marilyn

15 Aug   Start of shooting on *A Ticket to Tomahawk*

Johnny Hyde becomes Marilyn's agent

Marilyn films a small uncredited part in *Right Cross*

Oct   MGM give Marilyn a contract for a role in *The Asphalt Jungle*

10 Oct   *Life* magazine shows pictures of Marilyn in a feature on Hollywood's aspiring stars

1950

5 Jan   Marilyn begins shooting *The Fireball*

8 Apr   Release of *Love Happy*

27 Mar   Marilyn lands the part of a starlet in *All About Eve*

19 May   Release of *A Ticket to Tomahawk*

23 May   World première of *The Asphalt Jungle* at Grauman's Egyptian Theater

14 Oct   Release of *All About Eve*

9 Nov   Release of *The Fireball*

15 Nov   Release of *Right Cross*

10 Dec   Marilyn signs a contract with Twentieth Century Fox

18 Dec   Johnny Hyde dies of a heart attack

Dec   Marilyn has minor plastic surgery, possibly to remove a small lump from her nose

Dec   Marilyn appears in *As Young As You Feel* for Fox

Dec   Arthur Miller and Marilyn meet for the first time on the set of *As Young As You Feel* at Twentieth Century Fox

1951

Mar   After catching the attention of Spyros Skouras, president of Fox, Marilyn secures the renewal of her contract

29 Mar   Marilyn is a presenter at the 1951 Academy Awards ceremony

18 Apr   Starts shooting *The Love Nest* for Fox

11 May   The six-month contract with Fox is converted to a seven-year contract

        Release of *Hometown Story*

        Films a part in *Let's Make it Legal* for Fox

2 Aug   Release of *As Young As You Feel*

21 Aug   Fox agrees to loan Marilyn to RKO, to appear in *Clash by Night*

8 Sept   The first full-length feature on Marilyn appears in Colliers magazine

Autumn Marilyn tries to contact C. Stanley Gifford, the man she believed was her father, but he refuses to see her

        Marilyn enrols to study acting with coach Michael Chekov

        Filming of *Clash by Night*

        Filming of *Don't Bother to Knock*

10 Oct   Release of *Love Nest*

23 Oct   Marilyn appears on the cover of *Look* magazine for the first time

6 Nov   Release of *Let's Make It Legal*

15 Nov   *Quick* magazine has a feature on Marilyn as its cover story, designating her "The New Jean Harlow"

Dec   *Focus* magazine has a cover story on Marilyn, comparing her favourably with Lana Turner, Betty Grable and Rita Hayworth

1952

26 Feb   Marilyn begins filming *Monkey Business*

13 Mar   After the Press discover Marilyn's nude calendar picture, she admits publicly that she is the model

15 Mar   Joe DiMaggio and Marilyn meet for the first time

7 Apr   Marilyn features on her first *Life* magazine cover

28 Apr   Marilyn's appendix is removed at the Cedars of Lebanon hospital

3 May   Studio publicity about Marilyn had presented her as an orphan, but after it is discovered that her mother is still alive, she releases a short statement to the Press

1 Jun   Marilyn learns she has the part of Lorelei in *Gentlemen Prefer Blondes*

Jun   Start of filming of *Niagara*

18 Jun   Release of *Clash By Night*

12 Jul   General release of *We're Not Married*

18 Jul   Release of *Don't Bother to Knock*

Aug   New York première of *Don't Bother to Knock*

31 Aug	Marilyn's first live radio show is broadcast, in which she reads a role in a one-act play
1 Sept	The U.S. Army photographs Marilyn to use in a recruitment drive, but the pictures are withdrawn after the photographer shoots from a balcony, revealing too much of the Monroe cleavage
2 Sept	At the Miss America beauty pageant, Marilyn is a Grand Marshal
5 Sept	General release of *Monkey Business*
16 Oct	Release of *O Henry's Full House*
26 Oct	Marilyn is heard on ventriloquist Edgar Bergen's radio show
17 Nov	Filming begins on *Gentlemen Prefer Blondes*
22 Nov	An article titled "The Truth about Me" appears in The American Weekly, with Marilyn's name as the by-line

1953

Jan	The famous nude picture of Marilyn is republished as "Miss Golden Dreams" on the January page of a new calendar
21 Jan	*Niagara* is released
9 Feb	Gladys Baker is transferred to Rockhaven Sanatorium at Marilyn's expense
6 Mar	Filming on *Gentlemen Prefer Blondes* is completed
9 Mar	Scandal follows Marilyn's appearance at the *Photoplay* magazine awards in the tissue-thin gold lamé gown from *Gentlemen Prefer Blondes*
Mar	*Photoplay* features an article by Jim Dougherty, "Marilyn Monroe Was My Wife"
Apr	Start of filming on *How to Marry a Millionaire*
May	Marilyn is featured on the cover of *Cosmopolitan* magazine
26 Jun	Marilyn and Jane Russell both leave their prints outside Grauman's Chinese Theater
15 Jul	Release of *Gentlemen Prefer Blondes*
Aug	Filming of *River of No Return* in Canada
20 Aug	During filming, Marilyn slips and damages her leg
Aug	Official première of *Gentlemen Prefer Blondes* at Grauman's Chinese Theater
13 Sept	Marilyn's first television appearance on *The Jack Benny Show*
Oct	Marilyn signs a recording contract with RCA
10 Oct	Marilyn accompanies Joe DiMaggio to visit his family in San Francisco
4 Nov	Première of *How to Marry a Millionaire* in Los Angeles

Dec	The famous nude calendar shot appears in the first issue of *Playboy* magazine, as the first Sweetheart of the Month, and a clothed Marilyn also appears on the cover
15 Dec	Marilyn fails to report on the first day of rehearsals of *The Girl in Pink Tights*

1954

4 Jan	Fox suspends Marilyn for failing to appear for filming
14 Jan	Marilyn marries baseball player Joe DiMaggio at San Francisco City Hall
2 Feb	The couple arrive in Tokyo for their honeymoon
16 Feb	During their honeymoon, Marilyn takes time to entertain the troops in Korea
5 Mar	Marilyn arrives back in Los Angeles
14 Mar	Marilyn is voted Best New Actress of 1953 by *Photoplay* magazine
31 Mar	Charles Feldman at Famous Artists Agency officially becomes Marilyn's agent
14 Apr	After the lifting of her suspension, Marilyn returns to the studio
30 Apr	Release of *River of No Return*
28 May	Starts filming *There's No Business Like Show Business*
7 Jul	A representative of the armed forces presents Marilyn with a trophy and plaque for morale-building activities
10 Aug	Filming begins on *The Seven Year Itch*
9 Sept	Marilyn arrives in New York for location filming on *The Seven Year Itch*
10 Sept	Milton Greene photographs Marilyn as a ballerina
16 Sept	The famous skirt-blowing sequence for *The Seven Year Itch* is filmed on the streets of New York
5 Oct	Marilyn and Joe DiMaggio officially separate
27 Oct	A divorce from DiMaggio is granted, but not finalized for one year
4 Nov	Shooting finishes on *The Seven Year Itch*
5 Nov	Joe DiMaggio and Frank Sinatra carry out the "Wrong Door" raid, attempting to find Marilyn
6 Nov	Marilyn is honoured at a Hollywood party at Romanoff's
7 Nov	Marilyn enters the Cedars of Lebanon Hospital to undergo surgery for endometriosis
Dec	Leaving Hollywood, Marilyn heads for New York
16 Dec	Release of *There's No Business Like Show Business*
31 Dec	Marilyn Monroe Productions is officially formed

1955

7 Jan   Milton Greene and Marilyn hold a Press conference to announce the creation of Marilyn Monroe Productions

10 Jan   Marilyn returns briefly to Hollywood to film one scene of additional dialogue for *The Seven Year Itch*

15 Jan   Fox suspends Marilyn again

Feb   Marilyn begins to study under Lee Strasberg, founder of the Actors Studio in New York

9 Mar   At the première of East of Eden, Marilyn acts as an usherette in aid of the Actors Studio

30 Mar   At the opening of the Ringling Brothers Barnum & Bailey Circus, Marilyn appears riding a pink elephant in aid of the New York Arthritis & Rheumatism Foundation

8 Apr   Edward R. Murrow interviews Marilyn live on *Person to Person*

Summer   Marilyn briefly dates Marlon Brando, and when they split up they remain friends

1 Jun   World première of *The Seven Year Itch*

26 Jul Breaking her agency contract with Famous Artists, Marilyn signs with MCA

29 Sept Marilyn attends the opening night of Arthur Miller's play, *A View from the Bridge*, at New York's Coronet Theater

31 Oct The divorce from Joe DiMaggio is finalized

31 Dec Marilyn signs a new four-picture, seven-year contract with Fox

1956

4 Jan Twentieth Century Fox announce that they and Marilyn have come to terms, and that she will be returning to Hollywood

9 Feb At a Press conference in New York, Laurence Olivier announces their joint project, *The Prince and the Showgirl*

17 Feb Marilyn performs at the Actors' Studio, New York

23 Feb Norma Jeane legally changes her name to Marilyn Monroe

25 Feb Marilyn returns to Hollywood after her one-year exile in New York

3 Mar Filming begins on *Bus Stop*

12 Apr Suffering from bronchitis, Marilyn spends four days in St Vincent Hospital, Los Angeles

14 May *Time* magazine features Marilyn on the cover for the first and only time in her lifetime

11 Jun A divorce is granted to playwright Arthur Miller

29 Jun Marilyn marries Miller in a civil ceremony

1 Jul Marilyn and Miller have a Jewish wedding ceremony

14 Jul The Millers fly to London

7 Aug *The Prince and the Showgirl* starts filming in England

31 Aug Release of *Bus Stop*

Sept Marilyn becomes pregnant, but loses the baby within a few weeks

29 Oct Marilyn is presented to Queen Elizabeth II at the Royal Command Performance of *The Battle of the River Plate* in London

17 Nov Filming completed on *The Prince and the Showgirl*

20 Nov The Millers return to America

18 Dec Marilyn does a radio show broadcast from the Waldorf-Astoria

1957

18 Feb Miller is indicted by a federal grand jury on two counts of contempt of Congress

27 Feb Frank Sinatra testifies at an investigation into the "Wrong Door" raid carried out by Joe DiMaggio in 1954

1 Mar At a first hearing, Miller pleads not guilty

11 Apr A statement is released, accusing Greene of mismanaging Marilyn Monroe Productions

14 May After being called to Washington, Arthur Miller is put on trial for contempt of Congress; Marilyn accompanies him but stays out of sight

13 Jun Première of *The Prince and the Showgirl*

1 Aug Marilyn is rushed to Doctors Hospital, New York, with severe abdominal pain, which turns out to be an ectopic pregnancy that has to be terminated

10 Aug Marilyn leaves hospital under a barrage of Press attention

1958

28 Jan Marilyn attends the annual March of Dimes fashion show at the Waldorf-Astoria, New York

4 Apr After prevaricating, Marilyn signs the contract for *Some Like It Hot*

7 Jul Marilyn returns to Hollywood to prepare for filming

4 Aug Filming begins on *Some Like It Hot*

Oct Marilyn becomes pregnant again

6 Nov Filming on *Some Like It Hot* is completed

16 Dec Marilyn miscarries the baby, and is taken to Polyclinic Hospital in New York

1959

29 Mar Première of *Some Like It Hot* at Loew's Capitol Theater on Broadway

Jun Marilyn receives the David Di Donatello statuette from Italy for her performance in *The Prince and the Showgirl*

23 Jun Corrective gynaecological surgery is carried out on Marilyn at the Lennox Hill Hospital, New York, to try to cure her chronic endometriosis

18 Sept The Russian premier, Nikita Khrushchev, meets Marilyn at a luncheon in his honour at the Twentieth Century Fox studios in Hollywood

14 Oct Although Marilyn is due to begin rehearsing in New York for *The Billionaire* - later released as *Let's Make Love* - she fails to show

9 Nov Marilyn officially begins work on *Let's Make Love*

1960

25 Jan The first part of one of Marilyn's musical numbers in *Let's Make Love* is finally filmed

8 Mar Marilyn receives a Golden Globe award for Best Actress in a Comedy, for *Some Like It Hot*

Yves Montand and Marilyn have a brief affair during the filming of *Let's Make Love*

Jun Psychoanalyst Ralph Greenson begins seeing Marilyn on a daily basis

18 Jul Filming begins on *The Misfits*

27 Aug Marilyn is admitted to Westside Hospital in Los Angeles suffering from exhaustion

5 Sept Marilyn returns to Nevada to finish location filming on *The Misfits*

8 Sept Release of *Let's Make Love*

4 Nov Shooting finishes on *The Misfits*

Nov Yves Montand sees Marilyn briefly in New York, before returning to his wife in France

11 Nov Arthur Miller and Marilyn officially separate

16 Nov Clark Gable dies of a heart attack

1961

20 Jan A divorce from Arthur Miller is granted in Juarez, Mexico

31 Jan Première of *The Misfits*

7 Feb Marilyn enters the Payne-Whitney Clinic in New York under the name Faye Miller

11 Feb After three days, Joe DiMaggio arranges for Marilyn to be transferred to the Neurological Institute at Columbia-Presbyterian Hospital

5 Mar Marilyn leaves the Columbia-Presbyterian Hospital

Mar Margaret Parton interviews Marilyn for the *Ladies Home Journal*, but the interview is never published as it is deemed "too sympathetic" by the editor

May Again Marilyn enters the Cedars of Lebanon Hospital for a minor operation

Summer Frank Sinatra and Marilyn have a brief affair

28 June Marilyn enters Polyclinic Hospital in New York to have her gall bladder removed

11 Jul Marilyn leaves hospital

8 Aug Finally giving up on New York, Marilyn returns to Hollywood

Oct	Robert Kennedy and Marilyn begin an affair, after meeting at Peter Lawford's beach house
19 Nov	Marilyn attends a dinner at Peter Lawford's beach house, President John Kennedy is also present

1962

Feb	Marilyn buys a new home in Brentwood, California
21 Feb	With her housekeeper, Marilyn flies to Mexico to buy furniture and artefacts for her new home
2 Mar	Marilyn returns from Mexico
5 Mar	At the Golden Globe Awards, Marilyn is presented with a statuette as the World's Favorite Female Star
10 Apr	Marilyn attends costume and makeup tests for *Something's Got To Give*
23 Apr	Filming begins on *Something's Got To Give*
19 May	Marilyn sings "Happy Birthday" at a gala birthday party for President John Kennedy at Madison Square Garden
28 May	During filming, Marilyn is photographed swimming nude in a pool
1 Jun	Marilyn's last public appearance
8 Jun	Marilyn is fired from *Something's Got To Give* for persistent absenteeism
23 Jun	First *Vogue* photo session with Bert Stein
28 Jun	Negotiations with Fox begin about resuming work on *Something's Got To Give*
29 Jun	Start of a three-day photo session, with George Barris shooting Marilyn for *Cosmopolitan*
4 Jul	Richard Meryman begins an extensive interview with Marilyn, which turns out to be her last
12 Jul	Marilyn meets the studio chiefs at Fox
20 Jul	Marilyn enters the Cedars of Lebanon Hospital for an operation to cure her endometriosis

28 Jul	Marilyn spends the weekend at Cal-Neva Lodge
1 Aug	Fox revises Marilyn's contract, offering double her previous salary and agreeing to restart shooting on *Something's Got To Give*
3 Aug	Marilyn appears on the cover of *Life* magazine for the last time before her death
4 Aug	Dr Ralph Greenson spends six hours with Marilyn
5 Aug	Police are called after Marilyn is found dead in her Brentwood home
8 Aug	Marilyn's funeral, at Westwood Memorial Park, in Los Angeles, California

1995

1 Jun	A 32¢ commemorative postage stamp featuring Marilyn is issued in the US Legends of Hollywood series
Oct	Marilyn is voted UK's *Empire* magazine Sexiest Female Movie Star of All Time

1997

Oct	Marilyn is listed No.8 in the UK's *Empire* magazine The Top 100 Movie Stars of All Time

1998

Fall	Marilyn is voted *Playboy* magazine's Sexiest Female Star of the Twentieth Century

1999

Oct	At a Christie's auction of Marilyn memorabilia, the gown in which Marilyn sang "Happy Birthday" to John Kennedy is sold for over $1 million
Dec	*Playboy* magazine names Marilyn as Number One Sex Star of the Twentieth Century

Clark Gable
"Everything Marilyn does is different from any other woman, strange and exciting, from the way she talks to the way she uses that magnificent torso."

Billy Wilder
"She is a very great actress. Better Marilyn late than most of the others on time."

Barbara Stanwyck
"She wasn't disciplined, and she was often late but there was a sort of magic about her which we all recognized at once."

Edward Wagenknecht
"Marilyn played the best game with the worst hand of anybody I know."

Sam Shaw
"Everybody knows about her insecurities, but not everybody knows what fun she was, that she never complained about the ordinary things of life, that she never had a bad word to say about anyone, and that she had a wonderful spontaneous sense of humour."

Sammy Davis Jr.
"Still she hangs like a bat in the heads of men who have met her, and none of us will ever forget her."

Joe DiMaggio
"If it hadn't been for her friends she might still be alive."

Marilyn on Marilyn

"I'm not interested in money, I just want to be wonderful."

"I've been on a calendar, but never on time."

"Hollywood's a place where they'll pay you a thousand dollars for a kiss,
and fifty cents for your soul. I know, because I turned down the first offer
often enough and held out for the fifty."

"A sex-symbol becomes a thing, I just hate being a thing.
But if I'm going to be a symbol of something, I'd rather have it sex than some
of the other things we've got symbols of."

"If I had observed all the rules, I'd never have gotten anywhere."

"Some people have been unkind. If I say I want to grow as an actress,
they look at my figure. If I say I want to develop, to learn my craft, they laugh.
Somehow they don't expect me to be serious about my work."

"Dogs never bite me. Just humans."

Acknowlegements

All photographs in this book are reproduced
by kind permsission of
Corbis except those listed below.

Photographs on the following pages are reprodcued
by kind permission of
the Associated Newspapers Archive:

9, 183, 184, 185, 220, 221 (top and bottom),
222, 223, 224, 225 (top), 226, 227, 228, 229 (top and bottom), 230-1,
237 (bottom), 238 (top and bottom), 239, 240, 241, 242, 243, 244, 245,
246-7, 248, 250-1, 374, 375, 376 and 382

Robert Landau/Corbis: 87 bottom left
Jerry Ohlinger/Corbis: 115 top

Every effort has been made to ensure that the copyright details shown are correct,
but if there are any inaccuracies, please contact the publisher.

Bibliography

Marilyn Monroe   Barbara Leaming (Orion, London, 2002)

The Marilyn Encyclopedia   Adam Victor
(The Overlook Press, New York, 2001)

Norma Jean   Fred Lawrence Guiles
(Mayflower, St Albans, 1977)

My Story   Marilyn Monroe
(Stein & Day, New York, 1974)

The Pocket Essential Marilyn Monroe   Paul Donnelley
(Pocket Essentials, Harpenden, 2000)

Goddess, The Secret Lives of Marilyn Monroe   Anthony Summers
(Gollanz, London, 1985)

DiMaggio Setting the Record Straight   Morris Engleberg, Marv Schneider
(MBI, St Paul, 2003)

Blonde Heat   Richard Buskin
(Billboard Books, New York, 2001)

The Assassination of Marilyn Monroe   Donald H. Wolfe
(Time Warner Paperbacks, London 1998)

On Sunset Boulevard, The Life and Times of Billy Wilder   Ed Sikov
(Hyperion, New York, 1998)